WHO WROTE THAT SONG?

Dick Jacobs

BETTERWAY PUBLICATIONS, INC.
WHITE HALL, VIRGINIA

Published by Betterway Publications, Inc.
Box 219
Crozet, VA 22932

Cover design by Deborah Chapell
Photographs courtesy the author's collection and the collection of Jack Bradley.
Illustrations by Susan Reilly
Typography by TechType

Library of Congress Cataloging in Publication Data

Jacobs, Dick.
  Who wrote that song?

  Includes index.
  1. Popular music--United States--Bibliography.
I. Title.
ML120.U5J23   1988   784.5'00973   88-19351
ISBN 1-55870-108-7
ISBN 1-55870-100-1 (pbk)

Printed in the United States of America
098765432

To the Songwriters:
All those talented men and women who have
brightened our days, warmed our nights,
and enriched our lives beyond measure.

Contents

The Songs

Various symbols are used throughout the song listings to give you more information about a particular recording or the song itself. This is what each one indicates:

(w)   "Words by"
(m)   "Music by"
(wm)   "Words and Music by"
(I)   "Introduced by" (usually by recording)
(P)   "Popularized by"
(CR)   "Cover Record", i.e., a competing record made of the same song after the original record of the song has been issued.
(R)   "Revival recording"

A-TISKET A-TASKET (1938) (wm)Ella Fitzgerald—Al Feldman. (I)Ella Fitzgerald with Chick Webb and his Orchestra at The Savoy Ballroom in New York City. (P)Ella Fitzgerald. First record by Ella, made when she was fifteen.

"A" YOU'RE ADORABLE (The Alphabet Song) (1948) (wm)Buddy Kaye—Fred Wise—Sid Lippman. (P)Perry Como and The Fontaine Sisters. (CR)Jo Stafford and Gordon MacRae.

AARON LOVES ANGELA (1975) (wm)Jose and Janna Feliciano. (I)Film: *Aaron Loves Angela* by the voice of Jose Feliciano.

AIN'T GOT NO (1967) (w)Gerome Ragni—James Rado (m)Galt MacDermot. (I)Musical: Hair by Gerome Ragni, Walker Daniels, Steve Dean and Arnold Wilkerson. (off Broadway version). Broadway version by Melba Moore, Lamont Washington and Steve Curry. Recorded by Nina Simone.

AIN'T GOT NO HOME (1956) (wm)Clarence Henry. (P)Clarence "Frogman" Henry.

AIN'T IT DE TRUTH? (1942) (w)E. Y. Harburg (m)Harold Arlen. Originally in film *Cabin In The Sky*, but deleted. In musical *Jamaica* sung by Lena Horne.

AIN'T LOVE A BITCH (1978) (wm)Gary Grainger—Rod Stewart. (P)Rod Stewart.

AIN'T MISBEHAVIN' (1929) (w)Andy Razaf (m)Thomas "Fats" Waller—Harry Brooks. (I)Nightclub Revue: *Connie's Hot Chocolates* by Louis Armstrong. Recorded by Ruth Etting, Fats Waller, Louis Armstrong, Bill Robinson, Teddy Wilson.

AIN'T NO MOUNTAIN HIGH ENOUGH (1967) (wm)Nicholas Ashford—Valerie Simpson. (P)Marvin Gaye and Tammi Terrell. No. 1 Chart Record. (R)1970 by Diana Ross.

AIN'T NO ROAD TOO LONG (1985) (wm)Waylon Jennings. (I)Sesame Street film *Follow That Bird* by Waylon Jennings and muppet character Big Bird.

AIN'T NO STOPPING US NOW (1979) (wm)Jerry Cohen—Gene McFadden—John Whitehead. (P)McFadden and Whitehead.

AIN'T NO SUNSHINE (1971) (wm)Bill Withers. (P)Bill Withers. NARAS Award Winner.

AIN'T NO WAY (1968) (wm)Carolyn Franklin. (P)Aretha Franklin.

AIN'T NO WAY TO TREAT A LADY (1974) (wm)Harriet Shock. (P)Helen Reddy.

AIN'T NO WOMAN (Like The One I Got) (1973) (wm)Dennis Lambert—Brian Potter. (P)The Four Tops.

AIN'T NOBODY (1983) (wm)David Wolinski. (P)Rufus with Chaka Khan.

AIN'T NOBODY HERE BUT US CHICKENS (1947) (wm)Alex Kramer—Joan Whitney. (P)Louis Jordan and his Tympani Five.

AIN'T NOTHING LIKE THE REAL THING (1967) (wm)Nicholas Ashford—Valerie Simpson. (P)Marvin Gaye and Tammi Terrell. (R)1974 by Aretha Franklin. (R)1977 by Donny and Marie Osmond.

AIN'T NOTHING YOU CAN DO (1963) (wm)Deadric Malone—Joseph W. Scott. (P)Bobby Bland.

AIN'T SHE SWEET (1927) (w)Jack Yellen (m)Milton Ager. (I)Paul Ash and his Orchestra. Recorded by Ben Bernie and his Orchestra. Also, Gene Austin.

(R)1940s by Jimmy Lunceford and his Orchestra.

AIN'T THAT A SHAME (1955) (wm)Antoine "Fats" Domino—Dave Bartholomew. (I)Fats Domino. (CR)Pat Boone. No. 1 Chart Record.

AIN'T THAT JUST LIKE A MAN (1943) (wm)Don Raye—Gene de Paul. (I)Film: *What's Buzzin' Cousin*. (P)Freddie Slack and his Orchestra with vocal by Margaret Whiting.

AIN'T THAT JUST LIKE A WOMAN (1947) (wm)Fleecie Moore—Claude Demetrius. (P)Louis Jordan and his Tympani Five.

AIN'T THAT LOVIN' YOU BABY (1955) (wm)Jimmy Reed. (P)Jimmy Reed.

AIN'T THAT LOVING YOU (1961) (wm)Deadric Malone. (P)Bobby Bland.

AIN'T THAT PECULIAR (1965) (wm)William Robinson—Warren Moore—Marv Tarplin—Robert Rogers. (P)Marvin Gaye.

AIN'T TOO PROUD TO BEG (1966) (wm)Eddie Holland—Norman Whitfield. (P)The Temptations. (R)1974 by The Rolling Stones.

AIN'T WASTING TIME NO MORE (1972) (wm)Greg Allman. (P)The Allman Brothers.

AIN'T WE GOT FUN (1921) (w)Gus Kahn—Raymond B. Egan (m)Richard Whiting. (P)Van and Schenck. (CR)Billy Jones. (R)Film: *By The Light Of The Silvery Moon* by Gordon MacRae.

AIR (1967) (w)Gerome Ragni—James Rado (m)Galt MacDermot. (I)Sally Eaton in off Broadway and Broadway versions of musical *Hair*.

AIR MAIL SPECIAL (1941) (wm)Jimmie Mundy—Charlie Christian—Benny Goodman. (P)Benny Goodman and his Orchestra.

THE AIR THAT I BREATHE (1972) (wm)Albert and Mike Hazlewood. (P)The Hollies.

AIRPORT LOVE THEME (1970) (w)Paul Francis Webster (m)Alfred Newman. (P)Vincent Bell and his Orchestra. The last song written by Alfred Newman.

AL DI LA (1961) (w-Eng)Ervin Drake (m)C. Donida. (I)Film: Rome Adventure by Emilio Pericoli. San Remo Festival Winner.

ALABAM (1960) (wm)Lloyd Copas. (I)The Cowboy Copas. (CR)Pat Boone.

ALABAMA BARBECUE (1936) (wm)Benny Davis—J. Fred Coots. (I)Nightclub Revue: *Cotton Club Parade*.

ALABAMA JUBILEE (1915) (wm)Jack Yellen—George Cobb. (I)Arthur Collins and Byron Harlan. (R)1951 by Red Foley.

ALABAMA-SONG (1928) (w)Bertolt Brecht (m)Kurt Weill. (I)Lotte Lenya.

ALABAMY BOUND (1925) (w)B. G. De Sylva—Bud Green (m)Ray Henderson. (I)Al Jolson. In musical Kid Boots by Eddie Cantor. Recorded by Blossom Seeley, Isham Jones and his Orchestra. (R)1954 by The Mulcays.

ALBATROSS (1967) (wm)Judy Collins. (I)Judy Collins.

THE ALBUM OF MY DREAMS (1929) (w)Lou Davis (m)Harold Arlen. (I)Rudy Vallee and his Connecticut Yankees.

ALEXANDER THE SWOOSE (1941) (w)Ben Forrest—Glenn Burrs. (m)Frank Furlett—Leonard Keller. (P)Kay Kyser and his College of Musical Knowledge.

ALEXANDER'S RAGTIME BAND (1911) (wm)Irving Berlin. Recorded 1911 by Arthur Collins and Byron Harlan—Billy Murray. 1912 by Prince's Orchestra—Victor Military Band. 1927 by Bessie

Smith. 1935 by The Boswell Sisters. 1937 by Louis Armstrong. 1938 by Bing Crosby and Connee Boswell. 1947 by Bing Crosby and Al Jolson.

ALFIE (1966) (w)Hal David (m)Burt Bacharach. (I)Film: *Alfie* by voice of Cher. (P)Dionne Warwick. (CR)Cilla Black.

ALICE BLUE GOWN (1919) (w)Joseph McCarthy (m)Harry Tierney. (I)Musical: *Irene* by Edith Day. (R)1940 by Frankie Masters,Ozzie Nelson,Glenn Miller.

ALICE IN WONDERLAND (1963) (wm)Howard Greenfield—Neil Sedaka. (P)Neil Sedaka.

ALICE'S RESTAURANT (1966) (wm)Arlo Guthrie. (I)Film: *Alice's Restaurant* by Arlo Guthrie.

ALISON (1977) (wm)Elvis Costello. (I)Elvis Costello. (P)Linda Ronstadt.

ALIVE AGAIN (1978) (wm)James Pankow. (P)Chicago.

ALIVE AND KICKING (1985) (wm)Simple Minds. (P)Simple Minds.

ALL ALONE (1924) (wm)Irving Berlin. (I)*Music Box Revue of 1924* by Grace Moore and Oscar Shaw. Recorded by Al Jolson,Paul Whiteman,John McCormack,Abe Lyman.

ALL ALONE AM I (1962) (w-Eng)Arthur Altman (m)Manos Hadjidakis. (P)Brenda Lee.

ALL ALONG THE WATCHTOWER (1968) (wm)Bob Dylan. (I)Bob Dylan. (P)The Jimi Hendrix Experience.

ALL-AMERICAN BOY,THE (1976) (wm)Bill Parsons—Orville Lunsford. (P)Bill Parsons.

ALL AT ONCE (1937) (w)Lorenz Hart (m)Richard Rodgers. (I)Musical: *Babes In Arms* by Ray Heatherton and Mitzi Green. Ray Heatherton later became The Merry Mailman on TV.

ALL AT ONCE (1945) (w)Ira Gershwin (m)Kurt Weill. (I)Film: *Where Do We Go From Here* by Fred MacMurray

ALL AT ONCE (1986) (wm)Jeffrey Osborne—Michael Masser (P)Whitney Houston.

ALL AT ONCE YOU LOVE HER (1955) (w)Oscar Hammerstein II (m)Richard Rodgers. (I)Musical: *Pipe Dream.* (P)Perry Como.

ALL BY MYSELF (1921) (wm)Irving Berlin (I)Charles King. Recorded by Ted Lewis,Frank Crumit,Vaughn Deleath.

ALL BY MYSELF (1976) (wm)Eric Carmen. (P)Eric Carmen.

ALL CRIED OUT (1986) (wm)Full Force. (P)Lisa Lisa and Cult Jam.

ALL DARK PEOPLE (1937) (w)Lorenz Hart (m)Richard Rodgers. (I)Musical: *Babes In Arms* by Harold and Fayard Nicholas.

ALL DAY AND ALL OF THE NIGHT (1964) (wm)Ray Davies. (P)The Kinks.

ALL DRESSED UP (Spic and Spanish) (1939) (w)Lorenz Hart (m)Richard Rodgers (I)Musical: *Too Many Girls* by Diosa Costello. In film version by Desi Arnaz.

ALL ER NOTHIN' (1943) (w)Oscar Hammerstein II (m)Richard Rodgers. (I)Musical: *Oklahoma* by Celeste Holm and Lee Dixon. In film version (1955)by Gloria Grahame and Gene Nelson.

ALL FOR THE LOVE OF SUNSHINE (1970) (w)Mike Curb (m)Lalo Schifrin—Harley Hatcher. (I)Film: *Kelly's Heroes* by voice of Hank Williams,Jr.

ALL FOR YOU (1962) (w)Anne Crosswell (m)Lee Pockriss. (I)Musical: *Tovarich* by Vivien Leigh and Jean Pierre Aumont.

ALL GOD'S CHILLUN GOT RHYTHM (1937) (w)Gus Kahn (m)Bronislaw Kaper—Walter Jurmann. (I)Film: *A Day At The Races* by Ivie Anderson with Duke Ellington and his Orchestra.

ALL HIS CHILDREN (1971) (w)Alan and Marilyn Bergman (m)Henry Mancini. (I)Film: *Sometimes A Great Notion* by voice of Charlie Pride.

ALL I DO IS DREAM OF YOU (1934) (w)Arthur Freed (m)Nacio Herb Brown. (I)Film: *Sadie McKee* by Gene Raymond. Recorded by Jan Garber,Henry Busse,Freddy Martin. (R)1953 by Johnnie Ray.

ALL I EVER NEED IS YOU (1971) (wm)Jimmy Holiday—Eddie Reeves. (P)Sonny & Cher. (R)1979 by Kenny Rogers and Dottie West.

ALL I HAVE TO DO IS DREAM (1958) (wm)Boudleaux Bryant (P)The Everly Brothers. No. 1 Chart Record. (R)1981 by Andy Gibb.

ALL I KNOW (1973) (wm)Jim Webb. (P)Art Garfunkel.

ALL I NEED (1967) (wm)Eddie Holland—Frank Wilson—R. Dean Taylor. (P)The Temptations.

ALL I NEED (wm)Clifton Magness-Glen Ballard-David Robert Pack. (P)Jack Wagner.

ALL I NEED IS A MIRACLE (1985) (wm)Mike Rutherford—Christopher Neil. (P)Mike & The Mechanics.

ALL I NEED IS THE GIRL (1959) (w)Stephen Sondheim (m)Jule Styne. (I)Musical: *Gypsy* by Paul Wallace and Sandra Church.

ALL I NEED IS YOU (1942) (wm)Peter De Rose—Benny Davis—Mitchell Parish. (P)Dinah Shore.

ALL I OWE IOWAY (1945) (w)Oscar Hammerstein II (m)Richard Rodgers. (I)Film: *State Fair* by the entire cast.

ALL I REALLY WANT TO DO (1964) (wm)Bob Dylan. (I)Bob Dylan (P)Cher. (P)The Byrds.

ALL I REMEMBER IS YOU (1939) (w)Eddie De Lange (m)Jimmy Van Heusen. (P)Tommy Dorsey and his Orchestra.

ALL I SEE IS YOU (1966) (wm)Clive Westlake—Ben Weisman. (P)Dusty Springfield.

ALL I WANT FOR CHRISTMAS (Is My Two Front Teeth) (1950) (wm)Donald Yetter Gardner. (P)Spike Jones.

ALL I WANTED (1986) (wm)Steve Walsh—Steve Morse. (P)Kansas.

ALL IN FUN (1939) (w)Oscar Hammerstein II (m)Jerome Kern. (I)Musical: *Very Warm for May* by Frances Mercer and Jack Whiting.

ALL IN LOVE IS FAIR (1973) (wm)Stevie Wonder. (P)Barbra Streisand.

ALL I'VE GOT TO DO (1963) (wm)John Lennon—Paul McCartney. (P)The Beatles.

ALL I'VE GOT TO GET NOW IS MY MAN (1940) (wm)Cole Porter. (I)Musical: *Panama Hattie* by Betty Hutton.

ALL MY LIFE (1936) (w)Sidney Mitchell (m)Sammy Stept. (I)Film: *Laughing Irish Eyes* by Phil Regan. Recorded by Fats Waller,Teddy Wilson,Ted Fiorito.

ALL MY LOVE (1950) (wm)Mitchell Parish. (P)Patti Page. (CR)Bing Crosby,Percy Faith,Guy Lombardo,Doris Day.

(You Were Made For)ALL MY LOVE (1960) (wm)Jackie Wilson—Billy Myles. (P)Jackie Wilson.

ALL MY LOVING (1963) (wm)John Lennon—Paul McCartney. (P)The Beatles.

ALL NIGHT LONG (1980) (wm)Joe Walsh. (P)Joe Walsh.

ALL NIGHT LONG (All Night) (1983) (wm)Lionel Richie. (P)Lionel Richie. No. 1 Chart Record.

ALL OF A SUDDEN MY HEART SINGS (See MY HEART SINGS)

ALL OF ME (1931) (wm)Seymour Simons—Gerald Marks. (I)Belle Baker. Early recordings by Paul Whiteman,Louis Armstrong. (R)1943 by Count Basie. (R)1952 by Johnny Ray. Most popular recording by Frank Sinatra.

ALL OF MY LIFE (1944) (wm)Irving Berlin. (P)Kate Smith. (CR)Bing Crosby,The Three Suns,Sammy Kaye.

ALL OF YOU (1954) (wm)Cole Porter. (I)Musical: *Silk Stockings* by Don Ameche.

ALL OF YOU (1984) (w-Eng)Cynthia Weil. (m)Tony Renis—Julio Iglesias. (P)Julio Iglesias and Diana Ross.

ALL OR NOTHING AT ALL (1940) (wm)Jack Lawrence—Arthur Altman. (P)1943 by Harry James and his Orchestra,vocal by Frank Sinatra. (R)1954 by Joe Foley.

ALL OUT OF LOVE (1980) (wm)Graham Russell. (P)Air Supply.

ALL OVER THE WORLD (1962) (w)Charles Tobias (m)Al Frisch. (P)Nat "King" Cole.

ALL OVER THE WORLD (1980) (wm)Jeff Lynne. (P)ELO.

ALL RIGHT (1983) (wm)Christopher Cross. (P)Christopher Cross.

ALL RIGHT NOW (1970) (wm)Paul Rodgers—Andy Fraser. (P)Free.

ALL SHE WANTS TO DO IS DANCE (1985) (wm)Danny Kortchmar. (P)Don Henley.

ALL SHOOK UP (1957) (wm)Otis Blackwell—Elvis Presley. (P)Elvis Presley. No. 1 Chart Record.

ALL THAT GLITTERS IS NOT GOLD (1945) (w)Lee Kuhn (m)Alice Cornett—Eddie Asherman. (P)Dinah Shore.

ALL THAT I AM (1966) (wm)Sid Tepper—Roy C. Bennett. (I)Film: *Spinout* by Elvis Presley and male chorus. Also recorded by Presley.

ALL THAT LOVE WENT TO WASTE (1972) (w)Sammy Cahn (m)George Barrie. (I)Film: *A Touch Of Class* by voice of Madeline Bell.

ALL THAT MEAT AND NO POTATOES (1941) (wm)Thomas "Fats" Waller—Ed Kirkeby. (P)Fats Waller.

ALL THE CATS JOIN IN (1944) (w)Alec Wilder—Ray Gilbert (m)Eddie Sauter. (I)Film: *Make Mine Music* (cartoon)by Benny Goodman and his Orchestra.

ALL THE CHILDREN IN A ROW (1984) (w)Fred Ebb (m)John Kander. (I)Musical: *The Rink* by Liza Minnelli.

ALL THE GOLD IN CALIFORNIA (1979) (wm)Larry Gatlin (P)Larry Gatlin & The Gatlin Brothers Band.

ALL THE KING'S HORSES (1930) (wm)Alec Wilder—Edward Brandt—Howard Dietz. (I)Revue: *Three's A Crowd* by Margaret Lee.

ALL THE LOVE IN THE WORLD (1986) (wm)John Spinks (P)The Outfield.

ALL THE RIGHT MOVES (1983) (wm)Tom Snow—Barry Alfonso. (I)Film: *All the Right Moves*. (P)Jennifer Warnes and Chris Thompson.

ALL THE THINGS YOU ARE (1939) (w)Oscar Hammerstein II (m)Jerome Kern. (I)Musical: *Very Warm For May*. Recorded by Tommy Dorsey,Artie Shaw,Frankie Masters,Frank Sinatra.

ALL THE TIME (1945) (Ralph Freed) (m)Sammy Fain. (I)Film: *No Leave,No Love* by Guy Lombardo and his Royal Canadians,vocal by Pat Kirkwood.

ALL THE TIME (1958) (wm)Jay Livingston—Ray Evans. (I)Musical: *Oh Captain!* by Tony Randall and Jacquelyn McKeever.

ALL THE WAY (1957) (w)Sammy Cahn (m)Jimmy Van Heusen. (I)Film: *The Joker Is Wild* by Frank Sinatra. Academy Award Winner.

ALL THIS AND HEAVEN TOO (1939) (w)Eddie De Lange (m)Jimmy Van Heusen. Promo song for film All This And Heaven Too. Recorded by Jimmy Dorsey,Tommy Dorsey,Charlie Barnet.

ALL THIS LOVE (1982) (wm)Eldra DeBarge. (P)DeBarge.

ALL THOSE YEARS AGO (1981) (wm)George Harrison. (P)George Harrison. Song was written as a tribute to John Lennon.

ALL THROUGH THE NIGHT (1784)Traditional Welsh song. Early recording by Henry Burr.

ALL THROUGH THE NIGHT (1934) (wm)Cole Porter. (I)Musical: *Anything Goes*. First recording by Paul Whiteman and his Orchestra.

ALL THROUGH THE NIGHT (1984) (wm)Jules Shear. (P)Cyndi Lauper.

ALL THROUGH THE DAY (1946) (w)Oscar Hammerstein II (m)Jerome Kern. (I)Film: *Centennial Summer* by Cornel Wilde,Larry Stevens and the voice of Louanne Hogan dubbing for Jeanne Crain. Recorded by Frank Sinatra,Perry Como, Margaret Whiting.

ALL TOGETHER NOW (1968) (wm)John Lennon—Paul McCartney. (I)Film: *Yellow Submarine* by The Beatles.

ALL TOO SOON (1940) (w)Carl Sigman (m)Duke Ellington. (P)Duke Ellington and his Orchestra.

ALL YOU NEED IS A QUARTER (1960) (w)Betty Comden—Adolph Green (m)Jule Styne. (I)Musical: *Do Re Mi* by the male chorus.

ALL YOU NEED IS LOVE (1967) (wm)John Lennon—Paul McCartney. (I)Film: *Yellow Submarine* by The Beatles. Recorded by The Beatles. No. 1 Chart Record.

ALL YOU WANT TO DO IS DANCE (1937) (w)Johnny Burke (m)Arthur Johnston. (I)Film: *Double Or Nothing* by Bing Crosby.

ALLAH'S HOLIDAY (1916) (w)Otto Harbach (m)Rudolf Friml. (I)Musical: *Katinka.*

ALLEGHENY AL (1937) (w)Oscar Hammerstein II (m)Jerome Kern. (I)Film: *High, Wide And Handsome* by Dorothy Lamour and Irene Dunne.

ALLEGHENY MOON (1956) (wm)Al Hoffman—Dick Manning. (P)Patti Page.

ALLENTOWN (1981) (wm)Billy Joel. (P)Billy Joel.

ALLERGIES (1981) (wm)Paul Simon. (P)Paul Simon.

ALLEY CAT (1962) (w)Jack Harlen (m)Frank Bjorn. (P)Bent Fabric. Vocal version by David Thorne. NARAS Award Winner.

ALLEY OOP (1960) (wm)Dallas Frazier. (P)The Hollywood Argyles. No. 1 Chart Record.

ALLEZ-VOUS-EN, GO AWAY (1953) (wm)Cole Porter. (I)Musical: *Can Can* by Lilo. (P)Kay Starr.

ALLISON'S THEME FROM PARRISH (1961) (m)Max Steiner. (I)Film: *Parrish* as soundtrack theme.

ALMOST ALWAYS (1953) (wm)Katherine Lichty—Lew Douglas—Frank Lavere. (P)Joni James.

ALMOST IN YOUR ARMS (Love Theme From Houseboat) (1958) (wm)Jay Livingston—Ray Evans. (I)Film: *Houseboat* by Sophia Loren. Film also starred Cary Grant.

ALMOST LIKE BEING IN LOVE (1947) (Alan Jay Lerner

(m)Frederick Loewe. (I)Musical: *Brigadoon* by David Brooks and Marion Bell. In film version (1954) by Gene Kelly. Most popular recording by Frank Sinatra.

ALMOST PARADISE (1956) (wm)Norman Petty. (P)The Norman Petty Trio.

ALMOST PARADISE (Love Theme from Footloose) (1984) (w)Dean Pitchford (m)Eric Carmen. (I)Film: *Footloose*. (P)Mike Reno and Ann Wilson.

ALMOST PERSUADED (1966) (wm)Glenn Sutton—Billy Sherrill. (P)David Houston. NARAS Award Winner.

ALMOST THERE (1964) (wm)Jack Keller—Gloria Shayne. (I)Film: *I'd Rather Be Rich*. (P)Andy Williams.

ALOHA OE (1878) (wm)Queen Liliuokalani. Probably the most famous song of Hawaii. Best known record by Bing Crosby.

ALONE AGAIN (Naturally) (1972) (wm)Raymond O'-Sullivan. (P)Gilbert O'Sullivan. No. 1 Chart Record

ALONE AT A TABLE FOR TWO (1935) (wm)Billy Hill,Daniel Richman—Ted Fiorito. (P)Ted Fiorito and his Orchestra. (CR)Guy Lombardo.

ALONE AT LAST (1952) (w)Bob Hilliard (m)Victor Young. (I)Film: *Something To Live For*.

ALONE AT LAST (1960) (wm)Johnny Lehmann. Theme based on Tchaikovsky's Piano Concerto No. 1. (P)Jackie Wilson.

ALONE TOGETHER (1932) (w)Howard Dietz (m)Arthur Schwartz. (I)Revue: *Flying Colors* by Jean Sargent. Danced to by Clifton Webb and Tamara Geva. First recording by Leo Reisman and his Orchestra.

ALONE TOO LONG (1954) (w)Dorothy Fields (m)Arthur Schwartz. (I)Musical: *By The Beautiful Sea* by Shirley Booth and Wilbur Evans. (P)Nat "King" Cole.

ALONE (1935) (w)Arthur Freed (m)Nacio Herb Brown. (I)Film: *A Night At The Opera* by Allan Jones and Kitty Carlisle. Recorded by Tommy Dorsey,Hal Kemp,Al Donahue and their Orchestras.

ALONE (1987) (wm)B. Steinberg—T. Kelly. (P)Heart. No. 1 Chart Record.

ALONG CAME JONES (1959) (wm)Jerry Lieber—Mike Stoller. (P)The Coasters. (R)1969 by Ray Stevens.

ALONG COMES A WOMAN (1984) (wm)Peter Cetera—Mark Goldenberg. (P)Chicago.

ALONG COMES MARY (1965) (wm)Tandyn Almer. (P)The Association.

ALONG THE NAVAJO TRAIL (1942) (wm)Larry Markes—Dick Charles—Eddie De Lange. (I)Film: *Don't Fence Me In*. (P)Bing Crosby with The Andrews Sisters. (CR)Gene Autry,Dinah Shore,Glenn Miller,Gene Krupa.

ALONG THE SANTA FE TRAIL (1940) (w)Al Dubin—Edwina Coolidge (m)Will Grosz. (I)Film: *Santa Fe Trail*. (P)Glenn Miller and his Orchestra,vocal by Ray Eberle. (CR)Bing Crosby,Sammy Kaye,Dick Jurgens.

ALONG WITH ME (1946) (wm)Harold Rome. (I)Musical: *Call Me Mister* by Danny Scholl and Paula Bane. (P)Margaret Whiting.

ALOUETTE (1879)Author unknown. Traditional French folk song.

ALRIGHT, OKAY, YOU WIN (1955) (wm)Sid Wyche—Mayme Watts. (P)Count Basie and his Orchestra,vocal by Joe Williams.

ALSO SPRACH ZARATHUSTRA (2001 Space Odyssey)Originally written in 1896 by Richard Strauss as a classical composition. Used as theme in film *2001 Space Odyssey*. (P)Eumir Deodato (1971) as a popular disco record.

ALVIN'S HARMONICA (1959) (wm)Ross Bagdasarian. (P)David Seville and The Chipmunks. David Seville is Ross Bagdasarian.

ALWAYS AND ALWAYS (1937) (w)Bob Wright—Chet Forrest (m)Edward Ward. (I)Film: *Mannequin* by Joan Crawford. Recorded by Larry Clinton and his Orchestra.

ALWAYS AND FOREVER (1976) (wm)Rod Temperton. (I)Heatwave.

ALWAYS IN ALL WAYS (w)Leo Robin (m)Richard Whiting-W. Franke Harling. (I)Film: *Monte Carlo* by Jack Buchanan and Jeanette MacDonald.

ALWAYS IN MY HEART (1942) (w)Kim Gannon (m)Ernesto Lecuona. (I)Film: *Always In My Heart* by Gloria Warren. Recorded by Glenn Miller,Jimmy Dorsey and their Orchestras. Also,Kenny Baker.

ALWAYS ON MY MIND (1971) (wm)Johnny Christopher—Wayne Thompson—Mark James. (P)1982 by Willie Nelson. NARAS Award Winner. (R)1988 by Pet Shop Boys.

ALWAYS (1925) (wm)Irving Berlin. (I)Vaudeville: by Gladys Clark and Henry Bergman. Early recordings by Vincent Lopez, George Olsen, Nick Lucas. (R)1940s by Benny Goodman, Gordon Jenkins, Sammy Kaye, Guy Lombardo and their Orchestras.

ALWAYS (1987) (wm)J. Lewis—D. Lewis—W. Lewis. (P)Atlantic Starr. No. 1 Chart Record.

IRVING BERLIN

It is generally agreed that Irving Berlin has written the definitive popular songs that describe American life. Let's list them. Jazz song: *Alexander's Ragtime Band*. World War I song: *Oh How I Hate to Get Up in the Morning*. World War II Song: *This is the Army, Mr. Jones*. Love song: *Always*. Patriotic song: *God Bless America*. Easter Song: *Easter Parade*. Christmas song: *White Christmas*.

Certainly an entire book could be devoted to this great man and his music. All I can do in this space is say "Thank You, Irving Berlin, for the musical legacy you have left the world."

ALWAYS SOMETHING THERE TO REMIND ME (1964) (w)Hal David (m)Burt Bacharach. (I)Sandi Shaw. (R)1983 Naked Eyes.

ALWAYS TOGETHER (1968) (wm)Bobby Miller. (P)The Dells.

ALWAYS TRUE TO YOU IN MY FASHION (1948) (wm)Cole Porter (I)Musical: *Kiss Me, Kate* by Lisa Kirk. In film version (1953)by Ann Miller and Tommy Rall.

AM I ASKING TOO MUCH (1948) (wm)Fay Whitman—Helen Miller. (P)Dinah Washington.

AM I BLUE? (1929) (w)Grant Clarke (m)Harry Akst. (I)Film: *On With The Show* by Ethel Waters. Recorded by Libby Holman.

AM I IN LOVE (1952) (wm)Jack Brooks. (I)Film: *Son of*

Paleface by Bob Hope and Jane Russell.

AM I IN LOVE? (1937) (w)Al Dubin (m)Harry Warren. (I)Film: *Mr. Dodd Takes The Air* by Kenny Baker

AM I IN LOVE? (1954) (w)Ted Varnick (m)Nick Acquaviva. (P)Joni James.

AM I THAT EASY TO FORGET (1958) (wm)Carl Belew— W. S. Stevenson—Shelby Singleton. (P)Carl Belew (country record) (R)1963 by Jerry Wallace. (R)1967 by Engelbert Humperdinck.

AMANDA (1986) (wm)Tom Scholz. (P)Boston. No. 1 Chart Record.

AMAPOLA (Pretty Little Poppy) (1924) (w-Eng)Albert Gamse (m)Joseph M. Lacalle. (I)The Castillians. (R)1940 by Jimmy Dorsey and his Orchestra,vocal by Helen O'Connell and Bob Eberly. No. 1 Chart Record.

AMARILLO (1941) (w)Lorenz Hart (m)Richard Rodgers. (I)Film: *They Met In Argentina.*

AMAZING GRACE (1779) (wm)John Newton. Old hymn popularized first by The Weavers. (R)1971 by Judy Collins.

AMELIA (1976) (wm)Joni Mitchell. (P)Joni Mitchell.

AMEN (Yea-Man) (1942) (wm)Roger Segure—Bill Hardy—Vic Schoen. (P)Woody Herman and his Orchestra. (CR)Abe Lyman and his Orchestra.

AMEN (1964) (wm)John W. Pate, Sr. —Curtis Mayfield. (P)The Impressions.

AMEN (1968) (wm)Otis Redding. (P)Otis Redding.

AMERICA IS MY HOME (1968) (wm)James Brown— Hayward Moore. (P)James Brown.

AMERICA THE BEAUTIFUL (1895) (w)Katherine Lee Bates (m)Samuel Ward. Very popular American patriotic song. Early recording 1925 by Louise Homer.

AMERICA (1957) (w)Stephen Sondheim (m)Leonard Bernstein. (I)Musical: *West Side Story* by Chita Rivera,Reri Grist,Marilyn Cooper and The Shark Girls. Also in film version.

AMERICA (1968) (wm)Paul Simon. (P)Simon and Garfunkel. (R)1972 by Yes.

AMERICA (1981) (wm)Neil Diamond. (I)Film: *The Jazz Singer* by Neil Diamond. Recorded by Diamond.

AMERICA, I LOVE YOU (1915) (wm)Edgar Leslie—Archie Gottler. (I)Sam Ash and his Orchestra.

AMERICAN BEAUTY ROSE (1950) (wm)Hal David— Redd Evans—Arthur Altman. (P)Frank Sinatra. (CR)Eddy Howard.

AMERICAN HEARTBEAT (1982) (wm)Frank Sullivan— Jim Peterik. (P)Survivor.

AMERICAN IN PARIS,AN (1929) (m)George Gershwin. (P)Film: *Rhapsody In Blue.* (R)Film: *An American In Paris* danced by Gene Kelly. Premiere performance was by The New York Philharmonic Society, conducted by Walter Damrosch.

AMERICAN MUSIC (1982) (wm)Parker McGee. (P)The Pointer Sisters.

AMERICAN PATROL (1891) (m)F. W. Meacham. Very popular American patriotic song. First recording by Sousa's Band. (R)1942 by Glenn Miller and his Orchestra.

AMERICAN PIE (1971) (wm)Don McLean. (P)Don McLean. No. 1 Chart Record. This song was written as a tribute to Buddy Holly.

AMERICAN STORM (1986) (wm)Bob Seger. (P)Bob Seger and The Silver Bullet Band.

AMERICAN TUNE (1973) (wm)Paul Simon. (P)Paul Simon.

AMONG MY SOUVENIRS (1927) (w)Edgar Leslie (m)Horatio Nicholls. (I)In England by Jack Hylton and his Orchestra. In America by Paul Whiteman and his Orchestra. (CR)Ben Selvin,The Revelers,Roger Wolfe Kahn. (R)1959 by Connie Francis. (R)1976 by Marty Robbins.

AMOR (1943) (w-Eng)Sunny Skylar (m)Gabriel Ruiz. (I)Film: *Broadway Rhythm* by Ginny Simms. (P)Andy Russell. (CR)Bing Crosby,Xavier Cugat,The Four Aces.

AMSTERDAM (1967) (w-Eng)Mort Shuman—Eric Blau. (m)Jacques Brel. (I)Musical: *Jacques Brel Is Alive And Well And Living In Paris* by Mort Shuman.

AN AMERICAN DREAM (1976) (wm)Rodney Crowell. (P)The Dirt Band.

ANASTASIA (1956) (w)Paul Francis Webster (m)Alfred Newman. (I)Film: *Anastasia* as sound track theme. (P)Pat Boone.

ANATOLE (of Paris) (1939) (wm)Sylvia Fine. (I)Revue: *The Straw Hat Revue* by Danny Kaye. (R)1947 in film The Secret Life Of Walter Mitty by Danny Kaye.

ANCHORS AWEIGH (1906) (w)Alfred Hart Miles—R. Lovell (m)Charles A. Zimmerman. Official anthem of The United States Naval Academy. Recorded by The United States Naval Academy Band.

AND ALL THAT JAZZ (1975) (wm)Fred Ebb—John Kander. (I)Musical: *Chicago* by Chita Rivera.

AND HER TEARS FLOWED LIKE WINE (1943) (w)Joe Greene (m)Stan Kenton—Charles Lawrence. (P)Stan Kenton and his Orchestra,vocal by Anita O'Day. (CR)Ella Fitzgerald.

AND I AM TELLING YOU I'M NOT GOING (1981) (w)Tom Eyen (m)Henry Krieger. (I)Musical: *Dreamgirls* by Jennifer Holliday. Recorded by Ms. Holliday.

AND I LOVE HER (1964) (wm)John Lennon—Paul McCartney. (P)Film: *A Hard Day's Night* by The Beatles. Recorded by The Beatles.

AND I LOVE YOU SO (1970) (wm)Don McLean. (P)Perry Como.

AND LOVE WAS BORN (1932) (w)Oscar Hammerstein II (m)Jerome Kern. (I)Musical: *Music In The Air* by Reginald Werrenrath.

AND RUSSIA IS HER NAME (1943) (w)E. Y. Harburg (m)Jerome Kern. (I)Film: *And Russia Is Her Name.*

AND SO DO I (1940) (w)Eddie De Lange (m)Paul Mann— Stephen Weiss. (P)Jimmy Dorsey and his Orchestra,vocal by Helen O'Connell.

AND SO TO BED (1946) (w)Johnny Mercer (m)Robert Emmett Dolan. (P)Dinah Shore.

AND SO TO SLEEP AGAIN (1951) (wm)Joe Marsala— Sunny Skylar. (P)Patti Page. (CR)Dick Haymes.

AND THE ANGELS SING (1939) (w)Johnny Mercer (m)Ziggy Elman. (P)Benny Goodman and his Orchestra,vocal by Martha Tilton. Trumpet Solo by Ziggy Elman. Featured in film *The Benny Goodman Story* (1956). (CR)Bing Crosby.

AND THE BEAT GOES ON (1979) (wm)Leon Sylvers— Stephen Shockley—William Shelby. (P)The Whispers.

AND THE GREEN GRASS GREW ALL AROUND (1912) (w)William Jerome (m)Harry Von Tilzer. (I)Walter Van Brunt.

AND THEN THERE'S MAUDE (1972) (w)Alan and Marilyn Bergman (m)Dave Grusin. (I)TV show *Maude* starring Beatrice Arthur.

AND THEN YOU KISSED ME (1944) (w)Sammy Cahn (m)Jule Styne. (I)Film: *Step Lively* by Frank Sinatra.

AND THIS IS MY BELOVED (1953) (wm)Robert Wright—George Forrest. Adapted from a theme by Borodin. (I)Musical: *Kismet* by Richard Kiley, Alfred Drake, Doretta Morrow and Henry Calvin.

AND WHEN I DIE (1966) (wm)Laura Nyro—Jerry Sears. (P)Laura Nyro. (R)1969 by Blood, Sweat and Tears.

AND YOU'LL BE HOME (1950) (w)Johnny Burke (m)Jimmy Van Heusen. (I)Film: *Mr. Music* by Bing Crosby.

AND YOUR BIRD CAN SING (1966) (wm)John Lennon—Paul McCartney. (I)The Beatles.

ANDALUCIA (1928) (m)Ernesto Lecuona. Solo piano suite. Popular song version known as At The Crossroads.

ANDIAMO (1950) (w)Dorothy Fields (m)Harold Arlen. (I)Film: *Mr. Imperium* by Ezio Pinza.

ANEMA E CORE (1950) (w-Eng)Mann Curtis—Harry Akst (m)Salve d'Esposito. (I)Italian Film: *Anema E Core* by Ferrucia Tagliavani. (P)Eddie Fisher.

ANGEL (1945) (w)Arthur Freed (m)Harry Warren. (I)Film: *Yolanda And The Thief* by Lucille Bremer.

ANGEL (1964) (w)Jay Livingston—Ray Evans (m)Max Steiner. (I)Film: *Those Calloways*. (P)Johnny Tillotson.

ANGEL (1973) (wm)Rory Bourke—Gayle Barnhill. (P)Aretha Franklin.

ANGEL (1985) (wm)Madonna—Steve Bray. (P)Madonna.

ANGEL (1987) (wm)S. Tyler—D. Child. (P)Aerosmith.

ANGEL BABY (1958) (wm)Joe Penny. (P)Dean Martin.

ANGEL BABY (1960) (wm)Rose Hamlin. (P)Rosie And The Originals.

ANGEL EYES (1953) (w)Earl Brent (m)Matt Dennis. (I)Film: *Jennifer* by Matt Dennis.

ANGEL IN DISGUISE (1939) (w)Kim Gannon (m)Paul Mann—Stephen Weiss. (I)Film: *It All Came True*. (P)Dick Todd.

ANGEL IN YOUR ARMS (1977) (wm)Herbert Ivey—Terry Woodford—Thomas Brasfield. (P)Hot.

ANGEL OF THE MORNING (1967) (wm)Chip Taylor. (P)Merrilee Rush. (R)1981 by Juice Newton.

ANGEL SMILE (1958) (wm)Luther Dixon—Billy Dawn Smith—Bert Keyes. (P)Nat "King" Cole.

ANGELA MIA (My Angel) (1928) (w)Lew Pollack (m)Erno Rapee. (I)Film: *Street Angel* which starred Charles Farrell and Janet Gaynor. Recorded by Paul Whiteman, Vincent Lopez and their Orchestras.

ANGELINA (The Waitress at the Pizzeria) (1944) (wm)Allen Roberts—Doris Fisher. (P)Louis Prima and his Orchestra.

ANGELS IN THE SKY (1956) (wm)Dick Glasser. (P)The Crew Cuts.

ANGIE (1973) (wm)Keith Richards—Mick Jagger. (P)The Rolling Stones. No. 1 Chart Record.

ANGIE BABY (1974) (wm)Alan O'Day. (P)Helen Reddy. No. 1 Chart Record.

ANGRY (1933) (w)Dudley Mecum (m)Henry Brunies—Jules Cassard—Merritt Brunies. (I)New Orleans Rhythm Kings. (R)1939)Bob Crosby and his Orchestra. (R)1951 by Kay Starr.

ANIMAL (1987) (wm)Clark—Collen—Elliott—Lange—Savage. (P)Def Leppard.

ANIMAL CRACKERS IN MY SOUP (1935) (w)Ted Koehler—Irving Caesar (m)Ray Henderson. (I)Film: *Curly Top* by Shirley Temple. (CR)Don Bestor and his Or-

chestra.

ANITRA'S DANCE (1888) (m)Edvard Grieg. Classical selection from Peer Gynt Suite.

ANNA (El Negro Zambon) (w)F. Giordano (m)R. Vatro. (I)Italian Film: *Anna* by Flo Sandons dubbing for Silvana Mangano. (P)Silvana Mangano.

ANNA (Go to Him) (1962) (wm)Arthur Alexander. (I)The Beatles. (CR)Perez Prado, Ray Bloch and their Orchestras.

ANNIE DOESN'T LIVE HERE ANYMORE (1933) (w)Joe Young—Johnny Burke (m)Harold Spina. (P)Fred Waring's Pennsylvanians.

ANNIE LAURIE (1830) (w)William Douglas (m)Lady John Scott. Famous Scottish song. Recorded in 1910 by John McCormack.

ANNIE'S SONG (1974) (wm)John Denver (P)John Denver.

ANNIVERSARY SONG (1946) (wm)Saul Chaplin—Al Jolson. Based on Danube Waves. (P)Al Jolson. Film: *The Jolson Story* by dubbed in voice of Jolson.

ANNIVERSARY WALTZ, THE (1941) (wm)Al Dubin—Dave Franklin. (P)Bing Crosby.

ANOTHER AUTUMN (1951) (w)Alan Jay Lerner (m)Frederick Loewe. (I)Musical: *Paint Your Wagon* by Tony Bavaar.

ANOTHER BRICK IN THE WALL (1980) (wm)Roger Waters. (P)Pink Floyd. No. 1 Chart Record.

ANOTHER CUP OF COFFEE (1964) (w)Earl Shuman (m)Leon Carr. (P)Brook Benton.

ANOTHER DAY (1971) (wm)Paul and Linda McCartney. (P)Paul McCartney.

ANOTHER GIRL (1965) (wm)John Lennon—Paul McCartney. (I)Film: *Help* by The Beatles. Also on record.

ANOTHER HUNDRED PEOPLE (1970) (wm)Stephen Sondheim. (I)Musical: *Company* by Pamela Myers.

ANOTHER NIGHT (1966) (w)Hal David (m)Burt Bacharach. (I)Dionne Warwick. One of the few songs by this team that was not a smash hit.

ANOTHER NIGHT LIKE THIS (1947) (w-Eng)Harry Ruby (m)Ernesto Lecuona. (I)Film: *Carnival in Costa Rica* by Dick Haymes.

ANOTHER OP'NIN, ANOTHER SHOW (1948) (wm)Cole Porter (I)Musical: *Kiss Me, Kate* by Annabelle Hill and the ensemble.

ANOTHER PART OF ME (1986) (wm)Michael Jackson. (P)Michael Jackson. Written for Disney short film Captain Eo.

ANOTHER SATURDAY NIGHT (1963) (wm)Sam Cooke. (P)Sam Cooke. (R)1974 by Cat Stevens

ANOTHER SLEEPLESS NIGHT (1959) (w)Howard Greenfield (m)Neil Sedaka. (P)Jimmy Clanton.

(Hey Won't You Play)ANOTHER SOMEBODY DONE SOMEBODY WRONG SONG) (1975) (wm)Chips Moman—Larry Butler. (P)B. J. Thomas.

ANOTHER TIME, ANOTHER PLACE (1958) (wm)Jay Livingston—Ray Evans. (I)Film: *Another Time, Another Place*. (P)Don Cherry.

ANOTHER TIME, ANOTHER PLACE (1961) (wm)Richard Adler. (I)Musical: *Kwamina* by Sally Ann Howes.

ANOTHER TIME, ANOTHER PLACE (1971) (wm)Mike Leander—Edward Seago. (P)Englebert Humperdinck.

ANSWER ME, MY LOVE (1954) (w-Eng)Carl Sigman (m)Gerhard Winkler—Fred Rauch. (P)Nat "King" Cole.

ANTICIPATION (1972) (wm)Carly Simon (P)Carly Simon.

ANTONY AND CLEOPATRA THEME (1963) (m)Alex North. (I)Film: *Antony and Cleopatra* as the love theme.

ANVIL CHORUS (1853) (m)Giuseppe Verdi (I)Opera: *IL Trovatore.* (R)1941 by Glenn Miller and his Orchestra.

ANY BONDS TODAY (1941) (wm)Irving Berlin. The official song of the United States Treasury Department's savings bond campaign. (I)Barry Wood.

ANY DAY NOW (1962) (wm)Bob Hilliard—Burt Bacharach. (P)Chuck Jackson.

ANY MOMENT NOW (1944) (w)E. Y. Harburg (m)Jerome Kern. (I)Film: *Can't Help Singing* by Deanna Durbin.

ANY OLD PLACE WITH YOU (1919) (w)Lorenz Hart (m)Richard Rodgers. (I)Musical: *A Lonely Romeo.* This was the first published song of this great songwriting team.

ANY OLD TIME OF DAY (1964) (w)Hal David (m)Burt Bacharach. (P)Dionne Warwick.

ANY PLACE I HANG MY HAT IS HOME (1946) (w)Johnny Mercer (m)Harold Arlen. (I)Musical: *St. Louis Woman* by Robert Pope.

ANY TIME (1948) (wm)Herbert Happy Lawson. (P)1948 by Eddy Arnold (country record). (R)1951 by Eddie Fisher.

ANY TIME AT ALL (1964) (wm)John Lennon—Paul McCartney. (P)The Beatles. (R)1965 by Frank Sinatra.

ANY WAY THE WIND BLOWS (1959) (w)By Bunham (m)Marilyn Hooven—Joe Hooven. (I)Film: *Please Don't Eat The Daisies* by Doris Day.

ANY WAY YOU WANT IT (1964) (wm)Dave Clark. (P)The Dave Clark Five.

ANY WAY YOU WANT IT (1979) (wm)Steve Perry—Neil Schon. (P)Journey.

ANY WAY YOU WANT ME (1956) (wm)Aaron Schroeder—Cliff Owens. (P)Elvis Presley.

ANYBODY BUT ME (1960) (wm)Ronnie Self—Dub Allbritten. (P)Brenda Lee.

ANYONE CAN WHISTLE (1964) (wm)Stephen Sondheim. (I)Musical: *Anyone Can Whistle* by Lee Remick.

ANYONE WHO HAD A HEART (1964) (w)Hal David (m)Burt Bacharach. (P)Dionne Warwick. (CR)Cilla Black.

ANYONE WOULD LOVE YOU (1959) (wm)Harold Rome. (I)Musical: *Destry Rides Again* by Andy Griffith and Dolores Gray.

ANYTHING CAN HAPPEN-MAMBO (1954) (w)Sid Wayne (m)Joe Sherman. (P)Dolores Hawkins.

ANYTHING FOR YOU (1987) (wm)G. M. Estefan. (P)Gloria Estefan & Miami Sound Machine.

(I Would Do)ANYTHING FOR YOU (1932) (wm)Claude Hopkins—Alex Hill—Bob Williams. (I)Theme song of Claude Hopkins and his Orchestra.

ANYTHING GOES (1934) (wm)Cole Porter. (I)Musical: *Anything Goes* by Ethel Merman. (CR)Paul Whiteman and his Orchestra. (R)1967 by Harper's Bizarre.

ANYTHING THAT'S PART OF YOU (1962) (wm)Don Robertson. (P)Elvis Presley.

ANYTHING YOU CAN DO (1946) (wm)Irving Berlin. (I)Musical: *Annie Get Your Gun* by Ethel Merman and Ray Middleton. In film version (1950)by Betty Hutton and Howard Keel.

ANYTIME (I'll Be There) (1975) (wm)Paul Anka. (P)Frank Sinatra.

ANYTIME AT ALL (1961) (wm)Richard Adler. (P)Frank Sinatra.

ANYWHERE (1945) (w)Sammy Cahn (m)Jule Styne. (I)Film: *Tonight And Every Night* by Janet Blair.

ANYWHERE I WANDER (1952) (wm)Frank Loesser. (I)Film: *Hans Christian Andersen* by Danny Kaye. (P)Julius La Rosa.

APACHE (1960) (m)Jorgen Ingmann. (I)In England by The Shadows. (P)In America by Jorgen Ingmann.

APACHE DANCE (1861) (m)Jacques Offenbach. From ballet Le Papillon. Famous classical composition.

APALACHICOLA, FLA. (1947) (w)Johnny Burke (m)Jimmy Van Heusen. (I)Film: *Road To Rio* by Bob Hope and Bing Crosby.

APPLE DOESN'T FALL, THE (1984) (wm)Fred Ebb—John Kander. (I)Musical: *The Rink* by Liza Minnelli.

AN APPLE FOR THE TEACHER (1938) (w)Johnny Burke (m)James V. Monaco. (I)Film: *The Star Maker* by Bing Crosby and Linda Ware. (P)Bing Crosby and Connee Boswell.

APPLE HONEY (1944) (m)Woody Herman. (P)Woody Herman and his Orchestra.

APRIL FOOL (1925) (w)Lorenz Hart (m)Richard Rodgers. (I)Musical: *Garrick Gaieties* by Betty Starbuck and Romney Brent.

APRIL FOOLS, THE (1969) (w)Hal David (m)Burt Bacharach. (I)Film: *The April Fools* on the soundtrack by Percy Faith and his Orchestra. (P)Dionne Warwick.

APRIL IN PARIS (1932) (w)E. Y. Harburg (m)Vernon Duke. (I)Revue: *Walk A Little Faster* by Evelyn Hoey. First recording by Marian Chase. (CR)Freddy Martin, Henry King and their orchestras. (R)1951 by Count Basie and his Orchestra. Basie's arrangement was based on one by jazz organist Wild Bill Davis.

APRIL IN PORTUGAL (1953) (w-Eng)Jimmy Kennedy (m)Paul Ferrao. (P)Les Baxter and his Orchestra. Vocal versions by Vic Damone and Tony Martin.

APRIL LOVE (1957) (w)Paul Francis Webster (m)Sammy Fain. (I)Film: *April Love* by Pat Boone. (P)Pat Boone.

APRIL PLAYED THE FIDDLE (1940) (w)Johnny Burke (m)James V. Monaco. (I)Film: *If I Had My Way* by Bing Crosby. (P)Bing Crosby.

APRIL SHOWERS (1921) (w)B. G. De Sylva (m)Louis Silvers. (I)Musical: *Bombo* by Al Jolson. Recorded by Jolson. (CR)Paul Whiteman, Ernie Hare, Charles Harrison, Arthur Fields. (R)1947 by Guy Lombardo and his Royal Canadians.

APRIL SNOW (1944) (w)Dorothy Fields (m)Sigmund Romberg. (I)Musical: *Up In Central Park* by Maureen Cannon and Wilbur Evans.

APURKSADY (1938) (m)Chappie Willet—Gene Krupa. (P)Theme song of Gene Krupa and his Orchestra.

AQUARIUS (1967) (w)Gerome Ragni—James Rado. (m)Galt MacDermot. (I)Musical: *Hair* by the company in the off Broadway version. By Ronald Dyson in the Broadway version. (P)The Fifth Dimension in a medley with Let The Sunshine In. No. 1 Chart Record. NARAS Award Winner.

ARABY (1915) (wm)Irving Berlin. (I)Harry Macdonough. This song was not one of Berlin's big hits.

ARE YOU HAPPY? (1968) (wm)Kenny Gamble—Theresa Bell—Jerry Butler. (P)Jerry Butler.

ARE YOU HAVIN' ANY FUN? (1939) (w)Jack Yellen (m)Sammy Fain. (I)Revue: *George White's Scandals of 1939* by Ella Logan. Recorded by Tommy Dorsey and his Orchestra.

ARE YOU LONESOME TONIGHT? (1926) (wm)Roy Turk—Lou Handman. (I)Vaughn Deleath. (R)1950 by Blue Barron and his Orchestra. (R)1960 by Elvis Presley. No. 1 Chart Record. (R)1974 by Donny Osmond.

ARE YOU MAKIN' ANY MONEY? (1933) (wm)Herman Hupfeld. (I)Film: *Moonlight And Pretzels* by Lillian Miles. Recorded by Paul Whiteman and his Orchestra.

ARE YOU MAN ENOUGH (1973) (wm)Dennis Lambert—Brian Potter. (I)Film: *Shaft In Africa* by the voices of The Four Tops. (P)The Four Tops.

ARE YOU MY LOVE? (1936) (w)Lorenz Hart (m)Richard Rodgers. (I)Film: *Dancing Pirate* by Steffi Duna.

ARE YOU REALLY MINE? (1958) (wm)Al Hoffman—Dick Manning—Mark Markwell. (P)Jimmie Rodgers.

ARE YOU SINCERE? (1957) (wm)Wayne Walker. (P)Andy Williams.

ARE YOU SURE (1960) (wm)Meredith Willson. (I)Musical: *The Unsinkable Molly Brown* by Tammy Grimes,Jack Harrold and the Chorus.

ARE YOU THERE (With Another Girl) (1965) (w)Hal David (m)Burt Bacharach. (P)Dionne Warwick.

ARE YOU WITH IT? (1945) (w)Arnold B. Horwitt (m)Harry Revel. (I)Musical: *Are You With It?* by Dolores Gray.

AREN'T YOU GLAD YOU'RE YOU (1945) (w)Johnny Burke (m)Jimmy Van Heusen. (I)Film: *The Bells Of St. Mary's* by Bing Crosby. (P)Bing Crosby. (CR)The Pied Pipers,Les Brown,Tommy Dorsey.

AREN'T YOU KIND OF GLAD WE DID? (1946) (w)Ira Gershwin (m)George Gershwin. (I)Film: *The Shocking Miss Pilgrim* by Dick Haymes and Betty Grable.

ARIZONA (1969) (wm)Kenny Young. (P)Mark Lindsay.

ARKANSAS TRAVELER,THE (1851). Composers unknown. Early recording by Len Spencer. (R)Fiddlin' John Carson.

ARM IN ARM (1963) (wm)Meredith Willson. (I)Musical: *Here's Love* by Janis Paige.

ARMS FOR THE LOVE OF AMERICA (1941) (wm)Irving Berlin. Official Army Ordnance Song. No artist credited with introduction.

ARMY AIR CORPS SONG,THE (1942) (wm)Robert Crawford. Official song of the United States Air Corps. (I)Musical: *Winged Victory*. Recorded 1943 by Alvino Rey and his Orchestra.

AROUND THE CORNER (1930) (w)Gus Kahn (m)Art Kassel. (P)Art Kassel and his Orchestra. (CR)Leo Reisman and his Orchestra.

AROUND THE WORLD (1956) (w)Harold Adamson (m)Victor Young. (I)Film: *Around The World In Eighty Days* as soundtrack theme. (P)Victor Young and his Orchestra. Vocal version by Jane Morgan.

ARRIVEDERCI, ROMA (1954) (w-Eng)Carl Sigman (M)Renato Rascel. (I)In United States by The Three Suns. Recorded by Georgia Gibbs. In film *The Seven Hills Of Home* (1958)by Mario Lanza.

ARROW THROUGH ME (1979) (wm)Paul McCartney. (P)Wings.

ARTHUR MURRAY TAUGHT ME DANCING IN A HURRY (1942) (w)Johnny Mercer (m)Victor Schertzinger. (I)Film: *The Fleet's In* by Jimmy Dorsey and his Orchestra, vocal by Bob Eberly and Helen O'Connell. (CR)The King Sisters.

ARTHUR'S THEME (1981) (wm)Carole Bayer Sager—Christopher Cross—Burt Bacharach—Peter Allen. (I)Film: *Arthur*. (P)Christopher Cross. No. 1 Chart Record. Academy Award Winner.

ARTIFICIAL FLOWERS (1960) (w)Sheldon Harnick (m)Jerry Bock. (I)Musical: *Tenderloin* by Ron Husmann and The Parishioners. (P)Bobby Darin.

ARTISTRY IN RHYTHM (1941) (m)Stan Kenton. (P)Theme Song of Stan Kenton and his Orchestra.

ARTISTS LIFE (1867) (m)Johann Strauss. Famous Viennese Waltz.

AS I WENT OUT ONE MORNING (1968) (wm)Bob Dylan (P)Bob Dylan.

AS IF I DIDN'T HAVE ENOUGH ON MY MIND (1946) (w)Charles Henderson (m)Lionel Newman—Harry James. (I)Film: *Do You Love Me?* by Dick Haymes.

AS LONG AS HE NEEDS ME (1960) (wm)Lionel Bart. (I)Musical: *Oliver!* by Georgia Brown. (P)Shirley Bassey.

AS LONG AS I LIVE (1934) (w)Ted Koehler (m)Harold Arlen (I)Revue: *Cotton Club Parade* by Lena Horne and Avon Long. Recorded 1941 by Benny Goodman and his Orchestra.

AS LONG AS I LIVE (1945) (w)Charles Tobias (m)Max Steiner. Adaptation of a theme from Film: *Saratoga Trunk.*

AS LONG AS I'M DREAMING (1947) (w)Johnny Burke (m)Jimmy Van Heusen. (I)Film: *Welcome Stranger* by Bing Crosby. (P)Bing Crosby. (CR)Tex Beneke and his Orchestra.

AS LONG AS I'VE GOT MY MAMMY (1925) (w)B. G. De Sylva (m)Joseph Meyer—James F. Hanley. (I)Musical: *Big Boy* by Al Jolson.

AS LONG AS THERE'S MUSIC (1944) (w)Sammy Cahn (m)Jule Styne. (I)Film: *Step Lively* by Frank Sinatra.

AS LONG AS WE GOT EACH OTHER (1985) (w)John Bettis (m)Steven Dorff. (I)T. V. Series: *Growing Pains* by B. J. Thomas.

AS SIMPLE AS THAT (1961) (wm)Jerry Herman. (I)Musical: *Milk And Honey* by Robert Weede and Mimi Benzell.

AS TEARS GO BY (1966) (wm)Mick Jagger—Keith Richards—Andrew Oldham. (I)Marianne Faithfull. (P)The Rolling Stones.

AS THE BACKS GO TEARING BY (1909) (w)John Thomas Keady (m)Carl Blaisdell. Dartmouth University School Song.

AS THE GIRLS GO (1948) (w)Harold Adamson (m)Jimmy McHugh. (I)Musical: *As The Girls Go* by Bobby Clark.

AS TIME GOES BY (1931) (wm)Herman Hupfeld. (I)Revue: *Everybody's Welcome* by Frances Williams. Recorded by Rudy Vallee. (R)Film: *Casablanca* (1942)by Dooley Wilson. (R)1952 by Ray Anthony and his Orchestra.

AS YOU DESIRE ME (1932) (wm)Allie Wrubel. Promo song for Film: *As You Desire Me*. Recorded by Russ Columbo. (R)1940s by Tony Martin.

ASCOT GAVOTTE (1956) (w)Alan Jay Lerner (m)Frederick Loewe. (I)Musical: *My Fair Lady* by the ensemble.

ASIA MINOR (1951) (wm)Roger King Mozian. (I)Machito and his Orchestra. (R)1961 by Kokomo.

ASK ANYONE IN LOVE (1960) (wm)Mr. and Mrs. Ted Shapiro. (P)Tony Bennett.

ASK ANYONE WHO KNOWS (1947) (wm)Al Kaufman—

Sol Marcus—Eddie Seiler. (P)Eddy Howard. (CR)The Ink Spots,Margaret Whiting.

ASK ME (1956) (w-Eng)Sunny Skylar (m)Heino Gaze. (P)Nat "King" Cole

ASK ME (1964) (w-Eng)Bill Giant—Florence Kaye—Bernie Baum. (m)Domenico Modugno. (P)Elvis Presley.

ASK ME WHY (1963) (wm)John Lennon—Paul McCartney. (P)The Beatles.

ASK THE LONELY (1965) (wm)William Stevenson—Ivy Hunter. (P)The Four Tops.

ASKING FOR YOU (1960) (w)Betty Comden—Adolph Green (m)Jule Styne. (I)Musical: *Do Re Mi* by John Reardon.

ASLEEP IN THE DEEP (1897) (w)Arthur Lamb (m)Henry Petrie. Famous song usually performed by bass or baritone singers.

AT A GEORGIA CAMP MEETING (1897) (wm)Kerry Mills. (I)Vern Ossman.

AT A PERFUME COUNTER (On The Rue De La Paix) (1938) (w)Edgar Leslie (m)Joe Burke. (I)Morton Downey and Wini Shaw in nightclub. (P)Jimmy Dorsey and his Orchestra. (CR)Blue Barron.

AT DAWNING (1906) (w)Nelle Richmond Eberhart (m)Charles Wakefield Cadman. Popular American song. No artist credited with introduction.

AT LAST (1942) (w)Mack Gordon (m)Harry Warren. (I)Film: *Orchestra Wives* by Glenn Miller and his Orchestra. (P)Glenn Miller. (R)1952 by Ray Anthony and his Orchestra.

AT LAST! AT LAST! (1951) (w-Eng)Florence Miles (m)Charles Trenet. (P)Tony Martin.

AT LONG LAST LOVE (1938) (wm)Cole Porter. (I)Musical: *You Never Know* by Clifton Webb. Recorded by Ozzie Nelson, Larry Clinton and their Orchestras.

AT PEACE WITH THE WORLD (1926) (wm)Irving Berlin. (P)Al Jolson. (CR)Isham Jones and his Orchestra.

AT SEVENTEEN (1975) (wm)Janis Ian. (P)Janis Ian.

AT SUNDOWN (1927) (wm)Walter Donaldson. (I)Cliff Edwards at The Palace Theatre in New York City. (P)George Olsen and his Orchestra. No. 1 Chart Record.

AT THE BALALAIKA (1939) (w)Eric Maschwitz—Bob Wright—Chet Forrest (m)George Posford—Herbert Stothart. (I)Film: *Balalaika* by Ilona Massey and The Russian Art Choir. Recorded by Orrin Tucker, Abe Lyman and their Orchestras.

AT THE BALLET (1975) (w)Edward Kleban (m)Marvin Hamlisch. (I)Musical: *A Chorus Line* by Carole Bishop, Nancy Lane and Kay Cole.

AT A CANDLELIGHT CAFE (1947) (wm)Mack David. (I)Film: *Tisa.* (P)Gordon MacRae. (CR)Dinah Shore.

AT THE CLUB (1965) (wm)Gerry Goffin—Carole King. (P)The Drifters.

AT THE CODFISH BALL (1936) (w)Sidney Mitchell (m)Lew Pollack. (I)Film: *Captain January* by Shirley Temple and Buddy Ebsen.

AT THE CROSSROADS (1942) (w-Eng)Bob Russell (m)Ernesto Lecuona. Adapted from Malaguena from Andalucia Suite. (P)Jimmy Dorsey and his Orchestra.

AT THE DEVIL'S BALL (1912) (wm)Irving Berlin. (P)The Peerless Quartet.

AT THE FLYING "W" (1948) (wm)Allie Wrubel. (P)Tex Beneke and his Orchestra.

AT THE HOP (1957) (wm)A. Singer—J. Medora—D. White. (P)Danny And The Juniors. No. 1 Chart Record.

AT THE JAZZ BAND BALL (wm)Edwin Edwards—James La Rocca—Anthony Sparbaro—Larry Shields. (P)The Original Dixieland Jazz Band.

AT THE SCENE (1966) (wm)Dave Clark—Lenny Davidson. (P)The Dave Clark Five.

AT THE ZOO (1967) (wm)Paul Simon. (P)Simon and Garfunkel.

AT THIS MOMENT (1981) (wm)Billy Vera. (I)Billy Vera and The Beaters. Reintroduced in TV series: *Family Ties* by Billy And The Beaters (1985). (R)Billy and the Beaters. No. 1 Chart Record.

AT YOUR BECK AND CALL (1938) (wm)Eddie De Lange—Buck Ram. (P)Jimmy Dorsey and his Orchestra.

AT YOUR COMMAND (1931) (wm)Harry Tobias—Harry Barris—Bing Crosby. (P)Bing Crosby. No. 1 Chart Record.

ATHENA (1954) (wm)Bert Pollack—Hugh Martin—Ralph Blane. Film: *Athena* as soundtrack theme. (P)Don Cornell.

ATLANTA, G. A. (1945) (w)Sunny Skylar (m)Arthur Shaftel. (P)Woody Herman and his Orchestra. (CR)Sammy Kaye and his Orchestra.

ATLANTIS (1968) (wm)Donovan Leitch. (P)Donovan.

ATTACK (1965) (wm)Sandy Linzer—Denny Randell. (I)Film: *A Girl In Her Daddy's Bikini.* (P)The Toys

ATTITUDE DANCING (1975) (wm)Jacob Brackman—Carly Simon. (P)Carly Simon.

AU REVOIR AGAIN (1947) (w)Nikki Mason (m)Teri Josefovits. (P)Jean Sablon.

AU REVOIR BUT NOT GOODBYE (1927) (w)Raymond Klages (m)Louis Alter. (I)Joseph Knecht's Waldorf Astoria Orchestra with The Silver Masked Tenor.

AU REVOIR, PLEASANT DREAMS (1930) (w)Jack Meskill—Jean Schwartz. (P)Theme Song of Ben Bernie and his Orchestra.

AUBREY (1972) (wm)David Gates (P)Bread.

AUF WIEDERSEHN (1915) (w)Herbert Reynolds (m)Sigmund Romberg. (I)Musical: *The Blue Paradise.*

AUF WIEDERSEHN, MY DEAR (1932) (wm)Al Hoffman—Ed Nelson—Al Goodhart—Milton Ager. (P)Russ Columbo. (CR)Morton Downey,Abe Lyman and his Orchestra.

AUF WIEDERSEHN, SWEETHEART (1952) (w-Eng)John Sexton—John Turner (m)Eberhard Storch. (P)Vera Lynn. No. 1 Chart Record.

AULD LANG SYNE (1711) (w)Robert Burns (m)Traditional. Scottish song generally sung on New Year's Eve. Early Recording by Frank Stanley. Also,The Peerless Quartet.

AUNT HAGAR'S BLUES (1921) (w)J. Tim Brymn (m)W. C. Handy. (I)Erskine Tate and his Orchestra. (P)Ted Lewis and his Orchestra.

AURA LEE (1861) (w)W. W. Fosdick (m)George R. Poulton. Famous Civil War Song. Popular version known as Love Me Tender.

AUREET (1941) (wm)Fud Livingston—Arthur Russell—Bob Mosely. (P)Jimmy Dorsey and his Orchestra.

AURORA (1941) (w-Eng)Harold Adamson (m)Mario Lago—Roberto Roberti. (I)Film: *Hold That Ghost* by The Andrews Sisters. (P)The Andrews Sisters.

AUTHORITY SONG,THE (1983) (wm)John Cougar Mellencamp. (P)John Cougar Mellencamp.

AUTOMATIC (1984) (wm)Brock Walsh—Mark Goldenberg. (P)The Pointer Sisters.

AUTUMN (1964) (wm)Richard Maltby, Jr. —David Shire. (P)Barbra Streisand.

AUTUMN CONCERTO (1957) (w-Eng)Paul Siegel (m)Camillo Bargoni. (P)Richard Hayman and his Orchestra.

AUTUMN IN NEW YORK (1934) (wm)Vernon Duke (I)Revue: *Thumbs Up* by J. Harold Murray. (P)Frank Sinatra.

AUTUMN IN ROME (1954) (w)Sammy Cahn (m)Paul Weston. (I)Film: *Indiscretion Of An American Wife* on soundtrack.

AUTUMN LEAVES (1950) (w-Eng)Johnny Mercer (m)Joseph Kosma. (I)In United States by Roger Williams and his Orchestra.

AUTUMN NOCTURNE (1941) (w)Kim Gannon (m)Josef Myrow. (P)Claude Thornhill and his Orchestra.

AUTUMN OF MY LIFE (1968) (wm)Bobby Goldsboro. (P)Bobby Goldsboro.

AUTUMN SERENADE (1945) (w)Sammy Gallop (m)Peter De Rose. (P)Harry James and his Orchestra.

AVAILABLE SPACE (1978) (w)Van Dyke Parks (m)Perry Botkin,Jr. (I)Film: *Goin' South* by the voice of Ry Cooder.

AVALON (1920) (wm)Al Jolson—Vincent Rose. (P)Musical: *Sinbad* by Al Jolson. (P)Al Jolson. (CR)Harry Reser and The Cliquot Club Eskimos.

AVALON TOWN (1928) (w)Grant Clarke (m)Nacio Herb Brown. (P)Vincent Lopez and his Orchestra.

AVE MARIA (1826) (m)Franz Schubert. Well known religious song. Later recording by Perry Como.

AVE MARIA (1859) (m)Charles Gounod. Based on Bach's First Prelude. Recorded by Frances Alda with John McCormack.

AVE SATANI (1976) (m)Jerry Goldsmith. (I)Film: *The Omen* on soundtrack.

AWAKE IN A DREAM (1936) (w)Leo Robin (m)Frederick Hollander. (I)Film: *Desire* by Marlene Dietrich.

AWAY ALL BOATS (1956) (w)Lenny Adelson (m)Frank Skinner—Albert Skinner. Adapted from theme from Film: *Away All Boats*.

AWAY DOWN SOUTH IN HEAVEN (1927) (w)Bud Green (m)Harry Warren. (I)Revue: *Greenwich Follies of 1928* by Blossom Seeley.

AWAY FROM YOU (1975) (w)Sheldon Harnick (m)Richard Rodgers. (I)Musical: *Rex* by Nichol Williamson and Penny Fuller.

AWAY IN A MANGER (w)Unknown (m)James Ramsey Murray. Famous Christmas song.

AWFUL SAD (1929) (m)Duke Ellington. (P)Duke Ellington and his Orchestra.

AXEL F (1985) (wm)Harold Faltermeyer. (I)Film: *Beverly Hills Cop*. (P)Harold Faltermeyer.

AZURE (1937) (wm)Duke Ellington. (P)Duke Ellington and his Orchestra.

B-A-B-Y (1966) (wm)David Porter—Isaac Hayes. (P)Carla Thomas.

BABALU (1942) (w-Eng)S. K. Russell (m)Margarita Lecuona. (I)Xavier Cugat and his Orchestra. (P)Miguelito Valdes.

THE BABBITT AND THE BROMIDE (1927) (w)Ira Gershwin (m)George Gershwin. (I)Musical: *Funny Face* by Fred and Adele Astaire. (R)1945 Film: *Ziegfeld Follies* by Fred Astaire and Gene Kelly.

BABE (1979) (wm)Dennis DeYoung. (P)Styx.

BABES IN ARMS (1937) (w)Lorenz Hart (m)Richard Rodgers. (I)Musical: *Babes In Arms* by Mitzi Green, Alfred Drake and Ray Heatherton. (R)1939 in film version by Judy Garland, Mickey Rooney, Betty Jaynes and Douglas McPhail.

BABY (You've Got What It Takes) (1960) (wm)Clyde Otis—Murray Stein. (P)Brook Benton and Dinah Washington.

BABY, BABY ALL THE TIME (1946) (wm)Bobby Troup. (P)The King Cole Trio, featuring Nat Cole.

BABY,BABY,BABY (1950) (w)Mack David (m)Jerry Livingston. (I)Film: *Those Redheads From Seattle* by Teresa Brewer. (P)Teresa Brewer.

BABY, BABY, DON'T CRY (1969) (wm)Alfred Cleveland—William Robinson—Terry Johnson. (P)Smokey Robinson And The Miracles.

BABY BLUE (1972) (wm)William Peter Ham (P)Badfinger.

BABY BOY (1976) (wm)Mary Kay Place. (I)TV Show: *Mary Hartman*, Mary Hartman by Mary Kay Place. (P)Mary Kay Place.

BABY, COME BACK (1968) (wm)Edmund Grant. (P)The Equals.

BABY COME BACK (1978) (wm)Peter Beckett—John Crowley. (P)Player. No. 1 Chart Record.

BABY COME CLOSE (1973) (wm) (William Robinson—Pamela Moffett—Marvin Tarplin. (P)Smokey Robinson.

BABY, COME TO ME (1981) (wm)Rod Temperton. (P)Patti Austin and James Ingram. No. 1 Chart Record.

BABY DOLL (1927) (wm)Bessie Smith. (P)Bessie Smith.

BABY DOLL (1956) (w)Bernie Hanighen (m)Kenyon Hopkins. (I)Adaptation of the theme from Film: *Baby Doll*. (P)Andy Williams.

BABY DON'T GET HOOKED ON ME (1972) (wm)Mac Davis. (P)Mac Davis.

BABY, DON'T GO (1965) (wm)Sonny Bono. (P)Sonny And Cher.

BABY, DON'T TELL ON ME (1939) (wm)James Rushing—William Basie—Lester Young. (P)Count Basie and his Orchestra,Vocal by Jimmy Rushing.

BABY DREAM YOUR DREAM (1966) (w)Dorothy Fields (m)Cy Coleman. (I)Musical: *Sweet Charity* by Gwen Verdon. Shirley MacLaine appeared in the film version.

BABY ELEPHANT WALK (1962) (w)Hal David (m)Henry Mancini. (I)Film: *Hatari* on soundtrack. (P)Henry Mancini and his Orchestra. Vocal version by Pat Boone. NARAS Award Winner.

BABY FACE (1926) (wm)Benny Davis—Harry Akst. (P)Eddie Cantor. (CR)Jan Garber and his Orchestra.

(R)1948 by Art Mooney and his Orchestra.

BABY GRAND (1986) (wm)Billy Joel. (P)Billy Joel. This song was written as a tribute to Ray Charles.

BABY HOLD ON (1978) (wm)James Lyon—Edward Mahoney. (P)Eddie Money.

BABY I DON'T CARE (1957) (wm)Mike Stoller—Jerry Lieber. (I)Film: *Jailhouse Rock* by Elvis Presley. (P)Elvis Presley.

BABY, I LOVE YOU (1967) (wm)Ronnie Shannon. (P)Aretha Franklin.

BABY I LOVE YOUR WAY (1976) (wm)Peter Frampton. (P)Peter Frampton.

BABY, I NEED YOUR LOVING (1964) (wm)Eddie Holland—Brian Holland—Lamont Dozier. (P)The Four Tops. (R)1967 by Johnny Rivers.

BABY I'M A-WANT YOU (1971) (wm)David Gates. (P)Bread.

BABY, I'M FOR REAL (1969) (wm)Marvin and Anna Gaye. (P)The Originals.

BABY, I'M YOURS (1965) (wm)Van McCoy. (P)Barbara Lewis. (R)1978 by Debby Boone.

BABY, IT'S COLD OUTSIDE (1949) (wm)Frank Loesser. (I)Film: *Neptune's Daughter* by Esther Williams and Ricardo Montalban. (P)Dinah Shore and Buddy Clark. (CR)Johnny Mercer and Margaret Whiting. Academy Award Winner.

BABY, IT'S YOU (1962) (wm)Mack David—Burt Bacharach—Barney Williams. (P)The Shirelles. (R)1969 by Smith.

BABY JANE (1984) (wm)Rod Stewart—Jay Davis. (P)Rod Stewart.

BABY,LET ME HOLD YOUR HAND (1951) (wm)Ray Charles. (P)Ray Charles.

BABY LOVE (1964) (wm)Eddie Holland—Brian Holland—Lamont Dozier. (P)The Supremes. No. 1 Chart Record.

BABY LOVE (1986) (wm)Stephen Bray—Regina Richards—Mary Kessler. (P)Regina.

BABY,MAKE YOUR OWN SWEET MUSIC (1968) (wm)Sandy Linzer—Denny Randell. (P)Jay and The Techniques.

BABY MINE (1941) (w)Ned Washington— (m)Frank Churchill. (I)Cartoon Film: *Dumbo*.

BABY,NOW THAT I'VE FOUND YOU (1968) (wm)John MacLeod—Tony Macaulay. (P)The Foundations.

BABY, PLEASE DON'T GO (1935) (wm)Joe Williams. (P)Joe Williams.

BABY, SCRATCH MY BACK (1965) (wm)James Moore. (P)Slim Harpo.

BABY SITTIN' BOOGIE (1961) (wm)Johnny Parker. (P)Buzz Clifford.

BABY, TAKE A BOW (1934) (w)Lew Brown (m)Jay Gorney. (I)Film: *Stand Up And Cheer* by Shirley Temple, James Dunn and Patricia Lee.

BABY, TAKE ME IN YOUR ARMS (1970) (wm)Tony Macauley—John MacLeod. (P)Jefferson.

BABY TALK (1958) (wm)Melvin H. Schwartz. (P)Jan and Dean.

BABY, TALK TO ME (1960) (w)Lee Adams (m)Charles Strouse. (I)Musical: *Bye Bye Birdie* by Dick Van Dyke.

BABY THAT'S BACKATCHA (1975) (wm)William Robinson, Jr. (P)Smokey Robinson.

BABY, THE RAIN MUST FALL (1964) (w)Ernie Sheldon (m)Elmer Bernstein. (P)Film: *Baby, The Rain Must Fall* by The We Three.

BABY, WHAT A BIG SURPRISE (1977) (wm)Peter Cetera. (P)Chicago.

BABY, WHEN YOU AIN'T THERE (1932) (w)Mitchell Parish (m)Duke Ellington. (P)Duke Ellington and his Orchestra, vocal by Cootie Williams.

BABY, WON'T YOU PLEASE COME HOME (1922) (w)Charles Warfield (m)Clarence Williams. (P)Eva Taylor, with Clarence Williams at the piano. (R)1932 by The Mills Brothers.

BABY WORKOUT (1963) (wm)Alonzo Tucker—Jackie Wilson. (P)Jackie Wilson.

BABY, YOU BEEN ON MY MIND (1964) (wm)Bob Dylan. (P)Bob Dylan.

BABY, YOU'RE A RICH MAN (1967) (wm)John Lennon—Paul McCartney. (P)The Beatles.

BABY, YOU'RE RIGHT (1961) (wm)James Brown—Joe Tex. (P)James Brown.

BABY'S AWAKE NOW (1929) (w)Lorenz Hart (m)Richard Rodgers. (I)Musical: Spring Is Here by Thelma White and Inez Courtney.

BABY'S BEST FRIEND, A (1928) (w)Lorenz Hart (m)Richard Rodgers. (I)Musical: She's My Baby by Beatrice Lillie.

BABY'S BIRTHDAY PARTY (1930) (wm)Ann Ronnell. (P)Rudy Vallee. (CR)Guy Lombardo and his Royal Canadians.

BABY'S IN BLACK (1965) (wm)John Lennon—Paul McCartney. (P)The Beatles.

BACH GOES TO TOWN (1938) (m)Alec Templeton. (I)Alec Templeton as a piano solo. (P)Benny Goodman and his Orchestra.

BACHELOR BOY (1962) (wm)Cliff Richard—Bruce Welch. (P)Cliff Richard and The Shadows.

BACHELOR IN PARADISE (1961) (w)Mack David (m)Henry Mancini. (I)Film: Bachelor In Paradise on soundtrack.

BACK BAY POLKA (1947) (w)Ira Gershwin (m)George Gershwin. (I)Film: The Shocking Miss Pilgrim by The Outcasts.

BACK BAY SHUFFLE (1939) (m)Artie Shaw—Teddy McRae. (P)Artie Shaw and his Orchestra.

BACK BEAT BOOGIE (1940) (m)Harry James. (P)Harry James and his Orchestra.

BACK BY FALL (1976) (wm)Wendy Waldman. (P)Maria Muldaur.

BACK HOME AGAIN (1974) (wm)John Denver. (P)John Denver.

BACK IN LOVE AGAIN (1977) (wm)Len Hanks—Zane Grey. (P)L. T. D.

BACK IN MY ARMS AGAIN (1965) (wm)Lamont Dozier—Eddie Holland—Brian Holland. (P)The Supremes. No. 1 Chart Record.

BACK IN THE SADDLE AGAIN (1940) (wm)Gene Autry. (P)Theme song of Gene Autry. (CR)Art Kassel and his Orchestra.

BACK IN THE U. S. S. R. (1968) (wm)John Lennon—Paul McCartney. (P)The Beatles.

BACK IN YOUR OWN BACKYARD (1928) (wm)Al Jolson—Dave Dreyer—Billy Rose. (P)Al Jolson. (CR)Paul Ash and his Orchestra.

BACK O' TOWN BLUES (wm)Louis Armstrong-Luis Russell. (P)Louis Armstrong and his All-Stars.

BACK OFF BOOGALOO (1972) (wm)Richard Starkey. (P)Ringo Starr.

BACK ON THE CHAIN GANG (1982) (wm)Chrissie Hynde. (P)The Pretenders.

BACK ON THE CORNER (1961) (wm)Mose Allison. (P)Mose Allison.

BACK STABBERS (1972) (wm)Leon Huff—Gene McFadden—John Whitehead. (P)The O'Jays.

BACK STREET (1961) (w)Ken Darby (m)Frank Skinner. (I) Adaption of theme from Film: Back Street.

BACK STREET GIRL (1967) (wm)Mick Jagger—Keith Richard. (P)The Rolling Stones.

BACK TO BACK (1939) (wm)Irving Berlin. Film: Second Fiddle by Mary Healy. Recorded by Glenn Miller and his Orchestra.

BACK TO THE ISLAND (1975) (wm)Leon Russell. (P)Leon Russell.

BACK UP, TRAIN (1966) (w)Curtis Rogers (m)Palmer E. James. (P)Leon Russell.

BACK WATER BLUES (1927) (wm)Bessie Smith. (P)Bessie Smith, with James P. Johnson at the piano.

BACK WHEN MY HAIR WAS SHORT (1972) (wm)Glenn Leopold. (P)Gunhill Road.

BACK WHERE YOU BELONG (1983) (wm)Gary O'Connor. (P)38 Special.

BACKFIELD IN MOTION (1969) (wm)Herbert McPherson—Melvin Harden. (P)Mel and Tim.

BACKLASH BLUES (1966) (w)Langston Hughes (m)Nina Simone. (P)Nina Simone.

BACKSIDE OF THIRTY (1976) (wm)John Conlee. (P)John Conlee.

BACKSTAGE (1966) (wm)Fred Anisfield—Willie Denson. (P)Gene Pitney.

BACKSTREETS (1975) (wm)Bruce Springsteen. (P)Bruce Springsteen.

BACKWARD, TURN BACKWARD (1954) (wm)Dave Coleman. (P)Jane Froman.

BAD (1987) (wm)Michael Jackson. (P)Michael Jackson. No. 1 Chart Record.

BAD AND THE BEAUTIFUL, THE (1960) (w)Dory Langdon (m)David Raksin. (I)Film: The Bad And The Beautiful on soundtrack.

BAD, BAD, LEROY BROWN (wm)Jim Croce. (P)Jim Croce. No. 1 Chart Record.

BAD, BAD WHISKEY (1950) (P)Amos Milburn.

BAD BLOOD (1975) (w)Phil Cody (m)Neil Sedaka. (P)Neil Sedaka. No. 1 Chart Record.

BAD BOY (1986) (wm)Larry Dermer—Joe Galdo—Rafael Vigil. (P)Miami Sound Machine.

BAD CASE OF LOVIN' YOU (1978) (wm)John Martin. (P)Robert Palmer.

BAD GIRL (1963) (wm)Howard Greenfield—Neil Sedaka. (P)Neil Sedaka.

BAD GIRLS (1979) (wm)Joseph Esposito—Edward Hokenson—Bruce Sudano—Donna Summer. (P)Donna Summer. No. 1 Chart Record.

BAD LUCK (1956) (wm)Jules Taub—Sam Ling. (P)B. B. King.

BAD LUCK (Part 1) (1975) (wm)Victor Carstarphen—Gene McFadden—John Whitehead. (P)Harold Melvin and The Blue Notes.

BAD MOON RISING (1969) (wm)John C. Fogarty. (P)Creedence Clearwater Revival.

BAD SNEAKERS (1974) (wm)Donald Fagen—Walter Becker. (P)Steely Dan.

BAD TIME (1974) (wm)Mark Farner. (P)Grand Funk.

BAD TO ME (1964) (wm)John Lennon—Paul McCartney. (P)Billy J. Kramer and The Dakotas.

BADGE (1969) (wm)Eric Clapton—George Harrison. (P)Cream.

BADLANDS (1978) (wm)Bruce Springsteen. (P)Bruce Springsteen.

BADMAN'S BLUNDER (1960) (wm)Lee Hays—Cisco Houston. (P)The Kingston Trio.

BAGDAD (1918) (w)Harold Atteridge (m)Al Jolson. (I)Musical: *Sinbad* by Al Jolson.

BAGDAD (1924) (w)Jack Yellen—Milton Ager. (P)Fred Waring's Pennsylvanians.

BAG'S GROOVE (1962) (wm)Milt Jackson. (P)Milt Jackson, Miles Davis, Thelonius Monk, Percy Monk, Percy Heath and Kenny Clarke.

BAIA (1944) (w-Eng)Ray Gilbert (m)Ary Barroso. (I)Cartoon Film: *The Three Caballeros* by Nestor Amoral. (P)Bing Crosby.

BAION, THE (1953) (w)Ben Raleigh (m)Paulo Alencar. (P)Paulo Alencar and his Orchestra.

BAKER STREET (1978) (wm)Gerry Rafferty. (P)Gerry Rafferty.

BALBOA (1936) (w)Sidney Mitchell (m)Lew Pollack. (I)Film: *Pigskin Parade* by Judy Garland, Dixie Dunbar, Betty Grable, Johnny Downs, Jack Haley, Patsy Kelly and The Yacht Club Boys.

BALD HEADED LENA (1962) (w)Edward Sneed (m)Willie Perryman. (P)The Lovin' Spoonful.

BALI HA'I (1949) (w)Oscar Hammerstein II (m)Richard Rodgers. (I)Musical: *South Pacific* by Juanita Hall. Film version 1953 by Muriel Smith dubbing for Juanita Hall. (P)Perry Como. (CR)Bing Crosby, Peggy Lee, Frank Sinatra.

BALL AND CHAIN (1968) (wm)Willie Mae Thornton. (P)Big Brother and The Holding Company, with Janis Joplin.

BALL OF CONFUSION (1970) (wm)Norman Whitfield—Barrett Strong. (P)The Temptations.

BALL OF FIRE (1969) (wm)Tommy James—Mike Vale—Bruce Sudano—Woody Wilson—Paul Nauman. (P)Tommy James and The Shondells.

BALLAD FOR AMERICANS (1940) (w)John Latouche (m)Earl Robinson. (I)Radio Program: *Pursuit Of Happiness* in 1949. (P)Bing Crosby. (CR)Paul Robeson.

BALLAD FOR D (1982) (wm)Peabo Bryson—Roberta Flack—Ira Williams. (I)Film: *Bustin' Loose* by Peabo Bryson. (P)Peabo Bryson. The song is dedicated to Donny Hathaway.

BALLAD IN BLUE (1935) (w)Irving Kahal (m)Hoagy Carmichael. (P)Benny Goodman and his Orchestra.

BALLAD IN PLAIN D (1964) (wm)Bob Dylan. (P)Bob Dylan.

BALLAD OF A TEENAGE QUEEN (1958) (wm)Jack H. Clement. (P)Johnny Cash.

BALLAD OF A THIN MAN (1965) (wm)Bob Dylan. (P)Bob Dylan.

BALLAD OF BONNIE AND CLYDE, THE (1967) (wm)Mitch Murray—Peter Callander. (P)Georgie Fame.

BALLAD OF CAT BALLOU, THE (1965) (w)Mack David (m)Jerry Livingston. (I)Film: *Cat Ballou* by Nat "King" Cole and Stubby Kaye.

BALLAD OF DAVY CROCKETT, THE (1955) (w)Tom Blackburn (m)George Bruns. (I)Film: *Davy Crockett At The Alamo* by Fess Parker. (P)Bill Hayes. No. 1 Chart Record. (CR)Tennessee Ernie Ford.

BALLAD OF EASY RIDER (1969) (wm)Roger McGuinn. (I)Film: *Easy Rider* by The Birds. (P)The Byrds.

BALLAD OF FRANKIE LEE & JUDAS PRIEST, THE (1968) (wm)Bob Dylan. (P)Bob Dylan.

BALLAD OF GATOR McCLUSKY (1976) (wm)Jerry Reed Hubbard. (I)Film: *Gator* by the voice of Jerry Reed. (P)Jerry Reed.

BALLAD OF GILLIGAN'S ISLE,THE (1964) (wm)Sherwood Schwartz—George Wyle. (I)TV Series: *Gilligan's Isle* (theme song).

BALLAD OF HOLLIS BROWN (1963) (wm)Bob Dylan. (P)Bob Dylan.

BALLAD OF IRA HAYES (1962) (wm)Peter La Farge. (I)Peter La Farge. (P)Johnny Cash. Dedicated to Ira Hayes, the American Indian who raised the flag at Iwo Jima.

BALLAD OF JED CLAMPETT (1962) (wm)Paul Henning. (I)TV series: *The Beverly Hillbillies* by Flatt and Scruggs. (P)Flatt and Scruggs.

BALLAD OF JOHN AND YOKO, THE (1969) (wm)John Lennon—Paul McCartney. (P)The Beatles.

BALLAD OF PALADIN (1958) (wm)Richard Boone—Johnny Western—Sam Rolfe. (I)TV series: *Have Gun, Will Travel* by Johnny Western.

BALLAD OF THE ALAMO (1960) (w)Paul Francis Webster (m)Dimitri Tiomkin. (I)Film: *The Alamo*. (P)Marty Robbins.

BALLAD OF THE GREEN BERETS, THE (1966) (wm)Barry Sadler—Robin Moore. (P)S/Sgt. Barry Sadler. No. 1 Chart Record.

BALLAD OF THE SAD YOUNG MEN, THE (1959) (w)Fran Landesman (m)Tommy Wolf. (I)Musical: *The Nervous Set* by Tani Seitz. (P)Shirley Bassey.

BALLAD OF YOU AND ME AND POONEIL, THE (1967) (wm)Paul Kantner. (P)Jefferson Airplane.

BALLERINA (1947) (wm)Bob Russell—Carl Sigman. (P)Vaughn Monroe and his Orchestra. No. 1 Chart Record. (R)1955 by Nat "King" Cole.

BALLERINA GIRL (1987) (wm)Lionel Richie. (P)Lionel Richie.

BALLIN' THE JACK (1913) (w)James Henry Burris (m)Chris Smith. (I)Musical: *The Passing Show* of 1915. (P)Prince's Orchestra. (R)1940s by Georgia Gibbs.

BALLROOM BLITZ (1975) (wm)Mike Chapman—Nicky Chinn. (P)Sweet.

BALTIMORE (1977) (wm)Randy Newman. (P)Randy Newman.

BALTIMORE BUZZ (1921) (wm)Noble Sissle—Eubie Blake. (I)Musical: *Shuffle Along* by Noble Sissle.

BALTIMORE ORIOLE (1942) (w)Paul Francis Webster (m)Hoagy Carmichael. (I)Film: *To Have And Have Not*, by Hoagy Carmichael.

BAM, BAM BAMY SHORE (1925) (w)Mort Dixon (m)Ray Henderson.

BAMBALINA (1923) (w)Otto Harbach—Oscar Hammerstein II (m)Vincent Youmans—Herbert Stothart. (I)Musical: *Wildflower*, by Edith Day. (P)Paul Whiteman and his Orchestra.

BAMBOO (1950) (w)Buddy Bernier (m)Nat Simon. (P)Vaughn Monroe and his Orchestra.

BANANA BOAT SONG, THE (Day-O) (1956) (wm)Eric Darling—Bob Carey—Alan Arkin. (I)The Tarriers. (P)Harry Belafonte.

BANANA REPUBLIC (1976) (wm)Steve Goodman—Steve Burgh—Jim Rothermel. (P)Steve Goodman.

BAND OF ANGELS (1957) (w)Carl Sigman (m)Max Steiner. (I)Film: *Band Of Angels* on soundtrack.

BAND OF GOLD (1955) (w)Bob Musel (m)Jack Taylor. (I)Kit Carson. (P)Don Cherry. (R)1966 by Mel Carter.

BAND OF GOLD (1970) (wm)Ronald Dunbar—Edythe Wayne. (P)Freda Payne.

BAND OF THE HAND (wm)Bob Dylan. (I)Film: *Band Of The Hand* by Bob Dylan. (P)Bob Dylan.

BAND ON THE RUN (1974) (wm)Paul and Linda McCartney. (P)Paul McCartney and Wings. No. 1 Chart Record.

BAND PLAYED ON, THE (1895) (w)John Palmer (m)Charles Ward. (I)Dan Quinn. (R)1941)Guy Lombardo and his Orchestra. No. 1 Chart Record. (CR)The Jesters.

BANDANA DAYS (1921) (wm)Noble Sissle—Eubie Blake. (I)Musical: *Shuffle Along* by Arthur Porter. (P)Eubie Blake.

BANDIT, THE (1954) (w-Eng)John Turner—Michael Carr (m)Alfredo Ricardo de Nascimento. (I)Brazilian Film: *O Cangaceiro*. (P)Percy Faith and his Orchestra. (CR)Tex Ritter.

BANDIT, THE (1977) (wm)Dick Feller. (I)Film: *Smokey And The Bandit* by Jerry Reed. (P)Jerry Reed.

BANG BANG (My Baby Shot Me Down) (1966) (wm)Sonny Bono. (P)Cher. (CR)Joe Cuba.

BANG-SHANG-A-LANG (1968) (wm)Jeff Barry. (P)The Archies.

BANG THE DRUM SLOWLY (Theme) (1973) (w)Bruce Hart (m)Stephen Lawrence. (I)Film: *Bang The Drum Slowly*, by voice of Bobby Gosh on soundtrack.

BANGLA-DESH (1971) (wm)George Harrison. (I)Film: *Concert For Bangladesh*, by George Harrison. (P)George Harrison.

BANJO'S BACK IN TOWN, THE (1955) (wm)Earl Shuman—Alden Shuman—Marshall Brown. (P)Teresa Brewer.

BAR ROOM BUDDIES (1980) (wm)Snuff Garrett—Clifton Crofford—Stephen Dorff—Milton Brown. (I)Film: *Honky Tonk Man*. (P)Clint Eastwood with Merle Haggard.

BAR ROOM POLKA (1949) (wm)Vaughn Horton. (P)Russ Morgan and his Orchestra.

BARABAJAGAL (1969) (wm)Donovan Leitch. (P)Donovan with Jeff Beck.

BARABBAS (1962) (w-Eng)Earl Shuman (m)M. Nascimbene. Adapted from a theme from Film: *Barabbas*.

BARBARA ANN (1965) (wm)Fred Fassert. (P)The Beach Boys.

BARBER OF SEVILLE, THE (Overture) (1813) (m)G. Rossini. Famous classical overture from Opera: *The Barber Of Seville*.

BARCELONA (1970) (wm)Stephen Sondheim. (I)Musical: *Company*, by Susan Browning and Dean Jones.

BARE NECESSITIES, THE (1967) (wm)Terry Gilkyson. (I)Animated Film: *The Jungle Book*, by the voices of Phil Harris and Bruce Reitherman.

BAREFOOTIN' (1966) (m)Robert Parker. (P)Robert Parker.

BARETTA'S THEME (see Keep Your Eye On The Sparrow)

BARGAIN (1971) (wm)Peter Townshend. (P)The Who.

BARNACLE BILL THE SAILOR (1929) (wm)Carson Robison—Frank Luther. (P)Frank Luther.

BARNEY GOOGLE (1923) (wm)Billy Rose—Con Conrad. (I)Eddie Cantor. (P)Olsen and Johnson. (CR)Georgie Price.

BARNYARD BLUES (1919) (wm)Edwin B. Edwards—James D. LaRocca—Anthony Sparbaro—Larry Shields. (P)Original Dixieland Jazz Band.

BARRACUDA (1977) (wm)Michael Derosier—Roger Fisher—Ann Wilson—Nancy Wilson. (P)Heart.

NANCY WILSON

Pythian Temple was a building on West 70th Street that had been a meeting place for the Knights of Pythias. It was later taken over by the New York Institute of Technology and they would rent us the auditorium for our recording sessions. The control room was small but the room itself had a fantastic overall sound for orchestra.

There was a young black lady who worked as secretary to the president of The New York Institute of Technology who would wander in when we were recording. She used to tell us she wanted to be a singer someday and was interested in observing how record sessions were run. That lovely and talented lady was Nancy Wilson, and she has proved to be an excellent singer over the years.

BARRELHOUSE BESSIE FROM BASIN STREET (1942) (w)Herb Magidson (m)Jule Styne. (P)Bob Crosby and his Orchestra.

BARTERED BRIDE, THE (Overture) (1872) (m)Bedrich Smetena. Famous overture from Opera: *The Bartered Bride*.

BASIN STREET BLUES (1928) (wm)Spencer Williams. (I)Louis Armstrong and his Orchestra. (P)Jack Teagarden and his Orchestra. (R)1934 by Benny Goodman and his Orchestra. (R)1937 by Bing Crosby and Connee Boswell.

BATMAN THEME (1966) (wm)Neal Hefti (I)TV series: *Batman*. (P)Neal Hefti and his Orchestra. NARAS Award Winner.

BATTLE HYMN OF LIEUTENANT CALLEY (1971) (wm)Julian Wilson—James Smith. (P)C. Company featuring Terry Nelson.

BATTLE HYMN OF THE REPUBLIC (1862) (w)Julia Ward Howe (m)William Steffe. First popular recording by Columbia Stellar Quartet. (R)1959 by The Mormon Tabernacle Choir. (R)1968 by Andy Williams.

BATTLE OF KOOKAMONGA, THE (1959) (wm)J. J. Reynolds—Jimmy Driftwood. (P)Homer And Jethro.

BATTLE OF NEW ORLEANS, THE (1957) (wm)Jimmy Driftwood. (P)Johnny Horton. No. 1 Chart Record.

BAUBLES, BANGLES AND BEADS (1953) (wm)Robert Wright—George Forrest. Based on a theme by Borodin. (I)Musical: *Kismet*, by Doretta Morrow. (P)Peggy Lee. (R)1958 by The Kirby Stone Four.

BE (1973) (wm)Neil Diamond. (I)Film: *Jonathan Livingston Seagull*, by Neil Diamond. (P)Neil Diamond.

BE A CLOWN (1948) (wm)Cole Porter. (I)Film: *The Pirate*, by Judy Garland and Gene Kelly.

BE A GOOD SCOUT (1938) (w)Harold Adamson (m)Jimmy McHugh. (I)Film: *That Certain Age*, by Deanna Durbin.

BE A PERFORMER (1962) (wm)Carolyn Leigh—Cy Coleman. (I)Musical: *Little Me*, by Joey Faye, Mort Marshall and Virginia Martin.

BE A SANTA (1961) (w)Betty Comden—Adolph Green (m)Jule Styne. (I)Musical: *Subways Are For Sleeping*, by Sydney Chaplin and Chorus. Recorded by The McGuire Sisters.

BE ANYTHING (But Be Mine) (1952) (wm)Irving Gordon. (P)Eddy Howard. (CR)Peggy Lee, Helen O'Connell.

BE-BABA-LUBA (1945) (wm)Helen Humes. (P)Helen Humes.

BE BEAUTIFUL (1947) (w)Johnny Burke (m)Jimmy Van Heusen. (I)Film: *Road To Rio*, by Bing Crosby. (P)Bing Crosby

BE-BOP (1944) (wm)John Birks Gillespie. (P)Dizzy Gillespie.

BE-BOP-A-LULA (1956) (wm)Gene Vincent—Sheriff Tex Davis. (P)Gene Vincent.

BE-BOP BABY (1957) (wm)Pearl Lendhurst. (P)Ricky Nelson.

BE CAREFUL, IT'S MY HEART (1942) (wm)Irving Berlin. Film: *Holiday Inn*, by Bing Crosby. (P)Bing Crosby.

BE GOOD TO YOURSELF (1986) (wm)Steve Perry—Jonathan Cain—Neal Schon. (P)Journey.

BE HONEST WITH ME (1940) (wm)Gene Autry—Fred Rose. (I)Film: *Ridin' On A Rainbow* by Gene Autry. (P)Gene Autry. (CR)Bing Crosby, Freddy Martin and his Orchestra.

BE ITALIAN (1975) (wm)Maury Yeston. (I)Musical: *Nine*, by Kathi Moss.

BE KIND TO YOUR PARENTS (1954) (wm)Harold Rome (I)Musical: *Fanny*, by Florence Henderson and Lloyd Reese.

BE MINE (1950) (w)Jack Elliott (m)Harold Spina. (P)Mindy Carson.

BE MINE TONIGHT (Noche de Ronda) (1951) (w-Eng)Sunny Skylar. (m)Maria Teresa Lara. (I)In Mexico by Augustine Lara.

BE MY BABY (1963) (wm)Jeff Barry—Ellie Greenwich—Phil Spector. (P)The Ronettes. (R)1970 by Andy Kim.

BE MY HOST (1962) (wm)Richard Rodgers. (I)Musical: *No Strings*, by Richard Kiley, Bernice Massi, Don Chastain, Alvin Epstein and Ann Hodges.

BE MY LIFE'S COMPANION (1951) (wm)Bob Hilliard—Milton De Lugg. (P)The Mills Brothers. (CR)Rosemary Clooney.

BE MY LITTLE BABY BUMBLEBEE (1912) (w)Stanley Murphy (m)Henry I. Marshall. (I)Musical: *Ziegfeld Follies* of 1913.

BE MY LOVE (1950) (w)Sammy Cahn (m)Nicholas Brodszky. (I)Film: *The Toast Of New Orleans*, by Mario Lanza. (P)Mario Lanza. No. 1 Chart Record.

BE NEAR ME (1985) (wm)Martin Fry—Mark White. (P)ABC.

BE NICE TO ME (1971) (wm)Todd Rundgren. (P)Todd Rundgren.

BE PREPARED (1959) (w)Richard Quine (m)Fred Karger. (I)Film: *It Happened To Jane*, by Doris Day.

BE STILL MY BEATING HEART (1987) (wm)Sting. (P)Sting.

BE STILL, MY HEART! (1934) (wm)Allan Flynn—Jack Egan. (P)Freddy Martin and his Orchestra.

BE TRUE TO YOUR SCHOOL (1963) (wm)Brian Wilson. (P)The Beach Boys.

BEACH GIRL (1964) (wm)Terry Melcher—Bruce Johnson. (P)Pat Boone.

BEALE ST. BLUES (1916) (wm)W. C. Handy. (I)Prince's Orchestra. (R)1927 by Alberta Hunter. (R)1932 by Joe Venuti. (R)1942 by Guy Lombardo and his Royal Canadians.

BEALE STREET MAMA (1923) (wm)Roy Turk—J. Russel Robinson. (P)Sophie Tucker.

BEANS AND CORNBREAD (1949) (wm)Freddie Clark—Fleecie Moore. (P)Louis Jordan and his Tympani Five.

BEAST IN ME, THE (1985) (wm)Eric Kaz—Marvin Morrow. (I)Film: *Heavenly Bodies*, by The Pointer Sisters. (P)The Pointer Sisters.

BEAST OF BURDEN (1978) (wm)Mick Jagger—Keith Richards. (P)The Rolling Stones. (R)1984 by Bette Midler.

BEAT GOES ON, THE (1967) (wm)Sonny Bono. (P)Sonny and Cher.

BEAT IT (1982) (wm)Michael Jackson. (P)Michael Jackson. No. 1 Chart Record. NARAS Award Winner.

BEAT ME DADDY, EIGHT TO THE BAR (1940) (wm)Don Raye—Hughie Prince—Eleanore Sheehy. (P)Will Bradley and his Orchestra, vocal by Ray McKinley. (CR)The Andrews Sisters, Glenn Miller and his Orchestra.

BEAT OF MY HEART, THE (1934) (w)Johnny Burke (m)Harold Spina. (P)Paul Whiteman and his Orchestra. (CR)Ben Pollack and his Orchestra.

BEAT OUT THAT RHYTHM ON A DRUM (1943) (w)Oscar Hammerstein II (m)Georges Bizet. Adapted from a theme from the opera Carmen. (I)Musical: *Carmen Jones*, by June Hawkins with Cozy Cole on drums.

BEATNIK FLY (1960) (wm)Ira Mack—Tom King. (P)Johnny and The Hurricanes.

BEATS THERE A HEART SO TRUE (1958) (wm)Noel Sherman—Jack Keller. (P)Perry Como.

BEAUTIFUL (1962) (wm)James Goldman—John Kander—William Goldman. (I)Musical: *A Family Affair*, by Shelly Berman.

BEAUTIFUL (1971) (wm)Carole King. (P)Carole King.

BEAUTIFUL (1983) (wm)Stephen Sondheim. (I)Sunday In The Park With George, by Barbara Byrne and Mandy Patinkin.

BEAUTIFUL BROWN EYES (1951) (wm)Alton Delmore—Arthur Smith—Jerry Capehart. (P)Rosemary Clooney.

BEAUTIFUL CANDY (1961) (wm)Bob Merrill. (I)Musical: *Carnival!*, by Anna Marie Alberghetti, The Puppets and The Carnival People.

BEAUTIFUL DREAMER (1864) (wm)Stephen Collins Foster. One of Foster's most popular songs. No artist credited with introduction.

BEAUTIFUL GIRL (1933) (w)Arthur Freed (m)Nacio Herb Brown. (I)Film: *Going Hollywood*, by Bing Crosby. (P)Bing Crosby.

BEAUTIFUL LADY IN BLUE, A (1935) (w)Sam Lewis (m)J. Fred Coots. (I)Jan Peerce on radio. (P)Jan Garber and his Orchestra. No. 1 Chart Record. (CR)Ray Noble and his Orchestra.

BEAUTIFUL LAND, THE (1964) (wm)Leslie Bricusse—Anthony Newley. (I)Musical: *The Roar Of The Greasepaint—The Smell Of The Crowd* by The Urchins.

BEAUTIFUL LOSER (1974) (wm)Bob Seger. (P)Bob Seger.

BEAUTIFUL LOVE (1931) (w)Haven Gillespie (m)Victor Young—Wayne King—Egbert Van Alstyne. (P)Wayne King and his Orchestra. (R)1944 Film: *Sing A Jingle*, by Allan Jones.

BEAUTIFUL MORNING, A (1968) (wm)Felix Cavaliere—Edward Brigati, Jr. (P)The Rascals.

BEAUTIFUL OHIO (1918) (w)Ballard MacDonald (m)Mary Earl. Early recordings by Henry Burr, Waldorf-Astoria Dance Orchestra, Fritz Kreisler, Sam Ash and his Orchestra.

BEAUTIFUL PEOPLE (1967) (wm)Kenny O'Dell. (I)Kenny O'Dell. (P)Bobby Vee.

BEAUTY IS ONLY SKIN DEEP (1965) (wm)Eddie Holland—Norman Whitfield. (P)The Temptations.

BEAUTY SCHOOL DROPOUT (1972) (wm)Jim Jacobs—Warren Casey. (I)Musical: Grease, by Alan Paul, Marya Small and The Choir.

BEBE (1923) (w)Sam Coslow (m)Abner Silver. (P)Billy Jones. This song was dedicated to Bebe Daniels.

BECAUSE (1902) (w)Edward Teschemacher (m)Guy d'-Hardelot. (I)Enrico Caruso. (R)1948 by Perry Como. (R)1951 by Mario Lanza.

BECAUSE (1964) (wm)Dave Clark. (P)The Dave Clark Five.

BECAUSE (1969) (wm)John Lennon—Paul McCartney. (P)The Beatles.

BECAUSE, BECAUSE (1931) (w)Ira Gershwin (m)George Gershwin. (I)Musical: Of Thee I Sing by George Murphy and Grace Brinkley.

BECAUSE I LOVE YOU (1926) (wm)Irving Berlin. (I)Henry Burr.

BECAUSE OF YOU (1940) (wm)Arthur Hammerstein—Dudley Wilkinson. (P)Tony Bennett. No. 1 Chart Record. (CR)by Jan Peerce.

BECAUSE THE NIGHT (1978) (wm)Patti Smith—Bruce Springsteen. (P)Patti Smith.

BECAUSE THEY'RE YOUNG (1960) (w)Aaron Schroeder—Wally Gold (m)Don Costa. (I)Film: Because They're Young by Duane Eddy. (P)Duane Eddy.

BECAUSE YOU'RE MINE (1951) (w)Sammy Cahn (m)Nicholas Brodszky. (I)Film: Because You're Mine by Mario Lanza. (CR)Nat "King" Cole.

BECAUSE YOU'RE YOU (1906) (w)Henry Blossom (m)Victor Herbert. (I)Musical: The Red Mill. Recorded by Harry Macdonough and Elise Stevenson.

BEECHWOOD 4-5789 (1962) (wm)William Stevenson—George Gordy—Marvin Gaye. (P)The Marvelettes.

BEEN ON A TRAIN (1971) (wm)Laura Nyro. (P)Laura Nyro.

BEEN TO CANAAN (1972) (wm)Carole King. (P)Carole King.

BEEP, BEEP (1958) (wm)Donald Claps—Carl Cicchetti. (P)The Playmates.

BEER BARREL POLKA (1939) (w-Eng)Lew Brown (m)Jaromir Vejvoda. (I)In United States by Will Glahe and his Musette Orchestra. (P)The Andrews Sisters.

BEFORE AND AFTER (1965) (wm)Van McCoy. (I)The Fleetwoods. (P)Chad and Jeremy.

BEFORE I GAZE AT YOU AGAIN (1960) (w)Alan Jay Lerner (m)Frederick Loewe. (I)Musical: Camelot by Julie Andrews.

BEFORE I KISS THE WORLD GOODBYE (1963) (w)Howard Dietz (m)Arthur Schwartz. (I)Musical: Jennie by Mary Martin.

BEFORE THE DELUGE (1974) (wm)Jackson Browne (P)Jackson Browne.

BEFORE THE NEXT TEARDROP FALLS (1967) (wm)Ben Peters—Vivian Keith. (P)Freddy Fender. No. 1 Chart Record.

BEFORE THE PARADE PASSES BY (1963) (wm)Jerry Herman. (I)Musical: Hello, Dolly! by Carol Channing and The Company.

BEG, BORROW AND STEAL (1967) (wm)Lou Zerato—Joey Day. (P)Ohio Express.

BEG YOUR PARDON (1947) (wm)Francis Craig—Beasley Smith. (P)Francis Craig and his Orchestra. (CR)Frankie Carle and his Orchestra.

BEGAT, THE (1947) (w)E. Y. Harburg (m)Burton Lane. (I)Musical: Finian's Rainbow by Louis Sharp, Lorenzo Fuller, Jerry Laws and Robert Pitkin.

BEGGIN' (1967) (wm)Peggy Farina—Bob Gaudio. (P)The Four Seasons.

BEGGING FOR LOVE (1931) (wm)Irving Berlin. (P)Guy Lombardo and his Royal Canadians.

BEGIN THE BEGUINE (1935) (wm)Cole Porter. (I)Musical: Jubilee by June Knight. Recorded by Xavier Cugat and his Orchestra. (R)1938 by Artie Shaw and his Orchestra. (R)1946 by Frank Sinatra.

(I've Got)BEGINNER'S LUCK (1937) (w)Ira Gershwin (m)George Gershwin. (I)Film: Shall We Dance? by Fred Astaire. (P)Fred Astaire.

BEGINNINGS (1969) (wm)Robert Lamm (P)Chicago.

BEHIND BLUE EYES (1971) (wm)Peter Townshend. (P)The Who.

BEHIND CLOSED DOORS (1973) (wm)Kenny O'Dell. (P)Charlie Rich. NARAS Award Winner.

BEI MIR BIST DU SCHON (1937) (w-Eng)Sammy Cahn—Saul Chaplin (m)Sholom Secunda. (I)Yiddish Musical: I Would If I Could by Aaron Lebedoff. (P)The Andrews Sisters. No. 1 Chart Record. (CR)Guy Lombardo, Russ Morgan, Benny Goodman, Kate Smith.

BEIN' GREEN (1971) (wm)Joe Raposo. (I)TV series: Sesame Street by Jim Henson as the voice of Kermit The Frog. (P)Frank Sinatra.

BEING ALIVE (1970) (wm)Stephen Sondheim. (I)Musical: Company by Dean Jones and The Company.

BEING FOR THE BENEFIT OF MR. KITE (1967) (wm)John Lennon—Paul McCartney.

BEING IN LOVE (1961) (wm)Meredith Willson. (I)Film Version: The Music Man by Shirley Jones.

BEING WITH YOU (1981) (wm)William Robinson,Jr. (P)Smokey Robinson.

BELIEVE IN HUMANITY (1973) (wm)Carole King. (P)Carole King.

BELIEVE IN ME (1955) (w-Eng)Carl Sigman (m)Icini. (P)Connie Francis.

BELIEVE IT, BELOVED (1934)George Whiting—Nat Schwartz (m)J. C. Johnson. (P)Fats Waller.

BELIEVE ME IF ALL THOSE ENDEARING YOUNG CHARMS (1807) (w)Thomas Moore (m)Matthew Locke. Early recording by John McCormack.

BELIEVE WHAT YOU SAY (1958) (wm)Johnny and Dorsey Burnette. (P)Ricky Nelson.

BELL BOTTOM BLUES (1953) (w)Hal David (m)Leon Carr. (P)Teresa Brewer.

BELL BOTTOM BLUES (1970) (wm)Eric Clapton. (P)Eric Clapton.

BELL BOTTOM TROUSERS (1944) (wm)Moe Jaffe. (P)Tony Pastor and his Orchestra, vocal by Ruth McCullough and Tony Pastor. (CR)Jerry Colonna, Kay Kyser, Guy Lombardo.

BELLA BELLA MARIE (1947) (w-Eng)Don Pelosi—Leo Towers. (m)Gerhard Winkler. (P)The Andrews Sisters. (CR)Jan Garber and his Orchestra.

BELLE, BELLE (My Liberty Belle) (1931) (wm)Bob Merrill. (P)Guy Mitchell. (CR)Bobby Wayne.

BELLE OF THE BALL (1953) (w)Mitchell Parrish (m)Leroy Anderson. (P)Leroy Anderson and his Orchestra.

BELLS (1920) (wm)Irving Berlin. (I)Revue: *Ziegfeld Follies* of 1920 by Bernard Granville.

BELLS (1952) (wm)Billy Ward. (P)The Dominoes.

BELLS,THE (1963) (w)Edgar Allen Poe (m)Phil Ochs. (P)Phil Ochs.

BELLS,THE (1970) (wm)Marvin Gaye—Anna Gaye—Elgie Stover—Berry Gordy,Jr. (P)The Originals.

BELLS ARE RINGING (1956) (w)Betty Comden—Adolph Green (m)Jule Styne. (I)Musical: *Bells Are Ringing*, by The Chorus.

BELLS OF RHYMNEY (1960) (w)Idris Davies (m)Pete Seeger. (P)Pete Seeger.

BELLS OF ST. MARY'S, THE (1917) (w)Douglas Furber (m)Emmett Adams. Early recording by Frances Alda. (R)1946 Film: *The Bells of St. Mary's* by Bing Crosby. (P)Bing Crosby.

BELLS OF SAN RAQUEL (1941) (w-Eng)Fred Wise—Milton Leeds. (m)Lorenzo Barcelata. (I)Dick Jurgens and his Orchestra, vocal by Harry Cool. (CR)Glen Gray and the Casa Loma Orchestra, vocal by Kenny Sargent.

BELLY UP TO THE BAR, BOYS (1960) (wm)Meredith Willson. (I)Musical: *The Unsinkable Molly Brown* by Tammy Grimes. In film version (1964)by Debbie Reynolds.

BELOVED (1945) (w)George Waggner (m)Edward Ward. (I)Film: *Frisco Sal*, by Suzanna Foster.

BELOVED (1952) (w)Paul Francis Webster (m)Nicholas Brodszky. (I)Film: *The Student Prince* by voice of Mario Lanza dubbing for Edmund Purdom.

BELOVED, BE FAITHFUL (1950) (wm)Ervin Drake—Jimmy Shirl. (P)Russ Morgan and his Orchestra.

BEN (1972) (wm)Walter Scharf—Don Black. (I)Film: *Ben*, by Michael Jackson. (P)Michael Jackson. No. 1 Chart Record.

BEN CASEY, Theme From (1961) (m)David Raksin. (I)TV series: *Ben Casey* on soundtrack.

BEN HUR, Love Theme From (1959) (m)Miklos Rozsa. (I)Film: *Ben Hur* on soundtrack.

BENCH IN THE PARK, A (1930) (w)Jack Yellen (m)Milton Ager. (I)Film: *King of Jazz*, by Paul Whiteman and his Orchestra.

BEND DOWN SISTER (1931) (w)Ballard MacDonald—Dave Silverstein (m)Con Conrad. (I)Film: *Palmy Days*, by Charlotte Greenwood.

BEND ME, SHAPE ME (1967) (w)Scott English (m)Laurence Weiss. (P)The American Breed.

BENNIE AND THE JETS (1974) (wm)Elton John—Bernie Taupin. (P)Elton John. No. 1 Chart Record.

BERCEUSE (1888) (w)Paul Silvestre (m)Benjamin Godard. Famous aria for tenor singers from Opera: Jocelyn.

BERLIN MELODY, THE (1961) (m)Heino Gaze. (P)Billy Vaughn and his Orchestra.

BERMUDA (1952) (wm)Cynthia Strother—Eugene R. Strother. (P)The Bell Sisters with Henri Rene and his Orchestra.

BERNADETTE (1967) (wm)Brian Holland—Lamont Dozier—Eddie Holland. (P)The Four Tops.

BERNADINE (1957) (wm)Johnny Mercer. (I)Film: *Bernadine*, by Pat Boone. (P)Pat Boone.

BERNIE'S TUNE (1953) (wm)Bernie Miller—Mike Stoller—Jerry Lieber. (P)Gerry Mulligan as jazz instrumental. Vocal version by The Cheers.

BERRY TREE, THE (1954) (wm)Saul Chaplin. (I)Film: *Many Rivers To Cross* on soundtrack. (P)Bill Hayes.

BERTHA BUTT BOOGIE, THE (1975) (wm)Jimmy Castor—John Pruitt. (P)The Jimmy Castor Bunch.

BESAME MUCHO (1944) (w-Eng)Sunny Skylar (m)Consuelo Velazquez. (P)Jimmy Dorsey and his Orchestra, vocal by Kitty Kallen and Bob Eberly. No. 1 Chart Record. (CR)Andy Russell.

BESIDE A BABBLING BROOK (1923) (w)Gus Kahn (m)Walter Donaldson. (I)Marion Harris.

BESIDE AN OPEN FIREPLACE (1929) (wm)Paul Denniker—Will Osborne. (I)Will Osborne and his Orchestra.

BESIDE YOU (1947) (wm)Jay Livingston—Ray Evans. (I)Film: *My Favorite Brunette*, by Dorothy Lamour.

BESS, YOU IS MY WOMAN (1935) (w)Du Bose Heyward—Ira Gershwin (m)George Gershwin. (I)Opera: *Porgy and Bess*, by Todd Duncan and Anne Brown. Film version (1959)by Robert McFerrin dubbing for Sidney Poitier and Adele Addison dubbing for Dorothy Dandridge.

BEST IS YET TO COME, THE (1959) (w)Carolyn Leigh (m)Cy Coleman. (P)Tony Bennett.

BEST MAN, THE (1946) (wm)Roy Alfred—Fred Wise. (P)Les Brown and his Orchestra, vocal by Butch Stone.

BEST MAN IN THE WORLD, THE (1986) (wm)John Barry—Ann Wilson—Sue Ennis—Nancy Wilson. (I)Film: *The Golden Child*, by Ann Wilson.

BEST OF BOTH WORLDS (1968) (wm)Mark London—Don Black. (P)Lulu.

BEST OF EVERYTHING, THE (1959) (w)Sammy Cahn (m)Alfred Newman. (I)Film: *The Best Of Everything* by Johnny Mathis. (P)Johnny Mathis.

BEST OF MY LOVE (1975) (wm)Glenn Frey—Don Henley—John David Souther. (P)The Eagles. No. 1 Chart Record.

BEST OF MY LOVE (1977) (wm)Maurice White—Albert McKay. (P)The Emotions. No. 1 Chart Record.

BEST OF TIMES, THE (1981) (wm)Dennis DeYoung. (P)Styx.

BEST OF TIMES, THE (1983) (wm)Jerry Herman. (I)Musical: *La Cage Au Folles*, by George Hearn, Elizabeth Parrish and the Cast.

BEST THING FOR YOU, THE (1950) (wm)Irving Berlin. (I)Musical: *Call Me Madam*, by Ethel Merman and Paul Lukas.

BEST THINGS HAPPEN WHILE YOU'RE DANCING, THE (1953) (wm)Irving Berlin. (I)Film: *White Christmas*, by Danny Kaye.

BEST THINGS IN LIFE ARE FREE, THE (1927) (wm)B. G. De Sylva—Lew Brown—Ray Henderson. (I)Musical: *Good News*, by Mary Lawlor and John Price Jones. Recorded by Geroge Olsen and his Orchestra. (R)1948 by Dinah Shore, Jo Stafford. (R)1956 Film: *The Best Things In Life Are Free* by Dan Dailey, Ernest Borgnine, Sheree North and Gordon MacRae.

BETCHA BY GOLLY, WOW (1970) (wm)Thom Bell—Linda Creed. (P)The Stylistics.

BETH (1976) (wm)Peter Criscuola—Stanley Penridge—Bob Ezrin. (P)Kiss.

BETTE DAVIS EYES (1981) (w)Donna Weiss (m)Jackie DeShannon. (P)Kim Carnes. No. 1 Chart Record. NARAS Award Winner.

BETTER DAYS (1976) (wm)Carole Bayer Sager—Melissa Manchester. (P)Melissa Manchester.

BETTER LOVE NEXT TIME (1979) (wm)Larry Keith—Steve Pippin—Johnny Slate. (P)Dr. Hook.

BETTER LUCK NEXT TIME (1947) (wm)Irving Berlin. (P)Film: *Easter Parade*, by Judy Garland. Recorded by Jo Stafford.

BETTER PLACE TO BE (1976) (wm)Harry Chapin. (P)Harry Chapin.

BETTER THAN EVER (1979) (w)Carole Bayer Sager (m)Marvin Hamlisch. (I)Film: *Starting Over*, by Candice Bergen.

BETTY CO-ED (1930) (wm)J. Paul Fogarty—Rudy Vallee. (P)Rudy Vallee. (CR)Bob Haring and his Orchestra.

BETWEEN A KISS AND A SIGH (1938) (w)Johnny Burke (m)Arthur Johnston. (P)Bing Crosby. (CR)Artie Shaw and his Orchestra.

BETWEEN 18th AND 19th ON CHESTNUT STREET (1939) (wm)Will Osborne—Dick Rogers. (P)Bing Crosby and Connee Boswell. (CR)Bob Crosby and his Orchestra.

BETWEEN THE DEVIL AND THE DEEP BLUE SEA (1931) (w)Ted Koehler (m)Harold Arlen. (I)Nightclub Revue: *Rhythmania*, by Aida Ward. Recorded by Cab Calloway, Louis Armstrong, The Boswell Sisters.

BETWEEN YOU AND ME (1939) (wm)Cole Porter. (I)Film: *Broadway Melody Of 1940*, by George Murphy.

BEWARE MY HEART (1946) (wm)Sam Coslow. (I)Film: *Carnegie Hall* by Vaughn Monroe.

BEWARE OF IT (1954) (wm)Cy Coben. (P)Johnny and Jack.

BEWILDERED (1938) (w)Leonard Whitcup (m)Teddy Powell. (I)Amos Milburn. (P)Tommy Dorsey and his Orchestra. (CR)Billy Eckstine.

BEWITCHED (1941) (w)Lorenz Hart (m)Richard Rodgers. (I)Musical: *Pal Joey*, by Vivienne Segal. (P)Bill Snyder and his Orchestra. (CR)Doris Day. (R)1957 in film version by Frank Sinatra.

BEYOND THE BLUE HORIZON (1930) (w)Leo Robin (m)Richard A. Whiting—W. Franke Harling. (I)Film: *Monte Carlo*, by Jeanette MacDonald. Recorded by George Olsen and his Orchestra. (R)1951 by Hugo Winterhalter and his Orchestra.

BEYOND THE REEF (1949) (wm)Jack Pitman. (P)Bing Crosby.

BEYOND THE SEA (1947) (w-Eng)Jack Lawrence (m)Charles Trenet. (P)Charles Trenet. (R)1947 by Bobby Darin.

BEYOND THE VALLEY OF THE DOLLS (1970) (wm)Stu Phillips—Bob Stone. (I)Film: *Beyond The Valley Of The Dolls*, by The Sandpipers on the soundtrack.

BEYOND TOMORROW (1973) (w)Larry Kusik (m)Mikis Theodorakis. (I)Film: *Serpico* on soundtrack. (P)Perry Como.

BIANCA (1948) (wm)Cole Porter. (I)Musical: *Kiss Me Kate*, by Harold Lang.

BIBBIDI-BOBBIDI-BOO (The Magic Song) (1948) (wm)Mack David—Al Hoffman—Jerry Livingston. (I)Cartoon Film: *Cinderella* by voice of Verna Felton. (P)Jo Stafford and Gordon MacRae. (CR)Perry Como, Dinah Shore.

BIBLE TELLS ME SO, THE (1955) (wm)Dale Evans. (I)Roy Rogers and Dale Evans. (P)Don Cornell.

BICYCLE RACE (1978) (wm)Freddie Mercury. (P)Queen.

BIDIN' MY TIME (1930) (w)Ira Gershwin (m)George Gershwin. (I)Musical: *Girl Crazy*, by The Foursome, a male quartet.

BIG APPLE, THE (1937) (w)Buddy Bernier (m)Bob Emmerich. (I)Tommy Dorsey and his Orchestra. (CR)Clyde Lucas.

BIG BACK YARD, THE (1944) (w)Dorothy Fields (m)Sigmund Romberg. (I)Musical: *Up In Central Park*, by Wilbur Evans and the Chorus.

BIG BAD JOHN (1961) (wm)Jimmy Dean. (P)Jimmy Dean. No. 1 Chart Record. NARAS Award Winner.

BIG BLACK GIANT, THE (1953) (w)Oscar Hammerstein II (m)Richard Rodgers. (I)Musical: *Me And Juliet*, by Bill Hayes.

BIG BOSS MAN (1967) (wm)Al Smith—Luther Dixon. (P)Elvis Presley.

BIG BRASS BAND FROM BRAZIL (1947) (wm)Bob Hilliard—Carl Sigman. (I)Revue: *Angel In The Wings*, by the entire company. Recorded by Jack Smith.

BIG, BRIGHT GREEN PLEASURE MACHINE, THE (1966) (wm)Paul Simon. (I)Film: *The Graduate*, by Simon and Garfunkel on the soundtrack. (P)Simon and Garfunkel.

BIG CHIEF DE SOTA (1936) (wm)Andy Razaf—Fernando Arbelo. (I)Fletcher Henderson and his Orchestra. (P)Fats Waller.

BIG CITY BLUES (1929) (w)Sidney D. Mitchell—Archie Gottler (m)Con Conrad. (I)Film: *William Fox Movietone Follies* of 1929, by Lola Lane.

BIG CLOWN BALLOONS, THE (1963) (wm)Meredith Willson. (I)Musical: *Here's Love*, by The Paradesters.

BIG D (1956) (wm)Frank Loesser. (I)Musical: *The Most Happy Fella* by Shorty Long and Susan Johnson.

BIG DADDY (1958) (w)Peter Udell (m)Lee Pockriss. (I)Film: *Senior Prom* on soundtrack) (P)Jill Corey.

BIG GIRLS DON'T CRY (1962) (wm)Bob Crewe—Bob Gaudio. (P)The Four Seasons. No. 1 Chart Record.

BIG FUN (1982) (wm)Ronald Bell—Curtis Williams—Clifford Adams—James Taylor—Michael Ray—Claydes Smith—George Brown—Robert Mickens—Eumir Deodato—Robert Bell. (P)Kool and The Gang.

BIG GUITAR, THE (1958) (wm)Francis De Rosa—Robert Genovese—Larry Coleman. (P)Frank De Rosa and his D Men.

BIG HUNK 'O LOVE, A (1959) (wm)Aaron Schroeder—Sid Wyche. (P)Elvis Presley. No. 1 Chart Record.

BIG HURT, THE (1959) (wm)Wayne Shanklin. (P)Toni Fisher.

BIG IRON (1960) (wm)Marty Robbins (P)Marty Robbins.

BIG JOHN (Ain't You Gonna Marry Me?) (1961) (wm)John Patton—Amiel Summers. (P)The Shirelles.

BIG JOHN'S SPECIAL (1934) (m)Horace Henderson. (I)Fletcher Henderson and his Orchestra. (P)Benny Goodman and his Orchestra.

BIG LOG (1984) (wm)Robert Plant. (P)Robert Plant.

BIG LOVE (1987) (wm)L. Buckingmam. (P)Fleetwood Mac.

BIG MAMOU (1953) (wm)Link David. (P)Pete Hanley. (CR)Dolores Gray.

BIG MAN (1958) (wm)Glen Larson—Bruce Belland (P)The Four Preps.

BIG MAN IN TOWN (1964) (wm)Bob Gaudio. (P)The Four Seasons.

BIG MOLE (1949) (w)Maxwell Anderson (m)Kurt Weill.

(l)Musical: *Lost In The Stars*, by Herbert Coleman.

BIG MOVIE SHOW IN THE SKY (1949) (w)Johnny Mercer (m)Robert Emmett Dolan. (l)Musical: *Texas, L'il Darlin'*, by Danny Scholl.

BIG NOISE FROM WINNETKA (1940) (w)Gil Rodin—Bob Crosby (m)Bob Haggart—Ray Bauduc. (P)Bob Crosby and his Orchestra,featuring the whistling and bass playing of Haggart and the drumming of Bauduc.

BIG ROCK CANDY MOUNTAIN (1885) (wm)Unknown. Traditional American folk song.

BIG SHOT (1979) (wm)Billy Joel. (P)Billy Joel.

BIG SPENDER (1965) (w)Dorothy Fields (m)Cy Coleman. (l)Musical: *Sweet Charity*, by Helen Gallagher, Thelma Oliver and The Girls. In film version (1969)by Chita Rivera, Paula Kelly and The Girls. (P)Peggy Lee.

BIG TIME (1987) (wm)Peter Gabriel. (P)Peter Gabriel.

BIG WIDE WORLD (1962) (wm)Teddy Randazzo—Bobby Weinstein—Billy Barberis. (P)Teddy Randazzo.

BIG YELLOW TAXI (1970) (wm)Joni Mitchell. (P)Joni Mitchell.

BIGGEST ASPIDISTRA IN THE WORLD, THE (1938) (wm)James Hancock—W. G. Haines—Tommie Connor. (P)Gracie Fields.

BIGGEST PART OF ME, THE (1980) (wm)David Pack. (P)Ambrosia.

BIJOU (1944) (m)Ralph Burns. (P)Woody Herman and his Orchestra, trombone solo by Bill Harris.

BILBAO SONG, THE (1961) (w-Eng)Johnny Mercer (m)Kurt Weill. (l)In United States by Lotte Lenya. (P)Andy Williams.

BILL (1927) (w)P. G. Wodehouse—Oscar Hammerstein II. (m)Jerome Kern. (l)Musical: *Showboat*, by Helen Morgan. Also by Miss Morgan in first and second film versions (1929) and (1936). Third film version (1951)by Eileen Wilson dubbing for Ava Gardner. Also in film *The Helen Morgan Story* (1957)by Gogi Grant dubbing for Ann Blyth.

BILL BAILEY, WON'T YOU PLEASE COME HOME (1902) (wm)Hughie Cannon. First record by Arthur Collins. (P)Louis Armstrong. (R)1950s by Pearl Bailey.

BILLBOARD MARCH (1901) (m)John N. Klohr. Famous American march usually performed at circuses.

BILLIE (1928) (wm)George M. Cohan. (l)Musical: *Billie*, by Polly Walker.

BILLIE JEAN (1982) (wm)Michael Jackson. (P)Michael Jackson. No. 1 Chart Record. NARAS Award Winner.

BILLIE'S BOUNCE (1945) (m)Charlie Parker. (l)Charlie Parker with Dizzy Gillespie, Miles Davis, Curly Russell and Max Roach.

BILLION DOLLAR BABIES (1973) (wm)Alice Cooper—Michael Bruce. (P)Alice Cooper.

BILLY (For When I Walk) (1911) (w)Joe Goodwin (m)Kendis and Paley. No artist credited with introduction. (R)1939 by Orrin Tucker and his Orchestra, vocal by Bonnie Baker.

BILLY AND SUE (1965) (wm)Mark Charron. (P)B. J. Thomas.

BILLY BOY (1824) (wm)Unknown. Traditional English folk song.

BILLY, DON'T BE A HERO (1974) (wm)Peter Callender—Mitch Murray. (P)Bo Donaldson and The Heywoods. No. 1 Chart Record.

BIM BAM BABY (1952) (wm)Sammy Mysels. (P)Frank Sinatra.

BIMBOMBEY (1958) (wm)Mack David—Hugo Peretti—Luigi Creatore. (P)Jimmie Rodgers.

BIMINI BAY (1921) (w)Gus Kahn—Raymond B. Egan (m)Richard A. Whiting. (l)Benson Orchestra of Chicago.

BING! BANG! BONG! (1958) (wm)Jay Livingston—Ray Evans. (l)Film: *Houseboat*, by Sophia Loren.

BIRD DOG (1958) (wm)Boudleaux Bryant. (P)The Everly Brothers. No. 1 Chart Record.

BIRD IN A GILDED CAGE, A (1900) (w)Arthur J. Lamb (m)Harry Von Tilzer. (P)Jerry Mahoney. (CR)Steve Porter.

BIRD MAN, THE (1962) (w)Mack David (m)Elmer Bernstein. (l)Film: *Birdman Of Alcatraz*. (P)The Highwaymen.

BIRD ON THE WIRE (1968) (wm)Leonard Cohen. (P)Leonard Cohen. (CR)Judy Collins.

BIRDS AND THE BEES, THE (1965) (wm)Herb Newman. (P)Jewel Akens.

BIRDS OF A FEATHER (1941) (w)Johnny Burke (m)Jimmy Van Heusen. (l)Film: *Road To Zanzibar* by Bing Crosby. (P)Bing Crosby.

BIRMINGHAM (1974) (wm)Randy Newman. (P)Randy Newman.

BIRMINGHAM BREAKDOWN (1927) (m)Duke Ellington. (P)Duke Ellington and his Cotton Club Orchestra.

BIRMIN'HAM (1955) (wm)Hugh Martin—Ralph Blane. (l)Film: *The Girl Rush*, by Rosalind Russell and Eddie Albert.

BIRTH OF THE BLUES, THE (1926) (w)B. G. De Sylva—Lew Brown. (m)Ray Henderson. (l)Revue: *George White's Scandals of 1926* by Harry Richman. (P)Paul Whiteman and his Orchestra. No. 1 Chart Record. (CR)Harry Richman, The Revelers. (R)1952 by Frank Sinatra.

BIRTHDAY (1968) (wm)John Lennon—Paul McCartney. (P)The Beatles.

BIT OF SOUL, A (1961) (m)Ray Charles. (P)Ray Charles.

BITCH IS BACK, THE (1974) (wm)Elton John—Bernie Taupin. (P)Elton John.

BIT BY BIT (1985) (w)Frannie Golde (m)Harold Faltermeyer. (l)Film: *Fletch*, by Stephanie Mills. (P)Stephanie Mills.

BITS AND PIECES (1963) (wm)Dave Clark—Mike Smith. (P)The Dave Clark Five.

BITTER BAD (1973) (wm)Melanie Safka. (P)Melanie.

B. J. THE D. J. (1963) (wm)Hugh Lewis. (P)Stonewall Jackson.

BLACK AND TAN FANTASY (1927) (m)Bubber Miley—Duke Ellington. (P)Duke Ellington and his Orchestra.

BLACK & WHITE (1956) (w)David Arkin (m)Earl Robinson. (P)Three Dog Night. No. 1 Chart Record.

BLACK BEAUTY (1928) (m)Duke Ellington. (P)Duke Ellington as a piano jazz composition.

BLACK BETTY (1977) (wm)Kaye Dunham. (P)Ram Jam.

BLACK BOTTOM (1926) (w)B. G. De Sylva—Lew Brown (m)Ray Henderson. (l)Revue: *George White's Scandals of 1926*, by Ann Pennington, The McCarthy Sisters, Frances Williams and Tom Patricola. Recorded by Johnny Hamp and his Orchestra. (R)1956 Film: *The Best Things In Life Are Free*, by Sheree North

BLACK BOTTOM BALL (1927) (wm)Josephine Baker—Spencer Williams. (P)Josephine Baker.

BLACK BUTTERFLY (1937) (w)Ben Carruthers—Irving Mills (m)Duke Ellington. (P)Duke Ellington and his Orchestra.

BLACK COFFEE (1948) (wm)Paul Francis Webster—Sonny Burke. (P)Sarah Vaughan.

BLACK CROW BLUES (1963) (wm)Bob Dylan. (P)Bob Dylan.

BLACK DENIM TROUSERS AND MOTORCYCLE BOOTS (1955) (wm)Mike Stoller—Jerry Lieber. (P)The Cheers.

BLACK DOG (1972) (wm)Jimmy Page—Robert Plant—John Paul Jones. (P)Led Zeppelin.

BLACK EYED SUSAN BROWN (1933) (w)Herb Magidson (m)Al Hoffman—Al Goodhart. (P)Mark Fisher and his Orchestra.

BLACK IS BEAUTIFUL (1968) (wm)John Cacavas—Charles Wood. (P)Nancy Wilson.

BLACK IS BLACK (1966) (wm)Tony Hayes—Steve Wadey—M. Grainger. (P)Los Bravos.

BLACK IS THE COLOR OF MY TRUE LOVE'S HAIR (1875) (wm)Unknown. Traditional American folk song.

BLACK JAZZ (1932) (m)Eugene Gifford. (P)Glen Gray and The Casa Loma Orchestra.

BLACK LACE (1949) (w)Maria Shelton (m)Carl Fischer. (P)Frankie Laine.

BLACK LIMOUSINE (1981) (wm)Mick Jagger—Keith Richards—Ron Wood. (P)The Rolling Stones.

BLACK MAGIC WOMAN (1968) (wm)Peter Green. (P)Santana.

BLACK MAN (1976) (wm)Shatema Byrd—Stevie Wonder. (P)Stevie Wonder.

BLACK MARKET (1948) (wm)Frederick Hollander. (I)Film: A Foreign Affair, by Marlene Dietrich.

BLACK MOONLIGHT (1933) (wm)Sam Coslow—Arthur Johnston. (I)Film: Too Much Harmony, by Kitty Kelly. (P)Bing Crosby.

BLACK PEARL (1969) (wm)Phil Spector—Toni Wine—Irwin Levine. (P)Sonny Charles and The Checkmates.

BLACK SLACKS (1957) (wm)Joe Bennett—Jimmy Denton. (P)Joe Bennett and The Sparkletones.

BLACK SUPERMAN-"MUHAMMED ALI" (1974) (wm)Johnny Wakelin. (P)Jimmy Wakelin & The Kinshasha Band.

BLACK WATER (1975) (wm)Pat Simmons. (P)The Doobie Brothers. No. 1 Chart Record.

BLACKBIRD (1969) (wm)John Lennon—Paul McCartney. (P)The Beatles.

BLACKSMITH BLUES, THE (1952) (wm)Jack Holmes. (P)Ella Mae Morse.

BLAH-BLAH-BLAH (1931) (w)Ira Gershwin (m)George Gershwin. (I)Film: Delicious, by El Brendel.

BLAME IT ON MY LAST AFFAIR (1939) (wm)Henry Nemo—Irving Mills. (P)Mildred Bailey.

BLAME IT ON MY YOUTH (1934) (w)Edward Heyman (m)Oscar Levant. (P)Jan Garber and his Orchestra.

BLAME IT ON THE BOSSA NOVA (1962) (wm)Cynthia Weil—Barry Mann. (P)Eydie Gorme.

BLAME IT ON THE DANUBE (1937) (wm)Harry Akst—Frank Loesser. (I)Film: Fight For Your Lady, by Ida Lupino and reprised by John Boles.

BLAME IT ON THE RHUMBA (1936) (w)Harold Adamson (m)Jimmy McHugh. (I)Film: Top Of The Town, by Gertrude Niesen.

BLAME IT ON THE SAMBA (1948) (w-Eng)Ray Gilbert (m)Ernesto Nazareth. (I)Cartoon Film: Melody Time, by The Dinning Sisters with Ethel Smith on organ.

BLAZING SADDLES (1974) (w)Mel Brooks (m)John Morris. (I)Film: Blazing Saddles, by Frankie Laine on soundtrack.

BLEECKER STREET (1963) (wm)Paul Simon. (P)Simon and Garfunkel.

BLESS THE BEASTS AND CHILDREN (1971) (wm)Barry DeVorzon—Perry Botkin, Jr. (I)Film: Bless The Beasts And Children, by The Carpenters. (P)The Carpenters.

BLESS YOU (1961) (wm)Barry Mann—Cynthia Weil. (P)Tony Orlando.

BLESS YOUR BEAUTIFUL HIDE (1954) (w)Johnny Mercer (m)Gene de Paul. (I)Film: Seven Brides For Seven Brothers, by Howard Keel.

BLESS'EM ALL (1941) (wm)Jimmie Hughes—Frank Lake—Al Stillman. (P)In United States by The Jesters. (CR)The King Sisters.

BLIND MAN'S BUFF (1923) (wm)Jo Trent—Duke Ellington. (P)Duke Ellington. This was Ellington's first published song.

BLINDED BY THE LIGHT (1972) (wm)Bruce Springsteen. (P)Bruce Springsteen. (R)1977 by Manfred Mann. No. 1 Chart Record.

BLOB, THE (1958) (w)Mack David (m)Burt Bacharach. (I)Film: The Blob, by The Five Blobs.

BLOND SAILOR, THE (1945) (w-Eng)Mitchell Parish—Bell Leib (m)Jacob Pfeil. (P)The Andrews Sisters.

BLONDE IN THE BLEACHERS (1972) (wm)Joni Mitchell. (P)Joni Mitchell.

BLONDY (1929) (w)Arthur Freed (m)Nacio Herb Brown. (I)Film: Marianne.

BLOOD AND ROSES (1986) (wm)Pat DiNizio. (I)Film: Dangerously Close, by The Smithereens. (P)The Smithereens.

BLOODY MARY (1949) (w)Oscar Hammerstein II (m)Richard Rodgers. (I)Musical: South Pacific, by male chorus.

BLOOP, BLEEP! (1947) (wm)Frank Loesser. (P)Danny Kaye. (CR)Alvino Rey and his Orchestra.

BLOSSOM FELL, A (1955) (wm)Howard Barnes—Harold Cornelius—Dominic John. (P)Nat "King" Cole.

BLOSSOMS ON BROADWAY (1937) (wm)Leo Robin—Ralph Rainger. (I)Film: Blossoms On Broadway, by Shirley Ross.

BLOSSOMS ON THE BOUGH, THE (1949) (w)Sammy Gallop (m)Carl Sigman. (P)The Andrews Sisters.

BLOW AWAY (1979) (wm)George Harrison. (P)George Harrison.

BLOW, GABRIEL, BLOW (1934) (wm)Cole Porter. (I)Musical: Anything Goes, by Ethel Merman. Recorded by Enric Madriguera and his Orchestra. (R)1956 Film: Anything Goes, by Bing Crosby, Mitzi Gaynor, Donald O'Connor and Jeanmaire.

BLOW OUT THE CANDLE (1952) (wm)Phil Moore. (P)Jane Wyman.

BLOW THE MAN DOWN (1830) (wm)Unknown. Traditional song of the sea.

BLOWIN' IN THE WIND (1963) (wm)Bob Dylan. (I)Bob Dylan. (P)Peter, Paul and Mary. NARAS Award Winner. (R)1966 by Stevie Wonder.

BLOWING AWAY (1967) (wm)Laura Nyro. (P)1970 by The 5th Dimension.

BLOWTOP BLUES (1945) (wm)Leonard Feather—Jane

Feather. (P)Dinah Washington with Lionel Hampton and his Orchestra.

BLUE (And Broken Hearted) (1922) (w)Grant Clarke—Edgar Leslie (m)Lou Handman. (P)Marion Harris.

BLUE (1971) (wm)Joni Mitchell. (P)Joni Mitchell.

BLUE AGAIN (1930) (w)Dorothy Fields (m)Jimmy McHugh. (I)Revue: *The Vanderbilt Revue*, by Evelyn Hoey. (P)Guy Lombardo and his Royal Canadians. (CR)Red Nichols and his Five Pennies.

BLUE AND SENTIMENTAL (1939) (wm)Count Basie—Jerry Livingston—Mack David. (P)Count Basie and his Orchestra.

BLUE BAYOU (1963) (wm)Roy Orbison—Joe Melson. (P)Roy Orbison. (CR)Waylon Jennings. (R)1977 by Linda Ronstadt.

BLUE BIRD WALTZ (1954) (m)Frank Yankovic—Joe Trolli. (P)Frankie Yankovic.

BLUE CANARY (1953) (wm)Vincent Fiorino. (P)Dinah Shore.

BLUE CHAMPAGNE (1941) (wm)Grady Watts—Frank Ryerson. (P)Jimmy Dorsey and his Orchestra, vocal by Bob Eberly. No. 1 Chart Record.

BLUE CHRISTMAS (1945) (wm)Billy Hayes—Jay Johson. (P)Hugo Winterhalter and his Orchestra. (CR)Ernest Tubb, Russ Morgan and his Orchestra.

BLUE COLLAR MAN (1978) (wm)Tommy Shaw. (P)Styx.

BLUE DANUBE BLUES (1922) (w)Anne Caldwell (m)Jerome Kern. (I)Musical: *Good Morning Dearie*, by Louise Groody and Oscar Shaw.

BLUE DANUBE WALTZ, THE (1867) (m)Johann Strauss. Probably the most popular Viennese waltz. Early recording by Sousa's Band. (R)1933 by Wayne King and his Orchestra.

BLUE EVENING (1939) (wm)Gordon Jenkins—Joe Bishop. (P)Woody Herman and his Orchestra.

BLUE EYES (1982) (w)Gary Osborne (m)Elton John. (P)Elton John.

BLUE EYES CRYING IN THE RAIN (1945) (wm)Fred Rose. (R)1975 by Willie Nelson.

BLUE FEELING (1934) (m)Duke Ellington. (P)Duke Ellington and his Orchestra.

BLUE FLAME (1943) (w)Leo Corday (m)Jimmy Noble—Joe Bishop. (P)Theme song of Woody Herman and his Orchestra.

BLUE GARDENIA (1953) (wm)Bob Russell—Lester Lee. (I)Film: *Blue Gardenia* on soundtrack. (P)Nat "King" Cole.

BLUE GENIUS (1962) (wm)Ray Charles. (P)Ray Charles and Milt Jackson.

BLUE HAWAII (1937) (wm)Leo Robin—Ralph Rainger. (I)Film: *Waikiki Wedding*, by Bing Crosby and Shirley Ross. (P)Bing Crosby. Academy Award Winner. Song was originally introduced in Hawaii by Harry Owens and his Royal Hawaiian Orchestra. (R)1962 Film: *Blue Hawaii*, by Elvis Presley.

BLUE IS THE NIGHT (1930) (wm)Fred Fisher. (I)Film: *Their Own Desire*, by Norma Shearer.

BLUE JAY WAY (1967) (wm)George Harrison. (P)The Beatles.

BLUE JEAN (1984) (wm)David Bowie. (P)David Bowie.

BLUE LAMENT (1934) (w)Dave Franklin (m)Joe Bishop. (P)Isham Jones and his Orchestra, vocal by Eddie Stone.

BLUE LIGHT (1938) (m)Duke Ellington. (P)Duke Ellington and his Orchestra.

BLUE LIGHT BOOGIE (1950) (wm)Jessie Mae Robin-

son—Louis Jordan. (P)Louis Jordan.

BLUE LOU (1935) (wm)Edgar Sampson—Irving Mills. (I)Chick Webb and his Orchestra. (P)Benny Goodman and his Orchestra.

BLUE LOVEBIRD (1940) (w)Gus Kahn (m)Bronislaw Kaper. (I)Film: *Lillian Russell*, by Alice Faye and Don Ameche. (P)Kay Kyser and His College of Musical Knowledge. (CR)Mitchell Ayres and his Orchestra.

BLUE MIRAGE (1955) (w-Eng)Sam Coslow (m)Lotar Olias. (P)Guy Lombardo and his Orchestra.

BLUE MONDAY (1957) (wm)Dave Bartholomew—Antoine Domino. (I)Film: *The Girl Can't Help It*, by Fats Domino. (P)Fats Domino.

BLUE MONEY (1971) (wm)Van Morrison. (P)Van Morrison.

BLUE MONK (1954) (m)Thelonius Monk. (P)Thelonius Monk.

BLUE MOON (1934) (w)Lorenz Hart (m)Richard Rodgers. The only hit song written by them not intended for a musical or film. (P)Glen Gray and The Casa Loma Orchestra. No. 1 Chart Record. (CR)Benny Goodman and his Orchestra. (R)1949 Mel Torme, Billy Eckstine. (R)1961 by Elvis Presley. (R)1961 by The Marcels.

BLUE MOON OF KENTUCKY (1947) (wm)Bill Monroe. (I)Bill Monroe. This song was one of Elvis Presley's first recordings on Sun Records.

BLUE MORNING, BLUE DAY (1978) (wm)Lou Grammatico—Michael Jones. (P)Foreigner.

BLUE 'N BOOGIE (1945) (m)John Birks Gillespie—Frank Paparelli. (P)Dizzy Gillespie and his Sextet.

BLUE NIGHTFALL (1939) (w)Frank Loesser (m)Burton Lane. (I)Film: *St. Louis Blues*, by Lloyd Nolan and Dorothy Lamour.

BLUE OCEAN BLUES (1928) (w)Lorenz Hart (m)Richard Rodgers. (I)Musical: *Present Arms*, by Charles King.

BLUE ON BLUE (1963) (w)Hal David (m)Burt Bacharach. (P)Bobby Vinton.

BLUE ORCHIDS (1939) (wm)Hoagy Carmichael. (P)Glenn Miller and his Orchestra. (CR)Benny Goodman and his Orchestra.

BLUE PRELUDE (1933) (wm)Joe Bishop—Gordon Jenkins. (I)Isham Jones and his Orchestra. (P)Theme song of Woody Herman and his Orchestra.

BLUE RAIN (1939) (w)Johnny Mercer (m)Jimmy Van Heusen. (P)Theme song of Alvino Rey and his Orchestra.

BLUE, RED AND GRAY (1975) (wm)Peter Townshend. (P)The Who.

BLUE RHYTHM FANTASY (1936) (m)Teddy Hill—Chappie Willet. (P)Theme song of Teddy Hill and his Orchestra.

BLUE ROOM, THE (1926) (w)Lorenz Hart (m)Richard Rodgers. (I)Musical: *The Girl Friend*, by Eva Puck and Sammy White. First recordings by The Revelers, Sam Lanin and his Orchestra, The Melody Sheiks. (R)1949 Film: *Words And Music*, by Perry Como. Also recorded at this time by Como.

BLUE SHADOWS ON THE TRAIL (1948) (w)Johnny Lange (m)Eliot Daniel. (I)Cartoon Film: *Melody Time*, by Roy Rogers and The Sons Of The Pioneers. (P)Bing Crosby. (CR)Vaughn Monroe.

BLUE SKIES (1927) (wm)Irving Berlin. (I)Musical: *Betsy*, by Belle Baker. First recording by Ben Selvin and his Orchestra. No. 1 Chart Record. (CR)George Olsen and his Orchestra. Harry Richman, Vincent

Lopez and his Orchestra. (R)1941 by Johnny Long and his Orchestra. (R)1946 by Benny Goodman and his Orchestra. (R)1978 by Willie Nelson.

BLUE SKIRT WALTZ, THE (1948) (w-Eng)Mitchell Parish (m)Vaclav Blaha. (P)Frankie Yankovic and his Orchestra.

BLUE STAR (The Medic Theme) (1955) (w)Edward Heyman (m)Victor Young. (I)TV series: Medic as soundtrack theme. (P)Les Baxter and his Orchestra (instrumental). Vocal version by Felicia Sanders.

BLUE SUEDE SHOES (1955) (wm)Carl Lee Perkins. (I)Carl Perkins. (P)Elvis Presley.

BLUE TAIL FLY (see Jimmy Crack Corn).

BLUE TANGO (1951) (w)Mitchell Parish (m)Leroy Anderson. (P)Leroy Anderson and his Orchestra. (CR)Les Baxter, Hugo Winterhalter, Guy Lombardo and their Orchestras.

BLUE TURNING GRAY OVER YOU (1930) (w)Andy Razaf (m)Thomas "Fats" Waller. (P)Louis Armstrong.

BLUE TURNS TO GREY (1964) (wm)Mick Jagger—Keith Richard. (P)The Rolling Stones.

BLUE VELVET (1951) (wm)Bernie Wayne—Lee Morris. (P)Tony Bennett. (R)1963 by Bobby Vinton. No. 1 Chart Record.

BLUE VENETIAN WATERS (1937) (w)Gus Kahn (m)Bronislaw Kaper—Walter Jurmann. (I)Film: A Day At The Races, by Allan Jones.

BLUE VIOLINS (1951) (m)Ray Martin. (P)Hugo Winterhalter and his Orchestra.

BLUE WINTER (1963) (wm)Ben Raleigh—John Gluck, Jr. (P)Connie Francis.

BLUEBELL (1958) (w)Paul Francis Webster (m)Jerry Livingston. (P)Mitch Miller and his Chorus and Orchestra.

BLUEBERRY HILL (1940) (wm)Al Lewis—Larry Stock—Vincent Rose. (I)Film: The Singing Hill, by Gene Autry. (P)Glenn Miller and his Orchestra. No. 1 Chart Record. (CR)Kay Kyser and his Orchestra. (R)1957 by Fats Domino.

BLUEBIRD (1975) (wm)Leon Russell. (P)Helen Reddy.

BLUEBIRD OF HAPPINESS (1940) (w)Edward Heyman—Harry Parr Davies (m)Sandor Harmati. (P)Jan Peerce. (CR)Art Mooney and his Orchestra. (CR)Jo Stafford and Gordon MacRae.

BLUEBIRDS IN MY BELFRY (1944) (w)Johnny Burke (m)Jimmy Van Heusen.

BLUER THAN BLUE (1978) (wm)Randy Goodrum. (P)Michael Johnson.

BLUES IN ADVANCE (1952) (wm)Neil Drummond. (P)Dinah Shore.

BLUES IN MY HEART (1931) (wm)Benny Carter—Irving Mills. (P)Fletcher Henderson and his Orchestra.

BLUES IN THE NIGHT (1941) (w)Johnny Mercer (m)Harold Arlen. (I)Film: Blues In The Night, by William Gillespie. (P)Jimmy Lunceford and his Orchestra. (CR)Artie Shaw, Woody Herman, Dinah Shore, Cab Calloway, Benny Goodman. (R)1952 by Rosemary Clooney.

BLUES MY NAUGHTY SWEETIE GIVES TO ME (1919) (wm)Charles McCarron—Carey Morgan—Arthur Swanstrom. (P)Ted Lewis.

BLUES ON PARADE (1940) (m)Woody Herman—Toby Tyler. (P)Woody Herman and his Orchestra.

BLUES SERENADE, A (1935) (wm)Frank Signorelli—Jimmy Lytell—Vincente Grande—Mitchell Parish. (P)Theme song of Henry King and his Orchestra.

BLUE'S THEME (1966) (m)Mike Curb. (I)Film: The Wild Angels, by Davie Allan. (P)Davie Allan and The Arrows.

BLUES WITH A FEELING, THE (1929) (wm)Duke Ellington. (P)Duke Ellington and his Orchestra.

BLUESETTE (1963) (w)Norman Gimbel (m)Jean Thielemans. (P)Toots Thielemans. Vocal version by Sarah Vaughan.

BLUM BLUM (1949) (wm)Peggy Lee—Dave Barbour. (P)Peggy Lee.

BO DIDDLEY (1955) (wm)E. McDaniels. (P)Bo Diddley.

BO WEEVIL (1956) (wm)Dave Bartholomew—Antoine Domino. (P)Fats Domino.

BOA CONSTRICTOR (1962) (wm)Shel Silverstein. (P)Shel Silverstein.

BOA NOITE (1941) (w)Mack Gordon (m)Harry Warren. (I)Film: That Night In Rio, by Don Ameche.

BOB DYLAN'S 115th DREAM (1965) (P)Bob Dylan.

BOB WHITE (1937) (w)Johnny Mercer (m)Bernie Hanighen. (I)Guy Lombardo and his Royal Canadians. (P)Bing Crosby and Connee Boswell. (CR)Mildred Bailey.

BOBBY SHAFTO (1750) (wm)Unknown. Traditional sea chanty.

BOBBY SOX TO STOCKINGS (1959) (wm)Russell Faith—Clarence Wey Kehner—R. di Cicco. (P)Frankie Avalon.

BOBBY'S GIRL (1962) (wm)Henry Hoffman—Gary Klein. (P)Marcie Blane.

BODY AND SOUL (1930) (wm)Edward Heyman—Robert Sour—Frank Eyton—Johnny Green. (I)Revue: Three's A Crowd, by Libby Holman. First recording by Leo Reisman and his Orchestra with Eddy Duchin at the piano. (CR)Paul Whiteman, Ruth Etting, Helen Morgan, Ozzie Nelson, Louis Armstrong, Benny Goodman Trio. (R)1940 by Coleman Hawkins as a jazz tenor saxophone solo. Film: Body And Soul (1947) as soundtrack theme.

BODY LANGUAGE (1982) (wm)Freddy Mercury. (P)Queen.

BODY TALK (1986) (wm)Stephen Pearcy—Warren DeMartini—Juan Croucier. (I)Film: The Golden Child, by Ratt. (P)Ratt.

BOHEMIAN RHAPSODY (1976) (wm)Freddy Mercury. (P)Queen.

BOJANGLES OF HARLEM (1936) (w)Dorothy Fields (m)Jerome Kern. (I)Film: Swing Time, by Fred Astaire. (P)Fred Astaire.

BOLERO (1929) (m)Maurice Ravel. Very famous classical composition. (P)Film: Bolero, danced by George Raft and Carole Lombard.

BOLERO AT THE SAVOY (1939) (wm)Gene Krupa—Ray Biondi—Jimmy Mundy—Charles Carpenter. (P)Gene Krupa and his Orchestra, vocal by Anita O'Day.

BOLL WEEVIL SONG (1960) (wm)Clyde Otis—Brook Benton. (P)Brook Benton. (CR)Teresa Brewer.

BONANZA! (1959) (wm)Jay Livingston—Ray Evans. (I)TV series Bonanza!

BONAPARTE'S RETREAT (1949) (wm)Pee Wee King. (P)Pee Wee King. (CR)Kay Starr. (CR)Gene Krupa and his Orchestra.

BONEYARD SHUFFLE (1926) (m)Hoagy Carmichael—Irving Mills. (I)Curtis Hitch's Happy Harmonists with Carmichael at the piano. (P)Red Nichols and his Five Pennies.

BONGO ROCK (1959) (m)Preston Epps—Arthur Egnoian. (P)Preston Epps.

BONJOUR TRISTESSE (1957) (w)Arthur Laurents (m)Georges Auric. (I)Film: *Bonjour Tristesse* on soundtrack. (P)Gogi Grant.

BONNE NUIT-GOODNIGHT (1951) (wm)Jay Livingston—Ray Evans. (I)Film: *Here Comes The Groom*, by Bing Crosby. (P)Bing Crosby.

BONNIE BLUE GAL (1955) (w)William Engvick (m)Jessie Cavanaugh. (P)Mitch Miller and his Chorus and Orchestra.

BONNIE CAME BACK (1959) (m)Lee Hazlewood—Duane Eddy. (P)Duane Eddy.

BONY MORONIE (1957) (wm)Larry Williams. (P)Larry Williams.

BOO-HOO! (1937) (w)Edward Heyman (m)Carmen Lombardo—John Jacob Loeb. (P)Guy Lombardo and his Royal Canadians. (CR)Mal Hallet and his Orchestra.

BOOG-IT (1940) (wm)Cab Calloway—Buck Ram—Jack Palmer. (P)Glenn Miller and his Orchestra. (CR)Gene Krupa and his Orchestra. (CR)Cab Calloway and his Orchestra.

BOOGALOO DOWN BROADWAY (1967) (wm)Jesse James. (P)Fantastic Johnny C.

BOOGIE BLUES (1946) (wm)Gene Krupa—Ray Biondi. (P)Gene Krupa and his Orchestra, vocal by Anita O'Day.

BOOGIE CHILD (1976) (wm)Barry, Maurice and Robin Gibb. (I)Film: *Saturday Night Fever*, by the voices of The Bee Gees. (P)The Bee Gees.

BOOGIE CHILLUN (1949) (wm)John Lee Hooker. (P)John Lee Hooker.

BOOGIE DOWN (1973) (wm)Anita Poree—Frank Wilson—Leonard Caston. (P)Eddie Kendricks.

BOOGIE FEVER (1975) (wm)Freddy Perren—Kenny St. Louis. (P)The Sylvers. No. 1 Chart Record.

BOOGIE NIGHTS (1977) (wm)Rod Temperton. (P)Heatwave.

BOOGIE ON REGGAE WOMAN (1975) (wm)Stevie Wonder. (P)Stevie Wonder.

BOOGIE OOGIE OOGIE (1978) (wm)Janice Johnson—Perry Kibble. (P)A Taste Of Honey. No. 1 Chart Record.

BOOGIE SHOES (1975) (wm)Harry Casey—Richard Finch. (I)Film: *Saturday Night Fever*, by K. C. & The Sunshine Band. (P)K. C. & The Sunshine Band.

BOOGIE WONDERLAND (1979) (w)Allee Willis (m)Jonathan Lind. (P)Earth, Wind and Fire with The Emotions.

BOOGIE WOOGIE (1929) (m)Clarence "Pine Top" Smith. (I)Pine Top Smith. (R)1938 by Tommy Dorsey and his Orchestra.

BOOGIE WOOGIE BUGLE BOY (1941) (wm)Don Raye—Hughie Prince. (I)Film: *Buck Privates*, by The Andrews Sisters. (R)Bette Midler.

BOOGIE WOOGIE ETUDE (1943) (m)Morton Gould. (P)Jose Iturbi.

BOOGIE WOOGIE MAXIXE (1953) (wm)Sammy Gallop—Gil Rodin—Bob Crosby. (P)Bob Crosby and his Orchestra. Vocal version by The Ames Brothers.

BOOGIE WOOGIE PRAYER (1941) (m)Meade "Lux" Lewis, Albert Ammons, Pete Johnson. (I)Concert: Sprituals To Swing (Carnegie Hall)by Lewis, Ammons and Johnson.

BOOGIE WOOGIE STOMP (1941) (m)Albert Ammons. (P)Albert Ammons.

BOOGLIE WOOGLIE PIGGY, THE (1941) (wm)Roy Jacobs. (P)Glenn Miller and his Orchestra, vocal by Tex Beneke.

TOMMY DORSEY

When I had just been out of the army for a week or so, and was looking around the industry for something to do, I got a call from Bernie Pollock. Bernie was a song plugger for Tommy and Jimmy Dorsey's publishing firms and was familiar with my arranging work (and, I thought, my saxophone playing).

Bernie told me that Tommy Dorsey wanted to see me and subsequently an appointment was set up. I had never met Tommy before. Dressed in my best suit, I arrived at the Dorsey offices in the Brill Building. The Dorsey empire occupied the entire penthouse floor. I walked in, thinking I was about to be auditioned for a saxophone job in the band.

After a short interview, Tommy offered me a job. I asked whether he wanted me to play lead or second alto. He laughed and informed me he had hired me to be an arranger both for the band and for his publishing firms. This flattered me greatly since Dorsey had a reputation for picking good arrangers such as Axel Stordahl, Paul Weston, Sy Oliver, Nelson Riddle, and others. However, Tommy went on to explain that most of my arranging duties would be for the music publishing firms as a great backlog existed there.

Incidentally, my starting salary was $125 per week, and my first assignment to write an arranging book with Sy Oliver.

BOOK OF LOVE (1957) (wm)Warren Davis—Geroge Malone—Charles Patrick. (P)The Monotones.

BOOLA BOOLA (1898) (wm)Unknown. School song of Yale University.

BOOM BOOM BOOMERANG (1955) (wm)Lonnie Coleman. (P)The De Castro Sisters.

BOOMPS-A-DAISY (1940) (wm)Annette Mills. (I)In United States Revue: Hellzapoppin'.

BOOTS OF SPANISH LEATHER (1963) (wm)Bob Dylan. (P)Bob Dylan.

BOOZE AND BLUES (1924) (wm)J. Guy Suddoth. (P)Ma Rainey.

BOP! GOES MY HEART (1949) (w)Walter Bishop (m)Jule Styne. (P)Frank Sinatra.

BOP-TING-A-LING (1955) (wm)Winfield Scott. (P)LaVern Baker.

BORDER SONG (1970) (wm)Elton John—Bernie Taupin. (I)Elton John. (P)Aretha Franklin.

BORDERLINE (1983) (wm)Reginald Lucas. (P)Madonna.

BORN A WOMAN (1965) (wm)Martha Sharp. (P)Sandy Posey.

BORN AGAIN (1963) (wm)Howard Dietz—Arthur Schwartz. (I)Musical: *Jennie*, by Mary Martin, Jack De Lon and the Company.

BORN AND BRED IN OLD KENTUCKY (1925) (wm)B. G.

De Sylva—Joseph Meyer—James F. Hanley. (I)Musical: *Big Boy*, by Al Jolson.

BORN FREE (1966) (w)Don Black (m)John Barry. (I)Film: *Born Free* by Matt Monro. (P)Roger Williams. (CR)The Hesitations. Academy Award Winner.

BORN IN THE U. S. A. (1985) (wm)Bruce Springsteen. (P)Bruce Springsteen.

BORN TO BE ALIVE (1979) (wm)Patrick Hernandez. (P)Patrick Hernandez.

BORN TO BE BLUE (1947) (wm)Robert Wells—Mel Torme. (P)Mel Torme.

BORN TO BE WILD (1968) (wm)Mars Bonfire. (P)Steppenwolf. (R)1969 by Wilson Pickett.

BORN TO BE WITH YOU (1956) (wm)Don Robertson. (P)The Chordettes.

BORN TO LOSE (1943) (wm)Frankie Brown. (P)Ted Daffan.

BORN TO RUN (1975) (wm)Bruce Springsteen. (P)Bruce Springsteen.

BORN TO SING THE BLUES (1955) (w)Lenny Adelson (m)Imogene Carpenter. (P)Vic Damone.

BORN TO THE BREED (1975) (wm)Judy Collins. (P)Judy Collins.

BORN TO WANDER (1970) (wm)Tom Baird. (P)Rare Earth.

BORN TOO LATE (1958) (w)Fred Tobias (m)Charles Strouse. (P)The Poni Tails.

BORNING DAY, THE (1963) (wm)Fred Hellerman—Fran Minkoff. (P)Harry Belafonte.

BOSS, THE (1979) (wm)Nicholas Ashford—Valerie Simpson. (P)Diana Ross.

BOSS GUITAR (1963) (wm)Lee Hazlewood—Duane Eddy. (P)Duane Eddy.

BOSSA NOVA BABY (1963) (wm)Jerry Leiber—Mike Stoller. (P)Elvis Presley.

BOSSA NOVA U. S. A. (m)Dave Brubeck. (P)The Dave Brubeck Quartet.

BOSTON BEGUINE (1952) (wm)Sheldon Harnick. (I)Revue: *New Faces of 1952*, by Alice Ghostly.

BOTCH-A-ME (1952) (wm)Eddie Y. Stanley. (P)Rosemary Clooney.

BOTH SIDES NOW (also known as CLOUDS) (1967) (wm)Joni Mitchell. (P)Judy Collins.

BOTTLE OF WINE (1963) (wm)Tom Paxton. (I)Tom Paxton. (R)1968 by The Fireballs.

BOULEVARD (1980) (wm)Jackson Browne. (P)Jackson Browne.

BOULEVARD OF BROKEN DREAMS, THE (1933) (w)Al Dubin (m)Harry Warren. (I)Film: *Moulin Rouge*, by Constance Bennett. (P)Jan Garber and his Orchestra.

BOUNCE ME BROTHER WITH A SOLID FOUR (1941) (wm)Don Raye—Hughie Prince. (P)The Andrews Sisters.

BOUND FOR GLORY (1963) (wm)Phil Ochs. (P)Phil Ochs. This song is a tribute to Woody Guthrie.

BOUQUET OF ROSES (1948) (wm)Steve Nelson—Bob Hilliard. (P)Eddy Arnold.

BOURBON STREET BEAT (1959) (wm)Mack David—Jerry Livingston. (I)TV series: *Bourbon Street Beat.*

BOURBON STREET PARADE (1952) (m)Paul Barbarin. (P)Paul Barbarin and his New Orleans Band.

BOUTONNIERE (1950) (w)Bob Hilliard (m)Dave Mann. (P)Mindy Carson.

BOWERY, THE (1892) (w)Charles H. Hoyt (m)Percy Gaunt. (I)Musical: *A Trip To Chinatown*. Recorded by Dan Quinn.

BOXER, THE (1968) (wm)Paul Simon (P)Simon and Garfunkel.

BOY FROM NEW YORK CITY, THE (1964) (wm)John Taylor. (P)The Ad Libs. (R)1981 by Manhattan Transfer.

BOY I LEFT BEHIND ME, THE (1942) (w)Lorenz Hart (m)Richard Rodgers. (I)Musical: *By Jupiter*, by Jayne Manners.

BOY IN THE BUBBLE, THE (1986) (wm)Paul Simon—Forere Motlobelos. (P)Paul Simon. Song is based on roots music of South Africa.

BOY LIKE YOU, A (1947) (w)Langston Hughes (m)Kurt Weill. (I)Musical: *Street Scene*, by Polyna Stoska.

BOY MEETS HORN (1938) (w)Irving Mills (m)Duke Ellington—Rex Stewart. (P)Duke Ellington and his Orchestra, featuring Rex Stewart on trumpet.

BOY NAMED SUE, A (1969) (wm)Shel Silverstein. (P)Johnny Cash. NARAS Award Winner.

BOY NEXT DOOR, THE (1944) (wm)Hugh Martin—Ralph Blane. (I)Film: *Meet Me In St. Louis*, by Judy Garland. (P)Judy Garland.

BOY ON A DOLPHIN (1957) (w-Eng)Paul Francis Webster (m)Takis Morakis. (I)Film: *Boy On A Dolphin*, by Julie London. (P)Julie London.

BOY! WHAT LOVE HAS DONE TO ME (1930) (w)Ira Gershwin (m)George Gershwin. (I)Musical: *Girl Crazy*, by Ethel Merman.

BOY WITHOUT A GIRL, A (1959) (wm)Sid Jacobson—Ruth Sexter. (P)Frankie Avalon.

BOYS (1960) (wm)Luther Dixon—Wes Farrell. (P)The Shirelles. (R)1964 by The Beatles.

BOYS ARE BACK IN TOWN, THE (1976) (wm)Phil Lynott. (P)Thin Lizzy.

BOYS IN THE BACK ROOM, THE (1939) (w)Frank Loesser (m)Frederick Hollander. (I)Film: *Destry Rides Again*, by Marlene Dietrich. (P)Marlene Dietrich.

BOYS' NIGHT OUT, THE (1962) (w)Sammy Cahn (m)Jimmy Van Heusen. (I)Film: *The Boys' Night Out*. (P)Patti Page.

BOYS OF SUMMER, THE (1984) (wm)Don Henley—Mike Campbell. (P)Don Henley.

BRAHMS' LULLABY (1868) (w)Unknown (m)Johannes Brahms. Popular recording in 1941 by Bing Crosby.

BRAND NEW KEY (1971) (wm)Melanie Safka. (P)Melanie. No. 1 Chart Record.

BRAND NEW LOVER (1986) (wm)Dead or Alive. (P)Dead or Alive.

BRAND NEW ME, A (1969) (wm)Kenny Gamble—Jerry Butler—Theresa Bell. (I)Dusty Springfield. (P)Aretha Franklin.

BRANDY (You're A Fine Girl) (1972) (wm)Elliot Lurie. (P)Looking Glass. No. 1 Chart Record.

BRASS IN POCKET (I'm Special) (1979) (wm)Chryssie Hynde—James Scott. (P)The Pretenders.

BRAZIL (1942) (w-Eng)S. K. Russell (m)Ary Barroso. (I)In United States by Eddy Duchin and his Orchestra. (CR)Xavier Cugat and his Orchestra. (P)Jimmy Dorsey and his Orchestra, vocal by Helen O'Connell and Bob Eberly. (R)1975 by The Ritchie Family.

BREAD AND BUTTER (1964) (wm)Larry Parks—Jay Turnbow. (P)The Newbeats.

BREAKAWAY (1983) (wm)Jackie DeShannon—Sharon Sheeley. (I)Film: *Sylvester*, by Gail Davies.

BREAK IT TO ME GENTLY (1961) (wm)Diane Lampert—Joe Seneca. (P)Brenda Lee. (R)1982 by Juice Newton.

BREAK MY STRIDE (1983) (wm)Matthew Wilder—Greg Prestopino. (P)Matthew Wilder.

BREAK UP TO MAKE UP (1972) (wm)Thom Bell—Kenny Gamble—Linda Creed. (P)The Stylistics.

BREAKAWAY, THE (1929) (w)Sidney D. Mitchell—Archie Gottler (m)Con Conrad. (I)Film: *Fox Movietone Follies of 1929*, by Jeanette Dancey, Sue Carol and Chorus.

BREAKAWAY (1975) (wm)Benny Gallagher—Graham Lyle. (P)Art Garfunkel.

BREAKDANCE (1984) (w)Irene Cara—Bunny Hull (m)Giorgio Moroder. (I)Film: *Breakdance*, by Irene Cara. (P)Irene Cara.

BREAKDOWN (1977) (wm)Tom Petty. (P)Tom Petty And The Heartbreakers.

BREAKDOWN DEAD AHEAD (1980) (wm)Box Scaggs—David Foster. (P)Boz Scaggs.

BREAKFAST BALL (1934) (w)Ted Koehler (m)Harold Arlen. (I)Revue: *Cotton Club Parade*, by Jimmy Lunceford and His Orchestra.

BREAKIN' IN A PAIR OF SHOES (1935) (wm)Ned Washington—Dave Franklin—Sammy Stept. (P)Benny Goodman and his Orchestra.

BREAKIN'. . . THERE'S NO STOPPING US (1984) (wm)Ollie Brown—Jerry Knight. (I)Film: *Breakin'* on soundtrack. (P)Ollie and Jerry.

BREAKING IN A BRAND NEW BROKEN HEART (1961) (wm)Howard Greenfield—Jack Keller. (P)Connie Francis.

BREAKING UP IS HARD TO DO (1962) (wm)Howard Greenfield—Neil Sedaka. (P)Neil Sedaka. No. 1 Chart Record. (R)1972 by The Partridge Family.

BREAKING US IN TWO (1983) (wm)Joe Jackson. (P)Joe Jackson.

BREATHLESS (1958) (wm)Otis Blackwell. (P)Jerry Lee Lewis.

BREEZE, THE (That's Bringin' My Honey Back To Me) (1934) (wm)Tony Sacco—Al Lewis—Dick Smith. (P)Clarence Williams and his Orchestra. (CR)Anson Weeks and his Orchestra.

BREEZE AND I, THE (1940) (w-Eng)Al Stillman (m)Ernesto Lecuona—Tutti Camarata. Adapted from Lecuona's Andalucia Suite. (P)Jimmy Dorsey and his Orchestra, vocal by Bob Eberly. No. 1 Chart Record. (CR)Vic Damone. (CR)Xavier Cugat and his Orchestra.

BREEZIN' (1976) (m)Bobby Womack. (P)George Benson.

BREEZIN' ALONG WITH THE BREEZE (1926) (wm)Haven Gillespie—Seymour Simons—Richard A. Whiting. (P)Al Jolson. Theme song of Lou Breese and his Orchestra. (CR)Abe Lyman and his Orchestra.

BRIAN'S SONG (1972) (w)Alan and Marilyn Bergman (m)Michel Legrand. (I)TV Film: *Brian's Song* on soundtrack. (P)Michel Legrand and his Orchestra.

BRICK HOUSE (1977) (wm)William King,Jr. —Ronald La Pread—Thomas McClary—Walter Lee Orange—Lionel Richie—Milan Williams. (P)The Commodores.

BRIDAL CHORUS (Lohengrin) (1852) (m)Richard Wagner. From Opera: *Lohengrin*.

BRIDE AND GROOM POLKA (1948) (wm)Allan Roberts—Lester Lee. (P)The Andrews Sisters.

BRIDGE OVER TROUBLED WATER (1970) (wm)Paul Simon. (P)Simon and Garfunkel. No. 1 Chart Record.

NARAS Award Winner. (R)1971 by Aretha Franklin.

BRIDGES AT TOKO-RI, THE (1954) (m)Lyn Murray. (I)Film: *The Bridges At Toko-Ri* on soundtrack.

BRIGADOON (1947) (w)Alan Jay Lerner (m)Frederick Loewe. (I)Musical: *Brigadoon*, by The Chorus.

BRIGHT EYES (1920) (w)Harry Smith (m)Otto Motzan—M. K. Jerome. (P)Paul Whiteman and his Orchestra. (CR)Leo Reisman and his Orchestra.

BRILLIANT DISGUISE (1987) (wm)Bruce Springsteen. (P)Bruce Springsteen.

BRING BACK THE THRILL (1950) (w)Ruth Poll (m)Pete Rugolo. (P)Eddie Fisher.

BRING IT ON HOME TO ME (1962) (wm)Sam Cooke. (P)Sam Cooke.

BRING IT UP (1967) (wm)James Brown—Nat Jones. (P)James Brown.

BRING THE BOYS HOME (1971) (wm)Angelo Bond—Greg Perry—General Johnson. (P)Freda Payne.

BRISTOL STOMP, THE (1961) (wm)Kal Mann—Dave Appell. (P)The Dovells.

BROADWAY (1927) (w)B. G. De Sylva—Lew Brown (m)Ray Henderson. (I)Musical: *Manhattan Mary*, by Lou Holtz and The Embassy Boys.

BROADWAY (1940) (wm)Henry Woode—Teddy McRae—Bill Bird. (P)Count Basie and his Orchestra.

BROADWAY JAMBOREE (1937) (w)Harold Adamson (m)Jimmy McHugh. (I)Film: *You're A Sweetheart*, by Frances Hunt.

BROADWAY MELODY, THE (1929) (w)Arthur Freed (m)Nacio Herb Brown. (I)Film: *The Broadway Melody*, by Charles King. (P)Charles King. (CR)Nat Shilkret and his Orchestra.

BROADWAY RHYTHM (1935) (w)Arthur Freed (m)Nacio Herb Brown. (I)Film: *Broadway Melody Of 1936*, by Frances Langford. Recorded by Guy Lombardo and his Royal Canadians.

BROADWAY ROSE (1920) (wm)Eugene West—Martin Freed—Otis Spencer. (P)The Peerless Quartet.

BROADWAY'S GONE HAWAII (1937) (wm)Mack Gordon—Harry Revel. (I)Film: *Love And Hisses*, by Ruth Terry, The Peters Sisters and Ben Bernie and his Orchestra.

BROADWAY'S GONE HILL BILLY (1934) (w)Lew Brown (m)Jay Gorney. (I)Film: *Stand Up And Cheer*, by Sylvia Froos.

BROKEN DOWN MERRY-GO-ROUND (1950) (wm)Arthur Herbert—Fred Stryker. (P)Margaret Whiting and Jimmy Wakely.

BROKEN HEART AND A PILLOW FILLED WITH TEARS, A (1960) (wm)Paul Anka. (P)Patti Page.

BROKEN HEARTED ME, A (wm)Randy Goodrum. (P)Anne Murray.

BROKEN HEARTED MELODY (1922) (w)Gus Kahn (m)Isham Jones. (P)Isham Jones and his Orchestra.

BROKEN HEARTED MELODY (1959) (w)Hal David (m)Sherman Edwards. (P)Sarah Vaughan.

BROKEN RECORD, THE (1935) (wm)Cliff Friend—Charles Tobias—Boyd Bunch. (P)Guy Lombardo and his Royal Canadians.

BROKEN WINGS (1985) (wm)Richard Page—Steven George—John Lang. (P)Mr. Mister. No. 1 Chart Record.

BROOKLYN BRIDGE, THE (1947) (w)Sammy Cahn (m)Jule Styne. (I)Film: *It Happened In Brooklyn*, by Frank Sinatra. (P)Frank Sinatra.

BROOKLYN ROADS (1968) (wm)Neil Diamond. (P)Neil

Diamond.

BROTHER, CAN YOU SPARE A DIME? (1932) (w)E. Y. Harburg (m)Jay Gorney. (I)Revue: *Americana*, by Rex Weber. (P)Bing Crosby. (P)Rudy Vallee. Both records were No. 1 Chart Records.

BROTHER LOUIE (1973) (wm)Errol Brown—Anthony Wilson. (P)Stories. No. 1 Chart Record.

BROTHER LOVE'S TRAVELLING SALVATION SHOW (1969) (wm)Neil Diamond (P)Neil Diamond.

BROTHER RAPP (1970) (wm)James Brown (P)James Brown.

BROTHERHOOD OF MAN (1961) (wm)Frank Loesser. (I)Musical: *How To Succeed In Business Without Really Trying*, by Robert Morse, Sammy Smith, Ruth Kobart and the Company.

BROTHERS KARAMAZOV, THE (Love Theme) (1958) (m)Bronislau Kaper. (I)Film: *The Brothers Karamazov* on soundtrack.

BROWN EARTH (1971) (wm)Laura Nyro. (P)Laura Nyro.

BROWN EYED GIRL (1967) (wm)Van Morrison. (P)Van Morrison. (R)1972 by El Chicano.

BROWN EYED WOMAN (1968) (wm)Barry Mann—Cynthia Weill. (P)Bill Medley.

BROWN EYES, WHY ARE YOU BLUE? (1925) (w)Alfred Bryan (m)George W. Meyer. (P)Nick Lucas.

BROWN SUGAR (1971) (wm)Mick Jagger—Keith Richards. (P)The Rolling Stones. No. 1 Chart Record.

BRUCE (1981) (wm)Rick Springfield. (P)Rick Springfield.

BRUSH THOSE TEARS FROM YOUR EYES (1948) (wm)Oakley Haldeman—Al Trace—Jimmy Lee. (P)Al Trace and his Orchestra. (CR)Evelyn Knight.

BRUSH UP YOUR SHAKESPEARE (1948) (wm)Cole Porter. (I)Musical: *Kiss Me Kate*, by Harry Clark and Jack Diamond. In film version by Keenan Wynn and James Whitmore.

BUBBLE-LOO, BUBBLE-LOO (1948) (w)Paul Francis Webster (m)Hoagy Carmichael. (P)Hoagy Carmichael. (CR)Peggy Lee.

BUCKLE DOWN, WINSOCKI (1941) (wm)Hugh Martin—Ralph Blane. (I)Musical: *Best Foot Forward*, by Tommy Dix, Stuart Langley and Chorus.

BUDDIE, BEWARE (1934) (wm)Cole Porter. (I)Musical: *Anything Goes*, by Ethel Merman.

BUDS WON'T BUD (1937) (w)E. Y. Harburg (m)Harold Arlen. (I)Musical: *Hooray For What!*, by Hannah Williams. (R)Film: *Andy Hardy Meets Debutante* (1940)by Judy Garland.

BUENOS AIRES (1975) (m)Andrew Lloyd Webber (w)Tim Rice. (I)Musical: *Evita*, by Julie Covington in London version. Patti Lupone in American version.

BUFFALO GALS (1844) (wm)Cool White. Traditional American folk song.

BUGLE CALL RAG (1923) (m)Jack Pettis—Billy Meyers—Elmer Schoebel. (I)Friar's Society Orchestra. (R)1927 by Sophie Tucker. (R)1932 by The Mills Brothers. (R)1936 by Benny Goodman and his Orchestra.

BUILD ME UP, BUTTERCUP (wm)Tony McCauley-Michael D'Abo. (P)The Foundations.

BULLDOG, BULLDOG (1911) (wm)Cole Porter. This song written as a football song by Porter while a student at Yale University.

BUMBLE BOOGIE (1946) (m)Jack Fina. Adaptation of Rimsky—Korsakov's Flight Of The Bumblebee. (P)Freddy Martin and his Orchestra, featuring Jack

Fina on piano.

BUMBLEBEE (1959) (wm)Leroy Fullylove. (P)LaVern Baker. (R)1965 by The Searchers.

BUNDLE OF OLD LOVE LETTERS, A (1929) (w)Arthur Freed (m)Nacio Herb Brown. (I)Film: *Lord Byron Of Broadway*, by Charles Kaley. (P)Paul Whiteman and his Orchestra.

BUNGLE IN THE JUNGLE (1974) (wm)Ian Anderson. (P)Jethro Tull.

BUNNY HOP, THE (1952) (wm)Ray Anthony—Leonard Auletti. (P)Ray Anthony and his Orchestra.

BUON NATALE (Means Merry Xmas To You) (1959) (wm)Bob Saffer—Nat Cole. (P)Nat "King" Cole.

BURN ON, BIG RIVER (1970) (wm)Randy Newman. (P)Randy Newman.

BURN THAT CANDLE (1955) (wm)Winfield Scott. (P)Bill Haley and The Comets.

BURNING DOWN THE HOUSE (1983) (wm)David Byrne—Chris Frantz—Jerry Harrison—Tina Weymouth. (P)Talking Heads.

BURNING BRIDGES (1960) (wm)Melvin Miller. (P)Jack Scott.

BURNING HEART (1985) (wm)Frankie Sullivan—Jim Peterik. (I)Film: *Rocky IV* by Survivor. (P)Survivor.

BURNING LOVE (1972) (wm)Dennis Linde. (P)Elvis Presley.

BURNING OF ATLANTA, THE (1962) (wm)Chuck Taylor. (P)Claude King.

BUS STOP (1966) (wm)Graham Gouldman (P)The Hollies.

BUS STOP SONG, THE (1956) (wm)Ken Darby. (I)Film: *Bus Stop*, by The Four Lads on soundtrack. (P)The Four Lads.

BUSHEL AND A PECK, A (1950) (wm)Frank Loesser. (I)Musical: *Guys And Dolls*, by Vivian Blaine. (P)Betty Hutton and Perry Como. (CR)Doris Day.

BUSINESS IN F (1931) (m)Archie Bleyer. (P)Fletcher Henderson and his Orchestra.

BUSTED (1962) (wm)Harlan Howard. (I)Johnny Cash. (P)Ray Charles. NARAS Award Winner.

BUSY DOING NOTHING (1948) (w)Johnny Burke (m)Jimmy Van Heusen. (I)Film: *A Connecticut Yankee*, by Bing Crosby, William Bendix and Cedric Hardwicke.

BUT DEFINITELY (1936) (wm)Mack Gordon—Harry Revel. (I)Film: *Poor Little Rich Girl*, by Shirley Temple, Alice Faye and Jack Haley.

BUT I DID (1945) (w)Al Jacobs (m)Joseph Meyer. (P)Dinah Shore.

BUT I DO (1961) (wm)Robert Guidry—Paul Gayten. (P)Clarence "Frogman" Henry. (R)1973 by Bobby Vinton.

BUT IN THE MORNING, NO! (1939) (wm)Cole Porter. (I)Musical: *Du Barry Was A Lady*, by Ethel Merman and Bert Lahr.

BUT IT'S ALRIGHT (1966) (wm)Jerome Jackson—Pierre Tubbs. (P)J. J. Jackson.

BUT NOT FOR ME (1930) (w)Ira Gershwin (m)George Gershwin. (I)Musical: *Girl Crazy*, by Ginger Rogers and reprised by Willie Howard. (R)Film: *Girl Crazy* (1943)by Judy Garland. Recorded 1942 by Harry James and his Orchestra.

BUT WHERE ARE YOU (1936) (wm)Irving Berlin. (I)Film: *Follow The Fleet*, by Harriet Hilliard. Recorded by Ozzie Nelson and his Orchestra.

BUT YOU KNOW I LOVE YOU (1969) (wm)Mike Settle.

(P)Kenny Rogers and The First Edition. (CR)Bill Anderson.

BUT YOU'RE MINE (1965) (wm)Sonny Bono. (P)Sonny and Cher.

BUTTERFLIES (1953) (wm)Bob Merrill. (P)Patti Page.

BUTTERFLY (1957) (wm)Bernie Lowe—Kal Mann. (P)Andy Williams. (P)Charlie Gracie. Both No. 1 Chart Records.

BUTTON UP YOUR HEART (1930) (w)Dorothy Fields (m)Jimmy McHugh. (I)Revue: *The Vanderbilt Revue*, by Evelyn Hoey and Charles Barnes.

BUTTON UP YOUR OVERCOAT! (1928) (wm)B. G. De Sylva—Lew Brown (m)Ray Henderson. Early recordings by Helen Kane, Paul Whiteman, Ruth Etting, Fred Waring's Pennsylvanians.

BUTTONS AND BOWS (1948) (wm)Jay Livingston—Ray Evans. (I)Film: *Paleface*, by Bob Hope. Academy Award Winner. (P)Dinah Shore. (CR)Evelyn Knight.

BUY AND SELL (1966) (wm)Laura Nyro. (P)Laura Nyro.

BUY FOR ME THE RAIN (1967) (w)Greg Copeland (m)Steve Noonan. (P)The Nitty Gritty Dirt Band.

BUZZ BUZZ BUZZ (1957) (wm)J. Gray—R. Bird. (P)The Hollywood Flames.

BUZZ ME (1945) (wm)Danny Baxter—Fleecie Moore. (P)Louis Jordan and his Tympani Five.

BY A WATERFALL (1933) (w)Irving Kahal (m)Sammy Fain. (I)Film: *Footlight Parade*, by Ruby Keeler and Dick Powell. Recorded by Guy Lombardo, Rudy Vallee, Leo Reisman and their Orchestras.

BY HECK (1914) (w)L. Wolfe Gilbert (m)S. R. Henry. (I)Musical: *Push And Go*, by John Henning.

BY LOVE POSSESSED (1961) (w)Sammy Cahn (m)Elmer Bernstein. (I)Film: *By Love Possessed* on soundtrack.

BY MYSELF (1937) (w)Howard Dietz (m)Arthur Schwartz. (1937) (I)Musical: *Between The Devil*, by Jack Buchanan. (R)Film: *The Band Wagon* (1953)by Fred Astaire. (R)Film: *I Could Go On Singing* (1963)by Judy Garland.

BY STRAUSS (1936) (w)Ira Gershwin (m)George Gershwin. (I)Revue: *The Show Is On*, by Gracie Barrie and Robert Shafter. (R)Film: *An American In Paris* (1951)by Gene Kelly, Oscar Levant and Georges Guetary.

BY THE BEAUTIFUL SEA (1914) (w)Harold Atteridge (m)Harry Carroll. Early recordings by The Heidelberg Quintet, Ada Jones & Billy Watkins,Prince's Orchestra.

BY THE FIRESIDE (1932) (wm)Ray Noble—Jimmy Campbell—Reg Connelly. (P)Ray Noble and his Orchestra. (CR)George Olsen and his Orchestra.

BY THE LIGHT OF THE SILVERY MOON (1909) (w)Edward Madden (m)Gus Edwards. (I)Revue: *Ziegfeld Follies*. Early recordings by Billy Murray, Ada Jones, Peerless Quartet. (R)1942 by Ray Noble and his Orchestra.

BY THE MISSISSINEWAH (1942) (wm)Cole Porter. (I)Musical: *Something For The Boys*, by Ethel Merman and Paula Lawrence.

BY THE RIVER OF THE ROSES (1944) (w)Marty Symes (m)Joe Burke. (P)Woody Herman and his Orchestra.

BY THE RIVER SAINTE MARIE (1931) (w)Edgar Leslie (m)Harry Warren. (P)Kate Smith. (CR)Guy Lombardo and his Royal Canadians. (CR)Jimmy Lunceford and his Orchestra, vocal by Dan Grissom.

BY THE SYCAMORE TREE (1931) (w)Haven Gillespie (m)Pete Wendling. Early recordings by Bob Roberts, Harry Macdonough.

BY THE TIME I GET TO PHOENIX (1967) (wm)Jim Webb. (P)Glen Campbell. (R)1969 by Isaac Hayes.

BY THE WATERS OF MINNETONKA (1914) (w)J. M. Cavanass (m)Thurlow Lieurance. First recorded by Alice Nielsen.

BY THE WAY (1948) (w)Mack Gordon (m)Josef Myrow. (I)Film: *When My Baby Smiles At Me*.

BY-U, BY-O (The Lou'siana Lullaby) (1941) (wm)Jack Owens—Ted McMichael—Leo V. Killion. (P)Woody Herman and his Orchestra, vocal by Muriel Lane.

BYE AND BYE (1925) (w)Lorenz Hart (m)Richard Rodgers. (I)Musical: *Dearest Enemy*, by Helen Ford and Charles Purcell.

BYE BYE BABY (1936) (w)Walter Hirsch (m)Lou Handman. (P)Fats Waller (CR)Charlie Barnet and his Orchestra.

BYE BYE BABY (1949) (w)Leo Robin (m)Jule Styne. (I)Musical: *Gentlemen Prefer Blondes*, by Carol Channing and Jack McCauley. (R)Film version (1953)by Marilyn Monroe.

BYE BYE BABY (Baby Goodbye) (1965) (wm)Bob Gaudio—Bob Crewe. (P)The Four Seasons.

BYE BYE BIRDIE (1963) (w)Lee Adams (m)Charles Strouse. (I)Film: *Bye Bye Birdie*, by Ann Margret.

BYE BYE BLACKBIRD (1926) (w)Mort Dixon (m)Ray Henderson. (P)Eddie Cantor and The Duncan Sisters. Recorded by Gene Austin, Nick Lucas, Leo Reisman and his Orchestra. (R)1948 by Russ Morgan and his Orchestra. (R)Film: *The Eddie Cantor Story* (1953)by Eddie Cantor dubbing for Keefe Brasselle.

BYE BYE BLUES (1930) (wm)Bert Lown—Chauncey Gray—David Bennett—Fred Hamm. (P)Theme song of Bert Lown and his Orchestra. (CR)Leo Reisman and his Orchestra. (R)1941)by Cab Callloway and his Orchestra. (R)1953 by Les Paul and Mary Ford. (R)1965 by Bert Kaempfert and his Orchestra.

BYE BYE JOHNNY (1960) (wm)Chuck Berry. (P)Chuck Berry.

BYE BYE LOVE (1957) (wm)Felice and Boudleaux Bryant. (P)The Everly Brothers. (CR)The Everly Brothers.

"C" JAM BLUES (1942) (m)Duke Ellington. (P)Duke Ellington and his Orchestra.

C-I-T-Y (1985) (wm)John Cafferty. (P)John Cafferty and The Beaver Brown Band.

C-O-N-S-T-A-N-T-I-N-O-P-L-E (1928) (wm)Harry Carlton. Famous English novelty song.

(I'll See You In)C-U-B-A (1920) (wm)Irving Berlin. No artist credited with introduction. (R)1946)Film: *Blue Skies* by Bing Crosby and Olga San Juan.

CA, C'EST L'AMOUR (1957) (I)Film: *Les Girls*, by Taina Elg. (P)Tony Bennett.

CAB DRIVER (1968) (wm)Carson Parks. (P)The Mills Brothers.

CABARET (1949) (wm)Al Russell—Joel Cowan. (P)Rosemary Clooney.

CABARET (1966) (w)Fred Ebb (m)John Kander. (I)Musical: *Cabaret*, by Jill Haworth. Recorded by Herb Alpert and The Tijuana Brass. (R)1972 Film: *Cabaret*, by Liza Minnelli.

CABIN IN THE COTTON (1932) (w)Mitchell Parish (m)Frank Perkins. (P)Bing Crosby. (CR)Cab Calloway.

CABIN IN THE SKY (1940) (w)John Latouche (m)Vernon Duke. (I)Musical: *Cabin In The Sky*, by Ethel Waters and Dooley Wilson. In film version (1943)by Ethel Waters and Eddie "Rochester" Anderson.

CACTUS TREE (1968) (wm)Joni Mitchell. (P)Joni Mitchell.

CADILLAC CAR (1981) (w)Tom Eyen (m)Henry Krieger. (I)Musical: *Dreamgirls*, by Ben Harney, Cleavant Derricks and Obba Babatunde.

CAESAR AND CLEOPATRA THEME (see A World Of Love).

CAJUN QUEEN, THE (1962) (wm)Wayne Walker. (P)Jimmy Dean.

CAKE WALKING BABIES FROM HOME (1924) (wm)Chris Smith—Henry Troy—Clarence Williams. (P)Red Onion Jazz Babies, vocal by Alberta Hunter.

CAKEWALK YOUR LADY (1946) (w)Johnny Mercer (m)Harold Arlen. (I)Musical: *St. Louis Woman*, by Pearl Bailey.

CALCUTTA (1961) (w-Eng)Lee Pockriss—Paul Vance (m)Heino Gaze. (P)In United States by Lawrence Welk and his Orchestra. No. 1 Chart Record.

CALDONIA (What Makes Your Big Head So Hard?) (1945) (wm)Fleecie Moore. (P)Louis Jordan and his Tympani Five. (CR)Woody Herman and his Orchestra.

CALENDAR GIRL (1961) (wm)Howard Greenfield—Neil Sedaka. (P)Neil Sedaka.

CALICO DAYS (1933) (w)Ted Koehler (m)Harold Arlen. (I)Revue: *Cotton Club Parade*, by George Dewey Washington.

CALIFORN-I-AY (1946) (w)E. Y. Harburg (m)Jerome Kern. (I)Film: *Can't Help Singing*, by Deanna Durbin and Robert Paige.

CALIFORNIA DREAMING (1965) (wm)John and Michelle Phillips. (P)The Mamas and The Papas. (R)1969 by Bobby Womack. (R)1979 by America. (R)1986 by The Beach Boys.

CALIFORNIA GIRLS (1965) (wm)Brian Wilson. (P)The Beach Boys. (R)1985 by David Lee Roth.

CALIFORNIA, HERE I COME (1924) (wm)Al Jolson—B. G. De Sylva—Joseph Meyer. (I)Musical: *Bombo*, by Al Jolson. (P)Al Jolson. (CR)Theme song of Abe Lyman and his Orchestra. (R)1946 Film: *The Jolson Story* by voice of Jolson dubbing for Larry Parks. (R)1952 Film: *With A Song In My Heart*, by voice of Jane Froman dubbing for Susan Hayward.

RONALD REAGAN

Talk about big names ...

One day a gentleman named Jules Fields walked into my office. He had the rights to a soundtrack of a film narrated by Ronald Reagan (then the governor of California). My company agreed to purchase the rights to the sound track of *Freedom's Finest Hour*, in which Mr. Reagan narrated all the important speeches of American History (Lincoln's Gettysburg Address, for example). I added some music and got my name in the liner notes as co-producer.

Shortly after the album had been produced, a cruise was leaving New York with the governors of all the states on board plus a very large press contingent. Lynn Nofziger, Governor Reagan's right hand man, called asking if we could provide 500 copies of the album down to the ship. The governor wanted to pass them out as souvenirs of the cruise. Of course we did, at no charge, and later received a very nice thank you note from Mr. Reagan.

Sales of the album were pretty good, and when Mr. Reagan became President we put on a little publicity campaign and the album really started to sell well. It was a great kick for me to have my name on an album featuring the President of the United States.

CALIFORNIA NIGHTS (1967) (wm)Howard Liebling—Marvin Hamlisch. (P)Lesley Gore.

CALIFORNIA SAGA (Big Sur) (1973) (wm)Mike Love. (P)The Beach Boys.

CALIFORNIA SOUL (1967) (wm)Nicholas Ashford—Valerie Simpson. (P)The Fifth Dimension. (R)1970 by Marvin Gaye and Tammi Terrell.

CALIFORNIA SUN (1964) (wm)Morris Levy—Henry Glover. (P)The Rivieras.

CALL ME (1956) (wm)Clyde Otis—Belford C. Hendricks. (P)Johnny Mathis.

CALL ME (1965) (wm)Tony Hatch. (P)Chris Montez.

CALL ME (1970) (wm)Aretha Franklin. (P)Aretha Franklin.

CALL ME (1980) (wm)Debbie Harry—Georgio Moroder. (I)Film: *American Gigolo*, by Blondie. (P)Blondie.

CALL ME (1982) (wm)Randy Muller. (P)Skyy.

CALL ME DARLING (Call Me Sweetheart, Call Me Dear) (1931) (w-Eng)Dorothy Dick (m)Bert Reisfeld—Mart Fryberg—Rolf Marbot. (P)In United States by Russ Columbo. (CR)Ben Selvin and his Orchestra.

CALL ME IRRESPONSIBLE (1963) (w)Sammy Cahn (m)Jimmy Van Heusen. (I)Film: *Papa's Delicate Con-*

dition, by Jackie Gleason. Academy Award Winner. (P)Frank Sinatra. (CR)Jack Jones.

CALL ME MR. IN-BETWEEN. (1962) (wm)Harlan Howard (P)Burl Ives.

CALL ME UP SOME RAINY AFTERNOON (1910) (wm)Irving Berlin. (I)Ada Jones and The American Quartet. Not one of Berlin's hit songs.

CALL OF LIFE, THE (1929) (wm)Noel Coward. (I)Operetta: *Bitter Sweet,* by Peggy Wood in the London production and Evelyn Laye in the New York production.

CALL OF THE CANYON (1940) (wm)Billy Hill. (P)Tommy Dorsey and his Orchestra. (CR)Glenn Miller and his Orchestra. Film: *Call Of The Canyon,* by Gene Autry.

CALL OF THE FAR-AWAY HILLS, THE (1953) (w)Mack David (m)Victor Young. (I)Film: *Shane* on soundtrack.

CALL ON ME (1963) (wm)Deadric Malone. (P)Bobby Bland.

CALL ON ME (1974) (wm)Lee Loughrane. (P)Chicago.

CALL TO THE HEART (1984) (wm)Gregg Guiffria—David Eisley. (P)Guiffria.

CALLING DR. LOVE (1977) (wm)Gene Simmons. (P)Kiss.

CALLING OCCUPANTS OF INTERPLANETARY CRAFT (1977) (wm)Terry Draper—John Woloschuk. (P)The Carpenters. (CR)Klaatu.

CALYPSO (1975) (wm)John Denver. (P)John Denver.

CALYPSO BLUES (1950) (w)Don George (m)Nat "King" Cole. (P)Nat "King" Cole.

CALYPSO JOE (1957) (wm)Marge O'Neal—Fred Darian. (P)Nat "King" Cole.

CAMEL HOP (1938) (wm)Mary Lou Williams. (I)Andy Kirk and his Orchestra. (P)Benny Goodman and his Orchestra.

CAMELOT (1960) (w)Alan Jay Lerner (m)Frederick Loewe. (I)Musical: *Camelot,* by Richard Burton. In film version by Richard Harris.

CAMPBELLS ARE COMING (1745) (w)Robert Burns (m)Unknown. Traditional Scottish folk song.

CAMPTOWN RACES (See De Camptown Races)

CAN ANYONE EXPLAIN (No! No! No!) (1950) (wm)Bennie Benjamin—George Weiss. (P)The Ames Brothers. (CR)Ray Anthony and his Orchestra.

CAN BROADWAY DO WITHOUT ME? (1928) (wm)Jimmy Durante. (I)Musical: *Show Girl,* by Clayton, Jackson, and Durante. (R)1948 Film: *On An Island With You,* by Jimmy Durante with Xavier Cugat and his Orchestra. .

CAN CAN (1858) (m)Jacques Offenbach. (I)Opera: *Orpheus In The Underworld.*

CAN-CAN (1953) (wm)Cole Porter. (I)Musical: *Can—Can,* by Lilo and Gwen Verdon. In film version by Shirley MacLaine and company.

CAN I CHANGE MY MIND? (1968) (wm)Barry Despenza—Carl Wolfolk. . (P)Tyrone Davis.

CAN I FORGET YOU? (1937) (w)Oscar Hammerstein II (m)Jerome Kern. (I)Film: *High, Wide and Handsome* by Irene Dunne.

CAN I GET A WITNESS (1963) (wm)Eddie Holland—Lamont Dozier—Brian Holland. (P)Marvin Gaye. (R)1971 by Lee Michaels.

CAN THIS BE LOVE (1930) (w)Paul James (m)Kay Swift. (I)Musical: *Fine And Dandy,* by Alice Boulden.

CAN WE STILL BE FRIENDS (1978) (wm)Todd Rundgren. (P)Todd Rundgren. (R)1980 by Robert Palmer.

CAN YOU FIND IT IN YOUR HEART (1956) (w)Al Stillman (m)Robert Allen. (P)Tony Bennett.

CAN YOU PLEASE CRAWL OUT YOUR WINDOW? (1966) (wm)Bob Dylan. (P)Bob Dylan.

CAN YOU READ MY MIND (Love Theme From Superman) (1978) (w)Leslie Bricusse (m)John Williams. (I)Film: *Superman* on soundtrack. (P)Maureen McGovern.

CANADIAN CAPERS (1915) (wm)Gus Chandler—Gus White—Henry Cohen. Popular ragtime selection. No artist credited with introduction.

CANADIAN SUNSET (1956) (w)Norman Gimbel (m)Eddie Heywood. (P)Hugo Winterhalter and his Orchestra, with Eddie Heywood at the piano. Vocal version by Andy Williams.

CANCEL THE FLOWERS (1941) (w)Eddie Seiler (m)Sol Marcus—Bennie Benjamin. (P)Tommy Tucker and his Orchestra, vocal by Don Brown. (CR)Tony Martin.

CANDIDA (1970) (wm)Tony Wine—Irwin Levine (P)Dawn.

CANDLE IN THE WIND (1973) (wm)Elton John—Bernie Taupin. (P)Elton John. (R)1987 by Elton John.

CANDLE ON THE WATER (1977) (wm)Al Kasha—Joel Hirschorn. (I)Film: *Pete's Dragon,* by Helen Reddy. (P)Helen Reddy.

CANDLELIGHT AND WINE (1943) (w)Harold Adamson (m)Jimmy McHugh. (I)Film: *Around The World,* by Georgia Carroll and Harry Babbitt, with Kay Kyser and his Orchestra.

CANDY (1944) (wm)Mack David—Joan Whitney—Alex Kramer. (P)Jo Stafford, Johnny Mercer and The Pied Pipers. (CR)Dinah Shore. (CR)Johnny Long and his Orchestra.

CANDY (1987) (wm)L. Blackmon—T. Jenkins. (P)Cameo.

CANDY AND CAKE (1950) (wm)Bob Merrill. (P)Arthur Godfrey.

CANDY GIRL (1963) (wm)Larry Santos. (P)The Four Seasons.

CANDY KISSES (1949) (wm)George Morgan. (P)George Morgan.

CANDY MAN (1961) (wm)Fred Neil—Beverly Ross. (P)Roy Orbison.

CANDY MAN, THE (1971) (wm)Leslie Bricusse—Anthony Newley. (I)Film: *Wille Wonka And The Chocolate Factory,* by the voice of Aubrey Wood. (P)Sammy Davis, Jr. No. 1 Chart Record.

CANDY STORE BLUES (1949) (wm)Nick Castle—Herb Jeffries—Eddie Beal. (I)Film: *Manhattan Angel* by, Toni Harper. (P)Toni Harper.

CANNON BALL (1958) (m)Duane Eddy—Lee Hazlewood. (P)Duane Eddy.

CAN'T BUY ME LOVE (1964) (wm)John Lennon—Paul McCartney. (I)Film: *A Hard Day's Night* by The Beatles. (P)The Beatles.

CAN'T FIGHT THIS FEELING (1985) (wm)Kevin Cronin. (P)REO Speedwagon. No. 1 Chart Record.

CAN'T GET ENOUGH (1974) (wm)Mick Ralphs. (P)Bad Company.

CAN'T GET ENOUGH OF YOUR LOVE, BABE (1974) (wm)Barry White. (P)Barry White.

CAN'T GET INDIANA OFF MY MIND (1940) (w)Robert De Leon (m)Hoagy Carmichael. (P)Bing Crosby. (CR)Kate Smith.

CAN'T GET IT OUT OF MY HEAD (1974) (wm)Jeff Lynne. (P)Electric Light Orchestra.

CAN'T GET OUT OF THIS MOOD (1942) (w)Frank Loesser (m)Jimmy McHugh. (I)Film: *Seven Days' Leave*, by Ginny Simms. (P)Kay Kyser and his Orchestra. (CR)Johnny Long and his Orchestra.

CAN'T GET OVER (The Bossa Nova) (1964) (wm)Steve Lawrence—Eydie Gorme—Gims Marilyn. (P)Eydie Gorme.

CAN'T GET USED TO LOSING YOU (1963) (wm)Doc Pomus—Mort Shuman. (P)Andy Williams.

CAN'T HELP FALLING IN LOVE (1961) (wm)George Weiss—Hugo Peretti—Luigi Creatore. (I)Film: *Blue Hawaii*, by Elvis Presley. (P)Elvis Presley. (R)1970 by Al Martino. (R)1987 by Corey Hart.

CAN'T HELP LOVIN' DAT MAN (1927) (w)Oscar Hammerstein II (m)Jerome Kern. (I)Musical: *Show Boat*, by Helen Morgan, Tess Gardella—Norma Terris, Alan Campbell and Jules Bledsoe. (P)Helen Morgan. First film version (1929)by Miss Morgan. Second film version (1936)by Miss Morgan. Third film version (1951)by Kathryn Grayson and Eileen Wilson dubbing for Ava Gardner. (R)Film: *The Helen Morgan Story*, by Gogi Grant dubbing for Ann Blyth. (1957)

CAN'T HELP SINGING (1944) (w)E. Y. Harburg (m)Jerome Kern. (I)Film: *Can't Help Singing*, by Deanna Durbin and Robert Paige.

CAN'T I (1953) (wm)Leroy Lovett. (P)Nat "King" Cole. (CR)The Ames Brothers.

CAN'T SMILE WITHOUT YOU (1975) (wm)Geoff Morrow—Chris Arnold—David Martin. (I)Englebert Humperdinck. (P)Barry Manilow.

CAN'T STAY AWAY FROM YOU (1987) (wm) G. M. Estefan. (P)Gloria Estefan & Miami Sound Machine.

CAN'T STOP DANCIN (1976) (wm)John Pritchard, Jr. — Ray Stevens. (P)The Captain & Tennille.

CAN'T TAKE MY EYES OFF YOU (1967) (wm)Bob Crewe—Bob Gaudio. (P)Frankie Valli. (R)1968 by The Lettermen in a medley with Goin' Out Of My Head. (R)1969 by Nancy Wilson.

CAN'T WE BE FRIENDS? (1929) (w)James Warburg. (m)Kay Swift. (I)Revue: *The Little Show*, by Libby Holman. (R)1950 Film: *Young Man With A Horn*, on soundtrack.

CAN'T WE TALK IT OVER (1931) (w)Ned Washington (m)Victor Young. (I)Lee Wiley. (P)Bing Crosby with The Mills Brothers. (R)1950 by The Andrews Sisters.

CAN'T WE TRY (1987) (wm)D. Hill—B. Hill. (P)Dan Hill with Vonda Shepard.

CAN'T YOU DO A FRIEND A FAVOR? (1943) (w)Lorenz Hart (m)Richard Rodgers. (I)Musical: *A Connecticut Yankee* (revival)by Vivienne Segal and Dick Foran.

CAN'T YOU HEAR ME CALLING CAROLINE (1914) (wm)William Gardner—Caro Roma. Popular standard. No artist credited with introduction.

CAN'T YOU HEAR MY HEART BEAT? (1965) (wm)John Shakespeare—Kenneth Hawker. (P)Herman's Hermits.

CAN'T YOU JUST SEE YOURSELF (1947) (w)Sammy Cahn (m)Jule Styne. (I)Musical: *High Button Shoes*, by Lois Lee and Mark Dawson. Reprised by Phil Silvers and Lois Lee.

CAN'T YOU READ BETWEEN THE LINES? (1945) (w)Sammy Cahn (m)Jule Styne. (P)Charlie Spivak and his Orchestra, vocal by Irene Daye.

CAN'T YOU SEE IT? (w)Lee Adams (m)Charles Strouse. (I)Musical: *Golden Boy*, by Sammy Davis, Jr.

CAN'T YOU SEE THAT SHE'S MINE? (1964) (wm)Dave Clark—Mike Smith. (P)The Dave Clark Five.

CAN'TCHA SAY (You Believe In Me) (1987) (wm)J. Green—T. Scholz—B. Delp. (P)Boston.

CAPITAN, EL (1896) (m)John Philip Sousa. Famous American March. Recorded by Sousa's Band.

CAPRICCIO ESPAGNOL (1888) (m)N. Rimsky—Korsakov. Famous classical composition.

CAPRICE VIENNOIS (1910) (m)Fritz Kreisler. Famous classical composition originally written as a violin solo. (I)Fritz Kreisler.

CAPTAIN JACK (1971) (wm)Billy Joel. (P)Billy Joel.

CAPTAIN OF HER HEART (1986) (wm)Kurt Maloo—Felix Haug. (P)Double.

CAPTAINS OF THE CLOUDS (1942) (w)Johnny Mercer (m)Harold Arlen. (I)Film: *Captains Of The Clouds*, on soundtrack. Official song of Royal Canadian Air Force.

CAR ON A HILL (1973) (wm)Joni Mitchell. (P)Joni Mitchell.

CAR WASH (1977) (wm)Norman Whitfield. (I)Film: *Car Wash*, by Rose Royce. (P)Rose Royce. No. 1 Chart Record.

CARA MIA (1954) (wm)Tulio Trapani—Lee Lange. (P)David Whitfield. (R)1965 by Jay and The Americans.

CARAMBA! IT'S THE SAMBA! (1948) (wm)Irving Taylor—George Wyle—Eddie Pola. (P)Peggy Lee.

CARAVAN (1937) (w)Irving Mills (m)Juan Tizol—Duke Ellington. (P)Duke Ellington and his Orchestra. (CR)Barney Bigard and his Orchestra. (R)1949 by Billy Eckstine. (R)1953 by Ralph Marterie and his Orchestra.

CAREFREE HIGHWAY (1974) (wm)Gordon Lightfoot. (P)Gordon Lightfoot.

CARELESS (1939) (wm)Lew Quadling—Eddy Howard—Dick Jurgens. (P)Dick Jurgens and his Orchestra, vocal by Eddy Howard. (CR)Glenn Miller and his Orchestra.

CARELESS HANDS (1949) (wm)Carl Sigman—Bob Hilliard. (P)Mel Torme. No. 1 Chart Record (CR)Sammy Kaye, Bing Crosby.

CARELESS KISSES (1949) (wm)Tim Spencer. (P)Eddy Howard. (CR)Russ Morgan and his Orchestra.

CARELESS LOVE (1921) (wm)W. C. Handy—Spencer Williams. No artist credited with introduction. (R)Film: *St. Louis Blues*, by Nat "King" Cole and Eartha Kitt.

CARELESS RHAPSODY (1942) (w)Lorenz Hart (m)Richard Rodgers. (I)Musical: *By Jupiter*, by Ronald Graham and Constance Moore.

CARELESS WHISPER (1984) (wm)George Michael—Andrew Ridgely. (P)Wham, featuring George Michael. No. 1 Chart Record.

CAREY (1971) (wm)Joni Mitchell. (P)Joni Mitchell.

CARIBBEAN (1953) (wm)Mitchell Torok. (P)Mitchell Torok.

CARIBBEAN QUEEN (1984) (wm)Keith Diamond—Billy Ocean. (P)Billy Ocean. No. 1 Chart Record.

CARIOCA (1933) (w)Gus Kahn—Edward Eliscu. (m)Vincent Youmans. (I)Film: *Flying Down To Rio*, by Etta Moten and danced to by Fred Astaire and Ginger Rogers. Recorded by Enric Madriguera and his Orchestra. No. 1 Chart Record. (CR)Harry Sosnik and his Orchestra. (R)1952 by Les Paul.

CARNEGIE BLUES (1945) (m)Duke Ellington. (I)Duke Ellington and his Orchestra at Carnegie Hall.

CARNIVAL (Theme From) (Also called LOVE MAKES THE WORLD GO 'ROUND) (1961) (wm)Bob Merrill. (I)Musical: *Carnival,* by Anna Marie Alberghetti.

CARNIVAL (1945) (w)Bob Russell (m)Harry Warren. (P)Harry James and his Orchestra.

CARNIVAL OF VENICE (1854) (m)J. Bellak. Famous classical composition, usually performed as a trumpet or cornet solo.

CAROL (1958) (wm)Chuck Berry. (P)Chuck Berry. (R)1964 by Tommy Roe.

CAROLINA IN THE MORNING (1922) (w)Gus Kahn (m)Walter Donaldson. (I)Vaudeville, by William Frawley. (P)Van and Schenck. No. 1 Chart Record. (CR)Paul Whiteman and his Orchestra. (R)1949 Film: *The Jolson Story,* by voice of Jolson dubbing for Larry Parks.

CAROLINA IN THE PINES (1975) (wm)Michael Murphey. (P)Michael Murphey.

CAROLINA MOON (1928) (wm)Benny Davis—Joe Burke. (I)Gene Austin. (P)Theme song of Morton Downey. (CR)Guy Lombardo and his Royal Canadians.

CAROLINE, NO (1966) (wm)Tony Asher—Brian Wilson. (P)Brian Wilson.

CAROLYN (1971) (wm)Tommy Collins. (P)Merle Haggard.

CAROUSEL WALTZ, THE (1945) (m)Richard Rodgers. (I)Musical: *Carousel.*

CARPET MAN (1967) (wm)Jim Webb. (P)The Fifth Dimension.

CARRIE (1987) (wm)J. Tempest—M. Michaeli. (P)Europe.

CARRIE-ANNE (1967) (wm)Allan Clarke—Graham Nash—Tony Hicks. (P)The Hollies.

CARROUSEL IN THE PARK (1944) (w)Dorothy Fields (m)Sigmund Romberg. (I)Musical: *Up In Central Park,* by Maureen Cannon.

CARRY ME BACK (1969) (wm)Felix Cavaliere. (P)The Rascals.

CARRY ME BACK TO OLD VIRGINNY (1878 (wm)James A. Bland. Recorded in 1915 by soprano, Alma Gluck.

CARRY ME BACK TO THE LONE PRAIRIE (1934) (wm)Carson J. Robison. Adapted from American cowboy song. (P)Carson Robison. (R)Film: *Stars Over Broadway,* by James Melton. (1935)

CARRY ON WAYWARD SON (1976) (wm)Kerry Livgren. (P)Kansas.

CARRY THAT WEIGHT (1969) (wm)John Lennon—Paul McCartney. (P)The Beatles.

CARS (1979) (wm)Gary Numan (P)Gary Numan.

CASA LOMA STOMP (m)Eugene Gifford. (P)Glen Gary and The Casa Loma Orchestra.

CASANOVA (1987) (wm)R. Calloway. (P)Levert.

CASANOVA CRICKET (1947) (wm)Hoagy Carmichael— Larry Markes—Dick Charles. (P)Hoagy Carmichael.

CASEY AT THE BAT (1945) (wm)Ray Gilbert—Ken Darby—Eliot Daniel. (I)Cartoon Film: *Make Mine Music,* by Jerry Colonna.

CASEY JONES (1909) (w)T. Lawrence Seibert (m)Eddie Newton. Traditional song about railroad engineer. First recording by The American Quartet.

CASEY JUNIOR (1941) (w)Ned Washington (m)Frank Churchill. (I)Cartoon Film: *Dumbo.*

CASINO ROYALE (1965) (w)Hal David (m)Burt Bacharach. (I)Film: *Casino Royale,* by Herb Alpert and The Tijuana Brass on soundtrack. (P)Herb Alpert and The Tijuana Brass.

CAST YOUR FATE TO THE WIND (1960) (w)Carel Werber (m)Vincent Guaraldi. (P)Vince Guaraldi. NARAS Award Winner. (R)1965 by Sounds Orchestral.

CASTANETS AND LACE (1947) (wm)Bob Hilliard—Dave Mann—Milton Leeds. (P)Sammy Kaye and his Orchestra.

CASTLE ROCK (1951) (w)Ervin Drake—Jimmy Shirl (m)Al Sears. (P)Johnny Hodges and his Orchestra. Vocal version by Frank Sinatra with Harry James and his Orchestra.

CASTLES IN THE AIR (1972) (wm)Don McLean. (P)Don McLean.

CASUAL LOOK, A (1956) (wm)Ed Wells. (P)The Six Teens.

CAT, THE (1964) (m)Lalo Schifrin. (I)Film: *Joy House* on soundtrack. (P)Lalo Schifrin and his Orchestra. (CR)Jimmy Smith (organ). NARAS Award Winner.

CAT AND THE CANARY (1945) (w)Ray Evans (m)Jay Livingston. (I)Film: *Why Girls Leave Home,* on soundtrack.

CAT IN THE WINDOW, THE (1967) (wm)Garry Bonner— Alan Gordon. (P)Petula Clark.

CAT PEOPLE (Putting Out Fire) (1982) (wm)David Bowie—Georgio Moroder. (I)Film: *Cat People,* on soundtrack. (P)David Bowie.

CAT SCRATCH FEVER (1977) (wm)Ted Nugent. (P)Ted Nugent.

CATCH A FALLING STAR (1957) (wm)Paul Vance—Lee Pockriss. (P)Perry Como. No. 1 Chart Record.

CATCH ME (I'm Falling) (1987) (wm)J. Starling—W. Cooler (I)Film: *Hiding Out,* by Pretty Poison. (P)Pretty Poison.

CATCH THE WIND (1965) (wm)Donovan Leitch. (P)Donovan.

CATCH US IF YOU CAN (1965) (wm)Dave Clark—Lenny Davidson. (I)British Film: *Having A Wild Weekend* by The Dave Clark Five. (P)The Dave Clark Five.

CATERINA (1962) (wm)Earl Shuman—"Bugs" Bower. (P)Perry Como.

CATFISH SONG (1952) (w)Maxwell Anderson (m)Kurt Weill. (I)TV Show: *Huckleberry Finn.*

CATHEDRAL IN THE PINES (1938) (wm)Charles and Nick Kenny. (I)Shep Fields and his Orchestra. (R)1957 by Pat Boone.

CATHY'S CLOWN (1960) (wm)Don and Phil Everly. (P)The Everly Brothers. No. 1 Chart Record.

CAT'S IN THE CRADLE (1974) (wm)Harry and Sandra Chapin. (P)Harry Chapin.

CATTLE CALL (1934) (wm)Tex Owens. (I)Tex Owens. (R)1955 by Eddy Arnold. (CR)Dinah Shore.

CAUGHT UP IN YOU (1982) (wm)Jeff Carlisi—Jim Peterik—Richard Barnes—Frankie Sullivan. (P)38 Special.

CAUSING A COMMOTION (1987) (wm)Madonna—S. Bray. (P)Madonna.

CECILIA (1925) (w)Herman Ruby (m)Dave Dreyer. (P)Whispering Jack Smith. (R)1940 by Dick Jurgens and his Orchestra, vocal by Ronnie Kemper.

CECILIA (1970) (wm)Paul Simon. (P)Simon and Garfunkel.

CELEBRATE (1968) (wm)Gary Bonner—Alan Gordon. (P)Three Dog Night.

CELEBRATION (1980) (wm)Ronald Bell—Claydes

Smith—George Brown—Robert Bell—James Taylor—Eumir Deodato—Robert Mickens—Earl Toon—Dennis Thomas. (P)Kool and The Gang. No. 1 Chart Record.

CELERY STALKS AT MIDNIGHT (1941) (m)George Harris—Will Bradley. (P)Will Bradley and his Orchestra.

CEMENT MIXER (Put-ti, Put-ti) (1946) (wm)Slim Gaillard—Lee Ricks. (P)Slim Gaillard. (CR)Alvino Rey and his Orchestra.

CENTERFOLD (1982) (wm)Seth Justman. (P)J. Geils Band. No. 1 Chart Record.

CENTRAL PARK BALLAD (1985) (wm)Charles Strouse. (I)Musical: *Mayor*.

CERTAIN SMILE, A (1958) (w)Paul Francis Webster (m)Sammy Fain. (I)Film: *A Certain Smile*, by Johnny Mathis. (P)Johnny Mathis.

CERVEZA (1958) (m)Boots Brown (P)Boots Brown. (R)1968 by Bert Kaempfert and his Orchestra.

C'EST LA VIE (1955) (w)Stella Unger (m)Victor Young. (I)Musical: Seventh Heaven, by Robert Clary, Beatrice Arthur and Kurt Kasznar.

C'EST LA VIE (1955) (wm)Edward White—Mack Wolfson. (P)Sarah Vaughan.

C'EST LA VIE (1987) (wm)Nevil—Pain—Holding. (P)Robbie Nevil.

C'EST MAGNIFIQUE (1953) (wm)Cole Porter. (I)Musical: Can-Can, by Lilo and Peter Cookson. In film version by Frank Sinatra.

C'EST SI BON (1950) (w-Eng)Jerry Seelen (m)Henri Betti. (P)Johnny Desmond. (R)1953 by Eartha Kitt.

CHA CHA CHA, THE (1962) (wm)Kal Mann—Dave Appell. (P)Bobby Rydell.

CHAIN GANG (1956) (wm)Sol Quasha—Herb Yakus. (P)Bobby Scott. (R)1960 by Sam Cooke. (R)1968 by Jackie Wilson with Count Basie and his Orchestra.

CHAIN OF FOOLS (1967) (wm)Don Covay. (P)Aretha Franklin.

CHAIN STORE DAISY (1937) (wm)Harold Rome. (I)Musical: Pins And Needles, by Ruth Rubenstein.

CHAINED (1968) (wm)Frank Wilson. (P)Marvin Gaye.

CHAINS OF LOVE (1951) (w)Ahmet Ertegun— (m)Van Wells. (I)Joe Turner. (R)1956 by Pat Boone. (R)1969 by Bobby Bland.

CHAMPAGNE (1975) (wm)Peter Townshend. (I)Film: Tommy, by Ann Margret.

CHAMPAGNE POLKA (1945) (w)Norman Lee (m)Lawrence Welk. (P)Lawrence Welk and his Orchestra.

CHAMPAGNE WALTZ, THE (1934) (wm)Con Conrad—Ben Oakland—Milton Drake. (P)Jack Denny and his Orchestra. (CR)Glen Gray and The Casa Loma Orchestra. (R)1937)Film: The Champagne Waltz, danced by Veloz and Yolanda.

CHANCES ARE (1957) (w)Al Stillman (m)Robert Allen. (P)Johnny Mathis. No. 1 Chart Record.

CHANGE OF HEART (1943) (w)Harold Adamson (m)Jimmy McHugh. (I)Film: Hit Parade Of 1943.

CHANGE OF HEART (1978) (wm)Eric Carmen. (P)Eric Carmen.

CHANGE OF HEART (1986) (wm)Essra Mohawk—Cyndi Lauper. (P)Cyndi Lauper.

CHANGE PARTNERS (1938) (wm)Irving Berlin. (I)Film: Carefree, by Fred Astaire. (P)Fred Astaire. (CR)Jimmy Dorsey and his Orchestra. Both the Astaire and Dorsey records were No. 1 Chart Records.

CHANGE YOUR MIND (1935) (wm)Ray Noble. (I)Film:

Ship Cafe, by Carl Brisson.

CHANGING MY TUNE (1946) (w)Ira Gershwin (m)George Gershwin. (I)Film: The Shocking Miss Pilgrim, by Betty Grable.

CHANGING PARTNERS (1953) (w)Joe Darion (m)Larry Coleman. (P)Patti Page. (CR)Kay Starr, Dinah Shore, Bing Crosby.

CHANSON D'AMOUR (1958) (P)Art and Dotty Todd. (CR)The Fontane Sisters.

CHANSONETTE (See Donkey Serenade)

CHANT OF THE JUNGLE (1929) (w)Arthur Freed (m)Nacio Herb Brown. (I)Film: Untamed, by Joan Crawford. Recorded by Nat Shilkret and his Orchestra.

CHANT OF THE WEED (1932) (m)Don Redman. (P)Theme song of Don Redman and his Orchestra.

CHANTEZ, CHANTEZ (1957) (w)Albert Gamse (m)Irving Fields. (P)Dinah Shore.

CHANTILLY LACE (1958) (wm)J. P. Richardson. (P)Big Bopper (J. P. Richardson). (R)1972 by Jerry Lee Lewis.

CHAPEL BELLS (1938) (w)Harold Adamson (m)Jimmy McHugh. (I)Film: Mad About Music, by Deanna Durbin.

CHAPEL OF LOVE (1964) (wm)Phil Spector—Ellie Greenwich—Jeff Barry. (P)The Dixie Cups. No. 1 Chart Record. (R)1973 by Bette Midler.

CHARADE (1963) (w)Johnny Mercer (m)Henry Mancini. (I)Film: Charade, on soundtrack. (P)Henry Mancini and his Orchestra. Vocal version by Andy Williams.

CHARIOTS OF FIRE (1981) (w)Jon Anderson (m)Vangelis. (I)Film: Chariots Of Fire, on soundtrack. (P)Vangelis. No. 1 Chart Record. Vocal version by, Melissa Manchester.

CHARLESTON (1923) (wm)Cecil Mack—James P. Johnson. (I)Musical: Runnin' Wild, by Elisabeth Welch. Recorded by Paul Whiteman and his Orchestra. (R)1950 Film: Tea For Two, danced by Billy De Wolfe and Patrice Wymore.

CHARLESVILLE (1961) (wm)Ray Charles. (P)Ray Charles.

CHARLEY, MY BOY (1924) (wm)Gus Kahn—Ted Fiorito. (I)Russo and Fiorito's Oriole Orchestra. (P)Eddie Cantor. (R)1950 by The Andrews Sisters.

CHARLIE BROWN (1959) (wm)Jerry Leiber—Mike Stoller. (P)The Coasters.

CHARLIE'S ANGELS (1976) (wm)Jack Elliot—Allyn Ferguson. (I)TV Series: Charlie's Angels as soundtrack theme. (P)Henry Mancini and his Orchestra.

CHARM OF YOU, THE (1944) (w)Sammy Cahn (m)Jule Styne. (I)Film: Anchors Aweigh, by Frank Sinatra.

CHARMAINE (1913) (w)Lew Pollack (m)Erno Rapee. (I)Film: What Price Glory as soundtrack theme. (R)1951 by Mantovani and his Orchestra.

CHARMING (1929) (w)Clifford Grey (m)Herbert Stothart. (I)Film: Devil May Care, by Ramon Novarro.

CHARMING LITTLE FAKER (1940) (w)Johnny Burke (m)Frankie Masters—Keene Kahn. (P)Frankie Masters and his Orchestra.

CHARMS (1963) (wm)Howard Greenfield—Helen Miller. (P)Bobby Vee.

CHASE, THE (1978) (m)Giorgio Moroder. (I)Film: Midnight Express, by Giorgio Moroder on soundtrack. (P)Giorgio Moroder.

CHASING SHADOWS (1935) (w)Benny Davis (m)Abner

Silver. (P)Dorsey Brothers Orchestra. (CR)Henry King and his Orchestra.

CHATTANOOGA CHOO CHOO (1941) (w)Mack Gordon (m)Harry Warren. (I)Film: *Sun Valley Serenade*, by Glenn Miller and his Orchestra, vocal by Tex Beneke. (P)Glenn Miller. No. 1 Chart Record. (R)1967 by Harper's Bizarre.

CHATTANOOGIE SHOE SHINE BOY (1950) (wm)Henry Stone—Jack Stapp. (P)Red Foley. No. 1 Chart Record. (CR)Bing Crosby.

CHEAPER TO KEEP HER (1973) (wm)Mack Rice. (P)Johnnie Taylor.

CHEATER, THE (1965) (wm)John Mike Krenski. (P)Bob Kuban and The In—Men.

CHEATIN' ON ME (1925) (w)Jack Yellen (m)Lew Pollack. (I)Sophie Tucker. (CR)Ben Bernie and his Orchestra. (R)1939 by Jimmy Lunceford and his Orchestra.

CHECK IT OUT (1987) (wm)John Cougar Mellencamp.

CHEE CHE-OO CHEE (Sang The Little Bird) (1955) (w-Eng)John Turner—Geoffrey Parsons (m)Severio Seracini. San Remo Festival Winner. (P)Perry Como and Jane Morgan.

CHEEK TO CHEEK (1935) (wm)Irving Berlin. (I)Film: *Top Hat*, by Fred Astaire. Danced by Fred Astaire and Ginger Rogers. (P)Fred Astaire. No. 1 Chart Record. (CR)Eddy Duchin and his Orchestra.

CHEERFUL LITTLE EARFUL (1930) (w)Ira Gershwin—Billy Rose (m)Harry Warren. (I)Musical: Sweet And Low, by Hannah Williams and Jerry Norris. Recorded by Tom Gerun.

CHELSEA BRIDGE (1952) (m)Billy Strayhorn. (P)Duke Ellington and his Orchestra

CHELSEA MORNING (1967) (wm)Joni Mitchell. (I)Joni Mitchell. (R)1969 by Judy Collins.

CHERIE (1921) (w)Leo Wood (m)Irving Bibo. (P)Paul Whiteman and his Orchestra. No. 1 Chart Record. (CR)Nora Bayes.

CHERIE, I LOVE YOU (1926) (wm)Lillian Rosedale Goodman. (I)Grace Moore.

CHERISH (1965) (wm)Terry Kirkman. (P)The Association. No. 1 Chart Record. (R)1971 by David Cassidy.

CHERISH (1985) (wm)Ronald Bell—Charles Smith—Robert Bell—James Taylor—George Brown—Curtis Williams—James Bonneford. (P)Kool & The Gang.

CHEROKEE (1938) (m)Ray Noble. (I)Ray Noble and his Orchestra. (P)Charlie Barnet and his Orchestra.

CHERRY (1928) (wm)Don Redman. (I)McKinney's Cotton Pickers. (R)1944 by Harry James and his Orchestra.

CHERRY BOMB (1987) (wm)John Cougar Mellencamp. (P)John Cougar Mellencamp.

CHERRY, CHERRY (1966) (wm)Neil Diamond. (P)Neil Diamond.

CHERRY PIE (1954) (wm)Joe Josea—Marvin Phillips. (P)Skip and Flip.

CHERRY PIES OUGHT TO BE YOU (1950) (wm)Cole Porter. (I)Musical: *Out Of This World*, by William Redfield, Barbara Ashley, Charlotte Greenwood and David Burns.

CHERRY PINK AND APPLE BLOSSOM WHITE (1951) (w-Eng)Mack David (m)Louiguay. (I)Film: *Underwater* as love theme on soundtrack. (P)Perez Prado and his Orchestra. No. 1 Chart Record. Vocal version by Alan Dale. (R)1961 by Jerry Murad and his Harmonicats.

CHERRYHILL PARK (1969) (wm)Robert Nix—Billy Gil-

more. (P)Billy Joe Royal.

CHEVY VAN (1975) (wm)Sammy Johns. (P)Sammy Johns.

CHEW-CHEW-CHEW (Chew Your Bubble Gum) (1939) (wm)Buck Ram—Chick Webb—Ella Fitzgerald. (P)Chick Webb and his Orchestra, vocal by Ella Fitzgerald.

CHEWY, CHEWY (1968) (wm)Kris Resnick—Joey Levine. (P)Ohio Express.

CHEYENNE (w)Stan Jones-William Lava (1956) (I)T. V. Series: Cheyenne as soundtrack theme.

CHI-BABA CHI-BABA (My Bambino Go To Sleep) (wm)Mack David-Al Hoffman-Jerry Livingston. (P)Perry Como. No. 1 Chart Record.

CHICA CHICA BOOM CHIC (1941) (w)Mack Gordon—Harry Warren. (I)Film: *That Night In Rio*, by Carmen Miranda, Alice Faye and Don Ameche. Recorded by Xavier Cugat and his Orchestra.

CHICAGO (That Toddling Town) (1922) (I)Ben Selvin and his Orchestra. (R)1957 by Frank Sinatra.

CHICAGO (1971) (wm)Graham Nash. (P)Graham Nash.

CHICAGO, ILLINOIS (1981) (w)Leslie Bricusse (m)Henry Mancini. (I)Film: *Victor, Victoria*, by Lesley Ann Warren.

CHICAGO STYLE (1952) (w)Johnny Burke—Jimmy Van Heusen. (I)Film: *Road To Rio*, by Bing Crosby and Bob Hope.

CHICK-A-BOOM (1971) (wm)Janis Lee Guinn—Linda Martin. (P)Daddy Dewdrop.

CHICKEN AIN'T NOTHIN' BUT A BIRD, A (1940) (wm)Babe Wallace. (P)Ella Fitzgerald.

CHICKEN SONG, THE (1949) (wm)Terry Shand—Bob Merrill. (P)Guy Lombardo and his Royal Canadians.

CHICKEN SOUP WITH RICE (1975) (w)Maurice Sendak (m)Carole King. (I)Musical: *Really Rosie*, by The Children's Chorus. (P)Carole King.

CHICKERY CHICK (1945) (w)Sylvia Dee (m)Sidney Lippman. (P)Sammy Kaye and his orchestra, vocal by Nancy Norman and Billy Williams. (CR)Evelyn Knight.

CHICO AND THE MAN (Theme From)1974) (wm)Jose Feliciano. (I)TV Series: *Chico And The Man* by Jose Feliciano. (P)Jose Feliciano.

CHILD IN A UNIVERSE (1977) (wm)Laura Nyro. (P)Laura Nyro.

CHILD OF CLAY (1967) (wm)Jimmy Curtiss—Ernie Maresca. (P)Jimmie Rodgers.

CHILDREN AND ART (1983) (wm)Stephen Sondheim. (I)Musical: *Sunday In The Park With George*, by Bernadette Peters.

CHILDREN'S MARCHING SONG, THE (This Old Man) (1958) (wm)Malcolm Arnold. (I)Film: *Inn Of The Sixth Happiness*, by Ingrid Bergman and The Orphan's Chorus. (P)Mitch Miller and his Chorus and Orchestra.

CHIM CHIM CHER-EE (1963) (wm)Richard M. Sherman—Robert B. Sherman. (I)Film: *Mary Poppins*, by Julie Andrews, Dick Van Dyke, Karen Dotrice and Matthew Garber. Academy Award Winner. (P)New Christy Minstrels.

CHIME IN! (1961) (wm)Robert Wright—Geroge Forrest. (I)Musical: *Kean*, by Alfred De Sio, Christopher Hewitt, Robert Penn, Arthur Rubin and The Ensemble.

CHIMES OF FREEDOM (1964) (wm)Bob Dylan. (P)Bob Dylan.

CHIN UP! CHEERIO! CARRY ON! (1941) (w)E. Y. Harburg (m)Burton Lane. (I)Film: *Babes On Broadway*, by Judy Garland.

CHINA BOY (1929) (wm)Dick Winfree—Phil Boutelje. (P)Paul Whiteman and his Orchestra. (CR)Red Nichols and his Five Pennies. (R)1936 by Benny Goodman and his Trio.

CHINA DOLL (1960) (wm)Cindy Walker. (P)The Ames Brothers.

CHINA GATE (1957) (w)Harold Adamson (m)Victor Young. (I)Film: *China Gate*, by Nat "King" Cole. (P)Nat "King" Cole.

CHINA GIRL (1983) (wm)Iggy Pop—David Bowie. (P)David Bowie.

CHINA GROVE (1973) (wm)Tom Johnston (P)The Doobie Brothers.

CHINATOWN (1978) (wm)John Prine. (P)John Prine.

CHINATOWN, MY CHINATOWN (1906) (wm)William Jerome (m)Jean Schwartz. First recording by The American Quartet. (R)1932 by Louis Armstrong. (R)1932 by The Mills Brothers. (R)1935 by Ray Noble and his Orchestra.

CHINCHERINCHEE (1956) (wm)John Jerome. (P)Perry Como.

CHIP CHIP (1962) (wm)Jeff Barry—Cliff Crawford—Arthur Resnick. (P)Gene McDaniels.

CHIPMUNK SONG, THE (1958) (wm)Ross Bagdasarian. (P)David Seville (Bagdasarian)and The Chipmunks. No. 1 Chart Record.

CHIQUITA (1928) (w)L. Wolfe Gilbert (m)Mabel Wayne. (P)Paul Whiteman and his Orchestra.

CHIQUITA BANANA (1946) (wm)Leonard MacKenzie—Garth Montgomery—William Wirges. Adapted from radio commercial. (I)Film: *This Time For Keeps*, by Xavier Cugat and his Orchestra.

CHIQUITITA (1979) (wm)Benny Andersson—Buddy McCluskey—Bjoern Ulvaeus. (P)Abba.

CHIRPIN' THE BLUES (1923) (wm)Alberta Hunter—Lovie Austin. (P)Alberta Hunter.

CHIRPY CHIRPY CHEEP CHEEP (1971) (wm)Harold Stott. (P)Kate Kissoon and Mac Kissoon.

CHITTY CHITTY BANG BANG (1968) (wm)Richard M. Sherman—Robert B. Sherman. (I)Film: *Chitty Chitty Bang Bang*, by Dick Van Dyke, Adrian Hall and Arthur Ripley. Recorded by Paul Mauriat and his Orchestra.

CHIU, CHIU (1942) (w-Eng)Alan Surgal (m)Nicanor Molinare. (I)Film: *You Were Never Lovelier*, by Xavier Cugat and his Orchestra, vocal by Lina Romay.

CHLOE (1927) (w)Gus Kahn (m)Neil Moret. (I)Lee Barton Evans. (P)Paul Whiteman and his Orchestra. (R)1945 by Spike Jones. (R)1953 by Louis Armstrong.

CHOCOLATE SHAKE (1941) (w)Paul Francis Webster (m)Duke Ellington. (I)Musical: *Jump For Joy*.

CHOICE OF COLORS (1969) (wm)Curtis Mayfield. (P)The Impressions.

CHOKIN' KIND, THE (1967) (wm)Harlan Howard. (P)Waylon Jennings. (R)1969 by Joe Simon.

CHOO CHOO CH' BOOGIE (1945) (wm)Vaughn Horton—Denver Darling—Milt Gabler. (P)Louis Jordan and his Tympani Five.

CHOO CHOO TRAIN (1953) (w-Eng)Jack Lawrence (m)Marc Fontenoy. (P)Doris Day.

CHOO CHOO TRAIN (1968) (wm)Eddie Hinton—Donnie Fritts. (P)The Box Tops.

CHOO'N GUM (1952) (w)Mann Curtis (m)Vic Mizzy. (P)Teresa Brewer.

CHOPSTICKS (1877) (m)Arthur de Lulli. Popular novelty piano solo. Recorded by Kay Kyser in 1959 as an orchestral version.

CHRISTINE SIXTEEN (1977) (wm)Gene Simmons. (P)Kiss.

CHRISTMAS DREAM (1977) (w)Tim Rice (m)Andrew Lloyd Webber. (I)Film: *The Odessa File* by voices of Perry Como aand The London Boy Singers.

CHRISTMAS DREAMING (1947) (wm)Lester Lee—Irving Gordon. (P)Frank Sinatra.

CHRISTMAS IN KILLARNEY (1951) (wm)John Redmond—James Cavanaugh—Frank Weldon. (P)Dennis Day. (CR)Percy Faith and his Orchestra.

CHRISTMAS ISLAND (1946) (wm)Lyle L. Moraine. (P)The Andrews Sisters with Guy Lombardo and his Royal Canadians.

CHRISTMAS SONG, THE (Chestnuts Roasting On An Open Fire) (1946) (wm)Robert Wells—Mel Torme. (I)Mel Torme. (P)Nat "King" Cole. (CR)Les Brown and his Band Of Renown.

CHRISTOPHER COLUMBUS (1936) (w)Andy Razaf (m)Leon Berry. (P)Theme song of Fletcher Henderson and his Orchestra. Incorporated in arrangement of *Sing, Sing, Sing*, by Benny Goodman and his Orchestra.

CHRYSANTHEMUM TEA (1976) (wm)Stephen Sondheim. (I)Musical: *Pacific Overtures*, by The Cast.

CHUCK E'S IN LOVE (1978) (wm)Rickie Lee Jones. (P)Rickie Lee Jones.

CHUG-A-LUG (1964) (wm)Roger Miller. (P)Roger Miller.

CHURCH BELLS MAY RING (1956) (wm)Morty and The Willows Craft. (P)The Willows.

CHURCH OF THE POISON MIND (1983) (wm)Roy Hay—John Moss—Michael Craig—George O'Dowd. (P)Culture Club.

CIAO, CIAO, BAMBINA (1959) (w-Eng)Mitchell Parish (m)Domenico Modugno. San Remo Song Festival Award Winner. (P)Domenico Modugno. (CR)Jacky Noguez.

CIELITO LINDO (1919) (wm)Quirino Mendoza y Cortez. Traditional Mexican love song. No artist credited with introduction.

CIGAREETES, WHUSKY AND WILD, WILD WOMEN (1947) (I)Sons Of The Pioneers. (P)Red Ingle.

CIGARETTES, CIGARS (1931) (wm)Mack Gordon—Harry Revel. (I)Revue: *Ziegfeld Follies of 1931*, by Ruth Etting.

CIMARRON (Roll On) (1942) (wm)Johnny Bond. (P)Johnny Bond.

CINCINNATTI DANCING PIG (1950) (w)Al Lewis (m)Guy Wood. (P)Red Foley. (CR)Vic Damone.

CINCINNATI KID, THE (1965) (w)Dorcas Cochran (m)Lalo Schifrin. (I)Film: *The Cincinnati Kid*, by voice of Ray Charles on soundtrack.

CINCO ROBLES (1956) (w)Larry Sullivan (m)Dorothy Wright. (I)Russell Arms. (P)Les Paul and Mary Ford.

CINDERELLA (1949) (wm)Mack David—Al Hoffman—Jerry Livingston. (I)Cartoon Film: *Cinderella*, on soundtrack.

CINDERELLA, STAY IN MY ARMS (1938) (wm)Jimmy Kennedy—Michael Carr. (P)Guy Lombardo and his Royal Canadians. (CR)Glenn Miller and his Orchestra.

CINDERELLA'S FELLA (1933) (w)Arthur Freed (m)Nacio Herb Brown. (I)Film: *Going Hollywood*, by Fifi D'-Orsay. Later reprised by Marion Davies.

CINDY, OH CINDY (1956) (wm)Bob Barron—Burt Long. (I)Vince Martin and The Tarriers. (P)Eddie Fisher.

CINDY'S BIRTHDAY (1962) (wm)Jeff Hooven—Hal Winn. (P)Johnny Crawford.

CINNAMIN (1968) (wm)George Tobin—Johnny Cymbal. (P)Derek.

CINNAMON CINDER (1962) (wm)Russ Regan. (P)The Cinders.

CINNAMON SINNER (1954) (wm)Lincoln Chase. (P)Tony Bennett.

CINQUANTAINE, LA (1887) (m)Gabriel P. Marie. Famous light classical standard.

CIRCLE GAME (1967) (wm)Joni Mitchell. (I)Buffy Sainte—Marie. (R)1970 by Joni Mitchell.

CIRCUS (1949) (w)Bob Russell (m)Louis Alter. (P)Tony Martin.

CIRCUS ON PARADE, THE (1935) (w)Lorenz Hart (m)Richard Rodgers. (I)Musical: *Billy Rose's Jumbo*, by Henderson's Singing Razorbacks. In film version (1962), by Doris Day, Martha Raye and Jimmy Durante.

CIRIBIRIBIN (1898) (w)Rudolf Thaler (m)Alberto Pestalozza. Famous Italian song. (R)1940s by Harry James and his Orchestra as his theme song.

CISCO KID (1973) (wm)Sylvester Allen—Harold Brown—Morris Dickerson—Leroy Jordan—Charles Miller—Lee Oscar Levitin—Howard Scott. (P)War.

CISSY STRUT (1969) (m)Arthur Neville—Leo Nocentelli—George Porter, Jr. —Joseph Modeliste, Jr. (P)The Meters.

CITY OF ANGELS (1956) (wm)Nick Jovan—Bev Dusham. (P)The Highlights.

CITY OF NEW ORLEANS, THE (1973) (wm)Steve Goodman. (I)Judy Collins. (P)Arlo Guthrie. (P)Steve Goodman. (R)1984 by Rick Nelson.

CIVILIZATION (Bongo, Bongo, Bongo) (1947) (I)Revue: *Angels In The Wings*, by Elaine Stritch. (P)Danny Kaye and The Andrews Sisters.

CLAIR (1972) (wm)Raymond O'Sullivan. (P)Gilbert O'-Sullivan.

CLAIR DE LUNE (1905) (m)Claude Debussy. Famous classical composition. Popular recording by Jose Iturbi.

CLAP FOR THE WOLFMAN (1974) (wm)Burton Cummings—Bill Wallace—Kurt Winter. (P)Guess Who.

CLAP HANDS! HERE COMES CHARLEY! (1925) (w)Billy Rose—Ballard Macdonald. (m)Joseph Meyer. (I)Vaudeville: By "Salt and Pepper". First recording by Johnny Marvin. (R)1930s by Chick Webb and his Orchestra. (R)1940s as theme song for Charlie Barnet and his Orchestra.

CLAP YO' HANDS (1926) (w)Ira Gershwin (m)George Gershwin. (I)Musical: *Oh, Kay!*, by Harland Dixon, Betty Compton, Paulette Winston, Constance Carpenter and Janette Gilmore. Recorded by Roger Wolfe Kahn and his Orchestra.

CLAPPING SONG, THE (1965) (wm)Lincoln Chase—Mrs. James McCarthy—Mrs. Larry Kent. (P)Shirley Ellis.

CLARINET LAMENT (1936) (m)Duke Ellington—Barney Bigard. (P)Duke Ellington and his Orchestra, clarinet solo by Barney Bigard.

CLARINET MARMALADE (1918) (wm)Eddy Edwards—James La Rocca—Tony Sparbaro—Larry Shields. (P)Original Dixieland Jazz Band.

CLASSICAL GAS (1968) (m)Mason Williams. (P)Mason Williams. NARAS Award Winner.

CLEAN UP WOMAN (1971) (wm)Clarence Reid—Willie Clarke. (P)Betty Wright.

CLEAN UP YOUR OWN BACK YARD (1969) (wm)Scott Davis—Billy Strange. (I)Film: *The Trouble With Girls*. (P)Elvis Presley.

CLEAR OUT OF THIS WORLD (1940) (w)Al Dubin (m)Jimmy McHugh. (I)Musical: *Keep Off The Grass*, by Jane Froman, Robert Shackleton, The Morelli Singers and Virginia O'Brien.

(Oh My Darling)CLEMENTINE (1884) (wm)Percy Montrose. Traditional song of the American West. (R)Film: *My Darling Clementine*,on soundtrack.

CLEMENTINE (1960) (wm)Woody Harris (P)Bobby Darin. (CR)Jan and Dean.

CLEOPATRA JONES (1973) (wm)Joe Simon. (I)Film: *Cleopatra Jones* as soundtrack theme. (P)Joe Simon.

CLIMB EV'RY MOUNTAIN (1959) (w)Oscar Hammerstein II (m)Richard Rodgers. (I)Musical: *Sound Of Music*, by Patricia Neway.

CLINGING VINE (1964) (wm)Earl Shuman—Leon Carr—Grace Lane. (P)Bobby Vinton.

CLOSE (1937) (wm)Cole Porter. (I)Film: *Rosalie*, by Nelson Eddy.

CLOSE AS PAGES IN A BOOK (1945) (w)Dorothy Fields (m)Sigmund Romberg. (I)Musical: *Up In Central Park*, by Maureen Cannon and Wilbur Evans.

CLOSE ENCOUNTERS OF THE THIRD KIND (Theme From) (1977) (m)John Williams. (I)Film: *Close Encounters Of The Third Kind* on soundtrack. (P)John Williams and his Orchestra. Disco version by Meco.

CLOSE HARMONY (1964) (w)Betty Comden—Adolph Green (m)Jule Styne. (I)Musical: *Fade Out—Fade In*, by Jack Cassidy, Lou Jacobi, Tina Louise and The Nephews.

CLOSE THE DOOR (1978) (wm)Kenny Gamble—Leon Huff. (P)Teddy Pendergrass.

CLOSE TO CATHY (1962) (w)Earl Shuman (m)Bob Goodman. (P)Mike Clifford.

CLOSE TO ME (1936) (w)Sam M. Lewis (m)Peter De Rose. (P)Tommy Dorsey and his Orchestra.

(They Long To Be)CLOSE TO YOU (1970) (w)Hal David (m)Burt Bacharach. (P)The Carpenters. No. 1 Chart Record. (CR)Jerry Butler.

CLOSE YOUR EYES (1933) (wm)Bernice Petkere. (P)Ruth Etting.

CLOSE YOUR EYES (1955) (wm)Chuck Willis. (P)The Five Keys. (R)1967 by Peaches and Herb.

CLOSER I GET TO YOU,THE (1978) (wm)Reggie Lucas—James Mtume. (P)Roberta Flack and Donny Hathaway.

CLOSER THAN A KISS (1958) (w)Sammy Cahn (m)Jimmy Van Heusen. (P)Vic Damone.

CLOSER YOU ARE, THE (1956) (wm)Earle Lewis—Morgan C. Robinson. (P)The Channels.

CLOSEST THING TO PERFECT (1985) (wm)Michael Omartian—Bruce Sudano—Jermaine Jackson. (I)Film: *Perfect*, by Jermaine Jackson. (P)Jermaine Jackson.

CLOUD NINE (1968) (wm)Barrett Strong—Norman Whitfield. (P)The Temptations. (CR)Mongo Santamaria.

CLOUDS (1935) (w)Gus Kahn (m)Walter Donaldson.

(I)Ray Noble and his Orchestra. (P)Benny Goodman and his Orchestra.

C'MON AND SWIM (1964) (w)Thomas Coman (m)Sylvester Stewart. (P)Bobby Freeman.

C'MON EVERYBODY (1958) (wm)Eddie Cochran—Jerry Capehart. (P)Eddie Cochran.

C'MON MARIANNE (1967) (wm)L. Russell Brown—Raymond Bloodworth. (P)The Four Seasons. (R)1976 by Donny Osmond.

COAL MINER'S DAUGHTER (1971) (wm)Loretta Lynn. (I)Film: *Coal Miner's Daughter*, by Sissy Spacek. (P)Loretta Lynn.

COCA COLA COWBOY (1979) (wm)Irving Dain—Steven Dorff—James S. Pinkard,Jr. —Sam Atchley. (I)Film: *Every Which Way But Loose*, by the voice of Mel Tillis. (P)Mel Tillis.

COCK-EYED OPTIMIST, A (1949) (w)Oscar Hemmerstein II (m)Richard Rodgers. (I)Musical: *South Pacific*, by Mary Martin. In film version (1959)by Mitzi Gaynor.

COCKEYED MAYOR OF KAUNAKAKAI (1935) (wm)Al Stillman—R. Alex Anderson. (I)Clara Inter (Hilo Hattie). Film: *Song Of The Islands*, by Clara Inter (1942).

COCKTAILS FOR TWO (1934) (wm)Arthur Johnston—Sam Coslow. (I)Film: *Murder At The Vanities*, by Carl Brisson. Recorded by Duke Ellington and his Orchestra. (R)1945 by Spike Jones.

COCOANUT GROVE (1938) (wm)Harry Owens. (I)Film: *Cocoanut Grove*, by Harry Owens' Royal Hawaiian Orchestra. (P)Harry Owens.

COCOANUT SONG, THE (1945) (w)Charles Tobias (m)Nat Simon. (P)Guy Lombardo and his Royal Canadians.

COCOANUT SWEET (1957) (w)E. Y. Harburg (m)Harold Arlen. (I)Musical: Jamaica, by Lena Horne and Adelaide Hall.

COCOANUT WOMAN (1957) (wm)Harry Belafonte. (P)Harry Belafonte.

COCONUT (1972) (wm)Harry Nilsson. (P)Nilsson.

COD'INE (1964) (wm)Buffy Sainte-Marie. (P)Buffy Sainte—Marie.

COFFEE IN THE MORNING (And Kisses In The Night) (1933) (w)Al Dubin (m)Harry Warren. (I)Film: *Moulin Rouge*, by Russ Columbo and Constance Bennett. (P)The Andrews Sisters.

COFFEE SONG, THE (They've Got An Awful Lot Of Coffee In Brazil) (1946) (wm)Bob Hilliard—Dick Miles. (I)Revue: *Monte Proser's Copacabana Revue*. (P)Frank Sinatra.

COFFEE TIME (1945) (w)Arthur Freed—Harry Warren. (I)Film: *Yolanda And The Thief*, on soundtrack. No artist credited with introduction.

COLD AS ICE (1977) (wm)Lous Grammatico—Michael Jones. (P)Foreigner.

COLD BLUE STEEL AND SWEET FIRE (1972) (wm)Joni Mitchell. (P)Joni Mitchell.

COLD, COLD HEART (1951) (wm)Hank Williams. (P)Hank Williams. (P)Tony Bennett. Bennett record No. 1 Chart Record.

COLD IN HAND BLUES (1925) (wm)Jack Gee—Fred Longshaw. (P)Bessie Smith.

COLD SWEAT (1967) (wm)James Brown—Alfred Ellis. (P)James Brown and The Famous Flames.

COLD TURKEY (1969) (wm)John Lennon. (P)The Plastic Ono Band.

COLE SLAW (1949) (wm)Jesse Stone. (P)Louis Jordan and his Tympani Five.

COLLEGE RHYTHM (1934) (w)Mack Gordon (m)Harry Revel. (I)Film: *College Rhythm*, by Jack Oakie and Lyda Roberti.

COLLEGE SWING (1938) (w)Frank Loesser (m)Hoagy Carmichael. (I)Film: *College Swing*, by Betty Grable, Martha Raye and Skinnay Ennis.

COLLEGIATE (1926) (wm)Moe Jaffe—Nat Bonx. (P)Fred Waring's Pennsylvanians. (CR)Carl Fenton and his Orchestra.

COLONEL BOGEY MARCH (1916) (m)Kenneth J. Alford. (I)Famous British March. (P)Film: *The Bridge On The River Kwai*, known on the soundtrack as March From The River Kwai.

GENERAL DWIGHT D. EISENHOWER

During World War II I played piccolo with the Army Port of Authority Embarkation Band, which was stationed in Fort Hamilton in Brooklyn.

After VE Day, when General Eisenhower returned home, he was feted with a huge parade in New York City. It was our good fortune that our band was chosen to lead the parade from 59th Street to 34th Street on Fifth Avenue.

When the day of the parade arrived, the band's drum major woke up quite ill. I was pressed into service as his replacement and it was my honor to be at the head of the parade.

When we reached 34th Street, there was a short rest period to allow for changeover of the bands. As our band moved to the side, General Eisenhower alit from the car he was riding in and walked over to the band. The chief warrant officer and I both saluted him. General Eisenhower returned our salutes, thanked us, and warmly shook our hands. It was a thrill that will last forever in my memory.

COLOR HIM FATHER (1969) (wm)Richard Spencer. (P)The Winstons. NARAS Award Winner.

COLOR MY WORLD (1967) (wm)Tony Hatch—Jackie Trent. (P)Petula Clark.

COLORADO (1973) (wm)Rick Roberts. (I)The Flying Burrito Brothers. (P)Linda Ronstadt.

COLORADO, MY HOME (1960) (wm)Meredith Willson. (I)Musical: *The Unsinkable Molly Brown*, by Tammy Grimes, Harve Presnell and The Chorus. In film version (1964)by Harve Presnell.

COLORED LIGHTS (1984) (wm)Fred Ebb—John Kander. (I)Musical: *The Rink*, by Liza Minelli.

COLORFUL (1964) (w)Lee Adams (m)Charles Strouse. (I)Musical: Golden Boy, by Sammy Davis, Jr.

(You Can't Lose The Blues With)COLORS (1957) (wm)Irving Berlin. (P)Rosemary Clooney.

COLORS OF MY LIFE,THE (1980) (w)Michael Stewart (m)Cy Coleman. (I)Musical: Barnum, by Jim Dale and Glenn Close.

COLT . 45 (1958) (w)Douglas Heyes (m)Hal Hopper. (I)TV Series *Colt . 45* on soundtrack.

COLUMBIA, THE GEM OF THE OCEAN (1843) (wm)David T. Shaw—T. A. Beckett. Famous American patriotic song.

COMBINATION OF THE TWO (1968) (wm)S. Andrew. (P)Big Brother and The Holding Company, featuring Janis Joplin.

COME A LITTLE BIT CLOSER (1964) (wm)Tommy Boyce—Bobby Hart—Wes Farrell. (P)Jay and The Americans.

COME ALONG WITH ME (1953) (wm)Cole Porter. (I)Musical: Can-Can, by Erik Rhodes and Hans Conried.

COME AND GET IT (wm)Paul McCartney. (I)Film: *The Magic Christian*, by Badfinger. (P)Badfinger.

COME AND GET THOSE MEMORIES (1963) (wm)Brian Holland—Lamont Dozier—Eddie Holland. (P)Martha and The Vandellas.

COME AND GET YOUR LOVE (1974) (wm)Lolly Vegas. (P)Redbone.

COME AND STAY WITH ME (1965) (wm)Jackie DeShannon. (P)Marianne Faithull.

COME AND TAKE A RIDE IN MY BOAT (Come On Down To My Boat) (1967) (wm)Wes Farrell—Jerry Goldstein. (P)Every Mother's Son.

COME AWAY MELINDA (1962) (wm)Fred Hellerman—Fran Minkoff. (P)Harry Belafonte.

COME BACK (1980) (wm)Peter Wolf—Seth Justman. (P)J. Geils Band

COME BACK BABY (1955) (wm)Ray Charles. (P)Ray Charles.

COME BACK CHARLESTON BLUE (1972) (w)Al Cleveland—Quincy Jones (m)Donny Hathaway. (I)Film: *Come Back Charleston Blue*, by voices of Donny Hathaway and Valerie Simpson.

COME BACK SWEET PAPA (1926) (m)Paul Barbarin—Luis C. Russell. (P)Louis Armstrong and his Orchestra.

COME BACK TO ME (1965) (w)Alan Jay Lerner (m)Burton Lane. (I)Musical: *On A Clear Day You Can See Forever*, by John Cullum. In film version (1970)by Yves Montand.

COME BACK TO SORRENTO (1904) (wm)Ernesto de Curtis—Claude Aveling. Famous Italian song.

COME BACK WHEN YOU GROW UP (1967) (wm)Martha Sharp. (P)Bobby Vee and The Strangers.

COME BACK WITH THE SAME LOOK IN YOUR EYES (1986) (wm)Don Black—Andrew Lloyd Webber. (I)Musical: *Song And Dance*, by Bernadette Peters.

COME CLOSER TO ME (Acerate Mas) (1946) (w-Eng)Al Stewart (m)Osvaldo Farres. (I)Film: *Easy To Wed*, by Carlos Ramirez.

COME DANCING (1983) (wm)Ray Davies. (P)The Kinks.

COME GET TO THIS (1973) (wm)Marvin Gaye. (P)Marvin Gaye.

COME GO WITH ME (1957) (wm)C. E. Quick. (P)The Del Vikings. (R)1982 by The Beach Boys.

COME GO WITH ME (1987) (wm)L. A. Martinee. (P)Expose.

COME HOME (1947) (w)Oscar Hammerstein II (m)Richard Rodgers. (I)Musical: *Allegro*, by Annamary Dickey.

COME HOME (1965) (wm)Dave Clark—Mike Smith. (P)The Dave Clark Five.

COME IN FROM THE RAIN (1977) (wm)Melissa Manchester—Carole Bayer Sager. (P)The Captain and Tennille.

COME IN, MORNIN' (1952) (w)Maxwell Anderson (m)Kurt Weill. (I)TV Show, *Huckleberry Finn* (1964)by Franz Elkins and Randolph Symonette.

COME INTO MY HEART (1959) (wm)Lloyd Price—Harold Logan. (P)Lloyd Price.

COME JOSEPHINE (In My Flying Machine) (1910) (w)Alfred Bryan (m)Fred Fisher. First recording by Ada Jones, Billy Murray and The American Quartet.

COME MONDAY (1974) (wm)Jimmy Buffett. (P)Jimmy Buffett.

COME NEXT SPRING (1955) (w)Lenny Adelson (m)Max Steiner. (I)Film: *Come Next Spring*, by Tony Bennett. (P)Tony Bennett.

COME ON-A MY HOUSE (1951) (wm)William Saroyan—Ross Bagdasarian. (I)Kay Armen. (P)Rosemary Clooney. No. 1 Chart Record.

COME ON EILEEN (1983) (wm)Kevin Rowland—Jim Paterson—Kevin Adams. (P)Dexy's Midnight Runners. No. 1 Chart Record.

COME ON IN (1939) (wm)Cole Porter. (I)Musical: *Du Barry Was A Lady*, by Ethel Merman,

COME ON, LET YOURSELF GO (1964) (wm)Jan Berry—Artie Kornfeld. (I)Film: *The New Interns* on soundtrack.

COME ON, LET'S GO (1958) (wm)Richard Valenzuela. (P)Ritchie Valens. (R)1966 by The McCoys.

COME ON OVER (1976) (wm)Barry and Robin Gibb. (P)Olivia Newton—John.

COME PRIMA (For The First Time) (1958) (w-Eng)Buck Ram (m)Di Paola—Taccani. (P)Domenico Modugno. (CR)Polly Bergen.

COME RAIN OR COME SHINE (1946) (w)Johnny Mercer (m)Harold Arlen. (I)Musical: *St. Louis Woman*, by Ruby Hill and Harold Nicholas. Recorded by Margaret Whiting, Dick Haymes with Helen Forrest. Most popular recording by Frank Sinatra.

COME RUNNIN' BACK (1966) (wm)Dick Glasser. (P)Dean Martin.

COME RUNNING (1970) (wm)Van Morrison. (P)Van Morrison.

COME SAIL AWAY (1977) (wm)Dennis De Young. (P)Styx.

COME SATURDAY MORNING (1969) (w)Dory Previn (m)Fred Carlin. (I)Film: *The Sterile Cuckoo* by the voices of The Sandpipers on soundtrack. (P)The Sandpipers.

COME SEE ABOUT ME (1964) (wm)Brian Holland—Eddie Holland—Lamont Dozier. (P)The Supremes. No. 1 Chart Record. (R)1967 by Junior Walker and The All Stars.

COME SEPTEMBER (1961) (wm)Bobby Darin. (I)Film: *Come September*, on soundtrack. (P)Bobby Darin and his Orchestra.

COME SOFTLY TO ME (1959) (wm)Gary Troxel—Gretchen Christopher—Barbara Ellis. (P)The Fleetwoods. No. 1 Chart Record. (R)1973 by The New Seekers.

COME TO BABY, DO! (1945) (wm)Inez James—Sidney Miller. (P)Les Brown and his Band Of Renown, vocal by Doris Day.

COME TO ME (1931) (wm)B. G. De Sylva—Lew Brown (m)Ray Henderson. (I)Film: *Indiscreet*, by Gloria Swanson. Recorded by The High Hatters.

COME TO ME (1957) (w)Peter Lind Hayes (m)Robert Allen. (I)TV Show, *Come To Me* on soundtrack. (P)Johnny Mathis.

COME TO ME (1959) (wm)Marvin Johnson—Berry Gordy, Jr. (P)Marv Johnson.

COME TO ME (1976) (w)Don Black (m)Henry Mancini. (I)Film: *The Pink Panther Strikes Again*, by voice of Tom Jones. (P)Tom Jones.

COME TO ME (1979) (wm)Tony Green. (P)France Joli.

COME TO ME, BEND TO ME (1947) (w)Alan Jay Lerner (m)Frederick Loewe. (I)Musical: *Brigadoon*, by Lee Sullivan. In film version (1954)by voice of John Gustafson, dubbing for Jimmy Thompson.

COME TO THE MARDI GRAS (1947) (w-Eng)Ervin Drake—Jimmy Shirl (m)Max Bulhoes—Milton de Oliveira. (P)Freddy Martin and his Orchestra. (CR)Frankie Masters and his Orchestra.

COME TO THE SUNSHINE (1966) (wm)Van Dyck Parks (P)Harper's Bizarre.

COME TO THE SUPERMARKET (In Old Peking) (wm)Cole Porter. (I)TV Show *Aladdin* by Cyril Ritchard.

COME TOGETHER (1969) (wm)John Lennon—Paul McCartney. (P)The Beatles. No. 1 Chart Record. (CR)Ike and Tina Turner. (R)1978 in the Film: *Sergeant Pepper's Lonely Heart's Club Band*. by Aerosmith.

COME UP AND SEE ME SOMETIME (1933) (w)Arthur Swanstrom (m)Louis Alter. (I)Film: *Take A Chance*, by Lillian Roth.

COME UP TO MY PLACE (1943) (wm)Betty Comden—Adolph Green. (m)Leonard Bernstein. (I)Musical: *On The Town*, by Nancy Walker and Chris Alexander.

COME WEST, LITTLE GIRL, COME WEST (1928) (w)Gus Kahn (m)Walter Donaldson. (I)Musical: *Whoopee*, by Ethel Shutta.

COME WHAT MAY (w)Allen Schiller (m)Al Sanchez. (P)Patti Page.

COMEDY TONIGHT (wm)Stephen Sondheim. (I)Musical: *A Funny Thing Happened On The Way To The Forum*, by Zero Mostel and The Company.

COMES A-LONG A-LOVE (wm)Al Sherman. (P)Kay Starr.

COMES LOVE (1939) (wm)Sam H. Stept—Charles Tobias—Lew Brown. (I)Musical: *Yokel Boy*, by Judy Canova.

COMES ONCE IN A LIFETIME (1961) (wm)Betty Comden—Adolph Green (m)Jule Styne. Recorded by The McGuire Sisters.

COMIN' BACK BABY (1962) (w)Bob Dorough (m)Ben Tucker.

COMIN' HOME SOLDIER (1966) (wm)Bobby Vinton—Gene Allan. (P)Bobby Vinton.

COMIN' IN AND OUT OF YOUR LIFE (1981) (wm)Richard Parker—Bobby Whiteside. (P)Barbra Streisand.

COMIN' IN ON A WING AND A PRAYER (1943) (w)Harold Adamson (m)Jimmy McHugh. (I)Eddie Cantor. (P)The Song Spinners. No. 1 Chart Record.

COMIN' THRO' THE RYE (1796) (w)Robert Burns (m)Traditional. Famous folk type song. Recorded (1914)by Nelly Melba.

COMING ON STRONG (1966) (wm)David Wilkins. (P)Brenda Lee.

COMING AROUND AGAIN (1987) (wm)Carly Simon. (P)Carly Simon.

COMING UP (1981) (wm)Paul McCartney. (P)Paul McCartney. No. 1 Chart Record.

COMME CI, COMME CA (1949) (w-Eng)Joan Whitney—Alex Kramer. (m)Bruno Coquatrix. (P)Frank Sinatra.

COMMENT ALLEZ-VOUS? (1953) (w)Ralph Blane—Robert Wells (m)Josef Myrow. (I)Film: *The French Line*, by Gilbert Roland.

COMMOTION (1969) (wm)John C. Fogarty. (P)Creedence Clearwater Revival.

COMPANY WAY, THE (1961) (wm)Frank Loesser. (I)Musical: *How To Succeed In Business Without Really Trying*, by Robert Morse, Sammy Smith, Charles Nelson Reilly and The Company.

COMPOSER, THE (1967) (wm)William Robinson, Jr. (P)Diana Ross and The Supremes.

CONCENTRATIN' ON YOU (1931) (w)Andy Razaf (m)Thomas "Fats" Waller. (P)Fats Waller.

CONCERT IN THE PARK (1939) (wm)Cliff Friend—Dave Franklin. (P)Jan Garber and his Orchestra. (CR)Kay Kyser and his Orchestra.

CONCERTO FOR CLARINET (1941) (m)Artie Shaw. (I)Film: *Second Chorus*, by Artie Shaw and his Orchestra. (P)Artie Shaw.

CONCERTO FOR COOTIE (1940) (m)Duke Ellington. (P)Duke Ellington and his Orchestra, featuring Cootie Williams on trumpet. Lyrics added in 1943 under the title of *Do Nothin' Till You Hear From Me*.

CONCERTO FOR TWO (1941) (wm)Jack Lawrence. Adapted from Tchaikovsky's Piano Concerto No. 1. (P)Claude Thornhill and his Orchestra.

CONCERTO IN F (1925) (m)George Gershwin. (I)Paul Whiteman and his Orchestra. In Films: *An American In Paris*, danced by Gene Kelly. Rhapsody In Blue, by Oscar Levant.

CONCHITA, MARQUITA, LOLITA, PEPITA, ROSITA, JUANITA LOPEZ (1942) (w)Herb Magidson (m)Jule Styne. (I)Film: *Priorities On Parade*, by Johnny Johnston.

CONCRETE AND CLAY (1965) (wm)Tommy Moeller—Brian Parker. (P)The Unit Four Plus Two. (CR)Eddie Rambeau.

CONFESS (1948) (wm)Bennie Benjamin—George Weiss. (P)Patti Page. (CR)Tony Martin.

CONFESSIN' THE BLUES (1941) (wm)Jay McShann—Walter Brown. (P)Jay McShann and his Orchestra, vocal by Walter Brown.

CONFESSION (1931) (w)Howard Dietz (m)Arthur Schwartz. (I)Revue: *The Band Wagon*, by The Girls And The Boys.

CONFIDENCE (1964) (w)Earl Shuman (m)Leon Carr. (I)Musical: *The Secret Life Of Walter Mitty*, by Rudy Tronto, Cathryn Damon and Marc London. (P)The Kirby Stone Quartet.

CONFIDENTIALLY (1938) (w)Al Dubin—Johnny Mercer (m)Harry Warren. (I)Film: *Garden Of The Moon*, by John Payne and Mabel Todd.

CONFIRMATION (1953) (m)Charlie Parker. (P)Charlie Parker.

CONGA (1985) (wm)Enrique Garcia. (P)Miami Sound Machine.

COUNT YOUR BLESSINGS (1986) (wm)Nicholas Ashford—Valerie Simpson. (P)Ashford and Simpson. The song was also performed on a segment of the TV Show *The Equalizers*.

CONGRATULATIONS (1929) (wm)Maceo Pinkard—Coleman Goetz—Bud Green—Sam H. Stept. (P)Jack Denny and his Orchestra.

CONGRATULATIONS (1949) (wm)Paul Weston—Sid Robin. (P)Jo Stafford.

CONGRATULATIONS TO SOMEONE (1953) (w)Roy

Alfred (m)Al Frisch. (P)Tony Bennett. (CR)Gordon MacRae.

CONQUISTADOR (1972) (wm)Gary Booker—Keith Reid. (P)Procul Harum.

CONSCIENCE (1961) (wm)Barry Mann—Cynthia Weil. (P)James Darren.

CONSIDER YOURSELF (1960) (wm)Lionel Bart. (I)Musical: Oliver, by Keith Hamshere, Martin Horsey and the crowd in London production. In New York production, by Paul O'Keefe, David Jones and the crowd.

CONSTANTLY (1910) (w)Chris Smith—James Henry Burris (m)Bert Williams. (P)Bert Williams.

CONSTANTLY (1942) (w)Johnny Burke (m)Jimmy Van Heusen. (I)Film: Road To Morocco, by Bing Crosby. (P)Bing Crosby.

CONTENTED (1932) (wm)Roy Turk—Don Bestor. (P)Theme song of Don Bestor and his Orchestra on the Carnation Milk radio show.

CONTINENTAL, THE (1934) (w)Herb Magidson (m)Con Conrad. (I)Film: Gay Divorcee, by Ginger Rogers. Danced to by Fred Astaire and Ginger Rogers. Reprised by Erik Rhodes and Lillian Miles. First Academy Award Winning Song. First recording by Leo Reisman and his Orchestra.

CONTINUING STORY OF BUNGALOW BILL, THE (1968) (wm)John Lennon—Paul McCartney. (P)The Beatles.

CONTRASTS (1932) (m)Jimmy Dorsey. Adapted from saxophone solo Oodles Of Noodles. (P)Theme song of Jimmy Dorsey and his Orchestra.

CONTROL (1987)J. Harris III—T. Lewis—Janet Jackson. (P)Janet Jackson.

CONTROL YOURSELF (1962) (w)Dory Langdon (m)Andre Previn. (P)Doris Day.

CONVENTION '72 (1972) (wm)Nick Cenci—Nick Casel. (P)The Delegates.

CONVOY (1975) (w)William D. Fries (m)Louis Davis. (P)C. W. McCall. No. 1 Chart Record.

COOK WITH HONEY (1973) (wm)Valerie Carter. (P)Judy Collins.

COOKING BREAKFAST FOR THE ONE I LOVE (1930) (w)Billy Rose (m)Henry H. Rose. (I)Film: Be Yourself, by Fanny Brice.

COOL (1957) (w)Stephen Sondheim (m)Leonard Bernstein. (I)Musical: West Side Story, by Micky Calin and The Jets.

COOL, CALM AND COLLECTED (1967) (wm)Mick Jagger—Keith Richard. (P)The Rolling Stones.

COOL CHANGE (1979) (wm)Glen Shorrock. (P)The Little River Band.

COOL IT NOW (1984) (wm)Vincent Barntley—Rick Timas. (P)New Edition.

COOL JERK (1966) (wm)Donald Storball. (P)The Capitols.

COOL LOVE (1981) (wm)Cory Lerios—David Jenkins—John Pierce. (P)Pablo Cruise.

COOL NIGHT (1981) (wm)Paul Davis. (P)Paul Davis.

COOL WATER (1948) (wm)Bob Nolan. (I)The Sons Of The Pioneers. (P)Vaughn Monroe with The Sons Of The Pioneers.

COPACABANA (1978) (wm)Barry Manilow—Bruce Sussman—Jack Feldman. (P)Barry Manilow.

COPENHAGEN (1924) (w)Walter Melrose (m)Charlie Davis. (I)Benson Orchestra of Chicago.

COPPER CANYON (1949) (wm)Jay Livingston—Ray Evans. (I)Film: Copper Canyon as soundtrack theme.

COPPER KETTLE (1953) (wm)Albert F. Beddoe. (I)Oscar Brand. (R)1964 by Joan Baez.

COQUETTE (1928) (wm)Irving Berlin. Promo song for Film: Coquette.

COQUETTE (1928) (w)Gus Kahn (m)Carmen Lombardo—John Green. (P)Guy Lombardo and his Royal Canadians. (CR)Rudy Vallee. (R)1953, by Billy Eckstine.

CORAL SEA (1920) (wm)King Zany—Nacio Herb Brown. (P)Paul Whiteman and his Orchestra.

CORAZON (1973) (wm)Carole King. (P)Carole King.

CORN SILK (1940) (w)Irving Kahal (m)Wayne King—Hal Bellis. (P)Wayne King and his Orchestra.

CORNBELT SYMPHONY (1948) (wm)Nev Simons—Robert Mellin. (I)Nev Simons and The Ambassadors of Note. (R)1954 by Bing and Gary Crosby.

CORNER OF THE SKY (1972) (wm)Stephen Schwartz. (I)Film: Pippin, by John Rubinstein. (P)The Jackson Five.

CORNET MAN (1964) (w)Bob Merrill (m)Jule Styne. (I)Musical: Funny Girl, by Barbra Streisand.

CORNISH RHAPSODY (1944) (m)Hubert Bath. (I)Film: Love Story, on soundtrack.

CORNS FOR MY COUNTRY (1944) (wm)Leah Worth—Jean Barry—Dick Charles. (I)Film: Hollywood Canteen, by The Andrews Sisters.

CORRINE, CORRINA (1932) (wm)J. Mayo Williams—Bo Chatman. (I)Bo Chatman. (P)Cab Calloway and his Orchestra. New lyrics added in 1932 by Mitchell Parish. (R)1960 by Ray Peterson.

COSI COSA (1935) (w)Ned Washington— (m)Bronislaw Kaper—Walter Jurmann. (I)Film: A Night At The Opera, by Allan Jones. (P)Allan Jones.

COSSACK LOVE SONG (1926) (w)Otto Harbach—Oscar Hammerstein II (m)Herbert Stothart—George Gershwin. (I)Operetta: Song Of The Flame, by Tessa Kosta and Guy Robertson.

COTTAGE FOR SALE, A (1930) (w)Willard Robison—Larry Conley. (I)Willard Robison and his Deep River Orchestra. (CR)Guy Lombardo and his Royal Canadians. (R)1945 by Billy Eckstine. Most popular recording by Frank Sinatra.

COTTON CANDY (1964) (m)Russ Damon. (P)Al Hirt.

COTTON FIELDS (1962) (wm)Huddie Ledbetter (I)Huddie "Leadbelly" Ledbetter. (R)1962 by The Highwaymen.

COTTON JENNY (1969) (wm)Gordon Lightfoot. (P)Anne Murray.

COTTON TAIL (1940) (m)Duke Ellington. (P)Duke Ellington and his Orchestra.

COULD BE (1938) (w)Johnny Mercer (m)Walter Donaldson. (P)Johnny Messner and his Orchestra.

COULD I HAVE THIS DANCE (1980) (wm)Wayland Holyfield—Bob House. (I)Film: Urban Cowboy on soundtrack. (P)Anne Murray.

COULD IT BE I'M FALLING IN LOVE (wm)Melvin Steals-Mervin Steals. (P)The Spinners.

COULD IT BE MAGIC (1975) (wm)Barry Manilow—Adrienne Anderson. (P)Barry Manilow. (CR)Donna Summer.

COULD IT BE YOU? (1942) (wm)Cole Porter. (I)Musical: Something For The Boys, by Bill Johnson.

COULD THIS BE MAGIC (1957) (wm)Hiram Johnson—Richard Blandon. (P)The Dubs.

COULD YOU USE ME (1930) (w)Ira Gershwin (m)George

Gershwin. (I)Musical: Girl Crazy, by Allan Kearns and Ginger Rogers.

COULDN'T GET IT RIGHT (1977) (wm)Colin Cooper—John Cuffley—Peter Haycock—Derek Holt—Frederick Jones. (P)Climax Blues Band.

COULD'VE BEEN (1987) (wm)L. Blaisch. (P)Tiffany.

COUNT EVERY STAR (1950) (w)Sammy Gallop (m)Bruno Coquatrix. (P)Hugo Winterhalter and his Orchestra. (CR)Dick Haymes.

COUNT ME IN (1965) (wm)Glen D. Hardin. (P)Gary Lewis and The Playboys.

COUNT ON ME (1978) (wm)Jesse Barish. (P)Jefferson Starship.

COUNT YOUR BLESSINGS (1943) (wm)Cole Porter. (I)Musical: Mexican Hayride by June Havoc, Bobby Clark and George Givot.

COUNT YOUR BLESSINGS INSTEAD OF SHEEP (1952) (wm)Irving Berlin. (I)Film: White Christmas, by Bing Crosby. (P)Eddie Fisher. (CR)Rosemary Clooney. (CR)Bing Crosby.

COUNTRY BOY (You Got Your Feet In L. A.) (1975) (wm)Dennis Lambert—Brian Potter. (P)Glen Campbell.

COUNTRY GIRL-CITY MAN (1968) (wm)Ted Daryll—Chip Taylor. (P)Billy Vera with Judy Clay.

COUNTRY HONK (1969) (wm)Mick Jagger—Keith Richard. (P)The Rolling Stones.

COUNTRY PIE (1969) (wm)Bob Dylan. (P)Bob Dylan.

COUNTRY ROAD (1970) (wm)James Taylor. (P)James Taylor.

COUNTRY STYLE (1947) (w)Johnny Burke (m)Jimmy Van Heusen. (I)Film: Welcome Stranger, by Bing Crosby. (P)Bing Crosby.

COUPLE OF SONG AND DANCE MEN, A (1945) (wm)Irving Berlin. (I)Film: Blue Skies, by Fred Astaire and Bing Crosby.

COUPLE OF SWELLS, A (1947) (wm)Irving Berlin. (I)Film: Easter Parade by Fred Astaire and Judy Garland.

COVER ME (1984) (wm)Bruce Springsteen. (P)Bruce Springsteen.

COVER OF ROLLING STONE (1972) (wm)Shel Silverstein. (P)Dr. Hook.

COW-COW BLUES (1927) (wm)Charles "Cow Cow" Davenport. (I)Cow Cow Davenport. (R)1940 by Bob Crosby and his orchestra. Song was used as model for Cow Cow Boogie.

COW-COW BOOGIE (1941) (wm)Don Raye—Gene de Paul—Benny Carter. (I)Film: Reveille With Beverly by Ella Mae Morse. (P)Freddy Slack and his Orchestra, vocal by Ella Mae Morse. (CR)Ella Fitzgerald with The Ink Spots.

COWARD OF THE COUNTY (1979) (wm)Roger Bowling—Billy Edd Wheeler. (P)Kenny Rogers.

COWBOY AND THE LADY,THE (1938) (w)Arthur Quenzer (m)Lionel Newman. (I)Film: The Cowboy And The Lady, on soundtrack.

COWBOY AND THE LADY,THE (1977) (wm)Bobby Goldsboro. (P)Bobby Goldsboro. (R)1980 by Brenda Lee.

COWBOY FROM BROOKLYN (1938) (w)Johnny Mercer (m)Harry Warren. (I)Film: Cowboy From Brooklyn, by Dick Powell.

COWBOY SERENADE, THE (1941) (wm)Rich Hall. (P)Kay Kyser and his Orchestra, vocal by Harry Babbitt. (CR)Glenn Miller and his Orchestra, vocal by Ray Eberle. Film: Cowboy Serenade, by Gene Autry.

COWBOYS TO GIRLS (1968) (wm)Kenny Gamble—Leon Huff. (P)The Intruders.

COWBOY'S WORK IS NEVER DONE, A (1971) (wm)Sonny Bono. (P)Sonny and Cher.

CRACKERBOX PALACE (1977) (wm)George Harrison. (P)George Harrison.

CRACKLIN' ROSIE (1970) (wm)Neil Diamond. (P)Neil Diamond. No. 1 Chart Record.

CRADLE OF LOVE (1960) (wm)Jack Fautheree—Wayne Gray. (P)Johnny Preston.

CRAZE-OLOGY (1929) (m)Lawrence "Bud" Freeman. (P)Bud Freeman.

CRAZY (1961) (wm)Willie Nelson. (P)Patsy Cline.

CRAZY (1987) (wm)A. Qunta—I. Davies—R. Kretschmer. (P)Icehouse.

CRAZY AS A LOON (1940) (w)Al Dubin (m)Jimmy McHugh. (I)Musical: Keep Off The Grass, by Ray Bolger, Sunny O'Dea and Larry Adler.

CRAZY 'BOUT YA, BABY (1954) (w)Pat Barrett (m)Rudi Maugeri. (P)The Crew Cuts.

CRAZY FEET (1930) (wm)Sidney D. Mitchell—Con Conrad—Archie Gottler. (I)Film: Happy Days, by Dixie Lee.

CRAZY FOR YOU (1984) (w)John Bettis (m)Jon Lind. (P)Madonna. No. 1 Chart Record.

CRAZY, HE CALLS ME (1949) (w)Bob Russell (m)Carl Sigman. (P)Billie Holiday.

CRAZY HEART (1951) (wm)Fred Rose—Maurice Murray. (I)Guy Lombardo and his Royal Canadians. (CR)Hank Williams.

CRAZY HORSES (1972) (wm)Alan Osmond—Wayne Osmond—Merrill Osmond. (P)The Osmonds.

CRAZY IN THE NIGHT (Barking At Airplanes) (1985) (wm)Kim Carnes. (P)Kim Carnes.

CRAZY LITTLE THING CALLED LOVE (1979) (wm)Freddie Mercury/ (P)Queen. No. 1 Chart Record.

CRAZY LOVE (1958) (wm)Paul Anka. (P)Paul Anka.

CRAZY LOVE (1978) (wm)Russell Young. (P)Poco.

CRAZY MAMA (1972) (wm)Mick Jagger—Keith Richards. (P)J. J. Cale.

CRAZY MAN, CRAZY (1953) (wm)Bill Haley. (P)Bill Haley and The Comets.

CRAZY ON YOU (1976) (wm)Ann Wilson—Nancy Wilson—Roger Fisher. (P)Heart.

CRAZY OTTO RAG, THE (1955) (wm)Edward R. White—Mack Wolfson—Hugo Peretti—Luigi Creatore. (P)Crazy Otto.

CRAZY PEOPLE (1932) (wm)Edgar Leslie—James V. Monaco. (I)Film: The Big Broadcast, by The Boswell Sisters. (P)The Boswell Sisters.

CRAZY RHYTHM (1928) (w)Irving Caesar (m)Joseph Meyer—Roger Wolfe Kahn. (I)Musical: Here's Howe, by Ben Bernie, Peggy Chamberlain and June O'Dea. Recorded by Roger Wolfe Kahn and his Orchestra. (R)1948 Film: You Were Meant For Me, by Dan Dailey.

CRAZY WORDS-CRAZY TUNE (1927) (w)Jack Yellen (m)Milton Ager. (P)Frank Crumit.

CRAZY WORLD (1981) (w)Leslie Bricusse (m)Henry Mancini. (I)Film: Victor, Victoria, by Julie Andrews.

CREEPER, THE (1927) (m)Duke Ellington. (P)Duke Ellington and his Orchestra.

CREEQUE ALLEY (1967) (wm)John Phillips—Michelle Gilliam. (P)The Mamas and The Papas.

CREOLE RHAPSODY (1965) (m)Duke Ellington.

(P)Duke Ellington and his Orchestra.

CRESCENDO IN BLUE (1939) (m)Duke Ellington. (P)Duke Ellington and his Orchestra.

CRIED LIKE A BABY (1970) (w)Paul Williams (m)Craig Doerge. (P)Bobby Sherman.

CRIMSON AND CLOVER (1968) (wm)Peter Lucas—Tommy James. (P)Tommy James and The Shondells. No. 1 Chart Record. (R)1982 by Joan Jett and The Blackhearts.

CRINOLINE DAYS (1922) (wm)Irving Berlin, (I)Revue: *Music Box Revue of 1922*, by Grace La Rue. (P)Paul Whiteman and his Orchestra.

CROCE DI ORO (1955) (wm)Kim Gannon. (P)Patti Page. (CR)Joan Regan.

CROCODILE ROCK (1973) (wm)Elton John—Bernie Taupin. (P)Elton John. No. 1 Chart Record.

CROCODILE TEARS (1949) (wm)Jimmy MaDonald—Billie Weber. (P)Eddy Howard.

CROONING (1921) (w)Al Dubin (m)William F. Caesar. (P)Benson Orchestra of Chicago.

CROSBY, COLUMBO, AND VALLEE (1931) (wm)Al Dubin—Joe Burke. Song written about the popular crooners of the time.

CROSS MY BROKEN HEART (1987) (wm)S. Bray—T. Pierce. (I)Film: *Beverly Hills Cop II*, by The Jets. (P)The Jets.

CROSS OVER THE BRIDGE (1954) (wm)Bennie Benjamin—George Weiss. (P)Patti Page.

CROSS PATCH (1936) (w)Tot Seymour (m)Vee Lawnhurst. (P)Fats Waller.

CROSS YOUR FINGERS (1929) (w)Arthur Swanstrom—Benny Davis (m)J. Fred Coots. (I)Musical: *Sons O' Guns*, by Shirley Vernon and Milton Watson.

CROSS YOUR HEART (1926) (w)B. G De Sylva (m)Lewis E. Gensler. (I)Musical: *Queen High*, by Mary Lawlor and Clarence Nordstrom. Recorded by Roger Wolfe Kahn and his Orchestra.

CROSSFIRE (1959) (m)T. J. Fowler—Tom King. (P)Johnny and The Hurricanes.

CROSSROADS (1969) (wm)Robert Johnson. (P)Cream.

CROSSTOWN (1940) (wm)James Cavanaugh—John Redmond—Nat Simon. (P)Glenn Miller and his Orchestra. (CR)Guy Lombardo and his Royal Canadians.

CROWD, THE (1962) (wm)Roy Orbison—Joe Melson. (P)Roy Orbison.

CRUEL SUMMER (1984) (wm)Tony Swain—Steve Jolley. (P)Bananarama.

CRUEL TO BE KIND (1979) (wm)Robert Ian Gomm—Nick Lowe. (P)Nick Lowe.

CRUISIN' (1979) (wm)William Robinson—Marvin Tarplin. (P)Smokey Robinson.

CRUISING DOWN THE RIVER (1949) (wm)Eily Beadell—Neil Tollerton. (P)Blue Barron and his Orchestra. (P)Russ Morgan and his Orchestra. Both records No. 1 Chart Records.

CRUMBLIN' DOWN (1983) (wm)John Cougar Mellencamp—George Michael Green. (P)John Cougar Mellencamp.

CRUSH ON YOU (1986) (wm)Jerry Knight—Aaron Zigman. (P)The Jets.

CRY (1951) (wm)Churchill Kohlman. (P)Johnnie Ray. No. 1 Chart Record. (R)1965 by Ray Charles. (R)1972 by Lynn Anderson.

CRY (1985) (wm)Kevin Godley—Lol Creme. (P)Godley and Creme.

CRY BABY (1963) (wm)Bert Russell—Norman Meade. (P)Garnett Mimms and The Enchanters. (R)1971 by Janis Joplin.

CRY, BABY, CRY (1938) (wm)Jimmy Eaton—Terry Shand—Remus Harris—Irving Melsher. (P)Larry Clinton and his Orchestra. (CR)Dick Robertson.

CRY BABY CRY (1968) (wm)John Lennon—Paul McCartney. (P)The Beatles.

CRY LIKE A BABY (1968) (wm)Dan Penn—Spooner Oldham. (P)The Box Tops. (R)1980 by Kim Carnes.

CRY LIKE THE WIND (1960) (wm)Betty Comden—Adolph Green (m)Jule Styne. (I)Musical: Do Re Mi, by Nancy Dussault.

CRY ME A RIVER (wm)Arthur Hamilton. (P)Julie London. (R)1960 by Janice Harper. (R)1970 by Joe Cocker.

CRY OF THE WILD GOOSE,THE (wm)Terry Gilkyson. (P)Frankie Laine. No. 1 Chart Record. (CR)Tennessee Ernie Ford.

CRY TO ME (1962) (wm)Bert Russell. (P)Solomon Burke. (R)1963 by Betty Harris. (R)1970 by Freddie Scott.

CRYIN' FOR THE CAROLINES (1930) (wm)Joe Young—Sam M. Lewis (m)Harry Warren. (I)Film: *Spring Is Here*, by Lawrence Gray. (P)Guy Lombardo and his Royal Canadians. (CR)Ruth Etting.

CRYING (1961) (wm)Roy Orbison—Joe Melson. (I)Roy Orbison. (R)1966 by Jay and The Americans. (R)1981 by Don McLean.

CRYING FOR JOY (1948) (w)Billy Rose (m)James V. Monaco. (P)Dinah Shore.

CRYING IN THE CHAPEL (1953) (wm)Artie Glenn. (I)Darrell Glenn. (P)The Orioles. (CR)June Valli. (R)1965 by Elvis Presley.

CRYING IN THE RAIN (1961) (wm)Howard Greenfield—Carole King. (P)The Everly Brothers.

CRYING TIME (1965) (wm)Buck Owens. (P)Ray Charles. NARAS Award Winner.

CRYSTAL BLUE PERSUASION (1969) (wm)Tommy James—Mike Vale—Ed Gray. (P)Tommy James and The Shondells.

CUANDO CALIENTE EL SOL (Love Me With All Your Heart) (1964) (w-Eng)Michael Vaughn (m)Carlos Rigual. (P)The Ray Charles Singers. (R)1966 by The Bachelors.

CUANTO LE GUSTA (1948) (w-Eng)Ray Gilbert (m)Gabriel Ruiz. (I)Film: *A Date With Judy*, by Carmen Miranda. (P)Carmen Miranda with The Andrews Sisters. (CR)Xavier Cugat and his orchestra.

CUBAN LOVE SONG (1931) (wm)Dorothy Fields—Jimmy McHugh—Herbert Stothart. (I)Film: *Cuban Love Song*, by Lawrence Tibbett. Recorded by Paul Whiteman and his Orchestra. (CR)Ruth Etting.

CUBAN PETE (1936) (wm)Jose Norman. (I)Film: *Cuban Pete*, by Desi Arnaz and The King Sisters. (P)Desi Arnaz.

CUCARACHA, LA (1916) (wm)Unknown. Traditional Mexican folk song. Popular recording by Lud Gluskin and his Orchestra.

CUCKOO IN THE CLOCK (1939) (w)Johnny Mercer (m)Walter Donaldson. (P)Kay Kyser and his Orchestra.

CUDDLE UP A LITTLE CLOSER, LOVEY MINE (1908) (w)Otto Harbach (m)Karl Hoschna. (I)Musical: *The Three Twins*. (P)Ada Jones and Billy Murray. No. 1

Chart Record. (R)1943 by Kay Armen.

CUM ON FEEL THE NOIZE (1972) (wm)Noddy Holder—Jim Lea. (P)Quiet Riot.

CUMPARSITA, LA (1916) (w)Carol Raven (m)Matos Rodriguez. Popular Argentinian tango.

CUP OF COFFEE, A SANDWICH AND YOU, A (1925) (w)Al Dubin—Billy Rose (m)Joseph Meyer. (I)Revue: *Andre Charlot's Revue of 1926*, by Gertrude Lawrence and Jack Buchanan.

CUPID (1961) (wm)Sam Cooke. (P)Sam Cooke. (P)Sam Cooke. (R)1965 by Johnny Rivers. (R)1970 by Johnny Nash. (R)1970 by Tony Orlando and Dawn. (R)1980 by the Spinners.

CURLY SHUFFLE, THE (1983) (wm)Peter Quinn. (P)Jump 'n' The Saddle.

CURLY TOP (1935) (w)Ted Koehler (m)Ray Henderson. (I)Film: *Curly Top*, by John Boles.

CUT THE CAKE (1974) (wm)Roger Ball—Malcolm Duncan—Alan Gorrie—Robbie McIntosh—Owen McIntyre—Jamie Stuart. (P)Average White Band.

CUTE LITTLE THINGS YOU DO, THE (1931) (wm)James F. Hanley. (I)Film: *Young As You Feel*, by Fifi D'Orsay.

CUTTIN' THE CANE (1941) (w)Lorenz Hart (m)Richard Rodgers. (I)Film: *They Met In Argentina*, by Diosa Costello.

CYCLES (1968) (wm)Gayle Caldwell. (P)Frank Sinatra.

CYNTHIA'S IN LOVE (1946) (w)Jack Owens (m)Earl White—Billy Gish. (P)Tex Beneke and his Orchestra.

CZARDAS (1904) (m)Vittorio Monti. Written as a classical violin solo.

DA-DOO RON RON (1963) (wm)Jeff Barry—Ellie Greenwich—Phil Spector. (P)The Crystals. (R)1972 by Ian Mathews. (R)1977 by Shaun Cassidy. Cassidy No. 1 Chart Record.

DADDY (1941) (wm)Bob Troup (I)Film: *Two Latins From Manhattan*, by Joan Davis and Jinx Falkenburg. (P)Sammy Kaye and his Orchestra. No. 1 Chart Record. (CR)Joan Merrill.

DADDY COULD SWEAR, I DECLARE (1972) (wm)Johnny Bristol—Merald Knight, Jr. —Gladys Knight. (P)Gladys Knight and The Pips.

DADDY DON'T YOU WALK SO FAST (1970) (wm)Peter Callender—Geoff Stephens. (I)In England, by Daniel Boone. (P)Wayne Newton.

DADDY-O (I'm Gonna Teach You Some Blues) (1948) (wm)Don Raye—Gene de Paul. (I)Film: *A Song Is Born*, by Louis Jordan and his Tympani Five.

DADDY O (1955) (wm)Louie Innis—Buford Abner—Charlie Gore. (P)The Fontane Sisters. (CR)Bonnie Lou.

DADDY SANG BASS (1968) (wm)Carl Perkins. (P)Johnny Cash.

DADDY, YOU'VE BEEN A MOTHER TO ME (1920) (wm)Fred Fisher. (P)Henry Burr.

DADDY'S HOME (1961) (wm)James Sheppard—William Miller. (P)Shep and The Limelites. (R)1967 by Chuck Jackson and Maxine Brown. (R)1973 by Jermaine Jackson. (R)1982 by Cliff Richard.

DADDY'S LITTLE GIRL (1949) (wm)Bobby Burke—Horace Gerlach. (I)Henry Jerome and his Orchestra. (P)The Mills Brothers. (CR)Dick Todd. (R)1967 by Al Martino.

DAISY A DAY (1973) (wm)Jud Strunk. (P)Jud Strunk.

DAISY BELL (1892) (wm)Harry Dacre. (P)Dan Quinn. No. 1 Chart Record.

DAISY JANE (1975) (wm)Gerry Beckley. (P)America.

DAMES (1934) (w)Al Dubin (m)Harry Warren. (I)Film: *Dames*, by Dick Powell. Recorded by Eddy Duchin and his Orchestra.

DAMNED IF I DO (1978) (wm)Eric Woolfson. (P)Alan Parsons Project.

DANCE (Disco Heat) (1978) (wm)Victor Orsborn—Eric Robinson. (P)Sylvester.

DANCE, DANCE, DANCE (1964) (wm)Brian Wilson—Carl Wilson. (P)The Beach Boys.

DANCE, DANCE, DANCE (Yowsah, Yowsah, Yowsah) (1977) (wm)Nile Rodgers—Bernard Edwards—Kenny Lehman. (P)Chic.

DANCE, EVERYONE DANCE (1958) (wm)Sid Danoff. Adapted from Hebrew melody Hava Nagila. (P)Betty Madigan.

DANCE HALL DAYS (1984) (wm)Jack Hues. (P)Wang Chung.

DANCE, LITTLE LADY (1928) (wm)Noel Coward. (I)Revue: *This Year Of Grace*, London production by Sonnie Hale. New York production by Noel Coward.

DANCE ME LOOSE (1951) (w)Mel Howard (m)Lee Erwin. (P)Arthur Godfrey and The Chordettes. (CR)Russ Morgan and his Orchestra.

DANCE, MY DARLINGS (1935) (w)Oscar Hammerstein II (m)Sigmund Romberg. (I)Musical: *May Wine*, by Nancy McCord.

DANCE-O-MANIA (1920) (w)L. Wolfe Gilbert (m)Joe Cooper. (P)Ben Selvin and his Orchestra.

DANCE OF THE HOURS (1876) (m)A. Ponchielli. (I)Opera: *La Gioconda*. First popular recording by Arthur Pryor's Band.

DANCE OF THE SPANISH ONION (1942) (m)David Rose. (P)David Rose and his Orchestra.

DANCE ON LITTLE GIRL (1960) (wm)Paul Anka (P)Paul Anka.

DANCE ONLY WITH ME (1958) (w)Betty Comden—Adolph Green (m)Jule Styne. (I)Musical: *Say, Darling*, by Mitchell Gregg and Vivian Blaine.

DANCE THE NIGHT AWAY (1979) (wm)David Lee Roth—Michael Sobolewski, Alex Van Halen—Edward Van Halen. (P)Van Halen.

DANCE TO THE MUSIC (1968) (wm)Sylvester Stewart. (P)Sly and The Family Stone.

DANCE WITH A DOLLY (With A Hole In Her Stocking) (1944) (wm)Terry Shand—Jimmy Eaton—Mickey Leader. Adapted from folk song,Buffalo Gals. (P)Russ Morgan and his Orchestra. (CR)Evelyn Knight.

DANCE WITH ME (1959) (wm)Louis Lebish—Geroge Treadwell—Irv Nahan—Jerry Leiber—Mike Stoller. (P)The Drifters.

DANCE WITH ME (1975) (wm)John J. Hall—Johanna Hall. (P)Orleans.

DANCE WITH ME (1978) (wm)Peter Brown—Robert Rans. (P)Peter Brown and Betty Wright.

DANCE WITH ME HENRY (1955) (wm)Johnny Otis—Hank Ballard—Etta James. (I)Etta James. (P)Georgia Gibbs. No. 1 Chart Record.

DANCERS IN LOVE (1945) (m)Duke Ellington. From The Perfume Suite. (P)Duke Ellington and his Orchestra.

DANCIN' FOOL (1968) (wm)Frank Zappa. (P)Guess Who. (R)1975 by Frank Zappa.

DANCIN' MAN (1977) (wm)Vinnie Barrett—Yvonne Gray. (P)Q

DANCIN' PARTY (1962) (w)Kal Mann (m)Dave Appell. (P)Chubby Checker.

DANCIN' SHOES (1978) (wm)Carl Storie. (P)Nigel Olsson. (CR)Faith Band.

DANCIN' WITH SOMEONE (Longin' For You) (1953) (wm)Bennie Benjamin—George Weiss—Alex Alstone. (P)Teresa Brewer.

DANCING (1963) (wm)Jerry Herman. (I)Musical: *Hello, Dolly!*, by Carol Channing, Charles Nelson Reilly, Jerry Dodge, Sondra Lee, Eileen Brennan and The Company.

DANCING FOOL (1922) (w)Harry B. Smith—Francis Wheeler (m)Ted Snyder. (P)The Club Royal Orchestra.

DANCING IN THE DARK (1931) (w)Howard Dietz (m)Arthur Schwartz. (I)Revue: *The Band Wagon*, by John Barker. Recorded by Bing Crosby,Fred Waring's Pennsylvanians. (R)1941 by Artie Shaw and his Orchestra. (R)Film: *The Band Wagon*, danced by Fred Astaire and Cyd Charisse.

DANCING IN THE DARK (1984) (wm)Bruce Springsteen. (P)Bruce Springsteen.

DANCING IN THE MOONLIGHT (1973) (wm)Sherman Kelly. (P)King Harvest.

DANCING IN THE STREET (1964) (wm)William Stevenson—Marvin Gaye. (P)Martha and The Vandellas. (R)1967 by The Mamas & The Papas. (R)1982 by Van

Halen. (R)1985 by Mick Jagger & David Bowie.

DANCING IN THE SHEETS (1984) (w)Dean Pitchford—Bill Wolfer. (I)Film: *Footloose* on soundtrack. (P)Shalamar.

DANCING MACHINE (1974) (wm)Weldon Parks—Hal Davis—Donald Fletcher. (P)The Jackson Five.

DANCING ON A DIME (1940) (w)Frank Loesser (m)Burton Lane. (I)Film: *Dancing On A Dime*, by Robert Paige and Grace McDonald.

DANCING ON THE CEILING (1930) (w)Lorenz Hart (m)Richard Rodgers. (I)Musical: *Ever Green* (London production)by Jessie Matthews and Sonnie Hale. Recorded by Jack Hylton and his Orchestra.

DANCING ON THE CEILING (1986) (wm)Lionel Richie—Carlos Rios. (P)Lionel Richie.

DANCING QUEEN (1977) (wm)Benny Andersson—Bjorn Ulvaeus—Stig Anderson. (P)Abba. No. 1 Chart Record.

DANCING TAMBOURINE (1927) (w)Phil Ponce (m)W. C. Polla. (P)Fred Waring's Pennsylvanianas. (CR)Paul Whiteman and his Orchestra.

DANCING THE DEVIL AWAY (1927) (w)Bert Kalmar—Otto Harbach (m)Harry Ruby. (I)Musical: *Lucky*, by Mary Eaton. Recorded by Don Voorhees and his Orchestra.

DANCING WITH MR. D (1973) (wm)Mick Jagger—Keith Richards. (P)The Rolling Stones.

DANCING WITH TEARS IN MY EYES (1930) (w)Al Dubin (m)Joe Burke. (P)Rudy Vallee. (CR)Nat Shilkret and his Orchestra. (R)1952 by Mantovani and his Orchestra.

DANDELION (1967) (wm)Mick Jagger—Keith Richards. (P)The Rolling Stones.

DANDY (1966) (wm)Ray Davies. (P)Herman's Hermits.

DANG ME (1964) (wm)Roger Miller. (P)Roger Miller. NARAS Award Winner.

DANGER! HEARTBREAK AHEAD (1954) (wm)Carl Stutz—Carl Barefoot. (P)Jaye P. Morgan.

DANGER-LOVE AT WORK (1937) (wm)Mack Gordon—Harry Revel. (I)Film: *You Can't Have Everything*, by Louis Prima and Alice Faye. Film: *Danger— Love At Work*, by Jack Haley and Ann Sothern.

DANGER ZONE (1986) (wm)Giorgio Moroder—Tom Whitlock. (P)Kenny Loggins.

DANGLING CONVERSATION, THE (1966) (wm)Paul Simon. (P)Simon and Garfunkel.

DANIEL (1973) (wm)Elton John—Bernie Taupin. (P)Elton John.

DANIEL BOONE (1964) (w)Vera Matson (m)Lionel Newman. (I)TV series: *Daniel Boone* on soundtrack.

DANKE SCHOEN (1963) (w-Eng)Kurt Schwabach—Milt Gabler. (m)Bert Kaempfert. (P)Bert Kaempfert and his Orchestra. Vocal version by Wayne Newton.

DANNY BOY (1913) (wm)Fred Weatherly. Original recording by Madame Schumann—Heink. (R)1940 by Glenn Miller and his Orchestra. (R)1967 by Ray Price.

DANNY'S SONG (1970) (wm)Kenny Loggins. (P)Anne Murray.

DANSE MACABRE (1872) (m)Camille Saint—Saens. Famous classical composition.

DANSERO (1953) (w)Sol Parker (m)Richard Hayman—Lee Daniels. (P)Richard Hayman and his Orchestra.

DARDANELLA (1919) (w)Fred Fisher (m)Felix Bernard—Johnny S. Black. (I)Ben Selvin and his Orchestra. (CR)Prince's Orchestra.

DARING YOUNG MAN ON THE FLYING TRAPEZE, THE (1868) (w)George Leybourne (m)Alfred Lee. First popular recording by Walter O'Keefe (1934) Most popular recording by Rudy Vallee.

DARK EYES (1926) (wm)Arranged by Harry Horlick. Based on Russian folk song Otchi Tchorniya. (P)Harry Horlick and The A & P Gypsies on radio. (R)1937 by Tommy Dorsey and his Orchestra.

DARK HORSE (1974) (wm)George Harrison. (P)George Harrison.

DARK IS THE NIGHT (1950) (w)Sammy Cahn (m)Nicholas Brodszky. (I)Film: *Rich, Young And Pretty*, by Jane Powell.

DARK LADY (1973) (wm)John Durrill. (P)Cher. No. 1 Chart Record.

DARK MOON (1957) (wm)Ned Miller. (P)Gale Storm. (CR)Bonnie Guitar.

DARK NIGHT (1930) (w)Clifford Grey (m)Herbert Stothart. (I)Film: *In Gay Madrid*, by Ramon Novarro.

(When It's)DARKNESS ON THE DELTA (1932) (w)Marty Symes—Al J. Neiberg. (m)Jerry Livingston. (P)Mildred Bailey. (CR)Ted Fiorito and his Orchestra.

DARKNESS ON THE EDGE OF TOWN (1978) (wm)Bruce Springsteen. (P)Bruce Springsteen.

DARKTOWN STRUTTERS BALL (1917) (wm)Shelton Brooks. (I)Original Dixieland Jazz Band. (R)1927 by Ted Lewis and his Orchestra. (R)1948 by Alan Dale and Connie Haines. (R)1954 by Lou Monte.

DARLIN, (1968) (wm)Brian Wilson—Mike Love. (P)The Beach Boys. (R)1978 by Paul Davis and Susan Collins. (R)1980 by Yipes!!

DARLING BE HOME SOON (1967) (wm)John B. Sebastian. (I)Film: *You're A Big Boy Now*, by The Lovin' Spoonful on soundtrack. (P)The Lovin' Spoonful. (CR)Bobby Darin.

DARLING. JE VOUS AIME BEAUCOUP (1936) (wm)Anna Sosenko. (I)Hildegarde. Film: *Love And Hisses*, by Simone Simon. (R)1955 by Nat "King" Cole.

DARN THAT DREAM (1939) (w)Eddie De Lange (m)Jimmy Van Heusen. (I)Musical: *Swingin' The Dream*, by Maxine Sullivan, Louis Armstrong, Bill Bailey, The Dandridge Sisters, The Rhythmettes and The Deep River Boys. (P)Benny Goodman and his Orchestra. No. 1 Chart Record. (CR)Tommy Dorsey and his Orchestra.

DAT'S LOVE (1943) (w)Oscar Hammerstein II (m)Georges Bizet. Adapted from Habanera from opera *Carmen*. (I)Musical: *Carmen Jones*, by Muriel Smith.

DAUGHTER OF DARKNESS (1970) (wm)Les Reed—Geoff Stephens. (P)Tom Jones.

DAUGHTER OF ROSIE O'GRADY, THE (1918) (w)Monty C. Brice (m)Walter Donaldson. (I)Lewis James.

DAVENPORT BLUES (1925) (m)Bix Beiderbecke. (I)Bix Beiderbecke and his Rhythm Jugglers.

DAVID AND LISA'S LOVE SONG (1963) (w)Edward Heyman (m)Mark Lawrence. Adaptation of a theme from film *David And Lisa*.

DAWN (1927) (w)Otto Harbach—Oscar Hammerstein II (m)Robert Stolz—Herbert Stothart. (I)Operetta: *Golden Dawn*, by Louise Hunter and Paul Gregory.

DAWN (Go Away) (1964) (wm)Sandy Linzer—Bob Gaudio. (P)The Four Seasons.

DAY AFTER DAY (1972) (wm)William Peter Ham. (P)Badfinger.

DAY AFTER FOREVER, THE (1945) (w)Johnny Burke

(m)Jimmy Van Heusen. (I)Film: *Going My Way*, by Bing Crosby. (P)Bing Crosby.

DAY BEFORE SPRING, THE (1945) (w)Alan Jay Lerner (m)Frederick Loewe. (I)Musical: *The Day Before Spring*, by Irene Manning.

DAY BY DAY (1945) (wm)Sammy Cahn—Axel Stordahl—Paul Weston. (I)Jo Stafford. (P)Frank Sinatra. (CR)Les Brown and his Band of Renown.

DAY BY DAY (1971) (w)John Michael Tebelak (m)Stephen Schwartz. (I)Musical: *Godspell*, by The Cast. (P)Cast of Godspell.

DAY BY DAY (1986) (wm)Rob Hyman—Eric Bazilian—Rick Chertoff. (P)Hooters.

D. C. CAB (1984) (wm)Richard Feldman—Rich Kelly—Larry John McNally. (I)Film: *D. C. Cab* on soundtrack. (P)Peabo Bryson.

DAY DREAM (1941) (w)John Latouche (m)Duke Ellington—Billy Strayhorn. (P)Duke Ellington and his Orchestra.

DAY DREAMING (1941) (w)Gus Kahn (m)Jerome Kern. (P)Bing Crosby.

DAY DREAMING (1972) (wm)Aretha Franklin. (P)Aretha Franklin.

DAY DREAMS COME TRUE AT NIGHT (wm)Dick Jurgens. (P)Dick Jurgens and his Orchestra.

DAY IN-DAY OUT (1939) (w)Johnny Mercer (m)Rube Bloom. (P)Bob Crosby and his Orchestra, vocal by Helen Ward. No. 1 Chart Record. (CR)Artie Shaw and his Orchestra. Most popular recording by Frank Sinatra.

DAY IN THE LIFE, A (1967) (wm)John Lennon—Paul McCartney. (P)The Beatles.

DAY IN THE LIFE OF A FOOL, A (1966) (w-Eng)Carl Sigman (m)Luis Bonfa. English version of *Manha De Carnaval*. (P)Jack Jones.

DAY IS DONE (1969) (wm)Peter Yarrow. (P)Peter, Paul and Mary. (CR)Brooklyn Bridge.

DAY OF JUBILO, THE (1952) (wm)Terry Gilkyson. (P)Guy Mitchell.

DAY OF THE LOCUSTS (1970) (wm)Bob Dylan. (P)Bob Dylan.

DAY THE RAINS CAME, THE (1957) (w-Eng)Carl Sigman (m)Gilbert Becaud. (I)Gilbert Becaud. (P)Jane Morgan. (CR)Raymond Lefevre.

DAY TRIPPER (1966) (wm)John Lennon—Paul McCartney. (P)The Beatles. (R)1975 by Anne Murray.

DAY YOU CAME ALONG, THE (1933) (wm)Sam Coslow—Arthur Johnston. (I)Film: *Too Much Harmony*, by Bing Crosby and Judith Allen. (P)Bing Crosby.

DAYBREAK (1942) (w)Harold Adamson (m)Ferde Grofe. Based on *Mardi Gras* from Grofe's *Mississippi Suite*. (P)Tommy Dorsey and his Orchestra, vocal by Frank Sinatra. (CR)Harry James and his Orchestra.

DAYBREAK (1977) (wm)Barry Manilow—Adrienne Anderson. (P)Barry Manilow.

DAYBREAK EXPRESS (1934) (m)Duke Ellington. (P)Duke Ellington and his Orchestra.

DAYDREAM (1966) (wm)John B. Sebastian. (P)The Lovin' Spoonful.

DAYDREAM BELIEVER (1967) (wm)John Stewart. (P)The Monkees. No. 1 Chart Record.

DAYDREAMING (All Night Long) (1938) (w)Johnny Mercer (m)Harry Warren. (I)Film: *Gold Diggers In Paris*, by Rudy Vallee and Rosemary Lane. (P)Rudy Vallee.

DAYS GONE BY (1963) (w)Sheldon Harnick (m)Jerry Bock. (I)Musical: *She Loves Me*, by Ludwig Donath.

DAYS GONE DOWN (Still Got The Light In Your Eyes) (1979) (wm)Gerry Rafferty. (P)Gerry Rafferty.

DAYS OF THE WALTZ, THE (1962) (w-Eng)Will Holt (m)Jacques Brel. (I)Felicia Sanders. (P)Patti Page.

DAYS OF WINE AND ROSES (1962) (w)Johnny Mercer (m)Henry Mancini. (I)Film: *Days Of Wine And Roses*, by un—named vocal group. Academy Award Winner. (P)Henry Mancini and his Orchestra. Vocal version by Andy Williams. NARAS Award Winner.

DAYTIME FRIENDS (1976) (wm)Ben Peters. (P)Kenny Rogers.

DAZZ (1977) (wm)Reginald Hargis—Edward Irons—R. Ranson, Jr. (P)Bang.

DE CAMPTOWN RACES (1850) (wm)Stephen Collins Foster. One of Foster's most popular songs.

DE GLORY ROAD (1928) (w)Clement Wood (m)J. Russell Bodley. (P)Lawrence Tibbett.

DEACON BLUES (1978) (wm)Walter Becker—Donald Fagan. (P)Steely Dan.

DE DO DO DO, DE DA DA DA (1980) (wm)Gordon Sumner. (P)The Police.

DEAD END (1967) (w)Gerome Ragni—James Rado (m)Galt MacDermot. (I)Musical: *Hair*, by Jill O'Hara in off—Broadway version.

DEAD END STREET (1967) (w)Ben Raleigh (m)David Axelrod. (P)Lou Rawls.

DEAD MAN'S CURVE (1963) (wm)Roger Christian—Jan Berry—Artie Kornfeld. (P)Jan and Dean.

DEAD SKUNK (1973) (wm)Loudon Wainwright. (P)Loudon Wainwright.

DEAR DOCTOR (1968) (wm)Mick Jagger—Keith Richard. (P)The Rolling Stones.

DEAR FRIEND (1963) (w)Sheldon Harnick (m)Jerry Bock. (I)Musical: She Loves Me, by Barbara Cook.

DEAR HEART (1964) (w)Jay Livingston—Ray Evans (m)Henry Mancini. (I)Film: *Dear Heart*, by orchestra and chorus on soundtrack. (P)Andy Williams. (CR)Jack Jones.

DEAR HEARTS AND GENTLE PEOPLE (1950) (w)Bob Hilliard (m)Sammy Fain. (P)Dinah Shore. (P)Bing Crosby. (CR)Gordon MacRae. (CR)Doris Day.

DEAR IVAN (1962) (wm)Jimmy Dean (P)Jimmy Dean.

DEAR LANDLORD (1968) (wm)Bob Dylan. (P)Bob Dylan.

DEAR LITTLE CAFE (1929) (wm)Noel Coward. (I)Musical: *Bitter Sweet*, by Peggy Wood and Georges Metaxa in the London production. By Evelyn Laye and Gerald Nodin in the New York production. (R)1940 Film: *Bitter Sweet*, by Jeanette MacDonald and Nelson Eddy.

DEAR LITTLE GIRL (1926) (w)Ira Gershwin (m)George Gershwin. (I)Musical: *Oh, Kay!*, by Oscar Shaw. (R)1968 Film: Star!, by Julie Andrews and Daniel Massey.

DEAR LONELY HEARTS (I'm Writing To You) (1962) (wm)Bob Halley—Emil Anton. (P)Nat "King" Cole.

DEAR LOVE, MY LOVE (1920) (w)Brian Hooker (m)Rudolf Friml. (I)Musical: *June Love*, by Else Adler.

DEAR MOM (1941) (wm)Maury Coleman Harris. (P)Sammy Kaye and his Orchestra, vocal by Allan Foster.

DEAR OLD DONEGAL (1942) (wm)Steve Graham. (P)Bing Crosby.

DEAR OLD GIRL (1903) (w)Richard Henry Buck (m)Theodore F. Morse. (I)J. W. Myers.

DEAR OLD SOUTHLAND (1921) (w)Henry Creamer (m)Turner Layton. Adapted from the spiritual Deep River. (I)Sidney Bechet. (R)1939, by Benny Goodman and his Orchestra.

DEAR ONE (1962) (wm)John Lawrence Finneran—Vincent Finneran. (P)Larry Finneran.

DEAR PRUDENCE (1968) (wm)John Lennon—Paul McCartney. (P)The Beatles. (R)1970 by The Five Stairsteps.

DEAR LITTLE BOY OF MINE (1918) (w)J. Keirn Brennan (m)Ernest R. Ball. (I)Charles Harrison.

DEAREST, DAREST I (w)Johnny Burke (m)Jimmy Van Heusen. (I)Film: Love Thy Neighbor, by Eddie "Rochester" Anderson.

DEAREST LOVE (1938) (wm)Noel Coward. (I)Musical: Operette, by Muriel Barron and Max Oldaker (London). Revue: Set To Music, by Eva Ortega and Hugh French (New York).

DEARIE (1950) (wm)Bob Hilliard—Dave Mann. (P)Ray Bolger and Ethel Merman. (CR)Jo Stafford and Gordon MacRae. (CR)Lisa Kirk.

DEARLY BELOVED (1942) (w)Johnny Mercer (m)Jerome Kern. (I)Film: You Were Never Lovelier, by Fred Astaire. Recorded by Glenn Miller and his Orchestra, Dinah Shore, Alvino Rey and his Orchestra.

DEATH OF FLOYD COLLINS, THE (1925) (w)Rev. Andrew Jenkins (m)Irene Spain. (P)Vernon Dalhart on over fifteen different record labels.

DEATH OF LITTLE KATHY FISCUS, THE (1949) (wm)Jimmy Osborne. (P)Jimmy Osborne.

DECEMBER 1963 (Oh What A Night) (wm)Judy Parker-Bob Gaudio. (P)The Four Seasons. No. 1 Chart Record.

DECK OF CARDS, THE (1948) (wm)T. Texas Tyler. (I)T. Texas Tyler. (CR)Tex Ritter. (P)Phil Harris. (R)1959 by Wink Martindale.

DECK THE HALLS WITH BOUGHS OF HOLLY (1784) (wm)Unknown. Traditional Christmas Carol.

DEDE DINAH (1958) (w)Bob Marcucci (m)Peter De Angelis. (P)Frankie Avalon.

DEDICATED FOLLOWER OF FASHION (1966) (wm)Ray Davies. (P)The Kinks.

DEDICATED TO THE ONE I LOVE (1961) (wm)Lowman Pauling—Ralph Bass. (P)The Shirelles. (R)1967 by The Mamas & The Papas. (R)1981 by Bernadette Peters.

DEDICATED TO YOU (1936) (wm)Sammy Cahn—Saul Chaplin—Hy Zaret. (P)Andy Kirk and his Orchestra, vocal by Pha Terrell. (CR)Ella Fitzgerald with The Mills Brothers.

'DEED I DO (1926) (wm)Walter Hirsch—Fred Rose. (P)Ben Bernie and his Orchestra. (CR)Ruth Etting. (R)1948 by Lena Horne.

DEEP BLUE (1971) (wm)George Harrison. (P)George Harrison.

DEEP DOWN INSIDE (1962) (w)Carolyn Leigh (m)Cy Coleman. (I)Musical: Little Me, by Sid Caesar, Virginia Martin, Joey Faye and The Chorus.

DEEP FOREST (1933) (w)Andy Razaf (m)Reginald Foresyth—Earl Hines. (P)Theme song of Earl Hines and his Orchestra.

DEEP IN A DREAM (1938) (w)Eddie De Lange (m)Jimmy Van Heusen. (P)Artie Shaw and his Orchestra. (CR)Guy Lombardo, Russ Morgan, Bob Crosby and their Orchestras.

DEEP IN MY HEART, DEAR (1924) (w)Dorothy Donnelly (m)Sigmund Romberg. (I)Operetta: The Student Prince in Heidelberg, by Howard Marsh and Ilse Marvenga. (R)1954 Film: The Student Prince, by the voice of Mario Lanza dubbing for Edmund Purdom, and Ann Blyth.

DEEP IN THE HEART OF TEXAS (1942) (w)June Hershey (m)Don Swander. (P)Alvino Rey and his Orchestra. No. 1 Chart Record. (CR)Bing Crosby.

DEEP NIGHT (1929) (w)Rudy Vallee (m)Charles Henderson. (P)Rudy Vallee. (CR)Ruth Etting.

DEEP PURPLE (1934) (w)Mitchell Parish. (m)Peter De Rose. (I)Instrumentally. by Paul Whiteman and his Orchestra. (R)1939 by Larry Clinton and his Orchestra, vocal by Bea Wain. (CR)Bing Crosby (CR)Jimmy Dorsey and his Orchestra. (R)1957 by Billy Ward & His Dominoes. (R)1963 by Nino Tempo and April Stevens. No. 1 Chart Record. NARAS Award Winner. (R)1976 by Donny and Marie Osmond.

DEEP RIVER (1917) (wm)Unknown. Traditional Black Spiritual.

DEEP SONG (1947) (w)Douglass Cross (m)George Cory. (P)Billie Holiday.

DEEPER THAN THE NIGHT (1978) (wm)Tom Snow—John Vastano. (P)Olivia Newton—John.

DEJA VU (1979) (w)Adrienne Anderson (m)Isaac Hayes. (P)Dionne Warwick.

DELAWARE (1960) (wm)Irving Gordon. (P)Perry Como.

DELICADO (1952) (w)Jack Lawrence (m)Waldyr Azevado. (P)Percy Faith and his Orchestra. No. 1 Chart Record. (CR)Stan Kenton and his Orchestra. (CR)Dinah Shore.

DELILAH (1941) (w)Jimmy Shirl (m)Henry Manners. (P)Glenn Miller and his Orchestra, vocal by Tex Beneke and The Modernaires.

DELILAH (1968) (wm)Les Reed—Barry Mason. (P)Tom Jones.

DELIRIOUS (1983) (wm)Prince Rogers Nelson. (P)Prince.

DELISHIOUS (1931) (w)Ira Gershwin (m)George Gershwin. (I)Film: Delicious, by Raul Roulien. Recorded by Nat Shilkret and his Orchestra.

DELTA DAWN (1972) (wm)Alex Harvey—Larry Collins. (I)Bette Midler. (I)Tanya Tucker. (P)Helen Reddy. No. 1 Chart Record.

DEN OF INIQUITY (1940) (w)Lorenz Hart (m)Richard Rodgers. (I)Musical: Pal Joey, by Gene Kelly and Vivienne Segal.

DENISE (1963) (wm)Neil Levenson. (P)Randy and The Rainbows. (R)1977 by Blondie in a French version.

DENNIS THE MENACE (1952) (w)Dick Manning (m)Al Hoffman. Based on the comic strip, Dennis The Menace. (P)Jimmy Boyd and Rosemary Clooney.

DEPENDIN' ON YOU (1978) (wm)Michael McDonald—Pat Simmons. (P)The Doobie Brothers.

DER KOMMISSAR (1983) (w)Andrew Piercy (m)Robert Ponger. (P)After The Fire.

DER FUEHRER'S FACE (1942) (wm)Oliver Wallace. (I)Cartoon Film: Donald Duck In Nutzi Land on soundtrack. (P)Spike Jones.

DESAFINADO (Slightly Out Of Tune) (1959) (w-Eng)Jon Hendricks—Jessie Cavanaugh (m)Antonio Carlos Jobim. (P)Stan Getz and Charlie Byrd. Vocal version by Pat Thomas. NARAS Award Winner.

DESERT MOON (1984) (wm)Dennis De Young. (P)Dennis De Young.

DESERT SONG, THE (1926) (w)Otto Harbach—Oscar Hammerstein II (m)Sigmund Romberg. (I)Operetta: *The Desert Song*, by Vivienne Segal and Robert Halliday. First film version (1929)byJohn Boles and Carlotta King. Second film version (1943)by Dennis Morgan. Third film version (1953)by Gordon MacRae. Recorded by Nat Shilkret and his Orchestra.

DESIDERATA (1971) (w)Max Ehrman (m)Fred Werner, Jr. (P)Les Crane.

DESIRE (1980) (wm)Barry, Maurice, and Robin Gibb. (P)Andy Gibb.

DESIREE (1977) (wm)Neil Diamond. (P)Neil Diamond.

DESOLATION ROW (1965) (wm)Bob Dylan. (P)Bob Dylan.

DESPERADO (1973) (wm)Don Henley—Glenn Frey. (P)The Eagles. (R)1977 by Johnny Rodriguez. (R)1983 by Linda Ronstadt.

DESTINATION MOON (1951) (w)Roy Alfred (m)Marvin Fisher. (P)Nat "King" Cole.

DETOUR (1945) (wm)Paul Westmoreland. (I)Jimmy Walker. (P)Elton Britt. (R)1951 by Patti Page.

DETROIT CITY (1963) (wm)Mel Tillis—Danny Dill. (P)Bobby Bare. NARAS Award Winner. (R)1967 by Tom Jones.

DETROIT ROCK CITY (1976) (wm)Paul Stanley—Bob Ezrin. (P)Kiss.

DEVIL INSIDE (1987) (wm)A. Farriss—M. Hutchence. (P)INXS.

DEVIL MAY CARE (w)Johnny Burke (m)Harry Warren. (P)Bing Crosby.

DEVIL OR ANGEL (1955) (wm)Blanche Carter. (P)The Clovers. (R)1960 by Bobby Vee.

DEVIL WENT DOWN TO GEORGIA, THE (1979) (wm)Tommy Crain—Charlie Daniels—Taz DiGregorio—Fred Edwards—Charles Hayward—Jim Marshall. (P)The Charlie Daniels Band.

DEVIL WITH A BLUE DRESS ON (1966) (wm)Frederick Long—William Stevenson. (P)Mitch Ryder and the Detroit Wheels in a medley with *Good Golly Miss Molly*.

DEVIL WOMAN (1976) (wm)Marty Robbins. (P)Marty Robbins.

DEVIL WOMAN (1976) (wm)Terry Britten—Christine Authors. (P)Cliff Richard.

DEVOTED TO YOU (1958) (wm)Boudleaux Bryant. (P)The Everly Brothers.

DIAMOND GIRL (1973) (wm)James Seals—Darrell Crofts. (P)Seals and Croft.

DIAMOND HEAD (1963) (w)Mack David (m)Hugo Winterhalter. Adapted from a theme from the Film: Diamond Head.

DIAMONDS (1987) (wm)J. Jam—T. Lewis. (P)Herb Alpert.

DIAMONDS AND RUST (1975) (wm)Joan Baez. (P)Joan Baez.

DIAMONDS ARE A GIRL'S BEST FRIEND (1949) (w)Leo Robin (m)Jule Styne. (I)Musical: *Gentlemen Prefer Blondes*, by Carol Channing. (R)Film version 1953, by Marilyn Monroe.

DIAMONDS ARE FOREVER (wm)John Barry-Don Black. (I)Film: *Diamonds Are Forever*, by Shirley Bassey on soundtrack. (P)Shirley Bassey.

DIANA (1957) (wm)Paul Anka. (P)Paul Anka. No. 1 Chart Record. (R)1965 by Bobby Rydell.

(I'm In Heaven When I See You Smile)DIANE (1927) (wm)Lew Pollack—Erno Rapee. (I)Film: *Seventh Heaven* by unknown female vocalist on soundtrack. (R)1955 by Mantovani and his Orchestra. (R)1964 by The Bachelors.

DIARY, THE (1959) (w)Howard Greenfield (m)Neil Sedaka.

DIARY (1972) (wm)David Gates. (P)Bread.

DIAVALO (1935) (w)Lorenz Hart (m)Richard Rodgers. (I)Musical: *Billy Rose's Jumbo*, by Bob Lawrence and Henderson's Singing Razorbacks.

DICKEY-BIRD SONG, THE (1947) (w)Howard Dietz (m)Sammy Fain. (I)Film: *Three Daring Daughters*, by Jeanette MacDonald, Ann Todd, Eleanor Donahue and Jane Powell. (P)Freddy Martin and his Orchestra.

DICTY BLUES, THE (1923) (m)Fletcher Henderson. (P)Fletcher Henderson and his Orchestra. (CR)Larry Clinton and his Orchestra.

DICTY GLIDE, THE (1929) (m)Duke Ellington. (P)Duke Ellington and his Cotton Club Orchestra.

DID ANYONE EVER TELL YOU MRS. MURPHY (1949) (wm)Leah Worth—Lloyd Sloan—Karl Suessdorf. (P)Perry Como.

DID I REMEMBER? (1936) (w)Harold Adamson (m)Walter Donaldson. (I)Film: *Suzy*, by the voice of Virginia Verrill, dubbing for Jean Harlow and Cary Grant. (P)Tommy Dorsey and his Orchestra. (CR)Shep Fields and his Orchestra.

DID IT IN A MINUTE (1982) (wm)Daryl Hall—Sara Allen—Janna Allen. (P)Hall and Oates.

DID YOU EVER GET STUNG?1938) (w)Lorenz Hart (m)Richard Rodgers. (I)Musical: *I Married An Angel*, by Dennis Day, Vivienne Segal, and Charles Walters.

DID YOU EVER GET THAT FEELING IN THE MOONLIGHT (1944) (wm)James Cavanaugh—Larry Stock—Ira Schuster. (P)Perry Como. (CR)Gene Krupa and his Orchestra, vocal by Buddy Stewart and Anita O'Day.

DID YOU EVER HAVE TO MAKE UP YOUR MIND? (1966) (wm)John B. Sebastian. (P)The Lovin' Spoonful.

DID YOU EVER SEE A DREAM WALKING? (1933) (w)Mack Gordon (m)Harry Revel. (I)Film: *Sitting Pretty*, by Ginger Rogers and Art Jarrett. (P)Eddy Duchin and his Orchestra. No. 1 Chart Record. (CR)Bing Crosby.

DID YOU SEE JACKIE ROBINSON HIT THAT BALL (wm)Buddy Johnson. (P)Buddy Johnson and his Orchestra.

DID YOUR MOTHER COME FROM IRELAND? (1936) (wm)Jimmy Kennedy—Michael Carr. (P)Bing Crosby.

DIDJA EVER? (w)Mann Curtis (m)Vic Mizzy. (I)Film: Easy To Love, by Tony Martin.

DIDN'T I (Blow Your Mind This Time) (1970) (w)Thom Bell—William Hart (m)Thom Bell. (P)The Delfonics.

DIDN'T WE? (1969) (wm)Jim Webb. (P)Richard Harris. (R)1972 by Barbra Streisand.

DIDN'T WE ALMOST HAVE IT ALL (1987) (wm)Michael Masser—W. Jennings. (P)Whitney Houston. No. 1 Chart Record.

(I Just)DIED IN YOUR ARMS (1987) (wm)N. Eede. (P)Cutting Crew. No. 1 Chart Record.

DIFFERENT CORNER, A (1986) (wm)George Michael. (P)George Michael.

DIFFERENT WORLDS (1979) (w)Norman Gimbel

(m)Charles Fox. (I)TV Show: *Angie*, by voice of Maureen McGovern. (P)Maureen McGovern.

DIG YOU LATER (A Hubba-Hubba-Hubba) (1945) (w)Harold Adamson (m)Jimmy McHugh. (I)Film: *Doll Face*, by Perry Como. (P)Perry Como.

DIGA DIGA DOO (1928) (w)Dorothy Fields (m)Jimmy McHugh. (I)Revue: *Lew Leslie's Blackbirds of 1928*, by Adelaide Hall. (P)Duke Ellington and his Orchestra. (R)1943 Film: Stormy Weather, by Lena Horne.

DIGGING YOUR SCENE (1986) (wm)Robert Howard. (P)The Blow Monkeys.

DIM ALL THE LIGHTS (1979) (wm)Donna Summer. (P)Donna Summer.

DIM, DIM THE LIGHTS (1954) (wm)Beverly Ross—Julius Dixon. (P)Bill Haley and The Comets.

DIME A DOZEN (1949) (wm)Cindy Walker. (P)Margaret Whiting. (CR)Sammy Kaye.

DIMINUENDO IN BLUE (1937) (m)Duke Ellington. (P)Duke Ellington and his Orchestra.

DINAH (1925) (w)Sam M. Lewis—Joe Young (m)Harry Akst. (I)Revue: *Plantation Revue*, by Ethel Waters. (P)Ethel Waters. (CR)Cliff Edwards. (CR)Fletcher Henderson and his Orchestra. (R)1932 by Bing Crosby. No. 1 Chart Record. (R)1932 by The Mills Brothers. (R)1935 by The Boswell Sisters. (R)1936 by Fats Waller. Theme song of Dinah Shore.

DING-A-LING (1960) (wm)Kal Mann—Bernie Lowe—Dave Appell. (P)Bobby Rydell.

DING-DONG! THE WITCH IS DEAD (1939) (w)E. Y. Harburg (m)Harold Arlen. (I)Film: *The Wizard Of Oz*, by Judy Garland, Billie Burke, and The Singer Midgets. (R)1967 by The Fifth Estate.

DINNER AT EIGHT (1933) (w)Dorothy Fields (m)Jimmy McHugh. Promo song for Film: *Dinner At Eight*. (P)Frances Langford. (CR)Ben Selvin and his Orchestra.

DINNER FOR ONE PLEASE, JAMES (1935) (wm)Michael Carr. (I)London, by Leslie "Hutch" Hutchinson. (P)United States, by Hal Kemp and his Orchestra. (CR)Ray Noble and his Orchestra.

DINNER MUSIC FOR A PACK OF HUNGRY CANNIBALS (1938) (m)Raymond Scott. (P)The Raymond Scott Quintet.

DIPPER MOUTH BLUES (see Sugar Foot Stomp)

DIPSY DOODLE, THE (1937) (wm)Larry Clinton. (P)Theme song of Larry Clinton and his Orchestra. (CR)Tommy Dorsey and his Orchestra, vocal by Edythe Wright. (R)1953 by Johnny Maddox.

DIRTY HANDS, DIRTY FACE (1923) (w)Edgar Leslie—Grant Clarke—Al Jolson. (m)James V. Monaco. (I)Film: The Jazz Singer, by Al Jolson. (P)Al Jolson.

DIRTY LAUNDRY (1982) (wm)Don Henley—Danny Kortchmar. (P)Don Henley.

DIRTY WATER (1966) (wm)Ed Cobb. (P)The Standells. (R)1980 by The Inmates.

DIRTY WHITE BOY (1979) (wm)Lou Grammatico—Michael Jones. (P)Foreigner.

DIS-DONC, DIS-DONC (1958) (w-Eng)Julian More—David Heneker—Monty Norman (m)Marguerite Monnot. (I)Musical: *Irma La Douce*, by Colette Renard in the Paris version and by Elizabeth Seal in the London and New York productions.

DISCO DUCK (Part 1) (wm)Rick Dees. (P)Rick Dees and his Cast Of Idiots. No. 1 Chart Record.

DISCO INFERNO (1978) (wm)Leroy Green—Ron Kersey.

(I)Film: Saturday Night Fever, by Trammps on the soundtrack. (P)Trammps.

DISCO LADY (1976) (wm)Don Davis—Harvey Scales—Albert Vance. (P)Johnnie Taylor. No. 1 Chart Record.

DISCO LUCY (I Love Lucy Theme) (1977) (wm)Harold Adamson—Eliot Daniel. (P)Wilton Place Street Band.

DISCO NIGHTS (1979) (wm)Keith Crier—Paul Service—Herbert Lane—Emanuel Le Blanc. (P)G. Q.

DISCO QUEEN (1975) (wm)Errol Brown—Anthony Wilson. (P)Hot Chocolate.

DISORDERLY ORDERLY, THE (1964) (w)Earl Shuman (m)Leon Carr. (I)Film: *The Disorderly Orderly*, by Sammy Davis, Jr.

DISSERTATION ON THE STATE OF BLISS (Love And Learn) (1954) (w)Ira Gershwin (m)Harold Arlen. (I)Film: *The Country Girl*, by Bing Crosby.

DISTANT MELODY (1954) (w)Betty Comden—Adolph Green (m)Jule Styne. (I)Musical: *Peter Pan*, by Mary Martin.

DISTANT SHORES (1966) (wm)James Guercio. (P)Chad and Jeremy.

DITES-MOI (1949) (w)Oscar Hammerstein II (m)Richard Rodgers. (I)Musical: *South Pacific*, by Michael de Leon and Barbara Luna. (R)1958 in film version by Mitzi Gaynor.

DIXIE (1860) (wm)Daniel Decatur Emmett. Famous Civil War Song associated with The Confederacy.

DIXIELAND BAND (1935) (w)Johnny Mercer (m)Bernie Hanighen. (P)Benny Goodman and his Orchestra. (R)1957 by Teresa Brewer.

DIZZY (1969) (wm)Tommy Roe—Freddy Weller. (P)Tommy Roe. No. 1 Chart Record.

DIZZY FINGERS (1923) (m)Zez Confrey. (P)Zez Confrey as a piano solo. (R)1956 Film: *The Eddy Duchin Story*, as played by Carmen Cavallaro.

DO I DO (1982) (wm)Stevie Wonder. (P)Stevie Wonder.

DO DO DO (1926) (w)Ira Gershwin (m)George Gershwin. (I)Musical: *Oh, Kay!*, by Gertrude Lawrence and Oscar Shaw. Recorded by George Olsen and his Orchestra. (R)1950 Film: Tea For Two, by Doris Day and Gordon MacRae.

DO I HEAR A WALTZ? (1965) (w)Stephen Sondheim (m)Richard Rodgers. (I)Musical: *Do I Hear A Waltz?*, by Elizabeth Allen.

DO I HEAR YOU SAYING? (1928) (w)Lorenz Hart (m)Richard Rodgers. (I)Musical: *Present Arms*, by Charles King and Flora LeBreton.

DO I LOVE YOU BECAUSE YOU'RE BEAUTIFUL (1957) (w)Oscar Hammertstein II (m)Richard Rodgers. (I)TV Production: *Cinderella*, by Julie Andrews and Jon Cypher.

DO I LOVE YOU? (1939) (wm)Cole Porter. (I)Musical: *Du Barry Was A Lady*, by Ethel Merman and Ronald Graham. Recorded by Leo Reisman and his Orchestra. (R)1943 Film: Du Barry Was A Lady, by Gene Kelly. (R)1946 Film: Night And Day, by Ginny Simms.

DO I WORRY? (1941) (wm)Stanley Cowan—Bobby Worth. (P)The Ink Spots. (CR)Tommy Dorsey and his Orchestra. (CR)Bea Wain.

DO IT ('Til You're Satisfied) (1974) (wm)Billy Nichols. (P)B. T. Express.

DO IT AGAIN (1912) (wm)Irving Berlin. Not one of Berlin's hit songs. No artist credited with introduction.

DO IT AGAIN (1922) (w)B. G. De Sylva (m)George

Gershwin. (I)Musical: *The French Doll*, by Irene Bordoni. Recorded by Paul Whiteman and his Orchestra.

DO IT AGAIN (1970) (wm)Walter Becker—Donald Fagen. (P)Steely Dan.

DO IT AGAIN-A LITTLE BIT SLOWER (1967) (wm)Wayne Thompson. (P)Jon and Robin and The In Crowd.

DO IT ANY WAY YOU WANNA (1975) (wm)Leon Huff. (P)People's Choice.

DO IT BABY (1974) (wm)Christine Yarian—Freddy Perren. (P)The Miracles.

DO IT OR DIE (1979) (wm)Buddy Buie—J. R. Cobb—Ronnie Hammond. (P)Atlanta Rhythm Section.

DO IT THE HARD WAY (1940) (w)Lorenz Hart (m)Richard Rodgers. (I)Musical: *Pal Joey*, by June Havoc, Claire Anderson, and Jack Durant.

DO IT TO IT (1972) (wm)Quincy Jones. (I)Film: Dollars, by the voice of Little Richard.

DO NOTHIN' TILL YOU HEAR FROM ME (1943) (w)Bob Russell (m)Duke Ellington. Adapted from *Concerto For Cootie*. (I)Duke Ellington and his Orchestra. (P)Woody Herman and his Orchestra. (CR)Stan Kenton and his Orchestra.

DO-RE-MI (1959) (w)Oscar Hammerstein II (m)Richard Rodgers. (I)Musical: *The Sound Of Music*, by Mary Martin and The Children.

DO RIGHT (1980) (wm)Paul Davis (P)Paul Davis.

DO THAT TO ME ONE MORE TIME (1979) (wm)Toni Tennille. (P)The Captain & Tennille. No. 1 Chart Record.

DO THE BIRD (1963) (w)Kal Mann (m)Dave Appell. (P)Dee Dee Sharp.

DO THE CLAM (1965) (wm)Ben Weisman—Sid Wayne—Dolores Fuller. (I)Film: *Girl Happy*, by Elvis Presley, Gary Crosby, Joby Baker, Jimmy Hawkins and The Chorus. (P)Elvis Presley.

DO THE FREDDIE (1965) (wm)Lou Courtney—Dennis Lambert. (P)Freddie and The Dreamers.

DO THE NEW YORK (1931) (wm)J. P. Murray—Barry Trivers—Ben Oakland. (I)Revue: *Ziegfeld Follies of 1931*, by Harry Richman. Recorded by Glen Gray and The Casa Loma Orchestra.

DO THEY KNOW IT'S CHRISTMAS (1984) (wm)Bob Geldof—Midge Ure. (P)Band—Aid. Group comprises British All Star Rock Musicians. Proceeds donated to aid Ethiopian children.

DO-WACKA-DO (1964) (wm)Roger Miller (P)Roger Miller.

DO WAH DIDDY DIDDY (1964) (wm)Jeff Barry—Ellie Greenwich. (P)Manfred Mann. No. 1 Chart Record. (R)1964 by The Exciters.

DO WHAT YOU DO! (1929) (w)Gus Kahn—Ira Gershwin (m)George Gershwin. (I)Musical: *Show Girl*, by Ruby Keeler and Frank McHugh.

DO WHAT YOU DO (1984) (wm)Ralph Dino—Larry Di-Tomaso. (P)Jermaine Jackson.

DO WHAT YOU WANNA DO (1940) (w)John Latouche (m)Vernon Duke. (I)Musical: *Cabin In The Sky*, by Rex Ingram.

DO YA (1977) (wm)Jeff Lynne. (P)Electric Light Orchestra.

DO YA WANNA GET FUNKY WITH ME (1977) (wm)Peter Brown—Robert Rans. (P)Peter Brown.

DO YOU BELIEVE IN LOVE (1982) (wm)Robert John Lange. (P)Huey Lewis and The News.

DO YOU BELIEVE IN MAGIC (1965) (wm)John Sebastian. (P)The Lovin' Spoonful. (R)1978 by Shaun Cassidy.

DO YOU EVER THINK OF ME (1920) (w)Harry D. Kerr—John Cooper (m)Earl Burtnett. (P)Paul Whiteman and his Orchestra.

DO YOU FEEL LIKE WE DO (1976) (wm)Peter Frampton—Michael Gallagher—John Sidmos—Rick Wills. (P)Peter Frampton.

DO YOU KNOW THE WAY TO SAN JOSE? (1968) (w)Hal David (m)Burt Bacharach. (P)Dionne Warwick.

DO YOU KNOW WHAT I MEAN (1971) (wm)Lee Michaels. (P)Lee Michaels.

DO YOU KNOW WHAT IT MEANS TO MISS NEW ORLEANS (1946) (w)Eddie De Lange (m)Louis Alter. (I)Film: *New Orleans*, by Billie Holiday with Louis Armstrong and his Orchestra. Theme song of Pete Fountain.

PETE FOUNTAIN

When Lawrence Welk's contract came up for renewal, he decided to leave us and sign with Randy Wood's DOT label. Most of the band members and singers went with him, but Pete Fountain stayed with us. Pete is a wonderful guy who likes a drink now and then and Welk, of course, was a teetotaler. He did not approve of Pete and they never really did get along.

Pete recorded a couple of jazz albums with us in New Orleans. It was my pleasure to go down there with Bud Dant and record the albums in Pete's club. It was small (we had to use the men's room as the control room), but we had a good engineer with great equipment and the results were damn good. Both albums were big successes.

Pete stayed with the label for many years, but then he got into a contract dispute with our management. He left on very bad terms and a law suit in the bargain. Too bad. A good guy and a helluva player.

DO YOU KNOW WHERE YOU'RE GOING TO (1976) (w)Gerry Goffin (m)Michael Masser. (I)Film: *Mahogany*, by Diana Ross. (P)Diana Ross. No. 1 Chart Record.

DO YOU KNOW WHY (1940) (w)Johnny Burke (m)Jimmy Van Heusen. (I)Film: *Love Thy Neighbor*, by Mary Martin and The Merry Macs.

DO YOU LOVE ME (1946) (wm)Harry Ruby. (I)Film: *Do You Love Me*, by Dick Haymes with Harry James and his Orchestra.

DO YOU LOVE ME? (1962) (wm)Berry Gordy, Jr. (P)The Contours. (R)1964 by The Dave Clark Five.

DO YOU LOVE ME? (1964) (w)Sheldon Harnick (m)Jerry Bock. (I)Musical: *Fiddler On The Roof*, by Zero Mostel and Maria Karnilova.

DO YOU LOVE WHAT YOU FEEL (wm)David Wolinski. (P)Rufus with Chaka Khan.

DO YOU MIND? (1960) (wm)Lionel Bart. (I)Film: *Let's Get Married* on soundtrack. (I)Anthony Newley. (P)Andy Williams.

DO YOU REALLY WANT TO HURT ME (1983) (wm)Roy

Hay—John Moss—Michael Craig—George O'Dowd. (P)Culture Club.

DO (Da)YOU THINK I'M SEXY (1979) (wm)Carmine Appice, Jr. —Rod Stewart. (P)Rod Stewart. No. 1 Chart Record.

DO YOU WANNA JUMP, CHILDREN? (1938) (wm)Al Donahue—Jimmy Van Heusen—Willie Bryant—Victor Selsman. (P)Count Basie and his Orchestra, vocal by Jimmy Rushing.

DO YOU WANNA MAKE LOVE (1977) (wm)Peter McCann. (P)Peter McCann.

DO YOU WANNA TOUCH ME (1973) (wm)Gary Glitter—Mike Leander. (P)Joan Jett & The Blackhearts.

DO YOU WANT TO DANCE? (1958) (wm)Bobby Freeman. (P)Bobby Freeman. (R)1964 by Del Shannon. (R)1965 by The Beach Boys. (R)1973 by Bette Midler.

DO YOU WANT TO KNOW A SECRET? (1964) (wm)John Lennon—Paul McCartney. (P)The Beatles.

DO YOUR THING (1969) (wm)Charles Wright. (P)The Watts 103rd Street Rhythm Band.

DOATSY MAE (1978) (wm)Carol Hall. (I)Musical: *Best Little Whorehouse In Texas*, by Susan Mansur.

DOCTOR! DOCTOR! (1984) (wm)Thomas Bailet—Alanah Currie—Joe Leeway. (P)The Thompson Twins.

DOCTOR JAZZ (1927) (w)Walter Melrose (m)Joe "King" Oliver. (P)Jelly Roll Morton's Red Hot Peppers.

DR. KILDARE (Theme From) (*Three Stars Will Shine Tonight*) (1961) (w)Hal Winn (m)Jerry Goldsmith—Pete Rugolo. (I)TV series: *Dr. Kildare* on soundtrack. (P)Richard Chamberlain

DOCTOR, LAWYER, INDIAN CHIEF (1945) (w)Paul Francis Webster (m)Hoagy Carmichael. (I)Film: *Stork Club*, by Betty Hutton. (P)Betty Hutton. No. 1 Chart Record. (CR)Hoagy Carmichael.

DOCTOR MY EYES (1972) (wm)Jackson Browne. (P)Jackson Browne.

DOCTOR ROBERT (1966) (wm)John Lennon—Paul McCartney. (P)The Beatles.

DOCTOR'S ORDERS (1975) (wm)Roger Cook—Roger Greenaway—Geoff Stephens. (P)Carol Douglas.

DODGING A DIVORCEE (1935) (wm)Reginald Foresythe. (P)Reginald Foresythe and his Orchestra.

DOES ANYBODY REALLY KNOW WHAT TIME IT IS? (1969) (wm)Robert Lamm. (P)Chicago.

DOES GOODNIGHT MEAN GOODBYE (1963) (wm)Howard Greenfield—Gerry Goffin—Jack Keller. (I)Film: *The Victors*, on soundtrack. (P)Jane Morgan.

DOES YOUR CHEWING GUM LOSE IT'S FLAVOR ON THE BEDPOST OVER NIGHT? (1961) (wm)Billy Rose—Marty Bloom. (m)Ernest Breuer. (I)Harry Richman. (R)1961 by Lonnie Donegan.

DOES YOUR HEART BEAT FOR ME? (1936) (w)Mitchell Parish (m)Arnold Johnson—Russ Morgan. (P)Theme song of Russ Morgan and his Orchestra. (CR)Carl Lorch.

DOES YOUR MAMA KNOW ABOUT ME (1968) (wm)Tom Baird—Tommy Chong. (P)Bobby Taylor and The Vancouvers.

DOES YOUR MOTHER KNOW (1979) (wm)Benny Andersson—Bjoern Ulvaeus. (P)Abba.

DOESN'T SOMEBODY WANT TO BE WANTED (1971) (wm)Mike Appel—Jimmy Cretcos—Wes Farrell. (P)The Partridge Family.

DOG TOWN BLUES (1938) (wm)Bob Haggart. (P)Bob Crosby's Bobcats.

(How Much Is That)DOGGIE IN THE WINDOW (1953) (wm)Bob Merrill. (P)Patti Page. No. 1 Chart Record.

DOGGIN' AROUND (1960) (wm)Lena Agree. (P)Jackie Wilson. (R)1983 by Klique.

DOGGONE RIGHT (1969) (wm)William Robinson, Jr. —Al Cleveland—Marv Tarplin. (P)Smokey Robinson and The Miracles.

DOIN' THE NEW LOW-DOWN (1928) (w)Dorothy Fields (m)Jimmy McHugh. (I)Revue: *Lew Leslie's Blackbirds of 1928*, by Bill Robinson. (P)Duke Ellington and his Orchestra.

DOIN' THE RACCOON (1928) (w)Raymond Klages (m)J. Fred Coots. (P)George Olsen and his Orchestra.

DOIN' THE SUZI-Q (1936) (wm)Benny Davis—J. Fred Coots. (I)Revue: *Cotton Club Parade*.

DOIN' THE UPTOWN LOWDOWN (1933) (w)Mack Gordon (m)Harry Revel. (I)Film: *Broadway Thru A Keyhole*, by Frances Williams.

DOIN' THE VOOM VOOM (1929) (m)Bubber Miley—Duke Ellington. (P)The Jungle Band (Duke Ellington and his Orchestra).

DOIN' WHAT COMES NATUR'LLY (1946) (wm)Irving Berlin. (I)Musical: *Annie Get Your Gun*, by Ethel Merman. In film version (1950)by Betty Hutton. (P)Dinah Shore. (CR)Freddy Martin and his Orchestra.

DOING IT ALL FOR MY BABY (1987) (wm)P. Cody—M. Duke. (P)Huey Lewis & The News.

DOING THE REACTIONARY (1937) (wm)Harold Rome . (I)Revue: *Pins And Needles*, by Al Levy and Nettie Harary.

DOLCE FAR NIENTE (1960) (wm)Meredith Willson. (I)Musical: *The Unsinkable Molly Brown*, by Mitchell Gregg.

DOLL DANCE, THE (1927) (wm)Nacio Herb Brown. (I)Revue: *Hollywood Music Box Revue*, by Doris Eaton. (P)Vincent Lopez and his Orchestra. (CR)Earl Burtnett and his Orchestra.

DOLLY DAGGER (1971) (wm)Jimi Hendrix. (P)Jimi Hendrix.

DOLORES (1941) (w)Frank Loesser (m)Louis Alter. (I)Film: *Las Vegas Nights*, by Bert Wheeler. (P)Tommy Dorsey and his Orchestra.

DOMANI (Tomorrow) (1955) (w)Tony Velona (m)Ulpio Minucci. (P)Julius La Rosa.

DOMINIQUE (1963) (w-Eng)Noel Regney (m)Soeur Sourire. (P)The Singing Nun. No. 1 Chart Record. NARAS Award Winner.

DOMINO (1951) (w-Eng)Don Raye (m)Louis Ferrari. (P)Tony Martin. (CR)Bing Crosby. (CR)Doris Day.

DOMINOES (1987) (wm)Robbie Nevil—Eastman—Hart. (P)Robbie Nevil.

DON'CHA GO 'WAY MAD (1950) (w)All Stillman (m)Jimmy Mundy—Illinois Jacquet. (P)Ella Fitzgerald.

DONCHA' THINK IT'S TIME (1958) (wm)Clyde Otis—Willie Dixon. (P)Elvis Presley.

DONDI (1960) (w)Earl Shuman (m)Mort Garson. (I)Film: *Dondi*, by Patti Page. (P)Patti Page.

DONKEY SERENADE,THE (1923) (w)Robert Wright—Chet Forrest. (m)Rudolf Friml—Herbert Stothart. (I)Film: *The Firefly*, by Allan Jones. (P)Allan Jones.

DONNA (1958) (wm)Ritchie Valens. (P)Ritchie Valens.

DONNA LEE (1947) (m)Charlie Parker (P)Charlie Parker with Bud Powell, Miles Davis,Tommy Potter, and Max Roach.

DONNA THE PRIMA DONNA (1963) (wm)Dion Di Mucci—Ernie Maresca. (P)Dion.

DON'T (wm)Jerry Lieber-Mike Stoller. (P)Elvis Presley. No. 1 Chart Record.

DON'T ASK ME WHY (1958) (w)Fred Wise (m)Ben Weisman. (I)Film: *King Creole*, by Elvis Presley. (P)Elvis Presley.

DON'T ASK ME WHY (1980) (wm)Billy Joel. (P)Billy Joel.

DON'T ASK TO STAY UNTIL TOMORROW (1977) (w)Carol Connors (m)Artie Kane. (I)Film: *Looking For Mr. Goodbar*, by Marlena Shaw.

DON'T BE A BABY, BABY (1945) (w)Buddy Kaye (m)Howard Steiner. (P)The Mills Brothers. (CR)Benny Goodman and his Orchestra.

DON'T BE A WOMAN IF YOU CAN (1946) (w)Ira Gershwin (m)Arthur Schwartz. (I)Musical: *Park Avenue*, by Mary Wickes, Marthe Errolle, and Ruth Matteson.

DON'T BE AFRAID, LITTLE DARLIN' (1963) (wm)Cynthia Weil—Barry Mann. (P)Steve Lawrence.

DON'T BE AFRAID OF ROMANCE (1962) (wm)Irving Berlin. (I)Musical: *Mr. President*, by Jack Washburn.

DON'T BE ANGRY (1955) (wm)Napoleon Brown—Fred Madison—Rose Marie McCoy. (I)Nappy Brown. (P)The Crew Cuts.

DON'T BE CRUEL (To A Heart That's True) (1956) (wm)Otis Blackwell—Elvis Presley. (P)Elvis Presley. No. 1 Chart Record. (R)1960 by The Bill Black Combo.

DON'T BE SO MEAN TO BABY ('Cause Baby's So Good To You) (1947) (wm)Peggy Lee—Dave Barbour. (P)Peggy Lee.

DON'T BE THAT WAY (1938) (w)Mitchell Parish (m)Edgar Sampson—Benny Goodman. (I)Chick Webb and his Orchestra. (P)Benny Goodman and his Orchestra. No. 1 Chart Record.

DON'T BELIEVE EVERYTHING YOU DREAM (1943) (w)Harold Adamson (m)Jimmy McHugh. (I)Film: *Around The World*, on soundtrack. (P)The Ink Spots.

DON'T BET MONEY, HONEY (1961) (wm)Linda Scott. (P)Linda Scott.

DON'T BLAME ME (1933) (w)Dorothy Fields (m)Jimmy McHugh. (I)Revue: *Clowns In Clover*, by Jeanette Leff. Recorded by Ethel Waters, Guy Lombardo and his Royal Canadians. (R)1948 by Nat "King" Cole.

DON'T BLAME THE CHILDREN (1967) (w)Ivan Reeve (m)H. B. Barnum. (P)Sammy Davis, Jr.

DON'T BOTHER ME (1963) (wm)George Harrison. (P)The Beatles.

DON'T BREAK THE HEART THAT LOVES YOU (1962) (wm)Benny Davis—Ted Murry. (P)Connie Francis. No. 1 Chart Record. (R)1977 by Margo Smith.

DON'T BRING LULU (1925) (w)Billy Rose—Lew Brown (m)Ray Henderson. (P)Van and Schenck. (CR)Billy Jones and Ernie Hare.

DON'T BRING ME DOWN (1966) (wm)Gerry Goffin—Carole King. (P)The Animals.

DON'T BRING ME DOWN (1979) (wm)Jeff Lynne. (P)Electric Light Orchestra.

DON'T CALL IT LOVE (1947) (w)Ned Washington (m)Allie Wrubel. (I)Film: *I Walk Alone* on soundtrack. (P)Freddy Martin and his Orchestra.

DON'T CALL MY NAME (1953) (wm)Bennie Benjamin—George Weiss (P)Helene Dixon.

DON'T CALL US, WE'LL CALL YOU (1975) (wm)John Canter—Jerry Corbetta. (P)Sugarloaf.

DON'T COME AROUND HERE NO MORE (1985) (wm)Tom Petty—Dave Stewart. (P)Tom Petty & The Heartbreakers.

DON'T COME KNOCKIN' (1960) (wm)Antoine Domino. (P)Fats Domino.

DON'T CRY (1956) (wm)Frank Loesser. (I)Musical: *The Most Happy Fella*, by Art Lund and Jo Sullivan.

DON'T CRY (1983) (wm)John Wetten—Geoffrey Downes. (P)Asia.

DON'T CRY BABY (1929) (wm)Stella Unger—Saul Bernie—Jimmy Johnson. Not a hit when first published. (R)1961 by Etta James. (R)1962 by Aretha Franklin.

DON'T CRY DADDY (1969) (wm)Scott Davis (P)Elvis Presley in medley with Rubberneckin'.

DON'T CRY FOR ME ARGENTINA (1976) (w)Tim Rice (m)Andrew Lloyd Webber. (I)Musical: *Evita*, by Julie Covington in London production. By Patti Lupone in New York production.

DON'T CRY JOE (Let Her Go, Let Her Go, Let Her Go) (1949) (wm)Joe Marsala. (P)Gordon Jenkins and his Chorus and Orchestra. (CR)Frank Sinatra. (CR)Johnny Desmond.

DON'T CRY OUT LOUD (1979) (w)Carole Bayer Sager (m)Peter Allen. (P)Melissa Manchester.

DON'T DISTURB THIS GROOVE (1987) (wm)M. Murphy—D. Frank. (P)The System.

DON'T DO ME LIKE THAT (1979) (wm)Tom Petty. (P)Tom Petty and The Heartbreakers.

DON'T DREAM IT'S OVER (1987) (wm)N. Finn. (P)Crowded House.

DON'T EVER BE AFRAID TO GO HOME (1952) (w)Bob Hilliard (m)Carl Sigman. (P)Bing Crosby.

DON'T EVER BE LONELY (A Poor Little Fool Like Me) (1972) (wm)Eddie Cornelius. (P)The Cornelius Brothers and Sister Rose.

DON'T EVER LEAVE ME (1929) (w)Oscar Hammerstein II (m)Jerome Kern. (I)Musical: *Sweet Adeline*, by Helen Morgan and Robert Chisholm. (R)1934 in film version by Irene Dunne.

DON'T EXPECT ME TO BE YOUR FRIEND (1973) (wm)Kent La Voie. (P)Lobo.

DON'T EXPLAIN (1946) (w)Arthur Herzog, Jr. (m)Billie Holiday. (P)Billie Holiday.

DON'T FALL IN LOVE WITH A DREAMER (1980) (wm)Kim Carnes—Dave Ellington. (P)Kenny Rogers and Kim Carnes.

DON'T FALL IN LOVE WITH ME (1948) (wm)Ivory Joe Hunter. (P)Ivory Joe Hunter.

DON'T FENCE ME IN (1944) (wm)Cole Porter. (I)Film: *Hollywood Canteen*, by Roy Rogers and The Sons Of The Pioneers and reprised by The Andrews Sisters. (P)Bing Crosby and The Andrews Sisters. No. 1 Chart Record. (CR)Kate Smith.

DON'T FIGHT IT (1982) (wm)Kenny Loggins—Steve Perry. (P)Kenny Loggins with Steve Perry.

DON'T FORBID ME (1957) (wm)Charles Singleton. (P)Pat Boone. No. 1 Chart Record.

DON'T FORGET I STILL LOVE YOU (1964) (wm)Guy Louis. (P)Bobbi Martin.

DON'T FORGET 127th STREET (1964) (w)Lee Adams (m)Charles Strouse. (I)Musical: *Golden Boy*, by Sammy Davis, Jr. ,Johnny Brown, and The Company.

DON'T FORGET TO MESS AROUND WHEN YOU'RE DOING THE CHARLESTON (1926) (wm)Louis Armstrong—Paul Barbarin. (P)Louis Armstrong and his Hot Five.

DON'T FORGET TONIGHT, TOMORROW (1945) (wm)Jay Milton—Ukie Sherin. (P)Frank Sinatra.

DON'T GET AROUND MUCH ANYMORE (1942) (w)Bob Russell (m)Duke Ellington. (P)Duke Ellington and his Orchestra. (CR)The Ink Spots. (CR)Glen Gray and The Casa Loma Orchestra.

DON'T GET ME WRONG (1987) (wm)C. Hynde. (P)The Pretenders.

DON'T GIVE IN TO HIM (1969) (wm)Gary Usher. (P)Gary Puckett and The Union Gap.

DON'T GIVE UP ON US (1977) (wm)Tony Macaulay. (P)David Soul. No. 1 Chart Record.

DON'T GIVE UP THE SHIP (1935) (w)Al Dubin (m)Harry Warren. (I)Film: Shipmates Forever, by Dick Powell. Recorded by Tommy Dorsey and his Orchestra.

DON'T GO BREAKING MY HEART (1976) (wm)Elton John—Bernie Taupin. (P)Elton John with Kiki Dee. No. 1 Chart Record.

DON'T GO NEAR THE INDIANS (1962) (wm)Lorene Mann. (P)Rex Allen.

DON'T GO OUT INTO THE RAIN (1966) (wm)Kenny Young. (P)Herman's Hermits.

DON'T GO TO STRANGERS (1954) (w)Redd Evans (m)Arthur Kent—Dave Mann. (P)Vaughn Monroe and his Orchestra.

DON'T HANG UP (1963) (w)Kal Mann (m)Dave Appell. (P)The Orlons.

DON'T HOLD BACK (1979) (wm)James Jamerson, Jr. —David Williams. (P)Chanson.

DON'T HOLD EVERYTHING (1928) (wm)B. G. De Sylva—Lew Brown (m)Ray Henderson. (I)Musical: Hold Everything, by Alice Boulden, Buddy Harak, and Anna and Harry Locke. (R)Film: The Best Things In Life Are Free, by Gordon MacRae, Dan Dailey, and Ernest Borgnine (1956).

DON'T IT MAKE MY BROWN EYES BLUE (1977) (wm)Richard Leigh. (P)Crystal Gayle.

DON'T IT MAKE YOU WANT TO GO HOME (1969) (wm)Joe South. (P)Joe South. (CR)Brook Benton.

DON'T IT MAKE YOU WANNA DANCE (1980) (I)Film: Urban Cowboy, by Bonnie Raitt. (P)Bonnie Raitt.

DON'T JUST STAND THERE (What's On Your Mind?) (1965) (wm)Lor Crane—Bernice Ross. (P)Patty Duke.

DON'T KNOCK MY LOVE (1971) (w)Wilson Pickett (m)Brad Shapiro. (P)Wilson Pickett. (R)1974 by Diana Ross and Marvin Gaye.

DON'T LEAVE ME THIS WAY (1977) (wm)Cary Gilbert—Kenny Gamble—Leon Huff. (P)Thelma Houston. No. 1 Chart Record. (R)1987 by The Communards.

DON'T LET GO (1957) (wm)Jesse Stone. (P)Roy Hamilton. (CR)Billy Williams. (R)1975 by Commander Cody. (R)1980 by Isaac Hayes.

DON'T LET HER GO (1955) (w)Aaron Schroeder (m)Abner Silver. (P)Frank Sinatra.

DON'T LET IT BOTHER YOU (1934) (w)Mack Gordon (m)Harry Revel. (I)Film: The Gay Divorcee, by unknown singer and danced by Fred Astaire. Recorded by Fats Waller.

DON'T LET IT END (1983) (wm)Dennis De Young. (P)Styx.

DON'T LET IT GET YOU DOWN (1940) (w)E. Y. Harburg (m)Burton Lane. (I)Musical: Hold On To Your Hats, by Eunice Healey, Jack Whiting, Russ Brown, Gil Lamb, Margaret Irving, and The Radio Aces.

DON'T LET ME BE LONELY TONIGHT (1973) (wm)James Taylor. (P)James Taylor.

DON'T LET ME BE MISUNDERSTOOD (1964) (wm)Bennie Benjamin—Sol Marcus—Gloria Caldwell. (P)Nina Simone. (R)1965 by The Animals. (R)1978 by Santa Esmeralda.

DON'T LET ME DOWN (1969) (wm)John Lennon—Paul McCartney. (P)The Beatles.

DON'T LET THAT MOON GET AWAY (1938) (w)Johnny Burke (m)James V. Monaco. (I)Film: Sing You Sinners, by Bing Crosby. (P)Bing Crosby.

DON'T LET THE GREEN GRASS FOOL YOU (1971) (wm)Jerry Akines—Johnnie Bellmon—Victor Drayton—Reginald Turner. (P)Wilson Pickett.

DON'T LET THE JONESES GET YOU DOWN (1969) (wm)Norman Whitfield—Barrett Strong. (P)The Temptations.

DON'T LET THE RAIN COME DOWN (Crooked Little Man) (1964) (wm)Ersel Hickey—Ed Miller. (P)The Serendipity Singers.

DON'T LET THE STARS GET IN YOUR EYES (1953) (wm)Slim Willet—Cactus Pryor—Barbara Trammel. (I)Slim Willet. (P)Perry Como. No. 1 Chart Record.

DON'T LET THE SUN CATCH YOU CRYING (1964) (wm)Gerrard Marsden. (P)Gerry and The Pacemakers.

DON'T LET THE SUN GO DOWN ON ME (1974) (wm)Elton John—Bernie Taupin. (P)Elton John.

DON'T LET'S BE BEASTLY TO THE GERMANS (1943) (wm)Noel Coward. Written for Revue: Flying Colours, but deleted before opening.

DON'T LOOK AT ME THAT WAY (1928) (wm)Cole Porter. (I)Musical: Paris, by Irene Bordoni.

DON'T LOOK BACK (1978) (wm)Tom Scholz. (P)Boston.

DON'T LOSE MY NUMBER (1985) (wm)Phil Collins. (P)Phil Collins.

DON'T MAKE ME OVER (1963) (w)Hal David (m)Burt Bacharach. (P)Dionne Warwick. (R)1970 by Brenda and The Tabulations. (R)1980 by Jennifer Warnes.

DON'T MAKE ME WAIT FOR LOVE (1987) (wm)P. Glass—Afanasieff—Walden. (P)Kenny G. (Vocal by Lenny Williams).

DON'T MEAN NOTHING (1987) (wm)Richard Marx—B. Gaitsch. (P)Richard Marx.

DON'T MESS UP A GOOD THING (1965) (wm)Oliver Sain. (P)Fontella Bass with Bobby McClure.

DON'T MESS WITH BILL (1965) (wm)William Robinson. (P)The Marvelettes.

DON'T MIND THE RAIN (1924) (wm)Ned Miller—Chester Conn. (P)Blossom Seeley.

DON'T PASS ME BY (wm)Richard Starkey (Ringo Starr). (P)The Beatles.

DON'T PLAY THAT SONG (1962) (wm)Ahmet Ertegun—Betty Nelson. (P)Ben E. King. (R)1970 by Aretha Franklin.

DON'T PULL YOUR LOVE (1970) (wm)Dennis Lambert—Brian Potter. (P)Hamilton, Joe Frank and Reynolds.

DON'T PUT IT DOWN (1967) (w)Gerome Ragni—James Rado (m)Galt MacDermot. (I)Musical: Hair, by Gerome Ragni and Steve Curry.

DON'T RAIN ON MY PARADE (1964) (w)Bob Merrill (m)Jule Styne. (I)Musical: Funny Girl, by Barbra Streisand. (P)Barbra Streisand.

DON'T ROCK THE BOAT, DEAR (1950) (wm)Ralph Blane—Harold Arlen. (I)Film: My Blue Heaven, by Dan Dailey and Betty Grable.

DON'T SAY GOODNIGHT (1934) (w)Al Dubin (m)Harry Warren. (I)Film: *Wonder Bar*, by Dick Powell and The Chorus. Also, danced by Ricardo Cortez and Dolores Del Rio.

DON'T SAY NOTHIN' BAD (About My Baby) (1963) (wm)Gerry Goffin—Carole King. (P)The Cookies.

DON'T SAY YOU DON'T REMEMBER (1972) (wm)Helen Miller—Estelle Levitt. (P)Beverly Bremers.

DON'T SEND YOUR WIFE TO THE COUNTRY (1921) (w)Harold Atteridge—B. G. De Sylva (m)Con Conrad. (I)Musical: *Bombo*, by Al Jolson. (P)Al Jolson.

DON'T SHED A TEAR (1987) (wm)E. Schwartz—R. Friedman. (P)Paul Carrack.

DON'T SIT UNDER THE APPLE TREE (With Anyone Else But Me) (1942) (wm)Lew Brown—Charlie Tobias—Sam H. Stept. (I)Film: *Private Buckaroo*, by The Andrews Sisters. (P)Glenn Miller and his Orchestra. No. 1 Chart Record. (CR)The Andrews Sisters.

DON'T SLEEP IN THE SUBWAY (1967) (wm)Tony Hatch—Jackie Trent. (P)Petula Clark.

DON'T STAND SO CLOSE TO ME (1980) (wm)Gordon Sumner (Sting) (P)The Police.

DON'T STAY AWAY TOO LONG (1955) (wm)Al Hoffman—Dick Manning. (P)Eddie Fisher.

DON'T STOP (1977) (wm)Christine McVie. (P)Fleetwood Mac.

DON'T STOP BELIEVIN' (1976) (wm)John Farrar (P)Olivia Newton—John.

DON'T STOP BELIEVIN' (1981) (wm)Steve Perry—Neal Schon—Jonathan Cain. (P)Journey.

DON'T STOP THE MUSIC (1981) (wm)Lonnie Simmons—Alisa Peoples—Jonah Ellis. (P)Yarborough and Peoples.

DON'T STOP 'TIL YOU GET ENOUGH (1979) (wm)Michael Jackson. (P)Michael Jackson. No. 1 Chart Record.

DON'T SWEETHEART ME (1943) (wm)Cliff Friend—Charlie Tobias. (P)Lawrence Welk and his Orchestra.

LAWRENCE WELK

Back in the fifties, we had an early example of the selling power of television at Coral Records. Lawrence Welk and his orchestra were recording for us and, believe me, we couldn't give his records away (outside of a few minor sales to polka fans in the Midwest). Our sales department pleaded with our creative people to drop the Welk organization. However, inasmuch as we knew that Larry was going to start a TV show for Chrysler, we decided to wait, to see whether the TV exposure would have any effect on record sales.

Of course the rest is history. Welk became a household word and we couldn't press his records fast enough. But what might have happened to Lawrence Welk without the power of television?

DON'T TAKE IT SO HARD (1968) (wm)Mark Lindsay. (P)Paul Revere and The Raiders.

DON'T TAKE OUR CHARLIE FOR THE ARMY (1963) (wm)Noel Coward. (I)Musical: *The Girl Who Came To Supper*, by Tessie O'Shea, Sean Scully and The Ensemble.

DON'T TAKE YOUR GUNS TO TOWN (1959) (wm)Johnny Cash. (P)Johnny Cash.

DON'T TAKE YOUR LOVE FROM ME (1941) (wm)Henry Nemo. (P)Mildred Bailey. (CR)The Three Suns.

DON'T TALK TO STRANGERS (1965) (w)Bob Duran (m)Ron Elliott. (P)The Beau Brummels. (R)1982 by Rick Springfield.

DON'T TELL HER WHAT'S HAPPENED TO ME (1930) (wm)B. G. De Sylva—Lew Brown (m)Ray Henderson. (P)Ruth Etting.

DON'T TELL ME (1947) (wm)Buddy Pepper. (I)Film: *The Hucksters*, by voice of Eileen Wilson, dubbing for Ava Gardner.

DON'T TELL ME GOODNIGHT (1975) (wm)Roland Kent LaVoie. (P)Lobo.

DON'T TELL YOUR FOLKS (1930) (w)Lorenz Hart (m)Richard Rodgers. (I)Musical: *Simple Simon*, by Bobbe Arnst and Will Ahearn.

DON'T THINK IT AIN'T BEEN CHARMING (1940) (w)Johnny Mercer (m)Jimmy McHugh. (I)Film: *You'll Find Out*, by Kay Kyser and his College of Musical Knowledge.

DON'T THINK TWICE, IT'S ALL RIGHT (1963) (wm)Bob Dylan. (I)Bob Dylan. (P)Peter, Paul & Mary. (R)1965 by The Wonder Who.

(Our Love)DON'T THROW IT AWAY (1977) (wm)Barry Gibb—Blue Weaver. (P)Andy Gibb.

DON'T THROW YOUR LOVE AWAY (1964) (wm)Billy Jackson—Jim Wisner. (P)The Searchers.

DON'T WAIT TOO LONG (1963) (wm)Sunny Skylar. (P)Tony Bennett.

DON'T WAKE ME UP (Let Me Dream) (1925) (w)L. Wolfe Gilbert. (m)Mabel Wayne—Abel Baer.

DON'T WANT TO LIVE WITHOUT IT (1978) (wm)David Jenkins—Cory Lerios. (P)Pablo Cruise.

DON'T WORRY (1960) (wm)Marty Robbins. (P)Marty Robbins.

DON'T WORRY BABY (1964) (wm)Brian Wilson—Roger Christian. (P)The Beach Boys. (R)1979 by B. J. Thomas.

DON'T WORRY 'BOUT ME (1939) (w)Ted Koehler (m)Rube Bloom. (I)Revue: *Cotton Club Parade*, by Cab Calloway. Recorded by Hal Kemp and his Orchestra. Most popular recording by Frank Sinatra.

DON'T YOU (Forget About Me) (1985) (wm)Keith Forsey—Steve Schiff. (P)Simple Minds. No. 1 Chart Record.

DON'T YOU BELIEVE IT (1962) (w)Bob Hilliard (m)Burt Bacharach. (P)Andy Williams.

DON'T YOU CARE (1967) (wm)Gary Beisbier—Jim Holvay. (P)The Buckinghams.

DON'T YOU FORGET IT (1963) (w)Al Stillman (m)Henry Mancini. (P)Perry Como.

DON'T YOU KNOW (1954) (wm)Ray Charles. (P)Ray Charles.

DON'T YOU KNOW (1959) (wm)Bobby Worth. Adapted from Puccini's *Musetta's Waltz*. (P)Della Reese.

DON'T YOU KNOW I CARE (1944) (w)Mack David (m)Duke Ellington. (P)Duke Ellington and his Orchestra, vocal by Al Hibbler.

DON'T YOU LOVE ME ANYMORE? (1947) (wm)Mack David—Al Hoffman—Jerry Livingston. (P)Buddy Clark. (CR)Freddy Martin and his Orchestra.

DON'T YOU MISS YOUR BABY (1939) (wm)Ed Durham—William Basie—James Rushing. (P)Count

Basie and his Orchestra, vocal by Jimmy Rushing.

DON'T YOU WANT ME (1987 (wm)F. Golde-D. P. Bryant-Jody Watley. (P)Jody Watley.

DON'T YOU WORRY 'BOUT A THING (1974) (wm)Stevie Wonder. (P)Stevie Wonder.

DOO DOO DOO DOO DOO (Heartbreaker) (1973) (wm)Mick Jagger—Keith Richards. (P)The Rolling Stones.

DOODLE DOO DOO (1924) (wm)Art Kassel—Mel Stitzel. (P)Theme song of Art Kassel and his Orchestra.

DOOR IS STILL OPEN TO MY HEART, THE (1955) (wm)Chuck Willis. (P)The Cardinals. (R)1964 by Dean Martin. (CR)Don Cornell.

DOOR OF MY DREAMS, THE (1924) (w)Oscar Hammerstein II—Otto Harbach (m)Rudolf Friml. (I)Operetta: Rose Marie, by Mary Ellis.

DORMI, DORMI, DORMI (1958) (w)Sammy Cahn (m)Harry Warren. (I)Film: Rock-A-Bye-Baby on soundtrack. (P)Eydie Gorme.

DOUBLE CHECK STOMP (1930) (wm)Albany Bigard—Irving Mills. (P)Duke Ellington and his Orchestra.

DOUBLE LOVIN' (1971) (wm)George Jackson (m)Mickey Buckins. (P)The Osmonds.

DOUBLE SHOT (Of My Baby's Love) (1966) (wm)Don Smith—Cyril E. Vetter. (P)The Swinging Medallions.

DOUBLE TROUBLE (1935) (wm)Ralph Rainger—Leo Robin—Richard A. Whiting. (I)Film: Big Broadcast of 1936, by Lyda Roberti, Jack Oakie, and Henry Wadsworth. Recorded by Ray Noble and his Orchestra.

DOUBLE VISION (1978) (wm)Lou Grammatico—Michael Jones. (P)Foreigner.

DOWN ALONG THE COVE (1968) (wm)Bob Dylan. (P)Bob Dylan.

DOWN AMONG THE SHELTERING PALMS (1914) (w)James Brockman (m)Abe Olman. (P)The Lyric Quartet. (R)1949 by Sammy Kaye and his Orchestra.

DOWN ARGENTINA WAY (1940) (w)Mack Gordon (m)Harry Warren. (I)Film: Down Argentina Way, by Carmen Miranda. (P)Carmen Miranda. (CR)Eddy Duchin and his Orchestra.

DOWN AT LULU'S (1968) (wm)Joe Levine—Kris Resnick. (P)Ohio Express.

DOWN BY THE LAZY RIVER (1972) (wm)Alan R. Osmond (m)Merrill Osmond. (P)The Osmonds.

DOWN BY THE O-HI-O (1920) (w)Jack Yellen (m)Abe Olman. (I)Revue: Ziegfeld Follies of 1920, by Van and Schenck. Recorded by Billy Murray and Billy Jones. (R)1940 by The Andrews Sisters.

DOWN BY THE OLD MILL STREAM (1910) (wm)Tell Taylor. (I)Arthur Clough.

DOWN BY THE RIVERSIDE (1865) (wm)Unknown. Traditional Black American song. (R)1954 by Bing and Gary Crosby.

DOWN BY THE RIVER (1935) (w)Lorenz Hart (m)Richard Rodgers. (I)Film: Mississippi, by Bing Crosby. (P)Bing Crosby. (CR)Guy Lombardo and his Royal Canadians.

DOWN BY THE STATION (1948) (wm)Lee Ricks—Slim Gaillard. (P)Slim Gaillard. (P)Slim Gaillard. (CR)Tommy Dorsey and his Orchestra.

DOWN BY THE WINEGAR WORKS (1925) (wm)Don Bestor—Roger Lewis—Walter Donovan. (P)Don Bestor and his Orchestra.

DOWN HEARTED BLUES (1923) (w)Alberta Hunter (m)Lovie Austin. (P)Alberta Hunter.

DOWN IN OUR ALLEY BLUES (1927) (m)Duke Ellington—Otto Hardwick. (P)Duke Ellington and his Washingtonians.

DOWN IN THE BOONDOCKS (1965) (wm)Joe South. (P)Billy Joe Royal.

DOWN IN THE DEPTHS, ON THE NINETIETH FLOOR (1936) (wm)Cole Porter. (I)Musical: Red, Hot, and Blue, by Ethel Merman.

DOWN IN THE FLOOD (1967) (wm)Bob Dylan. (P)Bob Dylan.

DOWN IN THE VALLEY (1917) (wm)Unknown. Traditional American folk song. (R)1944 by The Andrews Sisters.

DOWN ON MACCONNACHY SQUARE (1947) (w)Alan Jay Lerner (m)Frederick Loewe. (I)Musical: Brigadoon, by The Chorus.

DOWN ON ME (1968) (wm)Janis Joplin. (P)Big Brother and The Holding Company, featuring Janis Joplin. (R)1972 by Janis Joplin.

DOWN ON THE CORNER (1969) (wm)John C. Fogarty. (P)Creedence Clearwater Revival, in medley with Fortunate Son.

DOWN SOUTH (1921) (W)B. G. De Sylva (m)Walter Donaldson. (I)Musical: Bombo, by Al Jolson. (P)Al Jolson.

DOWN SOUTH BLUES (1923) (wm)Alberta Hunter—Ethel Waters—Fletcher Henderson. (P)Alberta Hunter.

DOWN SOUTH CAMP MEETIN' (1935) (w)Irving Mills (m)Fletcher Henderson. (I)Fletcher Henderson and his Orchestra. (P)Benny Goodman and his Orchestra.

DOWN THE AISLE OF LOVE (1958) (wm)The Quin—Tones. (P)The Quin—Tones.

DOWN THE FIELD (1911) (w)Caleb O'Connor (m)Stanleigh Friedman. (I)Fight song of Yale University.

DOWN THE OLD OX ROAD (1933) (w)Sam Coslow (m)Arthur Johnston. (I)Film: College Humor, by Jack Oakie, Richard Arlen, Lona Andre, Mary Kornman, and Bing Crosby. (P)Bing Crosby.

DOWN THE RIVER OF GOLDEN DREAMS (1930) (wm)John Klenner—Nat Shilkret. (P)The Hilo Hawaiian Orchestra.

DOWN THE ROAD A PIECE (1941) (wm)Don Raye. (P)Will Bradley and his Orchestra, vocal by Ray McKinley. Freddie Slack on piano.

DOWN TO YOU (1973) (wm)Joni Mitchell. (P)Joni Mitchell.

DOWN T'UNCLE BILLS (1934) (wm)Johnny Mercer—Hoagy Carmichael. (P)Hoagy Carmichael.

DOWN UNDER (1982) (wm)Colin Hay—Roy Strykert. (P)Men At Work. No. 1 Chart Record.

DOWN WITH LOVE (1937) (w)E. Y. Harburg (m)Harold Arlen. (I)Musical: Hooray For What, by Vivian Vance, Jack Whiting, and June Clyde.

DOWN YONDER (1921) (wm)L. Wolfe Gilbert. (I)L. Wolfe Gilbert in vaudeville. (R)1951 by Del Wood.

DOWNHEARTED (1953) (w)Bob Hilliard (m)Dave Mann. (P)Eddie Fisher.

DOWNTOWN (1964) (wm)Tony Hatch. (P)Petula Clark. No. 1 Chart Record. NARAS Award Winner. (R)1984 by Dolly Parton.

DRAG CITY (1963) (wm)Roger Christian—Jan Berry—Brian Wilson. (P)Jan and Dean.

DRAGGIN' THE LINE (1971) (wm)Tommy James—

Robert L. King. (P)Tommy James and The Shondells.

DRAGNET (1953) (m)Walter Schumann. (I)TV series: *Dragnet*, as soundtrack theme. (P)Ray Anthony and his Orchestra.

DREAM (1945) (wm)Johnny Mercer. (P)The Pied Pipers. No. 1 Chart Record. (CR)Frank Sinatra. (CR)Jimmy Dorsey and his Orchestra.

DREAM A LITTLE DREAM OF ME (1931) (w)Gus Kahn (m)Wilbur Schwandt—Fabian Andre. (I)Wayne King and his Orchestra. (P)Kate Smith. (CR)Jack Owens. (R)1968 by Mama Cass Elliott.

DREAM ALONG WITH ME (1955) (wm)Carl Sigman. (P)Theme song of Perry Como.

DREAM BABY, HOW LONG MUST I DREAM? (1962) (wm)Cindy Walker. (P)Roy Orbison. (R)1971 by Glen Campbell.

DREAM DADDY (1923) (w)Louis Herscher (m)George Keefer. (P)Carl Fenton and his Orchestra.

DREAM DANCING (1941) (wm)Cole Porter. (I)Film: *You'll Never Get Rich*, by Fred Astaire.

DREAM, DREAM, DREAM (1946) (wm)John Redmond—Lou Ricca. (I)The Mills Brothers. (P)Perry Como.

DREAM, DREAM, DREAM (1954) (wm)Mitchell Parish—Jimmy McHugh. (P)Percy Faith and his Orchestra.

DREAM GIRL (1978) (wm)Stephen Bishop. (I)Film: *Animal House*, by Stephen Bishop. (P)Stephen Bishop.

A DREAM IS A WISH YOUR HEART MAKES. (1948) (wm)Mack David—Al Hoffman—Jerry Livingston. (I)Cartoon Film: *Cinderella*, by the voice of Ilene Woods as Cinderella.

DREAM LOVER (1929) (w)Clifford Grey (m)Victor Schertzinger. (I)Film: *The Love Parade*, by Jeanette MacDonald.

DREAM LOVER (1959) (wm)Bobby Darin. (P)Bobby Darin. (R)1964 by The Paris Sisters.

DREAM MERCHANT (1967) (wm)Larry Weiss—Jerry Ross. (P)Jerry Butler. (R)1975 by New Birth.

DREAM OF YOU (1934) (wm)Sy Oliver—Jimmie Lunceford—Edward P. Moran. (P)Jimmie Lunceford and his Orchestra, vocal by Sy Oliver.

DREAM ON (1973) (wm)Steve Tallarico. (P)Aerosmith. (R)1976 by Aerosmith.

DREAM ON LITTLE DREAMER (1964) (wm)Jan Crutchfield—Fred Burch. (P)Perry Como.

DREAM VALLEY (1940) (wm)Joe Burke—Charles Kenny—Nick Kenny. (P)Sammy Kaye and his Orchestra.

DREAM WEAVER (1976) (wm)Gary Wright. (P)Gary Wright.

(He's My)DREAMBOAT (1961) (wm)John D. Loudermilk. (P)Connie Francis.

DREAMER, THE (1943) (w)Frank Loesser (m)Arthur Schwartz. (I)Film: *Thank Your Lucky Stars*, by Dinah Shore. (P)Dinah Shore.

DREAMER, THE (1980) (wm)Roger Davies—Roger Hodgson. (P)Supertramp.

DREAMERS HOLIDAY, A (1949) (w)Kim Gannon (m)Mabel Wayne. (P)Perry Como. (CR)Buddy Clark.

DREAMIN' (1960) (wm)Ted Ellis—Barry DeVorzon. (P)Johnny Burnette. (R)1982 by John Schneider.

DREAMING (1979) (wm)Deborah Harry—Chris Stein. (P)Blondie.

DREAMING (1980) (wm)Alan Tarney—Leo Sayer. (P)Cliff Richard.

DREAMS (1977) (wm)Stephanie Nicks. (P)Fleetwood Mac. No. 1 Chart Record.

DREAMS OF THE EVERYDAY HOUSEWIFE (1968) (wm)Chris Gantry. (P)Glen Campbell. (CR)Wayne Newton.

DREAMSTREET (1961) (m)Erroll Garner. (P)Erroll Garner.

DREAMTIME (1986) (wm)Daryl Hall—John Beeby. (P)Daryl Hall.

DREAMY HAWAIIAN MOON (1938) (wm)Harry Owens. (I)Film: *Cocoanut Grove*, by Harry Owens and hi Royal Canadians. (P)Harry Owens.

DREIDEL (1973) (wm)Don McLean. (P)Don McLean.

DRESS YOU UP (1985) (wm)Peggy Stanziale—Andrea LaRusso. (P)Madonna.

DRIFT AWAY (1973) (wm)Mentor Williams. (P)Dobie Gray.

DRIFTER'S ESCAPE (1968) (wm)Bob Dylan. (P)Bob Dylan.

DRIFTING (1958) (w)Kim Gannon (m)Bronislau Kaper. Adapted from the theme from Film: *Auntie Mame*. (P)David Allen.

DRIFTING ALONG WITH THE TIDE (1921) (w)Arthur Jackson (m)George Gershwin. (I)Revue: *George White's Scandals of 1921*, by Lloyd Garrett and Victoria Herbert.

DRIFTING AND DREAMING (1925) (w)Haven Gillespie (m)Egbert Van Alstyne—Erwin Schmidt—Loyal Curtis. (P)Theme song of Orrin Tucker and his Orchestra. (CR)George Olsen and his Orchestra.

DRINK TO ME ONLY WITH THINE EYES (1780) (w)Ben Jonson (m)Unknown. Early recording by John McCormack.

DRINKIN' WINE, SPO-DEE-O-DEE (1949) (wm)Granville McGhee—J. Mayo Williams. (P)Stick McGhee. (R)1973 by Jerry Lee Lewis.

DRINKING SONG (1924) (w)Dorothy Donnelly (m)Sigmund Romberg. (I)Operetta: *The Student Prince in Heidelberg*, by Raymond Marlowe and The Chorus. (R)Film: *The Student Prince*, by the voice of Mario Lanza, dubbing for Edmund Purdom.

DRIP DROP (1963) (wm)Jerry Leiber—Mike Stoller. (P)Dion.

DRIVE (1984) (wm)Ric Ocasek. (P)The Cars.

DRIVE MY CAR (1965) (wm)John Lennon—Paul McCartney. (R)1966 by Bob Kuban. (R)1975 by Gary Toms Empire.

DRIVER'S SEAT (1979) (wm)Paul Roberts. (P)Sniff 'N' the Tears.

DROP ME OFF IN HARLEM (1933) (w)Nick Kenny (m)Duke Ellington. (P)Duke Ellington and his Orchestra.

DROWN IN MY TEARS (1956) (wm)Henry Glover. (P)Ray Charles.

DROWNIN' MY SORROWS (1963) (wm)Hunter Vincent—Bill Justis. (P)Connie Francis.

DROWNING IN THE SEA OF LOVE (1970) (wm)Kenny Gamble—Leon Huff. (P)Joe Simon.

DRUMBOOGIE (1941) (wm)Gene Krupa. (P)Gene Krupa and his Orchestra, vocal by Irene Daye.

DRUMMIN' MAN (1939) (wm)Tiny Parham—Gene Krupa. (P)Gene Krupa and his Orchestra, vocal by Irene Daye.

DRUMS IN MY HEART (1931) (w)Edward Heyman (m)Vincent Youmans. (I)Play with music: *Through The Years*, by Gregory Gaye. Recorded by Leo Reisman and his Orchestra.

DRY BONES (1865) (w)James Weldon Johnson (m)J. Rosamund Johnson. Based on a Black American Spiritual. (R)1949 by Tommy Dorsey and his Orchestra. Arrangement by Sy Oliver.

DRY YOUR EYES (1967) (w)Brenda Payton (m)Maurice Coates. (P)Brenda and The Tabulations.

DUCK, THE (1965) (wm)Earl Nelson—Fred Sledge Smith. (P)Jackie Lee.

DUDE (Looks Like A Lady) (1987) (wm)S. Tyler—J. Perry—D. Child. (P)Aerosmith.

DU, DU, LIEGST MIR IN HERZEN (1820) (wm)Unknown. Traditional German folk song.

DU UND DU (You And You Waltz) (1874) (m)Johann Strauss. Added words by Oscar Hammerstein for Film: *The Great Waltz.*

DUEL IN THE SUN (A Duel Of Two Hearts) (1947) (w)Stanley Adams—Maxson Judell (m)Dimitri Tiomkin. Adapted from theme from Film: *Duel In The Sun.*

DUELING BANJOS (1973) (m)Arthur Smith. (I)Film: *Deliverance,* by Eric Weissberg and Steve Mandel on soundtrack. (P)Weissberg and Mandel.

DUEL FOR ONE (The First Lady Of The Land) (w)Alan Jay Lerner (m)Leonard Bernstein. (I)Musical: *1600 Pennsylvania Ave.* ,by Patriciaa Routledge.

DUKE OF EARL (1962) (wm)Earl Edwards—Bernie Williams—Eugene Dixon. (P)Gene Chandler. No. 1 Chart Record.

DUKE STEPS OUT, THE (1929) (m)Duke Ellington. (P)Duke Ellington and his Orchestra.

DUKE'S PLACE (1958) (w)Ruth Roberts—Bill Katz—Bob Thiele. (m)Duke Ellington. Based on C Jam Blues.

DUM-DE-DA (1966) (wm)Merle Kilgore—Margie Singleton. (P)Bobby Vinton.

DUM DOT SONG, THE (1947) (wm)Julian Kay. (P)Frank Sinatra.

DUM DUM (1961) (wm)Jackie DeShannon—Sharon Sheeley. (P)Brenda Lee.

DUNA (1914) (wm)Marjorie Pickhall—Josephine McGill. Standard favorite about a place in Ireland.

DUNGAREE DOLL! (1955) (w)Ben Raleigh (m)Sherman Edwards. (P)Eddie Fisher.

DUSIC (1977) (wm)James B. Brown—Reginald Hargis—R. Ransom, Jr. (P)Brick.

DUSK IN UPPER SANDUSKY (1937) (m)Jimmy Dorsey—Larry Clinton. (P)Jimmy Dorsey and his Orchestra.

DUSK ON THE DESERT (1937) (wm)Irving Mills—Duke Ellington. (P)Duke Ellington and his Orchestra.

DUSKY STEVEDORE (1928) (w)Andy Razaf (m)J. C. Johnson. (I)Frankie Trumbauer and his Orchestra, featuring Bix Beiderbecke on cornet. Theme song of Nat Shilkret and his Orchestra.

DUST (1938) (wm)Johnny Marvin (I)Film: *Under Western Skies,* by Roy Rogers.

DUST IN THE WIND (1978) (wm)Kerry Livgren. (P)Kansas.

(Oh Suzanna)DUST OFF THAT OLD PIANNA (1935) (wm)Irving Caesar—Sammy Lerner—Gerald Marks. (P)Ozzie Nelson and his Orchestra.

D. W. Washburn (1968) (wm)Jerry Leiber—Mike Stoller. (P)The Monkees.

D'YE LOVE ME (1925) (w)Oscar Hammerstein II—Otto Harbach (m)Jerome Kern. (I)Musical: *Sunny,* by Marilyn Miller.

D'YER MAKER (1973) (wm)John Bonham—John Baldwin—Robert Plant. (P)Led Zeppelin.

DYING GAMBLER'S BLUES (1924) (wm)Jack Gee. (P)Bessie Smith.

DYING WITH THE BLUES (1921) (wm)W. Astor Morgan—Fletcher Henderson. (P)Ethel Waters.

DYNAMITE (1984) (wm)Andy Goldmark—Bruce Roberts. (P)Jermaine Jackson.

DYNOMITE (1975) (wm)Tony Camillo. (P)Bazuka.

EADIE WAS A LADY (1932) (w)B. G. De Sylva (m)Richard A. Whiting—Nacio Herb Brown. (I)Musical: *Take A Chance*, by Ethel Merman. Recorded by Paul Whiteman and his Orchestra. (R)1933 in Film: *Take A Chance*, by Lillian Roth

EAGER BEAVER (1962) (wm)Richard Rodgers. (I)Musical: *No Strings*, by Don Chastain and Bernice Massi.

EAGLE AND ME, THE (1944) (w)E. Y. Harburg (m)Harold Arlen. (I)Musical: *Bloomer Girl*, by Dooley Wilson and The Chorus.

EARACHE MY EYE (1974) (wm)Tommy Chong—Gaye DeLorme—Richard Moore. (P)Cheech and Chong.

EARFUL OF MUSIC, AN (1934) (w)Gus Kahn (m)Walter Donaldson. (I)Film: *Kid Millions*, by Ethel Merman.

EARLY AUTUMN (1948) (w)Johnny Mercer (m)Woody Herman—Ralph Burns. (P)Woody Herman and his Orchestra. (CR)Claude Thornhill and his Orchestra.

EARLY BIRD (1936) (w)Sidney Mitchell (m)Lew Pollack. (I)Film: *Captain January*, by Shirley Temple.

EARLY IN THE MORNING (1958) (wm)Bobby Darin. (P)The Rinky Dinks. (CR)Buddy Holly.

EARLY IN THE MORNING (1969) (wm)Mike Leander—Eddie Seago. (P)Vanity Fare.

EARLY IN THE MORNING (1982) (wm)Charles Wilson—Rudolph Taylor—Lonnie Simmons. (P)The Gap Band.

EARLY MORNIN' RAIN (1965) (wm)Gordon Lightfoot. (P)Peter, Paul, and Mary. (R)1966 by Chad & Jeremy.

EARTH AND THE SKY (1950) (wm)John Rox. (I)Revue: *John Murray Anderson's Almanac*, by Polly Bergen.

EARTH ANGEL (1955) (wm)Jesse Belvin. (I)The Penguins. (P)The Crew Cuts. (CR)Gloria Mann. (R)1960 by Johnny Tillotson. (R)1969 by The Vogues. (R)1986 by New Edition.

EARTHBOUND (1956) (wm)Jack Taylor—Clive Richardson—Bob Musel. (P)Sammy Davis, Jr. (CR)Mario Lanza.

EASE ON DOWN THE ROAD (1975) (wm)Charlie Smalls. (I)Musical: *The Wiz*, by Stephanie Mills. (P)Consumer Rapport. (R)1978 by Diana Ross and Michael Jackson.

EASIER SAID THAN DONE (1963) (wm)William Linton—Larry Huff. (P)The Essex. No. 1 Chart Record.

EAST BOUND AND DOWN (1977) (wm)Dick Feller—Jerry Reed Hubbard. (I)Film: *Smokey and The Bandit*, by Jerry Reed. (P)Jerry Reed.

EAST OF EDEN (Theme From) (1955) (m)Leonard Rosenman. (I)Film: *East Of Eden*, on soundtrack. (P)Dick Jacobs and his Orchestra.

EAST OF THE SUN (And West Of The Moon) (1934) (wm)Brooks Bowman. (I)Revue: *Stags At Bay* (Princeton University Triangle Club Production). Recorded by Tom Coakley and his Orchestra.

EAST ST. LOUIS TOODLE-O (1927) (m)Bubber Miley—Duke Ellington. (P)Duke Ellington and his Orchestra. This was Ellington's first theme song.

EAST SIDE OF HEAVEN (1939) (w)Johnny Burke (m)James V. Monaco. (I)Film: *East Side Of Heaven*, by Bing Crosby. (P)Bing Crosby.

EAST SIDE, WEST SIDE (The Sidewalks of New York) (1894) (wm)Charles B. Lawlor—James W. Blake.

(I)Dan Quinn. (R)1954 by a trio consisting of Alan Dale, Buddy Greco, and Johnny Desmond.

EAST, WEST (1966) (wm)Graham Gouldman. (P)Herman's Hermits.

EASTER PARADE (1933) (wm)Irving Berlin. (I)Revue: *As Thousands Cheer*, by Marilyn Miller and Clifton Webb. (R)1942 Film: *Holiday Inn*, by Bing Crosby. (P)Bing Crosby. (R)1942 by Harry James and his Orchestra. (R)1947 by Guy Lombardo and his Royal Canadians. (R)1954 by Liberace.

IRVING BERLIN

The story goes that when Irving Berlin first started to write he wrote only in the key of F-sharp, which meant he played only on the black keys. He had a piano with a lever that automatically changed keys for him. However, since he did not read or write music, someone else had to write the songs down on paper.

EASY (1977) (wm)Lionel Richie. (I)Film: *Thank God It's Friday*, by The Commodores. (P)The Commodores.

EASY COME, EASY GO (1934) (w)Edward Heyman (m)John Green. (I)Film: *Bachelor Of Arts*, as soundtrack theme. Recorded by Eddy Duchin and his Orchestra.

EASY COME, EASY GO. (1969) (wm)Diane Hilderbrand—Jack Keller. (P)Bobby Sherman.

EASY DOES IT (1940) (wm)Sy Oliver—Jimmy Young. (P)Tommy Dorsey and his Orchestra. (CR)Count Basie and his Orchestra.

EASY LOVER (1984) (wm)Philip Bailey—Phil Collins—Nathan East. (P)Philip Bailey with Phil Collins.

(Such An)EASY QUESTION (1962) (wm)Winfield Scott—Otis Blackwell. (P)Elvis Presley.

EASY STREET (1977) (w)Martin Charnin (m)Charles Strouse. (I)Musical: *Annie*, by Dorothy Loudon.

EASY TO BE HARD (1967) (w)Gerome Ragni—James Rado (m)Galt MacDermot. (I)Musical: *Hair*, by Suzannah Evans. Paul Jabara, Linda Compton, and The Company in off Broadway version. In Broadway version, by Lynn Kellogg. (P)1969 by Three Dog Night.

EASY TO LOVE (1936) (wm)Cole Porter. (I)Film: *Born To Dance*, by James Stewart and later reprised by Frances Langford. Danced to by Eleanor Powell.

EAT IT (1984) (wm)Michael Jackson (w)Al Yankovic. (P)Weird Al Yankovic. Parody on Michael Jackson's Beat It.

EAVESDROPPER'S BLUES (1924) (wm)J. C. Johnson. (P)Bessie Smith.

EBB TIDE (1953) (w)Carl Sigman (m)Robert Maxwell. (P)Frank Chacksfield and his Orchestra. Vocal version by Roy Hamilton. (R)1960 by The Platters. (R)1964 by Lenny Welch. (R)1966 by The Righteous Brothers.

EBONY AND IVORY (1982) (wm)Paul McCartney. (P)Paul McCartney with Stevie Wonder. No. 1 Chart Record.

EBONY EYES (1961) (wm)John Loudermilk. (P)The Everly Brothers.

EBONY EYES (1978) (wm)Robert Welch. (P)Bob Welch.

EBONY RHAPSODY (1934) (wm)Sam Coslow—Arthur

Johnston. Based on Liszt's Second Hungarian Rhapsody. (I)Film: *Murder At The Vanities*, by Duke Ellington and his Orchestra, vocal by Gertrude Michael. (P)Duke Ellington.

ECHO SAID NO, THE (1947) (wm)Art Kassel. (P)Guy Lombardo and his Royal Canadians. (CR)Sammy Kaye and his Orchestra.

ECHOES (1949) (wm)Bennie Benjamin—George Weiss. (P)Jo Stafford and Gordon MacRae. (CR)The Ink Spots.

ECHOES OF HARLEM (1936) (m)Duke Ellington. (P)Duke Ellington and his Orchestra, trumpet solo by Cootie Williams.

EDDIE, MY LOVE (1956) (wm)Aaron Collins—Maxwell Davis—Sam Ling. (P)The Fontane Sisters. (CR)The Chordettes. (CR)The Teen Queens.

EDELWEISS (1957) (w)Oscar Hammerstein II (m)Richard Rodgers. (I)Musical: *The Sound Of Music*, by Mary Martin. In film version by Julie Andrews.

EDGE OF HEAVEN, THE (1986) (wm)George Michael. (P)Wham!

EENY, MEENY, MINEY, MO (1935) (wm)Johnny Mercer—Matty Malneck. (I)Film: *To Beat The Band*, by Johnny Mercer. (P)Johnny Mercer with Ginger Rogers.

EGG AND I, THE (1947) (wm)Harry Akst—Herman Ruby—Bert Kalmar—Al Jolson. (I)Film: *The Egg And I* on soundtrack. (P)Sammy Kaye and his Orchestra. (CR)Dinah Shore.

EGYPTIAN ELLA (1931) (wm)Walter Doyle. (P)Ted Weems and his Orchestra. (CR)Ted Lewis and his Orchestra.

EH, CUMPARI! (1953) (wm)Julius La Rosa—Archie Bleyer. Adapted from Italian folk song. (P)Julius La Rosa.

8 1/2 (Theme from) (1963) (w)Tino Fornai (m)Nino Rota. (I)Italian Film: *8 1/2* on soundtrack.

EIGHT DAYS A WEEK (1965) (wm)John Lennon—Paul McCartney. (P)The Beatles. No. 1 Chart Record.

EIGHT MILES HIGH (1966) (wm)Gene Clark—David Crosby—Jim McGuinn. (P)The Byrds.

867-5309/JENNY (1982) (wm)Alex Call—James Keller. (P)Tommy Tutone.

EIGHTEEN (1971) (wm)Alice Cooper—Glen Buxton—Dennis Dunaway—Neal Smith—Michael Bruce. (P)Alice Cooper.

1812 OVERTURE (1882) (m)Peter I. Tchaikovsky. Very famous classical overture. Most popular recording by The Boston Pops Orchestra.

EIGHTEEN WITH A BULLET (1975) (wm)Barry Hammond—William Wingfield. (P)Pete Wingfield.

EIGHTEEN YELLOW ROSES (1963) (wm)Bobby Darin. (P)Bobby Darin.

EILEEN (1917) (w)Henry Blossom (m)Victor Herbert. (I)Musical: *Eileen*.

EL CID (Love Theme) (The Falcon and The Dove) (1961) (w)Paul Francis Webster (m)Miklos Rozsa. (I)Film: *El Cid* as soundtrack theme.

EL CUMBANCHERO (1943) (wm)Rafael Hernandez. Popular mexican song. No artist credited with introduction.

EL PASO (1959) (wm)Marty Robbins. (P)Marty Robbins. No. 1 Chart Record.

(Alla En)El RANCHO GRANDE (1934) (w-Eng)Bartley Costello (m)Silvano R. Ramos. (P)Bing Crosby.

EL RANCHO ROCK (1958) (w)Ben Raleigh (m)Silvano R. Ramos. (P)The Champs.

EL RELICARIO (see My Troubadour)

EL WATUSI (1962) (m)Ray Barretto. (P)Ray Barretto.

ELEANOR RIGBY (1966) (wm)John Lennon—Paul McCartney. (P)The Beatles. (R)1968 by Ray Charles. (R)1969 by Aretha Franklin.

ELECTION DAY (1985) (wm)Nick Rhodes—Roger Taylor—Simon LeBon. (P)Arcadia.

ELECTRIC AVENUE (1983) (wm)Eddy Grant. (P)Eddy Grant.

ELECTRIC BLUE (1987) (wm)I. Davies—J. Oates. (P)Icehouse.

ELEGANCE (1964) (wm)Jerry Herman. (I)Musical: *Hello Dolly*, by Charles Nelson Reilly, Eileen Brennan, Sondra Lee, and Jerry Dodge.

ELEGIE (1866) (m)Jules Massanet. Famous classical composition.

ELENA (1961) (wm)Robert Wright—George Forrest. (I)Musical: *Kean*, by Alfred Drake, Arthur Rubin and The Ensemble.

ELENORE (1968) (wm)Howard Kaylan—Mark Volman—Jim Pons—Al Nichol—John Barbata. (P)The Turtles.

ELEPHANTS TANGO, THE (1955) (wm)Bernie Landes. (P)Lawrence Welk and his Orchestra.

11th HOUR MELODY (1956) (w)Carl Sigman (m)King Palmer. (P)Al Hibbler. (CR)Lou Busch.

ELI'S COMING (1968) (wm)Laura Nyro. (I)Laura Nyro. (P)Three Dog Night. (R)1971 by The Fifth Dimension.

ELMER'S TUNE (1941) (wm)Elmer Albrecht—Sammy Gallop—Dick Jurgens. (I)Dick Jurgens and his Orchestra. (P)Glenn Miller and his Orchestra, vocal by Ray Eberle and The Modernaires.

No. 1 Chart Record.

ELUSIVE BUTTERFLY (1966) (wm)Bob Lind. (P)Bob Lind.

ELVIRA (1981) (wm)Dallas Frazier. (I)Dallas Frazier. (P)The Oak Ridge Boys.

ELVIRA MADIGAN (Theme From) (1969)Based on a theme by Mozart Op. 29, written in 1785. (P)Film: *Elvira Madigan* on soundtrack.

EMALINE (1934) (w)Mitchell Parish (m)Frank Perkins. (P)Mildred Bailey. (CR)Wayne King and his Orchestra.

EMBRACEABLE YOU (1930) (w)Ira Gershwin (m)George Gershwin. (I)Musical: *Girl Crazy*, by Ginger Rogers and Allan Kearns. Recorded by Red Nichols and his Five Pennies. (R)1943 Film: *Girl Crazy*, by Judy Garland. (R)1951 Film: *An American In Paris*, by Gene Kelly. (R)1952 Film: *With A Song In My Heart*, by the voice of Jane Froman dubbing for Susan Hayward.

EMILY (1964) (w)Johnny Mercer (m)Johnny Mandel. Adaptation of the soundtrack theme from Film: *The Americanization Of Emily*.

EMMA (1975) (wm)Errol Brown—Tony Wilson. (P)Hot Chocolate.

EMERGENCY (1985) (wm)George Brown—Ronald Bell—Charles Smith—James Taylor—Robert Bell—Curtis Williams—James Bonneford. (P)Kool and The Gang.

EMOTION (1975) (w-Eng)Patti Dahlstrom (m)Veronique Marie Sanson. (P)Helen Reddy.

EMOTION IN MOTION (1986) (wm)Ric Ocasek. (P)Ric Ocasek.

EMOTIONAL RESCUE (1980) (wm)Mick Jagger—Keith Richards. (P)The Rolling Stones.

EMOTIONS (1960) (wm)Mel Tillis—Ramsey Kearney. (P)Brenda Lee.

EMPIRE STRIKES BACK, THE (1980) (m)John Williams. (I)Film: *The Empire Strikes Back* on soundtrack.

EMPTY ARMS (1957) (wm)Ivory Joe Hunter. (P)Ivory Joe Hunter. (CR)Teresa Brewer. (R)1971 by Sonny James.

EMPTY BED BLUES (1928) (wm)J. C. Johnson. (P)Bessie Smith.

EMPTY GARDEN (Hey Hey Johnny) (1982) (wm)Elton John—Bernie Taupin. (P)Elton John.

EMPTY POCKETS FILLED WITH LOVE (1962) (wm)Irving Berlin. (I)Musical: *Mr. President*, by Anita Gillette and Jack Haskell.

EMPTY SADDLES (1936) (wm)Billy Hill. Based on a poem by J. Keirn Brennan. (I)Film: *Rhythm On The Range*, by Bing Crosby. (P)Bing Crosby.

EMPTY TABLES (1976) (w)Johnny Mercer (m)Jimmy Van Heusen. (P)Frank Sinatra.

ENCHANTED (1959) (wm)Buck Ram. (P)The Platters.

ENCHANTED ISLAND (1958) (w)Al Stillman (m)Robert Allen. (P)The Four Lads.

ENCHANTED MELODY, THE (1960) (m)Vic Mizzy. (I)TV Series: *The Shirley Temple Show*.

ENCHANTED SEA, THE (1959) (wm)Frank Metis—Randy Starr. (I)The Islanders. (P)Martin Denny.

ENCORE, CHERIE (1947) (w)Alice D. Simms (m)J. Fred Coots. (P)Tex Beneke and his Orchestra.

END, THE (1958) (wm)Sid Jacobson—Jimmy Krondes. (P)Earl Grant.

END, THE (1969) (wm)John Lennon—Paul McCartney. (P)The Beatles.

END OF A LOVE AFFAIR, THE (1950) (wm)Edward C. Redding. (I)Mabel Mercer. (P)Dinah Shore.

END OF OUR ROAD, THE (1968) (wm)Roger Penzabene—Barrett Strong—Norman Whitfield. (P)Gladys Knight and The Pips. (R)1970 by Marvin Gaye.

END OF THE WORLD, THE (1963) (w)Sylvia Dee (m)Arthur Kent. (P)Skeeter Davis.

ENDING WITH A KISS (1934) (w)Harlan Thompson (m)Lewis E. Gensler. (I)Film: *Melody In Spring*, by Lanny Ross.

ENDLESS LOVE (1981) (wm)Lionel Richie. (I)Film: *Endless Love* on soundtrack. (P)Diana Ross and Lionel Richie. No. 1 Chart Record.

ENDLESS SLEEP (1958) (wm)Jody Reynolds—Dolores Nance. (P)Jody Reynolds. (R)1964, by Hank Williams, Jr.

ENDLESS SUMMER NIGHTS(1987)(wm)Richard Marx.(P)Richard Marx.

ENDLESSLY (1959) (wm)Clyde Otis—Brook Benton. (P)Brook Benton. (R)1971 by Sonny James.

ENGINE, ENGINE NUMBER NINE (1965) (wm)Roger Miller. (P)Roger Miller.

ENGLAND SWINGS (1965) (wm)Roger Miller. (P)Roger Miller.

ENGLISH MUFFINS AND IRISH STEW (1956) (w)Bob Hilliard (m)Moose Charlap. (P)Sylvia Syms.

ENGLISH TEACHER, AN (1960) (w)Lee Adams (m)Charles Strouse. (I)Musical: *Bye Bye Birdie*, by Dick Van Dyke and Chita Rivera.

ENJOY YOURSELF (It's Later Than You Think) (1950) (w)Herb Magidson (m)Carl Sigman. (P)Guy Lombardo and his Royal Canadians. (CR)Doris Day.

ENJOY YOURSELF (1977) (wm)Kenny Gamble—Leon Huff. (P)The Jacksons.

ENTERTAINER, THE (1965) (wm)Tony Clarke. (P)Tony Clarke.

ENTERTAINER, THE (1903) (m)Scott Joplin. (I)Scott Joplin. (R)1973 Film: *The Entertainer*, piano performance by Marvin Hamlisch. (P)Marvin Hamlisch.

ENTERTAINER, THE (1974) (wm)Billy Joel. (P)Billy Joel.

ENVY (1948) (w)Eve London (m)David Gussin. (P)Fran Warren.

EPISTLE TO DIPPY (1967) (wm)Donovan Leitch. (P)Donovan.

EPISTROPHY (1942) (m)Thelonius Monk—Kenny Clarke—Cootie Williams. (P)Cootie Williams and his Orchestra.

ERES TU (Touch The Wind) (w-Eng)Jay Livingston-Ray Evans (m)Joan Calderon Lopes. (P)Mocedades.

ESCAPE (The Pina Colada Song) (wm)Rupert Holmes. (P)Rupert Holmes. No. 1 Chart Record.

ESO BESO (That Kiss) (1962) (wm)Joe Sherman—Noel Sherman. (P)Paul Anka.

ESPANA RHAPSODY (1884) (m)Emmanuel Chabrier. Famous classical composition.

ESPECIALLY FOR YOU (1938) (wm)Orrin Tucker—Phil Grogan. (I)Orrin Tucker and his Orchestra. (P)Jimmy Dorsey and his Orchestra.

ETERNALLY (Limelight) (1953) (w)Geoffrey Parsons (m)Charles Chaplin. (I)Film: *Limelight*, as soundtrack theme. (P)Frank Chacksfield and his Orchestra. Vocal version by Vic Damone.

EVANGELINE (1929) (w)Billy Rose (m)Al Jolson. (I)Film: *Evangeline*, by Dolores Del Rio.

EVE OF DESTRUCTION (1965) (wm)Phil F. Sloan (m)Steve Barri. (P)Barry McGuire. No. 1 Chart Record. (R)1970 by The Turtles.

EVELINA (1944) (w)E. Y. Harburg (m)Harold Arlen. (I)Musical: *Bloomer Girl*, by Celeste Holm and David Brooks.

EVEN NOW (1953) (wm)Richard Adler—Jerry Ross—Dan Howell. (P)Eddie Fisher.

EVEN NOW (1978) (w)Marty Panzer (m)Barry Manilow. (P)Barry Manilow.

EVEN NOW (1982) (wm)Bob Seger. (P)Bob Seger and The Silver Bullet Band.

EVEN THE NIGHTS ARE BETTER (1982) (wm)J. L. Wallace—Kenneth Bell—Terry Skinner. (P)Air Supply.

EVERYBODY HAVE FUN TONIGHT (1986) (wm)Wang Chung—Peter Wolf. (P)Wang Chung.

EVERYBODY'S GOT SOMETHING TO HIDE EXCEPT ME AND MY MONKEY (1968) (wm)John Lennon—Paul McCartney. (P)The Beatles.

EVERGREEN (1976) (w)Paul Williams (m)Barbra Streisand. (I)Film: *A Star Is Born*, by Barbra Streisand. (P)Barbra Streisand. No. 1 Chart Record. Academy Award Winner.

EVERLASTING LOVE (1967) (wm)James Cason—Mac Grayden. (P)Robert Knight. (R)1974 by Carl Carlton. (R)1981 by Rex Smith with Rachel Sweet.

EVERLASTING LOVE, AN (1978) (wm)Barry Gibb. (P)Andy Gibb.

EVERLOVIN' (1961) (wm)Dave Burgess. (I)Dave Burgess. (P)Rick Nelson.

EVERY BEAT OF MY HEART (wm)Johnny Otis. (P)The Pips. (R)1963 by James Brown.

EVERY BREATH YOU TAKE (1983) (wm)Gordon Sumner (Sting). (P)The Police. No. 1 Chart Record. NARAS

Award Winner.

EVERY DAY (1957) (wm)Buddy Holly—Norman Petty. (P)Buddy Holly. (R)1985 by James Taylor.

EVERY DAY I HAVE THE BLUES (1952) (wm)Peter Chatman. (P)Joe Williams with Count Basie and his Orchestra.

EVERY DAY IS LADIES DAY WITH ME (1906) (w)Henry Blossom (m)Victor Herbert. (I)Musical: *Blossom Time*.

EVERY DAY OF MY LIFE (1943) (wm)Morty Berk—Billy Hays—Harry James. (P)Harry James and his Orchestra, vocal by Frank Sinatra.

EVERY DAY OF MY LIFE (1956) (wm)Jimmie Crane—Al Jacobs. (P)The McGuire Sisters. (R)1972 by Bobby Vinton.

EVERY KINDA PEOPLE (1978) (wm)Andy Fraser. (P)Robert Palmer.

EVERY LITTLE KISS (1987) (wm)Bruce Hornsby (P)Bruce Hornsby and The Range.

EVERY LITTLE MOVEMENT (Has A Meaning All It's Own) (1910) (w)Otto Harbach (m)Karl Hoschna. (I)Musical: Madame Sherry. (R)1935 by Jimmy Dorsey and his Orchestra.

EVERY LITTLE THING (1964) (wm)John Lennon—Paul McCartney. (P)The Beatles.

EVERY LITTLE THING SHE DOES IS MAGIC (1981) (wm)Gordon Sumner (Sting). (P)The Police.

EVERY NOW AND THEN (1935) (wm)Al Sherman—Abner Silver—Al Lewis. (P)Ramona.

EVERY 1'S A WINNER (1979) (wm)Errol Brown. (P)Hot Chocolate.

EVERY STEP OF THE WAY (1962) (w)Al Stillman (m)Robert Allen. (P)Johnny Mathis.

EVERY TIME I FEEL THE SPIRIT (1865). Famous American Spiritual.

EVERY TIME I THINK OF YOU (1979) (wm)Ray Kennedy—Jack Conrad. (P)The Baby's.

EVERY TIME YOU GO AWAY (1985) (wm)Daryl Hall. (P)Paul Young. No. 1 Chart Record.

EVERY TIME YOU TOUCH ME (I Get High) (1976) (wm)Charlie Rich—Billy Sherrill. (P)Charlie Rich.

EVERY TUB (1938) (m)William Basie—Eddie Durham. (P)Count Basie and his Orchestra.

EVERY WHICH WAY BUT LOOSE (1978) (wm)Milton Brown—Stephen Dorff—Snuff Garrett. (I)Film: *Every Which Way But Loose*, by the voice of Eddie Rabbitt. (P)Eddie Rabbitt.

EVERY WOMAN IN THE WORLD (1981) (wm)Dominic Bugatti—Frank Musker. (P)Air Supply.

EVERYBODY (1963) (wm)Tommy Roe. (P)Tommy Roe.

EVERYBODY HAS A LAUGHING PLACE (1946) (w)Ray Gilbert (m)Allie Wrubel. (I)Film: *Song Of The South*, by Nicodemus Stewart and Johnny Lee.

EVERYBODY IS A STAR (1970) (wm)Sylvester Stewart. (P)Sly and The Family Stone.

EVERYBODY KNEW BUT ME (1946) (wm)Irving Berlin. (P)Woody Herman and his Orchestra.

EVERYBODY LOVES A CLOWN (1965) (wm)Gary Lewis—Thomas Lesslie—Leon Russell. (P)Gary Lewis and The Playboys.

EVERYBODY LOVES A LOVER (1958) (wm)Richard Adler—Jerry Ross. (P)Doris Day. (R)1963 by The Shirelles.

EVERYBODY LOVES ME BUT YOU (1962) (wm)Ronnie Self. (P)Brenda Lee.

EVERYBODY LOVES MY BABY, BUT MY BABY DON'T

LOVE NOBODY BUT ME (1924) (wm)Jack Palmer—Spencer Williams. (I)Clarence Williams' Blue Five, starring Louis Armstrong on trumpet. (P)Ruth Etting. (R)1955 Film: *Love Me Or Leave Me*, by Doris Day.

EVERYBODY LOVES SOMEBODY (1948) (w)Irving Taylor (m)Ken Lane. (I)Frank Sinatra. (P)Dean Martin. No. 1 Chart Record.

EVERYBODY NEEDS LOVE (1957) (wm)Eddie Holland—Norman Whitfield. (P)Gladys Knight and The Pips.

EVERYBODY NEEDS SOMEBODY TO LOVE (1964) (wm)Bert Berns—Solomon Burke—Jerry Wexler. (P)Solomon Burke. (R)1967 by Wilson Pickett.

EVERYBODY OUGHT TO HAVE A MAID (1962) (wm)Stephen Sondheim. (I)Musical: *A Funny Thing Happened On The Way To The Forum*, by Zero Mostel, David Burns, Jack Gilford, and John Carradine.

EVERYBODY PLAYS THE FOOL (1972) (wm)Kenneth Williams—Rudy Clark—Jim Bailey. (P)The Main Ingredient.

EVERYBODY SAYS DON'T (1964) (wm)Stephen Sondheim. (I)Musical: *Anyone Can Whistle*, by Harry Guardino.

EVERYBODY SING (1937) (w)Arthur Freed (m)Nacio Herb Brown. (I)Film: *Broadway Melody of 1938*, by Judy Garland. (P)Judy Garland.

EVERYBODY STEP (1921) (wm)Irving Berlin. (I)Revue: *Music Box Revue* by The Brox Sisters. (R)1938 Film: *Alexander's Ragtime Band*, by Ethel Merman. (R)1946 Film: *Blue Skies*, by Bing Crosby. Early recording by Paul Whiteman and his Orchestra.

EVERYBODY WANTS TO RULE THE WORLD (1985) (wm)Roy Orzabel—Ian Stanley—Chris Hughes. (P)Tears For Fears. No. 1 Chart Record.

EVERYBODY'S DOING IT (1911) (wm)Irving Berlin. (I)Musical: *Everybody's Doing It*. Recorded by Arthur Collins and Byron Harlan.

EVERYBODY'S EVERYTHING (1971) (wm)Carlos Santana—Milton Brown—Tyrone Moss. (P)Santana.

EVERYBODY'S GOT A HOME BUT ME (1955) (w)Oscar Hammerstein II (m)Richard Rodgers. (I)Musical: *Pipe Dream*, by Judy Tyler. (P)Eddie Fisher.

EVERYBODY'S GOT THE RIGHT TO LOVE (1970) (wm)Lou Stallman. (P)The Supremes.

EVERYBODY'S GOT TO LEARN SOMETIME (1980) (wm)James Warren. (P)Korgis.

EVERYBODY'S SOMEBODY'S FOOL (1960) (wm)Howard Greenfield—Jack Keller. (P)Connie Francis. No. 1 Chart Record.

EVERYBODY'S TALKIN (1969) (wm)Fred Neil. (I)Film: *Midnight Cowboy*, by voice of Nilsson. (P)Nilsson.

EVERYDAY PEOPLE (1969) (wm)Sylvester Stewart. (P)Sly and The Family Stone. No. 1 Chart Record. (R)1983 by Joan Jett and The Blackhearts.

EVERYDAY WITH YOU GIRL (1969) (wm)Buddy Buie—James B. Cobb. (P)The Classics IV. (CR)Dennis Yost.

EVERYONE'S GONE TO THE MOON (1965) (wm)Kenneth King. (P)Jonathan King.

EVERYTHING BUT YOU (1945) (wm)Don George—Duke Ellington—Harry James. (P)Duke Ellington and his Orchestra, vocal by Joya Sherrill.

EVERYTHING HAPPENS TO ME (1940) (w)Johnny Mercer (m)Hoagy Carmichael. (I)Musical: *Walk With Me*, by Frances Williams.

EVERYTHING HAPPENS TO ME (1941) (w)Tom Adair (m)Matt Dennis. (P)Tommy Dorsey and his Orchestra, vocal by Frank Sinatra.

EVERYTHING I HAVE IS YOURS (1933) (w)Harold Adamson (m)Burton Lane. (I)Film: *Dancing Lady*, by Joan Crawford and Art Jarrett. (P)Rudy Vallee. (CR)George Olsen and his Orchestra. (R)1948 by Billy Eckstine. (R)1952 by Eddie Fisher.

EVERYTHING IS BEAUTIFUL (1970) (wm)Ray Stevens. (P)Ray Stevens. No. 1 Chart Record.

EVERYTHING IS PEACHES DOWN IN GEORGIA (1918) (w)Grant Clarke (m)Milton Ager—George W. Meyer. (I)Prince's Orchestra.

EVERYTHING MAKES MUSIC WHEN YOU'RE IN LOVE (1965) (w)Sammy Cahn (m)Jimmy Van Heusen. (I)Film: *The Pleasure Seekers*, by Ann-Margret.

EVERYTHING SHE WANTS (1985) (wm)George Michael. (P)Wham! No. 1 Chart Record.

EVERYTHING THAT TOUCHES YOU (1968) (wm)Terry Kirkman. (P)The Association.

EVERYTHING'S ALRIGHT (1971) (w)Tim Rice (m)Andrew Lloyd Webber. (I)Musical: *Jesus Christ, Superstar*, by Ben Vereen, Yvonne Elliman, and Jeff Fenholt. In film version, by Yvonne Elliman.

EVERYTHING'S COMING UP ROSES (1959) (w)Stephen Sondheim (m)Jule Styne. (I)Musical: *Gypsy*, by Ethel Merman. In film version by the voice of Lisa Kirk dubbing for Rosalind Russell.

EVERYTHING'S GONNA BE ALL RIGHT (1936) (w)Benny Davis (m)Harry Akst. (I)Vaudeville, by Benny Davis. Recorded by The Ipana Troubadours.

EVERYTHING'S GREAT (1964) (w)Lee Adams (m)Charles Strouse. (I)Musical: *Golden Boy*, by Kenneth Tobey and Paula Wayne.

EVERYWHERE(1987)(wm)Christine McVie.(P)Fleetwood Mac.

EVERYWHERE YOU GO (1949) (wm)Larry Shay—Joe Goodwin—Mark Fisher. (P)Guy Lombardo and his Royal Canadians.

EVIL GAL BLUES (1944) (wm)Leonard Feather—Lionel Hampton. (P)Dinah Washington.

EVIL WAYS (1970) (wm)Clarence Henry. (P)Santana.

EVIL WOMAN (1969) (wm)Larry Wiegand—Richard Wiegand—David Waggoner. (P)Crow.

EVIL WOMAN (1975) (wm)Jeff Lynne. (P)Electric Light Orchestra.

EV'RY DAY (1935) (w)Irving Kahal (m)Sammy Fain. (I)Film: *Sweet Music*, by Rudy Vallee.

EV'RY DAY A HOLIDAY (1939) (wm)Cole Porter. (I)Musical: *Du Barry Was A Lady*, by Betty Grable and Charles Walters.

EV'RY DAY I LOVE YOU (Just A Little Bit More) (1948) (w)Sammy Cahn (m)Jule Styne. (I)Film: *Two Guys From Texas*, by Dennis Morgan.

EV'RY GIRL IS DIFF'RENT (1943) (w)Johnny Burke (m)Jimmy Van Heusen. (I)Film: *Belle Of The Yukon*.

EV'RY HOUR ON THE HOUR (1945) (w)Don George (m)Duke Ellington. (P)Duke Ellington and his Orchestra, vocal by Al Hibbler.

EV'RY NIGHT ABOUT THIS TIME (1942) (w)Ted Koehler (m)James V. Monaco. (P)The Ink Spots. (CR)Kay Kyser and his Orchestra.

EV'RY STREET'S A BOULEVARD IN OLD NEW YORK (1953) (w)Bob Hilliard (m)Jule Styne. (I)Musical: *Hazel Flagg*, by Jack Whiting.

EV'RY SUNDAY AFTERNOON (1940) (w)Lorenz Hart (m)Richard Rodgers. (I)Musical: *Higher and Higher*, by Marta Eggert and Leif Erickson.

EV'RY TIME (1941) (wm)Hugh Martin—Ralph Blane. (I)Musical: *Best Foot Forward*, by Maureen Cannon. Reprised by Rosemary Lane. In film version, by Virginia Weidler.

EV'RY TIME WE SAY GOODBYE (1944) (wm)Cole Porter. (I)Revue: *Seven Lively Arts*, by Nan Wynn and Jere McMahon. Recorded by Benny Goodman and his Orchestra.

EV'RYONE SAYS "I LOVE YOU" (1932) (w)Bert Kalmar (m)Harry Ruby. (I)Film: *Horse Feathers*, by The Marx Brothers.

EV'RYTHING BEAUTIFUL (1961) (wm)Jay Livingston—Ray Evans. (I)Musical: *Let It Ride*, by George Gobel and The Birthday Girls.

EV'RYTHING I LOVE (1941) (wm)Cole Porter. (I)Musical: *Let's Face It*, by Danny Kaye and Mary Jane Walsh.

EV'RYTHING IS HOTSY TOTSY NOW (1925) (wm)Jimmy McHugh—Irving Mills. (I)The Hotsy Totsy Boys (Jimmy McHugh and Irving Mills).

EV'RYTHING I'VE GOT (1942) (w)Lorenz Hart (m)Richard Rodgers. (I)Musical: *By Jupiter*, by Ray Bolger and Benay Venuta.

EXACTLY LIKE YOU (1930) (w)Dorothy Fields (m)Jimmy McHugh. (I)Revue: *Lew Leslie's International Review*, by Gertrude Lawrence and Harry Richman. (P)Harry Richman. (CR)Ruth Etting. (R)1936 by Benny Goodman.

EXODUS (1960) (m)Ernest Gold. (I)Film: *Exodus* as main theme. (P)Ferrante and Teicher. Lyrics written in 1961 by Pat Boone under the title: This Land Is Mine. (R)Pat Boone. NARAS Award Winner.

EXPERIENCE (1947) (w)Johnny Burke (m)Jimmy Van Heusen. (I)Film: *Road To Rio*, by Bing Crosby and Dorothy Lamour.

EXPERIENCE UNNECESSARY (1955) (wm)Gladys Shelley—Hugo Peretti—Luigi Creatore. (P)Sarah Vaughan.

EXPERIMENT (1933) (wm)Cole Porter. (I)London Musical: *Nymph Errant*, by Gertrude Lawrence.

EXPLOSION IN MY SOUL (1967) (wm)Kenny Gamble—Leon Huff. (P)The Soul Survivors.

EXPRESS (1975) (wm)Louis Risbrook—Barbara Lomas—William Risbrook—Orlando Woods—Richard Thompson—Carlos Ward—Dennis Rowe. (P)B. T. Express.

EXPRESS YOURSELF (1970) (wm)Charles Wright. (P)The Watts 103rd Street Band.

EXPRESSWAY TO YOUR HEART (1967) (wm)Kenny Gamble—Leon Huff. (P)The Soul Survivors.

EYES OF A NEW YORK WOMAN, THE (1968) (wm)Mark James. (P)B. J. Thomas.

EYE IN THE SKY (1982) (wm)Eric Woolfson—Alan Parsons. (P)The Alan Parsons Project.

EYE OF THE TIGER (1982) (wm)Frank Sullivan—Jim Peterik. (I)Film: *Rocky III*, by Survivor. (P)Survivor. No. 1 Chart Record.

EYES OF LAURA MARS (Prisoner) (1978) (I)Film: *The Eyes of Laura Mars*, by Barbra Streisand on soundtrack. (P)Barbra Streisand.

EYES OF LOVE, THE (1967) (w)Bob Russell (m)Quincy Jones. (I)Film: *Banning* on soundtrack.

EYES WITHOUT A FACE (1984) (wm)Billy Idol—Steve Stevens. (P)Billy Idol.

EYES OF TEXAS, THE (1903) (w)John L. Sinclair. Melody based on I've Been Working On The Railroad. Marching song of The University of Texas.

FA-FA-FA-FA-FA (1966) (Sad Song) (wm)Otis Redding—Steve Cropper. (P)Otis Redding.

FABLE OF THE ROSE, THE (1940) (w)Bickley Reichner (m)Josef Myrow. (P)Benny Goodman and his Orchestra, vocal by Helen Forrest.

FABULOUS (1957) (wm)Jon Sheldon—Harry Land. (P)Charlie Gracie. (CR)Steve Lawrence.

FABULOUS CHARACTER (1956) (wm)Bennie Benjamin—Sol Marcus. (P)Sarah Vaughan.

FACE IN THE CROWD, A (1957) (w)Budd Schulberg (m)Tom Glazer. (I)Film: *A Face In The Crowd*, by Andy Griffith.

FACE IT GIRL, IT'S OVER (1968) (w)Frank H. Stanton (m)Andy Badale. (P)Nancy Wilson.

FACE ON THE DIME, THE (1946) (wm)Harold Rome. (I)Revue: *Call Me Mister*, by Lawrence Winters.

FACE TO FACE (1953) (w)Sammy Cahn (m)Sammy Fain. (I)Film: *Three Sailors And A Girl*, by Jane Powell and Gordon MacRae.

FACTORY GIRL (1968) (wm)Mick Jagger—Keith Richard. (P)The Rolling Stones.

FACTS OF LIFE, THE (1960) (wm)Johnny Mercer. (I)Film: *The Facts Of Life*, by Steve Lawrence and Eydie Gorme on soundtrack.

FADE AWAY (1981) (wm)Bruce Springsteen. (P)Bruce Springsteen.

FADE AWAY AND RADIATE (1978) (wm)Chris Stein. (P)Blondie.

FADE OUT-FADE IN (1964) (w)Betty Comden—Adolph Green (m)Jule Styne. (I)Musical: *Fade Out—Fade In*, by Carol Burnett and Dick Patterson.

FADED SUMMER LOVE (1931) (wm)Phil Baxter. (P)Paul Whiteman and his Orchestra. (CR)Bing Crosby.

FANTAISIE IMPROMPTU (1855) (m)Frederic Chopin. Famous classical piano selection.

FAIR AND WARMER (1934) (w)Al Dubin (m)Harry Warren. (I)Film: *Twenty Million Sweethearts*, by Dick Powell with Ted Fiorito and his Orchestra.

FAIR WARNING (1959) (wm)Harold Rome. (I)Musical: *Destry Rides Again*, by Dolores Gray.

FAIRYTALE (1974) (wm)Anita and Bonnie Pointer. (P)The Pointer Sisters.

FAITH (1987) (wm)George Michael. (P)George Michael. No. 1 Chart Record.

FAITH CAN MOVE MOUNTAINS (1952) (w)Ben Raleigh (m)Guy Wood. (P)Nat "King" Cole. (CR)Johnnie Ray.

FAITHFUL FOREVER (1939) (wm)Leo Robin—Ralph Rainger. (I)Cartoon Film: *Gulliver's Travels*, by the voices of Lanny Ross and Jessica Dragonette. Recorded by Glenn Miller and his Orchestra.

FAITHFULLY (1983) (wm)Jonathan Cain. (P)Journey.

FAKIN' IT (1967) (wm)Paul Simon. (P)Simon and Garfunkel.

FALL IN LOVE WITH ME (1983) (wm)Maurice White—D. Vaughn—Wayne Vaughn. (P)Earth, Wind, and Fire.

FALLEN STAR, A (1957) (wm)James Joiner. (P)Nick Noble. (CR)Jimmy Newman. (CR)Ferlin Husky.

FALLIN' (1958) (w)Howard Greenfield (m)Neil Sedaka. (P)Connie Francis.

FALLIN' IN LOVE (Again) (1975) (wm)Danny and Ann Hamilton. (P)Hamilton, Joe Frank & Reynolds. No. 1 Chart Record.

FALLING (1978) (wm)Lenny Le Blanc—Edward Struzick. (P)Leblanc & Carr.

FALLING IN LOVE AGAIN (Can't Help It) (1930) (w-Eng)Sammy Lerner (m)Frederick Hollander. (I)Film: *The Blue Angel*, by Marlene Dietrich. (P)Marlene Dietrich.

FALLING IN LOVE WITH LOVE (1938) (w)Lorenz Hart (m)Richard Rodgers. (I)Musical: *The Boys From Syracuse*, by Muriel Angelus. In film version, by Allan Jones. Recorded by Frances Langford.

FALLING LEAVES (1940) (w)Mack David (m)Frankie Carle. (I)Horace Heidt and his Orchestra. (P)Glenn Miller and his Orchestra.

FAME (1975) (wm)John Lennon—David Bowie—Carlos Alomar. (P)David Bowie. No. 1 Chart Record.

FAME (1980) (w)Dean Pitchford (m)Michael Gore. (I)Film: *Fame*, by Irene Cara. (P)Irene Cara. NARAS Award Winner.

FAME AND FORTUNE (1960) (w)Fred Wise (m)Ben Weisman. (P)Elvis Presley.

FAMILY AFFAIR (1971) (wm)Sylvester Stewart. (P)Sly and The Family Stone. No. 1 Chart Record.

FAMILY MAN (1983) (wm)Mike Oldfield—Morris Pert—Tim Cross—Rick Fenn—Mike Frey—Maggie Reilly. (P)Hall and Oates.

FAMILY OF MAN (1972) (w)Paul Williams (m)Jack S. Conrad. (P)Three Dog Night.

FAN IT (1929) (wm)Frankie Jaxon—Dan Howell. (I)Frankie "Half Pint" Jaxon. (R)1945 by Woody Herman and his Orchestra.

FAN TAN FANNIE (1958) (w)Oscar Hammerstein II (m)Richard Rodgers. (I)Musical: *Flower Drum Song*, by Anita Ellis.

FAN THE FLAME (1964) (w)Earl Shuman (m)Leon Carr. (I)Musical: *The Secret Life Of Walter Mitty*, by Cathryn Damon.

FANCY (1969) (wm)Bobbie Gentry. (P)Bobbie Gentry.

FANCY FREE (1950) (w)Johnny Mercer (m)Harold Arlen. (I)Film: *The Pretty Girl*.

FANCY MEETING YOU (1936) (w)E. Y. Harburg (m)Harold Arlen. (I)Film: *Stage Struck*, by Dick Powell and Jeanne Madden. Recorded by Russ Morgan and his Orchestra.

FANCY OUR MEETING (1928) (w)Douglas Furber (m)Joseph Meyer—Philip Charig. (I)London Musical: *That's A Good Girl*, by Jack Buchanan and Elsie Randolph. American Revue: *Wake Up And Dream*, by Jessie Matthews and Jack Buchanan.

FANNY (1954) (wm)Harold Rome. (I)Musical: *Fanny*, by William Tabbert. (P)Eddie Fisher. (CR)Fred Waring's Pennsylvanians.

FANNY (Be Tender With My Love) (1976) (wm)Barry, Maurice, and Robin Gibb. (P)The Bee Gees.

FANTASY (1978) (wm)Maurice White—Verdine White—Eddie de Barrio. (P)Earth, Wind, and Fire.

FAR AWAY (1926) (w)Otto Harbach—Oscar Hammerstein II (m)Herbert Stothart—George Gershwin. (I)Operetta: *Song Of The Flame*, by Greek Evans and The Russian Art Choir.

FAR AWAY PLACES (1949) (wm)Joan Whitney—Alex Kramer. (P)Bing Crosby. (CR)Perry Como. (CR)Dinah Shore.

FAR, FAR AWAY (1938) (wm)Cole Porter. (I)Musical: *Leave It To Me*, by Tamara and William Gaxton.

FAR FROM OVER (1983) (wm)Frank Stallone—Vince DiCola. (I)Film: *Staying Alive*, by Frank Stallone on soundtrack. (P)Frank Stallone.

FAR FROM THE HOME I LOVE (1964) (w)Sheldon Harnick (m)Jerry Bock. (I)Musical: *Fiddler On The Roof*, by Zero Mostel and Julia Migenes.

FARAWAY BOY (1960) (wm)Frank Loesser. (I)Musical: *Greenwillow*, by Ellen McCown.

FARAWAY PART OF TOWN, THE (1960) (w)Dory Langdon (m)Andre Previn. (I)Film: *Pepe*, by Judy Garland on soundtrack. (P)Judy Garland.

FARE THEE WELL ANNABELLE (1934) (w)Mort Dixon (m)Allie Wrubel. (I)Film: *Sweet Music*, by Rudy Vallee. (P)Glen Gray and The Casa Loma Orchestra. (CR)Guy Lombardo and his Royal Canadians.

FARE-THEE-WELL TO HARLEM (1934) (w)Johnny Mercer (m)Bernie Hanighen. (P)Johnny Mercer and Jack Teagarden, with Paul Whiteman and his Orchestra.

FAREWELL (1964) (wm)Bob Dylan. (P)Bob Dylan.

FAREWELL AMANDA (1949) (wm)Cole Porter. (I)Film: *Adam's Rib*, by David Wayne.

FAREWELL, ANGELINA (1965) (wm)Bob Dylan. (P)Joan Baez.

FAREWELL BLUES (1923) (wm)Elmer Schoebel—Paul Mares—Leon Rappolo. (I)New Orleans Rhythm Kings. (CR)Isham Jones and his Orchestra. (CR)Ted Lewis.

FAREWELL, MY LOVELY (1935) (w)Howard Dietz (m)Arthur Schwartz. (I)Musical: *At Home Abroad*, by Woods Miller and The Continentals.

FAREWELL TO ARMS,A (Love Theme) (1957) (m)Mario Nascimbene. (I)Film: *A Farewell To Arms* as soundtrack theme.

FAREWELL TO ARMS (1933) (wm)Allie Wrubel—Abner Silver. Promo song for Film: *A Farewell To Arms*. Recorded by Paul Whiteman and his Orchestra.

FARMER AND THE COWMAN, THE (1943) (w)Oscar Hammerstein II (m)Richard Rodgers. (I)Musical: *Oklahoma!*, by Alfred Drake, Ralph Riggs, Betty Garde, Lee Dixon, and Celeste Holm. (R)1955 Film: *Oklahoma!*, by Gordon MacRae, Charlotte Greenwood, Gene Nelson, Jay C. Flippen, James Whitmore, and Gloria Grahame.

FARMING (1941) (wm)Cole Porter. (I)Musical: *Let's Face It*, by Danny Kaye, Benny Baker, Jack Williams, Sunny O'Dea, and Nanette Fabray.

FASCINATING RHYTHM (1924) (w)Ira Gershwin (m)George Gershwin. (I)Musical: *Lady Be Good!*, by Fred and Adele Astaire and Cliff Edwards. First recording by Cliff Edwards. (R)1945 Film: *Rhapsody In Blue*, by Hazel Scott.

FASCINATION (1957) (w-Eng)Dick Manning (m)F. D. Marchetti. (I)Film: *Love In The Afternoon*, as soundtrack theme. (P)Jane Morgan. (CR)Dick Jacobs and his Orchestra.

(Keep Feeling)FASCINATION (1983) (wm)Phil Oakey—Jo Callis. (P)The Human League.

FAT MAN,THE (195) (w)Antoine Domino (m)Dave Bartholomew. (P)Fats Domino.

FAT MEAT IS GOOD MEAT (1947) (wm)Irene Higginbotham. (P)Savannah Churchill.

FATE (1953) (wm)Robert Wright—George Forrest. Adapted from a theme by Borodin. (I)Musical: *Kismet*, by Alfred Drake and Doretta Morrow.

FATHER FIGURE (1987) (wm)George Michael. (P)George Michael. No. 1 Chart Record.

F. D. R. JONES (1938) (wm)Harold Rome. (I)Revue: *Sing Out The News*, by Rex Ingram.

FEATHERY FEELIN' THE (1948) (wm)Frank Loesser. (P)Freddy Martin and his Orchestra. (CR)Gordon MacRae.

FEED THE BIRDS (Tuppence A Bag) (1963) (wm)Richard M. Sherman (m)Robert B. Sherman. (I)Film: *Mary Poppins*, by Julie Andrews and The Chorus.

FEEL LIKE MAKIN' LOVE (1974) (wm)Gene McDaniels. (P)Roberta Flack. No. 1 Chart Record.

FEEL LIKE MAKIN' LOVE (1975) (wm)Michael Ralphs—Paul Rodgers. (P)Bad Company.

(I)FEEL SO BAD (1961) (wm)Sam "Lightnin" Hopkins. (P)Elvis Presley. (R)1967 by Little Milton. (R)1971 by Ray Charles.

FEEL SO FINE (1960) (wm)Leonard Lee. (P)Johnny Preston.

FEELIN' ALRIGHT (1968) (wm)David Mason. (P)Joe Cocker (R)1971 by Grand Funk Railroad.

FEELIN' HIGH (1934) (w)Howard Dietz (m)Walter Donaldson. (I)Film: *Hollywood Party*, by Shirley Ross and Harry Barris.

FEELIN' NO PAIN (1927) (m)Fud Livingston. (P)Red Nichols and his Five Pennies.

FEELIN' STRONGER EVERY DAY (1973) (wm)Peter Cetera—James Pankow. (P)Chicago.

FEELING GOOD (1964) (wm)Leslie Bricusse—Anthony Newley. (I)Musical: *The Roar Of The Greasepaint—The Smell Of The Crowd*, by Gilbert Price and The Urchins. (P)Joe Sherman and The Arena Brass.

FEELING I'M FALLING (1928) (w)Ira Gershwin (m)George Gershwin. (I)Musical: *Treasure Girl*, by Gertrude Lawrence and Paul Frawley.

FEELINGS (1975) (wm)Morris Albert—Mauricio Kaiserman. (P)Morris Albert. (R)1977 by Walter Jackson.

FEELS LIKE THE FIRST TIME (1977) (wm)Michael Jones. (P)Foreigner.

FEELS SO GOOD (1978) (wm)Chuck Mangione. (P)Chuck Mangione.

FEET UP (Pat Him On The Po-Po) (1952) (wm)Bob Merrill. (P)Guy Mitchell with Mitch Miller.

FELLA WITH AN UMBRELLA (1947) (wm)Irving Berlin. (I)Film: *Easter Parade*, by Judy Garland and Peter Lawford. (P)Bing Crosby.

FELLOW NEEDS A GIRL, A (1947) (w)Oscar Hammerstein II (m)Richard Rodgers. (I)Musical: *Allegro*, by William Ching and Annamary Dickey.

FELLOW ON A FURLOUGH,A (1943) (wm)Bobby Worth. (I)Albert Sack and his Orchestra. Film: *Meet Miss Bobby Sox*, by Bob Crosby.

FEMININITY (1958) (wm)Jay Livingston—Ray Evans. (I)Musical: *Oh Captain!*, by Abbe Lane.

FERDINAND THE BULL (1938) (w)Larry Morey (m)Albert Hay Malotte. (I)Cartoon Film: *Ferdinand The Bull*, by the voice of Sterling Holloway.

FERNANDO (1976) (wm)Benny Andersson—Stig Anderson—Bjorn Ulvaeus. (P)Abba.

FERRY BOAT SERENADE (1940) (w-Eng)Harold Adamson (m)E. di Lazzaro. (I)Gray Gordon and his Orchestra. (P)The Andrews Sisters. No. 1 Chart Record.

FERRY CROSS THE MERSEY (1964) (wm)Gerry Marsden. (I)British Film: *Ferry Cross The Mersey*, by Gerry and The Pacemakers. (P)Gerry and The Pacemakers.

FEUDIN' AND FIGHTIN' (1947) (wm)Al Dubin—Burton

Lane. (I)Revue: *Laffing Room Only*, by Pat Brewster. (P)Dorothy Shay. (CR)Jo Stafford.

FEVER (1956) (wm)John Davenport—Eddie Cooley. (P)Little Willie John. (R)1958 by Peggy Lee. (R)1965 by The McCoys. (R)1973 by Rita Coolidge.

FIDDLE FADDLE (1947) (m)Leroy Anderson. (P)Leroy Anderson and his Orchestra.

FIDDLER ON THE ROOF (1964) (m)Sheldon Harnick—Jerry Bock. (I)Musical: *Fiddler On The Roof*, as theme music.

FIDGETY FEET (1926) (w)Ira Gershwin (m)George Gershwin. (I)Musical: *Oh, Kay!*, by Harland Dixon and Marion Fairbanks. Recorded by Fletcher Henderson and his Orchestra.

FIE ON GOODNESS (1960) (w)Alan Jay Lerner (m)Frederick Loewe. (I)Musical: *Camelot*, by John Cullum, James Gannon and Bruce Yarnell.

FIFI (1937) (wm)Sam Coslow. (I)Film: *Every Day's A Holiday*, by Mae West.

FIFTEEN MINUTE INTERMISSION (1940) (wm)Sunny Skylar—Bette Cannon. (P)Cab Calloway and his Orchestra.

FIFTH OF BEETHOVEN, A (1976) (m)Walter Murphy. Adapted from Beethoven's Fifth Symphony. (P)Walter Murphy and The Big Apple Band. No. 1 Chart Record.

FIFTY MILLION FRENCHMEN CAN'T BE WRONG (1927) (w)Billy Rose—Willie Raskin (m)Fred Fisher. (P)Sophie Tucker.

59th STREET BRIDGE SONG, THE (Feelin' Groovy) (1966) (wm)Paul Simon. (P)Simon and Garfunkel. (CR)Harper's Bizarre.

FIFTY WAYS TO LEAVE YOUR LOVER (1976) (wm)Paul Simon. (P)Paul Simon. No. 1 Chart Record.

FIGHT THE POWER (Part 1) (1975) (wm)Ernest Isley—Marvin Isley—O'Kelly Isley—Ronald Isley—Rudolph Isley. (P)The Isley Brothers.

FINAL COUNTDOWN,THE (1987) (wm)J. Tempest. (P)Europe.

FINALLY GOT MYSELF TOGETHER (I'm A Changed Man) (1974) (wm)Edward Townshend. (P)The Impressions.

FIND ANOTHER FOOL (1982) (wm)Marv Ross. (P)Quarterflash.

FIND ANOTHER GIRL (1961) (wm)Jerry Butler—Curtis Mayfield. (P)Jerry Butler.

FIND ME A PRIMITIVE MAN (1929) (wm)Cole Porter. (I)Musical: *Fifty Million Frenchmen*, by Evelyn Hoey. Recorded by Libby Holman.

FIND YOURSELF A MAN (1964) (w)Bob Merrill (m)Jule Styne. (I)Musical: *Funny Girl*, by Kay Medford, Jean Stapleton, and Danny Meehan.

FINDING WORDS FOR SPRING (1965) (wm)Marian Grudeff—Raymond Jessel. (I)Musical: *Baker Street*, by Inga Swenson.

FINE AND DANDY (1930) (w)Paul James (m)Kay Swift. (I)Musical: *Fine And Dandy*, by Joe Cook and Alice Boulden.

FINE AND MELLOW (1940) (wm)Billie Holiday. (P)Billie Holiday.

FINE BROWN FRAME (1944) (wm)Guadalupe Cartiero—J. Mayo Williams. (I)Buddy Johnson and his Orchestra, vocal by Arthur Prysock. (R)1948 by Nellie Lutcher.

FINE ROMANCE, A (1936) (w)Dorothy Fields (m)Jerome Kern. (I)Film: *Swing Time*, by Fred Astaire and Ginger Rogers. (P)Fred Astaire. No. 1 Chart Record. (CR)Billie Holiday. (CR)Guy Lombardo and his Royal Canadians.

FINER THINGS, THE (1986) (wm)Steve Winwood—W. Jennings. (P)Steve Winwood.

FINGER POPPIN' TIME (1960) (wm)Hank Ballard. (P)Hank Ballard and The Midnighters.

FINGERTIPS (1963) (wm)Henry Cosby—Clarence Paul. (P)Little Stevie Wonder.

FINI (1953) (wm)Richard Adler—Jerry Ross. (I)Revue: *John Murray Anderson's Almanac*, by Polly Bergen. (P)Eydie Gorme.

FINISHING THE HAT (1983) (wm)Stephen Sondheim. (I)Musical: *Sunday In The Park With George*, by Mandy Patinkin.

FINLANDIA (1901) (m)Jean Sibelius. Famous classical composition.

FINS (1979) (wm)Jimmy Buffett—Barry Chance—Tom Corcoran—Deborah McColl. (P)Jimmy Buffett.

FIRE (1967) (wm)Jimi Hendrix. (I)Jimi Hendrix. (P)Five By Five.

FIRE (1974) (wm)Jim Williams—Clarence Satchell—Leroy Bonner—Marshall Jones—William Beck—Ralph Middlebrooks—Marvin Pierce. (P)Ohio Players. No. 1 Chart Record.

FIRE (1979) (wm)Bruce Springsteen. (P)The Pointer Sisters.

FIRE AND RAIN (1970) (wm)James Taylor. (P)James Taylor. (CR)Johnny Rivers.

FIREBIRD BALLET SUITE (1911) (m)Igor Stravinsky. Famous classical composition.

FIRE LAKE (1980) (wm)Bob Seger. (P)Bob Seger.

FIREFLY (1958) (w)Carolyn Leigh (m)Cy Coleman. (P)Tony Bennett.

FIREWORKS (1960) (w)Betty Comden—Adolph Green (m)Jule Styne. (I)Musical: *Do Re Mi*, by Nancy Dussault and John Reardon.

FIRST BORN (1956) (wm)John Lehman. (P)Tennessee Ernie Ford.

FIRST CUT IS THE DEEPEST, THE (1968) (wm)Cat Stevens. (P)Keith Hampshire. (R)1977 by Rod Stewart.

FIRST DATE, FIRST KISS, FIRST LOVE (1957) (wm)Mary Stovall—Dan Welch. (P)Sonny James.

FIRST LADY, THE (1962) (wm)Irving Berlin. (I)Musical: *Mr. President*, by Nanette Fabray.

FIRST NAME INITIAL (1959) (wm)Aaron Schroeder—Martin Kalmanoff. (P)Annette.

FIRST NOEL, THE (1833). Traditional English Christmas Carol.

FIRST OF MAY (1969) (wm)Robin, Maurice, and Barry Gibb. (P)The Bee Gees.

FIRST TIME EVER I SAW YOUR FACE, THE (1962) (wm)Ewan Mac Coll. (I)Kitty White. (P)1972 by Roberta Flack. No. 1 Chart Record. NARAS Award Winner.

FIRST TIME I SAW YOU, THE (1937) (wm)Allie Wrubel—Nathaniel Shilkret. (I)Film: *The Toast Of New York*, by Frances Farmer. Recorded by Bunny Berigan and his Orchestra.

FIRST TIME IT HAPPENS,THE (1981) (wm)Joe Raposo. (I)Film: *The Great Muppet Caper*.

FIRST YOU HAVE ME HIGH (Then You Have Me Low) (1935) (w)Lew Brown (m)Harold Arlen. (I)Film: *Strike Me Pink*, by Ethel Merman.

FISH, THE (1961) (wm)Kal Mann—Bernie Lowe—Dave

Appell. (P)Bobby Rydell.

FISHIN' HOLE, THE (1961) (w)Everett Sloane (m)Earle Hagen—Herb Spencer. (I)TV Series: Theme of *The Andy Griffith Show*.

FIT AS A FIDDLE (1932) (wm)Arthur Freed—Al Hoffman—Al Goodhart. (I)Revue: *George White's Music Hall Varieties*, by Harry Richman. Recorded by Fred Waring's Pennsylvanians. (R)1952 Film: *Singin' In The Rain*, by Gene Kelly and Donald O'Connor.

FIVE FOOT TWO, EYES OF BLUE (Has Anybody Seen My Girl) (1925) (w)Sam M. Lewis—Joe Young (m)Ray Henderson. (P)Gene Austin. No. 1 Chart Record.

FIVE GUYS NAMED MOW (1941) (w)Larry Wynn (m)Jerry Bresler. (P)Louis Jordan and his Tympani Five.

500 MILES AWAY FROM HOME (1963) (w)Bobby Bare—Hedy West (m)Charlie Williams—Hedy West. (P)Bobby Bare. (R)1972 by Heaven Bound with Tony Scotti.

FIVE MINUTES MORE (1940) (w)Sammy Cahn (m)Jule Styne. (I)Film: *Sweetheart Of Sigma Chi*, by Phil Brito. (P)Frank Sinatra. No. 1 Chart Record.

FIVE OAKS (see Cinco Robles)

FIVE O'CLOCK WHISTLE (1940) (wm)Josef Myrow—Kim Gannon—Gene Irwin. (P)Glenn Miller and his Orchestra. (CR)Ella Fitzgerald. (CR)Erskine Hawkins and his Orchestra.

FIVE O'CLOCK WORLD (1965) (wm)Allen Reynolds. (P)The Vogues.

FIVE PENNIES (1927) (m)Red Nichols. (P)Red Nichols and his Five Pennies.

FIVE SALTED PEANUTS (1945) (wm)Charlie Abbott. (P)Tony Pastor and his Orchestra.

5-10-15-20 (25-30 Years Of Love) (1970) (wm)Walter Boyd—Archie Powell. (P)The Presidents.

FIVE ZEROS (1978) (w)Betty Comden—Adolph Green (m)Jule Styne. (I)Musical: *On The Twentieth Century*, by Imogene Coca, John Cullum, George Coe and Dean Dittman.

FIXING A HOLE (1967) (wm)John Lennon—Paul McCartney. (P)The Beatles.

FLAMIN' MAMIE (1925) (wm)Fred Rose—Paul Whiteman. (P)Paul Whiteman and his Orchestra.

FLAMING YOUTH (1929) (m)Duke Ellington. (P)Duke Ellington and his Cotton Club Orchestra.

FLAMINGO (1941) (w)Ed Anderson (m)Ted Grouya. (P)Duke Ellington and his Orchestra, vocal by Herb Jeffries. (R)1966 by Herb Alpert and The Tijuana Brass.

FLAPPERETTE (1926) (m)Jesse Greer. (P)Vincent Lopez and his Orchestra. (CR)Nat Shilkret and his Orchestra.

FLASHDANCE (What A Feeling) (1983) (w)Keith Forsey—Irene Cara (m)Giorgio Moroder. (I)Film: *Flashdance*, by Irene Cara. (P)Irene Cara. No. 1 Chart Record. Academy Award Winner.

FLASH LIGHT (1978) (wm)George Clinton—Bernie Worrell—William Collins. (P)Parliament.

FLAT FOOT FLOOGIE, THE (1938) (wm)Slim Gaillard—Slam Stewart—Bud Green. (P)Slim and Slam. (CR)Wingy Mannone. (CR)Benny Goodman and his Orchestra. (CR)The Mills Brothers.

FLEET'S IN, THE (1942) (w)Johnny Mercer (m)Victor Schertzinger. (I)Film: *The Fleet's In*, by Betty Jane Rhodes.

FLIGHT OF THE BUMBLE BEE (1900) (m)N. Rimsky-Korsakov. Famous classical composition usually performed by a solo instrument. (R)1940 by Harry James as a trumpet solo with his Orchestra.

FLIM FLAM MAN (1966) (wm)Laura Nyro. (P)Laura Nyro. (R)1971 by Barbra Streisand.

FLIP FLOP AND FLY (1955) (wm)Charles Calhoun—Lou Willie Turner. (P)Joe Turner.

FLIRTATION WALK (1934) (wm)Mort Dixon—Allie Wrubel. (I)Film: *Flirtation Walk*, by Dick Powell and Ruby Keeler. (P)Dick Powell. (CR)Victor Young and his Orchestra.

FLOAT ON (1977) (wm)Arnold Ingram—James Mitchell, Jr. —Marvin Willis. (P)The Floaters.

FLORIDA, THE MOON AND YOU (1926) (w)Gene Buck (m)Rudolf Friml. (I)Revue: *No Foolin'* by Peggy Fears.

FLOW GENTLY, SWEET AFTON (1838) (w)Robert Burns (m)James E. Spilman. Well known Scottish folk song. Early recording by Henry Burr.

FLOWERS FOR MADAME (1935) (wm)Charlie Tobias—Charles Newman—Murray Mencher. (P)Ray Noble and his Orchestra.

FLOWERS MEAN FORGIVENESS (1956) (wm)Al Frisch—Mack Wolfson—Edward R. White. (P)Frank Sinatra.

FLOWERS ON THE WALL (1965) (wm)Lewis DeWitt. (P)The Statler Brothers.

FLOY JOY (1972) (wm)William Robinson, Jr. (P)The Supremes.

WILLIAM "SMOKEY" ROBINSON

Alonzo Tucker was a successful composer who wrote a number of songs for Jackie Wilson. Until the day he died, Alonzo swore to the veracity of the following story.

After Berry Gordy, Jr. had just started Motown, his office was in the same building and on the same floor on which Nate Tarnapol had his office. Tucker claimed he was walking on the street and bumped into somebody called Smokey Robinson, who said he was looking for a record deal. Tucker's story is that he directed Robinson to Tarnapol's office but that Robinson made an error and walked into the Motown office. Gordy promptly signed him to a contract, and the rest is history.

FLY, THE (1961) (wm)John Madera—Dave White. (P)Chubby Checker.

FLY AWAY (1976) (wm)John Denver. (P)John Denver.

FLY LIKE AN EAGLE (1977) (wm)Steve Miller. (P)The Steve Miller Band.

FLY ME TO THE MOON (In Other Words) (1954) (wm)Bart Howard. (I)Felicia Sanders. (R)1963 by Joe Harnell. (R)1965 by Tony Bennett. (R)1969 by Bobby Womack.

FLY, ROBIN, FLY (1975) (wm)Sylvester Levay—Stephen Prager. (P)Silver Convention. No. 1 Chart Record.

FLYING (1968) (wm)John Lennon—Paul McCartney—George Harrison—Ringo Starr. (P)The Beatles.

FLYING DOWN TO RIO (1933) (w)Gus Kahn—Edward Eliscu (m)Vincent Youmans. (I)Film: *Flying Down To Rio*, by Fred Astaire and The Chorus. First recording by Rudy Vallee and his Orchestra.

FLYING DUTCHMAN (Overture) (1844) (m)Richard Wagner. Famous operatic overture.

FLYING HOME (1941) (w)Sid Robin (m)Benny Goodman—Lionel Hampton. (P)Benny Goodman and his Orchestra. Theme song of Lionel Hampton and his Orchestra.

FM (No Static At All) (1978) (wm)Walter Becker—Donald Fagen. (I)Film: *FM*, by Steely Dan. (P)Steely Dan.

FOG AND THE GROG, THE (1961) (wm)Robert Wright—George Forrest. (I)Musical: *Kean, by Chris Hewitt*, Robert Penn, Arthur Rubin, Alfred Drake and The Ensemble.

FOGGY DAY, A (1937) (w)Ira Gershwin (m)George Gershwin. (I)Film: *A Damsel In Distress*, by Fred Astaire. Recorded by Bob Crosby and his Orchestra.

FOGGY MOUNTAIN BREAKDOWN (Ballad Of Bonnie and Clyde) (1950) (wm)Earl Scruggs. (I)Flatt and Scruggs. (R)1967 Film: *Bonnie and Clyde* by voices of Flatt and Scruggs. (P)Flatt and Scruggs.

FOLKS WHO LIVE ON THE HILL, THE (1937) (w)Oscar Hammerstein II (m)Jerome Kern. (I)Film: *High, Wide, and Handsome*, by Irene Dunne. (P)Guy Lombardo and his Royal Canadians.

GUY LOMBARDO

When I was a youngster, my parents would take me to Pavilion Royale, a restaurant on Long Island which featured the big name bands of the period.

Just about the time I was trying to start an orchestra, we went to see Guy Lombardo and the Royal Canadians. It was very difficult for my young band to get free copies of the stock orchestrations the music publishers printed and distributed to the name bands hoping, of course, the bands would perform these songs on the radio. Lombardo's orchestra had its own arrangers and no need whatsoever for the stuff the music publishers swamped him with. My parents persuaded me to go to Lombardo and ask him for suggestions as to how I might get some of these orchestrations from the publishers. Mr. Lombardo smiled at me and immediately sent someone to the band room; that person returned with enough stock orchestrations to fill the back of our car.

Guy Lombardo's kindness and generosity inspired a group of very young musicians to keep on playing.

FOLLOW IN MY FOOTSTEPS (1937) (w)Arthur Freed (m)Nacio Herb Brown. (I)Film: *Broadway Melody of 1938*, by Eleanor Powell, Buddy Ebsen, and George Murphy.

FOLLOW ME (1960) (w)Alan Jay Lerner (m)Frederick Loewe. (I)Musical: *Camelot*, by Marjorie Smith. (P)Tony Bennett.

FOLLOW THE BOYS (1963) (wm)Benny Davis—Ted Murry. (I)Film: *Follow The Boys*, as soundtrack theme. (P)Connie Francis.

FOLLOW THE DEAL ON DOWN (1924) (wm)Tom Delaney. (P)Bessie Smith.

FOLLOW THE FOLD (1950) (wm)Frank Loesser. (I)Musical: *Guys And Dolls*, by Isabel Bigley and Pat Rooney, Sr.

FOLLOW THE SWALLOW (1924) (w)Mort Dixon—Billy Rose (m)Ray Henderson. (P)Al Jolson.

FOLLOW THE SWALLOW (To Hideaway Hollow) (1949) (w)Paul Francis Webster (m)Hoagy Carmichael. (P)Vera Lynn.

FOLLOW YOU, FOLLOW ME (1978) (wm)Phil Collins—Mike Rutherford—Anthony Banks. (P)Genesis.

FOLLOWING THE SUN AROUND (1927) (w)Joseph McCarthy (m)Harry Tierney. (I)Musical: *Rio Rita*, by J. Harold Murray.

FOLSOM PRISON BLUES (1956) (wm)Johnny Cash. (P)Johnny Cash.

FOOD, GLORIOUS FOOD (1960) (wm)Lionel Bart. (I)Musical: *Oliver*, by Keith Hamshere and The Boys (London). Paul O'Keefe and The Boys (New York).

FOOL, THE (1956) (wm)Naomi Ford. (P)Sanford Clark. (CR)The Gallahads.

FOOL (If You Think It's Over) (1978) (wm)Chris Rea. (P)Chris Rea.

FOOL, FOOL, FOOL (1951) (wm)Ahmet Ertegun. (P)The Clovers. (CR)Kay Starr.

FOOL FOR YOU (1968) (wm)Curtis Mayfield. (P)The Impressions.

FOOL IN LOVE, A (Tell Me What's Wrong) (1960) (wm)Ike Turner. (P)Ike and Tina Turner.

FOOL IN THE RAIN (1980) (wm)John Paul Jones—Jimmy Page—Robert Plant. (P)Led Zeppelin.

FOOL KILLER, THE (1964) (w)Hal David (m)Burt Bacharach. Promo song for Film: *The Fool Killer*. (P)Gene Pitney.

FOOL NEVER LEARNS, A (1964) (wm)Sonny Curtis. (P)Andy Williams.

FOOL NO. 1 (1961) (wm)Kathryn R. Fulton. (I)Loretta Lynn. (P)Brenda Lee.

FOOL ON THE HILL, THE (1967) (wm)John Lennon—Paul McCartney. (P)The Beatles. (CR)Sergio Mendes and Brasil '66.

FOOL SUCH AS I, A (1953) (wm)Bill Trader. (P)Jo Stafford. (CR)Tommy Edwards. (R)1959 by Elvis Presley. (R)1974 by Bob Dylan.

FOOL TO CRY (1976) (wm)Mick Jagger—Keith Richards. (P)The Rolling Stones.

FOOL WAS I, A (1953) (w)Roy Alfred (m)Kurt Adams. (P)Nat "King" Cole.

FOOLED (1955) (w)Mann Curtis (m)Doris Tauber. (P)Perry Como.

FOOLED AROUND AND FELL IN LOVE (1976) (wm)Elvin Bishop. (P)Elvin Bishop.

FOOLISH HEART (1943) (w)Ogden Nash (m)Kurt Weill. (I)Musical: *One Touch Of Venus*, by Mary Martin.

FOOLISH HEART (1985) (wm)Steve Perry—Randy Goodrum. (P)Steve Perry.

FOOLISH LITTLE GIRL (1963) (wm)Howard Greenfield—Helen Miller. (P)The Shirelles.

FOOLS FALL IN LOVE (1940) (wm)Irving Berlin. (I)Musical: *Louisiana Purchase*, by William Gaxton and Zorina.

FOOLS' HALL OF FAME, THE (1959) (wm)Aaron Schroeder—Wally Gold. (P)Pat Boone.

FOOL'S PARADISE (1949) (wm)Bob Merrill. (P)Billy Eckstine.

FOOLS RUSH IN (Where Angels Fear To Tread) (1940) (w)Johnny Mercer (m)Rube Bloom. (I)Mildred Bailey. (P)Glenn Miller and his Orchestra. No. 1 Chart Record. (R)1963 by Rick Nelson.

FOOTLOOSE (1984) (w)Dean Pitchford (m)Kenny Loggins. (I)Film: *Footloose* on soundtrack. (P)Kenny Loggins.

FOOTSTEPS (1960) (wm)Barry Mann—Hank Hunter. (P)Steve Lawrence.

FOR A PENNY (1959) (wm)Charles Singleton. (P)Pat Boone.

FOR ALL WE KNOW (1934) (w)Sam M. Lewis (m)J. Fred Coots. (P)Morton Downey. (CR)Hal Kemp and his Orchestra.

FOR ALL WE KNOW (1970) (w)Robb Royer—James Griffin (m)Fred Carlin. (I)Film: *Lovers And Other Strangers* by the voice of Larry Meredith. (P)The Carpenters. Academy Award Winner.

FOR DANCERS ONLY (1937) (w)Don Raye—Vic Schoen (m)Sy Oliver. (P)Jimmie Lunceford and his Orchestra.

FOR EMILY, WHENEVER I MAY FIND HER (1966) (wm)Paul Simon. (P)Simon and Garfunkel.

FOR EVERY MAN THERE'S A WOMAN (1948) (w)Leo Robin (m)Harold Arlen. (I)Film: *Casbah*, by Tony Martin. (P)Tony Martin. (CR)Benny Goodman and his Orchestra, vocal by Peggy Lee.

FOR LOVE OF IVY (1968) (w)Bob Russell (m)Quincy Jones. (I)Film: *For Love Of Ivy*, by voice of Shirley Horn.

FOR LOVIN' ME (1964) (wm)Gordon Lightfoot. (I)Gordon Lightfoot. (P)Peter, Paul, and Mary. (R)1966 by Waylon Jennings.

FOR MAMA (1963) (w-Eng)Don Black (m)Charles Aznavour. (I)In France by Charles Aznavour. (P)1965 in US,by Connie Francis. (CR)Jerry Vale.

FOR ME AND MY GAL (1917) (w)Edgar Leslie—Ray Goetz (m)George W. Meyer. (I)Musical: *Here And There*. (P)Van and Schenck. (R)Film: *For Me And My Gal*, by Judy Garland and Gene Kelly.

FOR MY BABY (1961) (wm)Clyde Otis—Brook Benton. (P)Brook Benton.

FOR MY GOOD FORTUNE (1958) (wm)Otis Blackwell—Bobby Stevenson. (P)Pat Boone.

FOR NO ONE (1966) (wm)John Lennon—Paul McCartney. (P)The Beatles.

FOR NO RHYME OR REASON (1938) (wm)Cole Porter. (I)Musical: *You Never Know*, by Charles Kemper and Toby Wing.

FOR OLD TIMES' SAKE (1928) (w)B. G. De Sylva—Lew Brown (m)Ray Henderson. (P)Annette Hanshaw.

FOR ONCE IN MY LIFE (1967) (w)Ronald Miller (m)Orlando Murden. (I)Tony Bennett. (P)Stevie Wonder. (CR)Jackie Wilson.

(I Love You)FOR SENTIMENTAL REASONS (1947) (w)Deek Watson (m)William Best. (I)Eddy Howard. (P)Nat "King" Cole. No. 1 Chart Record. (CR)Dinah Shore.

FOR THE FIRST HUNDRED YEARS (1944) (w)Johnny Burke (m)Jimmy Van Heusen. (I)Film: *And The Angels Sing*, by Betty Hutton, Dorothy Lamour, Diana Lynn, and Mimi Chandler.

FOR THE FIRST TIME (I've Fallen In Love) (1945) (w)Charles Tobias (m)David Kapp. (I)Film: *Patrick The Great*, by Donald O'Connor. (P)Dick Haymes.

FOR THE FIRST TIME (see Come Prima).

FOR THE FIRST TIME (1961) (w)Howard Dietz (m)Arthur Schwartz. (I)Musical: *The Gay Life*, by Walter Chiari.

FOR THE GOOD TIMES (1970) (wm)Kris Kristofferson. (P)Ray Price.

FOR THE LOVE OF HIM (1970) (wm)Bobbi Martin—Al Mortimer. (P)Bobbi Martin.

FOR THE LOVE OF MONEY (1974) (wm)Kenny Gamble—Leon Huff—Anthony Jackson. (P)The O'Jays.

FOR THE LOVE OF YOU (1975) (wm)Ernest Isley—Marvin Isley—O'Kelly Isley—Ronald Isley—Rudolph Isley. (P)The Isley Brothers.

FOR THE ROSES (1972) (wm)Joni Mitchell. (P)Joni Mitchell.

FOR THE VERY FIRST TIME (1952) (wm)Irving Berlin. No artist credited with introduction.

FOR WHAT IT'S WORTH (1967) (wm)Stephen Stills. (P)Buffalo Springfield. (CR)The Staple Singers.

FOR YOU (1930) (w)Al Dubin (m)Joe Burke. (P)Glen Gray and The Casa Loma Orchestra, vocal by Kenny Sargent. (R)1964 by Rick Nelson.

FOR YOU (1972) (wm)Bruce Springsteen. (P)Bruce Springsteen.

FOR YOU BLUE (1970) (wm)George Harrison. (P)The Beatles.

FOR YOU, FOR ME, FOR EVERMORE (1946) (w)Ira Gershwin (m)George Gershwin. (I)Film: *The Shocking Miss Pilgrim*, by Dick Haymes. (P)Judy Garland aand Dick Haymes.

FOR YOU MY LOVE (1949) (wm)Paul Gayten. (P)Larry Darnell.

FOR YOUR EYES ONLY (1981) (wm)Bill Conti—M. Leeson. (I)Film: *For Your Eyes Only*, by Sheena Easton on soundtrack. (P)Sheena Easton.

FOR YOUR LOVE (1958) (wm)Ed Townsend. (P)Ed Townsend. (R)1965 by Sam and Bill. (R)1967 by Peaches and Herb. (R)1975 by Christopher, Paul, and Shawn.

FOR YOUR PRECIOUS LOVE (1958) (wm)Arthur Brooks—Richard Brooks—Jerry Butler. (P)Jerry Butler and The Impressions. (R)1964 by Garnett Mimms & The Enchanters. (R)1968 by Jerry Butler. (R)1967 by Oscar Toney, Jr. (R)1968 by Jackie Wilson with Count Basie and his Orchestra. (R)1972 by Linda Jones.

FOREVER (1960) (wm)Buddy Killen. (P)The Little Dippers. (CR)Billy Walker. (R)1964 by Pete Drake. (R)1969 by Mercy.

FOREVER AMBER (1947) (w)Johnny Mercer (m)David Raksin. Adapted from a theme from Film: *Forever Amber*.

FOREVER AND EVER (1928) (w)Jack Yellen (m)Milton Ager. (I)Musical: *Rain Or Shine*, by Warren Hull and Frances Shelley.

FOREVER AND EVER (1949) (w-Eng)Malia Rosa (m)Franz Winkler. (P)Russ Morgan and his Orchestra. No. 1 Chart Record. (CR)Perry Como.

FOREVER CAME TODAY (1968) (wm)Brian Holland—Lamont Dozier—Eddie Holland. (P)Diana Ross and The Supremes. (R)1975 by The Jackson Five.

FOREVER DARLING (1955) (w)Sammy Cahn (m)Bronislau Kaper. (I)Film: *Forever Darling*, by Desi Arnaz. (P)The Ames Brothers.

FOREVER IN BLUE JEANS (1979) (wm)Richard Bennett—Neil Diamond. (P)Neil Diamond.

FOREVER MY LOVE (1962) (w)Hal David (m)Burt Bacharach. (I)Film: *Forever My Love* on soundtrack.

FOREVER YOUNG (1974) (wm)Bob Dylan. (P)Bob Dylan.

FOREVER YOUNG (1977) (w)Rod McKuen (m)Lee Holdridge. (I)Film: *Forever Young, Forever Free*, by the voice of Bernadette Peters.

FORGET DOMANI (1965) (w)Norman Newell (m)Riz Ortolani. (P)Frank Sinatra. (CR)Connie Francis.

FORGET HIM (1963) (wm)Mark Anthony (Tony Hatch) (P)Bobby Rydell.

FORGIVE ME (1927) (w)Jack Yellen (m)Milton Ager. (P)Ruth Etting. (CR)Gene Austin. (R)1952 by Eddie Fisher. (R)1965 by Al Martino.

FORGIVE MY HEART (1955) (w)Sammy Gallop (m)Chester Conn. (P)Nat "King" Cole.

FORGOTTEN DREAMS (1957) (m)Leroy Anderson. (P)Leroy Anderson and his Orchestra.

FORTRESS AROUND YOUR HEART (1985) (wm)Gordon Sumner (Sting). (P)Sting.

FORTUNATE SON (1969) (wm)John C. Fogarty. (P)Creedence Clearwater Revival in medley with Down On The Corner.

FORTUNE TELLER, THE (1898) (w)Harry B. Smith (m)Victor Herbert. (I)Musical: *The Fortune Teller*.

FORTY DAYS AND FORTY NIGHTS (1956) (wm)Bernie Roth. (P)Muddy Waters.

FORTY FIVE MINUTES FROM BROADWAY (1905) (wm)George M. Cohan. (I)Musical: *Forty Five Minutes From Broadway*, by Victor Moore and Fay Templeton. First recording by Billy Murray.

FORTY MILES OF BAD ROADS. (1959) (m)Duane Eddy—Al Casey. (P)Duane Eddy.

FORTY-SECOND STREET (1933) (w)Al Dubin (m)Harry Warren. (I)Film: *Forty Second Street*, by Ruby Keeler. Recorded by Don Bestor and his Orchestra. (CR)Hal Kemp and his Orchestra.

FOUR BROTHERS (1948) (m)Jimmy Giuffre. (P)Woody Herman's Second Herd, featuring saxophonists Zoot Sims, Stan Getz, Herbie Steward, and Serge Chaloff.

FOUR HUNDRED YEARS (1975) (wm)Winston McIntosh. (P)Bob Marley and The Wailers.

FOUR IN THE MORNING (I Can't Take It Anymore) (1985) (wm)Jack Blades. (P)Night Ranger.

FOUR LITTLE ANGELS OF PEACE (1937) (wm)Harold Rome. (I)Revue: *Pins And Needles*, by Hy Goldstein, Al Eban, Murray Modick, and Paul Seymour.

FOUR OR FIVE TIMES (1927) (w)Marco H. Hellman (m)Byron Gay. (P)Theme song of Jimmie Noone and his Orchestra. (R)1937 by Jimmie Lunceford and his Orchestra, vocal and arrangement by Sy Oliver.

FOUR WALLS (1957) (wm)Marvin Moore—George Campbell. (P)Jim Reeves. (CR)Jim Lowe. (R)1962 by Kay Starr.

FOUR WINDS AND THE SEVEN SEAS, THE (1949) (w)Hal David (m)Don Rodney. (P)Sammy Kaye and his Orchestra. (CR)Mel Torme. (CR)Vic Damone.

4th OF JULY, ASBURY PARK (Sandy) (1973) (wm)Bruce Springsteen. (P)Bruce Springsteen.

FOURTH TIME AROUND (1966) (wm)Bob Dylan. (P)Bob Dylan.

FOX ON THE RUN (1976) (wm)Brian Connolly—Stephen Priest—Andrew Scott—Michael Tucker. (P)Sweet.

FOXEY LADY (1967) (wm)Jimi Hendrix. (P)Jimi Hendrix.

FRANK MILLS (1968) (w)Gerome Ragni—James Rado (m)Galt MacDermot. (I)Musical: *Hair*, by Shelley Plimpton.

FRANKENSTEIN (1973) (wm)Edgar Winter. (P)The Edgar Winter Group. No. 1 Chart Record.

FRANKIE (1959) (w)Howard Greenfield (m)Neil Sedaka. (P)Connie Francis.

FRANKIE AND JOHNNY (1870) (wm)Unknown. Traditional folk song. (R)1927 by Ted Lewis. (R)1927 by Frank Crumit. (R)1942 by Guy Lombardo and his Royal Canadians. (R)1959 by Johnny Cash. (R)1961 by Brook Benton. (R)1963 by Sam Cooke. (R)1966 by Elvis Presley. Song is most closely associated with Lena Horne.

FRANKLIN SHEPARD, INC. (1981) (wm)Stephen Sondheim. (I)Musical: *Merrily We Roll Along*, by Ronnie Price.

FRASQUITA SERENADE (see My Little Nest of Heavenly Blue).

FRAULEIN (1957) (wm)Lawton Williams. (P)Bobby Helms. (CR)Steve Lawrence.

FREDDY (1955) (wm)Sheldon Harnick—Peter Pan—Steve Kirk—Gisela Guenther. (I)In France by Annie Corday. (P)Connie Francis.

FREDDY AND HIS FIDDLE (1944) (wm)Robert Wright—George Forrest. Based on Grieg's Norwegian Dance. (I)Operetta: *Song Of Norway* by, Kent Edwards, Given Jones, and The Chorus.

FREDDIE'S DEAD (Theme from Superfly) (1972) (wm)Curtis Mayfield. (I)Film: *Superfly*, by voice of Curtis Mayfield. (P)Curtis Mayfield.

FREE (1947) (w)Sammy Gallop (m)David Saxon. (P)Billy Eckstine.

FREE (1971) (wm)Robert Lamm. (P)Chicago.

FREE (1976) (wm)Henry J. Redd—Nathan L. Watts. (P)Deniece Williams.

FREE AND EASY, THE (1930) (w)Roy Turk (m)Fred E. Ahlert. (I)Film: *Free And Easy*, by Buster Keaton.

FREE AS A BIRD (1971) (wm)Shel Silverstein. (I)Film: *Who Is Harry Kellerman*, by Dustin Hoffman.

FREE BIRD (1975) (wm)Allen Collins—Ronnie Van Zant. (P)Lynyrd Sknyrd.

FREE MAN IN PARIS (1973) (wm)Joni Mitchell. (P)Joni Mitchell.

FREE RIDE (1973) (wm)Dan Hartman. (P)The Edgar Winter Group.

FREEDOM (1971) (wm)Jimi Hendrix. (P)Jimi Hendrix.

FREEDOM (1985) (wm)George Michael. (P)Wham!

FREEDOM OVERSPILL (1986) (wm)Steve Winwood—George Fleming—Jake Hooker. (P)Steve Winwood.

FREEWAY OF LOVE (1985) (wm)Narada Michael Walden—Jeffrey Cohen. (P)Aretha Franklin. NARAS Award Winner.

FREEZE-FRAME (1982) (wm)Peter Wolf—Seth Justman. (P)J. Geils Band.

FREIGHT TRAIN (1957) (wm)Paul James—Fred Williams. (I)Peggy Seeger in England. (I)US, by Rusty Draper. (P)The Clyde McDevitt Skiffle Group, vocal by Nancy Wiskey.

FRENCH FOREIGN LEGION (1959) (w)Aaron Schroeder (m)Guy Wood. (P)Frank Sinatra.

FRENCH LESSON (1947) (wm)Betty Comden—Adolph Green—Roger Edens. (I)Film: *Good News*, by June Allyson and Peter Lawford.

FRENCH MARCHING SONG (1926) (w)Otto Harbach—Oscar Hammerstein II (m)Sigmund Romberg.

(I)Operetta: *The Desert Song*, by Vivienne Segal. First film version (1929) by Carlotta King. Second film version (1943)by Irene Manning.

FRENESI (1941) (w-Eng)Ray Charles—S. K. Russell (m)Alberto Dominguez. (P)Artie Shaw and his Orchestra. No. 1 Chart Record. (CR)Glenn Miller and his Orchestra.

FRERE JACQUES (1811) (wm)Unknown. Traditional French folk song.

FRESH (1985) (wm)James Taylor—Sandy Linzner—George Brown—Curtis Williams—Charles Smith—Ronald Bell—Robert Bell—James Bonneford. (P)Kool and The Gang.

FRESH AS A DAISY (1940) (wm)Cole Porter. (I)Musical: *Panama Hattie*, by Betty Hutton, Pat Harrington, and Frank Hyers.

FRESHIE (1925) (w)Jesse Greer—Harold Berg (m)Jesse Greer. (I)Film: *The Freshman*, as prologue played by Fred Waring's Pennsylvanians.

FRIDAY ON MY MIND (1967) (wm)Harry Wands—George Young. (P)The Easybeats.

FRIDAY'S CHILD (1966) (wm)Lee Hazlewood. (P)Nancy Sinatra.

FRIEND OF YOURS, A (1945) (w)Johnny Burke (m)Jimmy Van Heusen. (I)Film: *The Great John L.*, by Lee Sullivan. (P)Tommy Dorsey and his Orchestra.

FRIENDLIEST THING, THE (Two People Can Do) (1963) (wm)Ervin Drake. (I)Musical: *What Makes Sammy Run?*, by Bernice Massi. (P)Eydie Gorme.

FRIENDLY ISLANDS, THE (1950) (wm)Ralph Blane—Harold Arlen. (I)Film: *My Blue Heaven* on soundtrack.

FRIENDLY PERSUASION (Thee I Love) (1956) (w)Paul Francis Webster (m)Dimitri Tiomkin. (I)Film: *Friendly Persuasion*, on soundtrack. (P)Pat Boone. (CR)Pat Boone.

FRIENDLY STAR (1950) (w)Mack Gordon (m)Harry Warren. (I)Film: *Summer Stock*, by Judy Garland.

FRIENDLY TAVERN POLKA (1941) (wm)Jerry Bowne—Frank De Vol. (P)Horace Heidt and his Musical Knights.

FRIENDS (1971) (wm)Mark Klingman—Buzzy Linhart. (P)Bette Midler.

FRIENDS (1971) (wm)Elton John—Bernie Taupin. (P)Elton John.

FRIENDS AND LOVERS (Both To Each Other) (1986) (wm)Paul Gordon—Jay Gruska. (P)Gloria Loring and Carl Anderson. (CR)Eddie Rabbitt and Juice Newton.

FRIENDSHIP (1939) (wm)Cole Porter. (I)Musical: *Du Barry Was A Lady*, by Ethel Merman and Bert Lahr. (P)Kay Kyser and his Orchestra. (R)1943 Film: *Du Barry Was A Lady*, by Red Skelton, Lucille Ball, Gene Kelly, Virginia O'Brien, Rags Ragland, Zero Mostel, and Tommy Dorsey.

FRIENDSHIP TRAIN (1969) (wm)Norman Whitfield—Barrett Strong. (P)Gladys Knight and The Pips.

FRIM FRAM SAUCE, THE (1946) (wm)Joe Ricardel—Redd Evans. (P)Ella Fitzgerald and Louis Armstrong. (CR)Nat "King" Cole.

FRISCO FLO (1936) (wm)Benny Davis—J. Fred Coots. (I)Revue: *Cotton Club Parade*, by Cab Calloway.

FROGGY BOTTOM (1930) (wm)John Williams. (P)Andy Kirk and his Orchestra, piano solo by Mary Lou Williams.

FROM A BUICK 6 (1965) (wm)Bob Dylan. (P)Bob Dylan.

FROM A JACK TO A KING (1963) (wm)Ned Miller. (P)Ned Miller.

FROM A WINDOW (1964) (wm)John Lennon—Paul McCartney. (P)Billy J. Kramer and The Dakotas. (CR)Chad and Jeremy.

FROM ALPHA TO OMEGA (1938) (wm)Cole Porter (I)Musical: *You Never Know*, by Clifton Webb and Lupe Velez.

FROM ANOTHER WORLD (1940) (w)Lorenz Hart (m)Richard Rodgers. (I)Musical: *Higher and Higher*, by Marta Eggert, Jack Haley, Shirley Ross, Eva Condon, Robert Chisholm and The Company.

FROM HERE TO ETERNITY (1953) (w)Bob Wells (m)Fred Karger. Song inspired by film of the same name. (P)Frank Sinatra.

FROM ME TO YOU (1963) (wm)John Lennon—Paul McCartney. (P)The Beatles.

FROM MONDAY ON (1928) (wm)Harry Barris—Bing Crosby. (P)Paul Whiteman and his Orchestra, vocal by The Rhythm Boys (Bing Crosby, Harry Barris, Al Rinker).

FROM NOW ON (1938) (wm)Cole Porter. (I)Musical: *Leave It To Me!*, by William Gaxton and Tamara. (P)Eddy Duchin and his Orchestra. (CR)Isham Jones and his Orchestra.

FROM ONE LOVE TO ANOTHER (1941) (w-Eng)Albert Gamse (m)Ernesto Lecuona. (P)Glenn Miller and his Orchestra.

FROM RUSSIA WITH LOVE (1963) (wm)Lionel Bart. (I)Film: *From Russia With Love*, by the voice of Matt Monroe. (P)The Village Stompers.

FROM THE CANDY STORE ON THE CORNER (To The Chapel On The Hill) (1956) (wm)Bob Hilliard. (P)Tony Bennett.

FROM THE LAND OF THE SKY BLUE WATER (1909) (w)Nelle Richmond Eberhart (m)Charles Wakefield Cadman. Famous American light classical selection. (P)Alma Gluck.

FROM THE TERRACE (Love Theme) (1960) (m)Elmer Bernstein. (I)Film: *From The Terrace* as soundtrack theme.

FROM THE TOP OF YOUR HEAD TO THE TIP OF YOUR TOES (1935) (w)Mack Gordon (m)Harry Revel. (I)Film: *Two For Tonight*, by Bing Crosby. (P)Bing Crosby.

FROM THE VINE CAME THE GRAPE (1954) (w)Paul Cunningham (m)Leonard Whitcup. (P)The Gaylords.

FROM THIS DAY ON (1947) (w)Alan Jay Lerner (m)Frederick Loewe. (I)Musical: *Brigadoon*, by Marion Bell and David Brooks.

FROM THIS MOMENT ON (1950) (wm)Cole Porter. (I)Film: *Kiss Me Kate*. (P) Frank Sinatra.

FROSTY THE SNOW MAN (1951) (wm)Steve Nelson—Jack Rollins. (P)Gene Autry. (CR)Nat "King" Cole. (CR)Guy Lombardo and his Royal Canadians.

FUDDY DUDDY WATCHMAKER, THE (1943) (w)Frank Loesser (m)Jimmy McHugh. (I)Film: *Happy Go Lucky*, by Betty Hutton and The Sportsmen. (P)Kay Kyser and his Orchestra.

FUGUE FOR TINHORNS (1950) (wm)Frank Loesser. (I)Musical: *Guys And Dolls*, by Stubby Kaye, Johnny Silver and Douglas Deane.

FULL MOON (1942) (w-Eng)Bob Russell (m)Marcelene Odette. (P)Jimmy Dorsey and his Orchestra. (CR)Benny Goodman and his Orchestra.

FULL MOON AND AN EMPTY HEART, A (1942) (I)Film: *Beyond The Blue Horizon*, by Dorothy Lamour.

FULL MOON AND EMPTY ARMS (1946) (wm)Buddy Kaye—Ted Mossman. Adapted from Rachmaninoff's *Second Piano Concerto*. (P)Frank Sinatra. (CR)Ray Noble and his Orchestra.

FUN (Ffun) (1977) (wm)Michael Cooper. (P)Con Funk Shun.

FUN, FUN, FUN (1964) (wm)Brian Wilson. (P)The Beach Boys.

FUN TO BE FOOLED (1934) (w)Ira Gershwin—E. Y. Harburg (m)Harold Arlen. (I)Revue: *Life Begins At 8:40*, by Frances Williams and Bartlett Simmons. (P)Henry King and his Orchestra.

FUNERAL MARCH (1840) (m)Frederic Chopin. Famous classical composition.

FUNERAL MARCH OF A MARIONETTE (1872) (m)Charles Gounod. Classical selection used as theme music for TV Series: *Alfred Hitchcock Presents*.

FUNICULI-FUNICULA (1880) (wm)Luigi Denza. Popular Italian song.

FUNKY BROADWAY (1967) (wm)Arlester Christian. (P)Wilson Pickett. (CR)Dyke and The Blazers.

FUNKY NASSAU (1971) (wm)Ralph Munnings—Tyrone Fitzgerald. (P)Beginning Of The End.

FUNKY STREET (1968) (wm)Earl Simms—Arthur Conley. (P)Arthur Conley.

FUNKY WORM (1973) (wm)Andrew Noland—Walter Morrison—Marshall Jones—Leroy Bonner—Ralph Middlebrooks. (P)The Ohio Players.

FUNKYTOWN (1980) (wm)Steve Greenberg. (P)Lipps, Inc. No. 1 Chart Record. (R)1987 by Pseudo Echo.

FUNNIES, THE (wm)Irving Berlin. (I)Revue: *As Thousands Cheer*, by Marilyn Miller.

FUNNY (But I Still Love You) (1959) (wm)Ray Charles. (P)Ray Charles.

FUNNY (How Time Slips Away) (1961) (wm)Willie Nelson. (I)Jimmy Ellidge. (R)1963 by Johnny Tillotson. (R)1964 by Joe Hinton. (R)1976 by Dorothy Moore. (R)1983 by The Spinners.

FUNNY FACE (1972) (wm)Donna Fargo. (P)Donna Fargo.

FUNNY GIRL (1964) (w)Bob Merrill (m)Jule Styne. (I)Barbra Streisand as promo song for musical *Funny Girl*. (R)1968 Film: *Funny Girl*, by Barbra Streisand. (P)Barbra Streisand.

FUNNY OLD HILLS, THE (1939) (wm)Leo Robin—Ralph Rainger. (I)Film: *Paris Honeymoon*, by Bing Crosby and Edward Everett Horton. (P)Bing Crosby.

FUNNY THING (1954) (w)Carl Sigman (m)Arthur Williams. (P)Tony Bennett.

FUNNY THING HAPPENED, A (1962) (wm)Harold Rome. (I)Musical: *I Can Get It For You Wholesale*, by Elliott Gould and Marilyn Cooper.

FUNNY WAY OF LAUGHIN' (1962) (wm)Hank Cochran. (P)Burl Ives. NARAS Award Winner.

FUR ELISE (Albumblatt) (1810) (m)Ludwig van Beethoven. Famous classical selection.

FURRY SINGS THE BLUES (1976) (wm)Joni Mitchell. (P)Joni Mitchell.

FUTURE'S SO BRIGHT, I GOTTA WEAR SHADES, THE (1986) (wm)Pat MacDonald. (P)Timbuk 3.

FUTURISTIC RHYTHM (1928) (w)Dorothy Fields (m)Jimmy McHugh. (I)Musical: *Hello Daddy!*, by Wanda Goll and The Chorus.

FUZZY WUZZY (1944) (wm)Milton Drake—Al Hoffman—Jerry Livingston. (P)Al Trace and his Silly Symphonists. (CR)The Jesters.

GAL FROM JOE'S, THE (1939) (w)Irving Mills (m)Duke Ellington. (P)Duke Ellington and his Orchestra.

GAL IN CALICO, A (1946) (w)Leo Robin (m)Arthur Schwartz. (I)Film: *The Time, The Place And The Girl*, by Jack Carson, Martha Vickers, and Dennis Morgan. (P)Tex Beneke and his Orchestra. (CR)Johnny Mercer. (CR)Bing Crosby. (CR)Benny Goodman and his Orchestra.

GALVESTON (wm)Jimmy Webb. (1969) (P)Glen Campbell. (CR)Roger Williams and his Orchestra.

GALWAY BAY (1947) (wm)Arthur Colahan. (P)Bing Crosby. (CR)Clark Dennis.

GAMBLER, THE (1978) (wm)Don Schlitz. (P)Kenny Rogers. NARAS Award Winner.

GAMBLER'S GUITAR (1953) (wm)Jim Lowe. (I)Jim Lowe. (P)Rusty Draper.

GAME OF LOVE, THE (1956) (w)Matt Dubet (m)Harold Karr. (I)Musical: *Happy Hunting*, by Ethel Merman.

GAME OF LOVE, THE (1965) (wm)Clint Ballard. (P)Wayne Fontana and The Mindbenders. No. 1 Chart Record.

GAMES PEOPLE PLAY (1969) (wm)Joe South. (P)Joe South. (CR)Freddy Weller. NARAS Award Winner.

GAMES PEOPLE PLAY (1980) (wm)Eric Woolfson—Alan Parsons. (P)The Alan Parsons Project.

GAMES THAT LOVERS PLAY (1966) (w-Eng)Larry Kusik—Eddie Snyder (m)James Last. (P)Eddie Fisher. (CR)Wayne Newton.

GANDY DANCERS' BALL, THE (1952) (wm)Paul Weston—Paul Mason Howard. (P)Frankie Laine.

GARDEN IN THE RAIN, A (1929) (w)James Dyrenforth (m)Carroll Gibbons. (P)Gene Austin. (R)1946 by Perry Como. (R)1952 by The Four Aces.

GARDEN OF EDEN (1956) (wm)Dennise Haas Norwood. (P)Joe Valino.

GARDEN OF THE MOON (1938) (w)Al Dubin—Johnny Mercer (m)Harry Warren. (I)Film: *Garden Of The Moon*, by Mabel Todd. Recorded by Red Norvo.

GARDEN PARTY (1972) (wm)Rick Nelson. (P)Rick Nelson. (R)1983 by Herb Alpert and The Tijuana Brass.

GARDEN PATH TO HELL, THE (1985) (wm)Rupert Holmes. (I)Musical: *The Mystery Of Edwin Drood*, by Cleo Laine.

GATES OF EDEN (1965) (wm)Bob Dylan. (P)Bob Dylan.

GATHER THE ROSE (1927) (w)Brian Hooker (m)Rudolf Friml. (I)Musical: *The White Eagle*.

GAUCHO SERENADE, THE (1940) (wm)James Cavanaugh—John redmond—Nat Simon. (P)Sammy Kaye and his Orchestra. (CR)Dick Todd. (CR)Glenn Miller and his Orchestra.

GAY CABALLERO, A (1929) (wm)Frank Crumit—Lou Klein. (P)Frank Crumit.

GAY RANCHERO, A (1933) (wm)Abe Tuvim—Francia Luban (m)J. J. Espinosa. (I)Film: *King Of The Cowboys*, by Roy Rogers.

GEE! (1954) (wm)Viola Watkins—Daniel Norton—William Davis. (P)The Crows.

GEE BABY, AIN'T I GOOD TO YOU (1929) (wm)Don Redman—Andy Razaf. (I)McKinney's Cotton Pickers. (R)1946 by Nat "King" Cole.

GEE! BUT I HATE TO GO HOME ALONE (1922) (w)Joe Goodwin (m)James F. Hanley. (P)Billy Jones.

GEE, BUT IT'S LONELY (1958) (wm)Phil Everly. (P)Pat Boone.

GEE! BUT YOU'RE SWELL (1936) (w)Charlie Tobias (m)Abel Baer. (P)Benny Goodman and his Orchestra. (CR)Russ Morgan and his Orchestra.

GEE, OFFICER KRUPKE (1957) (w)Stephen Sondheim (m)Leonard Bernstein. (I)Musical: *West Side Story*, by Eddie Roll, Grove Dale, and The Jets.

GEE WHIZ! (Look At His Eyes) (1961) (wm)Carla Thomas. (P)Carla Thomas. (R)1980 by Bernadette Peters.

GEGETTA (1963) (wm)George David Weiss—Al Kasha. (I)Film: *Gidget Goes To Rome*, by James Darren.

GENTLE ON MY MIND (1967) (wm)John Hartford. (P)Glen Campbell. (CR)Patti Page. (R)1969 by Aretha Franklin. NARAS Award Winner.

GENTLEMAN IS A DOPE, THE (1947) (w)Oscar Hammerstein II (m)Richard Rodgers. (I)Musical: *Allegro*, by Lisa Kirk. Recorded by Jo Stafford.

GENTLEMAN JIMMY (1959) (w)Sheldon Harnick (m)Jerry Bock. (I)Musical: *Fiorello!*, by Eileen Rodgers and The Girls.

GENTLEMEN PREFER BLONDES 1926) (w)B. G. De Sylva (m)Lewis E. Gensler. (I)Musical: *Queen High*, by Luella Gear. (P)Billy Jones and Ernie Hare (The Happiness Boys).

GEORGE JACKSON (1971) (wm)Bob Dylan. (P)Bob Dylan.

GEORGETTE (1922) (w)Lew Brown. (m)Ray Henderson. (I)Revue: *Greenwich Follies of 1922*, by Ted Lewis. (P)Ted Lewis.

GEORGIA BLUES (1922) (w)Billy Higgins (m)W. Benton Overstreet. (P)Ethel Waters and her Jazz Masters.

GEORGIA BO BO (1926) (w)Jo Trent (m)Thomas Waller. (P)Lil's Hot Shots, featuring Louis Armstrong. Lil was Lil Hardin, who became Mrs. Louis Armstrong.

GEORGIA ON MY MIND (1930) (w)Stuart Gorrell (m)Hoagy Carmichael. (P)Mildred Bailey. (R)1960 by Ray Charles. No. 1 Chart Record. NARAS Award Winner. (R)1966 by The Righteous Brothers. (R)1968 by Wes Montgomery. (R)1978 by Willie Nelson.

GEORGY GIRL (1966) (w)Jim Dale (m)Tom Springfield. (I)British Film: *Georgy Girl*, by the voices of The Seekers. (P)The Seekers.

GERONIMO'S CADILLAC (1972) (wm)Michael Murphy—Charles Quarto. (P)Michael Murphy.

GET A JOB (1957) (wm)The Silhouettes. (P)The Silhouettes. No. 1 Chart Record. (CR)The Mills Brothers.

GET AWAY FOR A DAY (In The Country) (1947) (w)Sammy Cahn (m)Jule Styne. (I)Musical: *High Button Shoes*, by Jack McCauley, Johnny Stewart and The Singers.

GET BACK (1969) (wm)John Lennon—Paul McCartney. (P)The Beatles. No. 1 Chart Record. (R)1978 by Billy Preston.

GET CLOSER (1976) (wm)Jimmy Seals—Dash Crofts. (P)Seals and Crofts.

GET CLOSER (1981) (wm)Jonathan Carroll. (P)Linda Ronstadt.

GET DANCIN' (1975) (wm)Bob Crewe—Kenny Nolan. (P)Disco Tex & The Sex—O—Lettes.

GET DOWN (1973) (wm)Raymond O'Sullivan. (P)Gilbert O'Sullivan.

GET DOWN, GET DOWN (Get On The Floor) (1975)

(wm)Raeford Gerald—Joe Simon. (P)Joe Simon.

GET DOWN ON IT (1982) (wm)Ronald Bell—Eumir Deodato—Robert Mickens—James Taylor—Charles Smith—Robert Bell—George Brown. (P)Kool and The Gang.

GET DOWN TONIGHT (1975) (wm)Harry Casey—Richard Finch. (P)K. C. & The Sunshine Band. No. 1 Chart Record.

GET HAPPY (1930) (w)Ted Koehler (m)Harold Arlen. This was Harold Arlen's first published song. (I)Revue: 9:15 Revue, by Ruth Etting. Recorded by Nat Shilkret and his Orchestra. (R)1950 Film: Summer Stock, by Judy Garland. (R)1952 Film: With A Song In My Heart by Jane Froman dubbing for Susan Hayward.

GET IT RIGHT NEXT TIME (1979) (wm)Gerry Rafferty (P)Gerry Rafferty.

GET IT TOGETHER (1967) (wm)James Brown—Buddy Hobgood—Alfred Ellis. (P)James Brown.

GET ME TO THE CHURCH ON TIME (1956) (w)Alan Jay Lerner (M)Frederick Loewe. (I)Musical: My Fair Lady, by Stanley Holloway.

GET ME TO THE WORLD ON TIME (1967) (wm)Annette Tucker—Jill Jones. (P)Electric Prunes.

GET OFF (1979) (wm)Carlos Driggs—Ishmael Ledesma. (P)Foxy.

GET OFF OF MY CLOUD (1965) (wm)Mick Jagger—Keith Richard. (P)The Rolling Stones. No. 1 Chart Record.

GET ON THE GOOD FOOT (1972) (wm)James Brown—Fred Wesley—Joe Mims. (P)James Brown.

GET ON UP (1965) (wm)Gilbert Moorer—Johnny Taylor—Bill Sheppard. (P)The Esquires.

GET OUT AND GET UNDER THE MOON (1928) (w)Charlie Tobias—William Jerome (m)Larry Shay. (P)Paul Whiteman and his Orchestra. (CR)Helen Kane.

GET OUT OF TOWN (1938) (wm)Cole Porter. (I)Musical: Leave It To Me. (P)Eddy Duchin and his Orchestra. Most popular recording by Frank Sinatra.

GET OUT THOSE OLD RECORDS (1950) (wm)Carmen Lombardo—John Jacob Loeb. (P)Guy Lombardo and his Royal Canadians.

GET OUTTA MY DREAMS, GET INTO MY CAR (1987) (wm)R. J. Lange—B. Ocean. (P)Billy Ocean. No. 1 Chart Record.

GET READY (1966) (wm)William Robinson. (P)The Temptations. (R)1970 by Rare Earth.

GET THEE BEHIND ME SATAN (1936) (wm)Irving Berlin. (I)Film: Follow The Fleet, by Harriet Hilliard.

GET TOGETHER (1965) (wm)Chester Powers. (P)We Five. (R)1969 by The Youngbloods.

GET UP AND BOOGIE (1976) (w)Sylvester Levay—Stephen Prager. (P)Silver Convention.

GET USED TO IT (1979) (wm)Roger Voudouris—Michael Omartian. (P)Roger Voudouris.

GETAWAY (1976) (wm)Peter Cor—Beloyd Taylor. (P)Earth, Wind and Fire.

GETTIN' TOGETHER (1967) (wm)Ritchie Cordell. (P)Tommy James and The Shondells.

GETTING BETTER (1967) (wm)John Lennon—Paul McCartney. (P)The Beatles.

GETTING CLOSER (1979) (wm)Paul McCartney. (P)Wings.

(Running Around In Circles)GETTING NOWHERE (1945) (wm) Irving Berlin. (I)Film: Blue Skies, by Bing Crosby. (P)Bing Crosby.

GETTING SOME FUN OUT OF LIFE (1937) (w)Edgar Leslie (m)Joe Burke. (P)Billie Holiday.

GETTING TO KNOW YOU (1951) (w)Oscar Hammerstein II (m)Richard Rodgers. (I)Musical: The King And I, by Gertrude Lawrence and The Children. In film version by Deborah Kerr.

GHOSTBUSTERS (1984) (wm)Ray Parker, Jr. (I)Film: Ghostbusters on soundtrack. (P)Ray Parker, Jr.

(I Don't Stand A)GHOST OF A CHANCE WITH YOU (1932) (w)Ned Washington—Bing Crosby (m)Victor Young. (P)Bing Crosby. (CR)Ted Fiorito and his Orchestra.

GHOST RIDERS IN THE SKY (See Riders In The Sky).

GHOST TOWN (1956) (w)Ted Varnick (m)Nick Acquaviva. (P)Don Cherry.

G. I. JIVE (1943) (wm)Johnny Mercer. (I)Johnny Mercer. (P)Louis Jordan and his Tympani Five.

GIANNINA MIA (1912) (w)Otto Harbach (m)Rudolf Friml. (I)Musical: The Firefly, by Emma Trentini and Ray Atwell. In film version, by Jeanette MacDonald and Allan Jones.

GIANT (This Then Is Texas) (1956) (w)Paul Francis Webster (m)Dimitri Tiomkin. (I)Film: Giant as soundtrack theme.

GID-AP, GARIBALDI (1927) (w)Howard Johnson—Billy Moll (m)Harry Warren. (P)Fred Waring's Pennsylvanians.

GIDGET (1959) (w)Patti Washington (m)Fred Karger. (I)Film: Gidget, by James Darren.

GIFT TODAY, A (1962) (wm)Harold Rome. (I)Musical: I Can Get It For You Wholesale, by Steve Curry, Elliott Gould, Lillian Roth, Bambi Linn, Ken Le Roy, and Marilyn Cooper.

GIGI (1958) (w)Alan Jay Lerner (m)Frederick Loewe. (I)Film: Gigi, by Louis Jourdan. (P)Vic Damone. Academy Award Winner.

GILLY GILLY OSSENFEFFER KATZENELLEN BOGEN BY THE SEA (1954) (wm)Al Hoffman—Dick Manning. (P)The Four Lads.

GIMME A LITTLE KISS, WILL YA HUH? (1926) (wm)Roy Turk—Jack Smith—Maceo Pinkard. (I)Guy Lombardo and his Royal Canadians. (P)Whispering Jack Smith. No. 1 Chart Record. (R)1951 by April Stevens.

GIMME A PIGFOOT (1933) (wm)Wesley Wilson. (P)Bessie Smith.

GIMME DAT DING (1970) (wm)Albert Hammond—Mike Hazlewood. (P)Pipkins.

GIMME, GIMME, GOOD LOVIN' (wm)Joey Levine-Ritchie Cordell. (P)Crazy Elephant.

GIMME LITTLE SIGN (1967) (wm)Alfred Smith—Joseph Hooven—Jerry Winn. (P)Brenton Wood.

GIMME SHELTER (1969) (wm)Mick Jagger—Keith Richard. (I)The Rolling Stones. (CR)Merry Clayton. (R)1971 by Grand Funk Railroad.

GIMME SOME (1964) (w)Lee Adams (m)Charles Strouse. (I)Musical: Golden Boy by Sammy Davis, Jr. and Terrin Miles.

GIMME SOME LOVIN' (1967) (wm)Steve Winwood—Muff Winwood—Spencer Davis. (P)The Spencer Davis Group. (R)1971 by Traffic. (R)1978 by Kongas. (R)1980 by Blues Brothers.

GIMME SOME TRUTH (1971) (wm)John Lennon. (P)John Lennon.

GIN AND COCOANUT WATER (1946) (wm)Wilmoth Houdini. (P)Wilmoth Houdini.

GIN HOUSE BLUES, THE (1926) (w)Henry Troy (m)Fletcher Henderson. (P)Bessie Smith.

GIN MILL BLUES (1938) (m)Joe Sullivan, (I)Joe Sullivan as piano solo. (P)Bob Crosby and his Orchestra.

GINA (1960) (wm)Paul Vance—Leon Carr. (I)Johnny Janis. (P)Johnny Mathis.

GINGER BREAD (1958) (wm)Clint Ballard, Jr. —Hank Hunter. (P)Frankie Avalon.

GINGHAM AND YARN (1986) (wm)Joe Raposo. (I)Musical: *Raggedy Ann*, by Ivy Austin.

GINNY COME LATELY (1961) (w)Peter Udell (m)Gary Geld. (P)Brian Hyland.

GIRL (1965) (wm)John Lennon—Paul McCartney. (P)The Beatles.

GIRL AT THE IRONING BOARD, THE (1934) (w)Al Dubin (m)Harry Warren. (I)Film: *Dames*, by Joan Blondell.

GIRL CAN'T HELP IT (1986) (wm)Steve Perry—Jonathan Cain—Neal Schon. (P)Journey.

GIRL COME RUNNING (1965) (wm)Bob Crewe—Bob Gaudio. (P)The Four Seasons.

GIRL FRIEND, THE (1926) (w)Lorenz Hart (m)Richard Rodgers. (I)Musical: *The Girl Friend*, by Eva Puck and Sammy White. Recorded by George Olsen and his Orchestra.

GIRL FRIEND OF THE WHIRLING DERVISH, THE (1938) (w)Johnny Mercer—Al Dubin (m)Harry Warren. (I)Film: *Garden Of The Moon*, by John Payne, Jerry Colonna, Johnnie Davis, Joe Venuti, and Ray Mayer. (P)Guy Lombardo and his Royal Canadians.

GIRL FROM IPANEMA, THE (1964) (w-Eng)Norman Gimbel (m)Antonio Carlos Jobim. (I)Joao Gilberto. (P)Stan Getz, Joao Gilberto, Astrud Gilberto. NARAS Award Winner.

GIRL FROM THE NORTH COUNTRY (1963) (wm)Bob Dylan. (P)Bob Dylan and Johnny Cash.

GIRL IN LOVE (1966) (w)Chet Kelly (m)Tom King. (P)The Outsiders.

GIRL IN THE WOOD (1951) (wm)Terry Gilkyson—Neal Gilkyson—Stewart Gilkyson. (I)Film: *Rainbow 'Round My Shoulder*, by Frankie Laine. (P)Frankie Laine.

GIRL IS MINE, THE (1982) (wm)Michael Jackson. (P)Michael Jackson and Paul McCartney.

GIRL IS YOU AND THE BOY IS ME, THE (1926) (w)B. G. De Sylva—Lew Brown (m)Ray Henderson. (I)Revue: *George White's Scandals*, by Harry Richman.

GIRL LIKE YOU, A (1967) (wm)Felix Cavaliere—Edward Brigati, Jr. (P)The Young Rascals.

GIRL NAMED TAMIKO, A (1963) (w)Mack David (m)Elmer Bernstein. Adaptation of theme from Film: *A Girl Named Tamiko*. (P)Jackie Wilson.

GIRL OF MY DREAMS (1927) (wm)Sunny Clapp. (I)Blue Steele and his Orchestra. (P)Gene Austin.

GIRL OF MY DREAMS (1979) (wm)Ronald Thomas. (P)Bram Tchaikovsky.

GIRL OF THE MOMENT (1941) (w)Ira Gershwin (m)Kurt Weill. (I)Musical: *Lady In The Dark*, by The Ensemble.

GIRL ON A SWING (1966) (wm)Bob Miranda. (P)Gerry and The Pacemakers.

GIRL ON THE MAGAZINE COVER (1915) (wm)Irving Berlin. (I)Musical: *Follow The Crowd*. First recording by Harry Macdonough. (R)Film: *Easter Parade*, by Judy Garland and Fred Astaire.

GIRL ON THE POLICE GAZETTE, THE (1937) (wm)Irving Berlin. (I)Film: *On The Avenue*, by Dick Powell, Alice Faye and The Chorus. (P)Russ Morgan and his Orchestra.

GIRL THAT I MARRY, THE (1946) (wm)Irving Berlin. (I)Musical: *Annie Get Your Gun*, by Ray Middleton. (P)Frank Sinatra. (CR)Eddy Howard. (R)1950 Film: *Annie Get Your Gun*, by Howard Keel.

GIRL UPSTAIRS, THE (1955) (w)Sammy Cahn (m)Alfred Newman. Adaptation of theme from Film: *The Seven Year Itch*.

GIRL WATCHER (1968) (wm)Buck Trail (Ronald B. Killette). (P)The O'Kaysions.

GIRL WITH THE FLAXEN HAIR (1910) (m)Claude Debussy. Famous classical selection.

GIRL WITH THE GOLDEN BRAIDS, THE (1957) (wm)Stanley Kahan—Eddie Snyder. (P)Perry Como.

GIRL YOU'LL BE A WOMAN SOON (1967) (wm)Neil Diamond. (P)Neil Diamond.

GIRLFRIEND (1987) (wm)L. A. Reid—Babyface. (P)Pebbles.

GIRLS (1984) (wm)Dwight Twilley. (P)Dwight Twilley.

GIRLS CAN'T DO WHAT THE GUYS DO (1968) (wm)Clarence Reid—Willie Clark. (P)Betty Wright.

GIRLS, GIRLS, GIRLS (1907) (w)Adrian Ross (m)Franz Lehar. (I)Musical: *The Merry Widow*.

GIRLS, GIRLS, GIRLS (1987) (wm)Lee—Sixx—Mars. (P)Motley Crue.

GIRLS JUST WANT TO HAVE FUN (1984) (wm)Robert Hazard. (P)Cyndi Lauper.

GIRLS LIKE ME (1961) (w)Betty Comden—Adolph Green (m)Jule Styne. (I)Musical: *Subways Are For Sleeping*, by Carol Lawrence. (P)The McGuire Sisters.

GIRLS OF MY DREAMS, THE (1920) (wm)Irving Berlin. (I)Revue: *Ziegfeld Follies of 1920* by John Steel. (P)John Steel.

GIRLS OF SUMMER, THE (1981) (wm)Stephen Sondheim. (I)Musical: *Marry Me A Little*, by Craig Lucas.

GIRL'S SCHOOL (1978) (wm)Denny Laine—Paul McCartney. (P)Wings.

GIT ALONG LITTLE DOGIES (1880) (wm)Unknown. Traditional American Cowboy song.

GITARZAN (1969) (wm)Ray Stevens—Bill Justis. (P)Ray Stevens.

GIVE A LITTLE BIT (1977) (wm)Richard Davies—Roger Hodgson. (P)Supertramp.

GIVE A LITTLE WHISTLE (1940) (w)Ned Washington (m)Leigh Harline. (I)Cartoon Film: *Pinocchio*, by the voices of Cliff Edwards and Dickie Jones.

GIVE A LITTLE WHISTLE (1960) (w)Carolyn Leigh (m)Cy Coleman. (I)Musical: *Wildcat*, by Lucille Ball, Keith Andes, The Crew and The Townspeople.

GIVE HIM A GREAT BIG KISS (1964) (wm)George Morton. (P)The Shangri—Las.

GIVE HIM THE OO-LA-LA (1939) (wm)Cole Porter. (I)Musical: *Du Barry Was A Lady*, by Ethel Merman.

GIVE IRELAND BACK TO THE IRISH (1972) (wm)Paul and Linda McCartney. (P)Paul McCartney & Wings.

GIVE IT ALL YOU GOT (1980) (wm)Chuck Mangione. (P)Chuck Mangione.

GIVE IT ALL YOU'VE GOT (1958) (wm)Jay Livingston—Ray Evans. (I)Musical: *Oh Captain!*, by Susan Johnson.

GIVE IT BACK TO THE INDIANS (1939) (w)Lorenz Hart (m)Richard Rodgers. (I)Musical: *Too Many Girls*, by

Mary Jane Walsh.

GIVE IT TO ME (1973) (wm)Peter Wolf—Seth Justman. (P)The J. Geils Band.

GIVE IT TO THE PEOPLE (1974) (wm)Dennis Lambert—Brian Potter. (P)The Righteous Brothers.

GIVE IT UP (1984) (wm)Harry Casey—Deborah Carter. (P)K. C.

GIVE ME A MOMENT PLEASE (1930) (w)Leo Robin (m)Richard A. Whiting—W. Franke Harling. (I)Film: *Monte Carlo*, by Jeanette MacDonald and Jack Buchanan. Theme song of violinist Rubinoff.

GIVE ME A NIGHT IN JUNE (1927) (wm)Cliff Friend. (P)The Ipana Troubadours.

GIVE ME A SONG WITH A BEAUTIFUL MELODY (1949) (w)Sammy Cahn (m)Jule Styne. (I)Film: *It's A Great Feeling*, by Jack Carson.

GIVE ME JUST A LITTLE MORE TIME (1970) (wm)Brian Holland—Edythe Wayne. (P)Chairmen Of The Board.

GIVE ME LIBERTY OR GIVE ME LOVE (1933) (w)Leo Robin (m)Ralph Rainger. (I)Film: *Torch Singer*, by Claudette Colbert.

GIVE ME LOVE (Give Me Peace On Earth) (1973) (wm)George Harrison. (P)George Harrison. No. 1 Chart Record.

GIVE ME MY MAMMY (1921) (w)B. G. De Sylva (m)Walter Donaldson. (I)Musical: *Bombo*, by Al Jolson. (P)Al Jolson

GIVE ME THE NIGHT (1980) (wm)Rod Temperton. (P)George Benson.

GIVE ME THE SIMPLE LIFE (1945) (w)Harry Ruby (m)Rube Bloom. (I)Film: *Wake Up And Dream*, by John Payne and June Haver. (P)Bing Crosby with Jimmy Dorsey and his Orchestra. (CR)Benny Goodman.

GIVE ME YOUR TIRED, YOUR POOR (1949) (m)Irving Berlin (w)Emma Lazarus. The words are inscribed on The Statue Of Liberty. (I)Musical: *Miss Liberty*, by Allyn McLerie.

GIVE MY REGARDS TO BROADWAY (1904) (wm)George M. Cohan. (I)Musical: *Little Johnny Jones*. First recording by Billy Murray. (R)Musical: *George M.* by Joel Grey.

GIVE PEACE A CHANCE (1969) (wm)John Lennon—Paul McCartney. (P)Plastic Ono Band.

GIVE US THIS DAY (1956) (w)Buddy Kaye (m)Bobby Day. (P)Joni James.

GIVE US YOUR BLESSING (1965) (wm)Jeff Barry—Ellie Greenwich. (P)The Shangri—Las.

GIVING IT UP FOR YOUR LOVE (1980) (wm)Jerry Williams. (P)Delbert McClinton.

GIVING UP (1964) (wm)Van McCoy. (P)Gladys Knight and The Pips. (R)1972 by Donny Hathaway.

GLAD ALL OVER (1964) (wm)Dave Clark—Mike Smith. (P)The Dave Clark Five.

GLAD RAG DOLL (1929) (w)Jack Yellen (M)Milton Ager—Dan Dougherty. (I)Film: *The Glad Rag Doll*. (P)Ted Lewis. (CR)Ruth Etting.

GLAD TO BE HOME (1962) (wm)Irving Berlin. (I)Musical: *Mr. President*, by Nanette Fabray and The Ensemble.

GLAD TO BE UNHAPPY (1936) (w)Lorenz Hart (m)Richard Rodgers. (I)Musical: *On Your Toes*, by Doris Carson and David Morris. (R)1967 by The Mamas and The Papas.

GLADIATOR MARCH, THE (1886) (m)John Philip Sousa. Famous march generally performed at circuses throughout the world.

GLAMOROUS LIFE, THE (1984) (wm)Prince Rogers Nelson. (P)Sheila E.

GLASS ONION (1968) (wm)John Lennon—Paul McCartney. (P)The Beatles.

GLENDORA (1956) (wm)Ray Stanley. (P)Perry Como.

GLOOMY SUNDAY (1936) (w-Eng)Sam M. Lewis (m)Rezso Seress. (I)In United States, by Paul Robeson. (P)Bille Holiday. (CR)Hal Kemp and his Orchestra.

GLORIA (1966) (wm)Van Morrison. (P)Shadows Of Knight. (CR)Them.

GLORIA (1977) (wm)Emanuel Johnson—Michael Stokes. (P)Enchantment.

GLORIA (1982) (w-Eng)Trevor Veitch (m)Giancarlo Bigazzi—Umberto Tozzi. (P)Laura Branigan.

GLORY DAYS (1984) (wm)Bruce Springsteen. (P)Bruce Springsteen.

GLORY OF LOVE, THE (1936) (wm)Billy Hill. (P)Benny Goodman and his Orchestra. No. 1 Chart Record.

GLORY OF LOVE (Theme from The Karate Kid, Part 2) (1986) (wm)Peter Cetera—David Foster. (I)Film: *The Karate Kid*, Part 2, by Peter Cetera. No. 1 Chart Record.

GLORY ROAD (1969) (wm)Neil Diamond. (I)Film: *WUSA*, by Neil Diamond. (P)Neil Diamond.

GLOW WORM, THE (1952) (w-Eng)Johnny Mercer (m)Paul Lincke. Old German song. (R)1952 by The Mills Brothers, with arrangement by Sy Oliver. (CR)Johnny Mercer.

GO AHEAD AND CRY (1966) (wm)William T. Medley. (P)The Righteous Brothers.

GO ALL THE WAY (wm)Eric Carmen. (P)The Raspberries.

GO AWAY LITTLE GIRL (1963) (wm)Gerry Goffin—Carole King. (P)Steve Lawrence. No. 1 Chart Record. (R)1966 by The Happenings. (R)1971 by Donny Osmond. No. 1 Chart Record.

GO DOWN GAMBLIN' (1971) (w)David Clayton Thomas (m)Fred Lipsius. (P)Blood, Sweat & Tears.

GO DOWN MOSES (1860) (wm)Unknown. Traditional Black American Spiritual.

GO HOME (1986) (wm)Stevie Wonder. (P)Stevie Wonder.

GO HOME AND TELL YOUR MOTHER (1930) (w)Dorothy Fields (m)Jimmy McHugh. (I)Film: *Love In The Rough*, by Robert Montgomery and Dorothy Jordan. (P)Guy Lombardo and his Royal Canadians. (CR)Gus Arnheim and his Orchestra.

GO INTO YOUR DANCE (1935) (w)Al Dubin (m)Harry Warren. (I)Film: *Go Into Your Dance*, by Al Jolson. (P)Al Jolson.

GO, JIMMY, GO (1959) (wm)Doc Pomus—Mort Shuman. (P)Jimmy Clanton.

GO NOW! (1963) (wm)Larry Banks—Milton Bennett. (I)Bessie Banks. (P)The Moody Blues.

GO ON WITH THE WEDDING (1956) (wm)Arthur Korb—Charles Purvis—Milton Yakus. (P)Patti Page. (CR)Kitty Kallen and Georgie Shaw.

GO SLOW, JOHNNY (1961) (wm)Noel Coward. (I)Musical: *Sail Away*, by James Hurst.

GO TELL IT ON THE MOUNTAIN. (1865) (wm)Unknown. Traditional American Spiritual.

GO TO SLEEP, GO TO SLEEP, GO TO SLEEP (1950) (w)Sammy Cahn (m)Fred Spielman. (P)Arthur Godfrey and Mary Martin.

GO TO THE MIRROR, BOY (1969) (wm)Peter Townshend. (I)Rock Opera: Tommy, by The Who.

GO WHERE YOU WANNA GO (1967) (wm)John Phillips. (P)The 5th Dimension.

GO YOUR OWN WAY (1977) (wm)Lindsay Buckingham. (P)Fleetwood Mac.

GOD BLESS AMERICA (1939) (wm)Irving Berlin. (P)Kate Smith. (CR)Bing Crosby.

GOD BLESS THE CHILD (1941) (wm)Arthur Herzog, Jr.—Billie Holiday. (P)Billie Holiday. (R)1968 by Blood, Sweat & Tears.

GODFATHER (Love Theme) (Speak Softly Love) (1972) (w)Larry Kusik (m)Nono Rota. (I)Film: The Godfather as soundtrack theme. (P)Andy Williams. (CR)Al Martino.

GOD, LOVE AND ROCK 'N' ROLL (We Believe) (1970) (wm)S. Knape—D. Teegarden. (P)Teegarden & Van Winkle.

GOD ONLY KNOWS (1966) (w)Tony Asher—Brian Wilson (m)Brian Wilson. (P)The Beach Boys. (R)1978 by Marilyn Scott.

GOD REST YE MERRY GENTLEMEN (1827) (wm)Unknown. Traditional English Christmas Carol.

GOD'S COUNTRY (1938) (w)E. Y. Harburg (m)Harold Arlen. (I)Musical: Hooray For What!, by Jack Whiting. (R)Film: Babes In Arms, by Judy Garland, Mickey Rooney, Douglas McPhail, Betty Jaynes, and The Chorus.

GODS WERE ANGRY WITH ME, THE (1948) (wm)Bill and Roma Mackintosh. (P)Eddie Kirk. (R)1950 by Margaret Whiting and Jimmy Wakely.

GOIN' DOWN (1982) (wm)Greg Guidry—D. Martin. (P)Greg Guidry.

GOIN' HOME (1922) (wm)William Arms Fisher. Adapted from Dvorak's New World Symphony. No artist credited with introduction.

GOIN' HOME (1966) (wm)Mick Jagger—Keith Richard. (P)The Rolling Stones.

GOIN' OUT OF MY HEAD (1964) (wm)Teddy Randazzo—Bobby Weinstein. (P)Little Anthony and The Imperials. (R)1968 by The Lettermen in a medley with Can't Take My Eyes off You. (R)1969 by Frank Sinatra.

GOIN' TO CHICAGO BLUES (1941) (wm)Count Basie—Jimmy Rushing. (P)Count Basie and his Orchestra, vocal by Jimmy Rushing.

GOIN' TO HEAVEN ON A MULE (1934) (w)Al Dubin (m)Harry Warren. (I)Film: Wonder Bar, by Al Jolson. (P)Al Jolson.

GOING IN CIRCLES (1968) (w)Anita Porce (m)Jerry Peters. (P)The Friends Of Distinction.

GOING MY WAY (1944) (w)Johnny Burke (m)Jimmy Van Heusen. (I)Film: Going My Way, by Bing Crosby. (P)Bing Crosby.

GOING TO A GO-GO (1965) (wm)William Robinson—Warren Moore—Robert Rogers—Marv Tarplin. (P)The Miracles. (R)1982 by The Rolling Stones.

GOING UP THE COUNTRY (1968) (wm)Alan Wilson. (P)Canned Heat.

GOLD (1979) (wm)John Stewart. (P)John Stewart.

GOLD AND SILVER WALTZ (1904) (m)Franz Lehar. Famous Viennese Waltz.

GOLDEN BOY (1964) (w)Lee Adams (m)Charles Strouse. (I)Musical: Golden Boy, by Paula Wayne.

GOLDEN DAYS (1924) (w)Dorothy Donnelly (m)Sigmund Romberg. (I)Musical: The Student Prince in Heidelberg, by Greek Evans and Howard Marsh. (R)1954 Film: The Student Prince, by the voice of Mario Lanza dubbing for Edmund Purdom.

GOLDEN EARRINGS (1947) (w)Jay Livingston—Ray Evans (m)Victor Young. (I)Film: Golden Earrings, by Marlene Dietrich. (P)Peggy Lee. (CR)Dinah Shore.

(Oh Dem)GOLDEN SLIPPERS (1879) (wm)James A. Bland. Famous American folk song.

GOLDEN SLUMBERS (1969) (wm)John Lennon—Paul McCartney. (P)The Beatles.

GOLDEN YEARS (1976) (wm)David Bowie. (P)David Bowie.

GOLDFINGER (1965) (w)Lesley Bricusse—Anthony Newley (m)John Barry. (I)Film: Goldfinger, by voice of Shirley Bassey on soundtrack. (P)Shirley Bassey. (CR)Billy Strange.

GOLLIWOG'S CAKE WALK (1908) (m)Claude Debussy. Famous classical selection from the suite Children's Corner.

GOLONDRINA, LA (1883) (m)Narciso Serradell. Famous Mexican song.

GOMEN-NASAI (Forgive Me) (1953) (P)United States Soldier, Richard Bowers with The Columbia Tokyo Orchestra.

GONE (1957) (wm)Smokey Rogers. (P)Ferlin Husky. (R)1972 by Joey Heatherton.

GONE AT LAST (1975) (wm)Paul Simon. (P)Paul Simon and Phoebe Snow.

GONE FISHIN' (1950) (wm)Nick and Charles Kenny. (P)Bing Crosby and Louis Armstrong. (CR)Arthur Godfrey.

GONE TOO FAR (1977) (wm)John Ford Coley. (P)England Dan & John Ford Coley.

GONE WITH THE WIND (1937) (w)Herb Magidson (m)Allie Wrubel. This song has no association with the film. (P)Horace Heidt and his Orchestra. No. 1 Chart Record. (CR)Claude Thornhill and his Orchestra.

GONNA BUILD A BIG FENCE AROUND TEXAS (1944) (wm)Cliff Friend—Katherine Phillips—Phillips Olsen. (I)George Olsen and his Orchestra. (P)Gene Autry.

GONNA BUILD A MOUNTAIN (1962) (wm)Leslie Bricusse—Anthony Newley. (I)Musical: Stop The World—I Want To Get Off, by Anthony Newley. (P)Anthony Newley. (CR)Sammy Davis, Jr.

GONNA FIND ME A BLUEBIRD (1957) (wm)Marvin Rainwater. (P)Marvin Rainwater. (CR)Eddy Arnold.

GONNA FLY NOW (Theme from Rocky) (1976) (wm)Ayn Robbins—Bill Conti—Carol Connors. (I)Film: Rocky, by voice of DeEtta Little and Nelson Pigford on soundtrack. (P)Bill Conti and his Orchestra. No. 1 Chart Record. (CR)Maynard Ferguson and his Orchestra.

GONNA GET ALONG WITHOUT YOU NOW (1956) (I)Teresa Brewer. (P)Patience and Prudence. (R)1964 by Skeeter Davis. (R)1967 by Trini Lopez.

GONNA GIVE HER ALL THE LOVE I'VE GOT (1967) (wm)Barrett Strong—Norman Whitfield. (P)Jimmy Ruffin. (R)1970 by Marvin Gaye.

GOOBER PEAS (1864) (wm)Johnny Reb. Famous Civil War song.

GOOD BAIT (1945) (m)Tad Dameron—William Basie. (P)Dizzy Gillespie and his All Star Quintet.

GOOD-BYE (1935) (wm)Gordon Jenkins. (P)Closing theme of Benny Goodman and his Orchestra.

(R)1985, by Linda Ronstadt with Nelson Riddle and his Orchestra.

GOOD-BYE BLUES (1932) (wm)Jimmy McHugh—Dorothy Fields—Arnold Johnson. (P)The Mills Brothers.

GOOD-BYE BROADWAY, HELLO FRANCE (1917) (w)C. Francis Reisner—Benny Davis (m)Billy Baskette. (I)Musical: *The Passing Show of 1917*. Recorded by The American Quartet.

GOOD-BYE JONAH (1937) (w)Al Stillman (m)Arthur Schwartz. (I)Musical: *Virginia*, by John W. Bubbles.

GOOD CLEAN FUN (1960) (w)Sheldon Harnick (m)Jerry Bock. (I)Musical: *Tenderloin*, by Maurice Evans and The Parishioners.

GOOD DAY SUNSHINE (1966) (wm)John Lennon—Paul McCartney. (P)The Beatles. (CR)Caludine Longet.

GOOD EARTH, THE (1944) (m)Neal Hefti. (P)Woody Herman and his Orchestra.

GOOD EVENING FRIENDS (1931) (w-Eng)Irving Caesar (m)Robert Katscher. (I)Musical: *The Wonder Bar*, by Al Jolson. (P)Al Jolson.

GOOD FOR NOTHIN' (But Love) (1939) (w)Eddie De Lange (m)Jimmy Van Heusen.

GOOD FOR YOU, BAD FOR ME (1930) (w)B. G. De Sylva—Lew Brown (m)Ray Henderson. (I)Musical: *Flying High*, by Pearl Osgood and Russ Brown.

GOOD GIRLS DON'T (1979) (wm)Douglas Fieger. (P)The Knack.

GOOD GOLLY, MISS MOLLY (1958) (wm)Robert A. Blackwell—John Marascalco. (P)Little Richard. (R)1966 by Mitch Ryder and The Detroit Wheels in a medley with Devil With The Blue Dress On.

GOOD, GOOD, GOOD (1944) (wm)Allan Roberts—Doris Fisher. (P)Xavier Cugat and his Orchestra.

GOOD HEARTED WOMAN,A (1972) (wm)Waylon Jennings—Willie Nelson. (I)Waylon Jennings. (R)1976 by Waylon and Willie.

GOOD KING WENCESLAS (1853) (wm)Unknown. Traditional Christmas song based on a Swedish melody.

GOOD LIFE, THE (1963) (w)Jack Reardon (m)Sascha Distel. (I)Kathy Keegan. (P)Tony Bennett.

GOOD LOVIN' (1953) (wm)Leroy Kirkland—Danny Taylor—Ahmet Ertegub—Jesse Stone. (P)The Clovers.

GOOD LOVIN' (1966) (wm)Rudy Clark—Arthur Resnick. (P)The Young Rascals. No. 1 Chart Record.

GOOD LOVIN' AIN'T EASY TO COME BY (1969) (wm)Nicholas Ashford (m)Valerie Simpson. (P)Marvin Gaye and Tammi Terrell.

GOOD LUCK CHARM (1962) (wm)Aaron Schroeder—Wally Gold. (P)Elvis Presley. No. 1 Chart Record.

GOOD MAN IS HARD TO FIND, A (1927) (wm)Eddie Green. (I)Vaudeville, by Eddie Green. (P)Sophie Tucker. (CR)Ted Lewis. (CR)Bessie Smith.

GOOD MORNIN' (1937) (wm)Sam Coslow. (I)Film: *Mountain Music*, by Martha Raye.

GOOD MORNING (1939) (w)Arthur Freed (m)Nacio Herb Brown. (I)Film: *Babes In Arms*, by Judy Garland and Mickey Rooney. Recorded by Abe Lyman and his Orchestra. (R)1952 Film: *Singin' In The Rain*, by Debbie Reynolds, Gene Kelly, and Donald O'Connor.

GOOD MORNING BLUES (1938) (wm)William Basie—Ed Durham—James Rushing. (P)Count Basie and his Orchestra, vocal by Jimmy Rushing.

GOOD MORNING DEARIE (1921) (w)Anne Caldwell (m)Jerome Kern. (I)Musical: *Good Morning Dearie*, by Louise Groody.

GOOD MORNING GLORY (1933) (w)Mack Gordon (m)Harry Revel. (I)Film: *Sitting Pretty*, by Jack Haley, Jack Oakie, Art Jarrett, Ginger Rogers, and The Pickens Sisters.

GOOD MORNING, GOOD MORNING (1967) (wm)John Lennon—Paul McCartney. (P)The Beatles.

GOOD MORNING HEARTACHE (1946) (wm)Irene Higginbotham—Ervin Drake—Dan Fisher. (P)Billie Holiday. (R)1972 Film: *Lady Sings The Blues*, by Diana Ross.

GOOD MORNING STARSHINE (1967) (w)Gerome Ragni—James Rado (m)Galt MacDermot. (I)Musical: *Hair*, by Jill O'Hara and The Company in the off Broadway version. In Broadway version, by Lynn Kellogg, Melba Moore, James Rado, and Gerome Ragni. (P)Oliver. (CR)The Strawberry Alarm Clock.

GOOD NEWS (1927) (w)B. G. De Sylva—Lew Brown (m)Ray Henderson. (I)Musical: *Good News*, by Zelma O'Neal. (P)George Olsen and his Orchestra. (R)1956 Film: *The Best Things In Life Are Free*, by Gordon MacRae, Ernest Borgnine, and Dan Dailey.

GOOD NEWS (1964) (wm)Sam Cooke. (P)Sam Cooke.

GOOD NIGHT (1968) (wm)John Lennon—Paul McCartney. (P)The Beatles.

GOOD NIGHT ANGEL (1937) (w)Herb Magidson (m)Allie Wrubel. (I)Revue: *Radio City Revels*, by Ann Miller and Jack Oakie. (P)Artie Shaw and his Orchestra.

GOOD NIGHT LADIES (Merrily We Roll Along) (1853) (w)E. P. Christy (m)Unknown. Popular folk song.

GOOD NIGHT LITTLE GIRL OF MY DREAMS (1933) (wm)Charles Tobias—Joe Burke. (P)Henry King and his Orchestra.

GOOD NIGHT LOVELY LITTLE LADY (1934) (wm)Mack Gordon—Harry Revel. (I)Film: *We're Not Dressing*, by Bing Crosby. (P)Bing Crosby.

GOOD OLD FASHIONED COCKTAIL,A (With A Good Old Fashioned Girl) (1935) (w)Al Dubin (m)Harry Warren. (I)Film: *Go Into Your Dance*, by Ruby Keeler.

GOOD, THE BAD, AND THE UGLY. THE (1968) (m)Ennio Morricone. (I)Film: *The Good, The Bad, The Ugly* as Main Title Theme. (P)Hugo Montenegro and his Orchestra.

GOOD THING (1966) (wm)Terry Melcher—Mark Lindsay—Paul Revere. (P)Paul Revere and The Raiders.

GOOD THING GOING (Going Gone) (1981) (wm)Stephen Sondheim. (I)Musical: *Merrily We Roll Along*, by Lonny Price.

GOOD TIME BABY (1961) (w)Kal Mann (m)Bernie Lowe—Dave Appell. (P)Bobby Rydell.

GOOD TIME CHARLIE'S GOT THE BLUES (1972) (wm)Danny O'Keefe. (P)Danny O'Keefe.

GOOD TIMES (1979) (wm)Bernard Edwards—Niles Rodgers. (P)Chic. No. 1 Chart Record.

GOOD TIMIN' (1960) (wm)Clint Ballard, Jr. —Fred Tobias. (P)Jimmy Jones.

GOOD VIBRATIONS (1966) (wm)Mike Love—Brian Wilson. (P)The Beach Boys. No. 1 Chart Record.

GOODBYE (1969) (wm)John Lennon—Paul McCartney. (P)Mary Hopkin.

GOODBYE (1986) (wm)Jeff Watson—Jack Blades. (P)Night Ranger.

GOODBYE BABY (1959) (wm)Jack Scott. (P)Jack Scott.

GOODBYE CRUEL WORLD (1961) (wm)Gloria Shayne. (P)James Darren.

GOODBYE DOLLY GRAY (1900) (wm)Will D. Cobb—Paul Barnes. (I)Harry Macdonough.

GOODBYE GIRL (1977) (wm)David Gates. (I)Film: *The Goodbye Girl*, by voice of David Gates. (P)David Gates.

GOODBYE, JIMMY, GOODBYE (1959) (P)Kathy Linden.

GOODBYE, JOHN (1949) (w)Edward Eager (m)Alec Wilder. (P)Mabel Mercer. (CR)Peggy Lee.

GOODBYE, LITTLE DREAM, GOODBYE (1936) (wm)Cole Porter. (I)Musical: *Red, Hot, and Blue*, by Ethel Merman.

GOODBYE, MY LOVE (1968) (wm)James Brown. (P)James Brown.

GOODBYE, OLD GIRL (1955) (wm)Richard Adler—Jerry Ross. (I)Musical: *Damn Yankees*, by Robert Shafer and Stephen Douglass.

GOODBYE STRANGER (1979) (wm)Richard Davies—Roger Hodgson. (P)Supertramp.

GOODBYE SUE (1943) (wm)Lou Ricca—Jimmy Rule—Jules Loman. (P)Perry Como.

GOODBYE TO LOVE (1972) (w)John Bettis (m)Richard Carpenter. (P)The Carpenters.

GOODBYE TO ROME (see Arrivederci Roma).

GOODBYE YELLOW BRICK ROAD (1973) (wm)Elton John—Bernie Taupin. (P)Elton John.

GOODNIGHT (1965) (wm)Roy Orbison—Bill Dees. (P)Roy Orbison.

GOODNIGHT IRENE (1950) (wm)Huddie Ledbetter—John Lomax. (I)Leadbelly (Huddie Ledbetter). (P)The Weavers with Gordon Jenkins and his Orchestra. No. 1 Chart Record. (CR)Jo Stafford.

GOODNIGHT, MY LOVE (1936) (w)Mack Gordon (m)Harry Revel. (I)Film: *Stowaway*, by Shirley Temple and later reprised by Alice Faye. (P)Benny Goodman and his Orchestra. No. 1 Chart Record. (CR)Shep Fields and his Orchestra.

GOODNIGHT MY LOVE (1956) (wm)George Motola—John Manascalco. (P)The McGuire Sisters. (R)1959 by Ray Peterson. (R)1963 by The Fleetwoods. (R)1969 by Paul Anka.

GOODNIGHT MY SOMEONE (1957) (wm)Meredith Willson. (I)Musical: *The Music Man*, by Barbara Cook.

GOODNIGHT SWEETHEART (1931) (wm)Ray Noble—James Campbell—Reg Connelly—Rudy Vallee. (I)London, by Henry Hall's BBC Orchestra. (I)In US, by Rudy Vallee. (P)Guy Lombardo and his Royal Canadians. No. 1 Chart Record. (CR)Wayne King and his Orchestra.

GOODNIGHT SWEETHEART, WELL IT'S TIME TO GO (1954) (wm)Calvin Carter—James Hudson. (I)The Spaniels. (P)The McGuire Sisters. (CR)Sunny Gale.

GOODNIGHT TONIGHT (1979) (wm)Paul McCartney. (P)Wings.

GOODNIGHT, WHEREVER YOU ARE (1944) (wm)Dick Robertson—Al Hoffman—Frank Weldon. (P)Russ Morgan and his Orchestra.

GOODY GOODBYE (1939) (w)James Cavanaugh (m)Nat Simon. (P)Dolly Dawn. (CR)Ted Weems and his Orchestra.

GOODY-GOODY (1936) (wm)Johnny Mercer—Matt Malneck. (P)Benny Goodman and his Orchestra, vocal by Helen Ward. (CR)Freddy Martin and his Orchestra.

THE McGUIRE SISTERS

The McGuire Sisters had been appearing on the Arthur Godfrey Show. At this time, Milt Gabler was still head of Coral Records, just before he moved upstairs to Decca and Bob Thiele took over at Coral. Well, somebody brought the McGuires into Gabler's office. He took one look at them and said, "I don't care what they sound like. Any girls who look great have to sound great." So, the McGuire Sisters were signed to Coral Records.

The time came for their first recording session. Bob Thiele had to be in California, so I was given the assignment to produce the session. We hired Neal Hefti, a dear friend and superb arranger, to do the charts. The big song of the session was a cover record of a rhythm and blues hit called *Goodnight Sweetheart (Well It's Time To Go)*. The song was great, the arrangement was too, the girls sang their asses off, and we had a big hit. That established them immediately as a very important property in the recording industry.

GOODY GOODY GUMDROPS (1968) (wm)Billy Carl—Reid Whitelaw—Jeff Katz—Jerry Kasenetz. (P)The 1910 Fruitgum Company.

GOODY TWO SHOES (1982) (wm)Adam Ant—Marco Pirroni. (P)Adam Ant.

GOOFUS (1930) (w)Gus Kahn (m)Wayne King—William Harold. (P)Wayne King and his Orchestra. (CR)Red Nichols and his Five Pennies.

GOONIES 'R' GOOD ENOUGH, THE (1985) (wm)Cyndi Lauper—Stephen Lunt—Arthur Stead. (I)Film: *The Goonies* on the soundtrack. (P)Cyndi Lauper.

GOT A BRAN' NEW DADDY (1943) (w)Howard Dietz (m)Vernon Duke. (I)Musical: *Dancing In The Streets*, by Mary Martin.

GOT A BRAN' NEW SUIT (1935) (w)Howard Dietz (m)Arthur Schwartz. (I)Revue: *At Home Abroad*, by Ethel Waters.

GOT A DATE WITH AN ANGEL (1931) (w)Clifford Grey—Sonny Miller (m)Jack Waller—Joseph Tunbridge. (P)Hal Kemp and his Orchestra, vocal by Skinnay Ennis.

GOT A HOLD ON ME (1984) (wm)Christine McVie—Todd Sharp. (P)Christine McVie.

GOT A PAIR OF NEW SHOES (1937) (w)Arthur Freed (m)Nacio Herb Brown. (I)Film: *Thoroughbreds Don't Cry*, by Judy Garland.

GOT A RAINBOW (1928) (w)Ira Gershwin (m)George Gershwin. (I)Musical: *Treasure Girl*, by Walter Catlett, Charles Baron, Gertrude McDonald, Dorothy Jordan, Virginia Franck, and Peggy O'Neill.

GOT MY MIND SET ON YOU (1987) (wm)George Harrison—R. Clark. (P)George Harrison. No. 1 Chart Record.

GOT THE JITTERS (1934) (w)Billy Rose—Paul Francis Webster. (m)John Jacob Loeb. (P)Ben Pollack and his Orchestra.

GOT THE MOON IN MY POCKET (1942) (w)Johnny Burke (m)Jimmy Van Heusen. (I)Film: *My Favorite Spy*, by Kay Kyser and his Orchestra.

GOT TO BE REAL (1979) (wm)David Paich—Davis

Foster—Cheryl Lynn. (P)Cheryl Lynn.

GOT TO BE THERE (1971) (wm)Elliott Willensky. (P)Michael Jackson. (P)Michael Jackson. (R)1983 by Chaka Khan.

GOT TO GET YOU INTO MY LIFE (1966) (wm)John Lennon—Paul McCartney. (P)The Beatles. (R)1978 Film: *Sergeant Pepper's Lonely Hearts Club Band*, by Earth, Wind, and Fire.

GOT TO GET YOU OFF MY MIND (1965) (wm)Solomon Burks—Delores Burke—J. B. Moore. (P)Solomon Burke.

GOT TO GIVE IT UP (Part 1) (1977) (wm)Marvin Gaye. (P)Marvin Gaye. No. 1 Chart Record.

GOTTA BE THIS OR THAT (1945) (wm)Sunny Skylar. (P)Benny Goodman and his Orchestra. (CR)Sammy Kaye and his Orchestra.

GOTTA FEELIN' FOR YOU (1929) (w)Jo Trent (m)Louis Alter. (I)Film: *Hollywood revue of 1929*, by Joan Crawford and The Biltmore Quartet.

GOTTA GET ME SOMEBODY TO LOVE (1946) (wm)Allie Wrubel. (I)Film: *Duel In The Sun*, by Gregory Peck.

GOTTA HAVE ME GO WITH YOU (1954) (w)Ira Gershwin (m)Harold Arlen. (I)Film: *A Star Is Born*, by Judy Garland.

GOTTA HOLD ON TO THIS FEELING (1970) (wm)Joe Hinton—Pam Sawyer—Johnny Bristol. (P)Junior Walker and The All Stars.

GOTTA MOVE (1963) (wm)Peter Matz. (P)Barbra Streisand.

GOTTA SERVE SOMEBODY (1979) (wm)Bob Dylan. (P)Bob Dylan.

GOTTA TRAVEL ON (1958) (wm)Paul Clayton—Larry Ehrlich—Dave Lazer—Fred Hellerman—Pete Seeger—Lee Hays—Ronnie Gilbert. (P)Billy Grammar. (R)1963 by Timi Yuro.

GRACELAND (1986) (wm)Paul Simon. (P)Paul Simon. Song was written as a tribute to Elvis Presley's home in Tennessee, which was called Graceland.

GRADUATION DAY (1956) (wm)Joe Sherman—Noel Sherman. (P)The Rover Boys. (CR)The Four Freshmen. (R)1963 by Bobby Pickett. (R)1967 by The Arbors.

GRANADA (1932) (w-Eng)Dorothy Dodd (m)Augustin Lara. Most popular recording in 1961 by Frank Sinatra.

GRAND KNOWING YOU (1963) (w)Sheldon Harnick (m)Jerry Bock. (I)Musical: *She Loves Me*, by Jack Cassidy.

GRAND OLD IVY (1961) (wm)Frank Loesser. (I)Musical: *How To Succeed In Show Business Without Really Trying*, by Robert Morse and Rudy Vallee.

GRANDE VALSE BRILLIANTE (1834) (m)Frederic Chopin. Famous classical piano selection.

GRANDFATHER'S CLOCK (1876) (wm)Henry Clay Work. Famous American standard song. (R)1938 by Gene Krupa and his Orchestra.

GRANT AVENUE (1958) (w)Oscar Hammerstein II (m)Richard Rodgers. (I)Musical: *Flower Drum Song*, by Pat Suzuki.

GRASS IS ALWAYS GREENER, THE (1981) (w)Fred Ebb (m)John Kander. (I)Musical: *Woman Of The Year*, by Lauren Bacall and Marilyn Cooper.

GRASS IS GREENER, THE (1963) (wm)Barry Mann—Mike Anthony. (P)Brenda Lee.

GRAVITY (1985) (wm)Michael Sembello (I)Film: *Cocoon*, by Michael Sembello.

GRAVY (1962) (w)Kal Mann (m)Dave Appell. (P)Dee Dee Sharp.

GRAVY WALTZ (1963) (m)Steve Allen—Ray Brown. (P)Steve Allen. NARAS Award Winner.

GRAZING IN THE GRASS (1968) (w)Harry Elston (m)Philemon Hou. (P)Hugh Masakela. No. 1 Chart Record. (CR)Friends Of Distinction.

GREASE (1978) (wm)Barry Gibb. (I)Film: *Grease*, by voice of Frankie Valli. (P)Frankie Valli. No. 1 Chart Record.

GREAT AIRPLANE STRIKE OF 1966,THE (1966) (wm)Paul Revere—Mark Lindsay—Terry Melcher. (P)Paul Revere and The Raiders.

GREAT BALLS OF FIRE (1957) (wm)Jack Hammer—Otis Blackwell. (P)Jerry Lee Lewis. (R)1969 by Tiny Tim.

GREAT COME-AND-GET-IT DAY, THE (1947) (w)E. Y. Harburg (m)Burton Lane. (I)Musical: *Finian's Rainbow*, by Ella Logan and Donald Richards.

GREAT DAY! (1929) (w)Billy Rose—Edward Eliscu (m)Vincent Youmans. (I)Musical: *Great Day!*, by Lois Deppe and The Russell Wooding Jubilee Singers.

GREAT ESCAPE MARCH, THE (1963) (w)Al Stillman (m)Elmer Bernstein. (I)Film: *The Great Escape* as soundtrack theme.

GREAT IMPOSTER, THE (1961) (m)Henry Mancini. (I)Film: *The Great Imposter*, as soundtrack theme. (P)Henry Mancini and his Orchestra.

GREAT INDOORS, THE (1930) (wm)Cole Porter. (I)Musical: *The New Yorkers*, by Frances Williams.

GREAT PRETENDER, THE (1955) (wm)Buck Ram. (P)The Platters. No. 1 Chart Record.

GREAT SPECKLED BIRD, THE (1937) (wm)Rev. Guy Smith. (P)Roy Acuff.

GREATEST LOVE OF ALL (1977) (w)Linda Creed (m)Michael Masser. (I)Film: *The Greatest*, by the voice of George Benson. (R)1986 by Whitney Houston. No. 1 Chart Record.

GREATEST SHOW ON EARTH, THE (1952) (w)Ned Washington (m)Victor Young. (I)Film: *The Greatest Show On Earth* as soundtrack theme.

GREEN CARNATION (1929) (wm)Noel Coward. (I)Operetta: *Bitter Sweet*.

GREEN DOOR (1956) (w)Marvin Moore (m)Bob Davie. (P)Jim Lowe. No. 1 Chart Record.

GREEN EYED LADY (1970) (wm)Jerry Corbetta—J. C. Phillips—David Riordan. (P)Sugarloaf.

GREEN EYES (1931) (w-Eng)E. Rivera—Eddie Woods. (m)Nilo Menendez. (I)Don Azpiaza and his Orchestra. (R)1941 by Jimmy Dorsey and his Orchestra, vocal by Helen O'Connell and Bob Eberly. No. 1 Chart Record. (CR)Xavier Cugat and his Orchestra.

GREEN FIELDS (1956) (wm)Terry Gilkyson—Richard Dehr—Frank Miller. (I)The Easy Riders. (R)1959 by The Brothers Four. (R)1969 by The Vogues.

GREEN GRASS (1966) (wm)Tommy Boyce—Roger Atkins. (P)Gary Lewis and The Playboys.

GREEN GRASS STARTS TO GROW, THE (1971) (w)Hal David (m)Burt Bacharach. (P)Dionne Warwick.

GREEN GREEN (1963) (wm)Barry McGuire—Randy Sparks. (P)The New Christy Minstrels.

GREEN, GREEN GRASS OF HOME (1965) (wm)Curly Putnam. (I)Porter Wagoner. (P)Tom Jones.

GREEN LEAVES OF SUMMER, THE (1960) (w) (Paul Francis Webster (m)Dimitri Tiomkin. (I)Film: *The Alamo*, on soundtrack. (P)The Brothers Four.

GREEN ONIONS (1962) (wm)Steve Cropper—Al Jackson, Jr. —Lewie Steinberg-Booker T. Jones. (P)Booker T and the MGs.

GREEN RIVER (1969) (wm)John C. Fogarty. (P)Creedence Clearwater Revival.

GREEN TAMBOURINE (1967) (wm)Shelley Pinz—Paul Leka. (P)The Lemon Pipers. No. 1 Chart Record.

GREEN-UP TIME (1948) (w)Alan Jay Lerner (m)Kurt Weill. (I)Musical: *Love Life*, by Nanette Fabray.

GREEN YEARS (1954) (wm)Don Reid—Arthur Altman. (P)Eddie Fisher.

GREENBACK DOLLAR (1962) (wm)Hoyt Axton—Ken Ramsey. (P)The Kingston Trio.

GREENBACKS (1954) (wm)Renald Richard. (P)Ray Charles.

GRIEVIN' (1939) (w)Billy Strayhorn (m)Duke Ellington. (P)Duke Ellington and his Orchestra.

GROOVE LINE, THE (1978) (wm)Rod Temperton. (P)Heatwave.

GROOVE ME (1970) (wm)King Floyd. (P)King Floyd.

GROOVIN' (1967) (wm)Felix Cavaliere—Eddie Brigati. (P)The Young Rascals. No. 1 Chart Record. (CR)Booker T. and The MG'S.

GROOVIN' HIGH (1945) (m)John Birks Gillespie. (P)Dizzy Gillespie.

GROOVY GRUBWORM (1969) (m)Harlow Wilcox—Bobby Warren. (P)Harlow Wilcox.

GROOVY KIND OF LOVE,A (1966) (wm)Toni Wine—Carole Bayer Sager. (P)The Mindbenders.

GROOVY SITUATION (1970) (wm)Herman Davis—Russell R. Lewis. (P)Gene Chandler.

GROW SOME FUNK OF YOUR OWN (1976) (wm)Elton John—Bernie Taupin—David Johnstone. (P)Elton John.

GROWIN' UP (1972) (wm)Bruce Springsteen. (P)Bruce Springsteen.

G. T. O. (1964) (wm)John Wilkin. (P)Ronny and The Daytonas.

GUAGLIONI (The Man Who Plays The Mandolin) (1957) (w-Eng)Alan Bergman—Marilyn Bergman (m)Fanciulla. (I)Film: *10,000 Bedrooms* on soundtrack. (P)Renato Carasone. (CR)Perez Prado and his Orchestra. (CR)Vocal version by Don Cornell.

GUANTANAMERA (1963) (wm)Pete Seeger—Hector Angulo. (I)Pete Seeger. (R)1966 by The Sandpipers.

GUENEVERE (1960) (w)Alan Jay Lerner (m)Frederick Loewe. (I)Musical: *Camelot*, by The Ensemble.

GUESS I'LL HANG MY TEARS OUT TO DRY (1944) (w)Sammy Cahn (m)Jule Styne. (I)Musical: *Glad To See You.* (P)Dinah Shore. (CR)Harry James and his Orchestra. ,

GUESS THINGS HAPPEN THAT WAY (1958) (wm)Jack Clement. (P)Johnny Cash.

GUESS WHO (1949) (wm)Beatrice Hunter. (P)Ivory Joe Hunter.

GUILTY (1931) (wm)Gus Kahn—Harry Akst—Richard A. Whiting. (P)Russ Columbo. (CR)Ruth Etting. (R)1947 by Margaret Whiting. (CR)Ella Fitzgerald.

GUILTY (1980) (wm)Barry, Robin, and Maurice Gibb. (P)Barbra Streisand and Barry Gibb.

GUITAR BOOGIE (1946) (m)Arthur Smith. (P)Arthur Smith.

GUITAR MAN (1968) (wm)Jerry Reed. (P)Elvis Presley.

GUITAR MAN (1972) (wm)David Gates. (P)Bread.

GULF COAST BLUES (1923) (wm)Clarence Williams. (I)Monette Moore. (P)Bessie Smith. (CR)Fletcher Henderson and his Orchestra.

GUM DROP (1955) (wm)Rudy Toombs. (P)The Crew Cuts.

GUNS OF NAVARONE, THE (1961) (w)Paul Francis Webster (m)Dimitri Tiomkin. (I)Film: *The Guns Of Navarone* on soundtrack. (P)Joe Reisman and his Orchestra.

GUY IS A GUY, A (1951) (wm)Oscar Brand. (P)Doris Day. No. 1 Chart Record.

GUY WHAT TAKES HIS TIME, A (1933) (wm)Ralph Rainger. (I)Film: *She Done Him Wrong*, by Mae West.

G'WAN HOME. YOUR MUDDER'S CALLIN' (1945) (w)Ralph Freed (m)Sammy Fain. (I)Film: *Two Sisters From Boston*, by Jimmy Durante.

GYPSIES, TRAMPS, AND THIEVES (1971) (wm)Robert Stone. (P)Cher. No. 1 Chart Record.

GYPSY, THE (1945) (wm)Billy Reid. (P)The Ink Spots. No. 1 Chart Record. (CR)Dinah Shore.

GYPSY BLUES (1921) (wm)Noble Sissle—Eubie Blake. (I)Musical: *Shuffle Along*, by Lottie Gee, Gertrude Sanders, and Roger Mathews.

GYPSY IN ME (1934) (wm)Cole Porter. (I)Musical: *Anything Goes*, by Bettina Hall.

GYPSY IN MY SOUL, THE (1937) (w)Moe Jaffe (m)Clay Boland. (I)Revue: *University of Pennsylvania Mask And Wig Club* production, Fifty—Fifty.

GYPSY IN MY SOUL (1975) (w)Fred Ebb (m)Cy Coleman. (I)TV Show: *Gypsy In My Soul*, by Shirley MacLaine.

GYPSY LOVE SONG (1898) (w)Harry Smith (m)Victor Herbert. (I)Musical: *The Fortune Teller*.

GYPSY MAN (1973) (wm)Sylvester Allen—Harold R. Brown—Ronnie Dickerson—Leroy Jordan—Charles W. Miller—Lee Oscar Levitin—Howard Scott. (P)War.

GYPSY WITHOUT A SONG (1938) (w)Irving Gordon (m)Duke Ellington—Lou Singer—Juan Tizol. (P)Duke Ellington and his Orchestra.

GYPSY WOMAN (1961) (wm)Curtis Mayfield. (P)The Impressions. (R)1970 by Brian Hyland.

HAIL, HAIL, THE GANG'S ALL HERE (1917) (w)D. A. Estrom (m)Theodore Morse. Popular American party song. First recording by Irving Kaufman.

HAIL TO THE CHIEF (1812) (wm)Unknown. March played for The President Of The United States.

HAIR (1968) (w)Gerome Ragni—James Rado (m)Galt MacDermot. (I)Musical: *Hair*, by Walker Daniels, Gerome Ragni and The Company in off Broadway version. Broadway version by James Rado and Gerome Ragni. (P)The Cowsills.

HAIR OF GOLD, EYES OF BLUE (1948) (wm)Sunny Skylar. (I)Jack Emerson. (P)Gordon MacRae. (CR)The Harmonicats.

HAIR ON MY CHINNY-CHIN-CHIN (1966) (wm)Ronald Blackwell. (P)Sam the Sham and The Pharaohs.

HAJJI BABA (1954) (w)Ned Washington (m)Dimitri Tiomkin. (I)Film: *The Adventures Of Hajji Baba*, by Nat "King" Cole. (P)Nat "King" Cole.

HALF A HEART (1949) (wm)Al Morgan—William S. Walker—Tubby Rives. (P)Al Morgan. (CR)Eddy Howard.

HALF A MOON (1926) (w)Eddie Dowling—Herbert Reynolds. (m)James F. Hanley. (I)Musical: *Honeymoon Lane*, by Eddie Dowling.

HALF A PHOTOGRAPH (1953) (w)Bob Russell (m)Hal Stanley. (P)Kay Starr.

HALF A SIXPENCE (1965) (wm)David Heneker. (I)Musical: *Half A Sixpence*, by Tommy Steele and Polly James.

HALF AS MUCH (1952) (wm)Curley Williams. (I)Hank Williams. (P)Rosemary Clooney. (CR)Guy Lombardo and his Royal Canadians.

HALF-BREED (1973) (wm)Mary Dean—Al Capps. (P)Cher. No. 1 Chart Record.

HALF CASTE WOMAN (1931) (wm)Noel Coward. (I)Revue: *Ziegfeld Follies of 1931*, by Helen Morgan.

HALF MOON ON THE HUDSON (1938) (w)Walter Bullock (m)Harold Spina. (I)Film: *Sally, Irene, and Mary*, by Alice Faye, Joan Davis, The Brian Sisters, and Marjorie Weaver.

HALF OF IT DEARIE BLUES, THE (1924) (w)Ira Gershwin (m)George Gershwin. (I)Musical: *Lady, Be Good!*, by Fred Astaire and Kathlene Martyn.

HALF THE WAY (1979) (wm)Bobby Wood—Ralph Murphy. (P)Crystal Gayle.

HALFWAY TO PARADISE (1961) (wm)Gerry Goffin—Carole King. (P)Tony Orlando. (R)1968 by Bobby Vinton.

HALLELUJAH! (1927) (w)Leo Robin—Clifford Grey. (m)Vincent Youmans. (I)Musical: *Hit The Deck*, by Stella Mayhew and The Chorus. Recorded by Nat Shilkret and his Orchestra. (R)1955 Film: *Hit The Deck*, by Tony Martin, Vic Damone, and Russ Tamblyn.

HALLELUJAH CHORUS (1767) (m)George Frederic Handel. Famous choral work from The Messiah.

HALLELUJAH I LOVE HER SO (1956) (wm)Ray Charles. (P)Ray Charles.

HALLELUJAH, I'M A BUM (1933) (w)Lorenz Hart (m)Richard Rodgers. (I)Film: *Hallelujah, I'm A Bum*, by Al Jolson. (P)Al Jolson.

HALLOWE'EN (1950) (wm)Ralph Blane—Harold Arlen. (I)Film: *My Blue Heaven*, by Betty Grable, Jane Wyatt, Dan Dailey, and David Wayne.

HAMBONE (1952) (wm)Red Saunders—Leon Washington. (I)Red Saunders and his Orchestra, vocal by Dolores Hawkins. (P)Frankie Laine and Jo Stafford. (CR)Phil Harris and The Bell Sisters.

HAMP'S BOOGIE WOOGIE (1945) (wm)Lionel Hampton—Milt Buckner. (P)Lionel Hampton and his Orchestra.

HAND IN HAND (1947) (wm)Jack Lawrence. (P)Sammy Kaye and his Orchestra.

HAND ME DOWN MY WALKING CANE (1865) (wm)Unknown. Traditional American spiritual. Pop version 1930 by Paul Tremaine and his Orchestra.

HAND ME DOWN WORLD (1970) (wm)Kurt Winter. (P)The Guess Who.

HAND TO HOLD ONTO (1983) (wm)John Cougar Mellencamp. (P)John Cougar Mellencamp.

HANDFUL OF KEYS (1933) (m)Thomas Waller. (P)Fats Waller.

HANDFUL OF STARS, A (1940) (wm)Jack Lawrence—Ted Shapiro. (P)Glenn Miller and his Orchestra.

HANDS ACROSS THE BORDER (1943) (w)Ned Washington (m)Hoagy Carmichael. (P)Hal Kemp and his Orchestra. (CR)Lucienne Boyer.

HANDS ACROSS THE SEA (1899) (m)John Philip Sousa. Popular American march. Recorded by Sousa' Band.

HANDS ACROSS THE TABLE (1934) (w)Mitchell Parish (m)Jean Delettre. (I)Revue: *Continental Varieties*, by Lucienne Boyer. (P)Lucienne Boyer. (CR)Hal Kemp and his Orchestra.

HANDY MAN (1959) (wm)Otis Blackwell—Jimmy Jones. (P)Jimmy Jones. (R)1964 by Del Shannon. (R)1977 by James Taylor.

HANG 'EM HIGH (1968) (w)Jack Gold—Phil Zeller. (m)Dominic Frontiere. (I)Film: *Hang 'Em High* as Main Title Theme. (P)Hugo Montenegro and his Orchestra. (CR)Booker T. and The MG's.

HANG FIRE (1981) (wm)Mick Jagger—Keith Richard. (P)The Rolling Stones.

HANG ON IN THERE BABY (1974) (wm)Johnny Bristol. (P)Johnny Bristol.

HANG ON SLOOPY (1964) (wm)Bert Russell—Wes Farrell. (I)Vibrations. (P)The McCoys. No. 1 Chart Record. (CR)Ramsey Lewis. (R)1970 by The Lettermen. (R)1975 by Rick Derringer.

HANG ON TO ME (1924) (w)Ira Gershwin (m)George Gershwin. (I)Musical: *Lady, Be Good!*, by Fred and Adele Astaire.

HANG UP (1954) (w)Dorothy Fields (m)Arthur Schwartz. (I)Musical: *By The Beautiful Sea*, by Mae Barnes.

HANG UP MY ROCK AND ROLL SHOES (1958) (wm)Chuck Willis. (P)Chuck Willis.

HANG YOUR HEART ON A HICKORY LIMB (1939) (w)Johnny Burke (m)James V. Monaco. (I)Film: *East Side Of Heaven*, by Bing Crosby. (P)Bing Crosby.

HANGIN' AROUND WITH YOU (1930) (w)Ira Gershwin (m)George Gershwin. (I)Musical: *Strike Up The Band*, by Gordon Smith and Doris Carson.

HANGING ON THE TELEPHONE (1978) (wm)Jack Lee. (P)Blondie.

HANGING TREE, THE (1959) (w)Mack David (m)Jerry Livingston. (I)Film: *The Hanging Tree*, by Marty Robbins.

HANKY PANKY (1966) (wm)Jeff Barry—Ellie Greenwich.

(P)Tommy James and The Shondells.

HAPPENING, THE (1967) (wm)Eddie Holland—Lamont Dozier—Brian Holland. (P)The Supremes. No. 1 Chart Record. (CR)Herb Alpert and The Tijuana Brass.

HAPPENINGS TEN YEARS TIME AGO (1966) (wm)Keith Relf—James McCarty—Jeff Beck—Jimmy Page. (P)The Yardbirds.

HAPPIEST GIRL IN THE WHOLE U.S.A. (1972) (wm)Donna Fargo. (P)Donna Fargo.

HAPPINESS IS A THING CALLED JOE (1942) (w)E. Y. Harburg (m)Harold Arlen. (I)Film: Cabin In The Sky, by Ethel Waters. (P)Ethel Waters.

HAPPINESS IS A WARM GUN (1968) (wm)John Lennon—Paul McCartney. (P)The Beatles.

HAPPINESS STREET (Corner Sunshine Square) (1956) (wm)Mack Wolfson—Edward R. White. (P)Georgia Gibbs. (CR)Tony Bennett.

HAPPY (1972) (wm)Mick Jagger—Keith Richard. (P)The Rolling Stones.

HAPPY (Love Theme From Lady Sings The Blues) (1972) (w)William Robinson (m)Michel Legrand. (I)Film: Lady Sings The Blues on soundtrack. (P)Bobby Darin.

HAPPY (1987) (wm)D. Townsend—B. Jackson—D. Conley. (P)Surface.

HAPPY ANNIVERSARY (1959) (w)Al Stillman (m)Robert Allen. (I)Film: Happy Anniversary, by Mitzi Gaynor. (P)The Four Lads.

HAPPY ANNIVERSARY (1978) (wm)Beeb Birtles—David Briggs. (P)Little River Band.

HAPPY AS THE DAY IS LONG (1933) (w)Ted Koehler (m)Harold Arlen. (I)Revue: Cotton Club Parade, by Henry "Rubber Legs" Williams.

HAPPY BIRTHDAY, SWEET SIXTEEN (1961) (wm)Neil Sedaka—Howard Greenfield. (P)Neil Sedaka.

HAPPY BIRTHDAY TO YOU (1893) (wm)Patty Smith Hill—Mildred J. Hill. The all—time birthday song.

HAPPY DAYS (1974) (wm)Norman Gimbel—Charles Fox. (I)TV Series: Happy Days, by Pratt and McLain. (P)Pratt and McLain.

HAPPY DAYS AND LONELY NIGHTS (1930) (w)Billy Rose—Fred Fisher. (I)Musical: Simple Simon, by Ruth Etting. (R)1954 by The Fontane Sisters.

HAPPY DAYS ARE HERE AGAIN (1930) (w)Jack Yellen (m)Milton Ager. (I)Film: Chasing Rainbows, by Charles King, Bessie Love, and The Ensemble. Theme song of Lucky Strike Radio Show. Campaign song for Franklin D. Roosevelt, in 1932. (R)1963 by Barbra Streisand.

HAPPY FARMER, THE (1849) (m)Robert Schumann. Famous classical piano selection.

HAPPY FEET (1930) (w)Jack Yellen (m)Milton Ager. (I)Film: The King Of Jazz, by Paul Whiteman and his Orchestra and The Rhythm Boys.

HAPPY GO LUCKY (1943) (w)Frank Loesser (m)Jimmy McHugh. (I)Film: Happy Go Lucky, by Mary Martin and Dick Powell.

HAPPY GO LUCKY ME (1960) (w)Al Byron (m)Paul Evans. (P)Paul Evans.

HAPPY HABIT (1954) (w)Dorothy Fields (m)Arthur Schwartz. (I)Musical: By The Beautiful Sea, by Mae Barnes.

HAPPY, HAPPY BIRTHDAY BABY (1957) (wm)Margo Sylvia—Gilbert Lopez. (P)The Tune Weavers.

HAPPY HEART (1969) (w)Jackie Rae (m)James Last.

(P)Andy Williams. (CR)Petula Clark.

HAPPY HOLIDAY (1942) (wm)Irving Berlin. (I)Film: Holiday Inn, by Bing Crosby and Marjorie Reynolds. (P)Bing Crosby.

HAPPY HUNTING HORN (1940) (w)Lorenz Hart (m)Richard Rodgers. (I)Musical: Pal Joey, by Gene Kelly, June Fraser, and The Chorus.

HAPPY IN LOVE (1941) (w)Jack Yellen (m)Sammy Fain. (I)Revue: Sons O' Fun, by Ella Logan. (P)Dick Jurgens and his Orchestra.

HAPPY JACK (1967) (wm)Peter Townshend. (P)The Who.

HAPPY MUSIC (1976) (wm)David Laracuente—Richard Brown, Jr. (P)Blackbyrds.

HAPPY ORGAN, THE (1959) (wm)Ken Wood—David Clowney. (P)Dave "Baby" Cortez. No. 1 Chart Record.

HAPPY SONG (Dum Dum) (1968) (wm)Otis Redding—Steve Cropper. (P)Otis Redding.

HAPPY SUMMER DAYS (1966) (wm)Wes Farrell—Larry Kusik—Ritchie Adams. (P)Ronnie Dove.

HAPPY TALK (1949) (w)Oscar Hammerstein II (m)Richard Rodgers. (I)Musical: South Pacific, by Juanita Hall. Film version 1958 by Muriel Smith dubbing for Juanita Hall.

HAPPY TIMES (1949) (wm)Sylvia Fine. (I)Film: The Inspector General, by Danny Kaye.

HAPPY TO KEEP HIS DINNER WARM (1961) (wm)Frank Loesser. (I)Musical: How To Succeed In Business Without Really Trying, by Bonnie Scott.

HAPPY TO MAKE YOUR ACQUAINTANCE (1956) (wm)Frank Loesser. (I)Musical: The Most Happy Fella, by Robert Weede, Jo Sullivan, and Susan Johnson.

HAPPY TOGETHER (1967) (wm)Garry Bonner—Alan Gordon. (P)The Turtles. No. 1 Chart Record.

HAPPY WANDERER, THE (1954) (w-Eng)Antonia Ridge (m)Friedrich Wilhelm Moeller. (P)Frank Weir and his Orchestra. (CR)Henri Rene and his Orchestra. (CR)Tommy Leonetti.

HAPPY WHISTLER (1956) (m)Don Robertson. (P)Don Robertson.

HARBOR LIGHTS (1940) (w)Jimmy Kennedy (m)Will Grosz. (P)Rudy Vallee. Film: The Long Voyage Home, as background music. (R)1950 by Sammy Kaye and his Orchestra. No. 1 Chart Record. (R)1960 by The Platters.

HARD DAY'S NIGHT, A (1964) (wm)John Lennon—Paul McCartney. (P)The Beatles. No. 1 Chart Record.

HARD HABIT TO BREAK (1984) (wm)Steve Kipner—John Parker. (P)Chicago.

HARD HEADED WOMAN (1958) (wm)Claude De Metrius. (I)Film: King Creole by Elvis Presley. (P)Elvis Presley. No. 1 Chart Record.

HARD HEARTED HANNAH, THE VAMP OF SAVANNAH (1924) (wm)Jack Yellen—Bob Bigelow—Charles Bates. (I)Frances Williams. Recorded by Belle Baker, Cliff Edwards. (R)1955 Film: Pete Kelly's Blues, by Ella Fitzgerald.

HARD LUCK WOMAN (1977) (wm)Paul Stanley. (P)Kiss.

HARD RAIN'S A-GONNA FALL (1963) (wm)Bob Dylan. (P)Bob Dylan.

HARD TIMES (No One Knows Better Than I) (1961) (wm)Ray Charles. (P)Ray Charles.

HARD TO SAY I'M SORRY (1982) (wm)Peter Cetera—David Foster. (P)Chicago. No. 1 Chart Record.

HARD WAY, THE (1945) (w)Johnny Burke (m)Jimmy Van Heusen. (I)Film: Duffy's Tavern, by Betty Hutton.

HARDEN MY HEART (1981) (wm)Marv Ross. (P)Quarter Flash.

HARDER THEY COME, THE (1973) (wm)Jimmy Cliff. (I)Film: *The Harder They Come*, by Jimmy Cliff.

HARE KRISHNA (1967) (w)Gerome Ragni—James Rado (m)Galt MacDermot. (I)Musical: *Hair*, by The Company.

HARK THE HERALD ANGELS SING (1855) (w)Charles Wesley (m)Felix Mendelssohn. Famous Christmas song. Recording in 1912 by The Trinity Choir.

HARLEM NOCTURNE (1940) (m)Earle Hagen. (P)Ray Noble and his Orchestra. Theme song of Randy Brooks and his Orchestra. (R)1965 by The Viscounts.

HARLEM ON MY MIND (1933 (wm)Irving Berlin. (I)Musical: *As Thousands Cheer*, by Ethel Waters.

HARLEM SHUFFLE (1963) (wm)Keith Relf—Earl Nelson. (I)Bob and Earl. (R)1986 by The Rolling Stones.

HARLEM SPEAKS (1933) (m)Duke Ellington. (P)Duke Ellington and his Orchestra.

HARMONY (1945) (w)Johnny Burke (m)Jimmy Van Heusen. (I)Musical: *Nellie Bly*, by Victor Moore and William Gaxton. (P)Film: *Variety Girl*, by Bing Crosby and Bob Hope. (CR)Johnny Mercer with Nat "King" Cole.

HARMONY IN HARLEM (1938) (w)Irving Mills (m)Duke Ellington—Johnny Hodges. (P)Duke Ellington and his Orchestra.

HARPER VALLEY PTA, THE (1968) (wm)Tom T. Hall. (P)Jeannie C. Riley.

HARRIET (1945) (wm)Abel Baer—Paul Cunningham. (P)Gene Krupa and his Orchestra, vocal by Anita O'Day.

HARRIGAN (1907) (wm)George M. Cohan. (I)Musical: *Fifty Miles From Boston* by George M. Cohan. First recording by Billy Murray. (R)Film: *Yankee Doodle Dandy*, by James Cagney.

HARRY TRUMAN (1975) (wm)Robert Lamm. (P)Chicago.

HARVARD BLUES (1942) (w)George Frazier (m)Count Basie—Tab Smith. (P)Count Basie and his Orchestra, vocal by Jimmy Rushing.

HATARI! (1962) (m)Henry Mancini. (I)Film: *Hatari!* as Main Title Theme. (P)Henry Mancini and his Orchestra.

HATS OFF TO LARRY (1961) (wm)Del Shannon. (P)Del Shannon.

HAUNTED HEART (1948) (w)Howard Dietz (m)Arthur Schwartz. (I)Revue: *Inside U.S.A.*, by John Tyers.

HAUNTED HOUSE (1964) (wm)Robert Geddins. (P)Gene Simmons.

HAUNTED HOUSE BLUES (1924) (wm)J.C. Johnson. (P)Bessie Smith.

HAUNTED NIGHTS (1929) (m)Duke Ellington. (P)Duke Ellington and his Orchestra.

HAUNTING ME (1934) (w)Eddie De Lange (m)Josef Myrow. (P)Eddy Duchin and his Orchestra.

HAVE A DREAM (1962) (w)Lee Adams (m)Charles Strouse. (I)Musical: *All American*, by Fritz Weaver.

HAVE A GOOD TIME (1952) (wm)Felice and Boudleaux Bryant. (P)Tony Bennett.

HAVE A HEART (1931) (w)Harold Adamson (m)Burton Lane. (I)Revue: *Earl Carroll's Vanities*, by Lillian Roth and Woods Miller.

HAVE A LITTLE FAITH IN ME (1930) (w)Sam M. Lewis—Joe Young (m)Harry Warren. (I)Film: *Spring Is Here*, by Alexander Gray and Bernice Claire. (P)Guy Lombardo and his Royal Canadians.

HAVE I STAYED AWAY TOO LONG (1943) (wm)Frank Loesser. (P)Perry Como.

HAVE I THE RIGHT (1964) (wm)Alan Blaikley—Howard Blaikley. (P)The Honeycombs.

HAVE I TOLD YOU LATELY THAT I LOVE YOU (1945) (wm)Scott Wiseman. (I)Gene Autry. (P)Bing Crosby with The Andrews Sisters.

HAVE I TOLD YOU LATELY (1962) (wm)Harold Rome. (I)Musical: *I Can Get It For You Wholesale*, by Bambi Linn and Ken Le Roy.

HAVE MERCY (1939) (wm)Buck Ram—Chick Webb. (P)Chick Webb and his Orchestra, vocal by Ella Fitzgerald.

HAVE YOU EVER BEEN LONELY (Have You Ever Been Blue?) (1933) (w)Billy Hill (m)Peter De Rose. (P)Paul Whiteman and his Orchestra. (CR)Ted Lewis.

HAVE YOU EVER SEEN THE RAIN (1970) (wm)John C. Fogarty. (P)Creedence Clearwater Revival.

HAVE YOU GOT ANY CASTLES, BABY? (1937) (w)Johnny Mercer (m)Richard A. Whiting. (I)Film: *Varsity Show*, by Priscilla Lane. (P)Tommy Dorsey and his Orchestra. (CR)Dolly Dawn.

HAVE YOU HEARD (1953) (wm)Lew Douglas—Frank Lavere—Roy Rodde. (P)Joni James.

HAVE YOU LOOKED INTO YOUR HEART (1964) (wm)Teddy Randazzo—Bobby Weinstein—Billy Barberis. (P)Jerry Vale.

HAVE YOU MET MISS JONES? (1937) (w)Lorenz Hart (m)Richard Rodgers. (I)Musical: *I'd Rather Be Right*, by Joy Hodges and Austin Marshall.

HAVE YOU NEVER BEEN MELLOW (1975) (wm)John Farrar. (P)Olivia Newton-John. No. 1 Chart Record.

HAVE YOU SEEN HER (1971) (wm)Eugene Record—Barbara Acklin. (P)The Chi-Lites.

HAVE YOU SEEN YOUR MOTHER, BABY, STANDING IN THE SHADOW? (1966) (wm)Mick Jagger—Keith Richard. (P)The Rolling Stones.

HAVE YOURSELF A MERRY LITTLE CHRISTMAS (1944) (wm)Hugh Martin—Ralph Blane. (I)Film: *Meet Me In St. Louis*, by Judy Garland. (P)Judy Garland.

HAVEN'T GOT TIME FOR THE PAIN (1974) (wm)Jacob Brackman—Carly Simon. (P)Carly Simon.

HAVIN' MYSELF A TIME (1938) (wm)Leo Robin—Ralph Rainger. (I)Film: *Tropic Holiday*, by Martha Raye.

HAVING A PARTY (1962) (wm)Sam Cooke (P)Sam Cooke. (R)1973 by The Ovations.

(You're)HAVING MY BABY (1974) (wm)Paul Anka. (P)Paul Anka.

HAWAII (1966) (w)Mack David (m)Elmer Bernstein. (I)Film: *Hawaii*, as Main Title Theme. (P)Henry Mancini and his Chorus and Orchestra.

HAWAII FIVE-O (1969) (m)Mort Stevens. (I)TV Series: *Hawaii Five—O*. (P)The Ventures.

HAWAII TATTOO (1961) (wm)Michael Thomas. (P)The Waikikis.

HAWAIIAN EYE (1959) (wm)Mack David—Jerry Livingston. (I)TV Series: *Hawaiian Eye* as Main Title Theme.

HAWAIIAN WAR CHANT (1936) (w-Eng)Ralph Freed (m)Johnny Noble—Leleiohaku. (P)1939 by Tommy Dorsey and his Orchestra. (R)1946 by Spike Jones. (R)1951 by The Ames Brothers.

HAWAIIAN WEDDING SONG,THE (1958) (w)Al Hoffman—Dick Manning. (m)Charles E. King. (P)Andy

Williams.

HAWK, THE (1986) (wm)Kris Kristofferson. (I)Film: *Trouble In Mind*, by Marianne Faithfull.

HAWK-EYE (1955) (wm)Boudleaux Bryant (P)Frankie Laine.

HAY, STRAW (1928) (w)Oscar Hammerstein II (m)Vincent Youmans. (I)Musical: *Rainbow*, by Harland Dixon and Louise Brown.

HAYFOOT-STRAWFOOT (1942) (w)Harry Lenk—Ervin Drake (m)Paul McGrane. (P)Duke Ellington and his Orchestra, vocal by Ivie Anderson.

HAZY SHADE OF WINTER, A (1966) (wm)Paul Simon. (P)Simon and Garfunkel. (R)1987 by Bangles.

HE (1954) (w)Jack Mullan (m)Jack Richards. (P)The McGuire Sisters. (CR)Al Hibbler. (R)1966 by The Righteous Brothers.

HE AIN'T GOT RHYTHM (1937) (wm)Irving Berlin. (I)Film: *On The Avenue*, by Alice Faye, The Ritz Brothers, and The Girl's Chorus.

HE AIN'T HEAVY...HE'S MY BROTHER (1970) (w)Bob Russell (m)Bobby Scott. (P)The Hollies. (R)1970 by Neil Diamond. (R)1976 by Olivia Newton-John.

HE DON'T LOVE YOU (Like I Love You) (1960) (wm)Curtis Mayfield—Calvin Carter. (P)Jerry Butler. (R)1975 by Dawn. No. 1 Chart Record.

HE GIVES US ALL HIS LOVE (1971) (wm)Randy Newman. (I)Film: *Cold Turkey*, by the voice of Randy Newman. (P)Randy Newman.

HE HASN'T A THING EXCEPT ME (1936) (w)Ira Gershwin (m)Vernon Duke. (I)Revue: *Ziegfeld Follies of 1936*, by Fanny Brice.

HE IS AN ENGLISHMAN (1878) (w)Wm. S. Gilbert (m)Arthur Sullivan. (I)Operetta: *H.M.S. Pinafore*.

HE LOVES AND SHE LOVES (1927) (w)Ira Gershwin (m)George Gershwin. (I)Musical: *Funny Face*, by Adele Astaire and Allen Kearns. (R)1957 Film: *Funny Face*, by Fred Astaire.

HE MAKES ME BELIEVE HE'S MINE (1948) (w)John Latouche (m)Duke Ellington. (P)Duke Ellington and his Orchestra.

HE NEEDS ME (1955) (wm)Arthur Hamilton. (I)Film: *Pete Kelly's Blues*, by Peggy Lee. (P)Peggy Lee.

HE TOSSED A COIN (1970) (w)Sheldon Harnick (m)Jerry Bock. (I)Musical: *The Rothschilds*, by Hal Linden.

HE WAS MY BROTHER (1964) (wm)Paul Simon. (P)Simon and Garfunkel.

HE WEARS A PAIR OF SILVER WINGS (1942) (w)Eric Maschwitz (m)Michael Carr. (P)Kay Kyser and his Orchestra, vocal by Harry Babbitt. (CR)Dinah Shore.

HEAD GAMES (1979) (wm)Lou Grammatico—Michael Jones. (P)Foreigner.

HEAD OVER HEELS (1984) (wm)Charlotte Caffey—Kathy Valentine. (P)The Go—Go's.

HEAD OVER HEELS IN LOVE (1936) (w)Mack Gordon (m)Harry Revel. (I)British Film: *Head Over Heels*, by Jessie Matthews.

HEAD TO TOE (1987) (wm)Full Force. (P)Lisa Lisa & Cult Jam. No. 1 Chart Record.

HEAR ME TALKIN' TO YA (1928) (wm)Gertrude Rainey. (I)Ma Rainey. (P)Louis Armstrong.

HEAR MY SONG, VIOLETTA (1940) (w-Eng)Buddy Bernier—Bob Emmerich (m)Rudolf Luckesch—Othmar Klose. (I)Will Glahe and his Musette Orchestra. (P)Glenn Miller and his Orchestra. (CR)Tony Martin.

HEARD IT IN A LOVE SONG (1977) (wm)Toy Caldwell. (P)The Marshall Tucker Band.

HEART (1955) (wm)Richard Adler—Jerry Ross. (I)Musical: *Damn Yankees*, by Russ Brown, Jimmie Komack, Nat Frey, and Albert Linville. (P)Eddie Fisher. (CR)The McGuire Sisters.

HEART AND SOUL (1938) (w)Frank Loesser (m)Hoagy Carmichael. (I)Film Short: *A Song Is Born*, by Larry Clinton and his Orchestra. (P)Larry Clinton. No. 1 Chart Record. (R)1952 by The Four Aces.

HEART AND SOUL (1983) (wm)Mike Chapman—Nicky Chinn. (P)Huey Lewis and The News.

HEART AND SOUL (1987) (wm)C. Decker—R. Rogers. (P)T'Pau.

HEART FULL OF SOUL (1965) (wm)Graham Gouldman. (P)The Yardbirds.

HEART HOTELS (1980) (wm)Dan Fogelberg. (P)Dan Fogelberg.

HEART IN HAND (1962) (wm)Shari Sheeley—Jackie DeShannon. (P)Brenda Lee.

HEART IS QUICKER THAN THE EYE, THE (1936) (w)Lorenz Hart (m)Richard Rodgers. (I)Musical: *On Your Toes*, by Ray Bolger and Luella Gear.

HEART OF GLASS (1979) (wm)Deborah Harry—Chris Stein. (P)Blondie. No. 1 Chart Record.

HEART OF GOLD (1971) (wm)Neil Young. (P)Neil Young. No. 1 Chart Record.

(The Gang That Sang)HEART OF MY HEART (1946) (wm)Ben Ryan. No artist credited with introduction. (R)1954 by The Three D's (Don Cornell, Alan Dale, Johnny Desmond). (CR)The Four Aces.

HEART OF ROCK AND ROLL, THE (1983) (wm)Johnny Colla—Huey Lewis. (P)Huey Lewis & The News.

HEART OF STONE (1965) (wm)Mick Jagger—Keith Richard. (P)The Rolling Stones.

HEART OF THE COUNTRY (1971) (wm)Paul and Linda McCartney. (P)Paul McCartney and Wings.

HEART OF THE NIGHT (1979) (wm)Norman Cotton. (P)Poco.

HEART TO HEART (1982) (wm)Kenny Loggins—Michael McDonald—David Foster. (P)Kenny Loggins.

HEARTACHE TONIGHT (1979) (wm)Glen Frey—Don Henley—Bob Seger—John David Souther. (P)The Eagles. No. 1 Chart Record.

HEARTACHES (1931) (w)John Klenner (m)Al Hoffman. (P)Guy Lombardo and his Royal Canadians. (R)1947 by Ted Weems and his Orchestra. (R)1961 by The Marcels.

HEARTACHES BY THE NUMBER (1959) (wm)Harlan Howard. (I)Ray Price. (P)Guy Mitchell. No. 1 Chart Record. (R)1965 by Johnny Tillotson.

HEARTBEAT-IT'S A LOVEBEAT (1972) (wm)William Gregory Hudspeth—Michael Kennedy. (P)The DeFranco Family.

HEARTBREAK (It's Hurting Me) (1960) (wm)John Thomas—C. Hoyles. (P)Jon Thomas.

HEARTBREAK HOTEL (1956) (wm)Mae Boren Axton—Tommy Durden—Elvis Presley. (P)Elvis Presley. No. 1 Chart Record. (R)1971 by Frijid Pink.

HEARTBREAK HOTEL (1981) (wm)Michael Jackson. (P)The Jacksons.

HEARTBREAK KID, THE (Theme From)1972) (w)Sheldon Harnick (m)Cy Coleman. (I)Film: *The Heartbreak Kid*, by the voice of Bill Dean.

HEARTBREAKER (1947) (wm)Morty Berk—Frank Campano—Max C. Freedman. (I)The Ferko String Band. (P)The Andrews Sisters.

HEARTBREAKER (1978) (wm)Carole Bayer Sager—David Wolfert. (P)Dolly Parton.

HEARTBREAKER (1979) (wm)Geoff Gill—Cliff Wade. (P)Pat Benatar.

HEARTBREAKER (1982) (wm)Barry, Maurice, and Robin Gibb. (P)Dionne Warwick.

HEARTLESS (1978) (wm)Ann Wilson—Nancy Wilson. (P)Heart.

HEARTS (1981) (wm)Jeff Barish. (P)Marty Balin.

HEARTS AND FLOWERS (1899) (w)Mary D. Brine (m)Theodore Moses Tobani. (I)Harry MacDonough.

HEARTS OF STONE (1955) (w)Eddy Ray (m)Rudy Jackson. (I)Otis Williams and The Charms. (P)The Fontane Sisters. No. 1 Chart Record. (CR)Red Foley.

HEARTS OF STONE (1986) (wm)Bruce Springsteen. (P)Bruce Springsteen.

HEAT IS ON, THE (1985) (w)Keith Forsey (m)Harold Faltermeyer. (I)Film: Beverly Hills Cop, on soundtrack. (P)Glenn Frey.

HEAT OF THE NIGHT (1987) (w)Bryan Adams—J. Vallance. (P)Bryan Adams.

HEAT WAVE (1933) (wm)Irving Berlin. (I)Revue: As Thousands Cheer, by Ethel Waters. (P)Ethel Waters. (CR)Glen Gray and The Casa Loma Orchestra. (R)1954 Film: There's No Business Like Show Business, by Marilyn Monroe.

HEAT WAVE (1963) (wm)Eddie Holland—Brian Holland—Lamont Dozier. (P)Martha and The Vandellas. (R)1975 by Linda Ronstadt.

HEATHER HONEY (1969) (wm)Tommy Roe (P)Tommy Roe.

HEATHER ON THE HILL, THE (1947) (w)Alan Jay Lerner (m)Frederick Loewe. (I)Musical: Brigadoon, by David Brooks and Marion Bell. (R)1954 Film version by Gene Kelly.

HEAVEN (1985) (wm)Bryan Adams—Jim Vallance. (I)Film: A Night In Heaven. (P)Bryan Adams. No. 1 Chart Record.

HEAVEN CAN WAIT (1939) (w)Eddie De Lange (m)Jimmy Van Heusen. (P)Tommy Dorsey and his Orchestra, vocal by Jack Leonard. (CR)Kay Kyser and his Orchestra.

HEAVEN DROPS HER CURTAIN DOWN (1949) (wm)Sammy Mysels—George Mysels. (P)Freddy Martin and his Orchestra, vocal by Merv Griffin.

HEAVEN HELP US ALL (1970) (wm)Ronald Miller. (P)Stevie Wonder.

HEAVEN HOP, THE (1928) (wm)Cole Porter. (I)Play with Songs: Paris, by Irving Aaronson and his Commanders.

HEAVEN IN MY ARMS (1939) (w)Oscar Hammerstein II (m)Jerome Kern. (I)Musical: Very Warm For May, by Jack Whiting, Frances Mercer, and Hollace Shaw.

HEAVEN IN YOUR EYES (1986) (wm)Paul Dean—Mike Reno—Johnny Dexter—Debra Mae Moore. (I)Film: Top Gun, by Loverboy. (P)Loverboy.

HEAVEN IS A PLACE ON EARTH (1987) (wm)R. Nowels—E. Shipley. (P)Belinda Carlisle. No. 1 Chart Record.

HEAVEN KNOWS (1969) (wm)Dan Walsh—Harvey Price. (P)Grass Roots.

HEAVEN KNOWS (1979) (wm)Pete Bellotte—Giorgio Moroder—Donna Summer—Gregg Mathieson. (P)Donna Summer with Brooklyn Dreams.

HEAVEN MUST BE MISSING AN ANGEL (1976) (wm)Kenny St. Lewis—Freddy Perren. (P)Tavares.

HEAVEN MUST HAVE SENT YOU (1966) (wm)Eddie Holland—Lamont Dozier—Brian Holland. (P)The Elgins. (R)1979 by Bonnie Pointer.

HEAVEN ON THE SEVENTH FLOOR (1977) (wm)Dominic Bugatti—Frank Musker. (P)Paul Nicholas.

HEAVEN WILL PROTECT THE WORKING GIRL (1909) (w)Edgar Smith (m)A. Baldwin Sloane. (I)Musical: Tillie's Nightmare, by Marie Dressler.

HEAVENLY (1959) (w)Sydney Shaw (m)Burt Bacharach. (P)Johnny Mathis.

HEAVENLY FATHER (1952) (wm)Edna McGriff. (P)Edna McGriff.

HEAVENLY HIDEAWAY (1942) (w)Jules Loman (m)Lou Ricca. (P)Horace Heidt and his Musical Knights, vocal by Gordon MacRae, piano solo by Frankie Carle. (CR)Jimmy Dorsey and his Orchestra.

HEAVENLY PARTY, A (1938) (w)Dorothy Fields (m)Jerome Kern. (I)Film: Joy Of Living, by Irene Dunne.

HEEBIE JEEBIES (1926) (wm)Boyd Atkins. (P)Louis Armstrong and his Hot Five.

HEIGH-HO (The Dwarfs' Marching Song) (1938) (w)Larry Morey (m)Frank Churchill. (I)Cartoon Film: Snow White And The Seven Dwarfs, by The Dwarfs. Recorded by Horace Heidt and his Musical Knights.

HELEN POLA (1947) (wm)Walter Dana—Jimmy Carroll—Albert Gamse. (P)The Walter Dana Orchestra.

HELEN WHEELS (1974) (wm)Paul and Linda McCartney. (P)Paul McCartney and Wings.

HE'LL HAVE TO GO (1959) (wm)Joe Allison—Audrey Allison. (P)Jim Reeves. (CR)1960 by Jeanne Black under title of He'll Have To Stay.

HELLO (1984) (wm)Lionel Richie. (P)Lionel Richie. No. 1 Chart Record.

HELLO AGAIN (1980) (wm)Neil Diamond—Alan Lindgren. (I)Film: The Jazz Singer, by Neil Diamond. (P)Neil Diamond.

HELLO AGAIN (1984) (wm)R.C. Ocasek. (P)The Cars.

HELLO! BEAUTIFUL! (1931) (wm)Walter Donaldson. (I)Maurice Chevalier. (CR)Wayne King and his Orchestra.

HELLO, DOLLY! (1963) (wm)Jerry Herman. (I)Musical: Hello, Dolly!,by Carol Channing and The Company. (P)Louis Armstrong. No. 1 Chart Record. NARAS Award Winner.

HELLO FRISCO HELLO (1915) (w)Gene Buck (m)Louis A. Hirsch. (I)Revue: Ziegfeld Follies of 1915. Recorded by Olive Kline and Reginald Werrenrath.

HELLO, GOODBYE (1967) (wm)John Lennon—Paul McCartney. (P)The Beatles. No. 1 Chart Record.

HELLO, HELLO (1967) (wm)Peter Kraemer—Terry MacNeil. (P)Sopwith Camel.

HELLO-HOORAY (1968) (wm)Rolf Kempf. (I)Judy Collins. (R)1973 by Alice Cooper.

HELLO, I LOVE YOU (1968) (wm)Robert Krieger—James Morrison—John Densmore—Raymond Manzarek. (P)The Doors.

HELLO, I LOVE YOU, GOODBYE (1964) (w)Earl Shuman (m)Leon Carr. (I)Musical: The Secret Life Of Walter Mitty, by Eugene Roche, Marc London, and Rudy Tronto.

HELLO, IT'S ME (1968) (wm)Todd Rundgren. (I)The Nazz. (R)1973 by Todd Rundgren.

HELLO LITTLE GIRL (1963) (wm)John Lennon—Paul McCartney. (P)The Beatles.

A WRONG GUESS ...

Wrong guessing is habitual in the recording industry. When *Hello Dolly* opened, E. H. Morris Company, the publisher (now owned by Paul McCartney), could not get the title song recorded. In desperation, Jack Lee (one of the Morris Company song pluggers) went to Joe Glaser, Louis Armstrong's manager, and offered to pay for the recording session if Louis would record the song. Lee promised he would try to get the master released. So Louis recorded *Hello Dolly*. To save money, there was not even any arrangement; just a "head session", with the musicians pretty much improvising their parts.

Once he had the master tape, Jack Lee took it around to all the record companies. He was rebuffed by all of them. The reasons? Armstrong was cold, and music from shows didn't mean a thing. Finally Lee went to his buddy Dave Kapp, at Kapp Records. Kapp did his pal Lee a favor, and the rest is history. Just goes to show there are no geniuses when it comes to picking records.

HELLO, MARY LOU (1961) (wm)Gene Pitney. (P)Rick Nelson.

HELLO MUDDAH, HELLO FADDUH (1963) (w)Allen Sherman (m)Lou Busch. Music based on Dance Of The Hours by Ponchielli. NARAS Award Winner.

HELLO, MY LOVER, GOOD-BYE (1931) (w)Edward Heyman (m)John Green. (I)Musical: *Here Goes The Bride*, by Frances Langford.

HELLO OLD FRIEND (1976) (wm)Eric Clapton (P)Eric Clapton.

HELLO STRANGER (1963) (wm)Barbara Lewis. (P)Barbara Lewis. (R)1973 by Fire and Rain. (R)1977 by Yvonne Elliman.

HELLO! SWANEE, HELLO! (1926) (wm)Sam Coslow—Addy Britt. (P)Ben Bernie and his Orchestra. (CR)Fred Waring's Pennsylvanians.

HELLO TUCKY (1925) (w)B. G. De Sylva (m)Joseph Meyer—James F. Hanley. (I)Musical: *Big Boy*, by Al Jolson. (P)Al Jolson.

HELLO WALLS (1961) (wm)Willie Nelson. (P)Faron Young.

HELLO, YOUNG LOVERS (1951) (w)Oscar Hammerstein II (m)Richard Rodgers. (I)Musical: *The King and I*, by Gertrude Lawrence. In film version, by Deborah Kerr. (P)Perry Como.

HELP! (1965) (wm)John Lennon—Paul McCartney. (I)Film: *Help!*, by The Beatles. (P)The Beatles. No. 1 Chart Record.

HELP IS ON ITS WAY (1977) (wm)Glenn Shorrock. (P)Little River Band.

HELP ME (1973) (wm)Joni Mitchell. (P)Joni Mitchell.

HELP ME, GIRL (1974) (wm)Joni Mitchell. (P)Joni Mitchell.

HELP ME MAKE IT THROUGH THE NIGHT (1971) (wm)Kris Kristofferson. (I)Film: *Fat City*, by Sammi Smith. (P)Sammi Smith. (R)1971 by Joe Simon. (R)1972 by O. C. Smith.

HELP ME, RHONDA (1965) (wm)Brian Wilson. (P)The Beach Boys. No. 1 Chart Record. (R)1975 by Johnnie

Rivers.

HELP YOURSELF (1968) (w-Eng)Jack Fishman, (m)C. Donida. (P)Tom Jones.

HELP YOURSELF TO HAPPINESS (1931) (wm)Mack Gordon—Harry Revel—Harry Richman. (I)Revue: *Ziegfeld Follies of 1931*, by Harry Richman.

HELTER SKELTER (1968) (wm)John Lennon—Paul McCartney. (P)The Beatles.

HENDERSON STOMP (1926) (m)Fletcher Henderson. (P)Fletcher Henderson and his Orchestra.

HENNESEY (1960) (m)Sonny Burke. (I)T. V. Series: *Hennesey* as Main Title Theme. The series starred Jackie Cooper.

HER ROYAL MAJESTY (1962) (wm)Gerry Goffin—Carole King. (P)James Darren.

HER TOWN TOO (1981) (wm)James Taylor—John D. Souther—Waddy Wachtel. (P)James Taylor and J.D. Souther.

HERE (1954) (wm)Dorcas Cochran—Harold Grant. Melody based on Caro Nome from opera *Rigoletto* by Verdi. (P)Tony Martin.

HERE AM I-BROKEN HEARTED (1927) (wm)B.G. De Sylva—Lew Brown (m)Ray Henderson. (I)Revue: *Artists and Models of 1927*, by Jack Osterman. (P)Belle Baker. (R)1952 by Johnnie Ray. (R)1956 Film: *The Best Things In Life Are Free*, by Dan Dailey and Ernest Borgnine.

HERE AND NOW (1963) (wm)Noel Coward. (I)Musical: *The Girl Who Came To Supper*, by Florence Henderson.

HERE COME THE BRITISH (Bang! Bang!) (1934) (w)Johnny Mercer (m)Bernie Hanighen. No artist credited with introduction.

HERE COME THOSE TEARS AGAIN (1977) (wm)Nancy Farnsworth—Jackson Browne. (P)Jackson Browne.

(Lookie, Lookie, Lookie)HERE COMES COOKIE (1935) (wm)Mack Gordon. (I)Film: *Love In Bloom*, by Gracie Allen.

HERE COMES HEAVEN AGAIN (1945) (w)Harold Adamson (m)Jimmy McHugh. (I)Film: *Doll Face*, by Perry Como. (P)Perry Como.

HERE COMES MY BABY (1967) (wm)Cat Stevens. (P)The Tremeloes.

HERE COMES SANTA CLAUS (1947) (wm)Gene Autry—Oakley Haldeman. (P)Gene Autry.

HERE COMES SUMMER (1959) (wm)Jerry Keller. (P)Jerry Keller. (R)1977 by Wildfire.

HERE COMES THAT HEARTACHE AGAIN (1953) (w)Roy Alfred (m)Al Frisch. (P)Tony Bennett.

HERE COMES THAT RAINY DAY FEELING AGAIN (1971) (wm)Anthony Gordon Instone—Roger Cook—Roger Greenaway. (P)The Fortunes.

HERE COMES THE JUDGE (1968) (wm)Billie Jean Brown—Suzanne dePasse—Frederick Long. (P)Shorty Long (CR)Pigmeat Markham. (CR)The Magistrates.

HERE COMES THE NIGHT (1965) (wm)Bert Berns. (P)Them.

HERE COMES THE RAIN AGAIN (1984) (wm)Annie Lennox—David Stewart. (P)Eurythmics.

HERE COMES THE SHOW BOAT (1927) (w)Billy Rose (m)Maceo Pinkard. (I)Film: *Show Boat* by The Ensemble. Theme song of The Maxwell House Show Boat Radio Show. Recorded by Vaughn Deleath.

HERE COMES THE SUN (1930) (w)Arthur Freed (m)Harry Woods. (P)Vincent Lopez and his Orchestra. (CR)Bert Lown and his Orchestra.

HERE COMES THE SUN (1969) (wm)George Harrison. (P)The Beatles. (R)1971 by Richie Havens.

HERE GOES (A Fool) (1934) (w)Ted Koehler (m)Harold Arlen. (I)Nightclub Revue: *Cotton Club Parade*: by Jimmie Lunceford and his Orchestra.

HERE I AM (1965) (w)Hal David (m)Burt Bacharach. (I)Film: *What's New Pussycat?* (P)Dionne Warwick.

HERE I AM (1981) (wm)Norman Sallitt. (P)Air Supply.

HERE I GO AGAIN (1969) (wm)William Robinson—Al Cleveland—Terry Johnson—Warren Moore. (P)Smokey and The Miracles.

HERE I GO AGAIN (1987) (wm)Coverdale—Marsden. (P)Whitesnake. No. 1 Chart Record.

HERE I'LL STAY (1948) (w)Alan Jay Lerner (m)Kurt Weill. (I)Musical: *Love Life*, by Nanette Fabray and Ray Middleton. (P)Jo Stafford.

HERE IN MY ARMS (1925) (w)Lorenz Hart (m)Richard Rodgers. (I)Musical: *Dearest Enemy*, by Helen Ford and Charles Purcell. Recorded by Leo Reisman and his Orchestra.

HERE IN MY HEART (1952) (wm)Pat Genaro—Lou Levinson—Bill Borrelli. (P)Al Martino. No. 1 Chart Record. (CR)Vic Damone. (CR)Tony Bennett.

HERE IT COMES AGAIN (1965) (wm)Les Reed—Barry Mason. (P)The Fortunes.

HERE LIES LOVE (1932) (wm)Leo Robin—Ralph Rainger. (I)Film: *The Big Broadcast*, by Bing Crosby, Arthur Tracy, and Vincent Lopez and his Orchestra. (P)Bing Crosby.

HERE, THERE, AND EVERYWHERE (1966) (wm)John Lennon—Paul McCartney. (P)The Beatles. (R)1976 by Emmylou Harris.

HERE WE GO AGAIN (1967) (wm)Donnie H. Lanier—Russell Don Steagall. (P)Ray Charles. (R)1969 by Nancy Sinatra.

HERE YOU COME AGAIN (1977) (wm)Barry Mann—Cynthia Weil. (P)Dolly Parton.

HERE'S A HAND (1942) (w)Lorenz Hart (m)Richard Rodgers. (I)Musical: *By Jupiter*, by Ronnie Graham and Constance Moore.

HERE'S LOVE IN YOUR EYE (1936) (wm)Leo Robin—Ralph Rainger. (I)Film: *The Big Broadcast of 1937*, by Benny Fields. (P)Benny Goodman and his Orchestra.

HERE'S THAT RAINY DAY (1953) (w)Johnny Burke (m)Jimmy Van Heusen. (I)Musical: *Carnival In Flanders*, by John Raitt.

HERE'S TO LOVE (1949) (wm)Jay Livingston—Ray Evans. (I)Film: *My Friend Irma*, by Dean Martin. (P)Dean Martin.

HERE'S TO MY LADY (1951) (w)Johnny Mercer (m)Rube Bloom. (P)Nat "King" Cole.

HERE'S TO ROMANCE (1935) (w)Herb Magidson (m)Con Conrad. (I)Film: *Here's To Romance*, by Nino Martini. Recorded by Enric Madriguera and his Orchestra.

HERE'S TO US (1962) (w)Carolyn Leigh (m)Cy Coleman. (I)Musical: *Little Me*, by Nancy Andrews and The Chorus.

HERNANDO'S HIDEAWAY (1954) (wm)Richard Adler—Jerry Ross. (I)Musical: *The Pajama Game*, by Carol Haney. (P)Archie Bleyer and his Orchestra. (CR)Johnnie Ray.

HEROES AND VILLAINS (1967) (wm)Brian Wilson—Van Dyke Parks. (P)The Beach Boys.

HE'S A DEVIL IN HIS OWN HOME TOWN (1914) (wm)Grant Clark—Irving Berlin. One of the few songs in the Berlin corpus for which Berlin did not write both words and music. (I)Billy Morton.

HE'S A GOOD MAN TO HAVE AROUND (1929) (w)Jack Yellen (m)Milton Ager. (I)Film: *Honky Tonk*, by Sophie Tucker.

HE'S A LADIES MAN (1927) (wm)B.G. De Sylva—Lew Brown (m)Ray Henderson. (I)Musical: *Good News*, by Don Tomkins and The Chorus. (R)1947 Film: *Good News*, by Peter Lawford, Mel Torme, and Ray McDonald.

HE'S A RAG PICKER (1914) (wm)Irving Berlin. (I)Musical: *5064 Gerard*, by Jack Norworth. Recorded by The Peerless Quartet.

HE'S A REAL GONE GUY (1947) (wm)Nellie Lutcher. (P)Nellie Lutcher.

HE'S A REBEL (1962) (wm)Gene Pitney. (P)The Crystals. No. 1 Chart Record.

HE'S A TRAMP (1955) (wm)Peggy Lee—Sonny Burke. (I)Cartoon Film: *The Lady And The Tramp*, by Peggy Lee. (P)Peggy Lee.

HE'S GOOD FOR ME (1973) (w)Dorothy Fields (m)Michelle Lee. (I)Musical: *Seesaw*, by Michelle Lee.

HE'S GOT THE WHOLE WORLD IN HIS HANDS (1958) (wm)Geoff Love. Adaptation of a gospel song. (P)Laurie London. No. 1 Chart Record.

HE'S IN LOVE (1953) (wm)Robert Wright—George Forrest. Adapted from Polovetsian Dances by Borodin. (I)Musical: *Kismet*, by Hal Hackaday.

HE'S MY FRIEND (1964) (wm)Meredith Willson. (I)Film: *The Unsinkable Molly Brown*, by Harve Presnell.

HE'S MY GUY (1943) (wm)Don Raye—Gene de Paul. (P)Harry James and his Orchestra, vocal by Helen Forrest.

HE'S 1-A IN THE ARMY AND HE'S A-1 IN MY HEART (1941) (P)Harry James and his Orchestra, vocal by Helen Forrest.

HE'S SO FINE (1963) (wm)Ronnie Mack. (P)The Chiffons. No. 1 Chart Record. (R)1971 by Jody Miller.

HE'S SO SHY (1980) (w)Cynthia Weil (m)Tom Snow. (P)The Pointer Sisters.

HE'S SURE THE BOY I LOVE (1962) (wm)Barry Mann—Cynthia Weil. (P)The Crystals.

HE'S THE GREATEST DANCER (1979) (wm)Bernard Edwards—Nile Rodgers. (P)Sister Sledge.

HEY! BA-BA-RE-BOP (1945) (wm)Lionel Hampton—Curley Hamner. (I)Lionel Hampton and his Orchestra. (P)The Tex Beneke—Glenn Miller Orchestra.

HEY, BABE, HEY! (I'm Nuts About You) (1936) (wm)Cole Porter. (I)Film: *Born To Dance*, by Eleanor Powell, James Stewart, Una Merkel, and Buddy Ebsen.

HEY! BABY (1962) (wm)Bruce Channel—Margaret Cobb. (P)Bruce Channel. No. 1 Chart Record. (R)1977 by Ringo Starr.

HEY, BABY! THEY'RE PLAYIN' OUR SONG (1967) (wm)Jim Holvay—Gary Beisbier. (P)The Buckinghams.

HEY BIG BROTHER (1972) (wm)Dino Fekaris—Nick Zesses. (P)Rare Earth.

HEY BOBBA BEEDLE (1964) (wm)Kal Mann—Dave Appell. (P)Chubby Checker.

HEY BULLDOG (1968) (wm)John Lennon—Paul McCartney. (I)Film: *Yellow Submarine*, by The Beatles. (P)The Beatles.

HEY DEANIE (1977) (wm)Eric Carmen. (P)Shaun Cassidy.

HEY, DOLL BABY (1955) (wm)Titus Turner. (P)The Clovers.

HEY, GIRL (1963) (wm)Gerry Goffin—Carole King. (P)Freddie Scott. (R)1971 by Donny Osmond.

HEY, GOOD LOOKIN' (1942) (wm)Cole Porter. (I)Musical: *Something For The Boys*, by Ethel Merman, Bill Johnson, Betty Bruce, and Bill Callahan.

HEY GOOD LOOKIN' (1951) (wm)Hank Williams. (I)Hank Williams. (P)Frankie Laine and Jo Stafford.

HEY! JEALOUS LOVER (1956) (wm)Sammy Cahn—Kay Twomey—Bee Walker. (P)Frank Sinatra.

HEY JOE (1966) (wm)Dino Valenti. (P)The Leaves. (R)1967 by Cher. (R)1969 by Wilson Pickett.

HEY JUDE (1968) (wm)John Lennon—Paul McCartney. No. 1 Chart Record. (CR)Wilson Pickett.

HEY, LEROY, YOUR MAMA'S CALLIN' YOU (1967) (w)Johnnie Pruitt (m)Jimmy Castor. (P)Jimmy Castor.

HEY, LITTLE COBRA (1964) (wm)Marshal Howard Connors. (P)The Rip Chords.

HEY, LITTLE GIRL (1959) (wm)Bobby Stevenson—Otis Blackwell. (P)Dee Clark.

HEY LITTLE GIRL (1963) (wm)Curtis Mayfield. (P)Major Lance.

HEY, LOOK ME OVER (1960) (w)Carolyn Leigh (m)Cy Coleman. (I)Musical: *Wildcat*, by Lucille Ball and Paula Stewart.

HEY, MR. BANJO (1955) (wm)Freddy Morgan—Norman Malkin. (P)The Sunnysiders.

HEY, MR. POSTMAN (1946) (w)Don Raye (m)Paul Weston. (P)Ella Mae Morse with Freddie Slack.

HEY NINETEEN (1980) (wm)Walter Becker—Donald Fagen. (P)Steely Dan.

HEY, PAULA (1963) (wm)Ray Hildebrand. (P)Paul and Paula. No. 1 Chart Record.

HEY, SCHOOLGIRL (1957) (w)Arthur Garfunkel (m)Paul Simon. (P)Tom and Jerry. (Simon and Garfunkel).

HEY THERE (1954) (wm)Richard Adler—Jerry Ross. (I)Musical: *The Pajama Game*, by John Raitt. (P)Rosemary Clooney. No. 1 Chart Record. (CR)Sammy Davis, Jr. (CR)Johnnie Ray.

HEY THERE LONELY BOY (1963) (w)Earl Shuman (m)Leon Carr. (P)Ruby and The Romantics. (R)1970 by Eddie Holman. (R)1980 by Robert John. Both revivals under the title of *Hey There Lonely Girl*.

HEY, WESTERN UNION MAN (1968) (wm)Kenny Gamble—Leon Huff—Jerry Butler. (P)Jerry Butler.

HEY, WHAT DID THE BLUEBIRD SAY? (1936) (w)Ted Koehler (m)Jimmy McHugh. (I)Film: *Dimples*, by Shirley Temple.

HEY YOU (1975) (wm)Randy Bachman. (P)Bachman—Turner Overdrive.

HEY, YOUNG FELLA, CLOSE YOUR OLD UMBRELLA (1933) (I)Revue: *Clowns In Clover*, by Walter Woolf King.

HI-DE-HO (That Old Sweet Roll) (1970) (wm)Gerry Goffin—Carole King. (P)Blood, Sweat, and Tears.

HI-DIDDLE-DEE-DEE (An Actor's Life For Me) (1940) (w)Ned Wshington (m)Leigh Harline. (I)Cartoon Film: *Piocchio*, by the voices of Walter Catlett and Dickie Jones.

HI-HEEL SNEAKERS (1964) (wm)Robert Higgenbotham. (P)Tommy Tucker. (CR)Jerry Lee Lewis.

(R)1965 by Stevie Wonder. (R)1968 by Jose Feliciano.

HI HI HI (1973) (wm)Paul and Linda McCartney. (P)Paul McCartney and Wings.

HI-LILI, HI-LO (1952) (w)Helen Deutsch (m)Bronislau Kaper. (I)Film: *Lili*, by Leslie Caron and Mel Ferrer. (P)1956 by Dick Hyman Trio. (CR)Roger Williams and his Orchestra. (R)1963 by Richard Chamberlain.

HI, NEIGHBOR (1941) (wm)Jack Owens. (I)Film: *San Antonio Rose*, by Jane Frazee and The Merry Macs. (P)Orrin Tucker and his Orchestra.

HIDE AWAY-1962 (1962) (wm)Freddy King—Sonny Thompson. (P)Freddy King.

HIDEAWAY (1958) (wm)Robert Goodman. (P)The Four Esquires.

HIGH AND LOW (I've Been Looking For You) (1931) (w)Howard Dietz—Desmond Carter (m)Arthur Schwartz. (I)Revue: *The Band Wagon*, by John Barker and Roberta Robinson. (P)Fred Waring's Pennsylvanians.

HIGH AND THE MIGHTY, THE (1954) (w)Ned Washington (m)Dimitri Tiomkin. (I)Film: *The High And The Mighty*, as soundtrack theme. (P)Leroy Holmes and his Orchestra. (CR)Victor Young and his Orchestra. Vocal version by Johnny Desmond.

HIGH HAT (1927) (w)Ira Gershwin (m)George Gershwin. (I)Musical: *Funny Face*, by Fred Astaire.

HIGH HOPES (1959) (w)Sammy Cahn (m)Jimmy Van Heusen. (I)Film: *A Hole In The Head*, by Frank Sinatra and Eddie Hodges. (P)Sinatra and Hodges. Academy Award Winner.

HIGH LIFE (1929) (m)Duke Ellington. (P)Duke Ellington and his Cotton Club Orchestra.

HIGH NOON (Do Not Forsake Me) (1952) (w)Ned Washington (m)Dimitri Tiomkin. (I)Film: *High Noon*, by Tex Ritter. (P)Frankie Laine. Academy Award Winner.

HIGH ON A WINDY HILL (1941) (wm)Joan Whitney—Alex Kramer. (P)Jimmy Dorsey and his Orchestra. No. 1 Chart Record. (CR)Gene Krupa and his Orchestra.

HIGH ON YOU (1985) (wm)Frankie Sullivan—Jim Peterik. (P)Survivor.

HIGH SCHOOL CADETS (1891) (m)John Philip Sousa. One of Sousa's most popular marches.

HIGH SCHOOL CONFIDENTIAL (1958) (wm)Ron Hargrave—Jerry Lee Lewis. ()Film: *High School Confidential*, by Jerry Lee Lewis. (P)Jerry Lee Lewis.

HIGH SCHOOL DANCE (1977) (wm)Edmund, James, Joseph, and Leon Sylvers. (P)The Sylvers.

HIGH SOCIETY (1901) (wm)Walter Melrose—Porter Steele. Very popular Dixieland song. (R)1938 by Bob Crosby and his Orchestra.

HIGH, WIDE, AND HANDSOME (1937) (w)Oscar Hammerstein II (m)Jerome Kern. (I)Film: *High, Wide, and Handsome*, by Irene Dunne.

(Your Love Keeps Lifting Me)HIGHER AND HIGHER (1967) (wm)Gary L. Jackson—Carl Smith—Raynard Miner. (P)Jackie Wilson. (R)1977 by Rita Coolidge.

HIGHER GROUND (1973) (wm)Stevie Wonder. (P)Stevie Wonder.

HIGHER LOVE (1986) (w)Will Jennings (m)Steve Winwood. (P)Steve Winwood. No. 1 Chart Record. NARAS Award Winner.

HIGHWAY 61 REVISITED (1965) (wm)Bob Dylan.

(P)Bob Dylan.

HIGHWAYMAN (1977) (wm)Jim Webb. (P)Waylon Jennings, Willie Nelson, Johnny Cash, and Kris Kristofferson. NARAS Award Winner.

HIJACK (1975) (m)Jose Miro. (P)Herbie Mann.

HILLS OF COLORADO (1947) (wm)Bernie Bierman—Jack Manus. (P)Guy Lombardo and his Royal Canadians.

HILLS OF TOMORROW. THE (1981) (wm)Stephen Sondheim. (I)Musical: *Merrily We Roll Along*, by The Company.

HIM (1980) (wm)Rupert Holmes. (P)Rupert Holmes.

HIM OR ME, WHAT'S IT GONNA BE? (1967) (wm)Mark Lindsay—Terry Melcher. (P)Paul Revere and The Raiders.

HINDUSTAN (1918) (wm)Oliver Wallace. (I)Musical: *Joy Bells*. (R)1948 by Ted Weems and his Orchestra.

HINKY DINKY PARLAY VOO (1918) (wm)Unknown. Popular World War I song. Recorded by Billy Jones and Ernie Hare (The Happiness Boys).

HIP CITY, PART 2 (1968) (wm)Autry DeWalt—Janie Bradford. (P)Jr. Walker and The All Stars.

HIP TO BE SQUARE (1986) (wm)Bill Gibson—Sean Hopper—Huey Lewis. (P)Huey Lewis & The News.

HIS EYES-HER EYES (1968) (w)Alan and Marilyn Bergman (m)Michel Legrand. (I)Film: *The Thomas Crown Affair* on soundtrack. (R)1972 by Sarah Vaughan.

HIS FEET TOO BIG FOR DE BED (1946) (wm)Dick Sanford—Hernandez Brana—Sammy Mysels. (P)Stan Kenton and his Orchestra, vocal by June Christy.

HIS LATEST FLAME (Marie's The Name) (1961) (wm)Doc Pomus—Mort Shuman. (P)Elvis Presley.

HIS ROCKING HORSE RAN AWAY (1944) (w)Johnny Burke (m)Jimmy Van Heusen. (I)Film: *And The Angels Sing*, by Betty Hutton. (P)Betty Hutton.

HIT AND RUN AFFAIR (1954) (wm)Don Roseland—Ray Cormier—Mel Van. (P)Perry Como.

HIT ME WITH YOUR BEST SHOT (1980) (wm)Eddie Schwartz. (P)Pat Benatar.

HIT THE ROAD, JACK (1961) (wm)Percy Mayfield. (P)Ray Charles. No. 1 Chart Record. NARAS Award Winner. (R)1976 by The Stampeders.

HIT THE ROAD TO DREAMLAND (1942) (w)Johnny Mercer (m)Harold Arlen. (I)Film: *Star Spangled Rhythm*, by Dick Powell, Mary Martin, and The Golden Gate Quartet. (P)Bing Crosby. (CR)Freddie Slack and his Orchestra.

HITCHIN' A RIDE (1970) (wm)Peter Callendar—Mitch Murray. (P)Vanity Fair.

HITTIN' THE BOTTLE (1930) (w)Ted Koehler (m)Harold Arlen. (I)Revue: *Earl Carrolls's Vanities*. First recording by The Colonial Club Orchestra. (R)1937 by Jimmy Lunceford and his Orchestra.

HO HO SONG, THE (wm)Red Buttons-Joe Darion-Jack Wolf. (P)Red Buttons.

HO HUM (1931) (w)Edward Heyman (m)Dana Suesse. (I)Film: *Monkey Business*, by The Marx Brothers. Recorded by Gus Arnheim and his Orchestra. (CR)Ted Lewis.

HOBO ON PARK AVENUE (1935) (m)Will Hudson. (P)Theme Song of The Hudson-De Lange Orchestra.

HOCUS POCUS (1973) (wm)Jan Akkerman—Theis Van Leen. (P)Focus.

HOLD 'EM JOE (1954) (wm)Harry Thomas. (I)Revue: *John Murray Anderson's Almanac*, by Harry

Belafonte. (P)Harry Belafonte.

HOLD HER TIGHT (1972) (wm)Alan, Wayne, and Merrill Osmond. (P)The Osmonds.

HOLD ME (1920) (wm)Art Hickman—Ben Black. (P)Art Hickman and his Orchestra. No. 1 Chart Record.

HOLD ME (1933) (wm)Little Jack Little—Dave Oppenheim—Ira Schuster. (P)Little Jack Little.

HOLD ME (1982) (wm)Christine McVie—Robbie Patton. (P)Fleetwood Mac.

HOLD ME-HOLD ME-HOLD ME (1951) (w)Betty Comden—Adolph Green (m)Jule Styne. (I)Revue: *Two On The Aisle*, by Dolores Gray.

HOLD ME IN YOUR ARMS (1954) (wm)Ray Heindorf—Charles Henderson—Don Pippin. (I)Film: *Young At Heart*, by Doris Day. (P)Doris Day.

HOLD ME NOW (1984) (wm)Thomas Bailey—Alannah Currie—Joe Leeway. (P)The Thompson Twins.

HOLD ME, THRILL ME, KISS ME (1953) (wm)Harry Noble. (P)Karen Chandler. (R)1965 by Mel Carter.

HOLD ME TIGHT (1964) (wm)John Lennon—Paul McCartney. (P)The Beatles.

HOLD ME TIGHT (1968) (wm)Johnny Nash. (P)Johnny Nash.

HOLD MY HAND (1934) (wm)Irving Caesar—Jack Yellen—Ray Henderson. (I)Film: *George White's Scandals*. (P)Ray Noble and his Orchestra.

HOLD MY HAND (1950) (wm)Jack Lawrence—Richard Myers. (I)Film: *Susan Slept Here*, by Don Cornell on soundtrack. (P)Don Cornell.

HOLD ON (I'm Coming) (1966) (wm)Isaac Hayes—David Porter. (P)Sam and Dave. (CR)Chuck Jackson and Maxine Brown.

HOLD ON (1979) (wm)Ian Gomm. (P)Ian Gomm.

HOLD ON TIGHT (1981) (wm)Jeff Lynne. (P)ELO.

HOLD ONTO MY LOVE (1980) (wm)Robin Gibb—Blue Weaver. (P)Jimmy Ruffin.

HOLD THE LINE (1978) (wm)David Paich. (P)Toto.

HOLD TIGHT-HOLD TIGHT (Want Some Sea Food Mama) (1939) (wm)Leonard Kent—Edward Robinson—Leonard Ware—Jerry Brandow—Willie Spottswood. (P)The Andrews Sisters with Jimmy Dorsey and his Orchestra. (CR)Fats Waller.

HOLD WHAT YOU'VE GOT (1964) (wm)Joe Tex. (P)Joe Tex.

HOLD YOUR HEAD UP (1972) (wm)Rod Argent—Chris White. (P)Argent.

HOLD YOUR MAN (1933) (w)Arthur Freed (m)Nacio Herb Brown. (I)Film: *Hold Your Man*, by Jean Harlow. (P)Gertrude Niesen. (CR)Don Bestor and his Orchestra.

HOLDING BACK THE YEARS (1986) (wm)Mick Hucknall—Neil Moss. (P)Simply Red. No. 1 Chart Record.

HOLDIN' ON TO YESTERDAY (1974) (wm)Joseph Puerta, Jr.—David Pack. (P)Ambrosia.

HOLIDAY (1967) (wm)Barry, Robin, and Maurice Gibb. (P)The Bee Gees.

HOLIDAY FOR STRINGS (1943) (w)Sammy Gallop (m)David Rose. (P)David Rose and his Orchestra. (CR)Jimmy Dorsey and his Orchestra. (CR)Spike Jones.

HOLLY HOLY (1969) (wm)Neil Diamond. (P)Neil Diamond. (R)1971 by Jr. Walker and The All Stars.

HOLLY JOLLY CHRISTMAS, A (1962) (wm)Johnny Marks. (I)TV Show: *Rudolph The Red Nosed Reindeer*. (P)Burl Ives.

HOLLYWOOD NIGHTS (1978) (wm)Bob Seger. (P)Bob

Seger.

HOLLYWOOD SWINGING (1974) (wm)Ricky West—Claydes Smith—George Brown—Ronald Bell—Robert Bell—Robert Mickens—Dennis Thomas. (P)Kool and The Gang.

HOLY COW (1966) (wm)Allen Toussaint. (P)Lee Dorsey.

HOME (When Shadows Fall) (1931) (wm)Peter Van Steeden—Harry Clarkson—Jeff Clarkson. (P)Theme Song of Peter Van Steeden and his Orchestra. (R)1950 by Nat "King" Cole.

HOME (1974) (wm)Charlie Small. (I)Musical: *The Wiz*, by Stephanie Mills.

HOME COOKIN' (1950) (wm)Jay Livingston—Ray Evans. (I)Film: *Fancy Pants*, by Bob Hope and Lucille Ball.

(There's No Place Like)HOME FOR THE HOLIDAYS (1955) (w)Al Stillman (m)Robert Allen. (P)Perry Como.

HOME OF THE BRAVE (1965) (wm)Barry Mann—Cynthia Weil. (P)Jody Miller. (CR)Bonnie and The Treasures.

HOME ON THE RANGE (1873) (wm)Unknown. Traditional American Cowboy Song. (R)1933 by Bing Crosby.

HOME SWEET HOME (1823) (w)John Howard Payne. (m)Based on a Sicilian song. (P)Jenny Lind.

HOMELESS (1986) (wm)Paul Simon—Joseph Shabalala. (P)Paul Simon. Shabalala is one of South Africa's most famous musicians.

HOMESICK (1923) (wm)Irving Berlin. (P)Nora Bayes.

HOMESICK-THAT'S ALL (1945) (wm)Gordon Jenkins. (P)Frank Sinatra.

HOMEWARD BOUND (1966) (wm)Paul Simon. (P)Simon and Garfunkel.

HOMEWORK (1949) (wm)Irving Berlin. (I)Musical: *Miss Liberty*, by Mary McCarty.

HONEST AND TRULY (1924) (wm)Fred Rose—Leo Wood. (P)Henry Burr.

HONEST I DO (1957) (wm)Jimmy Reed—Ewart G. Abner, Jr. (P)Jimmy Reed.

HONESTLY (1933) (w)Charles Newman (m)Isham Jones. (P)Isham Jones and his Orchestra.

HONESTLY SINCERE (1960) (w)Lee Adams (m)Charles Strouse. (I)Musical: *Bye Bye Birdie*, by Dick Gautier and The Chorus. In film version (1963) by Jesse Pearson.

HONESTY (1979) (wm)Billy Joel. (P)Billy Joel.

HONEY (1928) (wm)Seymour Simons—Haven Gillespie—Richard A. Whiting. (P)Rudy Vallee. No. 1 Chart Record.

HONEY (1968) (wm)Bobby Russell. (P)Bobby Goldsboro. (CR)O.C. Smith.

HONEY-BABE (1955) (w)Paul Francis Webster (m)Max Steiner. (I)Film: *Battle Cry* on soundtrack. (P)Art Mooney and his Orchestra.

HONEY BUN (1949) (w)Oscar Hammerstein II (m)Richard Rodgers. (I)Musical: *South Pacific*, by Mary Martin. In film version (1958)by Mitzi Gayno.

HONEY CHILE (1967) (wm)Sylvia Moy—Richard Morris. (P)Martha and The Vandellas.

HONEY COME BACK (1965) (wm)Jim Webb. (P)Glen Campbell. (CR)Chuck Jackson.

HONEY IN THE HONEYCOMB (1940) (w)John Latouche (m)Vernon Duke. (I)Musical: *Cabin In The Sky*, Katherine Dunham. In film version (1943)by Ethel Waters and Lena Horne.

HONEY LOVE (1954) (wm)Clyde McPhatter—J. Gerald. (P)The Drifters.

HONEY PIE (1968) (wm)John Lennon—Paul McCartney. (P)The Beatles.

HONEYCOMB (1957) (wm)Bob Merrill. (P)Jimmie Rodgers. No. 1 Chart Record.

HONEYDRIPPER, THE (1945) (wm)Joe Liggins. (P)Joe Liggins. (CR)Jimmie Lunceford and his Orchestra.

HONEYMOON HOTEL (1933) (w)Al Dubin (m)Harry Warren. (I)Film: *Footlight Parade*, by Dick Powell and Ruby Keeler. Recorded by Leo Reisman and his Orchestra.

HONEYSUCKLE ROSE (1929) (wm)Andy Razaf—Thomas Waller. (I)Revue: *Load Of Coal*, as a dance routine. (I)On radio by Paul Whiteman and his Orchestra. Recordings by Fletcher Henderon, Fats Waller, Red Norvo, Dorsey Brothers, Bunny Berigan, Tommy Dorsey.

HONEYTHIEF THE (1987) (wm)A. McLeod—J. McElhone—G. Skinner—H. Travers. (P)Hipsway.

HONG KONG BLUES (1939) (wm)Hoagy Carmichael. (I)Film: *To Have And Have Not*, by Hoagy Carmichael. (P)Hoagy Carmichael.

HONKY CAT (1972) (wm)Elton John—Bernie Taupin. (P)Elton John.

HONKY TONK (1956) (w)Henry Glover (m)Bill Doggett—Billy Butler—Shape Sheppard—Clifford Scott. (P)Bill Doggett. (R)1965 by Lonnie Mack. (R)1972 by James Brown.

HONKY TONK TRAIN (1939) (m)Meade "Lux" Lewis. (I)Meade "Lux" Lewis as piano solo. (P)Bob Crosby and his Orchestra, featuring Bob Zurke on piano.

HONKY TONK WOMEN (1969) (wm)Mick Jagger—Keith Richard. (P)The Rolling Stones. No. 1 Chart Record.

HONOLULU (1939) (w)Gus Kahn (m)Harry Warren. (I)Film: *Honolulu*, by Gracie Allen. (P)Tommy Dorsey and his Orchestra.

HONOLULU LULU (1963) (wm)Jan Berry—Roger Christian—Spunky. (P)Jan and Dean.

HOODLE ADDLE (1946) (wm)Ray McKinley. (I)Ray McKinley and his Orchestra. (P)Tex Beneke and his Orchestra.

HOOKED ON A FEELING (1968) (wm)Mark James. (P)B.J. Thomas. (R)1974 by Blue Swede. No. 1 Chart Record.

HOOP-DEE-DO (1950) (w)Frank Loesser (m)Milton De Lugg. (P)Perry Como. (CR)Kay Starr. (CR)Doris Day.

HOOPS (1931) (w)Howard Dietz (m)Arthur Schwartz. (I)Revue: *The Band Wagon*, by Fred and Adele Astaire.

HOORAY FOR CAPTAIN SPAULDING (1928) (wm)Bert Kalmar—Harry Ruby. (I)Musical: *Animal Crackers*, by Zeppo Marx, Robert Greig, Margaret Dumont, Groucho Marx, and The Chorus. In film version (1930)by the same performers. (R)1950 Film: *Three Little Words*, by Fred Astaire and Red Skelton.

HOORAY FOR HAZEL (1966) (wm)Tommy Roe. (P)Tommy Roe.

HOORAY FOR HOLLYWOOD (1937) (w)Johnny Mercer (m)Richard A. Whiting. (I)Film: *Hollywood Hotel*, by Johnny "Scat" Davis, Frances Langford, and Benny Goodman and his Orchestra. (P)Johnny "Scat" Davis.

HOORAY FOR LOVE (1935) (w)Dorothy Fields (m)Jimmy McHugh. (I)Film: *Hooray For Love*, by Gene Raymond.

HOORAY FOR LOVE (1948) (w)Leo Robin (m)Harold Arlen. (I)Film: *Casbah*, by Tony Martin. (CR)Johnny Mercer.

HOORAY FOR SPINACH (1939) (w)Johnny Mercer (m)Harry Warren. (I)Film: *Naughty But Nice*, by Ann Sheridan.

HOOTIE BLUES (1942) (wm)Jay McShann—Charlie Parker. (P)Jay McShann and his Orchestra, vocal by Walter Brown. This was the first recording to feature Charlie Parker.

HOP SCOTCH POLKA (1949) (wm)William Whitlock—Carl Sigman—Gene Rayburn. (I)In England, by Billy Whitlock. (P)In United States, by Guy Lombardo and his Royal Canadians. (CR)Art Mooney.

HOPELESS (1963) (wm)Doc Pomus—Alan Jeffreys. (P)Andy Williams.

HOPELESSLY DEVOTED TO YOU (1978) (wm)John Farrar. (I)Film: *Grease*, by Olivia Newton-John. (P)Olivia Newton-John.

HOPPY, GENE, AND ME (1975) (wm)Thomas Garrett—Stephen Dorff—Milton Brown. (P)Roy Rogers.

HORA STACCATO (1930) (m)Grigoras Dinicu. Originally written in 1906 with arrangement by Jascha Heifetz in 1930. (P)Jascha Heifetz as violin solo.

HORSE, THE (1968) (m)Jesse James. (P)Cliff Nobles & Co.

HORSE TOLD ME, THE (1950) (w)Johnny Burke (m)Jimmy Van Heusen. (I)Film: *Riding High*, by Bing Crosby.

HORSE WITH NO NAME, A (1972) (wm)Lee Bunnell. (P)America. No. 1 Chart Record.

HORSE WITH THE DREAMY EYES, THE (1937) (w)Chet Forrest—Bob Wright (m)Walter Donaldson. (I)Film: *Saratoga*, by Cliff Edwards, Clark Gable, Una Merkel, Jean Harlow, and Hattie McDaniel.

HORSES (1926) (wm)Byron Gay—Richard A. Whiting. (P)George Olsen and his Orchestra. (CR)The Georgians.

HOSTESS WITH THE MOSTES' ON THE BALL, THE (1950) (wm)Irving Berlin. (I)Musical: *Call Me Madam*, by Ethel Merman. (P)Ethel Merman.

HOT AND BOTHERED (1929) (m)Duke Ellington. (P)Duke Ellington and his Orchestra.

HOT BLOODED (1978) (wm)Lou Grammatico. (P)Foreigner.

HOT CANARY, THE (1948) (w)Ray Gilbert (m)Paul Nero. (P)Florian Zabach. (CR)Paul Weston and his Orchestra.

HOT CHILD IN THE CITY (1978) (wm)James McColloch—Nick Gilder. (P)Nick Gilder. No. 1 Chart Record.

HOT DIGGITY (1956) (wm)Al Hoffman—Dick Manning. Melody based on Chabrier's Espana Rhapsody. (P)Perry Como. No. 1 Chart Record.

HOT FUN IN THE SUMMERTIME (1969) (wm)Sylvester Stewart. (P)Sly and The Family Stone. (R)1982 by Dayton.

HOT GIRLS IN LOVE (1983) (wm)Paul Dean—Bruce Fairbarn. (P)Loverboy.

HOT IN THE CITY (1982) (wm)Billy Idol. (P)Billy Idol.

HOT LEGS (1978) (wm)Rod Stewart. (P)Rod Stewart.

HOT LINE (1977) (wm)Kenny St. Lewis—Freddy Perren. (P)Sylvers.

HOT LIPS (1922) (wm)Henry Busse—Henry Lange—Lou Davis. (P)Paul Whiteman and his Orchestra, trumpet solo by Henry Busse. Theme song of Henry Busse

and his Orchestra. (CR)Ted Lewis.

HOT NUMBER (1979) (wm)Ishmael Ledesma. (P)Foxy.

HOT PASTRAMI (1963) (wm)Dessie Rozier. (P)The Dartells.

HOT ROD LINCOLN (1960) (wm)Charles Ryan—W.S. Stevenson. (P)Johnny Bond. (CR)Charlie Ryan. (R)1972 by Commander Cody.

HOT SMOKE AND SASSAFRAS (1969) (wm)Roy E. Cox, Jr.—William Rodney Prince. (P)Bubble Puppy.

HOT STUFF (1976) (wm)Mick Jagger—Keith Richard. (P)The Rolling Stones.

HOT STUFF (1979) (wm)Pete Bellotte—Harold Faltermeier—Keith Forsey. (P)Donna Summer. No. 1 Chart Record.

HOT SUMMER NIGHTS (1979) (wm)Walter Egan. (P)Night.

(There'll Be A)HOT TIME IN THE OLD TOWN TONIGHT (1896) (w)Joseph Hayden (m)Theodore M. Metz. (I)Dan Quinn,

(There'll Be A)HOT TIME IN THE TOWN OF BERLIN (When The Yanks Go Marching In) (1943) (w)John De Vries (m)Joe Bushkin. (I)Frank Sinatra. (P)Bing Crosby with The Andrews Sisters.

HOT TODDY (1952) (w)Herb Hendler (m)Ralph Flanagan. (P)Ralph Flanagan and his Orchestra. (CR)Cab Calloway and his Orchestra.

HOTEL CALIFORNIA (1977) (wm)Don Felder—Glenn Frey—Don Henley. (P)The Eagles. No. 1 Chart Record. NARAS Award Winner.

HOTEL HAPPINESS (1963) (w)Earl Shuman (m)Leon Carr. (P)Brook Benton.

HOTTA CHOCOLOTTA (1956) (w)Milton Drake (m)Vic Mizzy. (P)Ella Fitzgerald.

HOTTENTATE POTENTATE, THE (1935) (w)Howard Dietz (m)Arthur Schwartz. (I)Revue: *At Home Abroad*, by Ethel Waters.

HOUND DOG (1956) (wm)Jerry Leiber—Mike Stoller. (I)Willie Mae Thornton. (P)Elvis Presley. No. 1 Chart Record.

HOUND DOG MAN (1959) (wm)Doc Pomus—Mort Shuman. (I)Film: *Hound Dog Man*, by Fabian. (P)Fabian.

HOUR OF PARTING (1931) (w)Gus Kahn (m)Mischa Spoliansky. No artist credited with introduction. (R)1940 by Benny Goodman and his Orchestra.

HOUSE I LIVE IN, THE (That's America To Me) (1942) (wm)Lewis Allen—Earl Robinson. (I)Earl Robinson. (P)Frank Sinatra in film short *The House I Live In*. Also, on record.

HOUSE IS HAUNTED, THE (1934) (w)Billy Rose (m)Basil G. Adlam. (I)Revue: *Ziegfeld Follies of 1934*, by Jane Froman. (P)Jane Froman. (CR)Paul Whiteman and his Orchestra.

HOUSE IS NOT A HOME, A (1964) (w)Hal David (m)Burt Bacharach. (P)Dionne Warwick. (CR)Brook Benton.

HOUSE THAT JACK BUILT FOR JILL, THE (1936) (wm)Leo Robin—Frederick Hollander. (I)Film: *Rhythm On The Range*, by Bing Crosby. (P)Bing Crosby.

HOUSE OF BLUE LIGHTS (1946) (wm)Don Raye—Freddie Slack. (P)Ella Mae Morse with Freddie Slack. (R)1955 by Chuck Miller.

HOUSE OF FLOWERS (1954) (w)Truman Capote (m)Harold Arlen. (I)Musical: *House Of Flowers*, by Diahann Carroll and Rawn Spearman.

HOUSE OF THE RISING SUN, THE (1964) (wm)Alan

Price. Adapted from folk song. (P)The Animals. No 1 Chart Record. (R)1970 by Frijid Pink. (R)1978 by Santa Esmeralda. (R)1981 by Dolly Parton.

HOUSE RENT BALL (1924) (wm)Shelton Brooks. (P)Fletcher Henderson and his Orchestra.

HOUSE THAT JACK BUILT,THE (1968) (wm)Bobby Lance—Fran Robbins. (P)Aretha Franklin.

HOUSE WITH LOVE IN IT,A (1956) (w)Sylvia Dee (m)Sid Lippman. (P)The Four Lads.

HOUSTON (1965) (wm)Lee Hazlewood. (P)Dean Martin.

HOW ABOUT IT? (1931) (w)Lorenz Hart (m)Richard Rodgers. (I)Musical: *America's Sweetheart*, by Inez Courtney and Jack Whiting.

HOW ABOUT ME? (1928) (wm)Irving Berlin. (P)Fred Waring's Pennsylvanians.

HOW ABOUT YOU? (1941) (w)Ralph Freed (m)Burton Lane. (I)Film: *Babes On Broadway*, by Judy Garland and Mickey Rooney. (P)Tommy Dorsey and his Orchestra. (CR)Dick Jurgens and his Orchestra.

HOW AM I SUPPOSED TO LIVE WITHOUT YOU (1983) (wm)Michael Bolton—Doug James. (P)Laura Branigan.

HOW AM I TO KNOW? (1929) (w)Dorothy Parker (m)Jack King. (I)Film: *Dynamite*, by Russ Columbo. (P)Russ Columbo. (R)1939 by Tommy Dorsey and his Orchestra. (R)1951 Film: *Pandora And The Flying Dutchman*, by Ava Gardner.

HOW ARE THINGS IN GLOCCA MORRA? (1946) (w)E.Y. Harburg (m)Burton Lane. (I)Musical: *Finian's Rainbow*, by Ella Logan. (P)Dick Haymes. (CR)Buddy Clark. (CR)Tommy Dorsey and his Orchestra.

HOW BLUE THE NIGHT (1944) (w)Harold Adamson (m)Jimmy McHugh. (I)Film: *Four Jills In A Jeep*, by Dick Haymes. (P)Dick Haymes.

HOW 'BOUT US (1981) (wm)Dana Walden. (P)Champaign.

HOW CAN I BE SURE? (w)Felix Cavaliere-Edward Brigati, Jr. (P)The Rascals. (R)1973 by David Cassidy.

HOW CAN YOU DESCRIBE A FACE? (1961) (w)Betty Comden—Adolph Green (m)Jule Styne. (I)Musical: *Subways Are For Sleeping*, by Sydney Chaplin. (P)The McGuire Sisters.

HOW CAN YOU MEND A BROKEN HEART (1971) (wm)Barry Gibb—Robin Gibb. (P)The Bee Gees. No. 1 Chart Record.

HOW CAN YOU TELL AN AMERICAN? (1938) (w)Maxwell Anderson (m)Kurt Weill. (I)Musical: *Knickerbocker Holiday*, by Richard Kollmar and Ray Middleton.

HOW COME YOU DO ME LIKE YOU DO? (1924) (wm)Gene Austin—Roy Bergere. (P)Gene Austin. (CR)Marion Harris. (R)1955 Film: *Three For The Show*, by Betty Grable and Jack Lemmon.

HOW COULD WE BE WRONG (1933) (wm)Cole Porter. (I)London Musical: *Nymph Errant*, by Gertrude Lawrence.

HOW COULD YOU BELIEVE ME WHEN I SAID I LOVE YOU WHEN YOU KNOW I'VE BEEN A LIAR ALL MY LIFE (1950) (w)Alan Jay Lerner (m)Burton Lane. (I)Film: *Royal Wedding*, by Fred Astaire and Jane Powell. (P)Fred Astaire.

HOW COULD YOU? (1937) (w)Al Dubin (m)Harry Warren. (I)Film: *San Quentin*, by Ann Sheridan. (P)Billie Holiday with Teddy Wilson.

HOW DEEP IS THE OCEAN (1932) (wm)Irving Berlin. (P)Bing Crosby. (CR)Rudy Vallee. (CR)Ethel Merman. (R)1945 by Benny Goodman and his Orchestra.

HOW DEEP IS YOUR LOVE (1977) (wm)Barry, Maurice, and Robin Gibb. (I)Film: *Saturday Night Fever*, by the voices of The Bee Gees. (P)The Bee Gees. (P)The Bee Gees. No. 1 Chart Record.

HOW DO I MAKE YOU (1980) (wm)Billy Steinberg. (P)Linda Ronstadt.

HOW DO YOU CATCH A GIRL? (1967) (wm)Ronald Blackwell. (P)Sam The Sham and The Pharaohs.

HOW DO YOU DO (1924) (wm)Phil Fleming—Charlie Harrison—Cal De Voll. (P)Billy Jones and Ernie Hare (The Happiness Boys).

HOW DO YOU DO IT (1964) (wm)Mitch Murray. (P)Gerry and The Pacemakers.

HOW DO YOU DO? (1972) (w-Eng)Ronnie Ball (m)Van Hemert—Von Hoof. (P)Mouth & MacNeal.

HOW DO YOU SLEEP? (1971) (wm)John Lennon. (P)John Lennon. Song was written about Paul McCartney.

HOW DO YOU SPEAK TO AN ANGEL? (1953) (w)Bob Hilliard (m)Jule Styne. (I)Musical: *Hazel Flagg*, by John Howard. 1954 Film: *Living It Up*, by Dean Martin. (P)Eddie Fisher. (CR)Gordon MacRae.

HOW DOES THAT GRAB YOU DARLIN'? (1966) (wm)Lee Hazlewood. (P)Nancy Sinatra.

HOW DRY I AM (1921) (w)Phillip Dodridge (m)Edward F. Rimbault. Popular song during the prohibition era.

HOW D'YE TALK TO A GIRL (1966) (w)Sammy Cahn (m)Jimmy Van Heusen. (I)Musical: *Walking Happy*, by Norman Wisdom and Gordon Dilworth.

(You Don't Know)HOW GLAD I AM (1964) (wm)Jimmy Williams—Larry Harrison. (P)Nancy Wilson. NARAS Award Winner. (R)1975 by Kiki Dee.

HOW GREEN WAS MY VALLEY (1941) (w)Paul Francis Webster (m)Alfred Newman. (I)Film: *How Green Was My Valley*, as love theme.

HOW HIGH THE MOON (1940) (w)Nancy Hamilton (m)Morgan Lewis. (I)Revue: *Two For The Show*, by Alfred Drake and Frances Comstock. (P)Benny Goodman and his Orchestra, vocal by Helen Forrest.

LES PAUL

The make-up of recording sessions started to change dramatically in the fifties. Sessions used to take place with everything recorded live. The vocalist, the orchestra, and the background singers all would be present and all would be recorded simultaneously. But that began to change, and one man was responsible.

Les Paul was the musician who started multiple track recording and overdubs in the records he made with his wife, Mary Ford. They produced a lot of hits, starting with their great record of *How High the Moon*. Les Paul also was instrumental in the start of the development of the electric guitar and all the sounds and effects it could produce. In my opinion, Les Paul was and is a great musician and an electronics genius. His contribution to recorded music must be noted.

(CR)Larry Clinton and his Orchestra. (R)1951 by Les Paul and Mary Ford. No. 1 Chart Record.

HOW IMPORTANT CAN IT BE? (1955) (wm)Bennie Benjamin—George Weiss. (P)Joni James. (CR)Sarah Vaughan. (CR)Teresa Brewer.

HOW INSENSITIVE (1964) (w-Eng)Norman Gimbel (m)Antonio Carlos Jobim. (P)Astrud Gilberto.

HOW IT LIES, HOW IT LIES, HOW IT LIES (1950) (w)Paul Francis Webster (m)Sonny Burke. (P)Connie Haines. (CR)Kay Starr.

HOW LITTLE WE KNOW (1944) (w)Johnny Mercer (m)Hoagy Carmichael. (I)Film: *To Have And Have Not*, by Hoagy Carmichael.

HOW LITTLE WE KNOW (How Little It Matters How Little We Know) (1956) (w)Carolyn Leigh (m)Philip Springer. (P)Frank Sinatra.

HOW LONG (1975) (wm)Paul Carrack. (P)Ace. (R)1982 by Rod Stewart.

HOW LONG (Betcha' Got A Chick On The Side) (1975) (wm)Anita, Ruth, June, and Patricia Pointer. (P)The Pointer Sisters.

HOW LONG HAS THIS BEEN GOING ON? (1928) (W)Ira Gershwin (m)George Gershwin. (I)Musical: *Rosalie*, by Bobbe Arnst.

HOW LONG, HOW LONG BLUES (1929) (w)Ann Engberg (m)Leroy Carr. (P)Leroy Carr. (R)1936 by Count Basie and his Orchestra, vocal by Jimmy Rushing. (R)1966 by Ray Charles.

HOW LONG WILL IT LAST? (1931) (w)Max Lief (m)Joseph Meyer. (I)Film: *Possessed*, by Joan Crawford.

HOW LOVELY TO BE A WOMAN (1960) (w)Lee Adams (m)Charles Strouse. (I)Musical: *Bye Bye Birdie*, by Susan Watson. In film version (1963)by Ann—Margret.

HOW LUCKY CAN YOU GET (1975) (wm)John Kander—Fred Ebb. (I)Film: *Funny Lady*, by Barbra Streisand.

HOW MANY HEARTS HAVE YOU BROKEN (1944) (wm)Marty Symes—Al Kaufman. (P)The Three Suns. (CR)Stan Kenton and his Orchestra.

HOW MANY TIMES (1926) (wm)Irving Berlin. (I)Benny Krueger and his Orchestra.

HOW MANY TIMES CAN WE SAY GOODBYE (1983) (wm)Steve Goldman. (P)Dionne Warwick and Luther Vandross.

HOW MANY TIMES DO I HAVE TO TELL YOU (1944) (w)Harold Adamson (m)Jimmy McHugh. (I)Film: *Four Jills In A Jeep*, by Dick Haymes. (P)Dick Haymes.

HOW MUCH I FEEL (1978) (wm)David Pack. (P)Ambrosia.

HOW MUCH I LOVE YOU (1943) (w)Ogden Nash (m)Kurt Weill. (I)Musical: *One Touch Of Venus*, by Kenny Baker.

HOW MUCH LOVE (1977) (w)Leo Sayer (m)Barry Mann. (P)Leo Sayer.

HOW SAD (1962) (wm)Richard Rodgers. (I)Musical: *No Strings*, by Richard Kiley.

HOW SOON (Will I Be Seeing You) (1947) (wm)Carroll Lucas—Jack Owens. (P)Jack Owens. (CR)Vaughn Monroe. (CR)Bing Crosby. (CR)Dinah Shore.

HOW STRANGE (1939) (w)Gus Kahn (m)Herbert Stothart—Earl Brent. (I)Film: *Idiot's Delight*, by Norma Shearer. (P)Ted Fiorito and his Orchestra.

HOW SWEET IT IS (To Be Loved By You) (1965) (wm)Eddie Holland—Brian Holland—Lamont Dozier. (P)Marvin Gaye. (R)1966 by Junior Walker and The All Stars. (R)1975 by James Taylor.

HOW SWEET YOU ARE (1943) (w)Frank Loesser (m)Arthur Schwartz. (I)Film: *Thank Your Lucky Stars*, by Dinah Shore. (P)Dinah Shore. (CR)Jo Stafford. (CR)Kay Armen.

HOW THE TIME FLIES (1958) (wm)Tommy Jarrett. (P)Jerry Wallace.

HOW THE WEST WAS WON (1962) (w)Ken Darby (m)Alfred Newman. (I)Film: *How The West Was Won*, by the voices of The Ken Darby Chorus on the soundtrack.

HOW TO HANDLE A WOMAN (1960) (w)Alan Jay Lerner (m)Frederick Loewe. (I)Musical: Camelot, by Richard Burton. In film version, by Richard Harris.

HOW TO MURDER YOUR WIFE (1965) (m)Neal Hefti. (I)Film: *How To Murder Your Wife*, as soundtrack theme.

HOW TO SUCCEED IN BUSINESS WITHOUT REALLY TRYING (1961) (wm)Frank Loesser. (I)Musical: *How To Succeed In Business Without Really Trying*, by Robert Morse.

HOW TO WIN FRIENDS AND INFLUENCE PEOPLE (1938) (w)Lorenz Hart (m)Richard Rodgers. (I)Musical: *I Married An Angel*, by Charles Walters, Audrey Christie, and The Ensemble.

HOW WILL I KNOW (1985) (wm)Gary Merrill—Shannon Rubicam—Narada Michael Walden. (P)Whitney Houston. No. 1 Chart Record.

HOW WOULD YOU LIKE TO KISS ME IN THE MOONLIGHT? (1944) (w)Harold Adamson (m)Jimmy McHugh. (I)Film: *The Princesss And The Pirate*, by Virginia Mayo.

HOW YA GONNA KEEP 'EM DOWN ON THE FARM (1919) (w)Sam M. Lewis—Joe Young (m)Walter Donaldson. (I)Nora Bayes.

HOW YOU GONNA SEE ME NOW (1978) (wm)Alice Cooper—Dick Wagner—Bernie Taupin. (P)Alice Cooper.

HOW'D WE EVER GET THIS WAY? (1968) (wm)Jeff Barry—Andy Kim. (P)Andy Kim.

HOW'D YOU LIKE TO SPOON WITH ME (1906) (w)Edward Laska (m)Jerome Kern. (I)Musical: *The Earl And The Girl*. Recorded by Corrine Morgan.

HOWDJA LIKE TO LOVE ME (1938) (w)Frank Loesser (m)Burton Lane. (I)Film: *College Swing*, by Bob Hope and Martha Raye. (P)Jimmy Dorsey and his Orchestra. (CR)Dolly Dawn.

HOW'M I DOIN? (Hey, Hey!) (1932) (wm)Lem Fowler—Don Redman. (I)Film: *Twenty Million Sweethearts*, by The Mills Brothers. (P)The Mills Brothers.

HOW'M I DOIN' (1985) (wm)Charles Strouse. (I)Musical: *Mayor*, by Lenny Wolpe.

HOW'S CHANCES (1933) (wm)Irving Berlin. (I)Musical: *As Thousands Cheer*, by Marilyn Miller and Clifton Webb.

HOW'S YOUR ROMANCE? (1932) (wm)Cole Porter. (I)Musical: *Gay Divorcee*, by Erik Rhodes.

HUCKLE BUCK, THE (1948) (w)Roy Alfred (m)Andy Gibson. (I)Paul Williams and his Orchestra. (P)Tommy Dorsey and his Orchestra. Vocal version by Frank Sinatra.

HUCKLEBERRY DUCK (1939) (w)Jack Lawrence (m)Raymomd Scott. (P)Raymond Scott and his Quintet. Vocal version by Barry Wood.

HUGGIN' AND CHALKIN' (1946) (wm)Clancy Hayes—

Kermit Goell. (I)Clancy Hayes. (P)Hoagy Carmichael. No. 1 Chart Record. (CR)Johnny Mercer.

HUGUETTE WALTZ (1925) (w)Brian Hooker (m)Rudolf Friml. (I)Operetta: *The Vagabond King*, by Jane Carroll. Film version by Lillian Roth.

HULA HOOP SONG, THE (1959) (wm)Donna Kohler—Carl Maduri. (P)Georgia Gibbs. (CR)Teresa Brewer.

HULA LOVE (1957) (wm)Buddy Knox. (P)Buddy Knox.

HUMAN (1986) (wm)James Harris III—Terry Lewis. (P)Human League. No. 1 Chart Record.

HUMAN NATURE (1983) (w)John Bettis (m)Jeff Porcaro. (P)Michael Jackson.

HUMAN TOUCH (1983) (wm)Rick Springfield. (P)Rick Springfield.

HUMMINGBIRD (1955) (wm)Don Robertson. (I)Don and Lou Robertson. (P)Les Paul and Mary Ford. (CR)Frankie Laine.

HUMMINGBIRD (1972) (wm)James Seals—Darrell Crofts. (P)Seals and Crofts.

HUMORESQUE (1894) (m)Anton Dvorak. Famous classical composition. First recording by Mischa Elman as a violin solo. (R)1930s in a pop version by Guy Lombardo and his Royal Canadians.

HUMPTY DUMPTY (1928) (m)Fud Livingston. (P)Frankie Trumbauer and his Orchestra, featuring Bix Beiderbecke.

HUMPTY DUMPTY HEART (1941) (w)Johnny Burke (m)Jimmy Van Heusen. (I)Film: *Playmates*, by Kay Kyser and his Orchestra, vocal by Harry Babbitt. (P)Glenn Miller and his Orchestra.

HUNDRED AND SIXTY ACRES, A (1946) (wm)David Kapp. (P)Bing Crosby and The Andrews Sisters.

HUNDRED MILLION MIRACLES,A (1958) (w)Oscar Hammerstein II (m)Richard Rodgers. (I)Musical: *Flower Drum Song*, by Miyoshi Umeki, Conrad Yama, Keye Luke, Juanita Hall, and Rose Quong.

HUNDRED POUNDS OF CLAY, A (1961) (wm)Bob Elgin—Luther Dixon—Kay Roger. (P)Gene McDaniels.

HUNDRED YEARS FROM TODAY, A (1933) (w)Joe Young—Ned Washington (m)Victor Young. (I)Revue: *Lew Leslie's Blackbirds of 1933*, by Kathryn Perry. (P)Ethel Waters.

HUNGARIAN DANCE No. 1 (1869) (m)Johannes Brahms. Famous classical selection.

HUNGARIAN RHAPSODY No. 2 (1851) (m)Franz Liszt. Famous classical composition.

HUNGRY (1966) (wm)Barry Mann—Cynthia Weil. (P)Paul Revere and The Raiders.

HUNGRY EYES (1987) (wm)F. Previte—J. Denicola. (I)Film: *Dirty Dancing*, by Eric Carmen. (P)Eric Carmen.

HUNGRY HEART (1980) (wm)Bruce Springsteen. (P)Bruce Springsteen.

HUNGRY LIKE THE WOLF (1983) (wm)Duran Duran.

(P)Duran Duran.

HUNGRY YEARS, THE (1974) (wm)Neil Sedaka—Howard Greenfield. (P)Wayne Newton.

HUNTER GETS CAPTURED BY THE GAME, THE (1967) (wm)William Robinson. (P)The Marvelettes

HURDY GURDY MAN (1968) (wm)Donovan Leitch. (P)Donovan.

HURRICANE (Part 1) (1977) (wm)Bob Dylan—Jacques Levy. (P)Bob Dylan.

HURT (1953) (wm)Jimmy Crane—Al Jacobs. (P)Roy Hamilton. (R)1963 by Timi Yuro. (R)1966 by Elvis Presley.

HURT SO BAD (1965) (wm)Teddy Randazzo—Bobby Hart—Bobby Wilding. (P)Little Anthony and The Imperials. (R)1969 by The Lettermen. (R)1980 by Linda Ronstadt.

HURT SO GOOD (1982) (wm)John Cougar Mellencamp—George Michael Green. (P)John Cougar Mellencamp.

HURTING EACH OTHER (1972) (wm)Gary Geld—Peter Udell. (P)The Carpenters.

HURTS SO GOOD (1973) (wm)R. Michael Donovan. (P)Millie Jackson.

HUSBANDS AND WIVES (1966) (wm)Roger Miller. (P)Roger Miller.

HUSH-A-BYE ISLAND (1947) (w)Harold Adamson (m)Jimmy McHugh. (I)Film: *Smash-Up*, by Susan Hayward.

HUSHABYE (1959) (wm)Doc Pomus—Mort Shuman. (P)The Mystics. (R)1969 by Jay and The Americans. (R)1972 by Robert John.

HUSHABYE MOUNTAIN (1968) (wm)Richard M. Sherman—Robert B. Sherman. (I)Film: *Chitty Chitty Bang Bang*, by Dick Van Dyke.

HUSH HUSH, SWEET CHARLOTTE (1964) (w)Mack David (m)Frank De Vol. (I)Film : *Hush Hush, Sweet Charlotte*, by the voice of Al Martino on the soundtrack. (P)Patti Page.

HUSTLE, THE (1975) (wm)Van McCoy. (P)Van McCoy and The Soul City Symphony. No. 1 Chart Record.

HUT SUT SONG (1939) (wm)Leo Killion—Ted McMichael—Jack Owens. (P)Freddy Martin and his Orchestra. (R)1941 Film: *San Antonio Rose*, by The Merry Macs.

HYMN FOR A SUNDAY EVENING (1960) (w)Lee Adams (m)Charles Strouse. (I)Musical: *Bye Bye Birdie*, by Paul Lynde, Marijane Maricle, Susan Watson, and Johnny Borden. In film version (1963)by Ann-Margret, Paul Lynde, Mary LaRoche, and Bryan Russell.

HYPNOTIZED (1967) (wm)Gloria A. Spolan—Richard Poindexter. (P)Linda Jones.

HYSTERIA (1987) (wm)Clark—Collen—Elliott—Lange—Savage. (P)Def Leppard.

I ADORE HIM (1963) (wm)Jan Berry—Art Kornfeld. (P)The Angels.

I ADORE YOU (1958) (wm)Cole Porter. (I)TV show: *Aladdin*, by Anna Maria Alberghetti and Sal Mineo.

I AIN'T DOWN YET (1960) (wm)Meredith Willson. (I)Musical: *The Unsinkable Molly Brown*, by Tammy Grimes and Harve Presnell. Film version 1964, by Debbie Reynolds and Harve Presnell

I AIN'T GONNA STAND FOR IT (1980) (wm)Stevie Wonder. (P)Stevie Wonder.

I AIN'T GOT NOBODY (1916) (w)Roger Graham (m)Spencer Williams—Dave Peyton. (I)Marion Harris. (CR)Bessie Smith. (CR)Sophie Tucker. (R)1985 by David Lee Roth. (Medley)

I AIN'T GOT NOTHIN' BUT THE BLUES (1944) (w)Don George (m)Duke Ellington. (P)Duke Ellington and his Orchestra.

I AIN'T LAZY, I'M JUST DREAMING (1934) (wm)Dave Franklin. (P)Isham Jones and his Orchestra. (CR)Benny Goodman and his Orchestra.

I AIN'T NEVER (1959) (wm)Mel Tillis—Webb Pierce. (P)Webb Pierce. (CR)The Four Preps.

I ALMOST LOST MY MIND (1950) (wm)Ivory Joe Hunter. (I)Ivory Joe Hunter. (P)Pat Boone. No. 1 Chart Record. (CR)Nat "King" Cole.

I ALWAYS KNEW (1942) (wm)Cole Porter. (I)Film: *Something To Shout About*, by Don Ameche and Janet Blair.

I AM A LONESOME HOBO (1968) (wm)Bob Dylan. (P)Bob Dylan.

I AM A ROCK (1966) (wm)Paul Simon. (P)Simon and Garfunkel.

(Shout! Wherever You May Be)I AM AN AMERICAN (1940) (wm)Paul Cunningham—Ira Schuster—Leonard Whitcup. (P)Gray Gordon and his Orchestra, vocal by Meredith Blake.

I AM ASHAMED THAT WOMEN ARE SO SIMPLE (1948) (wm)Cole Porter. (I)Musical: *Kiss Me Kate*, by Patricia Morrison.

I AM BY YOUR SIDE (1986) (wm)Corey Hart. (P)Corey Hart.

I AM...I SAID (1971) (wm)Neil Diamond. (P)Neil Diamond.

I AM IN LOVE (1953) (wm)Cole Porter. (I)Musical: *Can-Can* by Peter Cookson.

I AM LOVE (Parts 1 & 2) (1975) (wm)Donald Fenceton—Mel Larson—Gerald Marcellino—Roderick Rancifer. (P)The Jackson Five.

I AM LOVED (1950) (wm)Cole Porter. (I)Musical: *Out Of This World*, by Patricia Gillette.

I AM ONLY HUMAN AFTER ALL (1930) (w)Ira Gershwin—E. Y. Harburg (m)Vernon Duke. (I)Revue: *The Garrick Gaities*, by James Norris, Velma Vavra, and Imogene Coca.

I AM SO EAGER (1932) (w)Oscar Hemmerstein II (m)Jerome Kern. (I)Musical: *Music In The Air*, by Tullio Carminati and Natalie Hall.

I AM THE WALRUS (1967) (wm)John Lennon—Paul McCartney. (P)The Beatles.

I AM WHAT I AM (1983) (wm)Jerry Herman. (I)Musical: *La Cage Au Folles*, by George Hearn.

I AM WOMAN (1972) (w)Helen Reddy (m)Ray Burton. (P)Helen Reddy. No. 1 Chart Record.

I APOLOGIZE (1931) (wm)Al Hoffman—Ed Nelson—Al Goodhart. (P)Bing Crosby. (R)1951 by Billy Eckstine. (CR)Tony Martin.

I BEG OF YOU (1958) (wm)Rose Marie McCoy—Kelly Owens. (P)Elvis Presley.

I BEGGED HER (1944) (w)Sammy Cahn (m)Jule Styne. (I)Film: *Anchors Aweigh*, by Frank Sinatra. (P)Frank Sinatra.

I BELIEVE (1947) (w)Sammy Cahn (m)Jule Styne. (I)Film: *It Happened In Brooklyn*, by Frank Sinatra, Jimmy Durante, and Billy Roy.

I BELIEVE (1953) (wm)Ervin Drake—Jimmy Shirl—Al Stillman—Irvin Graham. (I)Jane Froman on her TV show. (P)Frankie Laine.

I BELIEVE IN LOVE (1976) (w)Alan and Marilyn Bergman (m)Kenny Loggins. (I)Film: *A Star Is Born*, by Barbra Streisand. (P)Barbra Streisand.

I BELIEVE IN MIRACLES (1934) (w)Sam M. Lewis (m)Pete Wendling—George W. Meyer. (P)The Dorsey Brothers Orchestra. (CR)Fats Waller.

I BELIEVE IN MUSIC (1972) (wm)Mac Davis. (I)Mac Davis. (P)Gallery.

I BELIEVE IN YOU (1961) (wm)Frank Loesser. (I)Musical: *How To Succeed In Business Without Really Trying*, by Robert Morse.

I BELIEVE IN YOU (You Believe In Me) (1973) (wm)Don Davis. (P)Johnnie Taylor.

I BELIEVE YOU (1977) (wm)Robert Fischer (m)Ricci Mareno. (P)Dorothy Moore. (CR)The Carpenters.

I BELONG TO YOU (And Only You) (1975) (wm)Barry White. (P)Love Unlimited.

I BUILT A DREAM ONE DAY (1935) (w)Oscar Hammerstein II (m)Sigmund Romberg. (I)Musical: *May Wine*, by Walter Slezak—Walter Woolf King—Robert C. Fischer.

I CAIN'T SAY NO (1943) (w)Oscar Hammerstein II (m)Richard Rodgers. (I)Musical: *Oklahoma!*, by Celeste Holm. (R)Film version (1955)by Gloria Grahame.

I CALL YOUR NAME (1963) (wm)John Lennon—Paul McCartney. (P)The Beatles.

I CAME HERE TO TALK FOR JOE (1942) (wm)Charles Tobias—Lew Brown—Sam H. Stept. (P)Sammy Kaye and his Orchestra.

I CAN (1964) (wm)Walter Marks. (I)Musical: *Bajour*, by Chita Rivera and Nancy Dussault.

I CAN COOK TOO (1944) (w)Betty Comden—Adolph Green (m)Leonard Bernstein. (I)Musical: *On The Town*, by Nancy Walker.

I CAN DREAM ABOUT YOU (1983) (wm)Dan Hartman. (P)Dan Hartman.

I CAN DREAM, CAN'T I (1937) (w)Irving Kahal (m)Sammy Fain. (I)Revue: *Right This Way*, by Tamara. (P)Tommy Dorsey and his Orchestra. (R)1950 by The Andrews Sisters. No. 1 Chart Record.

I CAN HEAR MUSIC (1966) (wm)Jeff Barry—Ellie Greenwich—Phil Spector. (P)The Ronettes. (R)1969 by The Beach Boys.

I CAN HELP (1974) (wm)Billy Swan. (P)Billy Swan. No. 1 Chart Record.

I CAN MAKE IT WITH YOU (1966) (wm)Chip Taylor. (P)The Pozo—Seco Singers. (CR)Jackie De Shannon.

I CAN NEVER GO HOME ANYMORE (1965) (wm)George Morton—Jerry Grimaldi. (P)The Shangri—Las.

I CAN SEE CLEARLY NOW (1972) (wm)Johnny Nash. (P)Johnny Nash. No. 1 Chart Record. This was the first popular recording of Reggae music.

I CAN SEE FOR MILES (1967) (wm)Peter Townshend. (P)The Who.

THE WHO

I guess I have made known my feelings about the shortcomings of the management of Decca Records and their subsidiaries.

Only because of their English affiliation, the company was forced to release a single by a new British group called The Who. The title of the song was *I Can See For Miles*. Well, it was the usual thing. Decca didn't do a damn thing to promote the record but the record was so powerful it took off by itself.

So Decca was presented with a rock act they did not know how to handle. But when The Who came to the United States, the company was forced to throw a cocktail party for them at one of the big hotels. The disc jockeys and press were invited and it turned out to be one hell of an affair.

When I was introduced to Peter Townshend and company and they found out I was the guy who did all the arrangements for Buddy Holly I was bombarded with questions about Buddy from all the members of The Who. They were one of the great rock bands and it was a shame that Decca Records really didn't know what to do with them. But is was the usual course of events and naturally the group left the label.

I CAN SEE YOU (1950) (w)Sammy Fain (m)Nicholas Brodszky. (I)Film: *Rich, Young, and Pretty*, by Jane Powell.

I CAN TAKE OR LEAVE YOUR LOVING (1968) (wm)Rick Jones. (P)Herman's Hermits.

I CAN'T BE BOTHERED NOW (1937) (w)Ira Gershwin (m)George Gerswhin. (I)Film: *A Damsel In Distress*, by Fred Astaire.

I CAN'T BEGIN TO TELL YOU (1945) (w)Mack Gordon (m)James V. Monaco. (I)Film: *The Dolly Sisters*, by John Payne and reprised by Betty Grable.

I CAN'T BELIEVE I'M LOSING YOU (1968) (w)Phil Zeller (m)Don Costa. (P)Frank Sinatra.

I CAN'T BELIEVE IT'S TRUE (1932) (wm)Charles Newman—Ben Bernie—Isham Jones. (P)Isham Jones and his Orchestra. (CR)Ben Bernie and his Orchestra.

I CAN'T BELIEVE THAT YOU'RE IN LOVE WITH ME (1927) (wm)Clarence Gaskill—Jimmy McHugh. (I)Revue: *Gay Paree*, by Winnie Lightner. (P)Roger Wolfe Kahn and his Orchestra. (R)1953 by The Ames Brothers.

I CAN'T ESCAPE FROM YOU (1936) (wm)Leo Robin—Richard A. Whiting.

I CAN'T GET NEXT TO YOU (1969) (wm)Barrett Strong—Norman Whitfield. (P)The Temptations. No. 1 Chart Record. (R)1971 by Al Green.

I CAN'T GET STARTED WITH YOU (1935) (w)Ira Gershwin (m)Vernon Duke. (I)Revue: *Ziegfeld Follies of 1936*, by Bob Hope. (P)Hal Kemp and his Orchestra. (R)1930s by Bunny Berigan and his Orchestra.

I CAN'T GET YOU OUT OF MY HEART (Ti Amo-Ti Voglio Amor) (1958) (wm)Danny Di Minno—Jimmy Crane. (P)Al Martino.

I CAN'T GIVE YOU ANYTHING BUT LOVE (Baby) (1928) (w)Dorothy Fields (m)Jimmy McHugh. (I)Revue: *Lew Leslie's Blackbirds of 1928*, by Aida Ward and Willard McLean. (P)Cliff Edwards. No. 1 Chart Record. (CR)Gene Austin. (R)1936 by Billie Holiday with Teddy Wilson. (R)1948 by Rose Murphy. Film: *Stormy Weather* (1943)by Lena Horne and Bill Robinson.

I CAN'T GO FOR THAT (No Can Do) (1982) (wm)Daryl Hall—John Oates—Sara Allen. (P)Hall and Oates. No. 1 Chart Record.

I CAN'T HEAR YOU NO MORE (1976) (w)Gerry Goffin (m)Carole King. (P)Helen Reddy.

I CAN'T HELP IT (If I'm Still In Love With You) (1951) (wm)Hank Williams. (P)Hank Williams. (R)1958 by Margaret Whiting. (R)1960 by Adam Wade. (R)1962 by Johnny Tillotson. (R)1967 by B.J. Thomas. (R)1969 by Al Martino.

I CAN'T HELP IT (1979) (wm)Barry Gibb. (P)Andy Gibba and Olivia Newton—John.

I CAN'T HELP MYSELF (Sugar Pie, Honey Bunch) (1965) (wm)Eddie Holland—Lamont Dozier—Brian Holland. (P)The Four Tops. No. 1 Chart Record.

I CAN'T HOLD BACK (1984) (wm)Frank Sullivan—Jim Peterik. (P)Survivor.

I CAN'T LET GO (1966) (wm)Chip Taylor—Al Gorgoni. (P)The Hollies.

I CAN'T LOVE YOU ANY MORE (Any More Than I Do) (1940) (w)Herb Magidson (m)Allie Wrubel. (P)Benny Goodman and his Orchestra, vocal by Helen Forrest.

I CAN'T LOVE YOU ENOUGH (1956) (wm)Dorian Burton—Howard Plummer, Jr.—LaVern Baker. (P)LaVern Baker.

I CAN'T REMEMBER (1933) (wm)Irving Berlin. (P)Eddy Duchin and his Orchestra.

I CAN'T SEE MYSELF LEAVING YOU (1969) (wm)Ronnie Shannon. (P)Aretha Franklin.

I CAN'T STAND IT (1981) (wm)Eric Clapton. (P)Eric Clapton.

I CAN'T STAND IT NO MORE (1979) (wm)Peter Frampton. (P)Peter Frampton.

I CAN'T STAND MYSELF (When You Touch Me) (1967) (wm)James Brown. (P)James Brown.

I CAN'T STAND THE RAIN (1973) (wm)Donald Bryant—Ann Peebles—Bernard Miller. (P)Ann Peebles. (R)1978 by Eruption.

I CAN'T STAY MAD AT YOU (1963) (wm)Gerry Goffin—Carole King. (P)Skeeter Davis.

I CAN'T STOP LOVING YOU (1958) (wm)Don Gibson. (P)Don Gibson. (R)1962 by Ray Charles. No. 1 Chart Record. (R)1963 by Count Basie and his Orchestra.

I CAN'T TELL A WALTZ FROM A TANGO (1954) (wm)Al Hoffman—Dick Manning. (P)Patti Page.

I CAN'T TELL YOU WHY (1980) (wm)Glen Frey—Don Henley—Timothy Schmit. (P)The Eagles.

I CAN'T WAIT (1986) (wm)Stevie Nicks—Rick Nowels—Eris Pressly. (P)Stevie Nicks.

I CHOSE TO SING THE BLUES (I Choose To Sing The Blues) (1966) (wm)Jimmy Holiday—Ray Charles.

(P)Ray Charles.

I CONCENTRATE ON YOU (1939) (wm)Cole Porter. (I)Film: *Broadway Melody of 1940*, by Douglas McPhail and danced by Fred Astaire and Eleanor Powell. (P)Tommy Dorsey and his Orchestra. (CR)Eddy Duchin and his Orchestra.

I COULD BE HAPPY WITH YOU (1953) (wm)Sandy Wilson. (I)Musical: *The Boy Friend in London*, by Anne Rogers and Anthony Hayes. In New York production by, Julie Andrews and John Hewer.

I COULD GO ON SINGING (1963) (w)E.Y. Harburg (m)Harold Arlen. (I)Film: *I Could Go On Singing*, by Judy Garland.

I COULD HAVE DANCED ALL NIGHT (1956) (w)Alan Jay Lerner (m)Frederick Loewe. (I)Musical: *My Fair Lady*, by Julie Andrews. (P)Sylvia Syms. In film version by Marni Nixon dubbing for Audrey Hepburn.

I COULD NEVER LOVE ANOTHER (After Loving You) (1968) (wm)Barrett Strong—Norman Whitfield—Roger Penzabene. (P)The Temptations.

I COULD NEVER MISS YOU MORE THAN I DO (1981) (wm)Neil Harrison. (P)Lulu.

I COULD NEVER TAKE THE PLACE OF YOUR MAN (1987) (wm)Prince. (P)Prince.

I COULD USE A DREAM (1937) (w)Walter Bullock (m)Harold Spina. (I)Film: *Sally, Irene, and Mary* by Alice Faye and Tony Martin.

I COULD WRITE A BOOK (1940) (w)Lorenz Hart (m)Richard Rodgers. (I)Musical: *Pal Joey*, by Gene Kelly and Leila Ernst. Recorded by Eddy Duchin and his Orchestra. (R)Film version (1953)by Frank Sinatra.

I COULDN'T BELIEVE MY EYES (1935) (wm)Walter G. Samuels—Leonard Whitcup—Teddy Powell. (P)Freddy Martin and his Orchestra.

I COULDN'T LIVE WITHOUT YOUR LOVE (1966) (wm)Tony Hatch—Jackie Trent. (P)Petula Clark.

I COULDN'T SLEEP A WINK LAST NIGHT (1943) (w)Harold Adamson (m)Jimmy McHugh. (I)Film: *Higher and Higher*, by Frank Sinatra. (P)Frank Sinatra.

I COVER THE WATERFRONT (1933) (w)Edward Heyman (m)John Green. (I)Ben Bernie and his Orchestra on radio. Recorded by Eddy Duchin and his Orchestra. Later used as title theme for Film: *I Cover The Waterfront*.

I CRIED (1954) (wm)Michael Elias—Billy Duke. (I)Billy Duke. (P)Patti Page. (CR)Tommy Leonetti.

I CRIED A TEAR (1958) (wm)Al Julia—Fred Jay. (P)LaVern Baker.

I CRIED FOR YOU (Now It's Your Turn To Cry Over Me) (1923) (wm)Arthur Freed—Gus Arnheim—Abe Lyman. (I)Abe Lyman and his Orchestra. (P)Cliff Edwards. (R)1938 by Bunny Berigan and his Orchestra. (R)1939 by Glen Gary and The Casa Loma Orchestra. (R)1939 by Bing Crosby (R)1942 by Harry James and his Orchestra.

I CROSS MY FINGERS (1950) (wm)Walter Kent—Walter Farrar. (P)Percy Faith and his Orchestra. (CR)Perry Como. (CR)Bing Crosby.

(Last Night)I DIDN'T GET TO SLEEP AT ALL (1972) (wm)Tony Macauley. (P)The 5th Dimension.

I DIDN'T KNOW ABOUT YOU (1944) (w)Bob Russell (m)Duke Ellington. Adapted from Ellington's composition Sentimental Lady. (P)Duke Ellington and his Orchestra, vocal by Joya Sherrill.

I DIDN'T KNOW WHAT TIME IT WAS (1939) (w)Lorenz Hart (m)Richard Rodgers. (I)Musical: *Too Many Girls*, by Richard Kollmar and Marcy Westcott. (P)Benny Goodman and his Orchestra. (R)Film: *Pal Joey* (1957)by Frank Sinatra.

I DIDN'T MEAN TO TURN YOU ON (1985) (wm)James Harris III—Terry Lewis. (I)Cherelle. (P)Robert Palmer.

I DIDN'T RAISE MY BOY TO BE A SOLDIER (1915) (w)Alfred Bryan (m)Al Piantadosi. (P)Morton Harvey.

I DIDN'T SLIP, I WASN'T PUSHED, I FELL (1950) (wm)Eddie Pola—George Wyle. (P)Doris Day. (CR)Bing Crosby.

I DIG ROCK AND ROLL MUSIC (1967) (wm)Paul Stokey—James Mason—Dave Dixon. (P)Peter, Paul, and Mary.

I DO (1965) (wm)Jesse Smith—Johnny Paden—Frank Paden—Willie Stephenson—Melvin Mason. (P)The Marvelows. (R)1983 by The J. Geils Band.

I DO, I DO, I DO, I DO, I DO (1976) (wm)Benny Andersson—Stig Anderson—Bjorn Ulvaeus. (P)Abba.

I DO IT FOR YOUR LOVE (1975) (wm)Paul Simon. (P)Paul Simon.

I DO LOVE YOU (1965) (wm)Billy Stewart. (P)Billy Stewart. (R)1979 by GQ.

I DO NOT KNOW A DAY I DID NOT LOVE YOU (1970) (w)Martin Charnin (m)Richard Rodgers. (I)Musical: *Two By Two*, by Walter Willison.

I DO YOU (1987) (wm)L. Mallah—R. Kelly (P)The Jets.

I DON'T BELIEVE YOU (She Acts Like We Never Have Met) (1964) (wm)Bob Dylan. (P)Bob Dylan.

I DON'T BLAME YOU AT ALL (1971) (wm)William Robinson. (P)The Miracles.

I DON'T CARE (1905) (w)Jean Lenox (m)Harry O. Sutton. (I)Eva Tanguay. (R)Film: *In The Good Old Summertime*, by Judy Garland.

I DON'T CARE IF THE SUN DON'T SHINE (1949) (wm)Mack David (P)Patti Page. (R)1956 by Elvis Presley.

I DON'T CARE MUCH (1963) (w)Fred Ebb (m)John Kander. (P)Barbra Streisand.

I DON'T CARE WHO KNOWS IT (1945) (w)Harold Adamson (m)Jimmy McHugh. (I)Film: *Nob Hill*, by Vivian Blaine. (P)Harry James and his Orchestra.

I DON'T KNOW ENOUGH ABOUT YOU (1946) (wm)Peggy Lee—Dave Barbour. (P)Peggy Lee. (CR)The Mills Brothers. (CR)Benny Goodman and his Orchestra.

I DON'T KNOW HOW TO LOVE HIM (1971) (w)Tim Rice (m)Andrew Lloyd Webber. (I)Musical: *Jesus Christ Superstar*, by Yvonne Elliman and Jeff Fenholt. (P)Yvonne Elliman. (CR)Helen Reddy.

I DON'T KNOW IF IT'S RIGHT (1979) (wm)J. Fitch. (P)Evelyn "Champagne" King.

I DON'T KNOW WHY (I Just Do) (1931) (w)Roy Turk (m)Fred E. Ahlert. (P)Wayne King and his Orchestra. (R)1946 by Tommy Dorsey and his Orchestra.

I DON'T KNOW WHY (1969) (wm)Stevie Wonder—Paul Riser—Don Hunter—Lula Hardaway. (P)Stevie Wonder. (R)1975 by The Rolling Stones.

I DON'T LIKE TO SLEEP ALONE (1975) (wm)Paul Anka. (P)Paul Anka.

I DON'T NEED ANYTHING BUT YOU (1977) (w)Martin Charnin (m)Charles Strouse. (I)Musical: *Annie*, by Andrea McArdle, Reid Shelton, and Sandy Faison.

I DON'T NEED NO DOCTOR (1966) (wm)Nick Ashford—Valerie Simpson. (P)Ray Charles. (R)1971 by Humble Pie. (R)1972 by The New Riders Of The Purple Sage.

I DON'T NEED YOU (1981) (wm)Rick Christian. (P)Kenny Rogers.

I DON'T SEE ME IN YOUR EYES ANYMORE (1949) (wm)Bennie Benjamin—George Weiss. (P)Gordon Jenkins and The Starlighters. (CR)Perry Como. (R)1974 by Charlie Rich.

I DON'T THINK I'M IN LOVE (1966) (w)Sammy Cahn (m)Jimmy Van Heusen. (I)Musical: *Walking Happy*, by Norman Wisdom and Louise Troy.

I DON'T WANT NOBODY TO GIVE ME NOTHING (1969) (wm)James Brown. (P)James Brown.

I DON'T WANT TO CRY NO MORE (1961) (wm)Luther Dixon—Charles Jackson. (P)Chuck Jackson. (R)1969 by Ruby Winters. (R)1970 by Ronnie Dyson.

I DON'T WANT TO DO IT (1985) (wm)Bob Dylan. (I)Film: *Porky's Revenge*, by George Harrison. (P)George Harrison.

I DON'T WANT TO DO WRONG (1971) (wm)Johnny Bristol—William Guest—Gladys Knight—Merald Knight, Jr.—Catherine Shaffner—Walter Jones. (P)Gladys Knight & The Pips.

I DON'T WANT TO MAKE HISTORY (I Just Want To Make Love) (1936) (wm)Leo Robin—Ralph Rainger. (I)Film: *Palm Springs*, by Frances Langford. (P)Hal Kemp and his Orchestra.

I DON'T WANT TO SEE YOU AGAIN (1964) (wm)John Lennon—Paul McCartney. (P)Peter and Gordon.

I DON'T WANT TO SET THE WORLD ON FIRE (1941) (wm)Eddie Seiler—Sol Marcus—Bennie Benjamin—Eddie Durham. (I)Harlan Leonard and his Kansas City Rockets. (P)The Ink Spots. (CR)Horace Heidt and his Orchestra. (CR)The Mills Brothers.

I DON'T WANT TO SPOIL THE PARTY (1964) (wm)John Lennon—Paul McCartney. (P)The Beatles.

I DON'T WANT TO WALK WITHOUT YOU (1942) (w)Frank Loesser (m)Jule Styne. (I)Film: *Sweater Girl*, by Betty Jane Rhodes. (P)Harry James and his Orchestra, vocal by Helen Forrest.

I DOUBLE DARE YOU (1937) (wm)Terry Shand—Jimmy Eaton. (P)Freddy Martin and his Orchestra. (CR)Russ Morgan and his Orchestra.

I DREAM OF JEANIE WITH THE LIGHT BROWN HAIR (see Jeanie With The Light Brown Hair).

I DREAM OF YOU (More Than You Dream I Do) (1945) (wm)Marjorie Goetschius—Edna Osser. (P)Tommy Dorsey and his Orchestra, vocal by Freddy Stewart. (CR)Andy Russell. Most popular recording by Frank Sinatra.

I DREAM TOO MUCH (1935) (w)Dorothy Fields (m)Jerome Kern. (I)Film: *I Dream Too Much*, by Lily Pons. Recorded by Leo Reisman and his Orchestra.

I DREAMED (1956) (wm)Charles Grean—Marvin Moore. (P)Betty Johnson.

I DREAMED I SAW ST. AUGUSTINE (1968) (wm)Bob Dylan. (P)Bob Dylan.

I DREAMED OF A HILLBILLY HEAVEN (1961) (wm)Hal Sothern—Eddie Dean—Floyd Bartlett. (P)Tex Ritter.

I DREAMT I DWELT IN HARLEM (1941) (w)Robert B. Wright (m)Jerry Gray—Ben Smith—Leonard W. Ware. (P)Glenn Miller and his Orchestra.

I DREAMT I DWELT IN MARBLE HALLS (1843) (w)Alfred Bunn (m)Michael William Balfe. (I)Opera: *The Bohemian Girl*.

I ENJOY BEING A GIRL (1958) (w)Oscar Hammerstein II (m)Richard Rodgers. (I)Musical: *Flower Drum Song*, by Miyoshi Umeki.

I FALL IN LOVE TOO EASILY (1944) (w)Sammy Cahn (m)Jule Styne. (I)Film: *Anchors Aweigh*, by Frank Sinatra. (P)Frank Sinatra. (CR)Mel Torme.

I FALL IN LOVE WITH YOU EV'RY DAY (1946) (wm)Sam H. Stept. (P)Jimmy Dorsey and his Orchestra.

I FALL TO PIECES (1961) (w)Hank Cochran (m)Harlan Howard. (P)Patsy Cline.

I FAW DOWN AND GO BOOM! (1928) (w)James Brockman—Leonard Stevens (m)James Brockman. (P)Eddie Cantor.

I FEEL A SONG COMIN' ON (1935) (wm)Dorothy Fields—Jimmy McHugh—George Oppenheimer. (I)Film: *Every Night At Eight*, by Harry Barris and later reprised by Alice Faye, Frances Langford, and Patsy Kelly. (P)Frances Langford.

I FEEL AT HOME WITH YOU (w)Lorenz Hart (m)Richard Rodgers. (I)Musical: *A Connecticut Yankee*, by Jack Thompson and June Cochrane.

I FEEL FINE (1964) (wm)John Lennon—Paul McCartney. (P)The Beatles. No. 1 Chart Record.

I FEEL FOR YOU (1984) (wm)Prince Rogers Nelson. (P)Chaka Khan. NARAS Award Winner.

I FEEL LIKE A BULLET (In The Gun Of Robert Ford) (1976) (wm)Elton John—Bernie Taupin. (P)Elton John.

I FEEL LIKE A FEATHER IN THE BREEZE (1936) (w)Mack Gordon (m)Harry Revel. (I)Film: *Collegiate*, by The Girls' Chorus. (P)Jan Garber and his Orchestra.

I FEEL LIKE I'M GONNA LIVE FOREVER (1953) (w)Bob Hilliard (m)Jule Styne. (I)Musical: *Hazel Flagg*, by Helen Gallagher.

I FEEL LOVE (Benji's Theme) (1974) (w)Euel Box (m)Betty Box. (I)Film: *Benji*, by the voice of Charlie Rich.

I FEEL LOVE (1977) (wm)Donna Summer—Giorgio Moroder—Pete Bellotte. (P)Donna Summer.

I FEEL PRETTY (1957) (w)Stephen Sondheim (m)Leonard Bernstein. (I)Musical: *West Side Story*, by Carol Lawrence, Marilyn Cooper, Carmen Guiterrez, and Elizabeth Taylor.

I FEEL SO BAD (1961) (wm)Chuck Willis. (P)Elvis Presley. (R)1967 by Little Milton. (R)1971 by Ray Charles.

I FEEL SO SMOOCHIE (1947) (wm)Phil Moore. (P)Lena Horne.

I FEEL THE EARTH MOVE (1971) (wm)Carole King. (P)Carole King.

I FORGOT TO REMEMBER TO FORGET (1956) (wm)Stanley Kesler—Charles Feathers. (P)Elvis Presley.

I FOUGHT THE LAW (1961) (wm)Sonny Curtis. (P)Chuck Jackson.

I FOUND A FOUR LEAF CLOVER (1922) (w)B. G. De Sylva (m)George Gershwin. (I)Revue: *George White's Scandals of 1922*, by Coletta Ryan and Richard Bold.

I FOUND A GIRL (1965) (wm)P. F. Sloan—Steve Barri. (P)Jan and Dean.

I FOUND A LOVE (1962) (wm)Willie Schofield—Wilson Pickett—Robert West. (P)The Falcons. (R)1967 by Wilson Pickett.

I FOUND A MILLION DOLLAR BABY (In A Five And Ten

Cent Store) (1931) (w)Billy Rose—Mort Dixon (m)Harry Warren. (I)Revue: *Billy Rose's Crazy Quilt*, by Fanny Brice, Ted Healy, Phil Baker, and Lew Brice. (P)Fred Waring's Pennsylvanians. No. 1 Chart Record. (CR)Bing Crosby. (CR)The Boswell Sisters.

I FOUND SOMEONE (1987) (wm)M. Bolton—M. Mangold. (P)Cher.

I FOUND YOU AND YOU FOUND ME (1918) (w)P.G. Wodehouse (m)Jerome Kern. (I)Musical: *Oh Lady, Lady*.

I.G.Y. (What A Beautiful World) (wm)Donald Fagen. (P)Donald Fagen.

I GET A KICK OUT OF YOU (1934) (Cole Porter) (I)Musical: *Anything Goes*, by Ethel Merman and William Gaxton. (P)Ethel Merman. (CR)Paul Whiteman and his Orchestra. (R)1956 Film: *Night And Day*, by Ginny Simms. Most popular recording by Frank Sinatra.

I GET ALONG WITHOUT YOU VERY WELL (1939) (w)Jane Brown Thompson (m)Hoagy Carmichael. (I)On Radio, by Dick Powell. (P)Jimmy Dorsey and his Orchestra. (CR)Red Norvo. (R)1952 Film: *The Las Vegas Story*, by Hoagy Carmichael and Jane Russell.

I GET AROUND (1964) (wm)Brian Wilson. (P)The Beach Boys. No. 1 Chart Record.

I GET CARRIED AWAY (1944) (w)Betty Comden—Adolph Green (m)Leonard Bernstein. (I)Musical: *On The Town*, by Betty Comden and Adolph Green.

I GET IDEAS (1951) (w-Eng)Dorcas Cochran (m)Julio Sanders. Adapted from tango Adios Muchachos. (P)Tony Martin. (CR)Louis Armstrong. (CR)Peggy Lee.

I GET THE BLUES WHEN IT RAINS (1928) (w)Marcy Klauber (m)Harry Stoddard. (P)Guy Lombardo and his Royal Canadians.

I GET THE NECK OF THE CHICKEN (1942) (w)Frank Loesser (m)Jimmy McHugh. (I)Film: *Seven Days' Leave*, by Marcy McGuire.

I GET THE SWEETEST FEELING (1968) (wm)Van McCoy—Alicia Evelyn. (P)Jackie Wilson.

I GET WEAK (1987) (wm)D. Warren. (P)Delinda Carlisle.

I GIVE YOU MY WORD (1940) (wm)Al Kavelin—Merril Lyn. (P)Al Kavelin and his Orchestra. (CR)Eddy Duchin and his Orchestra. (CR)Jack Leonard.

I GO CRAZY (1978) (wm)Paul Davis. (P)Paul Davis.

I GO TO BED (1963) (w)Anne Croswell (m)Lee Pockriss. (I)Musical: *Tovarich*, by Jean Pierre Aumont.

I GO TO PIECES (1965) (wm)Del Shannon. (P)Peter and Gordon.

I GOT A "CODE" IN MY "DOZE" (1929) (wm)Arthur Fields—Fred Hall—Billy Rose. (P)Fields and Hall.

I GOT A FEELING (1958) (wm)Baker Knight. (P)Rick Nelson.

I GOT A LINE ON YOU (1969) (wm)Randy California. (P)Spirit.

I GOT A NAME (1973) (w)Norman Gimbel (m)Charles Fox. (I)Film: *The Last American Hero*, by the voice of Jim Croce. (P)Jim Croce.

I GOT A SONG (1944) (w)E. Y. Harburg (m)Harold Arlen. (I)Musical: *Bloomer Girl*, by Richard Huey, Dooley Wilson, Hubert Dilworth and The Chorus.

I GOT A WIFE (1959) (w)Erwin Wenzlaff (m)Eddie Mascari. (P)The Mark IV.

I GOT A WOMAN (I Got A Sweetie) (1955) (wm)Ray Charles—Renald J. Richard. (P)Jimmy McGriff. (R)1963 by Rick Nelson. (R)1965 by Ray Charles.

I GOT IT BAD (And That Ain't Good) (1941) (w)Paul Francis Webster (m)Duke Ellington. (I)Musical: *Jump For Joy*, by Ivie Anderson. (P)Duke Ellington and his Orchestra. (CR)Benny Goodman and his Orchestra.

I GOT LIFE (1967) (w)Gerome Ragni—James Rado (m)Galt MacDermot. (I)Musical: *Hair*, by Walker Daniels and Marijane Maricle in off Broadway version. In Broadway version, by James Rado and The Company.

I GOT LOST IN HIS ARMS (1946) (wm)Irving Berlin. (I)Musical: *Annie Get Your Gun*, by Ethel Merman. In film version by Betty Hutton. (1950)

I GOT LOVE (1935) (w)Dorothy Fields (m)Jerome Kern. (I)Film: *I Dream Too Much*, by Lily Pons.

I GOT LOVE (1970) (w)Peter Udell (m)Gary Geld. (I)Musical: *Purlie*, by Melba Moore. (P)Melba Moore.

I GOT LUCKY IN THE RAIN (1948) (w)Harold Adamson (m)Jimmy McHugh. (I)Musical: *As The Girls Go*, by Fran Warren and Bill Callahan.

I GOT MY MIND MADE UP (1979) (wm)Kim Miller—Scott Miller—Raymond Earl. (P)Instant Funk.

I GOT PLENTY O' NUTTIN' (1935) (w)Du Bose Heyward—Ira Gershwin (m)George Gershwin. (I)Opera: *Porgy and Bess*, by Todd Duncan. In film version by Robert McFerrin dubbing for Sidney Poitier. Early recording by Leo Reisman and his Orchestra.

I GOT RHYTHM (1930) (w)Ira Gershwin (m)George Gershwin. (I)Musical: *Girl Crazy*, by Ethel Merman. (P)Ethel Merman. (CR)Ethel Waters. (CR)Louis Armstrong. (R)1951 Film: *An American In Paris*, by Gene Kelly. (R)1967 by The Happenings.

I GOT SHOES (1865) (wm)Unknown. Traditional Black American spiritual.

I GOT STONED AND I MISSED IT (1973) (wm)Shel Silverstein. (P)Jim Stafford.

I GOT STUNG (1958) (wm)Aaron Schroeder—David Hill. (P)Elvis Presley.

I GOT THE FEELIN' (Oh No, No) (1966) (wm)Neil Diamond. (P)Neil Diamond.

I GOT THE FEELIN' (1968) (wm)James Brown. (P)James Brown and The Famous Flames.

I GOT THE SUN IN THE MORNING (1946) (wm)Irving Berlin. (I)Musical: *Annie Get Your Gun*, by Ethel Merman. (P)Ethel Merman. In film version, by Betty Hutton. (1950).

I GOT YOU (I Feel Good) (1966) (wm)James Brown. (P)James Brown.

I GOT YOU BABE (1965) (wm)Sonny Bono. (P)Sonny and Cher. No. 1 Chart Record.

I GOTCHA (1972) (wm)Joe Tex. (P)Joe Tex.

I GOTTA GAL I LOVE (In North and South Dakota) (1947) (w)Sammy Cahn (m)Jule Styne. (I)Film: *Ladies' Man*, by Eddie Bracken.

I GOTTA KNOW (1960) (wm)Paul Evans—Matt Williams. (P)Elvis Presley.

I GOTTA RIGHT TO SING THE BLUES (1932) (w)Ted Koehler (m)Harold Arlen. (I)Revue: *Earl Carrolls's Vanities*, by Lillian Shade. Theme song of Jack Teagarden and his Orchestra. (CR)Cab Calloway. (CR)Louis Armstrong. (CR)Benny Goodman and his Orchestra.

I GUESS I'LL GET THE PAPERS AND GO HOME (1946) (wm)Hughie Prince—Hal Kanner. (P)The Mills Brothers. (CR)Les Brown and his Band of Renown.

I GUESS I'LL HAVE TO CHANGE MY PLAN (The Blue Pajama Song) (1929) (w)Howard Dietz (m)Arthur Schwartz. (I)Revue: *The Little Show*, by Clifton Webb. (P)Rudy Vallee. (CR)Guy Lombardo and his Royal Canadians. (R)1953 Film: *The Band Wagon*, by Fred Astaire and Jack Buchanan.

I GUESS I'LL HAVE TO DREAM THE REST (1941) (w)Mickey Stoner—Martin Block (m)Harold Green. (P)Glenn Miller and his Orchestra,vocal by Ray Eberle and The Modernaires. (CR)Tommy Dorsey and his Orchestra, vocal by Frank Sinatra and The Pied Pipers.

I GUESS IT HAD TO BE THAT WAY (1933) (wm)Arthur Johnston—Sam Coslow. (I)Film: *Too Much Harmony*, by Bing Crosby. (P)Bing Crosby.

I GUESS THAT'S WHY THEY CALL IT THE BLUES (1983) (wm)Elton John—Bernie Taupin. (P)Elton John.

I HAD A DREAM (1967) (wm)Mark Lindsay—Terry Melcher. (P)Paul Revere and The Raiders.

I HAD MYSELF A TRUE LOVE (1946) (w)Johnny Mercer (m)Harold Arlen. (I)Musical: *St. Louis Woman*, by June Hawkins.

I HAD THE CRAZIEST DREAM (1942) (w)Mack Gordon (m)Harry Warren. (I)Film: *Springtime In The Rockies*. (P)Harry James and his Orchestra, vocal by Helen Forrest. No. 1 Chart Record. (R)1953 by The Skylarks.

I HAD TOO MUCH TO DREAM (Last Night) (1966) (wm)Nancie Mantz—Annette Tucker. (P)Electric Prunes.

I HADN'T ANYONE TILL YOU (1938) (wm)Ray Noble. (P)Ray Noble and his Orchestra. (CR)Tommy Dorsey and his Orchestra.

I HAPPEN TO LIKE NEW YORK (1931) (wm)Cole Porter. (I)Musical: *The New Yorkers*, by Oscar "Rags" Ragland.

I HATE MEN (1948) (wm)Cole Porter. (I)Musical: *Kiss Me Kate*, by Patricia Morrison. In film version (1953)by Kathryn Grayson.

I HATE YOU, DARLING (1941) (wm)Cole Porter. (I)Musical: *Let's Face It*, by Vivian Vance, James Todd, Mary Jane Walsh, and Danny Kaye.

I HAVE BUT ONE HEART (1945) (w-Eng)Marty Symes (m)Johnny Farrow. Adapted from O Marenariello. (I)Monica Lewis. (P)Frank Sinatra. (CR)Vic Damone.

I HAVE DREAMED (1951) (w)Oscar Hammerstein II (m)Richard Rodgers. (I)Musical: *The King And I*, by Doretta Morrow and Larry Douglas.

I HAVE EYES (1938) (wm)Leo Robin—Ralph Rainger. (I)Film: *Paris Honeymoon*, by Bing Crosby, Shirley Ross, and Franceska Gaal. (P)Bing Crosby. (CR)Benny Goodman and his Orchestra.

I HAVE NEVER FELT THIS WAY BEFORE (1985) (w)Don Black (m)Andrew Lloyd Webber. (I)Musical: *Song and Dance*, by Bernadette Peters.

I HAVE THE ROOM ABOVE (1936) (w)Oscar Hammerstein II (m)Jerome Kern. (I)Film: *Show Boat*, by Irene Dunne and Allan Jones.

I HAVE TO HAVE YOU (1929) (w)Leo Robin (m)Richard A. Whiting. (I)Film: *Pointed Heels*, by Helen Kane and Richard "Skeets" Gallagher.

I HAVE TO TELL YOU (1954) (wm)Harold Rome. (I)Musical: *Fanny*, by Florence Henderson.

I HAVEN'T GOT A WORRY IN THE WORLD (1946) (w)Oscar Hammerstein II (m)Richard Rodgers. (I)Play: *Happy Birthday*, by Helen Hayes. (P)Frances Langford.

I HAVEN'T TIME TO BE A MILLIONAIRE (1940) (w)Johnny Burke (m)James V. Monaco. (I)Film: *If I Had My Way*, by Bing Crosby. (P)Bing Crosby.

I HEAR A RHAPSODY (1940) (wm)George Fragos—Jack Baker—Dick Gasparre. (P)Jimmy Dorsey and his Orchestra. No. 1 Chart Record. (CR)Dinah Shore.

I HEAR A SYMPHONY (1965) (wm)Eddie Holland—Lamont Dozier—Brian Holland. (P)The Supremes. No. 1 Chart Record.

I HEAR MUSIC (1940) (w)Frank Loesser (m)Burton Lane. (I)Film: *Dancing On A Dime*, by Peter Lind Hayes, Eddie Quillan, Frank Jenks, and Robert Paige.

I HEAR TRUMPETS BLOW (1966) (wm)Mitchell Margo—Philip Margo—Henry Medress—Jay Siegel. (P)The Tokens.

I HEAR YOU KNOCKING (1955) (wm)Dave Bartholomew—Pearl King. (I)Smiley Lewis. (P)Gale Storm. (R)1961 by Fats Domino. (R)1971 by Dave Edmunds.

I HEARD A RUMOUR (1987) (wm)Dallin—Fahey—Woodward—Stock—Aitken—Waterman. (P)Bananarama.

I HEARD IT THROUGH THE GRAPEVINE (1967) (wm)Norman Whitfield—Barrett Strong. (P)Gladys Knight and The Pips. (R)1968 by Marvin Gaye. No. 1 Chart Record. (R)1976 by Creedence Clearwater Revival. (R)1981 by Roger.

I HEARD YOU CRIED LAST NIGHT (And So Did I) (1943) (w)Jerrie Kruger (m)Ted Grouya. (I)Film: *Cinderella Swings It*. (P)Harry James and his Orchestra, vocal by Helen Forrest. (CR)Dick Haymes.

I HIT A NEW HIGH (1937) (w)Harold Adamson (m)Jimmy McHugh. (I)Film: *Hitting A New High*, by Lily Pons.

I HONESTLY LOVE YOU (1974) (wm)Peter Allen—Jeff Barry. (P)Olivia Newton—John. No. 1 Chart Record. NARAS Award Winner.

I HOPE GABRIEL LIKES MY MUSIC (1935) (wm)David Franklin. (P)Louis Armstrong and his Orchestra.

I HUM A WALTZ (1937) (w)Mack Gordon (m)Harry Revel. (I)Film: *This is My Affair*, by Barbara Stanwyck.

I JUST CALLED TO SAY I LOVE YOU (1984) (wm)Stevie Wonder. (P)Stevie Wonder. No. 1 Chart Record. NARAS Award Winner.

I JUST CAN'T STOP DANCING (1968) (wm)Kenny Gamble—Leon Huff. (P)Archie Bell and The Drells.

I JUST CAN'T STOP LOVING YOU (1987) (wm)Michael Jackson. (P)Michael Jackson with Siedah Garrett. No. 1 Chart Record.

I JUST COULDN'T TAKE IT BABY (1933) (w)Mann Holiner (m)Alberta Nichols. (I)Revue: *Lew Leslie's Blackbirds of 1933*, by Gretchen Branch, Phil Scott, Kathryn Perry, The Duncan Sisters, and Eloise Uggams.

I JUST DON'T KNOW (1957) (w)Joseph Stone (m)Robert Allen. (P)The Four Lads.

I JUST DON'T KNOW WHAT TO DO WITH MYSELF (1966) (w)Hal David (m)Burt Bacharach. (P)Dionne Warwick. (CR)Gary Puckett.

I JUST DON'T UNDERSTAND (1961) (wm)Marijohn Wilkin—Kent Westbury. (P)Ann—Margret.

I JUST FALL IN LOVE AGAIN (1979) (wm)Stephen Dorff—Larry Herbstritt—Harry Lloyd—Gloria

Sklerov. (P)Anne Murray.

I JUST WANNA STOP (1978) (wm)Ross Vannelli. (P)Gino Vannelli.

I JUST WANT TO BE YOUR EVERYTHING (1977) (wm)Barry Gibb. (P)Andy Gibb. No. 1 Chart Record.

I KEEP FORGETTIN' (Every Time You're Near) (1962) (wm)Jerry Leiber—Mike Stoller. (P)Chuck Jackson. (R)1982 by Michael McDonald.

I KISS YOUR HAND, MADAME (1929) (w-Eng)Sam M. Lewis—Joe Young (m)Ralph Erwin. (I)Film: *The Emperor Waltz*, by Bing Crosby. (P)Bing Crosby. (R)1953 Film: *So This Is Love*, by Merv Griffin.

I KNEW YOU WERE WAITING FOR ME (1987) (wm)Climie—Morgan. (P)Aretha Franklin & George Michael. No. 1 Chart Record.

I KNEW YOU WHEN (1965) (wm)Joe South. (P)Billy Joe Royal. (R)1972 by Donny Osmond. (R)1983 by Linda Ronstadt.

I KNOW (You Don't Love Me No More) (1962) (wm)Barbara George. (P)Barbara George.

I KNOW A HEARTACHE WHEN I SEE ONE (1979) (wm)Kerry Chater—Rory Bourke—Charlie Black. (P)Jennifer Warnes.

I KNOW A PLACE (1965) (wm)Tony Hatch. (P)Petula Clark.

I KNOW ABOUT LOVE (1960) (w)Betty Comden—Adolph Green (m)Jule Styne. (I)Musical: *Do Re Mi* by John Reardon.

I KNOW NOW (1937) (w)Al Dubin (m)Harry Warren. (I)Film: *The Singing Marine*, by Doris Weston. (P)Guy Lombardo and his Royal Canadians. (CR)Dick Powell.

I KNOW THAT YOU KNOW (1926) (w)Anne Caldwell (m)Vincent Youmans. (I)Musical: *Oh, Please!*, by Beatrice Lillie and Charles Purcell. (R)1936 by Benny Goodman and his Orchestra. (R)1950 Film: *Tea For Two*, by Doris Day and Gordon MacRae. (R)1955 Film: *Hit The Deck*, by Vic Damone and Jane Powell.

I KNOW THE FEELING (1963) (w)Anne Croswell (m)Lee Pockriss. (I)Musical: *Tovarich*, by Vivien Leigh.

I KNOW THERE'S SOMETHING GOING ON (1982) (wm)Russ Ballard. (P)Frida.

I KNOW WHAT I LIKE (1987) (wm)Huey Lewis—C. Hayes. (P)Huey Lewis & The News.

I KNOW WHY (And So Do You) (1941) (w)Mack Gordon (m)Harry Warren. (I)Film: *Sun Valley Serenade*, by Glenn Miller and his Orchestra, vocal by Paula Kelly and The Modernaires. (P)Glenn Miller. (CR)Richard Himber and his Orchestra

I KNOW YOU BY HEART (1941) (wm)Hugh Martin—Ralph Blane. (I)Musical: *Best Foot Forward*, by Gil Stratton, Jr.

I LEFT MY HAT IN HAITI (1951) (w)Alan Jay Lerner (m)Burton Lane. (I)Film: *Royal Wedding*, by Fred Astaire.

I LEFT MY HEART AT THE STAGE DOOR CANTEEN. (1942) (wm)Irving Berlin. (I)Musical: *This Is The Army*, by Pvt. Earl Oxford and The Company. (P)Sammy Kaye and his Orchestra, vocal by Don Cornell. (CR)Charlie Spivak and his Orchestra.

I LEFT MY HEART IN SAN FRANCISCO (1954) (w)Douglass Cross (m)George Cory. (I)Claramae Turner. (R)1962 by Tony Bennett.

I LET A SONG GO OUT OF MY HEART (1938) (w)Henry Nemo—John Redmond—Irving Mills (m)Duke Ellington. (P)Duke Ellington and his Orchestra. Vocal version by Mildred Bailey. (CR)Benny Goodman and his Orchestra.

I LIKE DREAMIN (1977) (wm)Kenny Nolan Helfman. (P)Kenny Nolan.

I LIKE IT (1921) (wm)Irving Berlin. Not one of Berlin's hit songs.

I LIKE IT, I LIKE IT (1951) (w)Mann Curtis (m)Vic Mizzy. (P)Jane Turzy.

I LIKE IT LIKE THAT (1961) (wm)Chris Kenner—Alan Toussaint. (P)Chris Kenner. (R)1965 by The Dave Clark Five. (R)1975 by Loggins and Messina.

I LIKE MIKE (1946) (w)Mack Gordon (m)Josef Myrow. (I)Film: *Three Little Girls In Blue*, by Vera—Ellen.

I LIKE MOUNTAIN MUSIC (1933) (w)James Cavanaugh (m)Frank Weldon. (P)Ethel Shutta.

I LIKE MYSELF (1954) (w)Betty Comden—Adolph Green (m)Andre Previn. (I)Film: *It's Always Fair Weather*, by Gene Kelly.

I LIKE THE LIKES OF YOU (1934) (w)E.Y. Harburg (m)Vernon Duke. (I)Revue: *Ziegfeld Follies of 1934*, by Brice Hutchins and Judith Barron. Danced to by Vilma and Buddy Ebsen.

I LIKE THE SUNRISE (1947) (wm)Duke Ellington—Mercer Ellington. Adapted from Ellington's Liberian Suite. (I)At Carnegie Hall, by Duke Ellington and his Orchestra, vocal by Al Hibbler.

I LIKE THE WAY (1967) (wm)Ritchie Cordell—Bo Gentry. (P)Tommy James and The Shondells.

I LIKE TO RECOGNIZE THE TUNE (1939) (w)Lorenz Hart (m)Richard Rodgers. (I)Musical: *Too Many Girls*, by Eddie Bracken, Marcy Westcott, Mary Jane Walsh, Dick Kollmar, and Hal Le Roy. (R)1944 Film: *Meet The People*, by June Allyson, Vaughn Monroe, Virginia O'Brien, Ziggy Talent, and The Chorus.

I LIKE YOU (1954) (wm)Harold Rome. (I)Musical: *Fanny*, by Ezio Pinza and William Tabbert.

I LIKE YOUR KIND OF LOVE (1957) (wm)Melvin Endsley. (P)Andy Williams.

I LIVE FOR YOUR LOVE (1987) (wm)Reswick—Werfel—Rich. (P)Natalie Cole.

I LOOK AT HEAVEN (When I Look At You) (1942) (w)Bobby Worth (m)Ray Austin—Freddy Martin. Adapted from Grieg's Concerto in A Minor. (P)Dinah Shore with Freddy Martin and his Orchestra,

I LOST MY SUGAR IN SALT LAKE CITY (1942) (wm)Leon Rene—Johnny Lange. (I)Film: *Stormy Weather* on soundtrack. (P)Johnny Mercer.

I LOVE (1974) (wm)Tom T. Hall. (P)Tom T. Hall.

I LOVE A NEW YORKER (1950) (wm)Ralph Blane—Harold Arlen. (I)Film: *My Blue Heaven*, by Betty Grable and Dan Dailey.

I LOVE A PARADE (1931) (w)Ted Koehler (m)Harold Arlen. (I)Revue: *Rhythmania*, by Cab Calloway. (P)Harry Richman. (CR)The Ohman—Arden Orchestra.

I LOVE A PIANO (1915) (wm)Irving Berlin. Not a hit when first released. (R)1948 Film: *Easter Parade*, by Judy Garland and Fred Astaire.

I LOVE A RAINY NIGHT (1980) (wm)Eddie Rabbitt—Even Stevens—David Malloy. (P)Eddie Rabbitt. No. 1 Chart Record.

I LOVE HER, SHE LOVES ME (1922) (wm)Irving Caesar—Eddie Cantor. (I)Revue: *Make It Snappy*, by Eddie Cantor.

I LOVE HOW YOU LOVE ME (1961) (wm)Barry Mann—

Larry Kolber. (P)The Paris Sisters. (R)1968 by Bobby Vinton.

I LOVE LIFE (1923) (w)Irwin M. Cassel (m)Mme. Mana—Zucca. (I)Charles Hackett. (P)John Charles Thomas.

I LOVE LOUISA (1931) (w)Howard Dietz (m)Arthur Schwartz. (I)Revue: *The Band Wagon*, by Fred and Adele Astaire. (R)1953 Film: *The Band Wagon*, by Fred Astaire with Oscar Levant at the piano.

I LOVE MUSIC (Part 1) (1975) (wm)Kenny Gamble—Leon Huff. (P)The O'Jays.

I LOVE MY BABY (My Baby Loves Me) (1925) (w)Bud Green (m)Harry Warren. (P)Fred Waring's Pennsylvanians. (CR)Aileen Stanley.

I LOVE MY FRIEND (1974) (wm)Billy Sherrill—Norro Wilson. (P)Charlie Rich.

I LOVE PARIS (1953) (wm)Cole Porter. (I)Musical: *Can-Can*, by Lilo. (P)Les Baxter and his Orchestra. (CR)Michel Legrand and his Orchestra.

I LOVE ROCK AND ROLL (1984) (wm)Jake Hooker—Alan Merrill. (P)Joan Jett & The Blackhearts. No. 1 Chart Record.

I LOVE THE NIGHTLIFE (1978) (wm)Alicia Bridges—Susan Hutcheson. (P)Alicia Bridges. Featured in film *Love At First Bite*.

I LOVE THE WAY YOU LOVE (1960) (wm)Berry Gordy, Jr.—Mikaljohn. (P)Marv Johnson.

I LOVE THE WAY YOU SAY GOODNIGHT (1951) (wm)Eddie Pola—George Wyle. (I)Film: *Lullaby Of Broadway*, by Doris Day and Gene Nelson.

I LOVE TO LAUGH (1963) (wm)Richard M. Sherman—Robert B. Sherman. (I)Film: *Mary Poppins*, by Julie Andrews, Dick Van Dyke, and Ed Wynn.

I LOVE TO RHYME (1938) (w)Ira Gershwin (m)George Gershwin. (I)Film: *The Goldwyn Follies*, by Phil Baker and Edgar Bergen as Charlie McCarthy.

I LOVE TO SING-A (1936) (w)E.Y. Harburg (m)Harold Arlen. (I)Film: *The Singing Kid*, by Al Jolson and Cab Calloway.

I LOVE TO WALK IN THE RAIN (1938) (w)Walter Bullock (m)Harold Spina. (I)Film: *Just Around The Corner*, by Shirley Temple.

I LOVE TO WHISTLE (1938) (w)Harold Adamson (m)Jimmy McHugh. (I)Film: *Mad About Music*, by Deanna Durbin, Christian Rub, Helen Parrish, and Marcia Mae Jones. (P)Fats Waller.

I LOVE YOU (1923) (w)Harlan Thompson (m)Harry Archer. (I)Musical: *Little Jessie James*, by John Boles and Margaret Wilson. (P)Paul Whiteman and his Orchestra.

I LOVE YOU (1943) (wm)Cole Porter. (I)Musical: *Mexican Hayride*, by Wilbur Evans. (P)Bing Crosby. No. 1 Chart Record.

I LOVE YOU (1944) (wm)Robert Wright—George Forrest. Adapted from Grieg's Ich Liebe Dich. (I)Operetta: *Song Of Norway*, by Helena Bliss, Walter Kingsford, Ivy Scott, and The Chorus.

(P.S.)I LOVE YOU (1963) (wm)John Lennon—Paul McCartney. (P)The Beatles.

I LOVE YOU (1968) (wm)Chris White. (P)People.

I LOVE YOU (1981) (wm)Derek Holt. (P)The Climax Blues Band.

I LOVE YOU BECAUSE (1950) (wm)Leon Payne. (P)Ernest Tubb and Leon Payne. (R)1963 by Al Martino.

I LOVE YOU DROPS (1966) (wm)Bill Anderson (I)Bill Anderson. (P)Vic Dana.

I LOVE YOU FOR ALL SEASONS (1971) (wm)Sheila Young. (P)Fuzz.

I LOVE YOU MADLY (1954) (wm)Charles Jones (I)Charlie and Ray. (P)The Four Coins.

I LOVE YOU MORE AND MORE EVERY DAY (1964) (wm)Don Robertson. (P)Al Martino.

I LOVE YOU MUCH TOO MUCH (1940) (w)Don Raye (m)Alex Olshey—Chaim Towber. Adapted from the Yiddish version. (P)The Andrews Sisters.

I LOVE YOU 1000 TIMES (1966) (w)Inez Foxx (m)Luther Dixon. (P)The Platters.

I LOVE YOU, SAMANTHA (1956) (wm)Cole Porter (I)Film: *High Society*, by Bing Crosby.

I LOVE YOU SO MUCH IT HURTS (1948) (wm)Floyd Tillman. (I)Floyd Tillman. (P)The Mills Brothers. (CR)Buddy Clark.

I LOVE YOU SWEETHEART OF ALL MY DREAMS (1928) (wm)Art Fitch—Kay Fitch—Bert Lowe. (P)Rudy Vallee.

I LOVE YOU THIS MORNING (1945) (w)Alan Jay Lerner (m)Frederick Loewe. (I)Musical: *The Day Before Spring*, by Bill Johnson and Irene Manning.

I LOVE YOU TRULY (1912) (wm)Carrie Jacobs Bond. (I)Elsie Baker. Very popular song for weddings.

I LOVED YOU ONCE IN SILENCE (1960) (w)Alan Jay Lerner (m)Frederick Loewe. (I)Musical: *Camelot*, by Julie Andrews.

I LOVES YOU PORGY (1935) (w)Du Bose Heyward—Ira Gershwin (m)George Gershwin. (I)Opera: *Porgy and Bess*, by Anne Brown. In film version (1959) by Adele Addison dubbing for Dorothy Dandridge. (P)Nina Simone.

I MADE IT THROUGH THE RAIN (1980) (wm)Gerald Kenny—Drey Sheppard—Bruce Sussman—Jack Feldman—Barry Manilow. (P)Barry Manilow.

I MAKE A FOOL OF MYSELF (1967) (wm)Bob Crewe—Bob Gaudio. (P)Frankie Valli.

I MARRIED AN ANGEL (1938) (w)Lorenz Hart (m)Richard Rodgers. (I)Musical: *I Married An Angel*, by Dennis King. Recorded by Sammy Kaye and his Orchestra. (R)1942 Film version, by Nelson Eddy and Jeanette MacDonald.

I MAY BE WRONG (But I Think You're Wonderful) (1929) (w)Harry Ruskin (m)Henry Sullivan. (I)Revue: *John Murray Anderson's Almanac*, by Trixie Friganza and Jimmie Savo. (R)Film: *Young Man With A Horn*, by Doris Day.

I MAY NEVER PASS THIS WAY AGAIN (1958) (wm)Murray Wizell—Irving Melsher. (I)London, by Robert Earl. (P)Perry Como.

I MEAN TO SAY (1930) (w)Ira Gershwin (m)George Gershwin. (I)Musical: *Strike Up The Band*, by Doris Carson and Gordon Smith.

I MET HER ON MONDAY (1942) (w)Charles Newman (m)Allie Wrubel. (P)Horace Heidt and his Orchestra. (CR)Freddy Martin and his Orchestra. (CR)Guy Lombardo and his Royal Canadians.

I MIGHT FALL BACK ON YOU (1927) (w)Oscar Hammerstein II (m)Jerome Kern. (I)Musical: *Show Boat*, by Eva Puck and Sammy White. In third film version by Marge and Gower Champion.

I MISS MY SWISS, MY SWISS MISS MISSES ME (1922) (wm)L. Wolfe Gilbert—Abel Baer. (I)Revue: *Balieff's Chauve—Souris*. (P)Billy Jones and Ernie Hare (The Happiness Boys).

I MISS YOU (1985) (wm)Lynn Malsby. (P)Klymaxx.

I MUST BE SEEING THINGS AND HEARING THINGS (1965) (wm)Al Kooper—Bob Brass—Irwin Levine. (P)Gene Pitney.

I MUST HAVE THAT MAN (1928) (w)Dorothy Fields (m)Jimmy McHugh. (I)Revue: *Lew Leslie's Blackbirds of 1928*, by Adelaide Hall.

I MUST LOVE YOU (1928) (w)Lorenz Hart (m)Richard Rodgers. (I)Musical: *Chee—Chee*, by Helen Ford and William Williams.

I MUST SEE ANNIE TONIGHT (1938) (wm)Cliff Friend—Dave Franklin. (P)Guy Lombardo and his Royal Canadians. (CR)Benny Goodman and his Orchestra.

I NEED A LOVER (1979) (wm)John Cougar Mellencamp. (P)John Cougar Mellencamp.

I NEED LOVE (1987) (wm)J.T. Smith—B. Erving—D. Pierce—D. Simon—S. Ett. (P)L.L. Cool J.

I NEED SOMEBODY (1966) (wm)Francisco Lugo—Rudy Martinez—Robert Balderrana—Frank Rodriguez—Edward Serrato.

I NEED TO BE IN LOVE (1976) (wm)John Bettis—Albert Hammond (m)Richard Carpenter. (P)The Carpenters.

I NEED YOU (1965) (wm)George Harrison. (I)Film: *Help!*, by The Beatles. (P)The Beatles.

I NEED YOU (1972) (wm)Gerry Beckley. (P)America.

I NEED YOU NOW (1954) (wm)Jimmie Crane—Al Jacobs. (P)Eddie Fisher. No. 1 Chart Record.

I NEED YOUR LOVE TONIGHT (1959) (wm)Sid Wayne—Bix Reichner. (P)Elvis Presley.

I NEED YOUR LOVIN' (1962) (wm)Clarence Paul—Sonny Woods—Willie Jennings. First recording was by Conway Twitty in 1959. (P)Don Gardner and Dee Dee Ford.

I NEVER CRY (1976) (wm)Dick Wagner—Alice Cooper. (P)Alice Cooper.

I NEVER FELT THIS WAY BEFORE (1940) (w)Al Dubin (m)Duke Ellington. (P)Duke Ellington and his Orchestra.

I NEVER FELT THIS WAY BEFORE (1957) (w)Mack Gordon (m)Josef Myrow. (I)Film: *Bundle Of Joy*, by Eddie Fisher and Debbie Reynolds.

I NEVER HAD A CHANCE (1934) (wm)Irving Berlin. Not one of Berlin's hit songs.

I NEVER HAS SEEN SNOW (1954) (wm)Truman Capote—Harold Arlen. (I)Musical: *House Of Flowers*, by Diahann Carroll.

I NEVER KNEW HEAVEN COULD SPEAK (1939) (wm)Mack Gordon—Harry Revel. (I)Film: *Rose Of Washington Square*, by Alice Faye.

I NEVER KNEW I COULD LOVE ANYBODY LIKE I'M LOVING YOU (1920) (wm)Tom Pitts—Ray Egan—Roy Marsh. (P)Paul Whiteman and his Orchestra.

I NEVER LOVED A MAN (The Way I Love You) (1967) (wm)Ronnie Shannon. (P)Aretha Franklin.

I NEVER SEE MAGGIE ALONE (1926) (w)Harry Tilsley (m)Everett Lynton. (P)Irving Aaronson aand his Commanders. (R)1949 by Kenny Roberts. (CR)Art Mooney and his Orchestra.

I NEVER WILL MARRY (1958) (wm)Fred Hellerman. (P)Linda Ronstadt.

I ONLY HAVE EYES FOR YOU (1934) (w)Al Dubin (m)Harry Warren. (I)Film: *Dames*, by Dick Powell and Ruby Keeler. (P)Eddy Duchin and his Orchestra. (CR)Jane Froman. (R)1959 by The Flamingos. (R)1966 by The Lettermen. (CR)1972 by Jerry Butler. (R)1975 by Art Garfunkel.

I ONLY WANT TO BE WITH YOU (1963) (wm)Mike Hawker—Ivor Raymonde. (P)Dusty Springfield. (R)1976 by Bay City Rollers. (R)1980 by The Tourists. (R)1982 by Nicolette Larson.

I PITY THE POOR IMMIGRANT (1968) (wm)Bob Dylan. (P)Bob Dylan.

I PLAYED FIDDLE FOR THE CZAR (1932) (w)Mack Gordon (m)Harry Revel. (P)Ben Bernie and his Orchestra.

I PLEDGE MY LOVE (1980) (wm)Dino Fekaris—Freddy Perren. (P)Peaches & Herb.

I POURED MY HEART INTO A SONG (1939) (wm)Irving Berlin. (I)Film: *Second Fiddle*, by Tyrone Power and reprised by Rudy Vallee.

I PROMISE YOU (1944) (w)Johnny Mercer (m)Harold Arlen. (I)Film: *Here Come The Waves*, by Bing Crosby and Betty Hutton.

I PUT MY HAND IN (1963) (wm)Jerry Herman. (I)Musical: *Hello Dolly*, by Carol Channing and The Company.

I RAN (1982) (wm)Ali Score—Paul Reynolds—Mike Score—Frank Maudley. (P)A Flock Of Seagulls.

I RAN ALL THE WAY HOME (1951) (wm)Bennie Benjamin—George Weiss. (P)Eddy Howard. (CR)Sarah Vaughan. (CR)Buddy Greco.

I REALLY DON' T WANT TO KNOW. (1953) (w)Howard Barnes (m)Don Robertson. (I)Don Robertson. (R)1960 by Tommy Edwards. (R)1962 by Solomon Burke. (R)1963 by Esther Phillips. (CR)1966 by Ronnie Dove. (CR)1971 by Elvis Presley.

I REMEMBER IT WELL (1958) (w)Alan Jay Lerner (m)Frederick Loewe. (I)Film: *Gigi*, by Maurice Chevalier and Hermione Gingold.

I REMEMBER MAMA (1948) (wm)Charles Tobias—Henry Tobias. Adapted from La Cinquantaine by Gabriel P. Marie. (P)Claude Thornhill and his Orchestra, vocal by Fran Warren. (CR)Ziggy Lane.

I REMEMBER THE CORNFIELDS (1948) (wm)Martyn Mayne—Harry Ralton. (I)England, by Anne Shelton. In United States, by Evelyn Knight.

I REMEMBER YOU (1942) (w)Johnny Mercer (m)Victor Schertzinger. (I)Film: *The Fleet's In*, by Dorothy Lamour. (P)Jimmy Dorsey and his Orchestra. (CR)Harry James and his Orchestra. (R)1962 by Frank Ifeld.

I SAID MY PAJAMAS (And Put On My Pray'rs) (1949) (wm)Eddie Pola—George Wyle. (P)Fran Warren and Tony Martin with Henri Rene and his Orchestra. (CR)Ethel Merman and Ray Bolger. (CR)Doris Day. (CR)Margaret Whiting.

I SAID NO (1942) (w)Frank Loesser (m)Jule Styne. (I)Film: *Sweater Girl*, by Betty Jane Rhodes. (P)Jimmy Dorsey and his Orchestra, vocal by Helen O'Connell. (CR)Alvino Rey and his Orchestra.

I SAW HER AGAIN LAST NIGHT (1966) (wm)John Phillips—Dennis Doherty. (P)The Mamas and The Papas.

I SAW HER AT EIGHT O'CLOCK (1935) (w)Johnny Mercer (m)Matt Malneck. (I)Film: *To Beat The Band*, by Johnny Mercer, Evelyn Poe, and Fred Keating.

I SAW HER STANDING THERE (1964) (wm)John Lennon—Paul McCartney. (P)The Beatles. (R)1988 by Tiffany as "I Saw Him Standing There".

I SAW LINDA YESTERDAY (1962) (wm)Dickey Lee—Allen Reynolds. (P)Dickey Lee.

I SAW MOMMY KISSING SANTA CLAUS. (1952)

(wm)Tommie Connor. (P)Jimmy Boyd. No. 1 Chart Record. (CR)Spike Jones. (CR)Molly Bee.

I SAW STARS (1934) (wm)Maurice Sigler—Al Goodhart—Al Hoffman. (I)Paul Whiteman and his Orchestra. (CR)Freddy Martin and his Orchestra.

I SAW THE LIGHT (1972) (wm)Todd Rundgren. (P)Todd Rundgren.

I SAY A LITTLE PRAYER (1967) (w)Hal David (m)Burt Bacharach. (P)Dionne Warwick. (CR)Aretha Franklin.

I SAY HELLO (1959) (wm)Harold Rome. (I)Musical: *Destry Rides Again*, by Dolores Gray.

I SAY IT'S SPINACH (1932) (wm)Irving Berlin. (I)Musical: *Face The Music*, by J. Harold Murray and Katherine Carrington.

I SECOND THAT EMOTION (1967) (wm)William Robinson—Alfred Cleveland. (P)Smokey Robinson and The Miracles.

I SEE A MILLION PEOPLE (But All I Can See Is You) (1941) (w)Robert Sour (m)Una Mae Carlisle. (P)Una Mae Carlisle. (CR)Cab Calloway.

I SEE THE LIGHT (1966) (wm)Norman Ezell—Mike Rabon—John Durrill. (P)The Five Americans.

I SEE TWO LOVERS (1935) (w)Mort Dixon (m)Allie Wrubel. (I)Film: *Sweet Music*, by Helen Morgan.

I SEE YOUR FACE BEFORE ME (1937) (w)Howard Dietz (m)Arthur Schwartz. (I)Musical: *Between The Devil*, by Jack Buchanan, Evelyn Laye, and Adele Dixon.

I SHALL BE RELEASED (1968) (P)The Band. (R)1972 by Bob Dylan.

I SHALL SING (1974) (wm)Van Morrison. (P)Art Garfunkel.

I SHOT THE SHERIFF (1974) (wm)Bob Marley. (P)Eric Clapton. No. 1 Chart Record.

I SHOULD CARE (1945) (wm)Sammy Cahn—Axel Stordahl—Paul Weston. (I)Film: *Thrill Of A Romance*, by Robert Allen. (P)Tommy Dorsey and his Orchestra, vocal by Frank Sinatra. (CR)Martha Tilton.

I SHOULD HAVE KNOWN BETTER (1964) (wm)John Lennon—Paul McCartney. (I)Film: *A Hard Day's Night*, by The Beatles. (P)The Beatles.

I SOLD MY HEART TO THE JUNK MAN (1947) (wm)Otis Rene, Jr.—Leon Rene. (P)The Basin Street Boys.

I SPEAK TO THE STARS (1954) (w)Paul Francis Webster (m)Sammy Fain. (I)Film: *Lucky Me*, by Doris Day. (P)Doris Day.

I STARTED A JOKE (1969) (wm)Barry, Robin, and Maurice Gibb. (P)The Bee Gees.

I STAYED TOO LONG AT THE FAIR (1957) (wm)Billy Barnes. (I)Revue: *The Billy Barnes Revue*, by Joyce Jameson. (R)1963 by Barbra Streisand.

I STILL BELIEVE IN LOVE (1978) (w)Carole Bayer Sager (m)Marvin Hamlisch. (I)Musical: *They're Playing Our Song*, by Lucy Arnaz.

I STILL BELIEVE IN YOU (1930) (w)Lorenz Hart (m)Richard Rodgers. (I)Musical: *Simple Simon*, by Ruth Etting.

I STILL CAN'T GET OVER LOVING YOU (1984) (wm)Ray Parker, Jr. (P)Ray Parker, Jr.

I STILL GET A THRILL (Thinking Of You) (1930) (w)Benny Davis (m)J. Fred Coots. (P)Hal Kemp and his Orchestra. (CR)Guy Lombardo and his Royal Canadians. (CR)Ozzie Nelson and his Orchestra.

I STILL GET JEALOUS (1947) (w)Sammy Cahn (m)Jule Styne. (I)Musical: *High Button Shoes*, by Nanette Fabray and Jack McCauley. (P)The Three Suns.

(CR)Harry James and his Orchestra.

I STILL HAVEN'T FOUND WHAT I'M LOOKING FOR (1987) (wm)U2. (P)U2. No. 1 Chart Record.

I STILL LOOK AT YOU THAT WAY (1963) (w)Howard Dietz (m)Arthur Schwartz. (I)Musical: *Jennie*, by Mary Martin.

I STILL LOVE TO KISS YOU GOODNIGHT (1937) (w)Walter Bullock (m)Harold Spina. (I)Film: *Fifty-Second Street*, by Pat Paterson. (P)Bing Crosby. (CR)Shep Fields and his Orchestra.

I STILL SEE ELISA (1951) (w)Alan Jay Lerner (m)Frederick Loewe. (I)Musical: *Paint Your Wagon*, by James Barton.

I STILL SUITS ME (1936) (w)Oscar Hammerstein II (m)Jerome Kern. (I)Film: *Show Boat*, by Paul Robeson and Hattie McDaniel.

I SURRENDER, DEAR (1931) (w)Gordon Clifford (m)Harry Barris. (P)Gus Arnheim and his Orchestra, vocal by The Rhythm Boys, featuring Bing Crosby. (CR)Earl Burtnett and his Orchestra.

I TAKE IT BACK (1967) (wm)Perry C. Buie—James B. Cobb. (P)Sandy Posey.

I TAKE TO YOU (1941) (w)Mack Gordon (m)Harry Warren. (I)Film: *The Great American Broadcast*, by Alice Faye, John Payne, and Jack Oakie.

I TALK TO THE TREES (1951) (w)Alan Jay Lerner (m)Frederick Loewe. (I)Musical: *Paint Your Wagon*, by Tony Bavaar and Olga San Juan.

I TAUT I TAW A PUDDY TAT (I Thought I Saw A Pussy Cat) (1950) (wm)Alan Livingston—Billy May—Warren Foster. (P)Mel Blanc.

I THANK YOU (1968) (wm)David Porter—Isaac Hayes. (P)Sam and Dave. (R)1972 by Donny Hathaway and June Conquest. (R)1980 by ZZ Top.

I THINK I LOVE YOU (1970) (wm)Tony Romeo. (P)The Partridge Family. No. 1 Chart Record.

I THINK IT'S GOING TO RAIN TODAY (1966) (wm)Randy Newman. (P)Judy Collins. (R)1971 by Randy Newman.

I THINK IT'S LOVE (1986) (wm)Jermaine Jackson—Michael Omartian—Stevie Wonder. (P)Jermaine Jackson.

I THINK OF YOU (1941) (wm)Jack Elliott—Don Marcotte. Melody based on Rachmaninoff's Piano Concerto No. 2. (P)Tommy Dorsey and his Orchestra, vocal by Frank Sinatra.

I THINK WE'RE ALONE NOW (1967) (wm)Ritchie Cordell—Bo Gentry. (P)Tommy James and The Shondells. (R)1977 by Rubinoos. (R)Tiffany. No. 1 Chart Record.

I THOUGHT ABOUT YOU (1939) (w)Johnny Mercer (m)Jimmy Van Heusen. (P)Benny Goodman and his Orchestra, vocal by Mildred Bailey.

I THREW A KISS IN THE OCEAN (1942) (wm)Irving Berlin. (P)Kate Smith. (CR)Jimmy Dorsey and his Orchestra.

I THREW IT ALL AWAY (1969) (wm)Bob Dylan. (P)Bob Dylan.

I TURNED YOU ON (1969) (wm)Rudolph, O'Kelly, and Ronald Isley. (P)The Isley Brothers.

I UNDERSTAND (1941) (w)Kim Gannon (m)Mabel Wayne. (P)Jimmy Dorsey and his Orchestra, vocal by Bob Eberly.

I UNDERSTAND JUST HOW YOU FEEL (1953) (wm)Pat Best. (P)The Four Tunes. (R)1961 by The G—Clefs. (R)1965 by Freddie and The Dreamers.

I UPS TO HIM AND HE UPS TO ME (1929) (wm)Jimmy Durante. (I)Musical: *Show Girl*, by Jimmy Durante.

I USED TO BE COLOR BLIND. (1938) (wm)Irving Berlin. (I)Film: *Carefree*, by Fred Astaire.

I USED TO LOVE YOU BUT IT'S ALL OVER NOW. (1920) (w)Lew Brown (m)Albert Von Tilzer. (P)Frank Crumit.

I WAITED A LITTLE TOO LONG (1951) (wm)Sidney Miller—Donald O'Connor. (P)Kay Starr.

I WAITED TOO LONG (1959) (wm)Howard Greenfield—Neil Sedaka. (P)LaVern Baker.

I WAKE UP SMILING (1933) (w)Edgar Leslie (m)Fred E. Ahlert. (P)Guy Lombardo and his Royal Canadians.

I WALK THE LINE (1956) (wm)Johnny Cash. (P)Johnny Cash. (R)1959 by Don Costa and his Orchestra. (R)1960 by Jaye P. Morgan.

I WALK WITH MUSIC (1940) (w)Johnny Mercer (m)Hoagy Carmichael. (I)Musical: *Walk With Music*, by Kitty Carlisle and Jack Whiting.

I WALKED IN (With My Eyes Wide Open) (1945) (w)Harold Adamson (m)Jimmy McHugh. (I)Film: *Nob Hill*, by Vivian Blaine.

I WANNA BE A COWBOY (1986) (wm)Brian Chatton—Nico Ramsden—Nick Richards—Jeff Jeopardi. (P)The Cure.

I WANNA BE AROUND (1959) (wm)Johnny Mercer—Sadie Vimmerstedt. (P)In 1963 by Tony Bennett.

I WANNA BE IN WINCHELL'S COLUMN (1937) (w)Mack Gordon (m)Harry Revel. (I)Film: *Love and Hisses*, by Dick Baldwin.

I WANNA BE LOVED (1934) (w)Billy Rose—Edward Heyman (m)John Green. (I)Revue: *Casino de Paris*. (R)1950 by The Andrews Sisters. No. 1 Chart Record.

I WANNA BE LOVED BY YOU (1928) (w)Bert Kalmar (m)Harry Ruby—Herbert Stothart. (I)Musical: *Good Boy*, by Helen Kane and Dan Healy. (P)Helen Kane. (R)1950 Film: *Three Little Words*, by Fred Astaire and Helen Kane dubbing for Debbie Reynolds. (R)1959 Film: *Some Like It Hot*, by Marilyn Monroe.

I WANNA BE WHERE YOU ARE (1972) (wm)Arthur Ross—Leon Ware. (P)Michael Jackson.

I WANNA BE WITH YOU (1973) (wm)Eric Carmen. (P)The Raspberries.

I WANNA BE YOUR LOVER (1980) (wm)Prince Rogers Nelson. (P)Prince.

I WANNA BE YOUR MAN (1963) (wm)John Lennon—Paul McCartney. (P)The Rolling Stones.

I WANNA DANCE WIT CHOO (Doo Dat Dance) (1975) (wm)Bob Crewe—Denny Randell. (P)Disco Tex & The Sex—O—Lettes.

I WANNA DANCE WITH SOMEBODY (Who Loves Me) (1987) (wm)Merrill—Rubicam. (P)Whitney Houston. No. 1 Chart Record.

I WANNA GET MARRIED (1944) (wm)Dan Shapiro—Milton Pascal—Phil Charig. (I)Musical: *Follow The Girls*, by Gertrude Niesen. (P)Gertrude Niesen.

I WANNA GO BACK (1987) (wm)D. Chancey—M. Byrom—I. Walker. (P)Eddie Money

I WANNA GO BACK TO BALI (1938) (w)Al Dubin (m)Harry Warren. (I)Film: *Gold Diggers In Paris*, by Rudy Vallee.

I WANNA GO HOME (1949) (wm)Jack Joyce. (P)Perry Como and The Fontane Sisters.

I WANNA GO TO THE ZOO (1936) (w)Mack Gordon (m)Harry Revel. (I)Film: *Stowaway*, by Shirley Temple.

I WANNA GO WHERE YOU GO, DO WHAT YOU DO,

THEN I'LL BE HAPPY. (1925) (w)Sidney Clare—Lew Brown (m)Cliff Friend. (P)"Whispering" Jack Smith. (R)1945 by Tommy Dorsey and his Orchestra.

I WANNA LIVE (1968) (wm)John D. Loudermilk. (P)Glen Campbell.

I WANNA LOVE HIM SO BAD (1964) (wm)Jeff Barry—Ellie Greenwich. (P)The Jelly Beans.

I WANNA TESTIFY (1967) (wm)George Clinton—Deron Taylor. (P)The Parliaments. (R)1969 by Johnnie Taylor.

I WANT A BIG BUTTER AND EGG MAN (1926) (wm)Percy Venable—Louis Armstrong. (I)Cafe Revue: by Louis Armstrong and May Alix.

I WANT A KISS (w)Otto Harbach-Oscar Hammerstein II (m)Sigmund Romberg. (I)Operetta: *The Desert Song*, by Vivienne Segal, Glen Dale, and Robert Halliday.

I WANT A LITTLE DOGGIE (1945) (wm)Phil Moore—Milt Lance. (P)Lena Horne with The Phil Moore Five.

I WANT A LITTLE GIRL (1930) (w)Billy Moll (m)Murray Mencher. (P)McKinney's Cotton Pickers, vocal by George Thomas.

I WANT A LOVABLE BABY (1925) (w)B.G. De Sylva—Lew Brown (m)Ray Henderson. (I)Revue: *George White's Scandals of 1925*, by Helen Morgan.

I WANT A MAN (1928) (w)Oscar Hammerstein II (m)Vincent Youmans. (I)Musical: *Rainbow*, by Libby Holman.

I WANT A MAN (1931) (w)Lorenz Hart (m)Richard Rodgers. (I)Musical: *America's Sweetheart*, by Jeanne Aubert.

I WANT A NEW DRUG (1984) (wm)Christopher Hayes—Huey Lewis. (P)Huey Lewis & The News.

I WANT CANDY (1965) (wm)Bob Feldman—Jerry Goldstein—Richard Gottehrer—Bert Berns. (P)The Strangeloves.

I WANT HER (1987) (wm)K. Sweat—T. Riley. (P)Keith Sweat.

I WANT MY MAMA (Mama Yo Quiero) (1940) (w-Eng)Al Stillman (m)Jararaca Paiva—Vincente Paiva. (P)Carmen Miranda. (R)1941 Film: *Babes On Broadway*, by Mickey Rooney.

I WANT TO (Do Everything For You) (1965) (wm)Joe Tex. (P)Joe Tex. (R)1970 by The Raelettes.

I WANT TO BE BAD (1929) (w)B. G. De Sylva—Lew Brown (m)Ray Henderson. (I)Musical: *Follow Thru* by Zelma O'Neal. In film version by Nancy Carroll.

I WANT TO BE HAPPY (1924) (w)Irving Caesar (m)Vincent Youmans. (I)Musical: *No, No, Nanette*, by Charles Winniger and Louise Groody. Recorded by: Vincent Lopez and his Orchestra, Jan Garber and his Orchestra. (R)1937 by Benny Goodman and his Orchestra. (R)1950 Film: *Tea For Two*, by Doris Day and Gordon MacRae.

I WANT TO BE LOVED (But By Only You) (1947) (wm)Savannah Chuchill. (P)Savannah Churchill.

I WANT TO BE THE ONLY ONE (1948) (wm)Ernie Peterson. (P)Jon and Sandra Steele.

I WANT TO BE WANTED (1960) (w-Eng)Kim Gannon (m)Pino Spotti. (P)Brenda Lee. No. 1 Chart Record. (CR)Andy Williams.

I WANT TO BE WITH YOU (1964) (w)Lee Adams (m)Charles Strouse. (I)Film: *Golden Boy*, by Sammy Davis, Jr., and Paula Wayne. (P)1966 by Dee Dee Warwick.

I WANT TO BE YOUR MAN (1987) (wm)L. Troutman. (P)Roger.

I WANT TO CRY (1947) (w)Lille Randall (m)Harry Pirone. (P)Dinah Washington.

I WANT TO GO HOME (1938) (wm)Cole Porter. (I)Musical: *Leave It To Me*, by Victor Moore.

I WANT TO GO WITH YOU (1966) (wm)Hank Cochran. (P)Eddy Arnold.

I WANT TO HOLD YOUR HAND (1963) (wm)John Lennon—Paul McCartney. (P)The Beatles. No. 1 Chart Record. (CR)The Boston Pops Orchestra.

I WANT TO KNOW WHAT LOVE IS (1984) (wm)Mick Jones. (P)Foreigner.

I WANT TO RING BELLS (1933) (w)Maurice Sigler (m)J. Fred Coots. (P)Guy Lombardo and his Royal Canadians.

I WANT TO STAY HERE (1963) (wm)Gerry Goffin—Carole King. (P)Steve Lawrence and Eydie Gorme.

I WANT TO TAKE YOU HIGHER (1969) (wm)Sylvester Stewart. (P)Sly and The Family Stone. (R)1970 by Ike and Tina Turner.

I WANT TO TELL YOU (1966) (wm)George Harrison. (P)The Beatles.

I WANT TO THANK YOUR FOLKS (1947) (wm)Bennie Benjamin—George Weiss. (P)Perry Como.

I WANT TO WALK YOU HOME (1959) (wm)Antoine Domino. (P)Fats Domino.

I WANT YOU (1966) (wm)Bob Dylan. (P)Bob Dylan.

I WANT YOU (She's So Heavy) (1969) (wm)John Lennon—Paul McCartney. (P)The Beatles.

I WANT YOU (1976) (wm)Arthur Ross and Leon Ware. (P)Marvin Gaye.

I WANT YOU ALL TO MYSELF (1954) (wm)John Koch—Ray Carroll. (P)Kitty Kallen.

I WANT YOU BACK (1969) (wm)Freddy Perren—Al Mizell—Deke Richards—Berry Gordy, Jr. (P)The Jackson Five. No. 1 Chart Record. (R)1979 by Graham Parker.

I WANT YOU FOR MYSELF (1931) (wm)Irving Berlin. Not one of Berlin' hit songs.

I WANT YOU, I NEED YOU (1933) (wm)Ben Ellison—Harvey O. Brooks. (I)Film: *I'm No Angel*, by Mae West.

I WANT YOU, I NEED YOU, I LOVE YOU (1956) (w)Maurice Mysels (m)Ira Kosloff. (P)Elvis Presley. No. 1 Chart Record.

I WANT YOU TO BE MY BABY (1955) (wm)Jon Hendricks. (P)Georgia Gibbs. (CR)Lillian Briggs. (R)1967 by Ellie Greenwich.

I WANT YOU TO BE MY GIRL (1956) (wm)Richard Barrett—George Goldner. (P)Frankie Lymon and The Teenagers. (R)1965 by The Exciters.

I WANT YOU TO WANT ME (1979) (wm)Rick Nielsen. (P)Cheap Trick.

I WANT YOU TONIGHT (1979) (wm)Cory Lerios—David Jenkins—Allee Willis. (P)Pablo Cruise.

I WANT YOUR LOVE (1979) (wm)Bernard Edwards—Nile Rodgers. (P)Chic.

I WANT YOUR SEX (1987) (wm)George Michael. (I)Film: *Beverly Hills Cop II* on soundtrack. (P)George Michael.

I WANTA DO SOMETHING FREAKY TO YOU (1975) (wm)Leon Haywood. (P)Leon Haywood.

I WAS BORN IN LOVE WITH YOU (1970) (w)Alan and Marilyn Bergman (m)Michel Legrand. (I)Film: *Wuthering Heights* (1970)by The Chorus.

I WAS DOING ALL RIGHT (1938) (w)Ira Gershwin (m)George Gershwin. (I)Film: *The Goldwyn Follies*, by Ella Logan.

I WAS KAISER BILL'S BATMAN (wm)Roger Greenaway-Roger Cook. (P)Whistling Jack Smith.

I WAS LUCKY (1935) (w-Eng)Jack Meskill (m)Jack Stern. (I)Film: *Follies Bergere*, by Maurice Chevalier and Ann Sothern. (P)Benny Goodman and his Orchestra.

I WAS MADE FOR DANCIN' (1979) (wm)Michael Lloyd. (P)Leif Garret.

I WAS MADE FOR LOVING YOU (1979) (wm)Desmond Child—Vini Poncia—Paul Stanley. (P)Kiss.

I WAS MADE TO LOVE HER (1967) (wm)Henry Cosby—Lula Hardaway—Stevie Wonder. (P)Stevie Wonder. (CR)King Curtis.

I WAS ONLY JOKING (1978) (wm)Gary Grainger—Rod Stewart. (P)Rod Stewart.

I WAS THE ONE (1956) (wm)Aaron Schroeder—Claude De Metrius—Hal Blair—Bill Peppers. (P)Elvis Presley.

I WASHED MY HANDS IN MUDDY WATER (1965) (wm)Joe Babcock. (P)Stonewall Jackson. (R)1966 by Johnny Rivers.

I WASN'T BORN TO FOLLOW (1969) (wm)Gerry Goffin—Carole King. (I)Film: *Easy Rider*, by the voices of The Byrds. (P)The Byrds.

I WATCH THE LOVE PARADE (1931) (w)Otto Harbach (m)Jerome Kern. (I)Musical: *The Cat And The Fiddle*, by George Meader and Flora Le Breton. (R)1934 film version, by Jeanette MacDonald and Ramon Novarro.

I WENT TO A MARVELOUS PARTY (1939) (wm)Noel Coward. (I)Revue: *Set To Music*, by Beatrice Lillie.

I WENT TO YOUR WEDDING (1952) (wm)Jessie Mae Robinson. (P)Patti Page. No. 1 Chart Record. (CR)Spike Jones.

I WHISTLE A HAPPY TUNE (1951) (w)Oscar Hammerstein II (m)Richard Rodgers. (I)Musical: *The King And I*, by Gertrude Lawrence. Film version, by Deborah Kerr.

I WHO HAVE NOTHING (1966) (w-Eng)Jerry Leiber—Mike Stoller. (m)Carlo Donida. (I)Terry Knight and The Pack. (R)1970 by Tom Jones.

I WILL (1962) (wm)Dick Glasser. (P)Vic Dana. (R)1965 by Dean Martin.

I WILL (1969) (wm)John Lennon—Paul McCartney. (P)The Beatles.

I WILL ALWAYS THINK ABOUT YOU (1968) (wm)Ronald Rice—Leslie Kummel. (P)The New Colony Six.

I WILL FOLLOW HIM (1963) (w-Eng)Norman Gimbel—Arthur Altman. (m)J.W. Stole—Del Roma. (P)Little Peggy March. No. 1 Chart Record.

I WILL FOLLOW YOU (1961) (wm)Jerry Herman. (I)Musical: *Milk And Honey*, by Tommy Rall.

I WILL SURVIVE (1979) (wm)Dino Fekaris (m)Freddy Perren. (P)Gloria Gaynor. No. 1 Chart Record.

I WILL WAIT FOR YOU (1965) (w-Eng)Norman Gimbel. (m)Michel Legrand. (I)Film: *The Umbrellas Of Cherbourg*, on soundtrack. (P)Steve Lawrence.

I WISH (1945) (wm)Allan Roberts—Doris Fisher. (P)The Mills Brothers.

I WISH (1977) (wm)Stevie Wonder. (P)Stevie Wonder. No. 1 Chart Record.

I WISH I COULD SHIMMY LIKE MY SISTER KATE (1919) (wm)Armand Piron. (P)The Virginians. (CR)Harry Reser and his Orchestra. (R)1952 by The Mary Kaye Trio. No. 1 Chart Record.

I WISH I COULD TELL YOU (1946) (w)Harry Ruby (m)Rube Bloom. (I)Film: *Wake Up And Dream*, by June Haver.

I WISH I DIDN'T LOVE YOU SO (1947) (wm)Frank Loesser. (I)Film: *The Perils Of Pauline*, by Betty Hutton. (P)Dinah Shore. (CR)Vaughn Monroe and his Orchestra. (CR)Dick Haymes.

I WISH I KNEW (1945) (w)Mack Gordon (m)Harry Warren. (I)Film: *Diamond Horseshoe*, by Dick Haymes. (P)Dick Haymes.

I WISH I WAS EIGHTEEN AGAIN (1978) (wm)Sonny Throckmorton. (P)George Burns.

I WISH I WERE ALADDIN (1935) (wm)Mack Gordon—Harry Revel. (I)Film: *Two For Tonight*, by Bing Crosby. (P)Bing Crosby.

I WISH I WERE IN LOVE AGAIN (1937) (w)Lorenz Hart (m)Richard Rodgers. (I)Musical: *Babes In Arms*, by Grace McDonald and Rolly Pickert. (R)1948 Film: *Words And Music*, by Judy Garland and Mickey Rooney.

I WISH I WERE TWINS (So I Could Love You Twice As Much) (1934) (w)Frank Loesser—Eddie De Lange. (m)Joseph Meyer. (P)Fats Waller.

I WISH IT WOULD RAIN (1968) (wm)Barrett Strong—Roger Penzabene—Norman Whitfield. (P)The Temptations. (CR)Gladys Knight and The Pips.

I WISH THAT WE WERE MARRIED (1962) (wm)Marion Weiss—Edna Lewis. (P)Ronnie and The Hi—Lites.

I WISH YOU LOVE (1946) (w-Eng)Lee Wilson (m)Charles Trenet. (P)Felicia Sanders. (R)1964 by Gloria Lynne.

I WISHED ON THE MOON (1936) (w)Dorothy Parker (m)Ralph Rainger. (I)Film: *Big Broadcast of 1936*, by Bing Crosby. (P)Bing Crosby. (CR)Little Jack Little and his Orchestra.

I WOKE UP IN LOVE THIS MORNING (1971) (wm)Irwin Levine—L. Russell Brown. (P)The Partridge Family.

I WONDER (1945) (wm)Cecil Gant—Raymond Leveen. (P)Pvt. Cecil Gant.

I WONDER, I WONDER, I WONDER (1947) (wm)Daryl Hutchins. (I)The Vagabonds. (P)Eddy Howard. (CR)Guy Lombardo and his Royal Canadians. (CR)Martha Tilton.

I WONDER IF YOU STILL CARE FOR ME (1921) (w)Harry Smith—Francis Wheeler. (m)Ted Snyder. (P)Charles Hart.

I WONDER WHAT SHE'S DOING TONIGHT? (1967) (wm)Tommy Boyce—Bobby Hart. (P)Tommy Boyce and Bobby Hart.

I WONDER WHAT THE KING IS DOING TONIGHT? (196) (w)Alan Jay Lerner (m)Frederick Loewe. (I)Musical: *Camelot*, by Richard Burton. In film version by Richard Harris.

I WONDER WHAT'S BECOME OF SALLY (1924) (w)Jack Yellen (m)Milton Ager. (I)Van and Schenck. (P)Al Jolson. No. 1 Chart Record. (CR)Ted Lewis.

I WONDER WHERE MY BABY IS TONIGHT (1925) (w)Gus Kahn (m)Walter Donaldson. (P)Henry Burr and Billy Murray.

I WONDER WHO'S KISSING HER NOW (1909) (w)Will M. Hough—Frank R. Adams (m)Joseph E. Howard—Harold Orlob. (P)Henry Burr. (R)1947 by Perry Como with Ted Weems and his Orchestra.

I WONDER WHY (1958) (w)Ricardo Weeks (m)Melvin Anderson. (P)Dion and The Belmonts.

I WON'T CRY ANYMORE (1951) (w)Fred Wise (m)Al Frisch. (P)Tony Bennett.

I WON'T DANCE (1934) (w)Otto Harbach—Oscar Hammerstein II (m)Jerome Kern. (I)London Musical: *Three Sisters*, by Adele Dixon and Richard Dolman. Film: Roberta, by Fred Astaire and Ginger Rogers. (P)Eddy Duchin and his Orchestra. No. 1 Chart Record. (CR)George Hall and his Orchestra. (R)1952 Film: *Lovely To Look At*, by Marge and Gower Champion.

I WON'T GROW UP (1954) (w)Carolyn Leigh (m)Mark Charlap. (I)Musical: *Peter Pan*, by Mary Martin.

I WON'T HOLD YOU BACK (1982) (wm)Steve Lukather. (P)Toto.

I WON'T LAST A DAY WITHOUT YOU (1973) (wm)Roger Nichols—Paul Williams. (P)Maureen McGovern. (R)1974 by The Carpenters.

I WON'T SAY I WILL BUT I WON'T SAY I WON'T (1923) (w)B.G. De Sylva—Arthur Francis (Ira Gershwin) (m)George Gershwin. (I)Play with songs: *Little Miss Bluebeard*, by Irene Bordoni.

I WORSHIP YOU (1929) (wm)Cole Porter. (I)Musical: *Fifty Million Frenchmen*, by William Gaxton.

I WOULD DIE 4 U (1984) (wm)Prince Rogers Nelson. (P)Prince & The Revolution.

I WOULDN'T HAVE MISSED IT FOR THE WORLD (1982) (wm)Kye Fleming—Dennis Morgan—Charles Quillan. (P)Ronnie Milsap.

I WOULDN'T TRADE THE SILVER IN MY MOTHER'S HAIR (For All The Gold In The World) (1982) (wm)Little Jack Little—J. Fred Coots. (P)Little Jack Little and his Orchestra.

I WRITE THE SONGS (1976) (wm)Bruce Johnston. (P)Barry Manilow. No. 1 Chart Record. NARAS Award Winner.

I WUV A WABBIT (1948) (wm)Milton Berlin—Ervin Drake—Paul Martell. (P)Dick "Two—Ton" Baker.

I, YES ME, THAT'S WHO (1970) (w)Sammy Cahn (m)Jule Styne. (I)Musical: *Look To The Lilies*, by Al Freeman, Jr. and Shirley Booth.

I, YI, YI, YI, YI (I Like You Very Much) (1941) (w)Mack Gordon (m)Harry Warren. (I)Film: *That Night In Rio*, by Carmen Miranda. (P)Carmen Miranda.

(I Scream, You Scream, We All Scream For)ICE CREAM (1927) (wm)Howard Johnson—Billy Moll—Robert King. (P)Fred Waring's Pennsylvanians.

I'D CLIMB THE HIGHEST MOUNTAIN (1926) (wm)Lew Brown—Sidney Clare. (P)Sophie Tucker. (CR)Al Jolson. (CR)Lillian Roth.

I'D DO ANYTHING (1960) (wm)Lionel Bart. (I)Musical: *Oliver*, by Martin Horsey, Georgia Brown, Keith Hamshere, and The Cast in London production. In New York production, by David Jones, Georgia Brown, Paul O'Keefe, and The Cast.

I'D DO IT AGAIN (1965) (wm)Marian Grudeff—Raymond Jessel. (I)Musical: *Baker Street*, by Inga Swenson.

I'D KNOW YOU ANYWHERE (1940) (w)Johnny Mercer (m)Jimmy McHugh. (I)Film: *You'll Find Out*, by Harry Babbitt and Ginny Simms.

I'D LIKE TO SET YOU TO MUSIC (1943) (w)Paul Francis Webster (m)Harry Revel. (P)Film: *Hit The Ice*, by Ginny Simms.

I'D LIKE TO TEACH THE WORLD TO SING (1972) (wm)William Backer—Roger Cook—Roger Greenaway—Roquel Davis. Originally a Coca—Cola commercial. (P)The New Seekers. (CR)The Hillside Singers.

I'D LOVE TO FALL ASLEEP AND WAKE UP IN MY MAMMY'S ARMS (1920) (w)Sam M. Lewis—Joe Young. (m)Fred E. Ahlert. (P)The Peerless Quartet.

I'D LOVE TO LIVE IN LOVELAND (1912) (wm)Will Rossiter. (P)Walter Van Brunt.

I'D LOVE YOU TO WANT ME (1972) (wm)Kent Lavoie. (P)Lobo.

I'D RATHER BE BLUE OVER YOU (Than Be Happy With Somebody Else) (1928) (w)Billy Rose (m)Fred Fisher. (I)Film: *My Man*, by Fanny Brice. (P)Fanny Brice. (R)1968 Film: *Funny Girl*, by Barbra Streisand.

I'D RATHER BE RIGHT (1937) (w)Lorenz Hart (m)Richard Rodgers. (I)Musical: *I'd Rather Be Right*, by Austin Marshall, Joy Hodges, Mary Jane Walsh, George M. Cohan and The Company.

I'D RATHER LEAD A BAND (1936) (wm)Irving Berlin. (I)Film: *Follow The Fleet*, by Fred Astaire. (P)Fred Astaire.

I'D RATHER LEAVE WHILE I'M IN LOVE (1979) (wm)Peter Allen—Carole Bayer Sager. (P)Rita Coolidge.

I'D RATHER LISTEN TO YOUR EYES (1935) (w)Al Dubin (m)Harry Warren. (I)Film: *Shipmates Forever*, by Dick Powell.

I'D REALLY LOVE TO SEE YOU TONIGHT (1976) (wm)Parker McGee. (P)England Dan & John Ford Coley.

IDA, SWEET AS APPLE CIDER (1903) (wm)Eddie Leonard—Eddie Munson. (P)Theme Song of Eddie Cantor.

IDAHO (1942) (wm)Jesse Stone. (P)Alvino Rey and his Orchestra, vocal by Yvonne King and The Ensemble.

IDIOT WIND (1975) (wm)Bob Dylan. (P)Bob Dylan.

IDLE GOSSIP (1953) (w)Floyd Huddleston (m)Joseph Meyer. (P)Perry Como (England only). In United States by Tony Alamo.

IF (1950) (w)Robert Hargreaves—Stanley J. Damerell (m)Tochard Evans. (P)Perry Como. No. 1 Chart Record. (CR)Jo Stafford. (CR)Dean Martin. (CR)Billy Eckstine.

IF (1971) (wm)David Gates. (P)Bread.

IF A MAN ANSWERS (1962) (wm)Bobby Darin. (I)Film: *If A Man Answers*, by Bobby Darin.

IF ANYONE FALLS (1983) (wm)Sandy Stewart—Stephanie Nicks. (P)Stevie Nicks.

IF DREAMS COME TRUE (1934) (w)Irving Mills (m)Edgar Sampson—Benny Goodman. (P)Benny Goodman and his Orchestra.

IF DREAMS COME TRUE (1958) (w)Al Stillman (m)Robert Allen. (P)Pat Boone.

IF EVER I SEE YOU AGAIN (1977) (wm)Joe Brooks. (I)Film: *If Ever I See You Again*, on soundtrack. (P)Roberta Flack.

IF EVER I WOULD LEAVE YOU (1960) (w)Alan Jay Lerner (m)Frederick Loewe. (I)Musical: *Camelot*, by Robert Goulet. (P)Robert Goulet.

IF EVER YOU'RE IN MY ARMS AGAIN (1984) (wm)Cynthia Weil—Michael Masser—Tom Snow. (P)Peabo Bryson.

IF HE WALKED INTO MY LIFE (1966) (wm)Jerry Herman. (I)Musical: *Mame*, by Angela Lansbury. (P)Eydie Gorme.

IF I BECAME THE PRESIDENT (1930) (w)Ira Gershwin (m)George Gershwin. (I)Musical: *Strike Up The Band*, by Bobby Clark and Blanche Ring.

IF I CAN DREAM (1968) (wm)W. Earl Brown. (P)Elvis Presley.

IF I CAN'T HAVE YOU (1977) (wm)Barry, Robin, and Maurice Gibb. (I)Film: *Saturday Night Fever*, by the voice of Yvonne Elliman. (P)Yvonne Elliman.

IF I CARED A LITTLE BIT LESS (And You Cared A Little Bit More) (1942) (P)Sammy Kaye and his Orchestra, vocal by Don Cornell.

IF I COULD BE WITH YOU ONE HOUR TONIGHT (1926) (wm)Henry Creamer—Jimmy Johnson. (P)Theme song of McKinney's Cotton Pickers. (P)Ruth Etting. (CR)Louis Armstrong. (P)Maurice Chevalier.

IF I COULD BUILD MY WHOLE WORLD AROUND YOU (1967) (wm)Johnny Bristol—Vernon Bullock—Harvey Fuqua. (P)Marvin Gaye and Tammi Terrell.

IF I COULD REACH YOU (1972) (wm)Landy McNeill. (P)The 5th Dimension.

IF I DIDN'T CARE (1939) (wm)Jack Lawrence. (P)The Ink Spots. (R)1954 by The Hilltoppers. (R)1970 by The Moments.

IF I EVER LOVE AGAIN (1949) (wm)Russ Carlyle—Dick Reynolds. (P)Jo Stafford.

IF I FELL (1964) (wm)John Lennon—Paul McCartney. (I)Film: *A Hard Day's Night*, by The Beatles. (P)The Beatles.

IF I FORGET YOU (1933) (wm)Irving Caesar. (P)James Melton.

IF I GIVE MY HEART TO YOU (1954) (wm)Jimmie Crane—Al Jacobs—Jimmy Brewster. (I)Denise Lor. (P)Doris Day. (CR)Connee Boswell. (CR)Dinah Shore.

IF I HAD A DOZEN HEARTS (1945) (w)Paul Francis Webster (m)Harry Revel. (I)Film: *Stork Club*, by Betty Hutton.

IF I HAD A GIRL (1960) (wm)Sid Tepper—Roy C. Bennett. (P)Rod Lauren.

IF I HAD A GIRL LIKE YOU (1925) (wm)Billy Rose—Mort Dixon—Ray Henderson. (P)Rudy Vallee. (CR)Hal Kemp and his Orchestra.

IF I HAD A HAMMER (1958) (wm)Lee Hays—Pete Seeger. (P)The Weavers. (R)1962 by Peter, Paul, and Mary. (R)1963 by Trini Lopez.

IF I HAD A TALKING PICTURE OF YOU (1929) (w)B. G. De Sylva—Lew Brown (m)Ray Henderson. (I)Film: *Sunny Side Up*, by Janet Gaynor and Charles Farrell. (P)Paul Whiteman and his Orchestra. (R)1956 Film: *The Best Things In Life Are Free*, by Byron Palmer.

IF I HAD MY DRUTHERS (1956) (w)Johnny Mercer (m)Gene de Paul. (I)Musical: *L'il Abner*, by Peter Palmer.

IF I HAD MY WAY (1913) (wm)Lou Klein—James Kendis. (P)The Peerless Quartet. (R)1936 by Bunny Berigan and his Orchestra. (R)1939 by Glen Gray and The Casa Loma Orchestra.

IF I HAD YOU (1928) (wm)Ted Shapiro—Jimmy Campbell—Reg Connelly. (P)Rudy Vallee. (CR)Al Bowlly. (R)1948 Film: *You Were Meant For Me*, by Dan Dailey.

IF I KNEW (1960) (wm)Meredith Willson. (I)Musical: *The Unsinkable Molly Brown*, by Harve Presnell.

IF I KNEW THEN (What I Know Now) (1939) (wm)Dick Jurgens—Eddy Howard. (P)Dick Jurgens and his Orchestra, vocal by Eddy Howard.

IF I KNEW YOU WERE COMIN' I'D'VE BAKED A CAKE (1950) (wm)Al Hoffman—Bob Merrill—Clem Watts. (P)Eileen Barton. No. 1 Chart Record. (CR)Georgia Gibbs. (CR)Ethel Merman with Ray Bolger.

IF I LOVE AGAIN (1932) (w)Jack Murray (m)Ben Oakland. (I)Musical: *Hold Your Horses*, by Ona Munsen and Stanley Smith. (P)Rudy Vallee.

IF I LOVED YOU (1945) (w)Oscar Hammerstein (m)Richard Rodgers. (I)Musical: *Carousel*, by John Raitt and Jan Clayton. (P)Perry Como. (R)1957 Film version, by Shirley Jones and Gordon MacRae. (R)1965 by Chad and Jeremy.

IF I MAY (1955) (wm)Charles Singleton—Rose Marie McCoy. (P)Nat "King" Cole.

IF I NEEDED SOMEONE (1965) (wm)George Harrison. (P)The Beatles.

IF I ONLY HAD A BRAIN (1939) (w)E. Y. Harburg (m)Harold Arlen. (I)Film: *The Wizard of Oz*, by Ray Bolger.

IF I ONLY HAD A MATCH (1947) (wm)Lee Morris—Arthur Johnston—George W. Meyer. (P)Al Jolson.

IF I RULED THE WORLD (1964) (w)Leslie Bricusse (m)Cyril Ornadel. (I)Musical: *Oliver*, by Harry Secombe. (P)Tony Bennett.

IF I SHOULD LOSE YOU (1936) (wm)Leo Robin—Ralph Rainger. (I)Film: *Rose Of The Rancho*, by Gladys Swarthout and John Boles. (P)Richard Himber and his Orchestra.

IF I STEAL A KISS (1948) (w)Edward Heyman (m)Nacio Herb Brown. (I)Film: *The Kissing Bandit*, by Frank Sinatra. (P)Frank Sinatra.

IF I WERE A BELL (1950) (wm)Frank Loesser. (I)Musical: *Guys And Dolls*, by Isabel Bigley. In film version, by Jean Simmons.

IF I WERE A CARPENTER (1966) (wm)Tim Hardin. (I)Tim Hardin. (P)Bobby Darin. (R)1968 by The Four Tops. (R)1970 by Johnny Cash and June Carter. (R)1972 by Bob Seger. (R)1974 by Leon Russell.

IF I WERE A RICH MAN (1964) (w)Sheldon Harnick (m)Jerry Bock. (I)Musical: *Fiddler On The Roof*, by Zero Mostel. In film version, by Topol.

IF I WERE KING (1930) (wm)Leo Robin (m)Newell Chase—Sam Coslow. (I)Musical: *The Vagabond King*, by Dennis King.

IF I WERE YOU (1962) (w)Lee Adams (m)Charles Strouse. (I)Musical: *All American*, by Ray Bolger and Eileen Herlie.

IF I WERE YOUR WOMAN (1970) (wm)Gloria Jones—Pam Sawyer—Clay McMurray. (P)Gladys Knight & The Pips.

IF I'D BEEN THE ONE (1983) (wm)Don Barnes—Jeff Carlisi—Donnie Van Zant—Larry Steele. (P)38 Special.

IF I'M DREAMING, DON'T WAKE ME TOO SOON. (1929) (w)Al Dubin (m)Joe Burke. (I)Film: *Sally*, by Marilyn Miller and Alexander Gray.

IF I'M LUCKY (1946) (w)Eddie De Lange (m)Josef Myrow. (I)Film: *If I'm Lucky*, by Perry Como. (P)Perry Como.

IF IT'S THE LAST THING I DO (1937) (wm)Sammy Cahn—Saul Chaplin. (P)Tommy Dorsey and his Orchestra.

IF LOVE REMAINS (1945) (w)Ira Gershwin (m)Kurt Weill. (I)Film: *Where Do We Go From Here*, by Fred MacMurray and Joan Leslie.

IF LOVE WERE ALL (1929) (wm)Noel Coward. (I)Operetta: *Bitter Sweet* (London Production)by Ivy St. Helier. New York production by Mireille.

IF LOVING YOU IS WRONG I DON'T WANT TO BE RIGHT (1971) (wm)Homer Banks—Raymond Jackson—Carl Hampton. (P)Luther Ingram. (R)1975 by Millie Jackson. (R)1979 by Barbara Mandrell.

IF MY FRIENDS COULD SEE ME NOW (1965) (w)Dorothy Fields (m)Cy Coleman. (I)Musical: *Sweet Charity*, by Gwen Verdon. In film version 1969 by Shirley MacLaine.

IF NOT FOR YOU (1970) (wm)Bob Dylan. (I)Bob Dylan. (P)Olivia Newton—John.

IF SHE SHOULD COME TO YOU (La Montana) (1959) (w-Eng)Alec Wilder. (m)Augusto Alguero. (CR)Frank De Vol. (CR)Roger Williams.

IF THE MOON TURNS GREEN (1935) (w)Paul Coates (m)Bernie Hanighen. (P)Paul Whiteman and his Orchestra.

IF THERE IS SOMEONE LOVELIER THAN YOU (1934) (w)Howard Dietz (m)Arthur Schwartz. (I)Musical: *Revenge With Music*, by Georges Metaxa.

IF THIS IS IT (1984) (wm)John Colla—Huey Lewis. (P)Huey Lewis & The News.

IF THIS ISN'T LOVE (1947) (w)E. Y. Harburg (m)Burton Lane. (I)Musical: *Finian's Rainbow*, by Ella Logan and Donald Richards.

IF WE MAKE IT THROUGH DECEMBER (1974) (wm)Merle Haggard. (P)Merle Haggard.

IF WE ONLY HAVE LOVE (1968) (w-Eng)Mort Shuman—Eric Blau (m)Jacques Brel. (I)Musical: *Jacques Brel Is Alive And Well And Living In Paris*, by Elly Stone and company. (P)Dionne Warwick.

IF WE WERE IN LOVE (1982) (w)Alan and Marilyn Bergman. (m)John Williams. (I)Film: *Yes Giorgio*, by Placido Domingo.

IF YOU ARE BUT A DREAM (1941) (wm)Moe Jaffe—Jack Fulton—Nat Bonx. Adapted from Rubinstein's Romance. (P)Jimmy Dorsey and his Orchestra. Most popular recording by Frank Sinatra.

IF YOU BUILD A BETTER MOUSETRAP (1942) (w)Johnny Mercer (m)Victor Schertzinger. (I)Film: *The Fleet's In*, by Betty Hutton with Jimmy Dorsey and his Orchestra.

IF YOU CAN WANT (1968) (wm)William Robinson. (P)Smokey and The Miracles.

IF YOU COULD ONLY COME WITH ME (1929) (wm)Noel Coward. (I)Operetta: *Bitter Sweet*, by Georges Metaxa in London production. In New York Production, by Gerald Nodin. (R)1940 film version, by Nelson Eddy.

IF YOU COULD READ MY MIND (1969) (wm)Gordon Lightfoot. (P)Gordon Lightfoot.

IF YOU COULD SEE HER (The Gorilla Song) (1966) (w)Fred Ebb (m)John Kander. (I)Musical: *Cabaret*, by Joel Grey. Also, by Mr. Grey in the film version (1972).

IF YOU COULD SEE ME NOW (1946) (w)Carl Sigman (m)Tadd Dameron. (P)Sarah Vaughan.

IF YOU DON'T KNOW ME BY NOW (1972) (wm)Leon Huff—Kenny Gamble. (P)Harold Melvin and The Bluenotes.

IF YOU FEEL LIKE SINGING, SING (1950) (w)Mack Gordon (m)Harry Warren. (I)Film: *Summer Stock*, by Judy Garland.

IF YOU GO AWAY (1966) (w-Eng)Rod McKuen (m)Jacques Brel. (I)Jacques Brel. (P)Damita Jo.

IF YOU KNEW SUSIE LIKE I KNEW SUSIE (1925) (wm)B.G. De Sylva—Joseph Meyer. (I)Musical: *Big Boy*, by Al Jolson. (P)Eddie Cantor. (CR)Cliff Edwards. (R)1953 Film: *The Eddie Cantor Story*, by the voice of Eddie Cantor dubbing for Keefe Brasselle.

IF YOU KNOW WHAT I MEAN (1976) (wm)Neil Diamond. (P)Neil Diamond.

IF YOU LEAVE (1986) (wm)Orchestral Manoeuvres In The Dark. (I)Film: *Pretty In Pink*, by Orchestral Manoeuvres In The Dark. (P)Orchestral Manoeuvres In The Dark.

IF YOU LEAVE ME NOW (1976) (wm)Peter Cetera. (P)Chicago. No. 1 Chart Record.

IF YOU LOVE ME (Really Love Me) (1949) (w-Eng)Geoffrey Parsons (m)Marguerite Monnot. (P)Edith Piaf. (R)1954 by Kay Starr.

IF YOU LOVE ME (Let Me Know) (1974) (wm)John Rostill. (P)Olivia Newton—John.

IF YOU LOVE SOMEBODY SET THEM FREE (1985) (wm)Gordon Sumner (Sting). (P)Sting.

IF YOU LOVED ME TRULY (1953) (wm)Cole Porter (I)Musical: *Can-Can*, by The Ensemble.

IF YOU NEED ME (1963) (wm)Wilson Pickett—Robert Bateman—Sonny Sanders. (P)Solomon Burke. (CR)Wilson Pickett.

IF YOU ONLY HAVE LOVE (1968) (w-Eng)Mort Shuman—Eric Blau (m)Jacques Brel. (I)Jacques Brel. (R)1971 by Johnny Mathis.

IF YOU PLEASE (1943) (w)Johnny Burke (m)Jimmy Van Heusen. (I)Film: *Dixie*, by Bing Crosby. (P)Bing Crosby.

IF YOU REALLY KNEW ME (1978) (w)Carole Bayer Sager (m)Marvin Hamlisch. (I)Musical: *They're Playing Our Song*, by Lucy Arnaz.

IF YOU REALLY LOVE ME (1971) (wm)Stevie Wonder—Syreeta Wright. (P)Stevie Wonder.

IF YOU REMEMBER ME (1979) (w)Carole Bayer Sager (m)Marvin Hamlisch. (I)Film: *The Champ*, by the voices of Chris Thompson & Night. (P)Chris Thompson & Night.

IF YOU SMILE AT ME (1946) (wm)Cole Porter. (I)Musical: *Around The World*, by Victoria Cordova.

IF YOU STUB YOUR TOE ON THE MOON (1948) (w)Johnny Burke (m)Jimmy Van Heusen. (I)Film: *A Connecticut Yankee*, by Bing Crosby. (P)Bing Crosby.

IF YOU TALK IN YOUR SLEEP (1974) (wm)Bobby Red West—Johnny Christopher. (P)Elvis Presley.

IF YOU WANNA BE HAPPY (1963) (w)Carmela Guida—Frank Guida—Joseph Royster. (m)Frank Guida—Joseph Royster. (P)Jimmy Soul. No. 1 Chart Record.

IF YOU WANNA GET TO HEAVEN (1974) (wm)John Dillon—Steve Cash. (P)The Ozark Mountain Daredevils.

IF YOU WANT ME TO STAY (1973) (wm)Sylvester Stewart. (P)Sly & The Family Stone.

IF YOU WERE IN MY PLACE (What Would You Do?) (1938) (w)Irving Mills—Henry Nemo (m)Duke Ellington. (P)Duke Ellington and his Orchestra.

IF YOU WERE THE ONLY GIRL IN THE WORLD (1929) (w)Clifford Grey (m)Nat D. Ayer. (I)Film: *The Vagabond Lover*, by Rudy Vallee and his Connecticut Yankees. (R)1946 by Perry Como. (R)1957 Film: *The Helen Morgan Story*, by Gogi Grant dubbing for Ann Blyth.

IF YOU'RE EVER DOWN IN TEXAS (Look Me Up) (1946) (w)"By" Dunham (m)Terry Shand. (P)Phil Harris.

IF YOU'RE IN LOVE, YOU'LL WALTZ (1927) (w)Joseph McCarthy (m)Harry Tierney. (I)Musical: *Rio Rita*, by Ethelind Terry and J. Harold Murray.

IF YOU'RE READY (Come Go With Me) (1973) (wm)Ray Jackson—Carl Hampton—Homer Banks. (P)The Staple Singers.

IKO-IKO (1965) (wm)Marylin Jones—Sharon Jones—Joe Jones—Jessie Thomas. (P)The Dixie Cups. (R)1972 by Dr. John.

I'LL ALWAYS BE IN LOVE WITH YOU (1928) (wm)Herman Ruby—Bud Green—Sam H. Stept. (I)Film: *Syncopation*, by Morton Downey. (P)Morton Downey. (CR)Fred Waring's Pennsylvanians.

(Day After Day)I'LL ALWAYS LOVE YOU (1950) (wm)Jerry Livingston—Ray Evans. (I)Film: *My Friend Irma Goes West*, by Dean Martin. (P)Dean Martin.

I'LL BE ALRIGHT WITHOUT YOU (1987) (wm)S. Perry—J. Cain—N. Schon. (P)Journey.

I'LL BE AROUND (1942) (wm)Alec Wilder. (I)Cab Calloway and his Orchestra. (P)The Mills Brothers.

I'LL BE AROUND (1972) (wm)Earl Randle. (P)The Spinners.

I'LL BE BACK (1965) (wm)John Lennon—Paul McCartney. (P)The Beatles.

I'LL BE DOGGONE (1965) (wm)William Robinson—Warren Moore—Marv Tarplin. (P)Marvin Gaye.

I'LL BE GOOD TO YOU (1976) (wm)Louis Johnson—George Johnson—Senora Sam. (P)The Brothers Johnson.

I'LL BE HARD TO HANDLE (1933) (w)Bernard Dougall (m)Jerome Kern. (I)Musical: *Roberta*, by Lyda Roberti.

I'LL BE HOME (1955) (wm)Ferdinand Washington—Stan Lewis. (I)The Flamingos. (P)Pat Boone. (R)1966 by The Platters.

I'LL BE HOME FOR CHRISTMAS (1943) (wm)Walter Kent—Kim Gannon—Buck Ram. (P)Bing Crosby.

I'LL BE ON MY WAY (1963) (wm)John Lennon—Paul McCartney. (P)Billy J. Kramer and The Dakotas.

I'LL BE OVER YOU (1986) (wm)Steve Lukather—Randy Goodrum. (P)Toto.

I'LL BE SATISFIED (1959) (wm)Berry Gordy, Jr.—Gwen Gordy—Tyran Carlo.

I'LL BE SEEING YOU (1938) (w)Irving Kahal (m)Sammy Fain. (I)Revue: *Right This Way*, by Tamara. (P)Bing Crosby. No. 1 Chart Record. (CR)Tommy Dorsey and his Orchestra. Theme song of Liberace.

I'LL BE THERE (1960) (wm)Bobby Darin. (P)Bobby Darin. (R)1964 by Gerry and The Pacemakers.

I'LL BE THERE (1970) (wm)Bob West—Hal Davis—Willie Hutch—Berry Gordy, Jr. (P)The Jackson Five.

I'LL BE WITH YOU IN APPLE BLOSSOM TIME (1920) (w)Neville Fleeson (m)Albert Von Tilzer. (P)Nora Bayes. (R)1941 by The Andrews Sisters. (R)1965 by Wayne Newton.

I'LL BE YOUR BABY TONIGHT (1968) (wm)Bob Dylan. (P)Bob Dylan.

I'LL BE YOURS (J'Attendrai) (1945) (w-Eng)Anna Sosenko (m)Dino Olivieri. (P)Hildegarde.

I'LL BUILD A STAIRWAY TO PARADISE (1922) (w)B.G. De Sylva—Arthur Francis (Ira Gershwin) (m)George Gerswhin. (I)Revue: *George White's Scandals of 1922*, by Paul Whiteman and his Orchestra with The Cast. (P)Paul Whiteman. (CR)Ben Selvin and his Orchestra. (R)1951 Film: *An American In Paris*, by Georges Guetary.

I'LL BUY THAT DREAM (1945) (w)Herb Magidson (m)Allie Wrubel. (I)Film: *Sing Your Way Home*, by Anne Jeffreys. (P)Harry James and his Orchestra, vocal by Kitty Kallen.

I'LL BUY YOU A STAR (1951) (w)Dorothy Fields (m)Arthur Schwartz. (I)Musical: *A Tree Grows In Brooklyn*, by Johnny Johnston.

I'LL CRY INSTEAD (1964) (wm)John Lennon—Paul McCartney. (I)Film: *A Hard Day's Night*, by The Beatles. (P)The Beatles.

I'LL CRY TOMORROW (1955) (w)Johnny Mercer (m)Alex North. (I)Film: *I'll Cry Tomorrow* on soundtrack. (P)Lillian Roth. (CR)Susan Hayward.

I'LL DANCE AT YOUR WEDDING (1948) (w)Herb Magidson (m)Ben Oakland. (P)Buddy Clark with Ray Noble and his Orchestra. (CR)Tony Martin. (CR)Peggy Lee.

I'LL DREAM TONIGHT (1938) (w)Johnny Mercer (m)Richard A. Whiting. (I)Film: *Cowboy From Brooklyn*, by Dick Powell and Priscilla Lane. (P)Tommy Dorsey and his Orchestra.

I'LL FOLLOW MY SECRET HEART (1934) (wm)Noel Coward. (I)Musical: *Conversation Piece*, by Noel Coward and Yvonne Printemps.

I'LL FOLLOW THE SUN (1965) (wm)John Lennon—Paul McCartney. (P)The Beatles.

I'LL FORGET YOU (1921) (w)Annalu Burns (m)Ernest R. Ball. No artist credited with introduction. (R)1944 Film: *When Irish Eyes Are Smiling*, by Dick Haymes.

I'LL GET BY (As Long As I Have You) (1928) (w)Roy Turk (m)Fred E. Ahlert. (P)Ruth Etting. (CR)Nick Lucas. (R)1944 by Harry James and his Orchestra, vocal by Dick Haymes. (R)1948 Film: *You Were Meant For Me*, by Dan Dailey. (R)1960 by Billy Williams.

I'LL GET YOU (1963) (wm)John Lennon—Paul McCartney. (P)The Beatles.

I'LL GO HOME WITH BONNIE JEAN (1947) (w)Alan Jay Lerner (m)Frederick Loewe. (I)Musical: *Brigadoon*, by Lee Sullivan. In film version (1954) by John Gustafson dubbing for Jimmy Thompson.

I'LL HAVE TO SAY I LOVE YOU IN A SONG (1974) (wm)Jim Croce. (P)Jim Croce.

I'LL KEEP IT WITH MINE (1965) (wm)Bob Dylan. (P)Judy Collins. (R)1969 by Fairport Convention.

I'LL KEEP YOU SATISFIED (1964) (wm)John Lennon—Paul McCartney. (P)Billy J. Kramer and The Dakotas.

I'LL KNOW (1950) (wm)Frank Loesser. (I)Musical: *Guys And Dolls*, by Isabel Bigley and Robert Alda.

I'LL MAKE A MAN OF THE MAN (1966) (w)Sammy Cahn (m)Jimmy Van Heusen. (I)Musical: *Walking Happy*, by Louise Troy.

I'LL MAKE ALL YOUR DREAMS COME TRUE (1965) (wm)Bernice Ross—Wes Farrell. (P)Ronnie Dove.

I'LL MEET YOU HALFWAY (1971) (wm)Wes Farrell—Gerry Goffin. (P)The Partridge Family.

I'LL NEVER BE FREE (1950) (wm)Bennie Benjamin—George Weiss. (P)Kay Starr and Tennessee Ernie Ford. (CR)Paul Gayten and Annie Laurie.

I'LL NEVER BE THE SAME (1932) (w)Gus Kahn (m)Matty Malneck—Frank Signorelli. (I)Mildred Bailey. (P)Ruth Etting. (CR)Guy Lombardo and his Royal Canadians.

I'LL NEVER DANCE AGAIN (1962) (wm)Barry Mann—Mike Anthony. (P)Bobby Rydell.

(It Looks Like)I'LL NEVER FALL IN LOVE AGAIN (1967) (wm)Lonnie Donegan—Jimmy Currie. (P)Tom Jones.

I'LL NEVER FALL IN LOVE AGAIN (1968) (w)Hal David (m)Burt Bacharach. (I)Musical: *Promises, Promises*, by Jill O'Hara and Jerry Orbach. (P)Dionne Warwick.

I'LL NEVER FIND ANOTHER YOU (1965) (wm)Tom Springfield. (P)The Seekers. (R)1967 by Sonny James.

I'LL NEVER HAVE TO DREAM AGAIN. (1932) (w)Charles Newman (m)Isham Jones. (P)Isham Jones and his Orchestra.

I'LL NEVER LOVE AGAIN (1946) (w-Eng)Al Stewart. (m)Tata Nacho. (P)Dinah Shore with Xavier Cugat and his Orchestra.

I'LL NEVER SAY "NEVER AGAIN" AGAIN. (1935) (wm)Harry Woods. (P)Ozzie Nelson and his Orchestra. (CR)Dorsey Brothers Orchestra. (R)1953 by Benny Goodman and his Orchestra.

I'LL NEVER SAY NO (1960) (wm)Meredith Willson. (I)Musical: *The Unsinkable Molly Brown*, by Harve Presnell. Film version 1964 by Debbie Reynolds and Harve Presnell.

I'LL NEVER SMILE AGAIN (1939) (wm)Ruth Lowe. (P)Tommy Dorsey and his Orchestra, vocal by Frank Sinatra. No. 1 Chart Record. (CR)Glenn Miller and his Orchestra. (R)1953 by The Four Aces.

I'LL NEVER STOP LOVING YOU (1955) (w)Sammy Cahn (m)Nicholas Brodszky. (I)Film: *Love Me Or Leave Me*, by Doris Day. (P)Doris Day.

I'LL PLANT MY OWN TREE (1967) (w)Dory Previn (m)Andre Previn. (I)Film: *Valley Of The Dolls*, by Margaret Whiting dubbing for Susan Hayward.

I'LL PLAY FOR YOU (1970) (wm)Jimmy Seals—Dash Crofts. (P)Seals & Crofts.

I'LL PRAY FOR YOU (1942) (w)Roy King (m)Stanley Hill. (I)Vera Lynn. (P)The Andrews Sisters.

I'LL REMEMBER (In The Still Of The Nite) (1956) (wm)Fredericke Parris. (P)The Five Satins.

I'LL REMEMBER APRIL (1941) (wm)Don Raye—Gene de Paul—Pat Johnston. (I)Film: *Ride 'Em Cowboy*, by Dick Foran. (P)Woody Herman and his Orchestra.

I'LL REMEMBER HER (1963) (wm)Noel Coward. (I)Musical: *The Girl Who Came To Supper*, by Jose Ferrer.

I'LL REMEMBER TODAY (1956) (w)William Engvick (m)Edith Piaf. (I)Edith Piaf. (P)Patti Page.

I'LL SEE YOU AGAIN (1929) (wm)Noel Coward. (I)Operetta: *Bitter Sweet*, by Peggy Wood and Georges Metaxa (London). Evelyn Laye and Gerald Nodin (New York). (R)1940 Film: *Bitter Sweet*, by Nelson Eddy and Jeanette MacDonald.

I'LL SEE YOU IN MY DREAMS (1924) (w)Gus Kahn (m)Isham Jones. (P)Isham Jones and his Orchestra. No. 1 Chart Record. (CR)Lewis James. (R)1951 Film: *I'll See You In My Dreams*, by Doris Day.

I'LL SHARE IT ALL WITH YOU (1946) (wm)Irving Berlin. (I)Musical: *Annie Get Your Gun*, by Kenny Bowers and Betty Nyman.

I'LL SING YOU A THOUSAND LOVE SONGS (1936) (w)Al Dubin (m)Harry Warren. (I)Film: *Cain And Mabel*, by Robert Paige. (P)Eddy Duchin and his Orchestra. No. 1 Chart Record.

I'LL STILL BELONG TO YOU (1930) (w)Edward Eliscu (m)Nacio Herb Brown. (I)Film: *Whoopee*, by Eddie Cantor.

I'LL STRING ALONG WITH YOU (1934) (w)Al Dubin (m)Harry Warren. (I)Film: *Twenty Million Sweethearts*, by Dick Powell. (P)Ted Fiorito and his Orchestra. No. 1 Chart Record. (R)1953 Film: *The Jazz Singer*, by Danny Thomas.

I'LL TAKE AN OPTION ON YOU (1933) (w)Leo Robin (m)Ralph Rainger. (I)Revue: *Tattle Tales*, by Frank Fay and Betty Doree.

I'LL TAKE CARE OF YOUR CARES (1927) (w)Mort Dixon (m)James V. Monaco. No artist credited with introduction. (R)1967 by Frankie Laine.

I'LL TAKE GOOD CARE OF YOU (1966) (wm)Jerry Ragovoy—Bert Berns. (P)Garnet Mimms and The Enchanters.

I'LL TAKE ROMANCE (1937) (w)Oscar Hammerstein II (m)Ben Oakland. (I)Film: *I'll Take Romance* by Grace Moore. (P)Rudy Vallee.

I'LL TAKE TALLULAH (1942) (w)E.Y. Harburg (m)Burton Lane. (I)Film: *Ship Ahoy*, by Eleanor Powell, Red Skelton, Bert Lahr, and Tommy Dorsey and his Orchestra.

I'LL TAKE YOU HOME (1963) (wm)Cynthia Weil—Barry Mann. (P)The Drifters.

I'LL TAKE YOU HOME AGAIN KATHLEEN (1876) (wm)Thomas Westendorf. (P)John McCormack.

I'LL TAKE YOU THERE (1972) (wm)Alvertis Isbell. (P)The Staple Singers. No. 1 Chart Record.

I'LL TELL THE MAN IN THE STREET (1938) (w)Lorenz Hart (m)Richard Rodgers. (I)Musical: *I Married An Angel*, by Viveen Segal and Walter Slezak. Film version 1942 by Nelson Eddy and Jeanette MacDonald.

I'LL TRY ANYTHING (To Get You) (1966) (wm)Mark Barkan—Vic Millrose. (P)Dusty Springfield.

I'LL TRY SOMETHING NEW (1962) (wm)William Robinson. (P)The Miracles. (R)1969 by The Supremes and The Temptations. (R)1982 by A Taste Of Honey.

I'LL TUMBLE 4 YA (1983) (wm)Roy Hay—Jon Moss—Michael Craig—George O'Dowd. (P)Culture Club.

I'LL WAIT (1984) (wm)Eddie Van Halen—Alex Van Halen—Michael Anthony—David Lee Roth—Michael McDonald. (P)Van Halen.

I'LL WAIT FOR YOU (1958) (w)Bob Marcucci (m)Pete De Abgelis. (P)Frankie Avalon.

I'LL WALK ALONE (1944) (w)Sammy Cahn (m)Jule Styne. (I)Film: *Follow The Boys*, by Dinah Shore. (P)Dinah Shore. No. 1 Chart Record. (CR)Mary Martin. (CR)Jane Froman.

ILL WIND (You're Blowin' Me No Good) (1934) (w)Ted Koehler (m)Harold Arlen. (I)Revue: *Cotton Club Parade*, by Aida Ward.

ILLEGITIMATE DAUGHTER, THE (1931) (w)Ira Gershwin (m)George Gershwin. (I)Musical: *Of Thee I Sing*, by Florence Ames.

ILLUSION (1947) (w-Eng)Bob Russell—S.T. Gallagher (m)Xavier Cugat. (P)Xavier Cugat and his Orchestra.

ILONA (1963) (w)Sheldon Harnick (m)Jerry Bock. (I)Musical: *She Loves Me*, by Jack Cassidy.

I'M A BAD BAD MAN (1946) (wm)Irving Berlin. (I)Musical: *Annie Get Your Gun*, by Ray Middleton.

I'M A BELIEVER (1966) (wm)Neil Diamond. (P)The Monkees. No. 1 Chart Record. (R)1971 by Neil Diamond.

I'M A BETTER MAN (For Having Loved You) (1969) (w)Hal David (m)Burt Bacharach. (P)Engelbert Humperdinck.

I'M A BIG GIRL NOW (1946) (wm)Al Hoffman—Milton Drake—Jerry Livingston. (P)Sammy Kaye and his Orchestra, vocal by Betty Barclay. No. 1 Chart Record.

I'M A DING DONG DADDY FROM DUMAS (1928) (wm)Phil Baxter. (I)Phil Baxter and his Orchestra. (P)Louis Armstrong. (R)1937 Film: *Hollywood Hotel* by The Benny Goodman Quartet

I'M A DREAMER, AREN'T WE ALL (1929) (w)B.G. De Sylva (m)Ray Henderson. (I)Film: *Sunny Side Up*, by Janet Gaynor. (P)Paul Whiteman and his Orchestra.

I'M A FOOL (1965) (wm)Joey Cooper—Red West. (P)Dino, Desi, and Billy.

I'M A FOOL TO WANT YOU (1951) (wm)Jack Wolf—Joel Herron—Frank Sinatra. (P)Frank Sinatra.

I'M A GIGOLO (1929) (wm)Cole Porter. (I)Musical: *Wake Up And Dream*, by William Stephens.

I'M A HUNDRED PERCENT FOR YOU (1934) (wm)Irving Mills—Ben Oaklnad—Mitchell Parish. (I)Revue: *Cotton Club Parade*. (P)Benny Goodman and his Orchestra.

I'M A LITTLE BLACKBIRD LOOKING FOR A BLUEBIRD (1924) (w)Grant Clarke—Roy Turk (m)Geroge W. Meyer—Arthur Johnston. (I)Revue: *Dixie To Broadway*, by Florence Mills.

I'M A LOSER (1965) (wm)John Lennon—Paul McCartney. (P)The Beatles.

I'M A MAN (1955) (wm)E. McDaniel. (P)Gene McDaniel. (R)1965 by The Yardbirds.

I'M A MAN (1958) (wm)Doc Pomus—Mort Shuman. (P)Fabian.

I'M A MAN (1967) (wm)Steve Winwood—Jimmy Miller. (P)The Spencer Davis Group. (R)1969 by Chicago.

I'M A MIDNIGHT MOVER (1968) (wm)Wilson Pickett—Bobby Womack. (P)Wilson Pickett.

I'M A STRANGER HERE MYSELF (1943) (w)Ogden Nash (m)Kurt Weill. (I)Musical: *One Touch Of Venus*, by Mary Martin.

I'M A VAMP FROM EAST BROADWAY (1921) (wm)Bert Kalmar—Harry Ruby—Irving Berlin. One of the few songs that Berlin did not write by himself. (P)Fanny Brice.

I'M ALIVE (1980) (wm)Clint Ballard, Jr. (P)ELO.

I'M A WOMAN (1963) (wm)Jerry Leiber—Mike Stoller. (P)Peggy Lee. (R)1975 by Maria Muldaur.

I'M ALL DRESSED UP WITH A BROKEN HEART (1931) (wm)Fred Fisher—Stella Unger—Harold Stern. (P)Ted Lewis.

I'M ALL I'VE GOT (1962) (w)Ronny Graham (m)Milton Schafer. (I)Musical: *Bravo Giovanni*, by Michele Lee.

I'M ALRIGHT (1980) (wm)Kenny Loggins. (I)Film: *Caddyshack*, by Kenny Loggins on soundtrack. (P)Kenny Loggins.

I'M ALL SMILES (1964) (w)Herbert Martin (m)Michael Leonard. (I)Musical: *The Yearling*, by Carmen Alvarez. (P)Barbra Streisand.

I'M ALONE (1932) (w)Oscar Hammerstein II (m)Jerome Kern. (I)Musical: *Music In The Air*, by Natalie Hall.

I'M ALWAYS HEARING WEDDING BELLS (1955) (w-Eng)Robert Mellin (m)Herbert Jarczyk. (P)Eddie Fisher.

I'M AN INDIAN (1922) (w)Blanche Merrill (m)Leo Edwards. (I)Revue: *Ziegfeld Follies of 1920* by Fanny Brice. (P)Fanny Brice. (R)1928 Film: *My Man*, by Fanny Brice.

I'M AN INDIAN TOO (1946) (wm)Irving Berlin. (I)Musical: *Annie Get Your Gun*, by Ethel Merman.

I'M AN OLD COW HAND (From The Rio Grande) (1936) (wm)Johnny Mercer. (I)Film: *Rhythm On The Range*, by Bing Crosby. (P)BIng Crosby with Jimmy Dorsey and his Orchestra. (R)1943 Film: *King Of The Cowboys*, by Roy Rogers.

I'M AN ORDINARY MAN (1936) (w)Alan Jay Lerner (m)Frederick Loewe. (I)Musical: *My Fair Lady*, by Rex Harrison.

I'M AVAILABLE (1956) (wm)Jerry Bock—Larry Holofcener—George Weiss. (I)Musical: *Mr. Wonderful,* by Chita Rivera.

I'M AVAILABLE (1957) (wm)Dave Burgess. (P)Margie Rayburn.

I'M BEGINNING TO SEE THE LIGHT (1944) (wm)Harry James—Duke Ellington—Johnny Hodges—Don George. (I)Duke Ellington and his Orchestra. (P)Harry James and his Orchestra, vocal by Kitty Kallen. No. 1 Chart Record.

I'M BLUE (The Gong Gong Song) (1962) (wm)Ike Turner. (P)The Ikettes.

I'M BRINGING A RED, RED ROSE (1928) (w)Gus Kahn (m)Walter Donaldson. (I)Musical: *Whoopee,* by Paul Gregory and Frances Upton.

I'M BUILDING UP TO AN AWFUL LETDOWN (1938) (w)Johnny Mercer (m)Fred Astaire. (P)Fred Astaire.

I'M CALLED LITTLE BUTTERCUP (1878) (w)Wm. S. Gilbert (m)Arthur Sullivan. (I)Operetta: *H.M.S. Pinafore.*

I'M CHECKING OUT GOOMBYE (1939) (wm)Billy Strayhorn—Duke Ellington. (P)Duke Ellington and his Orchestra, vocal by Ivie Anderson and Sonny Greer.

I'M COMING OUT (1980) (wm)Bernard Edwards—Nile Rodgers. (P)Diana Ross.

I'M COMING VIRGINIA (1927) (w)Will Cook (m)Donald Heywood. (P)Ethel Waters. (CR)Frankie Trumbauer and his Orchestra. (R)1965 Film: *Mickey One,* by Warren Beatty.

I'M CONFESSIN' (That I Love You) (1930) (w)Al Neiburg (m)Doc Daugherty—Ellis Reynolds. (P)Rudy Vallee.

I'M CRAVING FOR THAT KIND OF LOVE (1921) (wm)Noble Sissle—Eubie Blake. (I)Musical: *Shuffle Along,* by Gertrude Saunders.

I'M CRAZY 'BOUT MY BABY (And My Baby's Crazy 'Bout Me) (1931) (wm)Thomas Waller—Alex Hill. (P)Fats Waller with Ted Lewis and his Band.

I'M CRYING (1964) (wm)Eric Burdon—Alan Price. (P)The Animals.

I'M DOIN' FINE NOW (1973) (wm)Sherman Marshall—Thom Bell. (P)New York City.

I'M EASY (1975) (wm)Keith Carradine. (I)Film: *Nashville,* by Keith Carradine. Academy Award Winner.

I'M EVERY WOMAN (1978) (wm)Nicholas Ashford—Valerie Simpson. (P)Chaka Khan.

I'M FALLING IN LOVE WITH SOMEONE (1910) (w)Rida Johnson Young (m)Victor Herbert. (I)Musical: *Naughty Marietta.* (R)1934 in film version by Nelson Eddy and Jeanette MacDonald. (R)1939 Film: *The Great Victor Herbert,* by Allan Jones and Mary Martin.

I'M FASCINATING (1962) (w)Lee Adams (m)Charles Strouse. (I)Musical: *All American,* by Ray Bolger.

I'M FEELIN' BLUE ('Cause I Got Nobody) (1931) (w)Dorothy Fields (m)Jimmy McHugh. (I)Revue: *Lew Leslie's Rhapsody In Black,* by Ethel Waters.

I'M FEELIN' LIKE A MILLION (1937) (w)Arthur Freed (m)Nacio Herb Brown. (I)Film: *Broadway Melody of 1938,* by Eleanor Powell and George Murphy.

I'M FLYING (1954) (w)Carolyn Leigh (m)Mark Charlap. (I)Musical: *Peter Pan,* by Mary Martin, Kathy Nolan, Richard Harrington, and Joseph Stafford.

I'M FOREVER BLOWING BUBBLES (1919) (wm)Jean Kenbrovin (m)John Kellette. (I)Musical: *Passing Show.* (P)Henry Burr & Albert Campbell. (R)1950 by Gordon Jenkins with Artie Shaw.

I'M FREE (1965) (wm)Mick Jagger—Keith Richard. (P)The Rolling Stones.

I'M GETTIN' SENTIMENTAL OVER YOU (1932) (w)Ned Washington (m)George Bassman. (P)Theme Song of Tommy Dorsey and his Orchestra. (R)1940 by The Ink Spots.

TOMMY DORSEY

Some years ago I worked for the great Tommy Dorsey as one of the music arrangers for his orchestra. Tommy's orchestra always would play the Capitol Theater during Christmas week, with the rehearsal generally taking place the day before the show opened. On this particular pre-Christmas afternoon, we were having a party in the office. A call came in asking me to rush right over to the theater. Dorsey wanted to see me. He explained that the arrangements for the opening acts were inadequate and that I would have to work all Christmas Eve to fix arrangements to meet the requirements and instrumentation of his orchestra.

Well, he was the boss, so I did it. At rehearsal the next morning, everything sounded fine - but all I received from Tommy was a fast "thank you." But when I walked into my office on Monday morning, I found an envelope on my desk containing a check from Dorsey and a most appreciative note. He really was a super guy.

I'M GETTING MYSELF READY FOR YOU (1930) (wm)Cole Porter. (I)Musical: *The New Yorkers,* by Frances Williams, Barrie Oliver, Ann Pennington, and Maurice Lapue.

I'M GETTING TIRED SO I CAN SLEEP (1942) (wm)Irving Berlin. (I)Revue: *This Is The Army,* by Pvt. William Horne.

I'M GLAD I WAITED (1930) (w)Clifford Grey—Harold Adamson (m)Vincent Youmans. (I)Musical: *Smiles,* by Fred Astaire and Marilyn Miller.

I'M GLAD I'M NOT YOUNG ANYMORE (1958) (w)Alan Jay Lerner (m)Frederick Loewe. (I)Film: *Gigi,* by Maurice Chevalier.

I'M GLAD THERE IS YOU (1941) (wm)Paul Madeira—Jimmy Dorsey. (P)Jimmy Dorsey and his Orchestra.

I'M GOIN' DOWN (1984) (wm)Bruce Springsteen. (P)Bruce Springsteen.

I'M GOIN' SOUTH (1921) (wm)Abner Silver—Harry Woods. (I)Musical: *Bombo,* by Al Jolson. (P)Musical: *Kid Boots,* by Eddie Cantor.

I'M GONE (1953) (wm)Leonard Lee—Dave Bartholomew. (P)Shirley and Lee.

I'M GONNA BE A WHEEL SOMEDAY (1957) (wm)Dave Bartholomew—Antoine Domino. (P)Fats Domino.

I'M GONNA BE STRONG (1963) (wm)Barry Mann—Cynthia Weil. (P)Gene Pitney.

I'M GONNA BE WARM THIS WINTER (1962) (wm)Hank Hunter—Mark Barkan. (P)Connie Francis.

I'M GONNA GET HIM (1956) (wm)Irving Berlin. (I)Musical: *Mr. President,* by Nanette Fabray and Anita Gillette.

I'M GONNA GET MARRIED (1959) (wm)Harold Logan—

Lloyd Price. (P)Lloyd Price.

I'M GONNA GO FISHIN' (1960) (w)Peggy Lee (m)Duke Ellington. Adapted from a theme from Film: *Anatomy Of A Murder*. (P)Peggy Lee.

I'M GONNA KNOCK ON YOUR DOOR (1961) (wm)Aaron Schroeder—Sid Wayne. (P)Eddie Hodges.

I'M GONNA LIVE TILL I DIE (195) (wm)Al Hoffman-Walter Kent-Mann Curtis. (I)Danny Scholl. (P)Frankie Laine.

I'M GONNA LOCK MY HEART (And Throw Away The Key) (1938) (wm)Jimmy Eaton—Terry Shand. (P)Billie Holiday. (CR)Henry Busse and his Orchestra.

I'M GONNA LOVE THAT GAL (1945) (wm)Frances Ash. (P)Perry Como.

I'M GONNA LOVE YOU JUST A LITTLE BIT MORE BABE (1973) (wm)Barry White. (P)Barry White.

I'M GONNA MAKE YOU LOVE ME (1966) (wm)Jerry Ross—Ken Gamble—Jerry Williams. (I)Dee Dee Warwick. (R)1978 by Madeleine Bell. (R)1969 by The Supremes and The Temptations.

I'M GONNA MAKE YOU MINE (1969) (wm)Tony Romeo. (P)Lou Christie.

I'M GONNA MOVE ON THE OUTSKIRTS OF TOWN (1937) (P)Count Basie and his Orchestra, vocal by Jimmy Rushing. (CR)Louis Jordan and his Tympani Five.

I'M GONNA PIN MY MEDAL ON THE GIRL I LEFT BEHIND (1918) (wm)Irving Berlin. Not one of Berlin's hit songs.

I'M GONNA SEE MY BABY (1945) (wm)Phil Moore. (I)The Phil Moore Four. (P)Film: *Eadie Was A Lady*, by Ann Miller.

I'M GONNA SIT RIGHT DOWN AND WRITE MYSELF A LETTER (1935) (w)Joe Young (m)Fred E. Ahlert. (P)Fats Waller. (CR)The Boswell Sisters. (R)1957 by Billy Williams.

I'M GONNA TEAR YOUR PLAYHOUSE DOWN (1972) (wm)Earl Randle. (P)Ann Peebles. (R)1985 by Paul Young.

I'M GONNA WASH THAT MAN RIGHT OUTA MY HAIR (1949) (w)Oscar Hammerstein II (m)Richard Rodgers. (I)Musical: *South Pacific*, by Mary Martin. In Film version (1958)by Mitzi Gaynor.

I'M HANS CHRISTIAN ANDERSON (1951) (wm)Frank Loesser. (I)Film: *Hans Christian Anderson*, by Danny Kaye.

I'M HAPPY ABOUT THE WHOLE THING (1939) (w)Johnny Mercer (m)Harry Warren. (I)Film: *Naughty But Nice*, by Dick Powell and Gale Page.

I'M HAPPY JUST TO DANCE WITH YOU (1964) (wm)John Lennon—Paul McCartney. (P)The Beatles.

I'M HENRY VIII, I AM (1965) (wm)Fred Murray—R.P. Weston. Song was originally published in 1911. (P)Herman's Hermits. No. 1 Chart Record.

I'M HUMMIN'-I'M WHISTLIN'-I'M SINGIN' (1934) (I)Film: *She Loves Me Not*, by Bing Crosby.

I'M HURTING (1966) (wm)Don Gibson. (P)Don Gibson.

I'M IN A DANCING MOOD (1936) (wm)Al Hoffman—Al Goodheart—Maurice Sigler. (I)British Film: *This'll Make You Whistle*, by Jack Buchanan and Elsie Randolph. (P)Tommy Dorsey and his Orchestra. (CR)Ambrose and his Orchestra.

I'M IN LOVE (1929) (wm)Cole Porter. (I)Musical: *Fifty Million Frenchmen*, by Genevieve Tobin.

I'M IN LOVE (1948) (w)Sammy Cahn (m)Jule Styne. (I)Film: *Romance On The High Seas*, by Doris Day.

(P)Doris Day.

I'M IN LOVE (1967) (wm)Bobby Womack. (P)Wilson Pickett. (R)1974 by Aretha Franklin.

I'M IN LOVE AGAIN (1925) (wm)Cole Porter. (I)Revue: *Greenwich Village Follies of 1924* by The Dolly Sisters. (R)1946 Film: *Night And Day*, by Jane Wyman. (R)1951 by April Stevens.

I'M IN LOVE AGAIN (1956) (wm)Antoine Domino—Dave Bartholomew. (P)Fats Domino. (CR)The Fontane Sisters. (R)1953 by Rick Nelson. (R)1982 by Pia Zadora.

I'M IN THE MOOD FOR LOVE (1935) (wm)Dorothy Fields—Jimmy McHugh. (I)Film: *Every Night At Eight*, by Frances Langford. (P)Little Jack Little and his Orchestra. No. 1 Chart Record. (CR)Louis Armstrong. (R)1946 by Billy Eckstine.

I'M IN YOU (1977) (wm)Peter Frampton. (P)Peter Frampton.

I'M INTO SOMETHING GOOD (1964) (wm)Gerry Goffin—Carole King. (P)Herman's Hermits. (CR)Earl—John.

I'M JIMMY THE WELL DRESSED MAN (1929) (wm)Jimmy Durante. (I)Musical: *Show Girl*, by Clayton, Jackson, and Durante. (P)Jimmy Durante.

I'M JUST A COUNTRY BOY (1954) (wm)Fred Brooks—Marshall Barer. (P)Harry Belafonte.

I'M JUST A LUCKY SO AND SO (1945) (w)Mack David (m)Duke Ellington. (P)Duke Ellington and his Orchestra, vocal by Al Hibbler.

I'M JUST A SINGER (In A Rock And Roll Band) (1973) (wm)John Lodge. (P)The Moody Blues.

I'M JUST A VAGABOND LOVER (1929) (wm)Rudy Vallee—Leon Zimmerman. (I)Film: *The Vagabond Lover*, by Rudy Vallee. (P)Rudy Vallee.

I'M JUST TAKING MY TIME (1961) (wm)Betty Comden—Adolph Green (m)Jule Styne. (I)Musical: *Subways Are For Sleeping*, by Sydney Chaplin and The Chorus. (P)The McGuire Sisters.

I'M JUST WILD ABOUT ANIMAL CRACKERS (1926) (wm)Freddie Rich—Sam Coslow—Harry Link. (P)Freddie Rich and his Orchestra.

I'M JUST WILD ABOUT HARRY (1921) (wm)Noble Sissle—Eubie Blake. (I)Musical: *Shuffle Along*, by Lottie Gee. (P)Marion Harris. (CR)Vincent Lopez and his Orchestra. (R)1939 Film: *Babes In Arms*, by Mickey Rooney and Judy Garland. (R)1949 Film: *Jolson Sings Again*, by Al Jolson dubbing for Larry Parks.

I'M LATE (1951) (w)Bob Hilliard (m)Sammy Fain. (I)Cartoon Film: *Alice In Wonderland*.

I'M LAUGHIN' (1934) (wm)Lew Brown—Jay Gorney. (I)Film: *Stand Up And Cheer*, by Dick Foran, Tess Gardella, and The Ensemble.

I'M LEAVING IT UP TO YOU (1963) (wm)Dewey Terry—Don F. Harris. (P)Dale and Grace. No. 1 Chart Record. (R)1974 by Donny and Marie Osmond.

I'M LIKE A FISH OUT OF WATER (1943) (w)Paul Francis Webster (m)Harry Revel. (I)Film: *Hit The Ice*, by Ginny Simms.

I'M LIKE A NEW BROOM (1951) (w)Dorothy Fields (m)Arthur Schwartz. (I)Musical: *A Tree Grows In Brooklyn*, by Johnny Johnston.

I'M LIVING IN A GREAT BIG WAY (1935) (w)Dorothy Fields (m)Jimmy McHugh. (I)Film: *Hooray For Love*, by Bill Robinson and Jeni Le Gon.

I'M LIVING IN SHAME (1969) (wm)Pam Sawyer—R.

Dean Taylor—Frank Wilson—Henry Cosby—Berry Gordy, Jr. (P)Diana Ross and The Supremes.

I'M LOOKING FOR A GUY WHO PLAYS ALTO AND BARITONE AND DOUBLES ON A CLARINET AND WEARS A SIZE 37 SUIT (1940) (wm)Ozzie Nelson. (P)Ozzie Nelson and his Orchestra.

I'M LOOKING OVER A FOUR LEAF CLOVER (1927) (w)Mort Dixon (m)Harry Woods. (P)Nick Lucas. (CR)Ben Bernie and his Orchestra. (R)1948 by Art Mooney and his Orchestra. No. 1 Chart Record. (CR)Arthur Godfrey. (R)1949 Film: *Jolson Sings Again*, by Al Jolson dubbing for Larry Parks. (R)1953 Film: *The Jazz Singer*, by Danny Thomas.

I'M LOOKING THROUGH YOU (1965) (wm)John Lennon—Paul McCartney. (P)The Beatles.

(I Know)I'M LOSING YOU (1966) (wm)Cornelius Grant—Norman Whitfield—Eddie Holland. (P)The Temptations. (R)1970 by Rare Earth. (R)1971 by Rod Stewart.

I'M MAKING BELIEVE (1944) (w)Mack Gordon (m)James V. Monaco. (I)Film: *Sweet and Low Down* on soundtrack by Benny Goodman and his Orchestra. (P)Ella Fitzgerald and The Ink Spots. No. 1 Chart Record.

I'M MAKING HAY IN THE MOONLIGHT (1932) (w)Tot Seymour (m)Jesse Greer. (I)Film: *Blessed Event*, by Dick Powell.

I'M MY OWN GRANDPAW (1948) (wm)Dwight Latham—Moe Jaffe. (P)Guy Lombardo and his Royal Canadians.

I'M NO ANGEL (1933) (wm)Gladys Du Bois—Ben Ellison—Harvey O. Brooks. (I)Film: *I'm No Angel*, by Mae West. (P)Mae West.

I'M NOBODY'S BABY (1921) (wm)Benny Davis—Milton Ager—Lester Santly. (P)Ruth Etting. (R)1940 Film: *Andy Hardy Meets A Debutante*, by Judy Garland. (CR)Bea Wain.

I'M NOT AT ALL IN LOVE (1954) (wm)Richard Adler—Jerry Ross. (I)Musical: *The Pajama Game*, by Janis Paige.

I'M NOT GONNA LET IT BOTHER ME TONIGHT (1978) (wm)Buddy Buie—Robert Nix—Dean Daugherty. (P)Atlanta Rhythm Section.

I'M NOT IN LOVE (1975) (wm)Graham Gouldman—Eric Stewart. (P)10cc.

I'M NOT LISA (1975) (wm)Jessi Colter. (P)Jessi Colter.

I'M OLD FASHIONED (1942) (w)Johnny Mercer (m)Jerome Kern. (I)Film: *You Were Never Lovelier*, by Fred Astaire and Nan Wynn dubbing for Rita Hayworth.

I'M ON FIRE (1975) (wm)David English—Glenn Leonard—Richard Street—Otis Williams—Benjamin Wright, Jr. (P)5000 Volts. (CR)Jim Gillstrap.

I'M ON FIRE (1975) (wm)Dwight Twilley. (P)Twilley Dwight Band.

I'M ON FIRE (1985) (wm)Bruce Springsteen. (P)Bruce Springsteen.

I'M ON MY WAY (1951) (w)Alan Jay Lerner (m)Frederick Loewe. (I)Musical: *Paint Your Wagon*, by The Cast and Chorus.

I'M ON MY WAY HOME (1926) (wm)Irving Berlin. (P)Whispering Jack Smith.

I'M ON THE CREST OF A WAVE (1928) (w)B.G. De Sylva—Lew Brown (m)Ray Henderson. (I)Revue: *George White's Scandals of 1928*, by Harry Richman. (P)Harry Richman. (CR)George Olsen and his Or-

chestra.

I'M ON THE OUTSIDE (Looking In) (1964) (wm)Teddy Randazzo—Bobby Weinstein. (P)Little Anthony and The Imperials.

I'M ONLY SLEEPING (1966) (wm)John Lennon—Paul McCartney. (P)The Beatles.

I'M PLAYING WITH FIRE (1932) (wm)Irving Berlin. Not one of Berlin's hit songs.

I'M POPEYE THE SAILOR MAN (1934) (wm)Sammy Lerner. (I)Cartoon Film: *Popeye The Sailor*. (P)Frank Luther

I'M PRAYIN' HUMBLE (1938) (m)Bob Haggart. (P)Bob Crosby and his Orchestra.

I'M PUTTING ALL MY EGGS IN ONE BASKET (1936) (wm)Irving Berlin. (I)Film: *Follow The Fleet*, by Fred Astaire and Ginger Rogers. (P)Fred Astaire. No. 1 Chart Record. (CR)Jan Garber and his Orchestra.

I'M READY (1959) (wm)Al Lewis—Sylvester Bradford—Antoine Domino. (P)Fats Domino.

I'M READY FOR LOVE (1966) (wm)Eddie Holland—Lamont Dozier—Brian Holland. (P)Martha and The Vandellas.

I'M RIDIN' FOR A FALL (1943) (w)Frank Loesser (m)Arthur Schwartz. (I)Film: *Thank Your Lucky Stars*, by Dennis Morgan and Joan Leslie.

I'M SATISFIED (1933) (w)Mitchell Parish (m)Duke Ellington. (P)Duke Ellington and his Orchestra.

I'M SHOOTING HIGH (1935) (w)Ted Koehler (m)Jimmy McHugh. (I)Film: *King Of Burlesque*, by Jack Oakie, Shaw & Lee, Warner Baxter, and Alice Faye. (P)Jan Garber and his Orchestra. (CR)Little Jack Little.

I'M SITTING HIGH ON A HILLTOP (1935) (w)Gus Kahn (m)Arthur Johnston. (I)Film: *Thanks A Million*, by Dick Powell. (P)Guy Lombardo and his Royal Canadians.

I'M SITTING ON TOP OF THE WORLD (1925) (w)Sam M. Lewis—Joe Young (m)Ray Henderson. (I)Film: *The Singing Fool*, by Al Jolson. (P)Al Jolson. (R)1946 Film: *The Jolson Story*, by Jolson dubbing for Larry Parks. (R)1953 by Les Paul and Mary Ford.

I'M SO EXCITED (1982) (wm)Anita Pointer—June Pointer—Trevor Lawrence—Ruth Pointer. (P)The Pointer Sisters.

I'M SO LONESOME I COULD CRY (1949) (wm)Hank Williams. (P)Hank Williams. (R)1962 by Johnny Tillotson. (R)1966 by B.J. Thomas. (R)1976 by Terry Bradshaw.

I'M SO PROUD (1964) (wm)Curtis Mayfield. (P)The Impressions. (R)1971 by Main Ingredient.

I'M SO TIRED (1969) (wm)John Lennon—Paul McCartney. (P)The Beatles.

I'M SO WEARY OF IT ALL (1938) (wm)Noel Coward. (I)Revue: *Set To Music*, by Beatrice Lillie.

I'M SORRY (1960) (wm)Ronnie Self—Dub Allbritten. (P)Brenda Lee. No. 1 Chart Record. (R)1973 by Joey Heatherton.

I'M SORRY (1975) (wm)John Denver. (P)John Denver. No. 1 Chart Record.

I'M SORRY DEAR (1931) (wm)Anson Weeks—Harry Tobias—Johnnie Scott. (P)Anson Weeks and his Orchestra.

I'M SORRY FOR MYSELF (1939) (wm)Irving Berlin. (I)Film: *Second Fiddle*, by Mary Healy.

I'M SORRY I MADE YOU CRY (1916) (wm)N.J. Clesi. (P)Henry Burr. (R)1937 by Fats Waller.

I'M STEPPING OUT WITH A MEMORY TONIGHT (1940)

(w)Herb Magidson (m)Allie Wrubel. (I)Kate Smith. (P)Glenn Miller and his Orchestra.

I'M STICKIN' WITH YOU (1957) (wm)Jimmy Bowen—Buddy Knox. (P)Jimmy Bowen. (CR)The Fontane Sisters.

I'M STILL IN LOVE WITH YOU (1972) (wm)Al Green—Willie Mitchell—Al Jackson. (P)Al Green.

I'M STILL STANDING (1983) (wm)Elton John—Bernie Taupin. (P)Elton John.

I'M STONE IN LOVE WITH YOU (1972) (wm)Thom Bell—Anthony Bell—Linda Creed. (P)The Stylistics.

I'M TELLING YOU NOW (1965) (wm)Freddy Garrity—Mitch Murray. (P)Freddie and The Dreamers.

I'M THE ECHO (You're The Song That I Sing) (1935) (w)Dorothy Fields (m)Jerome Kern. (I)Film: *I Dream Too Much*, by Lily Pons. Recorded by Paul Whiteman and his Orchestra.

I'M THE FIRST GIRL IN THE SECOND ROW (1947) (wm)Hugh Martin. (I)Musical: *Look Ma, I'm Dancing*, by Nancy Walker.

I'M THE GREATEST STAR (1964) (w)Bob Merrill (m)Jule Styne. (I)Musical: *Funny Girl*, by Barbra Streisand.

I'M THE LAST OF THE RED HOT MAMMAS (1929) (w)Jack Yellen (m)Milton Ager. (I)Film: *Honky Tonk*, by Sophie Tucker. (P)Sophie Tucker.

I'M THE MEDICINE MAN FOR THE BLUES (1929) (w)Grant Clarke (m)Harry Akst. (I)Film: *Is Everybody Happy?*, by Ted Lewis. (P)Ted Lewis.

(Remember Me)I'M THE ONE WHO LOVES YOU (1950) (wm)Stuart Hamblen. (P)Stuart Hamblen. (CR)Ernest Tubb. (R)1965 by Dean Martin.

(Come 'Round Here)I'M THE ONE YOU NEED (1966) (wm) Eddie Holland—Lamont Dozier—Brian Holland. (P)The Miracles.

I'M THINKING TONIGHT OF MY BLUE EYES (1930) (wm)A.P. Carter. (P)The Carter Family. (R)1942 by Bob Atcher. (R)1943 Film: *Man From Music Mountain*, by Roy Rogers.

I'M THRU WITH LOVE (1931) (w)Gus Kahn (m)Matt Malneck—Fud Livingston. (I)Mildred Bailey. (P)Bing Crosby. (CR)Henry Busse and his Orchestra. (R)1959 Film: *Some Like It Hot*, by Marilyn Monroe.

I'M TIRED (1945) (wm)Cecil Gant—W.S. Stevenson. (P)Pvt. Cecil Gant.

I'M TIRED OF EVERYTHING BUT YOU (1925) (wm)Isham Jones. (P)Isham Jones and his Orchestra. (CR)Ben Selvin and his Orchestra.

I'M TIRED OF TEXAS (1947) (wm)Hugh Martin (I)Musical: *Look Ma, I'm Dancin'!*, by Nancy Walker.

I'M UNLUCKY AT GAMBLING (1929) (wm)Cole Porter. (I)Musical: *Fifty Million Frenchmen*, by Evelyn Hoey.

I'M WAITING JUST FOR YOU (1951) (wm)Carolyn Leigh—Henry Glover—Lucky Millinder. (I)Lucky Millinder. (R)1951 by Rosemary Clooney. (R)1957 by Pat Boone.

I'M WALKIN' (1957) (wm)Antoine Domino—Dave Bartholomew. (P)Fats Domino. (CR)Rick Nelson.

I'M WALKING BEHIND YOU (1953) (wm)Billy Reid. (P)Eddie Fisher. No. 1 Chart Record. (CR)Frank Sinatra.

I'M WISHING (1937) (w)Larry Morey (m)Frank Churchill. (I)Cartoon Film: *Snow White And The Seven Dwarfs*, by the voice of Adrienne Caselotti as Snow White.

I'M WITH YOU! (wm)Walter Donaldson. (I)Revue: *Ziegfeld Follies of 1931*, by Helen Morgan and Harry Richman.

I'M WITH YOU (1964) (w)Betty Comden—Adolph Green. (m)Jule Styne. (I)Musical: *Fade Out—Fade In*, by Carol Burnett and Jack Cassidy.

I'M WONDERING (1967) (wm)Henry Cosby—Stevie Wonder—Sylvia Moy. (P)Stevie Wonder.

I'M YOUR BOOGIE MAN (1977) (wm)Harry Casey—Richard Finch. (P)K.C. & The Sunshine Band. No. 1 Chart Record.

I'M YOUR GIRL (1953) (w)Oscar Hammerstein II (m)Richard Rodgers. (I)Musical: *Me And Juliet*, by Isabel Bigley and Bill Hayes.

I'M YOUR PUPPET (1966) (wm)Lindon Oldham—Dan Pennington. (P)James and Bobby Purify.

I'M YOURS (1930) (w)E.Y. Harburg (m)John Green. (I)Musical: *Simple Simon*, by Ruth Etting. (P)Ben Bernie and his Orchestra.

I'M YOURS (1952) (wm)Robert Mellin. (P)Don Cornell. (CR)Eddie Fisher. (CR)The Four Aces.

I'M YOURS (1965) (wm)Don Robertson—Hal Blair. (P)Elvis Presley.

I'M YOURS TO COMMAND (1931) (wm)Russ Columbo. (P)Russ Columbo.

IMAGE OF A GIRL (1960) (w)Marvin Rosenberg (m)Richard Clasky. (P)The Safaris.

IMAGINARY LOVER (1978) (wm)Buddy Buie—Robert Nix—Dean Daugherty. (P)Atlanta Rhythm Section.

IMAGINATION (1940) (w)Johnny Burke (m)Jimmy Van Heusen. (I)Fred Waring's Pennsylvanians. (P)Glenn Miller and his Orchestra, vocal by Ray Eberle. (CR)Ella Fitzgerald. (CR)Kate Smith.

IMAGINE (1971) (wm)John Lennon. (P)John Lennon. No. 1 Chart Record.

IMITATION OF LIFE (1959) (w)Paul Francis Webster (m)Sammy Fain. (I)Film: *Imitation Of Life* on soundtrack.

IMMIGRANT, THE (1975) (wm)Neil Sedaka—Phil Cody. (P)Neil Sedaka.

IMMIGRANT SONG (1971) (wm)Robert Plant—Jimmy Page. (P)Led Zeppelin.

IMMIGRATION BLUES (1927) (m)Duke Ellington. (P)Duke Ellington and his Cotton Club Orchestra.

IMPATIENT YEARS, THE (1955) (w)Sammy Cahn (m)Jimmy Van Heusen. (I)TV production: *Our Town*, by Paul Newman and Eva Marie Saint.

IMPOSSIBLE (1956) (wm)Steve Allen. (P)Nat "King" Cole.

IMPOSSIBLE DREAM, THE (1965) (wm)Joe Darion (m)Mitch Leigh. (I)Musical: *Man Of La Mancha*, by Richard Kiley. In film version (1972)by voice of Simon Gilbert dubbing for Peter O'Toole. (P)Jack Jones. (CR)The Hesitations. (CR)Roger Williams and his Orchestra.

IN A BIG COUNTRY (1983) (wm)Big Country (P)Big Country.

IN A CHINESE TEMPLE GARDEN (1920) (m)Albert Ketelby. Popular light classical composition.

IN-A-GADDA-DA-VIDA (1968) (wm)Doug Ingle. (P)Iron Butterfly.

IN A LITTLE BOOKSHOP (1947) (wm)Kay Twomey—Al Goodhart—George Meyer. (P)Vaughn Monroe and his Orchestra.

IN A LITTLE DUTCH GARDEN (Down By The Zuider Zee) (1937) (w-Eng)Al Bryan (m)L. Rosenstock. (P)Jan Garber and his Orchestra.

IN A LITTLE GYPSY TEAROOM (1935) (w)Edgar Leslie

A WRONG GUESS

This was another situation where the producers and writers of a musical, *The Man of LaMancha*, not only could not find a company to do an original cast album they couldn't even find a music publisher. After being rejected by all the majors, they ended up with a small music publishing firm called Sam Fox Music.

The general consensus in the trade was that no show could be successful that was about Don Quixote and had a semi-classical score. Again, how wrong they were. And again, it was Dave Kapp of Kapp Records who took the chance (as he did with *Hello Dolly*) and came up with a huge winner ... and left all the other publishers and record companies on the sidelines, eating their hearts out.

(m)Joe Burke. (P)Bob Crosby and his Orchestra. No. 1 Chart Record. (CR)Jack Denny and his Orchestra. (CR)Louis Prima.

IN A LITTLE HULA HEAVEN (1937) (wm)Leo Robin—Ralph Rainger. (I)Film: *Waikiki Wedding*, by Bing Crosby and Shirley Ross.

IN A LITTLE SPANISH TOWN (1926) (w)Sam M. Lewis—Joe Young (m)Mabel Wayne. (P)Paul Whiteman and his Orchestra. (CR)Ben Selvin and his Orchestra. (R)1954 by David Carroll and his Orchestra.

IN A MELLOW TONE (1940) (m)Duke Ellington. (P)Duke Ellington and his Orchestra.

IN A MIST (1927) (m)Leon "Bix" Beiderbecke. (I)Bix Beiderbecke as a piano solo.

IN A MOMENT (1969) (wm)Alfred Brown—Ronald Hamilton—James Lee, Jr.—James Harris. (P)The Intrigues.

IN A MOMENT OF MADNESS (1944) (w)Ralph Freed (m)Jimmy McHugh. (I)Film: *Two Girls And A Sailor*, by Harry James and his orchestra, vocal by Helen Forrest.

IN A MOMENT OF WEAKNESS (1939) (w)Johnny Mercer (m)Harry Warren. (I)Film: *Naughty But Nice*, by Ann Sheridan and Gale Page.

IN A SENTIMENTAL MOOD (1935) (wm)Duke Ellington. (P)Duke Ellington and his Orchestra. (CR)Benny Goodman and his Orchestra.

IN A SHANTY IN OLD SHANTY TOWN (1932) (wm)Joe Young—John Siras—Little Jack Little. (I)Little Jack Little. (P)Ted Lewis and his Orchestra. No. 1 Chart Record. (R)1940 by Johnny Long and his Orchestra.

IN ACAPULCO (1945) (w)Mack Gordon (m)Harry Warren. (I)Film: *Diamond Horseshoe*, by Betty Grable and Carmen Cavallaro and his Orchestra.

IN AN EIGHTEENTH CENTURY DRAWING ROOM (1939) (w)Jack Lawrence (m)Raymond Scott. (P)The Raymond Scott Quintet.

IN AN OLD DUTCH GARDEN (By An Old Dutch Mill) (1940) (wm)Will Grosz. (P)Glenn Miller and his Orchestra. (CR)Dick Jurgens and his Orchestra.

IN AND OUT OF LOVE (1967) (wm)Brian Holland—Lamont Dozier—Eddie Holland. (P)Diana Ross and The Supremes.

IN-BETWEEN (1938) (wm)Roger Edens. (I)Film: *Love Finds Andy Hardy*, by Judy Garland.

IN CHI-CHI-CASTENANGO (1940) (w)Henry Myers (m)Jay Gorney. (I)Revue: *Meet The People*, by Josephine Del Mar, Robert Davis, and Doodles Weaver.

"IN" CROWD, THE (1964) (wm)Billy Page. (I)Dobie Gray. (P)The Ramsey Lewis Trio. NARAS Award Winner.

IN DREAMS (1963) (wm)Roy Orbison. (P)Roy Orbison.

IN EGERN ON THE TEGERN SEA (1932) (w)Oscar Hammerstein II (m)Jerome Kern. (I)Musical: *Music In The Air*, by Ivy Scott.

IN LOVE IN VAIN (1946) (w)Leo Robin (m)Jerome Kern. (I)Film: *Centennial Summer*, by Louanne Hogan dubbing for Jeanne Crain.

IN LOVE WITH LOVE (1923) (w)Anne Caldwell (m)Jerome Kern. (I)Musical: *Stepping Stones*.

IN MY ARMS (1944) (wm)Frank Loesser—Ted Grouya. (I)Film: *See Here, Private Hargrove* on soundtrack. (P)Dick Haymes.

IN MY HAREM (1913) (wm)Irving Berlin. Not one of Berlin's hit songs.

IN MY HOUSE (1985) (wm)Rick James. (P)The Mary Jane Girls.

IN MY LIFE (1965) (wm)John Lennon—Paul McCartney. (P)The Beatles. (CR)Judy Collins.

IN MY OWN LITTLE CORNER (1957) (w)Oscar Hammerstein II (m)Richard Rodgers. (I)TV production: *Cinderella*, by Julie Andrews.

IN MY MERRY OLDSMOBILE (1905) (w)Vincent Bryan (m)Gus Edwards. (P)Gus Edwards.

IN MY ROOM (1964) (wm)Brian Wilson—Gary Usher. (P)The Beach Boys. (R)1969 by Sagittarius.

IN OTHER WORDS, SEVENTEEN (1939) (w)Oscar Hammerstein II (m)Jerome Kern. (I)Musical: *Very Warm For May*, by Grace McDonald, Donald Brian, and Eve Arden.

IN OUR HIDE-AWAY (1962) (wm)Irving Berlin. (I)Musical: *Mr. President*, by Robert Ryan and Nanette Fabray.

IN PARIS AND IN LOVE (1954) (w)Leo Robin (m)Sigmund Romberg. (I)Musical: *The Girl In Pink Tights*, by Jeanmaire and David Atkinson.

IN THE AIR TONIGHT (1981) (wm)Phil Collins. (P)Phil Collins.

IN THE ARMS OF LOVE (1965) (w)Ray Evans—Jay Livingston (m)Henry Mancini. (I)Film: *What Did You Do In The War, Daddy?* on soundtrack. (P)Andy Williams.

IN THE BLUE OF EVENING (1943) (w)Tom Adair (m)Al D'Artega. (I)D'Artega and his Orchestra. (P)Tommy Dorsey and his Orchestra, vocal by Frank Sinatra. (R)1958 by Jackie Wilson.

IN THE CHAPEL IN THE MOONLIGHT (1936) (wm)Billy Hill. (P)Shep Fields and his Orchestra. (CR)Richard Himber and his Orchestra. (R)1954 by Kitty Kallen. (R)1967 by Dean Martin.

IN THE COOL, COOL, COOL OF THE EVENING (1951) (w)Johnny Mercer (m)Hoagy Carmichael. (I)Film: *Here Comes The Groom*, by Bing Crosby and Jane Wyman. (P)Bing Crosby. Academy Award Winner.

IN THE DARK (1931) (m)Bix Beiderbecke. (I)Bix Beiderbecke as a piano solo.

IN THE EVENING (When The Sun Goes Down) (1935) (wm)Leroy Carr. (P)Leroy Carr.

IN THE EVENING BY THE MOONLIGHT (1878) (wm)James A. Bland. No artist credited with introduction.

IN THE GARDEN (1912) (wm)C. Austin Miles. One of the most popular Protestant hymns.

IN THE GHETTO (The Vicious Circle) (1969) (wm)Mac Davis. (P)Elvis Presley. (R)1972 by Candi Staton.

IN THE GOOD OLD SUMMERTIME (1902) (w)Ren Shields (m)George Evans. (P)J.W. Myers. (R)1952 by Les Paul and Mary Ford.

IN THE HEART OF THE DARK (1939) (w)Oscar Hammerstein II (m)Jerome Kern. (I)Musical: *Very Warm For May*, by Hollace Shaw and later reprised by Frances Mercer.

IN THE HEAT OF THE NIGHT (1967) (w)Marilyn and Alan Bergman (m)Quincy Jones. (I)Film: *In The Heat Of The Night*, by voice of Ray Charles. (P)Ray Charles.

IN THE JAILHOUSE NOW (1928) (wm)Jimmie Rodgers. (P)Jimmie Rodgers. (R)1962 by Johnny Cash.

IN THE LAND OF BEGINNING AGAIN (1918) (w)Grant Clarke (m)George W. Meyer. (P)Charles Harrison. (R)1946 Film: *The Bells of St. Mary's*, by Bing Crosby.

IN THE LAND OF OO-BLA-DEE (1949) (wm)Mary Lou Williams—Milton Orent. (P)Mary Lou Williams and her Band, vocal by Pancho Hagood.

IN THE LITTLE RED SCHOOL HOUSE (1922) (wm)Al Wilson—James A. Brennan. (P)Billy Jones and Ernie Hare (The Happiness Boys).

IN THE MERRY MONTH OF MAYBE (1931) (w)Ira Gershwin—Billy Rose (m)Harry Warren. (I)Revue: *Billy Rose's Crazy Quilt*, by Ethel Norris and Tom Monroe.

IN THE MIDDLE OF A HEARTACHE (1961) (wm)Laurie Christenson—Pat Franzese—Wanda Jackson. (P)Wanda Jackson.

IN THE MIDDLE OF A KISS (1935) (wm)Sam Coslow. (I)Film: *College Scandal*, by Johnny Downs and Wendy Barrie. (P)Hal Kemp and his Orchestra.

IN THE MIDDLE OF AN ISLAND (1957) (wm)Nick Acquaviva—Ted Varnick. (P)Tony Bennett. (CR)Tennessee Ernie Ford.

IN THE MIDNIGHT HOUR (1965) (wm)Wilson Pickett—Steve Cropper. (P)Wilson Pickett. (R)1968 by The Mirettes. (R)1973 by Cross Country.

IN THE MISTY MOONLIGHT (1964) (wm)Cindy Walker. (P)Jerry Wallace. (R)1967 by Dean Martin.

IN THE MOOD (1938) (w)Andy Razaf (m)Joe Garland. (I)Edgar Hayes and his Orchestra. (R)1940 by Glenn Miller and his Orchestra. No. 1 Chart Record. (R)1959 by Ernie Fields. (R)1974 by Bette Midler. (R)1977 by The Henhouse Five Plus Too.

IN THE NAME OF LOVE (1964) (wm)Kenny Rankin—Estelle Levitt. (P)Peggy Lee.

IN THE NAVY (1979) (wm)Jacques Morali—Henri Belolo—Victor Willis. (P)Village People.

IN THE PARK IN PAREE (1933) (w)Leo Robin (m)Ralph Rainger. (I)Film: *A Bedtime Story*, by Maurice Chevalier. (P)Maurice Chevalier.

IN THE QUIET MORNING (For Janis Joplin) (1972) (wm)Mimi Farina. (P)Joan Baez.

IN THE RAIN (1971) (wm)Tony Hester. (P)The Dramatics.

IN THE SHADE OF THE OLD APPLE TREE (1905) (w)Harry H. Williams (m)Egbert Van Alstyne. (P)Henry Burr. (R)1933 by Duke Ellington and his Orchestra.

IN THE SHADE OF THE NEW APPLE TREE (1937) (w)E. Y. Harburg (m)Harold Arlen. (I)Musical: *Hooray For What!*, by Jack Whiting, Hugh Martin, Ralph Blane, Harold Cook, and John Smedburg.

IN THE STILL OF THE NIGHT (1937) (wm)Cole Porter. (I)Film: *Rosalie*, by Nelson Eddy. (P)Tommy Dorsey and his Orchestra. (CR)Leo Reisman and his Orchestra.

IN THE SUMMERTIME (1970) (wm)Ray Dorset. (P)Mungo Jerry.

IN THE SWEET BYE AND BYE (1902) (w)Vincent Bryan (m)Harry Von Tilzer. (P)The Haydn Quartet.

IN THE VALLEY (Where The Evening Sun Goes Down) (1945) (w)Johnny Mercer (m)Harry Warren. (I)Film: *The Harvey Girls*, by Judy Garland and Kenny Baker.

IN THE YEAR 2525 (1969) (wm)Rick Evans. (P)Zager and Evans. No. 1 Chart Record.

IN TOO DEEP (1987) (wm)Phil Collins—Mike Rutherford—A. Banks. (P)Genesis.

IN YOUR LETTER (1981) (wm)Gary Ricrath (P)REO Speedwagon.

IN YOUR OWN QUIET WAY (1936) (w)E.Y. Harburg (m)Harold Arlen. (I)Film: *Stage Struck*, by Dick Powell and later reprised by Jeanne Madden.

INCENSE AND PEPPERMINTS (1967) (wm)John Carter—Tim Gilbert. (P)Strawberry Alarm Clock. No. 1 Chart Record.

STRAWBERRY ALARM CLOCK

I have spoken often about the backward attitude of the management at Decca and their subsidiaries toward contemporary music. So it was sort of amusing when the company was forced to release a master by the group, Strawberry Alarm Clock. The title of the song (which became a #1 hit) was *Incense and Peppermints*.

Little did the bosses know that the song was about narcotics.

INCHWORM, THE (1951) (wm)Frank Loesser. (I)Film: *Hans Christian Anderson*, by Danny Kaye.

INDEPENDENCE DAY (1979) (wm)Bruce Springsteen. (P)Bruce Springsteen.

INDEPENDENT (On My Own) (1957) (wm)Betty Comden—Adolph Green (m)Jule Styne. (I)Musical: *Bells Are Ringing*, by Sydney Chaplin.

INDIAN GIVER (1969) (wm)Bobby Bloom—Bo Gentry—Ritchie Cordell. (P)The 1910 Fruitgum Company.

INDIAN LAKE (1968) (wm)Tony Romeo. (P)The Cowsills.

INDIAN LOVE CALL (1924) (w)Otto Harbach—Oscar Hammerstein II (m)Rudolf Friml. (I)Operetta: *Rose-Marie*, by Mary Ellis and Dennis King. Recorded by Paul Whiteman and his Orchestra. (R)1936 film version, by Jeanette MacDonald and Nelson Eddy. (P)Jeanette MacDonald and Nelson Eddy. (R)1954 film version, by Ann Blyth and Fernando Lamas. (R)1938 by Artie Shaw and his Orchestra, vocal by Tony Pastor. (R)1951 by Slim Whitman.

INDIAN RESERVATION (1968) (wm)John D. Loudermilk. (P)Don Fardon. (R)1971 by Paul Revere and The Raiders. No. 1 Chart Record.

INDIAN SUMMER (1939) (w)Al Dubin (m)Victor Herbert. (P)Tommy Dorsey and his Orchestra, vocal by Frank Sinatra. No. 1 Chart Record. (CR)Glenn Miller and his Orchestra.

(Back Home Again In)INDIANA (1917 (w)Ballard Mac-Donald (m)James F. Hanley. (P)Louis Armstrong.

INDIANA MOON (1923) (w)Benny Davis (m)Isham Jones. (P)Isham Jones and his Orchestra.

INDIANA WANTS ME (1970) (wm)R. Dean Taylor. (P)R. Dean Taylor.

INDISCREET (1958) (w)Sammy Cahn (m)Jimmy Van Heusen. (I)Film: *Indiscreet*, on soundtrack. (P)Barbara McNair.

INDISCRETION (1954) (wm)Sammy Cahn—Paul Weston. (I)Film: *Indiscretion Of An American Wife* on soundtrack. (P)Jo Stafford.

INFATUATION (1984) (wm)Rod Stewart—Duane Hitchings—Michael Omartian. (P)Rod Stewart.

INKA DINKA DOO (1933) (w)Ben Ryan (m)Jimmy Durante. (I)Film: *Palooka*, by Jimmy Durante. (P)Jimmy Durante.

INNAMORATA (1955) (w)Jack Brooks (m)Harry Warren. (I)Film: *Artists And Models*, by Dean Martin. (P)Dean Martin.

INNER CITY BLUES (Make Me Wanna Holler) (1971) (wm)Marvin Gaye—James Myx, Jr. (P)Marvin Gaye.

INNER LIGHT, THE (1968) (wm)George Harrison. (P)The Beatles.

INNOCENT MAN, AN (1984) (wm)Billy Joel. (P)Billy Joel.

INSEPERABLE (1975) (wm)Charles Jackson, Jr.—Marvin Yancy. (P)Natalie Cole.

INSIDE-LOOKING OUT (1966) (wm)Eric Burdon—Bryan Chandler—Alan Lomax. (P)Eric Burdon and The Animals.

INSPIRATION (1959) (w)Joe Lubin (m)I.J. Roth. (I)Film: *Pillow Talk*, by Doris Day.

INSTANT KARMA (1970) (wm)John Lennon. (P)John Ono Lennon.

INTERMEZZO (1890) (m)Pietro Mascagni.Classical selection from Opera: *Cavalleria Rusticana.*

INTERMEZZO (A Love Story) (1940) (w)Robert Henning (m)Heinz Provost. (I)Film: *Intermezzo* on soundtrack. (P)Guy Lombardo and his Royal Canadians. No. 1 Chart Record. (CR)Wayne King and his Orchestra. (CR)Benny Goodman and his Orchestra.

INTERMISSION RIFF (1946) (w)Steve Graham (m)Ray Wetzel. (P)Stan Kenton and his Orchestra.

INTO EACH LIFE SOME RAIN MUST FALL (1944) (wm)Allan Roberts—Doris Fisher. (P)Ella Fitzgerald and The Ink Spots. No. 1 Chart Record. (CR)Teresa Brewer.

INTO MY HEART (1930) (w)Roy Turk (m)Fred E. Ahlert, (I)Film: *In Gay Madrid*, by Ramon Novarro.

INTO THE NIGHT (1980) (wm)Paul Hewson—Larry Mullern—Adam Clayton—Dave Evans. (P)Benny Mardones.

INVINCIBLE (1985) (wm)Holly Knight—Simon Climie. (I)Film: *The Legend Of Billie Jean*, by voice of Pat Benatar. (P)Pat Benatar.

INVISIBLE TEARS (1964) (wm)Ned Miller—Sue Miller. (I)Ned Miller. (P)The Ray Conniff Singers.

INVISIBLE TOUCH (1986) (wm)Phil Collins—Mike Rutherford. (P)Genesis. No. 1 Chart Record.

INVITATION (1952) (m)Bronislau Kaper. (I)Film: *Invitation* on soundtrack.

INVITATION TO THE BLUES (1944) (wm)Doris Fisher—Allan Roberts—Arthur Gershwin. (P)Ella Mae Morse.

INVITATION TO THE DANCE (1821) (m)Carl Maria von Weber. Famous classical composition. Adapted in a swing version as opening theme song for Benny Goodman and his Orchestra.

IRENE (1919) (w)Joseph McCarthy (m)Harry Tierney. (I)Musical: *Irene*, by Edith Day. (P)Edith Day.

IRISH WASHERWOMAN, THE (1792) (wm)Unknown. Traditional Irish folk dance.

IRMA LA DOUCE (1956) (w-Eng)Julian More—David Heneker—Monty Norman (m)Marguerite Monnot. (I)Musical: *Irma La Douce*, by Colette Renard in Paris production. In London and New York productions by Elizabeth Seal.

IS HE THE ONLY MAN IN THE WORLD (1956) (wm)Irving Berlin. (I)Musical: *Mr. President*, by Nanette Fabray and Anita Gillette.

IS IT ANY WONDER (1953) (wm)Archie Gottler—Bob Hayes—Roy Rodde. (P)Joni James.

IS IT LOVE (1986) (wm)Richard Page—Steven George—Robert John Lange—Pat Mastellotto. (P)Mr. Mister.

IS IT SOMETHING YOU'VE GOT? (1969)wm)Barry Dispenza—Carl Wolfolk. (P)Tyrone Davis.

IS IT TRUE WHAT THEY SAY ABOUT DIXIE? (1936) (wm)Irving Calsar—Sammy Lerner—Gerald Marks. (P)Al Jolson. (CR)Jimmy Dorsey and his Orchestra. (CR)Ozzie Nelson and his Orchestra.

IS IT YOU (1981) (wm)Lee Ritenour—Eric Tagg—Bill Champlin. (P)Lee Ritenour.

IS MY BABY BLUE TONIGHT (1944) (w)William Tracey (m)Lou Handman. (P)Lawrence Welk and his Orchestra, vocal by Jayne Walton.

IS SHE REALLY GOING OUT WITH HIM? (1979) (wm)Joe Jackson. (P)Joe Jackson.

IS THAT ALL THERE IS? (1969) (wm)Jerry Leiber—Mike Stoller. (P)Peggy Lee.

IS THAT RELIGION? (1930) (wm)Maceo Pinkard—Mitchell Parish. (P)Mildred Bailey.

IS THERE SOMETHING I SHOULD KNOW (1983) (wm)Duran Duran. (P)Duran Duran.

IS THIS LOVE (1987) (wm)Jim Peterik—F. Sullivan (P)Survivor.

IS THIS LOVE (1987) (wm)David Coverdale—John Sykes. (P)White Snake.

IS YOU IS, OR IS YOU AIN'T (Ma' Baby) (1944) (wm)Billy Austin—Louis Jordan. (I)Film: *Follow The Boys*, by Louis Jordan. (P)Louis Jordan and his Tympani Five. (CR)The Delta Rhythm Boys.

I'SE A-MUGGIN' (1936) (wm)"Stuff" Smith. (P)Stuff Smith. (CR)Paul Whiteman and his Orchestra.

ISLAND GIRL (1975) (wm)Elton John—Bernie Taupin. (P)Elton John. No. 1 Chart Record.

ISLAND IN THE SUN (1956) (wm)Harry Belafonte—Irving Burgess. (I)Film: *Island In The Sun*, by Harry Belafonte. (P)Harry Belafonte.

ISLAND IN THE WEST INDIES (1936) (w)Ira Gershwin (m)Vernon Duke. (I)Revue: *Ziegfeld Follies of 1936*, by Gertrude Niesen.

ISLANDS IN THE STREAM (1983) (wm)Barry, Robin, and Maurice Gibb. (P)Kenny Rogers and Dolly Parton. No. 1 Chart Record.

ISLE OF CAPRI (1934) (w)Jimmy Kennedy (m)Will Grosz. (I)England, by Lew Stone and his Orchestra, vocal by Nat Gonella. (I)United States, by Guy Lombardo and his Royal Canadians. (P)Wingy Manone. (CR)Xavier Cugat and his Orchestra. (R)1954 by The

Gaylords.

ISN'T IT A PITY? (1932) (w)Ira Gershwin (m)George Gershwin. (I)Musical: *Pardon My English*, by George Givot and Josephine Houston.

ISN'T IT A PITY (1970) (wm)George Harrison. (P)George Harrison.

ISN'T IT KINDA FUN (1945) (w)Oscar Hammerstein II (m)Richard Rodgers. (I)Film: *State Fair*, by Dick Haymes and Vivian Blaine. (R)1962 Film: *State Fair*, by Ann—Margret and David Street.

ISN'T IT ROMANTIC? (1932) (w)Lorenz Hart (m)Richard Rodgers. (I)Film: *Love Me Tonight*, by Maurice Chevalier, Jeanette MacDonald, Bert Roach, Rolf Sedan, and Tyler Brook. (P)Harold Stern and his Orchestra.

ISN'T IT TIME (1977) (wm)Ray Kennedy—Jack Conrad. (P)The Babys.

ISN'T LIFE STRANGE (1972) (wm)John Lodge. (P)The Moody Blues.

ISN'T SHE LOVELY (1976) (wm)Stevie Wonder. (P)Stevie Wonder.

ISN'T THAT JUST LIKE LOVE (1940) (w)Johnny Burke (m)Jimmy Van Heusen. (I)Film: *Love Thy Neighbor*, by Mary Martin and The Merry Macs.

ISN'T THIS A LOVELY DAY (1935) (wm)Irving Berlin. (I)Film: *Top Hat*, by Fred Astaire. (P)Fred Astaire. (CR)Phil Ohman and his Orchestra.

ISRAELITES (1969) (wm)Desmond Dacres—Leslie Kong. (P)Desmond Dekker and The Aces.

ISTANBUL, NOT CONSTANTINOPLE (1953) (w)Jimmy Kennedy (m)Nat Simon. (P)The Four Lads.

"IT" (1926) (w)Otto Harbach—Oscar Hammerstein II (m)Sigmund Romberg. (I)Operetta: *The Desert Song*, by Eddie Buzzell and Nellie Breen. In film version (1929) by Louise Fazenda and Johnny Arthur.

IT AIN'T ENOUGH (1984) (wm)Corey Hart. (P)Corey Hart.

IT AIN'T GONNA RAIN NO MO' (1923) (wm)Wendell Hall. (P)Wendell Hall.

IT AIN'T ME, BABE (1964) (wm)Bob Dylan. (P)Bob Dylan. (CR)Johnny Cash. (CR)The Turtles.

IT AIN'T NECESSARILY SO (1935) (w)Ira Gershwin (m)George Gershwin. (I)Opera: *Porgy And Bess*, by John W. Bubbles. (R)1959 film version, by Sammy Davis, Jr.

IT ALL COMES BACK TO ME NOW (1940) (wm)Hy Zaret—Joan Whitney—Alex Kramer. (P)Hal Kemp and his Orchestra. (CR)Ted Weems and his Orchestra.

IT ALL DEPENDS ON YOU (1926) (w)B.G. De Sylva—Lew Brown (m)Ray Henderson. (I)Musical: *Big Boy*, by Al Jolson. Recorded by Paul Whiteman and his Orchestra. (CR)Ben Bernie and his Orchestra. (R)1955 Film: *Love Me Or Leave Me*, by Doris Day. (R)1956 Film: *The Best Things In Life Are Free*, by Sheree North and Gordon MacRae.

IT CAME UPON A MIDNIGHT CLEAR (1850) (w)Edmund Hamilton Sears (m)Richard Storrs Willis. Famous Christmas hymn.

IT CAN'T BE WRONG (1942) (w)Kim Gannon (m)Max Steiner. (I)Film: *Now, Voyager* on soundtrack. (P)Dick Haymes. No. 1 Chart Record.

IT COULD HAPPEN TO YOU (1944) (w)Johnny Burke (m)Jimmy Van Heusen. (I)Film: *And The Angels Sing*, by Dorothy Lamour and Fred MacMurray. (P)Jo Stafford. (CR)Bing Crosby.

IT DOESN'T MATTER ANY MORE (1959) (wm)Paul Anka. (P)Buddy Holly. (R)1975 by Linda Ronstadt.

IT DON'T COME EASY (1971) (wm)Richard Starkey (Ringo Starr) (P)Ringo Starr.

IT DON'T MATTER TO ME (1970) (wm)David Gates. (P)Bread.

IT DON'T MEAN A THING (If It Ain't Got That Swing) (1932) (w)Irving Mills (m)Duke Ellington. (P)Duke Ellington and his Orchestra, vocal by Ivie Anderson.

IT DON'T WORRY ME (1975) (wm)Keith Carradine. (I)Film: *Nashville*, by Barbara Harris.

IT GETS LONELY IN THE WHITE HOUSE (1962) (wm)Irving Berlin. (I)Musical: *Mr. President*, by Robert Ryan.

IT GOES LIKE IT GOES (1979) (w)Norman Gimbel (m)David Shire. (I)Film: *Norma Rae*, by voice of Jennifer Warnes. (P)Jennifer Warnes.Academy Award Winner.

IT GOES LIKE THIS (That Funny Melody) (1928) (w)Irving Caesar (m)Cliff Friend. (P)Johnny Johnson.

IT HAD TO BE YOU (1924) (w)Gus Kahn (m)Isham Jones. (I)Isham Jones and his Orchestra. (P)Cliff Edwards. (CR)Paul Whiteman and his Orchestra. (R)1941 by Artie Shaw. (R)1944 by Helen Forrest and Dick Haymes. (R)1951 Film: *I'll See You In My Dreams*, by Danny Thomas.

IT HAPPENED IN MONTEREY (1930) (w)Billy Rose (m)Mabel Wayne. (I)Film: *King Of Jazz*, by John Boles and Jeanette Loff. (P)Paul Whiteman and his Orchestra. (CR)Ruth Etting.

IT HAPPENED IN SUN VALLEY (1941) (w)Mack Gordon (m)Harry Warren. (I)Film: *Sun Valley Serenade*, by The Chorus.

IT HAPPENS EVERY SPRING (1949) (w)Mack Gordon (m)Josef Myrow. (I)Film: *It Happens Every Spring* on soundtrack. (P)Frank Sinatra.

IT HURTS TO BE IN LOVE (1964) (wm)Howard Greenfield—Helen Miller. (P)Gene Pitney. (R)1981 by Dan Hartman.

IT IS NO SECRET WHAT GOD CAN DO (1951) (wm)Stuart Hamblen. (P)Stuart Hamblen. (CR)Jo Stafford.

IT ISN'T FAIR (1933) (wm)Richard Himber—Frank Warshauer—Sylvester Sprigato. (I)Richard Himber and his Orchestra. (R)1950 by Sammy Kaye and his Orchestra, vocal by Don Cornell.

IT ISN'T RIGHT (1956) (wm)Robert Mellin. (P)The Platters.

IT KEEPS RIGHT ON A-HURTIN' SINCE I LEFT (1962) (wm)Johnny Tillotson—Lorene Mann. (P)Johnny Tillotson.

IT KEEPS YOU RUNNING (1976) (wm)Michael McDonald. (P)Carly Simon. (CR)The Doobie Brothers.

IT LOOKS LIKE RAIN IN CHERRY BLOSSOM LANE (1937) (wm)Edgar Leslie—Joe Burke. (P)Guy Lombardo and his Royal Canadians. No. 1 Chart Record. (CR)Shep Fields and his Orchestra

IT MAY SOUND SILLY (1954) (wm)Ivory Joe Hunter. (I)Ivory Joe Hunter. (P)The McGuire Sisters.

IT MIGHT AS WELL BE SPRING (1945) (w)Oscar Hammerstein II (m)Richard Rodgers. (I)Film: *State Fair*, by Louanne Hogan dubbing for Jeanne Crain. Academy Award Winner. (P)Dick Haymes. (R)1962 Film: *State Fair*, by Anita Gordon dubbing for Pamela Tiffin.

IT MIGHT AS WELL RAIN UNTIL SEPTEMBER (1962)

(wm)Gerry Goffin—Carole King. (P)Carole King.

IT MIGHT BE YOU (1982) (w)Alan and Marilyn Bergman (m)Dave Grusin. (I)Film: *Tootsie*, by voice of Stephen Bishop. (P)Stephen Bishop.

IT MIGHT HAVE BEEN (1942) (wm)Cole Porter. (I)Film: *Something To Shout About.* by Janet Blair.

IT MUST BE HIM (1967) (w-Eng)Mack David (m)Gilbert Becaud. (I)Gilbert Becaud. (P)Vicki Carr.

IT MUST BE JELLY ('Cause Jam Don't Shake Like That) (1942) (w)Sunny Skylar (m)George Williams—Chummy MacGregor. (P)Glenn Miller and his Orchestra.

IT MUST BE TRUE (1930) (w)Gus Arnheim—Gordon Clifford (m)Harry Barris. (P)Bing Crosby with The Rhythm Boys and Gus Arnheim and his Orchestra.

IT MUST BE YOU (1930) (w)Roy Turk (m)Fred E. Ahlert. (I)Film: *Free And Easy*, by Robert Montgomery.

IT NEVER ENTERED MY MIND (1940) (w)Lorenz Hart (m)Richard Rodgers. (I)Musical: *Higher And Higher*, by Shirley Ross. Most popular recording by Frank Sinatra.

IT NEVER RAINS IN SOUTHERN CALIFORNIA (1972) (wm)Albert Hammond—Mike Hazelwood. (P)Albert Hammond.

IT NEVER WAS YOU (1938) (w)Maxwell Anderson (m)Kurt Weill. (I)Musical: *Knickerbocker Holiday*, by Richard Kollmar and Jeanne Madden. (R)1963 film: *I Could Go On Singing*, by Judy Garland.

IT ONLY HAPPENS WHEN I DANCE WITH YOU (1947) (wm)Irving Berlin. (I)Film: *Easter Parade*, by Fred Astaire. (P)Fred Astaire. (CR)Frank Sinatra.

IT ONLY HURTS FOR A LITTLE WHILE (1956) (w)Mack David (m)Fred Spielman. (P)The Ames Brothers. (R)1978 by Margo Smith.

IT ONLY TAKES A MINUTE (1975) (wm)Dennis Lambert—Brian Potter. (P)Tavares.

IT ONLY TAKES A MOMENT (1964) (wm)Jerry Herman. (I)Musical: *Hello, Dolly!*, by Charles Nelson Reilly, Eileen Brennan and The Company.

IT SEEMS LIKE OLD TIMES (1937) (wm)Charles Tobias—Sam H. Stept. (P)Guy Lombardo and his Royal Canadians.Theme song of Arthur Godfrey. (R)1956 by The McGuire Sisters.

IT SEEMS TO BE SPRING (1930) (w)George Marion, Jr. (m)Richard A. Whiting. (I)Film: *Let's Go Native*, by Jeanette MacDonald and James Hall.

IT STARTED ALL OVER AGAIN (1942) (w)Bill Carey (m)Carl Fischer. (P)Tommy Dorsey and his Orchestra, vocal by Frank Sinatra.

IT TAKES A LOT TO LAUGH, IT TAKES A TRAIN TO CRY (1965) (wm)Bob Dylan. (P)Bob Dylan.

IT TAKES A WOMAN (1964) (wm)Jerry Herman. (I)Musical: *Hello, Dolly!* by David Burns and The Company.

IT TAKES TIME (1947) (wm)Arthur Korb. (P)Benny Goodman and his Orchestra, vocal by Johnny Mercer.

IT TAKES TWO (1967) (wm)William Stevenson—Sylvia Moy. (P)Marvin Gaye and Kim Weston.

IT TAKES TWO TO MAKE A BARGAIN (1935) (wm)Mack Gordon—Harry Revel. (I)Film: *Two For Tonight*, by Bing Crosby. (P)Bing Crosby.

IT TEARS ME UP (1966) (wm)Dan Penn—Dewey Lindon Oldham. (P)Percy Sledge.

IT WAS A NIGHT IN JUNE (1933) (w)Mack Gordon (m)Harry Revel. (P)Anson Weeks and his Orchestra.

IT WAS A VERY GOOD YEAR (1961) (wm)Ervin Drake.

(I)The Kingston Trio. (P)Frank Sinatra.NARAS Award Winner.

IT WAS ALMOST LIKE A SONG (1977) (w)Hal David (m)Archie Jordan. (P)Ronnie Milsap.

IT WAS ALWAYS YOU (1961) (wm)Bob Merrill. (I)Musical: *Carnival!*, by Kaye Ballard and James Mitchell.

IT WAS I (1959) (wm)Gary Paxton. (P)Skip and Flip.

IT WAS ONLY A SUN SHOWER (1927) (w)Irving Kahal—Francis Wheeler (m)Ted Snyder. (P)Ted Weems and his Orchestra.

IT WAS SO BEAUTIFUL (1932) (w)Arthur Freed (m)Harry Barris. (P)Harry Richman. (CR)Ruth Etting. (CR)Enric Madriguera and his Orchestra.

IT WAS WRITTEN IN THE STARS (1948) (wm)Cole Porter. (I)Musical: *Du Barry Was A Lady*, by Ronald Graham.

IT WAS WRITTEN IN THE STARS (1948) (w)Leo Robin (m)Harold Arlen. (I)Film: *Casbah*, by Tony Martin.

IT WON'T BE LONG (1963) (wm)John Lennon—Paul McCartney. (P)The Beatles.

IT WOULD HAVE BEEN WONDERFUL (1973) (wm)Stephen Sondheim. (I)Musical: *A Little Night Music*, by Len Cariou and Lawrence Guittard.

IT'S A PITY TO SAY GOODNIGHT (1946) (wm)Billy Reid. (P)Ella Fitzgerald with The Delta Rhythm Boys.

ITALIAN THEME, THE (1956) (w-Eng)Buddy Kaye (m)Angelo Giacomazzi—Clyde Hamilton.

ITCHY TWITCHY FEELING (1958) (wm)James Oliver. (P)Bobby Hendricks.

ITCHYCOO PARK (1967) (wm)Steve Marriott—Ronnie Lane. (P)The Small Faces.

IT'S A BIG WIDE WONDERFUL WORLD (1940) (wm)John Rox. (I)Revue: *All In Fun*, by Wynn Murray and Walter Cassell. (P)Buddy Clark.

IT'S A BLUE WORLD (1939) (wm)Robert Wright—Chet Forrest. (I)Film: *Music In My Heart*, by Tony Martin. (P)Tony Martin. (CR)Glenn Miller and his Orchestra.

IT'S A BOY (Overture From Tommy) (1969) (wm)Peter Townshend. (I)Rock opera: *Tommy*, by The Who. (P)The Assembled Multitude.

IT'S A CHEMICAL REACTION (1955) (wm)Cole Porter. (I)Musical: *Silk Stockings*, by Hildegarde Neff.

IT'S A GOOD DAY (1946) (wm)Peggy Lee—Dave Barbour. (P)Peggy Lee.

IT'S A GRAND NIGHT FOR SINGING (1945) (w)Oscar Hammerstein II (m)Richard Rodgers. (I)Film: *State Fair*, by The Cast. (P)Dick Haymes. (R)1962 Film: *State Fair*, by Pat Boone, Bobby Darin, and Anita Gordon dubbing for Pamela Tiffin and The Chorus.

IT'S A GREAT BIG WORLD (1946) (w)Johnny Mercer (m)Harry Warren. (I)Film: *The Harvey Girls*, by Virginia O'Brien and Betty Russell.

IT'S A GREAT DAY FOR THE IRISH (1940) (wm)Roger Edens. (I)Film: *Little Nellie Kelly*, by Judy Garland and Douglas MacPhail. (P)Freddy Martin and his Orchestra.

IT'S A GREAT FEELING (1949) (w)Sammy Cahn (m)Jule Styne. (I)Film: *It's A Great Feeling*, by Doris Day.

IT'S A GREAT LIFE (If You Don't Weaken) (1930) (w)Leo Robin (m)Richard A. Whiting—Newell Chase. (I)Film: *Playboy Of Paris*, by Maurice Chevalier. (P)Maurice Chevalier.

IT'S A HEARTACHE (1978) (wm)Ronnie Scott—Steve Wolfe. (P)Bonnie Tyler. (CR)Juice Newton.

IT'S A LAUGH (1978) (wm)Daryl Hall. (P)Hall and Oates.

IT'S A LONESOME OLD TOWN WHEN YOU'RE NOT

AROUND (1930) (wm)Charles Kisco—Harry Tobias. (P)Theme Song of Ben Bernie and his Orchestra.

IT'S A LONG LONG WAY TO TIPPERARY (1912) (wm)Jack Judge—Harry Williams. (I)Musical: *Chin Chin*. (P)John McCormack.

IT'S A LOVELY DAY TODAY (1950) (wm)Irving Berlin. (I)Musical: *Call Me Madam*, by Russell Nype and Galina Talva.

IT'S A LOVELY DAY TOMORROW (1939) (wm)Irving Berlin (I)Musical: *Louisiana Purchase*, by Irene Bordoni.

IT'S A MAD, MAD, MAD, MAD WORLD (1963) (w)Mack David (m)Ernest Gold. (I)Film: *It's A Mad, Mad, Mad, Mad World* on soundtrack.

IT'S A MAN'S, MAN'S, MAN'S WORLD (But It Wouldn't Be Without A Woman) (1966) (wm)James Brown—Betty Jean Newsome. (P)James Brown.

IT'S A MIRACLE (1975) (wm)Barry Manilow—Marty Panzer. (P)Barry Manilow.

IT'S A MIRACLE (1984) (wm)George O'Dowd—Jon Moss—Roy Hay—Mickey Craig—Phil Pickett. (P)Culture Club.

IT'S A MISTAKE (1983) (wm)Colin Hay. (P)Men At Work.

IT'S A MOST UNUSUAL DAY (1948) (w)Harold Adamson (m)Jimmy McHugh. (I)Film: *A Date With Judy*, by Jane Russell. (P)Ray Noble and his Orchestra.

IT'S A NEW WORLD (1954) (w)Ira Gershwin (m)Harold Arlen. (I)Film: *A Star Is Born*, by Judy Garland.

IT'S A SHAME (1970) (wm)Stevie Wonder—Lee Garrett—Syreeta Wright. (P)The Spinners.

IT'S A SIN (1987) (wm)N. Tennant—C. Lowe. (P)Pet Shop Boys.

IT'S A SIN TO TELL A LIE (1936) (wm)Billy Mayhew. (I)Kate Smith. (P)Fats Waller. No. 1 Chart Record. (R)1955 by Something Smith and The Redheads.

IT'S A SIN WHEN YOU LOVE SOMEBODY (1975) (wm)Jim Webb. (P)Joe Cocker.

IT'S A WOMAN'S WORLD (1954) (w)Sammy Cahn (m)Cyril Mockridge. (I)Film: *Woman's World*, by the voices of The Four Aces. (P)The Four Aces.

IT'S A WONDERFUL WORLD (1939) (w)Harold Adamson (m)Jan Savitt—Johnny Watson. (P)Theme Song of Jan Savitt and his Orchestra.

IT'S ALL DOWN TO GOODNIGHT VIENNA (1975) (wm)John Lennon. (P)Ringo Starr.

IT'S ALL IN THE GAME (1951) (w)Carl Sigman (m)Charles Gates Dawes. Dawes was the Vice President of The United States from 1925—1929. (P)Tommy Edwards. No. 1 Chart Record. (R)1963 by Cliff Richard. (R)1970 by The Four Tops.

IT'S ALL OVER NOW, BABY BLUE (1965) (wm)Bob Dylan. (P)Bob Dylan. (CR)Joan Baez.

IT'S ALL RIGHT! (1963) (wm)Curtis Mayfield. (P)The Impressions.

IT'S ALL RIGHT WITH ME (1953) (wm)Cole Porter. (I)Musical: *Can-Can*, by Peter Cookson. Most popular recording by Frank Sinatra.

IT'S ALL TOO MUCH (1968) (wm)George Harrison. (I)Film: *Yellow Submarine*, by The Beatles. (P)The Beatles.

IT'S ALMOST TOMORROW (1955) (w)Wade Buff (m)Eugene H. Adkinson. (I)Snooky Lanson. (P)The Dream Weavers. (CR)Jo Stafford.

IT'S ALRIGHT (1965) (wm)Chris Andrews. (P)Adam Faith.

IT'S ALRIGHT, MA (I'm Only Bleeding) (1965) (wm)Bob Dylan. (P)Bob Dylan.

IT'S ALWAYS FAIR WEATHER WHEN GOOD FELLOWS GET TOGETHER (1898) (w)Richard Hovey (m)Frederic Field Bullard. Famous American stein song.

IT'S ALWAYS YOU (1941) (w)Johnny Burke (m)Jimmy Van Heusen. (I)Film: *Road To Zanzibar*, by Bing Crosby. (P)Tommy Dorsey and his Orchestra, vocal by Frank Sinatra.

IT'S AN OLD SOUTHERN CUSTOM (1935) (w)Jack Yellen (m)Joseph Meyer. (I)Film: *George White's 1935 Scandals*, by Alice Faye, James Dunn, and Cliff Edwards.

IT'S ANYBODY'S SPRING (1945) (w)Johnny Burke (m)Jimmy Van Heusen. (I)Film: *Road To Utopia*, by Bing Crosby.

IT'S BEEN A LONG, LONG TIME (1945) (w)Sammy Cahn (m)Jule Styne. (I)Phil Brito. (P)Harry James and his Orchestra, vocal by Kitty Kallen. (CR)Bing Crosby with Les Paul. (CR)Charlie Spivak and his Orchestra.

IT'S BEEN SO LONG (1936) (w)Harold Adamson (m)Walter Donaldson. (P)Benny Goodman and his Orchestra, vocal by Helen Ward.

IT'S BEGINNING TO LOOK LIKE CHRISTMAS (1951) (wm)Meredith Willson. (P)Perry Como.

IT'S BETTER WITH A UNION MAN (1940) (wm)Harold Rome. (I)Revue: *Pins And Needles*, by Berni Gould, Harry Clark, Ella Gerber and The Ensemble.

IT'S DARK ON OBSERVATORY HILL (1934) (w)Johnny Burke (m)Harold Spina. (P)Ozzie Nelson and his Orchestra, vocal by Harriet Hilliard.

IT'S DELIGHFUL DOWN IN CHILE (1949) (w)Leo Robin (m)Jule Styne. (I)Musical: *Gentlemen Prefer Blondes*, by Carol Channing and Rex Evans.

IT'S DELIGHTFUL TO BE MARRIED (1907) (w)Anna Held (m)Vincent Scotto. (I)Musical: *The Parisian Model*.

IT'S D'LOVELY (1936) (wm)Cole Porter. (I)Musical: *Red, Hot And Blue*, by Ethel Merman and Bob Hope. (P)Ethel Merman. (R)Film: *Anything Goes*, by Mitzi Gaynor and Donald O'Connor.

IT'S EASY TO REMEMBER (1935) (w)Lorenz Hart (m)Richard Rodgers. (I)Film: *Mississippi*, by Bing Crosby. (P)Bing Crosby. No. 1 Chart Record.

IT'S EASY TO SAY (1979) (w)Robert Wells (m)Henry Mancini. (I)Film: *10* by Dudley Moore.

IT'S ECSTASY WHEN YOU LAY DOWN NEXT TO ME (1977) (wm)Nelson Pigford—Ekundayo Paris. (P)Barry White.

IT'S EVERY GIRL'S AMBITION (1931) (w)Edward Heyman (m)Vincent Youmans. (I)Musical: *Through The Years*, by Martha Mason.

IT'S FOR YOU (1964) (wm)John Lennon—Paul McCartney. (P)Cilla Black.

IT'S FUNNY TO EVERYONE BUT ME (1939) (wm)Jack Lawrence. (P)Harry James and his Orchestra, vocal by Frank Sinatra.

IT'S GETTING BETTER (1969) (wm)Barry Mann—Cynthia Weil. (P)Mama Cass Elliot.

IT'S GOING TO TAKE SOME TIME (1971) (wm)Carole King—Toni Stern. (P)The Carpenters.

IT'S GONNA BE ALL RIGHT (1965) (wm)Gerrard Marsden. (P)Gerry and The Pacemakers.

IT'S GONNA TAKE A MIRACLE (1965) (wm)Teddy Randazzo—Bobby Weinstein—Lou Stallman. (P)The Royalettes. (R)1982 by Deniece Williams.

IT'S GONNA WORK OUT FINE (1961) (wm)Rose Marie McCoy—Sylvia McKinney. (P)Ike and Tina Turner.

IT'S GOOD TO BE ALIVE (1957) (wm)Bob Merrill. (I)Musical: *New Girl In Town*, by Gwen Verdon.

IT'S GOT TO BE LOVE (1936) (w)Lorenz Hart (m)Richard Rodgers. (I)Musical: *On Your Toes*, by Ray Bolger and Doris Carson.

IT'S GROWING (1965) (wm)William Robinson—Warren Moore. (P)The Temptations.

IT'S HIGH TIME (1957) (w)Leo Robin (m)Jule Styne. (I)Musical: *Gentlemen Prefer Blondes*, by Yvonne Adair.

IT'S IMPOSSIBLE (1971) (w-Eng)Sid Wayne (m)Armando Manzanero. (P)Perry Como.

IT'S IN THE BOOK (1952) (wm)Johnny Standley—Art Thorsen. (P)Johnny Standley. No. 1 Chart Record.

IT'S JUST A MATTER OF TIME (1959) (wm)Brook Benton—Belford Hendricks—Clyde Otis. (P)Brook Benton. (R)1970 by Sonny James.

IT'S KIND OF LONESOME OUT TONIGHT (1947) (w)Don George (m)Duke Ellington. (P)The King Cole Trio.

IT'S LATE (1959) (wm)Dorsey Burnette. (P)Rick Nelson.

IT'S LIKE TAKIN' CANDY FROM A BABY (1948) (w)Bob Russell (m)Al Russell—Joel Cowan. (P)Tony Pastor and his Orchestra, vocal by Rosemary Clooney.

IT'S LOVE (1953) (w)Betty Comden—Adolph Green (m)Leonard Bernstein. (I)Musical: *Wonderful Town*, by Edith Adams and George Gaynes.

IT'S LOVE I'M AFTER (1936) (w)Sidney D. Mitchell (m)Lew Pollack. (I)Film: *Pigskin Parade*, by Judy Garland.

IT'S LOVE, LOVE, LOVE! (1944) (wm)Mack David—Joan Whitney—Alex Kramer. (P)Guy Lombardo and his Royal Canadians, vocal by Skip Nelson and The Lombardo Trio.

IT'S MAGIC (1948) (w)Sammy Cahn (m)Jule Styne. (I)Film: *Romance On The High Seas*, by Doris Day. (P)Doris Day. (CR)Dick Haymes. (CR)Vic Damone.

IT'S MAKE BELIEVE BALLROOM TIME (1940) (w)Mickey Stoner—Martin Block (m)Harold Green. (I)Theme song of disc jockey show: The Make Believe Ballroom on station WNEW in New York City. (P)Glenn Miller and his Orchestra, vocal by The Modernaires.

IT'S MY LIFE (1965) (wm)Roger Atkins—Carl D'Errico. (P)The Animals.

IT'S MY PARTY (1963) (wm)Herb Weiner—Wally Gold—John Gluck, Jr. (P)Leslie Gore. No. 1 Chart Record.

IT'S MY TURN (1980) (w)Carole Bayer Sager (m)Michael Masser. (I)Film: *It's My Turn*, on soundtrack. (P)Diana Ross.

IT'S NICE TO GET UP IN THE MORNING (1913) (wm)Sir Harry Lauder. (P)Sir Harry Lauder.

IT'S NOT EASY (1966) (wm)Mick Jagger—Keith Richard. (P)The Rolling Stones.

IT'S NOT FOR ME TO SAY (1957) (w)Al Stillman (m)Robert Allen. (I)Film: *Lizzie*, on soundtrack. (P)Johnny Mathis.

IT'S NOT OVER ('Til It's Over) (1987) (wm)R. Nevil—J. Van Tongeren—P. Galdston. (P)Starship.

IT'S NOT UNUSUAL (1965) (wm)Gordon Mills—Les Reed. (P)Tom Jones.

IT'S NOT WHERE YOU START (1972) (w)Dorothy Fields (m)Cy Coleman. (I)Musical: *Seesaw*, by Tommy Tune and The Company.

IT'S NOW OR NEVER (1960) (wm)Aaron Schroeder—Wally Gold. Based on O Solo Mio. (P)Elvis Presley.

No. 1 Chart Record.

IT'S NOW WINTER'S DAY (1967) (wm)Tommy Roe. (P)Tommy Roe.

IT'S ONLY A PAPER MOON (1933) (w)Billy Rose—E. Y. Harburg (m)Harold Arlen. (I)Film: *Take A Chance*, by June Knight and Buddy Rogers. (P)Nat "King" Cole. (CR)The Mills Brothers. (R)1945 by Benny Goodman and his Orchestra.

IT'S ONLY LOVE (1965) (wm)John Lennon—Paul McCartney. (I)The Beatles. (P)Tommy James and The Shondells.

IT'S ONLY LOVE (1969) (wm)Mark James—Steve Tyrell. (P)B.J. Thomas. (R)1971 by Elvis Presley.

IT'S ONLY LOVE (1985) (wm)Bryan Adams—Jim Valance. (P)Bryan Adams and Tina Turner.

IT'S ONLY MAKE BELIEVE (1958) (wm)Conway Twitty—Jack Nance. (P)Conway Twitty. No. 1 Chart Record. (R)1970 by Glen Campbell.

IT'S ONLY ROCK 'N' ROLL (But I Like It) (1974) (wm)Mick Jagger—Keith Richard. (P)The Rolling Stones.

IT'S OVER (1964) (wm)Roy Orbison—Bill Dees. (P)Roy Orbison.

IT'S RAINING AGAIN (1982) (wm)Rick Davies—Roger Hodgson. (P)Supertramp.

IT'S RAINING SUNBEAMS (1937) (w)Sam Coslow (m)Frederick Hollander. (I)Film: *100 Men And A Girl*, by Deanna Durbin.

IT'S SAD TO BELONG (1977) (wm)Randy Goodrum. (P)England Dan & John Ford Coley.

IT'S SO EASY (1958) (wm)Buddy Holly—Norman Petty. (P)Buddy Holly. (R)1977 by LInda Ronstadt.

IT'S SO NICE TO HAVE A MAN AROUND THE HOUSE. (1950) (w)Jack Elliott (m)Harold Spina. (P)Dinah Shore.

IT'S SO PEACEFUL IN THE COUNTRY (1941) (wm)Alec Wilder. (P)Mildred Bailey with The Delta Rhythm Boys.

IT'S STILL ROCK AND ROLL TO ME (1980) (wm)Billy Joel. (P)Billy Joel. No. 1 Chart Record.

IT'S SWELL OF YOU (1937) (w)Mack Gordon (m)Harry Revel. (I)Film: *Wake Up And Live*, by Buddy Clark dubbing for Jack Haley.

IT'S THE ANIMAL IN ME (1935) (w)Mack Gordon (m)Harry Revel. (I)The Big Broadcast of 1936, by Ethel Merman.

IT'S THE DREAMER IN ME (1938) (wm)Jimmy Dorsey—Jimmy Van Heusen. (P)Jimmy Dorsey and his Orchestra.

IT'S THE GIRL (1931) (w)Dave Oppenheim (m)Abel Baer. (P)The Boswell Sisters.

IT'S THE LITTLE THINGS IN TEXAS (1962) (wm)Richard Rodgers. (I)Film: *State Fair*, by Tom Ewell and Alice Faye.

IT'S THE NATURAL THING TO DO (1937) (w)Johnny Burke (m)Arthur Johnston. (I)Film: *Double Or Nothing*, by Bing Crosby. (P)Bing Crosby. (CR)Mildred Bailey.

IT'S THE SAME OLD DREAM (1947) (w)Sammy Cahn (m)Jule Styne. (I)Film: *It Happened In Brooklyn*, by Frank Sinatra. (P)Frank Sinatra.

IT'S THE SAME OLD SHILLELAGH (1940) (wm)Pat White. (P)Bing Crosby.

IT'S THE SAME OLD SONG (1965) (wm)Eddie Holland—Lamont Dozier—Brian Holland. (P)The Four Tops. (R)1978 by K.C. & The Sunshine Band.

IT'S THE STRANGEST THING (1977) (w)Fred Ebb (m)John Kander. (I)Musical: *The Act*, by Liza Minnelli.

IT'S THE TALK OF THE TOWN (1933) (w)Marty Symes—Al Neiberg (m)Jerry Livingston. (P)Glen Gray and The Casa Loma Orchestra, vocal by Kenny Sargent. (CR)Fletcher Henderson and his Orchestra.

IT'S TIME TO CRY (1959) (wm)Paul Anka. (P)Paul Anka.

IT'S TOO LATE (1971) (w)Toni Stern (m)Carole King. (P)Carole King. No. 1 Chart Record. NARAS Award Winner.

IT'S TOO SOON TO KNOW (1947) (wm)Deborah Chessler. (P)The Orioles. (CR)Dinah Washington. (R)1958 by Pat Boone. (R)1961 by Etta James. (CR)1966 by Roy Orbison.

IT'S UP TO YOU (1963) (wm)Jerry Fuller. (P)Rick Nelson.

IT'S WONDERFUL (1967) (w)Felix Cavaliere (m)Edward Brigati, Jr. (P)The Rascals.

IT'S YOU (1957) (wm)Meredith Willson. (I)Musical: *The Music Man*, by The Buffalo Bills.

IT'S YOU I LOVE (1957) (wm)Antoine Domino—Dave Bartholomew. (P)Fats Domino.

IT'S YOU OR NO ONE (1948) (w)Sammy Cahn (m)Jule Styne. (I)Film: *Romance On The High Seas*, by Doris Day. (P)Doris Day.

(LONELINESS MADE ME REALIZE)IT'S YOU THAT I NEED (1967) (wm)Norman Whitfield—Eddie Holland. (P)The Temptations.

IT'S YOUR THING (1969) (wm)Rudolph, Ronald, and O'-Kelly Isley. (P)The Isley Brothers.

ITALIAN STREET SONG (1910) (w)Rida Johnson Young (m)Victor Herbert. (I)Musical: *Naughty Marietta*. (P)Lucy Isabelle Marsh and The Victor Light Opera Company.

ITSY BITSY TEENIE WEENIE YELLOW POLKADOT BIKINI (1960) (wm)Paul J. Vance—Lee Pockriss. (P)Brian Hyland. No. 1 Chart Record.

I'VE A STRANGE NEW RHYTHM IN MY HEART (1937) (wm)Cole Porter. (I)Film: *Rosalie*, by Eleanor Powell.

I'VE BEEN HERE! (1966) (w-Eng)Earl Shuman (m)Charles Dumont. (P)Barbra Streisand.

I'VE BEEN IN LOVE BEFORE (1940) (w)Frank Loesser (m)Frederick Hollander. (I)Film: *Seven Sinners*, by Marlene Dietrich.

I'VE BEEN IN LOVE BEFORE (1987) (wm)N. Eede. (P)Cutting Crew.

I'VE BEEN INVITED TO A PARTY (1963) (wm)Noel Coward. (I)Musical: *The Girl Who Came To Supper*, by Florence Henderson.

I'VE BEEN LONELY TOO LONG (1967) (wm)Felix Cavaliere—Edward Brigati, Jr. (P)The Rascals.

I'VE BEEN LOVING YOU TOO LONG (1965) (wm)Otis Redding—Jerry Butler. (P)Otis Redding. (R)1969 by Ike and Tina Turner.

I'VE BEEN THIS WAY BEFORE (1975) (wm)Neil Diamond. (P)Neil Diamond.

I'VE BEEN WORKING ON THE RAILROAD (1894) (wm)Unknown. Traditional American folk song.

I'VE COME OF AGE (1959) (w)Sid Jacobson (m)Lou Stallman. (P)Billy Storm.

I'VE COME TO WIVE IT WEALTHILY IN PADUA. (1948) (wm)Cole Porter. (I)Musical: *Kiss Me Kate*, by Alfred Drake. (R)1953 in film version, by Howard Keel.

I'VE DONE EVERYTHING FOR YOU (1981) (wm)Rick Springfield. (P)Rick Springfield.

I'VE FOUND A NEW BABY (1926) (wm)Jack Palmer—Spencer Williams. (I)Clarence Williams' Blue Five. (P)Ted Lewis and his Orchestra. (CR)Ethel Waters. (R)1937 by Benny Goodman and his Orchestra.

I'VE FOUND SOMEONE OF MY OWN (1971) (wm)Frank K. Robinson. (P)Free Movement.

I'VE GONE ROMANTIC ON YOU (1937) (w)E. Y. Harburg (m)Harold Arlen. (I)Musical: *Hooray For What!*, by Jack Whiting and June Clyde.

I'VE GOT A CRUSH ON YOU (1928) (w)Ira Gershwin (m)George Gershwin. (I)Musical: *Treasure Girl*, by Clifton Webb and Mary Hay. (R)1952 Film: *Meet Danny Wilson*, by Frank Sinatra. (R)1955 Film: *Three For The Show*, by Betty Grable, Jack Lemmon, and Marge and Gower Champion. Most popular recording by Frank Sinatra.

I'VE GOT A DATE WITH A DREAM (1938) (w)Mack Gordon (m)Harry Revel. (I)Film: *My Lucky Star*, by Art Jarrett, Buddy Ebsen, Joan Davis, and The Girls. (P)Benny Goodman and his Orchestra. (CR)George Hall and his Orchestra.

I'VE GOT A FEELIN' YOU'RE FOOLIN' (1935) (w)Arthur Freed. (m)Nacio Herb Brown. (I)Film: *Broadway Melody of 1936*, by Robert Taylor, June Knight, and reprised by Frances Langford. (R)1952 Film: *With A Song In My Heart*, by Jane Froman dubbing for Susan Hayward.

I'VE GOT A FEELING I'M FALLING (1929) (w)Billy Rose (m)Harry Link—Thomas Waller. (P)Fats Waller.

I'VE GOT A GAL IN KALAMAZOO (1942) (w)Mack Gordon (m)Harry Warren. (I)Film: *Orchestra Wives*, by Glenn Miller and his Orchestra, vocal by Tex Beneke. (P)Glenn Miller. No. 1 Chart Record.

I'VE GOT A LOVELY BUNCH OF COCOANUTS (1949) (wm)Fred Heatherton. (I)Billy Cotton and his Orchestra (England). In United States, by Freddy Martin and his Orchestra, vocal by Merv Griffin. (CR)Danny Kaye.

I'VE GOT A ONE TRACK MIND (1944) (w)Howard Dietz (m)Vernon Duke. (I)Musical: *Jackpot*, by Allan Jones.

I'VE GOT A POCKETFUL OF DREAMS (1938) (w)Johnny Burke (m)James V. Monaco. (I)Film: *Sing You Sinners*, by Bing Crosby. (P)Bing Crosby. No. 1 Chart Record. (CR)Russ Morgan and his Orchestra.

I'VE GOT A POCKETFUL OF SUNSHINE (1935) (w)Gus Kahn (m)Arthur Johnston. (I)Film: *Thanks A Million* by Dick Powell.

I'VE GOT A ROCK AND ROLL HEART (1983) (wm)Troy Seals—Eddie Setser—Steve Diamond. (P)Eric Clapton.

I'VE GOT A TIGER BY THE TAIL (1965) (wm)Buck Owens—Harlan Howard. (P)Buck Owens.

I'VE GOT AN INVITATION TO A DANCE (1934) (wm)Marty Symes—Al Neiberg—Jerry Livingston. (P)Paul Pendarvis and his Orchestra.

I'VE GOT BONNIE (1961) (wm)Gerry Goffin—Carole King. (P)Bobby Rydell.

I'VE GOT FIVE DOLLARS (1931) (w)Lorenz Hart (m)Richard Rodgers. (I)Musical: *America's Sweetheart*, by Jack Whiting and Ann Sothern.Recorded by Emil Coleman and his Orchestra. (R)1955 Film: *Gentlemen Marry Brunettes*, by Jane Russell and Scott Brady.

I'VE GOT LOVE ON MY MIND (1977) (wm)Charles Jackson, Jr.—Marvin Yancy. (P)Natalie Cole.

I'VE GOT ME (1947) (w)John Latouche (m)Duke Ellington. (I)Musical: *Beggar's Holiday*, by Alfred Drake.

I'VE GOT MY CAPTAIN WORKING FOR ME NOW (1920) (wm)Irving Berlin. Not a hit when first released. (R)Film: *Blue Skies*, by Bing Crosby and Fred Astaire.

I'VE GOT MY EYES ON YOU (1939) (wm)Cole Porter. (I)Film: *Broadway Melody of 1940* by Fred Astaire. (P)Tommy Dorsey and his Orchestra. (CR)Bob Crosby and his Orchestra.

I'VE GOT MY EYES ON YOU (1954) (wm)Paul Winley. (P)The Clovers.

I'VE GOT MY FINGERS CROSSED (1935) (w)Ted Koehler (m)Jimmy McHugh. (I)Film: *King Of Burlesque*, by Fats Waller and Dixie Dunbar.

I'VE GOT MY LOVE TO KEEP ME WARM (1937) (wm)Irving Berlin. (I)Film: *On The Avenue*, by E.E. Clive, Dick Powell, and Alice Faye. Recorded by Billie Holiday, Ray Noble and his Orchestra, The Mills Brothers, Art Lund. (R)1949 by Les Brown and his Orchestra. No. 1 Chart Record.

I'VE GOT NO STRINGS (1940) (w)Ned Washington (m)Leigh Harline. (I)Cartoon film: *Pinocchio*, by voice of Dickie Jones.

I'VE GOT RINGS ON MY FINGERS (Bells On My Toes) (1909) (w)R.P. Weston (m)Maurice Scott. (I)Musical: *The Midnight Suns*. (P)Ada Jones. (R)1943 by Dick Kuhn and his Orchestra.

I'VE GOT SIXPENCE (1941) (wm)Box—Cox—Hall.Popular Marching Song of The Royal Air Force and The United States Army Air during World War II.

I'VE GOT THE MUSIC IN ME (1974) (wm)Bias Boshell. (P)Kiki Dee.

I'VE GOT THE WORLD ON A STRING (1932) (w)Ted Koehler (m)Harold Arlen. (I)Revue: *Cotton Club Parade*, by Aida Ward. (P)Cab Calloway. (CR)Bing Crosby. (R)1953 by Frank Sinatra.

I'VE GOT TO BE A RUG CUTTER (1937) (wm)Duke Ellington. (P)Duke Ellington and his Orchestra, vocal by Rex Stewart, Hayes Alvis, and Harry Carner.

I'VE GOT TO BE AROUND (1962) (wm)Irving Berlin. (I)Musical: *Mr. President*, by Javk Haskell.

I'VE GOT TO BE THERE (1933) (w)Ira Gershwin (m)George Gershwin. (I)Musical: *Pardon My English*, by Carl Randall and Barbara Newberry.

I'VE GOT TO CROW (1954) (w)Carolyn Leigh (m)Mark Charlap. (I)Musical: *Peter Pan*, by Mary Martin. (P)Eydie Gorme.

I'VE GOT TO GET HOT (1935) (w)Jack Yellen (m)Ray Henderson. (I)Revue: *George White's Scandals*, by Gracie Barrie.

I'VE GOT TO PASS YOUR HOUSE TO GET TO MY HOUSE (1933) (wm)Lew Brown. (I)Revue: *Paradise Revue*, by Gertrude Niesen. (P)Bing Crosby.

I'VE GOT TO SING A TORCH SONG (1933) (w)Al Dubin (m)Harry Warren. (I)Film: *Gold Diggers of 1933*, by Dick Powell. (P)Bing Crosby (CR)Hal Kemp and his Orchestra.

I'VE GOT TO USE MY IMAGINATION (1973) (wm)Gerry Goffin—Barry Goldberg. (P)Gladys Knight and The Pips.

I'VE GOT YOU ON MY MIND (1932) (wm)Cole Porter. (I)Musical: *Gay Divorcee*, by Fred Astaire and Claire Luce.

I'VE GOT YOU TO LEAN ON (1964) (wm)Stephen Sondheim. (I)Musical: *Anyone Can Whistle*, by Angela Lansbury, Gabe Dell, Arnold Soboloff, James Frawley, Sterling Clark, Harvey Evans, Larry Roquemore, and Tucker Smith.

I'VE GOT YOU UNDER MY SKIN (1936) (wm)Cole Porter. (I)Film: *Born To Dance*, by Virginia Bruce. (P)Hal Kemp and his Orchestra. Most popular recording by Frank Sinatra. (R)1946 Film: *Night And Day*, by Ginny Simms. (R)1966 by The Four Seasons.

I'VE GOT YOUR NUMBER (1962) (w)Carolyn Leigh (m)Cy Coleman.)I)Musical: *Little Me*, by Swen Swenson.

I'VE GOTTA BE ME (1967) (wm)Walter Marks. (I)Musical: *Golden Rainbow*, by Steve Lawrence. (P)Sammy Davis, Jr.

I'VE GROWN ACCUSTOMED TO HER FACE (1956) (w)Alan Jay Lerner (m)Frederick Loewe. (I)Musical: *My Fair Lady*, by Rex Harrison.

I'VE HAD ENOUGH (1978) (wm)Paul McCartney. (P)Wings.

I'VE HAD IT (1959) (wm)Ray Ceroni—Carl Bonura (m)Ray Ceroni. (P)The Bell Notes. (R)1974 by Fanny.

I'VE HEARD THAT SONG BEFORE (1942) (w)Sammy Cahn (m)Jule Styne. (I)Film: *Youth On Parade*, by Frank Sinatra. (P)Harry James and his Orchestra, vocal by Helen Forrest. No. 1 Chart Record.

I'VE HITCHED MY WAGON TO A STAR (1937) (w)Johnny Mercer (m)Richard A. Whiting. (I)Film: *Hollywood Hotel*, by Dick Powell with Raymond Paige and his Orchestra.

I'VE JUST SEEN A FACE (1965) (wm)John Lennon—Paul McCartney. (P)The Beatles.

I'VE JUST SEEN HER (1962) (w)Lee Adams (m)Charles Strouse. (I)Musical: *All American*, by Ron Husmann.

I'VE LOST YOU (1970) (wm)Ken Howard—Alan Blaikley. (P)Elvis Presley.

I'VE NEVER BEEN IN LOVE BEFORE (1950) (wm)Frank Loesser. (I)Musical: *Guys And Dolls*, by Robert Alda and Isabel Bigley. In film version, by Marlon Brando.

I'VE NEVER BEEN TO ME (1982) (wm)Ron Miller—Ken Hirsh. (P)Charlene.

I'VE NEVER FORGOTTEN (w)Sammy Cahn (m)Jule Styne. (I)Film: *Earl Carroll's Sketchbook*, by Constance Moore.

I'VE ONLY MYSELF TO BLAME (1947) (wm)Redd Evans—Dave Mann. (P)Doris Day.

I'VE PASSED THIS WAY BEFORE (1966) (wm)James Dean—William Witherspoon. (P)Jimmy Ruffin.

I'VE STILL GOT MY HEALTH (1940) (wm)Cole Porter. (I)Musical: *Panama Hattie*, by Ethel Merman.

I'VE TOLD EVERY LITTLE STAR (1932) (w)Oscar Hammerstein II (m)Jerome Kern. (I)Musical: *Music In The Air*, by Walter Slezak. In film version, by Gloria Swanson. (R)1961 by Linda Scott.

IVORY TOWER (1956) (wm)Jack Fulton—Lois Steele. (P)Cathy Carr. (CR)Gale Storm. (CR)Otis Williams.

IVY (1947) (wm)Hoagy Carmichael. (I)Film: *Ivy*, on soundtrack. (P)Vic Damone. (CR)Jo Stafford. (CR)Dick Haymes.

JACK AND DIANE (1982) (wm)John Cougar Mellencamp. (P)John Cougar Mellencamp. No. 1 Chart Record.

JACK AND JILL (1978) (wm)Ray Parker, Jr. (P)Raydio.

JACK THE BEAR (1940) (m)Duke Ellington. (P)P/Duke Ellington.

JACK, YOU'RE DEAD (1947) (wm)Richard Miles—Walter Bishop. (P)Louis Jordan and his Tympani Five.

JACKIE BLUE (1975) (wm)Larry Lee—Steve Cash. (P)The Ozark Mountain Daredevils.

JACKSON (1967) (wm)Gaby Rodgers—Billy Edd Wheeler. (P)Johnny Cash and June Carter. (CR)Nancy Sinatra and Lee Hazlewood.

JACOB'S LADDER (1987) (wm)B. Hornsby—J. Hornsby. (P)Huey Lewis & The News. No. 1 Chart Record.

JA-DA (1918) (wm)Bob Carleton. (I)Musical: *Bran Pie*, by Beatrice Lillie. (P)Arthur Fields.

JAIL HOUSE BLUES (1923) (wm)Bessie Smith—Clarence Williams. (P)Bessie Smith.

JAILHOUSE ROCK (1957) (wm)Jerry Leiber—Mike Stoller. (I)Film: *Jailhouse Rock*, by Elvis Presley. (P)Elvis Presley. No. 1 Chart Record.

ELVIS PRESLEY

Another "what might have been" Decca story ...

Back in the early fifties we had an A&R man by the name of Paul Cohen. Paul built Decca's country division into a formidable force in the record industry and signed most of the major artists to the label; Red Foley, Ernest Tubb, Kitty Wells, Loretta Lynn, Webb Pierce, Brenda Lee, Patsy Cline, and many others. Paul had a friend in Memphis, Sam Phillips, who had a label called Sun Records. Sam needed money and offered to his friend, Paul Cohen, the contract to a young singer Phillips had recording for him. The price was $30,000. Cohen brought the deal back to New York, where it was turned down. Management felt that was too much money for a weird looking rock-a-billy singer.

And that's how Decca lost Elvis Presley. That kind of thinking permeated the company and many other good, commercially successful artists were lost because of that kind of lack of vision.

JAM UP AND JELLY TIGHT (1969) (wm)Tommy Roe—Freddy Weller. (P)Tommy Roe.

JAMAICA FAREWELL (1955) (wm)Lord Burgess (P)Harry Belafonte.

JAMBALAYA (On The Bayou) (1952) (wm)Hank Williams. (I)Hank Williams. (P)Jo Stafford. (R)1960 by Bobby Comstock. (R)1962 by Fats Domino. (R)1972 by Nitty Gritty Dirt Band. (R)1973 by Blue Ridge Rangers.

JAMES (Hold The Ladder Steady) (1962) (wm)John D. Loudermilk. (P)Sue Thompson.

JAMES BOND THEME, THE (1963) (m)Monty Norman. (I)Film: *Dr. No*, on soundtrack. (P)Billy Strange and his Orchestra.

JAMIE (1962) (wm)Barrett Strong—William Stevenson. (P)Eddie Holland.

JAMIE (1984) (wm)Ray Parker, Jr. (P)Ray Parker, Jr.

JAMMIN' ME (1987) (wm)Tom Petty—M. Campbell—Bob Dylan. (P)Tom Petty & The Heartbreakers.

JANE (1980) (wm)David Friedberg—Jim McPherson—Craig Chaquico— Paul Kantner. (P)Jefferson Starship.

JAPANESE SANDMAN, THE (1920) (w)Raymond B. Egan (m)Richard A. Whiting. (I)Nora Bayes. (P)Paul Whiteman and his Orchestra. (R)1935 by Benny Goodman.

JAPANSY (1927) (w)Alfred Bryan (m)John Klenner. (P)Jimmy Noone and his Orchestra.

JAVA (1958) (m)Freddy Friday—Allen Toussaint—Alvin Tyler. (I)Floyd Cramer. (R)1964 by Al Hirt and his Orchestra.

JAVA JIVE (1940) (w)Milton Drake (m)Ben Oakland. (P)The Ink Spots.

JAWS (Theme From) (1975) (m)John Williams. (I)Film: *Jaws*, on soundtrack.

JAZZ ME BLUES, THE (1921) (wm)Tom Delaney. (I)Lucille Hegamin. (P)The Original Dixieland Jazz Band. (R)1951 by Les Paul.

JAZZMAN (1974) (wm)Carole King—Donald Palmer. (P)Carole King.

JAZZNOCRACY (1934) (m)Will Hudson. (P)Jimmie Lunceford and his Orchestra.

JE VOUS AIME (1947) (wm)Sam Coslow. (I)Film: *Copacabana,*, by Andy Russell.

JEALOUS (1924) (w)Tommy Malie—Dick Finch (m)Little Jack Little. (P)Little Jack Little. (CR)Marion Harris. (R)1941 by The Andrews Sisters.

JEALOUS HEART (1944) (wm)Jenny Lou Carson. (I)Jenny Lou Carson. (R)1949 by Al Morgan. (CR)Hugo Winterhalter and his Orchestra. (R)1965 by Connie Francis.

JEALOUS KIND OF FELLOW (1969) (wm)Josephine Armstead—Garfield Green—Maurice Dollison—Rudolph Browner. (P)Garland Green.

JEALOUS LOVER (1960) (m)Charles Williams. (I)Film: *The Apartment*, on soundtrack. (P)Ferrante and Teicher.

JEALOUS OF YOU (1951) (w-Eng)Marjorie Harper. (m)Vittorio Mascheroni. (P)Connie Francis.

JEALOUSY (Jalousie) (1938) (w-Eng)Vera Bloom (m)Jacob Gade. Originally introduced in Denmark. (P)The Boston Pops Orchestra. (CR)Frankie Laine. (CR)Harry James and his Orchestra.

JEAN (1969) (wm)Rod McKuen. (I)Film: *The Prime Of Miss Jean Brodie*, by voice of Rod McKuen. (P)Oliver.

JEANIE WITH THE LIGHT BROWN HAIR (1854) (wm)Stephen Collins Foster. One of Foster's most popular songs.

JEANNINE, I DREAM OF LILAC TIME (1928) (w)L. Wolfe Gilbert (m)Nathaniel Shilkret. (I)Film: *Lilac Time*, on soundtrack. (P)Gene Austin. No. 1 Chart Record. (CR)John McCormack. (CR)Ben Selvin and his Orchestra.

JEANS ON (1977) (wm)David Dundas—Roger Greenaway. (P)David Dundas.

JEEPERS CREEPERS (1938) (w)Johnny Mercer (m)Harry Warren. (I)Film: *Going Places*, by Louis

Armstrong. (P)Louis Armstrong. (CR)Al Donahue and his Orchestra.

JEEP'S BLUES (1938) (m)Duke Ellington—Johnny Hodges. (I)Duke Ellington and his Orchestra. (P)Johnny Hodges and his Orchestra.

JENIFER JUNIPER (1968) (wm)Donovan Leitch. (P)Donovan.

JENNY (The Saga of Jenny) (1941) (w)Ira Gershwin (m)Kurt Weill. (I)Musical: *Lady In The Dark*, by Gertrude Lawrence. (R)1944 Film version, by Ginger Rogers.

JENNY, JENNY (1957) (wm)Enotris Johnson—Richard Penniman. (P)Little Richard.

JENNY, TAKE A RIDE (1965) (wm)E. Johnson—R. Penniman. (P)Mitch Ryder and The Detroit Wheels.

JEOPARDY (1983) (wm)Greg Kihn—Steven Wright. (P)The Greg Kihn Band.

JERK, THE (1964) (wm)Don Julian. (P)The Larks.

JERSEY BOUNCE (1942) (w)Robert B. Wright (m)Bobby Plater—Tiny Bradshaw—Edward Johnson. (P)Glenn Miller and his Orchestra. (CR)Benny Goodman and his Orchestra.

JERU (1954) (m)Gerry Mulligan. (P)Miles Davis and his Orchestra.

JESSE (1972) (wm)Janis Ian. (P)Roberta Flack.

JESSIE'S GIRL (1981) (wm)Rick Springfield. (P)Rick Springfield. No. 1 Chart Record.

JET (1951) (w)Bennie Benjamin—George Weiss (m)Harry Revel. (I)Les Baxter and his Orchestra. (P)Nat "King" Cole.

JET (1974) (wm)Paul and Linda McCartney. (P)Paul McCartney and Wings.

JET AIRLINER (1977) (wm)Paul Pena. (P)The Steve Miller Band.

JEZEBEL (1951) (wm)Wayne Shanklin. (P)Frankie Laine.

JIG-SAW PUZZLE (1968) (wm)Mick Jagger—Keith Richard. (P)The Rolling Stones.

JIG WALK (1925) (w)Jo Trent (m)Duke Ellington. (P)Duke Ellington and his Orchestra. This was Ellington's first recording.

JILTED (1954) (wm)Robert Colby—Dick Manning. (P)Teresa Brewer. (CR)Red Foley.

JIM (1941) (w)Nelson Shawn (m)Caesar Petrillo—Edward Ross. (I)Dinah Shore. (P)Jimmy Dorsey and his Orchestra, vocal by Helen O'Connell.

JIM DANDY (1925) (w)Jo Trent (m)Duke Ellington. (I)German Revue: *Chocolate Kiddies*, by Lottie Gee.

JIM DANDY (1957) (wm)Lincoln Chase. (P)LaVern Baker. (R)1974 by Black Oak Arkansas.

JIMINY CRICKET (1939) (w)Ned Washington (m)Leigh Harline. Promo Song for Cartoon Film: *Pinocchio*.

JIMMY CRACK CORN (The Blue Tail Fly) (1846) (wm)Daniel Decatur Emmett. Popular song during the Civil War.

JIMMY MACK (1967) (wm)Brian Holland—Lamont Dozier—Eddie Holland. (P)Martha And The Vandellas. (R)1986 by Sheena Easton.

(Look Out For)JIMMY VALENTINE (1911) (w)Edward Madden (m)Gus Edwards. (P)Gus Edwards.

JIMMY'S GIRL (1960) (wm)Paul J. Vance—Lee Pockriss. (P)Johnny Tillotson.

JINGLE BELL ROCK (1957) (wm)Joe Beal—Jim Boothe. (P)Bobby Helms. (R)1961 by Bobby Rydell and Chubby Checker.

JINGLE BELLS (1857) (wm)J. S. Pierpont. The traditional Christmas Favorite. (R)1935 by Benny Goodman. (R)1941 by Glenn Miller. (R)1943 by Bing Crosby and The Andrews Sisters. (R)1952 by Les Paul.

JINGLE JANGLE (1969) (wm)Jeff Barry—Andy Kim. (P)The Archies.

JINGLE JANGLE JINGLE (1942) (w)Frank Loesser (m)Joseph J. Lilley. (I)Film: *Forest Rangers*, on soundtrack. (P)Kay Kyser and his Orchestra. No. 1 Chart Record. (CR)The Merry Macs. (CR)Freddy Martin and his Orchestra.

JITTER BUG (1934) (wm)Irving Mills—Cab Calloway—Ed Swayze. (P)Cab Calloway and his Orchestra.

JITTERBUG WALTZ, THE (1942) (m)Thomas Waller. (P)Fats Waller.

JIVE TALKIN (1975) (wm)Barry, Maurice, and Robin Gibb. (P)The Bee Gees, No. 1 Chart Record.

JO-ANN (1957) (wm)John Cunningham—James Cunnignham. (P)The Playmates.

JOANNA (1983) (wm)Charles Smith—James Taylor—James Bonneford— Ronald Bell—Curtis Williams—Robert Bell—George Brown— Clifford Adams. (P)Kool & The Gang.

JOANNE (1970) (wm)Michael Nesmith. (P)Michael Nesmith.

JOCKEY ON THE CAROUSEL, THE (1935) (w)Dorothy Fields (m)Jerome Kern. (I)Film: *I Dream Too Much*, by Lily Pons.

JOEY (1954) (wm)Herb Wiener—James J. Kriegsman—Salmirs— Bernstein. (P)Betty Madigan. (CR)Jeri Southern.

JOEY (1976) (wm)Bob Dylan—Jacques Levy. (P)Bob Dylan.

JOEY, JOEY, JOEY (1956) (wm)Frank Loesser. (I)Musical: *The Most Happy Fella*, by Art Lund. (P)Art Lund.

JOEY'S THEME (1953) (m)Eddy Manson. (I)Film: *The Little Fugitive* by harmonica player Eddy Manson.

JOHANNA (1978) (wm)Stephen Sondheim. (I)Musical: *Sweeney Todd*, by Victor Garber.

JOHN HENRY (1873) (wm)Unknown. Traditional American folk song.

JOHN PEEL (1820) (wm)John Woodcock Graves. Popular English folk song.

JOHN SILVER (1939) (m)Ray Krise—Jimmy Dorsey. (P)Jimmy Dorsey and his Orchestra.

JOHN WESLEY HARDING (1968) (wm)Bob Dylan. (P)Bob Dylan.

JOHHNY ANGEL (1962) (w)Lyn Duddy (m)Lee Pockriss. (P)Shelly Fabares. No. 1 Chart Record.

JOHNNY B. GOODE (1958) (wm)Chuck Berry (P)Chuck Berry. (R)1969 by Buck Owens. (R)1970 by Johnny Winter.

JOHNNY DOUGHBOY FOUND A ROSE IN IRELAND (1942) (wm)Al Goodhart— Kay Twomey. (I)Film: *Johnny Doughboy*, on soundtrack. (P)Kay Kyser and his Orchestra. (CR)Kenny Baker. (CR)Guy Lombardo and his Royal Canadians.

JOHNNY GET ANGRY (1962) (wm)Hal David—Sherman Edwards. (P)Joanie Sommers.

JOHNNY GUITAR (1954) (w)Peggy Lee (m)Victor Young. (I)Film: *Johnny Guitar*, by Peggy Lee. (P)Peggy Lee.

JOHNNY LOVES ME (1962) (wm)Barry Mann—Cynthia Weil. (P)Shelley Fabares.

JOHNNY ONE NOTE (1937) (w)Lorenz Hart (m)Richard Rodgers. (I)Musical: *Babes In Arms* by Wynn Murray. (P)Hal Kemp and his Orchestra. (R)1948 Film: *Words And Music*, by Judy Garland.

JOHNNY'S THEME (1962) (wm)Paul Anka—Johnny Carson. (P)Theme song of The Johnny Carson Show.

JOHN'S IDEA (1939) (m)William Basie—Ed Durham. (P)Count Basie and his Orchestra.

JOHNSON RAG (1940) (w)Jack Lawrence (m)Guy H. Hall—Henry Kleinkauf. (P)Glenn Miller and his Orchestra. (R)1949 by Russ Morgan and his Orchestra.

JOIN TOGETHER (1972) (wm)Peter Townshend. (P)The Who.

JOINT IS JUMPIN' THE (1937) (wm)Andy Razaf—Thomas Waller—James C. Johnson. (P)Fats Waller.

JOINT IS REALLY JUMPIN' IN CARNEGIE HALL, THE (1943) (wm)Roger Edens—Ralph Blane—Hugh Martin. (I)Film: Thousands Cheer, by Judy Garland.

JOKER, THE (1957) (wm)Billy Myles. (P)Billy Myles.

JOKER, THE (1964) (wm)Leslie Bricusse—Anthony Newley. (I)Musical: The Roar Of The Greasepaint—The Smell Of The Crowd, by Anthony Newley.

JOKER, THE (1974) (wm)Eddie Curtis—Steve Miller. (P)Steve Miller. No. 1 Chart Record.

JOKER WENT WILD, THE (1966) (wm)Bobby Russell. (P)Brian Hyland.

JOLLY GREEN GIANT, THE (1965) (wm)Lynn Easton—Don F. Harris— Dewey Terry. (P)The Kingsmen.

JOLLY HOLIDAY (1963) (wm)Richard M. Sherman—Robert B. Sherman. (I)Film: Mary Poppins, by Julie Andrews and Dick Van Dyke.

JOLLY TAR AND THE MILKMAID, THE (1937) (w)Ira Gershwin (m)George Gershwin. (I)Film: A Damsel In Distress, by Fred Astaire, Jan Duggan, Mary Dean, Pearl Amatore, Betty Rone, and The Chorus.

JOLTIN' JOE DI MAGGIO (1941) (w)Alan Courtney—Ben Homer. (P)Les Brown and his Orchestra, vocal by Betty Bonney.

JONES BOY, THE (1953) (w)Mann Curtis (m)Vic Mizzy. (P)The Mills Brothers.

JOOBALAI (1939) (wm)Leo Robin—Ralph Rainger. (I)Film: Paris Honeymoon, by Bing Crosby, Franceska Gaal, and The Chorus.

JOSEPH! JOSEPH! (1938) (w-Eng)Sammy Cahn—Saul Chaplin. (m)Nellie Casman—Sam Steinberg. (P)The Andrews Sisters.

JOSEPHINE (1937) (w)Gus Kahn (m)Wayne King—Bruce Bivens. (P)Wayne King and his Orchestra. (CR)Sammy Kaye and his Orchestra. (R)1951 by Les Paul.

JOSEPHINE (1955) (wm)Cole Porter. (I)Musical: Silk Stockings, by Gretchen Wyler.

JOSEPHINE PLEASE NO LEAN ON THE BELL (1945) (wm)Ed Nelson— Harry Pease—Duke Leonard. (P)Eddie Cantor. (R)1954 Film: The Eddie Cantor Story, by Eddie Cantor dubbing for Keefe Brasselle.

JOSHUA FIT DE BATTLE OF JERICHO (1865) (wm)Unknown. Traditional Black American spiritual.

JOSIE (1978) (wm)Walter Becker—Donald Fagen. (P)Steely Dan.

JOURNEY TO A STAR, A (1943) (w)Leo Robin (m)Harry Warren. (I)Film: The Gang's All Here, by Alice Faye.

JOURNEY TO THE CENTER OF THE MIND (1968) (wm)Ted Nugent—Steve Farmer. (P)The Amboy Dukes.

JOUSTS, THE (1960) (w)Alan Jay Lerner (m)Frederick Loewe. (I)Musical: Camelot, by Richard Burton and Julie Andrews.

JOY (Song Of Joy) (1972) (w-Eng)Ross Parker (m)Ludwig Von Beethoven. (P)Miguel Rios (R)Apollo 100. Adapted from the last movement of Beethoven's Ninth Symphony.

JOY TO THE WORLD (1839) (m)G. F. Handel. Famous hymn from The Messiah.

JOY TO THE WORLD (1971) (wm)Hoyt Axton. (P)Three Dog Night. No. 1 Chart Record.

JUANITA (1850) (wm)Unknown. Traditional Spanish folk song.

JU JU HAND (1965) (wm)Domingo Samudio. (P)Sam The Sham and The Pharaohs.

JUBILATION T. CORNPONE (1956) (w)Johnny Mercer (m)Gene de Paul. (I)Musical: L'il Abner, by Stubby Kaye.

JUBILEE (1937) (w)Stanley Adams (m)Hoagy Carmichael. (I)Film: Every Day's A Holiday, by Louis Armstrong.

JUDY IN DISGUISE (1967) (wm)John Fred—Andrew Bernard. (P)John Fred and His Playboy Band. No. 1 Chart Record.

JUDY'S TURN TO CRY (1963) (w)Edna Lewis (m)Beverly Ross. (P)Lesley Gore.

JUG OF WINE, A (1945) (w)Alan Jay Lerner (m)Frederick Loewe. (I)Musical: The Day Before Spring, by Patricia Marshall.

JUKE BOX BABY (1956) (wm)Joe Sherman—Noel Sherman. (P)Perry Como.

JUKE BOX SATURDAY NIGHT (1942) (w)Al Stillman (m)Paul McGrane. (I)Revue: Stars On Ice. (P)Glenn Miller and his Orchestra, vocal by Marion Hutton, Tex Beneke, and The Modernaires.

JULIA (1968) (wm)John Lennon—Paul McCartney. (P)The Beatles.

JULIE, DO YA LOVE ME (1970) (wm)Tom Bahler. (P)Bobby Sherman.

JUMP (1976) (wm)Curtis Mayfield. (I)Film: Sparkle, by Irene Cara and Lonette McKee. (P)Aretha Franklin.

JUMP (1983) (wm)Eddie Van Halen—Alex Van Halen—Michael Anthony— David Lee Roth. (P)Van Halen.

JUMP FOR JOY (1941) (w)Paul Francis Webster (m)Duke Ellington. (I)Musical: Jump For Joy. (P)Duke Ellington and his Orchestra, vocal by Al Hibbler.

JUMP (For My Love) (1983) (wm)Marti Sharron—Steve Mitchell—Gary Skardina. (P)The Pointer Sisters.

JUMP INTO THE FIRE (1972) (wm)Harry Nilsson. (P)Nilsson.

JUMP START (1987) (wm)R. Calloway—V. Calloway. (P)Natalie Cole.

JUMPIN' AT THE WOODSIDE (1938) (m)William Basie. (P)Count Basie and his Orchestra. (CR)Benny Goodman and his Orchestra.

JUMPIN' JACK FLASH (1968) (wm)Mick Jagger—Keith Richard. (P)The Rolling Stones. (R)1971 by Johnny Winter. (R)1986 by Aretha Franklin.

JUMPIN' JIVE (1939) (wm)Cab Calloway—Fred Froeba—Jack Palmer. (P)Cab Calloway and his Orchestra. (CR)Lionel Hampton and his Orchestra.

JUNE COMES AROUND EVERY YEAR (1945) (w)Johnny Mercer (m)Harold Arlen. (I)Film: Out Of This World, by the voice of Bing Crosby.

JUNE IN JANUARY (1934) (wm)Leo Robin—Ralph Rainger. (I)Film: Here Is My Heart, by Bing Crosby and Kitty Carlisle. (P)Bing Crosby. No. 1 Chart Record. (CR)Guy Lombardo and his Royal Canadians.

JUNE IS BUSTIN' OUT ALL OVER (1945) (w)Oscar Hammerstein II (m)Richard Rodgers. (I)Musical: *Carousel*, by Christine Johnson, Jan Clayton, and The Ensemble. In film version (1957)by Claramae Turner, Barbara Ruick, and The Chorus.

JUNGLE BOOGIE (1974) (wm)Ronald Bell—Robert Bell—George M. Brown—Richard Westfield—Clayton Smith—Robert Mickens—Donald Boyce—Dennis Thomas. (P)Kool & The Gang.

JUNGLE DRUMS (1930) (w-Eng)Carmen Lombardo—Charles O'Flynn (m)Ernesto Lecuona. (P)Guy Lombardo and his Royal Canadians. (R)1939 by Artie Shaw and his Orchestra.

JUNGLE FANTASY (1948) (m)Esy Morales. (P)Esy Morales and his Orchestra.

JUNGLE FEVER (1972) (wm)Bill Ador. (P)The Chakachas.

JUNGLE LOVE (1977) (wm)Greg Douglas—Leonard Turner. (P)The Steve Miller Band.

JUNGLE LOVE (1985) (wm)Jesse Johnson—Morris Day—Prince Rogers Nelson. (I)Film: *Purple Rain*, by Morris Day and The Time.

JUNGLELAND (1975) (wm)Bruce Springsteen. (P)Bruce Springsteen.

JUNIOR'S FARM (1974) (wm)Paul and Linda McCartney. (P)Paul McCartney & Wings.

JUNK FOOD JUNKIE (1976) (wm)Larry Groce. (P)Larry Groce.

JUNK MAN (1934) (w)Frank Loesser (m)Joseph Meyer. (P)Mildred Bailey.

JUPITER FORBID (1942 (w)Lorenz Hart (m)Richard Rodgers. (I)Musical: *By Jupiter*, by Benay Venuta,Martha Burnett, Rose Inghram, Kay Kimber, and Monica Moore.

JUST A BABY'S PRAYER AT TWILIGHT (1918) (w)Sam M. Lewis—Joe Young (m)M. K. Jerome. (P)Henry Burr. (CR)Prince's Orchestra.

JUST A BLUE SERGE SUIT (1945) (wm)Irving Berlin. (P)Vaughn Monroe.

JUST A COTTAGE SMALL BY A WATERFALL (1925) (w)B. G. De Sylva (m)James F. Hanley. (P)John McCormack.

JUST A DREAM (1958) (wm)Jimmy Clanton—Cosmo Matassa. (P)Jimmy Clanton.

JUST A GIGOLO (w-Eng)Irving Caesar (m)Leonello Casucci. (I)In United States, by Irene Bordoni. (P)Ted Lewis. No. 1 Chart Record. (CR)Vincent Lopez and his Orchestra. (CR)Bing Crosby. (R)1953 by Jaye P. Morgan. (R)1985 by David Lee Roth (In Medley).

JUST A GIRL THAT MEN FORGET (1923) (wm)Al Dubin—Fred Rath—Joe Garren. (P)Henry Burr. (CR)Lewis James.

JUST A KISS APART (1949) (w)Leo Robin (m)Jule Styne. (I)Musical: *Gentlemen Prefer Blondes*, by Yvonne Adair and Eric Brotherson.

JUST A LITTLE (1965) (wm)Ronald Elliott—Robert Durand. (P)The Beau Brummels.

JUST A LITTLE BIT BETTER (1965) (wm)Kenny Young. (P)Herman's Hermits.

JUST A LITTLE BIT OF YOU (1975) (wm)Eddie Holland—Brian Holland. (P)Michael Jackson.

JUST A LITTLE BIT SOUTH OF NORTH CAROLINA (1941) (wm)Sunny Skylar—Bette Cannon—Arthur Shaftel. (P)Gene Krupa and his Orchestra, vocal by Anita O'Day. (CR)Mitchell Ayres and his Orchestra.

JUST A LITTLE JOINT WITH A JUKE BOX (1941) (wm)Hugh Martin— Ralph Blane. (I)Musical: *Best Foot Forward*, by Nancy Walker and Kenneth Bowers.

JUST A LITTLE LOVIN' (Will Go A Long Way) (1948) (wm)Zeke Clements—Eddy Arnold. (P)Eddy Arnold. (R)1952 by Eddie Fisher.

JUST A LITTLE TOO MUCH (1959) (wm)Johnny Burnette. (P)Rick Nelson.

JUST A MEMORY (1927) (w)B. G. De Sylva—Lew Brown (m)Ray Henderson. (I)Musical: *Manhattan Mary*. (P)Paul Whiteman and his Orchestra. (R)1956 Film: *The Best Things In Life Are Free*, by Sheree North.

JUST A-SITTIN' AND A-ROCKIN' (1941) (w)Lee Gaines (m)Duke Ellington—Billy Strayhorn. (P)Duke Ellington and his Orchestra, vocal by Ivie Anderson.

JUST A SONG BEFORE I GO (1977) (wm)Graham Nash. (P)Crosby, Stills & Nash.

JUST A WEARYIN' FOR YOU (1910) (w)Frank Stanton (m)Carrie Jacobs Bond. (P)Lucy Isabelle Marsh.

JUST AN ECHO IN THE VALLEY (1933) (wm)Harry Woods—Jimmy Campbell—Reg Connelly. (I)Film: *Going Hollywood*, by Bing Crosby. (P)Bing Crosby. (CR)Rudy Vallee.

JUST ANOTHER NIGHT (1985) (wm)Mick Jagger. (P)Mick Jagger.

JUST ANOTHER POLKA (1953) (wm)Frank Loesser—Milton De Lugg. (P)Jo Stafford.

JUST AS I AM (1985) (wm)Dick Wagner—Robert Hegel. (P)Air Supply.

JUST AS MUCH AS EVER (1959) (wm)Charles Singleton—Larry Coleman. (P)Bob Beckham. (R)1963 by Bobby Vinton.

JUST AS THOUGH YOU WERE HERE (1942) (w)Eddie De Lange (m)John Benson Brooks. (P)Tommy Dorsey and his Orchestra, vocal by Frank Sinatra and The Pied Pipers.

JUST ASK YOUR HEART (1959) (w)Pete Damato—Joe Ricci (m)Diane De Nota. (P)Frankie Avalon.

JUST BECAUSE (1957) (wm)Lloyd Price. (P)Lloyd Price. (CR)The McGuire Sisters.

JUST BETWEEN YOU AND ME (1957) (wm)Lee Cathy—Jack Keller. (P)The Chordettes.

JUST BORN (To Be Your Baby) (1957) (P)Perry Como.

JUST DON'T WANT TO BE LONELY TONIGHT (1973) (wm)Vinnie Barrett— Bobby Eli—John C. Freeman. (I)Ronnie Dyson. (P)The Main Ingredient.

JUST DROPPED IN (To See What Condition My Condition Was In) (1968) (P)Kenny Rogers and The First Edition.

JUST FOR OLD TIMES' SAKE (1960) (wm)Hank Hunter—Jack Keller. (P)The McGuire Sisters.

JUST FOR ONCE (1959) (w)Dorothy Fields (m)Albert Hague. (I)Musical: *Redhead*, by Gwen Verdon, Richard Kiley, and Leonard Stone.

JUST FOR TONIGHT (1978) (w)Carole Bayer Sager (m)Marvin Hamlisch. (I)Musical: *They're Playing Our Song*, by Lucy Arnaz.

JUST FRIENDS (1931) (w)Sam M. Lewis (m)John Klenner. (P)Red McKenzie. (CR)Russ Columbo.

JUST GIVE ME A JUNE NIGHT, THE MOONLIGHT, AND YOU (June Night) (1924). (w)Cliff Friend (m)Abel Baer. (P)Cliff Edwards.

JUST IMAGINE (1927) (w)B. G. De Sylva—Lew Brown (m)Ray Henderson. (I)Musical: *Good News*, by Mary Lawlor, Shirley Vernon, and Ruth Mayon. (R)1947 Film: *Good News*, by June Allyson.

JUST IN TIME (1956) (w)Betty Comden—Adolph Green

(m)Jule Styne. (I)Musical: *Bells Are Ringing*, by Judy Holliday and Sydney Chaplin.

JUST KEEP IT UP (And See What Happens) (1959) (wm)Otis Blackwell. (P)Dee Clark.

JUST LET ME LOOK AT YOU (1938) (w)Dorothy Fields (m)Jerome Kern. (I)Film: *Joy Of Living*, by Irene Dunne.

JUST LIKE A BUTTERFLY THAT'S CAUGHT IN THE RAIN (1927) (wm)Mort Dixon—Harry Woods. (P)Blossom Seely. (CR)Vincent Lopez and his Orchestra.

JUST LIKE A MAN (1952) (w)Ogden Nash (m)Vernon Duke. (I)Revue: *Two's Company*, by Bette Davis.

JUST LIKE A MELODY OUT OF THE SKY (1928) (wm)Walter Donaldson. (P)Gene Austin. (CR)Paul Whiteman and his Orchestra.

JUST LIKE A WOMAN (1966) (wm)Bob Dylan. (P)Bob Dylan.

JUST LIKE ME (1966) (wm)Richard Dey—Roger Hart. (P)Paul Revere and The Raiders.

JUST LIKE PARADISE (1987) (wm)D. L. Roth—B. Tuggle. (P)David Lee Roth.

JUST LIKE TOM THUMB'S BLUES (1965) (wm)Bob Dylan. (P)Bob Dylan.

JUST MY IMAGINATION (Running Away With Me) (1971) (wm)Norman Whitfield—Barrett Strong. (P)The Temptations. No. 1 Chart Record.

JUST MY LUCK (1945) (w)Johnny Burke (m)Jimmy Van Heusen. (I)Musical: *Nellie Bly*, by William Gaxton and Joy Hodges.

JUST ONCE AROUND THE CLOCK (1935) (w)Oscar Hammmerstein II (m)Sigmund Romberg. (I)Musical: *May Wine*, by Walter Woolf King, Vera Van, and Leo G. Carroll.

JUST ONCE IN MY LIFE (1965) (wm)Gerry Goffin—Carole King—Phil Spector. (P)The Righteous Brothers.

JUST ONE LOOK (1963) (wm)Gregory Carroll—Doris Payne. (P)Doris Troy. (R)1967 by The Hollies. (R)1974 by Anne Murray. (R)1979 by Linda Ronstadt.

JUST ONE MORE CHANCE (1931) (w)Sam Coslow (m)Arthur Johnston. (P)Bing Crosby. No. 1 Chart Record. (CR)Russ Columbo. (CR)Abe Lyman and his Orchestra. (R)1951 by Les Paul and Mary Ford.

JUST ONE OF THOSE THINGS (1935) (wm)Cole Porter. (I)Musical: *Jubilee*, by June Knight and Charles Walters. (P)Richard Himber and his Orchestra. Most popular recording by Frank Sinatra. (R)1952 by Peggy Lee. (R)1960 Film: *Can Can*, by Maurice Chevalier.

JUST ONE TIME (1960) (wm)Don Gibson. (P)Don Gibson. (R)1971 by Connie Smith.

JUST ONE WAY TO SAY I LOVE YOU (1949) (wm)Irving Berlin. (I)Musical: *Miss Liberty*, by Eddie Albert and Allyn McLerie.

JUST PLAIN LONESOME (1942) (w)Johnny Burke (m)Jimmy Van Heusen. (I)Film: *My Favorite Spy*, by Kay Kyser and his Orchestra.

JUST REMEMBER I LOVE YOU (1977) (wm)Rick Roberts. (P)Firefall.

JUST SAY I LOVE HER (Dicitencello Vuie) (1950) (w-Eng)Martin Kalmanoff—Sam Ward. (m)Rodolfo Falvo—Jack Val—Jimmy Dale. (P)Vic Damone. (CR)Johnny Desmond.

JUST SQUEEZE ME (But Don't Tease Me) (1946) (w)Lee Gaines (m)Duke Ellington. (P)Duke Ellington and his Orchestra, vocal by Ray Nance.

JUST THE TWO OF US (1981) (wm)Bill Withers—William Salter— Ralph MacDonald. (P)Grover Washington, Jr. and Bill Withers. NARAS Award Winner.

JUST THE WAY YOU ARE (1978) (wm)Billy Joel. (P)Billy Joel. NARAS Award Winner.

JUST TO BE CLOSE TO YOU (1976) (wm)Lionel Richie. (P)The Commodores.

JUST TO SEE HER (1987) (wm)J. George—L. Pardin. (P)Smokey Robinson.

JUST TOO MANY PEOPLE (1975) (wm)Melissa Manchester—Vini Poncia. (P)Melissa Manchester.

JUST WALKING IN THE RAIN (1953) (wm)Johnny Bragg—Robert S. Riley. (I)The Prisonaires who were inmates of The Tennessee State Penitentiary. (P)Johnnie Ray.

JUST WE TWO (1924) (w)Dorothy Donnelly (m)Sigmund Romberg. (I)Operetta: *The Student Prince in Heidelberg*, by Roberta Beatty and John Coast.

JUST WHAT I NEEDED (1978) (wm)Ric Ocasek. (P)The Cars.

JUST WHEN I NEEDED YOU MOST (1979) (wm)Randy Van Warmer. (P)Randy Van Warmer.

JUST YOU (1965) (wm)Sonny Bono. (P)Sonny and Cher.

JUST YOU, JUST ME (1929) (w)Raymond Klages (m)Jesse Greer. (I)Film: *Marianne*, by Marion Davies and Lawrence Gray. (P)Cliff Edwards. (R)1935 by Benny Goodman.

JUST YOU 'N' ME (1973) (wm)James Pankow. (P)Chicago.

JUST YOU WAIT (1956) (w)Alan Jay Lerner (m)Frederick Loewe. (I)Musical: *My Fair Lady*, by Julie Andrews.

K-RA-ZY FOR YOU (1928) (w)Ira Gershwin (m)George Gershwin. (I)Musical: *Treasure Girl*, by Clifton Webb and Mary Hay.

(My Heart Goes)KA-DING-DONG (1956) (wm)Robert Jordan—John J. McDermott, Jr. (P)The G Clefs. (CR)The Diamonds. (CR)The Hilltoppers.

KA-LU-A (1922) (w)Anne Caldwell (m)Jerome Kern. (I)Musical: *Good Morning, Dearie*, by Oscar Shaw. (P)Elsie Baker. (R)1946 Film: *Till The Clouds Roll By*, by Van Heflin.

KAMENNOI OSTROW (1855) (m)Artur Rubinstein. Famous classical selection.

KANSAS CITY (1943) (w)Oscar Hammerstein II (m)Richard Rodgers. (I)Musical: *Oklahoma*, by Lee Dixon, Betty Garde, and The Chorus. (R)1955 Film: *Oklahoma*, by Gene Nelson, Charlotte Greenwood and The Men's Chorus.

KANSAS CITY (1959) (wm)Jerry Leiber—Mike Stoller. (P)Wilbert Harrison. (R)1964 by Trini Lopez. (R)1967 by James Brown.

KANSAS CITY KITTY (1929) (w)Edgar Leslie (m)Walter Donaldson. (P)Rudy Vallee.

KANSAS CITY STAR (1965) (wm)Roger Miller. (P)Roger Miller.

KARMA CHAMELEON (1983) (wm)George O'Dowd—Jon Moss—Roy Hay—Mickey Craig—Phil Pickett. (P)Culture Club. No. 1 Chart Record.

KASHMIRI LOVE SONG (1903) (w)Lawrence Hope (m)Amy Woodeforde-Finden. Famous light classical selection.

KATE (Have I Come Too Early, Too Late (1947) (wm)Irving Berlin. (P)Eddy Howard. (CR)Ray Bloch and his Orchestra.

KATHLEEN MINE (1931) (w)Edward Heyman (m)Vincent Youmans. (I)Musical: *Through the Years*, by Natalie Hall and Michael Bartlett.

KATHY-O (1958) (wm)Charles Tobias—Ray Joseph—Jack Sher. (I)Film: *Kathy-O*, by The Diamonds on soundtrack. (P)The Diamonds.

KATIE WENT TO HAITI (1939) (wm)Cole Porter. (I)Musical: *Du Barry Was A Lady*, by Ethel Merman. In film version 1943, by Jo Stafford, Dick Haymes, The Pied Pipers, and Tommy Dorsey and his Orchestra.

KATINKITSCHKA (1931) (w)Ira Gershwin (m)George Gershwin. (I)Film: *Delicious*, by Janet Gaynor, El Brendel, and The Chorus.

KATSUMI LOVE THEME (1957) (m)Franz Waxman. (I)Film: *Sayonara*, on soundtrack.

KAW-LIGA (1953) (wm)Fred Rose—Hank Williams. (P)Hank Williams. (CR)Dolores Gray. (R)1969 by Charlie Pride.

KEEM-O-SABE (1969) (m)Bernard Binnick—Bernice Borisoff. (P)Electric Indian.

KEEP A-KNOCKIN' (1957) (wm)Richard Penniman. (P)Little Richard.

KEEP IT A SECRET (1952) (wm)Jessie Mae Robinson. (P)Slim Whitman. (CR)Jo Stafford. (CR)Bing Crosby.

KEEP IT COMIN,LOVE (1977) (wm)Harry Casey—Richard Finch. (P)K. C. & The Sunshine Band.

KEEP IT GAY (1953) (w)Oscar Hammerstein II (m)Richard Rodgers. (I)Musical: *Me And Juliet*, by Mark Dawson and Bob Fortier. Later reprised by Joan McCracken and Buzz Miller.

KEEP ON DANCING (1965) (wm)Willie David Young. (P)The Gentrys.

KEEP ON LOVING YOU (1981) (wm)Kevin Cronin. (P)REO Speedwagon. No. 1 Chart Record.

KEEP ON PUSHING (1964) (wm)Curtis Mayfield. (P)The Impressions.

KEEP ON SINGING (1973) (wm)Danny Janssen—Bobby Hart. (I)Austin Roberts. (P)Helen Reddy.

KEEP ON SMILIN' (1974) (wm)Jack Hall—Maurice Hirsch—Lewis Ross—John Anthony—James Hall. (P)Wet Willie.

KEEP ON TRUCKIN' (1973) (wm)Frank Wilson—Leonard Caston—Anita Poree. (P)Eddie Kendricks.

KEEP ROMANCE ALIVE (1934) (w)Bert Kalmar (m)Harry Ruby. (I)Film: *Hips, Hips Hooray*, by Ruth Etting.

KEEP SEARCHIN' (1964) (wm)Del Shannon. (P)Del Shannon.

KEEP SMILING AT TROUBLE (1925) (w)Al Jolson—B. G. De Sylva (m)Lewis E. Gensler. (I)Musical: *Big Boy*, by Al Jolson. (P)Al Jolson.

KEEP THE BALL ROLLIN' (1967) (wm)Danny Randell—Sandy Linzer. (P)Jay and The Techniques. (CR)Al Hirt.

KEEP THE FIRE BURNIN' (1982) (wm)Kevin Cronin. (P)REO Speedwagon.

KEEP YOUNG AND BEAUTIFUL (1933) (w)Al Dubin (m)Harry Warren. (I)Film: *Roman Scandals*, by Eddie Cantor.

KEEP YOUR EYE ON THE SPARROW (Baretta's Theme) (1975) (I)TV series: *Baretta*, by Sammy Davis, Jr. (P)Sammy Davis, Jr. (CR)Merry Clayton. (CR)Rhythm Heritage.

KEEP YOUR HANDS OFF MY BABY (1962) (wm)Gerry Goffin—Carole King. (P)Little Eva.

KEEP YOUR HANDS TO YOURSELF (1987) (wm)D. Baird. (P)Georgia Satellites.

KEEPER OF THE CASTLE (1972) (wm)Dennis Lambert—Brian Potter. (P)The Four Tops.

KEEPIN' MYSELF FOR YOU (1930) (w)Sidney Clare (m)Vincent Youmans. (I)Film: *Hit The Deck*, by Jack Oakie and Polly Walker. (R)1955 Film: *Hit The Deck*, by Tony Martin, Ann Miller and The Girls.

KEEPING OUT OF MISCHIEF NOW (1932) (w)Andy Razaf (m)Thomas Waller. (P)Fats Waller. (CR)Louis Armstrong. (CR)Coon-Sanders Orchestra.

KEEPING THE FAITH (1985) (wm)Billy Joel. (P)Billy Joel.

KENTUCKIAN SONG, THE (1955) (wm)Irving Gordon. (I)Film: *The Kentuckian* on soundtrack. (P)The Hilltoppers.

KENTUCKY RAIN (1970) (wm)Eddie Rabbitt—Dick Heard. (P)Elvis Presley.

KENTUCKY WOMAN (1967) (wm)Neil Diamond. (P)Neil Diamond. (CR)Deep Purple.

KEWPIE DOLL (1958) (wm)Sid Tepper—Roy C. Bennett. (P)Perry Como.

KEY LARGO (1982) (wm)Sonny Limbo—Bertie Higgins. (P)Bertie Higgins.

KICKIN' THE GONG AROUND (1931) (w)Ted Koehler (m)Harold Arlen. (I)Revue: *Rhythmania*, by Cab Calloway. (P)Cab Calloway. (CR)Louis Armstrong.

KICKS (1966) (wm)Barry Mann—Cynthia Weil. (P)Paul Revere and The Raiders.

KIDDIO (1960) (wm)Brook Benton—Clyde Otis. (P)Brook Benton.

KIDS (1960) (w)Lee Adams (m)Charles Strouse. (I)Musical: *Bye Bye Birdie*, by Paul Lynde. In film version 1963 by Dick Van Dyke, Paul Lynde, Maureen Stapleton, and Bryan Russell.

KILLER QUEEN (1975) (wm)Freddie Mercury. (P)Queen.

KILLING ME SOFTLY WITH HIS SONG (1973) (wm)Norman Gimbel—Charles Fox. (I)Lori Lieberman. (P)Roberta Flack. No. 1 Chart Record. NARAS Award Winner.

KILLING OF GEORGIE (1977) (wm)Rod Stewart. (P)Rod Stewart.

KIND LOVIN' BLUES (1922) (wm)Ethel Waters—Fletcher Henderson—Lewis Mitchell. (P)Ethel Waters.

KIND OF A DRAG (1967) (wm)James Holvay. (P)The Buckinghams. No. 1 Chart Record.

KIND OF BOY YOU CAN'T FORGET, THE (1963) (wm)Jeff Barry—Ellie Greenwich. (P)The Raindrops.

KINDA LIKE YOU (1932) (w)Edward Heyman (m)Vincent Youmans. (I)Musical: *Through The Years*, by Martha Mason and Nick Long, Jr.

KIND'A LONESOME (1939) (wm)Leo Robin—Sam Coslow—Hoagy Carmichael. (I)Film: *St. Louis Blues*, by Maxine Sullivan and The Hall Johnson Choir.

KING COTTON (1895) (m)John Philip Sousa. March written for The Cotton States Exposition.

KING FOR A DAY (1986) (wm)T. Bailey—A. Currie—J. Leeway. (P)The Thompson Twins.

KING IS GONE, THE (1977) (wm)Lee Morgan—Ronnie McDowell. (P)Ronnie McDowell.

KING JOE (1941) (w)Richard Wright (m)William Basie. A tribute to Joe Louis. (P)Paul Robeson with Count Basie and his Orchestra.

KING OF KINGS THEME (1961) (m)Miklos Rozsa. (I)Film: *King Of Kings*, on soundtrack.

KING OF PAIN (1983) (wm)Gordon Sumner (Sting) (P)The Police.

KING OF THE ROAD (1964) (wm)Roger Miller. (P)Roger Miller. NARAS AWard Winner.

KING OF THE WHOLE WIDE WORLD (1962) (wm)Ruth Batchelor—Bob Roberts. (I)Film: *Kid Galahad*, by Elvis Presley. (P)Elvis Presley.

KING OF THE ZULUS, THE (1926) (wm)Lillian Hardin Armstrong. (P)Louis Armstrong and his Hot Five.

KING PORTER STOMP (1924) (m)Jelly Roll Morton. (I)Jelly Roll Morton. (P)Fletcher Henderson and his Orchestra. (R)1936 by Benny Goodman and his Orchestra, vocal by Bunny Berigan.

KING TUT (1978) (wm)Steve Martin. (P)Steve Martin & The Toots Uncommons.

KING'S HORSES, THE (And The King's Men) (1930) (wm)Noel Gay. (P)Ben Bernie and his Orchestra.

KINKAJOU, THE (1927) (w)Joseph McCarthy (m)Harry Tierney. (I)Musical: *Rio Rita*, by Ada May and The Chorus.

KISS (1986) (wm)Prince. (P)Prince and The Revolution. No. 1 Chart Record.

KISS AN ANGEL GOOD MORNING (1971) (wm)Ben Peters. (P)Charley Pride. NARAS Award Winner.

KISS AND SAY GOODBYE (1976) (wm)Winfred Lovett. (P)The Manhattans. No. 1 Chart Record.

KISS AWAY (1965) (wm)Billy Sherrill—Glenn Sutton. (P)Ronnie Dove.

KISS HIM GOODBYE (1987) (wm)D. Frashuer—G. De-Carlo—Paul Leka. (P)The Nylons.

KISS IN THE DARK, A (1922) (w)B. G. De Sylva (m)Victor Herbert. (I)Musical: *Orange Blossoms*, by Edith Day. (P)Amelita Galli—Curci. (R)1939 Film: *The Great Victor Herbert*, by Mary Martin.

KISS IN YOUR EYES, THE (1947) (w)Johnny Burke (m)Richard Heuberger. (I)Film: *The Emperor Waltz*, by Bing Crosby.

KISS ME AGAIN (1916) (w)Henry Blossom (m)Victor Herbert. (I)Musical: *Mlle. Modiste*, by Fritzi Scheff. (R)1939 Film: *The Great Victor Herbert*, by Mary Martin.

KISS ME ANOTHER (1956) (w)Fred Ebb (m)Charles Freidman (P)Georgia Gibbs.

KISS ME GOODBYE (1968) (wm)Les Reed—Barry Mason. (P)Petula Clark.

KISS ME QUICK (1961) (wm)Doc Pomus—Mort Shuman. (P)Elvis Presley.

KISS ME, SAILOR (1964) (wm)Eddie Rambeau—Bud Rehak. (P)Diane Renay.

KISS ME SWEET (1949) (wm)Milton Drake. (P)Sammy Kaye and his Orchestra. (CR)Kitty Kallen. (CR)Judy Valentine.

KISS OF FIRE (1952) (w-Eng)Lester Allen—Robert Hill (m)A. G. Villodo. Adapted from tango El Choclo. (P)Georgia Gibbs. (CR)Tony Martin. (CR)Louis Armstrong.

KISS ON MY LIST (1981) (wm)Janna Allen—Daryl Hall. (P)Hall and Oates. No. 1 Chart Record.

KISS POLKA, THE (w)Mack Gordon (m)Harry Warren. (I)Film: *Sun Valley Serenade*, by Sonja Henie.

KISS THE BOYS GOODBYE (1941) (w)Frank Loesser (m)Victor Schertzinger. (I)Film: *Kiss The Boys Goodbye*, by Mary Martin. (P)Tommy Dorsey and his Orchestra, vocal by Connie Haines. (CR)Bea Wain.

KISS THE BRIDE (1983) (wm)Elton John—Bernie Taupin. (P)Elton John.

KISS TO BUILD A DREAM ON, A (1935) (wm)Bert Kalmar—Harry Ruby—Oscar Hammerstein II. (P)Louis Armstrong. (CR)Hugo Winterhalter and his Orchestra.

KISS WALTZ, THE (1930) (w)Al Dubin (m)Joe Burke. (I)Film: *Dancing Sweeties*, by Sue Carol. (P)George Olsen and his Orchestra. (CR)Ben Bernie and his Orchestra.

KISS YOU ALL OVER (1978) (wm)Nicky Chinn—Mike Chapman. (P)Exile. No. 1 Chart Record.

KISSES SWEETER THAN WINE (1957) (w)Paul Campbell (The Weavers) (m)Huddie Ledbetter. (P)Jimmie Rodgers.

KISSIN' BUG BOOGIE (1951) (w)Allan Roberts (m)Robert Allen. (P)Jo Stafford.

KISSIN' COUSINS (1964) (wm)Fred Wise—Randy Starr. (I)Film: *Kissin' Cousins*, by Elvis Presley. (P)Elvis Presley.

KISSIN' TIME (1959) (wm)Leonard Frazier—James Frazier. (P)Bobby Rydell. (R)1974 by Kiss.

KITTEN ON THE KEYS (1921) (m)Zez Confrey. (I)Zez Confrey as piano solo. (P)Vincent Lopez and his Orchestra.

KITTY FROM KANSAS CITY (1921) (wm)Harry Rose—Jesse Greer—Rudy Vallee—George Bronson. Not a hit when first released. (R)1930 by Rudy Vallee.

K-K-K-KATY (1918) (wm)Geoffrey O'Hara. (P)Billy Murray. Very popular song during World War I.

KNEE DEEP IN THE BLUES (1957) (wm)Melvin

Endsley. (I)Marty Robbins. (P)Guy Mitchell.

KNIGHT IN RUSTY ARMOR (1966) (wm)Mike Leander—Charles Mills. (P)Peter and Gordon.

KNOCK, KNOCK. WHO'S THERE? (1936) (wm)Bill Tipton—Bill Davies—Johnny Morris—Vincent Lopez. (P)Vincent Lopez and his Orchestra.

KNOCK ME A KISS (1942) (wm)Andy Razaf—Mike Jackson. (P)Louis Jordan and his Tympani Five.

KNOCK ON WOOD (1966) (wm)Eddie Floyd—Steve Cropper. (P)Eddie Floyd. (CR)Otis and Carla. (R)1979 by Amii Stewart. No. 1 Chart Record.

KNOCK THREE TIMES (1971) (wm)Irwin Levine—L. Russell Brown. (P)Dawn. No. 1 Chart Record.

KNOCKIN' ON HEAVEN'S DOOR (1973) (wm)Bob Dylan. (I)Film: *Pat Garrett and Billy The Kid*, by voice of Bob Dylan. (P)Bob Dylan.

KNOWING ME, KNOWING YOU (1977) (wm)Benny Andersson—Stig Anderson—Bjorn Ulvaeus. (P)Abba.

KO KO MO, I LOVE YOU SO (1955) (wm)Forest Wilson—Jake Porter—Eunice Levy. (I)Gene and Eunice. (P)Perry Como. (CR)The Crew Cuts.

KODACHROME (1973) (wm)Paul Simon. (P)Paul Simon.

KOKOMO, INDIANA (1947) (w)Mack Gordon (m)Josef Myrow. (I)Film: *Mother Wore Tights*, by Betty Grable and Dan Dailey. (P)Vaughn Monroe and his Orchestra.

KOOKIE, KOOKIE, LEND ME YOUR COMB (1959) (wm)Irving Taylor. (P)Eddie Byrnes and Connie Stevens.

KOZMIC BLUES (1969) (wm)Janis Joplin—Gabriel Mekler. (P)Janis Joplin.

KUNG FU FIGHTING (1974) (wm)Carl Douglas. (P)Carl Douglas. No. 1 Chart Record.

KYRIE (1986) (wm)Richard Page—Steven George—Robert John Lange. (P)Mr. Mister. No. 1 Chart Record.

L-O-V-E (Love) (1975) (wm)Al Green—Willie Mitchell—Mabon Hodges. (P)Al Green.

LA BAMBA (1958) (wm)Ritchie Valens. (P)Ritchie Valens. (R)1962 by The Tokens. (R)1966 by Trini Lopez. (R)1987 Film: *La Bamba*, by Los Lobos. No. 1 Chart Record.

LA CUCARACHA (Date of origin unknown) (wm)Unknown. Popular Mexican folk song.

LA DEE DAH (1958) (wm)Frank C. Slay, Jr. —Bob Crewe. (P)Billy and Lillie.

LA DOLCE VITA (The Sweet Life) (1960) (w-Eng)Les Vandyke. (m)Nino Rota. (I)Film: *La Dolce Vita* on soundtrack.

LA ISLA BONITA (1987) (wm)Madonna—P. Leonard—B. Gaitsch. (P)Madonna.

LA LA LA (1962) (wm)Richard Rodgers. (I)Musical: *No Strings*, by Noelle Adams and Alvin Epstein.

LA LA LA (Means I Love You) (w)William Hart (m)Thomas Bell. (P)The Delfonics. (R)1981 by The Tierras.

LA PLUME DE MA TANTE (1959) (wm)Al Hoffman—Dick Manning. (P)Hugo and Luigi with their Orchestra and Children's Chorus.

LA ROSITA (1923) (w)Allan Stuart (m)Paul Dupont. No artist credited with introduction. (R)1953 by The Four Aces.

LA STRADA (Love Theme) (1954) (m)N. Rota. (I)Italian film: *La Strada*, on soundtrack.

L. A. SUNSHINE (1977) (wm)Sylvester Allen—Harold Ray Brown—Morris Dickerson—Gerald Goldstein—Leroy Jordan—Lee Oskar Levitan—Charles Miller—Howard Scott. (P)War.

LA VIE EN ROSE (1946) (w-Eng)Mack David (m)Louiguy. (I)Edith Piaf. (P)Tony Martin.

LADIES NIGHT (1979) (wm)Robert Bell—Ronald Bell—George Brown—Claydes Smith—James Taylor—Dennis Thomas—Meekaaeel Abdul Muhammad—Earl Toon, Jr. (P)Kool & The Gang.

LADIES OF THE TOWN (1929) (wm)Noel Coward. (I)Operetta: *Bitter Sweet*, by Zoe Gordon, Nancy Barnett, Dorothy Debenham, and Sylvia Leslie. (New York Production). (R)1940 film: *Bitter Sweet*, by Jeanette MacDonald, Muriel Goodspeed, and Pamela Randall.

LADIES WHO LUNCH, THE (1970) (wm)Stephen Sondheim. (I)Musical: *Company*, by Elaine Stritch.

LADY (1975) (wm)Dennis De Young. (P)Styx.

LADY (1979) (wm)Graham Goble. (P)Little River Band.

LADY (1980) (wm)Lionel Richie. (P)Kenny Rogers. No. 1 Chart Record.

LADY (You Bring Me Up) (1981) (wm)William King—Howard Hudson—S. King. (P)The Commodores.

LADY BIRD (1964) (wm)Buddy Killen—Billy Sherrill. (I)The Dawnbusters. (P)Nancy Sinatra and Lee Hazlewood.

LADY BLUE (1975) (wm)Howard Kaylan. (P)Leon Russell.

LADY FROM 29 PALMS (1947) (wm)Allie Wrubel. (P)Freddy Martin and his Orchestra. (CR)The Andrews Sisters.

LADY GODIVA (1966) (wm)Mike Leander—Charles Mills. (P)Peter and Gordon.

LADY IN RED, THE (1935) (w)Mort Dixon (m)Allie Wrubel. (I)Film: *In Caliente*, by Wini Shaw, Edward Everett Horton, George Humbert, and Judy Canova. (P)Xavier Cugat and his Orchestra. (CR)Louis Prima.

LADY IN RED, THE (1987) (wm)Chris De Burgh. (P)Chris De Burgh.

LADY IS A TRAMP, THE (1937) (w)Lorenz Hart (m)Richard Rodgers. (I)Musical: *Babes In Arms*, by Mitzi Green. Recorded by Tommy Dorsey and his Orchestra. Also, Sophie Tucker. (R)1939 film: *Words And Music*, by Lena Horne. (R)1957 film: *Pal Joey*, by Frank Sinatra. Most popular recording by Frank Sinatra.

LADY JANE (1966) (wm)Mick Jagger—Keith Richard. (P)The Rolling Stones.

LADY LOVE (1978) (wm)Yvonne Gray—Sherman Marshall. (P)Lou Rawls.

LADY LUCK (1960) (wm)Lloyd Price—Harold Logan. (P)Lloyd Price.

LADY MADONNA (1968) (wm)John Lennon—Paul McCartney. (P)The Beatles. (CR)Fats Domino.

LADY MARMALADE (1975) (wm)Bob Crewe—Kenny Nolan Helfman. (P)Patti Labelle. No. 1 Chart Record.

LADY MUST LIVE, A (1931) (w)Lorenz Hart (m)Richard Rodgers. (I)Musical: *America's Sweetheart*, by Jeanne Aubert.

LADY OF SPAIN (1931) (wm)Robert Hargreaves—Tolchard Evans—Stanley Damerell—Henry Tilsley. (I)Jack Payne and his Orchestra. (England) (CR)Ray Noble and his Orchestra. (R)1952 by Eddie Fisher. (R)1952 by Les Paul.

LADY OF THE EVENING (1922) (wm)Irving Berlin. (I)Revue: *Music Box Revue of 1922*, by John Steel. (P)Paul Whiteman and his Orchestra.

LADY, PLAY YOUR MANDOLIN (1930) (w)Irving Caesar (m)Oscar Levant. (I)Nick Lucas. (P)Blossom Seeley. (CR)Havana Novelty Orchestra.

LADY WILLPOWER (1969) (wm)Jerry Fuller. (P)Gary Puckett and The Union Gap.

LADYBIRD (1967) (wm)Lee Hazlewood. (P)Nancy Sinatra and Lee Hazlewood.

LADY'S IN LOVE WITH YOU, THE (1939) (w)Frank Loesser (m)Burton Lane. (I)Film: *Some Like It Hot*, by Bob Hope, Shirley Ross, and Gene Krupa and his Orchestra. (P)Glenn Miller and his Orchestra. (CR)Bob Crosby and his Orchestra.

LAMBETH WALK (1937) (wm)Noel Gay—Douglas Furber. (I)London musical: *Me And My Girl*, by Lupino Lane. (P)Russ Morgan and his Orchestra. (CR)Al Donahue and his Orchestra.

L'AMOUR, TOUJOURS, L'AMOUR (Love Everlasting) (1922) (w)Catherine Chisholm (m)Rudolf Friml. No artist credited with introduction. (1944)Film: *This Is The Life*, by Susanna Foster.

LAMP IS LOW, THE (1939) (w)Mitchell Parish (m)Peter De Rose—Bert Shefter. Adapted from Ravel's Pavane Pour Une Infante Defunte. (P)Larry Clinton and his Orchestra. (CR)Tommy Dorsey and his Orchestra.

LAMPLIGHT (1934) (wm)James Shelton. (I)Revue: *New Faces of 1934*, by James Shelton. (P)Hal Kemp and his Orchestra, vocal by Skinnay Ennis.

LAMPLIGHTER'S SERENADE, THE (1942) (w)Paul Francis Webster (m)Hoagy Carmichael. (P)Glenn Miller and his Orchestra, vocal by Ray Eberle and The Modernaires. (CR)Bing Crosby.

LAND OF A THOUSAND DANCES (1963) (wm)Chris Kenner. (I)Chris Kenner. (R)1965 by Cannibal & The

Headhunters. (R)1966 by Wilson Pickett. (R)1969 by Electric Indian. (R)1983 by J. Geils Band.

LAND OF CONFUSION (1987) (wm)Phil Collins—Mike Rutherford—A. Banks. (P)Genesis.

LAND OF DREAMS (1954) (w)Norman Gimbel (m)Eddie Heywood. (P)Hugo Winterhalter and his Orchestra, with Eddie Heywood at the piano.

LAND OF LOVE (Come My Love And Live With Me) (1949) (wm)Eden Ahbez. (P)Nat "King" Cole.

LAND OF MILK AND HONEY, THE (1966) (wm)John Hurley—Ronnie Wilkins. (P)The Vogues.

LAND OF THE PHARAOHS (1955) (w)Ned Washington (m)Dimitri Tiomkin. (I)Film: Land Of The Pharaohs, on soundtrack.

LANGUAGE OF LOVE, THE (1984) (wm)Dan Fogelberg. (P)Dan Fogelberg.

LARA'S THEME (See Somewhere My Love)

LAROO, LAROO, LILLI BOLERO (1948) (wm)Sylvia Dee—Elizabeth Moore—Sidney Lippman. (P)Peggy Lee. (CR)Perry Como.

LAST CALL FOR LOVE (1942) (wm)E. Y. Harburg—Margery Cummings—Lane Burton. (I)Film: Ship Ahoy, by Tommy Dorsey and his Orchestra, vocal by Frank Sinatra.

LAST CHANCE (To Turn Around) (1965) (wm)Vic Millrose—Tony Bruno—Bob Elgin. (P)Gene Pitney.

LAST CHILD (1976) (wm)Stephen Tyler—Brad Whitford. (P)Aerosmith.

LAST DANCE (1958) (w)Sammy Cahn (m)Jimmy Van Heusen. (P)Frank Sinatra. (R)1960 by The McGuire Sisters.

LAST DANCE (1978) (wm)Paul Jabara. (I)Film: Thank God It's Friday, by Donna Summer. (P)Donna Summer. NARAS Award Winner.

LAST DATE (1960) (wm)Floyd Cramer. (P)Floyd Cramer. (CR)Lawrence Welk and his Orchestra. Vocal version by Pat Boone.

LAST FAREWELL, THE (1975) (wm)R. A. Webster—Roger Whittaker. (P)Roger Whittaker.

LAST GAME OF THE SEASON, THE (A Blind Man In The Bleachers) (1975) (wm)Sterling Whipple. (P)David Geddes.

LAST KISS (1961) (wm)Wayne Cochran. (P)Wayne Cochran. (R)1964 by J. Frank Wilson with The Cavaliers.

LAST NIGHT (1961) (wm)The Mar—Keys. (P)The Mar—Keys.

LAST NIGHT I DREAMED OF YOU (1937) (w)Walter Hirsch (m)Lou Handman. (I)Film: The Hit Parade, by Frances Langford.

LAST NIGHT ON THE BACK PORCH, I LOVED HER BEST OF ALL (1923) (wm)Lew Brown—Carl Schraubstader. (I)Revue: George White' Scandals of 1923, by Winnie Lightner. (P)Billy Jones and Ernie Hare (The Happiness Boys).

LAST NIGHT WHEN WE WERE YOUNG (1936) (w)E. Y. Harburg (m)Harold Arlen. (P)Lawrence Tibbett.

LAST ROUND-UP, THE (1933) (wm)Billy Hill. (I)At Paramount Theatre in New York, by Joe Morrison. (P)Bing Crosby. (CR)Gene Autry. (CR)Guy Lombardo and his Royal Canadians.

LAST SONG (1973) (wm)Lawrence Wayne Evoy. (P)Edward Bear.

LAST TANGO IN PARIS (1973) (w)Dory Previn (m)Gato Barbieri. (I)Film: Last Tango In Paris, by Gato Barbieri on soundtrack. (P)Herb Alpert.

LAST TIME, THE (1965) (wm)Mick Jagger—Keith Richard. (P)The Rolling Stones.

LAST TIME I FELT LIKE THIS, THE (1978) (w)Alan and Marilyn Bergman (m)Marvin Hamlisch. (I)Film: Same Time, Next Year, by voices of Johnny Mathis and Jane Olivor. (P)Johnny Mathis.

LAST TIME I SAW HIM (1974) (wm)Michael Masser—Pam Sawyer. (P)Diana Ross.

LAST TIME I SAW PARIS, THE (1940) (w)Oscar Hammerstein II (m)Jerome Kern. (I)Film: Lady, Be Good, by Ann Sothern. (P)Kate Smith. Academy Award Winner.

LAST TRAIN TO CLARKSVILLE (1966) (wm)Tommy Boyce—Bobby Hart. (P)The Monkees. No. 1 Chart Record.

LAST WALTZ, THE (1967) (wm)Les Reed—Barry Mason. (P)Engelbert Humperdinck.

LASTING LOVE (1957) (wm)Hunt Stevens—Jack Ackerman. (P)Sal Mineo.

LATE IN THE EVENING (1980) (wm)Paul Simon. (I)Film: One Trick Pony, by Paul Simon. (P)Paul Simon.

LATER THAN SPRING (1961) (wm)Noel Coward. (I)Musical: Sail Away, by James Hurst.

LATIN TUNE, A MANHATTAN MOON AND YOU, A (1940) (w)Al Dubin (m)Jimmy McHugh. (I)Musical: Keep Off The Grass, by Ray Bolger and Betty Bruce.

LATINS KNOW HOW (1940) (wm)Irving Berlin. (I)Musical: Louisiana Purchase, by Irene Bordoni.

LAUGH AND CALL IT LOVE (1938) (w)Johnny Burke (m)James V. Monaco. (I)Film: Sing You Sinners, by Bing Crosby.

LAUGH AT ME (1965) (wm)Sonny Bono. (P)Sonny.

LAUGH! CLOWN! LAUGH! (1928) (w)Sam M. Lewis—Joe Young (m)Ted Fiorito. (P)Ted Fiorito and his Orchestra. (CR)Ted Lewis.

LAUGH, LAUGH (1965) (wm)Ronald C. Elliott (P)The Beau Brummels.

LAUGHING (1969) (wm)Randy Bachman—Burton Cummings. (P)The Guess Who.

LAUGHING BOY (1963) (wm)William Robinson. (P)Mary Wells.

LAUGHING ON THE OUTSIDE (Crying On The Inside) (1946) (w)Ben Raleigh (m)Bernie Wayne. (I)Sammy Kaye and his Orchestra. (P)Dinah Shore. (CR)Andy Russell. (CR)The Four Aces.

LAUGHTER IN THE RAIN (1975) (wm)Neil Sedaka—Phil Cody. (P)Neil Sedaka. No. 1 Chart Record.

LAURA (1945) (w)Johnny Mercer (m)David Raksin. (I)Film: Laura, as soundtrack theme. (P)Woody Herman and his Orchestra. (CR)Dick Haymes. (CR)Stan Kenton and his Orchestra.

LAURIE (Strange Things Happen) (1965) (wm)Milton C. Addington. (P)Dickey Lee.

LAVENDER BLUE (Dilly Dilly) (1948) (wm)Larry Morey (m)Eliot Daniel. (I)Film: So Dear To My Heart, by Dinah Shore. (R)1959 by Sammy Turner.

LAWD, YOU MADE THE NIGHT TOO LONG (1932) (w)Sam L. Lewis (m)Victor Young. (I)Guy Lombardo and his Royal Canadians. (CR)Louis Armstrong. (R)1966 by Barbra Streisand.

LAWDY MISS CLAWDY (1952) (wm)Lloyd Price. (P)Lloyd Price. (R)1967 by The Buckinghams.

LAWRENCE OF ARABIA (Theme) (1962) (m)Maurice Jarre. (I)Film: Lawrence of Arabia, on soundtrack.

LAWYERS IN LOVE (1983) (wm)Jackson Browne. (P)Jackson Browne.

LAY DOWN SALLY (1978) (wm)Eric Clapton—Marcy Levy—George Terry. (P)Eric Clapton.

LAY DOWN YOUR ARMS (1956) (w-Eng)Paddy Roberts. (m)Ake Gerhard—Leon Land. (I)Anne Shelton. (P)The Chordettes.

LAY DOWN YOUR WEARY TUNE (1964) (wm)Bob Dylan. (P)Bob Dylan.

LAY, LADY, LAY (1969) (wm)Bob Dylan. (P)Bob Dylan. (CR)Ferrante and Teicher. (R)1972 by The Isley Brothers.

LAY YOUR HANDS ON ME (1985) (wm)Tom Bailey—Alannah Currie—Joe Leeway. (I)Film: Perfect, by The Thompson Twins, on soundtrack. (P)The Thompson Twins.

LAYLA (1971) (wm)Eric Clapton—James Beck Gordon. (P)Derek and The Dominoes.

LAZIEST GAL IN TOWN, THE (1927) (wm)Cole Porter. Not a hit when first released. (R)1950 film: Stage Fright, by Marlene Dietrich.

LAZY (1924) (wm)Irving Berlin. (I)The Brox Sisters. (P)Blossom Seeley. (CR)Al Jolson. (R)1954 film: There's No Business Like Show Business, by Marilyn Monroe, Donald O' Connor, and Mitzi Gaynor.

LAZY DAY (1967) (wm)Tony Powers—George Fischoff. (P)Spanky and Our Gang.

(Love's Got Me In A)LAZY MOOD (1957) (w)Johnny Mercer (m)Eddie Miller.

(I)1937 by Bob Crosby's Bobcat's, tenor sax solo by Eddie Miller. Vocal version by Johnny Mercer.

LAZY RHAPSODY (1932) (w)Mitchell Parish (m)Duke Ellington. (P)Duke Ellington and his Orchestra, vocal by Cootie Williams.

LAZY RIVER (1931) (wm)Hoagy Carmichael—Sidney Arodin. (I)Haogy Carmichael and his Orchestra. (R)1946 film: The Best Years Of Our Lives, by Hoagy Carmichael. (R)1952 by The Mills Brothers. (R)1961 by Si Zentner and his Orchestra. NARAS Award Winner. (CR)1961 by Bobby Darin.

LAZY SUMMER NIGHT (1958) (wm)Harold Spina. (I)Film: Andy Hardy Comes Home, on soundtrack. (P)The Four Preps.

LAZYBONES (1933) (wm)Johnny Mercer—Hoagy Carmichael. (P)Mildred Bailey. (CR)Rudy Vallee. (CR)Ben Bernie and his Orchestra.

LE FREAK (1978) (wm)Bernard Edwards—Nile Rodgers. (P)Chic. No. 1 Chart Record.

LEAD, KINDLY LIGHT (1868) (w)John Henry Newman (m)John Bacchus Dykes. Famous hymn.

LEAD ME ON (1978) (w)Allee Willis (m)David Lasley. (P)Maxine Nightingale.

LEADER OF THE BAND (1981) (wm)Dan Fogelberg. (P)Dan Fogelberg.

LEADER OF THE LAUNDROMAT (1964) (wm)Paul Vance—Lee Pockriss. (P)The Detergents.

LEADER OF THE PACK (1964) (wm)George Morton—Jeff Barry—Ellie Grenwich. (P)The Shangri—Las. No. 1 Chart Record.

LEAN ON ME (1972) (wm)Bill Withers. (P)Bill Withers. (R)1987 by Club Nouveau.

LEANIN' ON THE OLE TOP RAIL (1940) (wm)Nick and Charles Kenny. (I)Film: Ride Tenderfoot Ride, by Gene Autry. (P)Gene Autry. (CR)Bob Crosby and his Orchestra.

LEANING ON THE LAMP POST (1937) (wm)Noel Gay. (I)British film: Feather Your Nest, by George Formby. (R)1966 by Herman's Hermits.

LEAP FROG (1941) (w)Leo Corday (m)Joe Garland. (P)Les Brown and his Orchestra.

LEARN TO CROON (1933) (w)Sam Coslow (m)Arthur Johnston. (I)Film: College Humor, by Bing Crosby. (CR)Fran Frey.

LEARN TO DO THE STRUT (1923) (wm)Irving Berlin. (I)Revue: Music Box Revue of 1923, by The Brox Sisters. (P)Vincent Lopez and his Orchestra.

LEARNIN' THE BLUES (1955) (wm)Dolores Vicki Silvers. (P)Frank Sinatra. No. 1 Chart Record.

LEATHER AND LACE (1981) (wm)Stephanie Nicks. (P)Stevie Nicks with Don Henley.

LEAVE IT TO JANE (1917) (w)P. G. Wodehouse (m)Jerome Kern. (I)Musical: Leave It To Jane.

LEAVE US FACE IT (We're In Love) (1944) (wm)Abe Burroughs—Frank Loesser. (I)Radio Show: Duffy's Tavern, by Ed Gardner. (P)Hildegarde.

LEAVES THAT ARE GREEN (1966) (wm)Paul Simon. (P)Simon and Garfunkel.

LEAVING ME (1973) (wm)M. Barge—Jimmie Jiles. (P)The Independents.

LEAVING ON A JET PLANE (1969) (wm)John Denver. (P)Peter, Paul, and Mary. No. 1 Chart Record.

LEFT ALL ALONE AGAIN BLUES (1920) (w)Anne Caldwell (m)Jerome Kern. (I)Musical: The Night Boat, by Stella Hoban.

LEFT RIGHT OUT OF YOUR HEART (1958) (w)Earl Shuman (m)Mort Garson. (P)Patti Page.

LEGACY, THE (1978) (w)Betty Comden—Adolph Green (m)Cy Coleman. (I)Musical: On The Twentieth Century, by John Cullum.

LEGALIZE MY NAME (1946) (wm)Johnny Mercer (m)Harold Arlen. (I)Musical: St. Louis Woman, by Pearl Bailey.

LEGEND, THE (1977) (wm)Jerry Reed Hubbard. (I)Film: Smokey And The Bandit, by Jerry Reed.

LEGEND OF BONNIE AND CLYDE, THE (1968) (wm)Merle Haggard—Bonnie Owens. (P)Merle Haggard.

LEGEND OF WYATT EARP, THE (1955) (w)Harold Adamson (m)Harry Warren. (I)TV series: The Life And Legend Of Wyatt Earp, on soundtrack.

LEGS (1984) (wm)Billy Gibbons—Dusty Hill—Frank Beard. (P)Z. Z. Top.

LEMON TREE (1961) (wm)Will Holt. (P)Peter, Paul, and Mary. (R)1964 by Trini Lopez.

LENNY BRUCE (1981) (wm)Bob Dylan. (P)Bob Dylan.

LES BICYCLETTES DE BELSIZE (1968) (wm)Les Reed—Barry Mason. (P)Engelbert Humperdinck.

LET A SMILE BE YOUR UMBRELLA (1927) (w)Irving Kahal—Francis Wheeler (m)Sammy Fain. (I)Vaudeville: by Fain and Dunn. (P)Roger Wolfe Kahn and his Orchestra. (CR)Sam Lanin and his Orchestra.

LET 'EM EAT CAKE (1933) (w)Ira Gershwin (m)George Gershwin. (I)Musical: Let 'Em Eat Cake, by William Gaxton and The Chorus.

LET 'EM IN (1976) (wm)Paul and Linda McCartney. (P)Wings.

LET HER IN (1976) (wm)Gary Benson. (P)John Travolta.

LET IT BE (1970) (wm)John Lennon—Paul McCartney. (P)The Beatles. No. 1 Chart Record.

LET IT BE ME (1955) (w-Eng)Mann Curtis (m)Gilbert Becaud. (I)Gilbert Becaud. (P)1960 by The Everly Brothers. (R)1964 by Jerry Butler and Betty Everett.

(R)1969 by Glen Campbell and Bobbie Gentry. (R)1982 by Willie Nelson.

LET IT BLEED (1969) (wm)Mick Jagger—Keith Richard. (P)The Rolling Stones.

LET IT OUT (1967) (wm)The Hombres. (P)The Hombres.

LET IT RIDE (1973) (wm)Randy Bachman—Charles Turner. (P)Bachman—Turner Overdrive.

LET IT SNOW! LET IT SNOW! LET IT SNOW! (1946) (w)Sammy Cahn (m)Jule Styne. (P)Vaughn Monroe and his Orchestra. (CR)The Boswell Sisters. (CR)Woody Herman and his Orchestra.

LET IT WHIP (1982) (wm)Reginald Andrews—Leon Chancler. (P)The Dazz Band.

LET LOVE COME BETWEEN US (1967) (wm)Joe Sobotka—Johnny Wyker, III. (P)James and Bobby Purify.

LET ME! (1969) (wm)Mark Lindsay. (P)Paul Revere and The Raiders.

LET ME BE (1965) (wm)P. F. Sloan. (P)The Turtles.

LET ME BE THE ONE (1987) (wm)L. A. Martinee. (P)Expose.

LET ME BE THERE (1973) (wm)John Rostill. (P)Olivia Newton—John.

LET ME BE YOUR CAR (1974) (wm)Elton John—Bernie Taupin. (P)Rod Stewart.

LET ME BELONG TO YOU (1961) (w)Peter Udell (m)Gary Geld. (P)Brian Hyland.

LET ME CALL YOU SWEETHEART (1910) (wm)Beth Slater Whitson—Leo Friedman. (I)The Peerless Quartet.

LET ME DANCE FOR YOU (1985) (w)Edward Kleban (m)Marvin Hamlisch. (I)Film: A Chorus Line, by The Cast.

LET ME ENTERTAIN YOU (1959) (w)Stephen Sondheim (m)Jule Styne. (I)Musical: Gypsy, by Sandra Church and The Company.

LET ME GO LOVER! (1954) (wm)Jenny Lou Carson (w)Al Hill. (I)TV show, Studio One, by Joan Weber on soundtrack. (P)Joan Weber. (CR)Teresa Brewer.

LET ME GO TO HIM (1970) (w)Hal David (m)Burt Bacharach. (P)Dionne Warwick.

LET ME IN (1951) (wm)Bob Merrill. (P)The Fontane Sisters. (CR)Blue Barrona and his Orchestra.

LET ME IN (1962) (wm)Yvonne Baker. (P)The Sensations.

LET ME LOVE YOU TONIGHT (No Te Importe Saber) (1939) (wm)Mitchell Parish—Rene Touzet. No artist credited with introduction. (R)1944 by Woody Herman and his Orchestra.

LET ME LOVE YOU TONIGHT (1980) (wm)Jeff Wilson—Dan Greer—Steve Woodard. (P)Pure Prairie League.

LET ME OFF UPTOWN (1941) (wm)Redd Evans—Earl Bostic. (P)Gene Krupa and his Orchestra, vocal by Anita O'Day and Roy Eldridge.

LET ME SERENADE YOU (1973) (wm)John Finley. (P)Three Dog Night.

LET ME SING AND I'LL BE HAPPY (1930) (wm)Irving Berlin. (I)Film: Mammy, by Al Jolson. (P)Al Jolson. (R)1954 film: White Christmas, by Bing Crosby and Danny Kaye.

LET ME TICKLE YOUR FANCY (1982) (wm)Jermaine Jackson—Paul M. Jackson, Jr. —Pam Sawyer—Marilyn McLeod. (P)Jermaine Jackson.

LET ME TRY AGAIN (1973) (w-Eng)Paul Anka—Sammy Cahn (m)Caravelli. (P)Frank Sinatra.

LET MY LOVE OPEN THE DOOR (1980) (w)Peter Townshend. (P)Pete Townshend.

LET THE BELLS KEEP RINGING (1958) (wm)Paul Anka. (P)Paul Anka.

LET THE FOUR WINDS BLOW (1961) (wm)Antoine Domino—Dave Bartholomew. (P)Fats Domino. (CR)Roy Brown.

LET THE GOOD TIMES ROLL (1956) (wm)Leonard Lee. (P)Shirley and Lee. (R)1960 by Shirley and Lee. NARAS Award Winner. (R)1960 by Ray Charles. (R)1965 by Roy Orbison.

LET THE MUSIC PLAY (1984) (wm)Chris Barbosa—Ed Chisolm. (P)Shannon.

LET THE REST OF THE WORLD GO BY (1919)9w)J. Keirn Brennan (m)Ernest Ball. (I)Elizabeth Spencer.

LET THE SUNSHINE IN (1968) (w)Gerome Ragni—James Rado (m)Galt MacDermot. (I)Musical: Hair, by James Rado, Lynn Kellogg, Melba Moore and The Company. (P)The 5th Dimension in a medley with Aquarius. No. 1 Chart Record. NARAS Award Winner.

LET THERE BE DRUMS (1961) (m)Sandy Nelson—Richard Podolor. (P)Sandy Nelson.

LET THERE BE LOVE (1940) (w)Ian Grant (m)Lionel Rand. (P)Sammy Kaye and his Orchestra. (CR)Al Donahue and his Orchestra.

LET YOUR LOVE FLOW (1976) (wm)Lawrence Williams. (P)The Bellamy Brothers. No. 1 Chart Record.

LET YOURSELF GO (1936) (wm)Irving Berlin. (I)Film: Follow The Fleet, by Fred Astaire and Ginger Rogers.

LET'S ALL SING LIKE THE BIRDIES SING (1932) (w)Robert Hargreaves—Stanley Damerell (m)Tolchard Evans. (P)Ben Bernie and his Orchestra.

LET'S ALWAYS LOVE (1972) (w)Bob Merrill (m)Jule Styne. (I)Musical: Sugar, by Tony Roberts.

LET'S BE BUDDIES (1940) (wm)Cole Porter. (I)Musical: Panama Hattie, by Ethel Merman and Joan Carroll.

LET'S BEGIN (1933) (w)Otto Harbach (m)Jerome Kern. (I)Musical: Roberta, by George Murphy.

LET'S CALL THE WHOLE THING OFF (1937) (w)Ira Gershwin (m)George Gershwin. (I)Film: Shall We Dance, by Fred Astaire and Ginger Rogers. (P)Fred Astaire. (CR)Eddy Duchin and his Orchestra.

LET'S DANCE (1935) (w)Fanny Baldridge (m)Gregory Stone—Joseph Bonine. Adapted from Von Weber's Invitation To The Dance. (P)Theme song of Benny Goodman and his Orchestra.

LET'S DANCE (1962) (wm)Jim Lee. (P)Chris Montez.

LET'S DANCE (1983) (wm)David Bowie. (P)David Bowie. No. 1 Chart Record.

LET'S DO IT (Let's Fall In Love) (1928) (wm)Cole Porter. (I)Play with words: Paris, by Irene Bordoni and Arthur Margetson. (P)Paul Whiteman and his Orchestra. (R)1960 film: Can-Can, by Frank Sinatra and Shirley MacLaine. Most popular recording by Frank Sinatra.

LET'S DO IT AGAIN (1975) (wm)Curtis Mayfield. (P)The Staple Singers. No. 1 Chart Record.

LET'S FACE THE MUSIC AND DANCE (1936) (wm)Irving Berlin. (I)Film: Follow The Fleet, by Fred Astaire. (P)Fred Astaire. (CR)Ted Fiorito and his Orchestra.

LET'S FALL IN LOVE (1933) (w)Ted Koehler (m)Harold Arlen. (I)Film: Let's Fall In Love, by Art Jarrett and reprised by Ann Sothern. (P)Eddy Duchin and his Orchestra. No. 1 Chart Record. (R)1956 film: The Eddy Duchin Story, by Carmen Cavallaro (piano) on the soundtrack. (R)1967 by Peaches and Herb.

LET'S FLY AWAY (1930) (wm)Cole Porter. (I)Musical:

The New Yorkers, by Charles King and Hope Williams.

LET'S GET AWAY FROM IT ALL (1941) (w)Tom Adair (m)Matt Dennis. (I)Fats Waller. (P)Tommy Dorsey and his Orchestra, vocal by Frank Sinatra, Connie Haines, Jo Stafford and The Pied Pipers.

LET'S GET IT ON (1973) (wm)Edward Townshend—Marvin Gaye. (P)Marvin Gaye. No. 1 Chart Record.

LET'S GET LOST (1943) (w)Frank Loesser (m)Jimmy McHugh. (I)Film: *Happy Go Lucky*, by Mary Martin. (P)Vaughn Monroe and his Orchestra. No. 1 Chart Record. (CR)Jimmy Dorsey and his Orchestra.

LET'S GET SERIOUS (1980) (wm)Stevie Wonder—Lee Garrett. (P)Jermaine Jackson.

LET'S GET TOGETHER (1934) (m)Chick Webb. (P)Theme Song of Chick Webb and his Orchestra.

LET'S GO (1979) (wm)Ric Ocasek. (P)The Cars.

LET'S GO (1987) (wm)Wang Chung. (P)Wang Chung.

LET'S GO ALL THE WAY (1986) (wm)Gary Cooper. (P)Sly Fox.

LET'S GO BACK TO THE WALTZ (1962) (wm)Irving Berlin. (I)Musical: *Mr. President*, by Nanette Fabray and The Ensemble.

LET'S GO BAVARIAN (1933) (w)Harold Adamson (m)Burton Lane. (I)Film: *Dancing Lady*, by Fred Astaire and Joan Crawford.

LET'S GO CRAZY (1984) (wm)Prine Rogers Nelson. (I)Film: *Purple Rain*, by Prince. (P)Prince. No. 1 Chart Record.

LET'S GO FLY A KITE (1963) (wm)Richard M. Sherman—Robert B. Sherman. (I)Film: *Mary Poppins*, by Dick Van Dyke and David Tomlinson.

LET'S GO GET STONED (1966) (wm)Nicholas Ashford—Valerie Simpson—Joseph Armstead. (P)Ray Charles.

LET'S GO, LET'S GO, LET'S GO (1960) (wm)Hank Ballard. (P)Hank Ballard and The Midnighters.

LET'S GO STEADY AGAIN (1963) (wm)Howard Greenfield—Neil Sedaka. (P)Neil Sedaka.

LET'S GO TO CHURCH (Next Sunday Morning) (1950) (wm)Steve Allen. (P)Jimmy Wakely and Margaret Whiting.

LET'S GROOVE (1981) (wm)Maurice White—Wayne Vaughn—W. Vaughn. (P)Earth, Wind, and Fire.

LET'S HANG ON (To What We've Got) (1965) (wm)Bob Crewe—Sandy Linzer—Denny Randell. (P)The Four Seasons. (R)1982 by Barry Manilow.

LET'S HAVE ANOTHER CUP OF COFFEE (1932) (wm)Irving Berlin. (I)Musical: *Face The Music*, by Katherine Carrington and J. Harold Murray. (P)Fred Waring's Pennsylvanians. (R)1954 film: *There's No Business Like Show Business*, by Ethel Merman.

LET'S HEAR IT FOR THE BOY (1984) (w)Dean Pitchford (m)Tom Snow. (P)Deniece Williams. No. 1 Chart Record.

LET'S KISS AND MAKE UP (1927) (w)Ira Gershwin (m)George Gershwin. (I)Musical: *Funny Face*, by Fred and Adele Astaire. (R)1957 film: *Funny Face*, by Fred Astaire.

LET'S LIVE FOR TODAY (1967) (w-Eng)Michael Julien (m)Mogol—D. Shapiro. (P)Grass Roots.

LET'S LOCK THE DOOR AND THROW AWAY THE KEY (1964) (wm)Roy Alfred—Wes Farrell. (P)Jay and The Americans.

LET'S MISBEHAVE (1928) (wm)Cole Porter. Written for Play: Paris,but deleted before New York opening. Recorded by Ben Bernie and his Orchestra.

LET'S NOT BE SENSIBLE (1962) (w)Sammy Cahn (m)Jimmy Van Heusen. (I)Musical: *The Road To Hong Kong*, by Bing Crosby and Dorothy Lamour.

LET'S NOT TALK ABOUT LOVE (1941) (wm)Cole Porter. (I)Musical: *Let's Face It*, by Danny Kaye and Eve Arden.

LET'S NOT WASTE A MOMENT (1961) (wm)Jerry Herman. (I)Musical: *Milk And Honey*, by Robert Weede.

LET'S PUT IT ALL TOGETHER (1974) (wm)Luigi Creatore—Hugo Peretti—George David Weiss. (P)The Stylistics.

LET'S PUT OUR HEADS TOGETHER (1937) (w)E. Y. Harburg (m)Harold Arlen. (I)Film: *Gold Diggers of 1937*, by Dick Powell.

LET'S PUT OUT THE LIGHTS AND GO TO SLEEP (1932) (wm)Herman Hupfeld. (I)Rudy Vallee. (P)Ozzie Nelson and Harriet Hilliard. (CR)Ben Bernie and his Orchestra.

LET'S SAY GOOD NIGHT TILL IT'S MORNING (1925) (w)Otto Harbach—Oscar Hammerstein II (m)Jerome Kern. (I)Musical: *Sunny*, by Jack Donahue and Mary Hay.

LET'S SAY GOODBYE (1932) (wm)Noel Coward. (I)London musical: *Words And Music*, by Rita Lyle and Edward Underdown.

LET'S SPEND THE NIGHT TOGETHER (1967) (wm)Mick Jagger—Keith Richard. (P)The Rolling Stones.

LET'S START ALL OVER AGAIN (1966) (wm)Al Kasha—Joel Hirschorn. (P)Ronnie Dove.

LET'S START THE NEW YEAR RIGHT (1942) (wm)Irving Berlin. (I)Film: *Holiday Inn*, by Bing Crosby. (P)Bing Crosby.

LET'S STAY TOGETHER (1972) (wm)Al Green—Willie Mitchell—Al Jackson. (P)Al Green. No. 1 Chart Record. (CR)Isaac Hayes. (R)1984 by Tina Turner.

LET'S STEP OUT (1930) (wm)Cole Porter. (I)Musical: *Fifty Million Frenchmen*, by Evelyn Hoey, Gertrude McDonald, and Reed and Duthers.

LET'S TAKE A WALK AROUND THE BLOCK (1934) (w)Ira Gershwin—E. Y. Harburg (m)Harold Arlen. (I)Revue: *Life Begins At 8:40* by Dixie Dunbar and Earl Oxford.

LET'S TAKE AN OLD FASHIONED WALK (1948) (wm)Irving Berlin. (I)Musical: *Miss Liberty*, by Eddie Albert and Allyn McLerie. (P)Perry Como. (CR)Doris Day. (CR)Frank Sinatra.

LET'S TAKE THE LONG WAY HOME (1944) (w)Johnny Mercer (m)Harold Arlen. (I)Film: *Here Come The Waves*, by Bing Crosby and Betty Hutton.

LET'S THINK ABOUT LIVING (1960) (wm)Boudleaux Bryant. (P)Bob Luman.

LET'S TURKEY TROT (1963) (wm)Gerry Goffin—Jack Keller. (P)Little Eva.

LET'S TWIST AGAIN (1961) (w)Kal Mann (m)Kal Mann—Dave Appell. (P)Chubby Checker. NARAS Award Winner.

LET'S WAIT AWHILE (1987) (wm)Janet Jackson—J. Harris—T. Lewis—M. Andrews. (P)Janet Jackson.

LETTER, THE (1969) (wm)Wayne Carson Thompson. (P)The Box Tops. No. 1 Chart Record. (R)1969 by The Arbors. (R)1970 by Joe Cocker.

LEVON (1972) (wm)Elton John—Bernie Taupin. (P)Elton John.

LIAR (1969) (wm)Russ Ballard. (I)Argent. (P)Three Dog Night.

LIAR, LIAR (1965) (wm)James J. Donna (P)The Castaways.

LIAISONS (1973) (wm)Stephen Sondheim. (I)Musical: *A Little Night Music*, by Len Cariou.

LIBERTY BELL (1893) (m)John Philip Sousa. Famous American march.

LICKING STICK-LICKING STICK (1968) (wm)James Brown—Bobby Byrd—Alfred Ellis. (P)James Brown.

LIDA ROSE (1957) (wm)Meredith Willson. (I)Musical: *The Music Man*, by Bill Spangenberg, Wayne Ward, Al Shea, and Vern Reed.

LIDO SHUFFLE (1970) (wm)David Paitch—William Scaggs. (P)Boz Scaggs.

LIE TO ME (1962) (wm)Brook Benton—Margie Singleton. (P)Brook Benton.

LIEBESFREUD (1910) (m)Fritz Kreisler. Famous classical violin solo. (P)Fritz Kreisler.

LIEBESLIED (1910) (m)Fritz Kreisler. Famous classical violin solo. (P)Fritz Kreisler.

LIEBESTRAUM (1847) (m)Franz Liszt. Famous classical selection.

LIECHTENSTEINER POLKA (1957) (wm)Edmund Koetscher—R. Lindt. (P)Will Glahe and his Orchestra.

LIES (1931) (w)George E. Springer (m)Harry Barris. (P)Russ Columbo. (R)1953 by Perry Como.

LIES (Are Breakin' My Heart) (1965) (wm)Buddy Randell—Beau Charles. (P)The Knickerbockers.

LIFE GOES TO A PARTY (1937) (m)Benny Goodman—Harry James. (P)Benny Goodman and his Orchestra.

LIFE I LEAD, THE (1963) (wm)Richard M. Sherman—Robert B. Sherman. (I)Film: *Mary Poppins*, by David Tomlinson.

LIFE IN A NORTHERN TOWN (1986) (wm)Nick Laird—Clowes—Gilbert Gabriel. (P)The Dream Academy.

LIFE IN ONE DAY (1985) (wm)Howard Jones. (P)Howard Jones.

LIFE IN THE FAST LANE (1977) (wm)Glenn Frey—Don Henley—Joe Walsh. (P)The Eagles.

LIFE IS A BEAUTIFUL THING (1951) (wm)Jay Livingston—Ray Evans. (I)Film: *Aaron Slick From Punkin Creek*, by Dinah Shore. (P)Dinah Shore.

LIFE IS A ROCK (But The Radio Rolled Me) (1974) (wm)Norman Dolph—Paul DiFranco. (P)Reunion.

LIFE IS A SONG (Let's Sing It Together) (1935) (w)Joe Young (m)Fred Ahlert. (I)Frank Parker. (P)Ruth Etting. No. 1 Chart Record. (CR)Freddy Martin and his Orchestra.

LIFE IS JUST A BOWL OF CHERRIES (1931) (w)Lew Brown (m)Ray Henderson. (I)Revue: *George White's Scandals*, by Ethel Merman. (P)Rudy Vallee. (CR)Bing Crosby. (R)1954 by Jaye P. Morgan.

LIFE IS SO PECULIAR (1950) (w)Johnny Burke (m)Jimmy Van Heusen. (I)Film: *Mr. Music*, by Bing Crosby, Peggy Lee, The Merry Macs, and Groucho Marx.

LIFE IS WHAT YOU MAKE IT (1971) (w)Johnny Mercer (m)Marvin Hamlisch. (I)Film: *Kotch*, by voice of Johnny Mathis.

LIFE OF A ROSE, THE (1923) (w)B. G. De Sylva (m)George Gershwin. (I)Revue: *George White's Scandals of 1923*, by Marga Waldron and Richard Bold.

LIFE UPON THE WICKED STAGE (1927) (w)Oscar Hammerstein II (m)Jerome Kern. (I)Musical: *Show Boat*, by Eva Puck. (R)1951 film: *Show Boat*, by Marge and Gower Champion.

LIFE'S A DANCE (1937) (w)E. Y. Harburg (m)Harold Arlen. (I)Musical: *Hooray For What!*, by Robert Shafer.

LIFE'S BEEN GOOD (1978) (wm)Joe Walsh. (P)Joe Walsh.

LIFE'S FULL OF CONSEQUENCE (1943) (w)E. Y. Harburg (m)Harold Arlen. (I)Film: *Cabin In The Sky*, by Lena Horne and Eddie "Rochester" Anderson.

LIGHT CAVALRY (Overture) (1868) (m)Franz Von Suppe. Famous classical composition.

LIGHT MY FIRE (1967) (wm)Jim Morrison, John Densmore, Robert Krieger, and Raymond Manzarek. (P)The Doors. No. 1 Chart Record. (R)1968 by Jose Feliciano. (R)1979 by Amii Stewart in a medley.

LIGHTNIN' STRIKES (1965) (w)Lou Christie (m)Twyla Herbert. (P)Lou Christie. No. 1 Chart Record.

LIGHTNING'S GIRL (1967) (wm)Lee Hazlewood. (P)Nancy Sinatra.

LIGHTS OUT (1935) (wm)Billy Hill. (P)Ozzie Nelson and Harriet Hilliard. (CR)Eddy Duchin and his Orchestra.

LIGHTS OUT (1984) (wm)Peter Wolf—Don Covay. (P)Peter Wolf.

LIKE A BABY (1966) (wm)John Madera—David White—Len Barry. (P)Len Barry.

LIKE A ROCK (1986) (wm)Bob Seger. (P)Bob Seger & The Silver Bullet Band.

LIKE A ROLLING STONE (1965) (wm)Bob Dylan. (P)Bob Dylan.

LIKE A SAD SONG (1976) (wm)John Denver. (P)John Denver. (CR)Frank Sinatra.

LIKE A VIRGIN (1984) (wm)Billy Steinberg—Tom Kelly. (P)Madonna. No. 1 Chart Record.

LIKE A YOUNG MAN (1961) (wm)Jerry Herman. (I)Musical: *Milk And Honey*, by Robert Weede.

LIKE AN OLD TIME MOVIE (1967) (wm)John Phillips. (P)Scott McKenzie.

LIKE DREAMERS DO (1964) (wm)John Lennon—Paul McCartney. (P)The Beatles.

LIKE HE LOVES ME (1926) (w)Anne Caldwell (m)Vincent Youmans. (I)Musical: *Oh, Please!*, by Beatrice Lillie.

LIKE NO OTHER NIGHT (1986) (wm)Don Barnes—Jon Bettis—Jim Vallance—Jeff Carlisi. (P)38 Special.

LIKE ORDINARY PEOPLE DO (1931) (w)Lorenz Hart (m)Richard Rodgers. (I)Film: *Hot Heiress*, by Ben Lyon, Inez Courtney, and Ona Munson.

LIKE SOMEONE IN LOVE (1944) (w)Johnny Burke (m)Jimmy Van Heusen. (I)Film: *Belle Of The Yukon*, by Dinah Shore. (P)Bing Crosby.

LIKE THE FELLA ONCE SAID (1940) (w)Johnny Mercer (m)Jimmy McHugh. (I)Film: *You'll Find Out*, by Kay Kyser and his College of Musical Knowledge.

LIKE TO GET TO KNOW YOU (1968) (wm)Stuart Scharf. (P)Spanky and Our Gang.

LI'L DARLIN' (1958) (m)Neal Hefti. (P)Count Basie and his Orchestra.

L'IL RED RIDING HOOD (1966) (wm)Ronald Blackwell. (P)Sam the Sham and The Pharaohs.

LILACS IN THE RAIN (1934) (w)Mitchell Parish (m)Peter De Rose. (P)Bob Crosby and his Orchestra. (CR)Charlie Barnet and his Orchestra.

LILLI MARLENE (1940) (w-Eng)Tommie Connor (m)Norbert Schultze. (I)England by Anne Shelton. (I)United States, by Marlene Dietrich. (R)1968 by Al Martino.

LILY BELLE (1945) (wm)Dave Franklin—Irving Taylor. (P)Freddy Martin and his Orchestra. (CR)The Pied

Pipers. (CR)Perry Como.

LILY OF LAGUNA (1942) (wm)Paul Francis Webster—Ted Fiorito. (P)Bing Crosby and Mary Martin.

LIMBO ROCK (1962) (wm)Jon Sheldon—Billy Strange. (P)Chubby Checker. (CR)The Champs.

LIMEHOUSE BLUES (1924) (w)Douglas Furber (m)Philip Braham. (I)Revue: *Andre Charlot's Revue of 1924*, by Gertrude Lawrence, Robert Hobbs, and Fred Leslie. (P)Paul Whiteman and his Orchestra. (R)1968 film: *Star!*, by Julie Andrews and The Male Chorus.

LINDA (1930) (w)Ted Koehler (m)Harold Arlen. (I)Revue: *Brown Sugar*. (P)Harold Arlen with Red Nichols and his Orchestra. (CR)Benny Goodman and his Orchestra.

LINDA (1947) (wm)Jack Lawrence. (P)Buddy Clark with Ray Noble and his Orchestra. (CR)Charlie Spivak and his Orchestra.

LING TING TONG (1954) (wm)Mable Godwin. (P)The Five Keys. (CR)Otis Williams and The Charms.

LINGER AWHILE (1923) (w)Harry Owens (m)Vincent Rose. (I)Lew Gold and his Orchestra. (P)Paul Whiteman and his Orchestra, with banjo solo by Mike Pingatore. (CR)Ted Lewis.

LIPS OF WINE (1957) (w)Shirley Wolfe (m)Sy Soloway. (P)Andy Williams.

LIPSTICK AND CANDY AND RUBBER SOLE SHOES (wm)Bob Haymes. (P)Julius La Rosa.

LIPSTICK ON YOUR COLLAR (1959) (w)Edna Lewis (m)George Goehring. (P)Connie Francis.

LISBON ANTIGUA (In Old Lisbon) (1956) (w-Eng)Harry Dupree (m)Raul Portela. (P)Nelson Riddle and his Orchestra. (CR)Mitch Miller and his Orchestra. Vocal version by Alan Dale.

LISTEN MY CHILDREN AND YOU SHALL HEAR (1937) (w)Ralph Freed (m)Burton Lane. (I)Film: *Double Or Nothing*, by Martha Raye.

LISTEN, PEOPLE (1966) (wm)Graham Gouldman. (I)Film: *When The Boys Meet The Girls*, by Herman's Hermits. (P)Herman's Hermits.

LISTEN TO THE MOCKING BIRD (1855) (w)Septimus Winner (m)Richard Milburn. First recording in 1891 by John Yorke Atlee.

LISTEN TO THE MUSIC (1972) (wm)Tom Johnston. (P)The Doobie Brothers.

LISTEN TO WHAT THE MAN SAID (1975) (wm)Paul and Linda McCartney. (P)Paul McCartney and Wings. No. 1 Chart Record.

LITTLE ANNIE ROONIE (1890) (wm)Michael Nolan. (I)Annie Hart.

LITTLE ARROWS (1968) (wm)Albert Hammond—Mike Hazlewood. (P)Leapy Lee.

LITTLE BIRD TOLD ME, A (1947) (wm)Harvey O. Brooks. (I)Paula Watson. (P)Evelyn Knight. No. 1 Chart Record.

LITTLE BIRDIE TOLD ME SO, A (1926) (w)Lorenz Hart (m)Richard Rodgers. (I)Musical: *Peggy Ann*, by Helen Ford.

LITTLE BISCUIT (1957) (w)E. Y. Harburg (m)Harold Arlen. (I)Musical: *Jamaica*, by Josephine Premice.

LITTLE BIT IN LOVE, A (1953) (w)Betty Comden—Adolph Green (m)Leonard Bernstein. (I)Musical: *On The Town*, by Edith Adams.

LITTLE BIT INDEPENDENT, A (1935) (w)Edgar Leslie (m)Joe Burke. (P)Fats Waller. No. 1 Chart Record. (CR)Freddy Martin and his Orchestra.

LITTLE BIT ME, A LITTLE BIT YOU, A (1967) (wm)Neil Diamond. (P)The Monkees.

LITTLE BIT MORE, A (1976) (wm)Bobby Gosh. (P)Dr. Hook.

LITTLE BIT O' SOUL (1967) (wm)John Shakespeare—Kenneth Lewis. (P)The Music Explosion.

LITTLE BIT OF HEAVEN, SURE THEY CALL IT IRELAND (1914) (w)J. Keirn Brennan (m)Ernest R. Ball. (I)Musical: *The Heart Of Paddy Whack*. (P)Bing Crosby.

LITTLE BIT OF HEAVEN, A (1966) (wm)Arthur Resnick—Kenny Young (P)Ronnie Dove.

LITTLE BIT OF SOAP, A (1961) (P)The Jarmels. (R)1965 by Garnet Mimms. (R)1965 by The Exciters. (R)1970 by Paul Davis. (R)1979 by Nigel Olsson.

LITTLE BITTY PRETTY ONE (1957) (wm)Robert Byrd. (P)Thurston Harris. (CR)Bobby Day. (R)1960 by Frankie Lymon. (R)1962 by Clyde McPhatter. (R)1972 by The Jackson Five.

LITTLE BITTY TEAR, A (1962) (wm)Hank Cochran. (P)Burl Ives. (CR)Wanda Jackson.

LITTLE BLACK BOOK (1962) (wm)Jimmy Dean.

LITTLE BLUE MAN, THE (1958) (wm)Fred Ebb—Paul Klein. (P)Betty Johnson.

LITTLE BOY AND THE OLD MAN, THE (1953) (wm)Wayne Shanklin. (P)Frankie Laine and Jimmy Boyd.

LITTLE BOY BLUES, THE (1948) (wm)Hugh Martin. (I)Musical: *Look Ma, I'm Dancin'!*, by Hugh Martin and Sandra Deel.

LITTLE BROWN BOOK (1944) (wm)Billy Strayhorn. (P)Duke Ellington and his Orchestra.

LITTLE BROWN JUG (1869) (wm)Joseph E. Winner. (P)In 1911 by The Weatherwax Brothers Quartet. (R)1939 by Glenn Miller and his Orchestra, arrangement by Bill Finegan.

LITTLE BUNGALOW, A (1925) (wm)Irving Berlin. (I)Musical: *The Cocoanuts*, by John Barker and Mabel Withee.

LITTLE BUTTERFLY (1923) (wm)Irving Berlin. (I)Revue: *Music Box Revue of 1923*.

LITTLE BY LITTLE (1929) (wm)Walter O'Keefe—Bobby Dolan. (I)Film: *The Sophomore*, by Sally O'Neil and Eddie Quillan. (P)Theme Song of Little Jack Little and his Orchestra.

LITTLE CHILD (1963) (wm)John Lennon—Paul McCartney. (P)The Beatles.

LITTLE CHILDREN (1964) (wm)Mort Shuman—J. Leslie McFarland. (P)Billy J. Kramer and The Dakotas.

LITTLE CURLY HAIR IN A HIGH CHAIR (1940) (w)Charles Tobias (m)Nat Simon. (I)Film: *Forty Little Mothers*, by Eddie Cantor.

LITTLE DARLIN' (1957) (wm)Maurice Williams. (P)The Diamonds.

LITTLE DARLING (I Need You) (1966) (wm)Eddie Holland—Lamont Dozier—Brian Holland. (P)Marvin Gaye. (R)1977 by The Doobie Brothers.

LITTLE DAVID, PLAY ON YOUR HARP (1921) (wm)Unknown. Traditional Black American spiritual.

LITTLE DEVIL (1961) (wm)Howard Greenfield—Neil Sedaka. (P)Neil Sedaka.

LITTLE DIANE (1962) (wm)Dion Di Mucci. (P)Dion.

LITTLE DIPPER (1959) (m)Robert Maxwell. (P)The Mickey Mozart Quintet.

LITTLE DROPS OF RAIN (1961) (w)E. Y. Harburg (m)Harold Arlen. (I)Cartoon film: *Gay Purr—ee*, by voices of Judy Garland and Robert Goulet.

LITTLE DRUMMER BOY, THE (1958) (wm)Katherine Davis—Henry Onorati—Harry Simeone. (P)The Harry Simeone Chorale.

LITTLE DUTCH MILL (1934) (w)Ralph Freed (m)Harry Barris. (P)Bing Crosby. No. 1 Chart Record. (CR)Don Bestor and his Orchestra.

LITTLE GIRL (1931) (wm)Madeline Hyde—Francis Henry. (P)Guy Lombardo and his Royal Canadians. (R)1948 by Nat "King" Cole.

LITTLE GIRL (1966) (wm)Don Baskin—Bob Gonzalez. (P)The Syndicate of Sound.

LITTLE GIRL BLUE (1935) (w)Lorenz Hart (m)Richard Rodgers. (I)Musical: *Billy Rose's Jumbo*, by Gloria Grafton. (R)1962 film: *Jumbo*, by Doris Day.

LITTLE GIRL FROM LITTLE ROCK, A (1949) (w)Leo Robin (m)Jule Styne. (I)Musical: *Gentlemen Prefer Blondes*, by Carol Channing. In film version 1953, by Marilyn Monroe.

LITTLE GIRL I ONCE KNEW, THE (1965) (wm)Brian Wilson. (P)The Beach Boys.

LITTLE GRAY HOUSE, THE (1949) (w)Maxwell Anderson (m)Kurt Weill. (I)Musical: *Lost In The Stars*, by Todd Duncan.

LITTLE GREEN APPLES (1968) (wm)Bobby Russell. (P)O. C. Smith. (CR)Roger Miller. (CR)Patti Page. NARAS Award Winner.

LITTLE HONDA (1964) (wm)Brian Wilson. (P)The Hondells. (CR)The Beach Boys.

LITTLE IN LOVE, A (1980) (wm)Alan Tarney. (P)Cliff Richard.

LITTLE JAZZ BIRD (1924) (w)Ira Gershwin (m)George Gershwin. (I)Musical: *Lady, Be Good!*, by Cliff Edwards.

LITTLE JEANNIE (1980) (w)Gary Osborne (m)Elton John. (P)Elton John.

LITTLE KISS AT TWILIGHT (1938) (wm)Leo Robin—Ralph Rainger. (I)Film: *Give Me A Sailor*, by Martha Raye.

LITTLE KISS EACH MORNING, A (A Little Kiss Each Night) (1929) (wm)Harry Woods. (I)Film: *The Vagabond Lover*, by Rudy Vallee. (P)Rudy Vallee. (CR)Guy Lombardo and his Royal Canadians.

LITTLE LADY MAKE BELIEVE (1936) (w)Charles Tobias (m)Nat Simon. (P)Guy Lombardo and his Royal Canadians.

LITTLE LAMB (1959) (w)Stephen Sondheim (m)Jule Styne. (I)Musical: *Gypsy*, by Sandra Church.

LITTLE LATIN LUPE LU (1962) (wm)Bill Medley. (P)Mitch Ryder and The Detroit Wheels. (CR)The Righteous Brothers.

LITTLE LIES (1987) (wm)Christine McVie—E. Quintela. (P)Fleetwood Mac.

LITTLE LOVE CAN GO A LONG, LONG WAY, A (1955) (w)Paul Francis Webster (m)Sammy Fain. (I)Film: *Ain't Misbehavin'*. (P)The Dream Weavers.

LITTLE MAMA (1954) (wm)Carmen Taylor—Willis Carroll—Ahmet Ertegun—Jerry Wexler. (P)The Clovers.

LITTLE MAN WITH A CANDY CIGAR (1941) (w)Frank Kilduff (m)Matt Dennis. (P)Tommy Dorsey and his Orchestra, vocal by Jo Stafford.

LITTLE MAN, YOU'VE HAD A BUSY DAY (1934) (w)Maurice Sigler—Al Hoffman (m)Mabel Wayne. (P)Isham Jones and his Orchestra. (CR)Emil Coleman and his Orchestra.

LITTLE ME (1962) (w)Carolyn Leigh (m)Cy Coleman. (I)Musical: *Little Me*, by Nancy Andrews and Virginia Martin.

LITTLE MORE LOVE, A (1979) (wm)John Farrar. (P)Olivia Newton—John.

LITTLE OLD LADY (1936) (w)Stanley Adams (m)Hoagy Carmichael. (I)Revue: *The Show Is On*, by Mitzi Mayfair and Charles Walters. (P)Abe Lyman and his Orchestra. (CR)Shep Fields and his Orchestra.

LITTLE OLD LADY, THE (From Pasadena) (1964) (wm)Roger Christian—Don Altfeld. (P)Jan and Dean.

LITTLE OLD MILL, THE (Went Round And Round) (1947) (wm)Don Pelosi—Lewis Ilda—Leo Towers. (P)Sammy Kaye and his Orchestra.

LITTLE OLD NEW YORK (1960) (w)Sheldon Harnick (m)Jerry Bock. (I)Musical: *Tenderloin*, by Eileen Rodgers, Lee Becker, and The Tenderloin Crowd.

LITTLE OLE MAN (Uptight Everything's Alright) (1967) (wm)Sylvia Moy—Stevie Wonder—Henry Cosby. (P)Bill Cosby.

LITTLE OLE WINEDRINKER ME (1967) (wm)Samuel Garrett—Dick Jennings. (P)Dean Martin. (CR)Robert Mitchum.

LITTLE ON THE LONELY SIDE, A (1944) (wm)Dick Robertson—James Cavanaugh—Frank Weldon. (P)Frankie Carle and his Orchestra, vocal by Paul Allen. (CR)Guy Lombardo and his Royal Canadians.

LITTLE PAL (1929) (wm)B. G. De Sylva—Lew Brown—Ray Henderson. (I)Film: *Say It With Songs*, by Al Jolson. (P)Al Jolson. No. 1 Chart Record. (CR)Gene Austin.

LITTLE PRINCE, THE (1974) (w)Alan Jay Lerner (m)Frederick Loewe. (I)Film: *The Little Prince*, by Richard Kiley.

LITTLE RED CORVETTE (1983) (wm)Prince Rogers Nelson. (P)Prince.

LITTLE RED FOX, THE (1939) (w)James V. Kern—Hy Heath—Johnny Lange (m)Lew Porter. (I)Film: *That's Right—You're Wrong*, by Kay Kyser and Harry Babbitt.

LITTLE RED ROOSTER (1961) (wm)Willie Dixon. (P)Sam Cooke.

LITTLE ROCK GETAWAY (1933) (m)Joe Sullivan. (I)Joe Sullivan as piano solo. (P)Bob Crosby and his Orchestra.

LITTLE SHOEMAKER, THE (1954) (w-Eng)Geoffrey Parsons—John Turner. (m)Rudi Revil. (P)the Gaylords. (CR)Hugo Winterhalter and his Orchestra.

LITTLE SIR ECHO (1939) (wm)Laura Smith—J. S. Fearis—Adele Girard Marsala—Joe Marsala. (P)Horace Heidt and his Musical Knights. (CR)Bing Crosby. (CR)Guy Lombardo and his Royal Canadians.

LITTLE SISTER (1961) (wm)Doc Pomus—Mort Shuman. (P)Elvis Presley.

LITTLE SKIPPER FROM HEAVEN ABOVE, A (1936) (wm)Cole Porter. (I)Musical: *Red, Hot and Blue*, by Jimmy Durante and The Chorus.

LITTLE STAR (1958) (wm)Vito Picone—Arthur Venosa. (P)The Elegants. No. 1 Chart Record.

LITTLE STREET WHERE OLD FRIENDS MEET, A (1932) (w)Gus Kahn—Harry Woods. (P)Guy Lombardo and his Royal Canadians.

LITTLE THINGS (1965) (wm)Bobby Goldsboro. (P)Bobby Goldsboro.

LITTLE THINGS IN LIFE, THE (1930) (wm)Irving Berlin. (P)Gus Arnheim and his Orchestra.

LITTLE THINGS MEAN A LOT (1954) (wm)Edith Lindeman—Carl Stutz. (P)Kitty Kallen. No. 1 Chart Record. (CR)Joni James.

LITTLE THINGS YOU USED TO DO, THE (1935) (w)Al Dubin (m)Allie Wrubel. (I)Film: Go Into Your Dance, by Helen Morgan.

LITTLE TOO LATE (1983) (wm)Alex Call. (P)Pat Benatar.

LITTLE TOWN FLIRT (1963) (wm)Marion McKenzie—Del Shannon. (P)Del Shannon.

LITTLE WHITE CLOUD THAT CRIED, THE (1951) (wm)Johnnie Ray. (P)Johnnie Ray.

LITTLE WHITE GARDENIA, A (1935) (wm)Sam Coslow. (I)Film: All The King's Horses, by Carl Brisson and Mary Ellis. (P)Hal Kemp and his Orchestra.

LITTLE WHITE LIES (1930) (wm)Walter Donaldson. (P)Guy Lombardo and his Royal Canadians. (CR)Fred Waring's Pennsylvanians. (R)1948 by Dick Haymes.

LITTLE WILLY (1973) (wm)Mike Day. (P)The Sweet.

LITTY BITTY GIRL (1960) (wm)Clint Ballard, Jr. —Fred Tobias. (P)Bobby Rydell.

LIVE AND LET DIE (1973) (wm)Paul and Linda McCartney. (I)Film: Live And Let Die, by Paul McCartney & Wings. (P)Paul Mc Cartney & Wings.

LIVE AND LET LIVE (1953) (wm)Cole Porter. (I)Musical: Can-Can, by Lilo.

LIVE TO TELL (1986) (wm)Madonna—Pat Leonard. (P)Madonna. No. 1 Chart Record.

LIVE WITH ME (1969) (wm)Mick Jagger—Keith Richard. (P)The Rolling Stones.

LIVELY UP YOURSELF (1975) (wm)Bob Marley. (P)Bob Marley.

LIVIN' FOR THE WEEKEND (1976) (wm)Cary Gilbert—Kenny Gamble—Leon Huff. (P)The O'Jays.

LIVIN' FOR YOU (1974) (wm)Al Green—Willie Mitchell. (P)Al Green.

LIVIN' IN THE SUNLIGHT-LOVIN' IN THE MOONLIGHT (1930) (w)Al Lewis (m)Al Sherman. (I)Film: The Big Pond, by Maurice Chevalier.

LIVIN' IT UP (Friday Night) (1979) (wm)Leroy Bell—Casey James. (P)Bell & James.

LIVIN' ON A PRAYER (1987) (wm)J. Bon Jovi—R. Sambora—D. Child. (P)Bon Jovi. No. 1 Chart Record.

LIVIN' THING (1976) (wm)Jeff Lynne. (P)Electric Light Orchestra.

LIVING DOLL (1959) (wm)Lionel Bart. (I)Film: Serious Charge, by Cliff Richard. (P)Cliff Richard.

LIVING FOR THE CITY (1974) (wm)Stevie Wonder. (P)Stevie Wonder. NARAS Award Winner. (CR)Ray Charles.

LIVING IN A BOX (1987) (wm)Vere—Piggot. (P)Living In A Box.

LIVING IN AMERICA (1985) (wm)Dan Hartman—Charlie Midnight. (I)Film: Rocky IV, by James Brown. (P)James Brown.

LIVING IN A HOUSE DIVIDED (1972) (wm)Tom Bahler. (P)Cher.

LIVING IN THE PAST (1972) (wm)Ian Anderson. (P)Jethro Tull.

LIVING INSIDE MYSELF (1981) (wm)Gino Vanelli. (P)Gino Vanelli.

LIVING NEXT DOOR TO ALICE (1977) (wm)Mike Chapman—Nicky Chinn. (P)Smokie.

LIVING THE BLUES (1970) (wm)Bob Dylan. (P)Bob Dylan.

LIVING TOGETHER, GROWING TOGETHER (1973)

(w)Hal David (m)Burt Bacharach. (I)Film: Lost Horizon, on soundtrack. (P)The 5th Dimension.

LIZA (All The Clouds'll Roll Away) (1929) (w)Ira Gershwin—Gus Kahn (m)George Gershwin. (I)Musical: Show Girl, by Nick Lucas and danced by Ruby Keeler. (P)Al Jolosn. (R)1946 film: The Jolson Story, by Jolson dubbing for Larry Parks.

LOAD OUT, THE (1978) (wm)Jackson Browne—Bryan Garafulo. (P)Jackson Browne.

LOADS OF LOVE (1962) (wm)Richard Rodgers. (I)Musical: No Strings, by Diahann Carroll.

LOCH LOMOND (1881) (wm)Unknown. Traditional Scottish folk song. (R)1937 by Maxine Sullivan. (R)1938 by Benny Goodman and his Orchestra.

LOCO-MOTION, THE (1962) (wm)Gerry Goffin—Carole King. (P)Little Eva. (R)1974 by Grand Funk. Both records were No. 1 Chart Records.

LOGICAL SONG, THE (1979) (wm)Richard Davies—Roger Hodgson. (P)Supertramp.

LOLA (1970) (wm)Ray Davies. (P)The Kinks.

LOLITA (Love Theme) (1962) (wm)Bob Harris. (I)Film: Lolita, on soundtrack.

LOLLIPOP (1958) (wm)Beverly Ross—Julius Dixon. (P)The Chordettes. (CR)Ronald and Ruby.

LOLLIPOPS AND ROSES (1960) (wm)Tony Velona. (P)Jack Jones. NARAS Award Winner. (CR)Paul Petersen.

LONDON (Is A Little Bit Of All Right) (1963) (wm)Noel Coward. (I)Musical: The Girl Who Came To Supper, By Tessie O'Shea, Sean Scully, and The Ensemble.

LONDON BRIDGE (Is Falling Down) (1744) (wm)Unknown. Traditional Children's song.

LONDON BY NIGHT (1950) (wm)Carroll Coates. (P)Frank Sinatra.

LONDON PRIDE (1941) (wm)Noel Coward. (I)London Revue: Up And Doing, by Binnie Hale.

LONDON TOWN (1978) (wm)Paul McCartney—Denny Laine. (P)Wings.

LONDONDERRY AIR (1855) (wm)Unknown. Traditional Irish folk melody. Used as melody for song Danny Boy.

LONELINESS OF EVENING (1949) (w)Oscar Hammerstein II (m)Richard Rodgers. Deleted from South Pacific (musical)before the opening. Recorded by Mary Martin. (R)1965 TV special: Cinderella, by Stuart Damon.

L-O-N-E-L-Y (1965) (wm)Bobby Vinton. (P)Bobby Vinton.

LONELY BLUE BOY (1959) (w)Fred Wise (m)Ben Wiseman. (P)Conway Twitty.

(I'm Just A)LONELY BOY (1959) (wm)Paul Anka. (P)Paul Anka. No. 1 Chart Record. (R)1972 by Donny Osmond.

(Hey There)LONELY BOY (1962) (w)Earl Shuman (m)Leon Carr. (P)Ruby and The Romantics. (R)1970 by Eddie Holman under the title of Hey There Lonely Girl.

LONELY BOY (1977) (wm)Andrew Gold. (P)Andrew Gold.

LONELY BULL, THE (1962) (m)Sol Lake. (P)Herb Alpert and The Tijuana Brass.

LONELY DAYS (1971) (wm)Barry, Maurice, and Robin Gibb. (P)The Bee Gees.

LONELY FOR YOU (1959) (wm)Gary Stites. (P)Gary Stites.

LONELY GOATHERD, THE (1959) (w)Oscar Hammerstein II (m)Richard Rodgers. (I)Musical: *The Sound Of Music*, by Mary Martin and The Children.

LONELY HEART (1933) (wm)Irving Berlin. (I)Musical: *As Thousands Cheer*, by Harry Stockwell.

LONELY HOUSE (1947) (w)Langston Hughes (m)Kurt Weill. (I)Musical: *Street Scene*, by Brian Sullivan.

LONELY ISLAND (1957) (wm)Eden Ahbez. (P)Sam Cooke.

LONELY LITTLE ROBIN (1951) (wm)Cy Coben. (P)Mindy Carson.

LONELY NIGHT (Angel Face) (1976) (wm)Neil Sedaka. (P)The Captain and Tennille.

LONELY OL' NIGHT (1985) (wm)John Cougar Mellencamp. (P)John Cougar Mellencamp.

LONELY ONE, THE (1958) (m)Lee Hazlewood—Duane Eddy. (P)Duane Eddy.

LONELY PEOPLE (1975) (wm)Catherine Peek—Dan Peek. (P)America.

LONELY STREET (1959) (wm)Kenny Sowder—W. S. Stevenson—Carl Belew. (P)Andy Williams.

LONELY TEARDROPS (1959) (wm)Berry Gordy, Jr. — Gwen Gordy—Tyran Carlo. (P)Jackie Wilson. (R)1971 by Brian Hyland. (R)1976 by Narvel Felts.

BERRY GORDY

(part of an interview from *Record World Magazine*)

RW: "You wrote songs for Jackie Wilson at one point, too. How did that happen?"

Gordy: "My sister sent me to a publishing company where the owners managed Jackie Wilson. They liked my songs and my ideas, so I got involved with that. We wrote the first six or seven Jackie Wilson hits: *Reet Petite*, *To Be Loved*, *Lonely Teardrops*, *That's Why I Love You*, and two or three others. A guy named Dick Jacobs, over at Decca Records, would always call me whenever they would record a song for Jackie. For *Lonely Teardrops*, they actually flew me into the company to be in on the session. I enjoyed working with Dick Jacobs quite a lot. Or at least I enjoyed talking to him - he always gave me a lot of credit, which built up my ego quite a lot."

LONELY TEENAGER (1971) (wm)Salvatore Pippa—Alfred DiPaola—Silvio Faraci. (P)Dion.

LONELY TOWN (1944) (w)Betty Comden—Adolph Green (m)Leonard Bernstein. (I)Musical: *On The Town*, by John Battles.

LONELY WEEKENDS (1960) (wm)Charlie Rich. (P)Charlie Rich.

LONELY WINE (1950) (wm)Roy Wells. (P)Les Baxter and his Orchestra.

LONELY WOMAM (1960) (w)Margo Guryan (m)Ornette Coleman. (P)Ornette Coleman. Vocal Version by June Christy.

LONESOME AND SORRY (1926) (wm)Benny Davis—Con Conrad. (I)Vaudeville: by Benny Davis. (P)Ruth Etting.

LONESOME DEATH OF HATTIE CARROLL (1964) (wm)Bob Dylan. (P)Bob Dylan.

LONESOME LOSER (1979) (wm)David Briggs. (P)Little River Band.

LONESOME NIGHTS (1934) (w)Irving Mills (m)Benny Carter. (P)Benny Carter and his Orchestra.

LONESOME POLECAT (1954) (w)Johnny Mercer (m)Gene de Paul. (I)Film: *Seven Brides For Seven Brothers*, by Bill Lee. (P)The McGuire Sisters. (CR)Freddy Martin and his Orchestra.

LONESOME ROAD, THE (1929) (w)Gene Austin (m)Nathaniel Shilkret. (I)Film: *Show Boat* (1929)by Jules Bledsoe dubbing for Stepin Fetchit. (P)Gene Austin. (CR)Ted Lewis. (R)1939 by Bing Crosby.

LONESOME TOWN (1958) (wm)Baker Knight. (P)Rick Nelson.

LONESOMEST GIRL IN TOWN, THE (1925) (w)Al Dubin (m)Jimmy McHugh—Irving Mills. (I)Vaudeville: by The Hotsy Totsy Boys (Jimmy McHugh and Irving Mills). (P)Morton Downey.

LONG ABOUT MIDNIGHT (1949) (wm)Roy Brown. (P)Roy Milton.

LONG AGO (And Far Away) (1944) (w)Ira Gershwin (m)Jerome Kern. (I)Film: *Cover Girl*, by Nan Wynn dubbing for Rita Hayworth. (P)Dick Haymes and Helen Forrest. (CR)Perry Como. (CR)Bing Crosby and Jo Stafford.

LONG AGO LAST NIGHT (1941) (w)Mack Gordon (m)Harry Warren. (I)Film: *The Great American Broadcast*, by Alice Faye.

LONG AGO TOMORROW (1971) (w)Hal David (m)Burt Bacharach. (I)Film: *Long Ago Tomorrow*, by voice of B. J. Thomas. (P)B. J. Thomas.

LONG AND WINDING ROAD, THE (1970) (wm)John Lennon—Paul McCartney. (I)Film: *Let It Be*, by The Beatles. (P)The Beatles. No. 1 Chart Record.

LONG AS I CAN SEE THE LIGHT (1970) (wm)John C. Fogarty. (P)Creedence Clearwater Revival.

LONG BEFORE I KNEW YOU (1956) (w)Betty Comden—Adolph Green (m)Jule Styne. (I)Musical: *Bells Are Ringing*, by Judy Holliday and Sydney Chaplin.

LONG BEFORE YOU CAME ALONG (1942) (w)E. Y. Harburg (m)Harold Arlen. (I)Film: *Rio Rita*, by John Carroll and Kathryn Grayson.

LONG COOL WOMAN (In A Black Dress) (1972) (wm)Roger Cook—Harold Clarke—Roger Greenaway. (P)The Hollies.

LONG DAY'S JOURNEY INTO NIGHT (1962) (m)Andre Previn. (I)Film: *Long Day's Journey Into Night*, as soundtrack theme.

LONG HOT SUMMER, THE (1957) (w)Sammy Cahn (m)Alex North. (I)Film: *The Long Hot Summer*, by voice of Jimmie Rodgers.

LONG LIVE OUR LOVE (1966) (wm)Sidney Barnes—J. J. Jackson (P)The Shangri—Las.

LONG LONELY NIGHTS (1957) (wm)Lee Andrews—Bernice Davis—Douglas Henderson—Mimi Uniman. (P)Lee Andrews & The Hearts. (CR)Clyde McPhatter. (R)1965 by Bobby Vinton. (R)1970 by The Dells.

LONG, LONG AGO (1833) (wm)Thomas Bayly. Traditional old favorite. Recorded by Geraldine Farrar in 1913.

LONG, LONG, LONG (1969) (wm)George Harrison. (P)The Beatles.

LONG LONG TIME (1970) (wm)Gary White. (P)Linda Ronstadt.

LONG, LONG WAY FROM HOME (1978) (wm)Lou Grammatico—Michael Jones—Ian McDonald. (P)Foreigner.

LONG TALL GLASSES (I Can Dance) (1975) (wm)David Courtney—Leo Sayer. (P)Leo Sayer.

LONG TALL SALLY (1956) (wm)Enotris Johnson—Richard Penniman—Robert Blackwell. (P)Little Richard. (CR)Pat Boone.

LONG TIME (1977) (wm)Tom Scholz. (P)Boston.

LONG TRAIN RUNNING (1973) (wm)Tom Johnston. (P)The Doobie Brothers.

LONGER (1979) (wm)Dan Fogelberg. (P)Dan Fogelberg.

LONGEST DAY, THE (1962) (wm)Paul Anka. (I)Film: *The Longest Day*, by Mitch Miller and his Chorus and Orchestra.

LONGEST TIME, THE (1984) (wm)Billy Joel. (P)Billy Joel.

LONGEST WALK, THE (1955) (w)Eddie Pola (m)Fred Spielman. (P)Jaye P. Morgan.

LONGFELLOW SERENADE (1974) (wm)Neil Diamond. (P)Neil Diamond.

LONGING FOR YOU (1951) (w)Bernard Jansen (m)Walter Dana. (P)Sammy Kaye and his Orchestra. (CR)Vic Damone. (CR)Teresa Brewer.

LOOK AT 'ER (1957) (wm)Bob Merrill. (I)Musical: *New Girl In Town*, by George Wallace.

LOOK AT THAT FACE (1964) (wm)Leslie Bricusse—Anthony Newley. (I)Musical: *The Roar Of The Greasepaint—The Smell Of The Crowd*, by Cyril Ritchard, Sally Smith and The Urchins.

LOOK FOR A STAR (1960) (wm)Tony Hatch. (I)British film: *Circus Of Horrors*, by Garry Miles. (P)Garry Miles. (CR)Billy Vaughn and his Orchestra.

LOOK FOR SMALL PLEASURES (1964) (w)Sidney Michaels (m)Mark Sandrich, Jr. (I)Musical: *Ben Franklin In Paris*, by Robert Preston and Ulla Sallert.

LOOK FOR THE SILVER LINING (1920) (w)B. G. De Sylva (m)Jerome Kern. (I)Musical: *Sally*, by Marilyn Miller and Irving Fisher. Recorded by Marion Harris. (R)1946 film: *Till The Clouds Roll By*, by Judy Garland. (R)1949 film: *Look For The Silver Lining*, by Gordon MacRae and June Haver.

LOOK IN MY EYES (1961) (wm)Richard Barrett. (P)The Chantels. (R)1966 by The Three Degrees.

LOOK IN MY EYES PRETTY WOMAN (1975) (wm)Dennis Lambert—Brian Potter. (P)Tony Orlando & Dawn.

LOOK INTO YOUR HEART (1976) (wm)Curtis Mayfield. (I)Film: *Sparkle*, by Irene Cara and Lonette McKee.

LOOK NO FURTHER (1962) (wm)Richard Rodgers. (I)Musical: *No Strings*, by Diahann Carroll and Richard Kiley.

LOOK OF LOVE (1965) (wm)Jeff Barry—Ellie Greenwich. (P)Lesley Gore.

LOOK OF LOVE, THE (1965) (w)Hal David (m)Burt Bacharach. (I)Film: *Casino Royale* by voice of Dusty Springfield. (P)Dusty Springfield. (CR)Sergio Mendes & Brasil '66. (R)1971 by Isaac Hayes.

LOOK OF LOVE, THE (1982) (wm)Martin Fry—Mark Lickley—Stephen Singleton—David Palmer. (P)ABC.

LOOK OVER THERE (1983) (wm)Jerry Herman. (I)Musical: *La Cage Au Folles*, by Gene Barry.

LOOK THROUGH ANY WINDOW (1965) (wm)Graham Gouldman—Charles Silverman. (P)The Hollies.

LOOK THROUGH MY WINDOW (1966) (wm)John E. A. Phillips. (P)The Mamas and The Papas.

LOOK TO THE RAINBOW (1947) (w)E. Y. Harburg (m)Burton Lane. (I)Musical: *Finian's Rainbow*, by Donald Richards and Ella Logan.

LOOK WHAT I FOUND (1946) (wm)Cole Porter. (I)Musical: *Around The World*, by Julie Warren and Larry Laurence.

LOOK WHAT THEY'VE DONE TO MY SONG, MA (See: What Have They Done To My Song, Ma).

LOOK WHAT YOU DONE FOR ME (1972) (wm)Al Green—Willie Mitchell—Al Jackson. (P)Al Green.

LOOK WHAT YOU DONE TO ME (1980) (wm)Boz Scaggs—David Foster. (P)Boz Scaggs. Performed in film: *Urban Cowboy*.

LOOK WHAT YOU'VE DONE (1967) (wm)Bob Johnston—Wes Farrell. (P)The Pozo-Seco Singers.

LOOK WHO'S DANCING (1951) (w)Dorothy Fields (m)Arthur Schwartz. (I)Musical: *A Tree Grows In Brooklyn*, by Shirley Booth and Marcia Van Dyke.

LOOKIN' FOR A LOVE (1962) (wm)James Alexander—Zelda Samuels. (P)The Valentinos. (R)1972 by J. Geils Band. (R)1974 by Bobby Womack.

LOOKIN' FOR LOVE (1980) (wm)Wanda Mallette—Patti Ryan—Bob Morrison. (P)Johnny Lee.

LOOKIN' OUT MY BACK DOOR (1970) (wm)John C. Fogerty. (P)Creedence Clearwater Revival.

LOOKIN' THROUGH THE WINDOWS (1971) (wm)Clifton Davis. (P)The Jackson Five.

LOOKING AT THE WORLD THRU ROSE COLORED GLASSES (1926) (wm)Tommy Malie—Jimmy Steiger. (I)Revue: *A Night In Paris*, by Jack Osterman. (P)Fred Waring's Pennsylvanians.

LOOKING AT YOU (1929) (wm)Cole Porter. (I)Musical: *Wake Up And Dream*, by Jessie Matthews and Dave Fitzgibbon.

LOOKING AT YOU (Across The Breakfast Table) (1929) (wm)Irving Berlin. (I)Film: *Mammy*, by Al Jolson.

LOOKING BACK (1958) (wm)Clyde Otis—Brook Benton—Belford Hendricks. (P)Nat "King" Cole. (R)1969 by Nat Simon.

LOOKING BACK (1974) (w)Betty Comden—Adolph Green (m)Jule Styne. (I)Musical: *Lorelei*, by Carol Channing.

LOOKING FOR A BOY (1925) (w)Ira Gershwin (m)George Gershwin. (I)Musical: *Tip-Toes*, by Queenie Smith.

LOOKING FOR A NEW LOVE (1987) (wm)Jody Watley—A. Cymone. (P)Jody Watley.

LOOKING FOR SPACE (1976) (wm)John Denver. (P)John Denver.

LOOKING FOR YESTERDAY (1940) (w)Eddie De Lange (m)Jimmy Van Heusen. (P)Woody Herman and his Orchestra. (CR)Glenn Miller and his Orchestra. (CR)Tommy Dorsey and his Orchestra.

LOOKING THROUGH THE EYES OF LOVE (1965) (wm)Barry Mann—Cynthia Weil. (P)Gene Pitney. (R)1973 by The Partridge Family.

LOOKING THROUGH THE EYES OF LOVE (1978) (w)Carole Bayer Sager (m)Marvin Hamlisch. (I)Film: *Ice Castles*, by Melissa Manchester.

LOOKS LIKE WE MADE IT (1977) (wm)Will Jennings—Richard Kerr. (P)Barry Manilow. No. 1 Chart Record.

LOOP DE LOOP (1963) (wm)Freddie Hart—Ann Lucas. (P)Johnny Thunder.

LORD'S PRAYER (1974) (m)Arnold Strals. (P)Sister Janet Meade.

LORELEI, THE (1920) (w)Anne Caldwell (m)Jerome Kern. (I)Musical: *Sally*, by Walter Catlett, Mary Hay, and Stanley Ridges.

LORELEI (1928) (wm)Noel Coward. (I)Revue: *This Year Of Grace*, by Rita Mackay and Queenie Leonard.

LORELEI (1933) (w)Ira Gershwin (m)George Gershwin. (I)Musical: *Pardon My English,* by Carl Randall and Barbara Newberry.

LORNA'S HERE (1964) (w)Lee Adams (m)Charles Strouse. (I)Musical: *Golden Boy,* by Paula Wayne.

LOSE THAT LONG FACE (1954) (w)Ira Gershwin (m)Harold Arlen. (I)Film: *A Star Is Born,* by Judy Garland.

LOSING YOU (1963) (w-Eng)Carl Sigman (m)Jean Renard. (P)Brenda Lee.

LOST (1936) (wm)Phil Ohman—Johnny Mercer—Macy O. Teetor. (P)Guy Lombardo and his Royal Canadians. (CR)Jan Garber and his Orchestra.

LOST BARBER SHOP CHORD, THE (1926) (w)Ira Gershwin (m)George Gershwin. (I)Musical: *Americana,* by Helen Morgan and Lew Brice.

LOST CHORD, THE (1877) (w)Adelaide Proctor (m)Sir Arthur Sullivan. Famous American song. First recording by Enrico Caruso.

LOST HORIZON (1973) (w)Hal David (m)Burt Bacharach. (I)Film: *Lost Horizon,* by Shawn Phillips.

LOST IN A DREAM (1949) (w)Edgar Leslie (m)Rube Bloom. (P)Billy Eckstine.

LOST IN EMOTION (1987) (wm)Full Force. (P)Lisa Lisa & Cult Jam. No. 1 Chart Record.

LOST IN A FOG (1934) (w)Dorothy Fields (m)Jimmy McHugh. (P)The Dorsey Brothers Orchestra. (CR)Rudy Vallee and his Connecticut Yankees.

LOST IN LOVE (1980) (wm)Graham Russell. (P)Air Supply.

LOST IN LOVELINESS (1954) (w)Leo Robin (m)Sigmund Romberg. (I)Musical: *The Girl In Pink Tights,* by Davie Atkinson.

LOST IN MEDITATION (1938) (w)Irving Mills (m)Duke Ellington—Juan Tizol—Lou Singer. (P)Duke Ellington and his Orchestra.

LOST IN THE FLOOD (1972) (wm)Bruce Springsteen. (P)Bruce Springsteen.

LOST IN THE STARS (1949) (w)Maxwell Anderson (m)Kurt Weill. (I)Musical: *Lost In The Stars,* by Todd Duncan. (R)1972 film: *Lost In The Stars,* by Brock Peters.

LOST WITHOUT YOUR LOVE (1977) (wm)David Gates. (P)Bread.

LOT OF LIVIN' TO DO, A (1960) (w)Lee Adams (m)Charles Strouse. (I)Musical: *Bye Bye Birdie,* by Dick Gautier and The Teenagers. In film Version (1963) by Jesse Pearson, Ann—Margaret, and Bobby Rydell.

LOTTA LOVE (1979) (wm)Neil Young. (P)Nicolette Larson.

LOUIE LOUIE (1963) (wm)Richard Berry. (P)The Kingsmen. (R)1966 by The Sandpipers. (R)1978 by John Belushi.

LOUISE (1929) (w)Leo Robin (m)Richard A. Whiting. (I)Film: *Innocents Of Paris,* by Maurice Chevalier. (P)Maurice Chevalier. (CR)Paul Whiteman and his Orchestra.

LOUISIANA (1927) (w)Andy Razaf—Bob Schafer (m)J. C. Johnson. (P)Paul Whiteman and his Orchestra, vocal by The Rhythm Boys (Bing Crosby, Al Rinker, Harry Barris). (R)1940 by Count Basie and his Orchestra.

LOUISIANA HAYRIDE (1932) (w)Howard Dietz (m)Arthur Schwartz. (I)Revue: *Flying Colors,* by Tamara Geva, Clifton Webb, and The Ensemble. (R)1953 film: *The Band Wagon,* by Nanette Fabray. First recording by Leo Reisman and his Orchestra, featuring Arthur Schwartz.

LOUISIANA PURCHASE (1940) (wm)Irving Berlin. (I)Musical: *Louisiana Purchase,* by Carol Bruce, The Martins, and The Buccaneers.

LOUISVILLE LOU, THE VAMPIN' LADY (1923) (w)Jack Yellen (m)Milton Ager. (P)Sophie Tucker.

LOVABLE AND SWEET (1929) (w)Sidney Clare (m)Oscar Levant. (I)Film: *Street Girl,* by Jack Oakie, John Harron, and Ned Sparks.

LOVABLE SORT OF PERSON (1941) (w)Frank Loesser (m)Victor Young. (I)Film: *Dancing On A Dime,* by Grace McDonald.

LOVE (1945) (wm)Ralph Blane—Hugh Martin. (I)Film: *Ziegfeld Follies,* by Lena Horne. (P)Lena Horne.

LOVE (Makes The World Go 'Round) (1962) (wm)Paul Anka. (P)Paul Anka.

LOVE (L-O-V-E) (1964) (w)Milt Gabler (m)Bert Kaempfert. (P)Nat "King" Cole.

LOVE (Can Make You Happy) (1969) (wm)Jack Sigler. (P)Mercy.

LOVE AMONG THE YOUNG (1955) (w)Norman Gimbel (m)Alec Wilder. (P)Rosemary Clooney.

LOVE AND A DIME (1935) (wm)Brooks Bowman. (I)Revue: *Stags At Bay* (Princeton University Triangle Club).

LOVE AND MARRIAGE (1955) (w)Sammy Cahn (m)Jimmy Van Heusen. (I)TV show: *Our Town,* by Frank Sinatra. (P)Frank Sinatra.

LOVE AND THE WEATHER (1947) (wm)Irving Berlin. (P)Kate Smith.

LOVE BALLAD (1975) (wm)Skip Scarborough. (P)LTD. (R)1979 by George Benson.

LOVE BIZARRE, A (1985) (wm)Sheila Escovedo—Prince Rogers Nelson. (P)Sheila E.

LOVE BOAT THEME (1976) (w)Paul Williams (m)Charles Fox. (I)TV series: *The Love Boat,* by voice of Jack Jones. (P)Jack Jones.

LOVE BUG LEAVE MY HEART ALONE (1967) (wm)Richard Morris—Sylvia Moy. (P)Martha and The Vandellas.

LOVE BUG WILL BITE YOU, THE (If You Don't Watch Out) (1937) (wm)Pinky Tomlin. (CR)Guy Lombardo and his Royal Canadians. (CR)Jimmy Dorsey and his Orchestra.

LOVE CAME TO ME (1962) (wm)Dion Di Mucci—John Falbo. (P)Dion.

LOVE CHILD (1968) (wm)Pam Sawyer—R. Dean Taylor—Frank Wilson—Deke Richards. (P)Diana Ross and The Supremes. No. 1 Chart Record.

LOVE COME DOWN (1982) (wm)Michael Jones. (P)Evelyn "Champagne" King.

LOVE DON'T LOVE NOBODY (1974) (wm)Joseph Jefferson—Charles Simmons. (P)The Spinners.

LOVE, DON'T TURN AWAY (1963) (w)Tom Jones (m)Harvey Schmidt. (I)Musical: *110 In The Shade,* by Inga Swenson.

LOVE EYES (1967) (wm)Lee Hazlewood. (P)Nancy Sinatra.

LOVE FOR SALE (1925) (w)Brian Hooker (m)Rudolf Friml. (I)Operetta: *The Vagabond King,* by Jane Carroll.

LOVE FOR SALE (1930) (wm)Cole Porter. (I)Musical: *The New Yorkers,* by Kathryn Crawford, June Shafer, Ida Pearson, Arline Judge. (P)Libby Holman. (CR)Hal

Kemp and his Orchestra.

LOVE FROM A HEART OF GOLD (1961) (wm)Frank Loesser. (I)Musical: *How To Succeed In Business Without Really Trying*, by Rudy Vallee and Virginia Martin.

LOVE GODDESS, THE (1965) (w)Mack David (m)Percy Faith. (I)Film: *The Love Goddesses*, on soundtrack. (P)Jerry Vale.

LOVE GROWS (Where My Rosemary Goes) (1970) (wm)Tony Macaulay—Barry Mason. (P)Edison Lighthouse.

LOVE HANGOVER (1976) (wm)Marilyn McLeod—Pam Sawyer. (P)Diana Ross. No. 1 Chart Record. (CR)The 5th Dimension.

LOVE HAS DRIVEN ME SANE (1971) (w)John Guare (m)Galt MacDermot. (I)Musical: *Two Gentlemen From Verona*, by Raul Julia.

LOVE HAS JOINED US TOGETHER (1955) (wm)Billy Dawn Smith—Teddy Powell. (P)Ruth Brown and Clyde McPhatter.

LOVE HELD LIGHTLY (1959) (w)Johnny Mercer (m)Harold Arlen. (I)Musical: *Saratoga*, by Odette Myrtil.

LOVE HER MADLY (1971) (wm)Robbie Krieger—Ray Manzarek—John Densmore. (P)The Doors.

LOVE HERE IS MY HEART (1915) (w)Adrian Ross (m)Lao Silesu. (P)John McCormack.

LOVE HURTS (1960) (wm)Boudleaux Bryant. (P)Nazareth. (CR)Jim Capaldi.

LOVE, I HEAR (1962) (wm)Stephen Sondheim. (I)Musical: *A Funny Thing Happened On The Way To The Forum*, by Brian Davies.

LOVE I LONG FOR, THE (1944) (w)Howard Dietz (m)Vernon Duke. (I)Musical: *Sadie Thompson*, by June Havoc and James Newill.

LOVE I LOST, THE (1973) (wm)Kenny Gamble—Leon Huff. (P)Harold Melvin & The Bluenotes.

LOVE I SAW IN YOU WAS JUST A MIRAGE, THE (1967) (wm)William Robinson, Jr. —Marvin Tarplin. (P)Smokey Robinson and The Miracles.

LOVE IN A HOME (1956) (w)Johnny Mercer (m)Gene de Paul. (I)Musical: *L'il Abner*, by Peter Palmer and Edith Adams.

LOVE IN BLOOM (1934) (wm)Leo Robin—Ralph Rainger. (I)Film: *She Loves Me Not*, by Bing Crosby and Kitty Carlisle. (P)Bing Crosby. (CR)Hal Kemp and his Orchestra. Paul Whiteman and his Orchestra. Theme Song of Jack Benny.

LOVE IN THE FIRST DEGREE (1982) (wm)Jim Hurt—James Dubois. (P)Alabama.

LOVE IN THE SHADOWS (1976) (wm)Neil Sedaka—Phil Cody. (P)Neil Sedaka.

LOVE IS A BATTLEFIELD (1983) (wm)Mike Chapman—Holly Knight. (P)Pat Benatar.

LOVE IS A BORE (1964) (w)Sammy Cahn (m)Jimmy Van Heusen. (P)Barbra Streisand.

LOVE IS A CHANCE (1964) (wm)Walter Marks. (I)Musical: Bajour, by Nancy Dussault.

LOVE IS A DANCING THING (1935) (w)Howard Dietz (m)Arthur Schwartz. (I)Revue: *At Home Abroad*, by The Male Chorus.

LOVE IS A GOLDEN RING (1957) (wm)Richard Dehr—Frank Miller—Terry Gilkyson. (P)Frankie Laine.

LOVE IS A HURTIN' THING (1966) (wm)Ben Raleigh—Dave Linden. (P)Lou Rawls.

LOVE IS A MANY SPLENDORED THING (1955) (w)Paul Francis Webster (m)Sammy Fain. Academy Award Winner. (P)The Four Aces. No. 1 Chart Record. (CR)Don Cornell. (CR)David Rose and his Orchestra.

LOVE IS A ROSE (1975) (wm)Neil Young. (P)Linda Ronstadt.

LOVE IS A SIMPLE THING (1952) (w)June Carroll (m)Arthur Siegel. (I)Revue: *New Faces of 1952*, by Rosemary O'Reilly, Robert Clary, Eartha Kitt, and June Carroll.

LOVE IS A STRANGER (1983) (wm)Annie Lennox—David Stewart. (P)Eurythmics.

LOVE IS A VERY LIGHT THING (1954) (wm)Harold Rome. (I)Musical: *Fanny*, by Ezio Pinza.

LOVE IS ALIVE (1976) (wm)Gary Wright. (P)Gary Wright.

LOVE IS ALL AROUND (1968) (wm)Reg Presley. (P)The Troggs.

LOVE IS ALL WE NEED (1958) (wm)Ben Raleigh—Don Wolf. (P)Tommy Edwards. (R)1964 by Vic Dana. (R)1966 by Mel Carter.

LOVE IS ALRITE TONITE (1982) (wm)Rick Springfield. (P)Rick Springfield.

LOVE IS BLUE (1968) (w-Eng)Brian Blackburn (m)Andre Popp. (P)Paul Mauriat and his Orchestra. No. 1 Chart Record. Vocal Version by Al Martino. (CR)Claudine Longet.

LOVE IS FOREVER (1987) (wm)Billy Ocean—W. Brathwaite—B. Eastmond. (P)Billy Ocean.

LOVE IS HERE AND NOW YOU'RE GONE (1967) (wm)Brian Holland—Lamont Dozier—Eddie Holland. (P)Diana Ross and The Supremes. No. 1 Chart Record.

(Our)LOVE IS HERE TO STAY (1938) (w)Ira Gershwin (m)George Gershwin. (I)Film: *The Goldwyn Follies*, by Kenny Baker. (R)1951 film: *An American In Paris*, by Gene Kelly. This was George Gershwin's last song before his death.

LOVE IS IN CONTROL (1982) (wm)Quincy Jones—Merria Ross—Rod Temperton. (P)Donna Summer.

LOVE IS IN THE AIR (1978) (wm)Harry Vanda—George Young. (P)John Paul Young.

LOVE IS JUST A FOUR LETTER WORD (1969) (wm)Bob Dylan. (P)Joan Baez.

LOVE IS JUST AROUND THE CORNER (1934) (wm)Leo Robin—Lewis Gensler. (I)Film: *Here Is My Heart*, by Bing Crosby. (P)Bing Crosby.

LOVE IS LIKE AN ITCHING IN MY HEART (1966) (wm)Eddie Holland—Lamont Dozier—Brian Holland. (P)The Supremes.

LOVE IS NEVER OUT OF SEASON (1937) (w)Lew Brown (m)Sammy Fain. (I)Film: *New Faces of 1937*, by Harriet Hilliard and William Brady.

LOVE IS STRANGE (1956) (wm)Mickey Baker—Ethel Smith. (P)Mickey and Sylvia. (R)1967 by Peaches and Herb.

LOVE IS SWEEPING THE COUNTRY (1931) (w)Ira Gershwin (m)George Gershwin. (I)Musical: *Of Thee I Sing*, by George Murphy and June O'Dea.

LOVE IS THE ANSWER (1979) (wm)Todd Rundgren. (P)England Dan & John Ford Coley.

LOVE IS THE DARNDEST THING (1946) (w)Johnny Burke (m)Jimmy Van Heusen. (I)Film: *Cross My Heart*, by Betty Hutton.

LOVE IS THE DRUG (1976) (wm)Roger Lewis. (P)Roxy Music.

LOVE IS THE REASON (1951) (w)Dorothy Fields (m)Arthur Schwartz. (l)Musical: *A Tree Grows In Brooklyn*, by Shirley Booth.

LOVE IS THE SEVENTH WAVE (1985) (wm)Gordon Sumner (Sting). (P)Sting.

LOVE IS THE SWEETEST THING (1933) (wm)Ray Noble. (l)Julia Sanderson. (P)Ray Noble and his Orchestra. (CR)Hal Kemp and his Orchestra.

LOVE IS THE THING (1933) (w)Ned Washington (m)Victor Young. (P)Ethel Waters.

LOVE IS WHERE YOU FIND IT (1938) (w)Al Dubin—Johnny Mercer (m)Harry Warren. (l)Film: *Garden Of The Moon*, by John Payne and Johnny "Scat" Davis.

LOVE IS WHERE YOU FIND IT (1948) (w)Earl K. Brent (m)Nacio Herb Brown. (l)Film: *The Kissing Bandit*, by Kathryn Grayson.

LOVE JONES (1972) (wm)Randolph Murph—Ralph Eskridge—Clarence Johnson. (P)Brighter Side Of Darkness.

LOVE LETTERS (1945) (w)Edward Heyman (m)Victor Young. (l)Film: *Love Letters*, as soundtrack theme. (P)Dick Brown. (R)1962 by Ketty Lester. (R)1966 by Elvis Presley.

LOVE LETTERS IN THE SAND (1931) (w)Nick and Charles Kenny (m)J. Fred Coots. (P)Russ Columbo. Theme song of George Hall and his Orchestra. (R)1957 by Pat Boone. No. 1 Chart Record.

LOVE LIES (1940) (wm)Carl Sigman—Ralph Freed—Joseph Meyer. (P)Tommy Dorsey and his Orchestra, vocal by Frank Sinatra.

LOVE LIGHT IN FLIGHT (1985) (wm)Stevie Wonder. (l)Film: *The Woman In Red*, by Stevie Wonder. (P)Stevie Wonder.

LOVE-LINE (1964) (wm)Walter Marks. (l)Musical: *Bajour*, by Chita Rivera.

LOVE LOCKED OUT (1933) (w)Max Kester (m)Ray Noble. (P)Ray Noble and his Orchestra. (CR)Ambrose and his Orchestra.

LOVE, LOOK AWAY (1958) (w)Oscar Hammerstein II (m)Richard Rodgers. (l)Musical: *Flower Drum Song*, by Arabella Hong.

LOVE! LOVE! LOVE! (1956) (wm)Teddy McRae—Sid Wyche—Sunny David. (P)The Clovers. (CR)The Diamonds.

LOVE MACHINE (Part 1) (1975) (wm)Billy Griffith—Peter Moore. (P)The Miracles. No. 1 Chart Record.

LOVE MAKES A WOMAN (1968) (wm)Eugene Record—William Sanders—Carl Davis. (P)Barbara Acklin.

LOVE MAKES SUCH FOOLS OF US ALL (1980) (w)Michael Stewart (m)Cy Coleman. (l)Musical: *Barnum*, by Marianne Tatum.

LOVE MAKES THE WORLD GO (1962) (wm)Richard Rodgers. (l)Musical: *No Strings*, by Polly Rowles and Bernice Massi.

LOVE MAKES THE WORLD GO 'ROUND (Yeah, Yeah) (1958) (wm)Ollie Jones. (P)Perry Como.

LOVE MAKES THE WORLD GO 'ROUND (See *Carnival!*, Theme)

LOVE MAKES THE WORLD GO 'ROUND (1966) (wm)Deon Jackson. (P)Deon Jackson.

LOVE ME (1934) (w)Ned Washington (m)Victor Young. (l)Lee Wiley. (P)Glen Gray and The Casa Loma Orchestra.

LOVE ME (1945) (w)Sammy Cahn (m)Jule Styne. (l)Film: *Stork Club*, by Andy Russell.

LOVE ME (1956) (wm)Jerry Leiber—Mike Stoller. (P)Elvis Presley.

LOVE ME (1976) (wm)Barry Gibb—Robin Gibb. (P)Yvonne Elliman.

LOVE ME DO (1964) (wm)John Lennon—Paul McCartney. (P)The Beatles. No. 1 Chart Record.

LOVE ME FOR A REASON (1974) (wm)Johnny Bristol—Wade Browd, Jr. —David Jones, Jr. (P)The Osmonds.

LOVE ME FOREVER (1935) (w)Gus Kahn (m)Victor Schertzinger. (P)Film: *Love Me Forever*, by Grace Moore. (P)Grace Moore.

LOVE ME FOREVER (1957) (wm)Beverly Guthrie—Gary Lynes. (P)Eydie Gorme. (CR)The Four Esquires. (R)1967 by Roger Williams.

LOVE ME, LOVE MY PEKINESE (1936) (wm)Cole Porter. (l)Film: *Born To Dance*, by Virginia Bruce.

LOVE ME OR LEAVE ME (1928) (w)Gus Kahn (m)Walter Donaldson. (l)Musical: *Whoopee*, by Ruth Etting. (P)Ruth Etting. (R)1934, by Benny Goodman and his Orchestra. (R)1951 film: *I'll See You In My Dreams*, by Patrice Wymore. (R)1955 film: *Love Me Or Leave Me*, by Doris Day.

LOVE ME TENDER (1956) (wm)Elvis Presley—Vera Matson. Adapted from Civil War song, Aura Lee. (P)Elvis Presley. No. 1 Chart Record. (R)1963 by Richard Chamberlain. (R)1967 by Percy Sledge.

LOVE ME TOMORROW (But Leave Me Alone Today) (1940) (w)John Latouche (m)Vernon Duke. (l)Musical: *Cabin In The Sky*, by Katherine Dunham and Dooley Wilson.

LOVE ME TONIGHT (1925) (w)Brian Hooker (m)Rudolf Friml. (l)Operetta: *The Vagabond King*, by Dennis King and Carolyn Thomson. (R)1930 film version by Dennis King and Jeanette MacDonald.

LOVE ME TONIGHT (1932) (w)Bing Crosby—Ned Washington (m)Victor Young. (P)Bing Crosby. (CR)George Olsen and his Orchestra.

LOVE ME TONIGHT (1932) (w)Lorenz Hart (m)Richard Rodgers. (l)Film: *Love Me Tonight*, by Jeanette MacDonald and Maurice Chevalier.

LOVE ME TONIGHT (1969) (w-Eng)Barry Mason (m)M. Panzeri. (P)Tom Jones.

LOVE ME TWO TIMES (1967) (wm)Raymomd Manzarek—Robert Krieger—James Morrison—John Densmore. (P)The Doors.

LOVE ME WARM AND TENDER (1962) (wm)Paul Anka. (P)Paul Anka.

LOVE ME WITH ALL YOUR HEART (See *Cuando Caliente El Sol*).

LOVE MINUS ZERO/NO LIMIT (1965) (wm)Bob Dylan. (P)Bob Dylan. (R)1970 by Turley Richards.

LOVE NEST, THE (1920) (w)Otto Harbach (m)Louis A. Hirsch. (l)Musical: *Mary*, by Janet Velie and Jack McGowan. (P)Art Hickman and his Orchestra. Theme song of Burns and Allen Radio Show. (R)1957 film: *The Helen Morgan Story*, by Gogi Grant dubbing for Ann Blyth.

LOVE NEVER WENT TO COLLEGE (1939) (w)Lorenz Hart (m)Richard Rodgers. (l)Musical: *Too Many Girls*, by Marcy Westcott and Dick Kollmar. In film version (1940)by Frances Langford.

LOVE OF MY LIFE (1940) (w)Johnny Mercer (m)Artie Shaw. (l)Film: *Second Chorus*, by Fred Astaire. (P)Fred Astaire.

LOVE OF MY LIFE, THE (1947) (w)Alan Jay Lerner (m)Frederick Loewe. (l)Musical: *Brigadoon*, by Pamela Britton.

LOVE OF MY LIFE (1948) (wm)Cole Porter. (I)Film: *The Pirate*, by Judy Garland.

LOVE OF MY MAN, THE (1963) (wm)Ed Townsend. (P)Theola Kilgore.

LOVE OF THE LOVED (1963) (wm)John Lennon—Paul McCartney. (P)Cilla Black.

LOVE OF THREE ORANGES (1919) (m)Serge Prokofieff. Famous modern classical composition.

LOVE ON A TWO-WAY STREET (1970) (wm)Sylvia Robinson—Bert Keyes. (P)The Moments. (R)1981 by Stacy Lattislaw.

LOVE ON MY MIND (1962) (m)Ray Charles. (P)Ray Charles and Milt Jackson.

LOVE ON THE ROCKS (1980) (wm)Neil Diamond. (I)Film: *The Jazz Singer*, by Neil Diamond. (P)Neil Diamond.

LOVE OR LET ME BE LONELY (1970) (wm)Anita Poree—C. "Skip" Scarborough. (P)The Friends Of Distinction.

LOVE OR SOMETHING LIKE IT (1978) (wm)Steven Glassmeyer—Kenny Rogers. (P)Kenny Rogers.

LOVE OVERBOARD (1987) (wm)R. Calloway (P)Gladys Knight & The Pips.

LOVE POTION NUMBER NINE (1959) (wm)Jerry Leiber—Mike Stoller. (P)The Clovers. (R)1965 by The Searchers.

LOVE POWER (1967) (wm)Teddy Vann. (P)The Sandpebbles.

LOVE POWER (1987) (w)Carole Bayer Sager (m)Burt Bacharach. (P)Dionne Warwick and Jeffrey Osborne.

LOVE REALLY HURTS WITHOUT YOU (1976) (wm)Les Charles—Benjamin Findon. (P)Billy Ocean.

LOVE ROLLERCOASTER (1975) (wm)Clarence Satchell—Leroy Bonner—Ralph Middlebrooks—William Beck—Marvin Pierce—Marshall Jones—Jim Williams. (P)The Ohio Players. No. 1 Chart Record.

LOVE SENDS A LITTLE GIFT OF ROSES (1919) (w)Leslie Cooke (m)John Openshaw. (P)John McCormack.

LOVE SHE CAN COUNT ON, A (1963) (wm)William Robinson. (P)The Miracles.

LOVE SO RIGHT (1976) (wm)Barry, Maurice, and Robin Gibb. (P)The Bee Gees.

LOVE SOMEBODY (1947) (wm)Joan Whitney—Alex Kramer (P)Doris Day and Buddy Clark. No. 1 Chart Record.

LOVE SOMEBODY (1984) (wm)Rick Springfield. (P)Rick Springfield.

LONG SONG FROM MUTINY ON THE BOUNTY (1962) (w)Paul Francis Webster (m)Bronislau Kaper. (I)Film: *Mutiny On The Bounty*, by The Chorus.

LOVE SONG OF TOM JONES (1964) (w)Mack Gordon (m)John Addison. (I)Film: *Tom Jones*, on soundtrack.

LOVE SONGS OF THE NILE (1933) (w)Arthur Freed (m)Nacio Herb Brown. (I)Film: *The Barbarian*, by Ramon Novarro.

LOVE STORY, A (Intermezzo) (1939) (w-Eng)Robert Henning (m)Heinz Provost. (I)Film: *Intermezzo—A Love Story*, as soundtrack theme. (P)1941 by Guy Lombardo and his Royal Canadians. (CR)Benny Goodman and his Orchestra.

LOVE STORY (Theme) (Where Do I Begin) (1970) (w)Carl Sigman (m)Francis Lai. (I)Film: *Love Story*, by Georges Pludermacher as a piano solo. (P)Andy Williams. (CR)Henry Mancini and his Orchestra.

LOVE TAKES TIME (1979) (wm)Marilyn Mason—Larry Hoppen. (P)Orleans.

LOVE THE WORLD AWAY (1980) (wm)Bob Morrison—Johnny Wilson. (P)Kenny Rogers.

LOVE THY NEIGHBOR (1934) (w)Mack Gordon (m)Harry Revel. (I)Film: *We're Not Dressing*, by Bing Crosby. (P)Bing Crosby. (CR)Raymond Paige and his Orchestra.

LOVE TO LOVE YOU BABY (1976) (wm)Pete Bellotte—Giorgio Moroder—Donna Summer. (P)Donna Summer.

LOVE TOUCH (1986) (wm)Mike Chapman—Holly Knight—Gene Black. (I)Film: *Legal Eagles*, by Rod Stewart. (P)Rod Stewart.

LOVE TRAIN (1973) (wm)Kenny Gamble—Leon Huff. (P)The O'Jays. No. 1 Chart Record.

LOVE WALKED IN (1938) (w)Ira Gershwin (m)George Gershwin. (I)Film: *The Goldwyn Follies*, by Kenny Baker. (P)Sammy Kaye and his Orchestra. No. 1 Chart Record. (CR)Louis Armstrong. (R)1953 by The Hilltoppers.

LOVE WALKS IN (1986) (wm)Eddie Van Halen—Michael Anthony—Sammy Hagar—Alex Van Halen. (P)Van Halen.

LOVE WILL CONQUER ALL (1986) (wm)Lionel Richie—Cynthia Weil—Greg Phillinganes. (P)Lionel Richie.

LOVE WILL FIND A WAY (1978) (wm)Cory Lerios—David Jenkins. (P)Pablo Cruise.

LOVE WILL KEEP US TOGETHER (1975) (w)Howard Greenfield (m)Neil Sedaka. (P)The Captain and Tennille. No. 1 Chart Record. NARAS Award Winner.

LOVE WILL TELL (1936) (w)Jack Yellen (m)Lew Pollack. (I)Film: *Sing, Baby, Sing*, by Alice Faye.

LOVE WILL TURN YOU AROUND (1982) (wm)Kenny Rogers—Even Stevens—Thom Schuyler—David Malloy. (P)Kenny Rogers.

LOVE WITH THE PROPER STRANGER (1964) (w)Jack Jones (m)Elmer Bernstein. (I)Film: *Love With The Proper Stranger*, by Jack Jones. (P)Jack Jones.

LOVE WON'T LET ME WAIT (1975) (wm)Bobby Eli—Vinnie Barrett. (P)Major Harris.

LOVE YA (1951) (w)Charles Tobias (m)Peter De Rose. (I)Film: *On Moonlight Bay*, by Doris Day.

LOVE, YOU DIDN'T DO RIGHT BY ME (1954) (wm)Irving Berlin. (I)Film: *White Christmas*, by Rosemary Clooney.

LOVE YOU DOWN (1987) (wm)M. Riley, Jr. (P)Ready For The World.

LOVE, YOU FUNNY THING (1932) (w)Roy Turk (m)Fred E. Ahlert. (P)Louis Armstrong.

LOVE YOU INSIDE OUT (1979) (wm)Barry, Maurice, and Robin Gibb. (P)The Bee Gees. No. 1 Chart Record.

LOVE YOU MOST OF ALL (1958) (wm)B. Campbell. (P)Sam Cooke.

LOVE YOU SAVE, THE (1970) (wm)Berry Gordy, Jr. —Fonce Mizell—Deke Richards—Freddy Perren. (P)The Jackson Five. No. 1 Chart Record.

LOVE YOU SO (1960) (wm)Ron Holden. (P)Ron Holden.

LOVE YOU TO (1966) (wm)George Harrison. (P)The Beatles.

LOVE, YOUR MAGIC SPELL IS EVERYWHERE (1929) (w)Elsie Janis (m)Edmund Goulding. (I)Film: *The Trespasser*, by Gloria Swanson.

LOVE ZONE (1986) (wm)Barry Eastmond—Wayne Braithwaite—Billy Ocean. (P)Billy Ocean.

LOVELESS LOVE (1921) (wm)W. C. Handy. Based on folk song *Careless Love*. (P)Noble Sissle and his Orchestra.

LOVELIER THAN EVER (1948) (wm)Frank Loesser. (I)Musical:
Where's Charley?, by Jane Lawrence, Paul England, and The Chorus.

LOVELIEST NIGHT OF THE YEAR, THE (1950) (w)Paul Francis Webster (m)Irving Aaronson. Adapted from Rosas waltz: Sobre Los Olas (Over The Waves). (I)Film: *The Great Caruso*, by Mario Lanza. (P)Mario Lanza.

LOVELIGHT (1984) (wm)O'Bryan Burnette—Don Cornelius. (P)O'Bryan.

LOVELINESS OF YOU, THE (1937) (w)Mack Gordon (m)Harry Revel. (I)Film: *You Can't Have Everything*, by Tony Martin. (P)Tony Martin.

LOVELY (1962) (wm)Stephen Sondheim. (I)Musical: *A Funny Thing Happened On The Way To The Forum*, by Brian Davies and Preshy Marker and later reprised by Zero Mostel and Jack Gilford.

LOVELY LADY (1935) (w)Ted Koehler (m)Jimmy McHugh. (I)Film: *King Of Burlesque*, by Kenny Baker. (P)Tommy Dorsey and his Orchestra.

LOVELY NIGHT, A (1957) (w)Oscar Hammerstein II (m)Richard Rodgers. (I)TV special: *Cinderella*, by Julie Andrews, Ilka Chase, Kaye Ballard, and Alice Ghostly.

LOVELY RITA (1967) (wm)John Lennon—Paul McCartney. (P)The Beatles.

LOVELY TO LOOK AT (1935) (w)Dorothy Fields—Jimmy McHugh (m)Jerome Kern. (I)Film: *Roberta*, by Irene Dunne. (P)Eddy Duchin and his Orchestra. No. 1 Chart Record. (CR)Leo Reisman and his Orchestra. (R)1952 film: *Lovely To Look At*, by Howard Keel.

LOVELY WAY TO SPEND AN EVENING, A (1943) (w)Harold Adamson (m)Jimmy McHugh. (I)Film: *Higher And Higher*, by Frank Sinatra.

LOVER (1932) (w)Lorenz Hart (m)Richard Rodgers. (I)Film: *Love Me Tonight*, by Jeanette MacDonald. (P)Paul Whiteman and his Orchestra. (CR)Greta Keller. (R)1948 by Les Paul. (R)1952 by Peggy Lee.

LOVER COME BACK (1962) (wm)Alan Spilton—Frank De Vol. (I)Film: *Lover Come Back*, by Doris Day.

LOVER, COME BACK TO ME (1928) (w)Oscar Hammerstein II (m)Sigmund Romberg. (I)Operetta: *The New Moon*, by Evelyn Herbert. Recorded by Rudy Vallee. (R)1930 film: *The New Moon*, by Grace Moore and Lawrence Tibbett. (R)1940 film: *The New Moon*, by Jeanette MacDonald and Nelson Eddy. (R)1953 by Nat "King" Cole.

LOVERGIRL (1985) (wm)Teena Marie Brockert. (P)Teena Marie.

LOVER MAN (Oh, Where Can You Be?) (1942) (wm)Jimmy Davis—Roger Ramirez—Jimmy Sherman. (P)Billie Holiday.

LOVER, PLEASE (1962) (wm)Bill Swan. (P)Clyde McPhatter.

LOVER'S CONCERTO, A (1965) (wm)Sandy Linzer—Denny Randell. (P)The Toys. (CR)Sarah Vaughan.

LOVER'S GOLD (1949) (w)Bob Merrill (m)Morty Nevins. (I)The Three Suns. (P)Dinah Shore.

LOVER'S LULLABY, A (1940) (wm)Frankie Carle—Andy Razaf—Larry Wagner. (P)Glen Gray and The Casa Loma Orchestra. (CR)Frankie Masters and his Orchestra.

LOVER'S QUESTION, A (1959) (wm)Brook Benton—Jimmy Williams. (R)1961 by Ernestine Anderson. (R)1969 by Otis Redding. (R)1975 by Loggins and Messina.

LOVERS WHO WANDER (1962) (wm)Dion Di Mucci—Ernest Maresca. (P)Dion.

LOVE'S BEEN A LITTLE BIT HARD ON ME (1982) (wm)Gary Burr. (P)Juice Newton.

LOVE'S GROWN DEEP (1977) (wm)Kenny Nolan Helfman. (P)Kenny Nolan.

LOVE'S LINES, ANGLES, AND RHYMES (1971) (wm)Dorothea Joyce. (P)The 5th Dimension.

LOVE'S MADE A FOOL OF YOU (1958) (wm)Buddy Holly—Bob Montgomery. (P)Buddy Holly. (R)1966 by The Bobby Fuller Four. (R)1971 by Cochise.

LOVES ME LIKE A ROCK (1973) (wm)Paul Simon. (P)Paul Simon.

LOVE'S THEME (1974) (wm)Barry White. (P)Love Unlimited Orchestra. No. 1 Chart Record.

LOVEY DOVEY (1954) (wm)Ahmet Ertegun—Memphis Curtis. (P)Clyde McPhatter. (R)1961 by Buddy Knox. (R)1968 by Otis & Carla.

LOVIN' SAM, THE SHEIK OF ALABAM' (1922) (I)Sophie Tucker. (P)Nora Bayes. (R)1950 film: *Young Man With A Horn*, by Kirk Douglas and Hoagy Carmichael.

LOVIN, TOUCHIN', SQUEEZIN' (1979) (wm)Steve Perry. (P)Journey.

LOVIN' YOU (1972) (wm)Richard Rudolph—Minnie Ripperton. (P)Minnie Riperton. No. 1 Chart Record.

LOVING ARMS (1974) (wm)Tom Jans. (P)Dobie Gray. (CR)Kris Kristofferson and Rita Coolidge.

LOVING HER WAS EASIER (Than Anything I'll Ever Do Again) (1970) (P)Kris Kristofferson.

LOVING YOU (1957) (wm)Jerry Leiber—Mike Stoller. (P)Elvis Presley.

LOW RIDER (1975) (wm)Sylvester Allen—Harold Ray Brown—Morris Dickerson—Gerald Goldstein—Leroy Jordan—Lee Oskar Levitan—Charles Miller—Howard Scott. (P)War.

LOWDOWN (1976) (wm)David Paich—William Scaggs. (P)Boz Scaggs. NARAS Award Winner.

LUCILLE (1957) (wm)Albert Collins—Richard Penniman. (P)Little Richard. (CR)The Everly Brothers.

LUCILLE (1977) (wm)Hal Bynum—Roger Bowling. (P)Kenny Rogers.

LUCK BE A LADY (1950) (wm)Frank Loesser. (I)Musical: *Guys and Dolls*, by Robert Alda. Most popular recording by Frank Sinatra.

LUCKENBACH, TEXAS (1977) (wm)Bobby Emmons—Chips Moman. (P)Waylon Jennings.

LUCKIEST MAN IN THE WORLD (1933) (w)Ira Gershwin (m)George Gershwin. (I)Musical: *Pardon My English*, by George Givot.

LUCKY DAY (1926) (w)B. G. De Sylva—Lew Brown (m)Ray Henderson. (I)Revue: *George White's Scandals of 1926* by Harry Richman. Recorded by George Olsen and his Orchestra. (R)1956 film: *The Best Things In Life Are Free*, by Dan Dailey.

LUCKY IN LOVE (1927) (w)B. G. De Sylva—Lew Brown (m)Ray Henderson. (I)Musical: *Good News*, by Mary Lawlor and John Price Jones. Recorded by George Olsen and his Orchestra. (R)1947 film: *Good News*, by Pat Marshall, Peter Lawford, and June Allyson. (R)1956 film: *The Best Things In Life Are Free*, by Gordon MacRae, Dan Dailey, and Ernest Borgnine.

LUCKY LADY (1975) (wm)John Kander—Fred Ebb. (I)Film: *Lucky Lady*, by Liza Minnelli.

LUCKY LADYBUG (1958) (wm)Frank Slay—Bob Crewe. (P)Billy and Lilli.

LUCKY LINDY! (1927) (w)L. Wolfe Gilbert (m)Abel Baer. (P)Vernon Dalhart.

LUCKY LIPS (1957) (wm)Jerry Leiber—Mike Stoller. (P)Ruth Brown. (CR)Gale Storm. (R)1963 by Cliff Richard.

LUCKY SEVEN (1930) (w)Howard Dietz (m)Arthur Schwartz. (I)Revue: *The Second Little Show*, by Joey Ray.

LUCKY STAR (1984) (wm)Madonna Ciccone. (P)Madonna.

LUCKY TO BE ME (1944) (w)Betty Comden—Adolph Green (m)Leonard Bernstein. (I)Musical: *On The Town*, by John Battles.

LUCY IN THE SKY WITH DIAMONDS (1968) (wm)John Lennon—Paul McCartney. (P)The Beatles. (R)1975 by Elton John. No. 1 Chart Record.

LUCY'S THEME (1961) (m)Max Steiner. (I)Film: *Parrish*, as soundtrack theme.

LUKA (1987) (wm)Suzanne Vega. (P)Suzanne Vega.

LULLABY IN BLUE (1957) (w)Mack Gordon (m)Josef Myrow. (I)Film: *Bundle of Joy*, by Eddie Fisher and Debbie Reynolds.

LULLABY IN RAGTIME (1958) (wm)Sylvia Fine. (I)Film: *The Five Pennies*, by Danny Kaye and the voice of Eileen Wilson.

LULLABY IN RHYTHM (1938) (w)Walter Hirsch (m)Benny Goodman—Edgar Sampson—Clarence Profit. (P)Benny Goodman and his Orchestra.

LULLABY OF BROADWAY (1935) (w)Al Dubin (m)Harry Warren. (I)Film: *Gold Diggers Of Broadway*, by Dick Powell and Wini Shaw. Recorded by The Dorsey Brothers Orchestra. Also, Hal Kemp and his Orchestra. Academy Award Winner.

LULLABY OF THE LEAVES (1932) (w)Joe Young (m)Bernice Petkere. (I)On Radio: By Freddie Berrens and his Orchestra. (P)George Olsen and his Orchestra. No. 1 Chart Record.

LULU'S BACK IN TOWN (1935) (w)Al Dubin (m)Harry Warren. (I)Film: *Broadway Gondolier*, by Dick Powell and The Mills Brothers. (P)Fats Waller.

LUMBERED (1962) (wm)Leslie Bricusse—Anthony Newley. (I)Musical: *Stop The World—I Want To Get Off*, by Anthony Newley.

LUNA ROSSA (Blushing Moon) (1952) (w-Eng)Kermit Goell (m)A. Vian. (P)Tony Martin.

LUSH LIFE (1938) (wm)Billy Strayhorn. (I)Billy Strayhorn. (R)1949 by Nat "King" Cole.

LUSTY MONTH OF MAY, THE (1960) (w)Alan Jay Lerner (m)Frederick Loewe. (I)Musical: *Camelot*, by Julie Andrews and The Ensemble.

LYDIA, THE TATTOOED LADY (1939) (w)E. Y. Harburg (m)Harold Arlen. (I)Film: *At The Circus*, by Groucho Marx.

LYGIA (1951) (w)Paul Francis Webster (m)Miklos Rozsa. (I)Film: *Quo Vadis*, as soundtrack love theme.

LYIN' EYES (1975) (wm)Glenn Frey—Don Henley. (P)The Eagles.

M-SQUAD (1959) (m)William "Count" Basie. (I)TV series: *M-Squad.*

MA! (He's Making Eyes At Me) (1921) (w)Sidney Clare (m)Con Conrad. (I)Revue: *The Midnight Rounders of 1921,* by Eddie Cantor. (P)Eddie Cantor. (R)1940 by Dick Robertson. (R)1974 by Lena Zavaroni.

MA BELLE (1928) (w)Clifford Grey (m)Rudolf Friml. (I)Operetta: *The Three Musketeers,* by Joseph Macauley.

MA BELLE AMIE (1970) (wm)Hans van Eijck—Peter Tetteroo. (P)The Tee Set.

MA SAYS, PA SAYS (1952) (wm)Josef Marais. (P)Doris Day. (CR)Johnnie Ray.

MACARTHUR PARK (1968) (wm)Jim Webb. (P)Richard Harris. (R)1978 by Donna Summer. No. 1 Chart Record.

MACHINE GUN (1974) (wn)Milan Williams. (P)The Commodores.

MACHO MAN (1978) (w-Eng)Henri Belolo—Victor Willis—Peter Whitehead (m)Jacques Morali. (P)The Village People.

MACK THE BLACK (1948) (wm)Cole Porter. (I)Film: *The Pirate,* by Judy Garland.

MACK THE KNIFE (Moritat) (1928) (w-Eng)Marc Blitzstein. (m)Kurt Weill. (I)Opera: *The Three Penny Opera,* by Lotte Lenya. (P)Lotte Lenya. (R)1956 by The Dick Hyman Trio. (CR)Richard Hayman and Jan August. (CR)Lawrence Welk. (CR)Les Paul. (R)1959 by Bobby Darin. No. 1 Chart Record. (R)1960 by Ella Fitzgerald. (R)1986 by Frank Sinatra.

MACNAMARA'S BAND (1917) (w)John J. Stamford (m)Shamus O'Connor. Famous Irish song. Most popular recording by Bing Crosby.

MACUSHLA (1910) (w)Josephine V. Rowe (m)Dermot MacMurrough. (P)John McCormack.

MAD ABOUT HIM, SAD WITHOUT HIM, HOW CAN I BE GLAD WITHOUT HIM BLUES (1941) (wm)Larry Markes—Dick Charles. (P)Dinah Shore.

MAD ABOUT YOU (1980) (wm)Paula Brown—James Whelan—Mitchell Young Evans. (P)Belinda Carlisle.

MAD ABOUT THE BOY (1935) (wm)Noel Coward. (I)Revue: *Words And Music,* by Joyce Barbour, Steffi Duna, Norah Howard, and Doris Hare.

MAD DOGS AND ENGLISHMEN (1931) (wm)Noel Coward. (I)Revue: *The Third Little Show,* by Beatrice Lillie.

(Girls, Girls, Girls,Were)MADE TO LOVE (1962) (wm)Phil Everly. (P)Eddie Hodges.

MADELON (1918) (w-Eng)Alfred Bryan (m)Camille Robert. Famous French song popular during World War I.

MADEMOISELLE DE PAREE (1948) (w-Eng)Mitchell Parish. (m)Paul Durang. (P)Jacqueline Francois.

MADEMOISELLE IN NEW ROCHELLE (1930) (w)Ira Gershwin (m)George Gershwin. (I)Musical: *Strike Up The Band,* by Bobby Clark and Paul McCullough.

MADISON TIME (1960) (w)Eddie Morrison (m)Ray Bryant. (P)Ray Bryant.

MAGGIE MAY (1971) (wm)Rod Stewart—Martin Quittenton. (P)Rod Stewart. No. 1 Chart Record.

MAGGIE'S FARM (1965) (wm)Bob Dylan (P)Bob Dylan.

MAGIC (1974) (wm)David Payton—William Lyall. (P)Pilot.

MAGIC (1980) (wm)John Farrar. (P)Olivia Newton—John. No. 1 Chart Record.

MAGIC (1984) (wm)Ric Ocasek. (P)The Cars.

MAGIC BUS, THE (1968) (wm)Peter Townshend. (P)The Who.

MAGIC CARPET RIDE (1968) (wm)Moreve Rushton—John Kay. (P)Steppenwolf.

MAGIC CIRCLE (1954) (wm)Bennie Benjamin—George Weiss. (P)Rusty Draper.

MAGIC IS THE MOONLIGHT (1930) (w-Eng)Charles Pasquale (m)Maria Grever. (I)Film: *Bathing Beauty,* by Carlos Ramirez. (R)1950 Film: *Nancy Goes To Rio,* by Jane Powell and later reprised by Ann Sothern.

MAGIC MAN (1976) (wm)Ann Wilson—Nancy Wilson. (P)Heart.

MAGIC MOMENT (1961) (w)Howard Dietz (m)Arthur Schwartz. (I)Musical: *The Gay Life,* by Barbara Cook.

MAGIC MOMENTS (1957) (w)Hal David (m)Burt Bacharach. (P)Perry Como.

MAGIC TOWN (1966) (wm)Barry Mann—Cynthia Weil. (P)The Vogues.

MAGICAL MYSTERY TOUR (1967) (wm)John Lennon—Paul McCartney. (P)The Beatles.

MAGNET AND STEEL (1978) (wm)Walter Egan. (P)Walter Egan.

MAGNIFICENT SEVEN, THE (1960) (m)Elmer Bernstein. (I)Film: *The Magnificent Seven,* as soundtrack theme.

MAHOGANY (THEME) (*See Do You Know Where You're Going To*).

MAHZEL (Means Good Luck) (1947) (wm)Artie Wayne—Jack Beekman. (P)Artie Wayne.

MAIN EVENT, THE (Fight) (1979) (wm)Paul Jabara—Bob Esty— Bruce Roberts. (I)Film: *The Main Event,* by Barbra Streisand. (P)Barbra Streisand.

MAIN STEM (1944) (m)Duke Ellington. (P)Duke Ellington and his Orchestra.

MAINE (1962) (wm)Richard Rodgers. (I)Musical: *No Strings,* by Diahann Carroll and Richard Kiley.

MAINSTREET (1977) (wm)Bob Seger. (P)Bob Seger.

MAIRZY DOATS (1943) (wm)Milton Drake—Al Hoffman—Jerry Livingston. (I)Al Trace and his Orchestra. (P)The Merry Macs.

MAJOR TOM (Coming Home) (1983) (wm)Peter Shilling—David Lodge. (P)Peter Shilling.

MAKE A MIRACLE (1948) (wm)Frank Loesser. (I)Musical: *Where's Charley?,* by Ray Bolger and Allyn McLerie.

MAKE A MOVE ON ME (1982) (wm)John Farrar—Tom Snow. (P)Olivia Newton—John.

MAKE A WISH (1937) (w)Louis Alter—Paul Francis Webster (m)Oscar Straus. (I)Film: *Make A Wish,* by Bobby Breen and Basil Rathbone.

MAKE BELIEVE (1927) (w)Oscar Hammerstein II (m)Jerome Kern. (I)Musical: *Show Boat,* by Howard Marsh and Norma Terris. (R)1936 Film: *Show Boat,* by Allan Jones and Irene Dunne. (R)1946 Film: *Till The Clouds Roll By,* by Tony Martin and Kathryn Grayson. (R)1951 Film: *Show Boat,* by Howard Keel and Kathryn Grayson.

MAKE BELIEVE (1969) (wm)Bo Gentry—Joey Levine. (P)Wind.

MAKE BELIEVE ISLAND (1940) (w)Nick and Charles Kenny (m)Will Grosz. (P)Mitchell Ayres and his Orchestra. (CR)Jan Savitt and his Orchestra.

MAKE IT ANOTHER OLD FASHIONED, PLEASE (1940) (wm)Cole Porter. (I)Musical: *Panama Hattie*, by Ethel Merman.

MAKE IT EASY ON YOURSELF (1962) (w)Hal David (m)Burt Bacharach. (P)Jerry Butler. (R)1965 by The Walker Brothers. (R)1970 by Dionne Warwick.

MAKE IT WITH YOU (1970) (wm)David Gates. (P)Bread. No. 1 Chart Record. (R)1977 by The Whispers.

MAKE LOVE TO ME (1954) (wm)Bill Norvas—Allan Copeland—Leon Rappolo—Paul Mares—Ben Pollack—George Brunies—Mel Stitzel— Walter Melrose. Adapted from *Tin Roof Blues*. (P)Jo Stafford. No. 1 Chart Record.

MAKE ME BELONG TO YOU (1966) (wm)Chip Taylor—Billy Vera. (P)Barbara Lewis.

MAKE ME SMILE (1970) (wm)James Pankow. (P)Chicago.

MAKE ME THE WOMAN THAT YOU GO HOME TO (1971) (wm)Clay McMurray. (P)Gladys Knight & The Pips.

MAKE ME YOUR BABY (1965) (wm)Roger Atkins—Helen Miller. (P)Barbara Lewis.

MAKE ME YOURS (1967) (wm)Bettye Jean Champion. (P)Bettye Swann.

MAKE SOMEONE HAPPY (1960) (w)Betty Comden—Adolph Green (m)Jule Styne. (I)Musical: *Do Re Mi*, by John Reardon.

MAKE THE MAN LOVE ME (1951) (w)Dorothy Fields (m)Arthur Schwartz. (I)Musical: *A Tree Grows In Brooklyn*, by Marcia Van Dyke and Johnny Johnston.

MAKE THE WORLD GO AWAY (1963) (wm)Hank Cochran. (P)Timi Yuro. (CR)Ray Price. (R)1965 by Eddy Arnold. (R)1975 by Donny and Marie Osmond.

MAKE WAY FOR TOMORROW (1944) (w)Ira Gershwin (m)Jerome Kern. (I)Film: *Cover Girl*, by Phil Silvers, Gene Kelly, and Nan Wynn dubbing for Rita Hayworth.

MAKE YOUR OWN KIND OF MUSIC (1969) (wm)Barry Mann—Cynthia Weil. (P)Mama Cass Elliot.

MAKE YOURSELF COMFORTABLE (1954) (wm)Bob Merrill. (P)Sarah Vaughan. (CR)Steve Lawrence and Eydie Gorme.

MAKIN' IT (1979) (wm)Dino Frekaris—Freddy Peren. (P)David Naughton.

MAKIN' LOVE (1959) (wm)Floyd Robinson. (P)Floyd Robinson.

MAKIN' WHOOPEE (1928) (w)Gus Kahn (m)Walter Donaldson. (I)Musical: *Whoopee*, by Eddie Cantor. (P)Eddie Cantor. (CR)Ben Bernie and his Orchestra. (R)1951 Film: *I'll See You In My Dreams*, by Doris Day and Danny Thomas. (R)1953 Film: *The Eddie Cantor Story*, by the voice of Eddie Cantor on soundtrack. (R)1965 by Ray Charles.

MAKING LOVE (1982) (wm)Carole Bayer Sager—Burt Bacharach— Bruce Roberts. (I)Film: *Making Love*, by voice of Roberta Flack. (P)Roberta Flack.

MAKING LOVE OUT OF NOTHING AT ALL (1983) (wm)Jim Steinman. (P)Air Supply.

MAKING OUR DREAMS COME TRUE (1976) (wm)Norman Gimbel—Charles Fox. (P)Cyndi Greco. Featured in TV Show: *Laverne & Shirley*.

MALAGUENA (1948) (w-Eng)Marian Banks (m)Ernesto Lecuona. From suite Andalucia. Popularized under title At The Crossroads.

MAMA (1960) (w-Eng)Harold Barlow—Phil Brito (m)C. A. Bixio. (I)Phil Brito. (P)Connie Francis.

MAMA (1966) (wm)Mark Charron. (P)B. J. Thomas.

MAMA CAN'T BUY YOU LOVE (1977) (wm)Leroy Bell—Casey James. (P)Elton John.

MAMA DOLL SONG, THE (1954) (w)Charles Tobias (m)Nat Simon. (P)Patti Page.

MAMA DON'T ALLOW NO EASY RIDERS HERE (1929) (wm)Charles Davenport. (P)Charles "Cow Cow" Davenport.

MAMA DON'T WANT NO PEAS AN' RICE AN' COCOANUT OIL (1931) (wm)L. Wolfe Gilbert—Charlie Lofthouse. Most popular recording by Count Basie and his Orchestra (1938).

MAMA FROM THE TRAIN (1956) (wm)Irving Gordon. (P)Patti Page.

MAMA INEZ (1931) (w-Eng)L. Wolfe Gilbert (M)Eliseo Grenet. (I)Maurice Chevalier. (P)Desi Arnaz.

MAMA LIKED THE ROSES (1970) (wm)Johnny Christopher. (P)Elvis Presley in medley with The Wonder Of You.

MAMA LOOK A BOOBOO (1957) (wm)Lord Melody. (P)Harry Belafonte.

MAMA SANG A SONG (1962) (wm)Bill Anderson. (CR)Stan Kenton and his Orchestra. (CR)Walter Brennan.

MAMA, TEACH ME TO DANCE (1956) (wm)Al Hoffman—Dick Manning. (P)Eydie Gorme.

MAMA TOLD ME (Not To Come) (1970) (wm)Randy Newman. (I)Randy Newman. (P)Three Dog Night. No. 1 Chart Record.

MAMA'S PEARL (1971) (wm)Berry Gordy, Jr—Fonce Mizell—Freddy Perren—Deke Richards. (P)The Jackson Five.

MAMBO BABY (1954) (wm)Charles Singleton—Rose Marie McCoy. (P)Ruth Brown.

MAMBO ITALIANO (1954) (wm)Bob Merrill. (P)Rosemary Clooney.

MAMBO, NO. 5 (1958) (m)Perez Prado. (P)Perez Prado and his Orchestra. (CR)Dick Jacobs and his Orchestra.

MAMBO ROCK (1955) (wm)Bix Reichner—Mildred Phillips—Jimmy Ayre. (P)Bill Haley and The Comets.

MAME (1966) (wm)Jerry Herman. (I)Musical: *Mame*, by Charles Braswell and The Company. (P)Louis Armstrong. (CR)Herb Alpert and The Tijuana Brass. (CR)Bobby Darin.

MAMIE IS MIMI (1949) (w)Leo Robin (m)Jule Styne. (I)Musical: *Gentlemen Prefer Blondes*, by Honi Coles and Cholly Atkins.

MAMMA GOES WHERE PAPA GOES OR PAPA DON'T GO OUT TONIGHT (1923) (wm)Jack Yellen—Milton Ager. (P)Sophie Tucker.

MAMMA LOVES PAPA, PAPA LOVES MAMMA (1923) (wm)Cliff Friend— Abel Baer. (P)Sophie Tucker.

MAMMA MIA (1975) (wm)Benny Andersson—Stig Anderson—Bjorn Ulvaeus. (P)Abba.

MAMMAS DON'T LET YOUR BABIES GROW UP TO BE COWBOYS (1978) (wm)Ed Bruce—Patsy Bruce. (I)Ed Bruce. (P)Waylon Jennings and Willie Nelson.

MAM'SELLE (1947) (w)Mack Gordon (m)Edmund Goulding. (I)Film: *The Razor's Edge* on soundtrack. (P)Art Lund. (CR)Frank Sinatra. (CR)Dick Haymes.

MAN AIN'T SUPPOSED TO CRY, A (1949) (wm)Frankie Laine—Norman Gimbel—Irving Reid. (P)Frankie Laine.

MAN AND A WOMAN, A (1967) (w-Eng)Jerry Keller—Francis Lai. (I)Film: *A Man And A Woman*, as soundtrack theme. (P)Francis Lai and his Orchestra.

MAN AND HIS DREAM, A (1939) (w)Johnny Burke (m)James V. Monaco. (I)Film: *The Star Maker*, by Bing Crosby.

MAN DOESN'T KNOW, A (1955) (wm)Richard Adler—Jerry Ross. (I)Musical: *Damn Yankees*, by Stephen Douglass.

MAN FROM MINTON'S, THE (1949) (m)George Shearing. (P)The George Shearing Trio.

MAN FROM THE SOUTH (With A Big Cigar In His Mouth) (1930) (wm)Rube Bloom—Harry Woods. (P)Ted Weems and his Orchestra.

MAN FROM U. N. C. L. E. (Theme) (1964) (m)Jerry Goldsmith. (I)TV series: *The Man From U. N. C. L. E.* as soundtrack theme.

MAN I LOVE, THE (1924) (w)Ira Gershwin (m)George Gershwin. (I)Marion Harris. (P)Paul Whiteman and his Orchestra. (R)1937 by The Benny Goodman Trio. (R)1945 Film: *Rhapsody In Blue*, by Hazel Scott. (R)1950 Film: *Young Man With A Horn* by Doris Day with Harry James and his Orchestra. (R)1957 Film: *The Helen Morgan Story*, by Gogi Grant dubbing for Ann Blyth.

MAN IN THE MIRROR (1987) (wm)S. Garrett—G. Ballardo (P)Michael Jackson. No. 1 Chart Record.

MAN IN THE RAINCOAT, THE (1955) (wm)Warwick Webster (P)Priscilla Wright.

MAN ON THE FLYING TRAPEZE, THE (1933) (wm)Walter O'Keefe. Adapted from old English song. (I)Walter O'Keefe. (P)Rudy Vallee.

MAN ON YOUR MIND (1982) (wm)Glenn Shorrock—Kerryn Tolhurst. (P)Little River Band.

MAN SIZE LOVE (1986) (wm)Rod Temperton. (I)Film: *Running Scared*, by Klymaxx on soundtrack. (P)Klymaxx.

MAN THAT GOT AWAY, THE (1954) (w)Ira Gershwin (m)Harold Arlen. (I)Film: *A Star Is Born*, by Judy Garland. (P)Judy Garland.

MAN WHO HAS EVERYTHING, THE (1962) (wm)Richard Rodgers. (I)Musical: *No Strings*, by Mitchell Gregg.

MAN WHO SHOT LIBERTY VALANCE, THE (1962) (w)Hal David (m)Burt Bacharach. Song did not appear in the film of the same name. (P)Gene Pitney.

MAN WITH A DREAM, A (1955) (w)Stella Unger (m)Victor Young. (I)Musical: *Seventh Heaven*, by Ricardo Montalban.

MAN WITH A HORN (1946) (w)Eddie De Lange (m)Bonnie Lake—Jack Jenney. (P)Theme song of Ray Anthony and his Orchestra.

MAN WITH THE BANJO (1954) (w-Eng)Robert Mellin (m)Fritz Schulz. (P)The Ames Brothers.

MAN WITH THE GOLDEN ARM, THE (Main Title) (1956) (m)Elmer Bernstein. (I)Film: *The Man With The Golden Arm*, as soundtrack theme. (P)Richard Maltby and his Orchestra. (CR)Elmer Bernstein and his Orchestra. (CR)Dick Jacobs and his Orchestra (In medley with Molly O). (CR)The McGuire Sisters as song: Delilah Jones, with lyric by Steve Allen.

MAN WITHOUT LOVE, A (1968) (w-Eng)Barry Mason (m)D. Pace—M. Panzeri—R. Livraghi. (P)Engelbert Humperdinck.

MANEATER (1982) (wm)Daryl Hall—John Oates—Sara Allen. (P)Hall and Oates. No. 1 Chart Record.

DICK JACOBS AND HIS ORCHESTRA

In the late fifties, management decided it was time for me to start recording under my own name. In 1958 Dick Jacobs and His Orchestra wound up in the *Cash Box* poll as the most promising orchestra of the year. My first record, a cover record on Kitty Kallen's smash hit, *Little Things Mean a Lot*, received nice reviews in the trade magazines, got quite a bit of air time, but didn't really sell all that well. The next record was another story ...

The new motion picture, *The Man With the Golden Arm*, had a fantastic score by the late Elmer Bernstein. However, the subject matter was such a taboo in those days the record companies were reluctant to release a record on such a touchy problem. However, Decca heard that RCA was coming out with a version by Richard Hayman; since they owned the soundtrack, Decca decided to release the Elmer Bernstein original.

Bob Thiele (bless him) thought that I could do a recording that would be better than the others so we planned for an immediate recording session. We had a gimmick; we would incorporate the love song *Molly-O* and make our recording stand out from the others. Our recording session was scheduled for 8:00 a.m.. Sandy Block, my musicians contractor, had gotten together a great band; marvelous players, including Billy Butterfield, Urbie Green, Hank Jones, Hymie Schertzer, Jimmy Nottingham, and Jimmy Maxwell. We had hired Louis Bellson to play drums, but Pearl Bailey (Louis' wife) called at 6:30 a.m. to say that Louis was ill and couldn't make it. An emergency call to Cliff Leeman got that great drummer in from Long Island only a few minutes late, and we were off and running.

The resulting record, *Main Title and Molly-O*, was my first success under my own name. The record made the charts well above the other two versions. Other successes followed, including the extremely popular (you couldn't turn on the radio without hearing it!) *Petticoats of Portugal*.

MANAGUA NICARAGUA (1947) (w)Albert Gamse (m)Irving Fields. (P)Freddy Martin and his Orchestra. No. 1 Chart Record. (CR)Glen Gray and The Casa Loma Orchestra.

MANANA (Is Soon Enough For me) (1948) (wm)Peggy Lee—Dave Barbour. (P)Peggy Lee. No. 1 Chart Record.

MANDOLIN RAIN (1987) (wm)Bruce Hornsby—J. Hornsby. (P)Bruce Hornsby & The Range.

MANDY (1919) (wm)Irving Berlin. (P)Van and Schenck. (R)1954 Film: *White Christmas*, by Bing Crosby and Danny Kaye.

MANDY (1975) (wm)Scott English—Richard Kerr. (P)Barry Manilow. No. 1 Chart Record.

MANDY, MAKE UP YOUR MIND (1924) (w)Grant Clark—Roy Turk (m)George W. Meyer—Arthur Johnston.

(I)Revue: *Dixie To Broadway*, by Florence Mills and The Ensemble. (P)Paul Whiteman and his Orchestra. (R)1943 by Tommy Dorsey and his Orchestra.

MANGOS (1957) (w)Sid Wayne (m)Dee Libbey. (I)Revue: *Ziegfeld Follies*, by Micki Marlo. (P)Rosemary Clooney.

MANHA DE CARNIVAL (1960) (wm)Antonio Maria (m)Luis Bonfa. (I)Film: *Black Orpheus*, by Breno Mello.

MANHATTAN (1925) (w)Lorenz Hart (m)Richard Rodgers. (I)Revue: *Garrick Gaieties*, by Sterling Holloway and June Cochran. (P)Ben Selvin and his Orchestra. (R)1948 Film: *Words And Music*, by Mickey Rooney, Tom Drake, and Marshall Thompson. (R)1957 Film: *Beau James*, by Bob Hope and Vera Miles.

MANHATTAN MADNESS (1932) (wm)Irving Berlin. (I)Musical: *Face The Music*, by J. Harold Murray and Catherine Carrington.

MANHATTAN MERRY GO ROUND (1936) (wm)Gustave Haenschen—Pinky Herman. (I)Radio Show: Manhattan Merry Go Round, as theme song.

MANHATTAN MOOD (1942) (w)Harold Adamson (m)Peter De Rose. (P)Glenn Miller and his Orchestra, vocal by The Modernaires.

MANHATTAN SERENADE (1942) (w)Harold Adamson (m)Louis Alter. (P)Paul Whiteman and his Orchestra. Theme song of Easy Aces radio show. (CR)Harry James and his Orchestra. (CR)Jimmy Dorsey and his Orchestra.

MANHATTAN SPIRITUAL (1959) (m)Billy Maxted. (P)Reg Owen and his Orchestra. (R)1975 by Mike Post and his Orchestra.

MANIAC (1983) (wm)Michael Sembello—Dennis Matkosky. (I)Film: *Flashdance*, by voice of Michael Sembello. (P)Michael Sembello. No. 1 Chart Record.

MANIC MONDAY (1986) (wm)Prince Rogers Nelson. (P)Bangles.

MANTECA (1948) (m)John Birks Gillespie—Gil Fuller. (P)Dizzy Gillespie and his Orchestra.

MANY A NEW DAY (1943) (w)Oscar Hammerstein II (m)Richard Rodgers. (I)Musical: *Oklahoma!*, by Joan Roberts. (R)1955 Film: *Oklahoma*, by Shirley Jones and The Girl's Chorus.

MANY TEARS AGO (1960) (wm)Winfield Scott. (P)Connie Francis.

MANY TIMES (1953) (w-Eng)Jessie Barnes (m)Felix Stahl. (P)Eddie Fisher.

MAPLE LEAF RAG (1899) (m)Scott Joplin. (I)Scott Joplin.

MARCH OF THE DWARFS (1891) (m)Edvard Grieg. Famous classical composition usually performed at circuses.

MARCH OF THE GRENADIERS (1929) (w)Clifford Grey (m)Victor Schertzinger. (I)Film: *The Love Parade*, by Jeanette MacDonald and The Male Chorus.

MARCH OF THE MUSKETEERS (1928) (w)P. G. Wodehouse—Clifford Grey (m)Rudolf Friml. (I)Operetta: *The Three Musketeers*, by Dennis King, Douglass Dumbrille, Detmar Poppen, Joseph Macauley and The Chorus.

MARCH OF THE SIAMESE CHILDREN, THE (1951) (m)Richard Rodgers. (I)Musical: *The King And I*.

MARCH OF THE TOYS (1903) (m)Victor Herbert. (I)Musical: *Babes In Toyland*.

MARCH OF THE YUPPIES (1985) (wm)Charles Strouse.

(I)Musical: *Mayor*, by Nancy Giles.

MARCHE MILITAIRE (1826) (m)Franz Schubert. Famous classical march.

MARCHE SLAV (1876) (m)Peter I. Tchaikovsky. Famous classical march.

MARCHETA (1913) (wm)Victor Schertzinger. (P)John McCormack.

MARCHING ALONG TOGETHER (1933) (wm)Edward Pola—Franz Steininger—Mort Dixon. (P)Kate Smith.

MARCHING THROUGH GEORGIA (1865) (wm)Henry Clay Work. Famous Civil War song.

MARGARITAVILLE (1977) (wm)Jimmy Buffett. (P)Jimmy Buffett.

MARGIE (1920) (w)Benny Davis (m)Con Conrad—J. Russel Robinson. (I)The Original Dixieland Jazz Band. (P)Eddie Cantor. (CR)Ted Lewis. (CR)Frank Crumit. (R)1937 by Jimmy Lunceford and his Orchestra. (R)1953 Film: *The Eddie Cantor Story*, by the voice of Eddie Cantor.

MARGOT (1926) (w)Otto Harbach—Oscar Hammerstein II (m)Sigmund Romberg. (I)Operetta: *The Desert Song*, by Glen Dale.

MARIA (1938) (wm)Cole Porter. (I)Musical: *You Never Know*, by Clifton Webb.

MARIA (1957) (w)Stephen Sondheim (m)Leonard Bernstein. (I)Musical: *West Side Story*, by Larry Kert. (P)Johnny Mathis. (R)1962 by Roger Williams and his Orchestra.

MARIA (1959) (w)Oscar Hammerstein II (m)Richard Rodgers. (I)Musical: *The Sound Of Music*, by Patricia Neway, Muriel O'Malley, Elizabeth Howell, and Karen Shepard.

MARIA ELENA (1941) (w-Eng)S. K. Russell. (m)Lorenzo Barcelata. (I)Lawrence Welk and his Orchestra. (P)Jimmy Dorsey and his Orchestra, vocal by Bob Eberly. No. 1 Chart Record.

MARIAN THE LIBRARIAN (1957) (wm)Meredith Willson. (I)Musical: *The Music Man*, by Robert Preston and The Boys and Girls.

MARIANNE (1928) (w)Oscar Hammerstein II (m)Sigmund Romberg. (I)Operetta: *The New Moon*, by Robert Halliday. (R)1940 Film: *The New Moon*, by Nelson Eddy and Jeanette MacDonald.

MARIANNE (1957) (wm)Terry Gilkyson—Frank Miller—Richard Dehr. (P)The Hilltoppers. (CR)Terry Gilkyson and The Easy Riders. (CR)Burl Ives.

MARIE (1928) (wm)Irving Berlin. (P)Rudy Vallee. (CR)Nat Shilkret and his Orchestra. (R)1937 by Tommy Dorsey and his Orchestra, vocal by Jack Leonard. (R)1947 Film: *The Fabulous Dorseys*, by Stuart Foster, Janet Blair, and Tommy Dorsey and his Orchestra. (R)1965 by The Bachelors.

MARIE FROM SUNNY ITALY (1909) (wm)Irving Berlin. Berlin's first published song, netting him royalties of thirty seven cents.

MARIE'S THE NAME, HIS LATEST FLAME (1961) (wm)Jerry Leiber— Mike Stoller. (P)Elvis Presley.

MARINA (1959) (w-Eng)Ray Maxwell (m)Rocco Granata. (P)Rocco Granata (CR)Willy Alberti. (CR)Jacky Noguez.

MARINE'S HYMN (From The Halls Of Montezuma To The Shores Of Tripoli) (1919) (w)Henry C. Davis. Based on a Jacques Offenbach melody. Official song of The United States Marine Corps.

MARMALADE, MOLASSES AND HONEY (1972) (w)Alan and Marilyn Bergman (m)Maurice Jarre. (I)Film: *The*

Life And Times Of Judge Roy Bean, by voice of Andy Williams. (P)Andy Williams.

MARRAKESH EXPRESS (1969) (wm)Graham Nash. (P)Crosby, Stills, and Nash.

MARRIAGE OF FIGARO (Overture) (1790) (m)Wolfgang Amadeus Mozart. From Opera: *The Marriage Of Figaro*.

MARRIAGE TYPE LOVE (1953) (w)Oscar Hammerstein II (m)Richard Rodgers. (I)Musical: *Me And Juliet*, by Arthur Maxwell and Helena Scott.

MARRIED (Heiraten) (1966) (w)Fred Ebb (m)John Kander. (I)Musical: *Cabaret*, by Lotte Lenya and Jack Gilford.

MARRIED I CAN ALWAYS GET (1956) (wm)Gordon Jenkins. From Manhattan Tower Suite. (P)Gordon Jenkins and his Chorus and Orchestra.

MARRIED MAN, A (1964) (wm)Marian Grudeff— Raymond Jessel. (I)Musical: *Baker Street*, by Peter Sallis. (P)Richard Burton.

MARRIED MEN (1979) (wm)Dominic Bugatti—Frank Musker. (P)Bette Midler.

MARRYING FOR LOVE (1950) (wm)Irving Berlin. (I)Musical: *Call Me Madam*, by Ethel Merman and Paul Lukas.

MARSEILLAISE, LA (1792) (wm)Claude Joseph Rouget de Lisle. French national anthem written after the French Revolution during France's war with Prussia and Austria.

MARSHMALLOW WORLD, A (1949) (w)Carl Sigman (m)Peter De Rose. (P)Bing Crosby.

MARTA (1931) (w-Eng)L. Wolfe Gilbert (m)Moises Simons. (P)Arthur Tracy (The Street Singer) (Theme Song).

MARTHA MY DEAR (1968) (wm)John Lennon—Paul McCartney. (P)The Beatles.

MARTIAN HOP (1963) (wm)John Spirt—Robert Lawrence Rappaport— Steve Rappaport. (P)The Ran—Dels.

MARTINS AND THE COYS, THE (1936) (wm)Ted Weems—Al Cameron. (P)Ted Weems and his Orchestra.

MARY HAD A LITTLE LAMB (1972) (wm)Paul and Linda McCartney (P)Wings.

MARY IN THE MORNING (1967) (wm)Johnny Cymbal— Mike Lendell. (P)Al Martino.

MARYLAND, MY MARYLAND (1861) (w)James Ryder Randall (m)Adapted from a drinking song. State song of Maryland.

MARY LOU (1926) (wm)Abe Lyman—George Waggner— J. Russel Robinson. (P)Abe Lyman and his Orchestra.

MARY LOU (1959) (wm)Ron Hawkins—Jacqueline Magill. (P)Ronnie Hawkins.

MARY MAKE BELIEVE (1928) (wm)Noel Coward. (I)Revue: *This Year Of Grace*, by Madeline Gibson and The Young Ladies (New York production).

MARY'S A GRAND OLD NAME (1905) (wm)George M. Cohan. (I)Musical: *Forty Five Minutes From Broadway*, by George M. Cohan. (P)George M. Cohan. (R)1942 Film: *Yankee Doodle Dandy*, by James Cagney.

MARY'S BOY CHILD (1956) (wm)Jester Hairston. (P)Harry Belafonte.

MARY'S LITTLE LAMB (1962) (wm)Cynthia Weil—Barry Mann. (P)James Darren.

M*A*S*H (Song From) (Suicide Is Painless) (1970) (w)Michael Altman (m)Johnny Mandel. (I)Film: *Mash*.

MASHED POTATO TIME (1962) (wm)R. Bateman—G. Dobbins—W. Garrett— F. C. Gorman—B. Holland. (P)Dee Dee Sharp.

MASQUERADE (1932) (w)Paul Francis Webster (m)John Jacob Loeb. (P)Ted Black and his Orchestra.

(I'm Afraid)MASQUERADE IS OVER, THE (1938) (w)Herb Magidson (m)Allie Wrubel. (P)Jimmy Dorsey and his Orchestra.

MASSACHUSETTS (The Lights Went Out In) (1969) (wm)Barry, Maurice, and Robin Gibb. (P)The Bee Gees.

MASSA'S IN DE COLD COLD GROUND (1852) (wm)Stephen Collins Foster. One of Foster's most popular songs.

MASTER BLASTER (1980) (wm)Stevie Wonder. (P)Stevie Wonder.

MASTERPIECE (See When I Paint My Masterpiece).

MASTERS OF WAR (1963) (wm)Bob Dylan. (P)Bob Dylan.

MATADOR, THE (1964) (wm)Carl Davis—William B. Butler—Major Lance. (P)Major Lance.

MATCHBOX (1957) (wm)Carl Perkins. (I)Carl Perkins. (R)1964 by The Beatles.

MATCHMAKER, MATCHMAKER (1964) (w)Sheldon Harnick (m)Jerry Bock. (I)Musical: *Fiddler On The Roof*, by Joanna Merlin, Julia Migenes, and Tanya Everett.

MATELOT (1945) (wm)Noel Coward. (I)Musical: *Sigh No More*, by Graham Payne.

MATERIAL GIRL (1984) (wm)Peter Brown—Robert Rans. (P)Madonna.

MATILDA, MATILDA (1953) (wm)Harry Thomas. (P)Harry Belafonte.

MATINEE (1948) (w)Bob Russell (m)Carl Sigman. (P)Vaughn Monroe and his Orchestra. (CR)Buddy Clark.

MATING GAME, THE (1959) (w)Lee Adams (m)Charles Strouse. (I)Film: *The Mating Game*, by Debbie Reynolds.

MATTER OF TRUST, A (1986) (wm)Billy Joel. (P)Billy Joel.

MAVERICK (1958) (w)Paul Francis Webster (m)David Buttolph. (I)TV series: *Maverick*, as soundtrack theme.

MAXIM'S (1907) (w)Adrian Ross (m)Franz Lehar. (I)Musical: *The Merry Widow*. (R)1934 Film: *The Merry Widow*, by Maurice Chevalier.

MAXWELL'S SILVER HAMMER (1969) (wm)John Lennon—Paul McCartney. (P)The Beatles.

MAY I (1934) (w)Mack Gordon (m)Harry Revel. (I)Film: *We're Not Dressing*, by Bing Crosby. (P)Bing Crosby.

MAY I HAVE THE NEXT ROMANCE WITH YOU (1936) (w)Mack Gordon (m)Harry Revel. (I)British Film: *Head Over Heels*, by Jessie Matthews and Louis Borrell. (P)Tommy Dorsey and his Orchestra.

MAY I SING TO YOU (1953) (wm)Charles Tobias—Harry Akst—Eddie Fisher. (P)Theme song of Eddie Fisher.

MAY THE BIRD OF PARADISE FLY UP YOUR NOSE (1965) (wm)Neal Merritt. (P)Little Jimmy Dickens.

MAY THE GOOD LORD BLESS AND KEEP YOU (1950) (wm)Meredith Willson. (P)Frankie Laine.

MAY YOU ALWAYS (1959) (wm)Larry Markes—Dick Charles. (P)The McGuire Sisters.

MAYBE (1926) (w)Ira Gershwin (m)George Gershwin. (I)Musical: *Oh, Kay!*, by Gertrude Lawrence and Oscar Shaw.

MAYBE (1935) (wm)Allan Flynn—Frank Madden. (P)The Ink Spots (1940). (R)1952 by Perry Como and Eddie Fisher.

PERRY COMO AND EDDIE FISHER

During the time Sy Oliver and I were in business together, Dave Kapp was the head of A&R at RCA Victor Records. One day Dave Kapp called Sy and asked him to recommend an arranger who was good but who had not done too much work for major artists. Sy promptly gave me a big endorsement and I was summoned to a secret night meeting with Kapp, Perry Como, and Eddie Fisher, where I learned that these were the artists for whom I would be doing arrangements. It was to be a duet record, with the big song a tune called *Watermelon Weather* and the other side, or throwaway, an old standard called *Maybe*.

The session went well, and naturally, as fate would have it, *Watermelon Weather* was a bomb and *Maybe* became a big hit. These were also the last arrangements I did for Como or Fisher, as they had strong loyalties to their previous arrangers, notably Hugo Winterhalter (a fine arranger). However, Dave Kapp liked my work and gave me a number of other assignments to work with Merv Griffin, Dorothy Loudon, Betty Clooney, Jimmy Wakely, and others.

MAYBE (1958) (wm)George Goldner. (P)The Chantels. (R)1965 by The Shangri—Las. (R)1970 by The Three Degrees.

MAYBE (1977) (w)Martin Charnin (m)Charles Strouse. (I)Musical: *Annie*, by Andrea McArdle.

MAYBE I KNOW (1964) (wm)Ellie Greenwich—Jeff Barry. (P)Lesley Gore. (R)1973)Ellie Greenwich.

MAYBE I SHOULD CHANGE MY WAYS (1947) (w)John Latouche (m)Duke Ellington. (I)Musical: *Beggar's Holiday*, by Alfred Drake.

MAYBE I'M A FOOL (1979) (wm)Lloyd Chiate—Lee Garrett—Edward Mahoney—Robert Taylor. (P)Eddie Money.

MAYBE I'M AMAZED (1977) (wm)Paul McCartney. (P)Wings.

MAYBE IT'S BECAUSE (I Love You Too Much) (1933) (wm)Irving Berlin. (P)Fred Astaire with Leo Reisman and his Orchestra.

MAYBE IT'S BECAUSE (1949) (w)Harry Ruby (m)Johnnie Scott. (P)Dick Haymes. (CR)Eddy Howard. (CR)Connie Haines.

MAYBE SOME OTHER TIME (1964) (wm)Ervin Drake. (I)Musical: *What Makes Sammy Run?*, by Robert Alda and Sally Ann Howes.

MAYBE THIS TIME (1972) (w) (w)Fred Ebb (m)John Kander. (I)Film: *Cabaret*, by Liza Minnelli.

MAYBE YOU'LL BE THERE (1948) (w)Sammy Gallop (m)Rube Bloom. (P)Gordon Jenkins and his Chorus and Orchestra.

MAYBELLENE (1955) (wm)Cuck Berry—Russ Fratto—Alan Freed. (P)Chuck Berry.

ME! (1931) (wm)Irving Berlin. (P)Ben Bernie and his Orchestra.

ME AND BABY BROTHER (1974) (wm)Sylvester Allen—Harold R. Brown— Dennis Dickerson—Leroy Jordan—Lee Oskar Levitan— Charles Miller—Howard Scott. (P)War.

ME AND BOBBY MCGEE (1971) (wm)Kris Kristofferson—Fred L. Foster. (P)Janis Joplin. No. 1 Chart Record. (CR)Jerry Lee Lewis.

ME AND JULIO DOWN BY THE SCHOOL YARD (1972) (wm)Paul Simon. (P)Paul Simon.

ME AND MARIE (1935) (wm)Cole Porter. (I)Musical: *Jubilee*, by Melville Cooper and Mary Boland.

ME AND MRS. JONES (1972) (wm)Leon Huff—Kenny Gamble—Cary Gilbert. (P)Billy Paul.

ME AND MY ARROW (1971) (wm)Harry Nilsson. (P)Nilsson.

ME AND MY SHADOW (1927) (w)Billy Rose (m)Al Jolson—Dave Dreyer. (I)Revue: *Harry Delmar's Revels*, by Frank Fay. (P)Ted Lewis.

ME AND THE MAN IN THE MOON (1928) (w)Edgar Leslie (m)James V. Monaco. (P)Helen Kane. (CR)Cliff Edwards.

ME AND THE MOON (1936) (w)Walter Hirsch (m)Lou Handman. (P)Bing Crosby. (CR)Hal Kemp and his Orchestra.

ME AND YOU AND A DOG NAMED BOO (1971) (wm)Kent Lavoie. (P)Lobo.

MEADOWLAND (1943) (w-Eng)Harold Rome (m)Lev Knipper. Soviet army song.

MEAN MR. MUSTARD (1969) (wm)John Lennon—Paul McCartney. (P)The Beatles.

MEAN TO ME (1929) (w)Roy Turk (m)Fred E. Ahlert. (P)Ruth Etting. (CR)Helen Morgan. (R)1937 by Billie Holiday and Teddy Wilson. (R)1955 Film: *Love Me or Leave Me*, by Doris Day.

MEAN WOMAN BLUES (1963) (wm)Jerry West—Whispering Smith. (P)Roy Orbison.

MEAT AND POTATOES (1962) (wm)Irving Berlin. (I)Musical: *Mr. President*, by Jack Haskell and Stanley Grover.

MECCA (1963) (wm)Neval Nader—John Gluck, Jr. (P)Gene Pitney.

MEDIC THEME (See Blue Star)

MEDICINE MAN (1969) (wm)Terry Cashman—Gene Pistilli—T. P. West. (P)The Buchanan Brothers.

MEDITATION (1963) (w-Eng)Norman Gimbel (m)Antonio Carlos Jobim. (P)Pat Boone. Most popular recording by Frank Sinatra with Antonio Carlos Jobim.

MEESKITE (1966) (w)Fred Ebb (m)John Kander. (I)Musical: *Cabaret*, by Jack Gilford.

MEET ME HALFWAY (1987) (wm)Giorgio Moroder—T. Whitlock. (P)Kenny Loggins.

MEET ME IN ST. LOUIS, LOUIS (1904) (w)Andrew B. Sterling (m)Kerry Mills. (P)Billy Murray. (R)1944 Film: *Meet Me In St. Louis*, by Judy Garland.

MEET ME TONIGHT IN DREAMLAND (1909) (w)Beth Slater Whitson (m)Leo Friedman. (P)Henry Burr. (R)1949 Film: *In The Good Old Summertime*, by Judy Garland and Van Johnson.

MEET MISTER CALLAGHAN (1952) (wm)Jimmy Shirl—Ervin Drake— Eric Spear. (P)Les Paul and Mary Ford.

MEIN HERR (1972) (w)Fred Ebb (m)John Kander.

(I)Film: *Cabaret*.

MELANCHOLY ME (1954) (wm)Joe Thomas—Howard Biggs. (P)Eddy Howard. (CR)Ella Fitzgerald.

MELANCHOLY RHAPSODY (1950) (w)Sammy Cahn (m)Ray Heindorf. (I)Film: *Young Man With A Horn*, by Harry James on soundtrack.

MELANCHOLY SERENADE (1953) (m)Jackie Gleason (I)TV series: *The Jackie Gleason Show* as theme song. (P)Jackie Gleason and his Orchestra.

MELINDA (1965) (w)Alan Jay Lerner (m)Burton Lane. (I)Musical: *On A Clear Day You Can See Forever*, by John Cullum. In film version (1970) by Yves Montand.

MELLOW YELLOW (1966) (wm)Donovan Leitch. (P)Donovan.

MELODIE D'AMOUR (1957) (w-Eng)Leo Johns (m)Henri Salvador. (I)Edmundo Ros and his Orchestra. (P)The Ames Brothers.

MELODY FROM THE SKY, A (1936) (w)Sidney D. Mitchell (m)Louis Alter. (I)Film: *The Trail Of The Lonesome Pine*, by Fuzzy Knight. (P)Jan Garber and his Orchestra. (CR)Eddy Duchin and his Orchestra.

MELODY IN F (1855) (m)Anton Rubenstein. Famous classical piano composition.

MELODY OF LOVE (1954) (w)Tom Glazer (m)H. Engelmann. (P)Billy Vaughn and his Orchestra. Vocal version by The Four Aces. (CR)Tony Martin and Dinah Shore.

MEMO FROM TURNER (1970) (wm)Mick Jagger—Keith Richard. (I)Film: *Performance*, by Mick Jagger. (P)Mick Jagger.

MEMORIES (1915) (w)Gus Kahn (m)Egbert Van Alstyne. (P)John Barnes Welles.

MEMORIES (1969) (wm)Billy Strange—Scott Davis. (P)Elvis Presley.

MEMORIES ARE MADE OF THIS (1955) (wm)Terry Gilkyson—Richard Dehr—Frank Miller. (P)Dean Martin. No. 1 Chart Record.

MEMORIES OF YOU (1930) (w)Andy Razaf (m)Eubie Blake. (I)Revue: *Lew Leslie's Blackbirds Of 1930*, by Minto Cato. (P)Louis Armstrong. (CR)The Ink Spots. (R)1930s by Glen Gray and The Casa Loma Orchestra, with trumpet solo by Sonny Dunham. (R)1956 Film: *The Benny Goodman Story*, by The Benny Goodman Trio.

MEMORY (1982) (w)Trevor Nunn—T. S. Eliot (m)Andrew Lloyd Webber. (I)Musical: *Cats*, by Betty Buckley. (P)Barbra Streisand. (CR)Barry Manilow.

MEMPHIS (1963) (wm)Chuck Berry. (P)Lonnie Mack. (CR)Johnny Rivers.

MEMPHIS BLUES, THE (1912) (w)George A. Norton (m)W. C. Handy. (I)Prince's Orchestra. (R)1927 by Ted Lewis. (R)1944 by Harry James and his Orchestra. (R)1958 Film: *St. Louis Blues*, by Nat "King" Cole and Eartha Kitt.

MEMPHIS IN JUNE (1945) (w)Paul Francis Webster (m)Hoagy Carmichael. (I)Film: *Johnny Angel*, by Hoagy Carmichael.

MEMPHIS SOUL STEW (1967) (wm)King Curtis. (P)King Curtis.

MEN, THE (Theme) (1972) (wm)Isaac Hayes—Ronny Scaife. (I)Film: *The Men*, by Isaac Hayes. (P)Isaac Hayes.

MEN ARE GETTIN' SCARCE (1968) (wm)Joe Tex. (P)Joe Tex.

MEN IN MY LITTLE GIRL'S LIFE, THE (1965) (w)Eddie V. Deane— Mary Candy (m)Gloria Shayne. (P)Mike Douglas.

MENDOCINO (1969) (wm)Douglas Sahm. (P)The Sir Douglas Quintet.

MENTION MY NAME IN SHEBOYGAN (1947) (wm)Bob Hilliard—Sammy Mysels—Dick Sanford. (P)Beatrice Kay.

MERCY (1969) (wm)Steven Feldman—Joey Levine. (P)Ohio Express.

MERCY MERCY ME (The Ecology) (1971) (wm)Marvin Gaye. (P)Marvin Gaye.

MERCY, MERCY, MERCY (1967) (w)Gail Levy—Vincent Levy (m)Joseph Zawinul. (P)The Buckinghams. (CR)Cannonball Adderly. (CR)Marlena Shaw. (CR)Larry Williams and Johnny Watson.

MERRY CHRISTMAS BABY (1947) (wm)Lou Baxter— Johnny Moore (P)Johnny Moore's Three Blazers. (CR)Lionel Hampton and his Orchestra.

MERRY-GO-ROUND (1935) (m)Duke Ellington. (P)Duke Ellington and his Orchestra.

MERRY-GO-ROUND BROKE DOWN, THE (1937) (wm)Cliff Friend—Dave Franklin. (P)Guy Lombardo and his Royal Canadians. (CR)Russ Morgan and his Orchestra. (CR)Jimmie Lunceford and his Orchestra.

MERRY OLD LAND OF OZ, THE (1939) (w)E. Y. Harburg (m)Harold Arlen. (I)Film: *The Wizard Of Oz*, by Singer's Midgets.

MERRY WIDOW WALTZ (1907) (w)Adrian Ross (m)Franz Lehar. (I)Musical: *The Merry Widow*. First recording by The Victor Orchestra.

MERRY WIVES OF WINDSOR, THE (Overture) (1850) (m)Otto Nicolai (I)Opera: *The Merry Wives Of Windsor*.

MESS O' BLUES, A (1960) (wm)Doc Pomus—Mort Shuman. (P)Elvis Presley.

MESSAGE TO MICHAEL (1966) (w)Hal David (m)Burt Bacharach. (P)Dionne Warwick.

METHOD OF MODERN LOVE (1985) (wm)Daryl Hall— Janna Allen. (P)Hall and Oates.

MEXICALI ROSE (1926) (w)Helen Stone (m)Jack B. Tenney. (I)The Cliquot Club Eskimos. (R)1938 by Bing Crosby.

MEXICAN HAT DANCE (Jarabe Tapatio) (1919) (wm)Unknown. Traditional Mexican folk song.

MEXICO (1961) (wm)Felice and Boudleaux Bryant. (P)Bob Moore.

MI CASA, SU CASA (My House Is Your House) (1957) (wm)Al Hoffman— Dick Manning. (P)Perry Como.

MIAMI BEACH RUMBA (1946) (w)Albert Gamse (m)Irving Fields. (P)The Irving Fields Trio.

MIAMI 2017 (Seen The Lights Go Out On Broadway) (1976) (wm)Billy Joel. (P)Billy Joel.

MIAMI VICE THEME (1984) (wm)Jan Hammer. (I)TV series: *Miami Vice*, by Jan Hammer on soundtrack. (P)Jan Hammer. No. 1 Chart Record.

MICHAEL (Row The Boat Ashore) (1961) (wm)Dave Fisher. (P)The Highwaymen. No. 1 Chart Record. (R)1966 by Trini Lopez.

MICHELLE (1966) (wm)John Lennon—Paul McCartney. (P)The Beatles. (CR)David and Jonathan. NARAS Award Winner.

MICKEY (1982) (wm)Nicky Chinn—Mike Chapman. (P)Toni Basil. No. 1 Chart Record.

MICKEY MOUSE'S BIRTHDAY PARTY (1936) (wm)Charles Tobias—Bob Rothberg—Joseph Meyer.

(P)Wayne King and his Orchestra.

MICKEY'S MONKEY (1963) (wm)Lamont Dozier—Brian Holland—Eddie Holland. (P)The Miracles.

MIDDLE OF THE ROAD (1984) (wm)Chrissie Hynde (P)The Pretenders.

MIDNIGHT AT THE OASIS (1974) (wm)David Nichtern. (P)Maria Muldaur.

MIDNIGHT BLUE (1975) (wm)Carole Bayer Sager—Melissa Manchester. (P)Melissa Manchester.

MIDNIGHT BLUE (1987) (wm)Lou Gramm—B. Turgon. (P)Lou Gramm.

MIDNIGHT CONFESSIONS (1968) (wm)Lou Josie. (P)Grass Roots.

MIDNIGHT COWBOY (1969) (m)John Barry. (I)Film: Midnight Cowboy, as soundtrack theme. (P)Ferrante and Teicher. NARAS Award Winner.

MIDNIGHT HOUR, THE (1952) (wm)Sam Sweet. (P)Ray Charles.

MIDNIGHT IN MOSCOW (1961) (wm)Kenny Ball—Jan Burgers. (P)Kenny Ball.

MIDNIGHT IN PARIS (1935) (wm)Con Conrad—Herb Magidson. (I)Film: Here's To Romance, by Nino Martini.

MIDNIGHT LACE (1960) (wm)Jerome Howard—Joe Lubin. (I)Film: Midnight Lace, on soundtrack. (P)Ray Ellis and his Orchestra. (CR)Ray Coniff and his Chorus and Orchestra.

MIDNIGHT MARY (1963) (wm)Artie Wayne—Ben Raleigh. (P)Joey Powers. (CR)Jerry Cole.

MIDNIGHT RAMBLER (1969) (wm)Mick Jagger—Keith Richard. (P)The Rolling Stones.

MIDNIGHT RIDER (1972) (wm)Greg Allman—Kim Payne. (P)Joe Cocker. (R)1974 by The Allman Brothers.

MIDNIGHT SPECIAL (1960) (wm)Johnny Rivers. (P)Paul Evans. (R)1965 by Johnny Rivers.

MIDNIGHT SUN (1947) (w)Johnny Mercer (m)Sonny Burke—Lionel Hampton. (P)Lionel Hampton and his Orchestra. Vocal version by Ella Fitzgerald. Also, Sarah Vaughan.

MIDNIGHT TRAIN TO GEORGIA (1973) (wm)Jim Weatherly (P)Gladys Knight & The Pips. No. 1 Chart Record.

MIDSUMMER'S EVE (1944) (wm)Robert Wright—George Forrest. Based on a theme by Edvard Grieg. (I)Operetta: Song Of Norway, by Kitty Carlisle and Robert Shafer.

MIGHTY LAK' A ROSE (1901) (w)Frank Stanton (m)Ethelbert Nevin. (P)Geraldine Farrar. This was the last song Miss Nevin wrote before her death.

MIGHTY LOVE, A (1974) (wm)Joseph P. Jefferson—Bruce Hawes— Charles Simmons. (P)The Spinners.

MIGHTY QUINN, THE (1970) (wm)Bob Dylan. (P)Bob Dylan. (R)1973 by Manfred Mann.

MILENBERG JOYS (1925) (w)Walter Melrose (m)Paul Mares—Leon Rappolo—Ferdinand "Jelly Roll" Morton. (P)The New Orleans Rhythm Kings, with Jelly Roll Morton at the piano. (R)1930s by Bob Crosby and his Orchestra.

MILITARY LIFE (The Jerk Song) (1946) (wm)Harold Rome. (I)Musical: Call Me Mister.

MILK AND HONEY (1961) (wm)Jerry Herman. (I)Musical: Milk And Honey, by Tommy Rall, Juli Arkin, and The Company.

MILKMAN, KEEP THOSE BOTTLES QUIET (1944) (wm)Don Raye—Gene de Paul. (I)Film: Broadway Rhythm, by Nancy Walker. (P)Ella Mae Morse. (CR)Woody Herman and his Orchestra. (CR)The King Sisters.

MILKMEN'S MATINEE, THE (1936) (wm)Paul Denniker—Joe Davis— Andy Razaf. (I)Radio Show: The Milkman's Matinee. All night program on WNEW, New York City.

MILLION AND ONE, A (1966) (wm)Yvonne Devaney. (P)Billy Walker. (CR)Dean Martin. (CR)Vic Dana.

MILLION DOLLAR BASH (1968) (wm)Bob Dylan. (P)Stone Country. (CR)The Fairport Convention. (R)1975 by Bob Dylan.

MILLION DREAMS AGO, A (1940) (wm)Lew Quadling—Eddy Howard— Dick Jurgens. (P)Dick Jurgens and his Orchestra. (CR)Glenn Miller and his Orchestra.

MILLION TO ONE, A (1960) (wm)Phil Medley. (P)Jimmy Charles. (R)1968 by The Five Stairsteps. (R)1969 by Brian Hyland. (R)1973 by Donny Osmond.

(How To Be A)MILLIONAIRE (1986) (wm)Martin Fry—Mark White. (P)ABC.

MILORD (1959) (w-Eng)Bunny Lewis (m)Marguerite Monnot. (P)Edith Piaf. (CR)Teresa Brewer. (R)1964 by Bobby Darin.

MIMI (1932) (w)Lorenz Hart (m)Richard Rodgers. (I)Film: Love Me Tonight, by Maurice Chevalier. (P)Maurice Chevalier. (R)1963 Film: A New Kind Of Love, by Maurice Chevalier.

MIND, BODY AND SOUL (1969) (wm)Ronald Dunbar—Edith Wayne. (P)The Flaming Ember.

MIND GAMES (1973) (wm)John Lennon. (P)John Lennon.

MIND IF I MAKE LOVE TO YOU (1956) (wm)Cole Porter. (I)Film: High Society, by Frank Sinatra.

MINE (1933) (w)Ira Gershwin (m)George Gershwin. (I)Musical: Let 'Em Eat Cake, by William Gaxton and Lois Moran.

MIND FOR ME (1974) (wm)Paul McCartney. (P)Rod Stewart.

MINNIE FROM TRINIDAD (1941) (wm)Roger Edens. (I)Film: Ziegfeld Girl, by Judy Garland and Tony Martin.

MINNIE THE MOOCHER (1931) (wm)Cab Calloway—Irving Mills— Clarence Gaskill. (P)Cab Calloway. No. 1 Chart Record.

MINNIE THE MOOCHER'S WEDDING DAY (1932) (w)Ted Koehler (m)Harold Arlen. (I)Nightclub Revue: Cotton Club Parade, by Cab Calloway.

MINUET IN G (1796) (m)Ludwig Van Beethoven. Famous classical piano selection.

MINUET IN G (1887) (m)Ignace Paderewski. Famous classical piano composition.

MINUTE BY MINUTE (1979) (wm)Lester Abrams—Michael McDonald. (P)The Doobie Brothers.

MIRA (Can You Imagine That?) (1961) (wm)Bob Merrill. (I)Musical: Carnival!, by Anna Maria Alberghetti.

MIRABELLE (1931) (wm)Noel Coward. (I)London play: Cavalcade, by Stella Wilson and Eric Purveur. (P)Noel Coward.

MIRACLE OF LOVE (1956) (wm)Bob Merrill. (P)Eileen Rodgers. (CR)Ginny Gibson.

MIRACLE OF MIRACLES (1964) (w)Sheldon Harnick (m)Jerry Bock. (I)Musical: Fiddler On The Roof, by Austin Pendleton.

MIRACLE WORKER, THE (Theme) (Hush, Little Baby) (1962) (wm)Arthur Siegel—Don Costa. (I)Film: The Miracle Worker, by Anne Bancroft.

MIRACLES (1975) (wm)Marty Balin. (P)Jefferson Starship.

MIRAGE (1967) (wm)Ritchie Cordell—Bo Gentry. (P)Tommy James and The Shondells.

MIRROR, MIRROR (1982) (wm)Michael Sembello—Dennis Natkosky. (P)Diana Ross.

MISCHA, JASCHA, TOSCHA, SASCHA (1921) (w)Ira Gerswhin (m)George Gershwin. (I)By the Gershwin's at parties and other gatherings.

MISERY (1963) (wm)John Lennon—Paul McCartney. (P)The Beatles.

MISIRLOU (1947) (w-Eng)Fred Wise—Milton Leeds—S. K. Russell (m)N. Roubanis. (P)Jan August.

MISLED (1985) (wm)Ronald Bell—James Taylor—Charles Smith— George Brown—Robert Bell—Curtis Williams—James Bonneford. (P)Kool & The Gang.

MISS AMERICA (1954) (wm)Bernie Wayne. (I)Miss America Pageant, by Bert Parks.

MISS ANNABELLE LEE (See Who's Wonderful, Who's Marvelous? Miss Annabelle Lee).

MISS BROWN TO YOU (1935) (wm)Leo Robin—Ralph Rainger—Richard A. Whiting. (I)Film: *The Big Broadcast of 1936*, by Ray Noble and his Orchestra and danced to by Bill Robinson and The Nicholas Brothers.

MISS CELIE'S BLUES (1985) (wm)Quincy Jones—Rod Temperton— Lionel Richie. (I)Film: *The Color Purple*, by Tata Vega.

MISS MARMELSTEIN (1962) (wm)Harold Rome. (I)Musical: *I Can Get It For You Wholesale*, by Barbra Streisand. (P)Barbra Streisand.

MISS ME BLIND (1984) (wm)George O'Dowd—Jon Moss—Roy Hay— Michael Craig. (P)Culture Club.

MISS OTIS REGRETS (1934) (wm)Cole Porter. Not originally written for a musical or film. (P)Ethel Waters. (R)1946 Film: *Night And Day*, by Monty Woolley.

MISS SUN (1980)wm)David Paich—Boz Scaggs. (P)Boz Scaggs.

MISS YOU (1929) (wm)Charles and Harry Tobias (m)Henry Tobias. (P)Rudy Vallee. (CR)Dinah Shore. (CR)Bing Crosby.

MISS YOU (1978) (wm)Mick Jagger—Keith Richard. (P)The Rolling Stones. No. 1 Chart Record.

MISSING YOU (1982) (wm)Dan Fogelberg. (P)Dan Fogelberg.

MISSING YOU (1984) (wm)John Waite—Chas Sanford—Mark Leonard. (P)John Waite. No. 1 Chart Record.

MISSING YOU (1985) (wm)Lionel Richie. (P)Diana Ross. The song is dedicated to Marvin Gaye.

MISSION: IMPOSSIBLE (1967) (m)Lalo Schifrin. (I)TV series: *Mission: Impossible*, as soundtrack theme. (P)Lalo Schifrin and his Orchestra. NARAS Award Winner.

MISSION TO MOSCOW (1942) (m)Mel Powell. (P)Benny Goodman and his Orchestra.

MISSIONARY MAN (1986) (wm)Dave Stewart—Annie Lennox. (P)The Eurythmics.

M-I-S-S-I-S-S-I-P-P-I (1916) (w)Bert Hanlon—Ben Ryan (m)Harry Tierney. (I)Musical: *Hitchy-Koo*. (P)Anna Wheaton.

MISSISSIPPI DREAM BOAT (1943) (w)Lew Brown—Ralph Freed (m)Sammy Fain. (I)Film: *Swing Fever*, by Kay Kyser and his Orchestra, vocal by Marilyn Maxwell.

MISSISSIPPI MOON (1929) (m)Duke Ellington. (P)Joe Turner and his Memphis Men. This group was an Ellington recording unit.

MISSISSIPPI MUD (1927) (wm)Harry Barris—James Cavanaugh. (P)Paul Whiteman and his Orchestra, vocal by The Rhythm Boys (Bing Crosby, Al Rinker, Harry Barris).

MISSISSIPPI SUITE (1926) (m)Ferde Grofe. Popular piano suite. The song *Daybreak* was adapted from this suite.

MISSOURI WALTZ, THE (1914) (w)James Royce Shannon (m)Frederick Knight Logan. (I)Victor Military Band. Favorite song of President Harry Truman.

MIST OVER THE MOON (1938) (w)Oscar Hammerstein II (m)Ben Oakland. (I)Film: *The Lady Objects*, by Lanny Ross.

MISTER AND MISSISSIPPI (1951) (wm)Irving Gordon. (P)Patti Page. (CR)Tennessee Ernie Ford.

MISTER AND MISSUS FITCH (1932) (wm)Cole Porter. (I)Musical: *Gay Divorcee*, by Luella Gear.

MR. AND MRS. IS THE NAME (1934) (w)Mort Dixon (m)Allie Wrubel. (I)Film: *Flirtation Walk*, by Dick Powell and Ruby Keeler. Recorded by Victor Young and his Orchestra.

MR. BIG STUFF (1971) (wm)Joe Broussard—Ralph Williams—Carrol Washington. (P)Jean Knight.

MR. BLUE (1959) (wm)Dewayne Blackwell. (P)The Fleetwoods. No. 1 Chart Record.

MR. BLUEBIRD (1935) (wm)Hoagy Carmichael. (P)Hoagy Carmichael.

MR. BOJANGLES (1968) (wm)Jerry Jeff Walker. (P)Jerry Jeff Walker. (CR)Bobby Cole. (R)1971 by The Nitty Gritty Dirt Band.

MR. BUSINESSMAN (1968) (wm)Ray Stevens. (P)Ray Stevens.

MR. CUSTER (1960) (wm)Fred Darian—Al DeLory—Joseph Van Winkle. (P)Larry Verne. No. 1 Chart Record.

MR. DIEINGLY SAD (1966) (wm)Don Ciccone. (P)The Critters.

MR. FIVE BY FIVE (1942) (wm)Don Raye—Gene de Paul. (I)Film: *Behind The 8 Ball*, by Sonny Dunham and his Orchestra, with Grace McDonald. (P)Freddie Slack and his Orchestra. (CR)Harry James and his Orchestra.

MISTER GALLAGHER AND MISTER SHEAN (1922) (wm)Ed Gallagher—Al Shean. (I)Revue: *Ziegfeld Follies of 1922*, by Ed Gallagher and Al Shean. (R)1938 by Bing Crosby and Johnny Mercer.

MR. GHOST GOES TO TOWN (1936) (w)Irving Mills—Mitchell Parish (m)Will Hudson. (P)The Hudson-De Lange Orchestra.

MR. JAWS (1975) (wm)B. Ramal—Dickie Goodman. (P)Dickie Goodman.

MR. LEE (1957) (wm)Heather Dixon—Helen Gathers—Emma Ruth Pought—Laura Webb—Jannie Pought. (P)The Bobbettes.

MR. LONELY (1965) (wm)Bobby Vinton—Gene Allan. (P)Bobby Vinton. No. 1 Chart Record. (CR)Buddy Greco.

MR. LUCKY (1960) (w)Jay Livingston—Ray Evans (m)Henry Mancini. (I)TV series: *Mr. Lucky*, as soundtrack theme. (P)Henry Mancini and his Orchestra.

MISTER MEADOWLARK (1940) (w)Johnny Mercer (m)Walter Donaldson. (P)Bing Crosby and Johnny Mercer.

MR. MOONLIGHT (1965) (wm)Roy Lee Johnson. (P)The Beatles.

MR. PAGANINI (See You'll Have To Swing It)

MR. PITIFUL (1965) (w)Otis Redding (m) Steve Cropper. (P)Otis Redding.

MR. ROBOTO (1983) (wm)Dennis De Young. (P)Styx.

MISTER SANDMAN (1954) (wm)Pat Ballard. (P)The Chordettes. No. 1 Chart Record. (CR)The Four Aces. (R)1981 by Emmy Lou Harris.

MISTER SNOW (1945) (w)Oscar Hammerstein II (m)Richard Rodgers. (I)Musical: *Carousel:* by Jean Darling. (R)1957 Film: *Carousel*, by Barbara Ruick.

MR. SPACEMAN (1966) (wm)Jim McGuinn. (P)The Byrds.

MR. SUN, MR. MOON (1969) (wm)Mark Lindsay. (P)Paul Revere and The Raiders.

MR. TAMBOURINE MAN (1964) (wm)Bob Dylan. (I)Bob Dylan. (P)The Byrds. No. 1 Chart Record.

MR. TELEPHONE MAN (1984) (wm)Ray Parker, Jr. (P)New Edition.

MR. TOUCHDOWN U. S. A. (1950) (wm)Ruth Roberts— Gene Pillar— William Katz. (P)Hugo Winterhalter and his Orchestra.

MR. WONDERFUL (1956) (wm)Jerry Bock—Larry Holofcener—George Weiss. (I)Musical: *Mr. Wonderful*, by Olga James.

MISTO CRISTOFO COLUMBO (1951) (wm)Jay Livingston—Ray Evans. (I)Film: *Here Comes The Groom*, by Bing Crosby, with Louis Armstrong, Dorothy Lamour, Cass Daley, and Phil Harris.

MISTY (1954) (w)Johnny Burke (m)Erroll Garner. (P)The Erroll Garner Trio. (R)1959 by Johnny Mathis. (R)1963 Lloyd Price. (R)1965 by The Vibrations. (R)1966 by Richard "Groove" Holmes. (R)1975 by Ray Stevens.

MISTY BLUE (1967) (wm)Bob Montgomery. (P)Eddy Arnold. (R)1972 by Joe Simon. (R)1976 by Dorothy Moore.

MISTY MORNIN' (1929) (m)Arthur Whetsol—Duke Ellington. (P)Duke Ellington and his Cotton Club Orchestra.

MISUNDERSTANDING (1980) (wm)Phil Collins. (P)Genesis.

MIXED EMOTIONS (1951) (wm)Stuart F. Louchheim. (P)Rosemary Clooney. (CR)Teresa Brewer.

M'LADY (1968) (wm)Sylvester Stewart. (P)Sly and The Family Stone.

MOANIN' IN THE MORNIN' (1937) (w)E. Y. Harburg (m)Harold Arlen. (I)Musical: *Hooray For What*, by Vivian Vance and The Singing Spies.

MOANIN' LOW (1929) (w)Howard Dietz (m)Ralph Rainger. (I)Revue: *The Little Show*, by Libby Holman. (P)Libby Holman. (CR)Billie Holiday and Teddy Wilson. (R)1950 Film: *Young Man With A Horn*, by Harry James and his Orchestra.

MOCKIN' BIRD HILL (1949) (wm)Vaughn Horton. (P)Les Paul and Mary Ford. (R)1950 by Patti Page. (R)1951 by The Pinetoppers. (CR)Russ Morgan and his Orchestra.

MOCKINGBIRD (1963) (wm)Inez and Charlie Foxx. (P)Inez Foxx. (R)1967 by Aretha Franklin. (R)1974 by Carly Simon and James Taylor.

MODERN GIRL (1981) (wm)Dominic Bugatti—Frank Musker. (P)Sheena Easton.

MODERN LOVE (1983) (wm)David Bowie. (P)David Bowie.

MODERN WOMAN (1986) (wm)Billy Joel. (I)Film: *Ruthless People*, by Billy Joel. (P)Billy Joel.

MOHAIR SAM (1965) (wm)Dallas Frazier. (P)Charlie Rich.

MOJO WOMAN BLUES (1928) (wm)"Blind" Lemon Jefferson. (P)Blind Lemon Jefferson.

MOLDAU, DIE (1879) (m)Bedrich Smetena. Famous classical composition.

MOLLY MALONE (1750) (wm)Unknown. Traditional Irish folk song.

MOMENT I SAW YOU, THE (1930) (w)Howard Dietz (m)Arthur Schwartz. (I)Revue: *Three's A Crowd*, by Clifton Webb.

MOMENT MUSICALE (1823) (m)Franz Schubert. Famous classical composition.

MOMENTS LIKE THIS (1938) (w)Frank Loesser (m)Burton Lane. (I)Film: *College Swing*, by Florence George.

MOMENTS TO REMEMBER (1955) (w)Al Stillman (m)Robert Allen. (P)The Four Lads. (R)1969 by The Vogues.

MOMMA MOMMA! (1962) (wm)Harold Rome. (I)Musical: *I Can Get It For You Wholesale*, by Elliot Gould and Lillian Roth.

MOMMA SAID (Mama Said) (1961) (wm)Luther Dixon— Willie Dennson. (P)The Shirelles.

MONA LISA (1949) (wm)Jay Livingston—Ray Evans. (I)Film: *Captain Carey,U. S. A. ,*on soundtrack. Academy Award Winner. (P)Nat "King" Cole. No. 1 Chart Record. (CR)Harry James and his Orchestra. (CR)Art Lund. (CR)Doris Day.

MONDAY, MONDAY (1966) (wm)John E. A. Phillips. (P)The Mamas and The Papas. No. 1 Chart Record.

MONEY (1973) (wm)Roger Waters. (P)Pink Floyd.

MONEY BURNS A HOLE IN MY POCKET (1954) (w)Bob Hilliard (m)Jule Styne. (I)Film: *Living It Up*, by Dean Martin.

MONEY CHANGES EVERYTHING (1983) (wm)Thomas Gray. (I)The Brains. (P)Cyndi Lauper.

MONEY FOR NOTHING (1985) (wm)Mark Knopfler— Gordon Sumner (Sting). (P)Dire Straits. No. 1 Chart Record.

MONEY HONEY (1953) (wm)Jesse Stone. (P)Clyde McPhatter. (R)1954 by The Drifters.

MONEY HONEY (1976) (wm)Eric Faulkner—Stuart Woods. (P)The Bay City Rollers.

MONEY IS THE ROOT OF ALL EVIL (1945) (wm)Joan Whitney—Alex Kramer. (P)The Andrews Sisters with Guy Lombardo and his Royal Canadians.

MONEY ISN'T EVERYTHING (1947) (w)Oscar Hammerstein II (m)Richard Rodgers. (I)Musical: *Allegro*, by Roberta Konay, Kathryn Lee, Patricia Bybell, June Humphries, and Sylvia Karlton.

MONEY SONG, THE (Money, Money) (1966) (w)Fred Ebb (m)John Kander. (I)Musical: *Cabaret*, by Joel Grey and The Cabaret Girls. (R)1972 Film: *Cabaret*, by Joel Grey, Liza Minelli, and The Girls.

MONEY, THAT'S WHAT I WANT (1960) (wm)Berry Gordy, Jr.—Janie Bradford. (P)Barrett Strong. (R)1964 by The Kingsmen. (R)1966 by Jr. Walker & The All Stars. (R)1980 by The Flying Lizards.

MONEY TREE, THE (1956) (w)Cliff Ferre (m)Mark McIntyre. (P)Margaret Whiting. (CR)Patience and Prudence.

MONKEY TIME, THE (1963) (wm)Curtis Mayfield. (P)Major Lance. (R)1983 by The Tubes.

MONSTER MASH (1962) (wm)Bobby Pickett—Leonard

Capizzi. (P)Bobby "Boris" Pickett and The Crypt Kickers.

MONTEGO BAY (1970) (wm)Jeff Barry—Bobby Bloom. (P)Bobby Bloom.

MONTEREY (1968) (wm)Eric Burdon—Victor Briggs— Johnny Weider— Barry Jenkins—Danny Mc-Culloch. (P)Eric Burdon and The Aninals.

MONY MONY (1968) (wm)Bobby Bloom—Ritchie Cordell—Bo Gentry— Tommy James. (P)Tommy James and The Shondells. (R)1987 by Billy Idol. No. 1 Chart Record.

MOOCHE, THE (1929) (m)Duke Ellington—Irving Mills. (P)Duke Ellington and his Orchestra.

MOOD INDIGO (1931) (wm)Duke Ellington—Irving Mills—Barney Bigard. (P)Duke Ellington and his Orchestra. (CR)Jimmie Lunceford and his Orchestra. (R)1954 Vocal version by The Four Freshmen.

MOOD THAT I'M IN, THE (1937) (wm)Abner Silver—Al Sherman. (P)Billie Holiday with Teddy Wilson. (CR)Lionel Hampton and his Orchestra.

MOODY BLUE (1976) (wm)Mark James. (P)Elvis Presley.

MOODY RIVER (1961) (wm)Gary D. Bruce. (P)Pat Boone. No. 1 Chart Record.

MOODY WOMAN (1969) (wm)Kenny Gamble—Jerry Butler—Theresa Bell. (P)Jerry Butler.

MOON COUNTRY (1934) (wm)Johnny Mercer—Hoagy Carmichael. (P)Hoagy Carmichael.

MOON-FACED, STARRY-EYED (1947) (w)Langston Hughes (m)Kurt Weill. (I)Musical: Street Scene, by Danny Daniels and Sheila Bond.

MOON GOT IN MY EYES, THE (1937) (w)Johnny Burke (m)Arthur Johnston. (I)Film: Double or Nothing, by Bing Crosby. (P)Bing Crosby.

MOON IS BLUE, THE (1953) (w)Sylvia Fine (m)Herschel Burke Gilbert. (I)Film: The Moon Is Blue, as title song. (P)The Sauter—Finegan Orchestra, vocal by Sally Sweetland.

MOON IS LOW, THE (1930) (w)Arthur Freed (m)Nacio Herb Brown. (I)Film: Montana Moon, by Cliff Edwards. (P)George Olsen and his Orchestra.

MOON LOVE (1939) (wm)Mack David—Mack Davis— Andre Kostelanetz. Adapted from Tchaikovsky's Fifth Symphony. (P)Glenn Miller and his Orchestra. No. 1 Chart Record. (CR)Al Donahue and his Orchestra. (CR)Mildred Bailey.

MOON MIST (1942) (wm)Mercer Ellington. (P)Duke Ellington and his Orchestra.

MOON OF MANAKOORA, THE (1937) (w)Frank Loesser (m)Alfred Newman. (I)Film: The Hurricane, by Dorothy Lamour. (P)Bing Crosby. (CR)Ray Noble and his Orchestra.

MOON OF MY DELIGHT (1928) (w)Lorenz Hart (m)Richard Rodgers. (I)Musical: Chee-Chee, by Betty Starbuck and Stark Patterson.

MOON OVER BURMA (1940) (w)Frank Loesser (m)Frederick Hollander. (I)Film: Moon Over Burma, by Dorothy Lamour.

MOON OVER MIAMI (1935) (w)Edgar Leslie (m)Joe Burke. (P)Eddy Duchin and his Orchestra. No. 1 Chart Record. (CR)Connee Boswell.

MOON OVER NAPLES (See Spanish Eyes).

MOON RIVER (1961) (w)Johnny Mercer (m)Henry Mancini. (I)Film: Breakfast At Tiffany's, by Audrey Hepburn. (P)Henry Mancini and his Orchestra. Vocal Version by Andy Williams. (CR)Jerry Butler. Academy Award Winner. NARAS Award Winner.

MOON SHADOW (1971) (wm)Cat Stevens. (P)Cat Stevens.

MOON SHINES ON THE MOONSHINE, THE (1920) (w)Francis De Witt (m)Robert Hood Bowers. (I)Revue: Broadway Brevities of 1920, by Bert Williams. (P)Bert Williams.

MOON SONG (That Wasn't Meant For Me) (1932) (w)Sam Coslow (m)Arthur Johnston. (I)Film: Hello, Everybody, by Kate Smith. (P)Kate Smith. (CR)Wayne King and his Orchestra.

MOON-TALK (1958) (wm)Al Hoffman—Dick Manning. (P)Perry Como.

MOONBEAMS (1906) (w)Henry Blossom (m)Victor Herbert. (I)Operetta: The Red Mill.

MOONBURN (1936) (w)Edward Heyman (m)Hoagy Carmichael. (I)Film: Anything Goes, by Bing Crosby. (P)Bing Crosby.

MOONFALL (1985) (wm)Rupert Holmes. (I)Musical: The Mystery Of Edwin Drood, by Howard McGillin.

MOONLIGHT AND ROSES BRING MEM'RIES OF YOU (1925) (wm)Ben Black— Neil Moret. Adapted from Lemare's Andantino In D Flat. (P)Lanny Ross. (CR)John McCormack. (R)1940 Film: Tin Pan Alley, by Betty Grable. (R)1954 by The Three Suns.

MOONLIGHT AND SHADOWS (1936) (wm)Leo Robin— Frederick Hollander. (I)Film: Jungle Princess, by Dorothy Lamour. (P)Dorothy Lamour. (CR)Bing Crosby. (CR)Shep Fields and his Orchestra.

(On)MOONLIGHT BAY (1912) (w)Edward Madden (m)Percy Wenrich. (P)The American Quartet. (R)1951 by Bing and Gary Crosby.

MOONLIGHT BECOMES YOU (1942) (w)Johnny Burke (m)Jimmy Van Heusen. (I)Film: Road To Morocco, by Bing Crosby. (P)Bing Crosby.

MOONLIGHT COCKTAIL (1941) (w)Kim Gannon (m)Lucky Roberts. (P)Glenn Miller and his Orchestra. No. 1 Chart Record.

MOONLIGHT FEELS RIGHT (1976) (wm)Michael Bruce Blackman. (P)Starbuck.

MOONLIGHT GAMBLER (1956) (w)Bob Hilliard (m)Phil Springer. (P)Frankie Laine.

MOONLIGHT IN VERMONT (1945) (w)John Blackburn (m)Karl Suessdorf. (I)Instrumentally, by Billy Butterfield and his Orchestra. (P)Margaret Whiting.

MOONLIGHT MASQUERADE (1941) (w)Jack Lawrence (m)Toots Camarata— Isaac Albeniz. Adapted from Tango In D by Albeniz. (P)Jimmy Dorsey and his Orchestra.

MOONLIGHT MILE (1971) (wm)Mick Jagger. (P)The Rolling Stones.

MOONLIGHT MOOD (1942) (w)Harold Adamson (m)Peter De Rose. (P)Glenn Miller and his Orchestra. (CR)Connee Boswell.

MOONLIGHT ON THE COLORADO (1930) (w)Billy Moll (m)Robert A. King. (P)Ben Selvin and his Orchestra.

MOONLIGHT ON THE GANGES (1926) (w)Chester Wallace (m)Sherman Myers. (P)Paul Whiteman and his Orchestra. (R)1965 by Vic Dana. Most popular recording by Frank Sinatra.

(There Ought To Be A)MOONLIGHT SAVINGS TIME (1931) (wm)Irving Kahal—Harry Richman. (P)Harry Richman.

MOONLIGHT SERENADE (1939) (w)Mitchell Parish (m)Glenn Miller. (P)Theme song of Glenn Miller and his Orchestra.

A WRONG GUESS

When I was selling arrangements to Gene Krupa, I often would attend the band's rehearsals. One time Glenn Miller was rehearsing his band in another studio in the same building. Young musicians made up the nucleus of both the Krupa and Miller bands and most of the guys became friendly with each other. During a break, Tex Beneke, the tenor saxophonist with Glenn Miller, walked into the Krupa rehearsal and started to rap with some of the fellows. Someone asked him how the Miller band was coming along and Tex answered that he personally was dubious about the success of the sound the Miller band was playing.

How pleasantly wrong he was.

MOONLIGHT SONATA (1802) (m)Ludwig Van Beethoven. Famous classical selection.

MOONLIGHTING (1985) (w)Al Jarreau (m)Lee Holdridge. (I)TV series: Moonlighting, by Al Jarreau. (P)Al Jarreau.

MOONRAKER (1979) (w)Hal David (m)John Barry. (I)Film: Moonraker, by voice of Shirley Bassey. (P)Shirley Bassey.

MOONSHINE LULLABY (1946) (wm)Irving Berlin. (I)Musical: Annie Get Your Gun, by Ethel Merman.

MOONSTRUCK (1933) (w)Sam Coslow (m)Arthur Johnston. (I)Film: College Humor, by Bing Crosby. (P)Bing Crosby.

MORE (1956) (w)Tom Glazer (m)Alex Alstone. (P)Perry Como.

MORE (Theme From Mondo Cane) (1963) (w-Eng)Norman Newell (m)Riz Ortolani—N. Oliviero. (I)Film: Mondo Cane, by Kathina Ortolani. (I)In United States, by Danny Williams. (P)Kai Winding and his Orchestra. Vocal Version by Vic Dana. NARAS Award Winner.

MORE AND MORE (1945) (w)E. Y. Harburg (m)Jerome Kern. (I)Film: Can't Help Singing, by Deanna Durbin. (P)Tommy Dorsey and his Orchestra. (CR)Perry Como.

MORE I CANNOT WISH YOU (1950) (wm)Frank Loesser. (I)Musical: Guys And Dolls, by Pat Rooney, Sr.

MORE I SEE YOU, THE (1945) (w)Mack Gordon (m)Harry Warren. (I)Film: Diamond Horseshoe, by Dick Haymes. (P)Dick Haymes. (CR)Harry James and his Orchestra. (R)1966 by Chris Montez.

MORE LOVE (1967) (wm)William Robinson. (P)Smokey Robinson and The Miracles. (R)1980 by Kim Carnes.

MORE LOVE THAN YOUR LOVE (1954) (w)Dorothy Fields (m)Arthur Schwartz. (I)Musical: By The Beautiful Sea, by Wilbur Evans.

MORE, MORE. MORE (Part 1) (1976) (wm)Gregg Diamond. (P)The Andrea True Connection.

MORE THAN A FEELING (1976) (wm)Tom Scholz. (P)Boston.

MORE THAN A WOMAN (1977) (wm)Barry, Maurice, and Robin Gibb. (I)Film: Saturday Night Fever, by the voices of The Bee Gees. (P)Tavares.

MORE THAN I CAN SAY (1980) (wm)Sonny Curtis—Jerry Allison. (P)Leo Sayer.

MORE THAN YOU KNOW (1929) (w)Billy Rose—Edward Eliscu (m)Vincent Youmans. (I)Musical: Great Day, by Mayo Methot. (P)Jane Froman. (CR)Mildred Bailey. (R)1946 by Perry Como. (R)1955 Film: Hit The Deck, by Tony Martin.

MORE TODAY THAN YESTERDAY (1969) (wm)Patrick N. Upton. (P)The Spiral Staircase.

MORGEN (One More Sunrise) (1959) (w-Eng)Noel Sherman (m)Peter Mosser. (P)Ivo Robic. (CR)Leslie Uggams.

MORITAT (See Mack The Knife).

MORNIN' (1983) (wm)Al Jarreau—Jay Graydon—David Foster. (P)Al Jarreau.

MORNIN' BEAUTIFUL (1975) (wm)Sandy Linzer—Dave Appell. (P)Tony Orlando & Dawn.

MORNING AFTER, THE (1972) (wm)Al Kasha—Joel Hirshhorn. (I)Film: The Poseidon Adventure, by Maureen McGovern. (P)Maureen McGovern. No. 1 Chart Record. Academy Award Winner.

MORNING DANCE (1979) (m)Jay Beckenstein. (P)Spyro Gyra.

MORNING GIRL (1969) (wm)Tupper Saussy. (P)Neon Philhomonic.

MORNING HAS BROKEN (1972) (w)Eleanor Farjeon (m)Cat Stevens.

MORNING MUSIC OF MONTMARTRE, THE (1958) (wm)Jay Livingston— Ray Evans. (I)Musical: Oh Captain!, by Susan Johnson.

MORNING TRAIN (1981) (wm)Florrie Palmer. (P)Sheena Easton. No. 1 Chart Record.

MORNINGSIDE OF THE MOUNTAIN, THE (1951) (wm)Dick Manning— Larry Stock. (P)Tommy Edwards. (CR)Merv Griffin. (R)1975 by Donny and Marie Osmond.

MOST BEAUTIFUL GIRL, THE (1973) (wm)Norro Wilson—Billy Sherrill—Rory Bourke. (P)Charlie Rich. No. 1 Chart Record.

MOST BEAUTIFUL GIRL IN THE WORLD, THE (1935) (w)Lorenz Hart (m)Richard Rodgers. (I)Musical: Billy Rose's Jumbo, by Donald Novis and Gloria Grafton. (R)1962 Film: Billy Rose's Jumbo, by Stephen Boyd and reprised by Jimmy Durante.

MOST GENTLEMEN DON'T LIKE LOVE (1938) (wm)Cole Porter. (I)Musical: Leave It To Me, by Sophie Tucker. (P)Mary Martin.

MOST HAPPY FELLA, THE (1956) (wm)Frank Loesser. (I)Musical: The Most Happy Fella, by Robert Weede.

MOST LIKELY YOU GO YOUR WAY (1966) (wm)Bob Dylan. (P)Bob Dylan.

MOST OF ALL (1955) (wm)Alan Freed—Harvey Fuqua. (P)The Moonglows. (CR)Don Cornell.

MOST PEOPLE GET MARRIED (1962) (w)Earl Shuman (m)Leon Carr.(P)Patti Page.

MOTEN STOMP (1927) (m)Bennie Moten. (P)Theme song of Bennie Moten's Kansas City Orchestra.

MOTEN SWING (1933) (m)Buster Moten—Bennie Moten. (P)Bennie Moten and his Orchestra.

MOTEN'S BLUES (1929) (m)Bennie Moten. (P)Bennie Moten's Kansas City Orchestra.

M-O-T-H-E-R (A Word That Means The World To Me) (1915) (w)Howard Johnson (m)Theodore F. Morse. (P)Henry Burr.

MOTHER (1927) (w)Dorothy Donnelly (m)Sigmund Romberg (I)Operetta: My Maryland, by Evelyn Herbert.

MOTHER (1971) (wm)John Lennon. (P)John Lennon.

(CR)Barbra Streisand.

MOTHER AND CHILD REUNION (1972) (wm)Paul Simon. (P)Paul Simon.

MOTHER-IN-LAW (1961) (w)Alan Toussaint. (P)Ernie K-Doe. No. 1 Chart Record.

MOTHER MACHREE (1910) (w)Rida Johnson Young (m)Theodore F. Morse. (P)Theme song of John McCormack.

MOTHER NATURE'S SON (1968) (wm)John Lennon—Paul McCartney. (P)The Beatles.

MOTHER POPCORN (1969) (wm)James Brown—Alfred Ellis. (P)James Brown.

MOTHERHOOD MARCH, THE (1964) (wm)Jerry Herman. (I)Musical: Hello, Dolly!, by Carol Channing, Eileen Brennan, and Sondra Lee.

MOTHER'S LITTLE HELPER (1966) (wm)Mick Jagger—Keith Richard. (P)The Rolling Stones.

MOTORCYCLE MAMA (1972) (wm)John Wyker. (P)Sailcat.

MOTORPSYCHO NIGHTMARE (1964) (wm)Bob Dylan. (P)Bob Dylan.

MOULIN ROUGE (See Song From Moulin Rouge).

MOUNTAIN GREENERY (1926) (w)Lorenz Hart (m)Richard Rodgers. (I)Revue: The Garrick Gaieties, by Sterling Holloway and Bobbie Perkins. (R)1948 Film: Words And Music, by Perry Como and Allyn McLerie.

MOUNTAIN OF LOVE (1959) (wm)Harold Dorman. (P)Harold Dorman. (R)1964 by Johnny Rivers. (R)1978 by Ronnie Dove.

MOUNTAINS BEYOND THE MOON, THE (1957) (w)Carl Sigman (m)Franz Waxman. (I)Film: Sayonara.

MOUNTAIN'S HIGH, THE (1961) (wm)Dick Gosting. (P)Dick and Deedee.

MOUNTIES, THE (1924) (w)Otto Harbach—Oscar Hammerstein II (m)Rudolf Friml. (I)Operetta: Rose—Marie, by Arthur Deagon and The Male Chorus. (R)1936

Film: Rose—Marie, by Nelson Eddy. (R)1954 Film: Rose—Marie, by Howard Keel.

MOVE AWAY (1986) (wm)Culture Club—Phil Pickett. (P)Culture Club.

MOVE ON (1983) (wm)Stephen Sondheim. (I)Musical: Sunday In The Park With George, by Mandy Patinkin and Bernadette Peters.

MOVE OVER (1969) (wm)John Kay—Gabriel Mekler. (P)Steppenwolf.

MOVIN' (1976) (wm)Randy Muller—Wade Williamston. (P)Brass Construction.

MOVIN' ON (1975) (wm)Mick Ralphs. (P)Bad Company.

MOVIN' ON UP (1975) (wm)Jeff Barry—Ja'net Dubois. (I)TV series: The Jeffersons, by voices of Ja'net Dubois and Oren Waters.

MOVING OUT (Anthony's Song) (1978) (wm)Billy Joel. (P)Billy Joel.

MOZAMBIQUE (1976) (wm)Bob Dylan—Jacques Levy. (P)Bob Dylan.

MRS. BROWN, YOU'VE GOT A LOVELY DAUGHTER (1965) (wm)Trevor Peacock. (I)In England, by Tom Courtenay. (P)Herman's Hermits. No. 1 Chart Record.

MRS. ROBINSON (1967) (wm)Paul Simon. (I)Film: The Graduate, by Simon and Garfunkel, on the soundtrack. (P)Simon and Garfunkel. No. 1 Chart Record. NARAS Award Winner.

MRS. WORTHINGTON (Don't Put Your Daughter On The Stage) (1935) (wm)Noel Coward. (P)Noel Coward.

M. T. A THE (1956) (wm)Jacqueline Steiner—Bess Hawes. Initials signify Metropolitan Transit Authority. (P)The Kingston Trio.

MUCHACHA (1935) (w)Al Dubin (m)Harry Warren. (I)Film: In Caliente, by Dolores Del Rio, Phil Regan, and The Chorus.

MUDDY WATER (1985) (wm)Roger Miller. (I)Musical: Big River, by Daniel Jenkins and Ron Richardson.

MUDDY WATERS (1926) (w)Jo Trent (m)Peter De Rose—Harry Richman. (P)Harry Richman.

MULE SKINNER BLUES (1931) (wm)Jimmie Rodgers—George Vaughn. (P)Jimmie Rodgers. (R)1960 by The Fendermen. (R)1970 by Dolly Parton.

MULE TRAIN (1949) (wm)Johnny Lange—Hy Heath—Fred Glickman. (I)Bill Butler. (P)Frankie Laine. No. 1 Chart Record. (CR)Tennessee Ernie Ford. (CR)Bing Crosby.

MULTIPLICATION (1961) (wm)Bobby Darin. (I)Film: Come September, by Bobby Darin.

MUNSTER'S THEME (1964) (m)Jack Marshall—Bob Mosher. (I)TV series: The Munsters, as soundtrack theme.

"MURDER" HE SAYS (1943) (w)Frank Loesser (m)Jimmy McHugh. (I)Film: Happy Go Lucky, by Betty Hutton. (P)Betty Hutton.

MUSCLES (1982) (wm)Michael Jackson. (P)Diana Ross.

MURDER ON THE ORIENT EXPRESS (1974) (m)Richard Rodney Bennett. (I)Film: Murder On The Orient Express, as soundtrack theme.

MUSETTA'S WALTZ (1898) (m)Giacomo Puccini. (I)Opera: La Boheme.

MUSIC AND THE MIRROR (1975) (w)Edward Kleban (m)Marvin Hamlisch. (I)Musical: A Chorus Line.

MUSIC BOX DANCER (1979) (m)Frank Mills. (P)Frank Mills.

MUSIC GOES 'ROUND AND AROUND, THE (1935) (w)Red Hodgson (m)Ed Farley—Mike Riley. (P)Riley and Farley and Their Band. No. 1 Chart Record. (CR)Tommy Dorsey and his Orchestra. (CR)Hal Kemp and his Orchestra.

MUSIC OF GOODBYE, THE (1985) (w)Alan and Marilyn Bergman (m)John Barry. (I)Film: Out Of Africa, by voices of Melissa Manchester and Al Jarreau.

MUSIC, MAESTRO, PLEASE! (1938) (w)Herb Magidson (m)Allie Wrubel. (I)Frank Parker and Frances Langford. (P)Tommy Dorsey and his Orchestra. No. 1 Chart Record. (CR)Art Kassel and his Orchestra.

MUSIC MAKERS (1941) (w)Don Raye (m)Harry James. (P)Harry James and his Orchestra.

MUSIC MAKES ME (1933) (w)Gus Kahn—Edward Eliscu (m)Vincent Youmans. (I)Film: Flying Down To Rio, by Ginger Rogers.

MUSIC! MUSIC! MUSIC! (Put Another Nickel In) (1950) (wm)Stephan Weiss—Bernie Baum. (P)Teresa Brewer. (CR)The Ames Brothers. (CR)Freddy Martin and his Orchestra.

MUSIC STOPPED, THE (1943) (w)Harold Adamson (m)Jimmy McHugh. (I)Film: Higher And Higher, by Frank Sinatra. (P)Frank Sinatra. (CR)Woody Herman and his Orchestra, vocal by Frances Wayne.

MUSIC THAT MAKES ME DANCE, THE (1964) (w)Bob Merrill (m)Jule Styne. (I)Musical: Funny Girl, by Barbra Sreisand.

MUSIC TO WATCH GIRLS BY (1967) (w)Tony Velona

(m)Sid Ramin. (P)The Bob Crewe Generation. (CR)Andy Williams.

MUSKRAT LOVE (1973) (wm)Willis Alan Ramsey. (P)America. (R)1976 by The Captain and Tennille.

MUSKRAT RAMBLE (1926) (w)Ray Gilbert (m)Edward "Kid" Ory. (P)Louis Armstrong and his Hot Five. (R)1954 by The McGuire Sisters.

MUST OF GOT LOST (1974) (wm)Seth Justman—Peter Wolf. (P)The J. Geils Band.

MUST TO AVOID, A (1966) (wm)P. F. Sloan—Steve Barri. (I)Film: *Hold On!,* by Herman's Hermits. (P)Herman's Hermits.

MUSTANG SALLY (1966) (wm)Bonny Rice. (P)Wilson Pickett.

MUTINY ON THE BOUNTY (Theme) (1962) (m)Bronislau Kaper. (I)Film: *Mutiny On The Bounty,* as soundtrack theme.

MUTUAL ADMIRATION SOCIETY (1956) (w)Matt Dubey (m)Harold Karr. (I)Musical: *Happy Hunting,* by Ethel Merman and Virginia Gibson. (P)Teresa Brewer.

MY ADOBE HACIENDA (1947) (wm)Louise Massey—Lee Penny. (P)Eddy Howard and his Orchestra. (CR)Kenny Baker. (CR)The Dinning Sisters.

MY ANGEL BABY (1978) (wm)Johnny Northern. (P)Toby Beau.

MY BABY (1965) (wm)Warren Moore—William Robinson—Robert Rogers. (P)The Temptations.

MY BABY JUST CARES FOR ME (1930) (w)Gus Kahn (m)Walter Donaldson. (I)Film: *Whoopee,* by Eddie Cantor. (P)Eddie Cantor. (CR)Ted Weems and his Orchestra.

MY BABY LEFT ME (1956) (wm)Arthur Crudup. (P)Elvis Presley.

MY BABY LOVES LOVIN' (1970) (wm)Roger Greenaway—Roger Cook. (P)White Plains.

MY BABY LOVES ME (1966) (wm)Sylvia Moy—William Stevenson—Ivy Hunter. (P)Martha and The Vandellas.

MY BABY MUST BE A MAGICIAN (1967) (wm)William Robinson. (P)The Marvelettes.

MY BACK PAGES (1964) (wm)Bob Dylan. (P)Bob Dylan (R)1967 by The Byrds.

MY BEST GIRL (1924) (wm)Walter Donaldson. (P)Isham Jones and his Orchestra. (CR)Nick Lucas.

MY BEST GIRL (1966) (wm)Jerry Herman. (I)Musical: *Mame,* by Frankie Michaels and Angela Lansbury.

MY BLUE HEAVEN (1924) (w)George Whiting (m)Walter Donaldson. (I)Vaudeville: by George Whiting. (P)1928 by Gene Austin. No. 1 Chart Record. (R)1939 by Jimmie Lunceford and his Orchestra. (R)1950 Film: *My Blue Heaven,* by Betty Grable and Dan Dailey. (R)1955 Film: *Love Me Or Leave Me,* by Doris Day.

MY BONNIE LASSIE (1955) (wm)Roy C. Bennett—Sid Tepper—Marion McClurg. (P)The Ames Brothers.

MY BONNIE LIES OVER THE OCEAN (1881) (wm)Unknown. Traditional Scottish folk song.

MY BOOMERANG WON'T COME BACK (1961) (wm)Max Diamond—Charlie Drake. (P)Charlie Drake.

MY BOY (1971) (w-Eng)Philip Coulter—Bill Martin (m)Jean Bourtayre—Claude Francois. (P)Richard Harris. (R)1975 by Elvis Presley.

MY BOY, FLAT TOP (1955) (wm)John F. Young, Jr. - Boyd Bennett. (I)Boyd Bennett. (P)Dorothy Collins.

MY BOYFRIEND'S BACK (1963) (wm)Robert Feldman— Gerald Goldstein— Richard Gottehrer. (P)The An-

gels. No. 1 Chart Record.

MY BUDDY (1922) (w)Gus Kahn (m)Walter Donaldson. (P)Al Jolson. (CR)Ben Bernie and his Orchestra. (R)1942 by Sammy Kaye and his Orchestra. (R)1951 Film: *I'll See You In My Dreams,* by Doris Day.

MY CHERIE AMOUR (1969) (wm)Stevie Wonder—Henry Cosby—Sylvia Moy. (P)Stevie Wonder.

MY COLORING BOOK (1962) (w)Fred Ebb (m)John Kander. (I)Kaye Ballard. (P)Sandy Stewart. (CR)Barbra Streisand. (CR)Kitty Kallen.

MY COUSIN IN MILWAUKEE (1933) (w)Ira Gershwin (m)George Gershwin. (I)Musical: *Pardon My English,* by Lyda Roberti.

MY CUP RUNNETH OVER (1966) (w)Tom Jones (m)Harvey Schmidt. (I)Musical: *I Do! I Do!,* by Mary Martin and Robert Preston. (P)Ed Ames.

MY DAD (1962) (wm)Barry Mann—Cynthia Weil. (P)Paul Peterson.

MY DANCING LADY (1933) (w)Dorothy Fields (m)Jimmy McHugh. (I)Film: *Dancing Lady,* by Art Jarrett and danced to by Joan Crawford.

MY DARLING (1932) (w)Edward Heyman (m)Richard Myers. (I)Revue: *Earl Carroll Vanities,* by John Hale and Josephine Houston. (P)Don Bestor and his Orchestra.

MY DARLING, MY DARLING (1948) (wm)Frank Loesser. (I)Musical: *Where's Charley?,* by Byron Palmer and Doretta Morrow. (P)Jo Stafford and Gordon MacRae. No. 1 Chart Record. (CR)Doris Day and Buddy Clark.

MY DEFENSES ARE DOWN (1946) (wm)Irving Berlin. (I)Musical: *Annie Get Your Gun,* by Ray Middleton. Film version 1950 by Howard Keel.

MY DEVOTION (1942) (wm)Roc Hillman—Johnny Napton. (P)Vaughn Monroe and his Orchestra. (CR)Jimmy Dorsey and his Orchestra.

MY DING-A-LING (1972) (wm)Chuck Berry. (P)Chuck Berry.

MY DREAM IS YOURS (1949) (w)Ralph Blane (m)Harry Warren. (I)Film: *My Dream Is Yours,* by Doris Day.

MY DREAMS ARE GETTING BETTER ALL THE TIME (1944) (w)Mann Curtis (m)Vic Mizzy. (I)Film: *In Society,* by Marion Hutton. (P)Les Brown and his Orchestra, vocal by Doris Day. No. 1 Chart Record. (CR)Johnny Long and his Orchestra.

MY ELUSIVE DREAMS (1967) (wm)Claude Putnam— Billy Sherrill. (P)David Houston and Tammy Wynette. (R)1970 by Bobby Vinton. (R)1975 by Charlie Rich.

MY EMPTY ARMS (1960) (wm)Al Kasha—Hank Hunter. Adapted from Vesti La Giubba, from Pagliacci. (P)Jackie Wilson.

MY EYES ADORED YOU (1975) (wm)Bob Crewe—Kenny Nolan Helfman. (P)Frankie Valli. No. 1 Chart Record.

MY FAIR SHARE (1977) (w)Paul Williams (m)Charles Fox. (I)Film: *One On One,* by voice of Seals & Crofts. (P)Seals & Crofts.

MY FATE IS IN YOUR HANDS (1929) (w)Andy Razaf (m)Thomas Waller. (P)Fats Waller.

MY FATHER'S HOUSE (1982) (wm)Bruce Springsteen. (P)Bruce Springsteen. (R)1986 by Emmylou Harris.

MY FAVORITE THINGS (1959) (w)Oscar Hammerstein II (m)Richard Rodgers. (I)Musical: *The Sound Of Music,* by Pat Neway and Mary Martin. (R)1968 by Herb Alpert and The Tijuana Brass. Jazz instrumental by John Coltrane.

MY FINE FEATHERED FRIEND (1937) (w)Harold Adamson (m)Jimmy McHugh. (I)Film: *You're A Sweetheart*, by Alice Faye.

MY FIRST LOVE SONG (1964) (wm)Leslie Bricusse—Anthony Newley. (I)Musical: *The Roar Of The Greasepaint—The Smell Of The Crowd*, by Anthony Newley and Joyce Jillson.

MY FOOLISH HEART (1950) (w)Ned Washington (m)Victor Young. (I)Film: *My Foolish Heart*, by Susan Hayward. (P)Gordon Jenkins and his Orchestra. (CR)Billy Eckstine. (CR)Mindy Carson. (CR)Margaret Whiting.

MY FUNNY VALENTINE (1937) (w)Lorenz Hart (m)Richard Rodgers. (I)Musical: *Babes In Arms*, by Mitzi Green. Most popular recording by Frank Sinatra.

MY FUTURE JUST PASSED (1930) (w)George Marion (m)Richard A. Whiting. (I)Film: *Safety In Numbers*, by Buddy Rogers.

MY GAL SAL (1905) (wm)Paul Dresser. (I)Byron G. Harlan.

MY GENTLE YOUNG JOHNNY (1960) (w)Sheldon Harnick (m)Jerry Bock. (I)Musical: *Tenderloin*, by Eileen Rodgers and The Girls.

MY GIRL (1964) (wm)William Robinson—Ronald White. (P)The Temptations. No. 1 Chart Record. (R)1968 by Bobby Vee (in medley) (R)1985 by Hall & Oates, David Ruffin, Eddie Kendricks (in medley).

MY GIRL BACK HOME (1958) (w)Oscar Hammerstein II (m)Richard Rodgers. (I)Film: *South Pacific*, by Bill Lee dubbing for John Kerr and Mitzi Gaynor.

MY GIRL BILL (1974) (wm)Jim Stafford. (P)Jim Stafford.

MY GIRL HAS GONE (1965) (wm)William Robinson—Marv Tarplin— Warren Moore—Ronald White. (P)The Miracles.

MY GIRL JOSEPHINE (1960) (wm)Antoine Domino—Dave Bartholomew. (P)Fats Domino. (R)1967 by Jerry Jaye.

MY GUY (1964) (wm)William Robinson. (P)Mary Wells. No. 1 Chart Record.

MY GUY'S COME BACK (1945) (w)Ray McKinley (m)Mel Powell. (I)Glenn Miller Army Air Force Band under title of: Oranges And Lemons. (P)Benny Goodman and his Orchestra, vocal by Liza Morrow.

MY HAPPINESS (1948) (w)Betty Peterson (m)Borney Bergantine. (P)Jon and Sondra Steele. (R)1953 by The Mulcays. (R)1959 by Connie Francis.

MY HEART AND I (1936) (w)Leo Robin (m)Frederick Hollander. (I)Film: *Anything Goes*, by Bing Crosby. (P)Bing Crosby.

MY HEART AT THY SWEET VOICE (19876) (m)Camille Saint— Saens. (I)Opera: *Samson And Delilah*.

MY HEART BELONGS TO DADDY (1938) (wm)Cole Porter. (I)Musical: *Leave It To Me*, by Mary Martin. (P)Mary Martin with Eddy Duchin and his Orchestra. (CR)Larry Clinton and his Orchestra. (R)1946 Film: *Night And Day*, by Mary Martin. (R)1946 by Artie Shaw and his Orchestra. (R)1960 Film: *Let's Make Love*, by Marilyn Monroe.

MY HEART BELONGS TO ME (1977) (wm)Alan Gordon. (P)Barbra Streisand.

MY HEART BELONGS TO ONLY YOU (1952) (wm)Frank and Dorothy Daniels. (P)Bette McLaurin. (R)1964 by Bobby Vinton.

MY HEART CRIES FOR YOU (1950) (wm)Carl Sigman—Percy Faith. (P)Guy Mitchell with Mitch Miller and his Orchestra. (CR)Dinah Shore. (CR)Vic Damone.

MY HEART HAS A MIND OF ITS OWN (1960) (w)Howard Greenfield (m)Jack Keller. (P)Connie Francis. No. 1 Chart Record.

MY HEART IS A HOBO (1947) (w)Johnny Burke (m)Jimmy Van Heusen. (I)Film: *Welcome Stranger*, by Bing Crosby. (P)Bing Crosby.

MY HEART IS AN OPEN BOOK (1957) (w)Hal David (m)Lee Pockriss. (P)Carl Dobkins, Jr.

(Don't Look Now, But)MY HEART IS SHOWING (w)Ann Ronell (m)Kurt Weill. (I)Film: *One Touch Of Venus*, by Eileen Wilson dubbing for Ava Gardner, Olga San Juan, and Dick Haymes.

MY HEART IS SO FULL OF YOU (1956) (wm)Frank Loesser. (I)Musical: *The Most Happy Fella*, by Robert Weede.

MY HEART IS TAKING LESSONS (1938) (w)Johnny Burke (m)James V. Monaco. (I)Film: *Doctor Rhythm*, by Bing Crosby.

MY HEART REMINDS ME (And That Reminds You) (1957) (P)Kay Starr. (P)Della Reese. (R)1969 by The Four Seasons.

(All Of A Sudden)MY HEART SINGS (1945) (w-Eng)Harold Rome (m)Herpin. (I)Film: *Anchors Aweigh*, by Kathryn Grayson. (R)1965 by Mel Carter.

MY HEART STOOD STILL (1927) (w)Lorenz Hart (m)Richard Rodgers. (I)English revue: *One Dam Thing After Another*, by Jessie Mathews and Richard Dolman. (I)US musical: *A Connecticut Yankee*, by William Gaxton and Constance Carpenter. (P)George Olsen and his Orchestra. (CR)Ben Selvin and his Orchestra.

MY HEART TELLS ME (1943) (w)Mack Gordon (m)Harry Warren. (I)Film: *Sweet Rosie O'Grady*, by Betty Grable. (P)Glen Gray and The Casa Loma Orchestra, vocal by Eugenie Baird. No. 1 Chart Record.

MY HEART'S SYMPHONY (1966) (wm)Glen D. Hardin (P)Gary Lewis and The Playboys.

MY HERO (1909) (w)Stanislaus Stange (m)Oscar Straus. (I)Musical: *The Chocolate Soldier*.

MY HEROES HAVE ALWAYS BEEN COWBOYS (1980) (wm)Sharon Vaughan. (I)Film: *The Electric Horseman*, by Willie Nelson. (P)Willie Nelson.

MY HOME TOWN (1960) (wm)Paul Anka. (P)Paul Anka.

MY HOME TOWN (1963) (I)Musical: *What Makes Sammy Run?* by, Steve Lawrence.

MY HOMETOWN (1984) (wm)Bruce Springsteen. (P)Bruce Springsteen.

MY HONEY'S LOVIN' ARMS (1922) (w)Herman Ruby (m)Joseph Meyer. (P)Isham Jones and his Orchestra. (R)1939 by Benny Goodman and his Orchestra. (R)1963 by Barbra Streisand.

MY IDEAL (1930) (w)Leo Robin (m)Richard A. Whiting—Newell Chase. (I)Film: *PLayboy Of Paris*, by Maurice Chevalier. (P)Maurice Chevalier. (CR)Maxine Sullivan. (CR)Jimmy Dorsey and his Orchestra.

MY KIND OF GIRL (1961) (wm)Leslie Bricusse. (P)Matt Monro.

MY KIND OF TOWN (1964) (w)Sammy Cahn (m)Jimmy Van Heusen. (I)Film: *Robin And The Seven Hoods*, by Frank Sinatra. (P)Frank Sinatra.

MY LADY LOVES TO DANCE (1952) (wm)Sammy Gallop—Milton De Lugg. (P)Julius La Rosa.

MY LAST AFFAIR (1936) (wm)Haven Johnson. (I)Revue: *New Faces Of 1936*, by Billie Haywood. (P)Mildred Bailey.

MY LAST GOODBYE (1939) (wm)Eddy Howard. (P)Dick

Jurgens and his Orchestra, vocal by Eddy Howard. (CR)Henry Busse and his Orchestra.

MY LAST LOVE (1943) (w)Alan Jay Lerner (m)Frederick Loewe. (I)Musical: *What's Up*, by Larry Douglas, Mary Roche, Lynn Gardner, Johnny Morgan, William Tabbert, and Gloria Warren.

MY LIFE (1979) (wm)Billy Joel. (P)Billy Joel.

MY LITTLE BUCKAROO (1937) (w)Jack Scholl (m)M. K. Jerome. (I)Film: *Cherokee Strip*, by Dick Foran. (P)Bing Crosby.

MY LITTLE CORNER OF THE WORLD (1960) (w)Bob Hilliard (m)Lee Pockriss. (P)Anita Bryant.

MY LITTLE TOWN (1974) (wm)Paul Simon. (P)Simon and Garfunkel.

MY LOVE (1966) (wm)Tony Hatch. (P)Petula Clark. No. 1 Chart Record. (R)1971 by Sonny James.

MY LOVE (1973) (wm)Paul and Linda McCartney. (P)Wings. No. 1 Chart Record.

MY LOVE AND DEVOTION (1951) (wm)Milton Carson. (P)Perry Como.

MY LOVE, FORGIVE ME (Amore, Scusami) (1964) (w-Eng)Sydney Lee (m)Gino Mescoli. (P)Robert Goulet.

MY LOVE, MY LOVE (1953) (w)Bob Haymes (m)Nick Acquaviva. (P)Joni James.

MY LOVE PARADE (1929) (w)Clifford Grey (m)Victor Schertzinger. (I)Film: *The Love Parade*, by Maurice Chevalier and Jeanette MacDonald.

MY LUCKY STAR (1929) (w)B. G. De Sylva—Lew Brown (m)Ray Henderson. (I)Musical: *Follow Thru*, by John Barker. (P)Paul Whiteman and his Orchestra.

MY MAMMY (1918) (w)Sam M. Lewis—Joe Young (m)Walter Donaldson. (I)Vaudeville: by William Frawley. (P)Musical: *Sinbad*, by Al Jolson. (CR)Paul Whiteman and his Orchestra. (R)1946 Film: *The Jolson Story*, by Jolson dubbing for Larry Parks. (R)1962 by Jackie Wilson. (R)1967 by The Happenings.

MY MAN (1920) (w-Eng)Channing Pollock (m)Maurice Yvain. (I)Revue: *Ziegfeld Girls of 1920*, by Fanny Brice. (P)Fanny Brice. (R)1928 Film: *My Man*, by Fanny Brice. (R)1938 Billie Holiday and Teddy Wilson. (R)1939 Film: *Rose Of Washington Square*, by Alice Faye. (R)1968 Film: *Funny Girl*, by Barbra Streisand.

MY MAN IS ON THE MAKE (1929) (w)Lorenz Hart (m)Richard Rodgers. (I)Musical: *Heads Up!*, by Alice Boulden. In film version, by Helen Kane.

MY MAN'S GONE NOW (1935) (w)Du Bose Heyward (m)George Gershwin. (I)Opera: *Porgy And Bess*, by Ruby Elzy. (R)1959 Film: *Porgy And Bess*, by Inez Matthews dubbing for Ruth Attaway.

MY MARIA (1973) (wm)B. W. Stevenson—Daniel Moore. (P)B. W. Stevenson.

MY MELANCHOLY BABY (1912) (w)George A. Norton (m)Ernie Burnett. (I)Walter Van Brunt. (R)1928 by Gene Austin. (R)1936 by Teddy Wilson. (R)1939 by Bing Crosby.

MY MELODY OF LOVE (1974) (wm)Bobby Vinton. (P)Bobby Vinton.

MY MISS MARY (1960) (w)Sheldon Harnick (m)Jerry Bock. (I)Musical: *Tenderloin*, by Ron Husmann, Wynne Miller, and The Ensemble.

MY MISTAKE (Was To Love You) (1974) (wm)Gloria Jones—Pam Sawyer. (P)Diana Ross and Marvin Gaye.

MY MOM (1932) (wm)Walter Donaldson. (P)Kate Smith.

MY MOONLIGHT MADONNA (1933) (w)Paul Francis Webster (m)William Scotti. Adapted From Poeme, by Fibich. (P)Rudy Vallee. (CR)Paul Whiteman and his Orchestra.

MY MOTHER WOULD LOVE YOU (1940) (wm)Cole Porter. (I)Musical: *Panama Hattie*, by Ethel Merman and James Dunn.

MY MOTHER'S EYES (1929) (w)L. Wolfe Gilbert (m)Abel Baer. (I)Film: *Lucky Boy*, by George Jessel. (P)George Jessel.

MY MOTHER'S WEDDIN' DAY (1947) (w)Alan Jay Lerner (m)Frederick Loewe. (I)Musical: *Brigadoon*, by Pamela Britton and The Chorus.

MY MUSIC (1973) (wm)Kenny Loggins—Jim Messina. (P)Loggins & Messina.

MY OLD FLAME (1934) (wm)Sam Coslow—Arthur Johnston. (I)Film: *Belle Of The Nineties*, by Mae West with Duke Ellington and his Orchestra.

MY OLD KENTUCKY HOME (1853) (wm)Stephen Collins Foster. One of Foster's most popular songs.

MY ONE AND ONLY (1927) (w)Ira Gershwin (m)George Gershwin. (I)Musical: *Funny Face*, by Fred Astaire, Gertrude McDonald, and Betty Compton. (R)1983 Musical: *My One And Only*, by Tommy Tune.

MY ONE AND ONLY HEART (1953) (w)Al Stillman (m)Robert Allen. (P)Perry Como.

MY ONE AND ONLY HIGHLAND FLING (1949) (w)Ira Gershwin (m)Harry Warren. (I)Film: *The Barkleys Of Broadway*, by Fred Astaire and Ginger Rogers.

MY ONE AND ONLY LOVE (1953) (w)Robert Mellin (m)Guy Wood. (P)Frank Sinatra.

MY OWN BEST FRIEND (1975) (w)Fred Ebb (m)John Kander. (I)Musical: *Chicago*, by Chita Rivera and Gwen Verdon.

MY OWN, MY ONLY, MY ALL (1949) (wm)Jay Livingston—Ray Evans. (I)Film: *My Friend Irma*, by Dean Martin. (P)Dean Martin.

MY OWN SPACE (1977) (w)Fred Ebb (m)John Kander. (I)Musical: *The Act*, by Liza Minnelli.

MY OWN TRUE LOVE (1954) (w)Mack David (m)Max Steiner. Based on Tara's Theme from Gone With The Wind. (P)Leroy Holmes and his Chorus and Orchestra. (CR)Johnny Desmond.

MY PET BRUNETTE (See Negra Consentida).

MY PLEDGE OF LOVE (1969) (wm)Joseph Stafford, Jr. (P)The Joe Jeffrey Group.

MY PRAYER (1939) (wm)Jimmy Kennedy—Georges Boulanger. (I)Vera Lynn. (P)Sammy Kaye and his Orchestra. (R)1956 by The Platters. No. 1 Chart Record.

MY RESISTANCE IS LOW (1951) (w)Harold Adamson (m)Hoagy Carmichael. (I)Film: *The Las Vegas Story*, by Hoagy Carmichael.

MY RESTLESS LOVER (Johnny Guitar) (1954) (wm)Pembroke Davenport. (P)Patti Page.

MY REVERIE (1938) (wm)Larry Clinton. Adapted from Reverie, by Debussy. (P)Larry Clinton and his Orchestra, vocal by Bea Wain. No. 1 Chart Record. (CR)Bing Crosby. (CR)Mildred Bailey.

MY ROMANCE (1935) (w)Lorenz Hart (m)Richard Rodgers. (I)Musical: *Billy Rose's Jumbo*, by Donald Novis and Gloria Grafton. (R)1962 Film: *Jumbo*, by Doris Day.

MY SHARONA (1934) (wm)Berton Averre—Pedro Berrios. (P)The Knack. No. 1 Chart Record.

MY SHAWL (1934) (w-Eng)Stanley Adams (m)Xavier

Cugat. (P)Theme song of Xavier Cugat and his Orchestra.

MY SHINING HOUR (1943) (w)Johnny Mercer (m)Harold Arlen. (I)Film: *The Sky's The Limit*, by Fred Astaire.

MY SHIP (1941) (w)Ira Gershwin (m)Kurt Weill. (I)Musical: *Lady In The Dark*, by Gertrude Lawrence. Film version 1944 by Ginger Rogers.

MY SILENT LOVE (1932) (w)Edward Heyman (m)Dana Suesse. (P)Ruby Newman and his Orchestra. (CR)Isham Jones and his Orchestra. Most popular recording by Frank Sinatra.

MY SIN (1930) (w)B. G. De Sylva—Lew Brown (m)Ray Henderson. (I)Film: *Show Girl In Hollywood.* (P)Belle Baker. (CR)Fred Waring's Pennsylvanians. (R)1954 by Georgia Gibbs.

MY SISTER AND I (1941) (wm)Hy Zaret—Joan Whitney—Alex Kramer. (P)Jimmy Dorsey and his Orchestra, vocal by Bob Eberly. No. 1 Chart Record.

MY SON, MY SON (1954) (wm)Bob Howard—Melville Farley—Eddie Calvert. (P)Vera Lynn.

MY SONG (1931) (wm)Lew Brown—Ray Henderson. (I)Revue: *George White's Scandals*, by Ethel Merman and Rudy Vallee. (P)Rudy Vallee.

MY SONG (1968) (wm)Stonewall Jackson. (P)Aretha Franklin.

MY SPECIAL ANGEL (1957) (wm)Jimmy Duncan. (P)Bobby Helms. (R)1968 by The Vogues.

MY SUMMER LOVE (1963) (w)Bob Hilliard (m)Mort Garson. (P)Ruby and The Romantics.

MY SUNNY TENNESSEE (1921) (wm)Bert Kalmar—Harry Ruby—Herman Ruby. (I)Revue: *The Midnight Rounders of 1921*, by Eddie Cantor. (P)Eddie Cantor. (CR)The Broadway Quartet. (R)1950 Film: *Three Little Words*, by Fred Astaire and Red Skelton.

MY SWEET LADY (1970) (wm)John Denver. (I)John Denver. (R)1974 by Cliff De Young. (R)1977 by John Denver.

MY SWEET LORD (1970) (wm)George Harrison. (P)George Harrison. No. 1 Chart Record.

MY TIME IS YOUR TIME (1927) (wm)Eric Little—Leo Dance. (P)Theme song of Rudy Vallee.

MY TIME OF DAY (1950) (wm)Frank Loesser. (I)Musical: *Guys And Dolls*, by Robert Alda.

MY TOREADOR (El Relicario) (1926) (w-Eng)William Cary Duncan (m)Jose Padilla. Famous Spanish composition.

MY TOWN, MY GUY, AND ME (1965) (wm)Paul Kaufman—Bob Elgin— Lesley Gore. (P)Lesley Gore.

MY TRUE LOVE (1958) (wm)Jack Scott. (P)Jack Scott.

MY TRUE STORY (1961) (wm)Eugene Pitt—Oscar Waltzer. (P)The Jive Five and Joe Rene.

MY TRULY, TRULY FAIR (1951) (wm)Bob Merrill. (P)Guy Mitchell with Mitch Miller and his Orchestra.

MY TWILIGHT DREAM (1939) (wm)Lew Sherwood—Eddy Duchin. Based on Chopin's Nocturne in E Flat. (P)Theme song of Eddy Duchin and his Orchestra.

(All I Want For Christmas Is)MY TWO FRONT TEETH. (1948) (wm)Don Gardner. (P)Spike Jones and his City Slickers.

MY VERY GOOD FRIEND, THE MILKMAN (1935) (w)Johnny Burke (m)Harold Spina. (P)Fats Waller.

MY WALKING STICK (1938) (wm)Irving Berlin. (I)Film: *Alexander's Ragtime Band*, by Ethel Merman.

MY WAY (1967) (w-Eng)Paul Anka (m)Jacques Revaux. (I)In United States, by Paul Anka. (P)Frank Sinatra (1969) (R)1977 by Elvis Presley.

MY WHOLE WORLD ENDED (1969) (wm)Johnny Bristol—Harvey Fuqua— Pam Sawyer—Jimmy Roach. (P)David Ruffin.

MY WILD IRISH ROSE (1899) (wm)Chauncey Olcott. (P)John McCormack.

MY WISH CAME TRUE (1959) (wm)Ivory Joe Hunter. (P)Elvis Presley.

MY WOMAN, MY WOMAN, MY WIFE (1969) (wm)Marty Robbins. (P)Marty Robbins. NARAS Award Winner.

MY WORLD (1972) (wm)Barry Gibb—Robin Gibb. (P)The Bee Gees.

MY WORLD IS EMPTY WITHOUT YOU (1966) (wm)Eddie Holland— Lamont Dozier—Brian Holland. (P)The Supremes. (R)1969 by The Supremes.

MY WUBBA DOLLY (1939) (wm)Kay Werner—Sue Werner. (P)Ella Fitzgerald.

MY YIDDISHE MOMME (1925) (wm)Jack Yellen—Lew Pollack. (P)Sophie Tucker. (R)1960 by Jackie Wilson.

MYSTERY LADY (1984) (wm)Keith Diamond—Billy Ocean—James Woodley. (P)Billy Ocean.

NADIA'S THEME (The Young And The Restless) (1976) (wm)Barry DeVorzon—Perry Botkin, Jr. (I)TV series: *The Young And The Restless*, as soundtrack theme. (P)Barry DeVorzon and Perry Botkin, Jr.

NADINE (Is It You?) (1964) (wm)Chuck Berry. (P)Chuck Berry.

NAGASAKI (1928) (w)Mort Dixon (m)Harry Warren. (P)The Ipana Troubadours. (R)1949 Film: *My Dream Is Yours*, by Doris Day.

NAME GAME, THE (1964) (wm)Shirley Elliston—Lincoln Chase. (P)Shirley Ellis.

NAME OF THE GAME, THE (1978) (wm)Benny Andersson—Stig Anderson— Bjorn Ulvaeus. (P)Abba.

NAMELY YOU (1956) (w)Johnny Mercer (m)Gene de Paul. (I)Musical: *L'il Abner*, by Peter Palmer and Edith Adams.

NA NA, HEY, HEY, KISS HIM GOODBYE (1969) (wm)Gary DeCarlo—Dale Frashuer—Paul Leka. (P)Steam. No. 1 Chart Record.

NANCY (With The Laughing Face) (1945) (w)Phil Silvers (m)Jimmy Van Heusen. (P)Frank Sinatra.

NAPOLEON (1957) (w)E. Y. Harburg (m)Harold Arlen. (I)Musical: *Jamaica*, by Lena Horne.

NARCISSUS (1891) (m)Ethelbert Nevin. Famous American light classical selection.

NASHVILLE CATS (1967) (wm)John B. Sebastian. (P)The Lovin' Spoonful.

NASHVILLE SKYLINE RAG (1969) (m)Bob Dylan. (P)Bob Dylan.

NASTY (1986) (wm)James Harris III—Terry Lewis—Janet Jackson. (P)Janet Jackson.

NATHAN JONES (1971) (wm)Leonard Caston—Kathy Wakefield. (P)The Supremes.

NATIONAL EMBLEM (1906) (m)E. E. Bagley. Famous American march.

NATIVE NEW YORKER (1977) (wm)Sandy Linzer—Denny Randell. (P)Odyssey.

NATURAL, THE (1984) (wm)Randy Newman. (I)Film: *The Natural*, on soundtrack.

NATURAL HIGH (1973) (wm)Charles E. McCormick. (P)Bloodstone.

NATURAL MAN, A (1970) (wm)Bobby Hebb—Sandy Baron. (P)Lou Rawls.

(You Make Me Feel Like)NATURAL WOMAN, A (1967) (wm)Carole King— Jerry Wexler—Gerry Goffin. (P)Aretha Franklin.

NATURE BOY (1948) (wm)Eden Ahbez. (P)Nat "King" Cole. No. 1 Chart Record. (CR)Frank Sinatra. (CR)Sarah Vaughan.

NAUGHTY LADY OF SHADY LANE, THE (1955) (wm)Sid Tepper—Roy C. Bennett. (P)The Ames Brothers.

NEAPOLITAN LOVE SONG (1915) (w)Henry Blossom, Jr. (m)Victor Herbert. (I)Musical: *The Princess Pat*.

NEAR TO YOU (1955) (wm)Richard Adler—Jerry Ross. (I)Musical: *Damn Yankees*, by Stephen Douglass and Shannon Bolin.

NEAR YOU (1947) (w)Kermit Goell (m)Francis Craig. (P)Francis Craig and his Orchestra. No. 1 Chart Record. (CR)The Andrews Sisters.

NEARER, MY GOD, TO THEE (1859) (w)Sarah Adams (m)Adapted from hymn Bethany. Famous hymn that was sung by the passengers as the Titanic was sinking.

NEARNESS OF YOU, THE (1940) (w)Ned Washington (m)Hoagy Carmichael. (P)Glenn Miller and his Orchestra. (CR)Bob Manning.

NECESSITY (1947) (w)E. Y. Harburg (m)Burton Lane. (I)Musical: *Finian's Rainbow*, by Dolores Martin.

NEED TO BE, THE (1974) (wm)Jim Weatherly (P)Jim Weatherly.

NEED YOU TONIGHT (1987) (wm)A. Farriss—M. Hutchence. (P)No. 1 Chart Record.

NEEDLE IN A HAYSTACK, A (1934) (I)Film: *The Gay Divorcee*, by Fred Astaire.

NEEDLES AND PINS (1963) (wm)Sonny Bono—Jack Nitzsche. (P)Jackie DeShannon. (R)1964 by The Searchers. (R)1977 by Smokie. (R)1986 by Tom Petty and Stevie Nicks.

NEGRA CONSENTIDA (My Pet Brunette) (1929) (w-Eng)Marjorie Harper (m)Joaquin Pardave. No artist credited with introduction. (R)1945 by Andy Russell.

NEIANI (1941) (wm)Axel Stordahl—Sy Oliver. (P)Tommy Dorsey and his Orchestra, vocal by Frank Sinatra and The Pied Pipers.

NEITHER ONE OF US (Wants To Be The First To Say Goodbye) (1973) (wm)Jim Weatherly. (P)Gladys Knight & The Pips.

NEL BLU, DIPINTO DI BLU (see: Volare).

NELLIE KELLY, I LOVE YOU (1922) (wm)George M. Cohan (I)Musical: *Little Nellie Kelly*, by Charles King. (R)1940 Film: *Little Nellie Kelly*, by Judy Garland and Douglas McPhail.

NEON RAINBOW (1967) (wm)Wayne Carson Thompson. (P)The Box Tops.

NEUTRON DANCE (1984) (wm)Allee Willis—David Sembello. (I)Film: *Beverly Hills Cop*, on soundtrack by The Pointer Sisters. (P)The Pointer Sisters.

NEVADA (1945) (wm)Mort Greene—Walter Donaldson. (P)Tommy Dorsey and his Orchestra, vocal by Stuart Foster and The Sentimentalists.

NEVER (1951) (w)Eliot Daniel (m)Lionel Newman. (I)Film: *Golden Girl*, by Dennis Day.

NEVER (1985) (wm)Holly Knight—Walter Bloch—Ann Wilson. (P)Heart.

NEVER AGAIN (1938) (wm)Noel Coward. (I)Revue: *Set To Music*, by Eva Ortega and Hugh French.

NEVER AS GOOD AS THE FIRST TIME (1986) (wm)Helen Folosade Adu— Stuart Matthewman. (P)Sade.

NEVER BE ANYONE ELSE BUT YOU (1959) (wm)Baker Knight. (P)Rick Nelson.

NEVER BE THE SAME (1980) (wm)Christopher Geppert. (P)Christopher Cross.

NEVER BEEN TO SPAIN (1972) (wm)Hoyt Axton. (P)Three Dog Night.

NEVER CAN SAY GOODBYE (1971) (wm)Clifton Davis. (P)The Jackson Five. (CR)Isaac Hayes. (R)1975 by Gloria Gaynor.

NEVER ENDING SONG OF LOVE (1971) (wm)Delaney Bramlett. (P)Delaney & Bonnie & Friends.

NEVER ENDING STORY (1985) (wm)Giorgio Moroder— Keith Forsey. (I)Film: *Never Ending Story*, on soundtrack. (P)Limahl.

NEVER GIVE ANYTHING AWAY (1953) (wm)Cole Porter. (I)Musical: *Can-an*, by Lilo.

NEVER GIVE YOU UP (Never Gonna Give You Up) (1968)

(wm)Kenny Gamble—Leon Huff—Jerry Butler. (P)Jerry Butler.

NEVER GONNA DANCE (1936) (w)Dorothy Fields (m)Jerome Kern. (I)Film: *Swing Time*, by Fred Astaire.

NEVER GONNA FALL IN LOVE AGAIN (1976) (wm)Eric Carmen. (P)Eric Carmen.

NEVER GONNA GIVE YOU UP (1987) (wm)Stock—Aitken— Waterman. (P)Rick Astley. No. 1 Chart Record.

NEVER GONNA LET YOU GO (1981) (w)Cynthia Weil (m)Barry Mann. (P)Sergio Mendes.

NEVER HAVE TO SAY GOODBYE AGAIN (We'll Never Have To Say Goodbye Again) (1977) (wm)Jeff Comanor. (I)Deardorff & Joseph. (P)England Dan & John Ford Coley.

NEVER IN A MILLION YEARS (1937) (w)Mack Gordon (m)Harry Revel. (I)Film: *Wake Up And Live*, by Buddy Clark dubbing for Jack Haley. (P)Bing Crosby with Jimmy Dorsey and his Orchestra. (CR)Mildred Bailey.

NEVER KNEW LOVE LIKE THIS BEFORE (1980) (wm)James Mtume— Reginald Lucas. (P)Stephanie Mills. NARAS Award Winner.

NEVER MY LOVE (1967) (wm)Don Addrisi—Dick Addrisi. (P)The Association. (CR)The Sandpebbles. (R)1971 by The 5th Dimension. (R)1974 by Blue Swede. (R)1977 by The Addrisi Brothers.

NEVER, NEVER GONNA GIVE YA UP (1973) (wm)Barry White. (P)Barry White.

NEVER-NEVER LAND (1954) (w)Betty Comden—Adolph Green (m)Jule Styne. (I)Musical: *Peter Pan*, by Mary Martin.

NEVER ON SUNDAY (1960) (w-Eng)Billy Towne (m)Mano Hadjadakis. (I)Film: *Never On Sunday*, by Melina Mercouri. (P)Don Costa and his Orchestra. Vocal version by The Chordettes. Academy Award Winner.

NEVER SAY "NO" (To A Man) (1962) (wm)Richard Rodgers. (I)Film: *State Fair*, by Alice Faye.

NEVER SURRENDER (1985) (wm)Corey Hart (P)Corey Hart.

NEVER THE LUCK (1986) (wm)Rupert Holmes. (I)Musical: *The Mystery Of Edwin Drood*, by Joe Grifasi. (P)Judy Collins.

NEVER WILL I MARRY (1960) (wm)Frank Loesser. (I)Musical: *Greenwillow*. by Anthony Perkins.

NEVERMORE (1934) (wm)Noel Coward. (I)London Musical: *Conversation Piece*, by Yvonne Printemps.

NEVERTHELESS (1931) (wm)Bert Kalmar—Harry Ruby. (P)Jack Denny and his Orchestra. (CR)Rudy Vallee. (R)1949 by The Mills Brothers. (R)1950 by Paul Weston and his Orchestra. (R)1950 by Frank Sinatra.

NEW ASHMOLEAN MARCHING SOCIETY AND STUDENTS CONSERVATORY BAND (1948) (wm)Frank Loesser. (I)Musical: *Where's Charley?*, by Byron Palmer, Allyn McLerie—Doretta Morrow—Bobby Harrell.

NEW ATTITUDE (1985) (wm)Sharon Robinson—Jonathan Gilutin—Bunny Hull. (P)Patti LaBelle.

NEW FANGLED TANGO, A (1956) (w)Matt Dubey (m)Harold Karr. (I)Musical: *Happy Hunting*, by Ethel Merman, Virginia Gibson, Leon Belasco, and The Chorus.

NEW GIRL IN TOWN (1976) (wm)Bob Merrick. (I)TV series: *Alice*, by voice of Linda Lavin on soundtrack.

NEW KID IN TOWN (1977) (wm)Glenn Frey—Don Henley—John David Souther. (P)The Eagles. No. 1 Chart Record.

NEW LOVE IS OLD, A (1931) (w)Otto Harbach (m)Jerome Kern. (I)Musical: *The Cat And The Fiddle*, by Georges Metaxa. In film version 1934 by Vivienne Segal and later reprised by Ramon Novarro and Jeanette MacDonald.

NEW MOON IS OVER MY SHOULDER, A (1934) (w)Arthur Freed (m)Nacio Herb Brown. (I)Film: *Student Tour*, by Phil Regan. (P)Phil Regan. (CR)Johnny Green and his Orchestra.

NEW MOON ON MONDAY (1984) (wm)Duran Duran. (P)Duran Duran.

NEW MORNING (1970) (wm)Bob Dylan. (P)Bob Dylan.

(Down In)NEW ORLEANS (1960) (wm)Frank J. Guida—Joseph F. Royster. (P)Gary "U. S. " Bonds.

NEW PAIR OF SHOES, A (1964) (wm)Ervin Drake. (I)Musical: *What Makes Sammy Run?*, by Steve Lawrence, Robert Alda, and The Ensemble.

NEW PRETTY BLONDE (New Jole Blon) (wm)Sidney Nathan—Moon Mullican. (P)Moon Mullican.

NEW SHADE OF BLUE, A (1948) (w)Ruth Poll (m)Andy Ackers—Johnny Farrow. (P)Billy Eckstine.

NEW SUN IN THE SKY (1931) (w)Howard Dietz (m)Arthur Schwartz. (I)Revue: *The Band Wagon*, by Fred Astaire. (R)1953: The Band Wagon, by India Adams dubbing for Cyd Charisse. (R)1949 Film: *Dancing In The Dark*, by Betsy Drake.

NEW TOWN IS A BLUE TOWN, A (1954) (wm)Richard Adler—Jerry Ross. (I)Musical: *The Pajama Game*, by John Raitt.

NEW WORLD MAN (1982) (w)Neil Peart (m)Alex Lifeson—Geddy Lee. (P)Rush.

NEW YORK GROOVE (1979) (wm)Russ Ballard. (P)Ace Frehley.

NEW YORK MINING DISASTER (1941) (wm)Barry, Maurice, and Robin Gibb. (P)The Bee Gees.

NEW YORK, NEW YORK (1945) (w)Betty Comden—Adolph Green (m)Leonard Bernstein. (I)Musical: *On The Town*, by John Battles, Cris Alexander, and Adolph Green.

NEW YORK, NEW YORK (Theme From) (1977) (wm)Fred Ebb—John Kander. (I)Film: *New York, New York*, by Liza Minnelli. (P)Frank Sinatra.

NEW YORK STATE OF MIND (1976) (wm)Billy Joel. (P)Billy Joel.

NEW YORK'S MY HOME (1946) (wm)Gordon Jenkins. (I)Manhattan Tower Suite: by Beverly Mahr.

NEXT DOOR TO AN ANGEL (1962) (wm)Howard Greenfield—Neil Sedaka. (P)Neil Sedaka.

NEXT PLANE TO LONDON (1967) (wm)Kenny Gist, Jr. (P)Rose Garden.

NEXT STEP IS LOVE, THE (1970) (wm)Paul Evans—Paul Parnes. (P)Elvis Presley.

NEXT TIME I FALL, THE (1986) (wm)Robert Caldwell—Paul Gordon. (P)Peter Cetera with Amy Grant. No. 1 Chart Record.

NEXT TIME IT HAPPENS, THE (1955) (w)Oscar Hammerstein II (m)Richard Rodgers. (I)Musical: *Pipe Dream*, by Judy Tyler and William Johnson.

NEXT TO YOUR MOTHER, WHO DO YOU LOVE? (1909) (w)Irving Berlin (m)Ted Snyder. One of the few songs for which Berlin did not write both words and music.

NICE 'N' EASY (1960) (w)Alan and Marilyn Bergman (m)Lew Spence. (P)Frank Sinatra.

NICE 'N' NASTY (1976) (m)Vincent Montana, Jr. (P)Salsoul Orchestra.

NICE TO BE WITH YOU (1972) (wm)Jim Gold. (P)Gallery.

NICE WORK IF YOU CAN GET IT (1937) (w)Ira Gershwin (m)George Gershwin. (I)Film: *A Damsel In Distress*, by Jan Duggan, Mary

Dea, Pearl Amatore, and Fred Astaire. (P)Fred Astaire. No. 1 Chart Record. (CR)The Andrews Sisters. (CR)Maxine Sullivan.

NIGHT (1960) (wm)Johnny Lehman—Herb Miller. Adapted from My Heart At Thy Sweet Voice, by Saint—Saens. (P)Jackie Wilson.

NIGHT AND DAY (1932) (wm)Cole Porter. (I)Musical: *Gay Divorcee*, by Fred Astaire and Claire Luce. (R)1934 Film: *The Gay Divorcee*, by Fred Astaire and Ginger Rogers. (R)1946 Film: *Night And Day*, by Cary Grant and Alexis Smith. Most popular recording by Frank Sinatra. (CR)Bing Crosby.

NIGHT BEFORE, THE (1965) (wm)John Lennon—Paul McCartney. (I)Film: *Help*, by The Beatles. (P)The Beatles.

NIGHT CHICAGO DIED, THE (1974) (wm)Peter Callendar—Lionel Stitcher. (P)Paper Lace. No. 1 Chart Record.

NIGHT FEVER (1977) (wm)Barry, Maurice and Robin Gibb. (I)Film: *Saturday Night Fever*, by The Bee Gees. (P)The Bee Gees. No. 1 Chart Record.

NIGHT HAS A THOUSAND EYES, THE (1948) (w)Buddy Bernier (m)Jerry Brainin. (I)Film: *The Night Has A Thousand Eyes*, on soundtrack. (R)1963 by Bobby Vee.

NIGHT IN TUNISIA,A (1944) (m)John Birks Gillespie—Frank Paparelli. (I)Earl Hines and his Orchestra. Recorded by Boyd Raeburn and his Orchestra. (P)Dizzy Gillespie.

NIGHT IS FILLED WITH MUSIC, THE (1938) (wm)Irving Berlin. (I)Film: *Carefree*: by Fred Astaire and Ginger Rogers. (P)Hal Kemp and his Orchestra.

NIGHT IS YOUNG AND YOU'RE SO BEAUTIFUL, THE (1936) (w)Billy Rose—Irving Kahal (m)Dana Suesse. (P)Jan Garber and his Orchestra. (CR)Wayne King and his Orchestra. (R)1951 by Ray Anthony and his Orchestra.

NIGHT LIGHTS (1956) (w)Sammy Gallop (m)Chester Conn. (P)Nat "King" Cole.

NIGHT MOVES (1977) (wm)Bob Seger. (P)Bob Seger.

NIGHT OF MY NIGHTS (1953) (wm)Robert Wright—George Forrest. Adapted from a theme by Borodin. (I)Musical: *Kismet*, by Richard Kiley.

NIGHT OWLS, THE (1981) (wm)Graham Goble. (P)Little River Band.

NIGHT SONG (1964) (w)Lee Adams (m)Charles Strouse. (I)Musical: *Golden Boy*, by Sammy Davis, Jr.

NIGHT THE LIGHTS WENT OUT IN GEORGIA, THE (1973) (wm)Bobby Russell. (P)Vickie Lawrence. No. 1 Chart Record.

NIGHT THEY DROVE OLD DIXIE DOWN, THE (1969) (wm)Jaime Robbie Robertson. (P)The Band. (R)1971 by Joan Baez.

NIGHT THEY INVENTED CHAMPAGNE, THE (1958) (w)Alan Jay Lerner (m)Frederick Loewe. (I)Film: *Gigi*, by Leslie Caron, Louis Jourdan, and Hermione Gingold.

NIGHT TIME (1966) (wm)Robert Feldman—Richard Gottehrer—Gerald Goldstein. (P)The Strangeloves.

NIGHT TRAIN (1952) (w)Oscar Washington—Lewis C. Simpkins (m)Jimmy Forrest. (P)Jimmy Forrest. (R)1960 by The Viscounts. (R)1961 by Richard Hayman. (R)1962 by James Brown.

NIGHT WALTZ (1973) (wm)Stephen Sondheim (I)Musical: *A Little Night Music*, by Glynnis Johns and Len Cariou.

NIGHT WAS MADE FOR LOVE, THE (1931) (w)Otto Harbach (m)Jerome Kern. (I)Musical: *The Cat And The Fiddle*, by George Meader. Film version 1934 by Ramon Novarro.

NIGHT WE CALLED IT A DAY, THE (1942) (w)Tom Adair (m)Matt Dennis. (P)Frank Sinatra.

NIGHTIE-NIGHT (1925) (w)Ira Gershwin (m)George Gershwin. (I)Musical: *Tip-Toes*, by Queenie Smith and Allen Kearns.

NIGHTINGALE (1942) (w-Eng)Fred Wise (m)Xavier Cugat—George Rosner. (P)Xavier Cugat and his Orchestra, vocal by Lina Romay.

NIGHTINGALE (1975) (wm)Carole King—David Palmer. (P)Carole King.

NIGHTINGALE SANG IN BERKELEY SQUARE,A (1940) (w)Eric Maschwitz (m)Manning

Sherwin. (I)London Revue: *New Faces*, by Judy Campbell. (P)Glenn Miller and his Orchestra.

NIGHTMARE (1937) (m)Artie Shaw. (P)Theme Song of Artie Shaw and his Orchestra.

NIGHTSHIFT (1985) (wm)Walter Orange—Dennis Lambert—Frannie Golde. (P)The Commodores. The song is a tribute to Sam Cooke, Jackie Wilson, and Marvin Gaye.

NIGHTS ARE FOREVER WITHOUT YOU (1976) (wm)Parker McGee. (P)England Dan & John Ford Coley.

NIGHTS IN WHITE SATIN (1972) (wm)Justin Hayward. (P)The Moody Blues.

NIGHTS ON BROADWAY (1975) (wm)Barry, Maurice, and Robin Gibb. (P)The Bee Gees.

NIKI HOEKY (1967) (wm)Pat Vegas—Lolly Vegas—Jim Ford. (P)P. J. Proby.

NIKITA (1986) (wm)Elton John—Bernie Taupin. (P)Elton John.

NINA (1948) (wm)Cole Porter. (I)Film: *The Pirate*, by Gene Kelly.

NINA NEVER KNEW (1952) (w)Milton Drake (m)Louis Alter. (P)The Sauter—Finegan Orchestra, vocal by Joe Mooney.

NINA, THE PINTA, THE SANTA MARIA, THE (1945) (w)Ira Gershwin (m)Kurt Weill. (I)Film: *Where Do We Go From Here?*

9 TO 5 (1981) (wm)Dolly Parton. (I)Film: *9 to 5* on soundtrack. (P)Dolly Parton. No. 1 Chart Record. NARAS Award Winner.

NINE TWENTY SPECIAL (1944) (w)Bill Engvick (m)Earl Warren. (P)Count Basie and his Orchestra.

19 (1985) (wm)Paul Hardcastle—W. Coutourie—J. McCord. (P)Paul Hardcastle.

19th NERVOUS BREAKDOWN (1966) (wm)Mick Jagger—Keith Richard. (P)The Rolling Stones.

98.6 (1966) (wm)Tony Powers—George Fischoff. (P)Keith.

99 (1979) (wm)David Paich. (P)Toto.

NINETY-NINE WAYS (1957) (wm)Anthony September. (P)Tab Hunter.

NINETY NINE YEARS (Dead Or Alive) (1956) (w)Sid Wayne (m)John Benson Brooks. (P)Guy Mitchell.

96 TEARS (1966) (wm)Rudy Martinez. (P)? and The Mysterians. No. 1 Chart Record. (CR)Big Maybelle.

NITTY GRITTY, THE (1963) (wm)Lincoln Chase. (P)Shirley Ellis. (R)1968 by Ricardo Ray. (R)1969 by Gladys Knight and The Pips.

NO ARMS CAN EVER HOLD YOU (Like These Arms Of Mine) (1955) (wm)Art Crafer—Jimmy Nebb. (P)Georgie Shaw (CR)Pat Boone. (R)1965 by The Bachelors. (R)1970 by Bobby Vinton.

NO CAN DO (1945) (w)Charles Tobias (m)Nat Simon. (P)Guy Lombardo and his Royal Canadians, vocal by Don Rodney and Rose Marie Lombardo.

NO CHEMISE, PLEASE! (1958) (wm)Gerry Granahan—Jodi D'Amour— Arnold Goland. (P)Gerry Granahan.

NO EXPECTATIONS (1968) (wm)Mick Jagger—Keith Richard. (P)The Rolling Stones.

(There Is)NO GREATER LOVE (1936) (w)Marty Symes (m)Isham Jones. (P)Isham Jones and his Orchestra.

NO LOVE (But Your Love) (1957) (wm)Billy Myles. (P)Johnny Mathis.

NO LOVE AT ALL (1971) (wm)Wayne Carson Thompson—Johnny Christopher. (P)B. J. Thomas.

NO LOVE, NO NOTHIN' (1953) (w)Leo Robin (m)Harry Warren. (I)Film: *The Gang's All Here*, by Alice Faye. (P)Johnny Long and his Orchestra, vocal by Patti Dugan. (CR)Ella Mae Morse. (CR)Jan Garber and his Orchestra.

NO MATTER WHAT (1970) (wm)William Peter Ham. (P)Badfinger.

NO MATTER WHAT SHAPE (Your Stomach's In) (1965) (wm)Sascha Burland. (P)The T-Bones.

NO MATTER WHAT SIGN YOU ARE (1969) (wm)Henry Cosby—Berry Gordy, Jr. (P)Diana Ross and The Supremes.

NO MOON AT ALL (1949) (wm)Redd Evans—Dave Mann. (P)The King Cole Trio. (CR)The Ames Brothers with Les Brown and his Orchestra.

(My Baby Don't Love Me)NO MORE (1955) (w)Julie De John—Dux De John (m)Leo J. De John. (P)The De John Sisters. (CR)The McGuire Sisters.

NO MORE (1964) (w)Lee Adams (m)Charles Strouse. (I)Musical: *Golden Boy*, by Sammy Davis Jr. , and The Company.

NO MORE LONELY NIGHTS (1984) (wm)Paul McCartney. (I)Film: *Give My Regards To Broad Street*, by Paul McCartney.

NO MORE LOVE (1933) (w)Al Dubin (m)Harry Warren. (I)Film: *Roman Scandals*, by Ruth Etting.

NO MORE TEARS (Enough Is Enough) (1979) (wm)Paul Jabara—Bruce Roberts. (P)Barbra Streisand and Donna Summer. No. 1 Chart Record.

NO NAME JIVE (1940) (m)Larry Wagner. (P)Glen Gray and The Casa Loma Orchestra.

NO NIGHT SO LONG (1980) (w)Will Jennings (m)Richard Kerr. (P)Dionne Warwick.

NO! NO! A THOUSAND TIMES NO! (1934) (wm)Al Sherman—Al Lewis— Abner Silver. Popular novelty song.

NO, NO, NANETTE (1924) (w)Otto Harbach (m)Vincent Youmans. (I)Musical: *No, No, Nanette*, by Louise Groody. (R)1950 Film: *Tea For Two*, by Doris Day and Gene Nelson.

NO NO SONG (1975) (wm)Hoyt Axton—David Jackson, Jr. (P)Ringo Starr.

NO NOT MUCH (1956) (w)Al Stillman (m)Robert Allen. (P)The Four Lads. (R)1969 by The Vogues.

NO ONE (1962) (wm)Doc Pomus—Mort Shuman. (P)Connie Francis. (R)1963 by Ray Charles. (R)1965 by Brenda Lee.

NO ONE IS TO BLAME (1985) (wm)Howard Jones. (P)Howard Jones.

NO ONE KNOWS (1958) (w)Ken Hecht (m)Ernie Maresca. (P)Dion and The Belmonts.

NO ORCHIDS FOR MY LADY (1948) (w)Alan Stranks (m)Jack Strachey. (P)Frank Sinatra.

NO OTHER ARMS, NO OTHER LIPS (1959) (wm)Joan Whitney—Alex Kramer—Hy Zaret. (P)The Chordettes. (CR)The Four Aces.

NO OTHER LOVE (1953) (w)Oscar Hammerstein II (m)Richard Rodgers. Adapted from Rodgers' Victory At Sea. (I)Musical: *Me And Juliet*, by Isabel Bigley and Bill Hayes. (P)Perry Como.

NO REGRETS (1936) (w)Harry Tobias (m)Roy Ingraham. (P)Glen Gray and The Casa Loma Orchestra. (CR)Tommy Dorsey and his Orchestra. (CR)Billie Holiday.

NO REPLY (1965) (wm)John Lennon—Paul McCartney. (P)The Beatles.

NO STRINGS (I'm Fancy Free) (1935) (wm)Irving Berlin. (I)Film: *Top Hat*, by Fred Astaire.

NO STRINGS (1962) (wm)Richard Rodgers. (I)Musical: *No Strings*, by Diahann Carroll and Richard Kiley.

NO TELL LOVER (1979) (wm)Peter Cetera—Lee Loughname—Daniel Seraphine. (P)Chicago.

NO TIME (1970) (wm)Randy Bachman—Burt Cummings. (P)The Guess Who.

NO TWO PEOPLE (1951) (wm)Frank Loesser. (I)Film: *Hans Christian Andersen*, by Danny Kaye and Jane Wyman. (P)Doris Day and Donald O'Connor.

NO WAY OUT (1984) (wm)Peter Wolf—Ina Wolf. (P)Jefferson Starship.

NOBODY (1905) (w)Alex Rogers (m)Bert Williams. (P)Bert Williams.

NOBODY (1982) (wm)Kye Fleming—Dennis W. Morgan. (P)Sylvia.

NOBODY BUT ME (1968) (wm)Rudolph Isley—O'Kelly Isley. (P)Human Beinz.

NOBODY BUT YOU (1919) (w)B. G. De Sylva (m)George Gershwin. (I)Musical: *La La Lucille*.

NOBODY BUT YOU (1958) (wm)Dee Clark. (P)Dee Clark.

NOBODY DOES IT BETTER (1977) (w)Carole Bayer Sager (m)Marvin Hamlisch. (I)Film: *The Spy Who Loved Me*, by the voice of Carly Simon. (P)Carly Simon.

NOBODY ELSE BUT ME (1946) (w)Oscar Hammerstein II (m)Jerome Kern. (I)Revival Musical: *Show Boat*, by Jan Clayton.

NOBODY I KNOW (1964) (wm)John Lennon—Paul McCartney. (P)Peter and Gordon.

NOBODY KNOWS AND NOBODY SEEMS TO CARE (1919) (wm)Irving Berlin. Not one of Berlin's better known songs.

NOBODY KNOWS DE TROUBLE I'VE SEEN (1865) (wm)Unknown. Traditional Black American spiritual.

NOBODY KNOWS YOU WHEN YOU'RE DOWN AND OUT (1923) (wm)Jimmie Cox. (I)Vaudeville:, by Jimmie Cox. (P)Bobby Baker. (R)1929 by Bessie Smith.

NOBODY MAKES A PASS AT ME (1937) (wm)Harold Rome (I)Revue: *Pins And Needles*, by Millie Weitz.

NOBODY SAID IT WAS EASY (1982) (wm)Tony Haseldon. (P)Le Roux.

NOBODY TOLD ME (1962) (wm)Richard Rodgers. (I)Musical: *No Strings*, by Diahann Carroll and Richard Kiley.

NOBODY TOLD ME (1984) (wm)John Lennon. (P)John Lennon.

NOBODY'S CHASING ME (1950) (wm)Cole Porter. (I)Musical: *Out Of This World*, by Charlotte Greenwood. (P)Dinah Shore.

NOBODY'S DARLIN' BUT MINE (1935) (wm)Jimmie Davis. (P)Jimmie Davis. (R)1949 by Bing Crosby.

NOBODY'S FOOL (1987) (wm)T. Keifer. (P)Cinderella.

NOBODY'S HEART (Belongs To Me) (1942) (w)Lorenz Hart (m)Richard Rodgers. (I)Musical: *By Jupiter*, by Constance Moore and later reprised by Ray Bolger.

NOBODY'S SWEETHEART (1923) (wm)Gus Kahn— Ernie Erdman—Billy Meyers—Elmer Schoebel. (I)Revue: *The Passing Show of 1923*, by Ted Lewis. (P)Isham Jones and his Orchestra. (R)1928 by Red Nichols and his Orchestra. (R)1931 by Cab Calloway. (R)1932 by The Mills Brothers. (R)1944 Film: *Atlantic City*, by Belle Baker. (R)1951 Film: *I'll See You In My Dreams*, by Doris Day.

NOCTURNE (Op. 9 No. 2) (1832) (m)Frederic Chopin. One of Chopin's most popular Nocturnes.

NOLA (1916) (m)Felix Arndt. (P)Theme Song of Vincent Lopez and his Orchestra.

NON DIMENTICAR (1952) (w-Eng)Shelley Dobbins. (m)P. G. Redi. (P)Nat "King" Cole.

NON-STOP FLIGHT (1939) (m)Artie Shaw. (P)Artie Shaw and his Orchestra.

NONE BUT THE LONELY HEART (1869) (m)Peter I. Tchaikovsky. Famous classical song.

NOODLIN' RAG (1952) (w)Allan Roberts (m)Robert Allen. (P)Perry Como.

NORMAL AMERICAN BOY (1960) (w)Lee Adams (m)Charles Strouse. (I)Musical: *Bye Bye Birdie*, by Dick Van Dyke, Chita Rivera and The Chorus.

NORMAN (1962) (wm)John D. Loudermilk. (P)Sue Thompson.

NORTH TO ALASKA (1960) (wm)Mike Phillips. (I)Film: *North To Alaska*, by Johnny Horton. (P)Johnny Horton.

NORTHWEST PASSAGE (1945) (m)Ralph Burns— Woody Herman—G. S. Jackson. (P)Woody Herman and his Orchestra.

NORWEGIAN DANCE (1881) (m)Edvard Grieg. Famous classical composition.

NORWEGIAN WOOD (1965) (wm)John Lennon—Paul McCartney. (P)The Beatles.

NOT A DAY GOES BY (1981) (wm)Stephen Sondheim. (I)Musical: *Merrily We Roll Along*, by Jim Walton.

NOT A SECOND TIME (1964) (wm)John Lennon—Paul McCartney. (P)The Beatles.

NOT AS A STRANGER (1955) (w)Buddy Kaye (m)Jimmy Van Heusen. (I)Film: *Not As A Stranger*, on soundtrack. (P)Frank Sinatra. (CR)Tony Bennett.

NOT FADE AWAY (1957) (wm)Buddy Holly—Norman Petty. (P)Buddy Holly. (R)1964 by The Rolling Stones.

NOT FOR ALL THE RICE IN CHINA (1933) (wm)Irving Berlin. (I)Revue: *As Thousands Cheer*, by Marilyn Miller, Clifton Webb, and The Ensemble. (R)1946 Film: *Blue Skies*, by Bing Crosby.

NOT ME (1960) (wm)Gary Anderson—Frank Guida. (P)Gary "U. S. " Bonds. (R)1963 by The Orlons.

NOT SINCE NINEVAH (1953) (wm)Robert Wright (m)George Forrest. Adapted from a theme by Borodin. (I)Musical: *Kismet*, by Joan Diener.

NOT THE LOVIN' KIND (1965) (wm)Lee Hazlewood. (P)Dino, Desi, and Billy.

NOT WHILE I'M AROUND (1978) (wm)Stephen Sondheim. (I)Musical: *Sweeney Todd*, by Angela Lansbury and Ken Jenning.

NOTHIN' AT ALL (1986) (wm)Mark Mueller. (P)Heart.

NOTHING (1975) (w)Edward Kleban (m)Marvin Hamlisch. (I)Musical: *A Chorus Line*.

NOTHING BUT HEARTACHES (1965) (wm)Eddie Holland—Lamont Dozier— Brian Holland. (P)The Supremes.

NOTHING BUT YOU (1940) (w)Lorenz Hart (m)Richard Rodgers. (I)Musical: *Higher And Higher*, by Marta Eggert, Leif Erickson, and The Singers.

NOTHING CAN STOP ME (1965) (wm)Curtis Mayfield. (P)Gene Chandler.

NOTHING CAN STOP ME NOW (1965) (wm)Leslie Bricusse—Anthony Newley. (I)Musical: *The Roar Of The Greasepaint—The Smell Of The Crowd*, by Anthony Newley.

NOTHING FROM NOTHING (1974) (wm)Billy Preston— Bruce Fisher. (P)Billy Preston. No. 1 Chart Record.

NOTHING IN COMMON (1958) (w)Sammy Cahn (m)Jimmy Van Heusen. (I)Film: *Paris Holiday*, by Bing Crosby and Bob Hope.

NOTHING WAS DELIVERED (1968) (wm)Bob Dylan. (P)The Byrds. (R)1975 by Bob Dylan.

NOTHING'S GONNA CHANGE MY LOVE FOR YOU (1987) (wm)Michael Masser—Gerry Goffin. (P)Glenn Medeiros.

NOTHING'S GONNA STOP US NOW (1987) (wm)D. Warren—Albert Hammond. (P)Starship. No. 1 Chart Record.

NOTHING'S TOO GOOD FOR MY BABY (1966) (wm)Sylvia Moy—Henry Cosby—William Stevenson. (P)Stevie Wonder.

NOTORIOUS (1987) (wm)John Taylor—Nick Rhodes— Simon LeBon. (P)Duran Duran.

NOW (1944) (wm)Robert Wright—George Forrest. Adapted from a melody by Grieg. (I)Operetta: *Song Of Norway*, by Kitty Carlisle and The Chorus.

NOW AND FOREVER (1941) (w)Al Stillman (m)Jan Savitt. Adapted from Tchaikovsky's Symphony No. 6. (P)Jan Savitt and his Orchestra. (R)1946 by Freddy Martin and his Orchestra.

NOW I HAVE EVERYTHING (1964) (w)Sheldon Harnick (m)Jerry Bock. (I)Musical: *Fiddler On The Roof*, by Bert Convy and Julia Migenes.

NOW I KNOW (1943) (w)Ted Koehler (m)Harold Arlen. (I)Film: *Up In Arms*, by Dinah Shore. (P)Dinah Shore.

NOW IS THE HOUR (Maori Farewell Song) (1946) (wm)Maewa Kaihan— Dorothy Stewart—Clement Scott. (I)Gracie Fields. (P)Bing Crosby. No. 1 Chart Record. (CR)Margaret Whiting. (CR)Buddy Clark. (CR)Kate Smith.

NOW IT CAN BE TOLD (1938) (wm)Irving Berlin. (I)Film: *Alexander's Ragtime Band*, by Don Ameche and later reprised by Alice Faye. (P)Bing Crosby. (CR)Tommy Dorsey and his Orchestra.

(Where Are You)NOW THAT I NEED YOU (1949) (wm)Frank Loesser. (I)Film: *Red, Hot, And Blue*, by Betty Hutton. (P)Doris Day. (CR)Frankie Laine.

NOW THAT YOU'VE GONE (1931) (w)Gus Kahn (m)Ted

Fiorito. (P)Guy Lombardo and his Royal Canadians. (CR)Ruth Etting.

NOW YOU HAS JAZZ (1956) (wm)Cole Porter. (I)Film: *High Society,* by Bing Crosby and Louis Armstrong.

NOWHERE MAN (1966) (wm)John Lennon—Paul McCartney. (P)The Beatles. Sung in Film: *Yellow Submarine* (1968)by The Beatles.

NOWHERE TO RUN (1965) (wm)Brian Holland—Lamont Dozier—Eddie Holland. (P)Martha and The Vandellas.

NOW'S THE TIME (1945) (m)Charlie Parker. (P)Charlie Parker, with Dizzy Gillespie, Miles Davis, Curly Russell, and Max Roach.

NOW'S THE TIME TO FALL IN LOVE (Potatoes Are Cheaper—Tomatoes Are Cheaper) (1931) (wm)Al Sherman—Al Lewis. (P)Eddie Cantor.

#9 DREAM (1975) (wm)John Lennon. (P)John Lennon.

NUTBUSH CITY LIMITS (1973) (wm)Tina Turner. (P)Ike & Tina Turner. (CR)Bob Seger.

NUTCRACKER SUITE (1892) (m)Peter I. Tchaikovsky. Famous Christmas ballet. In Disney Film: *Fantasia.*

NUTTIN' FOR CHRISTMAS (1955) (wm)Sid Tepper—Roy C. Bennett. (P)Barry Gordon with Art Mooney and his Orchestra. (CR)Joe Ward. (CR)The Fontane Sisters. (CR)Stan Freberg.

N. Y. C. (1977) (w)Martin Charnin (m)Charles Strouse. (I)Musical: *Annie,* by Dorothy Loudon and The Ensemble.

O COME ALL YE FAITHFUL (Adeste Fidelis) (1782) (w-Latin)John Francis Wade (w-Eng)Frederick Oakeley. (m)John Francis Wade. Famous Christmas Hymn.

O DIO MIO (1960) (wm)Al Hoffman—Dick Manning. (P)Annette.

O, KATHARINA! (1922) (w-Eng)L. Wolfe Gilbert (m)Richard Fall. (I)Revue: *Balieff's Chauve—Souris*. (P)Ted Lewis. (CR)Vincent Lopez and his Orchestra.

O LITTLE TOWN OF BETHLEHEM (1868) (w)Phillips Brooks (m)Lewis H. Redner. Famous Christmas Song.

O-O-H CHILD (1970) (wm)Stan Vincent. (P)The Five Stairsteps.

O SOLO MIO (1899) (w)Giovanni Capurro (m)Edorado di Capua. (P)Enrico Caruso. (See: There's No Tomorrow. Also, It's Now Or Never).

OBSESSION (1985 (wm)Holly Knight—Michael Desbarres. (P)Animotion.

OB-LA-DI, OB-LA-DA (1968) (wm)John Lennon—Paul McCartney. (P)The Beatles. (CR)Arthur Conley.

OBJECT OF MY AFFECTION, THE (1934) (wm)Pinky Tomlin—Coy Poe— Jimmy Grier. (P)Pinky Tomlin with Jimmy Grier and his Orchestra. (CR)The Boswell Sisters. (CR)Jan Garber and his Orchestra.

OBVIOUSLY FIVE BELIEVERS (1966) (wm)Bob Dylan. (P)Bob Dylan.

OCARINA, THE (Dance To The Music Of) (1930) (wm)Irving Berlin. (I)Musical: *Call Me Madam*, by Galina Talva.

OCCIDENTAL WOMAN (1936) (wm)Gene Austin. (I)Film: *Klondike Annie*, by Mae West.

OCTOPUS'S GARDEN (1969) (wm)Ringo Starr. (P)The Beatles.

ODD COUPLE, THE (Theme) (1968) (w)Sammy Cahn (m)Neal Hefti. (I)Film: *The Odd Couple* as soundtrack theme. Also on TV series.

ODDS AND ENDS (Of A Beautiful Love Affair) (1969) (w)Hal David (m)Burt Bacharach. (P)Dionne Warwick.

ODE TO BILLIE JOE (1967) (wm)Bobbie Gentry. (P)Bobbie Gentry. (CR)The Kingpins. (CR)Ray Bryant.

OF THEE I SING (1931) (w)Ira Gershwin (m)George Gershwin. (I)Musical: *Of Thee I Sing*, by William Gaxton and Lois Moran.

OFF SHORE (1953) (w)Steve Graham (m)Leo Diamond. (P)Leo Diamond. (CR)Richard Hayman.

OFF THE WALL (1980) (wm)Rod Temperton. (P)Michael Jackson.

OH BABE! (1950) (wm)Louis Prima—Milton Kabak. (P)Louis Prima and his Orchestra. (CR)Kay Starr. (CR)The Ames Brothers.

OH BABE, WHAT WOULD YOU SAY (1973) (wm)E. B. Smith. (P)Hurricane Smith.

OH, BABY MINE (I Get So Lonely) (1954) (wm)Pat Ballard. (P)The Four Knights.

OH BESS, OH WHERE'S MY BESS (1935) (w)Du Bose Heyward—Ira Gershwin (m)George Gershwin. (I)Opera: *Porgy And Bess*, by Todd Duncan.

OH BOY (1957) (wm)Buddy Holly—Norman Petty. (P)The Crickets.

OH BURY ME NOT ON THE LONE PRAIRIE (1849) (w)E. H. Chapin (m)George N. Allen. Traditional American cowboy song.

OH BY JINGO, OH BY GEE, YOU'RE THE ONLY GIRL FOR ME (1919) (w)Lew Brown (m)Albert Von Tilzer. (I)Musical: *Linger Longer, Letty*.

OH! CAROL (1959) (w)Howard Greenfield (m)Neil Sedaka. (P)Neil Sedaka.

OH! DARLING (1969) (wm)John Lennon—Paul McCartney. (P)The Beatles. (R)1978 by Robin Gibb.

OH, DIOGENES! (1938) (w)Lorenz Hart (m)Richard Rodgers. (I)Musical: *The Boys From Syracuse*, by Marcy Westcott.

OH, DONNA CLARA (1931) (w-Eng)Irving Caesar (m)J. Peterburski. (I)Musical: *The Wonder Bar*, by Al Jolson.

OH! GEE, OH! GOSH, OH! GOLLY, I'M IN LOVE (1923) (wm)Ole Olsen— Chick Johnson—Ernest Breuer. (P)Olsen and Johnson. (CR)Eddie Cantor.

OH GEE! OH JOY! (1928) (w)P. G. Wodehouse—Ira Gershwin (m)George Gershwin. (I)Musical: *Rosalie*, by Marilyn Miller and Jack Donahue.

OH GIRL (1971) (wm)Eugene Record. (P)The Chi—Lites. No. 1 Chart Record.

OH, HAPPY DAY (1952) (wm)Don Howard Koplow—Nancy Binns Reed. (P)Don Howard. (CR)Lawrence Welk and his Orchestra.

OH HOW HAPPY (1966) (wm)Charles Hatcher. (P)Shades Of Blue. (R)1969 by Edwin Starr and Blinky.

OH, HOW I HATE TO GET UP IN THE MORNING (1918) (wm)Irving Berlin. (I)World War I Revue: *Yip Yip Yaphank*.

OH HOW I LONG TO BELONG TO YOU (1932) (w)B. G. De Sylva (m)Vincent Youmans. (I)Musical: *Take A Chance*, by June Knight and Jack Whiting.

OH, HOW I MISS YOU TONIGHT (1925) (wm)Benny Davis—Joe Burke— Mark Fisher. (I)Vaudeville: By Benny Davis. (P)Ben Selvin and his Orchestra. (CR)The Benson Orchestra of Chicago.

OH JOHNNY, OH JOHNNY OH! (1917) (w)Ed Rose (m)Abe Olman. (I)Musical: *Follow Me*. (R)1940 by Orrin Tucker and his Orchestra, vocal by Bonnie Baker.

OH JULIE (1957) (wm)Kenneth R. Moffitt—Noel Ball. (CR)Sammy Salvo.

OH LADY, BE GOOD (1924) (w)Ira Gershwin (m)George Gershwin. (I)Musical: *Lady, Be Good!*, by Walter Catlett. (P)Paul Whiteman and his Orchestra. (CR)Cliff Edwards. (R)1941 Film: *Lady, Be Good*, by Ann Sothern, Robert Young, Red Skelton, and John Carroll. (R)1945 Film: *Rhapsody In Blue*, by Joan Leslie.

OH, LONESOME ME (1958) (wm)Don Gibson. (P)Don Gibson. (R)1961 by Johnny Cash.

OH! LOOK AT ME NOW! (1941) (w)John De Vries (m)Joe Bushkin. (P)Tommy Dorsey and his Orchestra, vocal by Frank Sinatra, Connie Haines, and The Pied Pipers.

OH! MA-MA (The Butcher Boy) (1938) (w-Eng)Lew Brown—Rudy Vallee. (m)Paolo Citorello. (P)Rudy Vallee and his Connecticut Yankees. (CR)The Andrews Sisters. (CR)Dick Robertson.

OH ME! OH MY! (1921) (wm)Arthur Francis (Ira Gershwin)-Vincent Youmans. (I)Musical: *Two Little Girls In Blue*. (R)1950 Film: *Tea For Two*, by Doris Day and Gene Nelson. (R)1953 Film: *So This Is Love*, by Kathryn Grayson.

OH ME OH MY (I'm A Fool For You, Baby) (1970) (wm)Jim Doris. (P)Lulu. (R)1973 by Aretha Franklin.

OH, MY GOODNESS! (1936) (w)Mack Gordon (m)Harry Revel. (I)Film: *Poor Little Rich Girl*, by Shirley Temple.

OH! MY PA-PA (1953) (w-Eng)John Turner—Geoffrey Parsons. (m)Paul Burkhard. (P)Instrumentally, by Eddie Calvert and his Orchestra. Vocal version, by Eddie Fisher. No. 1 Chart Record.

OH NO (1981) (wm)Lionel Richie. (P)The Commodores.

OH! NO, NOT MY BABY (1964) (wm)Gerry Goffin—Carole King. (P)Maxine Brown. (R)1973 by Rod Stewart. (R)1973 by Merry Clayton.

OH, OH, I'M FALLING IN LOVE AGAIN (1958) (wm)Al Hoffman—Dick Manning—Hugo Peretti—Luigi Creatore. (P)Jimmie Rodgers.

OH PRETTY WOMAN (1964) (wm)Roy Orbison—Bill Dees. (P)Roy Orbison. No. 1 Chart Record.

OH PROMISE ME (1890) (w)Clement Scott (M)Reginald De Koven. Famous song, usually performed at weddings.

OH SHEILA (1985) (wm)Mel Riley—Gordon Strozier—Gerald Valentine. (P)Ready For The World. No. 1 Chart Record.

OH, SHERRIE (1984) (wm)Steve Perry—Randy Goodrum—Bill Cuomo— Craig Krampf. (P)Steve Perry.

OH! SUSANNA (1848) (wm)Stephen Collins Foster. One of Foster's most popular songs.

OH, THAT BEAUTIFUL RAG (1910) (w)Irving Berlin (m)Ted Snyder. (I)Musical: *Up And Down Broadway*.

OH VERY YOUNG (1974) (wm)Cat Stevens. (P)Cat Stevens.

OH WELL (1970) (wm)Peter Green. (P)Fleetwood Mac. (R)1979 by The Rockets.

OH, WHAT A BEAUTIFUL MORNIN' (1943) (w)Oscar Hammerstein II (m)Richard Rodgers. (I)Musical: *Oklahoma!*, by Alfred Drake. (R)1955 Film: *Oklahoma!*, by Gordon MacRae. Most popular recording by Bing Crosby.

OH, WHAT A NIGHT (1956) (wm)Marvin Junior—John Funches. (P)The Dells. (R)1969 by The Dells.

OH WHAT A NIGHT FOR DANCING (1978) (wm)Barry White—Vance Wilson. (P)Barry White.

OH! WHAT A PAL WAS MARY (1919) (w)Edgar Leslie (m)Pete Wendling. (P)Henry Burr.

OH! WHAT IT SEEMED TO BE (1945) (wm)Bennie Benjamin—George Weiss—Frankie Carle. (P)Frankie Carle and his Orchestra. No. 1 Chart Record. (CR)Frank Sinatra. (CR)Helen Forrest and Dick Haymes.

OH YEAH (1966) (wm)Ellas McDaniel. (P)The Shadows Of Night.

OH YOU BEAUTIFUL DOLL (1911) (w)A. Seymour Brown (m)Nat D. Ayer. (P)The American Quartet.

OH, YOU CRAZY MOON (1939) (w)Johnny Burke (m)Jimmy Van Heusen. The first song they wrote together. (P)Tommy Dorsey and his Orchestra.

OHIO (1953) (w)Betty Comden—Adolph Green (m)Leonard Bernstein. (I)Musical: *On The Town*, by Rosalind Russell and Edith Adams.

OHIO (1970) (wm)Neil Young. (P)Crosby, Stills, Nash, and Young.

OKLAHOMA (1943) (w)Oscar Hammerstein II (m)Richard Rodgers. (I)Musical: *Oklahoma!*, by Alfred Drake, Joan Roberts, Betty Garde, Barry Kelley, Edwin Clay, and The Ensemble. (R)Film: *Oklahoma*, by Gordon MacRae, Charlotte Greenwood, James Whitmore, Shirley Jones, Jay C. Flippen, and The Chorus.

RICHARD RODGERS

It was the custom of Decca Records always to send a copy of a finished record to the songwriter. This was the practice for all songwriters, the little known and the famous. Whenever Richard Rodgers would receive a record of one of his songs, he would write the artist, the arranger, etc., thanking them and stating how much he enjoyed that particular version of the song.

OL' MAN MOSE (1938) (wm)Louis Armstrong—Zilner Randolph. (I)Louis Armstrong. (P)Eddy Duchin and his Orchestra, vocal by Patricia Norman.

OLD BLACK JOE (1860) (wm)Stephen Collins Foster. One of Foster's most popular songs.

OLD BROWN SHOE (1969) (wm)George Harrison. (P)The Beatles.

OLD CAPE COD (1956) (wm)Claire Rothrock—Milt Yakus—Allan Jeffrey. (P)Patti Page.

OLD CHISHOLM TRAIL, THE (1880) (wm)Unknown. Traditional American cowboy song.

OLD DAYS (1975) (wm)James Pankow. (P)Chicago.

OLD DEVIL MOON (1947) (w)E. Y. Harburg (m)Burton Lane. (I)Musical: *Finian's Rainbow*, by Ella Logan and Donald Richards.

OLD DOG TRAY (1853) (wm)Stephen Collins Foster. One of Foster's most popular songs.

OLD-FASHION LOVE (1980) (wm)Milan Williams. (P)The Commodores.

OLD FASHIONED GARDEN (1919) (wm)Cole Porter. (I)Revue: *Hitchy-Koo of 1919*, by Charles Howard and Joe Cook.

(There's Something About An)OLD FASHIONED GIRL (1930) (w)B. G. De Sylva—Lew Brown (m)Ray Henderson. (I)Film: *Just Imagine*, by John Garrick.

OLD FASHIONED LOVE SONG, AN (1971) (wm)Paul Williams (P)Three Dog Night.

OLD FASHIONED TUNE IS ALWAYS NEW, AN (1939) (wm)Irving Berlin. (I)Film: *Second Fiddle*, by Rudy Vallee.

OLD FOLKS (1938) (w)Dedette Lee Hill (m)Willard Robison. (P)Mildred Bailey. (CR)Larry Clinton and his Orchestra.

OLD FOLKS AT HOME (Way Down Upon The Swanee River) (1851) (wm)Stephen Collins Foster. First recording in 1892 by Len Spencer. (R)1936 by Jimmie Lunceford and his Orchestra. (R)1945 by Tommy Dorsey and his Orchestra.

OLD LAMP-LIGHTER, THE (1946) (w)Charles Tobias (m)Nat Simon. (P)Sammy Kaye and his Orchestra, vocal by Billy Williams. No. 1 Chart Record. (CR)Morton Downey. (CR)Kenny Baker.

OLD MACDONALD HAD A FARM (1917) (wm)Unknown. Traditional children's song.

OLD MAN (1972) (wm)Neil Young. (P)Neil Young.

OLD MAN AND THE SEA, THE (1958) (m)Dimitri Tiomkin. (I)Film: *The Old Man And The Sea*, as soundtrack theme.

OLD MAN DOWN THE ROAD, THE (1985) (wm)John Fogarty. (P)John Fogarty.

OLD MAN HARLEM (1933) (wm)Rudy Vallee—Hoagy Carmichael. (P)Rudy Vallee. (CR)Dorsey Brothers Orchestra.

OLD MAN OF THE MOUNTAIN, THE (1932) (w)Billy Hill (m)Victor Young. (P)The Boswell Sisters.

OLD MASTER PAINTER, THE (1949) (w)Haven Gillespie (m)Beasley Smith. (P)Richard Hayes. (CR)Snooky Lanson.

OLD OAKEN BUCKET, THE (1843) (w)Samuel Woodworth (m)George Kiallmark. First recording in 1894 by The Manhassett Quartet.

OLD PIANO ROLL BLUES, THE (1949) (wm)Cy Coben. (P)Lawrence Cook. (CR)Hoagy Carmichael and Cass Daley. (CR)Eddie Cantor and Lisa Kirk.

OLD REFRAIN, THE (1915) (m)Fritz Kreisler. Famous solo violin selection. (P)Fritz Kreisler.

OLD RIVERS (1962) (wm)Cliff Crofford. (P)Walter Brennan.

OLD RUGGED CROSS, THE (1913) (wm)Rev. George Bennard. One of the most popular Protestant hymns.

OLD SOFT SHOE, THE (1946) (w)Nancy Hamilton (m)Morgan Lewis. (I)Revue: Three To Make Ready, by Ray Bolger.

OLD SOLDIERS NEVER DIE (1951) (wm)Tom Glazer. (P)Vaughn Monroe.

OLD SONGS,THE (1980) (wm)David Pomeranz—Buddy Kaye. (I)David Pomeranz. (P)Barry Manilow.

OLD SPINNING WHEEL, THE (1933) (wm)Billy Hill. (P)Theme Song of Mary Small. (CR)Ray Noble and his Orchestra.

OLD TIME ROCK AND ROLL (1983) (wm)George Jackson—Tom Jones III. (I)Film: Risky Business, on soundtrack. (P)Bob Seger and The Silver Bullet Band.

OLDEST ESTABLISHED, THE (1950) (wm)Frank Loesser. (I)Musical: Guys And Dolls, by Sam Levene, Stubby Kaye, Johnny Silver, and The Ensemble.

OLE BUTTERMILK SKY (1946) (wm)Hoagy Carmichael—Jack Brooks. (I)Film: Canyon Passage, by Hoagy Carmichael. (P)Kay Kyser and his Orchestra. No. 1 Chart Record. (CR)Connee Boswell. (CR)Paul Weston and his Orchestra.

OLE FAITHFUL (1934) (wm)Michael Carr—Joseph Hamilton Kennedy. (P)The Original Hillbillies. (CR)Gene Autry.

OL' MAN RIVER (1927) (w)Oscar Hammerstein II (m)Jerome Kern. (I)Musical: Show Boat, by Jules Bledsoe and The Chorus. (P)Paul Robeson with Paul Whiteman and his Orchestra. Film version 1929 by Jules Bledsoe. Film version 1936 by Paul Robeson. Film version 1951 by William Warfield. Film: Till The Clouds Roll By (1946)by Caleb Peterson and reprised by Frank Sinatra.

ON A CAROUSEL (1967) (wm)Graham Nash—Tony Hicks—Allan Clarke. (P)The Hollies. (R)1982 by Glass Moon.

ON A CLEAR DAY (You Can See Forever) (1966) (w)Alan Jay Lerner (m)Burton Lane. (I)Musical: On A Clear Day You Can See Forever, by John Cullum. Film version (1970) by Yves Montand and reprised by Barbra Streisand.

ON A DESERT ISLAND WITH THEE (1927) (w)Lorenz Hart (m)Richard Rodgers. (I)Musical: A Connecticut Yankee, by Jack Thompson and June Cochran.

ON A LITTLE STREET IN SINGAPORE (1938) (w)Billy Hill (m)Peter De Rose. (P)Frank Sinatra with Harry James and his Orchestra. (CR)Jimmy Dorsey and his Orchestra.

ON A NIGHT LIKE THIS (1974) (wm)Bob Dylan. (P)Bob Dylan.

ON A ROOF IN MANHATTAN (1932) (wm)Irving Berlin. (I)Revue: Face The Music, by J. Harold Murray and Katherine Carrington.

ON A SLOW BOAT TO CHINA (1948) (wm)Frank Loesser. (P)Kay Kyser and his Orchestra, vocal by Harry Babbitt and Gloria Wood. (CR)Freddy Martin and his Orchestra. (CR)Benny Goodman and his Orchestra.

ON A SUNDAY AFTERNOON (1936) (w)Arthur Freed (m)Nacio Herb brown. (I)Film: Broadway Melody of 1936, by Vilma and Buddy Ebsen.

ON AND ON (1974) (wm)Curtis Mayfield. (I)Film: Claudine, on soundtrack. (P)Gladys Knight & The Pips.

ON AND ON (1977) (wm)Stephen Bishop. (P)Stephen Bishop.

ON AND ON AND ON (1933) (w)Ira Gershwin (m)George Gershwin. (I)Musical: Let 'Em Eat Cake, by the Chorus.

ON BEHALF OF THE VISITING FIREMEN (1940) (w)Johnny Mercer (m)Walter Donaldson. (P)Bing Crosby and Johnny Mercer.

ON BROADWAY (1963) (wm)Barry Mann—Cynthia Weil—Jerry Leiber— Mike Stoller. (P)The Drifters. (R)1978 by George Benson.

ON GREEN DOLPHIN STREET (1947) (w)Ned Washington (m)Bronislau Kaper. Adaptation of theme from Film: Green Dolphin Street. (P)Jimmy Dorsey and his Orchestra.

ON MY OWN (1986) (wm)Carole Bayer Sager—Burt Bacharach. (P)Patti LaBelle—Michael McDonald. No. 1 Chart Record.

ON REVIVAL DAY (1931) (wm)Andy Razaf. (P)Bessie Smith.

ON THE ALAMO (1922) (w)Gus Kahn—Joe Lyons (m)Isham Jones. (P)Isham Jones and his Orchestra. (R)1954 by The Norman Petty Trio.

ON THE ATCHISON, TOPEKA, AND THE SANTA FE (1946) (w)Johnny Mercer (m)Harry Warren. Academy Award Winner. (I)Film: The Harvey Girls, by Judy Garland and The Ensemble. (P)Johnny Mercer and The Pied Pipers. No. 1 Chart Record. (CR)Bing Crosby. (CR)Tommy Dorsey and his Orchestra.

ON THE BEACH AT BALI-BALI (1936) (wm)Al Sherman—Jack Meskill— Abner Silver. (P)Connee Boswell. (CR)Shep Fields and his Orchestra.

ON THE BEACH AT WAIKIKI (1915) (w)G. H. Stover (m)Henry Kailimaie. (I)Musical: The Bird Of Paradise.

ON THE BOARDWALK AT ATLANTIC CITY (1946) (w)Mack Gordon (m)Josef Myrow. (I)Film: Three Little Girls In Blue, by Vera—Ellen, June Haver, and Vivian Blaine. (P)Dick Haymes. (CR)The Charioteers.

ON THE BUMPY ROAD TO LOVE (1938) (wm)Al Hoffman—Al Lewis— Murray Mencher. (I)Film: Listen, Darling, by Judy Garland.

ON THE DARK SIDE (1982) (wm)John Cafferty. (I)Film: Eddie And The Cruisers, on soundtrack. (P)John

Cafferty & The Beaver Brown Band.

ON THE GOOD SHIP LOLLIPOP (1934) (wm)Sidney Clare—Richard A. Whiting. (I)Film: *Bright Eyes*, by Shirley Temple. (P)Shirley Temple. (R)1949 Film: *You're My Everything*, by Dan Dailey and Shari Robinson.

ON THE ISLE OF MAY (1940) (w)Mack David (m)Andre Kostelanetz. Adapted from Tchaikovsky's Andante Cantabile. (P)Connee Boswell. (CR)Dick Jurgens and his Orchestra.

ON THE MALL (1923) (m)Edwin Franko Goldman. Very popular American march.

ON THE OLD PARK BENCH (1940) (w)Howard Dietz (m)Jimmy McHugh. (I)Musical: *Keep Off The Grass*, by Jackie Gleason and Larry Adler.

ON THE RADIO (1980) (w)Donna Summer (m)Giorgio Moroder. (P)Donna Summer.

ON THE REBOUND (1961) (wm)Floyd Cramer. (P)Floyd Cramer.

ON THE ROAD AGAIN (1965) (wm)Bob Dylan. (P)Bob Dylan.

ON THE ROAD AGAIN (1968) (wm)Allen Wilson—Floyd Jones. (P)Canned Heat.

ON THE ROAD AGAIN (1980) (wm)Willie Nelson. (I)Film: *Honeysuckle Rose*, on soundtrack. (P)Willie Nelson. NARAS Award Winner.

ON THE ROAD TO MANDALAY (1907) (w)Rudyard Kipling (m)Oley Speaks. (I)Frank Croxton.

ON THE SENTIMENTAL SIDE (1938) (w)Johnny Burke (m)James V. Monaco. (I)Film: *Doctor Rhythm*, by Bing Crosby and Mary Carlisle. (P)Bing Crosby.

ON THE STREET WHERE YOU LIVE (1956) (w)Alan Jay Lerner (m)Frederick Loewe. (I)Musical: *My Fair Lady*, by Michael King. (P)Vic Damone.

ON THE SUNNY SIDE OF THE STREET (1930) (w)Dorothy Fields (m)Jimmy McHugh. (I)Revue: *Lew Leslie's International Revue*, by Harry Richman. (CR)Ted Lewis. (R)1945 by Tommy Dorsey and his Orchestra. (R)1951 Film: *On The Sunny Side Of The Street*, by Frankie Laine. (R)1956 Film: *The Benny Goodman Story*, by Benny Goodman and his Orchestra.

ON THE TRAIL (1933) (w)Harold Adamson (m)Ferde Grofe. From Grofe's Grand Canyon Suite. (P)Paul Whiteman and his Orchestra. (R)1948 by Sy Oliver and his Orchestra.

ON THE TWENTIETH CENTURY (1978) (w)Betty Comden—Adolph Green (m)Cy Coleman. (I)Musical: *On The Twentieth Century*, by John Cullum, Imogene Coca, and The Cast.

ON THE WINGS OF LOVE (1980) (wm)Peter Schless—Jeffrey Osborne. (P)Jeffrey Osborne.

ON THE WRONG SIDE OF THE RAILROAD TRACK (1947) (w)John Latouche (m)Duke Ellington. (I)Musical: *Beggar's Holiday*, by Marie Bryant, Avon Long, and Bill Dillard.

ON TOP OF OLD SMOKEY (1951) (wm)Pete Seeger. Adaptation of folk song. (P)The Weavers with Gordon Jenkins and his Orchestra.

ON TOP OF SPAGHETTI (1963) (wm)Tom Glazer. Adaptation of On Top Of Old Smokey. (P)Burl Ives.

ON TREASURE ISLAND (1935) (w)Edgar Leslie (m)Joe Burke. (P)Tommy Dorsey and his Orchestra. No. 1 Chart Record. (CR)Bing Crosby. (CR)Little Jack Little and his Orchestra.

ON WINGS OF SONG (1837) (m)Felix Mendelssohn.

Famous classical composition.

ON WITH THE DANCE (1920) (w)Clifford Grey (m)Jerome Kern. (I)Musical: *Sally*, by Mary Hay and Walter Catlett.

ON YOUR TOES (1936) (w)Lorenz Hart (m)Richard Rodgers. (I)Musical: *On Your Toes*, by Ray Bolger, Doris Carson, and David Morris. (P)Ruby Newman and his Orchestra.

ONCE AND FOR ALWAYS (1949) (w)Johnny Burke (m)Jimmy Van Heusen. (I)Film: *A Connecticut Yankee*, by Bing Crosby. (P)Bing Crosby. (CR)Jo Stafford.

ONCE IN A BLUE MOON (1923) (w)Anne Caldwell (m)Jerome Kern. (I)Musical: *Stepping Stones*, by Roy Hoyer, Evelyn Herbert, John Lambert, Lilyan and Ruth White.

ONCE IN A BLUE MOON (1934) (w)Mack Gordon (m)Harry Revel. (I)Film: *We're Not Dressing*, by Bing Crosby. (P)Bing Crosby.

ONCE IN A LIFETIME (1962) (wm)Leslie Bricusse—Anthony Newley. (I)Musical: *Stop The World—I Want To Get Off*, by Anthony Newley.

ONCE IN AWHILE (1937) (w)Bud Green (m)Michael Edwards. (P)Tommy Dorsey and his Orchestra, vocal by Jack Leonard. (CR)Louis Armstrong. (CR)Patti Page.

ONCE IN LOVE WITH AMY (1948) (wm)Frank Loesser. (I)Musical: *Where's Charley?*, by Ray Bolger. (P)Ray Bolger.

ONCE KNEW A FELLA (1959) (wm)Harold Rome. (I)Musical: *Destry Rides Again*, by Andy Griffith.

ONCE TOO OFTEN (1944) (w)Mack Gordon (m)James V. Monaco. (I)Film: *Pin Up Girl*, by Betty Grable with Charlie Spivak and his Orchestra. (P)Ella Fitzgerald.

ONCE UPON A TIME (1962) (w)Lee Adams (m)Charles Strouse. (I)Musical: *All American*, by Ray Bolger and Eileen Herlie.

ONCE UPON A TIME TODAY (1950) (wm)Irving Berlin. (I)Musical: *Call Me Madam*, by Ethel Merman.

ONCE YOU GET STARTED (1975) (wm)Gavin Wright. (P)Rufus, featuring Chaka Khan.

ONE (1969) (wm)Harry Nilsson. (P)Three Dog Night.

ONE (1975) (w)Edward Kleban (m)Marvin Hamlisch. (I)Musical: *A Chorus Line*, by The Company.

ONE ALONE (1926) (w)Otto Harbach—Oscar Hammerstein II (m)Sigmund Romberg. (I)Operetta: *The Desert Song*, by Robert Halliday. In 1929 film version, by John Boles. In 1943 film version, by Dennis Morgan and Irene Manning. In 1953 film version, by Gordon MacRae and Kathryn Grayson.

ONE BAD APPLE (Don't Spoil The Whole Bunch) (1971) (wm)George Jackson. (P)The Osmonds. No. 1 Chart Record.

ONE BIG UNION FOR TWO (1937) (wm)Harold Rome. (I)Revue: *Pins And Needles*, by The Ensemble.

ONE BOY (1960) (w)Lee Adams (m)Charles Strouse. (I)Musical: *Bye Bye Birdie*, by Susan Watson, Jessica Albright, Sharon Lerit, and Chita Rivera. In 1963 film version, by Ann-Margret, Janet Leigh, and Bobby Rydell.

ONE BROKEN HEART FOR SALE (1963) (wm)Otis Blackwell—Winfield Scott. (I)Film: *It Happened At The World's Fair*, on soundtrack. (P)Elvis Presley.

ONE DAY AT A TIME (1975) (wm)Jeff Barry—Nancy Barry. (I)TV series: *One Day At A Time*, by Polly Cutter, Cynthia Bullens, Valerie Carter, Fred Freeman, and Harry Nehls.

ONE DOZEN ROSES (1942) (wm)Roger Lewis—Country Washburn—Dick Jurgens—Walter Donovan. (P)Dick Jurgens and his Orchestra. (CR)Dinah Shore. (CR)Harry James and his Orchestra.

ONE EYED JACKS (Love Theme) (1961) (m)Hugo Friedhofer. (I)Film: One Eyed Jacks, as soundtrack theme. (P)Ferrante and Teicher.

ONE FINE DAY (Un Bel Di) (1904) (w)Luigi Illica—Giuseppe Giacosa (m)Giacomo Puccini. (I)Opera: Madame Butterfly.

ONE FINE DAY (1963) (wm)Gerry Goffin—Carole King. (P)The Chiffons. (R)1976 by Julie. (R)1979 by Rita Coolidge. (R)1980 by Carole King.

ONE FINE MORNING (1971) (wm)Skip Prokop. (P)Lighthouse.

ONE FOR MY BABY (And One More For The Road) (1943) (w)Johnny Mercer (m)Harold Arlen. (I)Film: The Sky's The Limit, by Fred Astaire. (P)Fred Astaire. Most popular recording by Frank Sinatra.

ONE HAND, ONE HEART (1957) (w)Stephen Sondheim (m)Leonard Bernstein. (I)Musical: West Side Story, by Larry Kert and Carol Lawrence.

ONE HAS MY NAME. . . THE OTHER HAS MY HEART (1948) (wm)Eddie Dean— Dearest Dean—Hal Blair. (P)Jimmy Wakely. (R)1965 by Barry Young. (R)1969 by Jerry Lee Lewis.

ONE HEARTBEAT (1987) (wm)S. Legassick—B. Ray. (P)Smokey Robinson.

ONE HELL OF A WOMAN (1974) (wm)Mac Davis—Mark James. (P)Mac Davis.

(I'd Love To Spend)ONE HOUR WITH YOU (1932) (w)Leo Robin (m)Richard A. Whiting. (I)Film: One Hour With You, by Maurice Chevalier, Jeanette MacDonald, Donald Novis, Charlie Ruggles, and Genevieve Tobin. (P)Maurice Chevalier. Closing theme of Eddie Cantor's radio show.

ONE HUNDRED WAYS (1982) (wm)Kathy Wakefield—Benjamin Wright— Tony Coleman. (P)James Ingram with Quincy Jones and his Orchestra.

ONE I LOVE, THE (1987) (wm)Berry—Buck—Mills—Stipe. (P)R. E. M.

ONE I LOVE BELONGS TO SOMEBODY ELSE, THE (1924) (w)Gus Kahn (m)Isham Jones. (P)Isham Jones and his Orchestra. (CR)Al Jolson. (CR)Sophie Tucker. (R)1938 by Tommy Dorsey and his Orchestra. (R)1957 Film: The Helen Morgan Story, by Gogi Grant dubbing for Ann Blyth.

ONE IN A MILLION YOU (1980) (wm)Sam Dees. (P)Larry Graham. (CR)Johnny Lee.

ONE KISS (1928) (w)Oscar Hammerstein II (m)Sigmund Romberg. (I)Operetta: The New Moon, by Evelyn Herbert. 1930 film version, by Grace Moore. 1940 film version, by Jeanette MacDonald.

ONE KISS FOR OLD TIMES' SAKE (1965) (w)Artie Resnick—Kenny Young. (P)Ronnie Dove.

ONE LAST KISS (1960) (w)Lee Adams (m)Charles Strouse. (I)Musical: Bye Bye Birdie, by Dick Gautier and The Company. 1963 film version, by Jesse Pearson.

ONE LESS BELL TO ANSWER (1970) (w)Hal David (m)Burt Bacharach. (P)The 5th Dimension, featuring Marilyn McCoo.

ONE LIFE TO LIVE (1941) (w)Ira Gershwin (m)Kurt Weill. (I)Musical: Lady In The Dark, by Gertrude Lawrence and Danny Kaye.

ONE LITTLE CANDLE (1952) (w)James Maloy Roach (m)George Mysels. (P)Perry Como.

ONE LONELY NIGHT (1985) (wm)Neal Doughty. (P)REO Speedwagon.

ONE LOVE IN MY LIFETIME (1976) (wm)Larry Brown—Theresa McFaddin—Leonard Perry. (P)Diana Ross.

ONE MAN BAND (1970) (wm)Billy Fox—Tommy Kaye—January Tyme. (P)Three Dog Night.

ONE MAN WOMAN/ONE MAN MAN (1975) (wm)Paul Anka. (P)Paul Anka with Odia Coates.

ONE MEAT BALL (1944) (wm)Hy Zaret—Lou Singer. (I)Josh White. (P)The Andrews Sisters.

ONE MINT JULEP (1952) (wm)Rudolph Toombs. (P)The Clovers. (CR)Louis Prima. (CR)Buddy Morrow and his Orchestra. (R)1961 by Ray Charles.

ONE MINUTE TO ONE (1933) (w)Sam M. Lewis (m)J. Fred Coots. (P)Harry Richman. Theme song of Gray Gordon and his Orchestra.

ONE MOMENT ALONE (1931) (w)Otto Harbach (m)Jerome Kern. (I)Musical: The Cat And The Fiddle, by Georges Metaxa. 1934 film version, by Ramon Novarro and Jeanette MacDonald.

ONE MONKEY DON'T STOP NO SHOW (1971) (wm)General Johnson—Greg S. Perry. (P)Honey Cone.

ONE MORE DANCE (1932) (w)Oscar Hammersetin II (m)Jerome Kern. (I)Musical: Music In The Air, by Tullio Carminati.

ONE MORE HEARTACHE (1966) (wm)William Robinson—Ronald White— Warren Moore—Robert Rogers—Marvin Tarplin. (P)Marvin Gaye.

ONE MORE HOUR (1981) (wm)Randy Newman. (I)Film: Ragtime, by Jennifer Warnes. (P)Jennifer Warnes.

ONE MORE NIGHT (1969) (wm)Bob Dylan. (P)Bob Dylan.

ONE MORE NIGHT (1985) (wm)Phil Collins. (P)Phil Collins. No. 1 Chart Record.

ONE MORNING IN MAY (1933) (w)Mitchell Parish (m)Hoagy Carmichael. (P)Hoagy Carmichael.

ONE NATION UNDER A GROOVE (1978) (wm)George Clinton—Gary Shider—Walter Morrison. (P)Funkadelic.

ONE NEVER KNOWS, DOES ONE? (1936) (w)Mack Gordon (m)Harry Revel. (I)Film: Stowaway, by Alice Faye.

ONE NIGHT (1958) (wm)Dave Bartholomew—Pearl King. (P)Elvis Presley.

ONE NIGHT IN BANGKOK (1985) (wm)Benny Andersson—Tim Rice—Bjorn Ulvaeus. (P)Murray Head. (CR)Robey.

ONE NIGHT OF LOVE (1934) (w)Gus Kahn (m)Victor Schertzinger. (I)Film: One Night Of Love, by Grace Moore. (P)Grace Moore.

ONE NIGHT LOVE AFFAIR (1985) (wm)Bryan Adams—Jim Vallance. (P)Bryan Adams.

ONE NIGHT ONLY (1981) (w)Tom Eyen (m)Henry Krieger. (I)Musical: Dreamgirls, by Jennifer Holliday and Vondee Curtis Hall. (CR)Sylvester.

ONE NOTE SAMBA (1961) (w-Eng)Jon Hendricks (m)Antonio Carlos Jobim. (P)Joao Gilberto. (CR)Pat Thomas. (CR)Herbie Mann with Antonio Carlos Jobim.

ONE O' CLOCK JUMP (1938) (m)William Basie. (P)Theme song of Count Basie and his Orchestra. (CR)Benny Goodman and his Orchestra. (CR)Metronome All Star Band.

ONE OF A KIND (Love Affair) (1973) (wm)Joseph B. Jefferson. (P)The Spinners.

ONE OF THE BOYS (1981) (w)Fred Ebb (m)John Kander. (I)Musical: *Woman Of The Year*, by Lauren Bacall.

ONE OF THE LIVING (1985) (wm)Holly Knight. (I)Film: *Mad Max Beyond Thunderdome*, by Tina Turner. (P)Tina Turner.

ONE OF THESE NIGHTS (1975) (wm)Glenn Frey—Don Henley. (P)The Eagles. No. 1 Chart Record.

ONE OF US (Will Weep Tonight) (1960) (wm)Clint Ballard, Jr. - Fred Tobias. (P)Patti Page.

ONE OF US MUST KNOW (1066) (wm)Bob Dylan. (P)Bob Dylan.

ONE ON ONE (1983) (wm)Daryl Hall. (P)Hall and Oates.

ONE PIECE AT A TIME (1976) (wm)Wayne Kemp. (P)Johnny Cash.

ONE ROSE, THE (That's Left In My Heart) (1936) (wm)Del Lyon— Lani McIntire. (P)Bing Crosby. (CR)Larry Clinton and his Orchestra.

ONE SONG (1937) (w)Larry Morey (m)Frank Churchill. (I)Cartoon film: *Snow White And The Seven Dwarfs*, by the voice of Harry Stockwell as the Prince.

ONE STEP UP (1987) (wm)Bruce Springsteen. (P)Bruce Springsteen.

ONE SUMMER NIGHT (1958) (wm)Danny Webb. (P)The Dandleers. (R)1961 by The Diamonds.

ONE SWEET LETTER FROM YOU (1927) (w)Lew Brown—Sidney Clare (m)Harry Warren. (P)Sophie Tucker. (CR)Kate Smith. (CR)Gene Austin.

ONE THAT YOU LOVE, THE (1981) (wm)Graham Russell. (P)Air Supply. No. 1 Chart Record.

1432 FRANKLIN PIKE CIRCLE HERO (1968) (wm)Bobby Russell. (P)Bobby Russell.

ONE THING LEADS TO ANOTHER (1983) (wm)Cy Curnin—Adam Woods— Jamie West—Oram—Rupert Greenall—Alfred Agius. (P)The Fixx.

ONE TIN SOLDIER (1969) (wm)Dennis Lambert—Brian Potter. (P)Original Caste. (R)1971 by Coven.

1999 (1983) (wm)Prince Rogers Nelson. (P)Prince.

ONE TRICK PONY (1980) (wm)Paul Simon. (I)Film: *One Trick Pony*, by Paul Simon. (P)Paul Simon.

ONE, TWO, BUTTON YOUR SHOE (1936) (w)Johnny Burke (m)Arthur Johnston. (I)Film: *Pennies from Heaven*, by Bing Crosby. (P)Bing Crosby. (CR)Shep Fields and his Orchestra.

ONE, TWO, THREE (1-2-3) (1965) (wm)John Madara—David White— Leonard Borisoff—Brian Holland—Lamont Dozier—Eddie Holland. (P)Len Barry. (R)1967 by Ramsey Lewis.

ONE-TWO-THREE-KICK (1939) (w)Al Stillman (m)Xavier Cugat. (P)Xavier Cugat and his Orchestra.

1,2,3, RED LIGHT (1968) (wm)Sal Trimachi—Bobbi Trimachi. (P)The 1910 Fruitgum Company.

ONE WAY OR ANOTHER (1979) (wm)Nigel Harrison—Deborah Harry. (P)Blondie.

ONE WHO REALLY LOVES YOU, THE (1962) (wm)William Robinson. (P)Mary Wells.

ONE YOU LOVE, THE (1980) (wm)Glenn Frey—Jack Tempchin. (P)Glenn Frey.

ONLY A NORTHERN SONG (1968) (wm)George Harrison. (I)Film: *Yellow Submarine*, by The Beatles. (P)The Beatles.

ONLY A PAWN IN THEIR GAME (1963) (wm)Bob Dylan. (P)Bob Dylan.

ONLY A ROSE (1925) (w)Brian Hooker (m)Rudolf Friml. (I)Operetta: *The Vagabond King*, by Carolyn Thomson and Dennis King. 1950 film version, by Jeanette MacDonald and Dennis King. (R)1953 by Bette McLaurin.

ONLY DANCE I KNOW, THE (Song For Belly Dancer) (1962) (wm)Irving Berlin. (I)Musical: *Mr. President*, by Wisa D'Orso.

ONLY FOR AMERICANS (1949) (wm)Irving Berlin. (I)Musical: *Miss Liberty*, by Eddie Albert and Ethel Griffies.

ONLY FOREVER (1940) (w)Johnny Burke (m)James V. Monaco. (I)Film: *Rhythm On The River*, by Bing Crosby. (P)Bing Crosby. No. 1 Chart Record. (CR)Tommy Dorsey and his Orchestra.

ONLY IN AMERICA (1963) (wm)Jerry Leiber—Cynthia Weil—Mike Stoller—Barry Mann. (P)Jay and The Americans.

ONLY IN MY DREAMS (1987) (wm)Debbie Gibson. (P)Debbie Gibson.

ONLY LOVE CAN BREAK A HEART (1962) (w)Hal David (m)Burt Bacharach. (R)1967 by Margaret Whiting. (R)1967 by Bobby Vinton.

ONLY LOVE IS REAL (1976) (wm)Carole King. (P)Carole King.

ONLY ONE, THE (1963) (w)Anne Croswell (m)Lee Pockriss. (I)Musical: *Tovarich*, by Vivien Leigh.

ONLY SIXTEEN (1959) (wm)Sam Cooke. (P)Sam Cooke. (R)1975 by Dr. Hook.

ONLY THE GOOD DIE YOUNG (1978) (wm)Billy Joel. (P)Billy Joel.

ONLY THE LONELY (1958) (w)Sammy Cahn (m)Jimmy Van Heusen. (P)Frank Sinatra.

ONLY THE LONELY (Know The Way I Feel) (1960) (wm)Roy Orbison— Joe Melson. (P)Roy Orbison. (R)1969 by Sonny James.

ONLY THE LONELY (1982) (wm)Martha Davis. (P)The Motels.

ONLY THE STRONG SURVIVE (1969) (wm)Kenny Gamble—Leon Huff— Jerry Butler. (P)Jerry Butler.

ONLY THE YOUNG (1985) (wm)Steve Perry—Jonathan Cain—Neal Schon. (P)Journey.

ONLY TIME WILL TELL (1982) (wm)John Wwtton—Geoffrey Downes. (P)Asia.

ONLY WOMEN (Bleed) (1975) (wm)Alice Cooper—Dick Wagner. (P)Alice Cooper.

ONLY YESTERDAY (1975) (wm)John Bettis—Richard Carpenter. (P)The Carpenters.

ONLY YOU (1955) (wm)Buck Ram—Ande Rand. (P)The Platters. (CR)The Hilltoppers. (R)1959 by Franck Pourcel's French Fiddles. (R)1963 by Mr. Acker Bilk. (R)1975 by Ringo Starr.

ONLY YOU KNOW AND I KNOW (1970) (wm)Dave Mason. (P)Dave Mason. (R)1971 by Delaney and Bonnie.

ONWARD CHRISTIAN SOLDIERS (1871) (w)Sabine Baring (m)Sir Arthur Sullivan.

OODLES OF NOODLES (1933) (m)Jimmy Dorsey. (P)The Dorsey Brothers Orchestra. Became the composition: Contrasts, which was the theme song of Jimmy Dorsey and his Orchestra.

OOH BABY BABY (1965) (wm)William Robinson—Warren Moore. (P)The Miracles. (R)1967 by The Five Stairsteps. (R)1979 by Linda Ronstadt.

OOH THAT KISS (1931) (w)Mort Dixon—Joe Young (m)Harry Warren. (I)Revue: *The Laugh Parade*, by Lawrence Gray, Jeanne Aubert and The Ensemble.

(P)The Dorsey Borthers Orchestra.

OOH! WHAT YOU SAID (1940) (w)Johnny Mercer (m)Hoagy Carmichael. (I)Musical: *Walk With Music*, by Mitzi Green and The Modernaires.

OOOH! LOOK-A-THERE,AIN'T SHE PRETTY? (1933) (wm)Clarence Todd— Carmen Lombardo. (P)Guy Lombardo and his Royal Canadians. (CR)Buddy Greco.

OOP BOP SH-BAM (1946) (m)Walter Fuller—Jay Roberts—John Birks Gillespie. (P)Dizzy Gillespie and his Orchestra.

OOP SHOOP (1954) (wm)Joe Josea. (P)The Crew Cuts. (CR)Helen Grayco.

OPEN A NEW WINDOW (1966) (wm)Jerry Herman. (I)Musical: *Mame*, by Angela Lansbury and The Company.

OPEN ARMS (1982) (wm)Steve Perry—Jonathan Cain. (P)Journey.

OPEN LETTER TO MY TEENAGE SON, AN (1967) (wm)Robert Tompson. (P)Victor Lundberg.

OPEN THE DOOR, RICHARD! (1947) (w)Dusty Fletcher—John Mason (m)Jack McVea—Don Howell. (I)Jack McVea. (P)Louis Jordan and his Tympani Five. (CR)Count Basie and his Orchestra. (CR)The Pied Pipers.

OPEN THE DOOR TO YOUR HEART (1966) (wm)Darrell Banks—Donnie Elbert. (P)Darrell Banks.

OPEN UP YOUR HEART (1955) (wm)Stuart Hamblen. (P)The Cowboy Church Sunday School Choir. (CR)Bing Crosby.

OPEN YOUR HEART (1986) (wm)Madonna—Gardner Cole—Peter Rafelson. (P)Madonna. No. 1 Chart Record.

OPERATOR (1975) (wm)William Spivey. (P)Manhattan Transfer.

OPERATOR (1985) (wm)Boaz Watson—Vincent Calloway—Belinda Lipscomb—Reggie Calloway. (P)Midnight Star.

OPPORTUNITIES (Let's Make Lots Of Money) (1986) (wm)Nick Tennant—Chris Lowe. (P)The Pet Shop Boys.

OPUS ONE (1945) (w)Sid Garris (m)Sy Oliver. (P)Tommy Dorsey and his Orchestra.

OPUS 17 (Don't Worry 'Bout Me) (1966) (wm)Denny Randall—Sandy Linzer. (P)The Four Seasons.

ORANGE COLORED SKY (1950) (wm)Milton De Lugg— Willie Stein. (P)Nat "King" Cole, with Stan Kenton and his Orchestra. (CR)Betty Hutton. (CR)Jerry Lester.

ORANGE GROVE IN CALIFORNIA, AN (1923) (wm)Irving Berlin. (I)Revue: *Music Box Revue of 1923*, by Grace Moore and John Steel.

ORCHID TO YOU, AN (1933) (wm)Mack Gordon—Harry Revel. (P)Eddy Duchin and his Orchestra. Song was dedicated to columnist Walter Winchell.

ORCHIDS FOR REMEMBRANCE (1940) (w)Mitchell Parish (m)Peter De Rose. (P)Eddy Howard.

ORCHIDS IN THE MOONLIGHT (1933) (w)Gus Kahn (m)Vincent Youmans. (I)Film: *Flying Down To Rio*, by Raul Roulien, and danced by Fred Astaire and Dolores Del Rio. (P)Rudy Vallee and his Connecticut Yankees. (CR)Enric Madriguera and his Orchestra.

ORGAN GRINDER'S SWING (1936) (w)Mitchell Parish— Irving Mills (m)Will Hudson. (I)The Hudson—De Lange Orchestra. (P)Chick Webb and his Orchestra, vocal by Ella Fitzgerald. (CR)Jimmie Lunceford and

his Orchestra.

ORIGINAL DIXIELAND ONE STEP (1918) (wm)Joe Jordan—James D. La Rocca—J. Russel Robinson. (P)The Original Dixieland Jazz Band.

ORNITHOLOGY (1946) (m)Charlie Parker—Benny Harris. (P)The Charlie Parker Septet.

ORTHODOX FOOL, AN (1962) (wm)Richard Rodgers. (I)Musical: *No Strings*, by Diahann Carroll.

OTHER GUY, THE (1983) (wm)Graham Goble. (P)Little River Band.

OTHER MAN'S GRASS IS ALWAYS GREENER, THE (1967) (wm)Tony Hatch— Jackie Trent. (P)Petula Clark.

OTHER SIDE OF THE TRACKS, THE (1962) (w)Carolyn Leigh (m)Cy Coleman. (I)Musical: *Little Me*, by Virginia Martin.

OTHER WOMAN, THE (1982) (wm)Ray Parker, Jr. (P)Ray Parker, Jr.

OUR BIG LOVE SCENE (1933) (w)Arthur Freed (m)Nacio Herb Brown. (I)Film: *Going Hollywood*, by Bing Crosby. (P)Bing Crosby.

OUR CHILDREN (1962) (w)Lee Adams (m)Charles Strouse. (I)Musical: *All American*, by Ray Bolger and Eileen Herlie.

OUR DAY WILL COME (1963) (w)Mort Garson (m)Bob Hilliard. (P)Ruby and The Romantics. No. 1 Chart Record. (R)1975 by Frankie Valli.

OUR DIRECTOR (1926) (m)F. E. Bigelow. Famous American march.

OUR HOUSE (1970) (wm)Graham Nash. (P)Crosby, Stills, Nash, and Young.

OUR HOUSE (1983) (wm)Charles Smyth—Chris Foreman. (P)Madness.

OUR LADY OF FATIMA (1950) (wm)Gladys Gollahon. (P)Kitty Kallen and Richard Hayes. (CR)Red Foley.

OUR LIPS ARE SEALED (1981) (wm)Jane Weidlin— Terry Hill. (P)The Go—Gos.

OUR LOVE (1939) (wm)Larry Clinton—Buddy Bernier— Bob Emmerich. Adapted from Tchaikovsky's Romeo And Juliet. (P)Larry Clinton and his orchestra. (CR)Tommy Dorsey and his Orchestra.

OUR LOVE (1978) (wm)Charles Jackson, Jr. -Marvin Yancy. (P)Natalie Cole.

OUR LOVE AFFAIR (1940) (wm)Arthur Freed—Roger Edens. (I)Film: *Strike Up The Band*, by Judy Garland and Mickey Rooney. (P)Tommy Dorsey and his Orchestra. (CR)Glenn Miller and his Orchestra.

OUR PRIVATE WORLD (1978) (w)Betty Comden— Adolph Green (m)Cy Coleman. (I)Musical: *On The Twentieth Century*, by John Cullum and Madeline Kahn.

OUR SONG (1937) (w)Dorothy Fields (m)Jerome Kern. (I)Film: *When You're In Love*, by Grace Moore.

OUR TIME (1981) (wm)Stephen Sondheim. (I)Musical: *Merrily We Roll Along*, by Jim Walton, Lonny Price, and Ann Morrison.

OUR WALTZ (1943) (w)Nat Burton (m)David Rose. (P)Theme song of David Rose's radio show.

OUR WINTER LOVE (1963) (w)Bob Tubert (m)John Cowell. (P)Bill Pursell.

OURS (1936) (wm)Cole Porter. (I)Musical: *Red, Hot And Blue*, by Dorothy Vernon, Thurston Crane, and The Hartmans.

OUT HERE ON MY OWN (1980) (wm)Michael Gore— Leslie Gore. (I)Film: *Fame*, by Irene Cara. (P)Irene Cara.

OUT IN THE COLD AGAIN (1934) (w)Ted Koehler (m)Rube Bloom. (P)Ruth Etting. (CR)Glen Gray and The Casa Loma Orchestra.

OUT IN THE COUNTRY (1970) (w)Paul Williams (m)Roger Nichols. (P)Three Dog Night.

OUT OF LIMITS (1963) (wm)Michael Z. Gordon. (P)The Marketts.

OUT OF MY DREAMS (1943) (w)Oscar Hammerstein II (m)Richard Rodgers. (I)Musical: *Oklahoma!*, by Joan Roberts and The Girls' Chorus. 1955 film version, by Shirley Jones and The Girl's Chorus.

OUT OF NOWHERE (1931) (w)Edward Heyman (m)John Green. (P)Bing Crosby. No. 1 Chart Record. (CR)Guy Lombardo and his Royal Canadians. (CR)Leo Reisman and his Orchestra.

OUT OF SIGHT, OUT OF MIND (1956) (wm)Ivory Joe Hunter—Clyde Otis. (P)The Five Keys. (R)1964 by Sunny & The Sunliners. (R)1969 by Little Anthony & The Imperials.

OUT OF SPACE (1934) (wm)Joe Bishop—Gene Gifford—Winston C. Tharp. (P)Jan Savitt and his Orchestra. (R)1939 by Glenn Miller and his Orchestra.

OUT OF THE BLUE (1987) (wm)D. Gibson. (P)Debbie Gibson.

OUT OF THE QUESTION (1973) (wm)Raymond O'-Sullivan. (P)Gilbert O'Sullivan.

OUT OF THIS WORLD (1945) (w)Johnny Mercer (m)Harold Arlen. (I)Film: *Out Of This World*, by the voice of Bing Crosby.

OUT OF TIME (1966) (wm)Mick Jagger—Keith Richard. (P)The Rolling Stones.

OUT OF TOUCH (1984) (wm)Daryl Hall—John Oates. (P)Hall and Oates. No. 1 Chart Record.

OUT OF WORK (1982) (wm)Bruce Springsteen. (P)Gary U. S. Bonds.

OUTA-SPACE (1972) (wm)Billy Preston—Joe Greene. (P)Billy Preston.

OUTLAW BLUES (1965) (wm)Bob Dylan. (P)Bob Dylan.

OUTSIDE OF HEAVEN (1952) (w)Sammy Gallop (m)Chester Conn. (P)Eddie Fisher.

OUTSIDE OF THAT I LOVE YOU (1940) (wm)Irving Berlin. (I)Musical: *Louisiana Purchase*, by William Gaxton and Zorina.

OVER AND OVER (1959) (wm)Robert Byrd. (P)Bobby Day. (R)1964 by The Dave Clark Five. No. 1 Chart Record.

OVER AND OVER AGAIN (1935) (w)Lorenz Hart (m)Richard Rodgers. (I)Musical: *Billy Rose's Jumbo*, by Bob Lawrence and Henderson's Singing Razorbacks. (R)1962 film: *Jumbo*, by Doris Day and The Chorus.

OVER MY HEAD (1976) (wm)Christine McVie. (P)Fleetwood Mac.

OVER SOMEBODY ELSE'S SHOULDER (1934) (wm)Al Lewis—Al Sherman. (P)Ozzie Nelson and his Orchestra. (CR)Isham Jones and his Orchestra.

OVER THE MOUNTAIN, ACROSS THE SEA (1957) (wm)Rex Garvin. (P)Johnnie and Joe. (R)1963 by Bobby Vinton.

OVER THE RAINBOW (1939) (w)E. Y. Harburg (m)Harold Arlen. (I)Film: *The Wizard Of Oz*, by Judy Garland. (P)Judy Garland. Academy Award Winner. (CR)Glenn Miller and his Orchestra. (CR)Bob Crosby and his Orchestra.

OVER THE WAVES (1888) (m)Juventino Rosas. Famous semi— classical waltz composition.

OVER THERE (1917) (wm)George M. Cohan. (I)George M. Cohan. (CR)Enrico Caruso. (CR)Nora Bayes. (R)1942 film: *Yankee Doodle Dandy*, by James Cagney.

OVER UNDER SIDEWAYS DOWN (1966) (wm)Cris Dreja—Keith Relf— Geoff Beck—James McCarty—Paul Samwell Smith. (P)The Yardbirds.

OVER YOU (1968) (wm)Jerry Fuller. (P)Gary Puckett and The Union Gap.

OVERJOYED (1986) (wm)Stevie Wonder. (P)Stevie Wonder.

OVERKILL (1983) (wm)Colin Hay. (P)Men At Work.

OVERNIGHT SENSATION (Hit Record) (1974) (wm)Eric Carmen. (P)The Raspberries.

OWNER OF A LONELY HEART (1983) (wm)Trevor Rabin—Jon Anderson— Chris Squire—Trevor Horn. (P)Yes. No. 1 Chart Record.

OYE COME VA (1963) (wm)Tito Puente. (P)Tito Puente and his Orchestra. (R)1971 by Santana.

OZARKS ARE CALLING ME HOME, THE (1936) (wm)Cole Porter. (I)Musical: *Red, Hot and Blue!*, by Ethel Merman.

PA-PAYA MAMA (1953) (wm)George Sandler—Larry Coleman—Norman Gimbel. (P)Perry Como.

PACK UP YOUR SINS AND GO TO THE DEVIL (1922) (wm)Irving Berlin. (I)Revue: *Music Box Revue of 1922*, by The McCarthy Sisters. (R)1938 Film: *Alexander's Ragtime Band*, by Ethel Merman.

PACK UP YOUR SORROWS (1964) (wm)Pauline Marden—Richard Farina. (P)Joan Baez.

PACK UP YOUR TROUBLES IN YOUR OLD KIT BAG AND SMILE, SMILE, SMILE (1915) (w)Geroge Asaf (m)Felix Powell. Popular song during World War I.

PAC-MAN FEVER (1982) (wm)Jerry Buckner—Gary Garcia. (P)Buckner and Garcia.

PADAM-PADAM (1952) (w-Eng)Mann Holiner—Alberta Nichols. (m)Norbert Glanzberg. (P)Tony Martin.

PADDLIN' MADELIN' HOME (1925) (wm)Harry Woods. (I)Cliff "Ukelele Ike" Edwards.

PADRE (1957) (w-Eng)Paul Francis Webster (m)Alain Romans. (I)Lola Dee. (P)Tony Arden.

PAGAN LOVE SONG (1929) (w)Arthur Freed (m)Nacio Herb Brown. (I)Film: *The Pagan.* (P)Bob Haring and his Orchestra. (R)1950 Film: *Pagan Love Song*, by Howard Keel.

PAGE MISS GLORY (1935) (w)Al Dubin (m)Harry Warren. (I)Film: *Page Miss Glory*, by Dick Powell and Marion Davies. (P)Hal Kemp and his Orchestra.

PAINT IT BLACK (1966) (wm)Mick Jagger—Keith Richard. (P)The Rolling Stones.

PAINTED, TAINTED ROSE (1963) (wm)Peter De Angelis—Jean Sawyer. (P)Al Martino.

PAINTING THE CLOUDS WITH SUNSHINE (1929) (w)Al Dubin (m)Joe Burke. (I)Film: *Gold Diggers of Broadway*, by Nick Lucas. (P)Nick Lucas. (CR)Jean Goldkette and his Orchestra. (R)1951 Film: *Painting The Clouds With Sunshine*, by Dennis Morgan.

PAL OF MY CRADLE DAYS (1925) (w)Marshall Montgomery (m)Al Piantadosi. (P)Lewis James.

PALESTEENA (1920) (wm)Con Conrad—J. Russel Robinson. (P)The Original Dixieland Jazz Band.

PALISADES PARK (1962) (wm)Chuck Barris. (P)Freddy Cannon.

PALOMA, LA (The Dove) (1864) (w)Unknown. (m)Sebastian Yradier. Traditional Spanish song.

PALOMA BLANCA (1976) (wm)Johannes Bowens. (P)George Baker Selection.

PANCHO MAXIMILIAN HERNANDEZ (The Best President We Ever Had) (1947) (wm)Bob Hilliard—Al Frisch. (P)Woody Herman and The Four Chips.

PAPA CAN YOU HEAR ME (1983) (w)Alan and Marilyn Bergman (m)Michel Legrand. (I)Film: *Yentl*, by Barbra Streisand. (P)Barbra Streisand.

PAPA DON'T PREACH (1986) (wm)Brian Elliot—Madonna Ciccone. (P)Madonna. (P)Madonna. No. 1 Chart Record.

(Down At)PAPA JOE'S (1963) (wm)Jerry Dean Smith. (P)The Dixiebelles.

PAPA LOVES MAMBO (1954) (wm)Al Hoffman—Dick Manning—Bix Reichner. (P)Perry Como.

PAPA NICCOLINI (1941) (wm)Anne Jean Edwards—Don George. (P)Glenn Miller and his Orchestra.

PAPA WAS A ROLLIN' STONE (1972) (wm)Norman Whitfield—Barrett Strong. (P)The Temptations. No. 1 Chart Record. NARAS Award Winner. (R)1983 by Wolf.

PAPA, WON'T YOU DANCE WITH ME (1947) (w)Sammy Cahn (m)Jule Styne. (I)Musical: *High Button Shoes*, by Nanette Fabray, Jack McCauley, and The Chorus.

PAPA'S GOT A BRAND NEW BAG (1965) (wm)James Brown. (P)James Brown. (R)1968 by Otis Redding.

PAPER DOLL (1930) (wm)Johnny Black. (P)Tommy Lyman. (R)1943 by The Mills Brothers. No. 1 Chart Record.

PAPER IN FIRE (1987) (wm)John Cougar Mellencamp. (P)John Cougar Mellencamp.

PAPER MACHE (1970) (w)Hal David (m)Burt Bacharach. (P)Dionne Warwick.

PAPER ROSES (1960) (w)Janice Torre (m)Fred Spielman. (P)Anita Bryant. (R)1973 by Marie Osmond.

PAPER SUN (1967) (wm)Steve Winwood—Jim Capaldi. (P)Traffic.

PAPERBACK WRITER (1966) (wm)John Lennon—Paul McCartney. (P)The Beatles.

PAPER TIGER (1965) (wm)John D. Loudermilk. (P)Sue Thompson.

PARACHUTE WOMAN (1968) (wm)Mick Jagger—Keith Richard. (P)The Rolling Stones.

PARADE IN TOWN, A (1964) (wm)Stephen Sondheim. (I)Musical: *Anyone Can Whistle*, by Angela Lansbury.

PARADE OF THE WOODEN SOLDIERS, THE (1922) (w-Eng)Ballard MacDonald (m)Leon Jessel. (P)Paul Whiteman and his Orchestra. (CR)Vincent Lopez and his Orchestra.

PARADIDDLE JOE (1941) (wm)Johnny Morris—Fred Parries—Jerry Pugsley. (P)Tony Pastor and his Orchestra.

PARADISE (1932) (wm)Gordon Clifford—Nacio Herb Brown. (I)Film: *A Woman Commands*, by Pola Negri. (P)Theme song of Russ Columbo. (CR)Guy Lombardo and his Royal Canadians.

PARDON MY SOUTHERN ACCENT (1934) (wm)Johnny Mercer—Matty Malneck. (P)Irving Aaronson and his Orchestra. (CR)Glen Gray and The Casa Loma Orchestra.

PAREE! (1927) (w-Eng)Leo Robin (m)Jose Padilla. (I)Paris Revue: *Ca C'est Paris*, by Mistinguett.

PAREE, WHAT DID YOU DO TO ME? (1929) (wm)Cole Porter. (I)Musical: *Fifty Million Frenchmen*, by Betty Compton and Jack Thompson.

PARIS BLUES (1961) (w)Billy Strayhorn—Harold Flender (m)Duke Ellington. (I)Film: *Paris Blues*, by Duke Ellington and his Orchestra.

PARIS IN THE SPRING (1935) (w)Mack Gordon (m)Harry Revel. (I)Film: *Paris In The Spring*, by Mary Ellis. (P)Ray Noble and his Orchestra. (CR)Freddy Martin and his Orchestra.

PARIS IS A LONELY TOWN (1961) (w)E. Y. Harburg (m)Harold Arlen. (I)Cartoon Film: *Gay Purr-ee*, by the voice of Judy Garland.

PARIS LOVES LOVERS (1954) (wm)Cole Porter. (I)Musical: *Silk Stockings*, by Don Ameche and Hildegarde Neff.

PARIS ORIGINAL (1961) (wm)Frank Loesser. (I)Musical: *How To Succeed In Business Without Really Trying*, by Bonnie Scott, Claudette Sutherland, Mara Landi, and The Company.

PARIS WAKES UP AND SMILES (1949) (wm)Irving Berlin. (I)Musical: *Miss Liberty*, by Johnny V. R. Thompson and Allyn McLerie.

PARISIAN PIERROT (1923) (wm)Noel Coward. (I)Revue: *Andre Charlot's Revue of 1924*, by Gertrude Lawrence, Barbara Roberts, and Jill Williams. (R)1968 Film: *Star!*, by Julie Andrews and Daniel Massey.

(I Don't Understand)PARISIENS, THE (1958) (w)Alan Jay Lerner (m)Frederick Loewe. (I)Film: *Gigi*, by Louis Jourdan.

PARLEZ-MOI-D'AMOUR (See: Speak To Me Of Love).

PART OF THE PLAN (1975) (wm)Dan Fogelberg. (P)Dan Fogelberg.

PART TIME LOVE (1963) (wm)Clay Hammond. (P)Little Johnny Taylor. (R)1970 by Ann Peebles.

PART-TIME LOVE (1975) (wm)David Gates. (P)Gladys Knight & The Pips.

PART-TIME LOVE (1978) (w)Elton John (m)Gary Osborne. (P)Elton John.

PART TIME LOVER (1985) (wm)Stevie Wonder. (P)Stevie Wonder. No. 1 Chart Record.

PARTY ALL THE TIME (1985) (wm)Rick James. (P)Eddie Murphy.

PARTY DOLL (1957) (wm)Jimmy Bowen—Buddy Knox. (P)Buddy Knox. (CR)Steve Lawrence.

PARTY LIGHTS (1962) (wm)Claudine Clark. (P)Claudine Clark.

PARTY'S OVER, THE (1956) (w)Betty Comden—Adolph Green (m)Jule Styne. (I)Musical: *Bells Are Ringing*, by Judy Holliday. (P)Judy Holliday.

PARTY'S OVER NOW, THE (1932) (wm)Noel Coward. (P)Cabaret theme of Noel Coward.

PASS THE DUTCHIE (1983) (wm)Jackie Mitoo—Lloyd Ferguson— Fitzroy Simpson. (P)Musical Youth.

PASSE (1946) (wm)Eddie De Lange—Carl Sigman— Joseph Meyer. (I)Jean Sablon. (P)Margaret Whiting.

PASSION (1980) (wm)Rod Stewart—Phil Chen—Jim Cregan—Gary Grainger—Kevin Savigar. (P)Rod Stewart.

PATA PATA (1967) (wm)Miriam Makeba—Jerry Ragovoy. (P)Miriam Makeba.

PATCHES (1962) (wm)Barry Mann—Larry Kolber. (P)Dickey Lee.

PATCHES (I'm Depending On You) (1970) (wm)General Johnson— Ronald Dunbar. (P)Clarence Carter. NARAS Award Winner.

PATRICIA (1958) (w)Bob Marcus (m)Perez Prado. (P)Perez Prado and his Orchestra.

PATTY CAKE, PATTY CAKE (Baker Man) (1938) (wm)Andy Razaf—J. C. Johnson—Thomas Waller. (P)Fats Waller.

PATTY DUKE THEME, THE (1963) (w)Bob Wells (m)Sid Ramin. (I)TV series: *The Patty Duke Show*.

PAVANNE (1938) (w)Gladys Shelley (m)Morton Gould. Adapted from Gould's American Symphonette No. 2. (P)Morton Gould and his Orchestra.

PAY TO THE PIPER (1970) (wm)General Johnson—Greg S. Perry— Ronald Dunbar. (P)The Chairmen Of The Board.

PAY YOU BACK WITH INTEREST (1967) (wm)Allan Clarke—Tony Hicks— Graham Nash. (P)The Hollies. (R)1981 by Gary O'.

PAYBACK, THE (1974) (wm)James Brown—Fred Wesley—John Starks. (P)James Brown.

PEACE LIKE A RIVER (1971) (wm)Paul Simon. (P)Paul Simon.

PEACE TRAIN (1971) (wm)Cat Stevens. (P)Cat Stevens.

PEACE WILL COME (According To Plan) (1970) (wm)Melanie Safka. (P)Melanie.

PEACEFUL (1973) (wm)Kenny Rankin. (P)Helen Reddy.

PEACEFUL EASY FEELING (1973) (wm)Jack Tempchin. (P)The Eagles.

PEANUT BUTTER (1961) (wm)H. B. Barnum—Martin J. Cooper—Cliff Goldsmith—Fred Smith. (P)The Marathons.

PEANUT VENDOR, THE (1932) (w-Eng)Marion Sunshine—L. Wolfe Gilbert (m)Moises Simons. (I)Don Azpiazu and his Orchestra. (CR)Louis Armstrong and his Orchestra. (R)1931 Film: *Cuban Love song*, by Lawrence Tibbett. (R)1954 Film: *A Star s Born*, by Judy Garland.

PEANUTS (1957) (wm)Joe Cook. (P)Little Joe and The Thrillers. (R)1961 by Rick and The Keens.

PEARLY SHELLS (1964) (wm)Webley Edwards—Leon Pober. (P)Burl Ives.

PECKIN' (1937) (wm)Ben Pollack—Harry James. (I)Ben Pollack and his Orchestra, vocal by Harry James. (P)Benny Goodman and his Orchestra, trumpet solo by Harry James.

PEEK-A-BOO (1958) (wm)Jack Hammer. (P)The Cadillacs.

PEG (1978) (wm)Walter Becker—Donald Fagen. (P)Steely Dan.

PEG O' MY HEART (1913) (w)Alfred Bryan (m)Fred Fisher. (I)Musical: *Ziegfeld Follies of 1913*. (P)Charles Harrison. (R)1947 by The Harmonicats. No. 1 Chart Record. (CR)Buddy Clark.

PEGGY DAY (1969) (wm)Bob Dylan. (P)Bob Dylan.

PEGGY O'NEIL (1921) (wm)Harry Pease—Ed Nelson— Gilbert Dodge. (P)Clara Norton. (R)1947 by Frankie Carle and his Orchestra.

PEGGY SUE (1958) (wm)Buddy Holly—Norman Petty— Jerry Allison. (P)Buddy Holly.

PENGUIN AT THE WALDORF (1947) (wm)Jimmy Eaton—Larry Wagner— Frank Shuman. (P)Frankie Carle and his Orchestra.

PENNIES FROM HEAVEN (1936) (wm)Johnny Burke— Arthur Johnston. (I)Film: *Pennies From Heaven*, by Bing Crosby. (P)Bing Crosby.

PENNSYLVANIA POLKA (1942) (wm)Lester Lee—Zeke Manners. (I)Film: *Give Out Sisters*, by The Andrews Sisters. (P)The Andrews Sisters.

PENNSYLVANIA 6-5000 (1940) (w)Carl Sigman (m)Jerry Gray. (P)Glenn Miller and his Orchestra.

PENNY A KISS, A PENNY A HUG, A (1950) (wm)Buddy Kaye—Ralph Care. (P)Dinah Shore and Tony Martin.

PENNY LANE (1967) (wm)John Lennon—Paul McCartney. (P)The Beatles. No. 1 Chart Record.

PENNY LOVER (1984) (wm)Lionel Richie—Brenda Harvey Richie. (P)Lionel Richie.

PENNY SERENADE (1938) (w)Hal Halifax (m)Melle Weersma. (P)Guy Lombardo and his Royal Canadians.

PENTHOUSE SERENADE (When We're Alone) (1931) (wm)Will Jason—Val Burton. (P)Ruth Etting.

PEOPLE (1964) (w)Bob Merrill (m)Jule Styne. (I)Musical: *Funny Girl*, by Barbra Streisand. (P)Barbra Streisand. NARAS Award Winner. (CR)Nat "King" Cole. (R)1968 by The Tymes.

PEOPLE ARE PEOPLE (1985) (wm)Martin K. Gore. (P)Depeche Mode.

PEOPLE ARE STRANGE (1967) (wm)Robert Krieger—

James Morrison—John Densmore—Raymond Manzarek. (P)The Doors.

PEOPLE, GET READY (1965) (wm)Curtis Mayfield. (P)The Impressions. (R)1985 by Jeff Beck and Rod Stewart.

PEOPLE GOT TO BE FREE (1968) (w)Felix Cavaliere (m)Edward Brigati, Jr. (P)The Rascals. No. 1 Chart Record.

PEOPLE OF THE SOUTH WIND (1979) (wm)Kerry Livgren. (P)Kansas.

PEOPLE SAY (1964) (wm)Jeff Barry—Ellie Greenwich. (P)The Dixie Cups.

PEOPLE WILL SAY WE'RE IN LOVE (1943) (w)Oscar Hammerstein II (m)Richard Rodgers. (I)Musical: Oklahoma!, by Alfred Drake and Joan Roberts. (R)1955 Film: Oklahoma!, by Gordon MacRae and Shirley Jones.

PEPINO, THE ITALIAN MOUSE (1963) (wm)Ray Allen—Wandra Merrell. (P)Lou Monte.

PEPPER-HOT BABY (1955) (wm)Alicia Evelyn. (P)Jaye P. Morgan. (CR)Giselle MacKenzie.

PEPPERMINT TWIST (1961) (wm)Joey Dee—Henry Glover. (P)Joey Dee and The Starlighters.

PERCOLATOR (1961) (m)Lou Bideu—Ernie Freeman. (P)Billy Joe and The Checkmates.

PERCY'S SONG (1985) (wm)Bob Dylan. (P)Bob Dylan.

PERDIDO (1942) (w)H. J. Lengsfelder—Ervin Drake (m)Juan Tizol. (P)Duke Ellington and his Orchestra.

PERFECT DAY, A (1910) (wm)Carrie Jacobs Bond. (P)Cecil Fanning.

PERFECT WAY (1985) (wm)Green Strohmeyer Gartside—David Gamson. (P)Scritti Politti.

PERFECT STRANGERS (1986) (wm)Rupert Holmes. (I)Musical: The Mystery Of Edwin Drood, by Betty Buckley and Patti Cohenour.

PERFIDIA (1941) (w-Eng)Milton Leeds (m)Alberto Dominguez. (P)Glenn Miller and his Orchestra. (R)1952 by The Four Aces.

PERHAPS LOVE (1980) (wm)John Denver. (P)Placido Domingo and John Denver.

PERHAPS, PERHAPS, PERHAPS (Quizas, Quizas, Quizas) (1947) (w—Eng)Joe Davis (m)Osvaldo Farres.

PERNAMBUCO (1948) (wm)Frank Loesser. (I)Musical: Where's Charley?, by Ray Bolger, Allyn McLerie, and The Pernambucans.

PERSONALITY (1946) (w)Johnny Burke (m)Jimmy Van Heusen. (I)Film: The Road To Utopia, by Dorothy Lamour. (P)Johnny Mercer. (CR)Bing Crosby. (CR)Dinah Shore.

PERSONALITY (1959) (wm)Harold Logan—Lloyd Price. (P)Lloyd Price.

PERSONALLY (1982) (wm)Paul Kelly. (P)Karla Bonoff.

PET ME, POPPA (1955) (wm)Frank Loesser. (I)Film: Guys And Dolls, by Vivian Blaine.

PETE KELLY'S BLUES (1955) (w)Sammy Cahn (m)Ray Heindorf. (I)Film: Pete Kelly's Blues, by Ella Fitzgerald.

PETER COTTONTAIL (195) (wm)Steve Nelsom—Jack Rollins. (P)Gene Autry. (CR)Merv Shiner.

PETER GUNN THEME (1958) (m)Henry Mancini. (I)TV series: Peter Gunn, on soundtrack. (P)Ray Anthony and his Orchestra.

PETITE FLEUR (1959) (m)Sidney Bechet. (I)In France, by Sidney Bechet. (P)Chris Barber.

PETITE WALTZ, THE (1950) (w-Eng)E. A. Ellington—

Phyllis Clare. (m)Joe Heyne. (P)The Three Suns.

PETTICOAT JUNCTION (1963) (wm)Paul Manning—Curt Massey. (I)TV series: Petticoat Junction, by Flatt and Scruggs. (P)Flatt and Scruggs.

PETTICOATS OF PORTUGAL (1956) (wm)Michael Durso—Mel Mitchell— Murl Kahn. (P)Dick Jacobs and his Orchestra. (CR)Billy Vaughn.

PHILADELPHIA FREEDOM (1975) (wm)Elton John—Bernie Taupin. (P)Elton John. No. 1 Chart Record.

PHILADELPHIA, U. S. A. (1958) (wm)Anthony Antonucci—Bill Borrelli, Jr. (P)The Nu—Tornados. (CR)Art Lund.

PHOENIX LOVE THEME, THE (1965) (w-Eng)Alec Wilder. (m)Gino Paoli. (I)Film: The Flight Of The Phoenix, on soundtrack. (P)The Brass Ring. (CR)Peggy Lee.

PHOTOGRAPH (1973) (wm)George Harrison—Ringo Starr. (P)Ringo Starr. No. 1 Chart Record.

PHOTOGRAPH (1983) (wm)Steve Clark—John Savage—Robert John Lange. (P)Def Leppard.

PHYSICAL (1981) (wm)Stephen Kipner—Terry Shaddick. (P)Olivia Newton—John. No. 1 Chart Record.

PHYSICIAN, THE (1933) (wm)Cole Porter. (I)London Musical: Nymph Errant, by Gertrude Lawrence.

PIANISSIMO (1947) (wm)George Weiss—Bennie Benjamin. (P)Perry Como.

PIANO MAN (1974) (wm)Billy Joel. (P)Billy Joel.

PICCOLINO, THE (1935) (wm)Irving Berlin. (I)Film: Top Hat, by Ginger Rogers.

PICCOLO PETE (1929) (wm)Phil Baxter. (P)Ted Weems and his Orchestra.

PICK UP THE PIECES (1975) (wm)Roger Ball—Malcolm Duncan—Alan Garrie—Robbie McIntosh—Owen McIntyre—Jamie Stuart. (P)The Average White Band. No. 1 Chart Record.

PICK YOURSELF UP (1936) (w)Dorothy Fields (m)Jerome Kern. (I)Film: Swing Time, by Fred Astaire and Ginger Rogers.

PICKIN' COTTON (1928) (w)B. G. De Sylva—Lew Brown (m)Ray Henderson. (I)Revue: George White's Scandals of 1928, by Frances Williams, Ann Pennington, and Tom Patricola.

PICKIN' WILD MOUNTAIN BERRIES (1968) (wm)Edward Thomas—Bob McRee—Clifton Thomas. (P)Peggy Scott and Jo Jo Benson.

PICNIC (Theme) (1955) (w)Steve Allen (m)George Duning. (I)Film: Picnic, in medley with Moonglow, on soundtrack. (P)The McGuire Sisters. (CR)Morris Stoloff and his Orchestra. (CR)George Cates and his Orchestra.

PICTURE ME WITHOUT YOU (1936) (w)Ted Koehler (m)Jimmy McHugh. (I)Film: Dimples, by Shirley Temple.

PICTURE OF ME WITHOUT YOU, A (1935) (wm)Cole Porter. (I)Musical: Jubilee, by June Knight and Charles Walters.

PICTURES OF MATCHSTICK MEN (1968) (wm)Francis Michael Rossi. (P)Status Quo.

PIECE OF MY HEART (1968) (wm)Bert Berns—Jerry Ragovoy. (P)Big Brother and The Holding Company, featuring Janis Joplin. (R)1982 by Sammy Hagar.

PIGGIES (1969) (wm)George Harrison. (P)The Beatles.

PIGTAILS AND FRECKLES (1962) (wm)Irving Berlin. (I)Musical: Mr. President, by Jack Haskell and Anita Gillette.

PILLOW TALK (1959) (wm)Buddy Pepper—Inez James.

(I)Film: *Pillow Talk*, by Rock Hudson and Doris Day.

PILLOW TALK (1973) (wm)Sylvia Robinson—Michael Burton. (P)Sylvia.

PILOT OF THE AIRWAVES (1980) (wm)Chairman Dore. (P)Charlie Dore.

PINBALL WIZARD (1969) (wm)Peter Townshend. (I)Rock Opera: *Tommy*, by The Who. (P)The Who.

PINEAPPLE PRINCESS (1960) (wm)Dick Sherman—Bob Sherman. (P)Annette.

PINK CADILLAC (1983) (wm)Bruce Springsteen. (P)Bruce Springsteen. (R)1988 by Natalie Cole.

PINK HOUSES (1983) (m)John Cougar Mellencamp. (P)John Cougar Mellencamp.

PINK PANTHER THEME (1963) (w)Johnny Mercer (m)Henry Mancini. (I)Film: *The Pink Panther*, on soundtrack. NARAS Award Winner.

PINK SHOELACES (1959) (wm)Mickie Grant. (P)Dodie Stevens.

PIPE-DREAMING (1946) (wm)Cole Porter. (I)Musical: *Around The World*, by Larry Laurence.

PIPELINE (1963) (m)Bob Spickard—Brian Carman. (P)The Chantays.

PIRATE JENNY (1928) (w)Bertolt Brecht (m)Kurt Weill. (P)1954 Musical: *The Threepenny Opera*, by Lotte Lenya.

PISTOL PACKIN' MAMA (1943) (wm)Al Dexter. (I)Al Dexter and his Troopers. (P)Bing Crosby and The Andrews Sisters.

PITTSBURGH, PENNSYLVANIA (1952) (wm)Bob Merrill. (P)Guy Mitchell with Mitch Miller and his Orchestra.

PLACE IN THE SUN, A (1951) (w)Jay Livingston—Ray Evans (m)Franz Waxman. (I)Film: *A Place In The Sun*, as soundtrack theme. Academy Award Winner.

PLACE IN THE SUN, A (1966) (w)Ronald Miller (m)Bryan Wells. (P)Stevie Wonder.

PLANT YOU NOW, DIG YOU LATER (1940) (w)Lorenz Hart (m)Richard Rodgers. (I)Musical: *Pal Joey*, by Jack Durant, June Havoc, and The Ensemble.

PLANTATION BOOGIE (1954) (m)Lenny Dee. (P)Lenny Dee.

PLAY A SIMPLE MELODY (1914) (wm)Irving Berlin. (P)Billy Murray and Elsie Baker. (R)1950 by Bing and Gary Crosby.

PLAY, FIDDLE, PLAY (1932) (w)Jack Lawrence (m)Emery Deutsch— Arthur Altman. (P)Emery Deutsch and his Orchestra.

PLAY GYPSIES-DANCE GYPSIES (1924) (w-Eng)Harry B. Smith (m)Emmerich Kalman. (I)Operetta: *Countess Maritza*, by Walter Woolf.

PLAY ME (1972) (wm)Neil Diamond. (P)Neil Diamond.

PLAY ME AN OLD FASHIONED MELODY (1945) (w)Mack Gordon (m)Harry Warren. (I)Film: *Billy Rose's Diamond Horseshoe*, by William Gaxton and Beatrice Kay.

PLAY ME HEARTS AND FLOWERS (I Wanna Cry) (1955) (w)Mann Curtis (m)Sanford Green. (I)TV special: *Play Me Hearts And Flowers*, by Johnny Desmond. (P)Johnny Desmond.

PLAY, ORCHESTRA, PLAY (1935) (wm)Noel Coward. (P)Play: Shadow Play, by Noel Coward.

PLAY THAT FUNKY MUSIC (1976) (wm)Robert Parissi. (P)Wild Cherry. No. 1 Chart Record.

PLAY THE GAME TONIGHT (1982) (wm)Kerry Livgren—Phil Ehart— Richard Williams— Robert Frazier—Danny Flower. (P)Kansas.

PLAY WITH FIRE (1965) (wm)Mick Jagger—Keith Richard—Bill Wyman. (P)The Rolling Stones.

PLAYBOY (1968) (wm)Gene Thomas. (P)Gene and Debbe.

PLAYBOYS AND PLAYGIRLS (1964) (wm)Bob Dylan. (P)Bob Dylan.

PLAYGROUND IN MY MIND (1973) (wm)Paul Vance—Lee Pockriss. (P)Clint Holmes.

PLAYMATES (1940) (wm)Saxie Dowell. (P)Kay Kyser and his College Of Musical Knowledge.

PLEASANT VALLEY SUNDAY (1967) (wm)Gerry Goffin—Carole King. (P)The Monkees.

PLEASE (1932) (w)Leo Robin (m)Ralph Rainger. (I)Film: *The Big Broadcast*, by Bing Crosby. (P)Bing Crosby.

PLEASE BE KIND (1938) (wm)Sammy Cahn—Saul Chaplin. (P)Mildred Bailey. (CR)Benny Goodman and his Orchestra.

PLEASE COME HOME FOR CHRISTMAS (1978) (wm)Charles Brown—Gene Redd. (P)The Eagles.

PLEASE COME TO BOSTON (1974) (wm)Dave Loggins. (P)Dave Loggins.

PLEASE DON'T ASK ABOUT BARBARA (1961) (wm)Bill Buchanan—Jack Keller. (P)Bobby Vee.

PLEASE DON'T EAT THE DAISIES (1960) (wm)Joe Lubin. (I)Film: *Please Don't Eat The Daisies*, by Doris Day. (P)Doris Day.

PLEASE DON'T GO (1979) (wm)Harry Casey—Richard Finch. (P)K. C. & The Sunshine Band. No. 1 Chart Record.

PLEASE DON'T LEAVE (1979) (wm)Lauren Wood. (P)Lauren Wood.

PLEASE DON'T SAY NO (1945) (w)Ralph Freed (m)Sammy Fain. (I)Film: *Thrill Of A Romance*, by Tommy Dorsey and his Orchestra, with The King Sisters.

PLEASE DON'T STOP LOVING ME (1966) (wm)Joy Byers. (I)Film: *Frankie And Johnny*, by Elvis Presley and The Jordanaires. (P)Elvis Presley.

PLEASE DON'T TALK ABOUT ME WHEN I'M GONE (1930) (w)Sidney Clare (m)Sam H. Stept. (P)Kate Smith. (CR)Gene Austin. (R)1953 by Johnnie Ray.

PLEASE HELP ME, I'M FALLING (1960) (wm)Don Robertson—Hal Blair. (P)Hank Locklin. (CR)Skeeter Davis.

PLEASE LOVE ME FOREVER (1959) (wm)Johnny Malone—Ollie Blanchard. (P)Tommy Edwards. (R)1961 by Cathy Jean & The Roommates. (R)1967 by Bobby Vinton.

PLEASE MR. PLEASE (1975) (wm)John Rostill—Bruce Welch. (P)Olivia Newton—John.

PLEASE MR. POSTMAN (1961) (wm)Brian Holland—Freddy C. Gorman. (P)The Marvelettes. No. 1 Chart Record. (R)1975 by The Carpenters. No. 1 Chart Record. (R)1983 by Gentle Persuasion.

PLEASE MR. SUN (1951) (w)Sid Frank (m)Ray Getzov. (P)Johnny Ray. (CR)Tommy Edwards. (R)1966 by The Vogues.

PLEASE NO SQUEEZA DA BANANA (1945) (wm)Jack Zero—Ben Jaffee. (P)Louis Prima and his Orchestra.

PLEASE PLEASE ME (1964) (wm)John Lennon—Paul McCartney. (P)The Beatles.

PLEASE RETURN YOUR LOVE TO ME (1968) (wm)Norman Whitfield— Barrett Strong. (P)The Temptations.

PLEASE SEND ME SOMEONE TO LOVE (1950) (wm)Percy Mayfield. (P)Percy Mayfield.

(Don't Go)PLEASE STAY (1961) (w)Bob Hilliard (m)Burt

Bacharach. (P)The Drifters.

PLEASE TELL ME WHY (1966) (wm)Dave Clark—Mike Smith. (P)The Dave Clark Five.

PLEASURE PRINCIPLE (1987) (wm)M. Moir. (P)Janet Jackson.

PLEASURE SEEKERS, THE (1965) (w)Sammy Cahn (m)Jimmy Van Heusen. (I)Film: *The Pleasure Seekers*, by Ann—Margret.

PLEDGING MY LOVE (1955) (wm)Ferdinand Washington—Don Robey. (P)Johnny Ace. (CR)Teresa Brewer.

PLEDGING MY TIME (1966) (wm)Bob Dylan. (P)Bob Dylan.

PLENTY TO BE THANKFUL FOR (1942) (wm)Irving Berlin. (I)Film: *Holiday Inn*, by Bing Crosby.

POCKETFUL OF MIRACLES (1961) (w)Sammy Cahn (m)Jimmy Van Heusen. (I)Film: *Pocketful of Miracles* by Frank Sinatra on soundtrack. (P)Frank Sinatra.

POET AND PEASANT OVERTURE (1854) (m)Franz Von Suppe. Famous classical overture.

POETRY IN MOTION (1960) (wm)Paul Kaufman—Mike Anthony. (P)Johnny Tillotson.

POETRY MAN (1975) (wm)Phoebe Snow Laub. (P)Phoebe Snow.

POINCIANA (1943) (w-Eng)Buddy Bernier. (m)Nat Simon. (P)David Rose and his Orchestra. Vocal version by Bing Crosby.

POINT OF NO RETURN (1961) (wm)Gerry Goffin—Carole King. (P)Gene McDaniels.

POISON IVY (1959) (wm)Jerry Leiber—Mike Stoller. (P)The Coasters.

POLITICS AND POKER (1959) (w)Sheldon Harnick (m)Jerry Bock. (I)Musical: *Fiorello*, by Howard Da Silva.

POLK SALAD ANNIE (1969) (wm)Tony Joe White. (P)Tony Joe White.

POLKA DOTS AND MOONBEAMS (1940) (w)Johnny Burke (m)Jimmy Van Heusen. (P)Tommy Dorsey and his Orchestra, vocal by Frank Sinatra. (CR)Glenn Miller and his Orchestra, vocal by Ray Eberle.

POLLY WOLLY DOODLE (1883) (wm)Unknown. Traditional American Minstrel song.

POLONAISE MILITAIRE (1840) (m)Frederic Chopin. Famous classical composition.

POLOVTSIAN DANCES (1888) (m)Alexander Borodin. (I)Opera: *Prince Igor*.

POLYTHENE PAM (1969) (wm)John Lennon—Paul McCartney. (P)The Beatles.

POMP AND CIRCUMSTANCE (1902) (w)Arthur Benson (m)Edward Elgar. March usually played at graduation exercises.

POMPTON TURNPIKE (1940) (wm)Will Osborne—Dick Rogers. (P)Charlie Barnet and his Orchestra.

PONY TIME (1961) (wm)Don Covay—J. Berry. (P)Chubby Checker.

POOR BOY (1959) (w)Mel Mitchell (m)David R. Sanderson. (P)The Royaltones.

POOR BUTTERFLY (1916) (w)John Golden (m)Raymond Hubbell. (P)The Victor Military Band. (R)1954 by The Hilltoppers.

POOR FOOL (1962) (wm)Ike Turner. (P)Ike and Tina Turner.

POOR JENNY (1959) (wm)Boudleaux and Felice Bryant. (P)The Everly Brothers.

POOR JUD (1943) (w)Oscar Hammerstein II (m)Richard Rodgers. (I)Musical: *Oklahoma!*, by Alfred Drake and Howard Da Silva. (R)1955 Film: *Oklahoma!*, by Gordon MacRae and Rod Steiger.

POOR LITTLE FOOL (1958) (wm)Shari Sheeley. (P)Rick Nelson.

POOR LITTLE HOLLYWOOD STAR (1962) (w)Carolyn Leigh (m)Cy Coleman. (I)Musical: *Little Me*, by Virginia Martin.

POOR LITTLE RHODE ISLAND (1944) (w)Sammy Cahn (m)Jule Styne. (I)Film: *Carolina Blues*, by Ann Miller.

POOR LITTLE RICH GIRL (1926) (wm)Noel Coward. (I)Revue: *Andre Charlot's Revue of 1926*, by Gertrude Lawrence.

POOR MAN'S ROSES, A (1957) (wm)Bob Hilliard—Milton De Lugg. (P)Patti Page.

POOR ME (1955) (wm)Antoine Domino—Dave Bartholomew. (P)Fats Domino.

POOR PEOPLE OF PARIS, THE (1954) (w-Eng)Jack Lawrence (m)Marguerite Monnot. (I)Edith Piaf. (P)Les Baxter and his Orchestra.

POOR PIERROT (1931) (w)Otto Harbach (m)Jerome Kern. (I)Musical: *The Cat And The Fiddle*, by Lucette Valsy and Peter Chambers. Film version 1934, by Jeanette MacDonald.

POOR POOR PITIFUL ME (1978) (wm)Warren Zevon. (I)Film: *F. M.*, by Linda Ronstadt. (P)Linda Ronstadt.

POOR SIDE OF TOWN (1966) (wm)Johnny Rivers—Lou Adler. (P)Johnny Rivers. No. 1 Chart Record

POOR YOU (1942) (w)E. Y. Harburg (m)Burton Lane. (I)Film: *Ship Ahoy*, by Frank Sinatra, Virginia O'-Brien, Red Skelton with Tommy Dorsey and his Orchestra.

POP GOES THE WEASEL (1853) (wm)Charles Twiggs. Very popular children's song.

POP LIFE (1985) (wm)Prince Rogers Nelson. (P)Prince & The Revolution.

POP MUZIK (1979) (wm)Robin Scott. (P)M. No. 1 Chart Record.

POPCORN, THE (1969) (m)James Brown. (P)James Brown.

POPCORN (1969) (wm)Gershon Kingsley. (P)Hot Butter.

POPEYE (The Hitchhiker) (1962) (w)Kal Mann (m)Dave Appell. (P)Chubby Checker.

(I'm)POPEYE THE SAILOR MAN (1931) (wm)Sammy Lerner. (I)Cartoon Film: *Popeye, The Sailor Man* on soundtrack. (P)Frank Luther.

POPPA DON'T PREACH TO ME (1947) (wm)Frank Loesser. (I)Film: *The Perils Of Pauline*, by Betty Hutton. (P)Betty Hutton.

POPSICLE (1966) (wm)Buzz Cason—Bobby Russell. (P)Jan and Dean.

POPSICLES AND ICICLES (1963) (wm)David Gates. (P)The Murmaids.

POR FAVOR (1955) (wm)Noel Sherman—Joe Sherman. (P)Vic Damone.

PORT-AU-PRINCE (1956) (wm)Bernie Wayne—Miriam Lewis. (P)Nelson Riddle and his Orchestra.

PORTRAIT OF MY LOVE (1961) (w)David West (m)Cyril Ornadel. (P)Steve Lawrence. (R)1967 by The Tokens.

PORTUGESE WASHERWOMEN, THE (1956) (m)Andre Popp—Roger Lucchesi. (P)Joe "Fingers" Carr and his Orchestra.

POSIN' (1937) (wm)Sammy Cahn—Saul Chaplin. (I)Nighclub revue: *The New Grand Terrace Revue*, by Fletcher Henderson and his Orchestra. (P)Tommy Dorsey and his Orchestra. (CR)Jimmie Lunceford and his Orchestra.

POSITIVELY 4th STREET (1965) (wm)Bob Dylan. (P)Bob Dylan.

POTATO HEAD BLUES (1927) (m)Louis Armstrong. (P)Louis Armstrong and his Hot Seven.

POWDER YOUR FACE WITH SUNSHINE (1948) (wm)Carmen Lombardo— Stanley Rochinski. (P)Evelyn Knight. No. 1 Chart Record. (CR)Dean Martin. (CR)Guy Lombardo and his Royal Canadians.

POWER OF GOLD, THE (1978) (wm)Dan Fogelberg. (P)Dan Fogelberg and Tim Weisberg.

POWER OF LOVE (1972) (wm)Kenny Gamble—Leon Huff—Joe Simon. (P)Joe Simon. (R)1974 by Martha Reeves.

POWER OF LOVE, THE (1985) (wm)Chris Hayes—Huey Lewis—Johnny Colla. (I)Film: Back To The Future on soundtrack. (P)Huey Lewis & The News. No. 1 Chart Record.

POWER OF LOVE (1987) (wm)C. DeRouge—G. Mende— J. Rush— M. Applegate. (P)Laura Branigan.

POWER TO THE PEOPLE (1971) (wm)John Lennon. (P)John Lennon.

POWERHOUSE (1937) (m)Raymond Scott. (P)The Raymond Scott Quintet.

PRACTICE MAKES PERFECT (1940) (wm)Don Roberts—Ernest Gold. (P)Bob Chester and his orchestra.

PRAISE THE LORD AND PASS THE AMMUNITION (1942) (wm)Frank Loesser. (P)Kay Kyser and his Orchestra. (CR)The Merry Macs.

PRECIOUS AND FEW (1972) (wm)Walter Nims. (P)Climax.

PRECIOUS ANGEL (1979) (wm)Bob Dylan. (P)Bob Dylan.

PRECIOUS LITTLE THING CALLED LOVE, A (1929) (wm)Lou Davis—J. Fred Coots. (I)Film: Shopworn Angel, by Nancy Carroll.

PRECIOUS LOVE (1979) (wm)Robert Welch. (P)Bob Welch.

PRELUDE IN C SHARP MINOR (1893) (m)Sergei Rachmaninoff. Famous classical piano composition.

PRELUDE TO A KISS (1938) (w)Irving Gordon—Irving Mills (m)Duke Ellington. (P)Duke Ellington and his Orchestra. (CR)Johnny Hodges.

PRESS (1986) (wm)Paul McCartney. (P)Paul McCartney.

PRESSURE (1980) (wm)Billy Joel. (P)Billy Joel.

PRETEND (1952) (wm)Lew Douglas—Cliff Parman— Frank Lavere. (P)Nat "King" Cole. (CR)Ralph Marterie and his Orchestra.

PRETTY BALLERINA (1967) (wm)Mike Brown. (P)The Left Banke.

PRETTY BLUE EYES (1959) (wm)Teddy Randazzo—Bob Weinstein. (P)Steve Lawrence.

PRETTY EYED BABY (1951) (wm)Mary Lou Williams— William Johnson— Snub Mosely. (P)Frankie Laine and Jo Stafford.

PRETTY FLAMINGO (1966) (wm)Mark Barkan. (P)Mark Barkan. (R)1976 by Rod Stewart.

PRETTY GIRL IS LIKE A MELODY, A (1919) (wm)Irving Berlin. (I)Revue: Ziegfeld Follies of 1919. (P)John Steel. (R)1956 Film: The Great Ziegfeld, by Dennis Morgan and The Chorus.

PRETTY LITTLE ANGEL EYES (1961) (wm)Tommy Boyce and Curtis Lee. (P)Curtis Lee.

PRETTY LITTLE BABY (1965) (wm)Clarence Paul—Mar-

vin Gaye—Dave Hamilton. (P)Marvin Gaye.

PRETTY TO WALK WITH (1957) (w)E. Y. Harburg (m)Harold Arlen. (I)Musical: Jamaica, by Lena Horne.

PRETTY WOMEN (1978) (wm)Stephen Sondheim. (I)Musical: Sweeney Todd, by Edmund Lyndeck— Len Cariou—Victor Garber.

PRIDE AND JOY (1963) (wm)Marvin Gaye—William Stevenson—Norman Whitfield. (P)Marvin Gaye.

PRIMROSE LANE (1959) (wm)George Callender— Wayne Shanklin. (P)Jerry Wallace. (R)1970 by O. C. Smith.

PRINCESS OF PURE DELIGHT (1941) (w)Ira Gershwin (m)Kurt Weill. (I)Musical: Lady In The Dark, by Gertrude Lawrence and The Children.

PRISONER OF LOVE (1931) (w)Leo Robin (m)Russ Columbo—Clarence Gaskill. (P)Russ Columbo. (R)1946 by Perry Como. (R)1963 by James Brown and The Famous Flames.

PRISONER'S SONG, THE (If I Had The Wings Of An Angel) (1924) (wm)Guy Massey. (P)Vernon Dalhart.

PRIVATE EYES (1981) (wm)Warren Pash—Sara Allen— Janna Allen— Daryl Hall. (P)Hall and Oates. No. 1 Chart Record.

PRIVATE DANCER (1985) (wm)Mark Knopfler. (P)Tina Turner.

PROBLEMS (1958) (wm)Boudleaux and Felice Bryant. (P)The Everly Brothers.

PROMISE ME LOVE (1958) (wm)Kay Thompson. (P)Andy Williams.

PROMISED LAND, THE (1964) (wm)Chuck Berry. (R)1974 by Elvis Presley.

PROMISES (1979) (wm)Richard Feldman—Roger Linn. (P)Eric Clapton.

PROMISES, PROMISES (1968) (w)Hal David (m)Burt Bacharach. (I)Musical: Promises, Promises, by Jerry Orbach. (P)Dionne Warwick.

PROMISES, PROMISES (1983) (wm)Pete Bryne—Rob Fisher. (P)Naked Eyes.

PROUD (1962) (wm)Barry Mann—Cynthia Weil. (P)Johnny Crawford.

PROUD MARY (1969) (wm)John C. Fogarty. (P)Creedence Clearwater

Revival. (CR)Solomon Burke. (CR)Sonny Charles and The Checkmates. (R)1971 by Ike and Tina Turner.

PROUD ONE, THE (1966) (wm)Bob Gaudio—Bob Crewe. (I)Frankie Valli. (R)1975 by The Osmonds.

PROVE IT ALL NIGHT (1978) (wm)Bruce Springsteen. (P)Bruce Springsteen.

PROVE YOUR LOVE (1987) (wm)S. Swirsky—A. Roman. (P)Taylor Dayne.

P. S. I LOVE YOU (1934) (w)Johnny Mercer (m)Gordon Jenkins. (P)Rudy Vallee. (R)1953 by The Hilltoppers.

P. S. I LOVE YOU (1964) (wm)John Lennon—Paul McCartney. (P)The Beatles.

PSYCHEDELIC SHACK (1970) (wm)Barrett Strong— Norman Whitfield. (P)The Temptations.

PSYCHOTIC REACTION (1966) (wm)Ken Ellner—Roy Chaney—Craig Atkinson—John Byrne—John Michalski. (P)The Count Five.

P. T. 109 (1962) (wm)Marijohn Wilkin—Fred Burch. (P)Jimmy Dean.

PUBLIC MELODY NUMBER ONE (1937) (w)Ted Koehler (m)Harold Arlen. (I)Film: Artists And Models, by Martha Raye and Louis Armstrong.

PUCKER UP, BUTTERCUP (1963) (wm)Johnny Bristol—Harvey Fuqua— Danny Coggins. (P)Jr. Walker and The All Stars.

PUFF (The Magic Dragon) (1963) (wm)Peter Yarrow—Leonard Lipton. (P)Peter, Paul, and Mary.

PUMP UP THE VOLUME (1987) (wm)S. Young—M. Young. (P)M/A/R/R/S.

PUPPET MAN (1970) (wm)Neil Sedaka—Howard Greenfield. (P)The 5th Dimension. (CR)Tom Jones.

PUPPET ON A STRING (1965) (wm)Sid Tepper—Roy Bennett. (P)Elvis Presley.

PUPPY LOVE (1960) (wm)Paul Anka. (P)Paul Anka. (R)1972 by Donny Osmond.

PURLIE (1970) (w)Peter Udell (M)Gary Geld. (I)Musical: Purlie, by Melba Moore.

PURPLE HAZE (1967) (wm)Jimi Hendrix. (P)Jimi Hendrix. (R)1969 by Dion.

PURPLE PEOPLE EATER, THE (1958) (wm)Sheb Wooley. (P)Sheb Wooley. No. 1 Chart Record.

PURPLE RAIN (1984) (wm)Prince Rogers Nelson. (I)Film: Purple Rain, by Prince. (P)Prince.

PUSH IT (1987) (wm)H. Azor. (P)Salt—N-Pepa.

PUSH THE BUTTON (1957) (w)E. Y. Harburg (m)Harold Arlen. (I)Musical: Jamaica, by Lena Horne.

PUSHOVER (1963) (wm)Roquel Davis—Tony Clarke. (P)Etta James.

PUSSY CAT (1958) (w)Sunny Skylar (m)Tom Glazer. (P)The Ames Brothers.

PUSSY CAT SONG, THE (Nyow! Nyot! Nyow!) (1948) (wm)Dick Manning. (P)Patti Andrews and Bob Crosby.

PUT A LIGHT IN THE WINDOW (1957) (w)Rhoda Roberts (m)Kenny Jacobson. (P)The Four Lads.

PUT A LITTLE LOVE IN YOUR HEART (1969) (wm)Jimmy Holiday—Randy Myers—Jackie DeShannon. (P)Jackie DeShannon.

PUT IT IN A BOX (Tie 'Em With A Ribbon And Throw 'Em In The Deep Blue Sea) (1948) (w)Sammy Cahn (m)Jule Styne. (I)Film: Romance On The High Seas, by Doris Day, with The Page Cavanaugh Trio.

PUT IT THERE, PAL (1945) (w)Johnny Burke (m)Jimmy Van Heusen. (I)Film: Road To Utopia, by Bob Hope and Bing Crosby.

PUT ME TO THE TEST (1944) (w)Ira Gershwin (m)Jerome Kern. (I)Film: Cover Girl, by Gene Kelly.

PUT ON A HAPPY FACE (1960) (w)Lee Adams (m)Charles Strouse. (I)Musical: Bye Bye Birdie, by Dick Van Dyke. 1963 Film version, by Dick Van Dyke and Janet Leigh.

PUT ON AN OLD PAIR OF SHOES (1935) (wm)Dedette Lee Hill—Billy Hill. (P)Ozzie Nelson and Harriet Hilliard.

PUT ON YOUR SUNDAY CLOTHES (1964) (wm)Jerry Herman. (I)Musical: Hello, Dolly!, by Charles Nelson Reilly, Carol Channing, Jerry Dodge, and Ivors Gavon.

PUT THE BLAME ON MAME (1946) (wm)Allan Roberts—Doris Fisher. (I)Film: Gilda, by Anita Ellis dubbing for Rita Hayworth.

PUT YOUR ARMS AROUND ME HONEY (1910) (w)Junie McCree (m)Albert Von Tilzer. (I)Byron Collins and Arthur Harlan. (R)1943 by Dick Haymes.

PUT YOUR DREAMS AWAY (For Another Day) (1942) (w)Ruth Lowe (m)Stephan Weiss—Paul Mann. (P)Theme song of Frank Sinatra.

PUT YOUR HAND IN THE HAND (1971) (wm)Gene Maclellan. (P)Ocean.

PUT YOUR HANDS TOGETHER (1974) (wm)Kenny Gamble—Leon Huff. (P)The O'Jays.

PUT YOUR HEAD ON MY SHOULDER (1958) (wm)Paul Anka. (P)Paul Anka. (R)1968 by The Lettermen.

PUT YOUR LITTLE FOOT RIGHT OUT (1945) (wm)Larry Spier. Adapted from a French folk song. (I)Film: San Antonio, by Ann Sheridan.

PUTTIN' ON THE RITZ (1930) (wm)Irving Berlin. (I)Film: Puttin' On The Ritz, by Harry Richman. (P)Harry Richman. (CR)Leo Reisman and his Orchestra. (R)1946 Film: Blue Skies, by Fred Astaire. (R)1983 by Taco.

PUTTING IT TOGETHER (1984) (wm)Stephen Sondheim. (I)Musical: Sunday In The Park With George. (R)1985 by Barbra Streisand.

PUZZLEMENT, A (1951) (w)Oscar Hammerstein II (m)Richard Rodgers. (I)Musical: The King And I, by Yul Brynner.

P. Y. T. (Pretty Young Thing) (1983) (wm)James Ingram—Quincy Jones. (P)Michael Jackson.

QUAKER CITY JAZZ (1937) (m)Jan Savitt—Jimmy Schultz. (P)Theme song of Jan Savitt and his Top Hatters.

QUANDO, QUANDO, QUANDO (Tell Me When) (1962) (w-Eng)Pat Boone (m)Tony Renis. (I)In Italy, by Emilio Pericoli. (P)Pat Boone.

QUARTER TO THREE (1961) (wm)Frank Guida—Joe Royster—Gene Barge—Gary Anderson. (P)Gary "U. S. " Bonds.

QUE SERA, SERA (Whatever Will Be, Will Be) (1935) (wm)Jay Livingston—Ray Evans. (I)Film: *The Man Who Knew Too Much*, by Doris Day. (P)Doris Day.

QUEEN BEE (1976) (wm)Rupert Holmes. (I)Film: *A Star Is Born*, by Barbra Streisand.

QUEEN JANE APPROXIMATELY (1965) (wm)Bob Dylan. (P)Bob Dylan.

QUEEN OF HEARTS (1981) (wm)Hank De Vito. (P)Juice Newton.

QUEEN OF THE HOP (1958) (wm)Woody Harris—Bobby Darin. (P)Bobby Darin.

QUEER NOTIONS (1933) (m)Coleman Hawkins. (P)Fletcher Henderson and his Orchestra, featuring Coleman Hawkins on tenor saxophone.

QUENTIN'S THEME (1969) (m)Robert W. Corbert. (I)TV series: *Dark Shadows*. (P)The Charles Randolph Grean Sounde.

QUESTION (1970) (wm)Justin Hayward. (P)Moody Blues.

QUESTIONS 67 and 68 (1968) (wm)Robert Lamm. (P)Chicago.

QUICK JOEY SMALL (Run, Joey, Run) (1968) (wm)Artie Resnick—Joe Levine. (P)The Kasenetz—Katz Singing Orchestral Circus.

QUICKSAND (1963) (wm)Eddie Holland—Brian Holland—Lamont Dozier. (P)Martha and The Vandellas.

QUIEN SABE? (Who Knows?) (1947) (wm)Jimmy O'Keefe—Jack Fulton—Dick Cunliffe. (P)Jimmy Dorsey and his Orchestra, vocal by Dee Parker and Bob Carroll.

QUIET GIRL, A (1953) (w)Betty Comden—Adolph Green (m)Leonard Bernstein. (I)Musical: *Wonderful Town*, by George Gaynes.

QUIET NIGHT (1936) (w)Lorenz Hart (m)Richard Rodgers. (I)Musical: *On Your Toes*, by Earl MacVeigh and The Ensemble.

QUIET NIGHTS OF QUIET STARS (Corcovado) (1962) (w-Eng)Gene Lees (m)Antonio Carlos Jobim. (I)Tony Bennett. Most popular recording by Frank Sinatra.

QUIET PLEASE (1940) (m)Sy Oliver. (P)Tommy Dorsey and his Orchestra.

QUIET VILLAGE (1951) (m)Les Baxter. (I)Les Baxter and his Orchestra. (R)1959 by Martin Denny.

R-O-C-K (In The U. S. A.) (1986) (wm)John Cougar Mellencamp. (P)John Cougar Mellencamp.

RACE IS ON, THE (1964) (wm)Don Rollins. (I)George Jones. (P)Jack Jones.

(When You're)RACING WITH THE CLOCK (1954) (wm)Richard Adler— Jerry Ross. (I)Musical: *The Pajama Game*, by Sydney Chaplin.

RACING WITH THE MOON (1941) (w)Vaughn Monroe—Pauline Pope. (P)Theme Song of Vaughn Monroe and his Orchestra.

RADAR LOVE (1974) (wm)Barry Hays—George Koogmans. (P)Golden Earring.

RAG DOLL (1964) (wm)Bob Crewe—Bob Gaudio. (P)The Four Seasons. No. 1 Chart Record.

RAG MOP (1950) (wm)Johnnie Lee Wells—Deacon Anderson. (P)The Ames Brothers.

RAGGEDY ANN (1923) (w)Anne Caldwell (m)Jerome Kern. (I)Musical: *Stepping Stones*, by Fred and Dorothy Stone, John Lambert, and The Tiller Sunshine Girls.

RAGGING THE SCALE (1915) (w)Dave Ringle (m)Edward B. Claypool. (P)Conway's Band.

RAGS TO RICHES (1953) (wm)Richard Adler—Jerry Ross. (P)Tony Bennett.

RAGTIME COWBOY JOE (1912) (wm)Lewis Muir—Grant Clarke—Maurice Abrahams. (P)Bob Roberts. (R)1939 by Pinky Tomlin. (R)1947 by Eddy Howard. (R)1949 by Jo Stafford.

RAGTIME VIOLIN (1911) (wm)Irving Berlin. (P)The American Quartet.

RAIN (1934) (w)Billy Hill (m)Peter De Rose. (I)On Radio by Major Bowes and his Capitol Theatre Family. (P)Jan Garber and his Orchestra.

RAIN (1966) (wm)John Lennon—Paul McCartney. (P)The Beatles.

RAIN DANCE (1971) (wm)Burton Cummings—Kurt Winter. (P)Guess Who.

RAIN IN SPAIN, THE (1956) (w)Alan Jay Lerner (m)Frederick Loewe. (I)Musical: *My Fair Lady*, by Rex Harrison, Julie Andrews, and Robert Coote.

RAIN ON THE ROOF (1932) (wm)Ann Ronell. (P)Paul Whiteman and his Orchestra.

RAIN ON THE ROOF (You And Me And Rain On The Roof) (1966) (wm)John B. Sebastian. (P)The Lovin' Spoonful.

RAIN ON THE SCARECROW (1986) (wm)John Cougar Mellencamp. (P)John Cougar Mellencamp.

RAIN, RAIN GO AWAY (1962) (wm)Gloria Shayne—Noel Regney. (P)Bobby Vinton.

RAIN, THE (1986) (wm)Vincent Bell. (P)Oran "Juice" Jones.

RAIN, THE PARK, AND OTHER THINGS, THE (1967) (wm)Artie Kornfield—Steve Duboff. (P)The Cowsills.

RAINBOW (1957) (wm)Russ Hamilton. (P)Russ Hamilton.

RAINBOW CONNECTION (1979) (wm)Kenny Ascher—Paul Williams. (I)Film: *The Muppet Movie*, by Jim Henson as Kermit The Frog.

RAINBOW ON THE RIVER (1936) (w)Paul Francis Webster (m)Louis Alter. (I)Film: *Rainbow On The River*, by Bobby Breen. Theme of radio series: Dr. Christian.

RAINBOW RHAPSODY (1943) (w)Allan Roberts (m)Benny Carter. (P)Glenn Miller and his Orchestra.

RAINDROPS (1961) (wm)Dee Clark. (P)Dee Clark.

RAINDROPS KEEP FALLIN' ON MY HEAD (1969) (w)Hal David (m)Burt Bacharach. (I)Film: *Butch Cassidy And The Sundance Kid*, by voice of B. J. Thomas. (P)B. J. Thomas. No. 1 Chart Record. Academy Award Winner.

A WRONG GUESS ...

People told B. J. Thomas that if he recorded *Raindrops Keep Falling on My Head* that it would totally ruin his career.

RAINS CAME, THE (1962) (wm)Huey P. Meaux. (P)The Sir Douglas Quintet.

RAINY DAY, A (1932) (w)Howard Dietz (m)Arthur Schwartz. (I)Musical: *Flying Colors*, by Clifton Webb.

RAINY DAY PEOPLE (1974) (wm)Gordon Lightfoot. (P)Gordon Lightfoot.

RAINY DAY WOMEN No. 12 & 35 (1966) (wm)Bob Dylan. (P)Bob Dylan.

RAINY DAYS AND MONDAYS (1971) (w)Paul Williams (m)Roger Nichols. (P)The Carpenters.

RAINY NIGHT IN GEORGIA (1979) (wm)Tony Joe White. (P)Brook Benton.

RAINY NIGHT IN RIO, A (1946) (w)Leo Robin (m)Arthur Schwartz. (I)Film: *The Time*, The Place And The Girl, by Dennis Morgan, Jack Carson, Janis Paige, and Martha Vickers.

RAMBLIN' GAMBLIN' MAN (1969) (wm)Bob Seger. (P)The Bob Seger System.

RAMBLIN MAN (1973) (wm)Richard Betts. (P)The Allman Brothers.

RAMBLIN' ROSE (1962) (wm)Noel Sherman—Joe Sherman. (P)Nat "King" Cole.

RAMONA (1927) (w)L. Wolfe Gilbert (m)Mabel Wayne. (I)Film: *Ramona*, by Dolores Del Rio. (P)Gene Austin. (CR)Paul Whiteman and his Orchestra.

RAMROD (1958) (m)Al Casey. (P)Duane Eddy.

RANGERS SONG, THE (1927) (w)Joseph McCarthy (m)Harry Tierney. (I)Musical: *Rio Rita*, by J. Harold Murray, Harry Ratcliffe. Donald Douglas, and The Chorus. (R)1929 film version by John Boles. (R)1942 film version by Kathryn Grayson, John Carroll, and The Chorus.

RASPBERRY BERET (1985) (wm)Prince Rogers Nelson. (P)Prince.

RAP TAP ON WOOD (1936) (wm)Cole Porter. (I)Musical: *Born To Dance*, by Eleanor Powell.

RAPPER, THE (1970) (wm)Don Iris. (P)The Jaggerz.

RAPTURE (1981) (w)Debbie Harry (m)Chris Stein. (P)Blondie. No. 1 Chart Record.

RAUNCHY (1957) (m)Bill Justis—Sidney Manker. (P)Bill Justis. (CR)Ernie Freeman. (CR)Billy Vaughn.

RAWHIDE (1958) (w)Milt Grant (m)Link Wray. (P)Link Wray.

RAWHIDE (1958) (w)Ned Washington (m)Dimitri Tiomkin. (I)TV series: *Rawhide*, on soundtrack by Frankie Laine.

RAY OF HOPE,A (1969) (wm)Felix Cavaliere—Edward Brigati, Jr. (P)The Rascals.

REACH OUT AND TOUCH (Somebody's Hand) (1970) (wm)Nick Ashford— Valerie Simpson. (P)Diana Ross.

REACH OUT FOR ME (1964) (w)Hal David (m)Burt Bacharach. (P)Dionne Warwick.

REACH OUT I'LL BE THERE (1966) (wm)Brian Holland—Lamont Dozier— Eddie Holland. (P)The Four Tops. (R)1971 by Diana Ross. (R)1975 by Gloria Gaynor.

REACH OUT FOR ME (1964) (w)Hal David (m)Burt Bacharach, (P)Dionne Warwick.

REACH OUT IN THE DARKNESS (1968) (wm)Jim Post. (P)Friend And Lover.

REACHING FOR THE MOON (1931) (wm)Irving Berlin. (I)Film: *Reaching For The Moon*, on soundtrack. (P)Ruth Etting.

READ' EM AND WEEP (1983) (wm)Jim Steinman. (P)Meat Loaf. (R)1983 by Barry Manilow.

READY (1975) (wm)Cat Stevens. (P)Cat Stevens.

READY TEDDY (1956) (wm)John Marascalco—Robert Blackwell. (P)Little Richard.

READY TO TAKE A CHANCE AGAIN (1978) (w)Norman Gimbel (m)Charles Fox. (I)Film: *Foul Play*, by voice of Barry Manilow. (P)Barry Manilow.

READY, WILLING, AND ABLE (1954) (wm)Al Rinker— Floyd Huddleston— Dick Gleason. (I)Film: *Young At Heart*, by Doris Day.

REAL LIVE GIRL (1962) (w)Carolyn Leigh (m)Cy Coleman. (I)Musical: *Little Me*, by Sid Caesar.

REAL LOVE (1980) (wm)Michael McDonald—Patrick Henderson. (P)The Doobie Brothers.

REAL NICE CLAMBAKE, A (1945) (w)Oscar Hammerstein II (m)Richard Rodgers. (I)Musical: *Carousel*, by Jean Darling, Christine Johnson, Jan Clayton, and Eric Mattson. (R)1957 Film: *Carousel*, by Barbara Ruick, Claramae Turner, Robert Rounseville, Cameron Mitchell and The Chorus.

REALLY WANNA KNOW YOU (1981) (wm)Gary Wright (m)Ali Thomson. (P)Gary Wright.

REASON TO BELIEVE (1966) (wm)Tim Hardin. (I)Tim Hardin. (P)1971 by Rod Stewart.

REBEL-ROUSER (1958) (m)Duane Eddy—Lee Hazlewood. (P)Duane Eddy.

RECKLESS (1935) (w)Oscar Hammerstein II (m)Jerome Kern. (I)Film: *Reckless*, by Virginia Merrill dubbing for Jean Harlow, Allan Jones, and Nina Mae McKinney.

RECONSIDER ME (1969) (wm)Myra Smith—Margaret Lewis. (P)Johnny Adams. (R)1975 by Narvel Felts.

RED BALL EXPRESS, THE (1946) (wm)Harold Rome. (I)Musical: *Call Me Mister*, by Lawrence Winters.

RED BANK BOOGIE (1943) (wm)William Basie—Buck Clayton. (P)Count Basie and his Orchestra.

RED HEADED WOMAN MAKES A CHOO CHOO JUMP ITS TRACK, A (1935) (w)Du Bose Heyward—Ira Gershwin (m)George Gershwin. (I)Opera: *Porgy And Bess*, by Warren Coleman. (R)1959 Film: *Porgy And Bess*, by Brock Peters.

RED, HOT AND BLUE (1936) (wm)Cole Porter. (I)Musical: *Red, Hot And Blue*, by Ethel Merman and The Chorus.

RED HOT MAMMA (1924) (wm)Gilbert Wells—Bud Cooper—Fred Rose. (P)Sophie Tucker.

RED RIVER ROCK (1959) (m)Tom King—Ira Mack— Fred Mendelsohn. (P)Johnny and The Hurricanes.

RED ROSES FOR A BLUE LADY (1948) (wm)Sid Tepper—Roy Brodsky. (P)Guy Lombardo and his Royal Canadians. (CR)Vaughn Monroe and his Orchestra. (R)1965 by Bert Kaempfert and his Orchestra.

RED RUBBER BALL (1966) (wm)Paul Simon—Bruce Woodley. (P)The Cyrkle.

RED RIVER VALLEY (1896) (wm)Unknown. Traditional American folk song.

RED SAILS IN THE SUNSET (1935) (w)Jimmy Kennedy (m)Hugh Williams. (P)Bing Crosby. No. 1 Chart Record. (CR)Ray Noble and his Orchestra. (CR)Guy Lombardo and his Royal Canadians. (R)1951 by Nat "King" Cole.

RED SILK STOCKINGS AND GREEN PERFUME (1947) (wm)Dick Sanford— Sammy Mysels—Bob Hilliard. (I)Ray McKinley and his Orchestra. (P)Sammy Kaye and his Orchestra, vocal by Don Cornell.

REDSKIN RHUMBA (1941) (m)Charlie Barnet. (I) Charlie Barnet and his Orchestra.

REEFER MAN (1932) (w)Andy Razaf (m)J. Russel Robinson. (I)Don Redman and his Orchestra. (P)Cab Calloway and his Orchestra.

REELIN' AND ROCKIN' (1965) (wm)Chuck Berry. (P)The Dave Clark Five. (R)1973 by Chuck Berry.

REELING IN THE YEARS (1973) (wm)Donald Fagen— Walter Becker. (P)Steely Dan.

REET PETITE (1957) (wm)Berry Gordy, Jr. —Tyran Carlo. (P)Jackie Wilson. This was Wilson's first solo record.

JACKIE WILSON

Bob Thiele was a great believer in the future of black music. In the mid-fifties - 1954 or 1955 - he wanted to sign Lavern Baker, a big star at the time, to a contract. Lavern's manager was a gentleman named Al Green. When Thiele contacted him, Green said he would give him Baker at the end of her current contract (in about one year), on one condition.

That condition was that Thiele also would have to sign a young male singer Green had under contract. The singer had been with Billy Ward and the Dominoes and Green wanted launch him on his own. Part of the deal would be that we would have to record him immediately.

The singer was Jackie Wilson, and our contract with him was the start of my friendship and love for one of the greatest singers and nicest human beings I had ever met. Ironically, during the waiting period, Al Green died and we never did get to record Lavern Baker.

REFLECTIONS (1967) (wm)Brian Holland—Lamont Dozier—Eddie Holland. (P)Diana Ross and The Supremes.

REFLEX, THE (1984) (wm)Duran Duran. (P)Duran Duran. No. 1 Chart Record.

REFUGEE (1980) (wm)Tom Petty—Mike Campbell. (P)Tom Petty & The Heartbreakers.

RELAX (1984) (wm)Peter Gill—William Johnson—Mark O'Toole. (I)Film: *Body Double*, on soundtrack. (P)Frankie Goes To Hollywood.

RELAX-AY-VOO (1955) (w)Sammy Cahn (m)Arthur

Schwartz. (I)Film: *You're Never Too Young*, by Dean Martin and Jerry Lewis.

RELEASE ME (And Let Me Love Again) (1954) (P)Ray Price. (CR)Kitty Wells. (R)1962 by "Little Esther" Phillips. (P)1967 by Engelbert Humperdinck.

REMEMBER (1925) (wm)Irving Berlin. First recording by Isham Jones and his Orchestra. (CR)Jean Goldkette and his Orchestra. (R)1938 Film: *Alexander's Ragtime Band*, by Alice Faye. (R)1954 Film: *There's No Business Like Show Business*, by Ethel Merman and Dan Dailey.

REMEMBER (Walking In The Sand) (1964) (wm)George F. Morton. (P)The Shangri-Las. (CR)Dean Martin.

REMEMBER ME (1937) (w)Al Dubin (m)Harry Warren. (I)Film: *Mr. Dodds Takes The Air*, by Kenny Baker. (P)Hal Kemp and his Orchestra, vocal by Skinnay Ennis.

REMEMBER ME (1971) (wm)Nicholas Ashford—Valerie Simpson. (P)Diana Ross.

REMEMBER MY FORGOTTEN MAN (1933) (w)Al Dubin (m)Harry Warren. (I)Film: *Gold Diggers of 1933*, by Joan Blondell, Etta Moten and Chorus.

REMEMBER PEARL HARBOR (1942) (wm)Don Reid— Sammy Kaye. (P)Sammy Kaye and his Orchestra.

REMEMBER WHAT I TOLD YOU TO FORGET (1975) (wm)Dennis Lambert— Brian Potter. (P)Tavares.

REMEMBER YOU'RE MINE (1957) (wm)Kal Mann— Bernie Lowe. (P)Pat Boone.

REMEMB'RING (1923) (wm)Rosetta Duncan—Vivian Duncan. (I)Musical: *Topsy And Eva*, by The Duncan Sisters. (P)The Duncan Sisters.

REMIND ME (1940) (w)Dorothy Fields (m)Jerome Kern. (I)Film: *One Night In The Tropics*, by Allan Jones.

REMINISCING (1978) (wm)Graham Goble. (P)Little River Band.

REMINISCING IN TEMPO (1935) (m)Duke Ellington. (P)Duke Ellington and his Orchestra.

RENDEZVOUS (1975) (wm)Bruce Johnston—Brett Hudson—Mark Hudson— William Hudson. (P)The Hudson Brothers.

RENEGADE (1979) (wm)Tommy Shaw. (P)Styx.

RENT PARTY BLUES (1929) (m)Duke Ellington— Johnny Hodges. (P)Duke Ellington and his Cotton Club Orchestra.

RESCUE ME (1965) (wm)Carl William Smith—Raynard Miner. (P)Fontella Bass.

RESPECT (1965) (wm)Otis Redding. (P)Otis Redding. (R)1967 by Aretha Franklin. No. 1 Chart Record.

RESPECT YOURSELF (1971) (wm)Mack Rice—Luther Ingram. (P)The Staple Singers. (R)1987 by Bruce Willis.

RESPECTABLE (1978) (wm)Mick Jagger—Keith Richard. (P)The Rolling Stones.

RESTLESS HEART (1954) (wm)Harold Rome. (I)Musical: *Fanny*, by William Tabbert.

RETURN OF THE RED BARON, THE (1967) (wm)James McCullough—John McCullough—Phil Gernhard. (P)The Royal Guardsmen.

RETURN TO ME (Ritorna A Me) (1957) (wm)Carmen Lombardo—Danny Di Minno. (P)Dean Martin.

RETURN TO PARADISE (1953) (wm)Ned Washington (m)Dimitri Tiomkin. (I)Film: *Return To Paradise*, as soundtrack theme. (P)Percy Faith and his Orchestra.

RETURN TO SENDER (1962) (wm)Otis Blackwell—Winfield Scott. (I)Film: *Girls! Girls! Girls!*, by Elvis Presley. (P)Elvis Presley.

REUNITED (1978) (wm)Dino Fekaris—Freddy Perren. (P)Peaches and Herb. No. 1 Chart Record.

REVEILLE ROCK (1959) (w)I. Mack (m)C. Conatser—J. King. (P)Johnny and The Hurricanes.

REVENGE (1961) (wm)Brook Benton—Marnie Ewald— Oliver Hall. (P)Brook Benton.

REVEREND MR. BLACK, THE (1963) (wm)Billy Wheeler. (P)The Kingston Trio.

REVOLUTION (1968) (wm)John Lennon—Paul McCartney. (P)The Beatles.

RHAPSODY IN BLUE (1924) (m)George Gershwin. (I)Paul Whiteman and his Orchestra, with Gershwin at the piano at Aeolian Hall in New York City. Theme song of Paul Whiteman and his Orchestra. (R)1943 by Glenn Miller and his Orchestra. (R)1945 Film: *Rhapsody In Blue*, by Oscar Levant with Paul Whiteman and his Orchestra.

GEORGE GERSHWIN

There is an interesting story told about George Gershwin, one of the greatest composers in American musical history. The story persists that, despite his genius musical talent as a composer, Mr. Gershwin needed help when it came to orchestrating his music. Supposedly this came to light when he had written *Rhapsody in Blue* and Ferde Grofé had to be called in to assist Gershwin in the orchestration. This association between the two continued until the time of Gershwin's untimely death.

Of course, Grofé went on to become a noted composer in his own right with such compositions as *Grand Canyon Suite* and *Mississippi Suite*. This story is not meant in anyway to detract from George Gershwin's enormous composing talent. He left us a wonderful musical legacy, a particularly remarkable achievement when you realize he was only thirty-eight when he died.

RHAPSODY IN THE RAIN (1966) (w)Lou Christie (m)Twyla Herbert. (P)Lou Christie.

RHIANNON (Will You Ever Win) (1976) (wm)Stephanie Nicks. (P)Fleetwood Mac.

RHINESTONE COWBOY (1974) (wm)Larry Weiss. (I)Larry Weiss. (P)Glen Campbell. No. 1 Chart Record.

RHUMBOOGIE (1940) (wm)Don Raye—Hughie Prince. (I)Film: *Argentine Nights*, by The Andrews Sisters. (P)The Andrews Sisters.

RHYTHM (1964) (wm)Curtis Mayfield (P)Major Lance.

RHYTHM AND ROMANCE (1935) (w)George Whiting— Nat Schwartz (m)J. C. Johnson. (P)Fats Waller.

(If I Had)RHYTHM IN MY NURSERY RHYMES (1935) (w)Sammy Cahn—Don Raye (m)Jimmie Lunceford— Saul Chaplin. (P)Jimmie Lunceford and his Orchestra.

RHYTHM IS GONNA GET YOU (1987) (wm)Gloria Estefan—E. E. Garcia. (P)Gloria Estefan and Miami Sound Machine.

RHYTHM IS OUR BUSINESS (1934) (w)Sammy Cahn— Saul Chaplin (m)Jimmie Lunceford. (P)Jimmie Lunceford and his Orchestra.

RHYTHM OF LIFE, THE (1965) (w)Dorothy Fields (m)Cy Coleman. (I)Musical: *Sweet Charity*, by Arnold Soboloff, Harold Pierson, Eddie Gasper, and The Worshippers. (R)1969 film version, by Sammy Davis,Jr. , and The Ensemble.

RHYTHM OF THE NIGHT (1985) (wm)Diane Warren. (I)Film: *The Last Dragon*, on soundtrack. (P)De-Barge.

RHYTHM OF THE RAIN (1935) (w)Jack Meskill (m)Jack Stern. (I)Film: *Folies Bergere*, by Maurice Chevalier and Ann Sothern.

RHYTHM OF THE RAIN (1963) (wm)John Gummoe. (P)The Cascades. (R)1969 by Gary
Lewis and The Playboys.

RHYTHM ON THE RIVER (1940) (w)Johnny Burke (m)James V. Monaco. (I)Film: *Rhythm On The River*, by Bing Crosby.

RIBBONS DOWN MY BACK (1964) (wm)Jerry Herman. (I)Musical: *Hello, Dolly!*, by Eileen Brennan.

RICH GIRL (1977) (wm)Daryl Hall. (P)Hall & Oates. No. 1 Chart Record.

RICOCHET (1953) (wm)Larry Coleman—Joe Darion—Norman Gimbel. (P)Teresa Brewer.

RIDE (1962) (wm)John Sheldon—David Leon. (P)Dee Dee Sharp.

RIDE AWAY (1965) (wm)Roy Orbison (m)Bill Dees.

RIDE CAPTAIN RIDE (1970) (wm)Frank Konte (m)Carlos Pinera. (P)Blues Image.

RIDE 'EM COWBOY (1974) (wm)Paul Davis (P)Paul Davis.

RIDE LIKE THE WIND (1980) (wm)Christopher Geppert. (P)Christopher Cross.

RIDE, TENDERFOOT, RIDE (1938) (w)Johnny Mercer (m)Richard A. Whiting. (I)Film: *Cowboy From Brooklyn*, by Dick Powell.

RIDE THROUGH THE NIGHT (1961) (w)Betty Comden—Adolph Green (m)Jule Styne. (I)Musical: *Subways Are For Sleeping*, by Sydney Chaplin—Carol Lawrence and The Chorus. (P)The McGuire Sisters.

RIDE YOUR PONY (1965) (wm)Naomi Neville. (P)Lee Dorsey.

RIDERS IN THE SKY (Ghost Riders In The Sky) (1949) (wm)Stan Jones (I)Burl Ives. (P)Vaughn Monroe and his Orchestra. (CR)Peggy Lee. (CR)Bing Crosby.

RIDERS ON THE STORM (1971) (wm)John Densmore—Jim Morrison— Robbie Krieger—Ray Manzarek. (P)The Doors.

RIDIN' AROUND IN THE RAIN (1934) (wm)Gene Austin—Carmen Lombardo. (P)Bing Crosby. (CR)Guy Lombardo and his Royal Canadians.

RIDIN' HIGH (1936) (wm)Cole Porter. (I)Musical: *Red, Hot and Blue!*, by Ethel Merman.

RIDIN' ON THE MOON (1946) (w)Johnny Mercer (m)Harold Arlen. (I)Musical: *St. Louis Woman*, by Harold Nicholas and The Ensemble.

RIFF SONG, THE (1926) (w)Otto Harbach—Oscar Hammerstein II (m)Sigmund Romberg. (I)Operetta: *The Desert Song*, by Robert Halliday, William O'Neal and The Male Chorus. (R)1943 Film: *The Desert Song*, by Dennis Morgan and The Male Chorus. (R)1953 Film: *The Desert Song*, by Gordon MacRae and The Male Chorus.

RIGHT AS THE RAIN (1944) (w)E. Y. Harburg (m)Harold Arlen. (I)Musical: *Bloomer Girl*, by Celeste Holm and David Brooks.

RIGHT BACK WHERE WE STARTED FROM (1976) (wm)Pierre Tubbs— Vincent Edwards. (P)Maxine Nightingale.

RIGHT DOWN THE LINE (1978) (wm)Gerry Rafferty. (P)Gerry Rafferty.

RIGHT GIRL FOR ME, THE (1949) (w)Betty Comden—Adolph Green (m)Roger Edens. (I)Film: *Take Me Out To The Ball Game*, by Frank Sinatra.

RIGHT ON TRACK (1987) (wm)S. Bray—Gilroy. (P)The Breakfast Club.

RIGHT OR WRONG, I'LL BE WITH YOU (1961) (wm)Wanda Jackson. (P)Wanda Jackson. (R)1964 by Ronnie Dove.

RIGHT SOMEBODY TO LOVE, THE (1936) (w)Jack Yellen (m)Lew Pollack. (I)Film: *Captain January*, by Shirley Temple.

RIGHT THING TO DO (1973) (wm)Carly Simon. (P)Carly Simon.

RIGHT TIME OF THE NIGHT (1977) (wm)Peter McCann. (P)Jennifer Warnes.

RIKKI DON'T LOSE THAT NUMBER (1974) (wm)Walter Becker—Donald Fagen. (P)Steely Dan.

RING DEM BELLS (1930) (wm)Duke Ellington—Irving Mills. (P)Duke Ellington and his Orchestra.

RING MY BELL (1979) (wm)Fredereick Knight. (P)Anita Ward. No. 1 Chart Record.

RING OF FIRE (1963) (wm)Merle Kilgore—June Carter. (P)Johnny Cash.

RING THE LIVING BELL (1972) (wm)Melanie Safka. (P)Melanie.

RINGO (1964) (w)Hal Blair—Don Robertson (m)Don Robertson. (P)Lorne Green. No. 1 Chart Record.

RINGS (1971) (wm)Alex Harvey—Eddie Reeves. (P)Cymarron. (R)1974 by Lobo.

RINKY DINK (1962) (wm)Paul Winley—David Clownet. (P)Dave "Baby" Cortez.

RIO (1983) (wm)Duran Duran. (P)Duran Duran.

RIO BRAVO (1959) (w)Paul Francis Webster (m)Dimitri Tiomkin. (I)Film: *Rio Bravo*, by Dean Martin.

RIO RITA (1926) (w)Joseph McCarthy (m)Harry Tierney. (I)Musical: *Rio Rita*, by Ethelind Terry and J. Harold Murray. (R)1929 film version, by Bebe Daniels and John Boles. (R)1942 film version, by John Carroll.

RIP IT UP (1956) (wm)Robert A. Blackwell—John Marascalco. (P)Little Richard.

RISE (1979) (wm)Andy Armer—Randy Alpert. (P)Herb Alpert and The Tijuana Brass. No. 1 Chart Record.

RISE 'N SHINE (1932) (w)B. G. De Sylva (m)Vincent Youmans. (I)Musical: *Take A Chance*, by Ethel Merman. 1933 film version, by Lillian Roth.

RITES OF SPRING (1911) (m)Igor Stravinsky. Famous classical composition. Performed in Disney film: *Fantasia*.

RITUAL FIRE DANCE (1924) (m)Manuel De Falla. Popular modern classical composition.

RIVER, THE (1953) (w-Eng)Robert Mellin (m)C. Concina. (P)Mitch Miller with Percy Faith and his Orchestra.

RIVER CHANTY (1952) (w)Maxwell Anderson (m)Kurt Weill. (I)TV Musical: *Huckleberry Finn*, by Franz Elkins and Randolph Symonette.

RIVER DEEP-MOUNTAIN HIGH (1966) (wm)Jeff Barry—Ellie Greenwich— Phil Spector. (P)Ike and Tina Turner. (R)1969 by Deep Purple. (R)1970 by The Supremes.

RIVER IS WIDE, THE (1967) (wm)Gary Knight—Billy Joe Admire. (P)Forum. (R)1969 by Grass Roots.

RIVER KWAI MARCH, THE (1957) (m)Malcolm Arnold. (I)Film: *The Bridge On The River Kwai*, on soundtrack. Adapted from Colonel Bogey March. (P)Mitch Miller and his Orchestra.

RIVER STAY 'WAY FROM MY DOOR (1931) (w)Mort Dixon (m)Harry Woods. (I)Revue: *Mum's The Word*, by Jimmy Savo. (P)Kate Smith with Guy Lombardo and his Royal Canadians. (CR)Ethel Waters.

RIVERBOAT SHUFFLE (1925) (wm)Dick Voynow—Hoagy Carmichael— Irving Mills—Mitchell Parish. (I)The Wolverines, featuring Bix Beiderbecke on trumpet.

RIVERS OF BABYLON (1978) (wm)F. Farian—G. Reyam—B. Dowe—F. McNaughton. (P)Boney M.

(I'm A)ROAD RUNNER (1966) (wm)Brian Holland—Lamont Dozier— Eddie Holland. (P)Jr. Walker and The All Stars.

ROAD TO HONG KONG, THE (1962) (w)Sammy Cahn (m)Jimmy Van Heusen. (I)Film: *The Road To Hong Kong*, by Bing Crosby and Bob Hope.

ROAD TO MOROCCO (1942) (w)Johnny Burke (m)Jimmy Van Heusen. (I)Film: *Road To Morocco*, by Bing Crosby and Bob Hope.

ROAD YOU DIDN'T TAKE (1971) (wm)Stephen Sondheim. (I)Musical: *Follies*, by Dick Latessa.

ROADHOUSE BLUES (1970) (wm)Jim Morrison—Robby Krieger—John Densmore—Ray Manzarek. (P)The Doors.

ROAMIN' IN THE GLOAMIN' (1911) (wm)Sir Harry Lauder. (I)Vaudeville: by Sir Harry Lauder.

ROBBIN' THE CRADLE (1959) (wm)Anthony J. Bellusci. (P)Tony Bellers.

ROBBINS NEST (1947) (m)Sir Chalres Thompson—Illinois Jacquet. Jazz instrumental dedicated to disc jockey Fred Robbins. (P)Count Basie and his Orchestra. (CR)Sam Donahue and his Orchestra.

ROBIN HOOD (1945) (wm)Louis Prima—Bob Miketta. (P)Louis Prima and his Orchestra.

ROBINS AND ROSES (1936) (w)Edgar Leslie (m)Joe Burke. (P)Bing Crosby.

ROCK-A-BILLY (1957) (wm)Woody Harris—Eddie V. Deane. (P)Guy Mitchell.

ROCK-A-BYE YOUR BABY WITH A DIXIE MELODY (1918) (w)Sam M. Lewis—Joe Young (m)Jean Schwartz. (I)Musical: *Sinbad*, by Al Jolson. (P)Al Jolson. (R)1956 by Jerry Lewis. (R)1961 by Aretha Franklin. Most popular recording by Judy Garland.

ROCK-A-HULA-BABY (1961) (wm)Fred Wise, Ben Weisman—Dolores Fuller. (I)Film: *Blue Hawaii*, by Elvis Presley. (P)Elvis Presley.

ROCK AND ROLL (Part II) (1972) (wm)Gary Glitter—Mike Leander. (P)Gary Glitter.

ROCK AND ROLL ALL NIGHT (1976) (wm)Stanley Eisen—Gene Simmons. (P)Kiss.

ROCK AND ROLL GIRLS (1985) (wm)John Fogarty. (P)John Fogarty.

ROCK AND ROLL HOOTCHIE KOO (1974) (wm)Rick Derringer. (P)Rick Derringer.

ROCK AND ROLL IS HERE TO STAY (1958) (wm)Danny And The Juniors. (P)Danny and The Juniors.

ROCK AND ROLL LULLABYE (1972) (wm)Barry Mann—Cynthia Weil. (P)B. J. Thomas.

ROCK AND ROLL MUSIC (1957) (wm)Chuck Berry. (P)Chuck Berry. (R)1976 by The Beach Boys.

ROCK AND ROLL WALTZ (1955) (w)Roy Alfred (m)Shorty Allen. (P)Kay Starr. No. 1 Chart Record.

ROCK AROUND THE CLOCK (1953) (wm)Max Freedman—Jimmy De Knight. (I)Film: *The Blackboard Jungle*, by Bill Haley and The Comets on soundtrack. (P)Bill Haley and The Comets. No. 1 Chart Record. (R)1974 by Bill Haley and The Comets.

MILT GABLER

Milt Gabler was one of our A&R producers at Decca. Milt had started his career owning Commodore Records, a great jazz label. He recorded many of the jazz greats, including the one and only Billie Holiday.

Most of Milt's work for Decca was with middle of the road pop singers and his record of hits was good as anyone around. He had an act called Bill Haley and The Comets, who came in with a song called *Rock Around the Clock*. Milt recorded Haley at Pythian Temple. It sticks in my memory because I happened to be at Pythian on that particular day. And of course the rest is history. *Rock Around the Clock* became a million seller on three different occasions and is now a smash nostalgia hit. It takes its place in music history as the first great white rock record.

ROCK ISLAND LINE (1956) (wm)Lonnie Donegan. Adapted from a folk song. (P)Lonnie Donegan. (CR)Don Cornell. (R)1970 by Johnny Cash.

ROCK LOVE (1955) (wm)Henry Glover (P)The Fontane Sisters.

ROCK ME (1969) (wm)John Kay. (I)Film: *Candy*, on soundtrack. (P)Steppenwolf.

ROCK ME AMADEUS (1986) (wm)Rob Bolland—Ferdi Bolland— Falco. (P)Falco. No. 1 Chart Record.

ROCK ME GENTLY (1974) (wm)Andy Kim. (P)Andy Kim. No. 1 Chart Record.

ROCK ME TONITE (1984) (wm)Billy Squier. (P)Billy Squier.

ROCK ME TONIGHT (For Old Times Sake) (1985) (wm)Paul Laurence. (P)Freddie Jackson.

ROCK AND ROLL FANTASY, A (1978) (wm)Ray Davies. (P)The Kinks.

ROCK 'N ROLL FANTASY (1979) (wm)Paul Rodgers. (P)Bad Company.

ROCK 'N ROLL IS KING (1983) (wm)Jeff Lynne. (P)ELO.

ROCK OF AGES (1832) (wm)Unknown. Famous hymn.

ROCK OF AGES (1983) (wm)Steve Clark—Robert John Lange—Joe Elliott. (P)Def Leppard.

ROCK ON (1974) (wm)David Essex. (P)David Essex.

ROCK STEADY (1971) (wm)Aretha Franklin. (P)Aretha Franklin.

ROCK STEADY (1987) (wm)Babyface—L. A. —D. Ladd—B. Watson. (P)The Whispers.

ROCK THE BOAT (1974) (wm)Waldo Humes. (P)The Hues Corporation. No. 1 Chart Record.

ROCK THE CASBAH (1982) (wm)Paul Simonon—Topper Headon—Joe Strummer—Mick Jones. (P)The Clash.

ROCK THIS TOWN (1982) (wm)Brian Setzer. (P)The Stray Cats.

ROCK WITH YOU (1979) (wm)Rod Temperton. (P)Michael Jackson. No. 1 Chart Record.

ROCK YOU LIKE A HURRICANE (1984) (wm)Rudolf Schenker—Klaus Meine—Herman Rarebell. (P)The Scorpions.

ROCK YOUR BABY (1974) (wm)Harry Casey—Richard Finch. (P)George McRae. No. 1 Chart Record.

ROCK YOUR LITTLE BABY TO SLEEP (1957) (wm)Buddy Knox. (P)Buddy Knox.

ROCKET 2 U (1987) (wm)B. Nunn. (P)The Jets.

ROCKET MAN (1972) (wm)Elton John—Bernie Taupin. (P)Elton John.

ROCKFORD FILES, THE (1975) (m)Peter Carpenter—Mike Post. (I)Film: TV Show: *The Rockford Files*, as soundtrack theme. (P)Mike Post and his Orchestra.

ROCKIN' ALL OVER THE WORLD (1975) (wm)John Fogarty. (P)John Fogarty.

ROCKIN' AROUND THE CHRISTMAS TREE (1960) (wm)Brenda Lee—Dub Allbritton. (P)Brenda Lee.

ROCKIN' CHAIR (1930) (wm)Hoagy Carmichael. (P)Mildred Bailey. (CR)Mills Brothers. (CR)Louis Armstrong with Hoagy Carmichael.

ROCKIN' GOOD WAY (To Mess Around And Fall In Love), A (1960) (P)Brook Benton and Dinah Washington.

ROCKIN' IN RHYTHM (1931) (m)Duke Ellington—Irving Mills—Harry Carney. (P)Duke Ellington and his Orchestra.

ROCKIN' PNEUMONIA AND THE BOOGIE WOOGIE FLU (1957) (wm)Huey Smith & The Clowns. (R)1972 by Johnny Rivers.

ROCKIN' ROBIN (1958) (wm)Jimmie Thomas. (P)Bobby Day. (R)1964 by The Rivieras. (R)1972 by Michael Jackson.

ROCKIN' ROLL BABY (1973) (wm)Linda Creed—Thom Bell. (P)The Stylistics.

ROCKIN' SOUL (1974) (wm)Waldo Holmes—Bruno Pallini—Lorenzo Raggi. (P)The Hues Corporation.

ROCKY (1975) (wm)Jay Stevens. (P)Dickie Lee. (CR)Austin Roberts.

ROCKY MOUNTAIN HIGH (1973) (wm)John Denver—Michael Taylor. (P)John Denver.

ROCKY MOUNTAIN WAY (1973) (wm)Joe Walsh—Joey Vitale—Kenny Passarelli—Roche Grace. (P)Joe Walsh.

ROCKY RACOON (1969) (wm)John Lennon—Paul McCartney. (P)The Beatles.

RODGER YOUNG (1945) (wm)Frank Loesser. Dedicated to Pvt. Rodger Young. (I)Earl Wrightson. (P)Burl Ives.

ROGUE SONG, THE (1929) (w)Clifford Grey (m)Herbert Stothart. (I)Film: *The Rogue Song*, by Lawrence Tibbett.

ROLENE (1979) (wm)Moon Martin. (P)Moon Martin.

ROLL 'EM (1937) (m)Mary Lou Williams. (P)Andy Kirk and his Orchestra, with Mary Lou Williams at the piano. (P)Benny Goodman and his Orchestra.

ROLL JORDAN ROLL (1865)Traditional Black American spiritual.

ROLL ME AWAY (1983) (wm)Bob Seger. (P)Bob Seger.

ROLL ON DOWN THE HIGHWAY (1975) (wm)Charles Turner—Randy Bachman. (P)Bachman—Turner Overdrive.

ROLL OVER BEETHOVEN (1956) (wm)Chuck Berry. (P)Chuck Berry. (R)1964 by The Beatles. (R)1973 by Electric Light Orchestra.

ROLLIN' STONE (1955) (wm)Robert S. Riley. (P)The Fontane Sisters. (CR)The Marigolds.

ROLLING HOME (1934) (wm)Cole Porter. (I)Film: *Born To Dance*, by Eleanor Powell.

ROMANCE (1926) (w)Otto Harbach—Oscar Hammerstein II (m)Sigmund Romberg. (I)Operetta: *The Desert Song*, by Vivienne Segal and The Women's Chorus. 1929 film version by Carlotta King. 1943 film version by Irene Manning. 1953 film version by Kathryn Grayson.

ROMANCE (1930) (w)Edgar Leslie (m)Walter Donaldson. (I)Film: *Cameo Kirby*, by J. Harold Murray.

ROMANCING THE STONE (1984) (wm)Eddy Grant. (P)Eddy Grant.

ROMANY LIFE (1898) (w)Harry Smith (m)Victor Herbert. (I)Musical: *The Fortune Teller*.

ROMEO AND JULIET (Overture) (1871) (m)Peter Tchaikovsky. (See, also, Our Love).

ROMEO AND JULIET (Love Theme) (See: A Time For Us)

(Just Like)ROMEO AND JULIET (1964) (wm)Bob Hamilton—Freddy Gorman. (P)The Reflections.

ROMEO'S TUNE (1979) (wm)Steve Forbert. (P)Steve Forbert.

RONNIE (1964) (wm)Bob Crewe—Bob Gaudio. (P)The Four Seasons.

ROOM FULL OF ROSES (1949) (wm)Tim Spencer. (P)Sammy Kaye and his Orchestra, vocal by Don Cornell. (CR)Eddy Howard. (CR)Dick Haymes. (CR)George Morgan. (R)1974 by Mickey Gilley.

ROOM WITH A VIEW, A (1928) (wm)Noel Coward. (I)Revue: *This Year Of Grace*, by Noel Coward, Madeline Gibson and The Young Ladies.

ROOM WITH A VIEW, A (1938) (w)Al Stillman (m)Einar Swan. (P)Tommy Dorsey and his Orchestra. (CR)Ben Selvin and his Orchestra.

ROOM WITHOUT WINDOWS, A (1964) (wm)Ervin Drake. (I)Musical: *What Makes Sammy Run?*, by Steve Lawrence and Sally Ann Howes.

ROOTS MEDLEY (Motherland) (1977) (m)Gerald Fried. (I)TV Show: *Roots*, on soundtrack. (P)Quincy Jones and his Orchestra.

ROSALIE (1937) (wm)Cole Porter. (I)Film: *Rosalie*, by Nelson Eddy.

ROSALITA (Come Out Tonight) (1973) (wm)Bruce Springsteen. (P)Bruce Springsteen.

ROSANNA (1982) (wm)David Paich. (P)Toto. NARAS Award Winner.

ROSARY, THE (1898) (w)Robert Cameron Rogers (m)Ethelbert Nevin. (I)William H. Thompson. (P)Ernestine Schumann—Heink. Also, John McCormack.

ROSE, THE (1979) (wm)Amanda McBroom. (I)Film: *The Rose*, by Bette Midler. (P)Bette Midler.

ROSE AND A BABY RUTH, A (1956) (wm)John Loudermilk. (P)George Hamilton IV.

(I Never Promised You A)ROSE GARDEN (1967) (wm)Joe South. (P)Lynn Anderson.

ROSE MARIE (1924) (w)Otto Harbach—Oscar Hammerstein II (m)Rudolf Friml. (I)Operetta: *Rose—Marie*, by Dennis King. 1936 film version by Nelson Eddy. 1954 film version by Howard Keel.

ROSE O'DAY (The Filla-Ga-Dusha Song) (1941) (wm)Charles Tobias— Al Lewis. (I)The Merry Macs. (P)Kate Smith.

ROSE OF MADRID (1924) (w)B. G. De Sylva (m)George Gershwin. (I)Revue: *George White's Scandals of 1924*, by Richard Bold.

ROSE OF THE RIO GRANDE (1922) (w)Edgar Leslie

(m)Harry Warren— Ross Gorman. (P)Paul Whiteman and his Orchestra.

ROSE OF TRALEE, THE (1912) (wm)Charles Glover—C. Mordaunt Spencer. (P)John McCormack.

ROSE OF WASHINGTON SQUARE (1920) (w)Ballard MacDonald (m)James F. Hanley. (P)Theme song of Fanny Brice.

ROSE ROOM (1917) (wm)Harry Williams (m)Art Hickman. (P)Art Hickman and his Orchestra. (CR)Duke Ellington and his Orchestra.

ROSE, ROSE, I LOVE YOU (1951) (w)Jack Brooks (m)Harry Warren. (P)Frankie Laine. (CR)Gordon Jenkins and his Orchestra.

ROSES ARE RED (My Love) (1962) (wm)Al Byron—Paul Evans. (P)Bobby Vinton. No. 1 Chart Record.

ROSES IN THE RAIN (1947) (w)Al Frisch—Fred Wise (m)Frankie Carle. (P)Frankie Carle and his Orchestra.

ROSES OF PICARDY (1916) (w)F. E. Weatherly (m)Haydn Wood. (P)John McCormack.

ROSE'S TURN (1959) (w)Stephen Sondheim (m)Jule Styne. (I)Musical: *Gypsy*, by Ethel Merman.

ROSES OF YESTERDAY (1928) (wm)Irving Berlin. (P)Fred Waring's Pennsylvanians.

ROSETTA (1935) (wm)Earl Hines—Henri Woode. (P)Earl Hines and his Orchestra.

ROSIE (1960) (w)Lee Adams (m)Charles Strouse. (I)Musical: *Bye Bye Birdie*, by Dick Van Dyke and Chita Rivera. 1963 film version by Ann—Margret, Janet Leigh, Dick Van Dyke, and Bobby Rydell.

ROSIE LEE (1957) (wm)Jerry Carr. (P)The Mello—Tones.

ROSIE THE RIVETER (1942) (wm)Redd Evans—John Jacob Loeb. (P)The Four Vagabonds.

ROSITA, LA (1923) (w)Allan Stuart (m)Paul Dupont. No artist credited with introduction. (R)1953 by The Four Aces.

ROUGH BOY (1986) (wm)Z. Z. Top (P)Z. Z. Top.

ROUND ABOUT (1952) (wm)Ogden Nash (m)Vernon Duke. (I)Revue: *Two's Company*, by Ellen Hanley.

ROUND AND ROUND (1956) (wm)Lou Stallman—Joe Shapiro. (P)Perry Como. No. 1 Chart Record.

ROUND AND ROUND (1984) (wm)Warren DeMartini—Stephen Pearcy— Robbin Crosby. (P)Ratt.

ROUND EVERY CORNER (1965) (wm)Tony Hatch. (P)Petula Clark.

'ROUND HER NECK SHE WORE A YELLOW RIBBON (1949) (wm)M. Ottner— Leroy Parker. Adaptation of American folk song. (I)Film: *She Wore A Yellow Ribbon* on soundtrack. Most popular recording by The Andrews Sisters with Russ Morgan and his Orchestra.

'ROUND MIDNIGHT (1944) (w)Bernie Hanighen (m)Cootie Williams— Thelonius Monk. (P)Cootie Williams and his Orchestra. (R)1986 by Linda Ronstadt.

ROUNDABOUT (1972) (wm)Jon Anderson—Steve Howe. (P)Yes.

(Get Your Kicks On)ROUTE 66! (1946) (wm)Bob Troup. (P)The King Cole Trio.

ROUTE 66 (Theme) (1966) (m)Nelson Riddle. (I)TV series: *Route 66* on soundtrack. (P)Nelson Riddle and his Orchestra.

ROVING KIND, THE (1951) (wm)Jessie Cavanaugh—Arnold Stanton. (P)Guy Mitchell with Mitch Miller and his Orchestra.

ROYAL GARDEN BLUES (1919) (wm)Spencer Williams—Clarence Williams. (P)The Original Dixieland Jazz Band.

RUB IT IN (1971) (wm)Layng Martine, Jr. (P)Layng Martine. (R)1974 by Billy "Crash" Craddock.

RUBBER BALL (1960) (wm)Aaron Schroeder—Anne Orlowski. (P)Bobby Vee.

RUBBER DUCKIE (1970) (wm)Jeffrey Moss. (I)TV Show: *Sesame Street* by Jim Henson as Ernie. (P)Ernie.

RUBBERBAND MAN, THE (1976) (wm)Thom Bell—Linda Creed. (P)The Spinners.

RUBBERNECKIN' (1970) (w)Dory Jones (m)Bunny Warren. (I)Film: *Change Of Habit*, by Elvis Presley. (P)Elvis Presley.

RUBY (1953) (w)Mitchell Parish (m)Heinz Roemheld. (I)Film: *Ruby Gentry*, as soundtrack theme. (P)Les Baxter and his Orchestra. (CR)Richard Hayman and his Orchestra.

RUBY BABY (1963) (wm)Jerry Leiber—Mike Stoller. (P)Dion. (R)1975 by Billy "Crash" Craddock.

RUBY, DON'T TAKE YOUR LOVE TO TOWN (1969) (wm)Mel Tillis. (P)Kenny Rogers and The First Edition.

RUBY-DU-DU (1960) (w)Sunny Skylar (m)Charles Wolcott. (P)Joanie Sommers.

RUBY TUESDAY (1967) (wm)Mick Jagger—Keith Richard. (P)The Rolling Stones. No. 1 Chart Record. (R)1970 by Melanie.

RUDOLPH THE RED NOSED REINDEER (1949) (wm)Johnny Marks. (P)Gene Autry. Subsequent recordings by most of the popular recording artists in the business. Over 300 different recordings with over 50, 000,000 records sold.

JOHNNY MARKS

Back in the 1940s. Johnny Marks and I shared offices in the Brill Building, the "heart" of Tin Pan Alley. Johnny had just composed *Rudolph the Red Nosed Reindeer* and he finally persuaded Gene Autry to record the song. Johnny had great faith that *Rudolph* and Gene's recording were going to prove successful.

However, he needed music arrangements, so he approached me with the following proposition. I was to do all the arrangements he needed. If *Rudolph* became a hit, he would pay me double the union scale for my efforts. If the song didn't make it, I would get nothing. I was not very busy at the time, so Johnny's offer was very welcome.

Of course *Rudolph* became one of the biggest song successes in history. Johnny not only paid me double scale, but added a handsome bonus as well. I lost a dear friend when Johnny passed away. *Rudolph the Red Nosed Reindeer* will live on forever in the hearts of young and old everywhere and so will the memory of Johnny Marks, for everyone whose life this gentle man touched.

RUG CUTTER'S SWING (1934) (m)Horace Henderson. (P)Fletcher Henderson and his Orchestra.

RUM AND COCA COLA (1944) (w)Morey Amsterdam

(m)Jeri Sullavan— Paul Baron. (P)The Andrews Sisters.

RUMANIAN RHAPSODY (1909) (m)Georges Enesco. Famous classical composition.

RUMBLE (1958) (m)Sy Oliver. (P)Link Wray.

RUMBLE, RUMBLE, RUMBLE (wm)Frank Loesser. (I)Film: *The Perils Of Pauline*, by Betty Hutton.

RUMORS (1986) (wm)Marcus Thompson—Michael Marshall—Alex Hill. (P)Timex Social Club.

RUMORS ARE FLYING (1946) (wm)Bennie Benjamin— George Weiss. (P)Frankie Carle and his Orchestra, vocal by Marjorie Hughes.

RUN, BABY, RUN (Back Into My Arms) (1965) (wm)Joe Melson—Don Gant. (P)The Newbeats.

RUN FOR THE ROSES (1982) (wm)Dan Fogelberg. (P)Dan Fogelberg.

RUN FOR YOUR LIFE (1965) (wm)John Lennon—Paul McCartney. (P)The Beatles.

RUN JOEY RUN (1975) (wm)Jack Perricone—Paul Vance. (P)David Geddes.

RUN, RABBIT, RUN (1939) (wm)Noel Gay—Ralph Butler. (I)London musical: *The Little Dog Laughed.*

RUN, RUN, LOOK AND SEE (1966) (wm)Marty Cooper— Ray Whitley. (P)Brian Hyland.

RUN RUN RUN (1972) (wm)Dominic Troiano—Roy Kenner. (P)Jo Jo Gunne.

RUN, RUNAWAY (1984) (wm)Noddy Holder—Jim Lea. (P)Slade.

RUN SAMSON RUN (1960) (w)Howard Greenfield (m)Neil Sedaka. (P)Neil Sedaka.

RUN THROUGH THE JUNGLE (1970) (wm)John C. Fogarty. (P)Creedence Clearwater Revival.

RUN TO HIM (1961) (wm)Gerry Goffin—Jack Keller. (P)Bobby Vee.

RUN TO ME (1972) (wm)Barry, Maurice, and Robin Gibb. (P)The Bee Gees.

RUN TO YOU (1985) (wm)Bryan Adams—Jim Vallance. (P)Bryan Adams.

RUNAROUND SUE (1961) (wm)Dion Di Mucci—Ernest Maresca. (P)Dion. No. 1 Chart Record. (R)1978 by Leif Garrett.

RUNAWAY (1961) (w)Del Shannon (m)Max Crook—Del Shannon. (P)Del Shannon. (CR)Lawrence Welk and his Orchestra. (R)1977 by Bonnie Raitt. (R)1986 by Luis Cardenas.

RUNAWAY (1978) (wm)Nicholas Dewey. (P)Jefferson Starship.

RUNNER, THE (1984) (wm)Ian Thomas. (P)Manfred Mann's Earth Band.

RUNNIN' AWAY (1972) (wm)Sylvester Stewart. (P)Sly & The Family Stone.

RUNNIN' WILD (1922) (w)Joe Grey—Leo Wood (m)A. Harrington Gibbs. (P)Art Hickman and his Orchestra. (R)1938 by Jimmie Lunceford and his Orchestra. (R)1959 Film: *Some Like It Hot*, by Marilyn Monroe.

RUNNING BEAR (1959) (wm)J. P. Richardson (P)Johnny Preston. (R)1969 by Sonny James.

RUNNING ON EMPTY (1978) (wm)Jackson Browne. (P)Jackson Browne.

RUNNING SCARED (1981) (wm)Roy Orbison—Joe Melson. (P)Roy Orbison. No. 1 Chart Record. (R)1981 by The Fools.

RUNNING WITH THE NIGHT (1983) (w)Cynthia Weil. (m)Lionel Richie. (P)Lionel Richie.

RUSSIAN LULLABY (1927) (wm)Irving Berlin. (P)Roger Wolfe Kahn and his Orchestra. (R)1938 by Bunny Berigan and his Orchestra. (R)1946 Film: *Blue Skies*, by Bing Crosby.

RUSSIANS (1986) (wm)Gordon Sumner (Sting). (P)Sting.

S-H-I-N-E (1924) (w)Cecil Mack—Lew Brown (m)Ford Dabney. (P)Louis Armstrong. (R)1943 Film: *Cabin In The Sky*, by John W. Bubbles. (R)1948 by Frankie Laine.

'S WONDERFUL (1927) (w)Ira Gershwin (m)George Gershwin. (I)Musical: *Funny Face*, by Adele Astaire and Allen Kearns. First recording by Frank Crumit. (R)1951 Film: *An American In Paris*, by Gene Kelly and Georges Guetary.

SABBATH PRAYER (1964) (w)Sheldon Harnick (m)Jerry Bock. (I)Musical: *Fiddler On The Roof*, by Zero Mostel, Maria Karnilova and The Chorus. Recorded by Dick Jacobs and his Orchestra.

SABRE DANCE BOOGIE (1948) (m)Aram Khachaturian. Adapted from Sabre Dance, from Gayne, Ballet Suite No. 1. (P)Freddy Martin and his Orchestra.

SACRED (1961) (w)William Landau (m)Adam Ross. (P)The Castells.

SAD EYED LADY OF THE LOWLANDS (1966) (wm)Bob Dylan. (P)Bob Dylan.

SAD EYES (1979) (wm)Robert John. (P)Robert John. No. 1 Chart Record.

SAD MOVIES (Make Me Cry) (1961) (wm)John D. Loudermilk. (P)Sue Thompson. (CR)The Lennon Sisters.

SAD, SAD GIRL (1965) (wm)Barbara Mason. (P)Barbara Mason.

SAD SWEET DREAMER (1975) (wm)Des Parton. (P)Sweet Sensation.

SADIE. SADIE (1964) (w)Beb Merrill (m)Jule Styne. (I)Musical: *Funny Girl*, by Barbra Streisand.

SAFETY DANCE, THE (1983) (wm)Ivan Doroschuk. (P)Men Without Hats.

SAGA OF JENNY (See: Jenny).

SAIL ALONG SILV'RY MOON (1937) (w)Harry Tobias (m)Percy Wenrich. (P)Bing Crosby. (R)1958 by Billy Vaughn and his Orchestra.

SAIL AWAY (1950) (wm)Noel Coward. (I)London Musical: *Ace Of Clubs*, by Graham Payn. (R)1961 Musical: *Sail Away*, by James Hurst.

SAIL ON (1979) (wm)Lionel Richie. (P)The Commodores.

SAILBOAT IN THE MOONLIGHT (1937) (wm)John Jacob Loeb—Carmen Lombardo. (P)Guy Lombardo and his Royal Canadians.

SAILING OVER THE BOUNDING MAIN (1880) (wm)Godfrey Marks. Popular folk song.

SAILING (1980) (wm)Christopher Cross. (P)Christopher Cross. NARAS Award Winner.

SAILOR (Your Home Is The Sea) (1960) (w-Eng)Alan Holt (m)Werner Scharfenberger. (P)Lolita.

SAILOR BEWARE (1936) (w)Leo Robin (m)Richard A. Whiting. (I)Film: *Anything Goes*, by Bing Crosby.

ST. ELMO'S FIRE (Man In Motion)1985) (wm)David Foster—John Parr. (I)Film: *St. Elmo's Fire* on soundtrack. (P)John Parr.

ST. GEORGE AND THE DRAGONET (1953) (w)Stan Freberg—Daws Butler. (m)Walter Schumann. (P)Stan Freberg.

ST. JAMES INFIRMARY (1930) (wm)Irving Mills. Adapted from traditional folk song. (P)Cab Calloway.

ST. THERESA OF THE ROSES (1956) (w)Remus Harris

(m)Arthur Strauss. (P)Billy Ward and The Dominoes, solo vocal by Jackie Wilson.

SALLY (1920) (w)Clifford Grey (m)Jerome Kern. (I)Musical: *Sally*, by Irving Fisher.

SALLY G (1975) (wm)Paul and Linda McCartney. (P)Paul McCartney & Wings.

SALLY GO 'ROUND THE ROSES (1963) (wm)Zell Sanders—Lona Spector. (P)The Jaynettes.

SALT OF THE EARTH, THE (1968) (wm)Mick Jagger—Keith Richard. (P)The Rolling Stones.

SALT PEANUTS (1945) (m)John Birks Gillespie—Kenny Clarke. (P)Dizzy Gillespie.

SALUDOS AMIGOS (1943) (w-Eng)Ned Washington (m)Charles Wolcott. (I)Cartoon film: *Saludos Amigos*.

SAME (1977) (wm)Don Black—John Farrar—Hank Marvin. (P)Olivia Newton—John.

SAM, THE OLD ACCORDION MAN (1927) (wm)Walter Donaldson. (P)Ruth Etting. (R)1955 Film: *Love Me Or Leave Me*, by Doris Day.

SAMBA DE ORFEU (1960) (w)Antonio Maria (m)Luis Bonfa. (I)French film: *Black Orpheus* on soundtrack.

SAME OLD LANG SYNE (1980) (wm)Dan Fogelberg. (P)Dan Fogelberg.

SAME OLD SATURDAY NIGHT (1955) (w)Sammy Cahn (m)Frank Reardon. (P)Frank Sinatra.

SAM'S SONG (The Happy Tune) (1950) (w)Jack Elliott (m)Lew Quadling. (P)Joe "Fingers" Carr. (CR)Bing and Gary Crosby.

SAN (1920) (wm)Lindsay McPhail—Walter Michels. (P)Paul Whiteman and his Orchestra. (CR)Ted Lewis. (R)1953 by Pee Wee Hunt.

SAN ANTONIO ROSE (1940) (wm)Bob Wills. (I)Bob Wills and his Texas Playboys. (P)Bing Crosby.

SAN FERNANDO VALLEY (1943) (wm)Gordon Jenkins. (P)Bing Crosby. (CR)Johnny Mercer.

SAN FRANCISCAN NIGHTS (1967) (wm)Eric Burdon—Victor Briggs— John Weider—Barry Jenkins—Danny McCulloch. (P)Eric Burdon and The Animals.

SAN FRANCISCO (1936) (w)Gus Kahn (m)Bronislaw Kaper—Walter Jurmann. (I)Film: *San Francisco*, by Jeanette MacDonald.

SAN FRANCISCO (Be Sure To Wear Some Flowers In Your Hair) (1967) (wm)John Phillips. (P)Scott McKenzie.

SANCTIFY YOURSELF (1986) (wm)Simple Minds. (P)Simple Minds.

SAND IN MY SHOES (1941) (w)Frank Loesser (m)Victor Schertzinger. (I)Film: *Kiss The Boys Goodbye*, by Connee Boswell. (P)Connee Boswell.

SANDMAN (1934) (w)Ralph Freed (m)Bonnie Lake. (I)Theme song of Dorsey Brothers Orchestra.

SANDS OF TIME (1953) (wm)Robert Wright—George Forrest. Adapted from Borodin's In The Steppes Of Central Asia. (I)Musical: *Kismet*, by Alfred Drake, Richard Oneto, and Doretta Morrow.

SANDY (1959) (wm)Terry Fell. (P)Larry Hall. (R)1965 by Ronny and The Daytonas.

SANDY (1978) (w)Scott Simon (m)Louis St. Louis. (I)Film: *Grease*, by John Travolta.

SANTA BABY (1953) (wm)Joan Javits—Phil Springer—Tony Springer. (P)Eartha Kitt.

SANTA CLAUS IS COMING TO TOWN (1934) (wm)Haven Gillespie—J. Fred Coots. (I)George Olsen and his Orchestra, vocal by Ethel Shutta. (P)Eddie Cantor. (R)1947 by Bing Crosby and The Andrews Sisters.

SANTO NATALE (1955) (wm)Al Hoffman—Dick Manning—Belle Nardone. (P)David Whitfield.

SARA (1976) (wm)Bob Dylan. (P)Bob Dylan.

SARA (1979) (wm)Stephanie Nicks. (P)Fleetwood Mac.

SARA (1986) (wm)Ina Wolf—Peter Wolf. (P)Starship. No. 1 Chart Record.

SARA SMILE (1976) (wm)Daryl Hall—John Oates. (P)Hall & Oates.

SATAN TAKES A HOLIDAY (1937) (m)Larry Clinton. (P)Tommy Dorsey and his Orchestra. No. 1 Chart Record.

SATIN AND SILK (1955) (wm)Cole Porter. (I)Musical: *Silk Stockings*, by Gretchen Wyler.

SATIN DOLL (1958) (w)Johnny Mercer (m)Bill Strayhorn—Duke Ellington. (P)Duke Ellington and his Orchestra. Most popular recording by Ella Fitzgerald.

SATIN PILLOWS (1965) (wm)Bob Tubert (m)Sonny James. (P)Bobby Vinton.

SATIN SOUL (1975) (wm)Barry White. (P)Love Unlimited Orchestra.

(I Can't Get No)SATISFACTION (1965) (wm)Mick Jagger—Keith Richard. (P)The Rolling Stones. No. 1 Chart Record. (R)1966 by Otis Redding.

SATURDAY IN THE PARK (1972) (wm)Robert Lamm. (P)Chicago.

SATURDAY NIGHT (Is The Loneliest Night In The Week) (1944) (w)Sammy Cahn (m)Jule Styne. (P)Frank Sinatra.

SATURDAY NIGHT (1976) (wm)Phil Coulter—Bill Martin. (P)The Bay City Rollers. No. 1 Chart Record.

SATURDAY NIGHT AT THE MOVIES (1964) (wm)Barry Mann—Cynthia Weil. (P)The Drifters.

SATURDAY NIGHT FISH FRY (1949) (wm)Ellis Walsh—Louis Jordan. (P)Louis Jordan and his Tympani Five.

SATURDAY NIGHT SPECIAL (1975) (wm)Edward King—Ronnie Van Zant. (P)Lynyrd Skynyrd.

SATURDAY NIGHT'S ALRIGHT (For Fighting) (1973) (wm)Elton John— Bernie Taupin. (P)Elton John.

SATURDAY NITE (1977) (wm)Philip Bailey—Albert McKay—Maurice White. (P)Earth, Wind & Fire.

SAVANNAH (1940) (wm)John Latouche (m)Vernon Duke. (I)Musical: *Cabin In The Sky*, by Ethel Waters.

SAVANNAH (1957) (w)E. Y. Harburg (m)Harold Arlen. (I)Musical: *Jamaica*, by Ricardo Montalban.

SAVE A PRAYER (1985) (wm)Duran Duran. (P)Duran Duran.

SAVE IT FOR A RAINY DAY (1977) (wm)Stephen Bishop. (P)Stephen Bishop.

SAVE IT FOR ME (1964) (wm)Bob Crewe—Bob Gaudio. (P)The Four Seasons.

SAVE ME, SISTER (w)E. Y. Harburg (m)Harold Arlen. (I)Film: *The Singing Kid*, by Al Jolson, Cab Calloway, and Wini Shaw.

SAVE THE COUNTRY (1968) (wm)Laura Nyro. (P)Laura Nyro. (R)1970 by The 5th Dimension. Also, Thelma Houston.

SAVE THE LAST DANCE FOR ME (1960) (wm)Doc Pomus—Mort Shuman. (P)The Drifters. (R)1974 by The De Franco Family.

SAVE YOUR HEART FOR ME (1965) (wm)Gary Geld—Peter Udell. (P)Gary Lewis and The Playboys.

SAVE YOUR KISSES FOR ME (1976) (wm)Anthony Hiller—Martin Lee— Lee Sheridan. (P)Brotherhood Of Man. (CR)Bobby Vinton.

SAVING ALL MY LOVE FOR YOU (1985) (wm)Michael Masser—Gerry Goffin. (P)Whitney Houston. No. 1 Chart Record.

SAVOY TRUFFLE (1969) (wm)George Harrison. (P)The Beatles.

SAY A PRAY'R FOR THE BOYS OVER THERE (1943) (w)Herb Magidson (m)Jimmy McHugh. (I)Film: *Hers To Hold*, by Deanna Durbin.

SAY, DARLING (1958) (w)Betty Comden—Adolph Green (m)Jule Styne. (I)Musical: *Say, Darling*, by Johnny Desmond.

SAY GOODBYE TO HOLLYWOOD (1976) (wm)Billy Joel. (P)Billy Joel.

SAY, HAS ANYBODY SEEN MY SWEET GYPSY ROSE (1973) (wm)Irwin Levine—L. Russell Brown. (P)Tony Orlando and Dawn.

SAY I AM (What I Am) (1966) (wm)George Tomsco—Barbara Tomsco. (P)Tommy James and The Shondells.

SAY IT (Over And Over Again) (1940) (w)Frank Loesser (m)Jimmy McHugh. (I)Film: *Buck Benny Rides Again*, by Ellen Drew, Virginia Dale, and Lillian Cornell. (P)Tommy Dorsey and his Orchestra, vocal by Frank Sinatra.

SAY IT ISN'T SO (1932) (wm)Irving Berlin. (P)Rudy Vallee. (CR)Connee Boswell. (CR)Ozzie Nelson and his Orchestra.

SAY IT ISN'T SO (1983) (wm)Daryl Hall. (P)Hall and Oates.

SAY IT LOUD-I'M BLACK AND I'M PROUD (1968) (wm)James Brown— Alfred Ellis. (P)James Brown and The Famous Flames.

SAY IT WITH MUSIC (1921) (wm)Irving Berlin. (I)Revue: *Music Box Revue*, by Wilda Bennett and Paul Frawley. (P)Paul Whiteman and his Orchestra. (R)1938 Film: *Alexander's Ragtime Band*, by Ethel Merman.

SAY, MAN (1959) (wm)E. McDaniel. (P)Bo Diddley.

SAY SAY SAY (1983) (wm)Paul McCartney—Michael Jackson. (P)Paul McCartney and Michael Jackson. No. 1 Chart Record.

SAY SI SI (1940) (w-Eng)Al Stillman (m)Ernesto Lecuona. (P)Xavier Cugat and his Orchestra, vocal by Lina Romay. Most popular recording by The Andrews Sisters.

SAY SO! (1928) (w)P. G. Wodehouse—Ira Gershwin (m)George Gershwin. (I)Musical: *Rosalie*, by Marilyn Miller and Oliver McLennan.

SAY SOMETHING FUNNY (1965) (wm)Bernice Ross—Lor Crane. (P)Patty Duke.

SAY YOU LOVE ME (1976) (wm)Christine McVie. (P)Fleetwood Mac.

SAY YOU, SAY ME (1985) (wm)Lionel Richie. (I)Film: *White Nights*, by Lionel Richie on soundtrack. (P)Lionel Richie. No. 1 Chart Record. Academy Award Winner.

SAY YOU WILL (1987) (wm)M. Jones—L. Gramm.

SAY YOU'LL BE MINE (1981) (wm)Christopher Cross. (P)Christopher Cross.

SAY YOU'LL STAY UNTIL TOMORROW (1976) (wm)Barry Mason—Roger Greenaway. (P)Tom Jones.

SAY YOU'RE WRONG (1985) (wm)Julian Lennon. (P)Julian Lennon.

SAYONARA (1957) (wm)Irving Berlin. (I)Film: *Sayonara* on soundtrack. (P)Eddie Fisher.

SAYS MY HEART (1938) (w)Frank Loesser (m)Burton Lane. (I)Film: *Cocoanut Grove*, by Harriet Hilliard with Harry Owens and his Orchestra. (P)Tommy

Dorsey and his Orchestra.

SCANDAL WALK (1920) (w)Arthur Jackson (m)George Gershwin. (I)Revue: *George White's Scandals of 1920* by Ann Pennington.

SCARBOROUGH FAIR-CANTICLE (1966) (wm)Paul Simon—Art Garfunkel. (I)Film: *The Graduate* on the soundtrack by Simon and Garfunkel. (P)Simon and Garfunkel.

SCARF DANCE (1888) (m)Cecile Chaminade. Famous classical composition.

SCARLET RIBBONS (For Her Hair) (1949) (w)Jack Segal (m)Evelyn Danzig. (I)Juanita Hall. (R)1956 by Harry Belafonte. (R)1960 by The Browns.

SCAT SONG, THE (1932) (w)Mitchell Parish (m)Frank Perkins—Cab Calloway. (P)Cab Calloway.

SCATTERBRAIN (1939) (wm)Johnny Burke—Frankie Masters—Kahn Keene—Carl Bean. (P)Theme song of Frankie Masters and his Orchestra. (CR)Benny Goodman and his Orchestra.

SCATTIN' AT THE KIT KAT (1937) (w)Irving Mills (m)Duke Ellington. (P)Duke Ellington and his Orchestra.

SCENES FROM AN ITALIAN RESTAURANT (1977) (wm)Billy Joel. (P)Billy Joel.

SCHEHERAZADE (1890) (m)Nikolai Rimsky—Korsakov. Famous classical composition.

SCHOOL DAY (Ring! Ring! Goes The Bell) (1957) (wm)Chuck Berry. (P)Chuck Berry.

SCHOOL DAYS (1907) (w)Will D. Cobb (m)Gus Edwards. (I)Byron C. Harlan.

SCHOOL IS OUT (1961) (wm)Gary Anderson—Gene Barge. (P)Gary "U. S. " Bonds.

SCHOOL'S OUT (1972) (wm)Alice Cooper—Michael Bruce. (P)Alice Cooper. (R)1986 by Krokus.

SCORPIO (1971) (m)Dennis Coffey. (P)Dennis Coffey,

SCRUB ME MAMA (With A Boogie Beat) (1940) (wm)Don Raye. (P)Will Bradley and his Orchestra.

SEA OF LOVE (1959) (wm)George Khoury—Phil Battiste. (P)Phil Phillips. (R)1982 by Del Shannon. (R)1985 by The Honeydrippers.

SEALED WITH A KISS (1962) (w)Peter Udell (m)Gary Geld. (P)Brian Hyland. (R)1968 by Gary Lewis and The Playboys. (R)1972 by Bobby Vinton.

SEARCH IS THROUGH, THE (1954) (w)Ira Gershwin (m)Harold Arlen. (I)Film: *The Country Girl*, by Bing Crosby.

SEARCHIN' (1957) (wm)Jerry Leiber—Mike Stoller. (P)The Coasters. (R)1964 by Ace Cannon.

(I've Been)SEARCHIN' SO LONG (1974) (wm)James Pankow. (P)Chicago.

SEARCHING FOR MY LOVE (1966) (wm)Robert Moore. (P)Bobby Moore and The Rhythm Aces.

SEASONS CHANGE (1987) (wm)L. A. Martinee. (P)Expose. No. 1 Chart Record.

SEASONS IN THE SUN (1964) (w-Eng)Rod McKuen (m)Jacques Brel. (I)In France by Jacques Brel under title of Le Moribond. (R)1974 by Terry Jacks. No. 1 Chart Record.

SECOND HAND LOVE (1962) (wm)Hank Hunter—Phil Spector. (P)Connie Francis.

SECOND HAND ROSE (w)Grant Clarke (m)James F. Hanley. (I)Revue: *Ziegfeld Follies of 1921*, by Fanny Brice. (P)Fanny Brice. (R)1928 Film: *My Man*, by Fanny Brice. (R)1968 Film: *Funny Girl*, by Barbra Streisand.

SECOND TIME AROUND, THE (1960) (w)Sammy Cahn

(m)Jimmy Van Heusen. (I)Film: *High Time*, by Bing Crosby. (P)Frank Sinatra.

SECRET, THE (1958) (wm)Joe Lubin—I. J. Roth. (P)Gordon MacRae.

SECRET AGENT MAN (1966) (wm)Phil Sloan—Steve Barri. (I)TV series: *Secret Agent* on soundtrack. (P)Johnny Rivers. (CR)The Ventures.

SECRET LOVE (1953) (w)Paul Francis Webster (m)Sammy Fain. (I)Film; *Calamity Jane*, by Doris Day. (P)Doris Day. Academy Award Winner. (R)1966 by Billy Stewart. (R)1975 by Freddy Fender.

SECRET SERVICE, THE (1962) (wm)Irving Berlin. (I)Musical: *Mr. President*, by Anita Gillette.

SECRETLY (1958) (wm)Al Hoffman—Dick Manning—Mark Markwell. (P)Jimmie Rodgers. (R)1965 by The Lettermen.

SEE (1969) (wm)Felix Cavaliere. (P)The Rascals.

SEE-SAW (1956) (wm)Roquel Davis—Charles Sutton—Harry Pratt. (P)The Moonglows. (CR)Don Cornell.

SEE SEE RIDER (1925) (wm)Ma Rainey. Adapted from a traditional blues song. (I)Gertrude "Ma" Rainey. (R)1966 by Eric Burdon and The Animals.

SEE THE FUNNY LITTLE CLOWN (1964) (wm)Bobby Goldsboro. (P)Bobby Goldsboro.

SEE WHAT IT GETS YOU (1964) (wm)Stephen Sondheim. (I)Musical: *Anyone Can Whistle*, by Lee Remick.

SEE YOU IN SEPTEMBER (1959) (w)Sid Wayne (m)Sherman Edwards. (P)The Tempos. (R)1966 by The Happenings.

SEE YOU LATER, ALLIGATOR (1955) (wm)Robert Guidry. (I)Film: *Rock Around The Clock*, by Bill Haley and The Comets. (P)Bill Haley and The Comets.

SEEMS LIKE OLD TIMES (1946) (wm)Carmen Lombardo—John Jacob Loeb. (I)Guy Lombardo and his Royal Canadians. (P)Theme song of Arthur Godrey. (R)1957 by The McGuire Sisters.

SEESAW (1965) (wm)Don Covay—Steve Cropper. (P)Don Covay and The Goodtimers. (R)1968 by Aretha Franklin.

SE LA (1987) (wm)Lionel Richie—G. Phillinganes. (P)Lionel Richie. (P)Lionel Richie.

SELF CONTROL (1984) (w-Eng)Steve Piccolo. (m)Raffaele Riefoli— Giancarlo Bigazzi. (P)Laura Branigan.

SEMPER FIDELIS (1888) (m)John Philip Sousa. Official march of the United States Marine Corps.

SEMPER PARATUS (1928) (wm)Francis Saltus Van Boskerck. Official song of the United States Coast Guard.

SEND FOR ME (1930) (w)Lorenz Hart (m)Richard Rodgers. (I)Musical: *Simple Simon*, by Doree Leslie—Alan Edwards, and The Chorus.

SEND FOR ME (1957) (wm)Ollie Jones. (P)Nat "King" Cole.

SEND IN THE CLOWNS (1973) (wm)Stephen Sondheim. (I)Musical: *A Little Night Music*, by Glynis Johns. (R)1977 by Judy Collins. NARAS Award Winner. (R)1987 by Barbra Streisand.

SEND ME NO FLOWERS (1964) (w)Hal David (m)Burt Bacharach. (I)Film: *Send Me No Flowers*, by Doris Day. (P)Doris Day.

SEND ME SOME LOVIN' (1957) (wm)Leo Price—John Marascalco. (P)Little Richard. (R)1963 by Sam Cooke.

SEND ME THE PILLOW YOU DREAM ON (1950) (wm)Hank Locklin. (P)Hank Locklin. (R)1960 by The

Browns. (R)1962 by Johnny Tillotson. (R)1965 by Dean Martin.

SEND ONE YOUR LOVE (1979) (wm)Stevie Wonder. (P)Stevie Wonder.

SENT FOR YOU YESTERDAY (And Here You Come Today) (1939) (wm)William Basie—Ed Durham—James Rushing. (P)Count Basie and his Orchestra, vocal by Jimmy Rushing.

SENTIMENTAL AND MELANCHOLY (1937) (w)Johnny Mercer (M)Richard A. Whiting. (I)Film: *Ready, Willing, And Able*, by Wini Shaw.

SENTIMENTAL GENTLEMAN FROM GEORGIA (1932) (w)Mitchell Parish (m)Frank Perkins. (P)The Boswell Sisters.

SENTIMENTAL JOURNEY (1944) (wm)Bud Green—Les Brown—Ben Homer. (P)Theme song of Les Brown and his Orchestra, with vocal by Doris Day. (R)1951 The Ames Brothers with Les Brown and his Orchestra.

SENTIMENTAL LADY (1972) (wm)Robert Welch. (P)Fleetwood Mac. (R)1977 by Bob Welch.

SENTIMENTAL ME (1925) (w)Lorenz Hart (m)Richard Rodgers. (I)Revue: *Garrick Gaieties*, by June Cochrane, James Norris, Edith Meiser, and Sterling Holloway.

SENTIMENTAL ME (1950) (wm)Jim Morehead—Jimmy Cassin. (P)The Ames Brothers. (CR)Russ Morgan and his Orchestra.

SENTIMENTAL STREET (1985) (wm)Jack Blades—Francis Fitzgerald. (P)Night Ranger.

SEPARATE LIVES (1985) (wm)Stephen Bishop. (I)Film: *White Nights* as soundtrack love theme. (P)Stephen Bishop. No. 1 Chart Record.

SEPARATE WAYS (1973) (wm)Bobby West—Richard Mainegra. (P)Elvis Presley.

SEPTEMBER (1979) (wm)Allee Willis—Maurice White—Albert McKay. (P)Earth, Wind & Fire.

SEPTEMBER IN THE RAIN (1937) (w)Al Dubin (m)Harry Warren. (I)Film: *Melody For Two*, by James Melton. (P)Guy Lombardo and his Orchestra. (R)1949 by The George Shearing Quintet.

SEPTEMBER MORN (1979) (wm)Neil Diamond—Gilbert Becaud. (P)Neil Diamond.

SEPTEMBER OF MY YEARS, THE (1965) (w)Sammy Cahn (m)Jimmy Van Heusen. (P)Frank Sinatra.

SEPTEMBER SONG (1938) (w)Maxwell Anderson (m)Kurt Weill. (I)Musical: *Knickerbocker Holiday*, by Walter Huston. 1944 Film version, by Charles Coburn. (P)Bing Crosby. (R)1984 by Willie Nelson.

SEQUEL (1980) (wm)Harry Chapin. (P)Harry Chapin.

SERENADE (1824) (m)Franz Schubert. Very famous classical selection.

SERENADE (1901) (m)Riccardo Drigo. From ballet: Les Millions D' Arlequin.

SERENADE (1901) (m)Enrico Toselli. Light classical selection. Theme song of radio series: The Rise Of The Goldbergs.

SERENADE (1924) (w)Dorothy Donnelly (m)Sigmund Romberg. (I)Operetta: *The Student Prince In Heidelberg*, by Howard Marsh, Raymond Marlowe—Frederic Wolff, Paul Kleeman, and The Chorus. (R)1954 Film: *The Student Prince*, by Mario Lanza dubbing for Edmund Purdom.

SERENADE FOR A WEALTHY WIDOW (1934) (w)Dorothy Fields—Jimmy McHugh (m)Reginald Foresythe. (P)Reginald Foresythe and his Orchestra

(London).

SERENADE IN BLUE (1942) (w)Mack Gordon (m)Harry Warren. (I)Film: *Orchestra Wives*, by Glenn Miller and his Orchestra, vocal by Ray Eberle and The Modernaires. (P)Glenn Miller.

SERENADE IN THE NIGHT (1936) (w-Eng)Jimmy Kennedy. (m)Cesare A. Bixio—B. Cherubini. (P)Mantovani and his Orchestra.

SERENADE OF THE BELLS (1948) (wm)Kay Twomey—Al Goodheart—Al Urbano. (P)Sammy Kaye and his Orchestra. (CR)Jo Stafford.

SERENADE TO AN OLD FASHIONED GIRL (1946) (wm)Irving Berlin. (I)Film: *Blue Skies*, by Joan Caulfield.

SERIOUS (1987) (wm)L. Pace—Donna Allen—P. Blitz. (P)Donna Allen.

SERPENTINE FIRE (1977) (wm)Reginald Burke—Maurice White— Verdine White. (P)Earth, Wind & Fire.

SET ME FREE (1965) (wm)Ray Davies. (P)The Kinks.

SET ME FREE (1980) (wm)Todd Rundgren—Roger Powell—Kasim Sulton— John Wilcox. (P)Utopia.

SEVEN DAY WEEKEND (1962) (wm)Doc Pomus—Mort Shuman. (P)Gary "U. S. " Bonds.

SEVEN DAYS (1956) (wm)Willis Carroll—Carmen Taylor. (P)Clyde McPhatter, (CR)The Crew Cuts. (CR)Dorothy Collins.

SEVEN DEADLY VIRTUES, THE (1960) (w)Alan Jay Lerner (m)Frederick Loewe. (I)Musical: *Camelot*, by Roddy McDowall.

SEVEN LITTLE GIRLS SITTING IN THE BACK SEAT (1959) (wm)Paul Evans. (P)Paul Evans.

SEVEN LONELY DAYS (1953) (wm)Earl Shuman—Alden Shuman—Marshall Brown. (P)Georgia Gibbs. (CR)Bonnie Lou.

7 ROOMS OF GLOOM (1967) (wm)Brian Holland—Lamont Dozier—Eddie Holland. (P)The Four Tops.

SEVEN TWENTY IN THE BOOKS (1939) (w)Harold Adamson (m)Jan Savitt—Johnny Watson. (P)Jan Savitt and his Orchestra.

SEVEN YEAR ACHE (1981) (wm)Rosanne Cash. (P)Rosanne Cash.

SEVENTEEN (1955) (wm)John Young, Jr. -Chuck Gorman—Boyd Bennett. (P)The Fontane Sisters. (CR)Boyd Bennett. (CR)Rusty Draper. (CR)1961 Frankie Ford.

SEVENTH SON, THE (1956) (wm)Willie Dixon. (P)Willie Dixon. (R)1965 by Johnny Rivers.

77 SUNSET STRIP (1959) (wm)Mack David—Jerry Livingston. (I)TV series: *Sunset Strip* as soundtrack theme.

SEVENTY SIX TROMBONES (1957) (wm)Meredith Willson. (I)Musical: *The Music Man*, by Robert Preston and The Girls and Boys.

SEWING MACHINE, THE (1947) (wm)Frank Loesser. (I)Film: *The Perils Of Pauline*, by Betty Hutton.

SEX MACHINE (1970) (wm)James Brown. (P)James Brown.

SEXUAL HEALING (1983) (wm)Marvin Gaye. (P)Marvin Gaye.

SEXY EYES (1980) (wm)Chris Dunn—Robert Mather—Keith Stegall. (P)Dr. Hook.

SEXY GIRL (1984) (wm)Jack Tempchin—Glenn Frey. (P)Glenn Frey.

SEXY MAMA (1974) (wm)Sylvia Robinson—Willie Goodman—Harry Milton Ray. (P)The Moments.

SEXY SADIE (1968) (wm)John Lennon—Paul McCartney. (P)The Beatles.

SGT. PEPPER'S LONELY HEARTS CLUB BAND (1967) (wm)John Lennon— Paul McCartney. (P)The Beatles. Also, in film: *Yellow Submarine* by The Beatles.

SH-BOOM (Life Could Be A Dream) (1954) (wm)James Keyes—Claude Feaster—Carl Feaster—Floyd McRae—James Edwards. (I)The Chords. (P)The Crew Cuts.

SHA-LA-LA (1964) (w)Robert Mosley (m)Robert Taylor. (P)The Shirelles. (CR)Manfred Mann.

SHA-LA-LA (Make Me Happy) (1974) (wm)Al Green. (P)Al Green.

SHADOW DANCING (1978) (wm)Robin, Barry, Maurice, and Andy Gibb. (P)Andy Gibb. No. 1 Chart Record.

SHADOW OF YOUR SMILE, THE (1965) (w)Paul Francis Webster (m)Johnny Mandel. (I)Film: *The Sandpiper* as love theme on soundtrack. Academy Award Winner. (P)Tony Bennett. NARAS Award Winner.

SHADOW WALTZ (1933) (w)Al Dubin (m)Harry Warren. (I)Film: *Gold Diggers of 1933*, by Dick Powell and Ruby Keeler. (P)Bing Crosby. No. 1 Chart Record. (CR)Rudy Vallee.

SHADOWS IN THE MOONLIGHT (1979) (wm)Charlie Black—Rory Bourke. (P)Anne Murray.

SHADOWS OF THE NIGHT (1982) (wm)David Leigh Byron. (P)Pat Benatar.

SHADRACK (Shadrach) (1938) (w)Robert MacGimsey. (P)Louis Armstrong. (R)1962 by Brook Benton.

SHADY LADY BIRD (1941) (wm)Hugh Martin—Ralph Blane. (I)Musical: *Best Foot Forward*, by Maureen Cannon.

SHAFT (Theme from)1971) (m)Isaac Hayes. (I)Film: *Shaft* on soundtrack. (P)Isaac Hayes. Academy Award Winner.

SHAKE (1965) (wm)Sam Cooke. (P)Sam Cooke. (R)1967 by Otis Redding.

SHAKE A HAND (1953) (wm)Joe Morris. (P)Red Foley and Faye Adams. (R)1963 by Jackie Wilson and Linda Hopkins.

SHAKE A TAIL FEATHER (1967) (w)Verlie Rice (M)Andre Williams— Otha Hayes. (P)James and Bobby Purify.

SHAKE AND FINGERPOP (1965) (wm)Lawrence Horn— Autry DeWalt— Willie Woods.

SHAKEDOWN (1987) (wm)Harold Faltermeyer—Keith Forsey—Bob Seger. (I)Film: *Beverly Hills Cop II*, by Bob Seger on soundtrack. (P)Bob Seger.

SHAKE DOWN THE STARS (1940) (w)Eddie De Lange (m)Jimmy Van Heusen. (P)Glenn Miller and his Orchestra. (CR)Ella Fitzgerald.

SHAKE IT (1979) (wm)Terence Boylan. (P)Ian Matthews.

SHAKE ME I RATTLE (Squeeze Me I Cry) (1957) (wm)Hal Hackaday— Charles Naylor. (P)Marion Worth. (CR)The Lennon Sisters.

SHAKE ME, WAKE ME (When It's Over) (1966) (wm)Brian Holland— Lamont Dozier—Eddie Holland. (P)The Four Tops.

SHAKE, RATTLE, AND ROLL (1954) (wm)Charles Calhoun. (P)Bill Haley and The Comets. (CR)Elvis Presley. (P)Joe Turner. (R)1967 by Arthur Conley.

SHAKE YOU DOWN (1987) (wm)Gregory Abbott. (P)Gregory Abbott. No. 1 Chart Record.

SHAKE YOUR BODY (Down To The Ground) (1979) (wm)Michael Jackson— Stephen Jackson. (P)The Jacksons.

(Shake, Shake, Shake)SHAKE YOUR BOOTY (1976) (wm)Harry Casey— Richard Finch. (P)K. C. & The Sunshine Band. No. 1 Chart Record.

SHAKE YOUR GROOVE THING (1979) (wm)Dino Fekaris—Freddy Perren. (P)Peaches & Herb.

SHAKE YOUR LOVE (1987) (wm)Debbie Gibson. (P)Debbie Gibson.

SHAKE YOUR RUMP TO THE FUNK (1976) (wm)F. Thomas—H. Henderson— C. Allen—J. Alexander— W. Stewart—L. Smith—L. Dodson—M. Beard. (P)The Bar—Kays.

SHAKEY GROUND (1975) (wm)Jeffrey Bowen—Alphonso Boyd—Edward Hazel. (P)The Temptations. (R)1977 by Phoebe Snow.

SHAKIN' ALL OVER (1965) (wm)Johnny Kidd. (P)The Guess Who.

SHAKING THE BLUES AWAY (1927) (wm)Irving Berlin. (I)Revue: *Ziegfeld Follies of 1927*, by Ruth Etting and The Chorus. (R)1948 Film: *Easter Parade*, by Ann Miller. (R)1955 Film: *Love Me Or Leave Me*, by Doris Day.

SHALL WE DANCE? (1937) (w)Ira Gershwin (m)George Gershwin. (I)Film: *Shall We Dance?* by Fred Astaire.

SHALL WE DANCE? (1951) (w)Oscar Hammerstein II (m)Richard Rodgers. (I)Musical: *The King And I*, by Gertrude Lawrence and Yul Brynner.

SHALOM (1961) (wm)Jerry Herman. (I)Musical: *Milk And Honey*, by Robert Weede and Mimi Benzell.

SHAMBALA (1973) (wm)Daniel Moore. (P)Three Dog Night. (CR)B. W. Stevenson.

SHAME (1978) (wm)John Fitch—Reuben Cross. (P)Evelyn "Champagne" King.

SHAME ON THE MOON (1982) (wm)Rodney Crowell. (P)Bob Seger & The Silver Bullet Band.

SHAME, SHAME (1968) (wm)Keith Colley—Linda Colley—Knox Henderson. (P)The Magic Lantern.

SHAME, SHAME, SHAME (1975) (wm)Sylvia Robinson. (P)Shirley & Company.

SHANE (See: The Call Of The Far—Away Hills)

(Why Did I Tell You I Was Going To)SHANGHAI (1951) (wm)Bob Hilliard—Milton De Lugg. (P)Doris Day.

SHANGHAI LIL (1933) (w)Al Dubin (m)Harry Warren. (I)Film: *Footlight Parade*, by James Cagney, Ruby Keeler, and The Chorus.

SHANGHAI SHUFFLE (1924) (wm)Larry Conley—Gene Rodemich. (I)Gene Rodemich and his Orchestra. (P)Fletcher Henderson and his Orchestra, featuring Louis Armstrong.

SHANGRI-LA (1946) (w)Carl Sigman (m)Robert Maxwell—Matty Malneck. (I)Robert Maxwell. (R)1957 by The Four Coins. (R)1964 by Robert Maxwell. (R)1964 by Vic Dana. (R)1969 by The Lettermen.

SHANNON (1976) (wm)Henry Gross. (P)Henry Gross.

SHAPE OF THINGS TO COME, THE (1968) (wm)Barry Mann—Cynthia Weil. (I)Film: *Wild In The Streets*, by unknown voice dubbing for Christopher Jones. (P)Max Frost and The Troopers.

SHAPES OF THINGS (1966) (wm)Paul Samwell—Smith—Keith Relf— James McCarty. (P)The Yardbirds.

SHARE THE LAND (1970) (wm)Burton Cummings. (P)Guess Who.

SHARE YOUR LOVE WITH ME (1963) (wm)Al Braggs— Deadric Malone. (P)Bobby Bland. (R)1969 by Aretha Franklin. (R)1981 by Kenny Rogers.

SHARING THE NIGHT TOGETHER (1978) (wm)Ava

Alderidge—Edward Struzick. (P)Dr. Hook.

SHATTERED (1978) (wm)Mick Jagger—Keith Richard. (P)The Rolling Stones.

SHE (1969) (wm)Tommy James—Mike Vale—Ritchie Cordell—Jeff Katz— Jerry Kasenetz. (P)Tommy James and The Shondells.

SHE BELIEVES IN ME (1979) (wm)Steve Gibb (P)Kenny Rogers.

SHE BELONGS TO ME (1965) (wm)Bob Dylan. (P)Bob Dylan. (R)1969 by Rick Nelson.

SHE BLINDED ME WITH SCIENCE (1983) (wm)Thomas Dolby—Joe Kerr. (P)Thomas Dolby.

SHE BOP (1984) (wm)Cyndi Lauper—Stephen Lunt—Gary Corbett— Richard Chertoff. (P)Cyndi Lauper.

SHE CAME IN THROUGH THE BATHROOM WINDOW (1969) (wm)John Lennon— Paul McCartney. (P)The Beatles. (CR)Joe Cocker.

SHE CAN'T FIND HER KEYS (1960) (w)Roy Alfred (m)Wally Gold. (P)Paul Petersen.

SHE CRIED (1962) (wm)Ted Daryll—Greg Richards. (I)Ted Daryll. (P)Jay & The Americans. (R)1966 by The Shangri—Las (He Cried). (R)1970 by The Lettermen.

SHE DID IT (1977) (wm)Eric Carmen. (P)Eric Carmen.

SHE DIDN'T SAY YES (1931) (w)Otto Harbach (m)Jerome Kern. (I)Musical: *The Cat And The Fiddle*, by Bettina Hall. 1934 Film version, by Jeanette MacDonald.

SHE HAD TO GO AND LOSE IT AT THE ASTOR (1939) (wm)Don Raye— Hughie Prince. (P)Johnny Messner and his Orchestra.

SHE IS STILL A MYSTERY (1967) (wm)John B. Sebastian. (P)The Lovin' Spoonful.

SHE LOVES ME (1963) (w)Sheldon Harnick (m)Jerry Bock. (I)Musical: *She Loves Me*, by Daniel Massey.

SHE LOVES YOU (1964) (wm)John Lennon—Paul McCartney. (P)The Beatles. No. 1 Chart Record.

SHE REMINDS ME OF YOU (1934) (w)Mack Gordon (m)Harry Revel. (I)Film: *We're Not Dressing*, by Bing Crosby.

SHE SAID SHE SAID (1966) (wm)John Lennon—Paul McCartney. (P)The Beatles.

SHE SAY (Oom Dooby Doom) (1959) (wm)Barry Mann—Mike Anthony. (P)The Diamonds.

SHE TOUCHED ME (He Touched Me) (1965) (w)Ira Levin (m)Milton Schafer. (I)Musical: *Drat! The Cat!*,by Elliott Gould. (P)Barbra Streisand.

SHE WASN'T YOU (He Isn't You) (1965) (w)Alan Jay Lerner (m)Burton Lane. (I)Musical: *On A Clear Day You Can See Forever*, by Clifford David. 1970 Film version, by Barbra Streisand.

SHE WORE A YELLOW RIBBON (See: 'Round Her Neck She Wore A Yellow Ribbon).

SHE WORKS HARD FOR THE MONEY (1983) (wm)Donna Summer—Michael Omartian. (P)Donna Summer.

SHE'D RATHER BE WITH ME (1967) (wm)Garry Bonner—Alan Gordon. (P)The Turtles.

SHEIK OF ARABY, THE (1921) (w)Harry B. Smith—Francis Wheeler (m)Ted Snyder. (P)The Club Royal Orchestra. (R)1939 by Jack Teagarden. (R)1943 by Spike Jones.

SHEILA (1962) (wm)Tommy Roe. (P)Tommy Roe. No. 1 Chart Record.

SHE'LL BE COMIN' ROUND THE MOUNTAIN (1899) (wm)Unknown. Traditional folk song.

SHELTER FROM THE STORM (1974) (wm)Bob Dylan. (P)Bob Dylan.

SHELTER OF YOUR ARMS, THE (1964) (wm)Jerry Samuels. (P)Sammy Davis, Jr.

SHENANDOAH (Across The Wide Missouri) (1826) (wm)Unknown. Traditional folk song of the Old West.

SHEPHERD SERENADE (1941) (w)Kermit Goell (m)Fred Spielman. (P)Horace Heidt and his Musical Knights. (CR)Bing Crosby.

SHERRY (1962) (wm)Bob Gaudio. (P)The Four Seasons. (R)1980 by Robert John.

SHE'S A BAD MAMA JAMA (1981) (wm)Leon Haywood. (P)Carl Carlton.

SHE'S A BEAUTY (1983) (wm)Steve Lukather—David Foster—Fee Waybill. (P)The Tubes.

SHE'S A HEARTBREAKER (1968) (wm)Jerry Williams—Charlie Foxx. (P)Gene Pitney.

SHE'S A LADY (1971) (wm)John B. Sebastian. (P)Tom Jones.

SHE'S A LATIN FROM MANHATTAN (1935) (w)Al Dubin (m)Harry Warren. (I)Film: *Go Into Your Dance*, by Al Jolson. (P)Al Jolson.

SHE'S A RAINBOW (1968) (wm)Mick Jagger—Keith Richard. (P)The Rolling Stones.

SHE'S A WOMAN (1964) (wm)John Lennon—Paul McCartney. (P)The Beatles.

SHE'S ABOUT A MOVER (1965) (wm)Doug Sahm. (P)The Sir Douglas Quintet. (R)1968 by Otis Clay.

SHE'S ALWAYS A WOMAN (1978) (wm)Billy Joel. (P)Billy Joel.

(I Got A Woman, Crazy For Me)SHE'S FUNNY THAT WAY (1928) (wm)Richard A. Whiting—Neil Moret. (I)Gene Austin. (CR)Ted Lewis. (R)1952 Film: *Meet Danny Wilson*, by Frank Sinatra. Most popular recording by Frank Sinatra.

SHE'S GONE (1974) (wm)Daryl Hall—John Oates. (P)Hall and Oates. (CR)Tavares.

SHE'S GOT A WAY (1981) (wm)Billy Joel. (P)Billy Joel.

SHE'S GOT YOU (1962) (wm)Hank Cochran. (P)Patsy Cline. (R)1977 by Loretta Lynn.

SHE'S JUST MY STYLE (1965) (wm)Gary Lewis—Leon Russell—Thomas Lesslie—Al Capps. (P)Gary Lewis and The Playboys.

SHE'S LEAVING HOME (1967) (wm)John Lennon—Paul McCartney. (P)The Beatles.

SHE'S LIKE THE WIND (1987) (wm)P. Swayze—S. Widelitz. (P)Patrick Swayze (Featuring Wendy Frazer).

SHE'S LOOKIN' GOOD (1968) (wm)Rodger Collins. (P)Wilson Pickett.

SHE'S MY GIRL (1967) (wm)Garry Bonner—Alan Gordon. (P)The Turtles.

SHE'S MY LOVE (1961) (wm)Bob Merrill. (I)Musical: *Carnival!*, by Jerry Orbach.

SHE'S NOT JUST ANOTHER WOMAN (1971) (wm)Ronald Dunbar—Clyde Wilson. (P)8th Day.

SHE'S NOT THERE (1964) (wm)Rod Argent. (P)The Zombies. (R)1977 by The Zombies.

SHE'S NOT YOU (1962) (wm)Doc Pomus—Jerry Leiber—Mike Stoller. (P)Elvis Presley.

SHE'S OUT OF MY LIFE (1980) (wm)Tom Bahler. (P)Michael Jackson.

SHE'S SEXY & 17 (1983) (wm)Brian Setzer. (P)The Stray Cats.

SHE'S SO COLD (1980) (wm)Mick Jagger—Keith

Richard. (P)The Rolling Stones.

SHIFTING, WHISPERING SANDS, THE (1955) (w)V. C. Gilbert (m)Mary M. Hadler. (P)Billy Vaughn and his Orchestra. (CR)Rusty Draper.

SHILO (1970) (wm)Neil Diamond. (P)Neil Diamond.

SHIMMY, SHIMMY, KO-KO-BOP (1960) (wm)Bob Smith. (P)Little Anthony and The Imperials.

SHINE IT ON (1977) (w)Fred Ebb (m)John Kander. (I)Musical: *The Act*, by Liza Minnelli.

SHINE ON HARVEST MOON (1908) (wm)Jack Norworth—Nora Bayes. (P)Ada Jones and Billy Murray. (R)1931 by Ethel Waters. (R)1943 by Kate Smith.

SHINE ON YOUR SHOES, A (1932) (w)Howard Dietz (m)Arthur Schwartz. (I)Revue: *Flying Colors*, by Buddy and Vilma Ebsen, Monette Moore, and Larry Adler.

SHININ' ON (1974) (wm)Mark Farner—Don Brewer. (P)Grand Funk.

SHINING STAR (1975) (wm)Maurice White—Philip Bailey—Larry Dunn. (I)Film: *Shining Star*, by Earth, Wind & Fire. (P)Earth, Wind & Fire.

SHINING STAR (1980) (wm)Leo Graham, Jr. -Paul Richmond. (P)The Manhattans.

SHIP WITHOUT A SAIL, A (1929) (w)Lorenz Hart (m)Richard Rodgers. (I)Musical: *Heads Up!*, by Jack Whiting. In Film version, by Buddy Rogers.

SHIPS (1979) (wm)Ian Hunter (P)Barry Manilow.

SHOE SHINE BOY (1936) (w)Sammy Cahn—Saul Chaplin. (I)Revue: *Connie's Hot Chocolates of 1936*, by Louis Armstrong. (P)Louis Armstrong.

SHOEIN' THE MARE (1934) (w)Ira Gershwin—E. Y. Harburg (m)Harold Arlen. (I)Revue: *Life Begins At 8:40*, by Adrienne Matzenauer.

SHOELESS JOE FROM HANNIBAL MO. (1955) (wm)Richard Adler—Jerry Ross. (I)Musical: *Damn Yankees*, by Rae Allen and Baseball Players.

SHOES WITH WINGS ON (1949) (w)Ira Gerswhin (m)Harry Warren. (I)Film: *The Barkleys Of Broadway*, by Fred Astaire.

SHOESHINE BOY (1974) (wm)Harry Booker—Linda Allen. (P)Eddie Kendricks.

SHOO-BE-DOO-BE-DOO-DA-DAY (1968) (wm)Henry Cosby—Sylvia Moy— Stevie Wonder. (P)Stevie Wonder.

SHOO-FLY-PIE AND APPLE PAN DOWDY (1946) (w)Sammy Gallop—Guy Wood. (P)Dinah Shore. (CR)Stan Kenton and his Orchestra. (CR)Guy Lombardo and his Royal Canadians.

SHOO-SHOO-BABY (1943) (wm)Phil Moore. (I)Film: *Three Cheers For The Boys*, by The Andrews Sisters. (P)The Andrews Sisters. (CR)Ella Mae Morse. (CR)Jan Garber and his Orchestra.

SHOOP, SHOOP SONG, THE (1964) (wm)Rudy Clark. (P)Betty Everett. (R)1977 by Kate Taylor.

SHOP AROUND (1961) (wm)Berry Gordy, Jr. -William Robinson. (P)The Miracles. (R)1976 by The Captain and Tennille.

SHORT FAT FANNIE (1957) (wm)Larry Williams. (P)Larry Williams.

SHORT PEOPLE (1978) (wm)Randy Newman. (P)Randy Newman.

SHORT SHORTS (1957) (w)Bob Gaudio—Bill Dalton (m)Bill Crandall— Tom Austin. (P)The Royal Teens.

SHORTEST DAY OF THE YEAR, THE (1938) (w)Lorenz Hart (m)Richard Rodgers. (I)Musical: *The Boys From Syracuse*, by Ronald Graham and Dolores Anderson.

SHORTNIN' BREAD (1928) (w)Clement Wood—Jacques Wolfe. Adaptation from folk song. (P)Lawrence Tibbett. (P)Paul Robeson. (P)Nelson Eddy.

SHOT-GUN BOOGIE (1951) (wm)Tennessee Ernie Ford. (P)Tennessee Ernie Ford.

SHOTGUN (1965) (wm)Autry DeWalt. (P)Jr. Walker and The All Stars. (R)1969 by Vanilla Fudge.

SHOULD I? (1930) (w)Arthur Freed (m)Nacio Herb Brown. (I)Film: *Lord Byron Of Broadway*, by Charles Kaley and later reprised by Ethelind Terry.

SHOULD I BE SWEET? (1932) (w)B. G. De Sylva (m)Vincent Youmans. (I)Musical: *Take A Chance*, by June Knight. Film version (1933)by Miss Knight.

SHOULD I DO IT (1982) (wm)Layng Martine, Jr. (P)The Pointer Sisters.

SHOULD I TELL YOU I LOVE YOU (1946) (wm)Cole Porter. (I)Musical: *Around The World*, by Mary Healy.

SHOULD'VE KNOWN BETTER (1987) (wm)Richard Marx. (P)Richard Marx.

SHOULD'VE NEVER LET YOU GO (1980) (wm)Neil Sedaka—Phil Cody. (P)Neil and Dara Sedaka.

SHOUT (Part 1 and 2) (1959) (wm)O'Kelly, Ronald, and Rudolph Isley. (P)The Isley Brothers. (R)1962 by Joey Dee & The Starliters. No. 1 Chart Record. (R)1962 by The Isley Brothers. (R)1964 by Lulu and the Lovers. (R)1969 by The Chambers Brothers.

SHOUT (1985) (wm)Roland Orzabel—Ian Stanley. (P)Tears For Fears.

SHOUT! SHOUT! KNOCK YOURSELF OUT! (1962) (wm)Ernie Maresca— Thomas F. Bogdany. (P)Ernie Maresca.

SHOW AND TELL (1974) (wm)Jerry Fuller. (P)Al Wilson. No. 1 Chart Record.

SHOW ME (1956) (w)Alan Jay Lerner (m)Frederick Loewe. (I)Musical: *My Fair Lady*, by Julie Andrews.

SHOW ME (1984) (wm)Chrissie Hynde. (P)The Pretenders.

SHOW ME THE WAY (1976) (wm)Peter Frampton. (P)Peter Frampton.

SHOW ME THE WAY TO GO HOME (1925) (wm)Irving King. (P)In U. S. , by Vincent Lopez and his Orchestra. (CR)Billy Jones and Ernie Hare (The Happiness Boys).

SHOW MUST GO ON, THE (1974) (wm)David Courtney—Leo Sayer. (P)Three Dog Night.

SHOWER THE PEOPLE (1976) (wm)James Taylor. (P)James Taylor.

SHRIMP BOATS (1951) (wm)Paul Mason Howard—Paul Weston. (P)Jo Stafford.

SHRINE OF ST. CECILIA (1941) (w-Eng)Carroll Loveday (m)"Jokern". (P)The Andrews Sisters. (CR)Al Donahue and his Orchestra, vocal by Phil Brito. (R)1957 by Faron Young.

SHUFFLE ALONG (1921) (wm)Noble Sissle—Eubie Blake. (I)Musical: *Shuffle Along*, by Charles Davis.

SHUFFLE OFF TO BUFFALO (1932) (w)Al Dubin (m)Harry Warren. (I)Film: *Forty Second Street*, by Ruby Keeler, Clarence Nordstrom, Ginger Rogers, and Una Merkel. (P)Hal Kemp and his Orchestra. (CR)Don Bestor and his Orchestra.

SHUT DOWN (1963) (w)Roger Christian (m)Brian Wilson. (P)The Beach Boys.

SHUTTERS AND BOARDS (1962) (wm)Audie Murphy—Scott Turner. (P)Jerry Wallace.

SIAMESE CAT SONG, THE (1955) (wm)Peggy Lee—Sonny Burke. (I)Cartoon Film: *The Lady And The*

Tramp, by Peggy Lee.

SIBERIA (1955) (wm)Cole Porter. (I)Musical: *Silk Stockings*.

SIBONEY (1929) (w-Eng)Dolly Morse (m)Ernesto Lecuona. (I)Alfredo Brito. (R)1937 Film: *When You're In Love*, by Grace Moore.

SIDE BY SIDE (1927) (wm)Harry Woods. (P)Nick Lucas. (CR)Paul Whiteman and his Orchestra. (R)1953 by Kay Starr.

SIDE BY SIDE BY SIDE (1970) (wm)Stephen Sondheim. (I)Musical: *Company*, by Dean Jones and The Company.

SIDESHOW (1974) (wm)Vinnie Barrett—Bobby Eli. (P)Blue Magic.

SIDEWALK TALK (1986) (wm)Madonna. (P)Jellybean.

SIDEWALKS OF CUBA (1934) (wm)Mitchell Parish—Irving Mills—Ben Oakland. (I)Revue: *Cotton Club Parade*, by The Ensemble. (R)1946 by Woody Herman and his Orchestra.

SIERRA SUE (1940) (wm)Joseph Buell Carey—Elliott Shapiro. (P)Bing Crosby. (CR)Gene Autry. (CR)Glenn Miller and his Orchestra.

SIGN OF THE TIMES, A (1966) (wm)Tony Hatch. (P)Petula Clark.

SIGN ON THE WINDOW (1970) (wm)Bob Dylan. (P)Bob Dylan.

SIGNED, SEALED, DELIVERED I'M YOURS (1970) (wm)Lila Mae Hardaway—Lee Garrett—Stevie Wonder—Syreeta Wright. (P)Stevie Wonder. (R)1977 by Peter Frampton.

SIGN O' THE TIMES (1987) (wm)Prince. (P)Prince.

SIGNS (1971) (wm)Arthur Thomas. (P)Five Man Electrical Band.

SILENCE IS GOLDEN (1967) (wm)Bob Crewe—Bob Gaudio. (P)The Tremeloes.

SILENT NIGHT, HOLY NIGHT (1818) (w)Joseph Mohr (m)Franz Gruber. One of the most popular Christmas songs. Most popular recording by Bing Crosby.

SILENT RUNNING (1985) (wm)Mike Rutherford—Brian Robertson. (P)Mike & The Mechanics.

SILHOUETTES (1957) (wm)Frank C. Slay, Jr. -Bob Crewe. (P)The Rays. (CR)The Diamonds. (R)1965 by Herman's Hermits.

SILK STOCKINGS (1955) (wm)Cole Porter. (I)Musical: *Silk Stockings*, by Don Ameche.

SILLY LOVE SONGS (1976) (wm)Paul and Linda McCartney. (P)Wings. No. 1 Chart Record.

SILVER BELLS (1950) (wm)Ray Evans—Jay Livinston. (I)Film: *The Lemon Drop Kid*, by Bob Hope. (P)Bing Crosby and Carol Richards.

SILVER THREADS AMONG THE GOLD (1873) (w)Eben E. Rexford (m)Hart Pease Danks. (I)Richard Jose. (P)John McCormack.

SILVER THREADS AND GOLDEN NEEDLES (1962) (wm)Dick Reynolds (m)Jack Rhodes. (P)The Springfields. (R)1965 by Jody Miller. (R)1969 by The Cowsills. (R)1974 by Linda Ronstadt.

SIMILAU (1948) (wm)Harry Coleman—Arden Clar. (P)Peggy Lee.

SIMON SAYS (1968) (wm)Elliot Chiprut. (P)The 1910 Fruitgum Company.

SIMPATICA (1941) (w)Lorenz Hart (m)Richard Rodgers. (I)Film: *They Met In Argentina*.

SIMPLE JOYS OF MAIDENHOOD, THE (1960) (w)Alan Jay Lerner (m)Frederick Loewe. (I)Musical: *Camelot*, by Julie Andrews.

SIMPLE TWIST OF FATE (1974) (wm)Bob Dylan. (P)Bob Dylan.

(It's No)SIN (1951) (w)Chester R. Shull (m)George Haven. (P)The Four Aces. (CR)Eddy Howard.

SINCE I DON'T HAVE YOU (1959) (w)James Beaumont—Janet Vogel— Joseph Verscharen—Walter Lester—John Taylor (m)Joseph Rock— Lennie Martin. (P)The Skyliners. (R)1964 by Chuck Jackson. (R)1979 by Art Garfunkel. (R)1981 by Don McLean.

SINCE I FELL FOR YOU (1948) (wm)Buddy Johnson. (P)The Paul Gayten Trio, with vocal by Annie Laurie. (R)1963 by Lenny Welch.

SINCE I KISSED MY BABY GOODBYE (1941) (wm)Cole Porter. (I)Film: *You'll Never Get Rich*, by The Delta Rhythm Boys.

SINCE I MET YOU BABY (1956) (wm)Ivory Joe Hunter. (P)Ivory Joe Hunter. (R)1969 by Sonny James.

SINCE MY BEST GAL TURNED ME DOWN (1927) (w)Howard Quicksell (m)Ray Lodwig—Howard Quicksell. (P)Bix Beiderbecke and his Gang.

SINCE YOU'VE BEEN GONE (Sweet, Sweet Baby) (1968) (wm)Aretha Franklin—Ted White. (P)Aretha Franklin. (CR)Ramsey Lewis.

SINCERELY (1955) (wm)Harvey Fuqua—Alan Freed. (I)The Moonglows. (P)The McGuire Sisters. (R)1964 by The Four Seasons. (R)1969 by Paul Anka.

McGUIRE SISTERS

They had some big hits but nothing that reached #1 on the charts until we covered another rhythm and blues hit called *Sincerely*. The original record was by The Moonglows and Gene Goodman (Benny's brother) brought the song into Thiele just about the time it was released. We were able to get on the market with the girls' version just about the same time as the original record.

The McGuires' record of *Sincerely* became a stone smash hit, reaching the #1 position on all the charts in the trade magazines. It made the girls major recording artists and gave me my first million seller record with my name on as arranger and conductor. It really was a very exciting moment.

SING (1926) (w)Lorenz Hart (m)Richard Rodgers. (I)Musical: *Betsy*, by Belle Baker.

SING (1972) (wm)Joe Raposo. (I)TV Show: *Sesame Street*, by Bob McGrath. (P)The Carpenters.

SING A TROPICAL SONG (1943) (w)Frank Loesser (m)Jimmy McHugh. (I)Film: *Happy Go Lucky*, by Dick Powell, Eddie Bracken, and Sir Lancelot. (P)The Andrews Sisters.

SING, BABY, SING (1936) (w)Jack Yellen (m)Lew Pollack. (I)Film: *Sing, Baby, Sing*, by Alice Faye.

SING BEFORE BREAKFAST (1936) (w)Arthur Freed (m)Nacio Herb Brown. (I)Film: *Broadway Melody of 1936*, by Vilma and Buddy Ebsen with Eleanor Powell.

SING BOY, SING (1957) (wm)Tommy Sands—Rod Mc-

Kuen. (I)Musical: *Sing Boy, Sing*, by Tommy Sands.

SING FOR YOUR SUPPER (1938) (w)Lorenz Hart (m)Richard Rodgers. (I)Musical: *The Boys From Syracuse*, by Marcy Westcott, Muriel Angelus, and Wynn Murray. 1940 Film version by Martha Raye.

SING ME A SONG OF THE ISLANDS (1942) (wm)Mack Gordon—Harry Owens. (I)Film: *Song Of The Islands*, by Betty Grable.

SING ME A SONG WITH SOCIAL SIGNIFICANCE (1937) (wm)Harold Rome. (I)Revue: *Pins And Needles*, by Harold Rome.

SING, SING, SING (1936) (wm)Louis Prima. (I)Louis Prima. (P)Benny Goodman and his Orchestra. This recording in two parts is one of Goodman's most popular and featured solos by Gene Krupa, Harry James, Vido Musso, and Goodman.

SING SOMETHING SIMPLE (1930) (wm)Herman Hupfeld. (I)Revue: *The Second Little Show*, by Ruth Tester, Arline Judge, and Fay Brady.

SING THIS ALL TOGETHER (1967) (wm)Mick Jagger—Keith Richard. (P)The Rolling Stones. (P)The Rolling Stones.

SING TO ME, GUITAR (1944) (wm)Cole Porter. (I)Musical: *Mexican Hayride*, by Corinna Mura.

SING YOU SINNERS (1930) (wm)Sam Coslow—W. Franke Harling. (I)Film: *Honey*, by Lillian Roth. (P)The High Hatters. (CR)Smith Ballew and his Orchestra.

SINGASONG (1976) (wm)Albert McKay—Maurice White. (P)Earth, Wind & Fire.

SINGER, NOT THE SONG, THE (1965) (wm)Mick Jagger—Keith Richard. (P)The Rolling Stones.

SINGIN' IN THE RAIN (1929) (w)Arthur Freed (m)Nacio Herb Brown. (I)Film: *Hollywood Revue of 1929*, by Cliff Edwards, The Brox Sisters, and The Rounders. (P)Cliff Edwards. (CR)Gus Arnheim and his Orchestra. (R)1952 Film: *Singin' In The Rain*, by Gene Kelly in one of the most popular film sequences in movie history.

SINGIN' THE BLUES (Till My Daddy Come Home) (1920) (w)Sam M. Lewis—Joe Young (m)Con Conrad—J. Russel Robinson. (P)The Original Dixieland Jazz Band.

SINGING A VAGABOND SONG (1929) (wm)Sam Messenheimer—Val Burton— Harry Richman. (I)Film: *Puttin' On The Ritz*, by Harry Richman. (P)Harry Richman.

SINGING HILLS, THE (1940) (wm)Mack David—Dick Sanford—Sammy Mysels. (P)Bing Crosby. (CR)Dick Todd.

SINGING THE BLUES (1954) (wm)Melvin Endsley. (P)Marty Robbins. (R)1957 by Guy Mitchell. No. 1 Chart Record.

SINGLE GIRL, THE (1966) (wm)Martha Sharp. (P)Sandy Posey.

SINK THE BISMARCK (1960) (wm)Tillman Franks—Johnny Horton. (P)Johnny Horton.

SINNER KISSED AN ANGEL, A (1941) (w)Mack David (m)Ray Joseph. (P)Tommy Dorsey and his Orchestra, vocal by Frank Sinatra.

SIOUX CITY SUE (1945) (w)Ray Freedman (m)Dick Thomas. (I)Dick Thomas. (P)Bing Crosby.

SIR DUKE (1977) (wm)Stevie Wonder. (P)Stevie Wonder. Stevie wrote this song as a tribute to Duke Ellington.

SISTER CHRISTIAN (1983) (wm)Kelly Keagy. (P)Night Ranger.

DICK JACOBS & THE HIT PARADE ORCHESTRA

Without my knowing anything about the plans that were being made, the people looking for a new musical conductor for the TV *Hit Parade* Orchestra decided I was the man. I guess the fact that I had a number of hit records at the time helped.

The *Hit Parade* staff had already decided that some changes had to be made in the orchestra, so I was able immediately to bring in some first class players: Don Lamond on drums; Dick Hyman on piano; Al Caiola on guitar; Jerome Richardson on tenor saxophone. Since we already had Jimmy Nottingham and Yank Lawson in the trumpet section, we were in great shape there.

TV was live in those day so you had to be sure there were no goofs. The president of American Tobacco, the sponsor, would call after each show and give his opinion. How happy I was when he called after that first show to say he had never heard the *Hit Parade* Orchestra sound better. I was in seventh heaven.

Remember this was in the late fifties. At that time it was not the practice to show a racially integrated orchestra on camera during a TV show. Well, we wanted to do the Benny Goodman arrangement of *Sing, Sing, Sing* (all fifteen minutes), featuring the orchestra and the singers. Two of the featured solos in the arrangement are for trumpet and tenor sax, and our soloists were black men - Jimmy Nottingham and Jerry Richardson. Bill Hobens, the director of the show, told Dan Lounsbury, the executive producer, that we would be showing two black men, close up and in long spots, on camera.

God bless Dan Lounsbury. His attitude was that if they were the soloists and the arrangement called for them to be featured on camera, that was the way it was going to be. So we went on the air that way. After the show, the expected call from the president of American Tobacco came. His words: *Sing, Sing, Sing* was one of the best (if not the best) productions he had ever seen on the show.

For what it is worth, I like to think that this happening made some contribution to the showing of integrated orchestras on national network television.

SISTER GOLDEN HAIR (1974) (wm)Gerry Beckley. (P)America. No. 1 Chart Record.

SISTER SUFFRAGETTE (1963) (wm)Richard M. Sherman—Robert B. Sherman. (I)Musical: *Mary Poppins*, by Glynis Johns.

SISTERS ARE DOIN' IT FOR THEMSELVES (1985) (wm)Annie Lennox— Dave Stewart. (P)The Eurythmics and Aretha Franklin.

SIT DOWN, YOU'RE ROCKIN' THE BOAT (1950) (wm)Frank Loesser. (I)Musical: *Guys And Dolls*, by Stubby Kaye.

SITTIN' IN THE BALCONY (1957) (wm)John Loudermilk. (P)Eddie Cochran. (CR)Johnny Dee.

SITTIN' ON A FENCE (1966) (wm)Mick Jagger—Keith Richard. (P)The Rolling Stones.

SITTIN' ON A LOG (Pettin' My Dog) (1933) (wm)Byron Gay—Edward E. Confrey. (P)Jack Denny and his Orchestra, vocal by Jeanie Lang.

SITTIN' ON THE DOCK OF THE BAY (1968) (wm)Otis Redding—Steve Cropper. (P)Otis Redding. No. 1 Chart Record. (CR)King Curtis. (R)1969 by The Dells. (R)1969 by Sergio Mendes & Brasil '66. (R)1979 by Sammy Hagar. (R)1982 by The Reddings. (R)1988 by Michael Bolton.

SITTING (1972) (wm)Cat Stevens. (P)Cat Stevens.

SITTING IN THE BACK SEAT (1959) (w)Bob Hilliard (m)Lee Pockriss. (P)Paul Evans and The Curls.

SITTING IN THE PARK (wm)Billy Stewart. (P)Billy Stewart.

SIX LESSONS FROM MADAME LA ZONGA (1939) (wm)Charles Newman— James V. Monaco. (P)Jimmy Dorsey and his Orchestra, vocal by Helen O'Connell.

634-5789 (1966) (wm)Steve Cropper—Eddie Floyd. (P)Wilson Pickett.

SIX O'CLOCK (1967) (wm)John B. Sebastian. (P)The Lovin' Spoonful.

SIXTEEN CANDLES (1959) (wm)Luther Dixon—Allyson R. Khent. (P)The Crests.

SIXTEEN GOING ON SEVENTEEN (1959) (w)Oscar Hammerstein II (m)Richard Rodgers. (I)Musical: *The Sound Of Music*, by Laurie Peters and Brian Davies.

SIXTEEN REASONS (Why I Love You) (1960) (wm)Bill Post—Doree Post. (P)Connie Stevens. (R)1976 by Laverne and Shirley.

SIXTEEN TONS (1947) (wm)Merle Travis. (P)Tennessee Ernie Ford. No. 1 Chart Record. (R)1967 by Tom Jones.

SIXTY FIVE LOVE AFFAIR (1982) (wm)Paul Davis. (P)Paul Davis

SIXTY MINUTE MAN (1951) (wm)William Ward—Rose Marks. (P)Billy Ward and The Dominoes.

SKATERS WALTZ, THE (1882) (m)Emile Waldteufel. Famous light classical selection.

SKELETON IN THE CLOSET (1936) (wm)Arthur Johnston—Johnny Burke. (I)Film: *Pennies From Heaven*, by Louis Armstrong. (P)Louis Armstrong.

SKIP TO MY LOU (1844) (wm)Unknown. Traditional American folk song.

SKELETONS (1987) (wm)Stevie Wonder. (P)Stevie Wonder.

SKIN TIGHT (1974) (wm)Marshall Jones—Marvin Pierce—Leroy Bonner—James Williams—Ronald Middlebrooks—Clarence Satchell. (P)The Ohio Players.

SKINNY LEGS AND ALL (1967) (wm)Joe Tex. (P)Joe Tex.

SKINNY MINNIE (1958) (wm)Bill Haley—Rusty Keefer— Catherine Cafra—Milt Gabler. (P)Bill Haley and The Comets.

SKIP A ROPE (1968) (wm)Jack Moran—Glenn D. Tubb. (P)Henson Cargill.

SKOKIAAN (1954) (w-Eng)Tom Glazer (m)August Msarurgwa. (P)The Four Lads. (CR)Ralph Marterie and his Orchestra.

SKY HIGH (1975) (wm)Des Dyer—Clive Scott. (P)Jigsaw.

SKY PILOT (1968) (wm)Eric Burdon—Victor Briggs— Johnny Weider— Barry Jenkins—Danny McCulloch. (P)Eric Burdon and The Animals.

SKYLARK (1942) (w)Johnny Mercer (m)Hoagy Carmichael. (P)Glenn Miller and his Orchestra, vocal by Ray Eberle.

SKYLINER (1944) (m)Charlie Barnet. (P)Charlie Barnet and his Orchestra.

SLAP THAT BASS (1937) (w)Ira Gershwin (m)George Gershwin. (I)Film: *Shall We Dance?*, by Fred Astaire.

SLAUGHTER ON TENTH AVENUE (1936) (m)Richard Rodgers. (I)Musical: *On Your Toes*, as danced by Ray Bolger and Tamara Geva. (R)1964 Film: *Words And Music*, by Gene Kelly.

SLEDGEHAMMER (1986) (wm)Peter Gabriel. (P)Peter Gabriel.

SLEEP (1923) (wm)Earl Lebieg. (P)Theme song of Fred Waring's Pennsylvanians.

SLEEP WALK (1959) (m)Ann Farina—John Farina—Santo Farina. (P)Santo and Johnny. No. 1 Chart Record.

SLEEPIN' BEE, A (1954) (w)Truman Capote (m)Harold Arlen. (I)Musical: *House Of Flowers*, by Diahann Carroll, Ada Moore, Dolores Harper, and Enid Mosier.

SLEEPING BAG (1985) (wm)Billy Gibbons—Dusty Hill—Frank Beard. (P)ZZ Top.

(By The)SLEEPY LAGOON (1930) (w)Jack Lawrence (m)Eric Coates. (I)Xavier Cugat and his Orchestra, vocal by Buddy Clark. (R)1942 by Harry James and his Orchestra. (CR)Tommy Dorsey and his Orchestra. (R)1960 by The Platters.

SLEEPY SERENADE (1941) (w)Mort Greene (m)Lou Singer. (I)Film: *Hold That Ghost*, by The Andrews Sisters with Ted Lewis and his Orchestra.

SLEEPY TIME GAL (1925) (w)Joseph R. Alden— Raymond B. Egan (m)Ange Lorenzo—Richard A. Whiting. (I)Ben Bernie and his Orchestra. (CR)Gene Austin. (CR)Nick Lucas. (R)1944 by Harry James and his Orchestra.

SLEIGH RIDE (1950) (w)Mitchell Parish (m)Leroy Anderson. (P)Leroy Anderson and his Orchestra.

SLEIGHRIDE IN JULY (1945) (I)Film: *Belle Of The Yukon*, by Dinah Shore. (P)Dinah Shore. (CR)Bing Crosby. (CR)Tommy Dorsey and his Orchestra.

SLIP AWAY (1968) (wm)William Armstrong—Wilbur Terrell—Marcus Daniel. (P)Clarence Carter.

SLIP SLIDIN AWAY (1977) (wm)Paul Simon. (P)Paul Simon.

SLIPPERY WHEN WET (1975) (wm)William King, Jr. , Ronald La Pread, Thomas McClary, Walter Orange, Lionel Richie, Milan Williams. (P)The Commodores.

SLIPPIN' AND SLIDIN' (1956) (wm)Richard Penniman— Edwin Bocage— James Smith—Albert Collins. (P)Little Richard.

SLIPPING AROUND (1949) (wm)Floyd Tillman. (P)Jimmy Wakely and Margaret Whiting. (CR)Ernest Tubb.

SLIPPING INTO DARKNESS (1972) (wm)Sylvester Allen—Morris Dickerson—Lee Oscar Levitan— Howard Scott—Lonnie Jordan. (P)War.

SLOOP JOHN B. (1966) (wm)Brian Wilson. (P)The Beach Boys.

SLOW DANCIN' DON'T TURN ME ON (1977) (wm)Donald J. Addrisi. (P)The Addrisi Brothers.

SLOW DANCING (Swayin' To The Music) (1977) (wm)Jack Tempchin. (P)Johnny Rivers. (CR)The Funky Kings.

SLOW DOWN (1964) (wm)Lawrence E. Williams. (P)The Beatles.

SLOW HAND (1981) (w)John Bettis (m)Michael Clark. (P)The Pointer Sisters.

SLOW POKE (1951) (wm)Pee Wee King—Redd Stewart—Chilton Price. (P)Pee Wee King. (CR)Helen O'Connell. (CR)Arthur Godfrey.

SLOW RIDE (1976) (wm)Dave Peverett. (P)Foghat.

SLOW TWISTIN' (1962) (wm)Jon Sheldon. (P)Chubby Checker.

SLOW WALK (1957) (wm)Sil Austin—Irving Siders—Connie Moore. (P)Sil Austin. (CR)Bill Doggett.

SLUEFOOT (1955) (wm)Johnny Mercer. (I)Film: *Daddy Long Legs*, by Fred Astaire and Ray Anthony and his Orchestra.

SLUMMING ON PARK AVENUE (1937) (wm)Irving Berlin. (I)Film: *On The Avenue*, by Alice Faye, The Ritz Brothers, and The Chorus.

SMACK DAB IN THE MIDDLE (1955) (wm)Charles E. Calhoun. (P)Count Basie and his Orchestra, vocal by Joe Williams.

SMACKWATER JACK (1971) (w)Gerry Goffin (m)Carole King. (P)Carole King.

SMALL FRY (1938) (wm)Frank Loesser—Hoagy Carmichael. (I)Film: *Sing You Sinners*, by Bing Crosby, Fred MacMurray, and Donald O'Connor. (P)Bing Crosby and Johnny Mercer. (CR)Mildred Bailey.

SMALL TALK (1954) (wm)Richard Adler—Jerry Ross. (I)Musical: *The Pajama Game*, by Janis Paige and John Raitt.

SMALL TOWN (1985) (wm)John Cougar Mellencamp. (P)John Cougar Mellencamp.

SMALL WORLD (1959) (w)Stephen Sondheim (m)Jule Styne. (I)Musical: *Gypsy*, by Ethel Merman and Jack Klugman.

SMELLIN' OF VANILLA (Bamboo Cage) (1954) (wm)Truman Capote— Harold Arlen. (I)Musical: *House Of Flowers*, by Enid Mosier, Dolores Harper, and Ada Mosier.

SMILE (1936) (w)John Turner—Geoffrey Parsons (m)Charles Chaplin. (I)Film: *Modern Times*, as soundtrack theme. (R)1959 by Tony Bennett. (R)1961 by Timi Yuro. (R)1962 by Ferrante and Teicher. (R)1965 by Jerry Butler and Betty Everett.

SMILE A LITTLE SMILE FOR ME (1969) (wm)Tony Macauley—Geoff Stephens. (P)The Flying Machine.

SMILE, DARN YA, SMILE (1931) (w)Charles O'Flynn—Jack Meskill (m)Max Rich. (I)Theme song of Fred Allen's radio show.

(There Are)SMILES (1917) (w)J. Will Callahan (m)Lee G. Roberts. (I)Joseph C. Smith's Orchestra.

SMOKE FROM A DISTANT FIRE (1977) (wm)Ed Sanford—John Townsend— Steven Stewart. (P)Sanford Townsend Band.

SMOKE GETS IN YOUR EYES (1933) (w)Otto Harbach (m)Jerome Kern. (I)Musical: *Roberta, by Tamara*. In film version, by Irene Dunne and danced to by Fred Astaire. (R)1959 by The Platters. No. 1 Chart Record. (CR)1973 by Blue Haze.

SMOKE ON THE WATER (1973) (w)Richard Blackmore—Ian Gillian— Roger Glover—Jon Lord—Ian Paice. (P)Deep Purple.

SMOKE RINGS (1933) (w)Ned Washington (m)Gene Gifford. (P)Theme song of Glen Gray and The Casa Loma Orchestra.

SMOKE! SMOKE! SMOKE! (That Cigarette) (1947) (wm)Merle Travis— Tex Williams. (P)Phil Harris. (CR)Tex Williams.

SMOKIE, (PART II) (1959) (wm)William P. Black. (P)Bill Black's Combo as instrumental. (CR)Bill Doggett. (R)1985 by Motley Crue.

SMOKIN' IN THE BOYS ROOM (1974) (wm)Michael Roda—Michael Lutz. (P)Brownsville Station.

SMOKIN' REEFERS (1932) (w)Howard Dietz (m)Arthur Schwartz. (I)Revue: *Flying Colors*, by Jean Sargent and The Ensemble.

SMOKY PLACES (1962) (wm)Abner Spector. (P)The Corsairs and Jay "Bird" Uzzell.

SMOOTH OPERATOR (1985) (wm)Helen Folosade Adu—St. John. (P)Sade.

SMOOTH SAILING (1951) (wm)Arnett Cobb. (P)Ella Fitzgerald.

SMUGGLER'S BLUES (1985) (wm)Glenn Frey—Jack Tempchin. (P)Glenn Frey. Featured in an episode of TV show *Miami Vice*.

SNAKE, THE (1968) (wm)Oscar Brown, Jr. (P)Al Wilson.

SNAP YOUR FINGERS (1962) (wm)Grady Martin—Alex Zanetis. (P)Joe Henderson. (R)1964 by Barbara Lewis.

SNOOPY VERSUS THE RED BARON (1967) (wm)Phil Gernhard—Richard L. Holler. (P)The Royal Guardsmen.

(You're A)SNOOTIE LITTLE CUTIE (1942) (wm)Bobby Troup. (P)Tommy Dorsey and his Orchestra, vocal by Frank Sinatra, Connie Haines, and The Pied Pipers.

SNOWBIRD (1970) (wm)Gene Maclellan. (P)Anne Murray.

SNOWFALL (1941) (m)Claude Thornhill. (P)Theme song of Claude Thornhill and his Orchestra.

SNUGGLED ON YOUR SHOULDER (Cuddled In Your Arms) (1931) (wm)Joe Young—Carmen Lombardo. (I)Guy Lombardo and his Royal Canadians. (P)Bing Crosby. (CR)Kate Smith. (CR)Eddy Duchin and his Orchestra.

SO AM I (1924) (w)Ira Gershwin (m)George Gershwin. (I)Musical: *Lady, Be Good*, by Adele Astaire and Alan Edwards.

SO BAD (1984) (wm)Paul McCartney. (P)Paul McCartney.

SO BEATS MY HEART FOR YOU (1930) (wm)Pat Ballard—Charles Henderson—Tom Waring. (P)Fred Waring's Pennsylvanians.

SO DEAR TO MY HEART (1948) (w)Irving Taylor (m)Ticker Freeman. (I)Film: *So Dear To My Heart*, by Dinah Shore. (P)Dinah Shore.

SO DO I (1932) (w)B. G. De Sylva (m)Vincent Youmans. (I)Musical: *Take A Chance*, by June Knight, Jack Whiting, and The Ensemble.

SO DO I (1936) (w)Johnny Burke (m)Arthur Johnston. (I)Film: *Pennies From Heaven*, by Bing Crosby. (P)Bing Crosby.

SO EMOTIONAL (1987) (wm)B. Steinberg—Kelly. (P)Whitney Houston. No. 1 Chart Record.

SO FAR (1947) (w)Oscar Hammerstein II (m)Richard Rodgers. (I)Musical: *Allegro*, by Gloria Wills.

SO FAR AWAY (1971) (wm)Carole King. (P)Carole King.

SO FAR AWAY (1986) (wm)Mark Knopfler. (P)Dire Straits.

SO FINE (1958) (wm)Johnny Otis. (P)The Fiestas.

SO HELP ME (1934) (wm)Irving Berlin. (P)Emil Coleman and his Orchestra.

SO HELP ME (If I Don't Love You) (1938) (w)Eddie De Lange (m)Jimmy Van Heusen. (P)Russ Morgan and his Orchestra. (CR)Mildred Bailey.

SO IN LOVE (1948) (wm)Cole Porter. (I)Musical: *Kiss me Kate*, by Patricia Morrison and later reprised by Alfred Drake. 1953 Film version, by Kathryn Grayson and Howard Keel.

SO IN LOVE (1985) (wm)Steve Hague. (P)Orchestral Manoeuvres In The Dark.

SO INTO YOU (1977) (wm)Buddy Buie—Dean Daughtry—Robert Nix. (P)The Atlanta Rhythm Section.

SO LONG (It's Been Good To Know Yuh) (1939) (wm)Woody Guthrie. (R)1950 by The Weavers.

SO LONG (1940) (wm)Russ Morgan—Remus Harris—Irving Melsher. (P)Closing Theme of Russ Morgan and his Orchestra.

SO LONG, DEARIE (1964) (wm)Jerry Herman. (I)Musical: *Hello, Dolly!*, by Carol Channing.

SO LONG! OH-LONG (How Long You Gonna Be Gone?) (1920) (wm)Bert Kalmar—Harry Ruby. No artist credited with introduction. (R)Film: *Three Little Words*, by Fred Astaire and Red Skelton.

SO LONG MARY (1905) (wm)George M. Cohan. (I)Musical: *Forty Five Minutes From Broadway*, by George M. Cohan.

SO MANY WAYS (1959) (wm)Bobby Stevenson. (P)Brook Benton.

SO MUCH IN LOVE (1963) (wm)William Jackson—George Williams—Roy Straigis. (P)The Tymes. No. 1 Chart Record.

SO NEAR AND YET SO FAR (1941) (wm)Cole Porter. (I)Film: *You'll Never Get Rich*, by Fred Astaire.

SO SAD (To Watch Good Love Go Bad) (1960) (wm)Don Everly. (P)The Everly Brothers.

SO THIS IS LOVE (1962) (wm)Herbert Newman. (P)The Castells.

SO TIRED (1948) (wm)Russ Morgan—Jack Stuart. (P)Russ Morgan and his Orchestra.

SO VERY HARD TO GO (1973) (wm)Emilio Castillo—Stephen Kupka. (P)Tower Of Power.

SO WHAT? (1933) (w)Ira Gershwin (m)George Gershwin. (I)Musical: *Pardon My English*, by Jack Pearl and Josephine Houston.

SO YOU WANT TO BE A ROCK 'N ROLL STAR (1967) (wm)Jim McGuinn— Chris Hillman. (P)The Byrds.

SOBBIN' WOMEN (1954) (w)Johnny Mercer (m)Gene De Paul. (I)Film: *Seven Brides For Seven Brothers*, by Howard Keel.

SOCIETY'S CHILD (1967) (wm)Janis Ian. (P)Janis Ian.

SOCK IT TO ME, BABY (1967) (wm)Bob Crewe—L. Russell Brown. (P)Mitch Ryder and The Detroit Wheels.

SOFT AS SPRING (1941) (wm)Alec Wilder. (P)Benny Goodman and his Orchestra, vocal by Peggy Lee.

SOFT LIGHTS AND SWEET MUSIC (1932) (wm)Irving Berlin. (I)Revue: *Face The Music*, by J. Harold Murray and Katherine Carrington. (P)Fred Waring's Pennsylvanians.

SOFT SUMMER BREEZE (1956) (w)Judy Spencer (m)Eddie Heywood. (P)Eddie Heywood.

SOFT WINDS (1940) (m)Benny Goodman. (P)The Benny Goodman Sextet.

SOFTLY, AS I LEAVE YOU (1962) (w-Eng)Hal Shaper (m)A. DeVita. (P)Frank Sinatra.

SOFTLY, AS IN A MORNING SUNRISE (1928) (w)Oscar Hammerstein II (m)Sigmund Romberg. (I)Operetta: *The New Moon*, by William O'Neal. (R)1940 Film: *The New Moon*, by Nelson Eddy. (R)1949 by Artie Shaw and his Orchestra.

SOLDIER BOY (1962) (wm)Florence Green—Luther Dixon. (P)The Shirelles. No. 1 Chart Record.

SOLDIERS CHORUS (1859) (m)Charles Gounod. (I)Opera: *Faust*.

SOLID (1985) (wm)Nicholas Ashford—Valerie Simpson. (P)Ashford And Simpson.

SOLILOQUY (1945) (w)Oscar Hammerstein II (m)Richard Rodgers. (I)Musical: *Carousel*, by John Raitt. (R)1957 Film: *Carousel*, by Gordon MacRae. Most popular recording by Frank Sinatra.

SOLITAIRE (1951) (w)Renee Borek—Carl Nutter (m)King Guion. (P)Tony Bennett.

SOLITAIRE (1973) (wm)Neil Sedaka—Phil Cody. (P)Andy Williams. (CR)The Carpenters.

SOLITAIRE (1983) (w-Eng)Diane Warren (m)Martine Clemenceau. (P)Laura Branigan.

SOLITARY MAN (1966) (wm)Neil Diamond. (P)Neil Diamond.

SOLITUDE (1934) (w)Eddie De Lange—Irving Mills (m)Duke Ellington. (P)Duke Ellington and his Orchestra. Most popular vocal record by Ella Fitzgerald.

SOLO FLIGHT (1944) (m)Charlie Christian—Jimmy Mundy—Benny Goodman. (P)Benny Goodman and his Orchestra.

SOLOMON (1933) (wm)Cole Porter. (I)London Musical: *Nymph Errant*, by Elisabeth Welch.

SOME DAY (1925) (w)Brian Hooker (m)Rudolf Friml. (I)Operetta: *The Vagabond King*, by Carolyn Thomson. 1930 Film version, by Jeanette MacDonald. 1956 Film version, by Kathryn Grayson.

SOME DAYS EVERYTHING GOES WRONG (1963) (wm)Ervin Drake. (I)Musical: *What Makes Sammy Run?*, by Steve Lawrence.

SOME ENCHANTED EVENING (1949) (w)Oscar Hammerstein II (m)Richard Rodgers. (I)Musical: *South Pacific*, by Ezio Pinza. (P)Perry Como. (R)1958 Film: *South Pacific*, by Giorgio Tozzi dubbing for Rossano Brazzi. (R)1965 by Jay and The Americans. (R)1977 by Jane Olivor.

SOME GIRLS (1978) (wm)Mick Jagger—Keith Richard. (P)The Rolling Stones.

SOME GUYS HAVE ALL THE LUCK (1973) (wm)Jeff Fortgang. (P)The Persuaders. (R)1985 by Rod Stewart.

SOME KIND-A-WONDERFUL (1961) (wm)Gerry Goffin—Carole King. (P)The Drifters.

SOME KIND OF FRIEND (1983) (w)Adrienne Anderson (m)Barry Manilow. (P)Barry Manilow.

SOME KIND OF LOVER (1987) (wm)A. Cymone—J. Watley. (P)Jody Watley.

SOME LIKE IT HOT (1985) (wm)Robert Palmer—Andy Taylor—John Taylor. (P)The Power Station.

SOME OF THESE DAYS (1910) (wm)Shelton Brooks. (P)Sophie Tucker.

SOME OTHER TIME (1944) (w)Betty Comden—Adolph Green (m)Leonard Bernstein. (I)Musical: *On The Town*, by Betty Comden, Adolph Green, Nancy Walker, and Cris Alexander.

SOME PEOPLE (1959) (w)Stephen Sondheim (m)Jule

RICHARD RODGERS

For many years it was my honor and pleasure to conduct the orchestra which played for the annual major gala the Friars Club holds to pay homage to someone in the entertainment industry. Top names of show business would appear and make up the great stage show that was presented each year. As part of one show, it was decided to have six of the top songwriters in musical history appear on stage; each of them was to sing a parody of one of their hits in tribute to the guest of honor.

There was no rehearsal for this part of the show, so the orchestra and I had no idea what song each composer was going to sing or in what key. Fortunately, the orchestra consisted of some of the top musicians in New York City and we were able to fake arrangements to back up each of the songwriters.

Everything went beautifully. When that part of the show was over, each composer walked off the stage to a standing ovation. All except one ... Richard Rodgers.

When the curtains were closed, he stood next to me and addressed the band. "I don't know how you boys did it, but the music you provided for all of us was just wonderful and I can't thank you enough. It was simply superb."

The entire orchestra and I gave Richard Rodgers our own standing ovation backstage, a tribute from a bunch of musicians to a great man.

Styne. (I)Musical: *Gypsy*, by Ethel Merman.

SOME SUNNY DAY (1922) (wm)Irving Berlin. (P)Marion Harris. (CR)Paul Whiteman and his Orchestra.

SOME THINGS ARE BETTER LEFT UNSAID (1985) (wm)Daryl Hall. (P)Hall and Oates.

SOME THINGS YOU NEVER GET USED TO (1968) (wm)Nicholas Ashford— Valerie Simpson. (P)Diana Ross and The Supremes.

SOME VELVET MORNING (1968) (wm)Lee Hazlewood. (P)Nancy Sinatra and Lee Hazlewood.

SOMEBODY (1960) (w)Jack Brooks (m)Harry Warren. (I)Film: *Cinderella*, by Jerry Lewis. (P)Tony Bennett.

SOMEBODY (1985) (wm)Bryan Adams—Jim Vallance. (P)Bryan Adams.

SOMEBODY BAD STOLE DE WEDDING BELL (1954) (w)Bob Hilliard (m)Dave Mann. (P)Georgia Gibbs.

SOMEBODY BIGGER THAN YOU AND I (1951) (wm)Johnny Lange—Hy Heath—Sonny Burke. (I)Film: *The Old West*, by Gene Autry.

SOMEBODY ELSE IS TAKING MY PLACE (1937) (wm)Dick Howard—Bob Ellsworth—Russ Morgan. (I)Russ Morgan and his Orchestra. (R)1941 by Benny Goodman and his Orchestra, vocal by Peggy Lee. (R)1965 by Al Martino.

SOMEBODY ELSE-NOT ME (1920) (w)Ballard Macdonald (m)James F. Hanley. (P)Bert Williams.

SOMEBODY FROM SOMEWHERE (1931) (w)Ira Gershwin (m)George Gershwin. (I)Film: *Delicious*, by Janet Gaynor. (R)1955 by Shannon Bolin.

SOMEBODY LOVES ME (1924) (w)B. G. De Sylva—Ballard Macdonald (m)George Gerswhin. (I)Revue: *George White's Scandals of 1924*, by Winnie Lightner. (P)Paul Whiteman and his Orchestra. (R)1945 Film: *Rhapsody In Blue*, by Robert Alda. (R)1952 by The Four Lads. (R)1957 Film: *The Helen Morgan Story*, by Gogi Grant dubbing for Ann Blyth.

SOMEBODY LOVES YOU (1932) (w)Charles Tobias (m)Peter De Rose. (P)Vincent Lopez and his Orchestra. (CR)Ted Lewis.

SOMEBODY, SOMEWHERE (1956) (wm)Frank Loesser (I)Musical: *The Most Happy Fella*, by Jo Sullivan.

SOMEBODY STOLE GABRIEL'S HORN (1932) (wm)Irving Mills—Ned Washington—Edgar Hayes. (I)The Mills Blue Rhythm Band. (P)Louis Armstrong.

SOMEBODY STOLE MY GAL (1918) (wm)Leo Wood. (P)Ted Lewis and his Orchestra. (R)1953 by Johnnie Ray.

SOMEBODY TO LOVE (1967) (wm)Darby Slick. (P)Jefferson Airplane.

SOMEBODY TO LOVE (1976) (wm)Freddie Mercury. (P)Queen.

SOMEBODY UP THERE LIKES ME (1956) (w)Sammy Cahn (m)Bronislau Kaper. (I)Film: *Somebody Up There Likes Me*, on soundtrack. (P)Perry Como.

SOMEBODY'S BABY (1982) (wm)Jackson Browne—Danny Kortchmar. (P)Jackson Browne.

SOMEBODY'S BEEN SLEEPING IN MY BED (1970) (wm)Greg S. Perry— General Johnson—Angelo Bond. (P)100 Proof.

SOMEBODY'S KNOCKIN' (1981) (wm)Ed Penny—Jerry Gillespie. (P)Terri Gibbs.

SOMEBODY'S WATCHING ME (1984) (wm)Rockwell. (P)Rockwell.

SOMEDAY (1987) (wm)Glass Tiger—J. Vallance. (P)Glass Tiger.

SOMEDAY (You'll Want Me To Want You) (1940) (wm)Jimmie Hodges. (P)Elton Britt. (R)1949 by Vaughn Monroe and his Orchestra.

SOMEDAY I'LL FIND YOU (1930) (wm)Noel Coward. (I)Play: Private Lives, by Noel Coward and Gertrude Lawrence.

SOMEDAY MY PRINCE WILL COME (1937) (wm)Larry Morey—Frank Churchill. (I)Cartoon film: *Snow White And The Seven Dwarfs*, by voice of Adrienne Caselotti as Snow White.

SOMEDAY NEVER COMES (1972) (wm)John C. Fogarty. (P)Creedence Clearwater Revival.

SOMEDAY SOON (1969) (wm)Ian Tyson. (P)Judy Collins.

SOMEDAY WE'LL BE TOGETHER (1969) (wm)Jackey Beavers—Johnny Bristol—Harvey Fuqua. (P)Diana Ross and The Supremes. No. 1 Chart Record.

SOMEONE COULD LOSE A HEART TONIGHT (1982) (wm)David Malloy— Eddie Rabbitt—Even Stephens. (P)Eddie Rabbitt.

SOMEONE NICE LIKE YOU (1962) (wm)Leslie Bricusse—Anthony Newley. (I)Musical: *Stop The World—I Want To Get Off*, by Anthony Newley.

SOMEONE SAVED MY LIFE TONIGHT (1975) (wm)Elton John—Bernie Taupin. (P)Elton John.

SOMEONE THAT I USED TO LOVE (1980) (w)Gerry Goffin (m)Michael Masser. (P)Natalie Cole.

SOMEONE TO LAY DOWN BESIDE ME (1976)

(wm)Karla Bonof (P)Linda Ronstadt.

SOMEONE TO WATCH OVER ME (1926) (w)Ira Gershwin (m)George Gershwin. (I)Musical: *Oh, Kay!*, by Gertrude Lawrence. (P)George Olsen and his Orchestra. (R)1954 Film: *Young At Heart*, by Frank Sinatra.

SOMEONE WHO BELIEVES IN YOU (1924) (w)B. G. De Sylva (m)George Gershwin. (I)Musical: *Sweet Little Devil*, by Constance Binney and Irving Beebe.

SOMEONE YOU LOVE (1955) (wm)Steven Michaels. (P)Nat "King" Cole.

SOMEONE'S ROCKING MY DREAMBOAT (1941) (wm)Leon Rene—Emerson Scott—Otis Rene. (P)The Ink Spots.

SOMETHIN' STUPID (1967) (wm)Carson C. Parks. (P)Nancy and Frank Sinatra. No. 1 Chart Record.

SOMETHING (1969) (wm)George Harrison. (P)The Beatles. No. 1 Chart Record. (CR)Shirley Bassey. (R)1974 by Johnny Rodriguez.

SOMETHING ABOUT YOU (1965) (wm)Eddie Holland—Lamont Dozier— Brian Holland. (P)The Four Tops.

SOMETHING ABOUT YOU (1986) (wm)Mark Lindup—Phil Gould—Boon Gould—Mark King—Walter Badarou. (P)Level 42.

SOMETHING BETTER TO DO (1975) (wm)John Farrar. (P)Olivia Newton— John.

SOMETHING FOR THE BOYS (1943) (wm)Cole Porter. (I)Musical: *Something For The Boys*, by Ethel Merman.

SOMETHING HAD TO HAPPEN (1933) (w)Otto Harbach (m)Jerome Kern. (I)Musical: *Roberta*, by Bob Hope, Lyda Roberti, and Ray Middleton.

SOMETHING HAPPENED TO ME YESTERDAY (1967) (wm)Mick Jagger— Keith Richard. (P)The Rolling Stones.

SOMETHING HE CAN FEEL (1976) (wm)Curtis Mayfield. (I)Film: *Sparkle*, by Irene Cara and Lonette McKee. (P)Aretha Franklin.

SOMETHING OLD, SOMETHING NEW (1946) (wm)Ramez Idriss—George Tibbles. (P)Frank Sinatra.

SOMETHING SO STRONG (1987) (wm)N. Finn—M. Froom. (P)Crowded House.

SOMETHING SORT OF GRANDISH (1947) (w)E. Y. Harburg (m)Burton Lane. (I)Musical: *Finian's Rainbow*, by Ella Logan and David Wayne.

SOMETHING TO DANCE ABOUT (1950) (wm)Irving Berlin. (I)Musical: *Call Me Madam*, by Ethel Merman.

SOMETHING TO LIVE FOR (1939) (wm)Duke Ellington—Billy Strayhorn. (P)Duke Ellington and his Orchestra, vocal by Jean Eldridge.

SOMETHING TO LIVE FOR (1963) (wm)Ervin Drake. (I)Musical: *What Makes Sammy Run?*, by Sally Ann Howes.

SOMETHING TO REMEMBER YOU BY (1930) (w)Howard Dietz (m)Arthur Schwartz. (I)Revue: *Three's A Crowd*, by Libby Holmam. (P)Libby Holman. (R)1943 by Dinah Shore.

SOMETHING TO SHOUT ABOUT (1943) (wm)Cole Porter. (I)Film: *Something To Shout About*, by Janet Blair.

SOMETHING WONDERFUL (1951) (w)Oscar Hammerstein II (m)Richard Rodgers. (I)Musical: *The King and I*, by Dorothy Sarnoff.

SOMETHING'S BURNING (1970) (wm)Mac Davis. (P)Kenny Rogers and The First Edition.

SOMETHING'S COMING (1957) (w)Stephen Sondhein (m)Leonard Bernstein. (I)Musical: *West Side Story*, by Larry Kert.

SOMETHING'S GOTTA GIVE (1955) (wm)Johnny Mercer. (I)Film: *Daddy Long Legs*, by Fred Astaire. (P)The McGuire Sisters. (CR)Sammy Davis, Jr.

McGUIRE SISTERS

Something's Gotta Give, words and music by Johnny Mercer, was sung by Fred Astaire in a movie. His original soundtrack record didn't mean much in terms of record sales, and so, even though we knew that Sammy Davis was going to record it for Decca we made a decision to cut it with the McGuires. We had a preliminary rehearsal in Phyllis McGuire's apartment in midtown Manhattan. My wife came along and Bob Thiele brought his wife, Jane Harvey. Jane, very pregnant at the time, was a fine singer with previous stints with Benny Goodman and others.

Well, we had some differences of opinion concerning tempos and feel for the arrangement of *Something's Gotta Give*. In the middle of a lively discussion, Jane jumped up, big belly and all, and sang a great version of the song. Believe, her tempo and her ideas were used in the recording.

When Thiele and I went to Chicago to record the McGuires on a Christmas album, Jane came along. We all went to see the movie *Picnic* together. When the theme of *Moonglow and Picnic* was played, Jane turned to Bob and urged him to record it like that as it would be a sure hit. We did it with Geroge Cates, our West Coast musical director, and it did become a big hit.

Jane Harvey was a great singer and she had a wonderful feel for making records. She should have been a record producer.

SOMETHING'S WRONG WITH ME (1972) (wm)Bobby Hart—Danny Harshman. (P)Austin Roberts.

SOMETIMES I FEEL LIKE A MOTHERLESS CHILD (1918) (wm)Unknown. Traditional Black American spiritual.

SOMETIMES I'M HAPPY (1927) (w)Leo Robin—Clifford Grey. (m)Vincent Youmans. (I)Musical: *Hit The Deck*, by Charles King and Louise Groody. (R)1955 Film: *Hit The Deck*, by Jane Powell and Vic Damone.

SOMETIMES WHEN WE TOUCH (1978) (w)Dan Hill (m)Barry Mann. (P)Dan Hill.

SOMEWHERE (1957) (w)Stephen Sondheim (m)Leonard Bernstein. (I)Musical: *West Side Story*, by Reri Grist. (R)1966 by Len Barry. (R)1986 by Barbra Streisand.

SOMEWHERE A VOICE IS CALLING (1911) (w)Eileen Newton (m)Arthur F. Tate. (P)John McCormack.

SOMEWHERE ALONG THE WAY (1952) (Sammy Gallop (m)Kurt Adams. (P)Nat "King" Cole.

SOMEWHERE DOWN THE ROAD (1981) (wm)Cynthia Weil—Tom Snow. (P)Barry Manilow.

SOMEWHERE IN THE NIGHT (1946) (w)Mack Gordon

(m)Josef Myrow. (I)Film: *Three Little Girls In Blue*, by Vivian Blaine. (P)Dick Haymes.

SOMEWHERE IN THE NIGHT (1975) (wm)Will Jennings—Richard Kerr. (P)Batdorf and Rodney. (R)1976 by Helen Reddy. (R)1978 by Barry Manilow.

SOMEWHERE MY LOVE (Lara's Theme) (1965) (w)Paul Francis Webster (m)Maurice Jarre. (I)Film: *Doctor Zhivago*, as soundtrack theme. (P)The Ray Conniff Singers. (CR)Roger Williams and his Orchestra.

SOMEWHERE THERE'S A SOMEONE (1966) (wm)Baker Knight. (P)Dean Martin.

SOMEWHERE OUT THERE (1987) (wm)Barry Mann—Cynthia Weil—J. Horner. (I)Film: *An American Tail* on soundtrack. (P)Linda Ronstadt and James Ingram.

SON-OF-A-PREACHER-MAN (1968) (wm)John Hurley—Ronnie Wilkins. (P)Dusty Springfield.

SONATA (1947) (w)Ervin Drake—Jimmy Shirl (m)Alex Alstone. (P)Perry Como.

SONATA PATHETIQUE (1799) (m)Ludwig Van Beethoven. Famous classical composition.

SONG FOR A SUMMER NIGHT (1956) (wm)Robert Allen. (I)TV Show: *Song For A Summer Night*, by Mitch Miller and his Orchestra. (P)Mitch Miller.

SONG FROM M*A*S*H (Suicide Is Painless) (1970) (wm)Mike Altman— Johnny Mandel. (I)Film: *M*A*S*H*, on soundtrack. (P)Al Delory and his Orchestra.

SONG FROM MOULIN ROUGE, THE (Where Is Your Heart) (1953) (w— Eng)Bill Engvick (m)Georges Auric. (I)Film: *Moulin Rouge*, on soundtrack. (P)Percy Faith and his Orchestra, vocal by Felicia Sanders. (CR)Mantovani and his Orchestra. (CR)Henri Rene and his Orchestra.

SONG FROM SOME CAME RUNNING (To Love And Be Loved) (1958) (w)Sammy Cahn (m)Jimmy Van Heusen. (I)Film: *Some Came Running*, on soundtrack. (P)Frank Sinatra.

SONG IS ENDED, BUT THE MELODY LINGERS ON, THE (1927) (wm)Irving Berlin. (P)Ruth Etting. (CR)"Whispering" Jack Smith. (R)1948 by Nellie Lutcher.

SONG IS YOU, THE (1932) (w)Oscar Hammerstein II (m)Jerome Kern. (I)Musical: *Music In The Air*, by Tullio Carminati and Natalie Hall. 1934 Film version, by John Boles.

SONG OF INDIA (1897) (m)Nikolai Rimsky—Korsakov. Famous classical composition. First popular recording in 1921 by Paul Whiteman and his Orchestra. (R)1937 by Tommy Dorsey and his Orchestra. (R)1953 by Mario Lanza.

SONG OF LOVE (1921) (w)Dorothy Donnelly (m)Sigmund Romberg. Based on Schubert's Unfinished Symphony. (I)Operetta: *Blossom Time*, by Bertram Peacock and Olga Cook. (P)Lucy Isabelle Marsh and Royal Dadmun.

SONG OF RAINTREE COUNTY, THE (1957) (w)Paul Francis Webster— Raymond B. Egan (m)Richard A. Whiting. (I)Film: *Raintree County*, by Nat "King" Cole, on soundtrack. (P)Nat "King" Cole.

SONG OF THE BAREFOOT CONTESSA (1954) (m)Mario Nascimbene. (I)Film: *The Barefoot Contessa*, as danced by Ava Gardner.

SONG OF THE BAYOU (1937) (wm)Rube Bloom. Popular selection introduced by Mr. Bloom.

SONG OF THE DREAMER (1955) (wm)Eddie Tex Curtis. (P)Eddie Fisher.

SONG OF THE FLAME (1925) (w)Otto Harbach—Oscar Hammerstein II (m)George Gershwin—Herbert Stothart. (I)Operetta: *Song Of The Flame*, by Greek Evans, Tessa Kosta, and The Russian Art Choir.

SONG OF THE ISLANDS (1915) (wm)Charles E. King. Popular Hawaiian song. (R)1930 by Wayne King and his Orchestra. (R)1936 by Bing Crosby.

SONG OF THE JET (1963) (w-Eng)Gene Lees (m)Antonio Carlos Jobim. (I)Italian film: *Copacabana*, on soundtrack. (P)Tony Bennett.

SONG OF THE METRONOME, THE (1939) (wm)Irving Berlin. (I)Film: *Second Fiddle*, by The Brian Sisters and The Children's Chorus.

SONG OF THE SOUTH (1946) (w)Sam Coslow (m)Arthur Johnston. (I)Film: *Song of the South* on soundtrack.

SONG OF THE VAGABONDS (1925) (w)Brian Hooker (m)Rudolf Friml. (I)Operetta: *The Vagabond King*, by Dennis King and The Chorus. 1930 Film version, by Dennis King. 1956 Film version, by Oreste.

SONG OF THE VOLGA BOATMAN (1867)Traditional Russian folk song. (R)1941 by Glenn Miller and his Orchestra. No. 1 Chart Record.

SONG OF THE WANDERER (Where Shall I Go?) (1926) (wm)Neil Moret. (P)Earl Burtnett and his Orchestra. (CR)Art Landry.

SONG OF THE WOODMAN (1936) (w)E. Y. Harburg (m)Harold Arlen. (I)Revue: *The Show Is On*, by Bert Lahr.

SONG ON THE RADIO (1979) (wm)Al Stewart. (P)Al Stewart.

SONG SUNG BLUE (1972) (wm)Neil Diamond. (P)Neil Diamond. No. 1 Chart Record.

SONG TO A SEAGULL (1967) (wm)Joni Mitchell. (P)Buffy Sainte— Marie. (R)1968 by Joni Mitchell.

SONG WAS BORN, A (1948) (wm)Don Raye—Gene De Paul. (I)Film: *A Song Is Born*, by Louis Armstrong, The Golden Gate Quartet, and Jeri Sullivan, dubbing for Virginia Mayo.

SONG WITHOUT WORDS (1868) (m)Peter I. Tchaikovsky. Famous classical composition.

SONGBIRD (1978) (wm)Dave Wolfert—Stephen Nelson. (P)Barbra Streisand.

SONGBIRD (1987) (wm)Kenny G. (P)Kenny G.

SONGS GOTTA COME FROM THE HEART, THE (1947) (w)Sammy Cahn (m)Jule Styne. (I)Film: *It Happened In Brooklyn*, by Jimmy Durante.

SONGS OF LONG AGO, THE (1920) (w)Arthur Jackson (m)George Gershwin. (I)Revue: *George White's Scandals of 1920* by Lester O'Keefe.

SONGS MY MOTHER TAUGHT ME (1880) (m)Anton Dvorak. Famous classical selection.

SONNY BOY (1928) (wm)Al Jolson—B. G. De Sylva—Lew Brown—Ray Henderson. (I)Film: *The Singing Fool*, by Al Jolson. (P)Al Jolson. (R)1949 Film: *Jolson Sings Again*, by Jolson dubbing for Larry Parks.

SONS OF KATIE ELDER, THE (w)Ernie Sheldon (m)Elmer Bernstein. (I)Film: *The Sons Of Katie Elder*, on soundtrack. (P)Johnny Cash.

SOON (1930) (w)Ira Gershwin (m)George Gershwin. (I)Musical: *Strike Up The Band*, by Maggie Schilling and Jerry Goff.

SOON (1935) (w)Lorenz Hart (m)Richard Rodgers. (I)Film: *Mississippi*, by Bing Crosby. (P)Bing Crosby.

SOONER OR LATER (1946) (w)Ray Gilbert (m)Charles

Wolcott. (I)Film: *Song Of The South*, by Hattie Mc-Daniel. (P)Sammy Kaye and his Orchestra, vocal by Betty Barclay.

SOONER OR LATER (1971) (wm)Gary Zekley—Mitch Bottler—Adenyi Paris—Ted McNamara—Ekundayo Paris. (P)Grass Roots.

SOPHISTICATED LADY (1933) (w)Mitchell Parish—Irving Mills (m)Duke Ellington. (P)Duke Ellington and his Orchestra. (CR)Glen Gray and The Casa Loma Orchestra. (R)1948 by Billy Eckstine.

SOPHISTICATED LADY (She's A Different Lady) (1976) (wm)Natalie Cole—Charles Jackson, Jr. -Marvin Yancy. (P)Natalie Cole.

SOPHISTICATED SWING (1936) (w)Mitchell Parish (m)Will Hudson. (P)The Hudson—De Lange Orchestra.

SORCERER'S APPRENTICE, THE (1897) (m)Paul Dukas. Famous classical composition featured in cartoon film: *Fantasia*.

SORGHUM SWITCH (1942) (m)Jesse Stone. (I)Doc Wheeler and his Orchestra. (P)Jimmy Dorsey and his Orchestra.

SORRY (1949) (w)Buddy Pepper (m)Richard A. Whiting. (P)Margaret Whiting.

SORRY, I RAN ALL THE WAY HOME (1959) (wm)Harry Giosasi—Artie Zwirn. (P)The Impalas.

SORRY SEEMS TO BE THE HARDEST WORD (1976) (wm)Elton John. (P)Elton John.

S. O. S. (1975) (wm)Stig Anderson—Bjorn Ulvaeus—Benny Andersson. (P)Abba.

(You're My) SOUL AND INSPIRATION (1966) (wm)Barry Mann—Cynthia Weil. (P)The Righteous Brothers.

SOUL DEEP (1969) (wm)Wayne Carson Thompson. (P)The Box Tops.

SOUL FINGER (1967) (m)Phalon Jones—Jimmy King—Carl Cunningham— Ben Cauley—Ronnie Caldwell—James Alexander. (P)The Bar—Keys.

SOUL HOOTENANNY (1964) (wm)Eugene Dixon. (P)Gene Chandler.

SOUL KISS (1985) (wm)Mark Goldenberg. (P)Olivia Newton—John.

SOUL-LIMBO (1968) (m)Booker T. Jones—Steve Cropper—Donald Dunn— Al Jackson. (P)Booker T. and The MG's.

SOUL MAN (1967) (wm)Isaac Hayes—David Porter. (P)Sam and Dave. (CR)The Ramsey Lewis Trio. (R)1969 by The Blues Brothers.

SOUL POWER (1971) (wm)James Brown. (P)James Brown.

SOUL SERENADE (1964) (wm)Curtis Ousley—Luther Dixon. (P)King Curtis. (R)1968 by Willie Mitchell.

SOUL TWIST (1962) (m)Curtis Ousley. (P)King Curtis.

SOULFUL STRUT (1968) (wm)Eugene Record—Sonny Sanders. (P)Young— Holt Unlimited. (CR)Barbara Acklin.

SOULS (1983) (wm)Rick Springfield. (P)Rick Springfield.

SOUND OF MUSIC, THE (1959) (w)Oscar Hammerstein II (m)Richard Rodgers. (I)Musical: *The Sound Of Music*, by Mary Martin.

SOUND OFF (1941) (wm)Willie Lee Duckworth. (P)Used by U. S. Army in close order training drills. (P)Vaughn Monroe and his Orchestra.

SOUNDS OF SILENCE, THE (1965) (wm)Paul Simon. Originally introduced by Simon and Garfunkel under their original name of Tom and Jerry. No. 1 Chart Record.

SOUTH AMERICA, TAKE IT AWAY (1946) (wm)Harold Rome. (I)Revue: *Call Me Mister*, by Betty Garrett. (P)Bing Crosby and The Andrews Sisters.

SOUTH AMERICAN WAY (1939) (w)Al Dubin (m)Jimmy McHugh. (I)Film: *Down Argentine Way*, by Carmen Miranda. (P)Carmen Miranda.

SOUTH OF THE BORDER (1939) (wm)Jimmy Kennedy—Michael Carr. (P)Shep Fields and his Orchestra. No. 1 Chart Record. (CR)Gene Autry. (CR)Tony Martin. (R)1953 by Frank Sinatra.

SOUTH RAMPART STREET PARADE (1938) (m)Ray Bauduc—Bob Haggart. (P)Bob Crosby and his Orchestra.

SOUTH SEA ISLAND MAGIC (1936) (wm)Andy Iona Long. (P)Bing Crosby.

SOUTH STREET (1963) (w)Kal Mann (m)Dave Appell. (P)The Orlons.

SOUTHERN CROSS (1982) (wm)Steve Stills—Richard Curtis—Michael Curtis. (P)Crosby, Stills and Nash.

SOUTHERN NIGHTS (1977) (wm)Allen Toussaint. (P)Glen Campbell. No. 1 Chart Record.

SOUTH'S GONNA DO IT, THE (1975) (wm)Charlie Daniels. (P)The Charlie Daniels Band.

SOUTHTOWN, U. S. A. (1964) (wm)Billy Sherrill. (P)The Dixiebelles.

SPACE ODDITY (1973) (wm)David Bowie. (P)David Bowie.

SPACE RACE (1973) (wm)Billy Preston. (P)Billy Preston.

SPACEMAN (1972) (wm)Harry Nilsson. (P)Nilsson.

SPAIN (1924) (w)Gus Kahn (m)Isham Jones. (P)Isham Jones and his Orchestra. (CR)Paul Whiteman and his Orchestra.

SPANIARD THAT BLIGHTED MY WIFE, THE (1911) (wm)Billy Merson. (P)Al Jolson.

SPANISH EYES (1965) (w)Eddie Snyder—Charlie Singleton (m)Bert Kaempfert. (P)Bert Kaempfert and his Orchestra. Vocal version by Wayne Newton.

SPANISH FLEA (1966) (m)Julius Wechter. (P)Herb Alpert and The Tijuana Brass.

SPANISH HARLEM (1961) (wm)Jerry Leiber—Phil Spector. (P)Ben E. King. (R)1966 by King Curtis. (R)1971 by Aretha Franklin.

SPANISH HARLEM INCIDENT (1964) (wm)Bob Dylan. (P)Bob Dylan.

SPANISH ROSE (1960) (w)Lee Adams (m)Charles Strouse. (I)Musical: *Bye Bye Birdie*, by Chita Rivera.

SPARROW IN THE TREETOP (1951) (wm)Bob Merrill. (P)Guy Mitchell with Mitch Miller and his Orchestra.

SPARTACUS (Love Theme) (1960) (m)Alex North. (I)Film: *Spartacus*, on soundtrack.

SPEAK LOW (1943) (w)Ogden Nash (m)Kurt Weill. (I)Musical: *One Touch Of Venus*, by Mary Martin and Kenny Baker. (P)Guy Lombardo and his Royal Canadians, vocal by Billy Leach. (R)1948 Film: *One Touch Of Venus*, by Dick Haymes and Eileen Wilson dubbing for Ava Gardner.

SPEAK SOFTLY LOVE (See: Love Theme From The Godfather).

SPEAK TO ME OF LOVE (Parlez—Moi D'Amour). (1932) (w-Eng)Bruce Sievier (m)Jean Lenoir. (P)Lucienne Boyer.

SPEAK TO THE SKY (1972) (wm)Richard Springthorpe. (P)Rick Springfield.

SPECIAL DELIVERY (1969) (wm)Bo Gentry—Bobby Bloom. (P)The 1910 Fruitgum Company.

SPECIAL LADY (1980) (wm)Harold Ray—Al Goodman—

L. Walter. (P)Ray, Goodman & Brown.

SPECIAL OCCASION (1968) (wm)Alfred Cleveland—William Robinson. (P)Smokey and The Miracles.

SPEEDOO (1955) (wm)Esther Navarro. (P)The Cadillacs.

SPEEDY GONZALEZ (1962) (wm)Buddy Kaye—Ethel Lee—David Hill. (I)In France by Dalida. (P)Pat Boone.

SPELLBOUND (1946) (m)Miklos Rozsa. (I)Film: *Spellbound* on soundtrack.

SPIDER AND THE FLY, THE (1966) (wm)Mick Jagger—Keith Richard. (P)The Rolling Stones.

SPIDERS AND SNAKES (1974) (wm)Jim Stafford—David Bellamy. (P)Jim Stafford.

SPIES LIKE US (1986) (wm)Paul McCartney. (P)Paul McCartney.

SPILL THE WINE (1970) (wm)Howard Scott—Morris Dickerson—Harold Brown—Charles Miller—Lonnie Jordan—Sylvester Allen—Lee Oscar Levitin. (P)Eric Burdon and War. (CR)The Isley Borthers.

SPINNING WHEEL (1969) (wm)David Clayton Thomas. (P)Blood, Sweat and Tears. (R)1971 by James Brown.

SPIRIT IN THE DARK (1970) (wm)Aretha Franklin. (P)Aretha Franklin.

SPIRIT IN THE NIGHT (1972) (wm)Bruce Springsteen. (P)Bruce Springsteen. (R)1976 by Manfred Mann's Earth Band.

SPIRIT IN THE SKY (1970) (wm)Norman Greenbaum. (P)Norman Greenbaum. (CR)Dorothy Morrison. (R)1986 by Doctor & The Medics.

SPIRITS IN THE MATERIAL WORLD (1982) (wm)Gordon Sumner (Sting). (P)The Police.

SPLISH SPLASH (1958) (wm)Bobby Darin—Jean Murray. (P)Bobby Darin.

SPOOKY (1967) (m)Harry Middlebrooks—Mike Shapiro. (P)Mike Sharpe. (R)1968 by The Classics IV. (R)1979 by The Atlanta Rhythm Section.

SPOONFUL OF SUGAR, A (1963) (wm)Richard M. Sherman—Robert B. Sherman. (I)Film: *Mary Poppins*, by Julie Andrews.

S'POSIN' (1929) (w)Andy Razaf (m)Paul Denniker. (P)Rudy Vallee. (CR)Fats Waller. (R)1953 by Don Cornell.

SPRING AGAIN (1938) (w)Ira Gerswhin (m)Vernon Duke. (I)Film: *The Goldwyn Follies*, by Kenny Baker.

SPRING IS HERE (1938) (w)Lorenz Hart (m)Richard Rodgers. (I)Musical: *I Married An Angel*, by Dennis King and Vivienne Segal.

SPRING SONG (1844) (m)Felix Mendelsohn. Famous classical composition.

SPRING SPRING SPRING (1954) (w)Johnny Mercer (m)Gene De Paul. (I)Film: *Seven Brides For Seven Brothers*, by The Chorus.

SPRING WILL BE A LITTLE LATE THIS YEAR (1944) (wm)Frank Loesser. (I)Film: *Christmas Holiday*, by Deanna Durbin. (P)Morton Downey.

SQUARE IN A SOCIAL CIRCLE, A (1945) (wm)Jay Livingston—Ray Evans. (I)Film: *Stork Club*, by Betty Hutton.

SQUEEZE BOX (1976) (wm)Peter Townshend. (P)The Who.

SQUEEZE ME (1925) (wm)Thomas Waller—Clarence Williams. (I)Clarence Williams' Blue Five, vocal by Eva Taylor. Most popular recording by Lena Horne.

ST. LOUIS BLUES (1914) (wm)W. C. Handy. (P)Marion Harris. No. 1 Chart Record. (R)1925 by Bessie Smith. (R)1930 by Louis Armstrong. (R)1930 by Cab Calloway. (R)1932 by The Mills Brothers. (R)1935 by The Boswell Sisters. (R)1936 by Benny Goodman and his Orchestra. (R)1953 by Billy Eckstine.

STAGGER LEE (1959) (wm)Harold Logan—Lloyd Price. (P)Lloyd Price. (R)1967 by Wilson Pickett.

STAIRWAY TO HEAVEN (1960) (w)Howard Greenfield (m)Neil Sedaka. (P)Neil Sedaka.

STAIRWAY TO HEAVEN (1972) (wm)Robert Plant—Jimmy Page. (P)Led Zeppelin. The song was never released as a single.

STAIRWAY TO THE STARS (1939) (w)Mitchell Parish (m)Matt Malneck— Frank Signorelli. (P)Paul Whiteman and his Orchestra.

STAMPEDE (1926) (m)Fletcher Henderson. (P)Fletcher Henderson and his Orchestra.

STAN' UP AN' FIGHT (1943) (w)Oscar Hammerstein II (m)Georges Bizet. Adapted from Bizet's Toreador Song. (I)Musical: *Carmen Jones*, by Glenn Bryant.

STAND (1969) (wm)Sylvester Stewart (P)Sly and The Family Stone.

STAND BACK (1983) (wm)Stephanie Nicks—Prince Rogers Nelson. (P)Stevie Nicks.

STAND BY ME (1961) (wm)Ben E. King—Jerry Leiber—Mike Stoller. (P)Ben E. King. (R)1967 by Spyder Turner. (R)1970 by David Ruffin. (R)1975 by John Lennon. (R)1987 Film: *Stand By Me*, by Ben E. King, on soundtrack.

STAND BY YOUR MAN (1968) (wm)Tammy Wynette—Billy Sherrill. (P)Tammy Wynette. (R)1970 by Candi Staton.

STAND TALL (1976) (wm)Burton Cummings. (P)Burton Cummings.

STANDING IN THE SHADOWS OF LOVE (1966) (wm)Eddie Holland— Lamont Dozier—Brian Holland. (P)The Four Tops.

STANDING ON THE CORNER (1956) (wm)Frank Loesser. (I)Musical: *The Most Happy Fella*, by Shorty Long, Alan Gilbert, John Henson, Roy Lazarus. (P)The Four Lads.

STANLEY STEAMER, THE (1948) (w)Ralph Blane (m)Harry Warren. (I)Film: *Summer Holiday*, by Gloria De Haven, Mickey Rooney, and Agnes Moorehead.

STAR! (1968) (w)Sammy Cahn (m)Jimmy Van Heusen. (I)Film: *Star!*, by Julie Andrews.

STAR DUST (1929) (w)Mitchell Parish (m)Hoagy Carmichael. (P)Isham Jones and his Orchestra. No. 1 Chart Record. (CR)Bing Crosby. (CR)Louis Armstrong. (CR)Wayne King and his Orchestra. (R)1935 by Jimmie Lunceford and his Orchestra. (R)1936 by Benny Goodman and his Orchestra. (R)1936 by Tommy Dorsey and his Orchestra. (R)1941 by Artie Shaw and his Orchestra. (R)1941 by Glenn Miller and his Orchestra. (R)1957 by Billy Ward & His Dominoes, vocal by Jackie Wilson. (R)1957 by Nat "King" Cole. (R)1962 by Frank Sinatra. (R)1964 by Nino Tempo and April Stevens.

STAR EYES (1943) (wm)Don Raye—Gene De Paul. (I)Film: *I Dood It*, by Jimmy Dorsey and his Orchestra, vocal by Bob Eberly and Helen O'Connell. (P)Jimmy Dorsey.

STAR SPANGLED BANNER, THE (1814) (w)Francis Scott Key (m)John Stafford Smith. Melody based on English song: Anacreon. National anthem of the United States of America.

STARS AND STRIPES FOREVER, THE (1897) (m)John Philip Sousa. The most popular patriotic march.

STAR WARS TITLE THEME (1977) (m)John Williams. (I)Film: *Star Wars*, by The London Symphony Orchestra, on soundtrack. (P)Meco and his Orchestra as a disco version. No. 1 Chart Record.

STARBRIGHT (1959) (wm)Lee Pockriss—Paul J. Vance. (P)Johnny Mathis.

STARLIT HOUR, THE (1940) (w)Mitchell Parish (m)Peter De Rose. (P)Ella Fitzgerald. (CR)Glenn Miller and his Orchestra.

STARS FELL ON ALABAMA (1934) (wm)Mitchell Parish (m)Frank Perkins. (P)Jack Teagarden.

STARS IN MY EYES (1936) (w)Dorothy Fields (m)Fritz Kreisler. (I)Film: *The King Steps Out*, by Grace Moore.

START ME UP (1981) (wm)Mick Jagger—Keith Richard. (P)The Rolling Stones.

START MOVIN' (1957) (wm)David Hill—Bobby Stevenson. (P)Sal Mineo.

START THE DAY RIGHT (1939) (wm)Charles Tobias—Al Lewis—Maurice Spitalny. (P)Bing Crosby and Connee Boswell.

STARTING ALL OVER AGAIN (1972) (wm)Phillip Mitchell (P)Mel & Tim.

STATE OF SHOCK (1984) (wm)Michael Jackson—Randy Hansen. (P)Michael Jackson and Mick Jagger.

STATE OF THE HEART (1985) (wm)Rick Springfield. (P)Rick Springfield.

STAY (1960) (wm)Maurice Williams. (P)Maurice Williams and The Zodiacs. No. 1 Chart Record. (R)1978 by Jackson Browne.

STAY AS SWEET AS YOU ARE (1934) (w)Mack Gordon (m)Harry Revel. (I)Film: *College Rhythm*, by Lanny Ross. (P)Jimmie Grier and his Orchestra. No. 1 Chart Record. (CR)Guy Lombardo and his Royal Canadians.

STAY AWAKE (1963) (wm)Richard M. Sherman—Robert B. Sherman. (I)Film: *Mary Poppins*, by Julie Andrews.

STAY AWHILE (1971) (wm)Ken Tobias. (P)The Bells.

STAY IN MY CORNER (1968) (wm)Wade Flemons—Bobby Miller—Barrett Strong. (P)The Dells.

STAY ON THE RIGHT SIDE SISTER (1933) (w)Ted Koehler (m)Rube Bloom. (P)Ruth Etting. (R)1955 Film: *Love Me Or Leave Me*, by Doris Day.

STAY THE NIGHT (1984) (wm)Peter Cetera—David Foster. (P)Chicago.

STAY THE NIGHT (1987) (wm)Benjamin Orr—D. G. Page. (P)Benjamin Orr.

STAY WITH ME (1972) (wm)Rod Stewart—Ron Wood. (P)Faces.

STAY WITH THE HAPPY PEOPLE (1950) (w)Bob Hilliard (m)Jule Styne. (I)Revue: *Michael Todd's Peep Show*, by Lina Romay.

STAYIN' ALIVE (1977) (wm)Barry, Maurice and Robin Gibb. (I)Film: *Saturday Night Fever* by the voices of The Bee Gees. (P)The Bee Gees. No. 1 Chart Record.

STEAL AWAY (1964) (wm)Jimmy Hughes. (P)Jimmy Hughes. (R)1970 by Johnnie Taylor.

STEAL AWAY (1980) (wm)Robbie Dupuis—Rick Chudacoff. (P)Robbie Dupree.

STEALIN' APPLES (1936) (w)Andy Razaf (m)Thomas Waller. (I)Fletcher Henderson and his Orchestra. (P)Benny Goodman and his Orchestra.

STEAM HEAT (1954) (wm)Richard Adler—Jerry Ross. (I)Musical: *The Pajama Game*, by Carol Haney, Buzz Miller and Pat Gennaro.

STEAMBOAT BILL (1910) (w)Ron Shields (m)Leighton Brothers. Traditional type folk song.

STEAMROLLER BLUES (1969) (wm)James Taylor. (P)James Taylor. (R)1973 by Elvis Presley.

(Maine)STEIN SONG (1910) (w)Lincoln Colcord (m)E. A. Fenstad. School song of the University of Maine. (P)Rudy Vallee.

STELLA BY STARLIGHT (1944) (w)Ned Washington (m)Victor Young. (I)Film: *The Uninvited*, on soundtrack. (P)Victor Young and his Orchestra. Most popular recording by Frank Sinatra.

STEP BY STEP (1960) (wm)Ollie Jones—Billy Dawn Smith. (P)The Crests.

STEP BY STEP (1981) (wm)Eddie Rabbitt—Even Stevens—David Malloy. (P)Eddie Rabbitt.

STEP IN TIME (1963) (wm)Richard M. Sherman—Robert B. Sherman. (I)Film: *Mary Poppins* by Dick Van Dyke and The Chimney Sweeps.

STEP INSIDE LOVE (1968) (wm)John Lennon—Paul McCartney. (P)Cilla Black.

STEP OUT OF YOUR MIND (1967) (wm)Al Gorgoni—Chip Taylor. (P)The American Breed.

STEPPIN' INTO SWING SOCIETY (1938) (w)Irving Mills—Henry Nemo. (m)Duke Ellington. (P)Duke Ellington and his Orchestra.

STEPPIN' OUT (1965) (wm)Paul Revere—Mark Lindsay. (P)Paul Revere and The Raiders.

STEPPIN' OUT (1982) (wm)Joe Jackson. (P)Joe Jackson.

STEPPIN' OUT (I'm Gonna Boogie Tonight) (1974) (wm)Irwin Levine— L. Russell Brown. (P)Tony Orlando and Dawn.

STEPPIN' OUT WITH MY BABY (1948) (wm)Irving Berlin. (I)Film: *Easter Parade*, by Fred Astaire.

(I'm Not Your)STEPPIN' STONE (1967) (wm)Tommy Boyce—Bobby Hart. (P)The Monkees.

STEREOPHONIC SOUND (1955) (wm)Cole Porter. (I)Musical: *Silk Stockings*.

STICK AROUND (1964) (w)Lee Adams (m)Charles Strouse. (I)Musical: *Golden Boy*, by Sammy Davis, Jr.

STICK SHIFT (1961) (m)Henry Bellinger. (P)The Duals.

STICK-UP (1971) (wm)General Johnson—Angelo Bond—Greg Perry. (P)Honey Cone.

STIFF UPPER LIP (1937) (w)Ira Gershwin (m)George Gershwin. (I)Film: *A Damsel In Distress*, by Gracie Allen

(I Love You)STILL (1963) (wm)Bill Anderson. (P)Bill Anderson.

STILL (1979) (wm)Lionel Richie. (P)The Commodores. No. 1 Chart Record.

STILL IN SAIGON (1982) (wm)Dan Daley. (P)The Charlie Daniels Band.

STILL THE ONE (1976) (wm)John J. Hall—Johanna Hall. (P)Orleans.

STILL THE SAME (1978) (wm)Bob Seger. (P)Bob Seger & The Silver Bullet Band.

STILL THEY RIDE (1982) (wm)Steve Perry—Neal Schon—Jonathan Cain. (P)Journey.

STILL WATER (Love) (1970) (wm)Frank Wilson—William Robinson. (P)The Four Tops.

STIR IT UP (1973) (wm)Bob Marley. (P)Johnny Nash.

STOMP (1980) (wm)Louis Johnson—George Johnson—

Rod Temperton— Valerie Johnson. (P)The Brothers Johnson.

STOMP OFF, LET'S GO (1925) (m)Elmer Schoebel. (P)Erskine Tate and his Orchestra, trumpet solo by Louis Armstrong.

STOMPIN' AT THE SAVOY (1934) (w)Andy Razaf (m)Benny Goodman— Edgar Sampson—Chick Webb. (I)Chick Webb and his Orchestra. (P)Benny Goodman and his Orchestra.

STONE COLD DEAD IN THE MARKET (1946) (wm)Wilmoth Houdini. (I)Wilmoth Houdini. (P)Ella Fitzgerald and Louis Jordan.

STONE FREE (1969) (wm)Jimi Hendrix. (P)The Jimi Hendrix Experience.

STONE LOVE (1987) (wm)Kool And The Gang. (P)Kool and The Gang.

STONED LOVE (1970) (wm)Frank Wilson—Yennik Samoht. (P)The Supremes.

STONED SOUL PICNIC (1968) (wm)Laura Nyro. (I)Laura Nyro. (P)The 5th Dimension.

STONES (1971) (wm)Neil Diamond. (P)Neil Diamond.

STONEWALL MOSKOWITZ MARCH (1926) (wm)Lorenz Hart—Irving Caesar— Richard Rodgers. (I)Musical: Betsy, by Al Shean.

STONY END (1967) (wm)Laura Nyro. (P)Laura Nyro. (R)1970 by Barbra Streisand.

STOOD UP (1958) (wm)Dub Dickerson—Erma Herrold. (P)Rick Nelson.

STOP AND SMELL THE ROSES (1974) (wm)Mac Davis— Doc Severinsen. (P)Mac Davis.

STOP AND THINK IT OVER (1964) (wm)Jake Graffagnino. (P)Dale and Grace.

STOP BEATIN' 'ROUND THE MULBERRY BUSH (1938) (w)Bickley Reichner (m)Clay Boland. Adapted from a nursery song. (P)Tommy Dorsey and his Orchestra.

STOP DRAGGIN' MY HEART AROUND (1981) (wm)Tom Petty—Mike Campbell. (P)Stevie Nicks with Tom Petty and The Heartbreakers.

STOP! IN THE NAME OF LOVE (1965) (wm)Brian Holland—Lamont Dozier—Eddie Holland. (P)The Supremes. No. 1 Chart Record. (R)1983 by The Hollies.

STOP, STOP, STOP (1966) (wm)Allan Clarke—Tony Hicks—Graham Nash. (P)The Hollies.

STOP TO LOVE (1987) (wm)Luther Vandross—Nat Adderly, Jr. (P)Luther Vandross.

STORMY (1968) (wm)Buddy Buie—James B. Cobb. (P)The Classics IV. (CR)Dennis Yost. (R)1979 by Santana.

STORMY WEATHER (1933) (w)Ted Koehler (m)Harold Arlen. (I)Leo Reisman and his Orchestra, vocal by Harold Arlen. (P)Ethel Waters. (CR)Guy Lombardo and his Royal Canadians. (CR)Duke Ellington and his Orchestra. (R)1943 Film: Stormy Weather, by Lena Horne. Most popular recording by Lena Horne.

STORY IN YOUR EYES (1971) (wm)Justin Hayward. (P)The Moody Blues.

STORY OF A STARRY NIGHT, THE (1941) (wm)Al Hoffman—Mann Curtis— Jerry Livingston. Adapted from Tchaikovsky's Pathetique Symphony. (P)Glenn Miller and his Orchestra, vocal by Ray Eberle.

STORY OF MY LIFE, THE (1957) (w)Hal David (m)Burt Bacharach. (P)Marty Robbins.

STORY OF MY LOVE, THE (1959) (wm)Jack Nance— Conway Twitty. (P)Conway Twitty.

STORY UNTOLD, A (1955) (wm)LeRoy Griffin—Marty Wilson. (P)The Crew Cuts. (CR)The Nutmegs.

STOUTHEARTED MEN (1928) (w)Oscar Hammerstein II (m)Sigmund Romberg. (I)Operetta: The New Moon, by Robert Halliday, William O'Neal, and The Male Chorus. 1930 Film version by Lawrence Tibbett. 1940 Film version by Nelson Eddy. (R)1967 by Barbra Streisand.

STRAIGHT FROM THE HEART (1983) (wm)Bryan Adams—Eric Kagna. (P)Bryan Adams.

STRAIGHT FROM THE SHOULDER (Right From The Heart) (1934) (w)Mack Gordon (m)Harry Revel. (I)Film: She Loves Me Not, by Bing Crosby and Kitty Carlisle. (P)Bing Crosby.

STRAIGHT ON (1978) (wm)Ann Wilson—Nancy Wilson. (P)Heart.

STRAIGHTEN UP AND FLY RIGHT. (1943) (wm)Nat Cole—Irving Mills. (I)Film: Here Comes Elmer, by The King Cole Trio. (P)The King Cole Trio.

STRANDED IN THE JUNGLE (1956) (wm)Ernestine Smith—James Johnson. (P)The Cadets. (CR)The Jayhawks.

STRANGE ENCHANTMENT (1939) (w)Frank Loesser (m)Frederick Hollander. (I)Film: Man About Town, by Dorothy Lamour. (P)Dorothy Lamour. (CR)Ozzie Nelson and his Orchestra.

STRANGE FRUIT (1939) (wm)Lewis Allan. (P)Billie Holiday.

STRANGE INTERLUDE (1932) (w)Ben Bernie—Walter Hirsch (m)Phil Baker. (P)Ben Bernie and his Orchestra. (CR)Rudy Vallee.

STRANGE MAGIC (1976) (wm)Jeff Lynne. (P)Electric Light Orchestra.

STRANGE MUSIC (1944) (wm)Robert Wright—George Forrest. Adapted from a theme by Grieg. (I)Operetta: Song Of Norway, by Lawrence Brooks and Helena Bliss.

STRANGE THINGS ARE HAPPENING (1953) (wm)Red Buttons—Allan Walker—Elliot Lawrence. (P)Red Buttons.

STRANGE WAY (1978) (wm)Rick Roberts. (P)Firefall.

STRANGER IN MY HOUSE (1983) (wm)Mike Reid. (P)Ronnie Milsap. NARAS Award Winner.

STRANGER IN PARADISE (1953) (wm)Robert Wright— George Forrest. Adapted from Borodin's Polovtsian Dances. (I)Musical: Kismet, by Doretta Morrow and Richard Kiley. (P)The Four Aces. No. 1 Chart Record.

STRANGER IN TOWN (1965) (wm)Del Shannon. (P)Del Shannon.

STRANGER ON THE SHORE (1961) (w)Robert Mellin (m)Acker Bilk. (P)Acker Bilk. Vocal Version by Andy Williams.

STRANGERS IN THE NIGHT (1966) (w)Charles Singleton—Eddie Snyder (m)Bert Kaempfert. (I)Film: A Man Could Get Killed, on soundtrack. (P)Bert Kaempfert and his Orchestra. Vocal Version by Frank Sinatra. No. 1 Chart Record. NARAS Award Winner.

STRAWBERRY FIELDS FOREVER (1967) (wm)John Lennon—Paul McCartney. (P)The Beatles.

STRAWBERRY LETTER 23 (1977) (wm)Shuggie Otis. (P)The Brothers Johnson.

STRAY CAT (1968) (wm)Mick Jagger—Keith Richard. (P)The Rolling Stones.

STRAY CAT STRUT (1983) (wm)Brian Setzer. (P)The Stray Cats.

STREAK, THE (1974) (wm)Ray Stevens. (P)Ray Stevens. No. 1 Chart Record.

STREET FIGHTING MAN (1968) (wm)Mick Jagger— Keith Richard. (P)The Rolling Stones.

STREET OF DREAMS (1932) (w)Sam Lewis (m)Victor Young. (P)Morton Downey. (CR)Bing Crosby. (R)1943 by Tommy Dorsey and his Orchestra.

STREET SCENE (1931) (m)Alfred Newman. (I)Film: *Street Scene* on soundtrack.

STRICTLY INSTRUMENTAL (1942) (wm)Eddie Seiler— Sol Marcus— Bennie Benjamin—Edgar Battle. (P)Harry James and his Orchestra.

STRICTLY U. S. A. (1949) (wm)Roger Edens. (I)Film: *Take Me Out To The Ball Game,* by Frank Sinatra, Gene Kelly, Esther Williams, and Betty Garrett.

STRIKE UP THE BAND (1927) (w)Ira Gershwin (m)George Gershwin. (I)Musical: *Strike Up The Band,* by Jim Townsend, Jerry Goff, The Chorus, all accompanied by Red Nichols and his Orchestra. (R)1940 Film: *Strike Up The Band* on soundtrack.

STRING ALONG (1952) (wm)Dave Coleman. (P)The Ames Brothers.

STRING OF PEARLS, A (1942) (w)Eddie De Lange (m)Jerry Gray. (P)Glenn Miller and his Orchestra. No. 1 Chart Record. (CR)Benny Goodman and his Orchestra.

STRIP POLKA (Take It Off—Take It Off) (1942) (wm)Johnny Mercer. (P)The Andrews Sisters. (CR)Alvino Rey and his Orchestra, vocal by The King Sisters.

STRIPPER, THE (1962) (m)David Rose. (P)David Rose and his Orchestra. No. 1 Chart Record.

STROKE, THE (1981) (wm)Billy Squier. (P)Billy Squier.

STROLL, THE (1958) (wm)Clyde Otis—Nancy Lee. (P)The Diamonds.

STRUT (1984) (wm)Charlene Dore—J. Littman. (P)Sheena Easton.

STRUTTIN' (1975) (wm)Jerry Reed Hubbard. (P)Billy Preston.

STRUTTIN' WITH SOME BARBECUE (1927) (wm)Lil

LOUIS ARMSTRONG

Some years before Louis Armstrong's death, I was given the assignment of writing the musical arrangements and supervising the production of his recording sessions. One of the record dates called for Louis to record several of the songs that were entered in the San Remo Music Festival. The lyrics of these songs were in Italian; inasmuch as Louis did not speak the language, we called in an interpreter to teach Louis the words phonetically.

The time for the recording session arrived and Armstrong did a marvelous job, caressing the lyrics with an Italian accent that could only have been Louis. At the conclusion of one of the songs, the interpreter instructed Louis to say "Ciao" at the conclusion of one song, as it meant goodbye. Louis looked at him with a wide grin and gave forth with one of those classic Armstrong remarks: "Man, when I say 'Chow', that means food and time to eat!"

Hardin Armstrong— Louis Armstrong. (P)Louis Armstrong.

STUCK IN THE MIDDLE WITH YOU (1973) (wm)Joe Egan—Gerry Rafferty. (P)Stealer's Wheel.

STUCK INSIDE OF MOBILE WITH THE MEMPHIS BLUES AGAIN. (1966) (wm)Bob Dylan. (P)Bob Dylan.

STUCK ON YOU (1960) (wm)Aaron Schroeder—J. Leslie McFarland. (P)Elvis Presley.

STUCK ON YOU (1984) (wm)Lionel Richie. (P)Lionel Richie.

STUCK WITH YOU (1986) (wm)Chris Hayes—Huey Lewis. (P)Huey Lewis & The News.

STUDY IN BROWN (1937) (m)Larry Clinton. (I)Bunny Berigan and his Orchestra. (CR)The Casa Loma Orchestra. Closing theme of Larry Clinton and his Orchestra.

STUFF IS HERE, THE (And It's Mellow) (1935) (wm)Walter Bishop— William H. Smith—Clarence Williams. (P)Cleo Brown.

STUFF LIKE THAT (1979) (wm)Nicholas Ashford— Valerie Simpson— Steve Gadd—Eric Gale—Quincy Jones—Ralph MacDonald—Richard Tee. (P)Quincy Jones and his Orchestra.

STUMBLIN' IN (1979) (wm)Mike Chapman—Nicky Chinn. (P)Suzi Quatro and Chris Norman.

STUMBLING (1922) (wm)Zez Confrey. (I)Zez Confrey as piano solo. (P)Paul Whiteman and his Orchestra.

STUPID CUPID (1958) (w)Howard Greenfield (m)Neil Sedaka. (P)Connie Francis.

STUPID GIRL (1966) (wm)Mick Jagger—Keith Richard. (P)The Rolling Stones.

SUAVECITO (1972) (wm)Richard Bean—Abel Zarate— Pablo Tellez. (P)Malo.

SUBTERRANEAN HOMESICK BLUES (1965) (wm)Bob Dylan. (P)Bob Dylan.

SUCH A NIGHT (1954) (wm)Lincoln Chase. (P)Johnny Ray. (CR)The Drifters.

SUCH A NIGHT (1973) (wm)Mac Rebennack. (P)Dr. John.

SUDDENLY (1934) (w)E. Y. Harburg—Billy Rose (m)Vernon Duke. (I)Revue: *Ziegfeld Follies of 1934,* by Jane Froman and Everett Marshall.

SUDDENLY (1980) (wm)John Farrar. (P)Olivia Newton—John & Cliff Richard.

SUDDENLY (1985) (wm)Billy Ocean—Keith Diamond. (P)Billy Ocean.

SUDDENLY IT'S SPRING (1944) (w)Johnny Burke (m)Jimmy Van Heusen. (I)Film: *Lady In The Dark,* by Ginger Rogers. (P)Glen Gray and The Casa Loma Orchestra, vocal by Eugenie Baird.

SUDDENLY LAST SUMMER (1983) (wm)Martha Davis. (P)The Motels.

SUDDENLY THERE'S A VALLEY (1955) (wm)Chuck Meyer—Biff Jones. (P)Gogi Grant. (CR)Jo Stafford.

SUE ME (1950) (wm)Frank Loesser. (I)Musical: *Guys And Dolls,* by Sam Levene and Vivian Blaine.

SUGAR (That Sugar Baby O' Mine) (1927) (w)Sidney Mitchell—Edna Alexander (m)Maceo Pinkard. (P)Ethel Waters. (R)1955 Film: *Pete Kelly's Blues,* by Peggy Lee.

SUGAR AND SPICE (1964) (wm)Fred Nightingale. (P)The Searchers. (R)1966 by The Cryin' Shames.

SUGAR BLUES (1923) (w)Lucy Fletcher. (m)Clarence Williams. (I)Sara Martin. (R)1936 by Clyde McCoy and his Orchestra. (R)1962 by Ace Cannon.

SUGAR DADDY (1971) (wm)Fonce Mizell—Freddy Perren—Berry Gordy, Jr. -Deke Richards. (P)The Jackson 5.

SUGAR DUMPLING (1965) (wm)Sam Cooke. (P)Sam Cooke.

SUGAR FOOT STOMP (Dipper Mouth Blues) (1926) (w)Walter Melrose. (m)Joe "King" Oliver. (I)Fletcher Henderson and his Orchestra, trumpet solo by Louis Armstrong. (R)1937 by Benny Goodman and his Orchestra.

SUGAR LIPS (1964) (wm)Buddy Killen—Billy Sherrill. (P)Al Hirt.

SUGAR MOON (1958) (wm)Danny Wolf. (P)Pat Boone.

SUGAR SHACK (1963) (wm)Keith McCormack—Faye Voss. (P)Jimmy Gilmer and The Fireballs. No. 1 Chart Record.

SUGAR, SUGAR (1969) (wm)Jeff Barry—Andy Kim. (P)The Archies. No. 1 Chart Record. (CR)Wilson Pickett.

SUGAR TOWN (1966) (wm)Lee Hazlewood. (P)Nancy Sinatra.

SUGAR WALLS (1985) (wm)Prince Rogers Nelson. (P)Sheena Easton.

SUGARTIME (1958) (wm)Charlie Phillips—Odis Echols. (I)Charlie Phillips. (P)The McGuire Sisters. No. 1 Chart Record.

SUITE: JUDY BLUE EYES (1969) (wm)Stephen Stills. (P)Crosby, Stills, and Nash.

SUKIYAKI (1961) (w-Eng)Tom Leslie—Buzz Cason (m)Hachidai Nakamura—Ei Rokusuke. (P)Kyu Sakamoto. (R)1981 by A Taste Of Honey.

SULTANS OF SWING (1979) (wm)Mark Knopfler. (P)Dire Straits.

SUMMER (1976) (wm)Sylvester Allen—Harold Ray Brown—Morris Dickerson—Gerald Goldstein—Lonnie Jordan—Lee Oskar Levitan— Charles Miller—Howard Scott. (P)War.

SUMMER BREEZE (1972) (w)James Seals (m)Darrell Crofts. (P)Seals & Crofts. (R)1974 by The Isley Brothers.

SUMMER IN THE CITY (1966) (wm)John B. Sebastian—Steve Boone— Mark Sebastian. (P)The Lovin' Spoonful. No. 1 Chart Record.

SUMMER KNOWS, THE (1942) (w)Marilyn and Alan Bergman (m)Michel Legrand. (I)Film: Summer of '42 on soundtrack. (P)Michel Legrand and his Orchestra.

SUMMER NIGHTS (1965) (wm)Brian Henderson—Liza Strike. (P)Marianne Faithful.

SUMMER NIGHTS (1972) (wm)Jim Jacobs—Warren Casey. (I)Musical: Grease, by Carole Demas and Barry Bostwick. (R)1978 Film: Grease, by John Travolta and Olivia Newton—John.

SUMMER PLACE, A (Theme From) (1960) (w)Mack Discant (m)Max Steiner. (I)Film: A Summer Place, on soundtrack. (P)Percy Faith and his Orchestra. NARAS Award Winner.

SUMMER RAIN (1967) (wm)James Hendricks. (P)Johnny Rivers.

SUMMER SAMBA (1966) (w-Eng)Norman Gimbel (m)Marcos Valle—Paulo Sergio Valle. (P)Walter Wanderly.

SUMMER SONG, A (1964) (wm)Clive Metcalfe—Keith Noble—David Stuart. (P)Chad & Jeremy.

SUMMER WIND (1966) (w-Eng)Johnny Mercer (m)Henry Mayer. (P)Frank Sinatra.

SUMMER'S GONE (1960) (wm)Paul Anka. (P)Paul Anka.

SUMMERTIME (1935) (w)Du Bose Heyward (m)George Gershwin. (I)Opera: Porgy and Bess, by Abbie Mitchell. (R)1959 Film version, by Loulie Jean Norman dubbing for Dorothy Dandridge. Theme song of Bob Crosby and his Orchestra. (R)1957 by Sam Cooke. (R)1971 by The Marcels. (R)1962 by Rick Nelson. (R)1966 by Billy Stewart.

SUMMERTIME BLUES (1958) (wm)Eddie Cochran—Jerry Capehart. (P)Eddie Cochran. (R)1968 by Blue Cheer. (R)1970 by The Who.

SUMMERTIME IN VENICE (1955) (w-Eng)Carl Sigman (m)Icini. (I)Film: Summertime, on soundtrack. (P)Dick Jacobs and his Chorus and Orchestra.

SUMMERTIME LOVE (1960) (wm)Frank Loesser. (I)Musical: Greenwillow, by Anthony Perkins.

SUMMERTIME, SUMMERTIME (1958) (wm)Tom Jameson—Sherm Feller. (P)The Jamies.

SUMMIT RIDGE DRIVE (1944) (m)Artie Shaw. (P)Artie Shaw and his Gramercy Five.

SUN ALWAYS SHINES ON TV (1985) (wm)Pal Waaktaar. (P)A-Ha.

SUNBONNET SUE (1906) (w)Will D. Cobb (m)Gus Edwards. (P)The Haydn Quartet.

SUN KING (1969) (wm)John Lennon—Paul McCartney. (P)The Beatles.

SUNDAY (1926) (wm)Ned Miller—Chester Conn—Jule Styne—Bennie Kreuger. First hit song by Jule Styne. (P)Cliff Edwards. (CR)Gene Austin.

SUNDAY (1958) (w)Oscar Hammerstein II (m)Richard Rodgers. (I)Musical: Flower Drum Song, by Pat Suzuki and Larry Blyden.

SUNDAY AND ME (1965) (wm)Neil Diamond. (P)Jay and The Americans.

SUNDAY FOR TEA (1967) (wm)Carter—Lewis (John Shakespeare). (P)Peter and Gordon.

SUNDAY IN THE PARK (1937) (wm)Harold Rome. (I)Revue: Pins and Needles, by The Ensemble.

SUNDAY KIND OF LOVE, A (1946) (wm)Barbara Belle—Louis Prima— Anita Leonard—Stan Rhodes. (P)Claude Thornhill and his Orchestra, vocal by Fran Warren.

SUNDAY, MONDAY, OR ALWAYS (1943) (w)Johnny Burke (m)Jimmy Van Heusen. (I)Film: Dixie, by Bing Crosby. (P)Bing Crosby.

SUNDAY MORNIN' (1968) (wm)Margo Guryan. (P)Spanky and Our Gang. (CR)Oliver.

SUNDOWN (1974) (wm)Gordon Lighfoot. (P)Gordon Lighfoot. No. 1 Chart Record.

SUNDOWNERS, THEME FROM (1960) (m)Dimitri Tiomkin. (I)Film: The Sundowners on soundtrack.

SUNFLOWER (1949) (wm)Mack David. (P)Russ Morgan and his Orchestra. (CR)Frank Sinatra.

SUNGLASSES AT NIGHT (1984) (wm)Corey Hart. (P)Corey Hart.

SUNNY (1925) (w)Otto Harbach—Oscar Hammerstein II (m)Jerome Kern. (I)Musical: Sunny, by Paul Frawley and The Male Chorus. (P)George Olsen and his Orchestra. (R)1946 Film: Till The Clouds Roll By, by The Chorus. (R)1949 Film: Look For The Silver Lining, by The Chorus and danced to by June Haver.

SUNNY (1966) (wm)Bobby Hebb. (P)Bobby Hebb.

SUNNY AFTERNOON (1966) (wm)Ray Davies. (P)The Kinks.

SUNNY SIDE UP (1929) (w)B. G. De Sylva—Lew Brown. (m)Ray Henderson. (I)Film: Sunny Side Up, by Janet

Gaynor. (P)Earl Burnett and his Orchestra. (R)1956 Film: *The Best Things In Life Are Free*, by Sheree North.

SUNRISE SERENADE (1938) (w)Jack Lawrence (m)Frankie Carle. (I)Glen Gray and The Casa Loma Orchestra. (P)Glenn Miller and his Orchestra. Theme song of Frankie Carle and his Orchestra.

SUNRISE, SUNSET (1964) (w)Sheldon Harnick (m)Jerry Bock. (I)Musical: *Fiddler On The Roof*, by Zero Mostel, Maria Karnilova and The Chorus. (P)Roger Williams and his Orchestra. (CR)Louis Armstrong.

SUNSET GRILL (1985) (wm)Don Henley—Dan Kortchmar—Ben Tench. (P)Don Henley.

SUNSHINE (1972) (wm)Andy Kim. (P)Jonathan Edwards.

SUNSHINE GIRL (1967) (wm)Jerry Riopelle—Fred Roberds—Murray MacLeod. (P)The Parade.

SUNSHINE, LOLLIPOPS AND ROSES (1965) (w)Howard Liebling (m)Marvin Hamlisch. (P)Lesley Gore.

SUNSHINE OF YOUR LOVE (1968) (wm)Jack Bruce—Peter Brown—Eric Clapton. (P)Cream.

SUNSHINE ON MY SHOULDERS (1974) (wm)Richard L. Kniss—Michael Taylor—John Denver. (P)John Denver. No. 1 Chart Record.

SUNSHINE SUPERMAN (1966) (wm)Donovan Leitch. (P)Donovan. No. 1 Chart Record.

SUPER BAD (1970) (wm)James Brown. (P)James Brown.

SUPERCALIFRAGILISTICEXPIALIDOCIOUS (1963) (wm)Richard M. Sherman—Robert B. Sherman. (I)Film: *Mary Poppins*, by Julie Andrews, Dick Van Dyke, and The Pearlies.

SUPERFLY (1972) (wm)Curtis Mayfield. (I)Film: *Superfly* by voice of Curtis Mayfield. (P)Curtis Mayfield.

SUPERSTAR (1971) (wm)Leon Russell—Bonnie Bramlett. (P)The Carpenters.

SUPERSTAR REMEMBER HOW YOU GOT WHERE YOU ARE (1971) (wm)Norman Whitfield—Barrett Strong. (P)The Temptations.

SUPERSTITION (1973) (wm)Stevie Wonder. (P)Stevie Wonder. No. 1 Chart Record. NARAS Award Winner.

SUPERWOMAN (Where Were You When I Needed You) (1972) (wm)Stevie Wonder. (P)Stevie Wonder.

SUPPER TIME (1933) (wm)Irving Berlin. (I)Revue: *As Thousands Cheer*, by Ethel Waters.

SURE AS I'M SITTIN' HERE (1974) (wm)John Hiatt. (P)Three Dog Night.

SURE GONNA MISS HER (1966) (wm)Bobby Russell. (P)Gary Lewis and The Playboys.

SURE THING (1944) (w)Ira Gershwin (m)Jerome Kern. (I)Film: *Cover Girl*, by Nan Wynn dubbing for Rita Hayworth.

SURF CITY (1963) (wm)Jan Berry—Brian Wilson. (P)Jan and Dean. No. 1 Chart Record.

SURFER GIRL (1963) (wm)Brian Wilson. (P)The Beach Boys.

SURFIN' BIRD (1964) (wm)Al Frazier—Carl White—John Earl Harris—Turner Wilson. (P)The Trashmen.

SURFIN' SAFARI (1962) (wm)Mike Love—Brian Wilson. (P)The Beach Boys.

SURFIN' U. S. A. (1963) (w)Brian Wilson (m)Chuck Berry. (P)The Beach Boys. (R)1977 by Leif Garrett.

SURFSIDE 6 (1960) (wm)Mack David—Jerry Livingston. (I)TV series: *Surfside 6*. on soundtrack.

SURPRISE SURPRISE (1985) (w)Edward Kleban (m)Marvin Hamlisch. (I)Film: *A Chorus Line*, by Greg Burge.

SURRENDER (1946) (wm)Bennie Benjamin—George Weiss. (P)Perry Como.

SURRENDER (1961) (wm)Doc Pomus—Mort Shuman. Adapted from: Torna A Sorrento. (P)Elvis Presley. No. 1 Chart Record.

SURREY WITH THE FRINGE ON TOP (1943) (w)Oscar Hammerstein II (m)Richard Rodgers. (I)Musical: *Oklahoma!*, by Alfred Drake, Joan Roberts and Betty Garde. (R)1955 Film: *Oklahoma*, by Shirley Jones, Gordon MacRae and Charlotte Greenwood.

SUSAN (1967) (wm)James Holvay—Gary Beisbier—James William Guercio. (P)The Buckinghams.

SUSIE DARLIN (1958) (wm)Robin Luke. (P)Robin Luke. (R)1962 by Tommy Roe.

SUSIE Q (1957) (wm)Dale Hawkins—Stan Lewis—Elly Broadwater. (P)Dale Hawkins. (R)1968 by Creedence Clearwater Revival.

SUSPICION (1964) (wm)Doc Pomus—Mort Shuman. (P)Terry Stafford.

SUSPICIONS (1979) (wm)David Malloy—Randy McCormick—Eddie Rabbitt—Even Stevens. (P)Eddie Rabbitt.

SUSPICIOUS MINDS (1969) (wm)Fred Zambon. (P)Elvis Presley. No. 1 Chart Record. (R)1970 by Waylon Jennings and Jesse Colter. (R)1971 by Dee Dee Warwick.

SUSSUDIO (1985) (wm)Phil Collins. (P)Phil Collins. No. 1 Chart Record.

SUZANNE (1986) (wm)Steve Perry—Jonathan Cain. (P)Journey.

SUZY SNOWFLAKE (1951) (wm)Sid Tepper—Roy Brodsky. (P)Rosemary Clooney.

SWAMP FIRE (1935) (m)Harold Mooney. (P)Ozzie Nelson and his Orchestra.

SWAN, THE (1887) (m)Camille Saint—Saens. Classical composition from Suite: The Carnival Of Animals.

SWANEE (1919) (w)Irving Caesar (m)George Gershwin. (I)Musical: *Sinbad*, by Al Jolson. (P)Al Jolson.

SWANEE SHUFFLE (1929) (wm)Irving Berlin. (I)Film: *Hallelujah*, by Nina Mae McKinney.

S. W. A. T. (Theme from) (1975) (m)Barry De Vorzon. (I)TV series: *S. W. A. T.*, on soundtrack. (P)Rhythm Heritage.

SWAY (Quien Sera) (1954) (w-Eng)Norman Gimbel (m)Pablo Beltran Ruiz. (P)Dean Martin. (CR)Eileen Barton. (R)1960 by Bobby Rydell.

SWEARIN' TO GOD (1975) (wm)Bob Crewe—Denny Randell. (P)Frankie Valli.

SWEDISH RHAPSODY (1954) (m)Hugo Alfven. (P)Percy Faith and his Orchestra.

SWEET ADELINE (1903) (w)Richard H. Gerard (m)Henry W. Armstrong. (P)The Peerless Quartet. (R)1939 by The Mills Brothers.

SWEET AND GENTLE (1955) (w-Eng)George Thorn (m)Otilio Portal. (P)Alan Dale. (CR)Georgia Gibbs.

SWEET AND HOT (1930) (w)Jack Yellen (m)Harold Arlen. (I)Musical: *You Said It*, by Lyda Roberti.

SWEET AND INNOCENT (1971) (wm)Rick Hall—Billy Sherrill. (P)Donny Osmond.

SWEET AND LOVELY (1931) (wm)Gus Arnheim—Harry Tobias—Jules Lemare. (I)Theme song of Gus Arnheim and his Orchestra. (P)Bing Crosby. (CR)Russ Columbo. (CR)Guy Lombardo and his Royal Canadians.

SWEET AND LOW (1863) (w)Alfred Tennyson (m)Joseph

Barnby. Famous lullaby.

SWEET AND LOW DOWN (1925) (w)Ira Gershwin (m)George Gershwin. (I)Musical: *Tip—Toes*, by Andrew Tombes, Lovey Lee, Gertrude McDonald and Amy Revere.

SWEET AS A SONG (1938) (w)Mack Gordon (m)Harry Revel. (I)Film: *Sally, Irene and Mary* by Tony Martin. (P)Horace Heidt and his Orchestra.

SWEET BABY (1981) (wm)George Duke. (P)Stanley Clarke and George Duke.

SWEET BABY JAMES (1969) (wm)James Taylor. (P)James Taylor. (CR)Tom Rush.

SWEET BEGINNING (1964) (wm)Leslie Bricusse—Anthony Newley. (I)Musical: *The Roar of The Greasepaint—The Smell Of The Crowd*, by Anthony Newley, Cyril Ritchard,and The Urchins.

SWEET BLINDNESS (1968) (wm)Laura Nyro. (P)Laura Nyro. (CR)The 5th Dimension.

SWEET CAROLINE (1969) (wm)Neil Diamond. (P)Neil Diamond. (R)1972 by Bobby Womack.

SWEET CHERRY WINE (1969) (wm)Tommy James—Richie Grasso. (P)Tommy James and The Shondells.

SWEET CITY WOMAN (1971) (wm)Richard Dodson. (P)The Stampeders.

SWEET CREAM LADIES, FORWARD MARCH (1969) (wm)Bobby Weinstein— Jon Stroll. (P)The Box Tops.

SWEET DREAMS (1956) (wm)Don Gibson (P)Faron Young. (R)1961 by Don Gibson. (R)1963 by Patsy Cline. (R)1976 by Tommy McLain. (R)1976, by Emmy Lou Harris.

SWEET DREAMS (1982) (wm)Graham Russell. (P)Air Supply. (P)Air Supply.

SWEET DREAMS (Are Made Of This) (1983) (wm)Annie Lennox—Dave Stewart. (P)The Eurythmics.

SWEET ELOISE (1942) (w)Mack David (m)Russ Morgan. (I)Russ Morgan and his Orchestra. (P)Glenn Miller and his Orchestra, vocal by Ray Eberle and The Modernaires.

SWEET FREEDOM (1986) (wm)Rod Temperton. (I)Film: *Running Scared*, by Michael McDonald. (P)Michael McDonald.

SWEET GENEVIEVE (1869) (wm)George Cooper—Henry Tucker. Popular American standard. No artist credited with introduction.

SWEET GEORGIA BROWN (1925) (wm)Ben Bernie—Maceo Pinkard—Ken Casey. (P)Ben Bernie and his Orchestra. (CR)Isham Jones and his Orchestra. (CR)Ethel Waters. (R)1932 by Bing Crosby. (R)1949 by Brother Bones.

SWEET HITCHHIKER (1971) (wm)John C. Fogarty. (P)Creedence Clearwater Revival.

SWEET HOME ALABAMA (1974) (wm)Ronnie Van Zant—Edward King—Gary Rossington. (P)Lynyrd Skynyrd.

SWEET INSPIRATIONS (1967) (wm)Dan Penn—Spooner Oldham. (P)The Sweet Inspirations. (R)1971 by Barbra Stresand in medley with: Where You Lead.

SWEET JENNIE LEE (1930) (wm)Walter Donaldson. (P)Guy Lombardo and his Royal Canadians. (CR)Isham Jones and his Orchestra.

SWEET LEILANI (1937) (wm)Harry Owens. (I)Film: *Waikiki Wedding*, by Bing Crosby. (P)Bing Crosby. Academy Award Winner.

SWEET LIFE (1978) (wm)Susan Collins—Paul Davis. (P)Paul Davis.

SWEET LITTLE SIXTEEN (1958) (wm)Chuck Berry. (P)Chuck Berry. (R)1962 by Jerry Lee Lewis.

SWEET LORRAINE (1928) (w)Mitchell Parish (m)Cliff Burwell. (P)Rudy Vallee. (R)1950s, by Nat "King" Cole.

SWEET LOVE (1975) (wm)William King, Jr. -Ronald La Pread—Thomas McClary—Walter Orange—Lionel Richie—Milan Williams. (P)The Commodores.

SWEET LOVE (1986) (wm)Anita Baker—Louis A. Johnson—Gary Bias. (P)Anita Baker. NARAS Award Winner.

SWEET MARY (1971) (wm)Steve Jablecki. (P)Wadsworth Mansion.

SWEET NOTHIN'S (1960) (wm)Ronnie Self. (P)Brenda Lee

SWEET OLD FASHIONED GIRL (1956) (wm)Bob Merrill. (P)Teresa Brewer.

(Let Me Get)SWEET ON YOU (1977) (wm)Graham Parker. (P)Graham Parker & The Rumour.

SWEET PEA (1966) (wm)Tommy Roe. (P)Tommy Roe.

SWEET PETER (1925) (w)Lorenz Hart (m)Richard Rodgers. (I)Musical: *Dearest Enemy*.

SWEET ROSIE O'GRADY (1896) (wm)Maude Nugent. (P)George J. Gaskin.

SWEET SEASONS (1972) (wm)Carole King—Toni Stern. (P)Carole King.

SWEET SIXTY-FIVE (1937) (w)Lorenz Hart (m)Richard Rodgers. (I)Musical: *I'd Rather be Right*, by Joy Hodges and Austin Marshall.

SWEET SOUL MUSIC (1967) (wm)Otis Redding—Arthur Conley—Sam Cooke. (P)Arthur Conley.

SWEET SUE-JUST YOU (1928) (w)Will J. Harris (m)Victor Young. (I)Sue Carol. (P)Ben Pollack and his Orchestra. (R)1932 by The Mills Brothers. (R)1939 by Tommy Dorsey and his Orchestra. (R)1949 by Johnny Long and his Orchestra.

SWEET SURRENDER (1972) (wm)David Gates. (P)Bread.

SWEET SURRENDER (1975) (wm)John Denver. (P)John Denver.

SWEET TALKIN' GUY (1966) (wm)Doug Morris—Elliot Greenberg— Barbara Baer—Robert Schwartz. (P)The Chiffons.

SWEET TALKIN' WOMAN (1978) (wm)Jeff Lynne. (P)Electric Light Orchestra.

SWEET THING (1975) (wm)Chaka Khan—Tony Maiden. (P)Rufus (Featuring Chaka Khan).

SWEET THURSDAY (1955) (w)Oscar Hammerstein II (m)Richard Rodgers. (I)Musical: *Pipe Dream*, by Helen Traubel.

SWEET VIOLETS (1951) (wm)Cy Coben—Charles Grean. Adapted from a folk song. (P)Dinah Shore.

SWEET WOMAN LIKE YOU, A (1965) (wm)Joe Tex. (P)Joe Tex.

SWEETER THAN YOU (1959) (wm)Baker Knight. (P)Rick Nelson.

SWEETEST GIFT, THE (1975) (wm)J. B. Coates. (P)Linda Ronstadt. (R)1976 by Linda Ronstadt and Emmy Lou Harris.

SWEETEST SOUNDS, THE (1962) (wm)Richard Rodgers. (I)Musical: *No Strings*, by Diahann Carroll and Richard Kiley.

SWEETEST TABOO, THE (1986) (wm)Helen Folasade Adu—Martin Ditcham. (P)Sade.

SWEETEST THING I'VE EVER KNOWN, THE (1981) (wm)Otha Young. (P)Juice Newton.

SWEETHEART (1981) (wm)Frankie Previte—W. Elworthy. (P)Franke & The Knockouts.

SWEETHEART OF SIGMA CHI, THE (1912) (w)Bryan Stokes (m)F. Dudleigh Vernor. (P)Fred Waring's Pennsylvanians.

SWEETHEART TREE, THE (1965) (w)Johnny Mercer (m)Henry Mancini. (I)Film: *The Great Race*, by Jackie Ward dubbing for Natalie Wood.

SWEETHEARTS (1913) (w)Robert B. Smith (m)Victor Herbert. (I)Musical: *Sweethearts*, by Tom MacNaughton and Christie MacDonald.

SWEETHEARTS ON PARADE (1928) (w)Charles Newman (m)Carmen Lombardo. (P)Guy Lombardo and his Royal Canadians. (R)1932 by Louis Armstrong. (R)1957 by Dick Jacobs and his Orchestra.

SWEETS FOR MY SWEET (1961) (wm)Doc Pomus—Mort Shuman. (P)The Drifters. (R)1979 by Tony Orlando.

SWEPT AWAY (1984) (wm)Daryl Hall—Sara Allen. (P)Diana Ross.

SWING LOW SWEET CHARIOT (1917) (wm)Unknown. Traditional Black American spiritual.

SWING LOW SWEET RHYTHM (1941) (w)Walter Bullock (m)Jule Styne. (I)Film: *Hit Parade of 1941* by Frances Langford.

SWING YOUR PARTNER ROUND AND ROUND (1945) (w)Johnny Mercer (m)Harry Warren. (I)Film: *The Harvey Girls*, by Judy Garland and The Chorus.

SWINGIN' DOWN THE LANE (1923) (w)Gus Kahn (m)Isham Jones. (I)Cliff Edwards. (P)Isham Jones and his Orchestra. (R)1951 Film: *I'll See You In My Dreams*, by Danny Thomas and Doris Day.

SWINGIN' IN A HAMMOCK (1930) (w)Tot Seymour—Charles O'Flynn (m)Pete Wendling. (P)Guy Lombardo and his Royal Canadians.

SWINGIN' SAFARI, A (1962) (m)Bert Kaempfert. (P)Billy Vaughn and his Orchestra.

SWINGIN' SCHOOL (1960) (wm)Kal Mann—Bernie Lowe—Dave Appell. (P)Bobby Rydell.

SWINGIN' SHEPHERD BLUES, THE (1958) (m)Moe Koffman. (P)Moe Koffman (jazz flute solo). (CR)David Rose and his Orchestra.

SWINGIN' THE BLUES (1939) (m)William Basie—Ed Durham. (P)Count Basie and his Orchestra.

SWINGIN' THE JINX AWAY (1936) (wm)Cole Porter. (I)Film: *Born To Dance*, by Frances Langford.

SWINGING ON A STAR (1944) (w)Johnny Burke (m)Jimmy Van Heusen. (I)Film: *Going My Way*, by Bing Crosby. (P)Bing Crosby. No. 1 Chart Record. Academy Award Winner.

SWINGTIME IN THE ROCKIES (1936) (m)Jimmy Mundy—Benny Goodman. (P)Benny Goodman and his Orchestra.

SWINGTOWN (1977) (wm)Chris McCarty—Steve Miller. (P)The Steve Miller Band.

SWISS MISS (1924) (w)Ira Gershwin (m)George Gershwin. (I)Musical: *Lady, Be Good!*, by Fred and Adele Astaire.

SWITCHAROO (1961) (wm)Al Kasha—Gordon Evans—Alonzo Tucker. (P)Hank Ballard and The Midnighters.

SYLVIA (1914) (w)Clinton Scollard (m)Oley Speaks. Famous American light classical song.

SYLVIA'S MOTHER (1972) (wm)Shel Silverstein. (P)Dr. Hook.

SYMPATHY FOR THE DEVIL (1968) (wm)Mick Jagger—Keith Richard. (P)The Rolling Stones.

SYMPHONY (1945) (w-Eng)Jack Lawrence (m)Alex Alstone. (P)Freddy Martin and his Orchestra, vocal by Clyde Rogers.

SYMPHONY IN RIFFS (1935) (wm)Irving Mills—Benny Carter. (P)Benny Carter and his Orchestra. (R)1938 by Gene Krupa and his Orchestra.

SYNCOPATED CLOCK, THE (1948) (m)Leroy Anderson. (P)Leroy Anderson and his Orchestra.

TA TA (1960) (wm)Jimmy Oliver—Clyde McPhatter. (P)Clyde McPhatter.

TABOO (1934) (w-Eng)S. K. Russell (m)Margarita Lecuona. Famous Cuban song. No artist credited with introduction.

'TAINT WHAT YOU DO (It's The Way That Cha Do It) (1939) (wm)Sy Oliver—James Young. (P)Jimmie Lunceford and his Orchestra.

TAINTED LOVE (1982) (wm)Ed Cobb. (P)Soft Cell.

TAKE A CHANCE ON ME (1978) (wm)Benny Andersson—Bjorn Ulvaeus. (P)Abba.

TAKE A LETTER, MARIA (1969) (wm)Sonny Childe. (P)R. B. Greaves.

TAKE A LITTLE RHYTHM (1980) (wm)Ali Thompson. (P)Ali Thompson.

TAKE A MESSAGE TO MARY (1959) (wm)Felice and Boudleaux Bryant. (P)The Everly Brothers.

TAKE A NUMBER FROM ONE TO TEN (1934) (w)Mack Gordon (m)Harry Revel. (I)Film: College Rhythm, by Lyda Roberti.

TAKE AND TAKE AND TAKE (1937) (w)Lorenz Hart (m)Richard Rodgers. (I)Musical: I'd Rather Be Right, by Mary Jane Walsh.

TAKE BACK YOUR MINK (1950) (wm)Frank Loesser. (I)Musical: Guys And Dolls, by Vivian Blaine.

TAKE CARE OF YOUR HOMEWORK (1969) (wm)Raymond Jackson—Homer Banks—Don Davis—Thomas Kelly. (P)Johnnie Taylor.

TAKE FIVE (1960) (m)Paul Desmond. (P)The Dave Brubeck Quartet.

TAKE GOOD CARE OF HER (1961) (wm)Ed Warren—Arthur Kent. (P)Adam Wade. (R)1966 by Mel Carter.

TAKE GOOD CARE OF MY BABY (1961) (wm)Gerry Goffin—Carole King. (P)Bobby Vee. No. 1 Chart Record. (R)1968 by Bobby Vinton.

TAKE HIM (1940) (w)Lorenz Hart (m)Richard Rodgers. (I)Musical: Pal Joey, by Vivienne Segal, Leila Ernst, and Gene Kelly.

TAKE IT AWAY (1982) (wm)Paul McCartney. (P)Paul McCartney.

TAKE IT EASY (1943) (wm)Albert De Bru—Irving Taylor—Vic Mizzy. (I)Film: Two Girls And A Sailor, by Lina Romay, Virginia O'Brien, The Wilde Twins, and Xavier Cugat and his Orchestra.

TAKE IT EASY (1986) (wm)Andy Taylor—Steve Jones. (I)Film: American Anthem, by Andy Taylor. (P)Andy Taylor.

TAKE IT EASY ON ME (1982) (wm)Graham Goble. (P)Little River Band.

TAKE IT ON THE RUN (1981) (wm)Gary Richrath. (P)REO Speedwagon.

TAKE IT SLOW, JOE (1957) (w)E. Y. Harburg (m)Harold Arlen. (I)Musical: Jamaica, by Lena Horne.

TAKE IT TO THE LIMIT (1976) (wm)Don Henley—Randy Meisner. (P)The Eagles.

TAKE ME (1942) (w)Mack David (m)Rube Bloom. (P)Tommy Dorsey and his Orchestra, vocal by Frank Sinatra.

TAKE ME ALONG (1959) (wm)Robert Merrill. (I)Musical: Take Me Along, by Jackie Gleason and Walter Pidgeon.

TAKE ME BACK (1965) (wm)Teddy Randazzo. (P)Little Anthony and The Imperials.

TAKE ME BACK TO MANHATTAN (1930) (wm)Cole Porter. (I)Musical: The New Yorkers, by Frances Williams.

TAKE ME BACK TO MY BOOTS AND SADDLES (1935) (wm)Walter G. Samuels—Leonard Whitcup—Teddy Powell. (P)Gene Autry. (CR)Tommy Dorsey and his Orchestra.

TAKE ME FOR A LITTLE WHILE (1965) (wm)Trade Martin. (P)Patti LaBelle. (R)1968 by Vanilla Fudge.

TAKE ME HOME (1979) (wm)Michele Aller—Bob Esty. (P)Cher.

TAKE ME HOME (1985) (wm)Phil Collins. (P)Phil Collins.

TAKE ME HOME. COUNTRY ROADS (1971) (wm)Bill Danoff—Taffy Nivert—John Denver. (P)John Denver.

TAKE ME HOME TONIGHT (1986) (wm)Mike Leeson—Peter Vale—Ellie Greenwich—Jeff Barry—Phil Spector. (P)Eddie Money with Ronnie Spector.

TAKE ME IN YOUR ARMS (1932) (w-Eng)Mitchell Parish (m)Fritz Rotter—Alfred Markush. (P)Ruth Etting.

TAKE ME IN YOUR ARMS (Rock Me A Little While) (1965) (wm)Eddie Holland—Lamont Dozier—Brian Holland. (P)Kim Weston. (R)1975 by The Doobie Brothers.

TAKE ME OUT TO THE BALL GAME (1908) (w)Jack Norworth (m)Albert Von Tilzer. (P)Billy Murray.

TAKE ME TO HEART (1983) (wm)Marv Ross. (P)Quarterflash.

TAKE ME TO THE RIVER (1973) (wm)Al Green—Mabon Hodges. (P)Syl Johnson. (R)1978 by Talking Heads.

TAKE MY BREATH AWAY (1986) (wm)Giorgio Moroder—Tom Whitlock. (I)Film: Top Gun, by Berlin on soundtrack. Academy Award Winner. (P)Berlin. No. 1 Chart Record.

TAKE MY HAND, PAREE. (1961) (w)E. Y. Harburg (m)Harold Arlen. (I)Cartoon Film: Gay Purr-ee, by the voice of Judy Garland.

TAKE MY HEART (1981) (wm)Charles Smith—James Taylor—George Brown—Eumir Deodato. (P)Kool & The Gang.

TAKE OFF (1982) (wm)Kerry Crawford—Jonathan Goldsmith—Mark Giacommelli—Rick Moranis—Dave Thomas. (P)Bob & Doug McKenzie.

TAKE ON ME (1985) (wm)Pal Weaktaar—Mags—Marten Harket. (P)A—Ha. No. 1 Chart Record.

TAKE THE "A" TRAIN (1941) (wm)Billy Strayhorn. (P)Theme Song of Duke Ellington and his Orchestra.

TAKE THE LONG WAY HOME (1979) (wm)Richard Davies—Roger Hodgson. (P)Supertramp.

TAKE THE MONEY AND RUN (1976) (wm)Steve Miller. (P)Steve Miller.

TAKE THESE CHAINS FROM MY HEART (1953) (wm)Fred Rose—Hy Heath. (P)Hank Williams. (R)1963 by Ray Charles.

TAKE TIME TO KNOW HER (1968) (wm)Steve Davis. (P)Percy Sledge.

TAKE YOUR TIME (Do It Right) (1980) (wm)Harold Clayton—Sigidi. (P)S. O. S. Band.

TAKES TWO TO MAKE A BARGAIN (1935) (w)Mack Gordon (m)Harry Revel. (I)Film: Two For Tonight, by Bing Crosby. (P)Bing Crosby.

TAKES TWO TO TANGO (1952) (wm)Al Hoffman—Dick Manning. (P)Pearl Bailey accompanied by Don Redman and his Orchestra.

TAKIN' CARE OF BUSINESS (1973) (wm)Randy Bachman. (P)Bachman—Turner Overdrive.

TAKIN' IT TO THE STREETS (1976) (wm)Michael Mc-Donald. (P)The Doobie Brothers.

TAKING A CHANCE ON LOVE (1940) (wm)John Latouche—Ted Fetter (m)Vernon Duke. (I)Musical: *Cabin In The Sky*, by Ethel Waters and later reprised by Ethel Waters and Dooley Wilson. 1943 Film Version, by Ethel Waters and Eddie "Rochester" Anderson.

TALE OF AN OYSTER, THE (1929) (wm)Cole Porter. (I)Musical: *Fifty Million Frenchmen*, by Helen Broderick.

TALES FROM THE VIENNA WOODS (1868) (m)Johann Strauss. Famous classical waltz.

TALK BACK TREMBLING LIPS (1963) (wm)John Loudermilk. (P)Johnny Tillotson. (CR)Debbie Stuart. (CR)Ernest Ashworth.

TALK DIRTY TO ME (1987) (wm)B. Dall—B. Michaels—R. Rockett. (P)Poison.

TALK, TALK (1966) (wm)Thomas Sear Bonniwell. (P)The Music Machine.

TALK TO ME (1985) (wm)Charles Sandford. (P)Stevie Nicks.

TALK TO ME (1987) (wm)N. Mundy—F. Golde—P. Fox. (P)Chico DeBarge.

TALK TO ME, TALK TO ME (1958) (wm)Joe Seneca. (P)Little Willie John. (R)1963 by Sunny and The Sunglows.

TALK TO THE ANIMALS (1967) (wm)Leslie Bricusse. (I)Film: *Doctor Doolittle*, by Rex Harrison. (P)Rex Harrison. (CR)Louis Armstrong.

TALKING IN YOUR SLEEP (1978) (wm)Roger Cook—Bobby Wood. (P)Crystal Gayle.

TALKING IN YOUR SLEEP (1983) (wm)Jimmy Marinos—Wally Palmer—Mike Skill—Coz Canler—Pete Solley. (P)The Romantics.

TALL PAUL (1959) (wm)Bob Roberts—Bob Sherman—Dick Sherman. (P)Annette.

TALLAHASSEE (1947) (wm)Frank Loesser. (I)Film: *Variety Girl*. (P)Bing Crosby and The Andrews Sisters.

TALLAHASSEE LASSIE (1959) (wm)Frank C. Slay, Jr.—Bob Crewe—A. Picariello. (P)Freddy Cannon.

TAMMANY (1905) (w)Vincent P. Bryan (m)Gus Edwards. Official song of The New York City Democratic Party.

TAMMY (1957) (wm)Jay Livingston—Ray Evans. (I)Film: *Tammy And The Bachelor*, by Debbie Reynolds. (P)Debbie Reynolds. No. 1 Chart Record. (CR)The Ames Brothers.

TAMPICO (1945) (wm)Allan Roberts—Doris Fisher. (P)Stan Kenton and his Orchestra, vocal by June Christy.

TANGERINE (1942) (w)Johnny Mercer (m)Victor Schertzinger. (I)Film: *The Fleet's In*, by Jimmy Dorsey and his Orchestra, vocal by Bob Eberly and Helen O'Connell. (P)Jimmy Dorsey. (R)1976 by The Salsoul Orchestra.

TANGLED UP IN BLUE (1974) (wm)Bob Dylan. (P)Bob Dylan.

TAPESTRY (1971) (wm)Carole King. (P)Carole King.

TA-RA-RA-BOOM-DER-E (1891) (wm)Henry J. Sayers. English song which spread to the United States.

TARA'S THEME (1931) (m)Max Steiner. (I)Film: *Gone With The Wind*, as principal soundtrack theme.

TARTER SONG, THE (1928) (w)Lorenz Hart (m)Richard Rodgers. (I)Musical: *Chee-Chee*, by George Houston.

TARZAN BOY (1986) (wm)Naimy Hackett—Maurizio Bassi. (P)Baltimora.

TASTE OF HONEY, A (1960) (w)Ric Marlow (m)Bobby Scott. (I)Martin Denny. (R)1964 by Tony Bennett. (R)1965 by Herb Alpert and The Tijuana Brass. NARAS Award Winner.

TAURUS (1972) (m)Dennis Coffey. (P)Dennis Coffey.

TAXI (1972) (wm)Harry Chapin. (P)Harry Chapin.

TAXMAN (1966) (wm)George Harrison. (P)The Beatles.

TEA FOR TWO (1925) (w)Irving Caesar (m)Vincent Youmans. (I)Musical: *No, No, Nanette*, by Louise Groody and John Barker. (P)Marion Harris. (R)1950 Film: *Tea For Two*, by Doris Day and Gordon MacRae. (R)1952 Film: *With A Song In My Heart*, by Jane Froman dubbing for Susan Hayward.

TEACH ME TONIGHT (1953) (w)Sammy Cahn (m)Gene De Paul. (P)The De Castro Sisters. (CR)Jo Stafford. (R)1962)George Maharis. (R)1982 by Al Jarreau.

TEACH YOUR CHILDREN (1970) (wm)Graham Nash. (P)Crosby, Stills, Nash, and Young.

TEACHER, TEACHER (1958) (w)Al Stillman (m)Robert Allen. (P)Johnny Mathis.

TEACHER TEACHER (1984) (wm)Bryan Adams—Jim Vallance. (P)38 Special.

TEACHER'S PET (1958) (wm)Joe Lubin. (I)Film: *Teacher's Pet*, by Doris Day. (P)Doris Day.

TEAMWORK (1962) (w)Sammy Cahn (m)Jimmy Van Heusen. (I)Film: *The Road To Hong King*, by Bing Crosby and Bob Hope.

TEAR DROP (1959) (m)Ann Farina—John Farina—Santo Farina. (P)Santo and Johnny.

TEAR FELL, A (1956) (wm)Dorian Burton—Eugene Randolph. (P)Teresa Brewer. (R)1964 by Ray Charles.

TEAR THE ROOF OFF THE SUCKER (Give Up The Funk) (1976) (wm)George Clinton—Bootsie Collins—Jerome Brailey. (P)Parliament.

TEARDROPS FROM MY EYES (1950) (wm)Rudolph Toombs. (P)Ruth Brown.

TEARS OF A CLOWN, THE (1970) (wm)Henry Cosby—Stevie Wonder—William Robinson. (P)The Miracles. No. 1 Chart Record.

TEARS ON MY PILLOW (1958) (wm)Sylvester Bradford—Al Lewis. (P)Little Anthony and The Imperials. (R)1961 by The McGuire Sisters.

TEDDY (1960) (wm)Paul Anka. (P)Connie Francis.

(Let Me Be Your)TEDDY BEAR (1957) (wm)Bernie Lowe—Kal Mann. (I)Film: *Loving You*, by Elvis Presley. (P)Elvis Presley. No. 1 Chart Record.

TEEN AGE CRUSH (1957) (wm)Audrey Allison—Joe Allison. (P)Tommy Sands.

TEEN AGE PRAYER (1956) (wm)Bickley Reichner—Bernie Lowe. (P)Gale Storm. (CR)Gloria Mann.

TEEN ANGEL (1960) (wm)Jean Surrey—Red Surrey. (P)Mark Dinning. (R)1974 by Wednesday.

TEEN BEAT (1959) (m)Sander Nelson—Arthur Egnoian. (P)Sandy Nelson.

TEENAGE IDOL, A (1962) (wm)Jack Lewis. (P)Rick Nelson.

TEENAGER IN LOVE, A (1959) (wm)Doc Pomus—Mort Shuman.

TEENAGER'S ROMANCE, A (1957) (wm)David Gillam. (P)Rick Nelson.

TELEFONE (Long Distance Love Affair. (1983) (wm)Greg Mathieson—Trevor Veitch. (P)Sheena Easton.

TELEPHONE LINE (1977) (wm)Jeff Lynne. (P)Electric Light Orchestra.

TELEPHONE MAN (1977) (wm)Meri Wilson. (P)Meri Wilson.

TELL HER ABOUT IT (1983) (wm)Billy Joel. (P)Billy Joel.

TELL HER IN THE SPRINGTIME (1924) (wm)Irving Berlin. (I)Revue: *Music Box Revue of 1924*, by Grace Moore.

TELL HER NO (1964) (wm)Rod Argente Petrillo—Chubby Cifelli. (P)The (P)The Zombies. (R)1983 by Juice Newton.

TELL HIM (1963) (wm)Bert Russell. (P)The Exciters.

TELL HIM NO (1959) (wm)Travis Pritchett. (P)Travis and Bob. (CR)Dean and Marc.

TELL IT ALL BROTHER (1970) (wm)Alex Harvey. (P)Kenny Rogers.

TELL IT LIKE IT IS (1967) (wm)George Davis—Lee Diamond. (P)Aaron Neville. (R)1976 by Andy Williams. (R)1981 by Heart.

TELL IT TO MY HEART (1987) (wm)S. Swirsky—E. Gold. (P)Taylor Dayne.

TELL IT TO THE RAIN (1966) (wm)Mike Petrillo—Chubby Cifelli. (P)The Four Seasons.

TELL LAURA I LOVE HER (1960) (wm)Jeff Barry—Ben Raleigh. (P)Ray Peterson. (R)1974 by Johnny T. Angel.

TELL MAMA (1967) (wm)Clarence Carter—Marcus Daniel—Wilbur Terrell. (P)Etta James.

TELL ME (1964) (wm)Mick Jagger—Keith Richard. (P)THe Rolling Stones.

TELL ME A STORY (1953) (wm)Terry Gilkyson. (P)Frankie Laine and Jimmy Boyd.

TELL ME, LITTLE GYPSY (1920) (wm)Irving Berlin. (I)Revue: *Ziegfeld Follies of 1920* by John Steel, Delyle. Alda, Albertine Marlowe, Juliet Compton, Gladys Loftus, Phoebe Lee, and Margaret Morris.

TELL ME MORE! (1925) (w)B. G. De Sylva—Ira Gershwin (m)George Gershwin. (I)Musical: *Tell Me More!*, by Phyllis Cleveland and Alexander Gray.

TELL ME PRETTY MAIDEN (Are There Any More At Home Like You) (1900) (w)Owen Hall (m)Leslie Stuart. (P)Byron G. Harlan, Joe Belmont & The Florodora Girls.

TELL ME SOMETHING GOOD (1974) (wm)Stevie Wonder. (P)Rufus.

TELL ME, TELL ME EVENING STAR (1944) (w)E. Y. Harburg (m)Harold Arlen. (I)Film: *Kismet*, by Marlene Dietrich.

TELL ME THAT IT ISN'T TRUE (1969) (wm)Bob Dylan. (P)Bob Dylan.

TELL ME THAT YOU LOVE ME (1935) (w-Eng)Al Stillman (m)Cesare A. Bixio. (P)Frank Parker. (CR)Freddy Martin and his Orchestra.

TELL ME WHAT YOU SEE (1965) (wm)John Lennon—Paul McCartney. (P)The Beatles.

TELL ME WHY (1951) (w)Al Alberts (m)Marty Gold. (P)The Four Aces.

TELL ME WHY (1956) (wm)Titus Turner. (P)The Crew Cuts. (CR)Gale Storm. (R)1966 by Elvis Presley.

TELL ME WHY (1964) (wm)John Lennon—Paul McCartney. (I)Film: *A Hard Day's Night*, by The Beatles.

TELL ME WITH A LOVE SONG (1931) (w)Ted Koehler (m)Harold Arlen. (P)Kate Smith.

TELL ME (You're Coming Back) (1964) (wm)Mick Jagger—Keith Richard.

TELSTAR (1962) (m)Joe Meek. (P)The Tornadoes. No. 1 Chart Record.

TEMPORARY LIKE ACHILLES (1966) (wm)Bob Dylan. (P)Bob Dylan.

TEMPTATION1933) (w)Arthur Freed (m)Nacio Herb Brown. (I)Film: *Going Hollywood*, by Bing Crosby. (P)Bing Crosby. (R)1944 by Artie Shaw and his Orchestra. (R)1945 by Perry Como. (R)1947 by Red Ingle.

TEMPTATION EYES (1971) (wm)Harvey Price—Dan Walsh. (P)Grass Roots.

TEN CENTS A DANCE (1930) (w)Lorenz Hart (m)Richard Rodgers. (I)Musical: *Simple Simon*, by Ruth Etting. (P)Ruth Etting. (R)1955 Film: *Love Me Or Leave Me*, by Doris Day.

TEN MINUTES AGO (1957) (w)Oscar Hammerstein II (m)Richard Rodgers. (I)T. V. Special: Cinderella.

TENDER IS THE NIGHT (1962) (w)Paul Francis Webster (m)Sammy Fain. (I)Film: *Tender Is The Night*, by Earl Grant. (P)Tony Bennett.

TENDER IS THE NIGHT (1983) (wm)Russ Kunkel—Danny Kortchmar—Jackson Browne. (P)Jackson Browne.

TENDER LOVE (1986) (wm)James Harris III—Terry Lewis. (I)Film: *Krush Groove*, by Force M. D. ,s. (P)Force M. D. ,s.

TENDER TRAP, THE (1955) (w)Sammy Cahn (m)Jimmy Van Heusen. (I)Film: *The Tender Trap*, by Frank Sinatra. (P)Frank Sinatra.

TENDERLY (1946) (w)Jack Lawrence (m)Walter Gross. (I)Clark Dennis. (P)Sarah Vaughan. (R)1955 by Rosemary Clooney.

TENEMENT SYMPHONY (1941) (w)Sid Kuller—Ray Golden (m)Hal Borne. (I)Film: *The Big Store*, by Tony Martin.

TENNESSEE BORDER (1969) (wm)Jack Blanchard. (P)Jack Blanchard and Misty Morgan.

TENNESSEE FISH FRY (1940) (w)Oscar Hammerstein II (m)Arthur Schwartz. (P)Kay Kyser and his College of Musical Knowledge.

TENNESSEE WALTZ (1948) (wm)Redd Stewart—Pee Wee King. (I)Erskine Hawkins and his Orchestra. (P)Patti Page. (R)1959 by Bobby Comstock. (R)1964 by Sam Cooke.

TENTING ON THE OLD CAMP GROUND (1864) (wm)Walter Kittredge. Popular Civil War Song.

TEQUILA (1958) (m)Chuck Rio, (P)The Champs. No. 1 Chart Record. (R)1964 by Bill Black's Combo.

TERRY THEME (See: Eternally)

TESS'S TORCH SONG (I Had A Man) (1944) (w)Ted Koehler (m)Harold Arlen. (I)Film: *Up In Arms*, by Dinah Shore. (P)Ella Mae Morse.

TEXAS TORNADO (1936) (w)Sidney D. Mitchell (m)Lew Pollack. (I)Film: *Pigskin Parade*, by Judy Garland.

THANK GOD I'M A COUNTRY BOY (1975) (wm)John Sommers. (P)John Denver. No. 1 Chart Record.

THAN GOD IT'S FRIDAY (1978) (wm)Robert Costandinos. (I)Film: *Thank God It's Friday*, by Love And Kisses. (P)Love And Kisses.

THANK HEAVEN FOR LITTLE GIRLS (1958) (w)Alan Jay Lerner (m)Frederick Loewe. (I)Film: *Gigi*, by Maurice Chevalier.

THANK YOU FALETTIN' ME BE MICE ELF AGAIN (1970) (wm)Sylvester Stewart. (P)Sly & The Family Stone. No. 1 Chart Record.

THANK YOU FOR A LOVELY EVENING (1934) (w)Dorothy Fields (m)Jimmy McHugh. (I)Nightclub Revue: by Phil Harris and Leah Ray. (P)Don Bestor and his Orchestra.

THANK YOU FOR BEING A FRIEND (1978) (wm)Andrew Gold. (P)Andrew Gold.

THANK YOU GIRL (1963) (wm)John Lennon—Paul McCartney. (P)The Beatles.

THANK YOU PRETTY BABY (1959) (wm)Clyde Otis—Brook Benton. (P)Brook Benton.

THANK YOUR FATHER (1930) (w)B. G. De Sylva—Lew Brown (m)Ray Henderson. (I)Musical: *Flying High*, by Oscar Shaw and Grace Brinkley.

THANKS (1933) (wm)Arthur Johnston—Sam Coslow. (I)Film: *Too Much Harmony*, by Bing Crosby and Judith Allen. (P)Bing Crosby.

THANKS A MILLION (1935) (w)Gus Kahn (m)Arthur Johnston. (I)Film: *Tanks A Million*, by Dick Powell. (P)Paul Whiteman and his Orchestra. (CR)Louis Armstrong.

THANKS FOR EVERYTHING (1938) (w)Mack Gordon (m)Harry Revel. (I)Film: *Thanks For Everything*, by Tony Martin. (P)Artie Shaw and his Orchestra. No. 1 Chart Record. (CR)Tommy Dorsey and his Orchestra.

THANKS FOR THE BUGGY RIDE (1925) (wm)Jules Buffano. (P)Billie Jones and Ernie Hare (The Happiness Boys.

THANKS FOR THE MEMORY (1937) (wm)Leo Robin—Ralph Rainger. (I)Film: *Big Broadcast of 1938*, by Bob Hope and Shirley Ross. (P)Theme Song of Bob Hope. (CR)Mildred Bailey. (CR)Shep Fields and his Orchestra.

THAT AIN'T LOVE (1987) (wm)K. Cronin. (P)REO Speedwagon.

THAT CERTAIN FEELING (1925) (w)Ira Gershwin (m)George Gershwin. (I)Musical: *Tip-Toes*, by Queenie Smith and Allen Kearns. (P)Paul Whiteman and his Orchestra. (R)1956 Film: *That Certain Feeling*, by Pearl Bailey and later reprised by Bob Hope and Eva Marie Saint.

THAT CHICK'S TOO YOUNG TO FLY (1946) (wm)Tommy Edwards—Jimmy Hilliard. (P)Louis Jordan and his Tympany Five.

THAT FACE (1957) (wm)Alan Bergman—Lew Spence. (P)Fred Astaire.

THAT FOOLISH FEELING (1936) (w)Harold Adamson (m)Jimmy McHugh. (I)Film: *Top Of The Town*, by Ella Logan.

THAT GIRL (1982) (wm)Stevie Wonder. (P)Stevie Wonder.

THAT GIRL COULD SING (1980) (wm)Jackson Browne. (P)Jackson Browne.

THAT GREAT COME-AND-GET-IT DAY (1947) (w)E. Y. Harburg (m)Burton Lane. (I)Musical: *Finian's Rainbow*, by Ella Logan, Donald Richards, and The Chorus.

THAT INTERNATIONAL RAG (1913) (wm)Irving Berlin. (I)Bonita, Lew Hearn, and Ethel Levey. (R)1953 Film: *Call Me Madam*, by Ethel Merman.

THAT LADY (1973) (wm)Christopher Isley—Ernest Isley—Marvin Isley. (P)The Isley Brothers.

THAT LITTLE DREAM GOT NOWHERE (1946) (w)Johnny Burke (m)Jimmy Van Heusen. (I)Film: *Cross My Heart*, by Betty Hutton.

THAT LOST BARBERSHOP CHORD (1926) (w)Ira Gershwin (m)George Gershwin. (I)Revue: *Americana of 1926*, by Louis Lazarin and The Pan—American Quartette.

THAT LUCKY OLD SUN (1949) (w)Haven Gillespie (m)Beasley Smith. (P)Frankie Laine. (CR)Vaughn Monroe. (R)1964 by Ray Charles.

THAT OLD BLACK MAGIC (1942) (w)Johnny Mercer (m)Harold Arlen. (I)Film: *Star Spangled Rhythm*, by Johnny Johnston. (P)Billy Daniels. (R)1955 by Sammy Davis, Jr. (R)1958 by Louis Prima and Keely Smith. (R)1961 by Bobby Rydell.

THAT OLD FEELING (1937) (wm)Lew Brown—Sammy Fain. (I)Film: *Walter Wanger's Vogues of 1938*, by Virgina Verrill. (P)Shep Fields and his Orchestra. (CR)Jan Garber and his Orchestra.

THAT OLD GANG OF MINE (1923) (w)Billy Rose—Mort Dixon (m)Ray Henderson. (I)Revue: *Ziegfeld Follies of 1923*, by Van and Schenck. (R)1938 by Dick Robertson.

THAT SLY OLD GENTLEMAN (From Featherbed Lane) (1939) (I)Film: *East Side Of Heaven*, by Bing Crosby.

THAT SUNDAY (That Summer) (1963) (w)George David Weiss (m)Joe Sherman. (P)Nat "King" Cole.

THAT TERRIFIC RAINBOW (1940) (w)Lorenz Hart (m)Richard Rodgers. (I)Musical: *Pal Joey*, by June Havoc and Van Johnson.

THAT WAS THEN, THIS IS NOW (1986) (wm)Vance Brescia—Ed Davis. (P)The Monkees.

THAT WAS YESTERDAY (1985) (wm)Mick Jones—Lou Gramm. (P)Foreigner.

THAT'LL BE THE DAY (1957) (wm)Jerry Allison—Buddy Holly—Norman Petty. (P)Buddy Holly and The Crickets. (R)1976 by Linda Ronstadt.

THAT'LL SHOW HIM (1962) (wm)Stephen Sondheim. (I)Musical: *A Funny Thing Happened On The Way To The Forum*, by Preshy Marker.

THAT'S A GOOD GIRL (1926) (wm)Irving Berlin. (P)Ben Selvin and his Orchestra.

THAT'S A PLENTY (1909) (w)Henry Creamer (m)Bert A. Williams. (P)Prince's Orchestra. Usually performed by jazz bands.

('Cause I Love Ya)THAT'S A WHY (1952) (wm)Bob Merrill. (P)Guy Mitchell and Mindy Carson.

THAT'S ALL (1952) (w)Alan Brandt (m)Bob Haymes. (P)Nat "King" Cole.

THAT'S ALL (1983) (wm)Tony Banks—Phil Collins—Mike Rutherfor. (P)Genesis.

THAT'S ALL I WANT FROM YOU (1955) (wm)M. Rotha. (P)Jaye P. Morgan. (CR)Dick Jacobs and his Orchestra.

THAT'S ALL THERE IS TO THAT (1956) (wm)Clyde Otis—Kelly Owens. (P)Nat "King" Cole.

THAT'S ALL YOU GOTTA DO (1960) (wm)Jerry Reed. (P)Brenda Lee.

THAT'S AMORE (1954) (wm)Jack Brooks—Harry Warren. (I)Film: *The Caddy*, by Dean Martin. (P)Dean Martin.

THAT'S FOR ME (1945) (w)Oscar Hammerstein II (m)Richard Rodgers. (I)Film: *State Fair*, by Vivian Blaine. (R)1962 Film: *State Fair*, by Pat Boone.

THAT'S HIM (1943) (w)Ogden Nash (m)Kurt Weill. (I)Musical: *One Touch Of Venus*, by Mary Martin. 1948 Film Version by Eileen Wilson dubbing for Ava Gardner, Olga San Juan, and Eve Arden.

THAT'S HOW I LOVE THE BLUES (1941) (wm)Hugh Martin—Ralph Blane. (I)Musical: *Best Foot Forward*, by Rosemary Lane and Marty May.

THAT'S HOW MUCH I LOVE YOU (1946) (wm)Eddy Arnold—Wally Fowler—J. Graydon Hall. (I)Eddy Arnold. (P)Bing Crosby.

THAT'S LIFE (1964) (wm)Dean Kay—Kelly Gordon. (I)Ocie Smith. (R)1966 by Frank Sinatra.

THAT'S LOVE (1934) (w)Lorenz Hart (m)Richard Rodgers. (I)Film: *Nana*, by Anna Sten.

THAT'S MY DESIRE (1931) (wm)Carroll Loveday—Helmy Kresa. (I)Lanny Ross. (R)1947 by Frankie Laine.

THAT'S MY WEAKNESS NOW (1928) (wm)Bud Green—Sam H. Stept. (P)Helen Kane.

THAT'S OLD FASHIONED (That's The Way Love Should Be) (1962) (wm)Bill Giant—Bernie Baum—Florence Kaye. (P)The Everly Brothers.

THAT'S ROCK 'N' ROLL (1977) (wm)Eric Carmen. (P)Shaun Cassidy.

THAT'S THE BEGINNING OF THE END (1947) (wm)Joan Whitney—Alex Kramer. (P)Perry Como.

THAT'S THE WAY (I Like It) (1975) (wm)Harry Casey—Richard Finch. (P)K. C. & The Sunshine Band. No. 1 Chart Record.

THAT'S THE WAY I'VE ALWAYS HEARD IT SHOULD BE (1971) (w)Jacob Brackman (m)Carly Simon. (P)Carly Simon.

THAT'S THE WAY LOVE IS (1969) (wm)Norman Whitfield—Barrett Strong. (P)Marvin Gaye.

THAT'S THE WAY OF THE WORLD (1975) (wm)Maurice White—Philip Bailey—Larry Dunn. (I)Film: *Shining Star*, by Earth, Wind,and Fire. (P)Earth, Wind and Fire.

THAT'S WHAT FRIENDS ARE FOR (1986) (wm)Carole Bayer Sager—Burt Bacharach. (I)In unknown film by Rod Stewart. (P)Dionne Warwick, Elton John, Gladys Knight, and Stevie Wonder. No. 1 Chart Record. NARAS Award Winner.

THAT'S WHAT GIRLS ARE FOR (1961) (wm)Harvey Fuqua—Gwen Gordy. (P)The Spinners.

THAT'S WHAT I LIKE (1954) (w)Bob Hilliard (m)Jule Styne. (I)Film: *Living It Up*, by Dean Martin. (P)Don, Dick, and Jimmy.

THAT'S WHAT I LIKE ABOUT THE SOUTH (1944) (wm)Andy Razaf. (P)Phil Harris.

THAT'S WHAT LOVE IS ALL ABOUT (1987) (wm)Michael Bolton—E. Kaz. (P)Michael Bolton.

THAT'S WHEN THE MUSIC TAKES ME (1975) (wm)Neil Sedaka. (P)Neil Sedaka.

THAT'S WHY (1959) (wm)Berry Gordy, Jr. —Gwen Gordy—Tyran Carlo (Billy Davis, Sr.) (P)Jackie Wilson.

THAT'S WHY DARKIES WERE BORN (1931) (w)Lew Brown (m)Ray Henderson. (I)Revue: *George White's Scandals*, by Everett Marshall.

(Ting-A-Ling)THE BAD HUMOR MAN (1940) (wm)Johnny Mercer—Jimmy McHugh. (I)Film: *You'll Find Out*, by Kay Kyser and his College of Musical Knowledge.

(Rock 'N' Roll I Gave You)THE BEST YEARS OF MY LIFE (1973) (wm)Kevin Johnson. (P)Kevin Johnson. (R)1975 by Mac Davis.

(You've Got)THE MAGIC TOUCH (1956) (wm)Buck Ram. (P)The Platters.

(I'm Afraid)THE MASQUERADE IS OVER (1938) (w)Herb Magidson (m)Allie Wrubel. (P)Larry Clinton and his Orchestra.

(There'll Be Blue Birds Over)THE WHITE CLIFFS OF DOVER (1941) (w)Nat Burton (m)Walter Kent. (P)Kay Kyser and his Orchestra. (CR)Glenn Miller and his Orchestra.

THEM THERE EYES (193) (wm)Maceo Pinkard-William Tracey-Doris Tauber. (I)Gus Arnheim and his Orchestra.

THEN CAME YOU (1974) (wm)Sherman Marshall—Phillip Pugh. (P)Dionne Warwick and The Spinners. No. 1 Chart Record.

THEN HE KISSED ME. 1963) (wm)Jeff Barry-Ellie Greenwich-Phil Spector.

THEN I'LL BE TIRED OF YOU (1934) (w)E. Y. Harburg (m)Arthur Schwartz. (P)Fats Waller. (CR)Freddy Martin and his Orchestra.

THEN YOU CAN TELL ME GOODBYE (1962) (wm)John D. Loudermilk. (I)John D. Loudermilk. (R)1967 by The Casinos. (R)1968 by Eddy Arnold. (R)1979 by Toby Beau.

THEN YOU MAY TAKE ME TO THE FAIR (1960) (w)Alan Jay Lerner (m)Frederick Loewe. (I)Musical: *Camelot*, by Julie Andrews, John Cullum, James Gannon, and Bruce Yarnell.

THEN YOU'VE NEVER BEEN BLUE (1935) (w)Sam Lewis—Joe Young (m)Ted Fiorito. (I)Film: *Every Night At Eight*, by Frances Langford.

THERE ARE SUCH THINGS (1942) (wm)Stanley Adams—Abel Baer—George W. Meyer. (P)Tommy Dorsey and his Orchestra, vocal by Frank Sinatra and The Pied Pipers.

THERE BUT FOR YOU GO I (1947) (w)Alan Jay Lerner (m)Frederick Loewe. (I)Musical: *Brigadoon*, by David Brooks.

THERE GOES MY BABY (1959) (wm)Benjamin Nelson—Lover Patterson—George Treadwell. (P)The Drifters. (R)1984 by Donna Summer.

THERE GOES MY EVERYTHING (1967) (wm)Dallas Frazier. (I)Jack Greene. (P)Engelbert Humperdick. (R)1971 by Elvis Presley.

THERE GOES MY HEART (1943) (w)Benny Davis (m)Abner Silver (I)Film: *The Heat's On*, by Xavier Cugat and his Orchestra, vocal by Lina Romay.

THERE GOES THAT SONG AGAIN (1944) (w)Sammy Cahn (m)Jule Styne. (I)Film: *Carolina Blues*, by Harry Babbitt, with Kay Kyser and his Orchestra.

THERE IS (1968) (wm)Bobby Miller—Raymond Miner. (P)The Dells.

THERE IS A MOUNTAIN (1967) (wm)Donovan Leitch. (P)Donovan.

THERE IS A TAVERN IN THE TOWN1883) (wm)Unknown. (R)1930's by Rudy Vallee.

THERE IS NOTHIN' LIKE A DAME (1949) (w)Oscar Hammerstein II (m)Richard Rodgers. (I)Musical: *South Pacific*, by The Sailors Chorus.

THERE ISN'T ANY LIMIT TO MY LOVE (1936) (wm)Al Hoffman—Al Goodhart—Maurice Sigler. (I)British Film: *This'll Make You Whistle*, by Jack Buchanan.

THERE, I'VE SAID IT AGAIN. (1941) (wm)Redd Evans—Dave Mann. (I)Benny Carter and his Orchestra. (R)1945 by Vaughn Monroe and his Orchestra. (R)1964 by Bobby Vinton. No. 1 Chart Record.

THERE MUST BE A WAY (1945) (wm)David Saxon—Sammy Gallop—Robert Cook. (P)Charlie Spivak and his Orchestra, vocal by Jimmy Saunders.

THERE MUST BE SOMEONE BETTER FOR ME (1944) (wm)Cole Porter. (I)Musical: *Mexican Hayride*, by June Havoc.

THERE ONCE WAS A MAN (1954) (wm)Richard Adler—Jerry Ross. (I)Musical: *The Pajama Game*, by John

Raitt and Janis Paige.

THERE WILL NEVER BE ANOTHER YOU (1942) (w)Mack Gordon (m)Harry Warren. (I)Film: *Iceland,* by John Payne. (P)Woody Herman and his Orchestra. (CR)Sammy Kaye and his Orchestra. (R)1966 by Chris Montez.

THERE WON'T BE ANYMORE (1974) (wm)Charlie Rich. (P)Charlie Rich.

THERE WON'T BE TRUMPETS (1964) (wm)Stephen Sondheim. (I)Musical: *Anyone Can Whistle,* by Lee Remick.

THERE'LL ALWAYS BE A LADY FAIR (1936) (wm)Cole Porter. (I)Musical: *Anything Goes,* by The Foursome. In film version, by Bing Crosby and Chill Wills.

THERE'LL ALWAYS BE AN ENGLAND (1939) (wm)Ross Parker—Hughie Charles. (I)In United States, by The Band Of The Coldstream Guards.

THERE'LL BE NO TEARDROPS TONIGHT (1949) (wm)Hank Williams—Nelson King. (R)1954 by Tony Bennett.

THERE'LL BE SAD SONGS (To Make You Cry) (1986) (wm)Wayne Braithwaite—Barry Eastmond—Billy Ocean. (P)Billy Ocean. No. 1 Chart Record.

THERE'LL BE SOME CHANGES MADE (1921) (w)Billy Higgins (m)W. Benton Overstreet. (I)Billy Higgins. (P)Ethel Waters. (CR)Ted Lewis. (R)1928 by Sophie Tucker. (R)1941 by Benny Goodman. (R)1947 by Ted Weems and his Orchestra.

THERE'LL COME A TIME (1969) (wm)Floyd Smith—Eugene Record. (P)Betty Everett.

THERE'S A BOAT DAT'S LEAVIN' SOON FOR NEW YORK (1935) (w)Ira Gershwin (m)George Gershwin. (I)Opera: *Porgy and Bess,* by John W. Bubbles. Film Version, by Sammy Davis, Jr.

THERE'S A BOY IN HARLEM (1938) (w)Lorenz Hart (m)Richard Rodgers. (I)Film: *Fool For Scandal,* by Jeni Le Gon.

THERE'S A CABIN IN THE PINES (1933) (wm)Billy Hill. (I)George Hall and his Orchestra, vocal by Loretta Lee.

THERE'S A FAR AWAY LOOK IN YOUR EYE (1938) (w)Irving Taylor (m)Vic Mizzy. (P)Jimmy Dorsey and his Orchestra.

THERE'S A GOLD MINE IN THE SKY (1938) (wm)Charles Kenny—Nick Kenny. (I)Film: *Gold Mine In The Sky,* by Gene Autry. (P)Bing Crosby. (CR)Horace Heidt and his Orchestra.

THERE'S A GREAT DAY COMING MANANA (1940) (w)E. Y. Harburg (m)Burton Lane. (I)Musical: *Hold On To Your Hats,* by Al Jolson.

THERE'S A KIND OF HUSH (1966) (wm)Les Reed—Geoff Stephens. (P)Herman's Hermits. (R)1976 by The Carpenters.

THERE'S LULL IN MY LIFE (1937) (w)Mack Gordon (m)Harry Revel. (I)Film: *Wake Up And Live,* by Alice Faye. (P)Alice Faye. (CR)George Hall and his Orchestra.

THERE'S A MOON OUT TONIGHT (1961) (wm)Al Striano—Joe Luccisano—Al Gentile. (P)The Capris.

THERE'S A PLACE (1963) (wm)John Lennon—Paul McCartney. (P)The Beatles.

THERE'S A RAINBOW 'ROUND MY SHOULDER (1928) (wm)Al Jolson—Billy Rose—Dave Dreyer. (I)Film: *The Singing Fool,* by Al Jolson. (P)Al Jolson. (R)1946 Film: *The Jolson Story* by voice of Jolson dubbing for Larry Parks.

THERE'S A SMALL HOTEL (1936) (w)Lorenz Hart (m)Richard Rodgers. (I)Musical: *On Your Toes,* by Doris Carson and Ray Bolger. (R)1957 Film: *Pal Joey* by Frank Sinatra.

THERE'S A STAR SPANGLED BANNER WAVING SOMEWHERE (1942) (wm)Paul Roberts—Shelley Daniels. (P)Elton Britt. (CR)Jimmy Wakely.

THERE'S DANGER IN YOUR EYES, CHERIE! (1929) (w)Jack Meskill (m)Pete Wendling. (I)Film: *Puttin' On The Ritz,* by Harry Richman. (P)Harry Richman. (CR)Fred Waring's Pennsylvanians.

THERE'S GOTTA BE SOMETHING BETTER THAN THIS (1965) (w)Dorothy Fields (m)Cy Coleman. (I)Musical: *Sweet Charity,* by Gwen Verdon, Helen Gallagher, and Thelma Oliver. 1969 Film Version, by Shirley Mac Laine, Chita Rivers, and Paula Kelly.

THERE'S NO BUSINESS LIKE SHOW BUSINESS (1946) (wm)Irving Berlin. (I)Musical: *Annie Get Your Gun,* by Ethel Merman, Ray Middleton, William O'Neal and Marty May. 1950 Film Version by Betty Hutton, Howard Keel, Keenan Wynn and Louis Calhern.

THERE'S NO TOMORROW (1949) (wm)Al Hoffman—Leo Corday—Leon Carr. Based on O Solo Mio. (P)Tony Martin.

THERE'S NO YOU (1945) (w)Tom Adair (m)Hal Hopper. (P)Jo Stafford.

(I Believe)THERE'S NOTHING STRONGER THAN OUR LOVE (1975) (wm)Paul Anka. (P)Paul Anka and Odia Coates.

THERE'S NOTHING TOO GOOD FOR MY BABY (1931) (wm)Eddie Cantor—Benny Davis—Harry Akst. (I)Film: *Palmy Days,* by Eddie Cantor.

THERE'S NOWHERE TO GO BUT UP (1938) (w)Maxwell Anderson (m)Kurt Weill. (I)Musical: *Knickerbocker Holiday,* by Richard Kollmar and Clarence Nordstrom.

THERE'S ONLY ONE OF YOU (1958) (w)Al Stillman (m)Robert Allen. (P)The Four Lads.

THERE'S SO MUCH MORE (1931) (w)Lorenz art (m)Richard Rodgers. (I)Musical: *America's Sweetheart,* by Jeanne Aubert and Gus Shy.

THERE'S SOMETHING ABOUT A SOLDIER (1933) (wm)Reginald M. Armitage. (I)British Film: *Soldiers Of The King,* by Cicely Courtneidge.

THERE'S SOMETHING IN THE AIR (1936) (w)Harold Adamson (m)Jimmy McHugh. (I)Film: *Banjo On My Knee,* by Tony Martin. (P)Tony Martin. (CR)Shep Fields and his Orchestra.

THERE'S SOMETHING ON YOUR MIND (1960) (wm)C. Jay Mc. Neely. (I)Big Jay McNeely & Band. (P)Bobby Marchan. (R)1966 by Baby Ray.

THERE'S THE GIRL (1987) (wm)H. Knight—Nancy Wilson. (P)Heart.

THERE'S YES! YES! IN YOUR EYES (1940) (w)Cliff Friend (m)Joseph Santly. (P)Guy Lombardo and his Royal Canadians.

THESE BOOTS ARE MADE FOR WALKING(1966) (wm)Lee Hazlewood. (P)Nancy Sinatra. No. 1 Chart Record.

THESE CHARMING PEOPLE (1925) (w)Ira Gershwin (m)George Gershwin. (I)Musical: *Tip-Toes,* by Andrew Tombes, Queenie Smith, and Harry Watson, Jr.

THESE DREAMS (1986) (wm)Bernie Taupin—Martin Page. (P)Heart.

THESE FOOLISH THINGS REMIND ME OF YOU (1936)

(w)Holt Marvell (m)Jack Strachey—Harry Link. (I)In London, by Leslie Hutchinson. (P)Benny Goodman and his Orchestra. (CR)Billie Holiday with Teddy Wilson.

THEY ALL FALL IN LOVE (1929) (wm)Cole Porter. (I)Film: *The Battle of Paris*, by Gertrude Lawrence.

THEY ALL LAUGHED (1937) (w)Ira Gershwin (m)George Gershwin. (I)Film: *Shall We Dance*, by Ginger Rogers.

THEY CALL IT DANCING (1921) (wm)Irving Berlin. (I)Revue: *Music Box Revue*, by Sam Bernard.

THEY CALL ME SISTER HONKY TONK (1933) (wm)Gladys Du Bois—Ben Ellison—Harvey Brooks. (I)Film: *I'm No Angel*, by Mae West.

THEY CALL THE WIND MARIA (1951) (w)Alan Jay Lerner (m)Frederick Loewe. (P)Musical: *Paint Your Wagon*, by Rufus Smith.

THEY CAN'T TAKE THAT AWAY FROM ME (1937) (w)Ira Gershwin (m)George Gershwin. (I)Film: *Shall We Dance?* by Fred Astaire. (P)Fred Astaire. (CR)Ozzie Nelson and his Orchestra. (CR)Tommy Dorsey and his Orchestra. (CR)Billie Holiday. Most popular recording by Frank Sinatra.

THEY DIDN'T BELIEVE ME (1914) (w)Herbert Reynolds (m)Jerome Kern. (I)Musical: *The Girl From Utah*, by Julia Sanderson and Donald Brian.

THEY DON'T KNOW (1984) (wm)Kirsty MacColl. (P)Tracey Ullman.

THEY JUST CAN'T STOP IT (The Games People Play) (1975) (wm)Joseph Jefferson—Bruce Hawes—Charles Simmons. (P)The Spinners.

THEY LOVE ME (1962) (wm)Irving Berlin. (I)Musical: *Mr. President*, by Nanette Fabray.

THEY MET IN RIO (1941) (w)Mack Gordon (m)Harry Warren. (P)Film: *That Night In Rio*, by Don Ameche and Alice Faye.

THEY SAY IT'S WONDERFUL (1946) (wm)Irving Berlin. (I)Musical: *Annie Get Your Gun*, by Ethel Merman and Ray Middleton. 1950 Film version by Betty Hutton and Howard Keel. (P)Perry Como.

THEY WERE DOIN' THE MAMBO (1954) (wm)Don Raye—Sonny Burke. (P)Vaughn Monroe.

THEY'RE COMING TO TAKE ME AWAY, HA-HAAA! (wm)Rosemary Djivre. (P)Napoleon XIV.

THEY'RE EITHER TOO YOUNG OR TOO OLD (1943) (w)Frank Loesser (m)Arthur Schwartz. (I)Film: *Thank Your Lucky Stars*, by Bette Davis.

THEY'RE PLAYING MY SONG (1979) (w)Carole Bayer Sager (m)Marvin Hamlisch. (I)Musical: *They're Playing Our Song*, by Lucy Arnaz and Robert Klein.

(Love Is)THICKER THAN WATER (1978) (wm)Barry Gibb—Andy Gibb. (P)Andy Gibb. No. 1 Chart Record.

THIN LINE BETWEEN LOVE AND HATE (1971) (wm)Richard Poindexter—Robert Poindexter—Jackie Members. (P)The Persuaders. (R)1984 by The Pretenders.

THING, THE (1950) (wm)Charles R. Grean. (P)Phil Harris.

THINGS (1962) (wm)Bobby Darin. (P)Bobby Darin.

THINGS AIN'T WHAT THEY USED TO BE (1953) (1943) (w)Ted Persons (m)Mercer Ellington. (I)Film: *Cabin In The Sky*, by Duke Ellington and his Orchestra.

THINGS ARE LOOKING UP (1937) (w)Ira Gershwin (m)George Gerswhin. (I)Film: *A Damsel In Distress*,by Fred Astaire and danced by Astaire and Joan Fontaine.

THINGS CAN ONLY GET BETTER (1985) (wm)Howard Jones. (P)Howard Jones.

THINGS I LOVE, THE (1941) (wm)Harold Barlow—Lew Harris. Adapted from a Tchaikovsky Melody. (P)Barry Wood.

THINGS I SHOULD HAVE SAID (1967) (wm)P. F. Sloan— Steve Barri. (P)Grass Roots.

THINGS I WANT, THE (1937) (w)Oscar Hammerstein II (m)Jerome Kern. (I)Film: *High, Wide and Handsome*, by Dorothy Lamour.

THINGS I'D LIKE TO SAY (1969) (w)Ronald Rice (m)Leslie Kummel. (P)The New Colony Six.

THINGS WE DID LAST SUMMER, THE (1946) (wm)Sammy Cahn—Jule Styne. (P)Frank Sinatra.

THINGS WE DO FOR LOVE, THE (1977) (wm)Graham Gouldman—Eric Stewart. (P)10cc.

THINGS WE SAID TODAY (1964) (wm)John Lennon—Paul McCartney. (P)The Beatles.

THINK (1957) (wm)Lowman Pauling. (I)The Five Royales. (P)James Brown and The Famous Flames.

THINK (1968) (wm)Aretha Franklin—Ted White. (P)Aretha Franklin.

THINK ABOUT ME (1980) (wm)Christine McVie. (P)Fleetwood Mac.

THINK FOR YOURSELF (1965) (wm)George Harrison. (P)The Beatles.

THINK I'LL GO SOMEWHERE AND CRY MYSELF TO SLEEP (1965) (wm)Bill Anderson. (I)Bill Anderson. (P)Al Martino.

THINK I'M IN LOVE (1982) (wm)Eddie Money—Randy Oda. (P)Eddie Money.

THINK OF LAURA (1984) (wm)Christopher Cross. (P)Christopher Cross.

THINK TWICE (1961) (wm)Joe Shapiro—Jimmy Williams—Clyde Otis. (P)Brook Benton. (R)1966 by Jackie Wilson and Lavern Baker.

BROOK BENTON

Some years ago, on a flight from Los Angeles to New York, I found myself sitting next to an old friend, singer Brook Benton. As we were waiting for takeoff, the captain announced there would be a three hour delay because of a mechanical problem. All the passengers were invited to the airport restaurant as guests of the airline.

When it came time to reboard, Brook hesitatingly said to me: "Dick, I don't know if I want to board that plane again. I'd rather me read about me in the papers instead of someone else reading about me." But we both got on and had a most pleasant flight to New York.

THINKING OF YOU (1927) (w)Bert Kalmar (m)Harry Ruby. (I)Musical: *The 5 O'Clock Girl*, by Oscar Shaw and Mary Eaton. Theme song of Kay Kyser and his Orchestra. (R)1950 Film: *Three Little Words*, by Vera— Ellen.

THINKING OF YOU (1972) (wm)Jim Messina. (P)Loggins and Messina.

THIRD MAN THEME,THE (The Harry Lime Theme) (1950) (m)Anton Karas. (I)Film: *The Third Man*, by Anton Karas playing zither on the soundtrack.

(P)Anton Karas. (CR)Guy Lombardo and his Royal Canadians.

THIRD RATE ROMANCE (1975) (wm)Howard Russell Smith. (P)Amazing Rhythm Aces.

THIRD TIME LUCKY (1979) (wm)Dave Peverett. (P)Foghat.

THIS BITTER EARTH (1960) (wm)Clyde Otis. (P)Dinah Washington. (R)1970 by The Satisfactions.

THIS BOY (Ringo's Theme) (1963) (wm)John Lennon—Paul McCartney. (I)Film: *A Hard Day's Night*, by The Beatles. (P)The Beatles.

THIS CAN'T BE LOVE (1938) (w)Lorenz Hart (m)Richard Rodgers. (I)Musical: *The Boys From Syracuse*, by Eddie Albert and Marcy Westcott. 1940 Film Version, by Rosemary Lane. (R)1962 Film: *Jumbo*, by Doris Day.

THIS COULD BE THE NIGHT (1986) (wm)Paul Dean—Jonathan Cain—Mike Reno—Bill Wray. (P)Loverboy.

THIS COULD BE THE START OF SOMETHING (Big) (1956) (wm)Steve Allen. (P)Les Brown and his Band of Renown. (P)Steve Lawrence and Eydie Gorme.

THIS DIAMOND RING (1964) (wm)Al Kooper—Irwin Levine—Bob Brass. (P)Gary Lewis and The Playboys. No. 1 Chart Record.

THIS DOOR SWINGS BOTH WAYS (1966) (wm)Don Thomas—Estelle Levitt. (P)Herman's Hermits.

THIS DREAM (1964) (wm)Leslie Bricusse—Anthony Newley. (I)Musical: *The Roar Of The Greaspaint—The Smell Of The Crowd*, by Anthony Newley and The Urchins.

THIS FRIENDLY WORLD (1959) (wm)Ken Darby. (I)Film: *Hound Dog MAN*, by Fabian. (P)Fabian.

THIS FUNNY WORLD (1926) (w)Lorenz Hart (m)Richard Rodgers. (I)Musical: *Betsy*, by Belle Baker.

THIS GIRL IS A WOMAN NOW (1969) (wm)Victor Millrose—Abe Bernstein. (P)Gary Puckett and The Union Gap.

THIS GUY'S IN LOVE WITH YOU (1968) (w)Hal David (m)Burt Bacharach. (P)Herb Alpert. Girls Version by Dionne Warwick.

THIS HAPPY FEELING (1958) (wm)Jay Livingston—Ray Evans. (I)Film: *This Happy Feeling*, by Debbie Reynolds.

THIS HEART OF MINE (1946) (w)Arthur Freed (m)Harry Warren. (I)Film: *Ziegfeld Follies*, by Fred Astaire. (P)Fred Astaire. (CR)Judy Garland.

THIS I SWEAR (1959) (wm)Joe Rock—Lennie Martin. (P)The Skyliners.

THIS IS A GREAT COUNTRY (1962) (wm)Irving Berlin. (I)Musical: *Mr. President*, by Robert Ryan.

THIS IS ALL I ASK (1963) (wm)Gordon Jenkins. (I)Burl Ives. (P)Tony Bennett.

THIS IS IT (1979) (wm)Kenny Loggins—Michael McDonald. (P)Kenny Loggins.

THIS IS MY COUNTRY (1940) (wm)Don Raye—Al Jacobs. (P)Fred Waring's Pennsylvanians.

THIS IS MY COUNTRY (1968) (wm)Curtis Mayfield. (P)The Impressions.

THIS IS MY NIGHT TO DREAM (1938) (w)Johnny Burke (m)James V. Monaco. (I)Film: *Doctor Rhythm*, by Bing Crosby. (P)Bing Crosby.

THIS IS MY SONG (1952) (wm)Dick Charles. (I)Theme song of Patti Page's Television Show.

THIS IS MY SONG (1966) (wm)Charles Chaplin. (I)Film: *A Countess In Hong Kong*, as soundtrack theme. (P)Petula Clark.

THIS IS NEW (1941) (w)Ira Gershwin (m)Kurt Weill. (I)Musical: *Lady In The Dark*, by Gertrude Lawrence and Victor Mature.

THIS IS NO LAUGHING MATTER (1941) (w)Buddy Kaye (m)Al Frisch. (P)Charlie Spivak and his Orchestra. (CR)Glenn Miller and his Orchestra.

THIS IS THE ARMY, MR. JONES (1942) (wm)Irving Berlin. (I)Revue: *This Is The Army*, by The Soldiers Chorus.

THIS IS THE BEGINNING OF THE END (1940) (wm)Mack Gordon, (I)Film: *Johnny Apollo*, by Dorothy Lamour. (R)1952 by Don Cornell.

THIS IS THE LIFE (1964) (w)Lee Adams (m)Charles Strouse. (I)Musical: *Golden Boy*, by Billy Daniels, Sammy Davis, Jr. ,and The Company.

THIS IS THE MISSUS (1931) (w)Lew Brown (m)Ray Henderson. (I)Revue: *George White's Scandals*, by Rudy Vallee. (R)1956 Film: *The Best Things In Life Are Free*, by Sheree North.

THIS IS THE NIGHT (1946) (wm)Redd Evans—Lewis Bellin.

THIS IS THE TIME (1987) (wm)Billy Joel. (P)Billy Joel.

THIS IS WHAT I CALL LOVE (1956) (w)Matt Dubey (m)Harold Karr. (I)Musical: *Happy Hunting*, by Ethel Merman.

THIS IS WORTH FIGHTING FOR (1942) (wm)Edgar De Lange—Sam H. Stept. (P)Jimmy Dorsey and his Orchestra.

THIS ISN'T HEAVEN (1962) (wm)Richard Rodgers. (I)Film: *State Fair*, by Bobby Darin.

THIS LAND IS YOUR LAND (1956) (wm)Woody Guthrie (I)The Weavers. (R)1963 by The New Christy Minstrels.

THIS LITTLE BIRD (1965) (wm)John D. Loudermilk. (P)Marianne Faithful.

THIS LITTLE GIRL (1963) (wm)Gerry Goffin—Carole King. (P)Dion.

THIS LITTLE GIRL (1980) (wm)Bruce Springsteen. (P)Gary U. S. Bonds.

THIS LITTLE GIRL OF MINE (1955) (wm)Ray Charles. (P)Ray Charles. (R)1958 by The Everly Brothers.

THIS LITTLE GIRL'S GONE ROCKIN' (1958) (wm)Bobby Darin—Mann Curtis. (P)Ruth Brown.

THIS LOVE OF MINE (1941) (w)Frank Sinatra (m)Sol Parker—Henry Sanicola. (P)Tommy Dorsey and his Orchestra, vocal by Frank Sinatra.

THIS MAGIC MOMENT (1960) (wm)Doc Pomus—Mort Shuman. (P)The Drifters. (R)1968 by Jay and The Americans.

THIS MASQUERADE (1976) (wm)Leon Russell. (P)George Benson. NARAS Award Winner.

THIS NEARLY WAS MINE (1949) (w)Oscar Hammerstein II (m)Richard Rodgers. (I)Musical: *South Pacific*, by Ezio Pinza. 1958 Film Version by Giorgio Tozzi dubbing for Rossano Brazzi.

THIS NIGHT WON'T LAST FOREVER (1976) (wm)Ron Freeland—Bill La Bounty. (P)Michael Johnson.

THIS OLD HEART OF MINE (Is Weak For You) (1966) (wm)Brian Holland—Lamont Dozier—Eddie Holland. (P)The Isley Brothers. (R)1969 by Tammi Terrell. (R)1975 by Rod Stewart.

THIS OLE HOUSE (1954) (wm)Stuart Hamblen. (I)Stuart Hamblen. (P)Rosemary Clooney.

THIS ONE'S FOR YOU (1976) (wm)Barry Manilow—Marty Panzer. (P)Barry Manilow.

THIS SONG (1976) (wm)George Harrison. (P)George

Harrison.

THIS TIME (1942) (wm)Irving Berlin. Not one of Berlins big hits.

THIS TIME (1958) (wm)Chips Moman. (P)Troy Shondell.

THIS TIME (1980) (wm)John Cougar Mellencamp. (P)John Cougar Mellencamp.

THIS TIME (1983) (wm)Bryan Adams—Jim Vallance. (P)Bryan Adams.

THIS TIME I'M IN IT FOR LOVE (1978) (wm)Steve Pippin—Larry Keith. (P)Player.

THIS TIME IT'S TRUE LOVE (1963) (wm)Noel Coward. (I)The Girl Who Came To Supper, by Florence Henderson and Jose Ferrer.

THIS TIME THE DREAM'S ON ME (1941) (w)Johnny Mercer (m)Harold Arlen. (I)Film: Blues In The Night, by Priscilla Lane. (P)Glenn Miller and his Orchestra, vocal by Ray Eberle.

THIS WAS A REAL NICE CLAMBAKE (1945) (w)Oscar Hammerstein (m)Richard Rodgers. (I)Musical: Carousel, by John Raitt and Jan Clayton. Film Version: by Shirley Jones and Gordon MacRae.

THIS WAY TO SESAME STREET (1970) (wm)Joe Raposo—Jeffrey Moss. (I)T. V. Show, by The Children of Sesame Street.

THIS WHEEL'S ON FIRE (1967) (w)Bob Dylan (m)Rick Danko. (P)The Band.

THIS WOMAN (1984) (wm)Barry Gibb—Albhy Galuten. (P)Kenny Rogers.

THIS YEAR'S KISSES (1937) (wm)Irving Berlin. (I)Film: On The Avenue, by Alice Faye.

THOROUGHLY MODERN MILLIE (1967) (w)Sammy Cahn (m)Jimmy Van Heusen. (I)Film: Thoroughly Modern Millie, by Julie Andrews. (CR)Louis Armstrong.

THOSE LAZY—HAZY—CRAZY—DAYS OF SUMMER (1964) (w)Charles Tobias (m)Hans Carste. (P)Nat "King" Cole.

THOSE OLDIES BUT GOODIES REMIND ME OF YOU (1961) (wm)Paul Politti—Nick Curinga. (P)Little Caesar and The Romans.

T'MORRA, T'MORRA (1944) (w)E. Y. Harburg (m)Harold Arlen. (I)Musical: Bloomer Girl by Joan McCracken.

T. S. O. P. (The Sound of Philadelphia) (1974) (wm)Kenny Gamble—Leon Huff. (P)M. F. S. B.

THOSE WERE THE DAYS (1968) (wm)Adapted from a folk song by Gene Raskin. (P)Mary Hopkin.

THOSE WERE THE DAYS or THEME FROM ALL IN THE FAMILY (1971) (wm)Charles Strouse—Lee Adams. (I)Theme of TV series All In The Family with Carroll O'Connor and Jean Stapleton.

THOU SHALT NOT STEAL (1962) (wm)John Loudermilk. (P)John Loudermilk. (R)1965 by Dick and Deedee.

THOU SWELL (1927) (w)Lorenz Hart (m)Richard Rodgers. (I)Musical: A Connecticut Yankee by William Gaxton and Constance Carpenter. Film: Words And Music (1948) by June Allyson and the Blackburn Twins.

THOUSAND STARS, A (1960) (wm)Eugene Pearson (P)Kathy Young and The Innocents.

THREE BELLS, THE (See WHILE THE ANGELUS WAS RINGING)

THREE CABALLEROS, THE (1944) (w—Eng)Ray Gilbert (m)Manuel Esperon. (I)Cartoon Film: The Three Caballeros by voices of Clarence Nash, Joaquin Garay, and Jose Oliveira.

THREE COINS IN THE FOUNTAIN (1954) (w)Sammy Cahn (m)Jule Styne. (I)Film: Three Coins In The Fountain. Frank Sinatra on soundtrack. Academy Award Winner. (P)Frank Sinatra. (P)The Four Aces. No. 1 Chart Record.

THREE KINGS OF ORIENT (See WE THREE KINGS OF ORIENT)

THREE LITTLE FISHIES (1939) (wm)Saxie Dowell. (P)Hal Kemp and his Orchestra, vocal by Saxie Dowell. (CR)Kay Kyser. No. 1 Chart Record.

THREE LITTLE SISTERS (1942) (wm)Irving Taylor—Vic Mizzy. (I)Film: Private Buckaroo by The Andrews Sisters.

THREE LITTLE WORDS (1930) (w)Bert Kalmar (m)Harry Ruby. (I)Film: Check And Double Check by Bing Crosby and The Rhythm Boys with Duke Ellington and his Orchestra. No. 1 Chart Record. (P)Rudy Vallee. Film: Three Little Words (1950) with Fred Astaire and Red Skelton.

THREE NIGHTS A WEEK (1960) (wm)Antoine Domino. (P)Fats Domino.

THREE O'CLOCK IN THE MORNING (1921) (w)Dorothy Terris (m)Julian Robledo. (I)Revue: Greenwich Village Follies Of 1921 by Richard Bold. Film: Presenting Lily Mars (1943) by Judy Garland. Film: That Midnight Kiss (1949) by J. Carrol Naish. (P)Paul Whiteman and His Orchestra (1922). No. 1 Chart Record.

THREE ON A MATCH (1932) (w)Raymond B. Egan (m)Ted Fiorito. (I)Film: Blondie Of The Follies with Marion Davies and Jimmy Durante.

THREE STARS WILL SHINE TONIGHT (See THE DOCTOR KILDARE THEME)

THREE TIMES A LADY (1978) (wm)Lionel B. Richie, Jr. (P)The Commodores. No. 1 Chart Record.

THREE TIMES IN LOVE (1979) (wm)Tommy James—Rick Serota. (P)Tommy James.

THREE'S A CROWD (1932) (w)Al Dubin—Irving Kahal (m)Harry Warren. (I)Film: The Crooner by David Manners.

THRILL IS GONE, THE (1931) (wm)Lew Brown—Ray Henderson. (I)Revue: George White'S Scandals by Rudy Vallee, Everett Marshall and Ross MacLean. (R)1970. B. B. King.

THRILLER (1984) (wm)Rod Temperton. (P)Michael Jackson.

THROUGH (How Can You Say We're Through) (1929) (w)Joe McCarthy (m)James V. Monaco. (P)Glen Gray and The Casa Loma Orchestra.

THROUGH A LONG AND SLEEPLESS NIGHT (1949) (w)Mack Gordon (m)Alfred Newman. (I)Film: Come To The Stable with Loretta Young and Celeste Holm.

THROUGH A THOUSAND DREAMS (1946) (w)Leo Robin (m)Arthur Schwartz. (I)Film: The Time, The Place And The Girl by Dennis Morgan and Martha Vickers and played by pianist Carmen Cavallaro.

THROUGH THE YEARS (1931) (w)Edward Heyman (m)Vincent Youmans. (I)Musical: Through The Years by Natalie Hall and Michael Bartlett.

THROW ANOTHER LOG ON THE FIRE (1934) (wm)Charles Tobias—Jack Scholl—Murray Mencher. (P)Morton Downey.

THROW ME A KISS (1922) (wm)Louis A. Hirsch—Gene Buck—Dave Stamper—Maurice Yvain. (I)Revue: Ziegfeld Follies Of 1922 by Mary Eaton.

THROWING IT ALL AWAY (1986) (wm)Anthony Banks—

Phil Collins—Michael Rutherford. (P)Genesis.

THRU THE COURTESY OF LOVE (1936) (w)Jack Scholl (m)M. K. Jerome. (I)Film: *Here Comes Carter* by Ross Alexander. (P)Ben Pollack and his Orchestra. (CR)Richard Himber and his Orchestra.

THUMBELINA (1952) (wm)Frank Loesser. (I)Film: *Hans Christian Andersen* by Danny Kaye.

THUNDER AND LIGHTNING (1972) (wm)Chi Coltrane. (P)Chi Coltrane.

THUNDER ISLAND (1978) (wm)Jay Ferguson. (P)Jay Ferguson.

THUNDERER, THE (1889) (m)John Philip Sousa. Famous American march.

TI—PI—TIN (1938) (w—Eng)Raymond Leveen (m)Maria Grever. (P)Horace Heidt and His Musical Knights.

TICKET TO RIDE (1965) (wm)John Lennon—Paul McCartney. (I)Film: *Help!* by The Beatles.

TICO TICO (1944) (w—Eng)Ervin Drake (m)Zequinha Abreu. (I)Cartoon Film: *Saludos Amigos* by Aloysio Oliveira. Film: *Bathing Beauty* (1944) by Xavier Cugat and his Orchestra. (P)Ethel Smith.

TIDE IS HIGH (1981) (wm)John Holt. (P)Blondie. Number one chart record.

TIE A YELLOW RIBBON ROUND THE OLE OAK TREE (1973) (wm)Irwin Levine—L. Russell Brown. (P)Tony Orlando and Dawn. No. 1 Chart Record.

TIE ME KANGAROO DOWN SPORT (1960) (wm)Rolf Harris. (P)Rolf Harris.

TIGER (1959) (wm)Ollie Jones. (P)Fabian.

TIGER RAG (1917) (m)Original Dixie and Jazz Band. (P)The Original Dixieland Jazz Band. Film: *Is Everybody Happy* with Ted Lewis. Film: *The Big Broadcast* with Bing Crosby and Kate Smith. Film: *Birth Of The Blues* with Bing Crosby and Mary Martin.

TIGHTEN UP (1968) (wm)Billy H. Buttier—Archie Bell. (P)Archie Bell and The Drells. No. 1 Chart Record.

TIGHTER TIGHTER (1970) (wm)Tommy James—Bob King. (P)Alive and Kicking.

TIJUANA JAIL, THE (1959) (wm)Denny Thompson. (P)The Kingston Trio.

'TIL I KISSED YOU (1959) (wm)Don Everly. (P)The Everly Brothers.

'TIL REVEILLE (1941) (wm)Stanley Cowan—Bobby Worth. (P)Kay Kyser.

TILL (1957) (w)Carl Sigman (m)Charles Danvers. (P)Tony Bennett.

TILL EULENSPIEGEL (1895) (m)Richard Strauss. Famous classical composition.

TILL I WALTZ AGAIN WITH YOU (1953) (wm)Sidney Prosen. (P)Teresa Brewer. No. 1 Chart Record.

TILL THE CLOUDS ROLL BY (1917) (wm)Guy Bolton—P. G. Wodehouse—Jerome Kern. (I)Musical: *Oh Boy!* (I)Musical: *Oh Joy.* Film: *Till The Clouds Roll By* with Judy Garland, Frank Sinatra and June Allyson.

TILL THE END OF TIME (1945) (wm)Buddy Kaye—Ted Mossman. Adapted from Chopin's Polonaise in A—Flat. (P)Perry Como.

TILL THE REAL THING COMES ALONG (See UNTIL THE REAL THING COMES ALONG)

TILL THEN (1933) (w)Ira Gershwin (m)George Gershwin. Not one of the Gershwins' hit songs.

TILL THEN (1944) (wm)Eddie Seiler—Sol Marcus—Guy Wood. Not a hit until revival in 1946 by The Classics.

TILL THERE WAS YOU (1957) (wm)Meredith Willson.

TERESA BREWER

One of the most important artists I worked with at Coral Records was Teresa Brewer. I think Teresa was a very underrated singer. Her versatility was amazing. She honestly could deliver a great performance with the proper feeling for contemporary, pop, old standards, country, rhythm and blues, Dixieland jazz ... you name it and she could do it. Her massive hit on *Til I Waltz Again With You* (on Decca) reached number one on the charts and advanced her to the status of a major recording artist. Incidentally, Sid Prosen, who wrote that song, made a fortune on it. But he spent all the money, never had another hit, and ended up driving a taxi. such is fate ... but Teresa Brewer kept on making lots of hits.

When Bob Thiele came in to head Coral, I became the arranger for Teresa Brewer. We had a number of big successes, including R & B hits like *You Send Me* and *Pledging My Love* and others like *Sweet Old Fashioned Girl* and *Mutual Admiration Society.* One big kick was a duet she did with Mickey Mantle on a song called *I Love Mickey.* That was a most interesting experience.

Both Mickey and Teresa were at the height of their careers. Bob Thiele, to whom I must give credit as a tireless innovator, someone arranged to get the two of them together. The fact that Teresa was a big Yankees fan helped.

When Mickey arrived at the session, accompanied only by his business agent, he promptly went into the control room to hide. However, when the band started to play. he came out and showed an intense interest in the guitar players. He played a little guitar and was fascinated by the dexterity and ability of our session players. After a few problems with getting Mickey to come in on time to say "Mickey Who", things worked out well and it became a fun session. The record took off pretty well and sold a couple of hundred thousand copies.

(I)Musical: *The Music Man* by Robert Preston and Barbara Cook. Film version by Robert Preston and Shirley Jones.

TILL TOMORROW (1959) (w)Sheldon Harnick (m)Jerry Bock. (I)Musical: *Fiorello* by Ellen Hanley and Company.

TILL WE MEET AGAIN (1918) (w)Raymond B. Egan (m)Richard A. Whiting. Popular standard. Film: *On Moonlight Bay* with Doris Day and Gordon MacRae. Film: *The Eddy Duchin Story* with Tyrone Power. Carmen Cavallero was the soundtrack pianist.

TILL WE TWO ARE ONE (1953) (w)Tom Glazer (m)Larry Martin—Billy Martin. (P)Georgie Shaw.

TIMBUCTOO (1920) (wm)Bert Kalmar—Harry Ruby. No artist credited with introduction.

TIME (CLOCK OF THE HEART) (1983) (wm)Roy Hay—John Moss—Michael Craig. (P)Culture Club.

TIME AFTER TIME (1947) (w)Sammy Cahn (m)Jule

Styne. (I)Film: *It Happened In Brooklyn* by Frank Sinatra.

TIME AFTER TIME (1984) (wm)Cyndi Lauper—Rob Hyman. (P)Cyndi Lauper. No. 1 Chart Record.

TIME ALONE WILL TELL (1944) (w)James V. Monaco (m)Harry Warren. (I)Film: *Pin Up Girl* by Charlie Spivak and his Orchestra.

TIME FOR US, A (See LOVE THEME FROM ROMEO AND JULIET)

TIME HAS COME TODAY (1967) (w)Joseph Chambers (m)Willie Chambers. (P)The Chambers Brothers.

TIME IN A BOTTLE (1974) (wm)Jim Croce. (P)Jim Croce. No. 1 Chart Record.

TIME IS ON MY SIDE (1964) (wm)Jerry Ragovoy. (P)The Rolling Stones.

TIME IS TIGHT (1969) (wm)Booker T. Jones—Al Jackson, Jr.—Steve Cooper—Donald V. Dunn. (P)Booker T. and The M. C.'s.

TIME OF MY LIFE, THE (1987) (wm)F. Previte—J. De-Nicola—D. Markowitz. (P)Bill Medley and Jennifer Warnes. Number one chart record.

TIME OF THE SEASON (1967) (wm)Red Argent. (P)The Zombies.

TIME ON MY HANDS (1930) (w)Harold Adamson—Mack Gordon (m)Vincent Youmans. (I)Musical: *Smiles* by Marilyn Miller and Paul Gregory. Film: *Look For The Silver Lining* with Ray Bolger, June Haver, and Gordon McRae.

TIME OUT FOR TEARS (1948) (wm)Abe Schiff—Irving Berman. (P)Savannah Churchill and The Four Tunes.

TIME PASSAGES (1978) (wm)Al Stewart—Peter White. (P)Al Stewart.

TIME WAITS FOR NO ONE (1944) (wm)Charlie Tobias—Cliff Friend. (I)Film: *Shine On Harvest Moon* with Ann Sheridan and Dennis Morgan. (P)Helen Forrest.

TIME WAS (1941) (w—Eng)S. K. Russell (m)Miguel Prado. Original title "Duerme." (P)Jimmy Dorsey and his Orchestra, vocal by Bob Eberly.

TIME WON'T LET ME (1966) (w)Chet Kelley (m)Tom King. (P)The Outsiders.

TIMES OF YOUR LIFE (1976) (wm)William M. Lane—Roger S. Nichols. (P)Paul Anka.

TIMOTHY (1970) (wm)Rupert Holmes. (P)The Buoys.

TIN MAN (1974) (wm)Lee Bunnell. (P)America.

TIN ROOF BLUES (1923) (w)Walter Melrose (m)George Brunies—Leon Rappolo—Paul Mares—Mel Stitzel—Ben Pollack. (P)The New Orleans Rhythm Kings. Words by Bill Norvas and Allan Copeland, entitled MAKE LOVE TO ME (1953) (P)Jo Stafford.

TINA MARIE (1954) (wm)Bob Merrill. (P)Perry Como.

TINY BUBBLES (1966) (wm)Leon Pober. Famous Hawaiian song. (R)Don Ho.

TINY LITTLE FINGERPRINTS (1935) (wm)Charles Newman—Sam H. Stept—Charles Tobias. (P)The Dorsey Brothers Orchestra.

TIP TOE THROUGH THE TULIPS (1926) (w)Al Dubin (m)Joe Burke. (I)Film: *Gold Diggers Of Broadway* by Nick Lucas. Film: *Painting The Clouds With Sunshine* (1951) by Gene Nelson, Lucille Norman, Virginia Mayo, and Virginia Gibson. (R)1968 by Tiny Tim.

TIPPERARY (See IT'S A LONG WAY TO TIPPERARY)

TIPPIN' IN (1945) (w)Marty Symes (m)Bobby Smith. (P)Erskine Hawkins and his Orchestra.

TIRED (1945) (wm)Allan Roberts—Doris Fisher. (P)Pearl Bailey. Film: *Variety Girl* (1947) by Pearl Bailey.

TIRED OF BEING ALONE (1971) (wm)Al Green. (P)Al Green.

TIRED OF TOEIN' THE LINE (1980) (wm)Rocky Burnette—Ron Coleman. (P)Rocky Burnette.

TIRED OF WAITING FOR YOU (1965) (wm)Roy Davies. (P)The Kinks.

'TIS AUTUMN (1941) (wm)Henry Nemo. (P)Les Brown and his Orchestra, with vocal by Ralph Young. (CR)Woody Herman and his Orchestra, with vocal by Woody Herman and Carolyn Grey.

TISHOMINGO BLUES (1918) (wm)Spencer Williams. Famous jazz composition.

TIT—WILLOW (1885) (w)W. S. Gilbert (m)Arthur Sullivan. (I)Operetta: *The Mikado.*

TITS AND ASS (1975) (w)Edward Kleban (m)Marvin Hamlisch. (I)Musical: *A Chorus Line.*

TO A WATER LILY (1896) (m)Edward MacDowell. Popular light classical selection. From WOODLAND SKETCHES.

TO A WILD ROSE (1896) (m)Edward MacDowell. Popular light classical selection from Woodland Sketches.

TO ALL THE GIRLS I'VE LOVED BEFORE (1984) (w)Hal David (m)Albert Hammond. (P)Julio Iglesias and Willie Nelson.

TO BE A LOVER (1962) (wm)William Bell—Booker T. Jones. (P)Gene Chandler (1962). (R)1968 Billy Idol.

TO BE FORGOTTEN (1928) (wm)Irving Berlin. Not one of Berlin's hits.

TO BE LOVED (1958) (wm)Tyran Carlo—Berry Gordy, Jr.—Gwen Gordy. (P)Jackie Wilson.

JACKIE WILSON

A touching incident occurred back in the late fifties. I was Jackie Wilson's arranger and conductor and went with him to Chicago to conduct a very big benefit show. Stevie Wonder, known then as Little Stevie Wonder, was also one of the featured acts.

After Stevie finished his performance, his entourage carried him on their shoulders off stage and down to the dressing room area, crowded with fans eager to greet their favorites. Suddenly a voice rang out: "Stevie, It's Jackie!" Stevie immediately had his people put him down and he embraced his idol, Jackie Wilson. To this day, I'm certain Stevie Wonder will acknowledge the tremendous influence Jackie Wilson had on his life.

TO EACH HIS OWN (1946) (wm)Jay Livingston—Ray Evans. (P)Eddy Howard. Inspired by film *To Each His Own* with Olivia De Haviland. No. 1 Chart Record.

TO KEEP MY LOVE ALIVE (1927) (w)Lorenz Hart (m)Richard Rodgers. (I)Musical: *Connecticut Yankee.* Also in film version (1931) with Will Rogers and Maureen O'Sullivan.

TO KNOW HIM IS TO LOVE HIM (1958) (wm)Phil Spector. (P)The Teddy Bears.

TO KNOW YOU IS TO LOVE YOU (1952) (w)Allan Roberts (m)Robert Allen. (P)Perry Como.

TO KNOW YOU IS TO LOVE YOU (1928) (w)B. G. De

Sylva—Lew Brown (m)Ray Henderson. (I)Musical: *Hold Everything.*

TO LIFE or L'CHAIM (1964) (w)Sheldon Harnick (m)Jerry Bock. (I)Musical: *Fiddler On The Roof* by Zero Mostel, Michael Granger and men. Film version with Topol.

TO LOVE SOMEBODY (1967) (wm)Barry Gibb—Robin Gibb—Maurice Gibb. (P)The Bee Gees.

TO MY MAMMY (1929) (wm)Irving Berlin. (I)Film: *Mammy* by Al Jolson. (P)Al Jolson.

TO SIR WITH LOVE (1967) (wm)Don Black—Mark London. (I)Film: *To Sir With Love* by Lulu. Sidney Poitier starred in the film. (P)Lulu. No. 1 Chart Record.

TO THE DOOR OF THE SUN (ALLE PORTE DEL SOLE) (1974) (w—Eng)Norman Newell (m)Mario Panzeri—Lorenzo Pilat—Corrado Conti. (P)Al Martino.

TO THINK YOU'VE CHOSEN ME (1950) (wm)Bernie Benjamin—George Weiss. (P)Eddy Howard.

TO YOU SWEETHEART ALOHA (1936) (wm)Harry Owens. (P)Harry Owens and His Royal Hawaiians.

TOAST AND MARMALADE FOR TEA (1971) (wm)Steve Groves. (P)Tin Tin.

TOBACCO ROAD (1960) (wm)John Loudermilk. (P)The Nashville Teens (1964).

TODAY (1964) (wm)Randy Sparks. (I)Film: *Advance To The Rear* on soundtrack. (P)The New Christy Minstrels.

TOGETHER (1928) (wm)B. G. De Sylva—Lew Brown (m)Ray Henderson. (P)Paul Whiteman and his Orchestra. (P)Nick Lucas. (P)Cliff "Ukelele Ike" Edwards. Film: *Since You Went Away* (1944). Film: *The Best Things In Life Are Free* (1956). (P)Connie Francis.

TOGETHER AGAIN (1963) (wm)Buck Owens. (P)Ray Charles (1966). (R)1976 by Emmy Lou Harris.

TOGETHER WHEREVER WE GO (1959) (w)Stephen Sondheim (m)Jule Styne. (I)Musical: *Gypsy* by Ethel Merman, Sandra Church and Jack Klugman. Film version with Rosalind Russell.

TOKAY (1929) (wm)Noel Coward. (I)Operetta: *Bitter Sweet* by Gerald Nodin and chorus. Film version (1940) by Nelson Eddy.

TOM DOOLEY (1958) (wm)Adapted from folk song by Dave Guard. (P)The Kingston Trio.

TOMORROW (1938) (wm)Cole Porter. (I)Musical: *Leave It To Me* by Sophie Tucker and chorus.

TOMORROW (1977) (w)Martin Charnin (m)Charles Strouse. (I)Musical: *Annie* by Andrea McArdle. Also in film version.

TOMORROW IS A LOVELY DAY (1940) (wm)Irving Berlin. (I)Musical: *Louisiana Purchase* with Victor Moore, William Gaxton and Irene Bordoni. Film version with Bob Hope and Irene Bordoni.

TOMORROW IS ANOTHER DAY (1937) (w)Gus Kahn (m)Bronislae Kaper—Walter Jurmann. (I)Film: *A Day At The Races* by Allan Jones.

TOMORROW NIGHT (1939) (w)Sam Coslow (m)Will Grosz. (P)Horace Heidt. (R)1948 by Lonnie Johnson.

TONIGHT (1957) (w)Stephen Sondheim (m)Leonard Bernstein. (I)Musical: *West Side Story* by Larry Kert and Carol Lawrence. Film version with Natalie Wood and Rita Moreno. (P)Instrumentally by Ferrante and Teicher.

TONIGHT IS MINE (1934) (w)Gus Kahn (m)W. Franke Harling. (I)Film: *Stingaree* by Irene Dunne. (P)Leo Reisman and his Orchestra.

TONIGHT SHE COMES (1986) (wm)Ric Ocasek. (P)Cars.

TONIGHT WE LOVE (1941) (wm)Bobby Worth—Ray Austin—Freddy Martin. Adapted from Tchaikovsky's First Piano Concerto in B—Flat. (P)Freddy Martin and his Orchestra.

TONIGHT YOU BELONG TO ME (1926) (w)Billy Rose (m)Lee David. (P)Gene Austin. (R)1956 by Patience and Prudence.

TONIGHT'S THE NIGHT (It's Gonna Be Alright) (1976) (wm)Rod Stewart. (P)Rod Stewart.

TONIGHT, TONIGHT, TONIGHT (1987) (wm)A. Banks—P. Collins—M. Rutherford. (P)Genesis.

TONY'S WIFE (1933) (w)Harold Adamson (m)Burton Lane. (P)Gertrude Niesen. Film: *Turn Back The Clock* by Lee Tracy.

TOO BAD (1955) (wm)Cole Porter. (I)Musical: *Silk Stockings.* Film version with Fred Astaire and Cyd Charisse.

TOO BUSY THINKING ABOUT MY BABY (1969) (wm)Norman Whitfield—Barrett Strong—Janie Bradford. (P)Marvin Gaye.

TOO CLOSE FOR COMFORT (1956) (wm)Jerry Bock—Larry Holofcener—George Weiss. (I)Musical: *Mr. Wonderful* by Sammy Davis, Jr.

TOO DARN HOT (1949) (wm)Cole Porter. (I)Musical: *Kiss Me Kate* by Lorenzo Fuller, Fred Davis and Eddie Sledge. Film version (1953) by Ann Miller.

TOO FAT POLKA (1947) (wm)Ross MacLean—Arthur Richardson. (P)Arthur Godfrey.

TOO GOOD FOR THE AVERAGE MAN (1936) (w)Lorenz Hart (m)Richard Rodgers. (I)Musical: *On Your Toes* by Monty Wooley and Luella Gear.

TOO HOT (1980) (wm)George Brown. (P)Kool and the Gang.

TOO LATE FOR GOODBYES (1985) (wm)Julian Lennon. (P)Julian Lennon.

TOO LATE NOW (1951) (w)Alan Jay Lerner (m)Burton Lane. (I)Film: *Royal Wedding* by Jane Powell.

TOO LATE TO TURN BACK NOW (1972) (wm)Eddie Cornelius. (P)Cornelius Brothers and Sister Rose.

TOO MANY MORNINGS (1971) (wm)Stephen Sondheim. (I)Musical: *Follies* with Alexis Smith and Yvonne De Carlo.

TOO MANY RINGS AROUND ROSIE (1924) (w)Irving Caesar (m)Vincent Youmans. (I)Musical: *No, No, Nanette* by Josephine Whittell and chorus.

TOO MANY RIVERS (1964) (wm)Harlan Howard. (P)Brenda Lee.

TOO MANY TEARS (1932) (w)Al Dubin (m)Harry Warren. (P)Guy Lombardo and his Royal Canadians. No. 1 Chart Record.

TOO MARVELOUS FOR WORDS (1937) (w)Johnny Mercer (m)Richard A. Whiting. (I)Film: *Ready, Willing And Able* by Wini Shaw and Ross Alexander. Film: *On The Sunny Side Of The Street* (1951) by Frankie Laine.

TOO MUCH (1956) (wm)Bernard Weinman. (P)Elvis Presley. No. 1 Chart Record.

TOO MUCH HEAVEN (1979) (wm)Barry Gibb—Maurice Gibb—Robin Gibb. (P)The Bee Gees. No. 1 Chart Record.

TOO MUCH TALK (AND NOT ENOUGH ACTION) (1968) (wm)Mark Lasley. (P)Paul Rever and the Raiders.

TOO MUCH TIME ON MY HANDS (1981) (wm)Tommy Shaw. (P)Styx.

TOO MUCH, TOO LITTLE, TOO LATE (1978) (wm)Nat

Kipner—John Vallins. (P)Johnny Mathis and Deniece Williams.

TOO OLD TO CUT THE MUSTARD (1951) (wm)Bill Carlisle. (P)Red Foley and Ernest Tubb. (P)Marlene Dietrich and Rosemary Clooney.

TOO ROMANTIC (1940) (w)Johnny Burke (m)James V. Monaco. (I)Film: *The Road To Singapore* by Bing Crosby and Dorothy Lamour.

TOO SHY (1983) (wm)Limahl Beggs—Nick Beggs. (P)Kajagoogoo.

TOO WEAK TO FIGHT (1968) (wm)John M. Keyes—Clarence Carter—Rick Hall—George Jackson. (P)Clarence Carter.

TOO YOUNG (1951) (w)Sylvia Dee (m)Sid Lippman. (P)Nat Cole.

TOO YOUNG TO GO STEADY (1955) (w)Harold Adamson (m)Jimmy McHugh. (I)Musical: *Strip For Action*. (P)Nat Cole.

TOO—RA—LOO—RA—LOO—RAL (That's An Irish Lullaby) (1914) (wm)James R. Shannon. (P)Chauncey Olcott. (R)Film: *Going My Way* by Bing Crosby.

TOODLE—OO, SO LONG, GOOD—BYE (1931) (wm)Rudy Vallee—Byron Gay. (I)Rudy Vallee.

TOOT TOOT TOOTSIE (1922) (wm)Gus Kahn—Ernie Erdman—Ted Fiorito—Robert A. King. (I)Musical: *Bombo* by Al Jolson. Film: *The Jazz Singer* (1927) by Al Jolson. Film: *Rose Of Washington Square* (1939) by Al Jolson. Film: *The Jolson Story* (1946) by Jolson dubbing for Larry Parks. Film: *Jolson Sings Again* (1949) by Jolson dubbing for Larry Parks. Film: *I'Ll See You In My Dreams* (1951) by Doris Day.

TOP HAT, WHITE TIE AND TAILS (1935) (wm)Irving Berlin. (I)Film: *Top Hat* by Fred Astaire.

TOP OF THE WORLD (1973) (wm)Richard Carpenter—John Bettis. (P)The Carpenters.

TOPSY (1958) (m)Edgar Battle—Eddie Durham. (P)Cozy Cole.

TORCH SONG, THE (1931) (w)Mort Dixon—Joe Young (m)Harry Warren. (I)Musical: *The Laugh Parade* by Bartlett Simmons.

TOREADOR SONG, THE (1875) (m)Georges Bizet. (I)Opera: *Carmen*. One of the most famous arias for baritone singers.

TORERO (1958) (w—Eng)Al Hoffman—Dick Manning (m)Renato Carosone. (P)Renato Carosone.

TORMENTED (1936) (wm)Will Hudson. (P)Richard Himber and his Orchestra. Also recorded by Wingy Manone and his Orchestra.

TORN BETWEEN TWO LOVERS (1977) (wm)Phil Jarrell—Peter Yarrow. (P)Mary MacGregor.

TORTURE (1962) (wm)John Loudermilk. (P)Kris Jensen.

TOSSIN' AND TURNIN' (1961) (wm)Malou Rene—Ritchie Adams. (P)Bobby Lewis.

TOTAL ECLIPSE OF THE HEART (1983) (wm)Jim Steinman. (P)Bonnie Tyler. Number one chart record.

TOTEM TOM TOM (1924) (w)Otto Harbach—Oscar Hammerstein II (m)Rudolf Friml. (I)Operetta: *Rose—Marie* by Pearl Regay and chorus. Film version 1936 by chorus. Film starred Nelson Eddy and Jeanette MacDonald

TOUCH ME (1969) (wm)James Morrison—John Densmore—Robert Krieger—Raymond Manzarek. (P)The Doors.

TOUCH ME (1974) (wm)Mike Hurst—Raymond Fenwick. (P)Fancy.

TOUCH ME (I Want Your Body) (1986) (wm)M. Shreeve—J. Astrop—P. Q. Harris. (P)Samantha Fox.

TOUCH ME IN THE MORNING (1973) (wm)Michael Masser—Ron Miller. (P)Diana Ross.

TOUCH OF GREY (1987) (wm)J. Garcia—R. Hunter. (P)The Grateful Dead.

TOUCH OF TEXAS, A (1942) (w)Frank Loesser (m)Jimmy McHugh. (I)Film: *Seven Days' Leave*. (P)Freddy Martin and his Orchestra.

TOUCH OF YOUR HAND, THE (1933) (w)Otto Harbach (m)Jerome Kern. (I)Musical: *Roberta* by Tamara and William Hain. Film version with Fred Astaire, Ginger Rogers and Irene Dunne. Film: *Lovely To Look At* with Howard Keel and Kathryn Grayson.

TOUCH OF YOUR LIPS, THE (1936) (wm)Ray Noble. (P)Ray Noble and his Orchestra, vocal by Al Bowlly.

TOWER OF STRENGTH (1961) (w)Bob Hilliard (m)Burt Bacharach. (P)Gene McDaniels.

TOWN WITHOUT PITY (1961) (w)Ned Washington (m)Dimitri Tiomkin. (I)Film: *Town Without Pity* by Gene Pitney. (P)Gene Pitney.

TOY TRUMPET, THE (1937) (w)Sidney D. Mitchell—Lew Pollack (m)Raymond Scott. (P)Instrumentally by The Raymond Scott Quintet. Words added 1938. Lyric version in film *Rebecca Of Sunnybrook Farm* by Shirley Temple, danced to by Bill Robinson, played by The Raymond Scott Quintet.

TOYLAND (1903) (w)Glen MacDonough (m)Victor Herbert. (I)Musical: *Babes In Toyland*. Film version with Laurel and Hardy.

TRACES (1969) (wm)Buddy Buie—Emory Gordy, Jr. —James B. Cobb, Jr. (P)The Classics IV.

TRACKS OF MY TEARS, THE (1967) (wm)Warren Moore—Wm. "Smokey" Robinson—Marvin Tarpin. (P)The Miracles. (R)1976 by Linda Ronstadt.

TRACY (1969) (wm)Lee Pockriss—Paul Vance. (P)The Cuff Links.

TRACY'S THEME (1960) (w)Roz Gordon (m)Robert Ascher. (I)TV Special: The Philadelphia Story. (P)Spencer Ross.

TRADE WINDS (1940) (wm)Charles Tobias—Cliff Friend. (P)Bing Crosby. No. 1 Chart Record.

TRADITION (1964) (w)Sheldon Harnick (m)Jerry Bock. (I)Musical: Fiddler On The Roof by Zero Mostel and chorus. Film version with Topol and chorus.

TRAFFIC JAM (1939) (m)Teddy McRae—Artie Shaw. (P)Artie Shaw and his Orchestra. Film: Dancing Co—Ed with Lana Turner and Richard Carlson, performed by Artie Shaw and his Orchestra.

TRAGEDY (1959) (wm)Gerald H. Nelson—Fred B. Burch. (P)Thomas Wayne.

TRAGEDY (1979) (wm)Barry Gibb—Maurice Gibb—Robin Gibb. (P)The Bee Gees.

TRAIL OF THE LONESOME PINE, THE (1913) (w)Ballard MacDonald (m)Harry Carroll. (P)Henry Burr and Albert Campbell.

TRAINS AND BOATS AND PLANES (1965) (w)Hal David (m)Burt Bacharach. (P)Dionne Warwick.

TRAMP! TRAMP! TRAMP! ALONG THE HIGHWAY (1910) (w)Rida Johnson Young (m)Victor Herbert. (I)Musical: Naughty Marietta with Emma Trentini and Orville Harold. Film version with Nelson Eddy and Jeanette MacDonald

TRAMP, TRAMP, TRAMP (The Boys Are Marching) (1864) (wm)George Frederic Root. Famous song during the Civil War.

TRANSFUSION (1956) (wm)Jimmy Drake. (P)Nervous Norvus.

TRAPPED BY A THING CALLED LOVE (1971) (wm)O. Denise Jones. (P)Denise LaSalle.

TRAUMEREI (1839) (m)Robert Schumann. Very famous classical selection. From suite *Children'S Scenes.*

TRAV'LIN' ALL ALONE (1930) (wm)J. C. Johnson. (I)Ethel Waters. (P)Jimmie Noone and his Orchestra. (R)1937 by Billie Holiday.

TRAVELIN' BAND (1970) (wm)John C. Fogarty. (P)Creedence Clearwater Revival.

TRAVELIN' MAN (1961) (wm)Jerry Fuller. (P)Ricky Nelson.

TREASURE OF LOVE (1956) (wm)J. Shapiro—Lou Stallman. (P)Clyde McPhatter.

TREAT HER LIKE A LADY (1971) (wm)Eddie Cornelius. (P)Cornelius Brothers and Sister Rose.

TREAT HER RIGHT (1965) (wm)Roy Head. (P)Roy Head.

TREAT ME NICE (1957) (wm)Mike Stoller—Jerry Leiber. (I)Film: Jailhouse Rock by Elvis Presley. (P)Elvis Presley.

TREAT ME ROUGH (1930) (w)Ira Gershwin (m)George Gershwin. (I)Musical: *Girl Crazy* by William Kent. Film version (1943) with Judy Garland, Mickey Rooney and June Allyson.

TREE IN THE MEADOW, A (1948) (wm)Billy Reid. (P)Margaret Whiting.

TREE IN THE PARK, A (1926) (w)Lorenz Hart (m)Richard Rodgers. (I)Musical: *Peggy Ann* by Lester Cole and Helen Ford.

TREES (1922) (w)Joyce Kilmer (m)Oscar Rasbach. The words are from a poem by Kilmer. (I)Film: *The Big Broadcast* (1932) by Donald Novis.

TROGLODYTE (Cave Man) (1972) (wm)Harry Jensen—Gerald Thomas—Douglas Gibson—Robert Manigault—James Castor—Langdon Fridie. (P)Jimmy Castor.

TROLLEY SONG, THE (1944) (wm)Hugh Martin—Ralph Blane. (I)Film: *Meet Me In St. Louis* by Judy Garland.

TROPICANA (1953) (m)Bernie Wayne. (P)Monty Kelly and his Orchestra.

TROUBLE (1982) (wm)Lindsey Buckingham. (P)Lindsey Buckingham.

TROUBLE IN PARADISE (1960) (wm)Allison R. Khent—Billy Dawn Smith. (P)The Crests.

TROUBLE IN RIVER CITY (1957) (wm)Meredith Willson. (I)Musical: *The Music Man* starring Robert Preston. Also in film version with Preston.

TRUCKIN' (1935) (w)Ted Koehler (m)Rube Bloom. (I)*Cotton Club Revue* by Cora La Redd and The Ensemble.

TRUE (1983) (wm)Gary Kemp. (P)Spandau Ballet.

TRUE (1934) (wm)Walter G. Samuels—Leonard Whitcup. (P)Enric Madriguera and his Orchestra. (R)1948 by Billy Eckstein.

TRUE BLUE (1986) (wm)Madonna—Steve Bray. (P)Madonna.

TRUE BLUE LOU (1929) (w)Sam Coslow (m)Richard A. Whiting. (I)Film: *The Dance Of Life* by Hal Skelly.

TRUE COLORS (1986) (wm)Tom Kelly—Billy Steinberg. (P)Cyndi Lauper. Number one chart record.

TRUE CONFESSION (1937) (wm)Sam Coslow—Frederick Hollander. (I)Theme of film *True Confession* with Carole Lombard and Fred MacMurray.

TRUE GRIT (1969) (w)Don Black (m)Elmer Bernstein. (I)Theme of film *True Grit* with John Wayne. (P)Glen Campbell.

TRUE LOVE (1956) (wm)Cole Porter. (I)Film: *High Society* by Bing Crosby and Grace Kelly.

TRUE LOVE (I Had Myself A) (1946) (w)Johnny Mercer (m)Harold Arlen. (I)Musical: *St. Louis Woman* by June Hawkins.

TRUE LOVE WAYS (1958) (wm)Norman Petty—Buddy Holly. (P)Peter and Gordon (1969).

TRULY (1982) (wm)Lionel Richie, Jr. (P)Lionel Richie. Number one chart record.

TRUST IN ME (1934) (w)Ned Wever (m)Jean Schwartz—Milton Ager. Not a hit when first published. (R)1961 by Etta James.

TRY A LITTLE TENDERNESS (1932) (wm)Harry Woods—Jimmy Campbell—Reg Connelly. (P)Ruth Etting. (R)1967 by Otis Redding.

TRY IT BABY (1964) (wm)Berry Gordy, Jr. (P)Marvin Gaye.

TRY ME ONE MORE TIME (1943) (wm)Ernest Tubb. (P)Ernest Tubb.

TRY TO FORGET (1931) (w)Otto Harbach (m)Jerome Kern. (I)Musical: *The Cat And The Fiddle* by Bettina Hall, Eddie Foy, Jr. and Doris Carson. Film version (1934) by Jeanette Ma

TRY TO REMEMBER (1960) (w)Tom Jones (m)Harvey Schmidt. (I)Off Broadway Musical: *The Fantasticks* by Jerry Ohrbach. (P)The Brothers Four. (P)Ed Ames. (R)Gladys Knight and The Pips, in medley with "The Way We Were."

TRY TOO HARD (1966) (wm)Dave Clark—Mike Smith. (P)The Dave Clark Five.

TRYIN' TO GET THE FEELIN' AGAIN (1976) (wm)David Pomeranz. (P)Barry Manilow.

TRYIN' TO LIVE MY LIFE WITHOUT YOU (1981) (wm)Eugene Williams. (P)J. Geils Band (1981). (P)Bob Seger.

TRYIN' TO LOVE TWO (1977) (wm)Paul Mitchell—William Bell. (P)William Bell.

TRYING (1952) (wm)Billy Vaughn. (P)The Hilltoppers.

TRYING TO HOLD ON TO MY WOMAN (1974) (wm)McKinley Jackson—James Reddick. (P)Lamont Dozier.

TSCHAIKOWSKY (1941) (w)Ira Gershwin (m)Kurt Weill. (I)Musical: *Lady In The Dark* by Danny Kaye.

TUBBY THE TUBA (1948) (w)George Kleinsinger (m)Paul Tripp. Popular composition for children.

TUBULAR BELLS (Exorcist Theme) (1974) (m)Mike Oldfield. (I)Theme from film *The Exorcist.* (P)Mike Oldfield.

TUCK ME TO SLEEP IN MY OLD 'TUCKY HOME (1921) (w)Sam M. Lewis—Joe Young (m)George W. Meyer. (P)Al Jolson.

TUFF (1961) (m)Ace Cannon. (P)Ace Cannon.

TUFF ENUF (1986) (wm)K. Wilson. (P)The Fabulous Thunderbirds.

TULIPS AND HEATHER (1951) (wm)Milton Carson. (P)Perry Como.

TUMBLING DICE (1972) (wm)Mick Jagger—Keith Richards. (P)The Rolling Stones.

TUMBLING TUMBLEWEEDS (1934) (wm)Bob Nolan. (I)Film: *Tumbling Tumbleweeds* by Gene Autry. (P)Bing Crosby. Film: *Don'T Fence Me In* (1945) by Gene Autry. Film: *Silver Spurs* (1943) by Roy Rogers. Film: *Hollywood Canteen* (1944) by The Sons of the Pioneers.

TUNNEL OF LOVE (1987) (wm)Bruce Springsteen. (P)Bruce Springsteen.

TURKEY IN THE STRAW or OLD ZIP COON (1834)Traditional folk song.

TURN AROUND, LOOK AT ME (1968) (wm)Jerry Capehart. (P)The Vogues.

TURN BACK THE HAND OF TIME (1951) (wm)Jimmy Eaton—Larry WagnerCon Hammond. (P)Eddie Fisher.

TURN BACK THE HANDS OF TIME (1970) (wm)Jack Daniels—Bonnie Thompson. (P)Tyrone Davis.

TURN DOWN THE DAY (1966) (wm)Jerry Keller—David Blume. (P)The Cyrkle.

TURN ME LOOSE (1959) (wm)Jerome "Doc" Pomus—Mort Shuman. (P)Fabian.

TURN OFF THE MOON (1937) (wm)Sam Coslow. (I)Film: *Turn Off The Moon* by Kenny Baker. (P)Mal Hallet.

TURN ON THE HEAT (1929) (w)B. G. De Sylva—Lew Brown (m)Ray Henderson. (I)Film: *Sunny Side Up* by Sharon Lynn and Frank Richardson. Film: *The Best Things In Life Are Free* (1956) danced by Gordon McRae and Sheree North.

TURN OUT THE LIGHT (1932) (w)B. G. De Sylva (m)Richard A. Whiting—Nacio Herb Brown. (I)Musical: *Take A Chance* by Sid Silvers, Jack Haley, June Knight and Jack Whiting. Film version with Charles "Buddy" Rogers and James Dunn.

TURN THE BEAT AROUND (LOVE TO HEAR PERCUSSION) (1975) (wm)Peter Jackson—Gerald Jackson. (P)Vickie Sue Robinson.

TURN TO STONE (1977) (wm)Jeff Lynne. (P)Electric Light Orchestra.

TURN YOUR LOVE AROUND (1982) (wm)Jay Graydon—Steve Lukather—Bill Champlin. (P)George Benson. NARAS award winner: R & B Song of the Year, 1982.

TURN! TURN! TURN! (1965) (wm)Pete Seeger. (P)The Byrds. No. 1 Chart Record.

TUSH (1975) (wm)Billy Gibbons—Joe Hill—Frank Beard. (P)ZZ Top.

TUSK (1979) (wm)Lindsey Buckingham. (P)Fleetwood Mac.

TUTTI—FRUTTI (1938) (wm)Doris Fisher—Slim Gaillard. (P)Slim and Slam (Slim Gaillard and Slam Stewart).

TUTTI—FRUTTI (1955) (wm)Richard Penniman—D. La-Bostrie—Joe Lubin. (P)Little Richard. (CR)Pat Boone.

TUXEDO JUNCTION (1940) (wm)Erskine Hawkins—Julian Dash—Buddy Feyne—William Johnson. (P)Erskine Hawkins and his Orchestra. (R)Glenn Miller and his Orchestra. Film: *The Glenn Miller Story* with James Stewart.

'TWAS NOT SO LONG AGO (1929) (w)Oscar Hammerstein, II (m)Jerome Kern. (I)Musical: *Sweet Adeline* by Helen Morgan. Film version (1934) by Irene Dunne, Phil Regan, Joseph Cawthorn, Hugh Herber

TWEEDLE—O—TWILL (1942) (wm)Gene Autry—Fred Rose. (I)Film: *Home In Wyoming* by Gene Autry. (P)Gene Autry.

TWEEDLEE DEE (1955) (wm)Winfield Scott. (P)Lavern Baker. (R)Georgia Gibbs.

TWELFTH OF NEVER, THE (1957) (w)Paul Francis Webster (m)Jerry Livingston. (P)Johnny Mathis.

TWELFTH STREET RAG (1914) (m)Euday L. Bowman. (P)Earl Fuller. Very popular jazz composition.

TWELVE DAYS OF CHRISTMAS (1700)Traditional Christmas song from England.

TWELVE THIRTY (YOUNG GIRLS ARE COMING TO THE CANYON) (1967) (wm)John Phillips. (P)The Mamas and The Papas.

TWENTIETH CENTURY BLUES (1931) (wm)Noel Coward. (I)Play: *Cavalcade* (English) by Binnie Barnes.

20 MILES (1963) (w)Kal Mann (m)Bernie Lowe. (P)Chubby Checker.

25 OR 6 TO 4 (1970) (wm)Robert Lamm (P)Chicago.

TWENTY—FIVE MILES (1969) (wm)Johnny W. Bristol—Harvey Fuqua—Edwin Starr—Jerry Wexler—Bert Berns. (P)Edwin Starr.

TWENTY—FOUR HOURS FROM TULSA (1963) (w)Hal David (m)Burt Bacharach. (P)Gene Pitney.

TWENTY—FOUR HOURS OF SUNSHINE (1949) (w)Carl Sigman (m)Peter De Rose. (P)Art Mooney and his Orchestra.

TWENTY—SIX MILES (1958) (wm)Glenn Larson—Bruce Belland. (P)The Four Preps.

(I LOVE YOU) TWICE AS MUCH (1953) (wm)Royce Swain. (P)The Mills Brothers.

TWILIGHT IN TURKEY (1937) (m)Raymond Scott. (P)The Raymond Scott Quintet. Film: *Ali Baba Goes To Town* with Eddie Cantor and Tony Martin.

TWILIGHT ON THE TRAIL (1936) (w)Sidney D. Mitchell (m)Louis Alter. (I)Film: *The Trail Of The Lonesome Pine* by Fuzzy Knight.

TWILIGHT TIME (1944) (w)Buck Ram (m)Morty Nevins—Al Nevins—Artie Dunn. (P)The Three Suns. (R)1958 by The Platters.

TWINE TIME (1965) (m)Andre Williams—Verlie Rice. (P)Alvin Cash and The Crawlers.

TWINKLE, TWINKLE LITTLE STAR (1936) (w)Herb Magidson (m)Ben Oakland. Not the traditional nursery song. (I)Film: *Hats Off* by John Payne and Mae Clarke.

TWIST AND SHOUT (1962) (wm)Bert Russell—Phil Medley. (P)The Isley Brothers. (R)1964 by The Beatles.

TWIST OF FATE (1984) (wm)Steven Kipner—Peter Beckett. (I)Film: *Two Of A Kind*, 1983. (P)Olivia Newton—John.

TWIST, THE (1960) (wm)Hank Ballard. (P)Hank Ballard (P)Chubby Checker. (R)1962 by Chubby Checker.

TWIST, TWIST SENORA (1962) (wm)Frank J. Guida—Gene Barge—Joseph Royster. (P)Gary U. S. Bonds.

TWISTIN' THE NIGHT AWAY (1962) (wm)Sam Cooke. (P)Sam Cooke.

TWISTIN' U. S. A. (1960) (wm)Kal Mann. (P)Danny and The Juniors.

TWIXT TWELVE AND TWENTY (1959) (wm)Aaron Schroeder—Fredda Gold. (P)Pat Boone.

TWO BLIND LOVES (1939) (w)E. Y. Harburg (m)Harold Arlen. (I)Film: *At The Circus* by Kenny Baker and Florence Rice. (P)Kenny Baker.

TWO BOUQUETS (1938) (wm)Jimmy Kennedy—Michael Carr. (I)Film: *Kickin' The Moon Around*. (P)Guy Lomabardo and his Royal Canadians.

TWO CIGARETTES IN THE DARK (1934) (w)Paul Francis Webster (m)Lew Pollack. (I)Play: *Kill That Story* by Gloria Grafton.

TWO DIFFERENT WORLDS (1956) (w)Sid Wayne (m)Al Frisch. (P)Don Rondo.

TWO DIVIDED BY LOVE (1971) (wm)Dennis Lambert—Brian Potter—Marty Kupps. (P)The Grass Roots.

TWO DOORS DOWN (1978) (wm)Dolly Parton. (P)Dolly Parton.

TWO DREAMS MET (1940) (w)Mack Gordon (m)Harry

Warren. (I)Film: *Down Argentina Way* by Six Hits and a Miss, Don Ameche, Betty Grable. (P)Mitchell Ayres and his Orchestra. (CR)Tommy Dorsey and his Orchestra.

TWO FACES HAVE I (1963) (wm)Twyla Herbert—Lou Sacco. (P)Lou Christie.

TWO FACES IN THE DARK (1958) (w)Dorothy Fields (m)Albert Hague. (I)Musical: *Redhead* by Bob Dixon.

TWO FOR THE ROAD (Theme from) (1967) (m)Henry Mancini. (I)Film: *Two For The Road* with Audrey Hepburn and Albert Finney.

TWO GUITARS (1925) (m)Harry Horlick. Traditional Russian Gypsy folk song. (I)Theme song of Harry Horlick and his Orchestra on the *Atlantic And Pacific Radio Hour.*

TWO HEARTS (1954) (wm)Otis Williams—Henry Stone. (P)Pat Boone.

TWO HEARTS ARE BETTER THAN ONE (1946) (w)Leo Robin (m)Jerome Kern. (I)Film: *Centennial Summer* with Cornel Wilde, Jeanne Crain and Walter Brennan.

TWO HEARTS IN THREE QUARTER TIME (1930) (w—Eng)Joe Young (m)Robert Stolz. Very popular waltz from Germany. German film *Two Hearts In Waltz Time* with Walter Janseen and Willy Forst.

TWO IN LOVE (1941) (wm)Meredith Willson. (P)Tommy Dorsey and his Orchestra with vocal by Frank Sinatra.

TWO LADIES (1972) (w)Fred Ebb (m)John Kander. (I)Film version only of *Cabaret* with Liza Minnelli and Joel Grey.

TWO LADIES IN DE SHADE OF DE BANANA TREE (1955) (wm)Truman Capote—Harold Arlen. (I)Musical: *House Of Flowers* by Ada Moore and Enid Mosier.

TWO LITTLE BABES IN THE WOODS (1928) (wm)Cole Porter. (I)Revue: *Greenwich Village Follies Of 1924* by Julia Silver and Georgie Hale. Play: PARIS by Irene Bordoni.

TWO LITTLE BLUEBIRDS (1925) (w)Oscar Hammerstein II (m)Jerome Kern. (I)Musical: *Sunny* by Clifton Webb and Mary Hay.

TWO LOST SOULS (1955) (wm)Richard Adler—Jerry Ross. (I)Musical: *Damn Yankees* by Gwen Verdon and Stephen Douglass. Film production with Gwen Verdon.

TWO LOVERS (1963) (wm)Wm. "Smokey" Robinson, Jr. (P)Mary Wells.

TWO LOVES HAVE I (1931) (w—Eng)J. P. Murray—Barry Trivers (m)Vincent Scotto. (P)In France by Josephine Baker, U. S. by Irene Bordoni.

TWO O'CLOCK JUMP (1941) (m)Harry James—Count Basie—Benny Goodman. (P)Harry James and his Orchestra.

TWO OF HEARTS (1986) (wm)John Mitchell—Sue Gatlin—Tim Greene. (P)Stacey Q (Stacey Swain).

TWO OUT OF THREE AIN'T BAD (1977) (wm)Jim Steinman. (P)Meat Loaf.

TWO SILHOUETTES (1945) (w)Ray Gilbert (m)Charles Wolcott. (I)Cartoon Film: *Make Mine Music* by voice of Dinah Shore.

TWO SLEEPY PEOPLE (1938) (w)Frank Loesser (m)Hoagy Carmichael. (I)Film: *Thanks For The Memory* with Bob Hope and Shirley Ross. (R)Musical: *Ain'T Misbehavin'*

TWO TICKETS TO GEORGIA (1933) (wm)Joe Young—Charles Tobias—J. Fred Coots. (P)Ted Lewis. (R)The Pickens Sisters.

TYPEWRITER, THE (1951) (m)Leroy Anderson. (I)Leroy Anderson.

TYPICAL MALE (1986) (wm)Terry Britten—Graham Lyle. (P)Tina Turner.

TYPICAL SELF—MADE AMERICAN, A (1930) (w)Ira Gershwin (m)George Gershwin. (I)Musical: *Strike Up The Band* by Dudley Clements, Jerry Goff and chorus.

TZENA, TZENA, TZENA (1950) (w—Eng)Mitchell Parish (m)Julius Grossman—Issachar Miron. From the book *Songs Of Israel.* (P)The Weavers with Gordon Jenkins and his Orchestra.

U GOT THE LOOK (1987) (wm)Prince. (P)Prince.

U. S. AIR FORCE SONG (See THE ARMY AIR CORPS SONG)

U. S. FIELD ARTILLERY MARCH or THE CAISSONS GO ROLLING ALONG (1918) (wm)Edmund L. Gruber. (I)Marching song of The U. S. Field Artillery.

UGLY DUCKLING, THE (1952) (wm)Frank Loesser. (I)Film: *Hans Christian Andersen* with Danny Kaye.

UH! OH! (The Nutty Squirrels) (1959) (wm)Granville Burland—Don Elliott. (P)The Nutty Squirrels.

UKELELE LADY (1925) (w)Gus Kahn (m)Richard A. Whiting. (P)Vaughn De Leath and Nick Lucas. Film: *I'LL See You In My Dreams* (1951) by the chorus.

UM, UM, UM, UM, UM, UM (1964) (wm)Curtis Mayfield. (P)Major Lance.

UMBRELLA MAN, THE (1938) (wm)James Cavanaugh—Vincent Rose—Larry Stock. (P)Guy Lombardo and his Royal Canadians. Film: *Garden Of The Moon* with Pat O'Brien and Margaret Lindsay.

UMBRELLAS OF CHERBOURG, THE (Theme from) (See I WILL WAIT FO

UN BEL DI or ONE FINE DAY (1904) (m)Giacomo Puccini. (I)Opera: *Madame Butterfly*. One of the most popular arias for soprano singers.

UNBORN CHILD (1974) (wm)Louise Bogan—James Seals. (P)Seals & Crofts.

UNCHAIN MY HEART (1961) (wm)Freddy James—Agnes Jones. (P)Ray Charles.

UNCHAINED MELODY (1955) (w)Hy Zaret (m)Alex North. (I)Theme from film *Unchained*. (P)Instrumentally by Les Baxter and his Orchestra. (P)Vocally by Al Hibbler.

UNCLE ALBERT/ADMIRAL HALSEY (1971) (wm)Paul McCartney—Linda McCartney. (P)Paul McCartney.

UNCLE JOHN'S BAND (1970) (wm)Robert Hunter—Jerry Garcia. (P)The Grateful Dead.

UNCLE PEN (1951) (wm)Bill Monroe. (P)Porter Wagoner.

UNCLE REMUS SAID (1946) (wm)Johnny Lange—Hy Heath—Eliot Daniel. (I)Film: *Song Of The South* by The Hall Johnson Choir.

UNDECIDED (1939) (w)Sid Robin (m)Charlie Shavers. (P)Chick Webb and his Orchestra, vocal by Ella Fitzgerald. (R)1951 by The Ames Brothers.

UNDER A BLANKET OF BLUE (1933) (w)Marty Symes—Al J. Neiberg (m)Jerry Livingston. (P)Glen Gray and The Casa Loma Orchestra.

UNDER A TEXAS MOON (1929) (w-Eng)Ray Perkins (w-Sp)Jimenez Gonzalez. (I)Film: *Under A Texas Moon* (1930) by Frank Fay, George E. Stone, and George Cooper. (P)Guy Lombardo.

UNDER MY THUMB (1966) (wm)Mick Jagger—Keith Richard. (P)The Rolling Stones.

UNDER PARIS SKIES (1953) (w-Eng)Kim Gannon (m)Hubert Giraud. (P)Mitch Miller and his Orchestra.

UNDER THE BAMBOO TREE (1902) (wm)Robert Cole—J. Rosamund Johnson. (P)Arthur Collins. Musicals: *Sally In Our Alley* and *Nancy Brown*. Film: *Meet Me In St. Louis* with Judy Garland.

UNDER THE BOARDWALK (1964) (wm)Arthur Resnick—Kenny Young. (P)The Drifters.

UNDER THE BRIDGES OF PARIS (1931) (wm)Vincent Scotto—Jean Rodor—Dorcas Cochran. No artist credited with introduction.

UNDER THE DOUBLE EAGLE (1850) (m)Josef Franz Wagner. Famous march.

UNDER THE YUM YUM TREE (1910) (w)Andrew B. Sterling (m)Harry Von Tilzer. (P)Arthur Collins and Byron Harlan. Film: *Wharf Angel* with Dorothy Dell and Preston Foster.

UNDER YOUR SPELL AGAIN (1960) (wm)Dusty Rhodes—Buck Owens. (P)Johnny Rivers (1965).

UNDERCOVER ANGEL (1977) (wm)Alan O'Day. (P)Alan O'Day.

UNDERCOVER OF THE NIGHT (1983) (wm)Mick Jagger—Keith Richards. (P)The Rolling Stones.

UNDERNEATH THE ARCHES (1933) (wm)Reg Connelly—Bud Flanagan—Joseph McCarthy. (P)England by Flanagan and Allen. (R)1948 in England by Primo Scala's Banjo and Accordion Orchestra.

UNDERNEATH THE HARLEM MOON (1932) (w)Mack Gordon (m)Harry Revel. (P)Joe Rines and his Orchestra. Other popular versions by Don Redman and his Orchestra, Chick Bullock and his Orchestra, and Fletcher Henderson and his Orchestra.

UNDERSTAND YOUR MAN (1964) (wm)Johnny Cash. (P)Johnny Cash.

UNDERSTANDING (IS THE BEST THING IN THE WORLD) (1967) (wm)Jimmy Holiday—Ray Charles. (P)Ray Charles (1968).

UNDUN (1969) (wm)Randall C. Bachman. (P)The Guess Who.

UNEASY RIDER (1973) (wm)Charlie Daniels. (P)Charlie Daniels.

UNFORGETTABLE (1951) (wm)Irving Gordon. (P)Nat Cole.

UNFORGIVEN, THE (The Need for Love) (1960) (w)Ned Washington (m)Dimitri Tiomkin. Adapted from theme from film *The Unforgiven* with Audrey Hepburn and Burt Lancaster. (P)Instrumentally by Don Costa and his Orchestra.

UNICORN, THE (1968) (wm)Shel Silverstein. (P)The Irish Rovers.

UNION MAN (1976) (wm)Earl Cate—Ernie Cate. (P)The Cate Brothers.

UNION OF THE SNAKE (1983) (wm)Duran Duran. (P)Duran Duran.

UNITED (1968) (wm)Kenny Gamble—Leon Huff. (P)Peaches and Herb.

UNITED WE STAND (1971) (wm)Tony Hiller—Peter Simons. (P)Brotherhood of Man.

UNIVERSAL SOLDIER, THE (1963) (wm)Buffy Sainte-Marie. (P)Buffy Sainte-Marie. (R)1965 Glen Campbell. (R)1965 Donovan.

UNLESS (1934) (wm)Robert Hargreaves—Stanley J. Damerell—Tolchard Evans—Henry B. Tilsley. (P)Henry Hall and the BBC Orchestra. (R)1951 Guy Mitchell. Also recorded by Eddie Fisher and Gordon Jenkins.

UNLOVED AND UNCLAIMED (1948) (wm)Roy Acuff—Vito Pellettieri. (P)Roy Acuff.

UNLUCKY IN LOVE (1924) (wm)Irving Berlin. (I)MUSIC BOX *Revue Of 1924* with Oscar Shaw, Fanny Brice and Grace Moore.

UNSQUARE DANCE (1961) (m)Dave Brubeck. (P)The Dave Brubeck Quartet.

UNSUSPECTING HEART (1955) (wm)Freddy James—Joe Beal—Bob Singer—Joe Shank. (P)Georgie Shaw.

UNTIL IT'S TIME FOR YOU TO GO (1965) (wm)Buffy Sainte Marie. (P)Buffy Sainte Marie. (R)In 1970s by Elvis Presley, Neil Diamond.

UNTIL THE REAL THING COMES ALONG (1936) (wm)Sammy Cahn—Saul Chaplin—L. E. Freeman—Mann Holiner (P)Andy Kirk and his Clouds of Joy, vocal by Pha Terrell.

UNTIL TODAY (1936) (w)Benny Davis (m)J. Fred Coots—Oscar Levant. (P)Fletcher Henderson and Nat Brandywynne.

UNTIL TOMORROW (1940) (wm)Sammy Kaye. (P)Sammy Kaye and his Orchestra.

UNTIL YOU COME BACK TO ME (1973) (wm)Clarence Paul—Morris Broadnax. (P)Aretha Franklin.

UNTOUCHABLES, THE (Theme from) (1959) (m)Nelson Riddle. (I)Theme of TV Series: *The Untouchables.*

UP A LAZY RIVER (See LAZY RIVER)

UP ABOVE MY HEAD, I HEAR MUSIC IN THE AIR (1949) (wm)Sister Rosetta Tharpe. (P)Sister Rosetta Tharpe.

UP AROUND THE BEND (1970) (wm)John C. Fogerty. (P)Creedence Clearwater Revival.

UP IN A PUFF OF SMOKE (1974) (wm)Gerald Shury—Philip Swern. (P)Polly Brown.

UP IN THE CLOUDS (1927) (w)Bert Kalmar (m)Harry Ruby. (I)Musical: *The Five O'Clock Girl* by Oscar Shaw and Mary Eaton. (P)Elizabeth Spencer and Lewis James. Film: *Three Little Words* (1950) by chorus.

UP ON CRIPPLE CREEK (1969) (wm)Jaime Robbie Robertson. (P)The Band.

UP ON THE ROOF (1963) (wm)Carole King—Gerry Goffin. (P)The Drifters.

UP THE LADDER TO THE ROOF (1970) (wm)Vincent Dimirco—Frank Wilson. (P)The Supremes.

UP WHERE WE BELONG (1982) (wm)Jack Nitzsche—Will Jennings—Buffy Sainte Marie. (I)Film: *An Officer And A Gentleman.* (P)Joe Cocker and Jennifer Warnes. Academy Award winner: Best Song, 1982. Number o

UP WITH THE LARK (1946) (w)Leo Robin (m)Jerome Kern. (I)Film: *Centennial Summer* by Dorothy Gish, Buddy Swan, Constance Bennett and Louanne Hogan dubbing for Jeanne Crain.

UP, UP AND AWAY or MY BEAUTIFUL BALLOON (1967) (wm)Jim Webb. (P)The Fifth Dimension.

UPSIDE DOWN (1980) (wm)Bernard Edwards—Nile Rodgers. (P)Diana Ross. Number one chart record.

UPTIGHT (Everything's Alright) (1966) (wm)Stevie Wonder—Sylvia Moy—Henry Cosby. (P)Stevie Wonder.

UPTOWN (1962) (wm)Barry Mann—Cynthia Weil. (P)The Crystals.

UPTOWN GIRL (1983) (wm)Billy Joel. (P)Billy Joel.

URGE FOR GOING (1966) (wm)Joni Mitchell. (P)George Hamilton IV (1967).

URGENT (1981) (wm)Mick Jones. (P)Foreigner.

USE ME (1972) (wm)Bill Withers. (P)Bill Withers.

USE TA BE MY GIRL (1978) (wm)Kenny Gamble—Leon Huff. (P)The O'Jays.

USE YOUR IMAGINATION (1950) (wm)Cole Porter. (I)Musical: *Out Of This World* by William Redfield and Patricia Gillette.

UTOPIA (1960) (w)Aaron Schroeder—Wally Gold—Martin Kalmanoff. (P)Frank Gari.

VACATION (1962) (wm)Gary Weston—Hank Hunter—Connie Francis. (P)Connie Francis.

VACATION (1982) (wm)Kathy Valentine (w)Charlotte Caffey—Jane Wiedlin. (P)Go-Gos.

VAGABOND DREAMS (1939) (w)Jack Lawrence (m)Hoagy Carmichael. (P)Glenn Miller and his Orchestra.

VAHEVELA (1971) (wm)Danny Loggins—Daniel Lottermoser. (P)Loggins and Messina.

VALENCIA (1926) (w-Eng)Clifford Grey (m)Jose Padilla. (I)In Paris revue by Mistinguett. In U. S. in revue: The Great Temptations by Hazel Dawn, Halfred Young and Charlotte Woodruff.

VALENTINE (1926) (w-Eng)Herbert Reynolds (m)H. Christine. (I)In Paris revue: Paris Qui Chante by Maurice Chevalier.

VALERIE (1987) (wm)Steve Winwood—W. Jennings. (P)Steve Winwood.

VALLERI (1968) (wm)Tommy Boyce—Bobby Hart. (P)The Monkees.

VALLEY OF TEARS (1957) (wm)Fats Domino—Dave Bartholomew. (P)Fats Domino.

VALLEY OF THE DOLLS (Theme from) (1968) (wm)Dory Previn—Andre Previn. (I)Theme of film: Valley Of The Dolls with Patty Duke.

VANESSA (1952) (m)Bernie Wayne. (P)Hugo Winterhalter and his Orchestra.

VANITY (1951) (w)Jack Manus—Bernard Bierman (m)Guy Wood. (P)Don Cherry. Also recorded by Tony Martin and Sarah Vaughan.

VARSITY DRAG, THE (1927) (w)B. G. De Sylva—Lew Brown (m)Ray Henderson. (I)Musical: Good News by Zelma O'Neal, Ruth Mayon, Don Tomkins and Wally Coyle. Film version (1930) by Penny Singleton

VAYA CON DIOS (1953) (wm)Larry Russell—Inez James—Buddy Pepper. (I)Anita O'Day. (P)Les Paul and Mary Ford.

VEHICLE (1969) (wm)James M. Peterik. (P)The Ides of March (1970).

VELVET GLOVE, THE (1953) (wm)Harold Spina. (P)Hugo Winterhalter and Henri Rene and their Orchestra.

VELVET MOON (1943) (w)Edgar De Lange (m)Josef Myrow. (P)Harry James and his Orchestra.

VENTURA HIGHWAY (1972) (wm)Lee Bunnell. (P)America.

VENUS (1959) (wm)Ed Marshall. (P)Frankie Avalon.

VENUS (1970) (wm)R. Leeuonen. (P)Shocking Blue, 1970, Number one chart record. (R)Banarama, 1986, Number one chart record.

VENUS AND MARS/ROCK SHOW (1975) (wm)Paul McCartney. (P)Paul McCartney and Wings.

VENUS IN BLUE JEANS (1962) (wm)Howard Greenfield—Jack Keller. (P)Jimmy Clanton.

VERY MERRY UN-BIRTHDAY TO YOU, A (1951) (wm)Al Hoffman—Jerry Livingston—Mack David. (I)Cartoon film: Alice In Wonderland with voices of Ed Wynn and Jerry Colonna.

VERY PRECIOUS LOVE, A (1958) (w)Paul Francis Webster (m)Sammy Fain. (I)Film: Marjorie Morningstar. (P)Doris Day.

VERY SOFT SHOES (1959) (w)Marshall Barer (m)Mary Rodgers. (I)Musical: Once Upon A Mattress with Carol Burnett.

VERY SPECIAL DAY, A (1953) (w)Oscar Hammerstein II (m)Richard Rodgers. (I)Musical: Me And Juliet by Isabel Bigley.

VERY SPECIAL LOVE SONG, A (1974) (wm)Norro Wilson—Billy Sherrill. (P)Charlie Rich. Grammy Award Winner, 1974.

VERY SPECIAL LOVE, A (1957) (wm)Robert Allen. (P)Johnny Nash.

VERY THOUGHT OF YOU, THE (1934) (wm)Ray Noble. (P)Ray Noble and his Orchestra. Film: Young Man With A Horn (1950) by Doris Day.

VESTI LA GIUBBA (1892) (wm)Ruggiero Leoncavallo. (I)Opera: Pagliacci. One of the most famous arias for tenors; most notably associated with Enrico Caruso.

VICT'RY POLKA (1943) (w)Samuel Cahn (m)Jule Styne. (P)Bing Crosby and The Andrews Sisters.

VICTORS, THE (1936) (wm)Louis Elbel. School Song of the University of Michigan. Also known as HAIL TO THE VICTORS VALIANT.

VICTORY (1986) (wm)R. Bell—J. Taylor. (P)Kool and the Gang.

VIDEO KILLED THE RADIO STAR (1979) (wm)Geoffrey Downs—Trevor Horn—Bruce Woolley. (P)The Buggles. Also Bruce Woolley & the Camera Club.

VIE EN ROSE, LA (1945) (w-French)Edith Piaf (w-Eng)Mack David (m)R. S. Lourgay. (P)Edith Piaf. Film: To The Victor with Dennis Morgan. Film: The Eddy Duchin Story with Tyrone Power.

VIENI, VIENI (1937) (w-Eng)Rudy Vallee (m)Vincent Scotto. (P)Rudy Vallee.

VIENNA LIFE (1873) (m)Johann Strauss. Famous light classical waltz.

VIEW TO A KILL, A (1985) (wm)Duran Duran (m)John Barry. (I)Film: A View To A Kill, 1985. (P)Duran Duran. Number one chart record.

VILIA (1907) (w)Adrian Ross (m)Franz Lehar. (I)Operetta: The Merry Widow. Film version (1934) with Maurice Chevalier and Jeanette MacDonald. Film version (1952) with Lana Turner and Fernando Lamas. New words were written for the 1934 version by Lorenz Hart.

VILLAGE OF SAINT BERNADETTE, THE (1960) (wm)Eula Parker. (P)In England by Anne Shelton, in U. S. by Andy Williams.

VINCENT (1971) (wm)Don McLean. (P)Don McLean.

VIOLINS FROM NOWHERE (1959) (w)Herb Magidson (m)Sammy Fain. (I)Revue: Michael Todd'S Peep Show by Art Carroll.

VIPER'S DRAG, THE (1934) (m)Thomas "Fats" Waller. (P)"Fats" Waller as a piano solo. (R)Musical: Ain'T Misbehavin' with Debbie Allen and Nell Carter.

VIRGINIA (1923) (w)B. G. De Sylva (m)George Gershwin. (I)Musical: Sweet Little Devil by Constance Binney and chorus.

VISIT PANAMA (1940) (wm)Cole Porter. (I)Musical: Panama Hattie by Ethel Merman.

VODKA (1926) (w)Otto Harbach—Oscar Hammerstein II (m)Herbert Stothart—George Gershwin. (I)Operetta: Song Of The Flame by Dorothy Mackaye.

VOICES CARRY (1985) (wm)Aimee Mann—Michael Hausman—Robert Holmes—Joseph Pesce. (P)'Til Tuesday.

VOICES OF SPRING (1883) (m)Johann Strauss. Famous light classical waltz. Film: The Great Waltz with lyrics added by Oscar Hammerstein II.

VOLARE or NEL BLU, DIPINTO DI BLU (1958) (w-Eng)Mitchell Parish (m)Domenico Modugno. (P)Domenico Modugno. Other versions by Bobby Vinton. Also, The McGuire Sisters.

VOLUNTEERS (1969) (wm)Marty Balin—Paul Kantner. (P)Jefferson Airplane.

VOO-IT! VOO-IT! (1946) (wm)Ulysses Banks—Frosty Pyles. (P)The Blues Woman.

VOYAGE TO THE BOTTOM OF THE SEA (1961) (m)Russell Faith. (I)Film: *Voyage To The Bottom Of The Sea* with Walter Pidgeon and Joan Fontaine.

W-O-L-D (1973) (wm)Harry Chapin. (P)Harry Chapin.

WABASH BLUES (1921) (wm)Dave Ringle—Fred Meinken. (P)Isham Jones and his Orchestra with Louis Panico playing trumpet solo.

WABASH CANNONBALL (1940) (wm)A. F. Carter. (P)Roy Acuff. Film: *Rolling Home To Texas* by Tex Ritter.

WABASH MOON (1931) (wm)Dave Dreyer—Morton Downey. (P)Morton Downey.

WACKY DUST (1938) (w)Stanley Adams (m)Oscar Levant. (P)Chick Webb and his Orchestra, with vocal by Ella Fitzgerald.

WADE IN THE WATER (1966) (m)Ramsey E. Lewis Jr. (P)The Ramsey Lewis Trio. Lewis's arrangement based on a pre-Civil War slave song.

WAGON TRAIN (1957) (wm)Henri Rene—Bob Russell. Title theme from TV series: *Wagon Train.*

WAGON WHEELS (1934) (wm)Billy Hill—Peter De Rose. (I)Revue: *Ziegfeld Follies Of 1934* by Everett Marshall. (P)George Olsen and his Orchestra.

WAH WATUSI, THE (1962) (wm)Dave Appell—Kal Mann. (P)The Orlons.

WAH-HOO! (1936) (wm)Cliff Friend. (I)Film: *Moonlight And Cactus* by The Andrews Sisters.

WAIL OF THE REEFER MAN, THE (1932) (w)Ted Koehler (m)Harold Arlen. (I)Revue: *Cotton Club Parade* by Cab Calloway.

WAIT 'TIL THE SUN SHINES NELLIE (1905) (w)Andrew B. Sterling (m)Harry Von Tilzer. (P)Byron Harlan. Also, Harry Talley. Film: *Birth Of The Blues* with Bing Crosby, Mary Martin. Film: *In The Good Old Summertime* with Judy Garland, Van Johnson. Film: *Wait Til The Sun Shines Nellie* with David Wayne.

WAIT 'TIL YOU SEE "MA CHERIE" (1929) (w)Leo Robin (m)Richard A. Whiting. (I)Film: *Innocents Of Paris* by Maurice Chevalier.

WAIT AND SEE (1945) (w)Johnny Mercer (m)Harry Warren. (I)Film: *The Harvey Girls* by Kenny Baker.

WAIT FOR ME (1979) (wm)Daryl Hall. (P)Hall & Oates.

WAIT FOR ME BABY (1943) (wm)Charlie Tobias—Nat Simon—Harry Tobias. (P)Dick Haymes.

WAIT FOR ME, MARY (1942) (wm)Charles Tobias—Nat Simon—Harry Tobias. (P)Dick Haymes.

WAIT TILL YOU SEE HER (1942) (w)Lorenz Hart (m)Richard Rodgers. (I)Musical: *By Jupiter* by Ronnie Graham.

WAIT UNTIL DARK (1968) (wm)Ray Evans—Jerry Livingston—Henry Mancini. (I)Film: *Wait Until Dark* with Audrey Hepburn.

WAITER AND THE PORTER AND THE UPSTAIRS MAID, THE (1941) (wm)Johnny Mercer. (I)Film: *Birth Of The Blues* by Mary Martin, Bing Crosby and Jack Teagarden.

WAITIN' AT THE GATE FOR KATY (1934) (w)Gus Kahn (m)Richard A. Whiting. (I)Film: *Bottoms Up* by John Boles and chorus. (P)Don Bestor and his Orchestra.

WAITIN' FOR MY DEARIE (1947) (w)Alan Jay Lerner (m)Frederick Loewe. (I)Musical: *Brigadoon* by Marion Bell. Film version 1954 sung by Carol Richards, dubbed for Cyd Charisse.

WAITIN' FOR THE TRAIN TO COME IN (1945) (wm)Sunny Skylar—Martin Block. (P)Peggy Lee.

WAITIN' IN SCHOOL (1957) (wm)Johnny Burnette—Dorsey Burnette. (P)Ricky Nelson.

WAITING AT THE END OF THE ROAD (1929) (wm)Irving Berlin. (I)Film: *Hallelujah* by Daniel Haynes and the Dixie Jubilee Singers. (P)Paul Whiteman and his Orchestra.

WAITING FOR A GIRL LIKE YOU (1981) (wm)Mick Jones—Lou Gramm. (P)Foreigner.

WAITING FOR THE GIRLS UPSTAIRS (1971) (wm)Stephen Sondheim. (I)Musical: *Follies* with Yvonne De Carlo and Alexis Smith.

WAITING FOR THE ROBERT E. LEE (1912) (w)L. Wolfe Gilbert (m)Lewis F. Muir. (P)The Heidelberg Quintet. Film: *The Story Of Vernon And Irene Castle* with Fred Astaire and Ginger Rogers. Film: *The Jolson Story* by Al Jolson dubbing for Larry Parks.

WAITING FOR THE SUN TO COME OUT (1920) (w)Arthur Francis (m)George Gershwin. (I)Musical: *The Sweetheart Shop* by Helen Ford and Joseph Lertora. (P)Lambert Murphy.

WAITING GAME, THE (1958) (w)Bob Hilliard (m)Robert Allen. (P)Harry Belafonte.

WAKE ME UP BEFORE YOU GO-GO (1984) (wm)George Michael. (P)Wham! Number one chart record.

WAKE ME WHEN IT'S OVER (1960) (w)Sammy Cahn (m)Jimmy Van Heusen. (I)Film: *Wake Me When It's Over.*

WAKE THE TOWN AND TELL THE PEOPLE (1955) (w)Sammy Gallop (m)Jerry Livingston. (P)Les Baxter and his Orchestra and Chorus.

WAKE UP AND LIVE (1937) (w)Mack Gordon (m)Harry Revel. (I)Film: *Wake Up And Live* by Alice Faye.

WAKE UP AND SING (1936) (wm)Cliff Friend—Carmen Lombardo—Charles Tobias. (P)Guy Lombardo and his Royal Canadians. (P)Bob Howard and his Orchestra.

WAKE UP LITTLE SUSIE (1957) (wm)Boudleaux Bryant—Felice Bryant. (P)The Everly Brothers.

WAKE UP, EVERYBODY (Part 1) (1976) (wm)Gene McFadden—John Whitehead—Vic Carstarphen. (P)Harold Melvin & The Blue Notes.

WALK - DON'T RUN (1960) (wm)Johnny Smith. (P)The Ventures.

WALK A MILE IN MY SHOES (1969) (wm)Joe South. (P)Joe South (1970).

WALK AWAY FROM LOVE (1975) (wm)Charles Kipps, Jr. (P)David Ruffin.

WALK AWAY, RENEE (1966) (wm)Mike Lookofsky—Tony Sansone—Bob Calilli. (P)Left Banke.

WALK HAND IN HAND (1956) (wm)Johnny Cowell. (P)Denny Vaughan. (R)Tony Martin.

WALK IN THE BLACK FOREST, A (1965) (m)Horst Janowski. (P)Horst Janowski.

WALK LIKE A MAN (1963) (wm)Bob Crewe—Bob Gaudio. (P)The Four Seasons.

WALK LIKE AN EGYPTIAN (1986) (wm)L. Sternberg. (P)Bangles. No. 1 Chart Record.

WALK OF LIFE (1986) (wm)Mark Knopfler. (P)Dire Straits.

WALK ON (1974) (wm)Neil Young. (P)Neil Young.

WALK ON BY (1961) (wm)Kendall Hayes. (P)Leroy Van Dyke.

WALK ON BY (1961) (w)Hal David (m)Burt Bacharach. (P)Dionne Warwick.

WALK ON THE WILD SIDE (1967) (w)Mack David

(m)Elmer Bernstein. (I)Film: *Walk On The Wild Side.* (P)Jimmy Smith.

WALK ON THE WILD SIDE (1972) (wm)Lou Reed. (P)Lou Reed.

WALK ON WATER (1972) (wm)Neil Diamond. (P)Neil Diamond.

WALK RIGHT BACK (1961) (wm)Sonny Curtis. (P)The Everly Brothers.

WALK RIGHT IN (1930) (w)Gus Cannon (m)H. Woods. (P)Gus Cannon's Jug Stompers. (R)1963 by The Rooftop Singers.

WALK THIS WAY (1977) (wm)S. Tyler—J. Perry. (P)Aerosmith. (R)Run-D. M. C. , 1986.

WALK, JENNY, WALK (1923) (w)Henry Creamer (m)Bob Schafer—Sam Wooding. (P)Sam Wooding's Orchestra. (P)Original Memphis Five.

WALKIN' AFTER MIDNIGHT (1956) (w)Don Hecht (m)Alan Block. (P)Patsy Cline.

WALKIN' BY THE RIVER (1940) (w)Robert Sour (m)Una Mae Carlisle. (P)Una Mae Carlisle. Other popular versions by Ginny Simms and Hal Kemp and his Orchestra. (R)1952 by Ella Fitzgerald.

WALKIN' IN THE RAIN WITH THE ONE I LOVE (1972) (wm)Barry White. (P)Love Unlimited.

WALKIN' MY BABY BACK HOME (1930) (wm)Roy Turk—Fred Ahlert. (P)Harry Richman. (R)1952 by Johnnie Ray. Film: *Walkin' My Baby Back Home* (1953) by Donald O'Connor.

WALKIN' TO MISSOURI (1952) (wm)Bob Merrill. (P)Sammy Kaye and his Orchestra.

WALKIN' WITH MY HONEY (Soon, Soon, Soon), I'LL BE (1945) (w)Buddy Kaye (m)Sam Medoff. (P)Sammy Kaye and his Orchestra.

WALKIN' WITH PENINNAH (1964) (w)Earl Shuman (m)Leon Carr. (I)Musical: *The Secret Life Of Walter Mitty* by Marc London and Christopher Norris.

WALKING AWAY WHISTLING (1959) (wm)Frank Loesser. (I)Musical: *Greenwillow* by Ellen McCown (1960).

WALKING DOWN YOUR STREET (1987) (wm)S. Hoffs—L. Gutierrez—D. Kahne. (P)Bangles.

WALKING HAPPY (1966) (w)Sammy Cahn (m)Jimmy Van Heusen. (I)Musical: *Walking Happy* by Norman Wisdom.

WALKING IN RHYTHM (1975) (wm)Barney Perry. (P)Blackbyrds.

WALKING IN SPACE (1967) (w)Gerome Ragni—James Rado (m)Galt MacDermot. (I)Musical: *Hair* by the company. (P)Instrumental by Quincy Jones.

WALKING IN THE RAIN (1964) (wm)Barry Mann—Cynthia Weil—Phil Spector. (P)The Ronettes. (R)1969-70 by Jay and The Americans.

WALKING ON SUNSHINE (1985) (wm)Kimberly Rew. (P)Katrina and the Waves.

WALKING PROUD (1963) (wm)Gerry Goffin—Carole King. (P)Steve Lawrence.

WALKING THE DOG (1963) (wm)Rufus Thomas. (P)Rufus Thomas.

WALKING THE FLOOR OVER YOU (1941) (wm)Ernest Tubb. (P)Ernest Tubb, also Bing Crosby with Bob Crosby and his Orchestra.

WALKING TO NEW ORLEANS (1960) (wm)Antoine Domino—Dave Bartholomew—Robert Guidry. (P)Fats Domino.

WALTZ COPPELIA (1870) (m)Leo Delibes. From the ballet COPPELIA.

WALTZ DREAM, A (1907) (wm)Adrian Ross—Oscar Strauss. (I)Musical: *A Waltz Dream.*

WALTZ FOR DEBBY (1964) (w)Gene Lees (m)Bill Evans. Adapted from jazz composition by Evans. (P)Tony Bennett.

WALTZ FROM THE COUNT OF LUXEMBOURG (1909) (m)Franz Lehar. Famous light classical waltz.

WALTZ HUGUETTE or THE VAGABOND KING WALTZ (1925) (w)Brian Hooker (m)Rudolf Friml. (I)Musical: *The Vagabond King* with Dennis King and Carolyn Thomson. Film version 1930 with Dennis King and Jeanette MacDonald.

WALTZ IN SWING TIME (1936) (w)Dorothy Fields (m)Jerome Kern. (I)Film: *Swing Time* by Fred Astaire and Ginger Rogers. (P)Johnny Green and his Orchestra.

WALTZ ME AROUND AGAIN WILLIE (1906) (w)Will D. Cobb (m)Ren Shields. (P)Billy Murray the The Haydn Quartet. Musical: *His Honour, The Mayor.*

WALTZ OF LONG AGO, THE (1923) (wm)Irving Berlin. (I)Revue: *Music Box Revue Of 1923* by Grace Moore. (P)Paul Specht.

WALTZ OF THE FLOWERS (1892) (m)Peter Tchaikovsky. From ballet *The Nutcracker Suite.* Film: *Fantasia.*

WALTZ YOU SAVED FOR ME, THE (1930) (w)Gus Kahn (m)Wayne King—Emil Flindt. (P)Wayne King (The Waltz King) and his Orchestra (theme song).

WALTZING CAT, THE (1951) (m)Leroy Anderson. (P)Leroy Anderson and his Orchestra.

WALTZING DOLL (See POUPEE VALSANTE)

WALTZING IN A DREAM (1932) (w)Bing Crosby—Ned Washington (m)Victor Young. (P)Bing Crosby. Also recorded by Guy Lombardo and his Royal Canadians.

WALTZING IN THE CLOUDS (1940) (w)Gus Kahn (m)Robert Stolz. (I)Film: *Spring Parade* by Deanna Durbin. Nominated for Academy Award.

WALTZING MATILDA (1903) (w)A. B. Patterson (m)Marie Cowan. Unofficial national anthem of Australia. Film: *On The Beach* with Fred Astaire and Gregory Peck.

WAND'RIN STAR (1951) (w)Alan Jay Lerner (m)Frederick Loewe. (I)Musical: *Paint Your Wagon* by Rufus Smith, Robert Penn, and Jared Reed.

WANDERER, THE (1961) (wm)Ernest Maresca. (P)Dion.

WANDERER, THE (1980) (w-Eng)Donna Summer (m)Giorgio Moroder. (P)Donna Summer.

WANDERIN' (1950) (wm)Sammy Kaye. Based on an American folk song discovered in Minnesota by Carl Sandburg. (P)Sammy Kaye and his Orchestra.

WANG WANG BLUES, THE (1921) (w)Leo Wood (m)Gus Muller—Buster Johnson—Henry Busse. (P)Paul Whiteman and his Orchestra, trumpet solo by Henry Busse. Revue: *Ziegfeld Follies Of 1921* by Van and Schenck.

WANNA BE STARTIN' SOMETHIN' (1983) (wm)Michael Jackson. (P)Michael Jackson. NARAS Award nominee, R & B Song of the Year, 1983.

WANT ADS (1971) (wm)General Johnson—Barney Perkins—Greg Perry. (P)Honey Cone.

WANTED (1954) (wm)Jack Fulton—Lois Steele. (P)Perry Como.

WANTED DEAD OR ALIVE (1987) (wm)J. Bon Jovi—R. Sambora. (P)Bon Jovi.

WANTING YOU (1928) (w)Oscar Hammerstein II (m)Sigmund Romberg. (I)Operetta: *The New Moon* by Evelyn Herbert and Robert Halliday. Film version 1930 by Lawrence Tibbett and Grace Moore.

WAR (1970) (wm)Norman Whitfield—Barrett Strong. (P)Edwin Starr. Number one chart record. (R)Bruce Springsteen and the E Street Band, 1986.

WAR AND PEACE (1956) (w)Wilson Stone (m)Nino Rota. Adapted from a theme from film: *War And Peace*. (P)Vic Damone.

WARM ALL OVER (1956) (wm)Frank Loesser. (I)Musical: *The Most Happy Fella* by Jo Sullivan.

WARM AND TENDER LOVE (Wrap Me in Your Warm and Tender Love) (1966) (wm)Bobby Robinson—Ida Irral Berger. (P)Percy Sledge.

WARM RED WINE, THE (1949) (wm)Cindy Walker. (P)Ernest Tubb.

WARRIOR, THE (1984) (wm)Holly Knight—Nick Gilder. (P)Scandal.

WARSAW CONCERTO (1942) (m)Richard Addinsell. (I)Film: *Suicide Squadron* by pianist Louis Kentner and The London Symphony Orchestra conducted by Muir Mathieson. (P)Freddy Martin and his Orchestra.

WAS IT A DREAM (1928) (wm)Sam Coslow—Larry Spier—Addy Britt. (P)Jan Garber and his Orchestra.

WAS IT RAIN? (1937) (w)Walter Hirsch (m)Lou Handman. (I)Film: *The Hit Parade* by Frances Langford.

WAS THAT THE HUMAN THING TO DO (1931) (w)Joe Young (m)Sammy Fain. (P)Guy Lombardo and The Royal Canadians.

WASHBOARD BLUES (1928) (wm)Hoagy Carmichael—Fred B. Callahan—Irving Mills. (P)Curtis Hitch's Happy Harmonists with Carmichael as piano soloist. (P)Red Nichols and his Five Pennies. Paul Whiteman and his Orchestra. (R)1938 by Mildred Bailey.

WASHINGTON AND LEE SWING (1910) (w)Thornton W. Allen—C. A. Robbins (m)Thornton W. Allen—M. W. Sheafe. School song for Washington and Lee University.

WASHINGTON POST MARCH (1889) (m)John Philip Sousa. One of Sousa's most popular marches.

WASHINGTON SQUARE (1963) (wm)Bob Goldstein—David Shire. (P)The Village Stompers.

WASHINGTON TWIST, THE (1962) (wm)Irving Berlin. (I)Musical: *Mr. President* by Anita Gillette. (P)Andre Kostelanetz.

WASTED DAYS WASTED NIGHTS (1975) (wm)Freddy Fender—Wayne Duncan. (P)Freddy Fender.

WASTED ON THE WAY (1982) (wm)Graham Nash. (P)Crosby, Stills & Nash.

WATCH OUT FOR LUCY (1978) (wm)Eric Clapton. (P)Eric Clapton.

WATCH WHAT HAPPENS (1964) (w-Eng)Norman Gimbel (m)Michel Legrand. (I)Film: *The Umbrellas Of Cherbourg*. English version by Jean-Paul Vignon.

WATCHIN' SCOTTY GROW (1970) (wm)Mac Davis. (P)Bobby Goldsboro.

WATCHING THE CLOUDS ROLL BY (1928) (wm)Bert Kalmar—Harry Ruby. (I)Musical: *Animal Crackers* by Bernice Ackerman and Milton Watson.

WATCHING THE RIVER FLOW (1971) (wm)Bob Dylan. (P)Bob Dylan.

WATCHING THE WHEELS (1981) (wm)John Lennon. (P)John Lennon.

WATER BOY (1922) (wm)Avery Robinson. Adaptation of folk song *Jack O'Diamonds*. Associated with Paul Robeson.

WATERLOO (1959) (wm)John Loudermilk—Marijohn Wilkins. (P)Stonewall Jackson.

WATERLOO (1974) (wm)Benny Anderson—Bjorn Ulvaeus—Stig Anderson. (P)Abba.

WATERMELON MAN (1963) (wm)(P)Mongo Santamaria.

WATERMELON WEATHER (1952) (w)Paul Francis Webster (m)Hoagy Carmichael. (P)Perry Como and Eddie Fisher.

WAVE TO ME, MY LADY (1945) (wm)William Stein—Frank Loesser. (P)Guy Lombardo and his Royal Canadians. (P)Elton Britt (1946).

WAVELENGTH (1978) (wm)Van Morrison. (P)Van Morrison.

WAVES OF THE DANUBE or DANUBE WAVES (1880) (m)Ion Ivanovici. Famous light classical waltz. See THE ANNIVERSARY SONG.

WAY BACK HOME (1935) (wm)Al Lewis—Tom Waring. (P)Fred Waring and his Pennsylvanians.

WAY DOWN (1977) (wm)Layng Martine. (P)Elvis Presley.

WAY DOWN UPON THE SWANEE RIVER (See OLD FOLKS AT HOME)

WAY DOWN YONDER IN NEW ORLEANS (1922) (wm)Henry Creamer—Turner Layton. (P)Creamer and Layton. Film: *The Story Of Vernon And Irene Castle* danced by Fred Astaire, Ginger Rogers, sung by the chorus. Film: *Somebody Loves Me* (1952) by Betty Hutton. (R)1960 by Freddie Cannon

WAY I FEEL TONIGHT, THE (1977) (w)Harvey Shields. (P)Bay City Rollers.

WAY I WANT TO TOUCH YOU, THE (1975) (wm)Toni Tenille. (P)The Captain and Tenille.

WAY IT IS, THE (1986) (wm)Bruce Hornsby. (P)Bruce Hornsby & The Range. No. 1 Chart Record.

WAY OF LOVE, THE (1972) (wm)Al Stillman—Jacques Dieval—Mariano Ruiz. (P)Cher.

WAY OUT WEST (1937) (w)Lorenz Hart (m)Richard Rodgers. (I)Musical: *Babes In Arms* by Wynn Murray, Alex Courtney, Clifton Darling, James Gillis and Robert Rounseville. Film version with Judy Garland and Mickey Rooney.

WAY WE WERE, THE (1973) (w)Alan Bergman—Marilyn Bergman (m)Marvin Hamlisch. (I)Film: *The Way We Were* by Barbra Streisand. Academy Award Winner 1973. Grammy Award Winner 1974. (R)1975 by Gladys Knight and The Pips, in medley with "*Try To Remember.*"

WAY YOU DO THE THINGS YOU DO, THE (1964) (wm)William Robinson—Bobby Rogers. (P)The Temptations. (R)1978 by Rita Coolidge. (R)1985 by Hall and Oates, David Ruffin, and Eddie Kendrick.

WAY YOU LOOK TONIGHT, THE (1936) (w)Dorothy Fields (m)Jerome Kern. (I)Film: *Swing Time* by Fred Astaire. Academy Award Winner 1936. (P)Fred Astaire.

WAY YOU MAKE ME FEEL, THE (1987) (wm)Michael Jackson. (P)Michael Jackson. No. 1 Chart Record.

WAYFARIN' STRANGER (1800)Traditional American folk song.

WAYS OF A WOMAN IN LOVE, THE (1958) (wm)Charlie Rich—Bill Justis. (P)Johnny Cash.

WAYWARD WIND, THE (1956) (wm)Stan Lebowsky—Herb Newman. (P)Gogi Grant.

WE AIN'T GOT NOTHING YET (1966) (wm)Emil Thielhelm—Michael Esposito—Ralph Scala—Ronald Gilbert. (P)The Blues Magoos.

WE ALMOST LOST DETROIT (1977) (wm)Gil Scott-Heron. (P)Gil Scott-Heron.

WE ARE FAMILY (1979) (wm)Bernard Rodgers—Nile Rodgers. (P)Sister Sledge.

WE ARE THE CHAMPIONS (1978) (wm)Freddie Mercury. (P)Queen.

WE ARE THE WORLD (1985) (wm)Michael Jackson—Lionel Richie. (P)USA for Africa. No. 1 Chart Record.

WE BELONG (1985) (wm)David Lowen—Daniel Navarro. (P)Pat Benatar.

WE BUILT THIS CITY (1985) (w)Bernie Taupin (wm)Martin Page—Dennis Lambert—Peter Wolf. (P)Starship. Number one chart record.

WE CAN WORK IT OUT (1966) (wm)John Lennon—Paul McCartney. (P)The Beatles.

WE COULD MAKE SUCH BEAUTIFUL MUSIC (Together) (1940) (w)Robert Sour (m)Henry Manners. (P)Vaughn Monroe and his Orchestra.

WE DID IT BEFORE (And We Can Do It Again) (1941) (wm)Cliff Friend—Charlie Tobias. (I)Musical: Banjo Eyes by Eddie Cantor. Film: Sweethearts Of The Fleet with Joan Davis and Joan Woodbury. (P)Dick Robertson and his Orchestra.

WE DON'T HAVE TO TAKE OUR CLOTHES OFF (1986) (wm)Preston Glass—Narada Michael Warden. (P)Jermaine Stewart.

WE DON'T NEED ANOTHER HERO (THUNDERDOME) (1985) (wm)Terry Britten—Graham Lyle. (I)Film: Mad Max: Beyond Thunderdome. (P)Tina Turner.

WE DON'T TALK ANYMORE (1979) (wm)Al- Tarney. (P)Cliff Richard.

WE GOT LOVE (1959) (w)Kal Mann (m)Bernie Lowe (P)Bobby Rydell.

WE GOT MORE SOUL (WE GOT LATIN SOUL) (1969) (wm)Arlester Christian. (P)Dyke and The Blazers.

WE GOT THE BEAT (1982) (wm)Charlotte Caffey. (P)Go-Gos.

WE GOT TO GET YOU A WOMAN (1970) (wm)Todd Rundgren. (P)Runt.

WE GOTTA GET OUT OF THIS PLACE (1965) (wm)Barry Mann—Cynthia Weil. (P)The Animals.

WE JUST COULDN'T SAY GOODBYE (1932) (wm)Harry Woods. (P)Paul Whiteman and his Orchestra and Guy Lombardo and his Royal Canadians.

WE JUST DISAGREE (1977) (wm)Jim Krueger. (P)Dave Mason.

WE KISS IN A SHADOW (1951) (w)Oscar Hammerstein II (m)Richard Rodgers. (I)Musical: The King And I by Doretta Morrow and Larry Douglas. Film version starring Deborah Kerr and Yul Brynner. Frank Sinatra.

WE LIVE IN TWO DIFFERENT WORLDS (1943) (wm)Fred Rose. (P)Tex Ritter.

WE MAY NEVER LOVE LIKE THIS AGAIN (1974) (wm)Al Kasha—Joel Hirschorn. (I)Film: The Towering Inferno by voice of Maureen McGovern. Academy Award Winner 1974. (P)Maureen McGovern.

WE MAY NEVER PASS THIS WAY (AGAIN) (1973) (wm)James Seals—Darrell Crofts. (P)Seals and Crofts.

WE MIGHT AS WELL FORGET IT (1944) (wm)Johnny Bond. (P)Bob Wills and his Texas Playboys.

WE MUST BE VIGILANT (See AMERICAN PATROL)

WE MUSTN'T SAY GOODBYE (1943) (w)Al Dubin (m)James V. Monaco. (P)Vaughn Monroe and his Or-chestra. Featured in film Stage Door Canteen. Nominated for Academy Award, 1943.

WE NEED A LITTLE CHRISTMAS (1966) (wm)Jerry Herman. (I)Musical: Mame starring Angela Lansbury. Film version starring Lucille Ball.

WE NEVER TALK MUCH (1951) (w)Sammy Cahn (m)Nicholas Brodszky. (I)Film: Rich, Young And Pretty by Jane Powell and Fernando Lamas.

WE OPEN IN VENICE (1948) (wm)Cole Porter. (I)Musical: Kiss Me Kate by Alfred Drake, Patricia Morison, Lisa Kirk, and Harold Lang. Film version 1953 sung by Kathryn Grayson, Howard Keel, Ann Miller, and Tommy Rall.

WE SAW THE SEA (1936) (wm)Irving Berlin. (I)Film: Swing Time by Fred Astaire and chorus. (P)Fred Astaire.

WE SHALL OVERCOME (1945) (wm)Anonymous. Song of the Black Civil Rights Movement.

WE THREE - MY ECHO, MY SHADOW AND ME (1940) (wm)Dick Robertson—Nelson Cogane—Sammy Mysels. (P)The Ink Spots.

WE THREE KINGS OF ORIENT (1857) (wm)John Henry Hopkins. Famous Christmas hymn.

WE WILL ALWAYS BE SWEETHEARTS (1932) (w)Leo Robin (m)Oscar Strauss. (I)Film: One Hour With You by Maurice Chevalier and Jeanette MacDonald.

WE'LL BE TOGETHER (1987) (wm)Sting. (P)Sting.

WE'LL BE TOGETHER AGAIN (1945) (wm)Frankie Laine—Carl Fischer. (P)Frankie Laine (theme song).

WE'LL GATHER LILACS (1945) (wm)Ivor Novello. (I)London musical: Perchance To Dream. Film: Lilacs In The Spring starring Errol Flynn. (P)Tommy Dorsey and his Orchestra.

WE'LL HAVE A KINGDOM (1926) (w)Otto Harbach—Oscar Hammerstein II (m)Rudolf Friml. (I)Musical: The Wild Rose.

WE'LL MAKE HAY WHILE THE SUN SHINES (1933) (w)Arthur Freed (m)Nacio Herb Brown. (I)Film: Going Hollywood by Bing Crosby and Marion Davies. (P)Bing Crosby.

WE'LL MEET AGAIN (1939) (wm)Ross Parker—Hughie Charles. (I)Film: Dr. Strangelove on soundtrack by Vera Lynn. (P)Vera Lynn.

WE'LL NEVER HAVE TO SAY GOODBYE AGAIN (1978) (wm)Jeffrey Comanor. (P)England Dan and John Ford Coley.

WE'LL SING IN THE SUNSHINE (1964) (wm)Gale Garnett. (P)Gale Garnett.

WE'RE ALL ALONE (1977) (wm)William "Boz" Scaggs. (P)Rita Coolidge.

WE'RE AN AMERICAN BAND (1973) (wm)Don Brewer. (P)Grand Funk Railroad.

WE'RE GONNA BE ALL RIGHT (1965) (w)Stephen Sondheim (m)Richard Rodgers. (I)Musical: Do I Hear A Waltz?

WE'RE HAVING A BABY (1941) (w)Harold Adamson (m)Vernon Duke. (I)Musical: Banjo Eyes by Eddie Cantor and June Clyde.

WE'RE IN THE MONEY or THE GOLD DIGGER SONG (1933) (w)Al Dubin (m)Harry Warren. (I)Film: Gold Diggers Of 1933 by Ginger Rogers.

WE'RE OFF TO SEE THE WIZARD (1939) (w)E. Y. Harburg (m)Harold Arlen. (I)Film: The Wizard Of Oz by Judy Garland, Bert Lahr, Jack Haley and Ray Bolger.

WE'RE READY (1986) (wm)T. Scholz. (P)Boston.

WE'RE THE COUPLE IN THE CASTLE (1941) (w)Frank Loesser (m)Hoagy Carmichael. (I)Cartoon film: *Mr. Bug Goes To Town.*

WE'VE GOT TONITE (1979) (wm)Bob Seger. (P)Bob Seger. (R)Kenny Rogers and Sheena Easton, 1983.

WE'VE ONLY JUST BEGUN (1970) (wm)Paul Williams. (P)The Carpenters.

WEAR MY RING AROUND YOUR NECK (1958) (wm)Bert Carroll—Russell Moody. (P)Elvis Presley.

WEARY RIVER (1929) (w)Grant Clarke (m)Louis Silvers. (I)Film: *Weary River* by unidentified vocalist dubbing for Richard Barthelmess. Popular versions by Rudy Vallee and Gene Austin.

WEAVER OF DREAMS (1951) (w)Jack Elliott (m)Victor Young. (P)Nat "King" Cole.

WEDDING BELL BLUES (1966) (wm)Laura Nyro. (P)Laura Nyro. (R)1969 by The Fifth Dimension.

WEDDING BELLS ARE BREAKING UP THAT OLD GANG OF MINE (1929) (wm)Irving Kahal—Willie Raskin—Sammy Fain. (P)Gene Austin. (R)1960s by The Four Aces.

WEDDING MARCH (1844) (m)Felix Mendelssohn. Famous composition played at weddings.

WEDDING MARCH (Bridal Chorus) (1852) (m)Richard Wagner. From opera *Lohengrin.* Also performed at weddings.

WEDDING OF LILLI MARLENE, THE (1949) (wm)Tommie Connor—Johnny Reine. (P)The Andrews Sisters (in U. S.).

WEDDING OF THE PAINTED DOLL, THE (1929) (w)Arthur Freed (m)Nacio Herb Brown. (I)Film: *Broadway Melody* by James Burrows. Film: *Singin' In The Rain* starring Gene Kelly, Debbie Reynolds and Donald O'Connor.

WEDDING SAMBA, THE (also known as THE WEDDING RHUMBA) (1947) (wm)Abraham Ellstein—Allan Small—Joseph Liebowitz. (P)The Andrews Sisters. (P)Edmundo Ros and his Orchestra. Film: *On An Island With You* starring Peter Lawford and Esther Williams.

WEDDING, THE (1961) (w-Eng)Fred Jay (m)Joaquin Prieto. (P)Julie Rogers.

WEE SMALL HOURS (Of the Morning), IN THE (1955) (w)Bob Hilliard (m)David Mann. (P)Frank Sinatra.

WEEKEND IN HAVANA, A (1941) (w)Mack Gordon (m)Harry Warren. (I)Film: *Weekend In Havana* by Carmen Miranda.

WEEKEND IN NEW ENGLAND (1977) (wm)Randy Edelman. (P)Barry Manilow.

WEEKEND IN THE COUNTRY, A (1973) (wm)Stephen Sondheim. (I)Musical: *A Little Night Music* with Len Cariou, Glynis Johns and Hermione Gingold. Film version with Len Cariou, Elizabeth Taylor, and Hermione Gingold.

WEEKEND OF A PRIVATE SECRETARY, THE (1938) (w)Johnny Mercer (m)Bernie Hanighen. (P)Mildred Bailey, with Red Norvo and his Orchestra.

WEEPING WOMAN BLUES (1928) (w)Bessie Smith (m)Gertrude "Ma" Rainey. (P)Ma Rainey.

WEIGHT, THE (1968) (wm)Jaime Robbie Robertson. (P)Jackie DeShannon. (P)The Band. (P)1969 Aretha Franklin; Diana Ross and The Supremes; The Temptations.

WELCOME BACK (1976) (wm)John Sebastian. (I)Theme of TV Series WELCOME BACK, KOTTER. (P)John Sebastian.

WELCOME HOME (1954) (wm)Harold Rome. (I)Musical: *Fanny* by Ezio Pinza.

WELCOME TO MY DREAM (1945) (w)Johnny Burke (m)James Van Heusen. (I)Film: *Road To Utopia* by Bing Crosby.

WELCOME TO MY WORLD (1961) (wm)Ray Winkler—John Hathcock. (P)Jim Reeves.

WELL ALL RIGHT! (Tonight's the Night) (1939) (wm)Frances Faye—Don Raye—Dan Howell. (P)The Andrews Sisters.

WELL RESPECTED MAN, A (1965) (wm)Ray Davies. (P)The Kinks.

WELL, DID YOU EVAH (1940) (wm)Cole Porter. (I)Musical: *Dubarry Was A Lady* by Betty Grable and Charles Walters. Film: *High Society* (1956) by Frank Sinatra and Bing Crosby.

WELL, GIT IT (1942) (m)Sy Oliver. (P)Tommy Dorsey and his Orchestra.

WELL, YOU NEEDN'T (1947) (m)Thelonious Monk. (P)Jazz instrumental by Thelonious Monk.

WENDY (1954) (w)Betty Comden—Adolph Green (m)Jule Styne. (I)Musical: *Peter Pan* by Mary Martin.

WERE THINE THAT SPECIAL FACE (1948) (wm)Cole Porter. (I)Musical: *Kiss Me Kate* by Alfred Drake. Film version 1953 sung by Howard Keel.

WERE YOU THERE WHEN THEY CRUCIFIED MY LORD? (1865)Traditional Black American spiritual.

WERE YOUR EARS BURNING, BABY? (1934) (wm)Mack Gordon—Harry Revel. (I)Film: *Shoot The Works* by Ben Bernie and his Orchestra.

WEREWOLVES OF LONDON (1978) (wm)Leroy Marinell—Robert Wachtel—Warren Zevon. (P)Warren Zevon.

WEST END BLUES (1928) (w)Clarence Williams (m)Joe Oliver. (P)King Oliver and his Dixie Syncopaters. (P)Louis Armstrong and his Hot Five.

WEST END GIRLS (1986) (wm)Nick Tennant—Chris Lowe. (P)Pet Shop Boys. Number one chart record.

WEST OF THE GREAT DIVIDE (1924) (w)George Whiting (m)Ernest R. Ball. (P)Henry Burr.

WESTERN MOVIES (1958) (w)Cliff Goldsmith (m)Fred Smith. (P)The Olympics.

WESTERN UNION (1967) (wm)Cliff Goldsmith—Norman Ezell—John Durrill (P)Five Americans.

WESTERN UNION BLUES (1928) (wm)Ida Cox. (P)Ida Cox.

WHAM BAM (Shang a Lang) (1975) (wm)Richard Giles. (P)Silver.

WHAT A DIFFERENCE A DAY MADE (1934) (w-Eng)Stanley Adams (m)Maria Grever. (P)Dorsey Brothers Orchestra. (R)1959 by Dinah Washington.

WHAT A DREAM (Oh What a Dream) (1954) (wm)Chuck Willis. (P)Patti Page.

WHAT A FOOL BELIEVES (1979) (wm)Kenny Loggins—Michael McDonald. (P)The Doobie Brothers. Grammy Award Winner 1979.

WHAT A LITTLE MOONLIGHT CAN DO (OOH) (1934) (wm)Harry Woods. (I)British film: *Roadhouse Nights*. (P)Billie Holiday.

WHAT A PERFECT COMBINATION (1932) (w)Bert Kalmar—Irving Caesar (m)Harry Ruby—Harry Akst. (I)Film: *The Kid From Spain* by Eddie Cantor.

WHAT A WOMAN IN LOVE WON'T DO (1966) (wm)John D. Loudermilk. (P)Sandy Posey.

WHAT A WONDERFUL WORLD (1968) (wm)George Douglas (m)George David Weiss. (P)Louis

Armstrong.

WHAT ABOUT LOVE? (1985) (wm)Sheron Alton—Brian Allen—Jim Vallance. (P)Heart.

WHAT AM I GONNA DO WITH YOU? (1975) (wm)Barry White. (P)Barry White.

WHAT AM I LIVING FOR? (1958) (wm)Fred Jay—Art Harris. (P)Chuck Willis.

WHAT ARE YOU DOING NEW YEAR'S EVE (1947) (wm)Frank Loesser. (P)Margaret Whiting.

WHAT ARE YOU DOING THE REST OF YOUR LIFE (1944) (w)Ted Koehler (m)Burton Lane. (I)Film: Hollywood Canteen with Eddie Cantor, Joan Crawford and Bette Davis.

WHAT ARE YOU DOING THE REST OF YOUR LIFE? (1969) (w)Alan Bergman—Marilyn Bergman (m)Michel Legrand. (I)Film: The Happy Ending by Michael Dees. Nominated for Academy Award. (P)J. P. Morgan.

WHAT BECOMES OF THE BROKEN HEARTED? (1966) (wm)James Dean—Paul Riser — William Weatherspoon. (P)Jimmy Ruffin.

WHAT CAN I SAY DEAR AFTER I SAY I'M SORRY (See AFTER I SAY I'M SORRY)

WHAT CAN YOU SAY IN A LOVE SONG? (1934) (w)Ira Gershwin—E. Y. Harburg (m)Harold Arlen. (I)Revue: Life Begins At 8:40 by Josephine Houston and Bartlett Simmons.

WHAT COLOR (IS A MAN) (1965) (wm)Marge Barton. (P)Bobby Vinton.

WHAT D'YA SAY? (1928) (wm)B. G. De Sylva—Lew Brown—Ray Henderson. (I)Revue: George White'S Scandals Of 1928 by Frances Williams and Harry Richman.

WHAT DID I DO TO BE SO BLACK AND BLUE (1933) (wm)Andy Razaf—Harry Brooks—Thomas "Fats" Waller. (P)Fats Waller. (R)Musical: Ain'T Misbehavin' with Debbie Allen and Nell Carter. Film: Satchmo The Great with Louis Armstrong.

WHAT DID I HAVE THAT I DON'T HAVE (1966) (w)Alan Jay Lerner (m)Burton Lane. (I)Musical: On A Clear Day You Can See Forever. Film version with Barbra Streisand.

WHAT DID YOU LEARN IN SCHOOL TODAY? (1962) (wm)Tom Paxton. (P)Tom Paxton.

WHAT DO I HAVE TO DO TO MAKE YOU LOVE ME? (1948) (wm)Inez James—Sidney Miller. (I)Film: Are You With It? (P)Vaughn Monroe and his Orchestra.

WHAT DO THE SIMPLE FOLKS DO? (1960) (w)Alan Jay Lerner (m)Frederick Loewe. (I)Musical: Camelot by Julie Andrews and Richard Burton. Film version with Vanessa Redgrave.

WHAT DO WE DO ON A DEW DEW DEWY DAY (1927) (wm)Howard Johnson—Charles Tobias—Al Sherman. (P)Ruth Etting.

WHAT DO YOU DO IN THE INFANTRY? (1943) (wm)Frank Loesser. Unofficial song of U. S. Infantry. (P)Bing Crosby.

WHAT DO YOU DO SUNDAY, MARY? (1923) (w)Irving Caesar (m)Stephen Jones. (I)Musical: Poppy by Luella Gear and Robert Woolsey. (P)American Quartet.

WHAT DO YOU WANT TO MAKE THOSE EYES AT ME FOR (1916) (wm)Joe McCarthy—Howard Johnson—James V. Monaco. (I)Musical: The Better 'Ole. Film: Incendiary Blonde with Betty Hutton. (P)Ada Jones and Billy Murray. Film: The Merry Monihans with Donald O'Connor.

WHAT DOES IT MATTER (1927) (wm)Irving Berlin. (P)Lucrezia Bori.

WHAT DOES IT TAKE (To Win Your Love) (1969) (wm)Harvey Fuqua—Vernon Bullock—Johnny Bristol. (P)Junior Walker and The All Stars.

WHAT GOES ON HERE IN MY HEART (1938) (wm)Leo Robin—Ralph Rainger. (I)Film: Give Me A Sailor by Betty Grable and Jack Whiting. (P)Benny Goodman and his Orchestra.

WHAT GOOD DOES IT DO (1957) (w)E. Y. Harburg (m)Harold Arlen. (I)Musical: Jamaica by Ricardo Montalban, Ossie Davis and Augustine Rios.

WHAT GOOD WOULD THE MOON BE? (1946) (w)Langston Hughes (m)Kurt Weill. (I)Musical: Street Scene by Anne Jeffreys (1947).

WHAT HAS BECOME OF HINKY DINKY PARLAY VOO (1924) (wm)Al Dubin—Irving Mills—Jimmy McHugh—Irwin Dash. (P)The Happiness Boys (Billie Jones and Ernie Hare).

WHAT HAVE I DONE TO DESERVE THIS (1987) (wm)Tennant— Lowe— Willis. (P)Pet Shop Boys and Dusty Springfield.

WHAT HAVE THEY DONE TO THE RAIN? (1962) (wm)Malvina Reynolds. (P)Malvina Reynolds. (P)1964-65 by The Searchers.

WHAT HAVE YOU DONE FOR ME LATELY (1986) (wm)Janet Jackson—Terry Lewis—James Harris III. (P)Janet Jackson.

WHAT HAVE YOU GOT THAT GETS ME? (1938) (wm)Leo Robin—Ralph Rainger. (I)Film: Artists And Models Abroad by The Yacht Club Boys, Joyce Compton, Joan Bennett, and Jack Benny.

WHAT I DID FOR LOVE (1975) (w)Edward Kleban (m)Marvin Hamlisch. (I)Musical: A Chorus Line by Donna McKechnie. Film version starring Michael Douglas.

WHAT IN THE WORLD'S COME OVER YOU (1960) (wm)Jack Scott. (P)Jack Scott.

WHAT IS HIP (1972) (wm)Emilio Castillo—John Garibaldi—Stephen Kupka. (P)Tower of Power.

WHAT IS LIFE (1970) (wm)George Harrison. (P)George Harrison.

WHAT IS LOVE? (1959) (wm)Lee Pockriss—Paul Vance. (P)The Playmates.

WHAT IS THERE TO SAY (1933) (w)E. Y. Harburg (m)Vernon Duke. (I)Ziegfeld Follies Of 1934 by Everett Marshall and Jane Froman. (P)Emil Coleman and his Orchestra.

WHAT IS THIS FEELING IN THE AIR? (1961) (w)Betty Comden—Adolph Green (m)Jule Styne. (I)Musical: Subways Are For Sleeping by Carol Lawrence and company.

WHAT IS THIS THING CALLED LOVE (1930) (wm)Cole Porter. (I)Musical: Wake Up And Dream. Film: Night And Day (1946) by Ginny Simms. Film: Young Man With A Horn (1950) by Harry James and his Orchestra. Film: Starflight (1951) by Gordon McRae, Lucille Gordon.

WHAT IS TRUTH (1970) (wm)Johnny Cash. (P)Johnny Cash.

WHAT IT WAS, WAS FOOTBALL (1954) (wm)Andy Griffith. A comedy monologue. (P)Andy Griffith.

WHAT KIND OF FOOL (Do You Think I Am) (1964) (wm)Ray Whitley. (P)The Tams.

WHAT KIND OF FOOL AM I (1962) (wm)Leslie Bricusse—Anthony Newley. (I)Musical: Stop The

PHYLLIS McGUIRE & SAM GIANCANA

A funny thing happened when we were recording *Subways Are for Sleeping* with the McGuire Sisters. At that time, Phyllis McGuire was going with Sam Giancana, reputed to be one of the major Mafia bosses. During the last session, Mr. Giancana came to the recording studio.

We had planned, at the end of the session, to record an overture similar to what is done in the theater prior to the show. But it would have cost us a small fortune - and we had already spent a small fortune. Everyone present, including Jule Styne, thought the album was great the way it was and that to record the overture would have been a ridiculous, unnecessary expense. Everyone, that is, except Phyllis Mcguire who kept insisting she wanted the overture recorded.

After much discussion and arguing, Giancana came up to me and asked what the trouble was. I explained it to him in great detail. He walked over to Phyllis and said: "Phyllis, these people are right and you're wrong. Put your coat on and let's go." And that's exactly what happened as I said to myself, "Thank you, Mr. Giancana."

World - I Want To Get Off by Anthony Newley. (P)Sammy Davis, Jr. Grammy Award Winner Best Song 1962.
WHAT KIND OF LOVE IS THIS? (1962) (wm)Johnny Nash. (P)Joey Dee and The Starliters.
WHAT MAKES THE SUNSET (1944) (w)Sammy Cahn (m)Jule Styne. (I)Film: *Anchors Aweigh* by Frank Sinatra.
WHAT MORE CAN A WOMAN DO? (1945) (wm)Peggy Lee—Dave Barbour. (P)Peggy Lee.
WHAT MORE CAN I ASK? (1932) (w)A. E. Wilkins (m)Ray Noble. (P)Ray Noble and his Orchestra.
WHAT NOW MY LOVE (1962) (w-Eng)Carl Sigman (m)Gilbert Becaud. Original French title "Et Maintenant." (P)France by Gilbert Becaud. (P)U. S. by Jane Morgan. (R)1966 Sonny and Cher. Also Herb Alpert and The Tijuana Brass.
WHAT TAKE MY FANCY (1960) (w)Carolyn Leigh (m)Cy Coleman. (I)Musical: *Wildcat* by Lucille Ball.
WHAT THE WORLD NEEDS NOW IS LOVE (1965) (w)Hal David (m)Burt Bacharach. (P)Dionne Warwick.
WHAT WILL I TELL MY HEART (1937) (wm)Peter Tinturin—Jack Lawrence—Irving Gordon. (P)Andy Kirk and his Clouds of Joy. . . Bing Crosby with Jimmy Dorsey and his Orchestra. . . Hal Kemp and his Orchestra.
WHAT WILL MY MARY SAY (1963) (wm)Paul Vance—Eddie Snyder. (P)Johnny Mathis.
WHAT WOULD WE DO WITHOUT YOU (1970) (wm)Stephen Sondheim. (I)Musical: *Company* with Elaine Stritch.
WHAT WOULDN'T I DO FOR THAT MAN! (1929) (w)E. Y. Harburg (m)Jay Gorney. (I)Film: *Applause* by Helen Morgan. Also film *Glorifying The American Girl.*

WHAT YOU GAVE ME (1969) (wm)Nicholas Ashford—Valerie Simpson. (P)Marvin Gaye and Tammi Terrell.
WHAT YOU GET IS WHAT YOU SEE (1987) (wm)T. Britten—G. Lyle. (P)Tina Turner.
WHAT YOU NEED (1986) (wm)Andrew Farriss—Michael Hutchence. (P)INXS.
WHAT YOU WON'T DO FOR LOVE (1979) (wm)Robert Caldwell—Alfons Kettner. (P)Bobby Caldwell.
WHAT YOU'RE DOING (1964) (wm)John Lennon—Paul McCartney. (P)Bobby Caldwell.
WHAT'D I SAY? (1959) (wm)Ray Charles. (P)Ray Charles. Also recorded by Jerry Lee Lewis, Elvis Presley, Bobby Darin and Rare Earth.
WHAT'LL I DO (1924) (wm)Irving Berlin. (I)*Music Box Revue Of 1923* by Grace Moore and John Steel. Film: *Alexander's Ragtime Band* (1938) by chorus. Film: *Big City* (1948) by Danny Thomas.
WHAT'S GOING ON (1971) (wm)Renaldo Benson—Marvin Gaye—Al Cleveland. (P)Marvin Gaye. (R)Cyndi Lauper (1987).
WHAT'S GOOD ABOUT GOOD NIGHT (1938) (w)Dorothy Fields (m)Jerome Kern. (I)Film: *Joy Of Living* by Irene Dunne.
WHAT'S GOOD ABOUT GOODBYE (1948) (w)Leo Robin (m)Harold Arlen. (I)Film: *Casbah* by Tony Martin. (P)Margaret Whiting.
WHAT'S GOOD FOR GENERAL BULLMOOSE (1956) (wm)Johnny Mercer—Gene De Paul. (I)Musical: *Li'L Abner* with Stubby Kaye.
WHAT'S IT GONNA BE? (1967) (wm)Mort Shuman—Jerry Ragovoy. (P)Dusty Springfield.
WHAT'S LOVE GOT TO DO WITH IT (1984) (wm)Terry Britten—Graham Lyle. (P)Tina Turner. NARAS Award nominee: Best Song of the Year, 1984. NARAS Award Winner: Best Record of the Year, 1984. No. 1 Chart Record.
WHAT'S NEW (1939) (w)Johnny Burke (m)Bob Haggart. Original title *I'M Free* and introduced and popularized by Bob Crosby and his Orchestra. (R)1985 by Linda Ronstadt.
WHAT'S NEW PUSSYCAT (1965) (w)Hal David (m)Burt Bacharach. (I)Film: *What's New Pussycat.* (P)Tom Jones.
WHAT'S THE REASON (I'M NOT PLEASIN' YOU) (1935) (wm)Pinky Tomlin—Coy Poe—Jimmie Grier—Earl Hatch. (I)Film: *Times Square Lady* by Pinky Tomlin.
WHAT'S THE USE OF BREAKING UP? (1969) (wm)Kenny Gamble—Jerry Butler—Theresa Bell. (P)Jerry Butler.
WHAT'S THE USE OF GETTING SOBER (1938) (wm)Bubsy Meyers. (P)1943 by Louis Jordan and his Tympany Five.
WHAT'S THE USE OF TALKING (1926) (w)Lorenz Hart (m)Richard Rodgers. (I)Revue: *The Garrick Gaieties Of 1926* by Betty Starbuck and Sterling Holloway.
WHAT'S THE USE OF WOND'RIN' (1945) (w)Oscar Hammerstein II (m)Richard Rodgers. (I)Musical: *Carousel* by Jan Clayton. Film version (1957) by Shirley Jones.
WHAT'S THIS (1945) (wm)Dave Lambert. (P)Dave Lambert and Buddy Stewart, with Gene Krupa and his Orchestra. First bop vocal recording according to jazz historian Leonard Feather.
WHAT'S WRONG WITH ME? (1948) (w)Edward Heyman (m)Nacio Herb Brown. (I)Film: *The Kissing Bandit* by Kathryn Grayson.

WHAT'S YOUR NAME (1962) (wm)Claude Johnson. (P)Don and Juan.

WHAT'S YOUR NAME (1977) (wm)Gary Rossington—Ronnie Van Zant. (P)Lynyrd Skynyrd.

WHAT'S YOUR STORY, MORNING GLORY? (1938) (wm)Jack Lawrence—Paul Francis Webster—Mary Lou Williams. (P)Andy Kirk and his Clouds of Joy, featuring Mary Lou Williams, pianist and arranger. (P)Jimmie Lunceford and his Orchestra.

WHATCHA GONNA DO (1977) (wm)Cory Lerios—David Jenkins. (P)Pablo Cruise.

WHATCHA KNOW JOE (1940) (wm)James "Trummy" Young. (P)Jimmie Lunceford and his Orchestra. (P)Charlie Barnet and his Orchestra.

WHATCHA SEE IS WHATCHA GET (1971) (wm)Tony Hester. (P)The Dramatics.

WHATEVER GETS YOU THROUGH THE NIGHT (1974) (wm)John Lennon—Yoko Ono. (P)John Lennon.

WHATEVER IT IS I'M AGAINST IT (1933) (w)Bert Kalmar (m)Harry Ruby. (I)Film: *Horse Feathers* by Groucho Marx.

WHATEVER LOLA WANTS (1955) (wm)Richard Adler—Jerry Ross. (I)Musical: *Damn Yankees* by Gwen Verdon. Also in film version by Miss Verdon.

WHEEL OF FORTUNE, THE (1952) (wm)Bennie Benjamin—George Weiss. (P)Kay Starr.

WHEEL OF HURT, THE (1966) (wm)Charles Singleton—Eddie Snyder. (P)Al Martino. (P)Margaret Whiting.

WHEELS (1961) (wm)Jimmy Tomes—Richard Stephens. (P)The String-A-Longs.

WHEN (1958) (wm)Paul Evans—Jack Reardon. (P)The Kalin Twins.

WHEN A GYPSY MAKES HIS VIOLIN CRY (1935) (w)Dick Smith—Frank Winegar—Jimmy Rogan (m)Emery Deutsch. (I)Theme song of Emery Deutsch and his Orchestra.

WHEN A MAID COMES KNOCKING AT YOUR HEART (1912) (w)Otto Harbach (m)Rudolf Friml. (I)Musical: *The Firefly*. Film version with Allan Jones and Jeanette MacDonald.

WHEN A MAN LOVES A WOMAN (1966) (wm)Calvin Lewis—Andrew Wright. (P)Percy Sledge.

WHEN A WOMAN LOVES A MAN (1930) (w)Billy Rose (m)Ralph Rainger. (I)Film: *Be Yourself* by Fanny Brice.

WHEN A WOMAN LOVES A MAN (1934) (w)Johnny Mercer (m)Bernie Hanighen—Gordon Jenkins. No artist credited with introduction.

WHEN BUDDHA SMILES (1921) (w)Arthur Freed (m)Nacio Herb Brown. (P)Paul Whiteman and his Orchestra.

WHEN DAY IS DONE (1926) (w)B. G. De Sylva (m)Robert Katscher. (P)In U. S. by Paul Whiteman and his Orchestra with trumpet solo by Henry Busse.

WHEN DID I FALL IN LOVE (1959) (wm)Sheldon Harnick—Jerry Bock. (I)Musical: *Fiorello* by Ellen Hanley.

WHEN DID YOU LEAVE HEAVEN (1936) (w)Walter Bullock (m)Richard A. Whiting. (I)Film: *Sing Baby Sing* by Tony Martin.

WHEN DOVES CRY (1984) (wm)Prince. (P)Prince. Number one chart record.

WHEN FRANCIS DANCES WITH ME (1921) (w)Benny Ryan (m)Sol Violinsky. Novelty song. (R)Film: *Give My Regards To Broadway* with Dan Dailey and Charles Winninger.

WHEN HEARTS ARE YOUNG (1922) (w)Cyrus Young (m)Sigmund Romberg—Alfred Goodman. (I)Operetta: *The Lady In Ermine* by Wilda Bennett.

WHEN I DIE (1969) (wm)Steve Kennedy—William Smith. (P)Motherlode.

WHEN I FALL IN LOVE (1951) (w)Edward Heyman (m)Victor Young. (I)Film: *One Minute To Zero* (P)Nat Cole. (R)1962 by The Lettermen.

WHEN I GET THRU WITH YOU, YOU'LL LOVE ME TOO (1962) (wm)Harlan Howard. (P)Patsy Cline.

WHEN I GROW TOO OLD TO DREAM (1935) (w)Oscar Hammerstein II (m)Sigmund Romberg. (I)Film: *The Night Is Young* by Ramon Novarro and Evelyn Laye. Film: *Deep In My Heart* (1954) by Jose Ferrer.

WHEN I GROW UP (To Be A Man) (1964) (wm)Brian Wilson. (P)The Beach Boys.

WHEN I LEAVE THE WORLD BEHIND (1915) (wm)Irving Berlin. (P)Henry Burr. (P)Sam Ash.

WHEN I LOOK AT YOU (1942) (w)Paul Francis Webster (m)Walter Jurmann. (I)Film: *Presenting Lily Mars* by Judy Garland.

WHEN I LOST YOU (1912) (wm)Irving Berlin. (P)Henry Burr.

WHEN I MARRY MISTER SNOW (1945) (w)Oscar Hammerstein II (m)Richard Rodgers. (I)Musical: *Carousel* by Jan Clayton. Film version by Shirley Jones.

WHEN I NEED YOU (1977) (w)Carole Bayer Sager (m)Albert Hammond. (P)Leo Sayer.

WHEN I SEE AN ELEPHANT FLY (1941) (wm)Ned Washington—Oliver Wallace. (I)Cartoon film: *Dumbo* by voice of Cliff Edwards as the voice of the crow.

WHEN I TAKE MY SUGAR TO TEA (1931) (wm)Irving Kahal—Sammy Fain—Pierre Norman Connor. (I)Film: *The Mating Season* with Gene Tierney and Miriam Hopkins. Film: *Monkey Business* with the Four Marx Brothers. (P)Connee Boswell.

WHEN I THINK OF YOU (1986) (wm)James Harris III—Terry Lewis—Janet Jackson. (P)Janet Jackson. Number one chart record.

WHEN I WALK WITH YOU (1947) (w)John Latouche (m)Duke Ellington. (I)Musical: *Beggar'S Holiday* by Jet MacDonald and Alfred Drake.

WHEN I WAS A LAD (1878) (w)W. S. Gilbert (m)Arthur Sullivan. (I)Operetta: *H. M. S. Pinafore*.

WHEN I WAS A LITTLE CUCKOO (1944) (wm)Cole Porter. (I)Revue: *Seven Lively Arts* by Beatrice Lillie.

WHEN I WAS YOUNG (1967) (wm)Eric Burdon—Victor Brigs—Barry Jenkins—Danny McCulloch—John Weider. (P)Eric Burdon and The Animals.

WHEN I'M LOOKING AT YOU (1929) (w)Clifford Grey (m)Herbert Stothart. (I)Musical: *The Rogue Song* by Lawrence Tibbett.

WHEN I'M NOT NEAR THE GIRL I LOVE (1946) (w)E. Y. Harburg (m)Burton Lane. (I)Musical: *Finian'S Rainbow* by David Wayne. Also in film version.

WHEN I'M SIXTY-FOUR (1964) (wm)John Lennon—Paul McCartney. (P)The Beatles.

WHEN I'M THE PRESIDENT (We Want Cantor) (1931) (wm)Al Lewis—Al Sherman. (P)Eddie Cantor.

WHEN I'M WITH YOU (1936) (w)Mack Gordon (m)Harry Revel. (I)Film: *Poor Little Rich Girl* by Shirley Temple and Tony Martin. Reprised by Alice Faye.

WHEN I'M WRONG (1975) (wm)B. B. King. (P)B. B. King.

WHEN IRISH EYES ARE SMILING (1912) (w)Chauncey Olcott—George Graff, Jr. (m)Ernest R. Ball. (I)Musical: *The Isle Of Dreams*. (P)Chauncey Olcott. (P)John

McCormack.

WHEN IS SOMETIME? (1948) (w)Johnny Burke (m)James Van Heusen. (I)Film: *A Connecticut Yankee* by Bing Crosby.

WHEN IT'S APPLE BLOSSOM TIME IN NORMANDY (1912) (wm)Harry Gifford—Huntley Trevor—Tom Mellor. (P)Elsie Baker and James F. Harrison. (R)Film: *Shine On Harvest Moon* with Ann Sheridan.

WHEN IT'S DARKNESS ON THE DELTA (See DARKNESS ON THE DELTA)

WHEN IT'S LAMP LIGHTIN' TIME IN THE VALLEY (1933) (wm)Joe Lyons—Sam C. Hart—Herald Goodman—Dean Upoon—Curt Poulton. (P)Wayne King and his Orchestra.

WHEN IT'S NIGHT TIME IN DIXIE LAND (1914) (wm)Irving Berlin. Not one of Berlin's hit songs.

WHEN IT'S NIGHT-TIME IN ITALY, IT'S WEDNESDAY OVER HERE (1923) (wm)James Kendis—Lew Brown. (P)James "Jimmy" Kendis. (P)Lew Holtz and his Orchestra.

WHEN IT'S SLEEPY TIME DOWN SOUTH (1931) (wm)Leon Rene—Otis Rene—Clarence Muse. (P)Theme song of Louis Armstrong.

WHEN IT'S SPRINGTIME IN THE ROCKIES (1929) (w)Mary Hale Woolsey (m)Robert Sauer. (P)Rudy Vallee. Film: *Silver Spurs* with Roy Rogers and Smiley Burnette.

WHEN JOHNNY COMES MARCHING HOME (1863) (wm)Patrick Gilmore. Famous song during the Civil War. (R)Film: *When Johnny Comes Marching Home* with Donald O'Connor and Allan Jones.

WHEN LIGHTS ARE LOW (1923) (wm)Ted Fiorito—Gus Kahn—Ted Koehler. (P)Ted Fiorito and his Orchestra.

WHEN LIKING TURNS TO LOVING (1965) (wm)Kenny Young—Jay Fishman. (P)Ronnie Dove.

WHEN LOVE IS YOUNG (1937) (w)Harold Adamson (m)Jimmy McHugh. (I)Film: *When Love Is Young* by Virginia Bruce. (P)Fats Waller.

WHEN MY BABY SMILES AT ME (1920) (wm)Andrew Sterling—Ted Lewis—Bill Munro. (P)Theme song of Ted Lewis and his Orchestra. Film: *Sing Baby Sing* (1936) by The Ritz Brothers. Film: *When My Baby Smiles At Me* with Dan Dailey and Betty Grable.

WHEN MY DREAM BOAT COMES HOME (1936) (wm)Cliff Friend—Dave Franklin. (P)Guy Lombardo and his Royal Canadians.

WHEN MY DREAMS COME TRUE (1929) (wm)Irving Berlin. (I)Film: *The Cocoanuts* by Oscar Shaw and Mary Eaton. (P)Paul Whiteman and his Orchestra.

WHEN MY LITTLE GIRL IS SMILING (1961) (wm)Gerry Goffin—Carole King. (P)The Drifters. (P)Jimmy Justice.

WHEN MY MAN COMES HOME (1944) (w)J. Mayo Williams (m)Buddy Johnson. (P)Buddy Johnson and his Orchestra.

WHEN MY SHIP COMES IN (1935) (w)Gus Kahn (m)Walter Donaldson. (I)Film: *Kid Millions* by Eddie Cantor.

WHEN MY SUGAR WALKS DOWN THE STREET ALL THE LITTLE BIRDIES GO TWEET-TWEET-T (1924) (wm)Gene Austin—Jimmy McHugh—Irving Mills. (P)Gene Austin. (P)Phil Harris and his Orchestra.

WHEN SHALL WE MEET AGAIN (1921) (w)Raymond B. Egan (m)Richard A. Whiting. (I)Musical: *Tip Top* by The Duncan Sisters.

WHEN SHE WALKS IN THE ROOM (1945) (w)Dorothy Fields (m)Sigmund Romberg. (I)Musical: *Up In Central Park*. Film version with Deanna Durbin and Vincent Price.

WHEN SMOKEY SINGS (1987) (wm)M. Fry—M. White. (P)ABC.

WHEN SOMETHING IS WRONG WITH MY BABY (1966) (wm)David Porter—Isaac Hayes. (P)Sam and Dave.

WHEN SUMMER IS GONE (Oh, How I'll Miss You) (1937) (wm)Hal Kemp. (P)Hal Kemp and his Orchestra.

WHEN SUNNY GETS BLUE (1956) (w)Jack Segal (m)Marvin Fisher. (P)Johnny Mathis.

WHEN THE BLACK SHEEP RETURNS TO THE FOLD (1916) (wm)Irving Berlin. Not one of Berlin's hit songs.

WHEN THE BOY IN YOUR ARMS (1961) (wm)Sid Tepper—Roy C. Bennett. (P)Connie Francis.

WHEN THE BOYS COME HOME (1944) (w)E. Y. Harburg (m)Harold Arlen. (I)Musical: *Bloomer Girl* by "The Five Daughters."

WHEN THE BOYS TALK ABOUT THE GIRLS (1958) (wm)Bob Merrill. (P)Valerie Carr.

WHEN THE CHILDREN ARE ASLEEP (1945) (w)Oscar Hammerstein II (m)Richard Rodgers. (I)Musical: *Carousel* by Eric Mattson and Jan Clayton. Film version (1957) by Barbara Ruick and Robert Rounseville.

WHEN THE GOING GETS TOUGH, THE TOUGH GET GOING (1986) (wm)Wayne Brathwaite—Barry Eastwood—Robert John Lange—Billy Ocean. (I)Film: *Jewel Of The Nile*, 1985. (P)Billy Ocean.

WHEN THE IDLE POOR BECOME THE IDLE RICH (1946) (w)E. Y. Harburg (m)Burton Lane. (I)Musical: *Finian'S Rainbow* by Ella Logan and chorus.

WHEN THE LIGHTS GO ON AGAIN (All Over The World) (1942) (wm)Eddie Seiler—Sol Marcus—Bennie Benjamin. (P)Vaughn Monroe and his Orchestra. Film: *When The Lights Go On Again* (1944) with Regis Toomey and Jimmy Lyon.

WHEN THE MIDNIGHT CHOO CHOO LEAVES FOR ALABAM' (1912) (wm)Irving Berlin. (P)Arthur Collins and Byron Harlan. Film: *Alexander's Ragtime Band* with Tyrone Power, Don Ameche and Alice Faye. Film:

WHEN THE MOON COMES OVER THE MOUNTAIN (1931) (w)Howard Johnson (m)Harry Woods. (P)Theme song of Kate Smith.

WHEN THE MOOR COMES OVER MADISON SQUARE (The Love Lament of a Western Gent) (1940) (w)Johnny Burke (m)James V. Monaco. (I)Film: *Rhythm On The River* by Bing Crosby.

WHEN THE MORNING COMES (1971) (wm)Hoyt Axton. (P)Hoyt Axton.

WHEN THE ONE YOU LOVE (Simply Won't Come Back) (1945) (w)Sammy Cahn (m)Jule Styne. (I)Film: *Cinderella Jones* with Robert Alda and Joan Leslie.

WHEN THE ORGAN PLAYED AT TWILIGHT (The Song That Reached My Heart) (1929) (w)Raymond Wallace (m)Jimmy Campbell—Reg Connelly. (P)Jesse Crawford.

WHEN THE RED, RED ROBIN COMES BOB, BOB BOBBIN' ALONG (1926) (wm)Harry Woods. (P)Sophie Tucker. (P)Lillian Roth. (P)Al Jolson. Film: *The Jolson Story* with Jolson dubbing for Larry Parks. Film: *Ha*

WHEN THE SAINTS GO MARCHING IN (1896)

(w)Katherine E. Purvis (m)James M. Black. Famous song which originated in New Orleans and became a jazz standard. Associated most with Louis Armstrong.

WHEN THE SPRING IS IN THE AIR (1932) (w)Oscar Hammerstein II (m)Jerome Kern. (I)Musical: *Music In The Air* by Katherine Carrington and full ensemble.

WHEN THE SUN COMES OUT (1940) (w)Ted Koehler (m)Harold Arlen. (P)Jimmy Dorsey and his Orchestra.

WHEN THE SWALLOWS COME BACK TO CAPISTRANO (1940) (wm)Leon Rene. (P)The Ink Spots.

WHEN THE WORLD WAS YOUNG (Ah The Apple Trees) (w-Eng)Johnny Mercer (m)M. Philippe Gerard. (P)U. S. by Peggy Lee.

WHEN THERE'S A BREEZE ON LAKE LOUISE (1942) (w)Mort Greene (m)Harry Revel. (I)Film: *The Mayor Of 44Th Street* by Joan Merrill. Nominated for Academy Award. (P)Freddy Martin and his Orchestra.

WHEN THERE'S NO YOU (1970) (wm)Les Reed—Jackie Rae. (P)Englebert Humperdinck. Based on "Vesti Law Giubba" from opera *Pagliacci.*

WHEN THEY ASK ABOUT YOU (1944) (wm)Sam H. Stept. (P)Jimmy Dorsey and his Orchestra, vocal by Kitty Kallen.

WHEN THEY PLAYED THE POLKA (1938) (w)Lou Holzer (m)Fabian Andre. (P)Horace Heidt and his Brigadiers. (P)Sammy Kaye and his Orchestra.

WHEN TOMORROW COMES (1933) (w)Irving Kahal (m)Sammy Fain. (I)Film: *Mandalay* by Kay Francis. (P)Freddy Martin and his Orchestra.

WHEN WE GET MARRIED (1961) (wm)Donald Hogan. (P)The Dreamlovers.

WHEN WE'RE ALONE or PENTHOUSE SERENADE (1931) (wm)Will Jason—Val Burton. (P)Ruth Etting. Film: *Beau James* with Bob Hope.

WHEN WILL I BE LOVED (1960) (wm)Phil Everly. (P)The Everly Brothers. (R)1975 by Linda Ronstadt.

WHEN WILL I SEE YOU AGAIN (1974) (wm)Kenny Gamble—Leon Huff. (P)The Three Degrees.

WHEN WINTER COMES (1939) (wm)Irving Berlin. (I)Film: *Second Fiddle* by Rudy Vallee. (P)Artie Shaw and his Orchestra.

WHEN YOU AND I WERE SEVENTEEN (1924) (w)Gus Kahn (m)Charles Rosoff. (P)Ruth Etting.

WHEN YOU AND I WERE YOUNG MAGGIE (1866) (w)George W. Johnson (m)James Austin Butterfield. (P)Frank Stanley and Corrine Morgan. (R)1923 by Van and Schenck. (R)1951 by Bing Crosby and Gary Crosby. (R)1951 by Margaret Whiting and Jimmy Wakely. Film: *Swing Time Johnny* with The Andrews Sisters.

WHEN YOU DANCE (1955) (wm)Andrew Jones—L. Kirkland. (P)The Turbans.

WHEN YOU LEAVE, DON'T SLAM THE DOOR (1946) (wm)Joe Allison. (P)Tex Ritter.

WHEN YOU WALKED OUT SOMEONE ELSE WALKED RIGHT IN (1923) (wm)Irving Berlin. (P)Isham Jones and his Orchestra. (P)Frank Crumit. *Music Box Revue Of 1923* with Grace Moore and Robert Benchley.

WHEN YOU WISH UPON A STAR (1940) (w)Ned Washington (m)Leigh Harline. (I)Cartoon film: *Pinocchio* by voice of Cliff Edwards as Jiminy Cricket.

Academy Award winning song 1940.

WHEN YOU WORE A TULIP AND I WORE A BIG RED ROSE (1914) (w)Jack Mahoney (m)Percy Wenrich. (P)The American Quartet. (R)Film: *For Me And My Gal* with Gene Kelly and Judy Garland. Film: *The Merry Monihans* with Donald O'Conner.

WHEN YOU'RE A LONG LONG WAY FROM HOME (1914) (w)Sam M. Lewis (m)George W. Meyer. (P)Henry Burr.

WHEN YOU'RE AWAY (1914) (w)Henry Blossom (m)Victor Herbert. (I)Operetta: *The Only Girl.*

WHEN YOU'RE HOT, YOU'RE HOT (1971) (wm)Jerry Reed. (P)Jerry Reed.

WHEN YOU'RE IN LOVE (1954) (w)Johnny Mercer (m)Gene de Paul. (I)Film: *Seven Brides For Seven Brothers* by Jane Powell and Howard Keel.

WHEN YOU'RE IN LOVE WITH A BEAUTIFUL WOMAN (1979) (wm)Evan Stevens. (P)Dr. Hook.

WHEN YOU'RE SMILING (The Whole World Smiles With You) (wm)Mark Fisher—Joe Goodwin—Larry Shay. (P)Seger Ellis. (P)Louis Armstrong. Film: *Meet Danny Wilson* with Frank Sinatra and Shelley Winters.

WHEN YOU'RE WITH SOMEBODY ELSE (1927) (w)L. Wolfe Gilbert (m)Ruth Etting—Abel Baer. (P)Ruth Etting.

WHEN YOU'RE YOUNG AND IN LOVE (1964) (wm)Van McCoy. (P)Ruby and The Romantics. (R)1967 by The Marvelettes.

WHEN YOUR HAIR HAS TURNED TO SILVER I WILL LOVE YOU JUST THE (1930) (w)Charles Tobias (m)Peter De Rose. (P)Russ Morgan and his Orchestra. (P)Rudy Vallee.

WHEN YOUR LOVER HAS GONE (1931) (wm)E. A. Swan. (I)Film: *Blonde Crazy* with James Cagney and Joan Blondell. Song was on soundtrack alone.

WHEN YUBA PLAYS THE RUMBA ON HIS TUBA (1931) (wm)Herman Hupfield. (I)Revue: *The Third Little Show* by Walter O'Keefe. (P)Rudy Vallee.

WHENEVER A TEENAGER CRIES (1964) (wm)Ernie Maresca. (P)Reparata and The Delrons.

WHENEVER HE HOLDS YOU (1964) (wm)Bobby Goldsboro. (P)Bobby Goldsboro.

WHENEVER I CALL YOU FRIEND (1978) (wm)Melissa Manchester—Kenny Loggins. (P)Kenny Loggins.

WHERE AM I GOING (1966) (w)Dorothy Fields (m)Cy Coleman. (I)Musical: *Sweet Charity* by Gwen Verdon. Film version by Shirley MacLaine. (R)1985 SWEET CHARITY with Debbie Allen.

WHERE AM I? (Am I in Heaven?) (1935) (w)Al Dubin (m)Harry Warren. (I)Film: *Stars Over Broadway* by James Melton. (P)Little Jack Little and his Orchestra. Other popular versions by Hal Kemp and his Orchestra and Ray Noble and his Orchestra.

WHERE ARE YOU (1936) (w)Harold Adamson (m)Jimmy McHugh. (I)Musical: *Top Of The Town* by Gertrude Nielsen. (P)Mildred Bailey and Gertrude Nielsen.

WHERE ARE YOU GOING (1970) (w)Danny Meehan (m)Bobby Scott. (I)Film: *Joe* by the voice of Jerry Butler.

WHERE CAN I GO WITHOUT YOU (1952) (w)Peggy Lee (m)Victor Young. (P)Nat "King" Cole. (R)1954 by Peggy Lee.

WHERE DID OUR LOVE GO (1964) (wm)Lamont Dozier—Brian Holland—Eddie Holland. (P)The Supremes.

WHERE DID ROBINSON CRUSOE GO WITH FRIDAY

ON SATURDAY NIGHT (1916) (wm)Joe Young—Sam M. Lewis—George W. Meyer. (I)Musical: *Robinson Crusoe, JR.* by Al Jolson. (P)Al Jolson. Musical: *Follow The Crowd* with Ethel Levey.

WHERE DID YOU GET THAT GIRL (1913) (w)Bert Kalmar (m)Harry Puck. (P)Walter Van Brunt. Film: *Three Little Words* with Fred Astaire and Red Skelton.

WHERE DO I BEGIN (See LOVE STORY)

WHERE DO I GO (1969) (w)Gerome Ragni—James Rado (m)Galt MacDermot. (I)Musical: *Hair.* Also film version.

WHERE DO THEY GO WHEN THEY ROW, ROW, ROW? (1920) (w)Bert Kalmar—George Jessel (m)Harry Ruby. (P)George Jessel.

WHERE DO WE GO FROM HERE! (1917) (wm)Howard Johnson—Percy Wenrich. Not a hit until revival in film *For Me And My Gal* with Judy Garland and Gene Kelly.

WHERE DO YOU GO? (1965) (wm)Sonny Bono. (P)Cher.

WHERE DO YOU WORK-A-JOHN (1926) (wm)Mortimer Weinberg—Charley Marks—Harry Warren. (P)Fred Waring and The Pennsylvanians.

WHERE HAVE ALL THE FLOWERS GONE (1961) (wm)Pete Seeger. (P)The Kingston Trio.

WHERE HAVE YOU BEEN (1930) (wm)Cole Porter. (I)Musical: *The New Yorkers* by Charles King and Hope Williams. (P)Emil Coleman and his Orchestra.

WHERE IN THE WORLD (1938) (wm)Harlan Howard. (I)Film: *Josette* by Don Ameche. (P)Hal Kemp and his Orchestra.

WHERE IS LOVE (1963) (wm)Lionel Bart. (I)Musical: *Oliver* London production by Keith Hamshere and reprised by Madeleine Newbury. New York production by Paul O'Connor and reprised by Dortha Duckworth.

WHERE IS THE LIFE THAT LATE I LED? (1948) (wm)Cole Porter. (I)Musical: *Kiss Me Kate* by Alfred Drake. Film version 1953 sung by Howard Keel.

WHERE IS THE LOVE (1975) (wm)Harry Wayne Casey—Richard Finch—Willy Clark—Betty Wright. (P)Betty Wright. 1975 NARAS Award Winner.

WHERE IS THE LOVE (1971) (wm)Ralph McDonald—William Salter. (P)Roberta Flack and Danny Hathaway.

WHERE IS THE MAN OF MY DREAMS? (1922) (w)B. G. De Sylva (m)George Gershwin. (I)Revue: *George White'S Scandals Of 1922* by Winnie Lightner and the Original Piano Trio.

WHERE IS THE SONG OF SONGS FOR ME (1928) (wm)Irving Berlin. (I)Film: *Lady Of The Pavements* (1929) by Lupe Velez.

WHERE IS YOUR HEART (See THE SONG FROM MOULIN ROUGE)

WHERE LOVE HAS GONE (1964) (w)Sammy Cahn (m)Jimmy Van Heusen. (I)Film: *Where Love Has Gone* by Jack Jones.

WHERE OR WHEN (1927) (w)Lorenz Hart (m)Richard Rodgers. (I)Musical: *Babes In Arms* by Ray Heatherton and Mitzi Green. Film version (1939) by Judy Garland. Film: *Words And Music* (1948) by Lena Horne. (R)1960 by Dion and The Belmonts.

WHERE THE BLACK EYED SUSANS GROW (1917) (w)Dave Radford (m)Richard A. Whiting. (I)Musical: *Robinson Crusoe, JR.* by Al Jolson. Musical: *Cheep* by Beatrice Lillie.

WHERE THE BLUE OF THE NIGHT MEETS THE GOLD OF THE DAY (1931) (wm)Roy Turk—Bing Crosby—Fred E. Ahlert. (I)Film: *The Big Broadcast* by Bing Crosby. Theme song of Bing Crosby.

WHERE THE BLUES WERE BORN IN NEW ORLEANS (1946) (w)Cliff Dixon (m)Bob Carleton. (I)Film: *New Orleans* by Louis Armstrong and his All-Stars.

WHERE THE BOYS ARE (1961) (w)Howard Greenfield (m)Neil Sedaka. (I)Film: *Where The Boys Are* by Connie Francis. (P)Connie Francis.

WHERE THE LAZY DAISIES GROW (1924) (wm)Cliff Friend. (P)Jean Goldkette and his Orchestra and Cliff Edwards.

WHERE THE LAZY RIVER GOES BY (1936) (w)Harold Adamson (m)Jimmy McHugh. (I)Film: *Banjo On My Knee* by Barbara Stanwyck and Tony Martin. (P)Teddy Wilson and his Orchestra, with vocal by Midge Williams.

WHERE THE MORNING GLORIES GROW (1917) (wm)Gus Kahn—Raymond Egan—Richard A. Whiting. (P)Elizabeth Spencer and The Spencer Trio.

WHERE THE MOUNTAINS MEET THE SKY (I'm Headin' for the Blue Horizon) (1942) (wm)Aston "Deacon" Williams. (P)Sammy Kaye and his Orchestra with vocal by Billy Williams.

WHERE THE SHY LITTLE VIOLETS GROW (1928) (w)Gus Kahn (m)Harry Warren. (P)Guy Lombardo and His Royal Canadians.

WHERE THE STREETS HAVE NO NAME (1987) (wm)U2. (P)U2.

WHERE WAS I? (1939) (w)Al Dubin (m)W. Franke Harling. (I)Film: *'Til We Meet Again.* (P)1940 by Charlie Barnet and his Orchestra; Jan Savitt and his Orchestra; Sammy Kaye and his Orchestra, vocal by Clyde Burke.

WHERE WOULD YOU BE WITHOUT ME (1965) (wm)Leslie Bricusse—Anthony Newley. (I)Musical: *The Roar Of The Greasepaint-The Smell Of The Crowd* with Anthony Newley and Cyril Ritchard.

WHERE'D YOU GET THOSE EYES? (1926) (wm)Walter Donaldson. (P)Ted Lewis and his Orchestra. (P)Vaughn Deleath and his Orchestra.

WHERE'S THAT RAINBOW (1927) (w)Lorenz Hart (m)Richard Rodgers. (I)Musical: *Peggy Ann* by Margaret Breen and Helen Ford. Film: *Words And Music* (1948) by Ann Sothern.

WHERE'S THE BOY? HERE'S THE GIRL! (1928) (w)Ira Gershwin (m)George Gershwin. (I)Musical: *Treasure Girl.*

WHERE, OH WHERE? (1950) (wm)Cole Porter. (I)Musical: *Out Of This World* by Barbara Ashley.

WHICH WAY YOU GOIN' BILLY (1970) (wm)Terry Jacks. (P)The Poppy Family.

WHIFFENPOOF SONG, THE (1911) (w)Meade Minnigerode—George S. Pomeroy (m)Tod B. Galloway. Theme song of The Whiffenpoof Club of Yale University. (P)Rudy Vallee. Film: *Winged Victory* (1935).

WHILE A CIGARETTE WAS BURNING (1938) (wm)Charles Kenny—Nick Kenny. (P)Joan Edwards. Theme of Fred Waring's Chesterfield radio show.

WHILE HEARTS ARE SINGING (1931) (w)Clifford Grey (m)Oscar Strauss. (I)Film: *The Smiling Lieutenant* by Claudette Colbert.

WHILE MY GUITAR GENTLY WEEPS (1969) (wm)George Harrison. (P)The Beatles.

WHILE STROLLING THROUGH THE PARK ONE DAY

(1884) (wm)Ed Haley—Robert A. Keiser. (P)The Du-Rell Twin Brothers. Film: *Hollywood Revue* with Joan Crawford, Marion Davies and Norma Shearer. Film: *Sunbonnet Sue* with Phil Regan and Gale Storm.

WHILE THE ANGELUS WAS RINGING or THE THREE BELLS or THE JIMMY BROWN SONG (1945) (w-Eng)Dick Manning (m)Jean Villard. (P)France by Edith Piaf and Les Compagnons de la Chanson. (P)U. S. by The Browns. No. 1 Chart Record. (CR)Dick Flood.

WHILE WE'RE YOUNG (1943) (wm)Bill Engvick—Alec Wilder—Morty Palitz. (P)Mabel Mercer. (P)Fred Waring and his Pennsylvanians.

WHILE YOU DANCED, DANCED, DANCED (1951) (wm)Stephan Weiss. (P)Georgia Gibbs.

WHILE YOU SEE A CHANCE (1981) (w)Will Jennings (m)Steve Winwood. (P)Steve Winwood.

WHIP-POOR-WILL (1921) (w)Clifford Grey (m)Jerome Kern. (I)Musical: *Sally* by Marilyn Miller and Irving Fisher. (P)Isham Jones and his Orchestra.

WHIPPED CREAM (1964) (m)Naomi Neville. (P)Herb Alpert and the Tijuana Brass.

WHISPERING (1920) (wm)John Schonberger—Richard Coburn—Vincent Rose. (P)Paul Whiteman and his Orchestra. Films: *Greenwich Village* (1944) by Vivian Blaine; *Ziegfeld Girl* with Judy Garland; *Belles On Their Toes* with Myna Loy; *The Eddie Duchin Story* With Tyrone Power.

Whispering Bells (1957) (wm)C. E. Quick. (P)The Del Vikings.

WHISPERING GRASS (Don't Tell the Trees) (1940) (w)Fred Fisher (m)Doris Fisher. (P)The Ink Spots. (P)Erskine Harris and his Orchestra, vocal by Jimmy Mitchelle.

WHISPERING HOPE (1868) (wm)Alice Hawthorne. (P)Alma Gluck and Louise Horner. (R)1949 by Gordon MacRae and Jo Stafford.

WHISPERING WINDS (1952) (wm)Corky Robbins. (P)Patti Page.

WHISPER'S GETTING LOUDER (WHISPERS), THE (1966) (wm)Barbara Acklin—David Scott. (P)Jackie Wilson.

WHISPERS IN THE DARK (1937) (w)Leo Robin (m)Frederick Hollander. (I)Film: *Artist And Models* by Connee Boswell with Andre Kostelanetz and his Orchestra. Film: *Desire* with Gary Cooper.

WHISTLE WHILE YOU WORK (1937) (w)Larry Morey (m)Frank Churchill. (I)Cartoon film: *Snow White And The Seven Dwarfs* by voice of Adrienne Castelotti as Snow White.

WHISTLER AND HIS DOG, THE (1905) (m)Arthur Pryor. Famous folk-like song. Film: *The Emperor Waltz* with Bing Crosby and Joan Fontaine. Theme of OUR GANG comedy series.

WHISTLING AWAY THE DARK (1970) (w)Johnny Mercer (m)Henry Mancini. (I)Film: *Darling Lili* by Julie Andrews. Nominated for Academy Award.

WHISTLING BOY, THE (1937) (w)Dorothy Fields (m)Jerome Kern. (I)Film: *When You'Re In Love* by Grace Moore.

WHISTLING IN THE DARK (1931) (w)Allen Boretz (m)Dana Suesse. (P)Guy Lombardo and his Royal Canadians.

WHITE CHRISTMAS (1942) (wm)Irving Berlin. (I)Film: *Holiday Inn* by Bing Crosby. Films: *Blue Skies* and *White Christmas*. Recordings by Bing Crosby, Charlie Spivak, Frank Sinatra, Jo Stafford, Perry Como, others. Academy Award winning song.

WHITE CLIFFS OF DOVER, THE (There'll Be Bluebirds Over) (1942) (w)Nat Burton (m)Walter Kent. (P)Kay Kyser and his Orchestra. (P)Glenn Miller and his Orchestra.

WHITE DOVE, THE (1930) (w)Clifford Grey (m)Franz Lehar. (I)Film: *The Rogue Song* with Lawrence Tibbett. (P)Lawrence Tibbett.

WHITE JAZZ (1933) (m)H. Eugene Gifford. (P)Glen Gray and the Casa Loma Orchestra.

WHITE ON WHITE (1964) (wm)Bernice Ross—Lor Crane. (P)Danny Williams.

WHITE RABBIT (1967) (wm)Grace Slick. (P)Jefferson Airplane.

WHITE ROOM (1968) (wm)Jack Bruce—Pete Brown. (P)Cream.

WHITE SILVER SANDS (1957) (wm)Charles G."Re" Matthews. (P)Dave Gardner. (P)Don Rondo. (R)1960 by Bill Black's Combo.

WHITE SPORT COAT AND A PINK CARNATION, A (1957) (wm)Marty Robbins. (P)Marty Robbins.

WHITER SHADE OF PALE, A (1967) (wm)Gary Brooker—Keith Reid. (P)Procol Harum.

WHITHER THOU GOEST (1954) (wm)Guy Singer. (P)Les Paul and Mary Ford.

WHO (1925) (w)Otto Harbach—Oscar Hammerstein II (m)Jerome Kern. (I)Musical: *Sunny* by Marilyn Miller and Paul Frawley. Film versions (1930) by Marilyn Miller and (1941) by Anna Neagle. Films: *Till The Clouds Roll By* (1946) *And Look For The Silver Lining* (1949).

WHO AM I? (1966) (wm)Tony Hatch—Jackie Trent. (P)Petula Clark.

WHO ARE YOU (1978) (wm)Peter Townsend. (P)The Who.

WHO ATE NAPOLEONS WITH JOSEPHINE WHEN BONAPARTE WAS AWAY (1920) (w)Alfred Bryan (m)E. Ray Goetz. (I)Musical: *As You Were*.

WHO CAN I TURN TO (When Nobody Needs Me) (1964) (wm)Leslie Bricusse—Anthony Newley. (I)Anthony Newley in Musical: *Roar Of The Greasepaint-The Smell Of The Crowd*. (P)Tony Bennett.

WHO CAN I TURN TO? (1941) (wm)Alec Wilder—Bill Engvick. (P)Tommy Dorsey and his Orchestra, vocal by Jo Stafford.

WHO CAN IT BE NOW? (1982) (wm)Colin Hay. (P)Men at Work. Number one chart record.

WHO CARES (1922) (w)Jack Yellen (m)Milton Ager. (I)Musical: *Bombo* by Al Jolson.

WHO CARES (1931) (w)Ira Gershwin (m)George Gershwin. (I)Musical: *Of Thee I Sing* by William Gaxton and Lois Moran. (R)1952 *Of Thee I Sing* by Jack Carson and Betty Oakes.

WHO DO YOU KNOW IN HEAVEN (That Made You the Angel You Are?) (1974) (wm)Desmond Dyer—C. K. Scott. (P)Bo Donaldson.

WHO DO YOU LOVE, I HOPE (1946) (wm)Irving Berlin. (I)Musical: *Annie Get Your Gun* by Betty Nyman and Kenny Bowers. Film version with Betty Hutton.

WHO DO YOU THINK YOU ARE (1947) (w)Sylvia Dee (m)Sidney Lippman. (I)Musical: *Barefoot Boy With Cheek* with Nancy Walker and Red Buttons.

WHO FOUND WHO (1987) (wm)P. Gurvitz. (P)Jellybean featuring Elisa Fiorillo.

WHO IS GONNA LOVE ME? (1967) (w)Hal David (m)Burt Bacharach. (P)Dionne Warwick.

WHO LOVES YOU (1975) (wm)Bob Gaudio—Judy Parker. (P)The Four Seasons.

WHO NEEDS YOU (1956) (w)Al Stillman (m)Robert Allen. (P)The Four Lads.

WHO PUT THE BOMP (In the Bomp-Bomp-Bomp) (1961) (wm)Barry Mann—Gerry Goffin. (P)Barry Mann.

WHO TAKES CARE OF THE CARETAKER'S DAUGHTER (While The Caretaker's Busy Taking Care) (1924) (wm)Paul Revere—Chick Endor. (I)Musical: *Lady, Be Good!* by Cliff "Ukelele Ike" Edwards.

WHO THREW THE OVERALLS IN MRS. MURPHY'S CHOWDER (1899) (wm)George L. Giefer. Popular novelty song.

WHO THREW THE WHISKEY IN THE WELL? (1945) (wm)Lucky Millinder—Eddie De Lange—Johnny Brooks. (P)Lucky Millinder and his Orchestra.

WHO WANTS TO BE A MILLIONAIRE (1956) (wm)Cole Porter. (I)Film: *High Society* with Bing Crosby, Frank Sinatra and Grace Kelly.

WHO WILL ANSWER (1967) (w-Eng)Sheila Davis (w-SpL. E. Aute. (P)Ed Ames. Original Spanish title "Aleluya #1."

WHO WILL BUY (1963) (wm)Lionel Bart. (I)Musical: *Oliver* by Keith Hamshere and chorus (London production). U. S. production by Paul O'Keefe and chorus. Also in film version.

WHO WILL YOU RUN TO (1987) (wm)D. Warren (P)Heart.

WHO WOULD HAVE DREAMED? (1940) (wm)Cole Porter. (I)Musical: *Panama Hattie* by Larry Douglas and Janis Carter.

WHO WOULDN'T BE BLUE? (1928) (w)Benny Davis (m)Joe Burke. (P)Ted Weems and his Orchestra.

WHO WOULDN'T LOVE YOU (1942) (w)Bill Carey (m)Carl Fischer. (P)Kay Kyser and his Orchestra.

WHO'D SHE COO (1976) (wm)William Beck—Jim Williams—Marshall Jones—Marvin Pierce—Ronald Middlebrooks—Clarence Satchell—Leroy Bonner.(P)The Ohio Players.

WHO'LL BE THE NEXT IN LINE? (1965) (wm)Ray Davies. (P)The Kinks.

WHO'LL BUY MY VIOLETS (1923) (w-Eng)E. Ray Goetz (m)Jose Padilla. (I)Play: Little Miss Bluebeard by Irene Bordoni. Film: CITY LIGHTS with Charlie Chaplin (on soundtrack).

WHO'LL STOP THE RAIN (1970) (wm)John C. Fogerty. (P)Creedence Clearwater Revival.

WHO'S AFRAID OF LOVE (1936) (w)Sidney D. Mitchell (m)Lew Pollack. (I)Film: *One In A Million* by Don Ameche and Leah Ray.

WHO'S AFRAID OF THE BIG BAD WOLF (1933) (wm)Frank Churchill. Additional lyric by Ann Ronell. (I)Cartoon film: *The Three Little Pigs*. Film: *Babes In Toyland* with Stan Laurel and Oliver Hardy. (R)1970's by Barbra Streisand.

WHO'S CHEATING WHO? (1965) (wm)Carl Smith—Billy Davis—Raynard Miner. (P)Little Milton.

WHO'S CRYING NOW (1981) (wm)Steve Perry—Jonathan Cain. (P)Journey.

WHO'S GONNA TAKE THE BLAME (1970) (wm)Nicholas Ashford—Valerie Simpson. (P)The Miracles.

WHO'S HOLDING DONNA NOW (1988) (wm)David Foster—Jay Graydon—Randy Goodrum. (P)DeBarge.

WHO'S JOHNNY ("Short Circuit" Theme) (1986) (wm)Peter Wolf—Ina Wolf. (I)Film: *Short Circuit.* (P)DeBarge.

WHO'S MAKING LOVE (1968) (wm)Homer Banks—Betty Crutcher—Don Davis—Raymond Jackson. (P)Johnny Taylor.

WHO'S SORRY NOW (1923) (wm)Bert Kalmar—Harry Ruby—Ted Snyder. (P)Van and Schenck. Film: *Three Little Words* (1950) by Gloria De Haven. (R)1957 by Connie Francis.

WHO'S THAT GIRL (1987) (wm)Madonna—P. Leonard. (P)Madonna. Number one chart record.

WHO'S WONDERFUL, WHO'S MARVELOUS? MISS ANNABELLE LEE (See MISS ANNABELLE LEE)

WHO'S YEHOODI (1940) (w)Bill Seckler (m)Matt Dennis. (P)Kay Kyser and his Orchestra.

WHO'S YOUR LITTLE WHO-ZIS (1931) (wm)Walter Hirsch—Al Goering—Ben Bernie. (P)Ben Bernie and his Orchestra. Film: *The Stooge* with Dean Martin, Jerry Lewis and Polly Bergen.

BARBRA STREISAND

With all that was going on in the late fifties it became a prestige situation for a label to record a act live at the Bon Soir in New York City. The Bon Soir was a small club in Greenwich Village. Their shows usually included three performers: an opening act, usually a boy or girl singer; a comedian for the second act; and the featured performer for the third act.

We had, under contract at Coral, a girl and boy team called Cindy and Lindy. They were semi-folk, semi-pop, and really quite good. They had a hit on another label before coming with us. Since they were going to be the featured act at Bon Soir, the company decided to record them live there (a very surprise decision by a usually very stingy management).

We arrived on a Friday afternoon to set up to record. Since we would not be able to rehearse, and needed to check for the correct musical balances and sounds, I asked the young girl singer who was the show opener if we could record her to make sure we were set up properly. She graciously gave her permission and even asked if she might hear the playback to hear how she sounded.

So I sat there, listened, and recorded Barbra Streisand doing her complete act. I thanked her and that was that. Everyone has laughed at me because of this story, wondering why the hell I didn't sign her at the time. There were a couple of reasons. One, I didn't know if she had a contract at the time. Two - or maybe this was one - she looked as though she hadn't bathed in a week. Knowing the Decca people, they might have thrown me out of the office with her if I had brought her up.

WHO'S ZOOMIN' WHO (1985) (wm)Narada Michael Walden—Preston Glass—Aretha Franklin. (P)Aretha Franklin.

WHODUNIT (1977) (wm)Kenny St. Lewis—Freddy Perren. (P)Tavares.

WHOEVER YOU ARE or SOMETIMES YOUR EYES LOOK BLUE TO ME (1968) (w)Hal David (m)Burt Bacharach. (I)Musical: *Promises, Promises* with Jerry Orbach.

WHOLE LOT OF LOVING (1959) (wm)Fats Domino—Dave Bartholomew. (P)Fats Domino.

WHOLE LOT OF SHAKIN' GOING ON (1957) (wm)Dave Williams—Sunny David. (P)Jerry Lee Lewis.

WHOLE LOT OF SHAKIN' IN MY HEART (Since I Met You) (1966) (wm)Frank Wilson. (P)The Miracles.

WHOLE LOTTA LOVE (1969) (wm)John Bonham—John Paul Jones—James Page—Robert Plant. (P)Led Zeppelin.

WHOLE LOTTA LOVING (1958) (wm)Antoine "Fats" Domino—Dave Bartholomew. (P)Fats Domino.

WHOLE WORLD IS SINGING MY SONG, THE (1946) (w)Mann Curtis (m)Vic Mizzy. (P)Les Brown and his Orchestra, vocal by Doris Day.

WHOSE BABY ARE YOU (1920) (w)Anne Caldwell (m)Jerome Kern. (I)Musical: *The Night Boat* by Louise Groody and Hal Skelly.

WHOSE HEART ARE YOU BREAKING TONIGHT? (1964) (wm)Benny Davis—Ted Murray. (P)Connie Francis.

WHOSE LITTLE HEART ARE YOU BREAKING NOW (1917) (wm)Irving Berlin. Not one of Berlin's big hits.

WHY (1960) (wm)Pete DeAngelis—Bob Marcucci. (P)Frankie Avalon.

WHY (Is There A Rainbow In The Sky) (1929) (wm)Arthur Swanstrom—Benny Davis—J. Fred Coots. (I)Musical: *Son'S O' Guns* by Lily Damita and Jack Donahue.

WHY AM I ME (1975) (w)Peter Udell (m)Gary Geld. (I)Musical: *Shenandoah* with John Cullum.

WHY BABY WHY (1957) (wm)Luther Dixon—Larry Harrison. (P)Pat Boone.

WHY CAN'T I (1929) (w)Lorenz Hart (m)Richard Rodgers. (I)Musical: *Spring Is Here* by Lillian Taiz and Inez Courtney. Film: *Billy Rose'S Jumbo* (1962) by Doris Day and Martha Raye.

WHY CAN'T THE ENGLISH (1956) (w)Alan Jay Lerner (m)Frederick Loewe. (I)Musical: *My Fair Lady* by Rex Harrison. Film version by Rex Harrison.

WHY CAN'T THIS BE LOVE (1986) (wm)Michael Anthony—Sammy Hagar—Alex Van Halen—Eddie Van Halen. (P)Van Halen.

WHY CAN'T WE BE FRIENDS (1975) (wm)Sylvester Allen—Harold Ray Brown—Morris D. Dickerson—Gerald Goldstein—Leroy "Lonnie" Jordan—Lee Oskar Levitin—Charles Miller—Howard E. Scott. (P)War.

WHY CAN'T WE LIVE TOGETHER (1973) (wm)Timmy Thomas. (P)Timmy Thomas.

WHY CAN'T YOU (Birdies Sing in Cages Too) (1929) (wm)B. G. De Sylva—Lew Brown—Ray Henderson—Al Jolson. (I)Film: *Say It With Songs* by Al Jolson.

WHY CAN'T YOU BEHAVE (1949) (wm)Cole Porter. (I)Musical: *Kiss Me Kate* by Lisa Kirk and Harold Lang. Film version (1953) by Ann Miller.

WHY DID I KISS THAT GIRL (1924) (w)Lew Brown (m)Robert King—Ray Henderson. (P)Paul Whiteman and his Orchestra.

WHY DO FOOLS FALL IN LOVE (1956) (wm)Frankie Lymon—George Goldner. (P)The Teenagers featuring Frankie Lymon. (R)1984 by Diana Ross.

WHY DO I (1926) (w)Lorenz Hart (m)Richard Rodgers. (I)Musical: *The Girl Friend* by Francis X. Donegan and June Cochran.

WHY DO I DREAM THOSE DREAMS (1934) (w)Al Dubin (m)Harry Warren. (I)Film: *Wonder Bar* by Dick Powell. (P)Eddy Duchin and his Orchestra.

WHY DO I LOVE YOU (1925) (w)B. G. De Sylva—Ira Gershwin (m)George Gershwin. (I)Musical: *Tell Me More*.

WHY DO I LOVE YOU (1927) (w)Oscar Hammerstein II (m)Jerome Kern. (I)Musical: *Show Boat* by Norma Terris, Howard Marsh, Charles Winninger, Edna May Oliver. First film version by Allan Jones and Irene Dunne; third by Howard Keel and Kathryn Grayson in 1951.

WHY DO LOVERS BREAK EACH OTHER'S HEARTS? (1962) (wm)Ellie Greenwich—Tony Powers—Phil Spector. (P)Bob B. Soxx and The Blue Jeans.

WHY DO YA ROLL THOSE EYES? (1926) (w)Morrie Ryskind (m)Philip Charig. (I)Revue: *Americana Of 1926* by Helen Morgan, Lyman Beck, Evelyn Bennett, and Betty Compton. (P)Paul Whiteman and his Orchestra.

WHY DO YOU SUPPOSE (1929) (w)Lorenz Hart (m)Richard Rodgers. (I)Musical: *Heads Up!* by Jack Whiting and Barbara Newberry.

WHY DOES IT GET SO LATE SO EARLY (1946) (wm)John Lehman—Allie Wrubel. (P)Helen Forrest and Dick Haymes.

WHY DON'T THEY DANCE THE POLKA ANYMORE (1914) (w)Harry B. Smith (m)Jerome Kern. (I)Musical: *The Girl From Utah*.

WHY DON'T THEY UNDERSTAND (1957) (wm)Jack Fishman—Joe Henderson. (P)George Hamilton IV.

WHY DON'T WE DO IT IN THE ROAD (1969) (wm)John Lennon—Paul McCartney. (P)The Beatles.

WHY DON'T WE DO THIS MORE OFTEN (1941) (w)Charles Newman (m)Allie Wrubel. (P)Freddy Martin and his Orchestra, vocal by Eddie Stone. (P)Kay Kyser and his Orchestra, vocal by Ginny Simms and Harry Babbitt.

WHY DON'T YOU BELIEVE ME (1952) (wm)Lew Douglas—King Laney—Roy Rodde. (P)Joni James.

WHY DON'T YOU DO RIGHT (1942) (wm)Joe McCoy. (P)Lil Green. Film: *Stage Door Canteen* (1943) by Peggy Lee with Benny Goodman and his Orchestra.

WHY DON'T YOU FALL IN LOVE WITH ME (1942) (w)Al Lewis (m)Mable Wayne. (P)Connie Boswell. Popular versions by Dinah Shore, Dick Jurgens and his Orchestra, and Johnny Long and his Orchestra.

WHY DON'T YOU HAUL OFF AND LOVE ME? (1949) (wm)Wayne Raney—Lonnie Glosson. (P)Wayne Raney.

WHY DON'T YOU WRITE ME (1955) (wm)Laura Hollins. (P)The Jacks. (P)Snooky Lanson.

WHY DREAM? (1935) (wm)Ralph Rainger—Leo Robin—Richard A. Whiting. (I)Film: *Big Broadcast Of 1936* by Henry Wadsworth.

WHY FIGHT THE FEELING (1950) (wm)Frank Loesser. (I)Film: *Let'S Dance* by Betty Hutton.

WHY I SING THE BLUES (1969) (wm)B. B. King—Dave Clark. (P)B. B. King.

WHY I'M WALKIN' (1960) (wm)Stonewall Jackson—Melvin Endsley. (P)Stonewall Jackson.

WHY ME (1972) (wm)Kris Kristofferson. (P)Kris Kristofferson.

WHY SHOULD I CARE (1937) (wm)Cole Porter. (I)Film: *Rosalie* by Eleanor Powell and Nelson Eddy.

WHY SHOULD I CRY OVER YOU? (1922) (wm)Ned Miller—Chester Conn. (P)Victor Roberts (Billy Jones).

WHY SHOULDN'T I (1935) (wm)Cole Porter. (I)Musical: *Jubilee* by Margaret Adams.

WHY TRY TO CHANGE ME NOW (1952) (wm)Cy Coleman—Joseph A. McCarthy. (P)Frank Sinatra.

WHY WAS I BORN (1929) (w)Oscar Hammerstein II (m)Jerome Kern. (I)Musical: *Sweet Adeline* by Helen Morgan. Film version (1934) by Wini Shaw and reprised by Irene Dunne. Films: *Till The Clouds Roll By* (1946) and *The Helen Morgan Story* (1957).

WHY WORRY? (1920) (wm)Seymour Simons. (I)Musical: *Her Family Tree* by Nora Bayes.

WICHITA LINEMAN (1968) (wm)Jim Webb. (P)Glen Campbell.

WICKED BLUES (1922) (wm)Perry Bradford. (P)Lizzie Miles.

WICKED MESSENGER, THE (1968) (wm)Bob Dylan. (P)Bob Dylan.

WIEDERSEH'N (1965) (w-Eng)Bert Kaempfert—Herbert Rehbein—Milt Gabler. (P)Al Martino.

WIENER BLUT (See VIENNA LIFE)

WIGWAM (1970) (wm)Bob Dylan. (P)Bob Dylan.

WILD BILLY'S CIRCUS STORY (1973) (wm)Bruce Springsteen. (P)Bruce Springsteen.

WILD BOYS (1984) (wm)Duran Duran. (P)Duran Duran.

WILD HONEY (1967) (wm)Brian Wilson—Mike Love. (P)The Beach Boys.

WILD HONEY PIE (1968) (wm)John Lennon—Paul McCartney. (P)The Beatles.

WILD HORSES (1953) (wm)Johnny Burke. (P)Perry Como.

WILD HORSES (1970) (wm)Mick Jagger—Keith Richards. (P)The Rolling Stones.

WILD IN THE COUNTRY (1961) (wm)George Weiss—Hugo Peretti—Luigi Creatore. (P)Elvis Presley.

WILD IS THE WIND (1957) (w)Ned Washington (m)Dimitri Tiomkin. (I)Film: *Wild Is The Wind* (P)Johnny Mathis.

WILD MAN BLUES (1927) (m)Louis Armstrong—Jelly Roll Morton. (P)Johnny Dodd's Black Bottom Stompers. (P)Louis Armstrong and his Hot Seven.

WILD NIGHT (1971) (wm)Van Morrison. (P)Van Morrison.

WILD ONE (1960) (wm)Dave Appell—Bernie Lowe—Kal Mann. (P)Bobby Rydell.

WILD ROSE, THE (1920) (w)Clifford Grey (m)Jerome Kern. (I)Musical: *Sally* by Marilyn Miller. Film: *Look For The Silver Lining* (1949) by June Haver.

WILD SIDE OF LIFE, THE (1952) (wm)W. Warren—A. A. Carter. (P)Hank Thompson. (P)Burl Ives.

WILD THING (1966) (wm)Chip Taylor. (P)The Troggs.

WILD WEEKEND (1963) (wm)Tom Shannon—Phil Todaro. (P)The Rebels.

WILD WORLD (1970) (wm)Cat Stevens (P)Cat Stevens.

WILDEST GAL IN TOWN, THE (1947) (w)Jack Yellen (m)Sammy Fain. (P)Billy Eckstine.

WILDFIRE (1975) (wm)Michael Murphey—Larry Cansler. (P)Michael Murphey.

WILDFLOWER (1923) (w)Otto Harbach—Oscar Hammerstein II (m)Herbert Stothart—Vincent Youmans. (I)Musical: *Wildflower* by Guy Robertson.

WILDFLOWER (1972) (wm)David Richardson—Doug Edwards. (P)Skylark.

WILDWOOD DAYS (1963) (w)Kal Mann (m)Dave Appell. (P)Bobby Rydell.

WILDWOOD WEED (1974) (wm)Jim Stafford. (P)Jim Stafford.

WILHELMINA (1950) (w)Mack Gordon (m)Joseph Myrow. (I)Film: *Wabash Avenue* with Betty Grable and Victor Mature.

WILKOMMEN (1967) (w)Fred Ebb (m)John Kander. (I)Musical: *Cabaret* by Joel Grey. Also by Mr. Grey in film version.

WILL HE LIKE ME (1963) (w)Sheldon Harnick (m)Jerry Bock. (I)Musical: *She Loves Me* by Barbara Cook.

WILL IT GO ROUND IN CIRCLES (1973) (wm)Billy Preston—Bruce Fisher. (P)Billy Preston.

WILL SHE COME FROM THE EAST? (EAST-NORTH-WEST OR SOUTH) (1922) (wm)Irving Berlin. (I)Revue: *Music Box Revue Of 1922* by John Steel.

WILL YOU BE STAYING AFTER SUNDAY? (1968) (wm)Al Kasha—Joel Hirschhorn. (P)The Peppermint Rainbow.

WILL YOU LOVE ME IN DECEMBER AS YOU DO IN MAY (1905) (w)James J. Walker (m)Ernest R. Ball. (P)The Haydn Quartet. (P)Albert Campbell. Film: *The Eddy Duchin Story* with Tyrone Power. Film: *Beau James* with Bob Hope.

WILL YOU LOVE ME TOMORROW (1961) (wm)Gerry Goffin—Carole King. (P)The Shirelles.

WILL YOU MARRY ME TOMORROW, MARIA (1937) (w)Oscar Hammerstein II (m)Jerome Kern. (I)Film: *High, Wide And Handsome* by William Frawley.

WILL YOU REMEMBER (Sweetheart) (1917) (w)Rida Johnson Young (m)Sigmund Romberg. (I)Musical: *Maytime* with Peggy Wood, Charles Purcell and William Norris. Film version with Nelson Eddy and Jeanette MacDonald. Film: *Deep In My Heart* with Jose Ferrer and Merle Oberon.

WILL YOU STILL BE MINE? (1941) (w)Tom Adair (m)Matt Dennis. (P)Tommy Dorsey and his Orchestra, vocal by Connie Haines.

WILL YOU STILL LOVE ME? (1986) (wm)D. Foster—T. Keane—R. Baskin. (P)Chicago.

WILLIAM TELL OVERTURE (1829) (m)G. Rossini. Famous classical composition. Theme song of LONE RANGER TV series.

WILLOW WEEP FOR ME (1932) (wm)Ann Ronell. (P)Paul Whiteman and his Orchestra, vocal by Irene Taylor.

WIMOWEH (See THE LION SLEEPS TONIGHT)

WIN YOUR LOVE FOR ME (1958) (wm)L. C. Cook. (P)Sam Cooke.

WINCHESTER CATHEDRAL (1966) (wm)Geoff Stephens. (P)The New Vaudeville Band.

WIND CRIES MARY, THE (1967) (wm)Jimi Hendrix. (P)The Jimi Hendrix Experience.

WINDMILLS OF YOUR MIND, THE or THE THEME FROM THE THOMAS CROWN AFFAIR (1968) (w)Alan Bergman—Marilyn Bergman (m)Michel Legrand. (I)Film: *The Thomas Crown Affair*. Academy Award winning song 1968. (R)Dusty Springfield (1969).

WINDOWS OF THE WORLD (1967) (w)Hal David (m)Burt Bacharach. (P)Dionne Warwick.

WINDY (1967) (wm)Ruthann Friedman. (P)The Association.

WINE, WOMEN AND SONG (1869) (m)Johann Strauss. Famous Viennese waltz.

WINE, WOMEN AND SONG (1946) (wm)Al Dexter—Aubrey Gass. (P)Al Dexter.

WINGS OF A DOVE (Also ON THE WINGS OF A DOVE) (1959) (wm)Robert B. Ferguson. (P)Ferlin Husky.

WINNER TAKES IT ALL (1981) (w-Eng)Benny Anderson—Bjorn Ulvaeus. (P)Abba.

WINNERS AND LOSERS (1976) (wm)Danny Hamilton—Ann Hamilton. (P)Hamilton, Joe Frank & Reynolds.

WINTER WEATHER (1941) (wm)Ted Shapiro. (P)Benny Goodman and his Orchestra, vocal by Peggy Lee.

WINTER WONDERLAND (1934) (w)Richard B. Smith (m)Felix Bernard. Popular Christmas season song. (P)Guy Lombardo and The Royal Canadians. (R)1946 by The Andrews Sisters.

WINTER WORLD OF LOVE (1969) (wm)Les Reed—Barry Mason. (P)Englebert Humperdinck.

WINTERGREEN FOR PRESIDENT (1932) (w)Ira Gershwin (m)George Gershwin. (I)Musical: Of Thee I Sing by the ensemble. William Gaxton and Victor Moore starred in the show.

WIPE OUT (1963) (wm)Ron Wilson—James Fuller—Robert Berryhill—Patrick Connolly. (P)The Surfaris. (R)Fat Boys & The Beach Boys (1987).

WISE OLD OWL (1940) (wm)Joe Ricardel. (P)Al Donahue and his Orchestra. Popular versions by Teddy Powell and his Orchestra and Kay Kyser and his Orchestra.

WISH ME A RAINBOW (1996) (wm)Jerry Livingston—Ray Evans. (I)Film: This Property Is Condemned by Mary Badham. (P)The Gunter Kallman Chorus.

WISH YOU DIDN'T HAVE TO GO (1965) (wm)Dan Pennington—Lindon Oldham. (P)James and Bobby Purify.

WISH YOU WERE HERE (1952) (wm)Harold Rome. (I)Musical: Wish You Were Here by Jack Cassidy. (P)Eddie Fisher.

WISH YOU WERE HERE, BUDDY (1966) (wm)Pat Boone. (P)Pat Boone.

WISHFUL, SINFUL (1968) (wm)James Morrison—John Densmore—Robert Krieger—Raymond Manzarek. (P)The Doors.

WISHIN' AND HOPIN' (1963) (w)Hal David (m)Burt Bacharach. (P)Dusty Springfield.

WISHING (Will Make It So) (1939) (wm)B. G. De Sylva. (I)Film: Love Affair by Irene Dunne.

WISHING FOR YOUR LOVE (1958) (wm)Sampson Horton. (P)The Voxpoppers.

WISHING RING (1952) (wm)Al Britt—Pete Maddux. (P)Joni James.

WISHING WELL (1987) (wm)T. T. D'Arby—S. Oliver. (P)Terence Trent D'Arby.

WISHING YOU WERE HERE (1974) (wm)Peter Cetera. (P)Chicago.

WITCH DOCTOR (1958) (wm)Ross Bagdasarian. (P)David Seville.

WITCH QUEEN OF NEW ORLEANS (1971) (wm)Patrick Vegas—Lolly Vegas. (P)Redbone.

WITCHCRAFT (1957) (w)Carolyn Leigh (m)Cy Coleman. (P)Frank Sinatra.

WITCHCRAFT (1955) (wm)Dave Bartholomew—Pearl King. (P)Elvis Presley.

WITH A LITTLE BIT OF LUCK (1956) (w)Alan Jay Lerner (m)Frederick Loewe. (I)Musical: My Fair Lady by Stanley Holloway. Film version also by Mr. Holloway.

WITH A LITTLE HELP FROM MY FRIENDS (1968) (wm)John Lennon—Paul McCartney. (P)The Beatles. (R)Joe Cocker.

WITH A LITTLE LUCK (1978) (wm)Paul McCartney—Linda McCartney. (P)Paul McCartney and Wings.

WITH A SMILE AND A SONG (1937) (w)Larry Morey (m)Frank Churchill. (I)Cartoon film: Snow White And The Seven Dwarfs by voice of Adrienne Caselotti as Snow White.

WITH A SONG IN MY HEART (1929) (w)Lorenz Hart (m)Richard Rodgers. (I)Musical: Spring Is Here. Film version (1930). Films: This Is The Life (1944); Words And Music (1948); Young Man With A Horn (1950); With A Song In My Heart (1952).

WITH ALL MY HEART (1935) (w)Gus Kahn (m)Jimmy McHugh. (I)Film: Her Master'S Voice by Peggy Conklin.

WITH ALL MY HEART (1957) (w)Bob Marcucci (wm)Pete De Angelis. (P)Jodie Sands.

WITH EVERY BREATH I TAKE (1934) (wm)Leo Robin—Ralph Rainger. (I)Film: Here Is My Heart by Bing Crosby.

WITH MY EYES WIDE OPEN I'M DREAMING (1934) (w)Mack Gordon (m)Harry Revel. (I)Film: Shoot The Works by Jack Oakie and Dorothy Dell. Film: The Stooge (1952) by Dean Martin.

WITH MY HEAD IN THE CLOUDS (1942) (wm)Irving Berlin. (I)Revue: This Is The Army by Pvt. Robert Stanley. Also in film version with Ronald Reagan and Kate Smith.

WITH OR WITHOUT YOU (1987) (wm)U2. (P)U2. Number one chart record.

WITH PEN IN HAND (1968) (wm)Bobby Goldsboro. (P)Billy Vera. (P)Johnny Darrell. (P)1969 by Vikki Carr.

WITH PLENTY OF MONEY AND YOU (1936) (w)Al Dubin (m)Harry Warren. (I)Film: Gold Diggers Of 1937 by Dick Powell. Film: My Dream Is Yours (1949) by Doris Day.

WITH SUMMER COMING ON (I'm Still A Sweetheart) (1932) (w)Roy Turk (m)Fred E. Ahlert. (P)Fred Waring's Pennsylvanians.

WITH THE WIND AND THE RAIN IN YOUR HAIR (1930) (wm)Jack Lawrence—Clara Edwards. (P)Kay Kyser and his Orchestra, vocal by Ginny Sims.

WITH THESE HANDS (1950) (w)Benny Davis (m)Abner Silver. (P)Nelson Eddy and Jo Stafford. (R)1953 by Eddie Fisher.

WITH THIS RING (1967) (wm)Luther Dixon—Richard Wylie—Anthony Hester. (P)The Platters.

WITH YOU (1929) (wm)Irving Berlin. (I)Film: Puttin' On The Ritz by Harry Richman. (P)Guy Lombardo and his Royal Canadians.

WITH YOU I'M BORN AGAIN (1979) (w)Carol Connors (m)David Shire. (P)Billy Preston and Syreeta.

WITH YOU ON MY MIND (1957) (w)Charlotte Hawkins (m)Nat "King" Cole. (P)Nat "King" Cole.

WITH YOUR LOVE (1976) (wm)Martyn Buchwald—Joey Covington—Victor Smith. (P)Jefferson Starship.

WITHIN YOU, WITHOUT YOU (1967) (wm)George Harrison. (P)The Beatles.

WITHOUT A SONG (1929) (w)Billy Rose—Edward Eliscu (m)Vincent Youmans. (I)Musical: Great Day by Lois Deppe and The Russell Wooding Jubilee

Singers. Theme song of Lawrence Tibbett.

WITHOUT A WORD OF WARNING (1935) (wm)Mack Gordon—Harry Revel. (I)Film: *Two For Tonight* by Bing Crosby.

WITHOUT HER (1965) (wm)Harry Nilsson. (P)1969 by Herb Alpert.

WITHOUT LOVE (1955) (wm)Cole Porter. (I)Musical: *Silk Stockings* by Hildegarde Neff.

WITHOUT LOVE (1970) (wm)Danny Small. (P)Tom Jones.

WITHOUT LOVE (1930) (w)B. G. De Sylva—Lew Brown (m)Ray Henderson. (I)Musical: *Flying High* by Grace Brinkley, reprised by Oscar Shaw and Kate Smith. Film: *The Best Things In Life Are Free* (1956) by Sheree North.

WITHOUT THAT CERTAIN THING (1933) (wm)Max Nesbitt—Harry Nesbitt. (P)Ambrose and his Orchestra.

WITHOUT YOU (1972) (wm)William Peter Ham—Tom Evans. (P)Nilsson.

WITHOUT YOU (1956) (w)Alan Jay Lerner (m)Frederick Loewe. (I)Musical: *My Fair Lady* by Rex Harrison and Julie Andrews. Film version with Rex Harrison and Audrey Hepburn.

WITHOUT YOU (1942) (w-Eng)Ray Gilbert (m)Osvaldo Farres. (I)Cartoon film: *Make Mine Music* by voice of Andy Russell.

WITHOUT YOU I'M NOTHING (1956) (wm)Jerry Bock—George Weiss—Larry Holofcener. (I)Musical: *Mr. Wonderful.*

WIVES AND LOVERS (Theme from) (1963) (w)Hal David (m)Burt Bacharach. Inspired by film: *Wives And Lovers.* (P)Jack Jones.

WOKE UP THIS MORNING (1953) (wm)Riley King—Jules Taub. (P)B. B. King.

WOLVERINE BLUES (1923) (wm)John Spikes—Benjamin Spikes—Jelly Roll Morton. (P)King Oliver's Creole Jazz Band and Jelly Roll Morton.

WOLVERTON MOUNTAIN (1962) (wm)Merle Kilgore—Claude King. (P)Claude King.

A WOMAN'S PREROGATIVE (1946) (w)Johnny Mercer (m)Harold Arlen. (I)Musical: *St. Louis Woman* by Pearl Bailey.

A WOMAN, A LOVER, A FRIEND (1959) (wm)Sid Wyche. (P)Jackie Wilson.

WOMAN (1981) (wm)John Lennon. (P)John Lennon.

WOMAN (1966) (wm)Bernard Webb. (P)Peter and Gordon.

WOMAN (1953) (wm)Dick Gleason. (P)Johnny Desmond. Popular version by Jose Ferrer and Rosemary Clooney.

WOMAN IN LOVE (1980) (wm)Barry Gibb—Robin Gibb. (P)Barbra Streisand. No. 1 Chart Record.

WOMAN IN LOVE, A (1955) (wm)Frank Loesser. (I)Film version of GUYS AND DOLLS by Frank Sinatra. (P)Frankie Laine.

WOMAN IN THE SHOE, THE (1929) (w)Arthur Freed (m)Nacio Herb Brown. (I)Film: *Lord Byron Of Broadway* by Ethelind Terry.

WOMAN IS A SOMETIME THING, A (1935) (w)DuBose Heyward (m)George Gershwin. (I)Opera: *Porgy And Bess* by Edward Mathews. Film version (1959) by Leslie Scott.

WOMAN IS ONLY A WOMAN, BUT A GOOD CIGAR IS A SMOKE, A (1905) (w)Harry B. Smith (m)Victor Herbert. (I)Musical: *Miss Dolly Dollars.*

WOMAN NEEDS LOVE, A (1981) (wm)Ray Parker, Jr. (P)Ray Parker, Jr. and Raydio.

WOMAN'S GOT SOUL (1963) (wm)Curtis Mayfield. (P)The Impressions.

WOMAN, WOMAN (1968) (wm)James W. Glaser—James O. Payne. (P)Gary Puckett and The Union Gap.

WON'T YOU COME HOME BILL BAILEY (See BILL BAILEY WON'T YOU PLEASE COME HOME)

WONDER BAR (1934) (w)Al Dubin (m)Harry Warren. (I)Film: *Wonder Bar* by Al Jolson.

WONDER OF YOU, THE (1971) (wm)Baker Knight. (P)Elvis Presley.

WONDER WHY (1950) (w)Sammy Cahn (m)Nicholas Brodszky. (I)Film: *Rich, Young And Pretty* by Jane Powell.

WONDERFUL COPENHAGEN (1952) (wm)Frank Loesser. (I)Film: *Hans Christian Andersen* by Danny Kaye.

WONDERFUL DAY LIKE TODAY, ON A (1965) (wm)Leslie Bricusse—Anthony Newley. (I)Musical: *The Roar Of The Greasepaint-The Smell Of The Crowd* by Cyril Ritchard and The Urchins.

WONDERFUL GUY, A (See I'M IN LOVE WITH A WONDERFUL GUY)

WONDERFUL ONE (My) (1922) (w)Dorothy Terriss (m)Paul Whiteman—Ferde Grofe. (P)Paul Whiteman and his Orchestra.

WONDERFUL SUMMER (1963) (wm)Gil Garfield—Perry Botkin, Jr. (P)Robin Ward.

WONDERFUL TONIGHT (1977) (wm)Eric Clapton. (P)Eric Clapton.

WONDERFUL WORLD (1965) (wm)Barbara Campbell—Lou Adler—Herb Alpert. (P)Herman's Hermits.

WONDERFUL WORLD, BEAUTIFUL PEOPLE (1969) (wm)Jimmy Cliff. (P)Jimmy Cliff.

WONDERFUL, WONDERFUL (1957) (w)Ben Raleigh (m)Sherman Edwards. (P)Johnny Mathis. (R)1963 by The Tymes.

WONDERING (1957) (wm)Jack Schafer. (P)Patti Page.

WONDERING (1952) (wm)Joe Werner. (P)Webb Pierce.

WONDERLAND BY NIGHT (1961) (w)Lincoln Chase (m)Klaus Gunter Neumann. (P)Bert Kaempfert and his Orchestra.

WOODEN HEART (1961) (w)Fred Wise—Ben Weisman—Kay Twomey—Bert Kaempfert. (I)Film: *G. I. Blues* by Elvis Presley. (P)Joe Dowell.

WOODEN SHIPS (1969) (wm)David Crosby—Stephen Stills—Paul Kantner. (P)Crosby, Stills and Nash.

WOODEN SOLDIER AND THE CHINA DOLL, THE (1932) (w)Charles Newman (m)Isham Jones. (P)Nat Shilkret and his Orchestra.

WOODMAN, WOODMAN SPARE THAT TREE (1911) (wm)Irving Berlin. Adapted from song and written as special material for Bert Williams.

WOODPECKER SONG, THE (1940) (w-Eng)Harold Adamson (m)Eldo di Lazzaro. (P)U. S. by Will Glahe and his Musette Orchestra. (P)Kay Kyser and his Orchestra. Film: *Ride Tenderfoot Ride* by Gene Autry.

WOODSTOCK (1969) (wm)Joni Mitchell. (P)Crosby, Stills, Nash and Young. Also recorded by Joni Mitchell. (R)1971 by Matthew's Southern Comfort.

WOODY WOODPECKER (1948) (wm)George Tibbles—Ramon Idriss. (I)Theme of WOODY WOODPECKER cartoon films.

WOOLY BULLY (1965) (wm)Domingo Samudio. (P)Sam The Sham.

WORD, THE (1965) (wm)John Lennon—Paul McCartney. (P)The Beatles.

WORD UP (1986) (wm)Larry Blackmon—Tomi Jenkins. (P)Cameo.

WORDS (1968) (wm)Barry Gibb—Maurice Gibb—Robin Gibb. (P)The Bee Gees.

WORDS (1966) (wm)Tommy Boyce—Bobby Hart. (P)The Monkees.

WORDS ARE IN MY HEART, THE (1935) (w)Al Dubin (m)Harry Warren. (I)Film: Gold Diggers OF 1935 by Dick Powell.

WORDS GET IN THE WAY (1986) (wm)Gloria M. Estefan. (P)Miami Sound Machine.

WORDS OF LOVE (1967) (wm)John Phillips. (P)The Mamas and the Papas.

WORDS OF LOVE (1960) (wm)Buddy Holly. (P)Buddy Holly.

WORDS WITHOUT MUSIC (1935) (w)Ira Gershwin (m)Vernon Duke. (I)Revue: Ziegfeld Follies Of 1936 by Gertrude Niesen.

WORK SONG (1960) (w)Oscar Brown Jr. (m)Vernon Duke. Adapted from jazz instrumental. Vocal version (P)Oscar Brown Jr. (R)1966 Herb Alpert and the Tijuana Brass.

WORK WITH ME ANNIE (1954) (wm)Henry "Hank" Ballard. (P)The Midnighters.

WORKIN' ON A GROOVY THING (1968) (wm)Neil Sedaka—Roger Atkins. (P)The 5th Dimension.

WORKING CLASS HERO (1970) (wm)John Lennon. (P)John Lennon. (R)1979 by Marianne Faithfull.

WORKING FOR THE MAN (1962) (wm)Roy Orbison. (P)Roy Orbison.

WORKING IN THE COAL MINE (1966) (wm)Allen Toussaint. (P)Lee Dorsey.

WORKING MY WAY BACK TO YOU (1966) (wm)Sandy Linzer—Denny Randell. (P)The Four Seasons.

WORLD (1969) (wm)James Brown. (P)James Brown.

WORLD IS A GHETTO (1973) (wm)Sylvester Allen—Harold R. Brown—Morris Dickerson—Leroy "Lonnie" Jordan—Charles Miller—Lee Oscar Levitin—Howard Scott. (P)War.

WORLD IS IN MY ARMS, THE (1940) (w)E. Y. Harburg (m)Burton Lane. (I)Musical: Hold On To Your Hats by Jack Whiting, Eunice Healey, The Ranchettes, The Tanner Sisters, The Radio Aces, and chorus.

WORLD IS MINE (TONIGHT), THE (1935) (w)Holt Marvell (m)George Posford. (I)Film: The Gay Desperado by Nino Martini.

WORLD IS WAITING FOR THE SUNRISE, THE (1919) (wm)Eugene Lockhart—Ernest Seitz. (P)Isham Jones and his Orchestra. (R)1951 by Les Paul and Mary Ford.

WORLD OF OUR OWN, A (1965) (wm)Tom Springfield. (P)The Seekers.

WORLD OWES ME A LIVING, THE (1934) (w)Larry Morey (m)Leigh Harline. (I)Cartoon film: The Grasshopper And The Ants.

WORLD WE KNEW, THE (Over and Over) (1967) (w-Eng)Carl Sigman (m)Bert Kaempfert—Herbert Rehbein. (P)Frank Sinatra.

WORLD WEARY (1928) (wm)Noel Coward. (I)Revue: This Year Of Grace by Beatrice Lillie.

WORLD WITHOUT LOVE, A (1964) (wm)John Lennon—Paul McCartney. (P)Peter and Gordon.

WORRIED MAN BLUES (1935) (wm)A. P. Carter. (P)The Carter Family.

WORRIED MIND (1941) (wm)Jimmie Davis—Ted Daffan. (P)Bob Wills.

WORRY, WORRY, WORRY (1948) (wm)Ramez Idriss—George Tibbles. (P)Hal Derwin.

WORST PIES IN LONDON, THE (1979) (wm)Stephen Sondheim. (I)Musical: Sweeney Todd with Angela Lansbury and Len Cariou.

WORST THAT COULD HAPPEN (1969) (wm)Jim Webb. (P)Brooklyn Bridge.

WOT'S IT TO YA (1987) (wm)R. Nevil—B. Walsh. (P)Robbie Nevil.

WOULD I LIE TO YOU? (1985) (wm)Annie Lennox—Dave Stewart. (P)Eurythmics.

WOULD I LOVE YOU (LOVE YOU, LOVE YOU) (1951) (w)Bob Russell (m)Harold Spina. (P)Patti Page.

WOULD YA? (1949) (wm)Bob Fellows. (P)Johnny Mercer.

WOULD YOU LIKE TO TAKE A WALK (1930) (w)Mort Dixon—Billy Rose (m)Harry Warren. (I)Revue: Sweet And Low by Hannah Williams.

WOULDN'T IT BE LOVERLY (1956) (w)Alan Jay Lerner (m)Frederick Loewe. (I)Musical: My Fair Lady by Julie Andrews. Film version by Marni Nixon dubbing for Audrey Hepburn.

WOULDN'T IT BE NICE (1966) (w)Tony Asher—Brian Wilson (m)Brian Wilson. (P)The Beach Boys.

WRAP YOUR TROUBLES IN DREAMS (And Dream Your Troubles Away) (1931) (w)Ted Koehler—Billy Moll (m)Harry Barris. (I)Bing Crosby. Film: Rainbow Round My Shoulder with Frankie Laine. Film: Top Man with Donald O'Connor and Lillian Gish.

WRAPPED AROUND YOUR FINGER (1984) (wm)Sting. (P)The Police.

WRAPPED UP IN A DREAM (1948) (wm)William Best—Irving Berman. (P)Do, Ray, and Me.

WRAPPIN' IT UP (The Lindy Glide) (1934) (m)Fletcher Henderson. (P)Fletcher Henderson and his Orchestra. (P)1938 by Benny Goodman and his Orchestra.

WRECK OF THE SHENANDOAH, THE (1925) (wm)Maggie Andrews. (P)Carson Robison. (P)Vernon Dalhart. Inspired by the wreck of a United States Army dirigible in Ohio.

WRECK OF THE EDMUND FITZGERALD, THE (1976) (wm)Gordon Lightfoot. (P)Gordon Lightfoot.

WRINGLE, WRANGLE (1956) (wm)Stan Jones. (I)Film: Westward Ho, The Wagons! by Fess Parker.

WRITE ME A LETTER (1947) (wm)Howard Biggs. (P)The Ravens.

WRITE ME SWEETHEART (1943) (wm)Roy Acuff. (P)Roy Acuff.

WRITING ON THE WALL (1961) (wm)Sandy Baron—Mark Barkan—George Eddy. (P)Adam Wade.

WRITTEN ON THE WIND (1956) (w)Sammy Cahn (m)Victor Young. (I)On opening soundtrack of film: Written On The Wind by The Four Aces.

WUNDERBAR (1949) (wm)Cole Porter. (I)Musical: Kiss Me Kate by Alfred Drake and Patricia Morrison. Film version (1953) by Kathryn Grayson and Howard Keel.

WYNKEN, BLYNKEN AND NOD (1938) (w)Eugene Field. (m)Leigh Harline. (I)Cartoon film: Wynken, Blynken And Nod.

X-RAY BLUES (1962) (m)Ray Charles. (P)Ray Charles and Milt Jackson.

XANADU (1980) (wm)Jeff Lynne. (I)Film: *Xanadu.* (P)Electric Light Orchestra with Olivia Newton-John.

Y. M. C. A. (1979) (wm)Henri Belolo—Jacques Morali—Victor Willis. (P)The Village People.

YA WANNA BUY A BUNNY? (1949) (wm)Carl Hoefle—Del Porter. (P)Spike Jones and his City Slickers.

YA-YA (1961) (wm)Lee Dorsey—Clarence Lewis—Morgan Robinson. (P)Lee Dorsey.

YAAKA HULAA HICKEY DULA (1916) (wm)E. Ray Goetz—Joe Young—Pete Wendling. (I)Musical: *Robinson Crusoe, Jr.* with Al Jolson. Film: *Applause* with Helen Morgan and Joan Peters.

YAH-TA-TA, YAH-TA-TA (TALK, TALK, TALK) (1945) (w)Johnny Burke (m)Jimmy Van Heusen. (P)Bing Crosby and Judy Garland.

YAKETY SAX (YAKETY AXE) (1963) (wm)Randy Randolph—James Rich. (P)As YAKETY SAX by Boots Randolph. (R)1965 as YAKETY AXE by Chet Atkins.

YAKETY YAK (1958) (wm)Jerry Leiber—Mike Stoller. (P)The Coasters.

YAM, THE (1938) (wm)Irving Berlin. (I)Film: *Carefree* by Fred Astaire and Ginger Rogers.

YANK ME, CRANK ME (1978) (wm)Ted Nugent. (P)Ted Nugent.

YANKEE DOODLE (1775)Traditional folk song popularized during the Revolutionary War.

YANKEE DOODLE BLUES, THE (1922) (w)Irving Caesar—B. G. De Sylva (m)George Gershwin. (I)Revue: *Spice Of 1922*. Film: *Rhapsody In Blue* (1945) by Hazel Scott. Film: *I'LL Get By* (1950) by June Haver.

YANKEE DOODLE BOY, I AM THE (1904) (wm)George M. Cohan. (I)Musical: *Little Johnny Jones*. Musical: *George M!* with Joel Grey and Bernadette Peters. Film: *Yankee Doodle Dandy* by James Cagney. Film: *The Seven Little Foys* with Bob Hope.

YANKEE ROSE (1926) (wm)Sidney Holden—Abe Frankl. (P)Sam Lanin and his Orchestra. (P)The Revelers.

YARD WENT ON FOREVER, THE (1968) (wm)Jim Webb. (P)Richard Harris.

YARDBIRD SUITE (1946) (m)Charlie Parker. (P)Charlie Parker, with Miles Davis, Dodo Marmarosa, Arv Garrison, Vic McMillan, and Roy Porter.

YEAR FROM TODAY, A (1924) (wm)Al Jolson—Ballard MacDonald—Dave Dreyer. (I)Film: *New York Nights* by Norma Talmadge.

YEAR OF THE CAT (1977) (wm)Peter Wood—Al Stewart. (P)Al Stewart.

YEARNING (Just For You) (1925) (wm)Benny Davis—Joe Burke. (P)Gene Austin.

YEARNING FOR LOVE (1936) (w)Mitchell Parish—Irving Mills (m)Edward "Duke" Ellington. (P)Duke Ellington and his Orchestra.

YEARS (1979) (wm)Kye Fleming—Dennis Morgan. (P)Barbara Mandrell. (P)1980 Wayne Newton.

YEH YEH (1963) (wm)Rodgers Grant—Pat Patrick—Jon Hendricks. (P)Mongo Santamaria. Also recorded by Georgie Fame.

YELLOW BALLOON (1967) (w)Dick St. John (wm)Gary Zekley—Jay Lee. (P)The Yellow Balloon.

YELLOW BIRD (1957) (wm)Norman Luboff—Marilyn Keith (Bergman)—Alan Bergman. Adapted from a West Indian folk song. (I)The Norman Luboff Choir.

YELLOW DOG BLUES (1928) (wm)W. C. Handy. Famous jazz standard. (R)Film: *St. Louis Blues* with Nat Cole and Eartha Kitt.

YELLOW RIVER (1970) (wm)Jeff Christie. (P)Christie.

YELLOW ROSE OF TEXAS, THE (1928)Traditional folk song adapted in 1955 by Don George. (P)Mitch Miller and his Chorus and Orchestra.

JOHNNY DESMOND

Another cover record story ...

Our local promotion guy in Cleveland said that Mitch Miller had just recorded a song called *The Yellow Rose of Texas* and it looked as though it might be a smash. It was on Columbia and the only records that were around were a few disc jockey acetates that Columbia had sent to some of the more important jocks around the country.

Bob Thiele (who was never asleep) had Thompson, our Cleveland guy, get hold of the copy that had been sent to Bill Randle, the top Cleveland DJ. Thompson called me on the phone and played the record over and over until I was able to copy down the melody and the lyrics. This was sometime very early in the morning. At the same time, Thiele placed a call to Johnny Desmond, who was in Florida at the time. He told Desmond to fly in immediately, that we would cut the record that night and give Columbia a stiff fight.

Well, I wrote the arrangement, Desmond flew in, we recorded the song, and actually had finished product in the stores before Columbia did. Mitch Miller, of course, had the big hit, but we sold about 300,000 records. Not too bad.

Cover records were a lot of fun because our sales and promo departments would bust their chops to make our record a hit. Our Coral sale and promotional people were a little different from their counterparts at Decca.

YELLOW SUBMARINE (1966) (wm)John Lennon—Paul McCartney. (P)The Beatles.

YER BLUES (1968) (wm)John Lennon—Paul McCartney. (P)The Beatles.

YES, I'M READY (1979) (wm)Barbara Mason. (P)Teri De Sario with KC.

YES INDEED (1943) (wm)Sy Oliver. (P)Tommy Dorsey and his Orchestra, vocal by Sy Oliver and Jo Stafford.

YES IT IS (1965) (wm)John Lennon—Paul McCartney. (P)The Beatles.

YES MY DARLING DAUGHTER (1941) (wm)Jack Lawrence. (I)Revue: *Crazy With The Heat* by Gracie Barrie. (P)Dinah Shore.

YES SIR, THAT'S MY BABY (1925) (w)Gus Kahn (m)Walter Donaldson. (P)Eddie Cantor. Film: *Yes Sir, That'-S My Baby* (1949) by Donald O'Connor; *I'll See You In My Dreams* (1951) by Doris Day; *The Eddie Cantor Story* (1953) by voice of Eddie Cantor dubbing for

Keefe Braselle.

YES TONIGHT, JOSEPHINE (1957) (wm)Roy Irwin. (P)Johnnie Ray.

YES WE CAN CAN (1970) (wm)Allan Toussaint. (P)The Pointer Sisters.

YES! WE HAVE NO BANANAS (1923) (wm)Frank Silver—Irving Cohn. (P)Frank Silver's Music Masters. Revue: *Make It Snappy* (1922) by Eddie Cantor. Film: *Luxury Liner* (1948) by The Pied Pipers. Film: *The Eddie Cantor Story* (1953) by voice of Eddie Cantor on soundtrack.

YES, YES, YES (1975) (wm)Michael Hazlewood. (P)Bill Cosby.

YESTER LOVE (1968) (wm)William "Smokey" Robinson—Alfred Cleveland. (P)Smokey Robinson and The Miracles.

YESTER-ME YESTER-YOU YESTERDAY (1969) (wm)Ron Miller—Bryan Wells. (P)Stevie Wonder.

YESTERDAY (1965) (wm)John Lennon—Paul McCartney. (P)The Beatles.

YESTERDAY ONCE MORE (1973) (wm)John Bettis—Richard Carpenter. (P)The Carpenters.

YESTERDAY WHEN I WAS YOUNG (1969) (wm)Charles Aznavour—Herbert Kretzmer. (P)In France, Charles Aznavour. (P)In U. S. , Roy Clark.

YESTERDAY'S DREAMS (1968) (wm)Pamela Sawyer—Ivy Hunter—Vernon Bullock—Jack Goga. (P)The Four Tops.

YESTERDAY'S GARDENIAS (1942) (wm)Dick Robertson—Nelson Cogane—Sammy Mysels. (P)Glenn Miller and his Orchestra, vocal by Ray Eberle and The Modernaires.

YESTERDAY'S HERO (1976) (wm)Harry Vanda—George Young. (P)John Paul Young. (P)Bay City Rollers.

YESTERDAY'S PAPERS (1967) (wm)Mick Jagger—Keith Richard. (P)The Rolling Stones.

YESTERDAY'S TEARS (1943) (wm)Ernest Tubb. (P)Ernest Tubb.

YESTERDAYS (1933) (w)Otto Harbach (m)Jerome Kern. (I)Musical: *Roberta* by Fay Templeton. Film version with Fred Astaire and Ginger Rogers. Film: *Till The Clouds Roll By* with Frank Sinatra, June Allyson, van Johnson, Judy Garland.

YESTERTHOUGHTS (1940) (w)Stanley Adams (m)Victor Herbert. Adaptation of Herbert's instrumental composition of same name, originally published in 1900. (P)Glenn Miller and his Orchestra, vocal by Ray Eberle.

YIP-I-ADDY-I-AY (1909) (wm)Will D. Cobb—John H. Flynn. (I)Musical: *Our Miss Gibbs*. Film: *New York Town* with Fred MacMurray and Mary Martin. Film: *Sunbonnet Sue* with Phil Regan and Gale Storm.

YO-YO (1971) (wm)Joe South (P)The Osmonds.

YOGI (1963) (wm)Lou Stallman—Sid Jacobson—Charles Koppelman. (P)The Ivy Three.

YOO-HOO (1921) (w)B. G. De Sylva (m)Al Jolson. (I)Musical: *Bombo* by Al Jolson.

YOU (1975) (wm)George Harrison. (P)George Harrison.

YOU (1975) (wm)Tom Snow. (P)Rita Coolidge.

YOU (1968) (wm)Ivy Hunter—Jack Goga—Jeffrey Bowen. (P)Marvin Gaye.

YOU (Gee But You're Wonderful) (1936) (w)Harold Adamson (m)Walter Donaldson. (I)Film: *The Great Ziegfeld* by The Ziegfeld Brides and Grooms.

YOU AIN'T HEARD NOTHIN' YET (1919) (wm)Al Jolson—Gus Kahn—B. G. De Sylva. (P)Al Jolson.

YOU AIN'T SEEN NOTHIN' YET (1974) (wm)Randy Bachman. (P)Bachman-Turner Overdrive. No. 1 Chart Record.

YOU ALONE (Sole Tu) (1953) (w)Al Stillman (m)Robert Allen. (P)Perry Como.

YOU ALWAYS HURT THE ONE YOU LOVE (1944) (wm)Allan Roberts—Doris Fisher. (P)The Mills Brothers.

YOU AND I (1941) (wm)Meredith Willson. (P)Glenn Miller and his Orchestra, vocal by Ray Eberle. Theme song of radio show *Maxwell House Coffee Time.*

YOU AND I (1945) (w)Arthur Freed (m)Nacio Herb Brown. (I)Film: *Meet Me In St. Louis* by voice of Arthur Freed dubbing for Leon Ames and Mary Astor.

YOU AND I (1983) (wm)Frank Myers. (P)Eddie Rabbitt and Crystal Gayle.

YOU AND I (1978) (wm)James Johnson Jr. (P)Rick James.

YOU AND I KNOW (1937) (w)Albert Stillman—Laurence Stallings (m)Arthur Schwartz. (I)Musical: *Virginia* by Anne Booth and Ronald Graham. (P)Tommy Dorsey and his Orchestra.

YOU AND ME (1977) (wm)Alice Cooper—Dick Wagner. (P)Alice Cooper.

YOU AND ME AGAINST THE WORLD (1974) (wm)Kenneth Lee Asher—Paul Williams. (P)Helen Reddy.

YOU AND THE NIGHT AND THE MUSIC (1934) (w)Howard Dietz (m)Arthur Schwartz. (P)Conrad Thibault. Musical: *Revenge With Music* by Georges Metaxa and Libby Holman.

YOU ARE (1983) (wm)Lionel Richie, Jr. —Brenda Richie. (P)Lionel Richie.

YOU ARE ALWAYS IN MY HEART (See ALWAYS IN MY HEART)

YOU ARE BEAUTIFUL (1958) (w)Oscar Hammerstein II (m)Richard Rodgers. (I)Musical: *Flower Drum Song* by Ed Kenny and Juanita Hall. Also in film version by Nancy Kwan.

YOU ARE EVERYTHING (1972) (wm)Thom Bell—Linda Creed. (P)The Stylistics.

YOU ARE LOVE (1928) (w)Oscar Hammerstein II (m)Jerome Kern. (I)Musical: *Show Boat* by Norma Terris and Howard Marsh. Film version 1936 by Irene Dunne and Allan Jones. Film version (1951) by Kathryn Grayson and Howard Keel.

YOU ARE MY DESTINY (1958) (wm)Paul Anka. (P)Paul Anka.

YOU ARE MY LOVE (1955) (wm)Jimmie Nabbie. (P)Joni James.

YOU ARE MY LUCKY STAR (1935) (w)Arthur Freed (m)Nacio Herb Brown. (I)Film: *Broadway Melody Of 1936*, Frances Langford. Films: *Singin' In The Rain* (1953) Gene Kelly, Debbie Reynolds; *Babes In Arms*, Judy Garland; *Broadway Melody Of 1936* with Jack Benny, Eleanor Powell.

YOU ARE MY SUNSHINE (1940) (wm)Jimmie Davis—Charles Mitchell. (P)Jimmie Davis during his campaign for Governor of Louisiana. Film: *Take Me Back To Oklahoma* by Tex Ritter. (P)Bing Crosby. (R)1962 by Ray Charles.

YOU ARE NEVER AWAY (1947) (w)Oscar Hammerstein II (m)Richard Rodgers. (I)Musical: *Allegro* by John Battles, Roberta Jonay and chorus.

YOU ARE SIXTEEN (1959) (w)Oscar Hammerstein II (m)Richard Rodgers. (I)Musical: *The Sound Of Music* with Mary Martin. Film version with Julie Andrews.

Irving Berlin has long been recognized as the greatest and most prolific writer of songs (words and music) in the history of American popular music. He is pictured here with Dinah Shore a pleasing singer of popular songs in the 40s and 50s. **(JB)**

Mr. and Mrs. Harold Arlen, with Lena Horne and Ruth DuBonnet, at whose home this photograph was taken. A top composer from the late 20s through the 50s, one of Mr. Arlen's greatest successes has been *Stormy Weather*, a song most associated with Lena Horne. **(JB)**

In addition to being a gifted and enduring bandleader and arranger over a career that spanned more than five decades, Duke Ellington composed a staggering number of jazz and popular songs of enduring popularity. **(JB)**

A gifted lyricist of the 20s and 30s, Irving Mills collaborated often with Duke Ellington on such hits as *Sophisticated Lady* and *Solitude*. Mills also organized an all-star band that recorded under the name, Irving Mills & His Hotsy Totsy Gang. **(JB)**

A leading lyricist from the 30s into the 60s, Johnny Mercer's credits include more than one thousand songs. He collaborated with such giants as Hoagy Carmichael, Harry Warren, Jerome Kern, Harold Arlen, and Arthur Schwartz. Also successful songwriter and an engagingly distinctive vocalist. **(JB)**

An exceptional jazz pianist, a most entertaining singer, and one of the most exuberant performers in American musical history, Fats Waller also composed many songs of lasting value – notably *Honeysuckle Rose* and *Ain't Misbehavin'*. **(JB)**

Dorothy Collins, a star of the TV Hit Parade in the late 50s, and one of the many popular performers recorded by Dick Jacobs when he was A & R Director for the Coral label.

Author, producer, arranger, and orchestra leader Dick Jacobs at one of his many recording sessions. His career embraced many categories of American popular music, from jazz through the big band era to the advent of rock.

The McGuire Sisters were one of the country's most popular singing groups in the 50s and 60s. They enjoyed many popular chart hits, a number of them produced and directed by Dick Jacobs. *Sincerely*, for example, sold over a million copies.

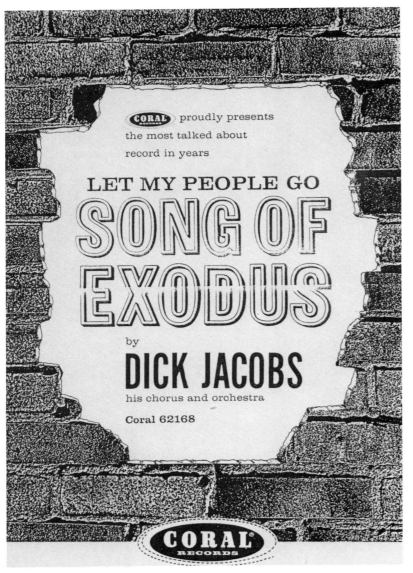

Song of Exodus, chorus and orchestra under the direction of Dick Jacobs, was one of Dick's chart successes during his stint at Coral Records.

When the movie, *The Man with the Golden Arm*, became a box office hit, the soundtrack by the brilliant Elmer Bernstein also became very popular. Dick Jacobs arrangement of Bernstein's *Main Title* – incorporating the love song, *Molly–O*, made all the music magazine charts.

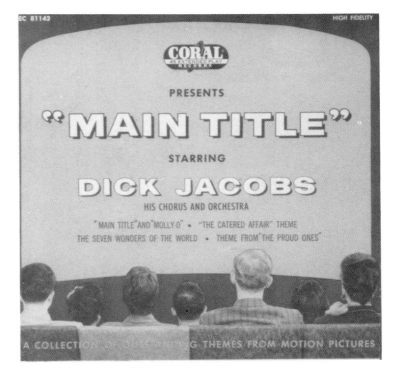

The

Buddy Holly
Memorial Society

"DEDICATED TO THE MUSIC & MEMORY OF BUDDY HOLLY"

Dick Jacobs (Guest of Honor)

WAS IN ATTENDANCE AT THE **FIRST**
INTERNATIONAL CONVENTION OF THE

Buddy Holly MEMORIAL SOCIETY

HELD AUGUST 26-27, 1978 IN WETHERSFIELD, CONNECTICUT.

WILLIAM F. GRIGGS
president

In a career that included working with such great performers as Louis Armstrong, Tommy and Jimmy Dorsey, and Jackie Wilson, Dick Jacobs found some of the greatest satisfaction arranging and producing for Buddy Holly. One of the seminal white rock performers, Holly died at a very early age in the same plane crash that took the life of Richie Valens, another young and gifted performer. The importance of Dick Jacobs' involvement in Buddy Holly's life was recognized by the Buddy Holly Memorial Society.

cresc.

Dick Jacobs and others at a meeting of the Buddy Holly Memorial society.

Dick Jacobs worked often with Eydie Gorme and Steve Lawrence in the late 60s, during his stint as A & R Director, often doubling as arranger and orchestra leader, at Coral Records.

Dick Jacobs directing Eydie Gorme in a recording session. A marvelous performer, as comfortable with an up-tempo jazz number as she is with a ballad, Eydie's early reputation stemmed from her work as a regular (with husband Steve Lawrence) on Steve Allen's *Tonight Show.*

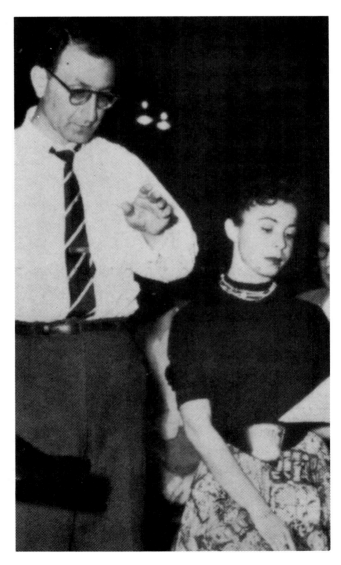

A Steve Lawrence album (45 rpm), produced and directed by Dick Jacobs. **(JB)**

When "THE STARS WERE OUT ON CORAL", Dick Jacobs was one of them.

In another confirmation of the value and commercial success Dick Jacobs and His Orchestra were enjoying, the Juke Box Operators of America voted him "The Most Promising New Orchestra of 1956", in the eleventh annual poll conducted by *The Cash Box*.

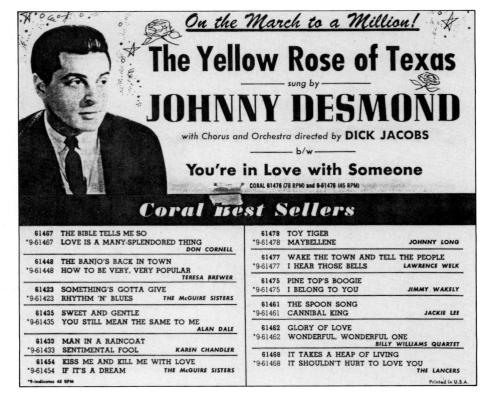

Johnny Desmond's record of *The Yellow Rose of Texas*, arranged and directed by Dick Jacobs, was a big commercial success – and undoubtedly one of the great "cover record" stories of the period (you can read about it in this book).

Let My People Go, SONG OF EXODUS!, was arranged by Dick Jacobs. The record, orchestra and chorus directed by Dick Jacobs, was an important achievement at the time for the Coral label.

DICK CLARK

Dear Dick,

Many thanks for your tireless patience and help last Sunday. Without your valuable assistance, the "Record Years" would not have been possible.

Again, thank you.

Gratefully,

Dick

A gracious thank you note to Dick Jacobs from Dick Clark.

DECCA News

FOR IMMEDIATE RELEASE

Lenny Salidor
DIRECTOR OF PUBLICITY

DICK JACOBS TO DECCA SPECIAL MARKETS AS EXECUTIVE PRODUCER

Martin P. Salkin, Vice President of Special Markets for Decca Records, announced the appointment of Dick Jacobs to the post of Executive Producer, Special Markets Department. "This expansion move is another step in the overall strengthening of the special markets department," stated Salkin, "so that we will have a self-contained department that can function completely under its own auspices."

Jacobs will be responsible for directing the development and producing of records necessary for all Decca Special Markets activities. He will also be involved in the creative development of this product, working in conjunction with Martin L. Weiss, Director of Special Markets, and Don Hobens, Manager of Operations, Decca Special Markets. In making the announcement, Salkin said, "We are fortunate in having the services of Dick Jacobs whose career in the recording industry has been devoted to writing, producing and arranging record sessions for many of the top names in our business. His experience will be an invaluable asset in creating and developing the kind of product that will be aimed specifically at the ever increasing Special Markets field."

-1-

Decca Records • A Division of MCA, Inc. • 445 Park Ave., New York, N. Y. 10022 • 759-7500

Another milestone in the Dick Jacobs career. Page two of the *NEWS* Release cites many of Dick's accomplishments, including his stint as musical director and orchestra conductor for the TV *Hit Parade Show* in 1957 and 1958.

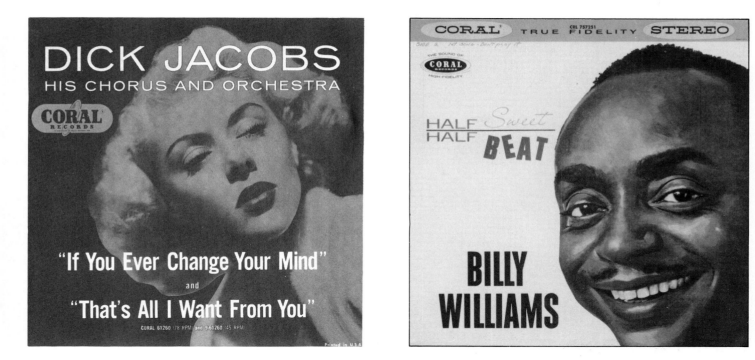

Fine

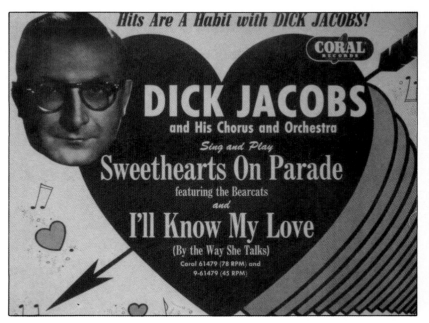

As the poster says, "Hits Are a Habit With Dick Jacobs"... both with his own orchestra and other performing artists of the day. (The Billy Williams album cover is from the collection of Jack Bradley.)

Photographs and album covers noted **(JB)** are from the collection of Jack Bradley.

Dick Jacobs with Sid Caesar, then at the peak of his career starring in the wonderful, long-running TV hit, *Your Show of Shows.* **(JB)**

Vince Edwards not only starred as TV's popular *Dr. Ben Casey*, he also sang very well. Dick Jacobs produced and directed his first record.

Dick Jacobs with Cozy Cole, one of the great jazz drummers of all time. Like many artists, Cozy was versatile; in the mid-40s, he starred in *Carmen Jones*, a modern remake of the opera *Carmen*.

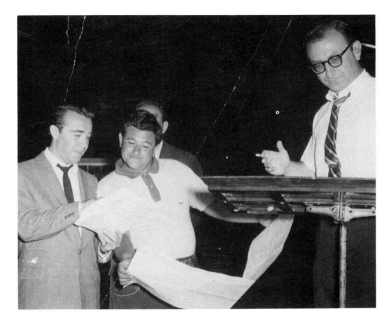

Alan Dale, a very popular singer of romantic ballads, enjoyed many hits arranged by, and under the baton of Dick Jacobs. Comedian Buddy Hackett, a pal of Dale's, was a guest/kibitzer at this session.

Louis Armstrong sang in Italian for this recording session, arranged, produced, and directed by Dick Jacobs. An interesting footnote: an instructor from the Berlitz School was on the set to whisper each line in Louis' ear – in phonetic Italian – before he sang it. **(JB)**

This record was the result, produced for the San Remo Music Festival.

Famed jazz clarinetist, Pete Fountain and Dick Jacobs became good friends as well as collaborators. Dick produced a number of records with Pete, recording them in Mr. Fountain's New Orleans club. Space was so tight the recording equipment was set up in the men's room. **(JB)**

$\frac{2}{4}$

Pete Fountain's New Orleans includes many of the great songs associated with the Birthplace of Jazz, including *Basin Street Blues* and *Do You Know What It Means to Miss New Orleans.*

Jackie Wilson, another great performer who died much too soon, represented one of the professional and personal highlights of Dick Jacobs' career. His vocal talent and range, his charisma, and his innate decency made him a Jacobs favorite.

One of the Jackie Wilson records arranged and produced by Dick Jacobs when he was an executive producer at Decca Records. **(JB)**

Dick Jacobs conducting while Jackie Wilson sings. Jacobs was an early champion of rock and roll.

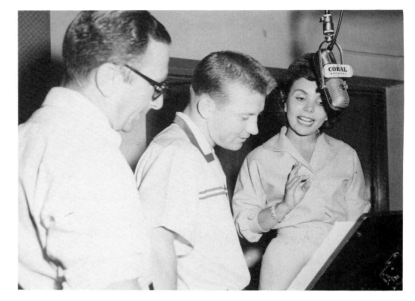

Teresa Brewer started on the *Major Bowes Amateur Hour* on the radio, as a five year old. Her first big hit, *Music! Music! Music!,* came in 1950, when she was nineteen. A petite, attractive lady with a big voice, she is equally at home with jazz, ballads, country ... even novelties like *I Love Mickey* (which she wrote). This album was produced and directed by Dick Jacobs. **(JB)**

Dick Jacobs, Mickey, Mantle, and Teresa Brewer recording *I Love Mickey*. Mantle, New York Yankee centerfielder and properly celebrated as one of baseball's all-time greats, had only to chime in with "Mickey Who?" when cued by Dick. **(JB)**

Steve Allen, another Coral artist produced and directed by Dick Jacobs (on piano, not clarinet!) starred in the title role in *The Benny Goodman Story* in 1955. **(JB)**

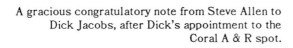

A gracious congratulatory note from Steve Allen to Dick Jacobs, after Dick's appointment to the Coral A & R spot.

STEVE ALLEN

January 26, 1959

Dear Dick:

Congratulations on your new spot. If you ever have any ideas about all my old Coral albums, or need anything in the way of material give me a buzz.

Best regards,

Steve

STEVE ALLEN

SA:nw

Mr. Dick Jacobs
Coral Records
50 West 57th St.
New York, New York

Duke Ellington and Tommy Dorsey, two of the giants of the Big Band Era. **(JB)**

The Jimmy Dorsey Orchestra in a live performance. **(JB)**

Tommy Dorsey and Frank Sinatra with the Pied Pipers. Some of Dick Jacobs early arranging work was done for Tommy and Jimmy Dorsey, right after the end of World War II. Shortly after that, Dick and Sy Oliver formed a partnership that lasted eight years. **(JB)**

Frank Sinatra at the onset of his career, performing with the Tommy Dorsey Orchestra. **(JB)**

Louis Armstrong, taking a break at a Brunswick record date. **(JB)**

Johnny Mercer and Bob Crosby in a rare duet. **(JB)**

Screamin' Jay Hawkins and his wife, Ginny. A big hit every time he appeared in Harlem's fabled Apollo Theater, Hawkins was a highly regarded rhythm and blues performer, who was recorded by Dick Jacobs on the Roulette label in 1963. **(JB)**

YOU ARE SO BEAUTIFUL (1975) (wm)Billy Preston—Bruce Fisher. (P)Joe Cocker.

YOU ARE THE GIRL (1987) (wm)Ric Ocasek. (P)The Cars.

YOU ARE THE SUNSHINE OF MY LIFE (1973) (wm)Stevie Wonder. (P)Stevie Wonder.

YOU ARE THE WOMAN (1976) (wm)Richard Roberts. (P)Firefall.

YOU ARE TOO BEAUTIFUL (1932) (w)Lorenz Hart (m)Richard Rodgers. (I)Film: *Hallelujah, I'M A Bum* (1933) by Al Jolson.

YOU ARE WOMAN (I Am Man) (1964) (w)Bob Merrill (m)Jule Styne. (I)Musical: *Funny Girl* with Barbra Streisand and Sydney Chaplin. Also in film version with Barbra Streisand.

YOU BEAT ME TO THE PUNCH (1962) (wm)Wm."Smokey" Robinson—Ronald White. (P)Mary Wells.

YOU BELONG TO ME (1952) (wm)Pee Wee King—Rodd Stewart—Chilton Price. (P)Joni James (her first recording). (P)Jo Stafford. (P)Patti Page. (R)1962 by The Duprees.

YOU BELONG TO ME (1978) (wm)Michael McDonald. (P)Carly Simon.

YOU BELONG TO MY HEART or SOLAMENTE UNA VEZ (1943) (w-Eng)Ray Gilbert (m)Agustin Lara. (I)Cartoon film: *The Three Caballeros* by voice of Dora Luz. (P)1945 by Bing Crosby with Xavier Cugat and his Orchestra. Films: *The Gay Ranchero* with Roy Rogers; *Mr. Imperium* with Ezio Pinza.

YOU BELONG TO THE CITY (1985) (wm)Glenn Frey. (P)Glenn Frey.

YOU BETTER GET IT (1965) (wm)Joe Tex. (P)Joe Tex.

YOU BETTER GO NOW (1936) (wm)Bix Reichner—Irvin Graham. (I)Revue: *New Faces Of 1936* by Nancy Nolan and Tom Rutherford. (R)1945 by Billie Holiday. (P)Jeri Sothern.

YOU BETTER KNOW IT (1959) (wm)Jackie Wilson—Norm Henry. (P)Jackie Wilson.

YOU BETTER RUN (1966) (wm)Felix Cavaliere—Eddie Brigati. (P)The Rascals. (R)1980 Pat Benatar.

YOU BETTER SIT DOWN KIDS (1967) (wm)Sonny Bono. (P)Cher.

YOU BETTER THINK TWICE (1970) (wm)Jim Messina. (P)Poco.

YOU BROUGHT A NEW KIND OF LOVE TO ME (1930) (wm)Sammy Fain—Irving Kahal—Pierre Norman Connor. (I)Film: *The Big Pond* by Maurice Chevalier. Film: *A New Kind Of Love* (1963) as theme. Film: *Monkey Business* with The Marx Brothers.

YOU CALL EVERYBODY DARLING (1946) (wm)Sam Martin—Ben Trace—Clem Watts. (P)Al Trace and his Orchestra.

YOU CALL IT MADNESS (Ah, But I Call It Love) (1931) (wm)Con Conrad. (P)Theme song of Russ Columbo.

YOU CAME A LONG WAY FROM ST. LOUIS (1948) (w)Bob Russell (m)John Benson Brooks. (P)Ray McKinley and his Orchestra.

YOU CAME ALONG FROM OUT OF NOWHERE (See OUT OF NOWHERE)

YOU CAN ALL JOIN IN (1968) (wm)David Mason. (P)Traffic.

YOU CAN DEPEND ON ME (1932) (wm)Charles Carpenter—Louis Dunlap—Earl Hines. (P)Louis Armstrong. (R)1961 by Brenda Lee.

YOU CAN DO MAGIC (1982) (wm)Russ Ballard. (P)America.

YOU CAN DO NO WRONG (1948) (wm)Cole Porter. (I)Film: *The Pirate* by Judy Garland.

YOU CAN GET IT IF YOU REALLY WANT (1970) (wm)Jimmy Cliff. (I)Film: *The Harder They Come* by Jimmy Cliff.

YOU CAN HAVE HER (1960) (wm)Bill Cook. (P)Roy Hamilton.

YOU CAN'T ALWAYS GET WHAT YOU WANT (1969) (wm)Mick Jagger—Keith Richard. (P)The Rolling Stones.

YOU CAN'T BE TRUE DEAR (1948) (w-Eng)Hal Cotton (m)Ken Griffin. Music adapted from German song, *"Du Kannst Nicht Treu Sein."* (P)Ken Griffin and Jerry Wayne.

YOU CAN'T CHANGE THAT (1979) (wm)Ray Parker, Jr. (P)Raydio.

YOU CAN'T DO THAT (1964) (wm)John Lennon—Paul McCartney. (P)The Beatles. Also in film *Help!* by The Beatles.

YOU CAN'T GET A MAN WITH A GUN (1946) (wm)Irving Berlin. (I)Musical: *Annie Get Your Gun* by Ethel Merman. Film version by Betty Hutton.

YOU CAN'T GET THAT NO MORE (1944) (wm)Louis Jordan—Sam Theard. (P)Louis Jordan and his Tympany Five.

YOU CAN'T HAVE EVERYTHING (1937) (w)Mack Gordon (m)Harry Revel. (I)Film: *You Can'T Have Everything* by Alice Faye.

YOU CAN'T HURRY LOVE (1966) (wm)Eddie Holland—Brian Holland—Lamont Dozier. (P)The Supremes.

YOU CAN'T KEEP A GOOD MAN DOWN (1920) (wm)Perry Bradford. (P)Mamie Smith and her Jazz Hounds.

YOU CAN'T PULL THE WOOL OVER MY EYES (1936) (wm)Milton Ager—Charles Newman—Murray Mencher. (P)Benny Goodman and his Orchestra, vocal by Helen Ward.

YOU CAN'T RUN AWAY FROM IT (1956) (w)Johnny Mercer (m)Gene de Paul. (I)Film: *You Can'T Run Away From It.* (P)The Four Aces.

YOU CAN'T SEE THE SUN WHEN YOU'RE CRYIN' (1946) (wm)Allen Roberts—Doris Fisher. (P)Vaughn Monroe and his Orchestra.

YOU CAN'T SIT DOWN (1963) (wm)Dee Clark—Cornell Muldrow—Kal Mann. (P)The Dovells.

YOU CAN'T STOP ME FROM DREAMING (1937) (wm)Cliff Friend—Dave Franklin. (P)Guy Lombardo and his Royal Canadians.

YOU CAN'T STOP ME FROM LOVIN' YOU (1931) (w)Mann Holiner (m)Alberta Nichols. (I)Revue: *Rhapsody In Black* by Ethel Waters and Blue McAllister. (P)Ethel Waters.

YOU CAN'T TURN ME OFF (1977) (wm)Marilyn McLeod—Pam Sawyer. (P)High Energy.

YOU CANNOT MAKE YOUR SHIMMY SHAKE ON TEA (1919) (wm)Irving Berlin. Written by Berlin in anticipation of Prohibition but not a hit.

YOU CHEATED (1958) (wm)Don Burch. (P)The Shields.

YOU COULD DRIVE A PERSON CRAZY (1970) (wm)Stephen Sondheim. (I)Musical: *Company* with Elaine Stritch.

YOU COULDN'T BE CUTER (1938) (w)Dorothy Fields (m)Jerome Kern. (I)Film: *Joy Of Living* by Irene Dunne.

YOU DECORATED MY LIFE (1979) (wm)Bob Morrison—

Debbie Hupp. (P)Kenny Rogers. Grammy Award Winner 1979.

YOU DID IT (1956) (w)Alan Jay Lerner (m)Frederick Loewe. (I)Musical: *My Fair Lady* by Rex Harrison. Film version also by Rex Harrison.

YOU DIDN'T HAVE TO BE SO NICE (1966) (mw)John Sebastian—Steve Boone. (P)The Lovin' Spoonful.

YOU DO (1947) (w)Mack Gordon (m)Josef Myrow. (I)Film: *Mother Wore Tights* by Dan Dailey. (P)Bing Crosby with Carmen Cavallaro and his Orchestra. (P)Vaughn Monroe.

YOU DO SOMETHING TO ME (1929) (wm)Cole Porter. (I)Musical: *Fifty Million Frenchmen* by William Gaxton. Films: *Night And Day* (1946), by Jane Wyman; *Starlift* (1951), by Doris Day; *The Helen Morgan Story* (1957); *Can Can* (1960) by Louis Jourdan.

YOU DO THE DARNDEST THINGS, BABY (1936) (w)Sidney D. Mitchell (m)Lew Pollack. (I)Film: *Pigskin Parade* by Jack Haley.

YOU DON'T BRING ME FLOWERS (1978) (w)Alan Bergman—Marilyn Bergman—Neil Diamond (m)Neil Diamond (P)Barbra Streisand and Neil Diamond.

YOU DON'T HAVE TO BE A BABY TO CRY (1963) (wm)(P)The Caravelles.

YOU DON'T HAVE TO BE A STAR (To Star In My Show) (1977) (wm)James Dean—John Henry Glover, Jr. (P)Marilyn McCoo and Billy Davis, Jr.

YOU DON'T HAVE TO KNOW THE LANGUAGE (1947) (w)Johnny Burke (m)Jimmy Van Heusen. (I)Film: *The Road To Rio* by Bing Crosby and The Andrews Sisters.

YOU DON'T HAVE TO PAINT ME A PICTURE (1966) (wm)Roger Carroll Tillison—Leon Russell—Thomas Garrett. (P)Gary Lewis and They Playboys.

YOU DON'T HAVE TO SAY YOU LOVE ME (1966) (w-Eng)Vicki Wickham—Simon Napier-Bell (m)P. Donaggio. (P)Dusty Springfield.

YOU DON'T KNOW (1987) (wm)R. Hild. (P)Scarlett and Black.

YOU DON'T KNOW ME (1955) (wm)Cindy Walker—Eddy Arnold. (P)Eddy Arnold. (R)1962 by Ray Charles. (R)Elvis Presley.

YOU DON'T KNOW PAREE (1929) (wm)Cole Porter. (I)Musical: *Fifty Million Frenchmen* by William Gaxton.

YOU DON'T KNOW WHAT LOVE IS (1941) (wm)Don Raye—Gene DePaul. (I)Film: *Keep 'Em Flying* by Carol Bruce.

YOU DON'T KNOW WHAT YOU MEAN TO ME (1968) (wm)Eddie Floyd—Steve Cropper. (P)Sam and Dave.

YOU DON'T KNOW WHAT YOU'VE GOT (1961) (wm)Paul Hampton—George Barton. (P)Ral Donner.

YOU DON'T LIKE IT--NOT MUCH (1927) (wm)Ned Miller—Art Kahn—Chester Conn. (P)Art Kahn and his Orchestra. Also recorded by Ernest Hare and Billy Jones.

YOU DON'T LOVE ME ANYMORE (1977) (wm)Alan Ray—Jeffrey Raymond. (P)Eddie Rabbitt.

YOU DON'T LOVE ME WHEN I CRY (1969) (wm)Laura Nyro. (P)Laura Nyro.

YOU DON'T MESS AROUND WITH JIM (1972) (wm)Jim Croce. (P)Jim Croce.

YOU DON'T OWE ME A THING (1956) (wm)Marty Robbins. (P)Marty Robbins. (P)1957 by Johnnie Ray.

YOU DON'T OWN ME (1964) (wm)John Madara—David White. (P)Leslie Gore.

YOU FORGOT YOUR GLOVES (1931) (w)Edward Eliscu (m)Ned Lehac. (I)Revue: *The Third Little Show* by Constance Carpenter and Jerry Norris.

YOU GAVE ME A MOUNTAIN (1968) (wm)Marty Robbins. (P)Johnny Bush. (P)Frankie Laine.

YOU GIVE LOVE A BAD NAME (1986) (wm)Jon Bon Jovi—Ritchie Sambora—Desmond Child. (P)Bon Jovi. Number one chart record.

YOU GO TO MY HEAD (1938) (w)Haven Gillespie (m)J. Fred Coots. (P)Glen Gray and The Casa Loma Orchestra. Also recorded by Larry Clinton and his Orchestra, vocal by Bea Wain.

YOU GOT IT ALL (1986) (wm)R. Holmes. (P)The Jets.

YOU GOT THE LOVE (1974) (wm)Chaka Khan—Ray Parker Jr. (P)Rufus.

YOU GOT WHAT IT TAKES (1959) (wm)Berry Gordy, Jr.—Gwen Gordy—Tyran Carlo—Marv Johnson. (R)Dave Clark Five.

YOU GOTTA BE A FOOTBALL HERO (To Get Along With The Beautiful Girls) (1933) (wm)Al Lewis—Al Sherman—Buddy Fields. (P)Ben Bernie and his Orchestra.

YOU GOTTA EAT YOUR SPINACH BABY (1936) (w)Mack Gordon (m)Harry Revel. (I)Film: *Poor Little Rich Girl* with Jack Haley and Shirley Temple.

YOU GOTTA HAVE A GIMMICK (1959) (wm)Stephen Sondheim. (I)Musical: *Gypsy* with Ethel Merman. Film version with Rosalind Russell.

YOU HAVE CAST YOUR SHADOW ON THE SEA (1938) (w)Lorenz Hart (m)Richard Rodgers. (I)Musical: *The Boys From Syracuse* with Zero Mostel and Jimmy Savo. Also in film version.

YOU HAVE EVERYTHING (1937) (w)Howard Dietz (m)Arthur Schwartz. (I)Musical: *Between The Devil* by Charles Walters and Vilma Ebsen.

YOU HAVE TAKEN MY HEART (1933) (w)Johnny Mercer (m)Gordon Jenkins. (P)Lanny Ross.

YOU HAVEN'T CHANGED AT ALL (1945) (w)Alan Jay Lerner (m)Frederick Loewe. (I)Musical: *The Day Before Spring* by Irene Manning.

YOU HAVEN'T DONE NOTHIN' (1974) (wm)Stevie Wonder. (P)Stevie Wonder.

YOU HIT THE SPOT (1936) (w)Mack Gordon (m)Harry Revel. (I)Film: *Collegiate* by Mack Gordon, Frances Langford and Jack Oakie.

YOU IRRITATE ME SO (1941) (wm)Cole Porter. (I)Musical: *Let'S Face It* by Jack Williams and Nanette Fabray.

YOU KEEP COMING BACK LIKE A SONG (1943) (wm)Irving Berlin. (I)Film: *Blue Skies* by Bing Crosby.

YOU KEEP ME HANGIN' ON (1966) (wm)Eddie Holland—Brian Holland—Lamont Dozier. (P)The Supremes. (R)Kim Wilde (1987), number one chart record.

YOU KEEP RUNNING AWAY (1967) (wm)Eddie Holland—Lamont Dozier—Brian Holland. (P)The Four Tops.

YOU KNOW I LOVE YOU. . . DON'T YOU (1986) (wm)Howard Jones. (P)Howard Jones.

YOU KNOW WHAT I MEAN (1967) (wm)Garry Bonner—Alan Gordon. (P)The Turtles.

YOU KNOW YOU BELONG TO SOMEBODY ELSE SO WHY DON'T YOU LEAVE ME ALONE (1922) (w)Eugene West (m)James V. Monaco. (P)Henry Burr.

YOU LEAVE ME BREATHLESS (1938) (w)Ralph Freed

(m)Frederick Hollander. (I)Film: *Cocoanut Grove* by Fred MacMurray.

YOU LET ME DOWN (1935) (w)Al Dubin (m)Harry Warren. (I)Film: *Stars Over Broadway* by Jane Froman.

YOU LIGHT UP MY LIFE (1977) (wm)Joe Brooks. (I)Film: *You Light Up My Life* by Kacey Cisyk. (P)Debby Boone. Academy Award Winner 1977. Grammy Award Winner 1977.

YOU LITTLE TRUSTMAKER (1973) (wm)Christopher Jackson. (P)The Tymes.

YOU LOVE THE THUNDER (1977) (wm)Jackson Browne. (P)Jackson Browne.

YOU MADE ME BELIEVE IN MAGIC (1977) (wm)Leonard Boone. (P)Bay City Rollers.

YOU MADE ME LOVE YOU (I Didn't Want To Do It) (1913) (w)Joseph McCarthy (m)James V. Monaco. (P)Al Jolson. Films: *Wharf Angel*, Dorothy Dell, Preston Foster; *Broadway Melody Of 1938*, Judy Garland with special lyric ("Dear Mr. Gable"); *Syncopation; The Jolson Story* and *Jolson Sings Again; Private Buckaroo*, The Andrews Sisters; *Love Me Or Leave Me* by Doris Day. (R)1941 by Harry James and his Orchestra.

YOU MAKE LOVING FUN (1977) (wm)Christine McVie. (P)Fleetwood Mac.

YOU MAKE ME FEEL BRAND NEW (1974) (wm)Linda Creed—Thom Bell. (P)The Stylistics.

YOU MAKE ME FEEL LIKE A NATURAL WOMAN (See NATURAL WOMAN, A)

YOU MAKE ME FEEL LIKE DANCING (1977) (wm)Leo Sayer—Vini Poncia. (P)Leo Sayer. Grammy Award Winner 1977.

YOU MAKE ME FEEL SO YOUNG (1946) (w)Mack Gordon (m)Josef Myrow. (I)Film: *Three Little Girls In Blue* by Vera Ellen and Frank Lattimore. Film: *I'll Get By* with June Haver, George Montgomery and Vivian Blaine. Film *I'll Get By* with Doris Day and June Haver.

YOU MAKE ME REAL (1970) (wm)Jim Morrison. (P)The Doors.

YOU MAKE MY DREAMS (1981) (wm)Daryl Hall (w)John Oates—Sara Allen. (P)Daryl Hall and John Oates.

YOU MAY BE RIGHT (1980) (wm)Billy Joel. (P)Billy Joel.

YOU MEAN EVERYTHING TO ME (1960) (wm)Neil Sedaka—Howard Greenfield. (P)Neil Sedaka.

YOU MET YOUR MATCH. . . (1968) (wm)Don Hunter—Stevie Wonder—Lula Hardaway. (P)Stevie Wonder.

YOU MIGHT THINK (1984) (wm)Ric Ocasek. (P)The Cars.

YOU MUST HAVE BEEN A BEAUTIFUL BABY (1938) (w)Johnny Mercer (m)Harry Warren. (I)Film: *Hard To Get* by Dick Powell. Film: *My Dream Is Yours* (1949) by Doris Day. (R)1961 by Bobby Darin.

YOU MUST MEET MY WIFE (1973) (wm)Stephen Sondheim. (I)Musical: *A Little Night Music* with Glynis Johns, Len Cariou and Hermione Gingold. Film version with Elizabeth Taylor, Len Cariou, Hermione Gingold.

YOU MUSTN'T KICK IT AROUND (1940) (w)Lorenz Hart (m)Richard Rodgers. (I)Musical: *Pal Joey* by Gene Kelly, June Havoc, Diane Sinclair, Sondra Barrett and chorus. Film version with Frank Sinatra and Kim Novak.

YOU NEED HANDS (1957) (wm)Roy Irwin. (I)Musical: *Queen O'Hearts* by Nora Bayes and Arthur Uttry.

YOU NEED SOMEONE, SOMEONE NEEDS YOU (1922)

(w)Oscar Hammerstein II (m)Lewis E. Gensler. (I)Musical: *Queen O'Hearts* by Nora Bayes and Arthur Uttry.

YOU NEEDED ME (1978) (wm)Randy Goodrum. (P)Anne Murray.

YOU NEVER DONE IT LIKE THAT (1978) (wm)Howard Greenfield—Neil Sedaka. (P)The Captain and Tenille.

YOU NEVER GIVE ME YOUR MONEY (1969) (wm)John Lennon—Paul McCartney. (P)The Beatles.

YOU NEVER KNOW (1938) (wm)Cole Porter. (I)Musical: *You Never Know* by Libby Holman.

YOU NEVER MISS THE WATER TILL THE WELL RUNS DRY (1946) (w)Paul Secon (m)Arthur Kent. (P)The Mills Brothers.

YOU ONLY LIVE TWICE (Theme from) (1967) (wm)Leslie Bricusse—John Barry. Theme from film: *You Only Live Twice* with Sean Connery.

YOU OUGHT TO BE WITH ME (1972) (wm)Al- Green—Willie Mitchell—Al- Jackson. (P)Al Green.

YOU OUGHTA BE IN PICTURES (1934) (w)Edward Heyman (m)Dana Suesse. (I)Revue: *Ziegfeld Follies Of 1934* by Jane Froman. Film: *Starlift* (1951) by Doris Day.

YOU RASCAL YOU (I'll Be Glad When You're Dead) (1931) (wm)Sam Theard. (P)Louis Armstrong.

YOU REALLY GOT ME (1964) (wm)Ray Davies. (P)The Kinks.

YOU REALLY KNOW HOW TO HURT A GUY (1965) (wm)Roger Christian—Jan Berry—Jill Gibson. (P)Jan and Dean.

YOU REMIND ME OF MY MOTHER (1922) (wm)George M. Cohan. (I)Musical: *Little Nellie Kelly* by Charles King and Elizabeth Hines.

YOU SAID A BAD WORD (1972) (wm)Joe Tex. (P)Joe Tex.

YOU SAY THE NICEST THINGS, BABY (1948) (w)Harold Adamson (m)Jimmy McHugh. (I)Musical: *As The Girls Go* by Bill Callahan and Betty Jane Watson. Reprised by Irene Rich and Bobby Clark.

YOU SEND ME (1957) (wm)L. C. Cooke. (P)Sam Cooke.

YOU SEXY THING (1975) (wm)E. A. G. Brown—Tony Wilson. (P)Hot Chocolate.

YOU SHOULD BE DANCING (1976) (wm)Barry Gibb—Maurice Gibb—Robin Gibb. (P)The Bee Gees.

YOU SHOULD HEAR HOW SHE TALKS ABOUT YOU (1982) (wm)Tom Snow—Dean Pritchard. (P)Melissa Manchester.

YOU SHOWED ME (1969) (wm)Gene Clark—Jim McGuinn. (P)The Turtles.

YOU SHOWED ME THE WAY (1937) (wm)Bud Green—Ella Fitzgerald—Teddy McRae—Chick Webb. (P)Chick Webb and his Orchestra, vocal by Ella Fitzgerald.

YOU STARTED SOMETHING (1941) (w)Leo Robin (m)Ralph Rainger. (I)Film: *Moon Over Miami* by Don Ameche, Betty Grable and Robert Cummings.

YOU STARTED SOMETHING (1947) (wm)Al Rinker—Floyd Huddleston. (P)Tony Pastor and his Orchestra.

YOU STEPPED INTO MY LIFE (1976) (wm)Barry Gibb—Robin Gibb—Maurice Gibb. (P)Wayne Newton. (P)Melba Moore.

YOU STEPPED OUT OF A DREAM (1940) (w)Gus Kahn (m)Nacio Herb Brown. (I)Film: *Ziegfeld Girl* by Tony Martin.

YOU TAKE MY BREATH AWAY (1979) (wm)Bruce Hart—Stephen Lawrence. (P)Rex Smith.

YOU TALK TOO MUCH (1960) (wm)Joe Jones—Reggie Hall. (P)Joe Jones.

YOU TELL ME WHY (1965) (wm)Ronald Elliott. (P)The Beau Brummels.

YOU TELL ME YOUR DREAM or I HAD A DREAM, DEAR (1908) (wm)Charles N. Daniels—Jay Blackton—A. H. Brown—Seymour Rice. Popular standard. (R)1931 by The Mills Brothers.

YOU TOLD A LIE (I BELIEVED YOU) (1949) (wm)Teepee Mitchell—Lew Porter. (P)Marjorie Hughes.

YOU TOOK ADVANTAGE OF ME (1928) (w)Lorenz Hart (m)Richard Rodgers. (I)Musical: *Present Arms* by Busby Berkeley and Joyce Barbour. Film: *A Star Is Born* with Judy Garland and James Mason.

YOU TOOK THE WORDS RIGHT OUT OF MY MOUTH (1977) (wm)Jim Steinman. (P)Meat Loaf.

YOU TRY SOMEBODY ELSE, AND I'LL TRY SOMEBODY ELSE (1931) (w)Lew Brown—B. G. De Sylva (m)Ray Henderson. (P)Russ Columbo. Film: *The Best Things In Life Are Free* (1951) by Sheree North.

YOU TURN ME ON (1965) (wm)Ian Whitcomb. (P)Ian Whitcomb.

YOU TURN ME ON, I'M A RADIO (1972) (wm)Joni Mitchell. (P)Joni Mitchell.

YOU TURNED THE TABLES ON ME (1936) (w)Sidney D. Mitchell (m)Louis Alter. (I)Film: *Sing, Baby, Sing* by Alice Faye. (P)Benny Goodman and his Orchestra, vocal by Helen Ward. Film: *The Benny Goodman Story* with Steve Allen.

YOU WALK BY (1940) (w)Ben Raleigh (m)Bernie Wayne. (P)Guy Lombardo and his Royal Canadians. (P)Eddy Duchin and his Orchestra.

YOU WAS (1949) (w)Paul Francis Webster (m)Sonny Burke. (P)Doris Day and Buddy Clark.

YOU WEAR IT WELL (1972) (wm)Rod Stewart—Martin Quittenton. (P)Rod Stewart.

YOU WERE MEANT FOR ME (1924) (wm)Noble Sissle—Eubie Blake. (I)London revue: *London Calling!* by Noel Coward and Gertrude Lawrence. U. S. in revue: *Andre Charlot'S Revue Of 1924* by Gertrude Lawrence and Jack Buchanan.

YOU WERE MEANT FOR ME (1929) (w)Arthur Freed (m)Nacio Herb Brown. (I)Film: *The Broadway Melody* (1929) by Charles King. Films: *Hollywood Revue Of 1929*; *The Show Of Shows* (1929); *Hullabaloo* (1940); *You Were Meant For Me* (1948); *Singin' In The Rain* with Gene Kelly.

YOU WERE MINE (1959) (wm)Paul Giacalone. (P)The Fireflies.

YOU WERE NEVER LOVELIER (1924) (w)Johnny Mercer (m)Jerome Kern. (I)Film: *Something To Shout About* by Don Ameche and Janet Blair. Film: *You Were Never Lovelier* with Fred Astaire and Rita Hayworth.

YOU WERE ON MY MIND (1965) (wm)Sylvia Fricker. (P)We Five.

YOU WERE ONLY FOOLING (1946) (w)William E. Faber—Fred Meadows (m)Larry Fotine. (P)Blue Barron and his Orchestra.

YOU WERE THERE (1935) (wm)Noel Coward. (I)England play: SHADOW PLAY by Noel Coward and Gertrude Lawrence.

YOU WILL HAVE TO PAY FOR YOUR YESTERDAY (1945) (w)Bonnie Dodd—Sarah Jane Cooper (m)Tex Ritter. (P)Tex Ritter.

YOU WON'T BE SATISFIED (Until You Break My Heart) (1945) (wm)Freddy James—Larry Stock. (P)Les Brown and his Orchestra, vocal by Doris Day.

YOU WON'T SEE ME (1966) (wm)John Lennon—Paul McCartney. The Beatles. (R)1974 by Anne Murray.

YOU WONDERFUL YOU (1950) (w)Jack Brooks—Saul Chaplin (m)Harry Warren. (I)Film: *Summer Stock* by Gene Kelly and Judy Garland.

YOU WOULDN'T FOOL ME, WOULD YOU? (1928) (w)B. G. De Sylva—Lew Brown (m)Ray Henderson. (I)Musical: *Follow Thru* by Irene Delroy and John Barker.

YOU WOULDN'T LISTEN (1966) (wm)Millas— Peterik—Borch. (P)The Ides of March.

YOU'D BE SO EASY TO LOVE (See EASY TO LOVE)

YOU'D BE SO NICE TO COME HOME TO (1942) (wm)Cole Porter. (I)Film: *Something To Shout About* (1943) by Don Ameche and Janet Blair.

YOU'D BE SURPRISED (1919) (wm)Irving Berlin. (I)Ziegfeld Follies of 1919 with Eddie Cantor. Film: *Blue Skies* with Bing Crosby and Fred Astaire. Film: *There'S No Business Like Show Business* with Ethel Merman and Marilyn Monroe.

YOU'D BETTER COME HOME (1965) (wm)Tony Hatch. (P)Petula Clark.

YOU'LL ALWAYS BE THE ONE I LOVE (1947) (w)Sunny Skylar (m)Ticker Freeman. (P)Frank Sinatra.

YOU'LL ANSWER TO ME (1961) (w)Hal David (m)Sherman Edwards. (P)Patti Page.

YOU'LL BE SORRY (1942) (wm)Fred Rose—Gene Autry. (P)Gene Autry.

YOU'LL HAVE TO SWING IT (See IF YOU CAN'T SING IT, YOU'LL HAVE TO SWING IT)

YOU'LL LOSE A GOOD THING (1962) (wm)Barbara Lynn Ozen. (P)Barbara Lynn.

YOU'LL NEVER FIND ANOTHER LOVE LIKE MINE (1976) (wm)Kenny Gamble—Leon Huff. (P)Lou Rawls.

YOU'LL NEVER GET AWAY (1952) (wm)Joan Whitney—Alex Kramer—Hy Zaret. (P)The Paulette Sisters. (P)Teresa Brewer and Don Cornell.

YOU'LL NEVER GET AWAY FROM ME (1959) (w)Stephen Sondheim (m)Jule Styne. (I)Musical: *Gypsy* by Jack Klugman and Ethel Merman.

YOU'LL NEVER GET TO HEAVEN (1964) (w)Hal David (m)Burt Bacharach. (P)Dionne Warwick. (R)1973 by The Stylistics.

YOU'LL NEVER KNOW (1943) (w)Mack Gordon (m)Harry Warren. (I)Film: *Hello, Frisco, Hello* by Alice Faye. Film: *Four Jills In A Jeep* (1944) by Alice Faye. (P)Dick Haymes. Academy Award Winning Song 1943.

YOU'LL NEVER WALK ALONE (1945) (w)Oscar Hammerstein II (m)Richard Rodgers. (I)Musical: *Carousel* by Christine Johnson. Film version (1957) by Claramae Turner.

YOU'RE A BUILDER UPPER (1934) (w)Ira Gershwin—E. Y. Harburg (m)Harold Arlen. (I)Revue: *Life Begins At 8:40* by Ray Bolger and Dixie Dunbar.

YOU'RE A GOOD MAN, CHARLIE BROWN (1967) (wm)Clark Gesner. (I)Musical: *You'Re A Good Man, Charlie Brown.*

YOU'RE A GRAND OLD FLAG (1906) (wm)George M. Cohan. (I)Musical: *George Washington, Jr.* by George M. Cohan. Musical: *George M!* by Joel Grey. Film: *Yankee Doodle Dandy* by James Cagney.

YOU'RE A HEAVENLY THING (1935) (wm)Joe Young—

Little Jack Little. (P)Little Jack Little and his Orchestra.

YOU'RE A PART OF ME (1975) (wm)Kim Carnes. (P)Susan Jacks. (R)1976 Kim Carnes. (R)1979 Charlie McLain.

YOU'RE A SPECIAL PART OF ME (1973) (wm)Gregory Wright—Harold Johnson—Andrew Porter. (P)Diana Ross and Marvin Gaye.

YOU'RE A SWEET LITTLE HEADACHE (1938) (wm)Leo Robin—Ralph Rainger. (I)Film: *Paris Honeymoon* by Bing Crosby. (P)Bing Crosby.

YOU'RE A SWEETHEART (1937) (w)Harold Adamson (m)Jimmy McHugh. (I)Film: *You're A Sweetheart* by Alice Faye. Film: *Meet Danny Wilson* (1952) by Frank Sinatra.

YOU'RE A WONDERFUL ONE (1964) (wm)Eddie Holland—Brian Holland—Lamont Dozier. (P)Marvin Gaye.

YOU'RE ALL I NEED TO GET BY (1968) (wm)Valerie Simpson—Nicholas Ashford. (P)Marvin Gaye and Tammi Terrell.

YOU'RE ALL I WANT FOR CHRISTMAS (1948) (wm)Glen Moore—Seger Ellis. (P)Frank Gallagher. Also recorded by Frankie Laine.

YOU'RE ALWAYS IN MY ARMS (But Only In My Dreams) (1929) (w)Joseph McCarthy (m)Harry Tierney. (I)Film: *Rio Rita* by John Boles and Bebe Daniels.

YOU'RE AN ANGEL (1935) (w)Dorothy Fields (m)Jimmy McHugh. (I)Film: *Hooray For Love* by Ann Sothern and Gene Raymond.

YOU'RE AN OLD SMOOTHIE (1932) (wm)B. G. De Sylva—Richard A. Whiting—Nacio Herb Brown. (I)Musical: *Take A Chance* by Jack Haley and Ethel Merman.

YOU'RE BLASE (1932) (w)Bruce Sivier (m)Ord Hamilton. (I)London in musical: *Bow Bells* by Binnie Hale. (P)In U. S. by Gus Arnheim and his Orchestra.

YOU'RE BREAKING MY HEART (1949) (wm)Pat Genaro—Sunny Skylar. Adapted from Leoncavallo's "La Mattinata." (P)Vic Damone. Also recorded by Buddy Clark.

YOU'RE CLEAR OUT OF THIS WORLD (See OUT OF THIS WORLD)

YOU'RE DEVASTATING (1933) (w)Otto Harbach (m)Jerome Kern. (I)Musical: *Roberta* by Bob Hope and Tamara. Film: *Lovely To Look At* with Kathryn Grayson, Howard Keel, Red Skelton and Ann Miller.

YOU'RE DRIVING ME CRAZY (What Did I Do) (1930) (wm)Walter Donaldson. (I)Musical: *Smiles* by Adele Astaire and Eddie Foy, Jr. (P)Guy Lombardo and his Royal Canadians.

YOU'RE EVERYWHERE (1947) (w)Paul Francis Webster (m)Harry Revel. (I)Film: *It Happened On 5Th Avenue.*

YOU'RE EVERYWHERE (1932) (w)Edward Heyman (m)Vincent Youmans. (I)Musical: *Through The Years* by Natalie Hall and Michael Bartlett.

YOU'RE GETTING TO BE A HABIT WITH ME (1932) (w)Al Dubin (m)Harry Warren. (I)Film: *Forty-Second Street* by Bebe Daniels. Film: *Lullaby Of Broadway* by Doris Day.

YOU'RE GONNA HURT YOURSELF (1965) (wm)Bob Crewe—Charles Calello. (P)Frankie Valli.

YOU'RE GONNA LOSE THAT GIRL (1965) (wm)John Lennon—Paul McCartney. (P)The Beatles. Also in film *Help!* by The Beatles.

YOU'RE GONNA LOSE YOUR GAL (1933) (wm)Joe

Young—James V. Monaco. (P)Jan Garber and his Orchestra. Film: *Starlift* (1951) by Doris Day and Gordon MacRae.

YOU'RE GONNA MISS ME (1959) (wm)Eddie Curtis. (P)Connie Francis.

YOU'RE HAVING MY BABY (See HAVING MY BABY)

YOU'RE IN MY HEART (1972) (wm)Rod Stewart. (P)Rod Stewart.

YOU'RE JUST IN LOVE (1950) (wm)Irving Berlin. (I)Musical: *Call Me Madam* by Ethel Merman and Russell Nype. (P)Perry Como. Also in film version by Ethel Merman.

YOU'RE JUST TOO TOO (1957) (wm)Cole Porter. Not one of Porter's hit songs.

YOU'RE LAUGHING AT ME (1937) (wm)Irving Berlin. (I)Film: *On The Avenue* by Dick Powell.

YOU'RE LONELY AND I'M LONELY (1941) (wm)Irving Berlin. (I)Musical: *Louisiana Purchase* by Victor Moore and Zorina.

YOU'RE MINE YOU (1933) (w)Edward Heyman (m)John Green. No artist credited with introduction.

YOU'RE MOVING OUT TODAY (1977) (wm)Carole Bayer Sager—Bruce Roberts—Bette Midler. (P)Bette Midler. (P)Carole Bayer Sager.

YOU'RE MY BEST FRIEND (1975) (wm)John Deacon. (P)Queen.

YOU'RE MY EVERYTHING (1931) (w)Mort Dixon—Joe Young (m)Harry Warren. (I)Revue: *The Laugh Parade*. Films: *You're My Everything* (1949) by Dan Dailey; *Painting The Clouds With Sunshine* with Dennis Morgan, Virginia Mayo; *The Eddie Duchin Story.*

YOU'RE MY EVERYTHING (1967) (wm)Norman Whitfield—Roger Penzabene—Cornelius Grant. (P)The Temptations.

YOU'RE MY GIRL (1947) (w)Sammy Cahn (m)Jule Styne. (I)Musical: *High Button Shoes* by Mark Dawson and Lois Lee.

YOU'RE MY PAST, PRESENT AND FUTURE (1933) (w)Mack Gordon (m)Harry Revel. (I)Film: *Broadway Thru A Keyhole* by Russ Columbo.

YOU'RE MY SOUL AND INSPIRATION (See SOUL AND INSPIRATION)

YOU'RE MY THRILL (1934) (w)Ned Washington (m)Burton Lane. (I)Film: *Here Comes The Band* by Ted Lewis.

YOU'RE MY WORLD (1963) (w-Eng)Carl Sigman (w-It)Gino Paoli (m)Umberto Bindi. Original title "Il Mio Mondo." (P)Cilla Black. (R)1977 by Helen Reddy.

YOU'RE NO GOOD (1975) (wm)Clint Ballard, Jr. (P)Linda Ronstadt.

YOU'RE NOBODY 'TIL SOMEBODY LOVES YOU (1944) (wm)Russ Morgan—Larry Stock—James Cavanaugh. (P)Russ Morgan and his Orchestra. (R)1965 by Dean Martin.

YOU'RE NOT THE KIND (1936) (wm)Will Hudson—Irving Mills. (P)Fats Waller.

YOU'RE ONLY HUMAN (SECOND WIND) (1985) (wm)Billy Joel. (P)Billy Joel.

YOU'RE ONLY LONELY (1979) (wm)John David Souther. (P)J. D. Souther.

YOU'RE SENSATIONAL (1956) (wm)Cole Porter. (I)Film: *High Society* by Frank Sinatra.

YOU'RE SIXTEEN (1960) (wm)Richard Sherman—Robert Sherman. (P)Johnny Burnette. (R)1974 by Ringo Starr.

YOU'RE SLIGHTLY TERRIFIC (1936) (w)Sidney D.

Mitchell (m)Lew Pollack. (I)Film: *Pigskin Parade* by Tony Martin and Dixie Dunbar.

YOU'RE SO FINE (1959) (wm)Lance Finney—Bob West—Willie Schofield. (P)The Falcons.

YOU'RE SO UNDERSTANDING (1949) (wm)Bernie Wayne—Ben Raleigh. (P)Blue Barron and his Orchestra.

YOU'RE SO VAIN (1973) (wm)Carly Simon. (P)Carly Simon.

YOU'RE STILL A YOUNG MAN (1972) (wm)Emilio Castillo—Stephen Kupka. (P)Tower of Power.

YOU'RE SUCH A COMFORT TO ME (1933) (w)Mack Gordon (m)Harry Revel. (I)Film: *Sitting Pretty* by Ginger Rogers, Jack Oakie, Thelma Todd and Jack Haley.

YOU'RE THE CREAM IN MY COFFEE (1928) (w)B. G. De Sylva—Lew Brown (m)Ray Henderson. (I)Musical: *Hold Everything!* by Jack Whiting and Ona Munson. Film: *The Cockeyed World* with Stuart Erwin and Joe E. Brown.

YOU'RE THE DEVIL IN DISGUISE (1963) (wm)Bill Giant—Bernie Baum—Florence Kaye. (P)Elvis Presley.

YOU'RE THE FIRST, THE LAST, MY EVERYTHING (1974) (wm)Barry White—Tony Sepe—Peter Radcliffe. (P)Barry White.

YOU'RE THE INSPIRATION (1985) (wm)Peter Cetera—David Foster. (P)Chicago.

YOU'RE THE ONE (1965) (wm)Petula Clark—Tony Hatch. (P)The Vogues.

YOU'RE THE ONE (1966) (wm)William Robinson. (P)The Marvelettes.

YOU'RE THE ONE (FOR ME) (1940) (w)Johnny Mercer (m)Jimmy McHugh. (I)Film: *You're The One* by Orrin Tucker and Bonnie Baker. (P)Orrin Tucker and his Orchestra.

YOU'RE THE ONE I CARE FOR (1930) (w)Harry Link (m)Bert Lown—Chauncey Gray. (P)Bert Lown and his Orchestra.

YOU'RE THE ONE THAT I WANT (1978) (wm)John Farrar. (I)Film: *Grease* by John Travolta and Olivia Newton-John.

YOU'RE THE ONLY ONE (1979) (wm)Seth Justman—Peter Wolf. (P)J. Geils Band.

YOU'RE THE ONLY STAR IN MY BLUE HEAVEN (1938) (wm)Gene Autry. (I)Film: *The Old Barn Dance* by Gene Autry. Films: *Mexicali Rose* and *Rim Of The Canyon* both by Gene Autry.

YOU'RE THE REASON (1960) (wm)Bobby Edwards—Mildred Imes—Fred Henley—Terry Fell. (P)Bobby Edwards.

YOU'RE THE REASON I'M LIVING (1963) (wm)Bobby Darin. (P)Bobby Darin.

YOU'RE THE TOP (1934) (wm)Cole Porter. (I)Musical: *Anything Goes* by Ethel Merman, William Gaxton. Film versions: (1936) by Ethel Merman, Bing Crosby; (1956) by Bing Crosby, Mitzi Gaynor. Film: *Night And Day* by Ginny Sims, Cary Grant.

YOU'VE BEEN CHEATIN' (1965) (wm)Curtis Mayfield. (P)The Impressions.

YOU'VE BEEN IN LOVE TOO LONG (1965) (wm)Ivy Hunter—Clarence Paul—William Stevenson. (P)Martha and The Vandellas.

YOU'VE CHANGED (1942) (w)Bill Carey (m)Carl Fischer. (P)Harry James and his Orchestra, vocal by Dick Haymes.

YOU'VE GOT A FRIEND (1971) (wm)Carole King. (P)James Taylor.

YOU'VE GOT EVERYTHING (1933) (w)Gus Kahn (m)Walter Donaldson. (I)Film: *The Prizefighter And The Lady* with Myrna Loy and Jack Dempsey.

YOU'VE GOT ME CRYING AGAIN (1933) (w)Charles Newman (m)Isham Jones. (P)Ruth Etting.

YOU'VE GOT ME DANGLING ON A STRING (1970) (wm)Ronald Dunbar—Edythe Wayne. (P)The Chairmen of the Board.

YOU'VE GOT ME THIS WAY (Whatta-Ya-Gonna Do About It) (1940) (w)Johnny Mercer (m)Jimmy McHugh. (I)Film: *You'll Find Out* by Kay Kyser and his College of Musical Knowledge. (P)Kay Kyser and his Orchestra. Also recorded by Glenn Miller, Tommy Dorsey, Jimmy Dorsey and their Orchestras.

YOU'VE GOT THAT THING (1929) (wm)Cole Porter. (I)Musical: *Fifty Million Frenchmen* by Jack Thompson and Betty Compton.

YOU'VE GOT TO BE CAREFULLY TAUGHT (1949) (w)Oscar Hammerstein II (m)Richard Rodgers. (I)Musical: *South Pacific* by William Tabbert. Film version (1958) by Bill Lee dubbing for John Kerr.

YOU'VE GOT TO HIDE YOUR LOVE AWAY (1965) (wm)John Lennon—Paul McCartney. (P)The Beatles.

YOU'VE GOT TO PICK A POCKET OR TWO (1963) (wm)Lionel Bart. (I)Musical: *Oliver* with Ron Moody. Also in film version with Ron Moody.

YOU'VE GOT TO SEE MAMMA EV'RY NIGHT OR YOU CAN'T SEE MAMMA AT ALL (1923) (wm)Billy Rose—Con Conrad. (P)Sophie Tucker.

YOU'VE GOT YOUR TROUBLES (1965) (wm)Roger Greenaway—Roger Cook. (P)The Fortunes.

YOU'VE LOST THAT LOVIN' FEELIN' (1965) (wm)Barry Mann—Cynthia Weill—Phil Spector. (P)The Righteous Brothers. (R)1985 by Daryl Hall and John Oates.

PHIL SPECTOR

After Les Paul, one of the pioneers of multi-track recording was Phil Spector. He created what was known as "The Wall of Sound" in his fantastic production of the Righteous Brothers recording of *You've Lost That Lovin' Feeling*.

YOU'VE MADE ME SO VERY HAPPY (1969) (wm)Berry Gordy, Jr. —Frank E. Wilson—Brenda Holloway—Patrice Holloway. (P)Brenda Holloway. (P)Blood, Sweat and Tears.

YOU'VE REALLY GOT A HOLD ON ME (1963) (wm)(P)The Miracles.

YOU, BABY (NOBODY BUT YOU) (1965) (wm)P. F. Sloan—Steve Barri. (P)The Turtles.

YOU, I (1968) (wm)Steve McNicol. (P)The Rugbys.

YOU, YOU, YOU (1953) (w-Eng)Robert Mellin (m)Lotar Olias. (P)The Ames Brothers.

YOU, YOU, YOU ARE THE ONE (1948) (w)Fred Wise—Milton Leeds (m)Tetos Demey. (P)Russ Morgan. Also recorded by The Ames Brothers and The Three Suns.

YOUNG AND FOOLISH (1954) (w)Arnold B. Horwitt (m)Albert Hague. (I)Musical: *Plain And Fancy* by David Daniels and Gloria Marlowe.

YOUNG AND HEALTHY (1932) (w)Al Dubin (m)Harry

Warren. (I)Film: *Forty-Second Street* by Dick Powell.

YOUNG AND THE RESTLESS, THE (See NADIA'S THEME)

YOUNG AND WARM AND WONDERFUL (1958) (wm)Hy Zaret—Lou Singer. (P)Tony Bennett.

YOUNG AT HEART (1954) (w)Carolyn Leigh (m)Johnny Richards. (P)Frank Sinatra. Later used as theme for film: *Young At Heart*.

YOUNG BLOOD (1958) (wm)Jerry Leiber—Mike Stoller—Doc Promus. (P)The Coasters.

YOUNG EMOTIONS (1962) (w)Mack David (m)Jerry Livingston. (P)Ricky Nelson.

YOUNG GIRL (1968) (wm)Jerry Fuller. (P)Gary Puckett and The Union Gap.

YOUNG IDEAS (1955) (w)Chuck Sweeney (m)Moose Charlap. (I)TV musical: *The King And Mrs. Candle*. (P)Tony Martin.

YOUNG LOVE (1957) (wm)Carole Joyner—Ric Cartey. (P)Sonny James. Also recorded by Tab Hunter. (R)1966 by Lesley Gore.

YOUNG LOVERS (1963) (wm)Ray Hildebrand—Jill Jackson. (P)Paul and Paula.

YOUNG MAN'S FANCY, A (1920) (w)John Murray Anderson—Jack Yellen (m)Milton Ager. (I)Revue: *What'S In A Name* by Rosalind Fuller.

YOUNG TURKS (1981) (w)Rod Stewart (m)Carmine Appice—Kevin Savigar—Duane Hitchings. (P)Rod Stewart.

YOUNG WORLD (1962) (wm)Jerry Fuller. (P)Rick Nelson.

YOUNGBLOOD (1979) (wm)Rickie Lee Jones. (P)Rickie Lee Jones.

YOUNGER GIRL (1965) (wm)John Sebastian. (P)The Critters. (P)The Hondells.

YOUNGER THAN SPRINGTIME (1949) (w)Oscar Hammerstein II (m)Richard Rodgers. (I)Musical: *South Pacific* by William Tabbert. Film version (1958) by Bill Lee dubbing for John Kerr.

YOUR BULLDOG DRINKS CHAMPAGNE (1975) (wm)David Bellamy—Jim Stafford. (P)Jim Stafford.

YOUR CHEATIN' HEART (1953) (wm)Hank Williams. (P)Hank Williams. Also recorded by Joni James. (R)1962 by Ray Charles.

YOUR EYES HAVE TOLD ME SO (1919) (wm)Gus Kahn—Walter Blaufuss—Egbert Van Alstyne. (P)John McCormack. Film: *Sing Me A Love Song* with Zasu Pitts and Patricia Ellis and James Melton. Film: *I'Ll See You In My Dreams* with Doris Day and Danny Thomas.

YOUR FEET'S TOO BIG (1935) (wm)Ada Benson—Fred Fisher. (P)Fats Waller. (R)Musical: *Ain'T Misbehavin'* with Debbie Allen and Nell Carter.

YOUR GOOD THING (IS ABOUT TO END) (1966) (wm)David Porter—Isaac Hayes. (P)Mable John. (P)1969 Lou Rawls.

YOUR HUSBAND, MY WIFE (1969) (wm)Toni Wine—Irwin Levine. (P)Brooklyn Bridge.

YOUR LAND AND MY LAND (1927) (w)Dorothy Donnelly (m)Sigmund Romberg. (I)Nathaniel Wagner and the Chorus in Operetta: *My Maryland*.

YOUR LETTER (1977) (wm)Joan Armatrading. (P)Joan Armatrading.

YOUR LOVE (1986) (wm)John Spinks. (P)The Outfield.

YOUR LOVE KEEPS LIFTING ME HIGHER AND HIGHER (1966) (wm)Gary L. Jackson—Carl Smith—Raynard Miner. (P)Jackie Wilson. (R)1977 by Rita Coolidge.

YOUR MAMA DON'T DANCE (1973) (wm)Kenny Loggins—Jim Messina. (P)Loggins and Messina.

YOUR MOTHER AND MINE (1929) (w)Joe Goodwin (m)Gus Edwards. (I)Film: *Hollywood Revue Of 1929* by Charles King. Film: *The Show Of Shows* by Frank Fay, Beatrice Lillie, Louise Fazenda and Lloyd Hamilton.

YOUR MOTHER SHOULD KNOW (1968) (wm)John Lennon—Paul McCartney. (P)The Beatles.

YOUR OLD STANDBY (1963) (wm)Janie Bradford—Wm."Smokey" Robinson, Jr. (P)Mary Wells.

YOUR OWN SPECIAL WAY (1977) (wm)Mike Rutherford. (P)Genesis.

YOUR PRECIOUS LOVE (1967) (wm)Valerie Simpson—Nicholas Ashford. (P)Marvin Gaye and Tammi Terrell.

YOUR RED WAGON (1940) (w)Don Raye (m)Gene de Paul—Richard M Jones. Based on an instrumental blues composition by Richard M. Jones. (P)The Andrews Sisters. Also recorded by Ray McKinley and his Orchestra.

YOUR SMILING FACE (1977) (wm)James Taylor. (P)James Taylor.

YOUR SOCKS DON'T MATCH (1941) (wm)Leon Carr—Leo Corday. (P)Fats Waller. Also recorded by Bing Crosby and Louis Jordan.

YOUR SONG (1970) (wm)Elton John—Bernie Taupin. (P)Elton John.

YOUR TIME TO CRY (1970) (wm)Joe Simon—Raeford Gerald—Dock Price Jr. (P)Joe Simon.

YOUR TRUE LOVE (1957) (wm)Carl Lee Perkins. (P)Carl Perkins.

YOUR UNCHANGING LOVE (1965) (wm)Brian Holland—Lamont Dozier—Eddie Holland. (P)Marvin Gaye.

YOUR WILDEST DREAMS (1986) (wm)Justin Hayward. (P)The Moody Blues.

YOURS (1931) (w-Eng)Jack Sherr (m)Gonzalo Roig. Original title "Quierme Mucho." (P)In Spanish by Tito Schipa. Film: *Sioux City Sue* (1946) by Gene Autry. (P)Jimmy Dorsey and his Orchestra, vocal by Helen O'Connell and Bob Eberly.

YOURS AND MINE (1937) (w)Arthur Freed (m)Nacio Herb Brown. (I)Film: *Broadway Melody Of 1938* by Judy Garland and later reprised by Eleanor Powell.

YOURS FOR A SONG (1939) (w)Billy Rose—Ted Fetter (m)Dana Suesse. (I)At New York World's Fair in *Billy Rose'S Aquacade* by Morton Downey.

YOURS IS MY HEART ALONE (1931) (w-Eng)Harry B. Smith (m)Franz Lehar. (I)Germany by Richard Tauber in operetta: *The Land Of Smiles*.

YOURS SINCERELY (1929) (w)Lorenz Hart (m)Richard Rodgers. (I)Musical: *Spring Is Here* by Glenn Hunter and Bernice Claire. Film version (1930) by Alexander Gray and Bernice Claire.

YUMMY YUMMY YUMMY (1968) (wm)Arthur Resnick—Joe Levine. (P)The Ohio Express.

ZABADAK (1967) (wm)Howard Blaikley. (P)Dave, Dozy, Beaky, Mick, and Tich Dee.

ZIGEUNER (1929) (wm)Noel Coward. (I)London musical: *Bitter Sweet* by Peggy Wood. New York production by Evelyn Laye. Film version (1940) by Jeanette MacDonald.

ZING A LITTLE ZONG (1952) (w)Leo Robin (m)Harry Warren. (I)Film: *Just For You* by Bing Crosby and Jane Wyman.

ZING WENT THE STRINGS OF MY HEART (1935) (wm)James Hanley. (I)Revue: *Thumbs Up* by Hal Le Roy and Eunice Healy. Film: *Listen Darling* (1938) by Judy Garland. Film: *Lullaby Of Broadway* (1951) by Gene Nelson. (Judy Garland auditioned at MGM with this song.)

ZING ZING — ZOOM ZOOM (1950) (w)Charles Tobias (m)Sigmund Romberg. (P)Perry Como.

ZIP (1940) (w)Lorenz Hart (m)Richard Rodgers. (I)Musical: *Pal Joey* by Jean Castro. Also in film version.

ZIP CODE (1967) (wm)Mike Rabon—Norman Ezell—John Durrill. (P)The Five Americans.

ZIP-A-DEE-DOO-DAH (1945) (w)Ray Gilbert (m)Allie Wrubel. (I)Film: *Song Of The South* by James Baskett. (P)Johnny Mercer with the Pied Pipers. (R)1962 by Bob B. Soxx and the Blue Jeans. 1947 Academy Award Winner.

ZONKY (1929) (w)Andy Razaf (m)Thomas "Fats" Waller. (I)Revue: *Load Of Coal.*

ZOOT SUIT (For My Sunday Gal), A (1941) (wm)Ray Gilbert (m)Bob O'Brien. (P)Kay Kyser and his Orchestra, vocal by Harry Babbitt.

ZORBA THE GREEK (Theme from) (1965) (m)Mikos Theodorakis. (I)Film: *Zorba The Greek* with Anthony Quinn. (P)Herb Alpert and the Tijuana Brass.

ZSA ZSA (1953) (m)Bernie Wayne. Dedicated to Zsa Zsa Gabor. (P)Bernie Wayne and his Orchestra.

ZUYDER ZEE (1944) (w)Sammy Cahn (m)Jule Styne. (I)Film: *Knickerbocker Holiday* with Nelson Eddy and Constance Dowling.

The Songwriters

Songwriters often have their works recorded under varying forms of their names. For example, "David Songwriter" might appear under that name on one record or song sheet, "D. Songwriter" on another, perhaps "David Charles Songwriter" on yet a third. If you don't find the composer or lyricist you are seeking under his most commonly used name, check for other possible variations of the name.

The information presented here is based on the listings in the "Songs" section. Clearly no single volume could include all the American Popular Songs ever written. Some lesser-known works and songwriters have necessarily been omitted. Also, the information presented here has been gathered from many sources. Your indulgence is requested for any duplications or misspellings that may have resulted.

A

AARONSON, IRVING — Loveliest Night Of The Year

ABBOTT, CHARLIE — Five Salted Peanuts

ABBOTT, GREGORY — Shake You Down

ABGELIS, PETE DE — I'll Wait For You

ABNER JR., EWART G. — Honest I Do

ABNER, BUFORD — Daddy O

ABRAHAMS, MAURICE — Ragtime Cowboy Joe

ABRAMS, LESTER — Minute By Minute

ABREU, ZEQUINHA — Tico Tico

ACKERMAN, JACK — Lasting Love

ACKERS, ANDY — New Shade Of Blue

ACKLIN, BARBARA — Have You Seen Her; The Whisper's Getting Louder (Whispers)

ACQUAVIVA, NICK — Am I In Love?; Ghost Town; In The Middle Of An Island; My Love, My Love

ACUFF, ROY — Unloved And Unclaimed; Write Me Sweetheart

ADAIR, TOM — Everything Happens To Me; In The Blue Of Evening; Lets Get Away From It All; Night We Called It A Day; Will You Still Be Mine?

ADAMS, BRYAN — Heat Of The Night; Heaven; It's Only Love; One Night Love Affair; Run To You; Somebody; Straight From The Heart

ADAMS, CLIFFORD — Big Fun

ADAMS, EMMETT — Bells Of St. Mary's

ADAMS, FRANK R. — I Wonder Who's Kissing Her Now

ADAMS, KEVIN — Come On Eileen; Come Prima(For The First Time)

ADAMS, KURT — Fool Was I; Somewhere Along The Way

ADAMS, LEE — Baby, Talk To Me; Bye Bye Birdie; Can't You See It?; Colorful; Don't Forget 127th Street; English Teacher, An; Everything's Great; Gimme Some; Golden Boy; Have A Dream; Honestly Sincere; How Lovely To Be A Woman; Hymn For A Sunday Evening; I Want To Be With You; I'm Fascinating; I've Just Seen Her; If I Were You; Kids; Lorna's Here; Lot Of Livin' To Do; Mating Game; Night Song; No More; Normal American Boy; Once Upon A Time; One Boy; One Last Kiss; Our Children; Put On A Happy Face; Rosie; Spanish Rose; Stick Around; Those Were The Days Or Theme From All In The Family

ADAMS, RITCHIE — Happy Summer Days; Tossin' And Turnin'

ADAMS, SARAH — Nearer, My God, To Thee

ADAMS, STANLEY — Duel In The Sun(A Duel Of Two Hearts); Jubilee; Little Old Lady; My Shawl; Wacky Dust; What A Difference A Day Made; Yesterthoughts

ADAMSON, HAROLD — Around The World; As The Girls Go; Aurora; Be A Good Scout; Blame It On The Rhumba; Broadway Jamboree; Candlelight And Wine; Change Of Heart; Chapel Bells; China Gate; Comin' In On A Wing And A Prayer; Daybreak; Did I Remember?; Dig You Later(a Hubba-hubba-hubba); Disco Lucy(I Love Lucy Theme); Don't Believe Everything You Dream; Everything I Have Is Yours; Have A Heart; Here Comes Heaven Again; How Blue The Night; How Many Times Do I Have To Tell You; How Would You Like To Kiss Me In The Moonlight?; Hush-A-Bye Island; I Couldn't Sleep A Wink Last Night; I Don't Care Who Knows It; I Got Lucky In The Rain; I Hit A New High; I Love To Whistle; I Walked In(With My Eyes Wide Open); I'm Glad I Waited; It's A Most Unusual Day; It's A Wonderful World; It's Been So Long; Legend Of Wyatt Earp; Let's Go Bavarian; Lovely Way To Spend An Evening; Manhattan Mood; Manhattan Serenade; Moonlight Mood; Music Stopped; My Fine Feathered Friend; My Resistance Is Low; On The Trail; Seven Twenty In The Books; Time On My Hands; Tony's Wife; Too Young To Go Steady; We're Having A Baby; When Love Is Young; Where Are You; Where The Lazy River Goes By; Woodpecker Song; You (Gee But You're Wonderful); You Say The Nicest Things, Baby; You're A Sweetheart

ADDERLY JR., NAT — Stop To Love

ADDINGTON, MILTON C. — Laurie(Strange Things Happen)

ADDINSELL, RICHARD — Warsaw Concerto

ADDISON, JOHN — Love Song Of Tom Jones

ADDRISI, DICK — Never My Love

ADDRISI, DON — Never My Love; Slow Dancin' Don't Turn Me On

ADELSON, LENNY — Away All Boats; Born To Sing The Blues; Come Next Spring

ADKINSON, EUGENE H. — It's Almost Tomorrow

ADLAM, BASIL G. — House Is Haunted

ADLER, LOU — Poor Side Of Town; Wonderful World

ADLER, RICHARD — (When You're)Racing With The Clock; Another Time, Another Place; Anytime At All; Even Now; Everybody Loves A Lover; Fini; Goodbye, Old Girl; Heart; Hernando's Hideaway; Hey There; I'm Not At All In Love; Man Doesn't Know,a; Near To You; New Town Is A Blue Town; Rags To Riches; Shoeless Joe From Hannibal Mo.; Small Talk; Steam Heat; Two Lost Souls; Whatever Lola Wants

ADMIRE, BILLY JOE — River Is Wide

ADOR, BILL — Jungle Fever

ADU, HELEN FOLASADE — Sweetest Taboo

ADU, HELEN FOLOSADE — Never As Good As The First Time; Smooth Operator

AGER, MILTON — Ain't She Sweet; Auf Wiedersehn, My Dear; Bagdad; Bench In The Park; Crazy Words-Crazy Tune; Everything Is Peaches Down In Georgia; Forever And Ever; Forgive Me; Glad Rag Doll; Happy Days Are Here Again; Happy Feet; He's A Good Man To Have Around; I Wonder What's Become Of Sally; I'm Nobody's Baby; I'm The Last Of The Red Hot Mammas; Louisville Lou, The Vampin' Lady; Mamma Goes Where Papa Goes Or Papa Don't Go Out Tonight; Trust In Me; Who Cares; You Can't Pull The Wool Over My Eyes; Young Man's Fancy

AGREE, LENA — Doggin' Around

AHBEZ, EDEN — Land Of Love(Come My Love And Live With Me); Lonely Island; Nature Boy

AHLERT, FRED — Life Is A Song(Let's Sing It Together); Walkin' My Baby Back Home

AHLERT, FRED E. — Free And Easy; I Don't Know Why(I Just Do); I Wake Up Smiling; I'd Love To Fall Asleep And Wake Up In My Mammy's Arms; I'll Get By(As Long As I Have You); I'm Gonna Sit Right Down And Write Myself A Letter; Into My Heart; It Must Be You; Love, You Funny Thing; Mean To Me; Where The Blue Of The Night Meets The Gold Of The Day; With Summer Coming On (I'm Still A Sweetheart)

AKINES, JERRY — Don't Let The Green Grass Fool You

AKKERMAN, JAN — Hocus Pocus

AKST, HARRY — Am I Blue?; Anema E Core; Baby Face; Blame It On The Danube; Dinah; Egg And I; Everything's Gonna Be All Right; Guilty; I'm The Medicine Man For The Blues; May I Sing To You; What A Perfect Combination

ALBENIZ, ISAAC — Moonlight Masquerade

ALBERT, MORRIS — Feelings

ALBRECHT, ELMER — Elmer's Tune

ALDEN, JOSEPH R. — Sleepy Time Gal

ALDERIDGE, AVA — Sharing The Night Together

ALENCAR, PAULO — Baion

ALEXANDER, ARTHUR — Anna(Go To Him)

ALEXANDER, EDNA — Sugar(That Sugar Baby O' Mine)

ALEXANDER, J. — Shake Your Rump To The Funk

ALEXANDER, JAMES — Lookin' For A Love

ALFONSO, BARRY — All The Right Moves

ALFORD, KENNETH J. — Colonel Bogey March

ALFRED, ROY — Best Man; Congratulations To Someone; Destination Moon; Fool Was I; Here Comes That Heartache Again; Huckle Buck; Let's Lock The Door And Throw Away The Key; Rock And Roll Waltz; She Can't Find Her Keys

ALFVEN, HUGO — Swedish Rhapsody

ALGUERO, AUGUSTO — If She Should Come To You(La Montana)

ALIVE, DEAD OR — Brand New Lover

ALLAN, GENE — Comin' Home Soldier; Mr. Lonely

ALLAN, LEWIS — Strange Fruit

ALLBRITTEN, DUB — Anybody But Me; I'm Sorry

ALLBRITTON, DUB — Rockin' Around The Christmas Tree

ALLEN, BRIAN — What About Love?

ALLEN, C. — Shake Your Rump To The Funk

ALLEN, DONNA — Serious

ALLEN, GEORGE N. — Oh Bury Me Not On The Lone Prairie

ALLEN, JANNA — Did It In A Minute; Kiss On My List; Method Of Modern Love; Private Eyes

ALLEN, LESTER — Kiss Of Fire

ALLEN, LEWIS — House I Live In, The(That's America To Me)

ALLEN, LINDA — Shoeshine Boy

ALLEN, PETER — Arthur's Theme; Don't Cry Out Loud; I Honestly Love You; I'd Rather Leave While I'm In Love

ALLEN, RAY — Pepino, The Italian Mouse

ALLEN, ROBERT — (There's No Place Like)Home For The Holidays; Can You Find It In Your Heart; Chances Are; Come To Me; Enchanted Island; Every Step Of The Way; Happy Anniversary; I Just Don't Know; If Dreams Come True; It's Not For Me To Say; Kissin' Bug Boogie; Moments To Remember; My One And Only Heart; No Not Much; Noodlin' Rag; Song For A Summer Night; To Know You Is To Love You; Very Special Love; Waiting Game; Who Needs You; You Alone (Sole Tu)

ALLEN, SARA — Did It In A Minute; I Can't Go For That(No Can Do); Maneater; Private Eyes; Swept Away; You Make My Dreams

ALLEN, SHORTY — Rock And Roll Waltz

ALLEN, STEVE — Gravy Waltz; Impossible; Let's Go To Church(Next Sunday Morning); Picnic(Theme)

ALLEN, SYLVESTER — Cisco Kid; Gypsy Man; L. A. Sunshine; Low Rider; Me And Baby Brother; Slipping Into Darkness; Summer; Why Can't We Be Friends; World Is A Ghetto

ALLEN, THORNTON W. — Washington And Lee Swing

ALLISON, AUDREY — He'll Have To Go

ALLISON, JERRY — More Than I Can Say; Peggy Sue

ALLISON, JOE — He'll Have To Go; When You Leave, Don't Slam The Door

ALLISON, MOSE — Back On The Corner

ALLMAN, GREG — Ain't Wasting Time No More; Midnight Rider

ALMER, TANDYN — Along Comes Mary

ALOMAR, CARLOS — Fame

ALPERT, HERB — Wonderful World

ALPERT, RANDY — Rise

ALSTONE, ALEX — Dancin' With Someone(longin' For You); More; Sonata; Symphony

ALSTYNE, EGBERT VAN — Beautiful Love; Drifting And Dreaming; In The Shade Of The Old Apple Tree; Memories

ALTER, LOUIS — Au Revoir But Not Goodbye; Circus; Come Up And See Me Sometime; Do You Know What It Means To Miss New Orleans; Dolores; Gotta Feelin' For You; Make A Wish; Manhattan Serenade; Melody From The Sky; Nina Never Knew; Rainbow On The River; You Turned The Tables On Me

ALTFELD, DON — Little Old Lady, The(From Pasadena)

ALTMAN, ARTHUR — All Alone Am I; All Or Nothing At All; American Beauty Rose; Green Years; I Will Follow Him; Play, Fiddle, Play

ALTMAN, MICHAEL — M*A*S*H(song From)(Suicide Is Painless)

ALTON, SHERON — What About Love?

AMER, SAMUEL WARD — America The Beautiful

AMMONS, ALBERT — Boogie Woogie Prayer; Boogie Woogie Stomp

AMSTERDAM, MOREY — Rum And Coca Cola

ANDERSON, ADRIENNE — Could It Be Magic; Daybreak; Deja Vu; Some Kind Of Friend

ANDERSON, BENNY — Waterloo; Winner Takes It All

ANDERSON, BILL — (I Love You)Still; I Love You Drops; Mama Sang A Song

ANDERSON, DEACON — Rag Mop

ANDERSON, ED — Flamingo

ANDERSON, GARY — Not Me; Quarter To Three; School Is Out

ANDERSON, IAN — Bungle In The Jungle; Living In The Past

ANDERSON, JOHN MURRAY — Young Man's Fancy

ANDERSON, JON — Chariots Of Fire; Owner Of A Lonely Heart; Roundabout

ANDERSON, LEROY — Belle Of The Ball; Blue Tango; Fiddle Faddle; Forgotten Dreams; Sleigh Ride; Syncopated Clock; Typewriter; Waltzing Cat

ANDERSON, MAXWELL — Big Mole; Catfish Song; Come In, Mornin'; How Can You Tell An American?; It Never Was You; Little Gray House; Lost In The Stars; River Chanty; September Song

ANDERSON, MELVIN — I Wonder Why

ANDERSON, R. ALEX — Cockeyed Mayor Of Kaunakakai

ANDERSON, STIG — Dancing Queen; Fernando; I Do, I Do, I Do, I Do, I Do; Knowing Me, Knowing You; Mamma Mia; Name Of The Game; S. O. S.; Waterloo

ANDERSSON, BENNY — Chiquitita; Dancing Queen; Does Your Mother Know; Fernando; I Do, I Do, I Do, I Do, I Do; Knowing Me, Knowing You; Mamma Mia;

Name Of The Game; One Night In Bangkok; S. O. S.

ANDRE, FABIAN — Dream A Little Dream Of Me; When They Played The Polka

ANDREW, S. — Combination Of The Two

ANDREWS, CHRIS — It's Alright

ANDREWS, LEE — Long Lonely Nights

ANDREWS, M. — Let's Wait Awhile

ANDREWS, MAGGIE — The Wreck Of The Shenandoah

ANDREWS, REGINALD — Let It Whip

ANGELIS, PETER DE — Dede Dinah; Painted, Tainted Rose

ANGULO, HECTOR — Guantanamera

ANISFIELD, FRED — Backstage

ANKA, PAUL — (I'm Just A)Lonely Boy; (You're)Having My Baby; Anytime(I'll Be There); Broken Heart And A Pillow Filled With Tears; Crazy Love; Dance On Little Girl; Diana; I Don't Like To Sleep Alone; It Doesn't Matter Any More; It's Time To Cry; Johnny's Theme; Let Me Try Again; Let The Bells Keep Ringing; Longest Day; Love Me Warm And Tender; Love(Makes The World Go 'round); My Home Town; My Way; One Man Woman/one Man Man; Puppy Love; Put Your Head On My Shoulder; Summer's Gone; You Are My Destiny

ANONYMOUS, — We Shall Overcome

ANT, ADAM — Goody Two Shoes

ANTHONY, JOHN — Keep On Smilin'

ANTHONY, MICHAEL — I'll Wait; Jump; Love Walks In; Why Can't This Be Love

ANTHONY, MIKE — Grass Is Greener; I'll Never Dance Again; Poetry In Motion; She Say(Oom Dooby Doom)

ANTHONY, RAY — Bunny Hop

ANTON, EMIL — Dear Lonely Hearts(I'm Writing To You)

ANTONUCCI, ANTHONY — Philadelphia, U. S. A.

APPEL, MIKE — Doesn't Somebody Want To Be Wanted

APPELL, DAVE — Bristol Stomp; Cha Cha Cha; Dancin' Party; Ding-A-Ling; Do The Bird; Don't Hang Up; Fish; Good Time Baby; Gravy; Hey Bobba Beedle; Let's Twist Again; Mornin' Beautiful; Popeye(The Hitchhiker); South Street; Swingin' School; Wah Watusi; Wild One; Wildwood Days

APPICE JR., CARMINE — Do(Da)You Think I'm Sexy

APPICE, CARMINE — Young Turks

APPLEGATE, M. — Power Of Love

ARBELO, FERNANDO — Big Chief De Sota

ARCHER, HARRY — I Love You

ARGENT, RED — Time Of The Season

ARGENT, ROD — Hold Your Head Up; She's Not There

ARKIN, ALAN — Banana Boat Song, The(Day-O)

ARKIN, DAVID — Black & White

ARLEN, HAROLD — A Woman's Prerogative; Ain't It De Truth?; Andiamo; Any Place I Hang My Hat Is Home; As Long As I Live; Between The Devil And The Deep Blue Sea; Blues In The Night; Breakfast Ball; Buds Won't Bud; Cakewalk Your Lady; Calico Days; Captains Of The Clouds; Cocoanut Sweet; Come Rain Or Come Shine; Ding-Dong! The Witch Is Dead; Dissertation On The State Of Bliss(Love And Learn); Don't Rock The Boat, Dear; Down With Love; Eagle And Me; Evelina; Fancy Free; Fancy Meeting You; First You Have Me High(Then You Have Me Low); For Every Man There's A Woman; Friendly Islands; Fun To Be Fooled; Get Happy; God's Country; Gotta Have Me Go With You; Hallowe'en; Happiness Is A Thing Called Joe; Happy As The Day Is Long; Here Goes(A

Fool); Hit The Road To Dreamland; Hittin' The Bottle; Hooray For Love; House Of Flowers; I Could Go On Singing; I Got A Song; I Gotta Right To Sing The Blues; I Had Myself A True Love; I Love A New Yorker; I Love A Parade; I Love To Sing-A; I Never Has Seen Snow; I Promise You; I've Gone Romantic On You; I've Got The World On A String; If I Only Had A Brain; Ill Wind(You're Blowin' Me No Good); In The Shade Of The New Apple Tree; In Your Own Quiet Way; It Was Written In The Stars; It's A New World; It's Only A Paper Moon; June Comes Around Every Year; Kickin' The Gong Around; Last Night When We Were Young; Legalize My Name; Let's Fall In Love; Let's Put Our Heads Together; Let's Take A Walk Around The Block; Let's Take The Long Way Home; Life's A Dance; Life's Full Of Consequence; Linda; Little Biscuit; Little Drops Of Rain; Long Before You Came Along; Lose That Long Face; Love Held Lightly; Lydia, The Tattooed Lady; Man That Got Away; Merry Old Land Of Oz; Minnie The Moocher's Wedding Day; Moanin' In The Mornin'; My Shining Hour; Napoleon; Now I Know; One For My Baby(And One More For The Road); Out Of This World; Over The Rainbow; Paris Is A Lonely Town; Pretty To Walk With; Public Melody Number One; Push The Button; Ridin' On The Moon; Right As The Rain; Savannah; Save Me, Sister; Search Is Through; Shoein' The Mare; Sleepin' Bee; Smellin' Of Vanilla(Bamboo Cage); Song Of The Woodman; Stormy Weather; Sweet And Hot; T'morra, T'morra; The Album Of My Dreams; True Love (I Had Myself A); Two Blind Loves; Two Ladies In De Shade Of De Banana Tree; We're Off To See The Wizard; What Can You Say In A Love Song?; What Good Does It Do; What's Good About Goodbye; When The Boys Come Home; When The Sun Comes Out; You're A Builder Upper

ARMATRADING, JOAN — Your Letter

ARMER, ANDY — Rise

ARMSTEAD, JOSEPH — Let's Go Get Stoned

ARMSTEAD, JOSEPHINE — Jealous Kind Of Fellow

ARMSTRONG, HENRY W. — Sweet Adeline

ARMSTRONG, LIL HARDIN — King Of The Zulus; Struttin' With Some Barbecue

ARMSTRONG, LOUIS — Back O' Town Blues; Don't Forget To Mess Around When You're Doing The Charleston; I Want A Big Butter And Egg Man; Ol' Man Mose; Potato Head Blues; Struttin' With Some Barbecue; Wild Man Blues

ARMSTRONG, WILLIAM — Slip Away

ARNDT, FELIX — Nola

ARNHEIM, GUS — I Cried For You(Now It's Your Turn To Cry Over Me); It Must Be True; Sweet And Lovely

ARNOLD, CHRIS — Can't Smile Without You

ARNOLD, EDDY — Just A Little Lovin'(Will Go A Long Way); You Don't Know Me

ARNOLD, MALCOLM — Children's Marching Song, The(This Old Man); River Kwai March

ARODIN, SIDNEY — Lazy River

ASAF, GEORGE — Pack Up Your Troubles In Your Old Kit Bag And Smile, Smile, Smile

ASCHER, KENNY — Rainbow Connection

ASCHER, ROBERT — Tracy's Theme

ASH, FRANCES — I'm Gonna Love That Gal

ASHER, KENNETH LEE — You And Me Against The World

ASHER, TONY — Caroline, No; God Only Knows; God Rest Ye Merry Gentlemen; Wouldn't It Be Nice

ASHERMAN, EDDIE — All That Glitters Is Not Gold

ASHFORD, NICHOLAS — Ain't No Mountain High Enough; Ain't Nothing Like The Real Thing; Boss; California Soul; Count Your Blessings; Good Lovin' Ain't Easy To Come By; I'm Every Woman; Let's Go Get Stoned; Remember Me; Solid; Some Things You Never Get Used To; Stuff Like That; What You Gave Me; Who's Gonna Take The Blame; You're All I Need To Get By; Your Precious Love

ASHFORD, NICK — I Don't Need No Doctor; Reach Out And Touch(Somebody's Hand)

ASTAIRE, FRED — I'm Building Up To An Awful Let-down

ASTROP, J. — Touch Me (I Want Your Body)

ATCHLEY, SAM — Coca Cola Cowboy

ATKINS, BOYD — Heebie Jeebies

ATKINS, ROGER — Green Grass; It's My Life; Make Me Your Baby; Workin' On A Groovy Thing

ATKINSON, CRAIG — Psychotic Reaction

ATTERIDGE, HAROLD — Bagdad; By The Beautiful Sea; Don't Send Your Wife To The Country; Don't Shed A Tear

AULETTI, LEONARD — Bunny Hop

AURIC, GEORGES — Bonjour Tristesse; Song From Moulin Rouge, The(Where Is Your Heart)

AUSTIN, BILLY — Is You Is, Or Is You Ain't(Ma' Baby)

AUSTIN, GENE — How Come You Do Me Like You Do?; Lonesome Road; Occidental Woman; Ridin' Around In The Rain; When My Sugar Walks Down The Street

AUSTIN, LOVIE — Chirpin' The Blues; Down Hearted Blues

AUSTIN, RAY — I Look At Heaven(When I Look At You); Tonight We Love

AUSTIN, SIL — Slow Walk

AUSTIN, TOM — Short Shorts

AUTE, L. E. — Who Will Answer

AUTHORS, CHRISTINE — Devil Woman

AUTRY, GENE — Back In The Saddle Again; Be Honest With Me; Here Comes Santa Claus; Tweedle-o-Twill; You'll Be Sorry; You're The Only Star In My Blue Heaven

AVELING, CLAUDE — Come Back To Sorrento

AVERRE, BERTON — My Sharona

AXELROD, DAVID — Dead End Street

AXTON, HOYT — Greenback Dollar; Joy To The World; Juanita; Never Been To Spain; No No Song; When The Morning Comes

AXTON, MAE BOREN — Heartbreak Hotel

AYER, NAT D. — If You Were The Only Girl In The World; Oh You Beautiful Doll

AYRE, JIMMY — Mambo Rock

AZEVADO, WALDYR — Delicado

AZNAVOUR, CHARLES — For Mama; Yesterday When I Was Young

AZOR, H. — Push It

BABCOCK, JOE — I Washed My Hands In Muddy Water

BACHARACH, BURT — (Don't Go) Please Stay; (They Long To Be)Close To You; Alfie; Always Something There To Remind Me; Another Night; Any Day Now; Any Old Time Of Day; Anyone Who Had A Heart; April Fools; Are You There(with Another Girl); Arthur's Theme; Baby, It's You; Blob; Blue On Blue; Casino Royale; Do You Know The Way To San Jose?; Don't Make Me Over; Don't Make Me Wait For Love; Don't You Believe It; Fool Killer; Forever My Love; Green Grass Starts To Grow; Heavenly; Here I Am; House Is Not A Home; I Just Don't Know What To Do With Myself; I Say A Little Prayer; I'll Never Fall In Love Again; I'm A Better Man(For Having Loved You); Let Me Go To Him; Living Together, Growing Together; Long Ago Tomorrow; Look Of Love; Lost Horizon; Love Power; Magic Moments; Make It Easy On Yourself; Making Love; Man Who Shot Liberty Valance; Message To Michael; Odds And Ends(Of A Beautiful Love Affair); On My Own; One Less Bell To Answer; Only Love Can Break A Heart; Paper Mache; Promises, Promises; Raindrops Keep Fallin' On My Head; Reach Out For Me; Send Me No Flowers; Story Of My Life; Tower Of Strength; Trains And Boats And Planes; Twenty-Four Hours From Tulsa; Walk On By; What The World Needs Now Is Love; What's New Pussycat; Who Is Gonna Love Me?; Whoever You Are Or Sometimes Your Eyes Look Blue To Me; Windows Of The World; Wishin' And Hopin'; Wives And Lovers (Theme From); You'll Never Get To Heaven

BACHMAN, RANDALL C. — Undun

BACHMAN, RANDY — Hey You; Laughing; Let It Ride; No Time; Roll On Down The Highway; You Ain't Seen Nothin' Yet

BACKER, WILLIAM — I'd Like To Teach The World To Sing

BADALE, ANDY — Face It Girl, It's Over

BADAROU, WALTER — Something About You

BAER, ABEL — Don't Wake Me Up(Let Me Dream); Gee! But You're Swell; Harriet; I Miss My Swiss; It's The Girl; Just Give Me A June Night, The Moonlight, And You(June Night); Lucky Lindy!; Mamma Loves Papa, Papa Loves Mamma; My Mother's Eyes; When You're With Somebody Else

BAER, BARBARA — Sweet Talkin' Guy

BAEZ, JOAN — Diamonds And Rust

BAGDASARIAN, ROSS — Alvin's Harmonica; Chipmunk Song; Come On-A My House; Witch Doctor

BAGLEY, E. E. — National Emblem

BAHLER, TOM — Julie, Do Ya Love Me; Living In A House Divided; She's Out Of My Life

BAILET, THOMAS — Doctor! Doctor!

BAILEY, JIM — Everybody Plays The Fool

BAILEY, PHILIP — Easy Lover; Saturday Nite; Shining Star

BAILEY, T. — King For A Day

BAILEY, THOMAS — Hold Me Now

BAILEY, TOM — Lay Your Hands On Me

BAIRD, D. — Keep Your Hands To Yourself

BAIRD, TOM — Born To Wander; Does Your Mama Know About Me

BAKER, ANITA — Sweet Love

BAKER, JACK — I Hear A Rhapsody

BAKER, JOSEPHINE — Black Bottom Ball

BAKER, LAVERN — I Can't Love You Enough

BAKER, MICKEY — Love Is Strange

BAKER, PHIL — Strange Interlude

BAKER, YVONNE — Let Me In

BALDERRANA, ROBERT — I Need Somebody

BALDRIDGE, FANNY — Let's Dance

BALDWIN, JOHN — D'yer Maker

BALFE, MICHAEL WILLIAM — I Dreamt I Dwelt In Marble Halls

BALIN, MARTY — Miracles; Volunteers

BALL, ERNEST R. — Dear Little Boy Of Mine; I'll Forget You; Let The Rest Of The World Go By; Little Bit Of Heaven, Sure They Call It Ireland; West Of The Great Divide; When Irish Eyes Are Smiling; Will You Love Me In December As You Do In May

BALL, KENNY — Midnight In Moscow

BALL, NOEL — Oh Julie

BALL, ROGER — Cut The Cake; Pick Up The Pieces

BALLARD JR., CLINT — Ginger Bread; Good Timin'; I'm Alive; Litty Bitty Girl; One Of Us(Will Weep Tonight)

BALLARD, CLINT — Game Of Love

BALLARD, HANK — Dance With Me Henry; Finger Poppin' Time; Let's Go, Let's Go, Let's Go; Twist

BALLARD, HENRY "HANK" — Work With Me Annie

BALLARD, JR, CLINT — You're No Good

BALLARD, PAT — Mister Sandman; Oh, Baby Mine(I Get So Lonely); So Beats My Heart For You

BALLARD, RUSS — I Know There's Something Going On; Liar; New York Groove; You Can Do Magic

BALLARDO, G. — Man In The Mirror

BANKS, A. — In Too Deep; Land Of Confusion; Tonight, Tonight, Tonight

BANKS, ANTHONY — Follow You, Follow Me; Throwing It All Away

BANKS, DARRELL — Open The Door To Your Heart

BANKS, HOMER — If Loving You Is Wrong I Don't Want To Be Right; If You're Ready(Come Go With Me); Who's Making Love

BANKS, LARRY — Go Now!

BANKS, MARIAN — Malaguena

BANKS, ULYSSES — Voo-It! Voo-It!

BARBARIN, PAUL — Bourbon Street Parade; Come Back Sweet Papa; Don't Forget To Mess Around When You're Doing The Charleston

BARBATA, JOHN — Elenore

BARBERIS, BILLY — Big Wide World; Have You Looked Into Your Heart

BARBIERI, GATO — Last Tango In Paris

BARBOSA, CHRIS — Let The Music Play

BARBOUR, DAVE — Blum Blum; Don't Be So Mean To Baby('cause Baby's So Good To You); I Don't Know Enough About You; It's A Good Day; Manana(Is Soon Enough For Me); What More Can A Woman Do?

BARCELATA, LORENZO — Maria Elena

BARE, BOBBY — 500 Miles Away From Home

BAREFOOT, CARL — Danger! Heartbreak Ahead

BARER, MARSHALL — I'm Just A Country Boy; Very Soft Shoes

BARGE, GENE — Quarter To Three; School Is Out; Twist, Twist Senora

BARGE, M. — Leaving Me

BARGONI, CAMILLO — Autumn Concerto

BARING, SABINE — Onward Christian Soldiers

BARISH, JEFF — Hearts

BARISH, JESSE — Count On Me

BARKAN, MARK — I'll Try Anything(To Get You); I'm Gonna Be Warm This Winter; Pretty Flamingo; Writing On The Girl

BARLOW, HAROLD — Mama

BARNBY, JOSEPH — Sweet And Low

BARNES, BILLY — I Stayed Too Long At The Fair

BARNES, DON — If I'd Been The One; Like No Other Night

BARNES, HOWARD — Blossom Fell; I Really Don't Want To Know

BARNES, JESSIE — Many Times

BARNES, PAUL — Goodbye Dolly Gray

BARNES, RICHARD — Caught Up In You

BARNES, SIDNEY — Long Live Our Love

BARNET, CHARLIE — Redskin Rhumba; Skyliner

BARNHILL, GAYLE — Angel

BARNTLEY, VINCENT — Cool It Now

BARNUM, H. B. — Don't Blame The Children; Peanut Butter

BARON, PAUL — Rum And Coca Cola

BARON, SANDY — Natural Man; Writing On The Wall

BARRETT, PAT — Crazy 'bout Ya, Baby

BARRETT, RICHARD — I Want You To Be My Girl; Look In My Eyes

BARRETT, VINNIE — Dancin' Man; Just Don't Want To Be Lonely Tonight; Love Won't Let Me Wait; Sideshow; Sidewalk Talk

BARRETTO, RAY — El Watusi

BARRI, STEVE — Eve Of Destruction; I Found A Girl; Must To Avoid; Secret Agent Man; You, Baby (Nobody But You)

BARRIE, GEORGE — All That Love Went To Waste

BARRIO, EDDIE DE — Fantasy

BARRIS, CHUCK — Palisades Park; Paloma, La(The Dove)

BARRIS, HARRY — At Your Command; From Monday On; I Surrender, Dear; It Must Be True; It Was So Beautiful; Lies; Little Dutch Mill; Mississippi Mud; Wrap Your Troubles In Dreams (And Dream Your Troubles Away)

BARRON, BOB — Cindy, Oh Cindy

BARROSO, ARY — Baia; Brazil

BARRY, JEAN — Corns For My Country

BARRY, JEFF — Bang-Shang-A-Lang; Be My Baby; Chapel Of Love; Chip Chip; Da-Doo Ron Ron; Do Wah Diddy Diddy; Give Us Your Blessing; Hanky Panky; How'd We Ever Get This Way?; I Can Hear Music; I Honestly Love You; I Wanna Love Him So Bad; Jingle Jangle; Kind Of Boy You Can't Forget; Leader Of The Pack; Look Of Love; Maybe I Know; Montego Bay; Movin' On Up; One Day At A Time; People Say; River Deep-Mountain High; Sugar, Sugar

BARRY, JOHN — Best Man In The World; Born Free; Diamonds Are Forever; Goldfinger; Midnight Cowboy; Moonraker; Music Of Goodbye; View To A Kill; You Only Live Twice (Theme From)

BARRY, LEN — Like A Baby

BARRY, NANCY — One Day At A Time

BART, LIONEL — As Long As He Needs Me; Consider Yourself; Do You Mind?; Food, Glorious Food; From Russia With Love; I'd Do Anything; Living Doll; Where Is Love; Who Will Buy; You've Got To Pick A Pocket Or Two

BARTHOLOMEW, DAVE — Ain't That A Shame; Blue Monday; Bo Weevil; Fat Man, The(195); I Hear You Knocking; I Heard A Rumour; I'm Gone; I'm Gonna Be A Wheel Someday; I'm In Love Again; I'm Walkin'; It's You I Love; Let The Four Winds Blow; My Girl Josephine; One Night; Poor Me; Valley Of Tears; Walking To New Orleans; Whole Lot Of Loving; Whole Lotta Loving; Witchcraft

BARTLETT, FLOYD — I Dreamed Of A Hillbilly Heaven

BARTON, GEORGE — You Don't Know What You've Got

BARTON, MARGE — What Color (Is A Man)

BASIE, WILLIAM "COUNT" — Baby, Don't Tell On Me; Blue And Sentimental; Don't You Miss Your Baby; Every Tub; Goin' To Chicago Blues; Good Bait; Good Morning Blues; Harvard Blues; John's Idea; Jumpin' At The Woodside; King Joe; M-Squad; One O' Clock Jump; Red Bank Boogie; Sent For You Yesterday(And Here You Come Today); Swingin' The Blues; Two O'clock Jump

BASKETTE, BILLY — Good-bye Broadway, Hello France

BASKIN, DON — Little Girl

BASKIN, R. — Will You Still Love Me?

BASS, RALPH — Dedicated To The One I Love

BASSMAN, GEORGE — I'm Gettin' Sentimental Over You

BATCHELOR, RUTH — King Of The Whole Wide World

BATEMAN, R. — Mashed Potato Time

BATEMAN, ROBERT — If You Need Me

BATES, CHARLES — Hard Hearted Hannah, The Vamp Of Savannah

BATES, KATHERINE LEE — America The Beautiful

BATH, HUBERT — Cornish Rhapsody

BATTISTE, PHIL — Sea Of Love

BATTLE, EDGAR — Strictly Instrumental

BAUDUC, RAY — Big Noise From Winnetka; South Rampart Street Parade

BAUM, BERNIE — Ask Me; Music! Music! Music!(Put Another Nickel In); You're The Devil In Disguise

BAXTER, DANNY — Buzz Me

BAXTER, LES — Quiet Village

BAXTER, LOU — Merry Christmas Baby

BAXTER, PHIL — Faded Summer Love; I'm A Ding Dong Daddy From Dumas; Piccolo Pete

BAYES, NORA — Shine On Harvest Moon

BAYLY, THOMAS — Long, Long Ago

BAZILIAN, ERIC — Day By Day

BEADELL, EILY — Cruising Down The River

BEAL, EDDIE — Candy Store Blues

BEAL, JOE — Jingle Bell Rock; Unsuspecting Heart

BEAN, CARL — Scatterbrain

BEAN, RICHARD — Suavecito

BEARD, FRANK — Legs; Sleeping Bag; Tush

BEAUMONT, JAMES — Since I Don't Have You

BEAVERS, JACKEY — Someday We'll Be Together

BECAUD, GILBERT — Day The Rains Came; It Must Be Him; Let It Be Me; September Morn; What Now My Love

BECHET, SIDNEY — Petite Fleur

BECK, GEOFF — Over Under Sideways Down

BECK, JEFF — Happenings Ten Years Time Ago

BECK, WILLIAM — Fire; Love Rollercoaster; Who'd She Coo

BECKENSTEIN, JAY — Morning Dance

BECKER, WALTER — Bad Sneakers; Deacon Blues; Do

It Again; Fm(No Static At All); Hey Nineteen; Josie; Peg; Reeling In The Years; Rikki Don't Lose That Number

BECKETT, PETER — Baby Come Back; Twist Of Fate

BECKETT, T. A. — Columbia, The Gem Of The Ocean

BECKLEY, GERRY — Daisy Jane; I Need You; Sister Golden Hair

BEDDOE, ALBERT F. — Copper Kettle

BEEBY, JOHN — Dreamtime

BEEKMAN, JACK — Mahzel(Means Good Luck)

BEETHOVEN, LUDWIG VON — Fur Elise(Albumblatt); Joy(Song Of Joy); Minuet In G; Moonlight Sonata; Sonata Pathetique

BEGGS, LIMAHL — Too Shy

BEGGS, NICK — Too Shy

BEIDERBECKE, LEON "BIX" — Davenport Blues; In A Mist; In The Dark

BEISBIER, GARY — Don't You Care; Hey, Baby! They're Playin' Our Song; Susan

BELAFONTE, HARRY — Cocoanut Woman; Island In The Sun

BELEW, CARL — Am I That Easy To Forget; Lonely Street

BELL, ANTHONY — I'm Stone In Love With You

BELL, KENNETH — Even The Nights Are Better

BELL, LEROY — Livin' It Up(Friday Night); Mama Can't Buy You Love

BELL, R. — Victory

BELL, ROBERT — Celebration; Cherish; Emergency; Hollywood Swinging; Jungle Boogie; Ladies Night; Misled

BELL, RONALD — Big Fun; Celebration; Cherish; Emergency; Get Down On It; Hollywood Swinging; Joanna; Joey; Jungle Boogie; Ladies Night; Misled

BELL, THERESA — Are You Happy?; Brand New Me; Moody Woman; What's The Use Of Breaking Up?

BELL, THOM — Betcha By Golly, Wow; Break Up To Make Up; Didn't I(Blow Your Mind This Time); I'm Doin' Fine Now; I'm Stone In Love With You; Rockin' Roll Baby; Rubberband Man; You Are Everything; You Make Me Feel Brand New

BELL, THOMAS — La La La(Means I Love You)

BELL, VINCENT — Rain

BELL, WILLIAM — To Be A Lover; Tryin' To Love Two

BELLAMY, DAVID — Spiders And Snakes; Your Bulldog Drinks Champagne

BELLAND, BRUCE — Big Man; Twenty-Six Miles

BELLE, BARBARA — Sunday Kind Of Love

BELLINGER, HENRY — Stick Shift

BELLIS, HAL — Corn Silk

BELLMON, JOHNNIE — Don't Let The Green Grass Fool You

BELLOTTE, PETE — Heaven Knows; Hot Stuff; I Feel Love; Love To Love You Baby

BELLUSCI, ANTHONY J. — Robbin' The Cradle

BELOLO, HENRI — In The Navy; Macho Man; Y.M.C.A.

BELVIN, JESSE — Earth Angel

BENJAMIN, BENNIE — Can Anyone Explain(No! No! No!); Cancel The Flowers; Confess; Cross Over The Bridge; Dancin' With Someone(longin' For You); Don't Call My Name; Don't Let Me Be Misunderstood; Echoes; Fabulous Character; How Important Can It Be?; I Don't See Me In Your Eyes Anymore; I Don't Want To Set The World On Fire; I Ran All The Way Home; I Want To Thank Your Folks; I'll Never Be Free; Jet; Magic Circle; Oh! What It

Seemed To Be; Pianissimo; Rumors Are Flying; Strictly Instrumental; Surrender; Wheel Of Fortune; When The Lights Go On Again (All Over The World)

BENJAMIN, BERNIE — To Think You've Chosen Me

BENNARD, REV. GEORGE — Old Rugged Cross

BENNETT, BOYD — My Boy, Flat Top; Seventeen

BENNETT, DAVID — Bye Bye Blues

BENNETT, JOE — Black Slacks

BENNETT, MILTON — Go Now!

BENNETT, RICHARD — Forever In Blue Jeans

BENNETT, RICHARD RODNEY — Murder On The Orient Express

BENNETT, ROY C. — All That I Am; If I Had A Girl; Kewpie Doll; My Bonnie Lassie; My Bonnie Lies Over The Ocean; Naughty Lady Of Shady Lane; Nuttin' For Christmas; Puppet On A String; When The Boy In Your Arms

BENSON, ADA — Your Feet's Too Big

BENSON, ARTHUR — Pomp And Circumstance

BENSON, GARY — Let Her In

BENSON, RENALDO — What's Going On

BENTON, BROOK — Boll Weevil Song; Endlessly; For My Baby; It's Just A Matter Of Time; Kiddio; Lie To Me; Looking Back; Lover's Question; Revenge

BERG, HAROLD — Freshie

BERGANTINE, BORNEY — My Happiness

BERGER, IDA IRRAL — Warm And Tender Love (Wrap Me In Your Warm And Tender Love)

BERGERE, ROY — How Come You Do Me Like You Do?

BERGMAN, ALAN AND MARILYN — All His Children; And Then There's Maude; Brian's Song; Guaglioni(The Man Who Plays The Mandolin); His Eyes-Her Eyes; I Believe In Love; I Was Born In Love With You; If We Were In Love; In The Heat Of The Night; It Might Be You; Last Time I Felt Like This; Marmalade, Molasses And Honey; Music Of Goodbye; Nice 'n' Easy; Papa Can You Hear Me; Summer Knows; Way We Were; Windmills Of Your Mind, The Or The Theme From The Thomas Crown Affair; Yellow Bird; You Don't Bring Me Flowers

BERK, MORTY — Every Day Of My Life; Heartbreaker

BERLIN, IRVING — (I'll See You In)C-U-B-A; (Running Around In Circles)Getting Nowhere; (You Can't Lose The Blues With)Colors; Alexander's Ragtime Band; All Alone; All By Myself; All Of My Life; Always; Any Bonds Today; Anything You Can Do; Araby; Arms For The Love Of America; At Peace With The World; At The Devil's Ball; Back To Back; Be Careful, It's My Heart; Because I Love You; Begging For Love; Bells; Best Thing For You; Best Things Happen While You're Dancing; Better Luck Next Time; Blue Skies; But Where Are You; Call Me Up Some Rainy Afternoon; Change Partners; Cheek To Cheek; Coquette; Count Your Blessings Instead Of Sheep; Couple Of Song And Dance Men; Couple Of Swells; Crinoline Days; Do It Again; Doin' What Comes Natur'lly; Don't Be Afraid Of Romance; Easter Parade; Empty Pockets Filled With Love; Everybody Knew But Me; Everybody Step; Everybody's Doing It; Fella With An Umbrella; First Lady; Fools Fall In Love; For The Very First Time; Funnies; Get Thee Behind Me Satan; Girl On The Magazine Cover; Girl On The Police Gazette; Girl That I Marry; Girls Of My Dreams; Give Me Your Tired, Your Poor; Glad To Be Home; God Bless America; Happy Holiday; Harlem On My Mind; He Ain't Got Rhythm; He's A Devil In

His Own Home Town; He's A Rag Picker; Heat Wave; Homesick; Homework; Hostess With The Mostes' On The Ball; How About Me?; How Deep Is The Ocean; How Many Times; How's Chances; I Can't Remember; I Got Lost In His Arms; I Got The Sun In The Morning; I Left My Heart At The Stage Door Canteen; I Like It; I Love A Piano; I Never Had A Chance; I Poured My Heart Into A Song; I Say It's Spinach; I Threw A Kiss In The Ocean; I Used To Be Color Blind; I Want You For Myself; I'd Rather Lead A Band; I'll Share It All With You; I'm A Bad Bad Man; I'm A Vamp From East Broadway; I'm An Indian Too; I'm Getting Tired So I Can Sleep; I'm Gonna Get Him; I'm Gonna Pin My Medal On The Girl I Left Behind; I'm On My Way Home; I'm Playing With Fire; I'm Putting All My Eggs In One Basket; I'm Sorry For Myself; I've Got My Captain Working For Me Now; I've Got My Love To Keep Me Warm; I've Got To Be Around; In My Harem; In Our Hide-away; Is He The Only Man In The World; Isn't This A Lovely Day; It Gets Lonely In The White House; It Only Happens When I Dance With You; It's A Lovely Day Today; It's A Lovely Day Tomorrow; Just A Blue Serge Suit; Just One Way To Say I Love You; Kate(Have I Come Too Early, Too Late); Lady Of The Evening; Latins Know How; Lazy; Learn To Do The Strut; Let Me Sing And I'll Be Happy; Let Yourself Go; Let's Face The Music And Dance; Let's Go Back To The Waltz; Let's Have Another Cup Of Coffee; Let's Start The New Year Right; Let's Take An Old Fashioned Walk; Little Bungalow; Little Butterfly; Little Things In Life; Lonely Heart; Looking At You(Across The Breakfast Table); Louisiana Purchase; Love And The Weather; Love, You Didn't Do Right By Me; Mandy; Manhattan Madness; Marie; Marie From Sunny Italy; Marrying For Love; Maybe It's Because(I Love You Too Much); Me!; Meat And Potatoes; Moonshine Lullaby; My Defenses Are Down; My Walking Stick; Next To Your Mother, Who Do You Love?; Night Is Filled With Music; No Strings(I'm Fancy Free); Nobody Knows And Nobody Seems To Care; Nobody Knows De Trouble I've Seen; Not For All The Rice In China; Now It Can Be Told; Ocarina, The(Dance To The Music Of); Oh, How I Hate To Get Up In The Morning; Oh, That Beautiful Rag; Old Fashioned Tune Is Always New, An; On A Roof In Manhattan; Once Upon A Time Today; Only Dance I Know, The(Song For Belly Dancer); Only For Americans; Orange Grove In California, An; Outside Of That I Love You; Pack Up Your Sins And Go To The Devil; Paris Wakes Up And Smiles; Piccolino; Pigtails And Freckles; Play A Simple Melody; Plenty To Be Thankful For; Pretty Girl Is Like A Melody; Puttin' On The Ritz; Ragtime Violin; Reaching For The Moon; Remember; Roses Of Yesterday; Russian Lullaby; Say It Isn't So; Say It With Music; Sayonara; Secret Service; Serenade To An Old Fashioned Girl; Shaking The Blues Away; Slumming On Park Avenue; So Help Me; Soft Lights And Sweet Music; Some Sunny Day; Something To Dance About; Song Is Ended, But The Melody Lingers On; Song Of The Metronome; Steppin' Out With My Baby; Supper Time; Swanee Shuffle; To Be Forgotten; To My Mammy; Tomorrow Is A Lovely Day; Top Hat, White Tie And Tails; Unlucky In Love; Waiting At The End Of The Road; Waltz Of Long Ago; Washington Twist; We Saw The Sea; What Does It Matter; What'll I Do; When I Leave The World Behind; When I Lost You; When It's Night Time In Dixie Land; When My Dreams Come True; When The Black Sheep Returns To The Fold; When The Midnight Choo Choo Leaves For Alabam'; When Winter Comes; When You Walked Out Someone Else Walked Right In; Where Is The Song Of Songs For Me; White Christmas; Who Do You Love, I Hope; Whose Little Heart Are You Breaking Now; Will She Come From The East? (East-North-West Or South); With My Head In The Clouds; With You; Woodman, Woodman Spare That Tree; Yam; You Can't Get A Man With A Gun; You Cannot Make Your Shimmy Shake On Tea; You Keep Coming Back Like A Song; You'd Be Surprised; You're Just In Love; You're Laughing At Me; You're Lonely And I'm Lonely

BERLIN, MILTON — I Wuv A Wabbit

BERMAN, IRVING — Time Out For Tears; Wrapped Up In A Dream

BERNARD, ANDREW — Judy In Disguise

BERNARD, FELIX — Dardanella; Winter Wonderland

BERNIE, BEN — I Can't Believe It's True; Strange Interlude; Sweet Georgia Brown; Who's Your Little Whozis

BERNIE, SAUL — Don't Cry Baby

BERNIER, BUDDY — Bamboo; Big Apple; Hear My Song, Violetta; Night Has A Thousand Eyes; Our Love; Poinciana

BERNS, BERT — Everybody Needs Somebody To Love; Here Comes The Night; I Want Candy; I'll Take Good Care Of You; Piece Of My Heart

BERNSTEIN, ELMER — Baby, The Rain Must Fall; Bird Man; By Love Possessed; From The Terrace(Love Theme); Girl Named Tamiko,a; Great Escape March; Hawaii; Love With The Proper Stranger; Magnificent Seven; Man With The Golden Arm, The(Main Title); Sons Of Katie Elder; True Grit; Walk On The Wild Side

BERNSTEIN, LEONARD — America; Come Up To My Place; Cool; Duel For One(The First Lady Of The Land); Gee, Officer Krupke; I Can Cook Too; I Feel Pretty; I Get Carried Away; It's Love; Little Bit In Love; Lonely Town; Lucky To Be Me; Maria; New York, New York; Ohio; One Hand, One Heart; Quiet Girl; Some Other Time; Something's Coming; Somewhere; Tonight

BERRIOS, PEDRO — My Sharona

BERRY, CHUCK — Bye Bye Johnny; Carol; Johnny B. Goode; Maybellene; Memphis; My Ding-a-Ling; Nadine(Is It You?); Promised Land; Reelin' And Rockin'; Rock And Roll Music; Roll Over Beethoven; School Day(Ring! Ring! Goes The Bell); Surfin' U. S. A.; Sweet Little Sixteen

BERRY, J. — Pony Time

BERRY, JAN — Come On, Let Yourself Go; Dead Man's Curve; Drag City; Honolulu Lulu; Surf City; You Really Know How To Hurt A Guy

BERRY, LEON — Christopher Columbus

BERRY, RICHARD — Louie Louie

BERRYHILL, ROBERT — Wipe Out

BEST, PAT — I Understand Just How You Feel

BEST, WILLIAM — (I Love You)For Sentimental Reasons; Wrapped Up In A Dream

BESTOR, DON — Contented; Down By The Winegar Woiks

BETHANY, ADAPTED FROM HYMN — Nearer, My God,

To Thee

BETTI, HENRI — C'est Si Bon

BETTIS, JOHN — As Long As We Got Each Other; Crazy For You; Goodbye To Love; Human Nature; I Need To Be In Love; Only Yesterday; Slow Hand; Top Of The World; Yesterday Once More

BETTIS, JON — Like No Other Night

BETTS, RICHARD — Ramblin Man

BIAS, GARY — Sweet Love

BIBO, IRVING — Cherie

BIDEU, LOU — Percolator

BIERMAN, BERNARD — Vanity

BIERMAN, BERNIE — Hills Of Colorado

BIGARD, ALBANY — Double Check Stomp

BIGARD, BARNEY — Clarinet Lament; Mood Indigo

BIGAZZI, GIANCARLO — Self Control

BIGELOW, BOB — Hard Hearted Hannah, The Vamp Of Savannah

BIGELOW, F. E. — Our Director

BIGGS, HOWARD — Melancholy Me; Write Me A Letter

BILK, ACKER — Stranger On The Shore

BINDI, UMBERTO — You're My World

BINNICK, BERNARD — Keem-O-Sabe

BIONDI, RAY — Bolero At The Savoy; Boogie Blues

BIRD, BILL — Broadway

BIRD, R. — Buzz Buzz Buzz

BIRTLES, BEEB — Happy Anniversary

BISHOP, ELVIN — Fooled Around And Fell In Love

BISHOP, JOE — Blue Evening; Blue Flame; Blue Lament; Blue Prelude; Out Of Space

BISHOP, STEPHEN — Dream Girl; On And On; Save It For A Rainy Day; Separate Lives

BISHOP, WALTER — Bop! Goes My Heart; Jack, You're Dead; Stuff Is Here, The(and It's Mellow)

BIVENS, BRUCE — Josephine

BIXIO, C. A. — Mama

BIXIO, CESARE A. — Serenade In The Night

BIZET, GEORGES — Beat Out That Rhythm On A Drum; Dat's Love; Stan' Up An' Fight; Toreador Song

BJORN, FRANK — Alley Cat

BLACK, BEN — Hold Me; Moonlight And Roses Bring Mem'ries Of You

BLACK, CHARLIE — I Know A Heartache When I See One; Shadows In The Moonlight

BLACK, DON — Ben; Best Of Both Worlds; Born Free; Come Back With The Same Look In Your Eyes; Come To Me; Diamonds Are Forever; For Mama; I Have Never Felt This Way Before; Same; To Sir With Love; True Grit

BLACK, GENE — Love Touch

BLACK, JAMES M. — When The Saints Go Marching In

BLACK, JOHNNY — Paper Doll

BLACK, JOHNNY S. — Dardanella

BLACK, WILLIAM P. — Smokie,(Part II)

BLACKBURN, BRIAN — Love Is Blue

BLACKBURN, JOHN — Moonlight In Vermont

BLACKBURN, TOM — Ballad Of Davy Crockett

BLACKMAN, MICHAEL BRUCE — Moonlight Feels Right

BLACKMON, L. — Candy

BLACKMON, LARRY — Word Up

BLACKMORE, RICHARD — Smoke On The Water

BLACKTON, JAY — You Tell Me Your Dream Or I Had A Dream, Dear

BLACKWELL, DEWAYNE — Mr. Blue

BLACKWELL, OTIS — (such An)Easy Question; All Shook Up; Breathless; Don't Be Cruel(to A Heart That's True); For My Good Fortune; Great Balls Of Fire; Handy Man; Hey, Little Girl; Just Keep It Up(And See What Happens); One Broken Heart For Sale; Return To Sender

BLACKWELL, ROBERT — Long Tall Sally; Ready Teddy

BLACKWELL, ROBERT A. — Good Golly, Miss Molly; Rip It Up

BLACKWELL, RONALD — Hair On My Chinny-Chin-Chin; How Do You Catch A Girl?; L'il Red Riding Hood

BLADES, JACK — Four In The Morning(I Can't Take It Anymore); Goodbye; Sentimental Street

BLAIKLEY, ALAN — Have I The Right; I've Lost You

BLAIKLEY, HOWARD — Have I The Right; Zabadak

BLAIR, HAL — I Was The One; I'm Yours; One Has My Name. . . The Other Has My Heart; Please Help Me, I'm Falling; Ringo

BLAISCH, L. — Could've Been

BLAISDELL, CARL — As The Backs Go Tearing By

BLAKE, EUBIE — Baltimore Buzz; Bandana Days; Gypsy Blues; I'm Craving For That Kind Of Love; I'm Just Wild About Harry; Memories Of You; Shuffle Along; You Were Meant For Me; You're Lucky To Me

BLAKE, JAMES W. — East Side, West Side(the Sidewalks Of New York)

BLANC, EMANUEL LE — Disco Nights

BLANC, LENNY LE — Falling

BLANCHARD, OLLIE — Please Love Me Forever

BLAND, JAMES A. — (Oh Dem)Golden Slippers; Carry Me Back To Old Virginny; In The Evening By The Moonlight

BLANDON, RICHARD — Could This Be Magic

BLANE, RALPH — Athena; Birmin'ham; Boy Next Door; Buckle Down, Winsocki; Comment Allez-vous?; Don't Rock The Boat, Dear; Ev'ry Time; Friendly Islands; Hallowe'en; Have Yourself A Merry Little Christmas; I Know You By Heart; I Love A New Yorker; Joint Is Really Jumpin' In Carnegie Hall; Just A Little Joint With A Juke Box; Love; My Dream Is Yours; Shady Lady Bird; Stanley Steamer; Trolley Song

BLAU, ERIC — Amsterdam; If We Only Have Love; If You Only Have Love

BLAUFUSS, WALTER — Your Eyes Have Told Me So

BLEYER, ARCHIE — Business In F; Eh, Cumpari!

BLITZ, P. — Serious

BLITZSTEIN, MARC — Mack The Knife(Moritat)

BLOCH, WALTER — Never

BLOCK, ALAN — Walkin' After Midnight

BLOCK, MARTIN — I Guess I'll Have To Dream The Rest; It's Make Believe Ballroom Time; Waitin' For The Train To Come In

BLOODWORTH, RAYMOND — C'mon Marianne

BLOOM, BOBBY — Indian Giver; Montego Bay; Mony Mony; Special Delivery

BLOOM, MARTY — Does Your Chewing Gum Lose It's Flavor On The Bedpost Over Night?

BLOOM, RUBE — Day In-Day Out; Don't Worry 'bout Me; Fools Rush In(Where Angels Fear To Tread); Give Me The Simple Life; Here's To My Lady; I Wish I Could Tell You; Lost In A Dream; Man From The South(With A Big Cigar In His Mouth); Maybe You'll Be There; Out In The Cold Again; Song Of The Bayou; Stay On The Right Side Sister; Truckin'

BLOOM, VERA — Jealousy(Jalousie)

BLOSSOM JR., HENRY — Neapolitan Love Song

BLOSSOM, HENRY — Because You're You; Eileen; Every Day Is Ladies Day With Me; Kiss Me Again; Moonbeams; When You're Away

BLUME, DAVID — Turn Down The Day

BOCAGE, EDWIN — Slippin' And Slidin'

BOCK, JERRY — Artificial Flowers; Days Gone By; Dear Friend; Do You Love Me?; Far From The Home I Love; Fiddler On The Roof; Gentleman Jimmy; Good Clean Fun; Grand Knowing You; He Tossed A Coin; I'm Available; If I Were A Rich Man; Ilona; Little Old New York; Matchmaker, Matchmaker; Miracle Of Miracles; Mr. Wonderful; My Gentle Young Johnny; My Miss Mary; Now I Have Everything; Politics And Poker; Sabbath Prayer; She Loves Me; Sunrise, Sunset; Till Tomorrow; To Life Or L'chaim; Too Close For Comfort; Tradition; When Did I Fall In Love; Will He Like Me; Without You I'm Nothing

BODLEY, J. RUSSELL — De Glory Road

BOGAN, LOUISE — Unborn Child

BOGDANY, THOMAS F. — Shout! Shout! Knock Yourself Out!

BOIS, GLADYS DU — I'm No Angel

BOLAND, CLAY — Gypsy In My Soul; Stop Beatin' 'round The Mulberry Bush

BOLLAND, FERDI — Rock Me Amadeus

BOLLAND, ROB — Rock Me Amadeus

BOLTON, GUY — Till The Clouds Roll By

BOLTON, M. — I Found Someone

BOLTON, MICHAEL — How Am I Supposed To Live Without You

BON JOVI, JON — Wanted Dead Or Alive; You Give Love A Bad Name Livin' On A Prayer

BOND, ANGELO — Bring The Boys Home; Somebody's Been Sleeping In My Bed; Stick-Up

BOND, CARRIE JACOBS — I Love You Truly; Just A Wearyin' For You; Perfect Day

BOND, JOHNNY — Cimarron(Roll On); We Might As Well Forget It

BONFA, LUIS — Carl Sigman; Manha De Carnival; Samba De Orfeu

BONFIRE, MARS — Born To Be Wild

BONHAM, JOHN — D'yer Maker; Whole Lotta Love

BONINE, JOSEPH — Let's Dance

BONNEFORD, JAMES — Joanna; Joey

BONNER, GARRY — Cat In The Window; Happy Together; She'd Rather Be With Me; She's My Girl; You Know What I Mean

BONNER, GARY — Celebrate

BONNER, LEROY — Fire; Funky Worm; Love Rollercoaster; Skin Tight

BONO, SONNY — Baby, Don't Go; Bang Bang(My Baby Shot Me Down); Beat Goes On; But You're Mine; Cowboy's Work Is Never Done; I Got You Babe; Just You; Laugh At Me; Needles And Pins; Where Do You Go?

BONOF, KARLA — Someone To Lay Down Beside Me

BONURA, CARL — I've Had It

BONX, NAT — Collegiate; If You Are But A Dream

BOOKER, GARY — Conquistador

BOOKER, HARRY — Shoeshine Boy

BOONE, LEONARD — You Made Me Believe In Magic

BOONE, PAT — Quando, Quando, Quando(Tell Me When); Wish You Were Here, Buddy

BOONE, RICHARD — Ballad Of Paladin

BOONE, STEVE — Summer In The City; You Didn't Have To Be So Nice

BOOTHE, JIM — Jingle Bell Rock

BORCH, — You Wouldn't Listen

BOREK, RENEE — Solitaire

BORETZ, ALLEN — Whistling In The Dark

BORISOFF, BERNICE — Keem-O-Sabe

BORISOFF, LEONARD — One, Two, Three(1-2-3)

BORODIN, ALEXANDER — Polovtsian Dances

BORRELLI JR., BILL — Philadelphia, U. S. A.

BORRELLI, BILL — Here In My Heart

BOSHELL, BIAS — I've Got The Music In Me

BOSKERCK, FRANCIS VAN — Semper Paratus

BOSTIC, EARL — Let Me Off Uptown

BOTKIN JR., PERRY — Available Space; Bless The Beasts And Children; Nadia's Theme(The Young And The Restless)

BOTKIN, JR., PERRY — Wonderful Summer

BOTTLER, MITCH — Sooner Or Later

BOULANGER, GEORGES — My Prayer

BOURKE, RORY — Angel; I Know A Heartache When I See One; Most Beautiful Girl; Shadows In The Moonlight

BOURTAYRE, JEAN — My Boy

BOUTELJE, PHIL — China Boy

BOWEN, JEFFREY — Shakey Ground; You

BOWEN, JIMMY — I'm Stickin' With You; Party Doll

BOWENS, JOHANNES — Paloma Blanca

BOWER, "BUGS" — Caterina

BOWERS, ROBERT HOOD — Moon Shines On The Moonshine

BOWIE, DAVID — Blue Jean; Cat People(Putting Out Fire); China Girl; Fame; Golden Years; Let's Dance; Modern Love; Space Oddity

BOWLING, ROGER — Coward Of The County; Lucille

BOWMAN, BROOKS — East Of The Sun(and West Of The Moon); Love And A Dime

BOWMAN, EUDAY L. — Twelfth Street Rag

BOWNE, JERRY — Friendly Tavern Polka

BOX, BETTY — I Feel Love(Benji's Theme)

BOX, EUEL — I Feel Love(Benji's Theme)

BOYCE, TOMMY — (I'm Not Your)Steppin' Stone; Come A Little Bit Closer; Green Grass; I Wonder What She's Doing Tonight?; Last Train To Clarksville; Valleri; Words

BOYD, ALPHONSO — Shakey Ground

BOYD, WALTER — 5-10-15-20(25-30 Years Of Love)

BOYLAN, TERENCE — Shake It

BRACKMAN, JACOB — Attitude Dancing; Haven't Got Time For The Pain

BRADFORD, JANIE — Hip City, Part 2; Money, That's What I Want; Too Busy Thinking About My Baby; Your Old Standby

BRADFORD, PERRY — Wicked Blues; You Can't Keep A Good Man Down

BRADFORD, SYLVESTER — I'm Ready

BRADSHAW, TINY — Jersey Bounce

BRAGG, JOHNNY — Just Walking In The Rain

BRAGGS, AL — Share Your Love With Me

BRAHAM, PHILIP — Limehouse Blues

BRAHMS, JOHANNES — Brahms' Lullaby; Hungarian Dance No. 1

BRAININ, JERRY — Night Has A Thousand Eyes

BRAMLETT, BONNIE — Superstar

BRAMLETT, DELANEY — Never Ending Song Of Love

BRANA, HERNANDEZ — His Feet Too Big For De Bed

BRAND, OSCAR — Guy Is A Guy
BRANDOW, JERRY — Hold Tight-Hold Tight(Want Some Sea Food Mama)
BRANDT, EDWARD — All The King's Horses
BRASFIELD, THOMAS — Angel In Your Arms
BRASS, BOB — I Must Be Seeing Things And Hearing Things
BRATHWAITE, WAYNE — Love Is Forever; Love Zone; When The Going Gets Tough, The Tough Get Going
BRAY, STEPHEN — Baby Love; Causing A Commotion; Cross My Broken Heart; Right On Track
BRAY, STEVE — Angel; True Blue
BRECHT, BERTOLT — Alabama-Song; Pirate Jenny
BREL, JACQUES — Amsterdam; Days Of The Waltz; If We Only Have Love; If You Go Away; If You Only Have Love; Seasons In The Sun
BRENNAN, J. KEIRN — Dear Little Boy Of Mine; Little Bit Of Heaven, Sure They Call It Ireland
BRENNAN, JAMES A. — In The Little Red School House
BRENT, EARL K. —Angel Eyes; How Strange; Love Is Where You Find It
BRESLER, JERRY — Five Guys Named Moe
BREUER, ERNEST — Does Your Chewing Gum Lose It's Flavor On The Bedpost Over Night?; Oh! Gee, Oh! Gosh, Oh! Golly, I'm In Love
BREWER, DON — Shinin' On
BREWSTER, JIMMY — If I Give My Heart To You
BRICE, MONTY C. — Daughter Of Rosie O'grady
BRICUSSE, LESLIE — I Ruled The World"; Beautiful Land; Can You Read My Mind(Love Theme From Superman); Candy Man; Chicago, Illinois; Crazy World; Feeling Good; Goldfinger; Gonna Build A Mountain; Joker; Look At That Face; Lumbered; My First Love Song; My Kind Of Girl; Nothing Can Stop Me Now; Once In A Lifetime; Someone Nice Like You; Sweet Beginning; What Kind Of Fool Am I; Where Would You Be Without Me; Who Can I Turn To (When Nobody Needs Me); Wonderful Day Like Today, On A; You Only Live Twice (Theme From)
BRIDGES, ALICIA — I Love The Nightlife
BRIGATI JR., EDWARD — Beautiful Morning; Girl Like You,a; I've Been Lonely Too Long; It's Wonderful; People Got To Be Free; Ray Of Hope,a
BRIGATI, EDDIE — Groovin'; You Better Run
BRIGATI, EDWARD — How Can I Be Sure?
BRIGGS, DAVID —Happy Anniversary; Lonesome Loser
BRIGGS, VICTOR — Monterey; San Franciscan Nights; Sky Pilot; When I Was Young
BRINE, MARY D. — Hearts And Flowers
BRISTOL, JOHNNY — Daddy Could Swear, I Declare; Gotta Hold On To This Feeling; Hang On In There Baby; I Don't Want To Do Wrong; If I Could Build My Whole World Around You; Love Me For A Reason; My Whole World Ended; Pucker Up, Buttercup; Someday We'll Be Together; What Does It Take (To Win Your Love)
BRISTOL, JOHNNY W. — Twenty-Five Miles
BRITO, PHIL — Mama
BRITT, ADDY — Hello! Swanee-Hello!; Was It A Dream
BRITT, AL — Wishing Ring
BRITTEN, TERRY — Devil Woman; Typical Male; We Don't Need Another Hero (Thunderdome); What You Get Is What You See
BROADNAX, MORRIS — Until You Come Back To Me
BROADWATER, ELLY — Susie Q

BROCKERT, TEENA MARIE — Lovergirl
BROCKMAN, JAMES — Down Among The Sheltering Palms; I Faw Down And Go Boom!
BRODSKY, ROY — Red Roses For A Blue Lady; Suzy Snowflake; Swan
BRODSZKY, NICHOLAS — Be My Love; Because You're Mine; Beloved; Dark Is The Night; I Can See You; I'll Never Stop Loving You; We Never Talk Much; Wonder Why
BRONSON, GEORGE — Kitty From Kansas City
BROOKER, GARY — Whiter Shade Of Pale
BROOKS, ARTHUR — For Your Precious Love
BROOKS, FRED — I'm Just A Country Boy
BROOKS, HARRY — Ain't Misbehavin'; What Did I Do To Be So Black And Blue
BROOKS, HARVEY O. — I Want You, I Need You; I'm No Angel; Little Bird Told Me
BROOKS, JACK — Am I In Love; Innamorata; Ole Buttermilk Sky; Rose, Rose, I Love You; Somebody; You Wonderful You
BROOKS, JOE — If Ever I See You Again; You Light Up My Life
BROOKS, JOHN BENSON — Just As Though You Were Here; Ninety Nine Years(Dead Or Alive); You Came A Long Way From St. Louis
BROOKS, JOHNNY — Who Threw The Whiskey In The Well?
BROOKS, MEL — Blazing Saddles
BROOKS, PHILLIPS — O Little Town Of Bethlehem
BROOKS, RICHARD — For Your Precious Love
BROOKS, SHELTON — Darktown Strutters Ball; House Rent Ball; Some Of These Days
BROTHERS, LEIGHTON — Steamboat Bill
BROUSSARD, JOE — Mr. Big Stuff
BROWD JR., WADE — Love Me For A Reason
BROWN JR, OSCAR — Work Song
BROWN JR., OSCAR — Snake
BROWN JR., RICHARD — Happy Music
BROWN, A. H. — You Tell Me Your Dream Or I Had A Dream, Dear
BROWN, A. SEYMOUR — Oh You Beautiful Doll
BROWN, ALFRED — In A Moment
BROWN, BILLIE JEAN — Here Comes The Judge
BROWN, BOOTS — Cerveza
BROWN, CHARLES — Please Come Home For Christmas
BROWN, E. A. G. — You Sexy Thing
BROWN, ERROL — Brother Louie; Disco Queen; Emma; Every 1's A Winner
BROWN, FRANKIE — Born To Lose
BROWN, GEORGE — C'est La Vie; Celebration; Cherish; Emergency; Fresh; Hollywood Swinging; Ladies Night; Misled; Too Hot
BROWN, GEORGE M. — Jungle Boogie
BROWN, HAROLD — Cisco Kid; Spill The Wine
BROWN, HAROLD R. — Gypsy Man; Me And Baby Brother; World Is A Ghetto
BROWN, HAROLD RAY — L. A. Sunshine; La Vie En Rose; Low Rider; Summer; Why Can't We Be Friends
BROWN, JAMES — America Is My Home; Baby, You're Right; Bring It Up; Brother Rapp; Cold Sweat; Get It Together; Get On The Good Foot; Goodbye, My Love; I Can't Stand Myself(When You Touch Me); I Don't Want Nobody To Give Me Nothing; I Got The Feelin'; I Got You(I Feel Good); It's A Man's, Man's, Man's World(But It Wouldn't Be Without A Woman); Lick-

ing Stick-Licking Stick; Mother Popcorn; Papa's Got A Brand New Bag; Payback; Popcorn; Say It Loud-I'm Black And I'm Proud; Sex Machine; Soul Power; Super Bad; World

BROWN, JAMES B. — Dusic

BROWN, L. RUSSELL — C'mon Marianne; I Woke Up In Love This Morning; Knock Three Times; Say, Has Anybody Seen My Sweet Gypsy Rose; Sock It To Me, Baby; Steppin' Out(I'm Gonna Boogie Tonight); Tie A Yellow Ribbon Round The Ole Oak Tree

BROWN, LARRY — One Love In My Lifetime

BROWN, LES — Sentimental Journey

BROWN, LEW — (There's Something About An)Old Fashioned Girl; Baby, Take A Bow; Beer Barrel Polka; Best Things In Life Are Free; Birth Of The Blues; Black Bottom; Broadway; Broadway's Gone Hill Billy; Button Up Your Overcoat!; Come To Me; Comes Love; Don't Bring Lulu; Don't Hold Everything; Don't Sit Under The Apple Tree(With Anyone Else But Me); Don't Tell Her What's Happened To Me; First You Have Me High(Then You Have Me Low); For Old Times' Sake; Georgette; Girl Is You And The Boy Is Me; Good For You, Bad For Me; Good News; He's A Ladies Man; Here Am I-Broken Hearted; I Came Here To Talk For Joe; I Used To Love You But It's All Over Now; I Wanna Go Where You Go, Do What You Do, Then I'll Be Happy; I Want A Lovable Baby; I Want To Be Bad; I'd Climb The Highest Mountain; I'm Laughin'; I'm On The Crest Of A Wave; I've Got To Pass Your House To Get To My House; If I Had A Talking Picture Of You; It All Depends On You; Just A Memory; Just Imagine; Last Night On The Back Porch, I Loved Her Best Of All; Life Is Just A Bowl Of Cherries; Little Pal; Love Is Never Out Of Season; Lucky Day; Lucky In Love; Mississippi Dream Boat; My Lucky Star; My Sin; My Song; Oh By Jingo, Oh By Gee, You're The Only Girl For Me; Oh! Ma-Ma(The Butcher Boy); One Sweet Letter From You; Pickin' Cotton; S-H-I-N-E; Sonny Boy; Sunny Side Up; Thrill Is Gone; Together; Turn On The Heat; Varsity Drag; What D'ya Say?; When It's Night-Time In Italy, It's Wednesday Over Here; Why Can't You (Birdies Sing In Cages Too); Why Did I Kiss That Girl; Without Love; You Try Somebody Else, And I'll Try Somebody Else; You Wouldn't Fool Me, Would You?; You're The Cream In My Coffee

BROWN, MARSHALL — Banjo's Back In Town; Seven Lonely Days

BROWN, MIKE — Pretty Ballerina

BROWN, MILTON — Bar Room Buddies; Every Which Way But Loose; Everybody's Everything; Hoppy, Gene, And Me

BROWN, NACIO HERB — All I Do Is Dream Of You; Alone; Avalon Town; Beautiful Girl; Blondy; Broadway Melody; Broadway Rhythm; Bundle Of Old Love Letters; Chant Of The Jungle; Cinderella's Fella; Coral Sea; Doll Dance; Eady Was A Lady; Everybody Sing; Follow In My Footsteps; Good Morning; Got A Pair Of New Shoes; Hold Your Man; I'll Still Belong To You; I'm Feelin' Like A Million; I've Got A Feelin' You're Foolin'; If I Steal A Kiss; Love Is Where You Find It; Love Songs Of The Nile; Moon Is Low; New Moon Is Over My Shoulder; On A Sunday Afternoon; Our Big Love Scene; Pagan Love Song; Paradise; Should I?; Sing Before Breakfast; Singin' In The Rain; Turn Out The Light; We'll Make Hay While The Sun Shines; Wedding Of The Painted Doll; What's Wrong With Me?; When Buddha Smiles; Woman In The Shoe; You And I; You Are My Lucky Star; You Stepped Out Of A Dream; You Were Meant For Me; You're An Old Smoothie; Yours And Mine

BROWN, NAPOLEON — Don't Be Angry

BROWN, OLLIE — Breakin'...There's No Stopping Us

BROWN, PAULA — Mad About You

BROWN, PETE — White Room

BROWN, PETER — Dance With Me; Do Ya Wanna Get Funky With Me; Material Girl; Sunshine Of Your Love

BROWN, RAY — Gravy Waltz

BROWN, ROY — Long About Midnight

BROWN, W. EARL — If I Can Dream

BROWN, WALTER — Confessin' The Blues

BROWNE, JACKSON — Before The Deluge; Boulevard; Doctor My Eyes; Here Come Those Tears Again; Lawyers In Love; Load Out; Running On Empty; Somebody's Baby; You Love The Thunder

BROWNER, RUDOLPH — Jealous Kind Of Fellow

BRUBECK, DAVE — Bossa Nova U.S.A; Unsquare Dance

BRUCE, ED — Mammas Don't Let Your Babies Grow Up To Be Cowboys

BRUCE, GARY D. — Moody River

BRUCE, JACK — Sunshine Of Your Love; White Room

BRUCE, MICHAEL — Billion Dollar Babies; Eighteen; School's Out

BRUCE, PATSY — Mammas Don't Let Your Babies Grow Up To Be Cowboys

BRUNIES, GEORGE — Tin Roof Blues

BRUNIES, HENRY — Angry; Animalclark

BRUNIES, MERRITT — Angry; Animalclark

BRUNO, TONY — Last Chance(To Turn Around)

BRUNS, GEORGE — Ballad Of Davy Crockett

BRYAN, ALFRED — Brown Eyes, Why Are You Blue?; Come Josephine(In My Flying Machine); I Didn't Raise My Boy To Be A Soldier; In A Little Dutch Garden(Down By The Zuider Zee); Japansy; Madelon; Peg O' My Heart; Who Ate Napoleons With Josephine When Bonaparte Was Away

BRYAN, VINCENT — In My Merry Oldsmobile; In The Sweet Bye And Bye

BRYANT, BOUDLEAUX — All I Have To Do Is Dream; Bird Dog; Devoted To You; Hawk-Eye; Let's Think About Living; Love Hurts; Wake Up Little Susie

BRYANT, BOUDLEAUX AND FELICE — Bye Bye Love; Have A Good Time; Mexico; Poor Jenny; Problems

BRYANT, D. P. — Don't You Want Me

BRYANT, DONALD — I Can't Stand The Rain

BRYANT, FELICE — Wake Up Little Susie

BRYANT, RAY — Madison Time

BRYANT, WILLIE — Do You Wanna Jump, Children?

BRYMN, J. TIM — Aunt Hagar's Blues

BRYNE, PETE — Promises, Promises

BRYSON, PEABO — Ballad For D

BUCHANAN, BILL — Please Don't Ask About Barbara

BUCHWALD, MARTYN — With Your Love

BUCK, GENE — Florida, The Moon And You; Hello Frisco Hello; Throw Me A Kiss

BUCK, RICHARD HENRY — Dear Old Girl

BUCKINGHAM, LINDSAY — Big Love; Go Your Own Way; Trouble; Tusk

BUCKINS, MICKEY — Double Lovin'

BUCKNER, JERRY — Pac-man Fever

BUCKNER, MILT — Hamp's Boogie Woogie

BUFF, WADE — It's Almost Tomorrow

BUFFETT, JIMMY — Come Monday; Fins; Margaritaville

BUGATTI, DOMINIC — Every Woman In The World; Heaven On The Seventh Floor; Married Men; Modern Girl

BUIE, BUDDY — Do It Or Die; Everyday With You Girl; I'm Not Gonna Let It Bother Me Tonight; Imaginary Lover; So Into You; Stormy; Traces

BUIE, PERRY C. — I Take It Back

BULHOES, MAX — Come To The Mardi Gras

BULLARD, FREDERIC FIELD — It's Always Fair Weather When Good Fellows Get Together

BULLOCK, VERNON — If I Could Build My Whole World Around You; What Does It Take (To Win Your Love); Yesterday's Dreams

BULLOCK, WALTER — Half Moon On The Hudson; I Could Use A Dream; I Love To Walk In The Rain; I Still Love To Kiss You Goodnight; Swing Low Sweet Rhythm; When Did You Leave Heaven

BUNCH, BOYD — Broken Record

BUNHAM, BY — Any Way The Wind Blows

BUNN, ALFRED — I Dreamt I Dwelt In Marble Halls

BUNNELL, LEE — Horse With No Name; Tin Man; Ventura Highway

BURCH, DON — You Cheated

BURCH, FRED B. — Dream On Little Dreamer; P. T. 109; Tragedy

BURDON, ERIC — I'm Crying; Inside-Looking Out; Monterey; San Franciscan Nights; Sky Pilot; When I Was Young

BURGERS, JAN — Midnight In Moscow

BURGESS, DAVE — Everlovin'; I'm Available

BURGESS, IRVING — Island In The Sun

BURGESS, LORD — Jamaica Farewell

BURGH, CHRIS DE — Lady In Red

BURGH, STEVE — Banana Republic

BURKE, BOBBY — Daddy's Little Girl

BURKE, DELORES — Got To Get You Off My Mind

BURKE, JOE — At A Perfume Counter(on The Rue De La Paix); Carolina Moon; Crosby, Columbo, And Vallee; Dancing With Tears In My Eyes; Dream Valley; For You; Getting Some Fun Out Of Life; Good Night Little Girl Of My Dreams; If I'm Dreaming, Don't Wake Me Too Soon; In A Little Gypsy Tearoom; It Looks Like Rain In Cherry Blossom Lane; Kiss Waltz; Little Bit Independent; Moon Over Miami; Oh, How I Miss You Tonight; On Treasure Island; Painting The Clouds With Sunshine; Robins And Roses; Tip Toe Through The Tulips; Who Wouldn't Be Blue?; Yearning (Just For You)

BURKE, JOHNNY — All You Want To Do Is Dance; An Apple For The Teacher; And You'll Be Home; Annie Doesn't Live Here Anymore; Apalachicola, Fla.; April Played The Fiddle; Aren't You Glad You're You; As Long As I'm Dreaming; Be Beautiful; Beat Of My Heart; Between A Kiss And A Sigh; Birds Of A Feather; Bluebirds In My Belfry; Busy Doing Nothing; Charming Little Faker; Chicago Style; Constantly; Country Style; Day After Forever; Dearest, Darest I; Devil May Care; Do You Know Why; Don't Let That Moon Get Away; East Side Of Heaven; Ev'ry Girl Is Diff'rent; Experience; For The First Hundred Years; Friend Of Yours; Going My Way; Got The Moon In My Pocket; Hang Your Heart On A Hickory Limb; Hard Way; Harmony; Here's That Rainy Day; His Rocking Horse Ran Away; Horse Told Me; Humpty Dumpty Heart; I Haven't Time To Be A Millionaire; I've Got A Pocketful Of Dreams; If You Please; If You Stub Your Toe On The Moon; Imagination; Isn't That Just Like Love; It Could Happen To You; It's Always You; It's Anybody's Spring; It's Dark On Observatory Hill; It's The Natural Thing To Do; Just My Luck; Just Plain Lonesome; Kiss In Your Eyes; Laugh And Call It Love; Life Is So Peculiar; Like Someone In Love; Love Is The Darndest Thing; Man And His Dream; Misty; Moon Got In My Eyes; Moonlight Becomes You; My Heart Is A Hobo; My Heart Is Taking Lessons; My Very Good Friend, The Milkman; Oh, You Crazy Moon; On The Sentimental Side; Once And For Always; One, Two, Button Your Shoe; Only Forever; Pennies From Heaven; Personality; Polka Dots And Moonbeams; Polly Wolly Doodle; Put It There, Pal; Rhythm On The River; Road To Morocco; Scatterbrain; Skeleton In The Closet; So Do I; Suddenly It's Spring; Sunday, Monday, Or Always; Swinging On A Star; Too Romantic; Welcome To My Dream; What's New; When Is Sometime?; When The Moor Comes Over Madison Square (The Love Lament Of A Western Gent); Wild Horses; Yah-Ta-Ta, Yah-Ta-Ta (Talk, Talk, Talk); You Don't Have To Know The Language

BURKE, REGINALD — Serpentine Fire

BURKE, SOLOMON — Everybody Needs Somebody To Love

BURKE, SONNY — Black Coffee; He's A Tramp; Hennesey; How It Lies, How It Lies, How It Lies; Midnight Sun; Siamese Cat Song; Somebody Bigger Than You And I; You Was

BURKHARD, PAUL — Oh! My Pa-Pa

BURKS, SOLOMON — Got To Get You Off My Mind

BURLAND, GRANVILLE — Uh! Oh! (The Nutty Squirrels)

BURLAND, SASCHA — No Matter What Shape(Your Stomach's In)

BURNETT, ERNIE — My Melancholy Baby

BURNETTE, DORSEY — It's Late; Waitin' In School

BURNETTE, JOHNNY — Just A Little Too Much; Waitin' In School

BURNETTE, JOHNNY AND DORSEY — Believe What You Say

BURNETTE, O'BRYAN — Lovelight

BURNETTE, ROCKY — Tired Of Toein' The Line

BURNS, ANNALU — I'll Forget You

BURNS, RALPH — Bijou; Early Autumn; Northwest Passage

BURNS, ROBERT — Auld Lang Syne; Campbells Are Coming; Comin' Thro' The Rye; Flow Gently, Sweet Afton

BURR, GARY — Love's Been A Little Bit Hard On Me

BURRIS, JAMES HENRY — Ballin' The Jack; Constantly

BURROUGHS, ABE — Leave Us Face It(We're In Love)

BURRS, GLENN — Alexander The Swoose

BURTNETT, EARL — Do You Ever Think Of Me

BURTON, DORIAN — I Can't Love You Enough

BURTON, MICHAEL — Pillow Talk

BURTON, NAT — Our Waltz; White Cliffs Of Dover, The (There'll Be Bluebirds Over)

BURTON, RAY — I Am Woman

BURTON, VAL — Penthouse Serenade(When We're

Alone); Singing A Vagabond Song; When We're Alone Or Penthouse Serenade

BURWELL, CLIFF — Sweet Lorraine

BUSCH, LOU — Hello Muddah, Hello Fadduh

BUSHKIN, JOE — (There'll Be A)Hot Time In The Town Of Berlin; Oh! Look At Me Now!

BUSSE, HENRY — Hot Lips; Wang Wang Blues

BUTLER, BILLY — Honky Tonk; Honolulu Lulu

BUTLER, DAWS — St. George And The Dragonet

BUTLER, JERRY — Are You Happy?; Brand New Me; Find Another Girl; For Your Precious Love; Hey, Western Union Man; I've Been Loving You Too Long; Moody Woman; Never Give You Up(Never Gonna Give You Up); Never Gonna Give You Up; Only The Strong Survive; What's The Use Of Breaking Up?

BUTLER, LARRY — (Hey Won't You Play)another Somebody Done Somebody Wrong Song)

BUTLER, RALPH — Run, Rabbit, Run

BUTLER, WILLIAM B. — Matador

BUTTERFIELD, JAMES AUSTIN — When You And I Were Young Maggie

BUTTOLPH, DAVID — Maverick

BUTTONS, RED — Ho Ho Song; Strange Things Are Happening

BUXTON, GLEN — Eighteen

BYERS, JOY — Please Don't Stop Loving Me

BYNUM, HAL — Lucille

BYRD, BOBBY — Licking Stick-Licking Stick

BYRD, ROBERT — Little Bitty Pretty One; Over And Over

BYRD, SHATEMA — Black Man

BYRNE, DAVID — Burning Down The House

BYRNE, JOHN — Psychotic Reaction

BYROM, M. — I Wanna Go Back

BYRON, AL — Happy Go Lucky Me; Roses Are Red(My Love)

BYRON, DAVID LEIGH — Shadows Of The Night;

CACAVAS, JOHN — Black Is Beautiful

CADMAN, CHARLES — From The Land Of The Sky Blue Water

CAESAR, IRVING — (Oh Suzanna)Dust Off That Old Pianna; Animal Crackers In My Soup; Crazy Rhythm; Good Evening Friends; Hold My Hand; I Love Her, She Loves Me; I Want To Be Happy; If I Forget You; Is It True What They Say About Dixie?; It Goes Like This(That Funny Melody); Just A Gigolo; Lady, Play Your Mandolin; Oh, Donna Clara; Stonewall Moskowitz March; Swanee; Too Many Rings Around Rosie; What A Perfect Combination; What Do You Do Sunday, Mary?; Yankee Doodle Blues

CAESAR, WILLIAM F. — Crooning

CAFFERTY, JOHN — C-I-T-Y; On The Dark Side

CAFFEY, CHARLOTTE — Head Over Heels; We Got The Beat

CAFRA, CATHERINE — Skinny Minnie

CAHN, SAMMY — (If I Had)Rhythm In My Nursery Rhymes; All That Love Went To Waste; All The Way; And Then You Kissed Me; Anywhere; As Long As There's Music; Autumn In Rome; Be My Love; Because You're Mine; Bei Mir Bist Du Schon; Best Of Everything; Boys' Night Out; Brooklyn Bridge; By Love Possessed; Call Me Irresponsible; Can't You Just See Yourself; Can't You Read Between The Lines?; Charm Of You; Closer Than A Kiss; Dark Is The Night; Day By Day; Dedicated To You; Dormi, Dormi, Dormi; Ev'ry Day I Love You(Just A Little Bit More); Everything Makes Music When You're In Love; Face To Face; Five Minutes More; Forever Darling; Get Away For A Day(In The Country); Girl Upstairs; Give Me A Song With A Beautiful Melody; Go To Sleep, Go To Sleep, Go To Sleep; Guess I'll Hang My Tears Out To Dry; Hey! Jealous Lover; High Hopes; How D'ye Talk To A Girl; I Begged Her; I Believe; I Don't Think I'm In Love; I Fall In Love Too Easily; I Gotta Gal I Love(in North And South Dakota); I Should Care; I Still Get Jealous; I Still Haven't Found What I'm Looking For; I'll Make A Man Of The Man; I'll Never Stop Loving You; I'll Walk Alone; I'm In Love; I've Heard That Song Before; I've Never Forgotten; I, Yes Me, That's Who; If It's The Last Thing I Do; Impatient Years; Indiscreet; Indiscretion; It's A Great Feeling; It's A Woman's World; It's Been A Long, Long Time; It's Magic; It's The Same Old Dream; It's You Or No One; Joseph! Joseph!; Last Dance; Let It Snow! Let It Snow! Let It Snow!; Let Me Try Again; Let's Not Be Sensible; Long Hot Summer; Love And Marriage; Love Is A Bore; Love Me; Melancholy Rhapsody; My Kind Of Town; Nothing In Common; Odd Couple, The(Theme); Only The Lonely; Papa, Won't You Dance With Me; Pete Kelly's Blues; Please Be Kind; Pleasure Seekers; Pocketful Of Miracles; Poor Little Rhode Island; Posin'; Put It In A Box(Tie 'em With A Ribbon And Throw 'em In The Deep Blue Sea); Relax-Ay-Voo; Rhythm Is Our Business; Road To Hong Kong; Same Old Saturday Night; Saturday Night(Is The Loneliest Night In The Week); Second Time Around; September Of My Years; Shoe Shine Boy; Somebody Up There Likes Me; Song From Some Came Running(To Love And Be Loved); Songs Gotta Come From The Heart; Star!;

Three Coins In The Fountain; Time After Time; Until The Real Thing Comes Along; Wake Me When It's Over; Walking Happy; We Never Talk Much; What Makes The Sunset; When The One You Love (Simply Won't Come Back); Where Love Has Gone; Wonder Why; Written On The Wind; You're My Girl; Zuyder Zee

CAHN, SAMUEL — Vict'ry Polka

CAIN, J. — I'll Be Alright Without You

CAIN, JONATHAN — Be Good To Yourself; Don't Stop Believin'; Faithfully; Girl Can't Help It; Only The Young; Open Arms; Still They Ride; Suzanne; Who's Crying Now

CALDWELL, ANNE — Blue Danube Blues; Good Morning Dearie; I Know That You Know; In Love With Love; Ka-Lu-A; Left All Alone Again Blues; Like He Loves Me; Lorelei; Once In A Blue Moon; Raggedy Ann; Whose Baby Are You

CALDWELL, GAYLE — Cycles

CALDWELL, GLORIA — Don't Let Me Be Misunderstood

CALDWELL, ROBERT — Next Time I Fall; What You Won't Do For Love

CALDWELL, RONNIE — Soul Finger

CALDWELL, TOY — Heard It In A Love Song

CALELLO, CHARLES — You're Gonna Hurt Yourself

CALHOUN, CHARLES E. — Flip Flop And Fly; Shake, Rattle, And Roll; Smack Dab In The Middle

CALIFORNIA, RANDY — I Got A Line On You

CALILLI, BOB — Walk Away, Renee

CALL, ALEX — 867-5309/Jenny; Little Too Late

CALLAHAN, FRED B. — Washboard Blues

CALLAHAN, J. WILL — (There Are)Smiles

CALLANDER, PETER — Ballad Of Bonnie And Clyde

CALLENDAR, PETER — Hitchin' A Ride; Night Chicago Died

CALLENDER, GEORGE — Primrose Lane

CALLENDER, PETER — Billy, Don't Be A Hero; Daddy Don't You Walk So Fast

CALLIS, JO — (Keep Feeling)Fascination

CALLOWAY, CAB — Boog-It; Jitter Bug; Jumpin' Jive; Minnie The Moocher; Scat Song

CALLOWAY, R. — Casanova; Jump Start; Love Overboard

CALLOWAY, REGGIE — Operator

CALLOWAY, V. — Jump Start

CALLOWAY, VINCENT — Operator

CALVERT, EDDIE — My Son, My Son

CAMARATA, ERNESTO LECUONA-TUTT — Breeze And I

CAMARATA, TOOTS — Moonlight Masquerade

CAMERON, AL — Martins And The Coys

CAMILLO, TONY — Dynomite

CAMPANO, FRANK — Heartbreaker

CAMPBELL, B. — Love You Most Of All

CAMPBELL, BARBARA — Wonderful World

CAMPBELL, GEORGE — Four Walls

CAMPBELL, JIMMY — By The Fireside; Goodnight Sweetheart; If I Had You; Just An Echo In The Valley; Try A Little Tenderness; When The Organ Played At Twilight (The Song That Reached My

CAMPBELL, MIKE — Boys Of Summer; Jammin' Me; Refugee; Stop Draggin' My Heart Around

CAMPBELL, PAUL — Kisses Sweeter Than Wine

CANDY, MARY — Men In My Little Girl's Life

CANNON, ACE — Tuff

CANNON, BETTE — Fifteen Minute Intermission; Just A Little Bit South Of North Carolina

CANNON, GUS — Walk Right In

CANNON, HUGHIE — Bill Bailey, Won't You Please Come Home

CANSLER, LARRY — Wildfire

CANTER, JOHN — Don't Call Us, We'll Call You

CANTOR, EDDIE — I Love Her, She Loves Me

CAPALDI, JIM — Paper Sun

CAPEHART, JERRY — Beautiful Brown Eyes; C'mon Everybody; Summertime Blues; Summertime In Venice; Turn Around, Look At Me

CAPIZZI, LEONARD — Monster Mash

CAPOTE, TRUMAN — House Of Flowers; I Never Has Seen Snow; Sleepin' Bee; Smellin' Of Vanilla(Bamboo Cage); Two Ladies In De Shade Of De Banana Tree

CAPPS, AL — Half-Breed; She's Just My Style

CAPUA, EDORADO DI — O Solo Mio

CAPURRO, GIOVANNI — O Solo Mio

CARA, IRENE — Breakdance; Flashdance(What A Feeling)

CARE, RALPH — Penny A Kiss, A Penny A Hug

CAREY, BILL — It Started All Over Again; Who Wouldn't Love You

CAREY, BOB — Banana Boat Song, The(Day-O)

CAREY, JOSEPH BUELL — Sierra Sue

CARL, BILLY — Goody Goody Gumdrops

CARLE, FRANKIE — Falling Leaves; Lover's Lullaby; Oh! What It Seemed To Be; Roses In The Rain; Sunrise Serenade

CARLETON, BOB — Ja-Da; Where The Blues Were Born In New Orleans

CARLIN, FRED — Come Saturday Morning; For All We Know

CARLISI, JEFF — Caught Up In You; Causing A Commotion; If I'd Been The One; Like No Other Night

CARLISLE, BILL — Too Old To Cut The Mustard

CARLISLE, UNA MAE — I See A Million People(But All I Can See Is You); Walkin' By The River

CARLO, TYRAN — I'll Be Satisfied; Lonely Teardrops; Reet Petite; To Be Loved; You Got What It Takes

CARLTON, HARRY — C-O-N-S-T-A-N-T-I-N-O-P-L-E

CARLYLE, RUSS — If I Ever Love Again

CARMAN, BRIAN — Pipeline

CARMEN, ERIC — All By Myself; Almost Paradise(Love Theme From Footloose); Change Of Heart; Go All The Way; Hey Deanie; I Wanna Be With You; Never Gonna Fall In Love Again; Never Gonna Give You Up; Overnight Sensation(Hit Record); She Did It

CARMICHAEL, HOAGY — Ballad In Blue; Baltimore Oriole; Blue Orchids; Boneyard Shuffle; Bubble-Loo, Bubble-Loo; Can't Get Indiana Off My Mind; Casanova Cricket; College Swing; Doctor, Lawyer, Indian Chief; Everything Happens To Me; Follow The Swallow(To Hideaway Hollow); Georgia On My Mind; Hands Across The Border; Heart And Soul; Hong Kong Blues; How Little We Know; I Get Along Without You Very Well; I Walk With Music; In The Cool, Cool, Cool Of The Evening; Ivy; Jubilee; Kind'a Lonesome; Lamplighter's Serenade; Lazy River; Lazybones; Little Old Lady; Memphis In June; Moon Country; Moonburn; Mr. Bluebird; My Resistance Is Low; N Tuncle Bills"; Nearness Of You; Old Man Harlem; Ole Buttermilk Sky; One Morning In May; Ooh! What You Said; Riverboat Shuffle; Rockin'

Chair; Skylark; Small Fry; Star Dust; Two Sleepy People; Vagabond Dreams; Washboard Blues; Watermelon Weather; We're The Couple In The Castle

CARNES, KIM — Crazy In The Night(Barking At Airplanes); Don't Fall In Love With A Dreamer; You're A Part Of Me

CARNEY, HARRY — Rockin' In Rhythm

CAROSONE, RENATO — Torero

CARPENTER, CHARLES — Bolero At The Savoy; You Can Depend On Me

CARPENTER, IMOGENE — Born To Sing The Blues

CARPENTER, PETER — Rockford Files

CARPENTER, RICHARD — Goodbye To Love; I Need To Be In Love; Only Yesterday; Top Of The World; Yesterday Once More

CARR, JERRY — Rosie Lee

CARR, LEON — (Hey There)Lonely Boy; Another Cup Of Coffee; Bell Bottom Blues; Clinging Vine; Confidence; Disorderly Orderly; Fan The Flame; Gina; Hello, I Love You, Goodbye; Hey There Lonely Boy; Hotel Happiness; Most People Get Married; Walkin' With Peninnah; Your Socks Don't Match

CARR, LEROY — How Long, How Long Blues; In The Evening(When The Sun Goes Down)

CARR, MICHAEL — Cinderella, Stay In My Arms; Did Your Mother Come From Ireland?; Dinner For One Please, James; He Wears A Pair Of Silver Wings; Ole Faithful; South Of The Border; Two Bouquets

CARRACK, PAUL — How Long

CARRADINE, KEITH — I'm Easy; It Don't Worry Me

CARROLL, BERT — Wear My Ring Around Your Neck

CARROLL, GREGORY — Just One Look

CARROLL, HARRY — By The Beautiful Sea; Trail Of The Lonesome Pine

CARROLL, JIMMY — Helen Pola

CARROLL, JONATHAN — Get Closer

CARROLL, JUNE — Love Is A Simple Thing

CARROLL, RAY — I Want You All To Myself

CARROLL, WILLIS — Little Mama; Seven Days

CARRUTHERS, BEN — Black Butterfly

CARSON, JENNY LOU — Jealous Heart; Let Me Go Lover!

CARSON, JOHNNY — Johnny's Theme

CARSON, MILTON — My Love And Devotion; Tulips And Heather

CARSTARPHEN, VICTOR — Bad Luck(part 1); Wake Up, Everybody (Part 1)

CARTER, A. A. — Wild Side Of Life

CARTER, A. F. — Wabash Cannonball

CARTER, A. P. — I'm Thinking Tonight Of My Blue Eyes; Worried Man Blues

CARTER, BENNY — Blues In My Heart; Cow-Cow Boogie; Crazy; Lonesome Nights; Rainbow Rhapsody; Symphony In Riffs

CARTER, BLANCHE — Devil Or Angel

CARTER, CALVIN — Goodnight Sweetheart, Well It's Time To Go; He Don't Love You(Like I Love You)

CARTER, CLARENCE — Too Weak To Fight

CARTER, DEBORAH — Give It Up

CARTER, DESMOND — High And Low(I've Been Looking For You)

CARTER, JOHN — Incense And Peppermints

CARTER, JUNE — Ring Of Fire

CARTER, VALERIE — Cook With Honey

CARTEY, RIC — Young Love

CARTIERO, GUADALUPE — Fine Brown Frame

CASEL, NICK — Convention '72

CASEY, AL — Forty Miles Of Bad Roads; Ramrod

CASEY, HARRY — (Shake, Shake, Shake)Shake Your Booty; Boogie Shoes; Get Down Tonight; Give It Up; I'm Your Boogie Man; Keep It Comin,love; Please Don't Go; Rock Your Baby

CASEY, HARRY WAYNE — Where Is The Love

CASEY, KEN — Sweet Georgia Brown

CASEY, WARREN — Beauty School Dropout; Summer Nights

CASH, JOHNNY — Don't Take Your Guns To Town; Folsom Prison Blues; I Walk The Line; Understand Your Man; What Is Truth

CASH, ROSANNE — Seven Year Ache

CASH, STEVE — If You Wanna Get To Heaven; Jackie Blue

CASHMAN, TERRY — Medicine Man

CASMAN, NELLIE — Joseph! Joseph!

CASON, BUZZ — Popsicle; Sukiyaki

CASON, JAMES — Everlasting Love

CASSARD, JULES — Angry; Animalclark

CASSEL, IRWIN M. — I Love Life

CASSIN, JIMMY — Sentimental Me

CASTILLO, EMILIO — So Very Hard To Go; What Is Hip; You're Still A Young Man

CASTLE, NICK — Candy Store Blues

CASTON, LEONARD — Boogie Down; Keep On Truckin'; Nathan Jones

CASTOR, JIMMY — Bertha Butt Boogie; Hey, Leroy, You're Mama's Callin' You

CASUCCI, LEONELLO — Just A Gigolo

CATE, EARL — Union Man

CATE, ERNIE — Union Man

CATHY, LEE — Just Between You And Me

CAULEY, BEN — Soul Finger

CAVALIERE, FELIX — Beautiful Morning; Carry Me Back; Girl Like You,a; Groovin'; How Can I Be Sure?; I've Been Lonely Too Long; It's Wonderful; People Got To Be Free; Ray Of Hope,a; See; You Better Run

CAVANASS, J. M. — By The Waters Of Minnetonka

CAVANAUGH, JAMES — Christmas In Killarney; Crosstown; Did You Ever Get That Feeling In The Moonlight; Gaucho Serenade; Goody Goodbye; I Like Mountain Music; Little On The Lonely Side; Mississippi Mud; Umbrella Man; You're Nobody 'til Somebody Loves You

CAVANAUGH, JESSIE — Bonnie Blue Gal; Desafinado (Slightly Out Of Tune); Roving Kind

CENCI, NICK — Convention '72

CERONI, RAY — I've Had It

CETERA, PETER — Along Comes A Woman; Baby, What A Big Surprise; Feelin' Stronger Every Day; Glory Of Love(Theme From The Karate Kid, Part 2); Hard To Say I'm Sorry; If You Leave Me Now; No Tell Lover; Stay The Night; Wishing You Were Here; You're The Inspiration

CHABRIER, EMMANUEL — Espana Rhapsody

CHAMBERS, JOSEPH — Time Has Come Today

CHAMBERS, WILLIE — Time Has Come Today

CHAMINADE, CECILE — Scarf Dance

CHAMPION, BETTYE JEAN — Make Me Yours

CHAMPLIN, BILL — Is It You; Turn Your Love Around

CHANCE, BARRY — Fins

CHANCEY, D. — I Wanna Go Back

CHANCLER, LEON — Let It Whip

CHANDLER, BRYAN — Inside-Looking Out

CHANDLER, GUS — Canadian Capers

CHANEY, ROY — Psychotic Reaction

CHANNEL, BRUCE — Hey! Baby

CHAPIN, E. H. — Oh Bury Me Not On The Lone Prairie

CHAPIN, HARRY — Better Place To Be; Sequel; W-O-L-D

CHAPIN, HARRY AND SANDRA — Cat's In The Cradle

CHAPLIN, CHARLES — Eternally(Limelight); Smile

CHAPLIN, SAUL — (If I Had)Rhythm In My Nursery Rhymes; Anniversary Song; Bei Mir Bist Du Schon; Berry Tree; Dedicated To You; If It's The Last Thing I Do; Joseph! Joseph!; Please Be Kind; Posin'; Rhythm Is Our Business; Shoe Shine Boy; Until The Real Thing Comes Along; You Wonderful You

CHAPMAN, MIKE — Ballroom Blitz; Heart And Soul; Kiss You All Over; Living Next Door To Alice; Love Is A Battlefield; Love Touch; Mickey; Stumblin' In

CHAQUICO, CRAIG — Jane

CHARIG, PHIL — I Wanna Get Married

CHARIG, PHILIP — Fancy Our Meeting; Why Do Ya Roll Those Eyes?

CHARLAP, MARK — I Won't Grow Up; I'm Flying; I've Got To Crow

CHARLAP, MOOSE — English Muffins And Irish Stew; Young Ideas

CHARLES, BEAU — Lies(Are Breakin' My Heart)

CHARLES, DICK — Along The Navajo Trail; Casanova Cricket; Corns For My Country; Mad About Him, Sad Without Him, How Can I Be Glad Without Him Blues; May You Always

CHARLES, HUGHIE — We'll Meet Again

CHARLES, LES — Love Really Hurts Without You

CHARLES, RAY — Baby,let Me Hold Your Hand; Bit Of Soul; Blue Genius; Charlesville; Come Back Baby; Don't You Know; Frenesi; Frere Jacques; Funny(But I Still Love You); Hallelujah I Love Her So; Hard Times(No One Knows Better Than I); I Chose To Sing The Blues(I Choose To Sing The Blues); I Got A Woman(I Got A Sweetie); Love On My Mind; Understanding (Is The Best Thing In The World); What'd I Say?; X-Ray Blues

CHARNIN, MARTIN — Easy Street; I Do Not Know A Day I Did Not Love You; I Don't Need Anything But You; Maybe; N. Y. C.; Tomorrow

CHARRON, MARK — Billy And Sue; Billy Boy; Mama

CHASE, LINCOLN — Cinnamon Sinner; Clapping Song; Jim Dandy; Name Game; Nitty Gritty; Such A Night; Wonderland By Night

CHASE, NEWELL — If I Were King; It's A Great Life(If You Don't Weaken); My Ideal

CHATER, KERRY — I Know A Heartache When I See One

CHATMAN, BO — Corrine, Corrina

CHATMAN, PETER — Every Day I Have The Blues

CHATTON, BRIAN — I Wanna Be A Cowboy

CHEN, PHIL — Passion

CHERTOFF, RICK — Day By Day; She Bop

CHERUBINI, B. — Serenade In The Night

CHESSLER, DEBORAH — It's Too Soon To Know

CHIATE, LLOYD — Maybe I'm A Fool

CHILD, D. — Angel; Dude(Looks Like A Lady); Livin' On A Prayer

CHILD, DESMOND — I Was Made For Loving You; You Give Love A Bad Name

CHINN, NICKY — Ballroom Blitz; Heart And Soul; Kiss

You All Over; Living Next Door To Alice; Mickey; Stumblin' In

CHIPRUT, ELLIOT — Simon Says

CHISHOLM, CATHERINE — L'amour, Toujours, L'amour(Love Everlasting)

CHISOLM, ED — Let The Music Play

CHONG, TOMMY — Does Your Mama Know About Me; Earache My Eye

CHOPIN, FREDERIC — Fantaisie Impromptu; Funeral March; Grande Valse Brilliante; Nocturne(op. 9 No. 2); Polonaise Militaire

CHRISTENSON, LAURIE — In The Middle Of A Heartache

CHRISTIAN, ARLESTER — Funky Broadway; We Got More Soul (We Got Latin Soul)

CHRISTIAN, CHARLIE — Air Mail Special; Solo Flight

CHRISTIAN, RICK — I Don't Need You

CHRISTIAN, ROGER — Dead Man's Curve; Don't Worry Baby; Drag City; Honolulu Lulu; Little Old Lady, The(From Pasadena); Shut Down; You Really Know How To Hurt A Guy

CHRISTIE, JEFF — Yellow River

CHRISTIE, LOU — Lightnin' Strikes; Rhapsody In The Rain

CHRISTINE, H. — Valentine

CHRISTOPHER, GRETCHEN — Come Softly To Me

CHRISTOPHER, JOHNNY — Always On My Mind; If You Talk In Your Sleep; Mama Liked The Roses; No Love At All

CHRISTY, E. P. — Good Night Ladies(Merrily We Roll Along)

CHUDACOFF, RICK — Steal Away

CHUNG, WANG — Everybody Have Fun Tonight; Let's Go

CHURCHILL, FRANK — Baby Mine; Casey Junior; Heigh-Ho(The Dwarfs' Marching Song); I'm Wishing; One Song; Someday My Prince Will Come; Whistle While You Work; Who's Afraid Of The Big Bad Wolf; With A Smile And A Song

CHURCHILL, SAVANNAH — I Want To Be Loved(But By Only You)

CICCHETTI, CARL — Beep, Beep

CICCO, R. DI — Bobby Sox To Stockings

CICCONE, DON — Mr. Dieingly Sad

CICCONE, MADONNA — Lucky Star; Papa Don't Preach

CITORELLO, PAOLO — Oh! Ma-Ma(The Butcher Boy)

CLANTON, JIMMY — Just A Dream

CLAPP, SUNNY — Girl Of My Dreams

CLAPS, DONALD — Beep, Beep

CLAPTON, ERIC — Badge; Bell Bottom Blues; Hello Old Friend; I Can't Stand It; Lay Down Sally; Layla; Sunshine Of Your Love; Watch Out For Lucy; Wonderful Tonight

CLAR, ARDEN — Similau

CLARE, PHYLLIS — Petite Waltz

CLARE, SIDNEY — I Wanna Go Where You Go, Do What You Do, Then I'll Be Happy; I'd Climb The Highest Mountain; Keepin' Myself For You; Lovable And Sweet; Ma!(He's Making Eyes At Me); On The Good Ship Lollipop; One Sweet Letter From You; Please Don't Talk About Me When I'm Gone

CLARK, CLAUDINE — Party Lights

CLARK, DAVE — Any Way You Want It; At The Scene; Because; Bits And Pieces; Can't You See That She's Mine?; Catch Us If You Can; Come Home; Glad All Over; Please Tell Me Why; Try Too Hard; Why I Sing The Blues

CLARK, DEE — Nobody But You; Raindrops; You Can't Sit Down

CLARK, FREDDIE — Beans And Cornbread

CLARK, GENE — Eight Miles High; You Showed Me

CLARK, GRANT — He's A Devil In His Own Home Town; Mandy, Make Up Your Mind

CLARK, MICHAEL — Slow Hand

CLARK, PETULA — You're The One

CLARK, R. — Got My Mind Set On You

CLARK, RUDY — Everybody Plays The Fool; Good Lovin'; Shoop, Shoop Song

CLARK, STEVE — Photograph; Rock Of Ages

CLARK, WILLIE — Girls Can't Do What The Guys Do

CLARK, WILLY — Where Is The Love

CLARKE, ALLAN — Carrie-Anne; On A Carousel; Pay You Back With Interest; Stop, Stop, Stop

CLARKE, GRANT — Am I Blue?; Avalon Town; Blue(and Broken Hearted); Dirty Hands, Dirty Face; Everything Is Peaches Down In Georgia; I'm A Little Blackbird Looking For A Bluebird; I'm The Medicine Man For The Blues; In The Land Of Beginning Again; Ragtime Cowboy Joe; Second Hand Rose; Weary River

CLARKE, HAROLD — Long Cool Woman(In A Black Dress)

CLARKE, KENNY — Epistrophy; Salt Peanuts

CLARKE, TONY — Entertainer; Pushover

CLARKE, WILLIE — Clean Up Woman

CLARKSON, HARRY — Home(When Shadows Fall)

CLARKSON, JEFF — Home(When Shadows Fall)

CLASKY, RICHARD — Image Of A Girl

CLAYPOOL, EDWARD B. — Ragging The Scale

CLAYTON, ADAM — Into The Night

CLAYTON, BUCK — Red Bank Boogie

CLAYTON, PAUL — Gotta Travel On

CLEMENCEAU, MARTINE — Solitaire

CLEMENT, JACK H. — Ballad Of A Teenage Queen; Guess Things Happen That Way

CLEMENTS, ZEKE — Just A Little Lovin'(Will Go A Long Way)

CLESI, N. J. — I'm Sorry I Made You Cry

CLEVELAND, AL — Come Back Charleston Blue; Doggone Right; Here I Go Again; What's Going On

CLEVELAND, ALFRED — Baby, Baby, Don't Cry; I Second That Emotion; Special Occasion; Yester Love

CLIFF, JIMMY — Harder They Come; Wonderful World, Beautiful People; You Can Get It If You Really Want

CLIFFORD, GORDON — I Surrender, Dear; It Must Be True; Paradise

CLIMIE, SIMON — Invincible

CLINTON, GEORGE — Flash Light; I Wanna Testify; One Nation Under A Groove

CLINTON, LARRY — Dipsy Doodle; Dusk In Upper Sandusky; My Reverie; Our Love; Satan Takes A Holiday; Study In Brown

CLOWNEY, DAVID — Happy Organ; Rinky Dink

CLOWNS, HUEY SMITH & THE — Rockin' Pneumonia And The Boogie Woogie Flu

CLUB, CULTURE — Move Away

COATES, CARROLL — London By Night

COATES, ERIC — (By The)Sleepy Lagoon

COATES, J. B. — Sweetest Gift

COATES, MAURICE — Dry Your Eyes

COATES, PAUL — If The Moon Turns Green

COBB JR., JAMES B. — Traces

COBB, ARNETT — Smooth Sailing
COBB, ED — Dirty Water
COBB, GEORGE — Alabama Jubilee
COBB, J. R. — Do It Or Die
COBB, JAMES B. — Everyday With You Girl; I Take It Back; Stormy
COBB, MARGARET — Hey! Baby
COBB, WILL D. — Goodbye Dolly Gray; School Days; Sunbonnet Sue; Waltz Me Around Again Willie; Yip-I-Addy-I-Ay
COBEN, CY — Beware Of It; Lonely Little Robin; Old Piano Roll Blues; Sweet Violets
COBURN, RICHARD — Whispering
COCHRAN, DORCAS — Cincinnati Kid; Here; I Get Ideas; Under The Bridges Of Paris
COCHRAN, EDDIE — C'mon Everybody; Summertime Blues
COCHRAN, HANK — Funny Way Of Laughin'; I Fall To Pieces; I Want To Go With You; Little Bitty Tear; Make The World Go Away; She's Got You
COCHRAN, WAYNE — Last Kiss
CODY, P. — Doing It All For My Baby
CODY, PHIL — Bad Blood; Immigrant; Laughter In The Rain; Love In The Shadows; Should've Never Let You Go; Solitaire
COFFEY, DENNIS — Scorpio
COGANE, NELSON — We Three - My Echo, My Shadow And Me; Yesterday's Gardenias
COGGINS, DANNY — Pucker Up, Buttercup
COHAN, GEORGE M. — Billie; Forty Five Minutes From Broadway; Give My Regards To Broadway; Harrigan; Mary's A Grand Old Name; Nellie Kelly, I Love You; Over There; So Long Mary; Yankee Doodle Boy, I Am The; You Remind Me Of My Mother; You're A Grand Old Flag
COHEN, HENRY — Canadian Capers
COHEN, JEFFREY — Freeway Of Love
COHEN, JERRY — Ain't No Stopping Us Now
COHEN, LEONARD — Bird On The Wire
COHN, IRVING — Yes! We Have No Bananas
COLAHAN, ARTHUR — Galway Bay
COLBY, ROBERT — Jilted
COLCORD, LINCOLN — (Maine)Stein Song
COLE, GARDNER — Open Your Heart
COLE, NAT "KING" — Buon Natale(Means Merry Xmas To You); Calypso Blues; Straighten Up And Fly Right; With You On My Mind
COLE, NATALIE — Sophisticated Lady(She's A Different Lady)
COLE, ROBERT — Under The Bamboo Tree
COLEMAN, CY — Baby Dream Your Dream; Be A Performer; Best Is Yet To Come; Big Spender; Colors Of My Life; Deep Down Inside; Firefly; Give A Little Whistle; Gypsy In My Soul; Heartbreak Kid; Here's To Us; Hey, Look Me Over; I've Got Your Number; If My Friends Could See Me Now; It's Not Where You Start; Legacy; Little Me; Love Makes Such Fools Of Us All; On The Twentieth Century; Other Side Of The Tracks; Our Private World; Poor Little Hollywood Star; Real Live Girl; Rhythm Of Life; What Take My Fancy; Where Am I Going; Why Try To Change Me Now; Witchcraft
COLEMAN, DAVE — Backward, Turn Backward; String Along
COLEMAN, HARRY — Similau
COLEMAN, LARRY — Big Guitar; Changing Partners;

Just As Much As Ever; Pa-Paya Mama; Ricochet
COLEMAN, LONNIE — Boom Boom Boomerang
COLEMAN, ORNETTE — Lonely Woman
COLEMAN, RON — Tired Of Toein' The Line
COLEMAN, TONY — One Hundred Ways; One I Love
COLEY, JOHN FORD — Gone Too Far
COLL, EWAN MAC — First Time Ever I Saw Your Face
COLLA, JOHNNY — Heart Of Rock And Roll; If This Is It; Power Of Love
COLLEY, KEITH — Shame, Shame
COLLEY, LINDA — Shame, Shame
COLLINS, AARON — Eddie, My Love
COLLINS, ALBERT — Lucille; Slippin' And Slidin'
COLLINS, ALLEN — Free Bird
COLLINS, JUDY — Albatross; Born To The Breed
COLLINS, LARRY — Delta Dawn
COLLINS, P. — Tonight, Tonight, Tonight
COLLINS, PHIL — Don't Lose My Number; Easy Lover; Follow You, Follow Me; In The Air Tonight; In Too Deep; Invisible Touch; Land Of Confusion; Misunderstanding; One More Night; Sussudio; Throwing It All Away
COLLINS, RODGER — She's Lookin' Good
COLLINS, SUSAN — Sweet Life
COLLINS, TOMMY — Carolyn
COLLINS, WILLIAM — Flash Light
COLTER, JESSI — I'm Not Lisa
COLTRANE, CHI — Thunder And Lightning
COLUMBO, RUSS — I'm Yours To Command; Prisoner Of Love
COMAN, THOMAS — C'mon And Swim
COMANOR, JEFFREY — Never Have To Say Goodbye Again(We'll Never Have To Say Goodbye Again); We'll Never Have To Say Goodbye Again
COMDEN, BETTY — All You Need Is A Quarter; Asking For You; Be A Santa; Bells Are Ringing; Close Harmony; Come Up To My Place; Cry Like The Wind; Dance Only With Me; Distant Melody; Fade Out-Fade In; Fireworks; Five Zeros; French Lesson; Girls Like Me; Hold Me-Hold Me-Hold Me; How Can You Describe A Face?; I Can Cook Too; I Get Carried Away; I Know About Love; I Like Myself; I'm Just Taking My Time; I'm With You; Independent(On My Own); It's Love; Just In Time; Legacy; Little Bit In Love; Lonely Town; Long Before I Knew You; Looking Back; Lucky To Be Me; Make Someone Happy; Never-Never Land; New York, New York; Ohio; On The Twentieth Century; Our Private World; Party's Over; Quiet Girl; Ride Through The Night; Right Girl For Me; Say, Darling; Some Other Time; Wendy; What Is This Feeling In The Air?
CONATSER, C. — Reveille Rock
CONCINA, C. — River
CONFREY, EDWARD E. — Sittin' On A Log(Pettin' My Dog)
CONFREY, ZEZ — Dizzy Fingers; Kitten On The Keys; Stumbling
CONLEE, JOHN — Backside Of Thirty
CONLEY, ARTHUR — Funky Street; Sweet Soul Music
CONLEY, D. — Happy
CONLEY, LARRY — Cottage For Sale; Shanghai Shuffle
CONN, CHESTER — Don't Mind The Rain; Forgive My Heart; Night Lights; Outside Of Heaven; Sunday; Why Should I Cry Over You?; You Don't Like It—Not Much
CONNELLY, REG — By The Fireside; Goodnight

Sweetheart; If I Had You; Just An Echo In The Valley; Try A Little Tenderness; Underneath The Arches; When The Organ Played At Twilight (The Song That Reached My

CONNOLLY, BRIAN — Fox On The Run

CONNOLLY, PATRICK — Wipe Out

CONNOR, PIERRE NORMAN — When I Take My Sugar To Tea; You Brought A New Kind Of Love To Me

CONNOR, TOMMIE — Biggest Aspidastra In The World; I Saw Mommy Kissing Santa Claus; Lilli Marlene; Wedding Of Lilli Marlene

CONNORS, CAROL — Don't Ask To Stay Until Tomorrow; Gonna Fly Now(Theme From Rocky); With You I'm Born Again

CONNORS, MARSHAL HOWARD — Hey, Little Cobra

CONRAD, CON — Barney Google; Bend Down Sister; Big City Blues; Breakaway; Champagne Waltz; Continental; Crazy Feet; Don't Send Your Wife To The Country; Here's To Romance; Lonesome And Sorry; Ma!(He's Making Eyes At Me); Margie; Midnight In Paris; Palesteena; Singin' The Blues(Till My Daddy Come Home); You Call It Madness (Ah, But I Call It Love); You've Got To See Mamma Ev'ry Night Or You Can't See Mamma At All

CONRAD, JACK — Every Time I Think Of You; Isn't It Time

CONRAD, JACK S. — Family Of Man

CONTI, BILL — For Your Eyes Only; Gonna Fly Now(Theme From Rocky)

CONTI, CORRADO — To The Door Of The Sun (Alle Porte Del Sole)

COOK, BILL — You Can Have Her

COOK, JOE — Peanuts

COOK, L. C. — Win Your Love For Me

COOK, ROGER — Doctor's Orders; Here Comes That Rainy Day Feeling Again; I Was Kaiser Bill's Batman; I'd Like To Teach The World To Sing; Long Cool Woman(In A Black Dress); My Baby Loves Lovin'; You've Got Your Troubles

COOK, WILL — I'm Coming Virginia

COOKE, L. C. — You Send Me

COOKE, LESLIE — Love Sends A Little Gift Of Roses

COOKE, SAM — Another Saturday Night; Bring It On Home To Me; Cupid; Good News; Having A Party; Only Sixteen; Shake; Sugar Dumpling; Sweet Soul Music; Twistin' The Night Away

COOLER, W. — Catch Me(I'm Falling)

COOLEY, EDDIE — Fever

COOLIDGE, EDWINA — Along The Santa Fe Trail

COOPER, ALICE — Billion Dollar Babies; Eighteen; How You Gonna See Me Now; I Never Cry; Only Women(Bleed); School's Out; You And Me

COOPER, BUD — Red Hot Mamma

COOPER, COLIN — Couldn't Get It Right

COOPER, GARY — Let's Go All The Way

COOPER, GEORGE — Sweet Genevieve

COOPER, JOE — Dance-O-Mania

COOPER, JOEY — I'm A Fool

COOPER, JOHN — Do You Ever Think Of Me

COOPER, MARTIN J. — Peanut Butter

COOPER, MARTY — Run, Run, Look And See

COOPER, MICHAEL — Fun(1977)

COOPER, SARAH JANE — You Will Have To Pay For Your Yesterday

COOPER, STEVE — Time Is Tight

COOTS, J. FRED — Alabama Barbecue; Beautiful Lady In Blue,a; Cross Your Fingers; Doin' The Raccoon; Doin' The Suzi-Q; Encore, Cherie; For All We Know; Frisco Flo; I Still Get A Thrill(Thinking Of You); I Want To Ring Bells; I Wouldn't Trade The Silver In My Mother's Hair(for All The Gold In The World; Love Letters In The Sand; One Minute To One; Precious Little Thing Called Love; Santa Claus Is Coming To Town; Two Tickets To Georgia; Until Today; Why (Is There A Rainbow In The Sky)

COPAS, LLOYD — Alabam

COPELAND, ALLAN — Make Love To Me

COPELAND, GREG — Buy For Me The Rain

COQUATRIX, BRUNO — Comme Ci, Comme Ca; Count Every Star

COR, PETER — Getaway

CORBERT, ROBERT W. — Quentin's Theme

CORBETT, GARY — She Bop

CORBETTA, JERRY — Don't Call Us, We'll Call You; Green Eyed Lady

CORCORAN, TOM — Fins

CORDAY, LEO — Blue Flame; Leap Frog; Your Socks Don't Match

CORDELL, RITCHIE — Gettin' Together; Gimme, Gimme, Good Lovin'; I Like The Way; I Think We're Alone Now; Indian Giver; Mirage; Mony Mony; She

CORMIER, RAY — Hit And Run Affair

CORNELIUS, DON — Lovelight

CORNELIUS, EDDIE — Don't Ever Be Lonely(A Poor Little Fool Like Me); Too Late To Turn Back Now; Treat Her Like A Lady

CORNELIUS, HAROLD — Blossom Fell

CORNETT, ALICE — All That Glitters Is Not Gold

CORTEZ, QUIRINO MENDOZA Y — Cielito Lindo

CORY, GEORGE — Deep Song; I Left My Heart In San Francisco

COSBY, HENRY — Fingertips; I Was Made To Love Her; I'm Living In Shame; I'm Wondering; Little Ole Man(Uptight Everything's Alright); My Cherie Amour; No Matter What Sign You Are; Nothing's Too Good For My Baby; Shoo-Be-Foo-Be-Doo-Da-Day; Uptight (Everything's Alright)

COSLOW, SAM — Bebe; Beware My Heart; Black Moonlight; Blue Mirage; Cocktails For Two; Day You Came Along; Down The Old Ox Road; Ebony Rhapsody; Fifi; Good Mornin'; Hello! Swanee-Hello!; I Guess It Had To Be That Way; I'm Just Wild About Animal Crackers; If I Were King; In The Middle Of A Kiss; It's Raining Sunbeams; Je Vous Aime; Just One More Chance; Kind'a Lonesome; Learn To Croon; Little White Gardenia; Moon Song(That Wasn't Meant For Me); Moonstruck; My Old Flame; Sing You Sinners; Song Of The South; Tomorrow Night; True Blue Lou; True Confession; Turn Off The Moon; Was It A Dream

COSTA, DON — Because They're Young; I Can't Believe I'm Losing You; Miracle Worker, The(Theme)(Hush, Little Baby)

COSTELLO, BARTLEY — (alla En)el Rancho Grande

COSTELLO, ELVIS — Alison

COTTON, HAL — You Can't Be True Dear

COTTON, NORMAN — Heart Of The Night

COULTER, PHILIP — My Boy; Saturday Night

COUNTRY, BIG — In A Big Country

COURTNEY, ALAN — Joltin' Joe Di Maggio

COURTNEY, DAVID — Long Tall Glasses(I Can Dance); Show Must Go On

COURTNEY, LOU — Do The Freddie

COUTOURIE, W. — 19

COVAY, DON — Chain Of Fools; Lights Out; Pony Time; Seesaw

COVERDALE, DAVID — Is This Love

COVINGTON, JOEY — With Your Love

COWAN, JOEL — Cabaret; It's Like Takin' Candy From A Baby

COWAN, MARIE — Waltzing Matilda

COWAN, STANLEY — 'Til Reveille; Do I Worry?

COWARD, NOEL — Call Of Life; Dance, Little Lady; Dear Little Cafe; Dearest Love; Don't Let's Be Beastly To The Germans; Don't Take Our Charlie For The Army; Go Slow, Johnny; Go Tell It On The Mountain; Green Carnation; Half Caste Woman; Here And Now; I Went To A Marvelous Party; I'll Follow My Secret Heart; I'll Remember Her; I'll See You Again; I'm So Weary Of It All; I've Been Invited To A Party; If Love Were All; If You Could Only Come With Me; Ladies Of The Town; Later Than Spring; Let's Say Goodbye; London Bridge(Is Falling Down); London Pride; London(Is A Little Bit Of All Right); Lorelei; Mad About The Boy; Mad Dogs And Englishmen; Mary Make Believe; Matelot; Mirabelle; Mrs. Worthington(Don't Put Your Daughter On The Stage); Never Again; Nevermore; Parisian Pierrot; Party's Over Now; Play, Orchestra, Play; Poor Little Rich Girl; Room With A View; Sail Away; Someday I'll Find You; Tokay; Twentieth Century Blues; World Weary; You Were There; Zigeuner

COWELL, JOHN — Our Winter Love

COWELL, JOHNNY — Walk Hand In Hand

COX JR., ROY E. — Hot Smoke And Sassafras

COX, IDA — Western Union Blues

COX, JIMMIE — Nobody Knows You When You're Down And Out

CRAFER, ART — No Arms Can Ever Hold You(Like These Arms Of Mine)

CRAFT, MORTY AND THE WILLOWS — Church Bells May Ring

CRAIG, FRANCIS — Beg Your Pardon; Near You

CRAIG, MICHAEL — Church Of The Poison Mind; Do You Really Want To Hurt Me; I'll Tumble 4 Ya; Miss Me Blind; Time (Clock Of The Heart)

CRAIG, MICKEY — It's A Miracle; Karma Chameleon

CRAIN, TOMMY — Devil Went Down To Georgia

CRAMER, FLOYD — Last Date; On The Rebound

CRANDALL, BILL — Short Shorts

CRANE, JIMMY — Every Day Of My Life; Hurt; I Can't Get You Out Of My Heart(Ti Amo-ti Voglio Amor); I Need You Now; If I Give My Heart To You

CRANE, LOR — Don't Just Stand There(What's On Your Mind?); Say Something Funny; White On White

CRAWFORD, CLIFF — Chip Chip

CRAWFORD, ROBERT — Army Air Corps Song

CREAMER, HENRY — Dear Old Southland; If I Could Be With You One Hour Tonight; Walk, Jenny, Walk; Way Down Yonder In New Orleans

CREATORE, LUIGI — Bimbombey; Can't Help Falling In Love; Crazy Otto Rag; Experience Unnecessary; Let's Put It All Together; Oh, Oh, I'm Falling In Love Again; Wild In The Country

CREED, LINDA — Betcha By Golly, Wow; Break Up To Make Up; Greatest Love Of All; I'm Stone In Love With You; Rockin' Roll Baby; Rubberband Man; You Are Everything; You Make Me Feel Brand New

CREGAN, JIM — Passion

CREME, LOL — Cry

CRETCOS, JIMMY — Doesn't Somebody Want To Be Wanted

CREWE, BOB — Big Girls Don't Cry; Bye Bye Baby(Baby Goodbye); Can't Take My Eyes Off You; Get Dancin'; Girl Come Running; I Make A Fool Of Myself; I Wanna Dance Wit' Choo(Doo Dat Dance); I Wanna Dance With Somebody(Who Loves Me); La Dee Dah; Lady Marmalade; Let's Hang On(To What We've Got); Lucky Ladybug; My Eyes Adored You; Proud One; Rag Doll; Ronnie; Save It For Me; Silence Is Golden; Silhouettes; Sock It To Me, Baby; Swearin' To God; Walk Like A Man; You're Gonna Hurt Yourself

CRIER, KEITH — Disco Nights

CRISCUOLA, PETER — Beth

CROCE, JIM — Bad, Bad, Leroy Brown; I'll Have To Say I Love You In A Song; Time In A Bottle; You Don't Mess Around With Jim

CROFFORD, CLIFF — Old Rivers

CROFFORD, CLIFTON — Bar Room Buddies

CROFTS, DARRELL — Diamond Girl; Hummingbird; Summer Breeze; We May Never Pass This Way (Again)

CROFTS, DASH — Get Closer; I'll Play For You

CRONIN, KEVIN — Can't Fight This Feeling; Keep On Loving You; Keep The Fire Burnin'

CROOK, MAX — Runaway

CROPPER, STEVE — 634-5789; Fa-Fa-Fa-Fa-Fa(Sad Song); Green Onions; Happy Song(Dum Dum); In The Midnight Hour; Knock On Wood; Mr. Pitiful; Seesaw; Sittin' On The Dock Of The Bay; Soul-Limbo; You Don't Know What You Mean To Me

CROSBY, BING — (I Don't Stand A)Ghost Of A Chance With You; At Your Command; From Monday On; Love Me Tonight; Waltzing In A Dream; Where The Blue Of The Night Meets The Gold Of The Day

CROSBY, BOB — Big Noise From Winnetka; Boogie Woogie Maxixe

CROSBY, DAVID — Eight Miles High; Wooden Ships

CROSBY, ROBBIN — Round And Round

CROSS, CHRISTOPHER — All Right; Arthur's Theme; Sailing; Say You'll Be Mine

CROSS, DOUGLASS — Deep Song; I Left My Heart In San Francisco

CROSS, REUBEN — Shame

CROSS, TIM — Family Man

CROSSWELL, ANNE — All For You; I Go To Bed; I Know The Feeling; Only One

CROUCIER, JUAN — Body Talk

CROWELL, RODNEY — An American Dream; Shame On The Moon

CROWLEY, JOHN — Baby Come Back

CRUDUP, ARTHUR — My Baby Left Me

CRUMIT, FRANK — Gay Caballero,a

CRUTCHER, BETTY — Who's Making Love

CRUTCHFIELD, JAN — Dream On Little Dreamer

CUFFLEY, JOHN — Couldn't Get It Right

CUGAT, XAVIER — Illusion; My Shawl; Nightingale; One-Two-Three-Kick

CUMMINGS, BURTON — Clap For The Wolfman; Laughing; No Time; Rain Dance; Share The Land; Stand Tall

CUMMINGS, MARGERY — Last Call For Love

CUNLIFFE, DICK — Quien Sabe?(Who Knows?)

CUNNIGNHAM, JAMES — Jo-Ann
CUNNINGHAM, CARL — Soul Finger
CUNNINGHAM, JOHN — Jo-Ann
CUNNINGHAM, PAUL — (Shout! Wherever You May Be)I Am An American; From The Vine Came The Grape; Harriet
CUOMO, BILL — Oh, Sherrie
CURB, MIKE — All For The Love Of Sunshine; Blue's Theme
CURNIN, CY — One Thing Leads To Another
CURRIE, A. — King For A Day
CURRIE, ALANNAH — Doctor! Doctor!; Hold Me Now; Lay Your Hands On Me
CURRIE, JIMMY — (It Looks Like)I'll Never Fall In Love Again
CURTIS, EDDIE — Joker; You're Gonna Miss Me
CURTIS, EDDIE TEX — Song Of The Dreamer
CURTIS, ERNESTO DE — Come Back To Sorrento

CURTIS, KING — Memphis Soul Stew
CURTIS, LOYAL — Drifting And Dreaming
CURTIS, MANN — Anema E Core; Choo'n Gum; Didja Ever?; Fooled; I Like It, I Like It; Jones Boy; Let It Be Me; My Dreams Are Getting Better All The Time; Play Me Hearts And Flowers(I Wanna Cry); Story Of A Starry Night; Whole World Is Singing My Song
CURTIS, MEMPHIS — Lovey Dovey
CURTIS, MICHAEL — Southern Cross
CURTIS, RICHARD — Southern Cross
CURTIS, SONNY — Fool Never Learns; I Fought The Law; More Than I Can Say; Walk Right Back
CURTISS, JIMMY — Child Of Clay
CYMBAL, JOHNNY — Cinnamin; Mary In The Morning
CYMONE, A. — Looking For A New Love; Some Kind Of Lover;

D

D'ABO, MICHAEL — Build Me Up, Buttercup; Bumble Boogie

D'AMOUR, JODI — No Chemise, Please!

D'ARBY, T. T. — Wishing Well

D'ARTEGA, AL — In The Blue Of Evening

D'ERRICO, CARL — It's My Life

D'ESPOSITO, SALVE — Anema E Core

D'HARDELOT, GUY — Because

DABNEY, FORD — S-H-I-N-E

DACRE, HARRY — Daisy Bell

DACRES, DESMOND — Israelites

DAHLSTROM, PATTI — Emotion

DAIN, IRVING — Coca Cola Cowboy

DALE, JIM — Georgy Girl

DALE, JIMMY — Just Say I Love Her(Dicitencello Vuie)

DALEY, DAN — Still In Saigon

DALTON, BILL — Short Shorts

DAMATO, PETE — Just Ask Your Heart

DAMERELL, STANLEY — Lady Of Spain; Let's All Sing Like The Birdies Sing

DAMERELL, STANLEY J. — If; Unless

DAMERON, TAD — Good Bait

DAMERON, TADD — If You Could See Me Now

DAMON, RUSS — Cotton Candy

DANA, WALTER — Helen Pola; Longing For You

DANCE, LEO — My Time Is Your Time

DANIEL, ELIOT — Blue Shadows On The Trail; Casey At The Bat; Disco Lucy(I Love Lucy Theme); Lavender Blue(Dilly Dilly); Never; Uncle Remus Said

DANIEL, MARCUS — Slip Away

DANIELS, CHARLES N. — You Tell Me Your Dream Or I Had A Dream, Dear

DANIELS, CHARLIE — Devil Went Down To Georgia; South's Gonna Do It; Uneasy Rider

DANIELS, FRANK AND DOROTHY — My Heart Belongs To Only You

DANIELS, JACK — Turn Back The Hands Of Time

DANIELS, LEE — Dansero

DANKS, HART PEASE — Silver Threads Among The Gold

DANOFF, SID — Dance, Everyone Dance

DANVERS, CHARLES — Till

DANZIG, EVELYN — Scarlet Ribbons(For Her Hair)

DARBY, KEN — Back Street; Bus Stop Song; Casey At The Bat; How The West Was Won

DARIAN, FRED — Calypso Joe; Mr. Custer

DARIN, BOBBY — Come September; Dream Lover; Early In The Morning; Eighteen Yellow Roses; I'll Be There; If A Man Answers; Multiplication; Queen Of The Hop; Splish Splash; You're The Reason I'm Living

DARION, JOE — Changing Partners; Ho Ho Song; Impossible Dream; Ricochet

DARLING, DENVER — Choo Choo Ch' Boogie

DARLING, ERIC — Banana Boat Song, The(Day-O)

DARYLL, TED — Country Girl-City Man; She Cried

DASH, IRWIN — What Has Become Of Hinky Dinky Parlay Voo

DASH, JULIAN — Tuxedo Junction

DAUGHERTY, DEAN — I'm Not Gonna Let It Bother Me Tonight; Imaginary Lover

DAUGHERTY, DOC — I'm Confessin'(That I Love You)

DAUGHTRY, DEAN — So Into You

DAVENPORT, CHARLES — Mama Don't Allow No Easy Riders Here

DAVENPORT, CHARLES "COW COW" — Cow-Cow Blues

DAVENPORT, JOHN — Fever

DAVENPORT, PEMBROKE — My Restless Lover (Johnny Guitar)

DAVID, HAL — (They Long To Be)Close To You; Alfie; Always Something There To Remind Me; American Beauty Rose; Another Night; Any Old Time Of Day; Anyone Who Had A Heart; April Fools; Are You There(with Another Girl); Baby Elephant Walk; Bell Bottom Blues; Blue On Blue; Broken Hearted Melody; Casino Royale; Do You Know The Way To San Jose?; Don't Make Me Over; Fool Killer; Forever My Love; Four Winds And The Seven Seas; Green Grass Starts To Grow; Here I Am; House Is Not A Home; I Just Don't Know What To Do With Myself; I Say A Little Prayer; I'll Never Fall In Love Again; I'm A Better Man(For Having Loved You); It Was Almost Like A Song; Johnny Get Angry; Let Me Go To Him; Living Together, Growing Together; Long Ago Tomorrow; Look Of Love; Lost Horizon; Magic Moments; Make It Easy On Yourself; Man Who Shot Liberty Valance; Message To Michael; Moonraker; My Heart Is An Open Book; Odds And Ends(Of A Beautiful Love Affair); One Less Bell To Answer; Only Love Can Break A Heart; Paper Mache; Promises, Promises; Raindrops Keep Fallin' On My Head; Reach Out For Me; Send Me No Flowers; Story Of My Life; To All The Girls I've Loved Before; Trains And Boats And Planes; Twenty-Four Hours From Tulsa; Walk On By; What The World Needs Now Is Love; What's New Pussycat; Who Is Gonna Love Me?; Whoever You Are Or Sometimes Your Eyes Look Blue To Me; Windows Of The World; Wishin' And Hopin'; Wives And Lovers (Theme From); You'll Answer To Me; You'll Never Get To Heaven

DAVID, LEE — Tonight You Belong To Me

DAVID, LINK — Big Mamou

DAVID, MACK — 77 Sunset Strip; A Dream Is A Wish Your Heart Makes; Ali-Baba Chi-Baba(My Bambino Go To Sleep); At A Candlelight Cafe; Baby, It's You; Baby,baby,baby; Bachelor In Paradise; Ballad Of Cat Ballou; Bibbidi-Bobbidi-Boo(the Magic Song); Bimbombey; Bird Man; Blob; Blue And Sentimental; Bourbon Street Beat; Call Of The Far-Away Hills; Candy; Cherry Pink And Apple Blossom White; Cinderella; Diamond Head; Don't You Know I Care; Don't You Love Me Anymore?; Falling Leaves; Girl Named Tamiko,a; Hanging Tree; Hawaii; Hawaiian Eye; Hush Hush, Sweet Charlotte; I Don't Care If The Sun Don't Shine; I'm Just A Lucky So And So; It Must Be Him; It Only Hurts For A Little While; It's A Mad, Mad, Mad, Mad World; It's Love, Love, Love!; La Vie En Rose; Love Goddess; Moon Love; My Own True Love; On The Isle Of May; Singing Hills; Sinner Kissed An Angel; Sunflower; Surfside 6; Sweet Eloise; Very Merry Un-Birthday To You; Vie En Rose, La; Walk On The Wild Side; Young Emotions

DAVID, SUNNY — Love! Love! Love!; Whole Lot Of Shakin' Going On

DAVIDSON, LENNY — At The Scene; Catch Us If You Can

DAVIE, BOB — Green Door

DAVIES, BILL — Knock, Knock. Who's There?

DAVIES, HARRY PARR — Bluebird Of Happiness

DAVIES, IDRIS — Bells Of Rhymney

DAVIES, RAY — All Day And All Of The Night; Come Dancing; Dandy; Dedicated Follower Of Fashion; Lola; Rock And Roll Fantasy; Set Me Free; Sunny Afternoon; Well Respected Man; Who'll Be The Next In Line?; You Really Got Me

DAVIES, RICHARD — Give A Little Bit; Goodbye Stranger; Logical Song

DAVIES, RICK — It's Raining Again

DAVIES, ROGER — Dreamer

DAVIES, ROY — Tired Of Waiting For You

DAVIS, BENNY — Alabama Barbecue; All I Need Is You; Baby Face; Carolina Moon; Chasing Shadows; Cross Your Fingers; Doin' The Suzi-Q; Don't Break The Heart That Loves You; Everything's Gonna Be All Right; Follow The Boys; Frisco Flo; Good-bye Broadway, Hello France; I Still Get A Thrill(Thinking Of You); I'm Nobody's Baby; Indiana Moon; Lonesome And Sorry; Margie; Oh, How I Miss You Tonight; Until Today; Who Wouldn't Be Blue?; Whose Heart Are You Breaking Tonight?; Why (Is There A Rainbow In The Sky); With These Hands; Yearning (Just For You)

DAVIS, BERNICE — Long Lonely Nights

DAVIS, BILLY — Who's Cheating Who?

DAVIS, CARL — Love Makes A Woman; Matador

DAVIS, CHARLIE — Copenhagen

DAVIS, CLIFTON — Lookin' Through The Windows; Never Can Say Goodbye

DAVIS, DON — Disco Lady; I Believe In You(You Believe In Me); Who's Making Love

DAVIS, HAL — Dancing Machine; I'll Be There

DAVIS, HENRY C. — Marine's Hymn(From The Halls Of Montezuma To The Shores Of Tripoli)

DAVIS, HERMAN — Groovy Situation

DAVIS, JAY — Baby Jane

DAVIS, JIMMIE — Nobody's Darlin' But Mine; You Are My Sunshine

DAVIS, JIMMY — Lover Man(Oh, Where Can You Be?)

DAVIS, JOE — Milkmen's Matinee; Perhaps, Perhaps, Perhaps(Quizas, Quizas, Quizas)

DAVIS, KATHERINE — Little Drummer Boy

DAVIS, LOU — Hot Lips; Precious Little Thing Called Love; The Album Of My Dreams

DAVIS, LOUIS — Convoy

DAVIS, MAC — Baby Don't Get Hooked On Me; I Believe In Music; In The Ghetto(The Vicious Circle); One Hell Of A Woman; Something's Burning; Stop And Smell The Roses; Watchin' Scotty Grow

DAVIS, MACK — Moon Love

DAVIS, MARTHA — Only The Lonely; Suddenly Last Summer

DAVIS, MAXWELL — Eddie, My Love

DAVIS, PAUL — Cool Night; Do Right; I Go Crazy; Ride 'em Cowboy; Sixty Five Love Affair; Sweet Life

DAVIS, ROQUEL — I'd Like To Teach The World To Sing; Pushover; See-Saw

DAVIS, SCOTT — Clean Up Your Own Back Yard; Don't Cry Daddy; Memories

DAVIS, SHEILA — Who Will Answer

DAVIS, SHERIFF TEX — Be-Bop-A-Lula

DAVIS, SPENCER — Gimme Some Lovin'

DAVIS, WARREN — Book Of Love; Boola Boola

DAVIS, WILLIAM — Gee!

DAWES, CHARLES GATES — It's All In The Game

DAY, BOBBY — Give Us This Day

DAY, JOEY — Beg, Borrow And Steal

DAY, MIKE — Little Willy

DAY, MORRIS — Jungle Love

DE ANGELIS, PETE — With All My Heart

DE LANGE, EDDIE — Who Threw The Whiskey In The Well?

DE LANGE, EDGAR — Velvet Moon

DE PAUL, GENE — What's Good For General Bullmoose; When You're In Love; You Can't Run Away From It; Your Red Wagon

DE ROSE, PETER — Twenty-Four Hours Of Sunshine; Wagon Wheels; When Your Hair Has Turned To Silver I Will Love You Just The Same

DE SYLVA, B. G. — Turn On The Heat; Turn Out The Light; Varsity Drag; Virginia; What D'ya Say?; When Day Is Done; Where Is The Man Of My Dreams?; Why Can't You (Birdies Sing In Cages Too); Why Do I Love You; Wishing (Will Make It So); Without Love; Yankee Doodle Blues; Yoo-Hoo; You Ain't Heard Nothin' Yet; You Try Somebody Else, And I'll Try Somebody Else; You Wouldn't Fool Me, Would You?; You're An Old Smoothie; You're The Cream In My Coffee

DEACON, JOHN — You're My Best Friend

DEAN, DEAREST — One Has My Name. . . The Other Has My Heart

DEAN, EDDIE — I Dreamed Of A Hillbilly Heaven; One Has My Name. . . The Other Has My Heart

DEAN, JAMES — I've Passed This Way Before; What Becomes Of The Broken Hearted?; You Don't Have To Be A Star (To Star In My Show)

DEAN, JIMMY — Big Bad John; Dear Ivan; Little Black Book

DEAN, MARY — Half-Breed

DEAN, PAUL — Heaven In Your Eyes; Hot Girls In Love

DEANE, EDDIE V. — Men In My Little Girl's Life; Rock-A-Billy

DEANGELIS, PETE — Why

DEBARGE, ELDRA — All This Love

DEBUSSY, CLAUDE — Clair De Lune; Girl With The Flaxen Hair; Golliwog's Cake Walk

DECARLO, G. — Kiss Him Goodbye

DECARLO, GARY — Na Na, Hey, Hey, Kiss Him Goodbye

DECKER, C. — Heart And Soul

DEE, JOEY — Peppermint Twist

DEE, LENNY — Plantation Boogie

DEE, SYLVIA — Chickery Chick; End Of The World; House With Love In It,a; Laroo, Laroo, Lilli Bolero; Too Young; Who Do You Think You Are

DEES, BILL — Goodnight; It's Over; Oh Pretty Woman; Ride Away

DEES, RICK — Disco Duck(part 1)

DEES, SAM — One In A Million You

DEHR, RICHARD — Green Fields; Love Is A Golden Ring; Marianne; Memories Are Made Of This

DELANEY, TOM — Follow The Deal On Down; Jazz Me Blues

DELETTRE, JEAN — Hands Across The Table

DELIBES, LEO — Waltz Coppelia

DELMORE, ALTON — Beautiful Brown Eyes

DELORME, GAYE — Earache My Eye

DELORY, AL — Mr. Custer

DELP, B. — Can'tcha Say(You Believe In Me)

DEMARTINI, WARREN — Body Talk; Round And Round

DEMETRIUS, CLAUDE — Ain't That Just Like A

Woman

DEMEY, TETOS — You, You, You Are The One

DENICOLA, J. — Hungry Eyes; Time Of My Life

DENNIKER, PAUL — Beside An Open Fireplace; Milkmen's Matinee; S'posin'

DENNIS, MATT — Angel Eyes; Everything Happens To Me; Lets Get Away From It All; Little Man With A Candy Cigar; Night We Called It A Day; Who's Yehoodi; Will You Still Be Mine?

DENNSON, WILLIE — Momma Said(Mama Said)

DENSMORE, JOHN — Hello, I Love You; Love Her Madly; Love Me Two Times; People Are Strange; Riders On The Storm; Roadhouse Blues; Touch Me; Wishful, Sinful

DENSON, WILLIE — Backstage

DENTON, JIMMY — Black Slacks

DENVER, JOHN — Annie's Song; Back Home Again; Calypso; Fly Away; I'm Sorry; Leaving On A Jet Plane; Like A Sad Song; Looking For Space; My Sweet Lady; Perhaps Love; Rocky Mountain High; Sunshine On My Shoulders; Sweet Surrender

DENZA, LUIGI — Funiculi-Funicula

DEODATO, EUMIR — Get Down On It

DEPASSE, SUZANNE — Here Comes The Judge

DEPAUL, GENE — You Don't Know What Love Is

DERMER, LARRY — Bad Boy

DEROSIER, MICHAEL — Barracuda

DEROUGE, C. — Power Of Love

DERRINGER, RICK — Rock And Roll Hootchie Koo

DESBARRES, MICHAEL — Obsession

DESHANNON, JACKIE — Bette Davis Eyes; Breakaway; Come And Stay With Me; Dum Dum; Heart In Hand; Put A Little Love In Your Heart

DESPENZA, BARRY — Can I Change My Mind?

DEUTSCH, EMERY — Play, Fiddle, Play; When A Gypsy Makes His Violin Cry

DEUTSCH, HELEN — Hi-Lili, Hi-lo

DEVANEY, YVONNE — Million And One

DEVITA, A. — Softly, As I Leave You

DEVORZON, BARRY — Bless The Beasts And Children; Dreamin'; Nadia's Theme(The Young And The Restless)

DEWALT, AUTRY — Hip City, Part 2; Shake And Fingerpop; Shotgun

DEWEY, NICHOLAS — Runaway

DEWITT, LEWIS — Flowers On The Wall

DEXTER, AL — Pistol Packin' Mama; Wine, Women And Song

DEXTER, JOHNNY — Heaven In Your Eyes

DEY, RICHARD — Just Like Me

DEYOUNG, DENNIS — Babe; Best Of Times

DI LAZZARO, ELDO — Woodpecker Song

DIAMOND, GREGG — More, More, More(part 1)

DIAMOND, KEITH — Caribbean Queen; Mystery Lady; Suddenly

DIAMOND, LEO — Off Shore

DIAMOND, MAX — My Boomerang Won't Come Back

DIAMOND, NEIL — America; Be; Brooklyn Roads; Brother Love's Travelling Salvation Show; Cherry, Cherry; Cracklin' Rosie; Desiree; Forever In Blue Jeans; Girl You'll Be A Woman Soon; Glory Road; Hello Again; Holly Holy; I Am. . . I Said; I Got The Feelin'(Oh No, No); I'm A Believer; I've Been This Way Before; I've Been Working On The Railroad; If You Know What I Mean; Kentucky Woman; Little Bit Me, A Little Bit You; Longfellow Serenade; Love On The

Rocks; Play Me; September Morn; Shilo; Solitary Man; Song Sung Blue; Stones; Sunday And Me; Sunday For Tea; Sweet Caroline; Walk On Water; You Don't Bring Me Flowers

DIAMOND, STEVE — I've Got A Rock And Roll Heart

DICK, DOROTHY — Call Me Darling(Call Me Sweetheart, Call Me Dear)

DICKERSON, DENNIS — Me And Baby Brother

DICKERSON, DUB — Stood Up

DICKERSON, MORRIS — Cisco Kid; L. A. Sunshine; Low Rider; Slipping Into Darkness; Spill The Wine; Summer; World Is A Ghetto

DICKERSON, MORRIS D. — Why Can't We Be Friends

DICKERSON, RONNIE — Gypsy Man

DICOLA, VINCE — Far From Over

DIETZ, HOWARD — All The King's Horses; Alone Together; Before I Kiss The World Goodbye; Born Again; By Myself; Confession; Dancing In The Dark; Dickey-bird Song; Farewell, My Lovely; Feelin' High; For The First Time; Got A Bran' New Daddy; Got A Bran' New Suit; Haunted Heart; High And Low(I've Been Looking For You); Hoops; Hottentate Potentate; I Guess I'll Have To Change My Plan(the Blue Pajama Song); I Love Louisa; I See Your Face Before Me; I Still Look At You That Way; I've Got A One Track Mind; If There Is Someone Lovelier Than You"; Louisiana Hayride; Love I Long For; Love Is A Dancing Thing; Lucky Seven; Magic Moment; Moanin' Low; Moment I Saw You; New Sun In The Sky; On The Old Park Bench; Rainy Day; Shine On Your Shoes; Smokin' Reefers; Something To Remember You By; You And The Night And The Music; You Have Everything

DIEVAL, JACQUES — Way Of Love

DIFRANCO, PAUL — Life Is A Rock(But The Radio Rolled Me)

DIGREGORIO, TAZ — Devil Went Down To Georgia

DILL, DANNY — Detroit City

DILLON, JOHN — If You Wanna Get To Heaven

DIMIRCO, VINCENT — Up The Ladder To The Roof

DINICU, GRIGORAS — Hora Staccato

DINIZIO, PAT — Blood And Roses

DINO, RALPH — Do What You Do

DIPAOLA, ALFRED — Lonely Teenager

DISCANT, MACK — Summer Place, A(Theme From)

DITCHAM, MARTIN — Sweetest Taboo

DITOMASO, LARRY — Do What You Do

DIXON, CLIFF — Where The Blues Were Born In New Orleans

DIXON, DAVE — I Dig Rock And Roll Music

DIXON, EUGENE — Duke Of Earl; Soul Hootenanny

DIXON, HEATHER — Mr. Lee

DIXON, JULIUS — Dim, Dim The Lights; Lollipop

DIXON, LUTHER — Angel Smile; Big Boss Man; Boys; Hundred Pounds Of Clay; I Don't Want To Cry No More; I Love You 1000 Times; Momma Said(Mama Said); Sixteen Candles; Soldier Boy; Soul Serenade; Why Baby Why; With This Ring

DIXON, MORT — Bam, Bam Bamy Shore; Bye Bye Blackbird; Fare Thee Well Annabelle; Flirtation Walk; Follow The Swallow; I Found A Million Dollar Baby(in A Five And Ten Cent Store); I See Two Lovers; I'll Take Care Of Your Cares; I'm Looking Over A Four Leaf Clover; If I Had A Girl Like You; Just Like A Butterfly That's Caught In The Rain; Lady In Red; Marching Along Together; Mr. And Mrs.

Is The Name; Nagasaki; Ooh That Kiss; River Stay 'way From My Door; Torch Song; Would You Like To Take A Walk; You're My Everything
DIXON, WILLIE — Doncha' Think It's Time; Little Red Rooster; Seventh Son
DOBBINS, G. — Mashed Potato Time
DOBBINS, SHELLEY — Non Dimenticar
DODD, BONNIE — You Will Have To Pay For Your Yesterday
DODD, DOROTHY — Granada
DODGE, GILBERT — Peggy O'neil
DODRIDGE, PHILLIP — How Dry I Am
DODSON, RICHARD — Sweet City Woman
DOERGE, CRAIG — Cried Like A Baby
DOGGETT, BILL — Honky Tonk
DOHERTY, DENNIS — I Saw Her Again Last Night
DOLAN, BOBBY — Little By Little
DOLAN, ROBERT EMMETT — And So To Bed; Big Movie Show In The Sky
DOLBY, THOMAS — She Blinded Me With Science
DOLLISON, MAURICE — Jealous Kind Of Fellow
DOLPH, NORMAN — Life Is A Rock(But The Radio Rolled Me)
DOMINGUEZ, ALBERTO — Frenesi; Perfidia
DOMINO, ANTIONE "FATS" — Valley Of Tears; Whole Lot Of Loving
DOMINO, ANTOINE "FATS" — Ain't That A Shame; Blue Monday; Bo Weevil; Don't Come Knockin'; Fat Man, The(195); I Want To Walk You Home; I'm Gonna Be A Wheel Someday; I'm In Love Again; I'm Ready; I'm Walkin'; It's You I Love; Let The Four Winds Blow; My Girl Josephine; Poor Me; Three Nights A Week; Walking To New Orleans; Whole Lotta Loving
DONAGGIO, P. — You Don't Have To Say You Love Me
DONAHUE, AL — Do You Wanna Jump, Children?
DONALDSON, WALTER — At Sundown; Beside A Babbling Brook; Carolina In The Morning; Clouds; Come West, Little Girl, Come West; Could Be; Cuckoo In The Clock; Daughter Of Rosie O'grady; Did I Remember?; Down South; Earful Of Music, An; Feelin' High; Give Me My Mammy; Hello! Beautiful!; Horse With The Dreamy Eyes; How Ya Gonna Keep 'em Down On The Farm; I Wonder Where My Baby Is Tonight; I'm Bringing A Red, Red Rose; I'm With You!; It's Been So Long; Just Like A Melody Out Of The Sky; Kansas City Kitty; Little White Lies; Love Me Or Leave Me; Makin' Whoopee; Mister Meadowlark; My Baby Just Cares For Me; My Best Girl; My Blue Heaven; My Buddy; My Mammy; My Mom; Nevada; On Behalf Of The Visiting Firemen; Romance; Sam, The Old Accordion Man; Sweet Jennie Lee; When My Ship Comes In; Where'd You Get Those Eyes?; Yes Sir, That's My Baby; You (Gee But You're Wonderful); You're Driving Me Crazy (What Did I Do); You've Got Everything
DONEGAN, LONNIE — (It Looks Like)I'll Never Fall In Love Again; Rock Island Line
DONIDA, CARLO — Al Di La; Help Yourself; I Who Have Nothing
DONNA, JAMES J. — Liar, Liar
DONNELLY, DOROTHY — Deep In My Heart, Dear; Drinking Song; Golden Days; Just We Two; Mother; Serenade; Song Of Love; Your Land And My Land
DONOVAN, R. MICHAEL — Hurts So Good
DONOVAN, WALTER — Down By The Winegar Woiks;

One Dozen Roses; One I Love
DORE, CHAIRMAN — Pilot Of The Airwaves
DORE, CHARLENE — Strut
DORFF, STEPHEN — Bar Room Buddies; Every Which Way But Loose; Hoppy, Gene, And Me; I Just Fall In Love Again
DORFF, STEVEN — As Long As We Got Each Other; Coca Cola Cowboy
DORIS, JIM — Oh Me Oh My(I'm A Fool For You, Baby)
DORMAN, HAROLD — Mountain Of Love
DOROSCHUK, IVAN — Safety Dance
DOROUGH, BOB — Comin' Back Baby
DORSET, RAY — In The Summertime
DORSEY, JIMMY — Contrasts; Dusk In Upper Sandusky; I'm Glad There Is You; It's The Dreamer In Me; John Silver; Oodles Of Noodles
DORSEY, LEE — Ya-Ya
DOUGALL, BERNARD — I'll Be Hard To Handle
DOUGHERTY, DAN — Glad Rag Doll
DOUGHTY, NEAL — One Lonely Night
DOUGLAS, CARL — Kung Fu Fighting; Kyrie
DOUGLAS, GEORGE — What A Wonderful World
DOUGLAS, GREG — Jungle Love
DOUGLAS, LEW — Almost Always; Have You Heard; Pretend; Why Don't You Believe Me
DOUGLAS, WILLIAM — Annie Laurie
DOWE, B. — Rivers Of Babylon
DOWELL, SAXIE — Playmates; Three Little Fishies
DOWLING, EDDIE — Half A Moon
DOWNES, GEOFFREY — Don't Cry; Only Time Will Tell
DOWNEY, MORTON — Wabash Moon
DOWNS, GEOFFREY — Video Killed The Radio Star
DOYLE, WALTER — Egyptian Ella
DOZIER, LAMONT — (Come 'round Here)I'm The One You Need; (I'm A)Road Runner; 7 Rooms Of Gloom; Baby Love; Baby, I Need Your Loving; Back In My Arms Again; Bernadette; Can I Get A Witness; Come And Get Those Memories; Come See About Me; Forever Came Today; Happening; Heat Wave; Heaven Must Have Sent You; How Sweet It Is(To Be Loved By You); I Can't Help Myself(Sugar Pie, Honey Bunch); I Hear A Symphony; I'm Ready For Love; In And Out Of Love; It's The Same Old Song; Jimmy Mack; Little Darling(I Need You); Love Is Here And Now You're Gone; Love Is Like An Itching In My Heart; Mickey's Monkey; My World Is Empty Without You; Nothing But Heartaches; Nowhere To Run; One, Two, Three(1-2-3); Quicksand; Reach Out I'll Be There; Reflections; Shake Me, Wake Me(When It's Over); Something About You; Standing In The Shadows Of Love; Stop! In The Name Of Love; Where Did Our Love Go; You Can't Hurry Love; You Keep Me Hangin' On; You Keep Running Away; You're A Wonderful One; Your Unchanging Love
DRAKE, CHARLIE — My Boomerang Won't Come Back
DRAKE, ERVIN — Al Di La; Beloved, Be Faithful; Castle Rock; Come To The Mardi Gras; Friendliest Thing, The(Two People Can Do); Good Morning Heartache; Hayfoot-Strawfoot; I Believe; I Wuv A Wabbit; It Was A Very Good Year; Maybe Some Other Time; Meet Mister Callaghan; My Home Town; New Pair Of Shoes; Perdido; Room Without Windows; Some Days Everything Goes Wrong; Something To Live For; Sonata; Tico Tico
DRAKE, JIMMY — Transfusion
DRAKE, MILTON — Champagne Waltz; Fuzzy Wuzzy;

Hotta Chocolotta; I'm A Big Girl Now; Java Jive; Kiss Me Sweet; Mairzy Doats; Nina Never Knew

DRAPER, TERRY — Calling Occupants Of Interplanetary Craft

DRAYTON, VICTOR — Don't Let The Green Grass Fool You

DREJA, CRIS — Over Under Sideways Down

DRESSER, PAUL — My Gal Sal

DREYER, DAVE — Back In Your Own Backyard; Cecilia; Me And My Shadow; Wabash Moon; Year From Today

DRIFTWOOD, JIMMY — Battle Of Kookamonga; Battle Of New Orleans

DRIGGS, CARLOS — Get Off

DRIGO, RICCARDO — Serenade

DRUMMOND, NEIL — Blues In Advance

DUBEY, MATT — Game Of Love; Mutual Admiration Society; New Fangled Tango

DUBIN, AL — Along The Santa Fe Trail; Am I In Love?; Anniversary Waltz,the; Boulevard Of Broken Dreams; Clear Out Of This World; Coffee In The Morning(and Kisses In The Night); Confidentially; Crazy As A Loon; Crooning; Crosby, Columbo, And Vallee; Cup Of Coffee, A Sandwich And You; Dames; Dancing With Tears In My Eyes; Don't Give Up The Ship; Don't Say Goodnight; Fair And Warmer; Feudin' And Fightin'; For You; Forty-Second Street; Garden Of The Moon; Girl At The Ironing Board; Girl Friend Of The Whirling Dervish,the; Go Into Your Dance; Goin' To Heaven On A Mule; Good Old Fashioned Cocktail, A(With A Good Old Fashioned Girl); Honeymoon Hotel; How Could You?; I Know Now; I Never Felt This Way Before; I Only Have Eyes For You; I Wanna Go Back To Bali; I'd Rather Listen To Your Eyes; I'll Sing You A Thousand Love Songs; I'll String Along With You; I've Got To Sing A Torch Song; If I'm Dreaming, Don't Wake Me Too Soon; Indian Summer; Just A Girl That Men Forget; Keep Young And Beautiful; Kiss Waltz; Latin Tune, A Manhattan Moon And You; Little Things You Used To Do; Lonesomest Girl In Town; Love Is Where You Find It; Lullaby Of Broadway; Lulu's Back In Town; Muchacha; No More Love; Page Miss Glory; Painting The Clouds With Sunshine; Remember Me; Remember My Forgotten Man; September In The Rain; Shadow Waltz; Shanghai Lil; She's A Latin From Manhattan; Shuffle Off To Buffalo; South American Way; Three's A Crowd; Tip Toe Through The Tulips; Too Many Tears; We Mustn't Say Goodbye; We're In The Money Or The Gold Digger Song; What Has Become Of Hinky Dinky Parlay Voo; Where Am I? (Am I In Heaven?); Where Was I?; Why Do I Dream Those Dreams; With Plenty Of Money And You; Wonder Bar; Words Are In My Heart; You Let Me Down; You're Getting To Be A Habit With Me; Young And Healthy

DUBOFF, STEVE — Rain, The Park, And Other Things

DUBOIS, JA'NET — Movin' On Up

DUBOIS, JAMES — Love In The First Degree

DUCHIN, EDDY — My Twilight Dream

DUCKWORTH, WILLIE LEE — Sound Off

DUDDY, LYN — Johhny Angel

DUKAS, PAUL — Sorcerer's Apprentice

DUKE, BILLY — I Cried

DUKE, GEORGE — Sweet Baby

DUKE, M. — Doing It All For My Baby

DUKE, VERNON — April In Paris; Autumn In New York; Cabin In The Sky; Do What You Wanna Do; Got A Bran' New Daddy; He Hasn't A Thing Except Me; Honey In The Honeycomb; I Am Only Human After All; I Can't Get Started With You; I Like The Likes Of You; I've Got A One Track Mind; Island In The West Indies; Just Like A Man; Love I Long For; Love Me Tomorrow(But Leave Me Alone Today); Round About; Savannah; Spring Again; Suddenly; We're Having A Baby; What Is There To Say; Words Without Music; Work Song

DUMONT, CHARLES — I've Been Here!

DUNAWAY, DENNIS — Eighteen

DUNBAR, RONALD — Band Of Gold; Mind, Body And Soul; Patches(I'm Depending On You); Pay To The Piper; She's Not Just Another Woman; You've Got Me Dangling On A String

DUNCAN, JIMMY — My Special Angel

DUNCAN, MALCOLM — Cut The Cake; Pick Up The Pieces

DUNCAN, ROSETTA — Rememb'ring

DUNCAN, VIVIAN — Rememb'ring

DUNCAN, WAYNE — Wasted Days Wasted Nights

DUNCAN, WILLIAM CARY — My Toreador(El Relicario)

DUNDAS, DAVID — Jeans On

DUNHAM, "BY" — If You're Ever Down In Texas(Look Me Up)

DUNHAM, KAYE — Black Betty

DUNING, GEORGE — Picnic(Theme)

DUNLAP, LOUIS — You Can Depend On Me

DUNN, ARTIE — Twilight Time

DUNN, CHRIS — Sexy Eyes

DUNN, DONALD V. — Soul-Limbo; Time Is Tight

DUNN, LARRY — Shining Star

DUPONT, PAUL — La Rosita; Rosita, La

DUPREE, HARRY — Lisbon Antigua(In Old Lisbon)

DUPUIS, ROBBIE — Steal Away

DURAN, BOB — Don't Talk To Strangers

DURAN, DURAN — Hungry Like The Wolf; Is There Something I Should Know; New Moon On Monday; Reflex; Rio; Save A Prayer; Union Of The Snake; View To A Kill; Wild Boys

DURAND, ROBERT — Just A Little

DURANG, PAUL — Mademoiselle De Paree

DURANTE, JIMMY — Can Broadway Do Without Me?; I Ups To Him And He Ups To Me; I'm Jimmy The Well Dressed Man; Inka Dinka Doo

DURDEN, TOMMY — Heartbreak Hotel

DURHAM, ED — Don't You Miss Your Baby; Don't You Want Me; Good Morning Blues; John's Idea; Sent For You Yesterday(And Here You Come Today); Swingin' The Blues

DURHAM, EDDIE — Every Tub; I Don't Want To Set The World On Fire

DURRILL, JOHN — Dark Lady; I See The Light; Western Union; Zip Code

DURSO, MICHAEL — Petticoats Of Portugal

DUSHAM, BEV — City Of Angels

DVORAK, ANTON — Humoresque; Songs My Mother Taught Me

DYER, DESMOND — Sky High; Who Do You Know In Heaven (That Made You The Angel You Are?)

DYKES, JOHN BACCHUS — Lead, Kindly Light

DYLAN, BOB — All Along The Watchtower; All I Really Want To Do; As I Went Out One Morning; Baby, You Been On My Mind; Ballad In Plain D; Ballad Of A

Thin Man; Ballad Of Frankie Lee & Judas Priest; Ballad Of Hollis Brown; Band Of The Hand; Black Crow Blues; Blowin' In The Wind; Boots Of Spanish Leather; Can You Please Crawl Out Your Window?; Chimes Of Freedom; Country Pie; Day Of The Locusts; Dear Landlord; Desolation Row; Don't Think Twice,it's All Right; Down Along The Cove; Down In The Flood; Down In The Valley; Drifter's Escape; Farewell; Farewell, Angelina; Forever Young; Fourth Time Around; From A Buick 6; Gates Of Eden; George Jackson; Girl From The North Country; Gotta Serve Somebody; Hard Rain's A-Gonna Fall; Highway 61 Revisited; Hurricane(part 1); I Am A Lonesome Hobo; I Don't Believe You(She Acts Like We Never Have Met); I Don't Want To Do It; I Dreamed I Saw St. Augustine; I Pity The Poor Immigrant; I Threw It All Away; I Want You; I'll Be Your Baby Tonight; I'll Keep It With Mine; Idiot Wind; If Not For You; It Ain't Me, Babe; It Takes A Lot To Laugh, It Takes A Train To Cry; It's All Over Now, Baby Blue; It's Alright, Ma(I'm Only Bleeding); Jammin' Me; Joey; John Wesley Harding; Just Like A Woman; Just Like Tom Thumb's Blues; Knockin'
On Heaven's Door; Lay Down Your Weary Tune; Lay, Lady, Lay; Lenny Bruce; Like A Rolling Stone; Living The Blues; Lonesome Death Of Hattie Carroll; Love Is Just A Four Letter Word; Love Minus Zero/no Limit; Maggie's Farm; Masters Of War; Mighty Quinn; Million Dollar Bash; Most Likely You Go Your Way; Motorpsycho Nightmare; Mozambique; Mr. Tambourine Man; My Back Pages; Nashville Skyline Rag; New Morning; Nothing Was Delivered; Obviously Five Believers; On A Night Like This; On The Road Again; One More Night; One Of Us Must Know; Only A Pawn In Their Game; Outlaw Blues; Peggy Day; Percy's Song; Playboys And Playgirls; Pledging My Time; Positively 4th Street; Precious Angel; Queen Jane Approximately; Rainy Day Women No. 12 & 35; Sad Eyed Lady Of The Lowlands; Sara; She Belongs To Me; Shelter From The Storm; Sign On The Window; Simple Twist Of Fate; Spanish Harlem Incident; Stuck Inside Of Mobile With The Memphis Blues Again; Subterranean Homesick Blues; Watching The River Flow; Wicked Messenger; Wigwam

DYRENFORTH, JAMES — Garden In The Rain,a

EAGER, EDWARD — Goodbye, John

EARL, MARY — Beautiful Ohio

EARL, RAYMOND — I Got My Mind Made Up

EAST, NATHAN — Easy Lover

EASTMOND, BARRY — Love Is Forever; Love Zone

EASTON, LYNN — Jolly Green Giant

EASTWOOD, BARRY — When The Going Gets Tough, The Tough Get Going

EATON, JIMMY — Cry, Baby, Cry; Dance With A Dolly(with A Hole In Her Stocking); I Double Dare You; I'm Gonna Lock My Heart(and Throw Away The Key); Penguin At The Waldorf; Turn Back The Hand Of Time

EBB, FRED — All The Children In A Row; And All That Jazz; Apple Doesn't Fall,the; Cabaret; Colored Lights; Grass Is Always Greener; Gypsy In My Soul; How Lucky Can You Get; I Don't Care Much; If You Could See Her(The Gorilla Song); It's The Strangest Thing; Kiss Me Another; Little Blue Man; Lucky Lady; Married(Heiraten); Maybe This Time; Meeskite; Mein Herr; Money Song, The(Money, Money); My Coloring Book; My Own Best Friend; My Own Space; New York, New York(Theme From); One Of The Boys; Shine It On; Two Ladies; Wilkommen

EBERHART, NELLE RICHMOND — At Dawning; From The Land Of The Sky Blue Water

ECHOLS, ODIS — Sugartime

EDDY, DUANE — Bonnie Came Back; Boss Guitar; Cannon Ball; Forty Miles Of Bad Roads; Lonely One; Rebel-Rouser

EDDY, GEORGE — Writing On The Wall

EDELMAN, RANDY — Weekend In New England

EDENS, ROGER — French Lesson; In-Between; It's A Great Day For The Irish; Joint Is Really Jumpin' In Carnegie Hall; Minnie From Trinidad; Our Love Affair; Right Girl For Me; Strictly U. S. A.

EDWARDS, ANNE JEAN — Papa Niccolini

EDWARDS, BERNARD — Dance, Dance, Dance(yowsah, Yowsah, Yowsah); Good Times; He's The Greatest Dancer; I Want Your Love; I'm Coming Out; Le Freak; Upside Down

EDWARDS, BOBBY — You're The Reason

EDWARDS, CLARA — With The Wind And The Rain In Your Hair

EDWARDS, DOUG — Wildflower

EDWARDS, EARL — Duke Of Earl

EDWARDS, EDWIN B. — At The Jazz Band Ball; Barnyard Blues; Clarinet Marmalade

EDWARDS, FRED — Devil Went Down To Georgia

EDWARDS, GUS — (Look Out For)Jimmy Valentine; By The Light Of The Silvery Moon; In My Merry Oldsmobile; School Days; Sunbonnet Sue; Your Mother And Mine

EDWARDS, JAMES — Sh-Boom(Life Could Be A Dream)

EDWARDS, LEO — I'm An Indian

EDWARDS, MICHAEL — Once In Awhile

EDWARDS, SHERMAN — Broken Hearted Melody; Dungaree Doll!; Johnny Get Angry; See You In September; Wonderful, Wonderful; You'll Answer To Me

EDWARDS, VINCENT — Right Back Where We Started From

EDWARDS, WEBLEY — Pearly Shells

EEDE, N. — (I Just)Died In Your Arms; I've Been In Love Before

EGAN, JACK — Be Still, My Heart!

EGAN, JOE — Stuck In The Middle With You

EGAN, RAY — I Never Knew I Could Love Anybody Like I'm Loving You

EGAN, RAYMOND B. — Ain't We Got Fun; Bimini Bay; Japanese Sandman; Sleepy Time Gal; Song Of Raintree County; Three On A Match; Till We Meet Again; When Shall We Meet Again; Where The Morning Glories Grow

EGAN, WALTER — Hot Summer Nights; Magnet And Steel

EGNOIAN, ARTHUR — Bongo Rock

EHART, PHIL — Play The Game Tonight

EHRLICH, LARRY — Gotta Travel On

EHRMAN, MAX — Desiderata

EIJCK, HANS VAN — Ma Belle Amie

EISEN, STANLEY — Rock And Roll All Night

EISLEY, DAVID — Call To The Heart

ELBEL, LOUIS — Victors

ELBERT, DONNIE — Open The Door To Your Heart

ELGAR, EDWARD — Pomp And Circumstance

ELGIN, BOB — Hundred Pounds Of Clay; Last Chance(To Turn Around); My Town, My Guy, And Me

ELI, BOBBY — Just Don't Want To Be Lonely Tonight; Love Won't Let Me Wait; Sideshow

ELIAS, MICHAEL — I Cried

ELIOT, T. S. — Memory

ELISCU, EDWARD — Carioca; Flying Down To Rio; Great Day!; I'll Still Belong To You; More Than You Know; Music Makes Me; Without A Song; You Forgot Your Gloves

ELLINGTON, DAVE — Don't Fall In Love With A Dreamer

ELLINGTON, E. A. — Petite Waltz

ELLINGTON, EDWARD "DUKE" — "C" Jam Blues; All Too Soon; Awful Sad; Azure; Baby, When You Ain't There; Birmingham Breakdown; Black And Tan Fantasy; Black Beauty; Black Butterfly; Blind Man's Buff; Blue Feeling; Blue Light; Blues With A Feeling; Boy Meets Horn; Caravan; Carnegie Blues; Chocolate Shake; Clarinet Lament; Concerto For Cootie; Cotton Tail; Creeper; Creole Rhapsody; Crescendo In Blue; Dancers In Love; Day-Dream; Daybreak Express; Dicty Glide; Diminuendo In Blue; Do Nothin' Till You Hear From Me; Doin' The Voom Voom; Don't Get Around Much Anymore; Don't You Know I Care; Down In Our Alley Blues; Drop Me Off In Harlem; Duke Steps Out; Duke's Place; Dusk On The Desert; East St. Louis Toodle-O; Echoes Of Harlem; Ev'ry Hour On The Hour; Everything But You; Flaming Youth; Gal From Joe's; Grievin'; Gypsy Without A Song; Harlem Speaks; Harmony In Harlem; Haunted Nights; He Makes Me Believe He's Mine; High Life; Hot And Bothered; I Ain't Got Nothin' But The Blues; I Didn't Know About You; I Got It Bad(and That Ain't Good); I Let A Song Go Out Of My Heart; I Like The Sunrise; I Never Felt This Way Before; I'm Beginning To See The Light; I'm Checking Out Goombye; I'm Gonna Go Fishin'; I'm Just A Lucky So And So; I'm Satisfied; I've Got Me; I've Got To Be A Rug Cutter; If You Were In My Place(What Would You Do?); Immigration Blues; In A Mellow Tone; In A Sentimental Mood; It Don't Mean A Thing(If It Ain't Got That Swing); It's Kind Of Lonesome Out Tonight; Jack The

Bear; Jeep's Blues; Jig Walk; Jim Dandy; Jump For Joy; Just A-Sittin' And A-Rockin'; Just Squeeze Me(But Don't Tease Me); Lazy Rhapsody; Lost In Meditation; Main Stem; Maybe I Should Change My Ways; Merry-go-round; Mississippi Moan; Misty Mornin'; Mooche; Mood Indigo; On The Wrong Side Of The Railroad Track; Paris Blues; Prelude To A Kiss; Reminiscing In Tempo; Rent Party Blues; Ring Dem Bells; Rockin' In Rhythm; Satin Doll; Scattin' At The Kit Kat; Scheherazade; Solitude; Something To Live For; Sophisticated Lady; Steppin' Into Swing Society; When I Walk With You; Yearning For Love

ELLINGTON, MERCER — I Like The Sunrise; Moon Mist

ELLIOT, BRIAN — Papa Don't Preach

ELLIOTT, DON — Uh! Oh! (The Nutty Squirrels)

ELLIOTT, JACK — Be Mine; Charlie's Angels; I Think Of You; It's So Nice To Have A Man Around The House.; Sam's Song(The Happy Tune); Weaver Of Dreams

ELLIOTT, JOE — Rock Of Ages

ELLIOTT, RONALD C. — Don't Talk To Strangers; Just A Little; Laugh, Laugh; You Tell Me Why

ELLIS, ALFRED — Cold Sweat; Get It Together; Licking Stick-Licking Stick; Mother Popcorn; Say It Loud-I'm Black And I'm Proud

ELLIS, BARBARA — Come Softly To Me

ELLIS, JONAH — Don't Stop The Music

ELLIS, SEGER — You're All I Want For Christmas

ELLIS, TED — Dreamin'

ELLISON, BEN — I Want You, I Need You; I'm No Angel

ELLISTON, SHIRLEY — Name Game

ELLNER, KEN — Psychotic Reaction

ELLSTEIN, ABRAHAM — Wedding Samba, The (Also Known As The Wedding Rhumba)

ELLSWORTH, BOB — Somebody Else Is Taking My Place

ELMAN, ZIGGY — And The Angels Sing

ELSTON, HARRY — Grazing In The Grass

ELWORTHY, W. — Sweetheart

EMMERICH, BOB — Big Apple; Hear My Song, Violetta; Our Love

EMMETT, DANIEL DECATUR — Dixie; Jimmy Crack Corn(The Blue Tail Fly)

EMMONS, BOBBY — Luckenbach, Texas

ENDOR, CHICK — Who Takes Care Of The Caretaker's Daughter (While The Caretaker's Busy Taki

ENDSLEY, MELVIN — I Like Your Kind Of Love; I Live For Your Love; Knee Deep In The Blues; Singing The Blues

ENESCO, GEORGES — Rumanian Rhapsody

ENGBERG, ANN — How Long, How Long Blues

ENGELMANN, H. — Melody Of Love

ENGLISH, DAVID — I'm On Fire

ENGLISH, SCOTT — Bend Me, Shape Me; Mandy

ENGVICK, BILL — Bonnie Blue Gal; I'll Remember Today; Nine Twenty Special; Song From Moulin Rouge, The(Where Is Your Heart); While We're Young; Who Can I Turn To?

ENNIS, SUE — Best Man In The World

EPPS, PRESTON — Bongo Rock

ERDMAN, ERNIE — Nobody's Sweetheart; Toot Toot Tootsie

ERTEGUN, AHMET — Chains Of Love; Don't Play That Song; Fool, Fool, Fool; Good Lovin'; Little Mama; Lovey Dovey

ERVING, B. — I Need Love

ERWIN, LEE — Dance Me Loose

ERWIN, RALPH — I Kiss Your Hand, Madame

ESCOVEDO, SHEILA — Love Bizarre

ESKRIDGE, RALPH — Love Jones

ESPERON, MANUEL — Three Caballeros

ESPINOSA, J. J. — Gay Ranchero

ESPOSITO, JOSEPH — Bad Girls

ESPOSITO, MICHAEL — We Ain't Got Nothing Yet

ESSEX, DAVID — Rock On

ESTEFAN, GLORIA M. — Anything For You; Rhythm Is Gonna Get You; Words Get In The Way

ESTROM, D. A. — Hail To The Chief; Hail, Hail, The Gang's All Here

ESTY, BOB — Main Event, The(Fight)

ETT, S. — I Need Love

ETTING, RUTH — When You're With Somebody Else

EVANS, BILL — Waltz For Debby

EVANS, DALE — Bible Tells Me So

EVANS, DAVE — Into The Night

EVANS, GEORGE — In The Good Old Summertime

EVANS, GORDON — Switcharoo

EVANS, MITCHELL YOUNG — Mad About You

EVANS, PAUL — Happy Go Lucky Me; I Gotta Know; Next Step Is Love; Roses Are Red(My Love); Seven Little Girls Sitting In The Back Seat; When

EVANS, RAY — (Day After Day)I'll Always Love You; All The Time; Almost In Your Arms(Love Theme From Houseboat); Angel; Another Time, Another Place; Beside You; Bing! Bang! Bong!; Bonanza!; Bonne Nuit-Goodnight; Buttons And Bows; Cat And The Canary; Copper Canyon; Dear Heart; Eres Tu(Touch The Wind); Ev'rything Beautiful; Femininity; Give It All You've Got; Golden Earrings; Here's To Love; Home Cookin'; In The Arms Of Love; Life Is A Beautiful Thing; Misto Cristofo Columbo; Mona Lisa; Morning Music Of Montmartre; Mr. Lucky; My Own, My Only, My All; Place In The Sun; Que Sera, Sera(Whatever Will Be, Will Be); Silver Bells; Square In A Social Circle; To Each His Own; Wait Until Dark; Wish Me A Rainbow

EVANS, REDD — American Beauty Rose; Don't Go To Strangers; Frim Fram Sauce; I've Only Myself To Blame; Let Me Off Uptown; No Moon At All; Rosie The Riveter

EVANS, RICK — In The Year 2525

EVANS, TOLCHARD — If; Lady Of Spain; Let's All Sing Like The Birdies Sing; Unless

EVANS, TOM — Without You

EVELYN, ALICIA — I Get The Sweetest Feeling; Pepper-Hot Baby

EVERLY, DON — 'Til I Kissed You; So Sad(To Watch Good Love Go Bad)

EVERLY, DON AND PHIL — Cathy's Clown

EVERLY, PHIL — (Girls, Girls, Girls,Were)(Made To Love); Gee, But It's Lonely; When Will I Be Loved

EVOY, LAWRENCE WAYNE — Last Song

EWALD, MARNIE — Revenge

EYEN, TOM — And I Am Telling You I'm Not Going; Cadillac Car; One Night Only

EYTON, FRANK — Body And Soul

EZELL, NORMAN — I See The Light; Western Union; Zip Code

EZRIN, BOB — Beth; Detroit Rock City; Devil Inside

FABER, WILLIAM E. — You Were Only Fooling
FAGAN, DONALD — Deacon Blues
FAGEN, DONALD — Bad Sneakers; Do It Again; Fm(No Static At All); Hey Nineteen; I. G. Y. (What A Beautiful World); Josie; Peg; Reeling In The Years; Rikki Don't Lose That Number
FAIN, SAMMY — All The Time; April Love; Are You Havin' Any Fun?; By A Waterfall; Certain Smile; Dear Hearts And Gentle People; Dickey-bird Song; Ev'ry Day; Face To Face; G'wan Home, Your Mudder's Callin'; Happy In Love; I Can Dream, Can't I; I Can See You; I Speak To The Stars; I'll Be Seeing You; I'm Late; Imitation Of Life; Let A Smile Be Your Umbrella; Little Love Can Go A Long, Long Way; Love Is A Many Splendored Thing; Love Is Never Out Of Season; Mississippi Dream Boat; Please Don't Say No; Secret Love; Very Precious Love; Violins From Nowhere; Was That The Human Thing To Do; Wedding Bells Are Breaking Up That Old Gang Of Mine; When I Take My Sugar To Tea; When Tomorrow Comes; Wildest Gal In Town; You Brought A New Kind Of Love To Me
FAIRBARN, BRUCE — Hot Girls In Love
FAITH, PERCY — Love Goddess; My Heart Cries For You
FAITH, RUSSELL — Bobby Sox To Stockings; Voyage To The Bottom Of The Sea
FALBO, JOHN — Love Came To Me
FALL, RICHARD — O, Katharina!
FALLA, MANUEL DE — Ritual Fire Dance
FALTERMEIER, HAROLD — Hot Stuff
FALTERMEYER, HAROLD — Axel F; Bit By Bit; Heat Is On; Shakedown
FALVO, RODOLFO — Just Say I Love Her(Dicitencello Vuie)
FAMOUS CLASSICAL — Danse Macabre
FARACI, SILVIO — Lonely Teenager
FARGE, PETER LA — Ballad Of Ira Hayes
FARGO, DONNA — Funny Face; Happiest Girl In The Whole U. S. A.
FARIAN, F. — Rivers Of Babylon
FARINA, ANN — Sleep Walk
FARINA, JOHN — Sleep Walk
FARINA, MIMI — In The Quiet Morning(For Janis Joplin)
FARINA, PEGGY — Beggin'
FARINA, RICHARD — Pack Up Your Sorrows
FARINA, SANTO — Sleep Walk
FARJEON, ELEANOR — Morning Has Broken
FARLEY, ED — Music Goes 'round And Around
FARLEY, MELVILLE — My Son, My Son
FARMER, STEVE — Journey To The Center Of The Mind
FARNER, MARK — Bad Time"; Shinin' On
FARNSWORTH, NANCY — Here Come Those Tears Again
FARRAR, JOHN — Don't Stop Believin'; Have You Never Been Mellow; Hopelessly Devoted To You; Little More Love; Magic; Make A Move On Me; Same; Something Better To Do; Suddenly; You're The One That I Want
FARRAR, WALTER — I Cross My Fingers
FARRELL, WES — Boys; Come A Little Bit Closer; Come And Take A Ride In My Boat(Come On Down To My Boat); Doesn't Somebody Want To Be Wanted; Hang On Sloopy; Happy Summer Days; I'll Make All Your Dreams Come True; I'll Meet You Halfway; Let's Lock The Door And Throw Away The Key; Look What You've Done
FARRES, OSVALDO — Come Closer To Me(Acerate Mas); Perhaps, Perhaps, Perhaps(Quizas, Quizas, Quizas); Without You
FARRISS, ANDREW — Devil Inside; Need You Tonight; What You Need
FARROW, JOHNNY — I Have But One Heart; New Shade Of Blue
FASSERT, FRED — Barbara Ann
FAULKNER, ERIC — Money Honey
FAUTHEREE, JACK — Cradle Of Love
FAYE, FRANCES — Well All Right! (Tonight's The Night)
FEARIS, J. S. — Little Sir Echo
FEASTER, CARL — Sh-Boom(Life Could Be A Dream)
FEASTER, CLAUDE — Sh-Boom(Life Could Be A Dream)
FEATHER, JANE — Blowtop Blues
FEATHER, LEONARD — Blowtop Blues; Evil Gal Blues
FEATHERS, CHARLES — I Forgot To Remember To Forget
FEKARIS, DINO — Hey Big Brother; I Pledge My Love; I Will Survive; Reunited; Shake Your Groove Thing
FELDER, DON — Hotel California
FELDMAN, AL — A-Tisket A-Tasket
FELDMAN, BOB — I Want Candy
FELDMAN, JACK — Copacabana; I Made It Through The Rain
FELDMAN, RICHARD — D.C. Cab; Promises
FELDMAN, ROBERT — My Boyfriend's Back; Night Time
FELDMAN, STEVEN — Mercy
FELICIANO, JOSE — Chico And The Man(theme From)
FELICIANO, JOSE AND JANNA — Aaron Loves Angela
FELL, TERRY — Sandy; You're The Reason
FELLER, DICK — Bandit; East Bound And Down
FELLER, SHERM — Summertime, Summertime
FELLOWS, BOB — Would Ya?
FENCETON, DONALD — I Am Love(parts 1 & 2)
FENDER, FREDDY — Wasted Days Wasted Nights
FENN, RICK — Family Man
FENSTAD, E. A. — (Maine)Stein Song
FENWICK, RAYMOND — Touch Me
FERGUSON, ALLYN — Charlie's Angels
FERGUSON, JAY — Thunder Island
FERGUSON, LLOYD — Pass The Dutchie
FERRAO, PAUL — April In Portugal
FERRARI, LOUIS — Domino; Dominoes
FERRE, CLIFF — Money Tree
FETTER, TED — Yours For A Song
FEYNE, BUDDY — Tuxedo Junction
FIEGER, DOUGLAS — Good Girls Don't
FIELD, EUGENE — Wynken, Blynken And Nod
FIELDS, ARTHUR — I Got A "code" In My "doze"
FIELDS, BUDDY — You Gotta Be A Football Hero (To Get Along With The Beautiful Girls)
FIELDS, DOROTHY — Alone Too Long; Andiamo; April Snow; Baby Dream Your Dream; Big Back Yard; Big Spender; Blue Again; Bojangles Of Harlem; Button Up Your Heart; Carrousel In The Park; Close As Pages In A Book; Cuban Love Song; Diga Diga Doo; Dinner At Eight; Doin' The New Low-down; Don't Blame Me; Exactly Like You; Fine Romance; Futuris-

tic Rhythm; Go Home And Tell Your Mother; Good-bye Blues; Hang Up; Happy Habit; He's Good For Me; Heavenly Party; Hooray For Love; I Can't Give You Anything But Love; I Dream Too Much; I Feel A Song Comin' On; I Got Love; I Must Have That Man; I'll Buy You A Star; I'm Feelin' Blue('cause I Got Nobody); I'm In The Mood For Love; I'm Like A New Broom; I'm Living In A Great Big Way; I'm The Echo(You're The Song That I Sing); If My Friends Could See Me Now; It's Not Where You Start; Jockey On The Carousel; Just For Once; Just Let Me Look At You; Look Who's Dancing; Lost In A Fog; Love Is The Reason; Lovely To Look At; Make The Man Love Me; More Love Than Your Love; My Dancing Lady; Never Gonna Dance; On The Sunny Side Of The Street; Our Song; Pick Yourself Up; Remind Me; Rhythm Of Life; Serenade For A Wealthy Widow; Stars In My Eyes; Two Faces In The Dark; Waltz In Swing Time; Way You Look Tonight; What's Good About Good Night; When She Walks In The Room; Where Am I Going; Whistling Boy; You Couldn't Be Cuter; You're An Angel

FIELDS, IRVING — Chantez, Chantez; Managua Nicaragua; Miami Beach Rumba

FINA, JACK — Bumble Boogie

FINCH, DICK — Jealous

FINCH, RICHARD — (Shake, Shake, Shake)Shake Your Booty; Boogie Shoes; Get Down Tonight; I'm Your Boogie Man; Keep It Comin,love; Please Don't Go; Rock Your Baby; Where Is The Love

FINDON, BENJAMIN — Love Really Hurts Without You

FINE, SYLVIA — Anatole(of Paris); Happy Times; Lullaby In Ragtime; Moon Is Blue

FINLEY, JOHN — Let Me Serenade You

FINN, N. — Don't Dream It's Over; Something So Strong

FINNERAN, JOHN LAWRENCE — Dear One

FINNERAN, VINCENT — Dear One

FINNEY, LANCE — You're So Fine

FIORINO, VINCENT — Blue Canary

FIORITO, TED — Alone At A Table For Two; Charley, My Boy; Laugh! Clown! Laugh!; Lily Of Laguna; Now That You've Gone; Three On A Match; Toot Toot Tootsie; When Lights Are Low

FISCHER, CARL — Black Lace; It Started All Over Again; We'll Be Together Again; Who Wouldn't Love You

FISCHER, ROBERT — I Believe You

FISCHOFF, GEORGE — 98. 6; Lazy Day

FISHER, BRUCE — Nothing From Nothing; Will It Go Round In Circles; You Are So Beautiful

FISHER, DAN — Good Morning Heartache

FISHER, DAVE — Michael(Row The Boat Ashore)

FISHER, DORIS — Angelina(the Waitress At The Pizzeria); Good, Good, Good; I Wish; Into Each Life Some Rain Must Fall; Invitation To The Blues; Put The Blame On Mame; Tired; Tutti-Frutti; Whispering Grass (Don't Tell The Trees); You Always Hurt The One You Love; You Can't See The Sun When You're Cryin'

FISHER, EDDIE — May I Sing To You

FISHER, FRED — Blue Is The Night; Come Josephine(In My Flying Machine); Daddy, You've Been A Mother To Me; Dardanella; Fifty Million Frenchmen Can't Be Wrong; Happy Days And Lonely Nights; I'd Rather Be Blue Over You(Than Be Happy With Somebody Else); I'm All Dressed Up With A Broken Heart; Peg O' My Heart; Whispering Grass (Don't Tell The Trees); Your Feet's Too Big

FISHER, MARK — Everywhere You Go; Oh, How I Miss You Tonight; When You're Smiling (The Whole World Smiles With You)

FISHER, MARVIN — Destination Moon; When Sunny Gets Blue

FISHER, ROB — Promises, Promises

FISHER, ROGER — Barracuda; Crazy On You

FISHER, WILLIAM ARMS — Goin' Home

FISHMAN, JACK — Help Yourself; Why Don't They Understand

FISHMAN, JAY — When Liking Turns To Loving

FITCH, ART — I Love You Sweetheart Of All My Dreams

FITCH, J. — I Don't Know If It's Right

FITCH, JOHN — Shame

FITCH, KAY — I Love You Sweetheart Of All My Dreams

FITZGERALD, ELLA — A-Tisket A-Tasket; Chew-Chew-Chew(Chew Your Bubble Gum); You Showed Me The Way

FITZGERALD, FRANCIS — Sentimental Street

FITZGERALD, TYRONE — Funky Nassau

FLACK, ROBERTA — Ballad For D

FLANAGAN, BUD — Underneath The Arches

FLANAGAN, RALPH — Hot Toddy

FLEESON, NEVILLE — I'll Be With You In Apple Blossom Time

FLEMING, GEORGE — Freedom Overspill

FLEMING, KYE — I Wouldn't Have Missed It For The World; Nobody; Years

FLEMING, PHIL — How Do You Do

FLEMONS, WADE — Stay In My Corner

FLENDER, HAROLD — Paris Blues

FLETCHER, DONALD — Dancing Machine

FLETCHER, DUSTY — Open The Door, Richard!

FLETCHER, LUCY — Sugar Blues

FLINDT, EMIL — Waltz You Saved For Me

FLOWER, DANNY — Play The Game Tonight

FLOYD, EDDIE — 634-5789; Knock On Wood; You Don't Know What You Mean To Me

FLOYD, KING — Groove Me

FLYNN, ALLAN — Be Still, My Heart!; Maybe

FLYNN, JOHN H. — Yip-I-Addy-I-Ay

FOGARTY, J. PAUL — Betty Co-ed

FOGARTY, JOHN C. — Bad Moon Rising; Commotion; Down On The Corner; Fortunate Son; Green River; Have You Ever Seen The Rain; Long As I Can See The Light; Lookin' Out My Back Door; Old Man Down The Road; Proud Mary; Rock And Roll Girls; Rockin' All Over The World; Run Through The Jungle; Someday Never Comes; Sweet Hitchhiker; Travelin' Band; Up Around The Bend; Who'll Stop The Rain

FOGELBERG, DAN — Heart Hotels; Language Of Love; Leader Of The Band; Longer; Missing You; Part Of The Plan; Power Of Gold; Run For The Roses; Same Old Lang Syne

FONTENOY, MARC — Choo Choo Train

FORBERT, STEVE — Romeo's Tune

FORCE, FULL — All Cried Out; Head To Toe; Lost In Emotion

FORD, FRED HAMM — Bye Bye Blues

FORD, JIM — Niki Hoeky

FORD, NAOMI — Fool

FORD, TENNESSEE ERNIE — Shot-Gun Boogie

FOREMAN, CHRIS — Our House

FORESYTH, REGINALD — Deep Forest

FORESYTHE, REGINALD — Dodging A Divorcee; Serenade For A Wealthy Widow

FORNAI, TINO — 8 1/2(theme From)

FORREST, BEN — Alexander The Swoose

FORREST, CHET — Always And Always; At The Balalaika; Donkey Serenade,the; Horse With The Dreamy Eyes; It's A Blue World

FORREST, GEORGE — And This Is My Beloved; Baubles, Bangles And Beads; Chime In!; Elena; Fate; Fog And The Grog; Freddy And His Fiddle; He's In Love; I Love You; Midsummer's Eve; Night Of My Nights; Not Since Ninevah; Now; Sands Of Time; Strange Music; Stranger In Paradise

FORREST, JIMMY — Night Train

FORSEY, KEITH — Don't You(Forget About Me); Flashdance(What A Feeling); Heat Is On; Hot Stuff; Never Ending Story; Shakedown

FORTGANG, JEFF — Some Guys Have All The Luck

FOSDICK, W. W. — Aura Lee

FOSTER, D. — Will You Still Love Me?

FOSTER, DAVID — Breakdown Dead Ahead; Glory Of Love(Theme From The Karate Kid, Part 2); Hard To Say I'm Sorry; Heart To Heart; Look What You Done To Me; Mornin'; She's A Beauty; St. Elmo's Fire(Man In Motion); Stay The Night; Who's Holding Donna Now; You're The Inspiration

FOSTER, DAVIS — Got To Be Real

FOSTER, FRED L. — Me And Bobby Mcgee

FOSTER, STEPHEN COLLINS — Beautiful Dreamer; De Camptown Races; Jeanie With The Light Brown Hair; Massa's In De Cold Cold Ground; My Old Kentucky Home; Oh! Susanna; Old Black Joe; Old Dog Tray; Old Folks At Home(Way Down Upon The Swanee River)

FOSTER, WARREN — I Taut I Taw A Puddy Tat(I Thought I Saw A Pussy Cat)

FOTINE, LARRY — You Were Only Fooling

FOWLER, LEM — How'm I Doin?(Hey, Hey!)

FOWLER, T. J. — Crossfire

FOX, BILLY — One Man Band

FOX, CHARLES — Different Worlds; Happy Days; I Got A Name; Killing Me Softly With His Song; Love Boat Theme; Making Our Dreams Come True; My Fair Share; Ready To Take A Chance Again

FOXX, CHARLIE — She's A Heartbreaker

FOXX, INEZ — I Love You 1000 Times

FOXX, INEZ AND CHARLIE — Mockingbird

FRAGOS, GEORGE — I Hear A Rhapsody

FRAMPTON, PETER — Baby I Love Your Way; Do You Feel Like We Do; I Can't Stand It No More; I'm In You; Show Me The Way

FRANCIS, ARTHUR — Waiting For The Sun To Come Out

FRANCIS, CONNIE — Vacation

FRANCOIS, CLAUDE — My Boy

FRANK, D. — Don't Disturb This Groove

FRANK, SID — Please Mr. Sun

FRANKL, ABE — Yankee Rose

FRANKLIN, ARETHA — Call Me; Day Dreaming; Rock Steady; Since You've Been Gone(Sweet, Sweet Baby); Spirit In The Dark; Who's Zoomin' Who

FRANKLIN, CAROLYN — Ain't No Way

FRANKLIN, DAVE — Anniversary Waltz,the; Blue Lament; Breakin' In A Pair Of Shoes; Concert In The Park; I Ain't Lazy, I'm Just Dreaming; I Hope Gabriel Likes My Music; I Must See Annie Tonight; Lily Belle;

Merry-go-round Broke Down; When My Dream Boat Comes Home; You Can't Stop Me From Dreaming

FRANKS, TILLMAN — Sink The Bismarck

FRANTZ, CHRIS — Burning Down The House

FRANZESE, PAT — In The Middle Of A Heartache

FRASER, ANDY — All Right Now; Every Kinda People

FRASHUER, D. — Kiss Him Goodbye

FRASHUER, DALE — Na Na, Hey, Hey, Kiss Him Goodbye

FRATTO, RUSS — Maybellene

FRAZIER, AL — Surfin' Bird

FRAZIER, DALLAS — Alley Oop; Elvira; Mohair Sam

FRAZIER, GEORGE — Harvard Blues

FRAZIER, JAMES — Kissin' Time

FRAZIER, LEONARD — Kissin' Time

FRAZIER, ROBERT — Play The Game Tonight

FREBERG, STAN — St. George And The Dragonet

FRED, JOHN — Judy In Disguise

FREED, ALAN — Maybellene; Most Of All; Sincerely

FREED, ARTHUR — All I Do Is Dream Of You; Alone; Angel; Beautiful Girl; Blondy; Broadway Melody; Broadway Rhythm; Bundle Of Old Love Letters; Chant Of The Jungle; Cinderella's Fella; Coffee Time; Everybody Sing; Fit As A Fiddle; Follow In My Footsteps; Good Morning; Got A Pair Of New Shoes; Here Comes The Sun; Hold Your Man; I Cried For You(Now It's Your Turn To Cry Over Me); I'm Feelin' Like A Million; I've Got A Feelin' You're Foolin'; It Was So Beautiful; Love Songs Of The Nile; Moon Is Low; New Moon Is Over My Shoulder; On A Sunday Afternoon; Our Big Love Scene; Our Love Affair; Pagan Love Song; Should I?; Sing Before Breakfast; Singin' In The Rain; We'll Make Hay While The Sun Shines; Wedding Of The Painted Doll; When Buddha Smiles; Woman In The Shoe; You And I; You Are My Lucky Star; You Were Meant For Me; Yours And Mine

FREED, MARTIN — Broadway Rose

FREED, RALPH — G'wan Home, Your Mudder's Callin'; Hawaiian War Chant; How About You?; In A Moment Of Madness; Listen My Children And You Shall Hear; Little Dutch Mill; Love Lies; Mississippi Dream Boat; Please Don't Say No; Sandman; You Leave Me Breathless

FREEDMAN, MAX C. — Heartbreaker; Rock Around The Clock

FREEDMAN, RAY — Sioux City Sue

FREEMAN, BOBBY — Do You Want To Dance?

FREEMAN, ERNIE — Percolator

FREEMAN, JOHN C. — Just Don't Want To Be Lonely Tonight

FREEMAN, L. E. — Until The Real Thing Comes Along

FREEMAN, LAWRENCE "BUD" — Craze-ology

FREEMAN, TICKER — So Dear To My Heart; You'll Always Be The One I Love

FREIDMAN, CHARLES — Kiss Me Another

FREKARIS, DINO — Makin' It

FREY, GLEN — Heartache Tonight; I Can't Tell You Why

FREY, GLENN — Best Of My Love; Desperado; Hotel California; Life In The Fast Lane; Lyin' Eyes; New Kid In Town; One Of These Nights; One You Love; Sexy Girl; Smuggler's Blues; You Belong To The City

FREY, MIKE — Family Man

FRICKER, SYLVIA — You Were On My Mind

FRIDAY, FREDDY — Java

FRIED, GERALD — Roots Medley(Motherland)

FRIEDBERG, DAVID — Jane
FRIEDHOFER, HUGO — One Eyed Jacks(Love Theme)
FRIEDMAN, LEO — Let Me Call You Sweetheart; Meet Me Tonight In Dreamland
FRIEDMAN, R. — Don't Shed A Tear
FRIEDMAN, RUTHANN — Windy
FRIEDMAN, STANLEIGH — Down The Field
FRIEND, CLIFF — Broken Record; Concert In The Park; Don't Sweetheart Me; Give Me A Night In June; Gonna Build A Big Fence Around Texas; I Must See Annie Tonight; I Wanna Go Where You Go, Do What You Do, Then I'll Be Happy; It Goes Like This(That Funny Melody); Just Give Me A June Night, The Moonlight, And You (June Night); Mamma Loves Papa, Papa Loves Mamma; Merry-Go-Round Broke Down; Time Waits For No One; Trade Winds; Wahhoo!; Wake Up And Sing; We Did It Before (and We Can Do It Again); When My Dream Boat Comes Home; Where The Lazy Daisies Grow; You Can't Stop Me From Dreaming
FRIES, WILLIAM D. — Convoy
FRIML, RUDOLF — Allah's Holiday; Dear Love, My Love; Donkey Serenade,the; Door Of My Dreams; Florida, The Moon And You; Gather The Rose; Giannina Mia; Huguette Waltz; Indian Love Call; L'amour, Toujours, L'amour(Love Everlasting); Love For Sale; Love Me Tonight; Ma Belle; March Of The Musketeers; Mounties; Only A Rose; Rose Marie; Some Day; Song Of The Vagabonds; Totem Tom Tom; Waltz Huguette Or The Vagabond King Waltz; We'll Have A Kingdom; When A Maid Comes Knocking At Your Heart
FRISCH, AL — All Over The World; Congratulations To Someone; Flowers Mean Forgiveness; Here Comes

That Heartache Again; I Won't Cry Anymore; Pancho Maximilian Hernandez(The Best President We Ever Had); Roses In The Rain; Two Different Worlds
FRITTS, DONNIE — Choo Choo Train
FROEBA, FRED — Jumpin' Jive
FRONTIERE, DOMINIC — Hang 'em High
FROOM, M. — Something So Strong
FRY, M. — When Smokey Sings
FRY, MARTIN — (How To Be A)Millionaire; Be Near Me; Look Of Love
FRYBERG, MART — Call Me Darling(Call Me Sweetheart, Call Me Dear)
FULLER, DOLORES — Do The Clam; Rock-A-Hula-Baby
FULLER, GIL — Manteca
FULLER, JAMES — Wipe Out
FULLER, JERRY — It's Up To You; Lady Willpower; Over You; Show And Tell; Travelin' Man; Young Girl; Young World
FULLER, WALTER — Oop Bop Sh-bam
FULLYLOVE, LEROY — Bumblebee
FULTON, JACK — If You Are But A Dream; Ivory Tower; Quien Sabe?(Who Knows?); Wanted
FULTON, KATHRYN R. — Fool No. 1
FUNCHES, JOHN — Oh, What A Night
FUQUA, HARVEY — If I Could Build My Whole World Around You; Most Of All; My Whole World Ended; Pucker Up, Buttercup; Sincerely; Someday We'll Be Together; Twenty-Five Miles; What Does It Take (To Win Your Love)
FURBER, DOUGLAS — Bells Of St. Mary's; Fancy Our Meeting; Lambeth Walk; Limehouse Blues
FURLETT, FRANK — Alexander The Swoose

G, KENNY — Songbird

GABLER, MILT — Choo Choo Ch' Boogie; Love(L-O-V-E); Skinny Minnie; Wiederseh'n

GABRIEL, GILBERT — Life In A Northern Town

GABRIEL, PETER — Big Time; Sledgehammer

GADD, STEVE — Stuff Like That

GADE, JACOB — Jealousy(Jalousie)

GAILLARD, SLIM — Cement Mixer(Put-ti, Put-ti); Down By The Station; Flat Foot Floogie; Tutti-Frutti

GAINES, LEE — Just A-Sittin' And A-Rockin'; Just Squeeze Me(But Don't Tease Me)

GAITSCH, B. — Don't Mean Nothing; La Isla Bonita

GALDO, JOE — Bad Boy

GALDSTON, P. — It's Not Over('Til It's Over)

GALE, ERIC — Stuff Like That

GALLAGHER, BENNY — Breakaway

GALLAGHER, ED — Mister Gallagher And Mister Shean

GALLAGHER, MICHAEL — Do You Feel Like We Do

GALLAGHER, S. T. — Illusion

GALLOP, SAMMY — Autumn Serenade; Blossoms On The Bough; Boogie Woogie Maxixe; Count Every Star; Elmer's Tune; Forgive My Heart; Free; Holiday For Strings; Maybe You'll Be There; My Lady Loves To Dance; Night Lights; Outside Of Heaven; Shoo-Fly-Pie And Apple Pan Dowdy; Wake The Town And Tell The People

GALLOWAY, TOD B. — Whiffenpoof Song

GAMBLE, KENNY — Are You Happy?; Brand New Me; Break Up To Make Up; Close The Door; Cowboys To Girls; Don't Leave Me This Way; Drowning In The Sea Of Love; Enjoy Yourself; Espressway To Your Heart; Explosion In My Soul; For The Love Of Money; Hey, Western Union Man; I Just Can't Stop Dancing; I Love Music(part 1); I'm Gonna Make You Love Me; If You Don't Know Me By Now; Livin' For The Weekend; Love I Lost; Love Train; Me And Mrs. Jones; Moody Woman; Never Give You Up(Never Gonna Give You Up); Only The Strong Survive; Power Of Love; Put Your Hands Together; T.S.O.P. (The Sound Of Philadelphia); United; Use Ta Be My Girl; What's The Use Of Breaking Up?; When Will I See You Again; You'll Never Find Another Love Like Mine

GAMSE, ALBERT — Amapola(Pretty Little Poppy); Chantez, Chantez; From One Love To Another; Helen Pola; Managua Nicaragua; Miami Beach Rumba

GAMSON, DAVID — Perfect Way

GANG, KOOL AND THE — Stone Love

GANNON, KIM — Always In My Heart; Angel In Disguise; Autumn Nocturne; Croce Di Oro; Dreamers Holiday; Drifting; Five O'clock Whistle; I Understand; I Want To Be Wanted; I'll Be Home For Christmas; It Can't Be Wrong; Moonlight Cocktail; Under Paris Skies

GANT, CECIL — I Wonder; I'm Tired

GANT, DON — Run, Baby, Run(Back Into My Arms)

GANTRY, CHRIS — Dreams Of The Everyday Housewife

GARAFULO, BRYAN — Load Out

GARCIA, E. E. — Rhythm Is Gonna Get You

GARCIA, ENRIQUE — Conga

GARCIA, GARY — Pac-man Fever

GARCIA, J. — Touch Of Grey

GARCIA, JERRY — Uncle John's Band

GARDNER, DON — All I Want For Christmas(Is My Two Front Teeth)

GARDNER, WILLIAM — Can't You Hear Me Calling Caroline

GARFIELD, GIL — Wonderful Summer

GARFUNKEL, ART — Hey, Schoolgirl; Scarborough Fair-Canticle

GARIBALDI, JOHN — What Is Hip

GARLAND, JOE — In The Mood; Leap Frog

GARNER, ERROLL — Dreamstreet; Misty

GARNETT, GALE — We'll Sing In The Sunshine

GARREN, JOE — Just A Girl That Men Forget

GARRETT, LEE — It's A Shame; Let's Get Serious; Maybe I'm A Fool; Signed, Sealed, Delivered I'm Yours

GARRETT, S. — Man In The Mirror

GARRETT, SAMUEL — Little Ole Winedrinker Me

GARRETT, SNUFF — Bar Room Buddies; Every Which Way But Loose

GARRETT, THOMAS — Hoppy, Gene, And Me; You Don't Have To Paint Me A Picture

GARRETT, W. — Mashed Potato Time

GARRIE, ALAN — Pick Up The Pieces

GARRIS, SID — Opus One

GARRITY, FREDDY — I'm Telling You Now

GARSON, MORT — Dondi; Left Right Out Of Your Heart; My Summer Love; Our Day Will Come

GARTSIDE, GREEN STROHMEYER — Perfect Way

GARVIN, REX — Over The Mountain, Across The Sea

GASKILL, CLARENCE — I Can't Believe That You're In Love With Me; Minnie The Moocher; Prisoner Of Love

GASPARRE, DICK — I Hear A Rhapsody

GASS, AUBREY — Wine, Women And Song

GATES, DAVID — Aubrey; Baby I'm A-Want You; Diary; Goodbye Girl; Guitar Man; If; It Don't Matter To Me; Lost Without Your Love; Make It With You; Part-Time Love; Popsicles And Icicles; Sweet Surrender

GATHERS, HELEN — Mr. Lee

GATLIN, LARRY — All The Gold In California

GATLIN, SUE — Two Of Hearts

GAUDIO, BOB — Beggin'; Big Girls Don't Cry; Big Man In Town; Bye Bye Baby(Baby Goodbye); Can't Take My Eyes Off You; Dawn(Go Away); Girl Come Running; I Make A Fool Of Myself; Proud One; Rag Doll; Ronnie; Save It For Me; Sherry; Short Shorts; Silence Is Golden; Walk Like A Man; Who Loves You

GAUNT, PERCY — Bowery

GAY, BYRON — Four Or Five Times; Horses; Sittin' On A Log(Pettin' My Dog); Toodle-oo, So Long, Good-bye

GAY, NOEL — King's Horses, The(And The King's Men); Lambeth Walk; Leaning On The Lamp Post; Run, Rabbit, Run

GAYE, ANNA — Bells

GAYE, MARVIN — Beechwood 4-5789; Bells; Come Get To This; Dancing In The Street; Got To Give It Up(part 1); Inner City Blues(Make Me Wanna Holler); Let's Get It On; Mercy Mercy Me(The Ecology); Pretty Little Baby; Pride And Joy; Sexual Healing; What's Going On

GAYE, MARVIN AND ANNA — Baby, I'm For Real

GAYTEN, PAUL — But I Do; For You My Love

GAZE, HEINO — Ask Me; Berlin Melody; Calcutta

GEDDINS, ROBERT — Haunted House

GEE, JACK — Cold In Hand Blues; Dying Gambler's Blues

GELD, GARY — Ginny Come Lately; Hurting Each Other; I Got Love; Let Me Belong To You; Purlie; Save Your Heart For Me; Sealed With A Kiss; Why Am I Me

GELDOF, BOB — Do They Know It's Christmas

GENARO, PAT — Here In My Heart; You're Breaking My Heart

GENOVESE, ROBERT — Big Guitar

GENSLER, LEWIS E. — Cross Your Heart; Ending With A Kiss; Gentlemen Prefer Blondes1926); Keep Smiling At Trouble; Love Is Just Around The Corner; You Need Someone, Someone Needs You

GENTRY, BO — I Like The Way; I Think We're Alone Now; Indian Giver; Make Believe; Mirage; Mony Mony; Special Delivery

GENTRY, BOBBIE — Fancy; Ode To Billie Joe

GEORGE, BARBARA — I Know(You Don't Love Me No More)

GEORGE, DON — Calypso Blues; Ev'ry Hour On The Hour; Everything But You; I Ain't Got Nothin' But The Blues; I'm Beginning To See The Light; It's Kind Of Lonesome Out Tonight; Papa Niccolini

GEORGE, J. — Just To See Her

GEORGE, STEVEN — Broken Wings; Is It Love

GEPPERT, CHRISTOPHER — Never Be The Same; Ride Like The Wind

GERALD, J. — Honey Love

GERALD, RAEFORD — Get Down, Get Down(Get On The Floor); Your Time To Cry

GERARD, M. PHILIPPE — When The World Was Young (Ah The Apple Trees)

GERARD, RICHARD H. — Sweet Adeline

GERHARD, AKE — Lay Down Your Arms

GERLACH, HORACE — Daddy's Little Girl

GERNHARD, PHIL — Return Of The Red Baron; Snoopy Versus The Red Baron

GERSHWIN, GEORGE — 'S Wonderful; (I've Got)Beginner's Luck; (Our) Love Is Here To Stay; (Our)Love Is Here To Stay; American In Paris,an; Aren't You Kind Of Glad We Did?; Back Bay Polka; Because, Because; Bess, You Is My Woman; Bidin' My Time; Blah-Blah-Blah; Boy! What Love Has Done To Me; But Not For Me; By Strauss; Changing My Tune; Clap Yo' Hands; Concerto In F; Cossack Love Song; Could You Use Me; Dear Little Girl; Delishious; Do Do Do; Do It Again; Do What You Do!; Drifting Along With The Tide; Embraceable You; Far Away; Fascinating Rhythm; Feeling I'm Falling; Fidgety Feet; Foggy Day; For You, For Me, For Evermore; Got A Rainbow; Half Of It Dearie Blues; Hang On To Me; Hangin' Around With You; He Loves And She Loves; High Hat; How Long Has This Been Going On?; I Can't Be Bothered Now; I Found A Four Leaf Clover; I Got Plenty O' Nuttin'; I Got Rhythm; I Love To Rhyme; I Loves You Porgy; I Mean To Say; I Was Doing All Right; I Won't Say I Will But I Won't Say I Won't; I'll Build A Stairway To Paradise; I've Got A Crush On You; I've Got To Be There; If I Became The President; Illegitimate Daughter; Isn't It A Pity?; It Ain't Necessarily So; Jolly Tar And The Milkmaid; K-Ra-Zy For You"; Katinkitschka; Let 'em Eat Cake; Let's Call The Whole Thing Off; Let's Kiss And Make Up; Let's Live For Today; Life Of A Rose; Little Jazz Bird; Liza(All The Clouds'll Roll Away); Looking For A Boy; Lorelei; Lost Barber Shop Chord; Love Is Sweeping The Country; Love Walked In; Luckiest

Man In The World; Mademoiselle In New Rochelle; Man I Love; Maybe; Mine; Mischa, Jascha, Toscha, Sascha; My Cousin In Milwaukee; My Man's Gone Now; My One And Only; Nice Work If You Can Get It; Nightie-night; Nobody But You; Of Thee I Sing; Oh Bess, Oh Where's My Bess; Oh Gee! Oh Joy!; Oh Lady, Be Good; On And On And On; Red Headed Woman Makes A Choo Choo Jump Its Track; Rhapsody In Blue; Rose Of Madrid; Say So!; Scandal Walk; Shall We Dance?; Slap That Bass; So Am I; So What?; Somebody From Somewhere; Somebody Loves Me; Someone To Watch Over Me; Someone Who Believes In You; Song Of The Flame; Songs Of Long Ago; Soon; Stiff Upper Lip; Strike Up The Band; Summertime; Swanee; Sweet And Low Down; Swiss Miss; The Babbitt And The Bromide; Till Then; Treat Me Rough; Typical Self-Made American; Virginia; Vodka; Waiting For The Sun To Come Out; Where Is The Man Of My Dreams?; Where's The Boy? Here's The Girl!; Who Cares; Why Do I Love You; Wintergreen For President; Woman Is A Sometime Thing; Yankee Doodle Blues

GERSHWIN, IRA — 'S Wonderful; (I've Got)Beginner's Luck; (Our) Love Is Here To Stay; (Our)Love Is Here To Stay; All At Once; Aren't You Kind Of Glad We Did?; Back Bay Polka; Because, Because; Bess, You Is My Woman; Bidin' My Time; Blah-Blah-Blah; Boy! What Love Has Done To Me; But Not For Me; By Strauss; Changing My Tune; Cheerful Little Earful; Clap Yo' Hands; Could You Use Me; Dear Little Girl; Delishious; Dissertation On The State Of Bliss(Love And Learn); Do Do Do; Do What You Do!; Don't Be A Woman If You Can; Embraceable You; Fascinating Rhythm; Feeling I'm Falling; Fidgety Feet; Foggy Day; For You, For Me, For Evermore; Fun To Be Fooled; Girl Of The Moment; Got A Rainbow; Gotta Have Me Go With You; Half Of It Dearie Blues; Hang On To Me; Hangin' Around With You; He Hasn't A Thing Except Me; He Loves And She Loves; High Hat; How Long Has This Been Going On?; I Am Only Human After All; I Can't Be Bothered Now; I Can't Get Started With You; I Got Plenty O' Nuttin'; I Got Rhythm; I Got Shoes; I Love To Rhyme; I Loves You Porgy; I Mean To Say; I Was Doing All Right; I Won't Say I Will But I Won't Say I Won't; I'll Build A Stairway To Paradise; I've Got A Crush On You; I've Got To Be There; If I Became The President; If Love Remains; Illegitimate Daughter; In The Merry Month Of Maybe; Invitation To The Blues; Island In The West Indies; Isn't It A Pity?; It Ain't Necessarily So; It's A New World; Jenny(The Saga Of Jenny); Jolly Tar And The Milkmaid; K-Ra-Zy For You"; Katinkitschka; Let 'em Eat Cake; Let's Call The Whole Thing Off; Let's Kiss And Make Up; Let's Take A Walk Around The Block; Little Jazz Bird; Liza(All The Clouds'll Roll Away); Long Ago(And Far Away); Looking For A Boy; Lorelei; Lose That Long Face; Lost Barber Shop Chord; Love Is Sweeping The Country; Love Walked In; Luckiest Man In The World; Mademoiselle In New Rochelle; Make Way For Tomorrow; Man I Love; Man That Got Away; Maybe; Mine; Mischa, Jascha, Toscha, Sascha; My Cousin In Milwaukee; My One And Only; My One And Only Highland Fling; My Ship; Nice Work If You Can Get It; Nightie-night; Nina, The Pinta, The Santa Maria; Of Thee I Sing; Oh Bess, Oh Where's My Bess; Oh

Gee! Oh Joy!; Oh Lady, Be Good; Oh Me! Oh My!; On And On And On; One Life To Live; Princess Of Pure Delight; Put Me To The Test; Red Headed Woman Makes A Choo Choo Jump Its Track; Say So!; Search Is Through; Shall We Dance?; Shoein' The Mare; Shoes With Wings On; Slap That Bass; So Am I; So What?; Somebody From Somewhere; Someone To Watch Over Me; Soon; Spring Again; Stiff Upper Lip; Strike Up The Band; Sure Thing; Sweet And Low Down; Swiss Miss; The Babbitt And The Bromide; Till Then; Treat Me Rough; Tschaikowsky; Typical Self-Made American; What Can You Say In A Love Song?; Where's The Boy? Here's The Girl!; Who Cares; Why Do I Love You; Wintergreen For President; Words Without Music; You're A Builder Upper

GESNER, CLARK — You're A Good Man, Charlie Brown

GETZOV, RAY — Please Mr. Sun

GIACALONE, PAUL — You Were Mine

GIACOMAZZI, ANGELO — Italian Theme

GIACOSA, GIUSEPPE — One Fine Day(Un Bel Di)

GIANT, BILL — Ask Me; You're The Devil In Disguise

GIBB, BARRY — (Our Love)Don't Throw It Away; Everlasting Love, An; Grease; How Can You Mend A Broken Heart; I Can't Help It; I Just Want To Be Your Everything; Love Me; My World; To Love Somebody; Too Much Heaven; Tragedy; Woman In Love; Words; You Should Be Dancing; You Stepped Into My Life

GIBB, BARRY AND ROBIN — Come On Over

GIBB, BARRY, MAURICE AND ROBIN — Boogie Child; Desire; Fanny(Be Tender With My Love); First Of May; Guilty; Heartbreaker; Holiday; How Deep Is Your Love; I Started A Joke; If I Can't Have You; Islands In The Stream; Jive Talkin; Lonely Days; Love So Right; Love You Inside Out; Massachusetts(The Lights Went Out In); More Than A Woman; New York Mining Disaster; Night Fever; Nights On Broadway; Run To Me; Stayin' Alive

GIBB, MAURICE — To Love Somebody; Too Much Heaven; Tragedy; Words; You Should Be Dancing; You Stepped Into My Life

GIBB, ROBIN — Hold Onto My Love; How Can You Mend A Broken Heart; Love Me; My World; To Love Somebody; Too Much Heaven; Tragedy; Woman In Love; Words; You Should Be Dancing; You Stepped Into My Life

GIBB, STEVE — She Believes In Me

GIBBONS, BILLY — Legs; Sleeping Bag; Tush

GIBBONS, CARROLL — Garden In The Rain,a

GIBBS, A. HARRINGTON — Runnin' Wild

GIBSON, ANDY — Huckle Buck

GIBSON, BILL — Hip To Be Square

GIBSON, DEBBIE — Only In My Dreams; Out Of The Blue; Shake Your Love

GIBSON, DON — I Can't Stop Loving You; I'm Hurting; Just One Time; Oh, Lonesome Me; Sweet Dreams

GIBSON, DOUGLAS — Troglodyte (Cave Man)

GIBSON, JILL — You Really Know How To Hurt A Guy

GIEFER, GEORGE L. — Who Threw The Overalls In Mrs. Murphy's Chowder

GIFFORD, H. EUGENE — Black Jazz; Casa Loma Stomp; Out Of Space; Smoke Rings; White Jazz

GILBERT, CARY — Don't Leave Me This Way; Livin' For The Weekend; Me And Mrs. Jones

GILBERT, HERSCHEL BURKE — Moon Is Blue

GILBERT, L. WOLFE — By Heck; Chiquita; Dance-O-Mania; Don't Wake Me Up(Let Me Dream); Down Yonder; I Miss My Swiss; Jeannine, I Dream Of Lilac Time; Lucky Lindy!; Mama Don't Want No Peas An' Rice An' Cocoanut Oil; Mama Inez; Marta; My Mother's Eyes; O, Katharina!; Peanut Vendor; Ramona; Waiting For The Robert E. Lee; When You're With Somebody Else

GILBERT, RAY — All The Cats Join In; Baia; Blame It On The Samba; Casey At The Bat; Everybody Has A Laughing Place; Hot Canary; Muskrat Ramble; Sooner Or Later; Three Caballeros; Two Silhouettes; Without You; You Belong To My Heart Or Solamente Una Vez; Zip-A-Dee-Doo-Dah; Zoot Suit (For My Sunday Gal)

GILBERT, RONALD — We Ain't Got Nothing Yet

GILBERT, TIM — Incense And Peppermints

GILBERT, V. C. — Shifting, Whispering Sands

GILBERT, WM. S. — He Is An Englishman; I'm Called Little Buttercup; Tit-Willow; When I Was A Lad

GILDER, NICK — Hot Child In The City; Warrior

GILES, RICHARD — Wham Bam (Shang A Lang)

GILKYSON, NEAL — Girl In The Wood

GILKYSON, STEWART — Girl In The Wood

GILKYSON, TERRY — Bare Necessities; Cry Of The Wild Goose,the; Day Of Jubilo; Girl In The Wood; Green Fields; Love Is A Golden Ring; Marianne; Memories Are Made Of This

GILL, GEOFF — Heartbreaker

GILL, PETER — Relax

GILLESPIE, HAVEN — Beautiful Love; Breezin' Along With The Breeze; By The Sycamore Tree; Drifting And Dreaming; Honey; Old Master Painter; Santa Claus Is Coming To Town

GILLESPIE, JERRY — Somebody's Knockin'

GILLESPIE, JOHN BIRKS — Be-Bop; Blue 'n Boogie; Groovin' High; Manteca; Night In Tunisia,a; Oop Bop Sh-bam; Salt Peanuts

GILLIAM, MICHELLE — Creeque Alley

GILLIAN, IAN — Smoke On The Water

GILMORE, BILLY — Cherryhill Park

GILMORE, PATRICK — When Johnny Comes Marching Home

GILUTIN, JONATHAN — New Attitude

GIMBEL, NORMAN — Bluesette; Canadian Sunset; Different Worlds; Girl From Ipanema; Happy Days; How Insensitive; I Got A Name; I Will Follow Him; I Will Wait For You; It Goes Like It Goes; Killing Me Softly With His Song; Land Of Dreams; Love Among The Young; Making Our Dreams Come True; Man Ain't Supposed To Cry; Meditation; Pa-Paya Mama; Ready To Take A Chance Again; Ricochet; Summer Samba; Sway(Quien Sera); Watch What Happens

GIORDANO, F. — Anna(El Negro Zambon)

GIOSASI, HARRY — Sorry, I Ran All The Way Home

GIRAUD, HUBERT — Under Paris Skies

GISH, BILLY — Cynthia's In Love

GIST JR., KENNY — Next Plane To London

GIUFFRE, JIMMY — Four Brothers

GLANZBERG, NORBERT — Padam-Padam

GLASER, JAMES W. — Woman, Woman

GLASS, PRESTON — Don't Make Me Wait For Love; We Don't Have To Take Our Clothes Off; Who's Zoomin' Who

GLASSER, DICK — Angels In The Sky; Come Runnin' Back; I Will

GLASSMEYER, STEVEN — Love Or Something Like It

GLAZER, TOM — Face In The Crowd; Melody Of Love;

More; Old Soldiers Never Die; On Top Of Spaghetti; Pussy Cat; Skokiaan; Till We Two Are One

GLEASON, DICK — Ready, Willing, And Able; Woman

GLEASON, JACKIE — Melancholy Serenade

GLENN, ARTIE — Crying In The Chapel

GLICKMAN, FRED — Mule Train

GLITTER, GARY — Do You Wanna Touch Me; Rock And Roll(part II)

GLOSSON, LONNIE — Why Don't You Haul Off And Love Me?

GLOVER, CHARLES — Rose Of Tralee

GLOVER, HENRY — California Sun; Drown In My Tears; Honky Tonk; I'm Waiting Just For You; Peppermint Twist; Rock Love

GLOVER, JR, JOHN HENRY — You Don't Have To Be A Star (To Star In My Show)

GLOVER, ROGER — Smoke On The Water

GLUCK JR., JOHN — Blue Winter; It's My Party; Mecca

GOBLE, GRAHAM — Lady; Night Owls; Other Guy; Reminiscing

GODARD, BENJAMIN — Berceuse

GODLEY, KEVIN — Cry

GODWIN, MABLE — Ling Ting Tong

GOEHRING, GEORGE — Lipstick On Your Collar

GOELL, KERMIT — Huggin' And Chalkin'; Luna Rossa(Blushing Moon); Near You; Shepherd Serenade

GOERING, AL — Who's Your Little Who-zis

GOETSCHIUS, MARJORIE — I Dream Of You(More Than You Dream I Do)

GOETZ, COLEMAN — Congratulations

GOETZ, RAY — For Me And My Gal; Who Ate Napoleons With Josephine When Bonaparte Was Away; Yaaka Hulaa Hickey Dula

GOFFIN, GERRY — (You Make Me Feel Like)Natural Woman; At The Club; Do You Know Where You're Going To; Does Goodnight Mean Goodbye; Don't Bring Me Down; Don't Say Nothin' Bad(About My Baby); Go Away Little Girl; Halfway To Paradise; Her Royal Majesty; Hey, Girl; Hi-De-Ho(That Old Sweet Roll); I Can't Hear You No More; I Can't Stay Mad At You; I Want To Stay Here; I Wasn't Born To Follow; I'll Meet You Halfway; I'm Into Something Good; I've Got Bonnie; I've Got To Use My Imagination; It Might As Well Rain Until September; Just Once In My Life; Keep Your Hands Off My Baby; Let's Turkey Trot; Loco-Motion; Nothing's Gonna Change My Love For You; Oh! No, Not My Baby; One Fine Day; Pleasant Valley Sunday; Point Of No Return; Run To Him; Saving All My Love For You; Smackwater Jack; Some Kind-A-Wonderful; Someone That I Used To Love; Up On The Roof; When My Little Girl Is Smiling; Who Put The Bomp (In The Bomp-Bomp-Bomp); Will You Love Me Tomorrow

GOGA, JACK — Yesterday's Dreams; You

GOLAND, ARNOLD — No Chemise, Please!

GOLD, ANDREW — Lonely Boy

GOLD, ERNEST — Exodus; It's A Mad, Mad, Mad, Mad World; Practice Makes Perfect

GOLD, FREDDA — Twixt Twelve And Twenty

GOLD, JACK — Hang 'em High

GOLD, JIM — Nice To Be With You

GOLD, WALLY — Because They're Young; Fools' Hall Of Fame; Good Luck Charm; It's My Party; It's Now Or Never; She Can't Find Her Keys; Utopia

GOLDBERG, BARRY — I've Got To Use My Imagination

GOLDE, FRANNIE — Bit By Bit; Nightshift

GOLDEN, JOHN — Poor Butterfly

GOLDENBERG, MARK — Along Comes A Woman; Automatic; Soul Kiss

GOLDMAN, EDWIN FRANKO — On The Mall

GOLDMAN, JAMES — Beautiful

GOLDMAN, STEVE — How Many Times Can We Say Goodbye

GOLDMAN, WILLIAM — Beautiful

GOLDMARK, ANDY — Dynamite

GOLDNER, GEORGE — I Want You To Be My Girl; Maybe; Why Do Fools Fall In Love

GOLDSBORO, BOBBY — Autumn Of My Life; Cowboy And The Lady,the; Little Things; See The Funny Little Clown; Whenever He Holds You; With Pen In Hand

GOLDSMITH, CLIFF — Peanut Butter; Western Movies; Western Union

GOLDSMITH, JERRY — Ave Satani; Dr. Kildare(Theme from)(Three Stars Will Shine Tonight); Man From U. N. C. L. E. (Theme)

GOLDSTEIN, BOB — Washington Square

GOLDSTEIN, GERALD — L. A. Sunshine; Low Rider; My Boyfriend's Back; Night Time; Summer; Why Can't We Be Friends

GOLDSTEIN, JERRY — Come And Take A Ride In My Boat(Come On Down To My Boat); I Want Candy

GOLLAHON, GLADYS — Our Lady Of Fatima

GOMM, IAN — Cruel To Be Kind; Hold On

GONZALEZ, BOB — Little Girl

GONZALEZ, JIMENEZ — Under A Texas Moon

GOODHART, AL — Auf Wiedersehn, My Dear; Black Eyed Susan Brown; Fit As A Fiddle; I Apologize; I Saw Stars; I'm In A Dancing Mood; In A Little Bookshop; Johnny Doughboy Found A Rose In Ireland; Serenade Of The Bells

GOODMAN, AL — Special Lady

GOODMAN, ALFRED — When Hearts Are Young

GOODMAN, BENNY — Air Mail Special; Don't Be That Way; Flying Home; If Dreams Come True; Life Goes To A Party; Lullaby In Rhythm; Soft Winds; Solo Flight; Stompin' At The Savoy; Swingtime In The Rockies; Two O'clock Jump

GOODMAN, BOB — Close To Cathy

GOODMAN, DICKIE — Mr. Jaws

GOODMAN, HERALD — When It's Lamp Lightin' Time In The Valley

GOODMAN, LILLIAN ROSEDALE — Cherie, I Love You

GOODMAN, ROBERT — Hideaway

GOODMAN, STEVE — Banana Republic; City Of New Orleans

GOODMAN, WILLIE — Sexy Mama

GOODRUM, RANDY — Bluer Than Blue; Broken Hearted Me; Foolish Heart; I'll Be Over You; It's Sad To Belong; Oh, Sherrie; Who's Holding Donna Now; You Needed Me

GOODWIN, JOE — Billy(For When I Walk); Everywhere You Go; Gee! But I Hate To Go Home Alone; When You're Smiling (The Whole World Smiles With You); Your Mother And Mine

GORDON, ALAN — Cat In The Window; Celebrate; Happy Together; My Heart Belongs To Me; She'd Rather Be With Me; She's My Girl; You Know What I Mean

GORDON, IRVING — Be Anything(but Be Mine); Christmas Dreaming; Delaware; Gypsy Without A

Song; Kentuckian Song; Mama From The Train; Mister And Mississippi; Prelude To A Kiss; Unforgettable; What Will I Tell My Heart

GORDON, JAMES BECK — Layla

GORDON, MACK — (Lookie, Lookie, Lookie)Here Comes Cookie; At Last; Boa Noite; Broadway's Gone Hawaii; But Definitely; By The Way; Chattanooga Choo Choo; Chica Chica Boom Chic; Cigarettes, Cigars; College Rhythm; Danger-Love At Work; Did You Ever See A Dream Walking?; Doin' The Uptown Lowdown; Don't Let It Bother You; Down Argentina Way; Friendly Star; From The Top Of Your Head To The Tip Of Your Toes; Good Morning Glory; Good Night Lovely Little Lady; Goodnight, My Love; Head Over Heels In Love; Help Yourself To Happiness; I Can't Begin To Tell You; I Feel Like A Feather In The Breeze; I Had The Craziest Dream; I Hum A Waltz; I Know Why(and So Do You); I Like Mike; I Never Felt This Way Before; I Never Knew Heaven Could Speak; I Played Fiddle For The Czar; I Take To You; I Wanna Be In Winchell's Column; I Wanna Go To The Zoo; I Wish I Knew; I Wish I Were Aladdin; I'm Making Believe; I've Got A Date With A Dream; I've Got A Gal In Kalamazoo; I, Yi, Yi, Yi, Yi(I Like You Very Much); If You Feel Like Singing, Sing; In Acapulco; It Happened In Sun Valley; It Happens Every Spring; It Takes Two To Make A Bargain; It Was A Night In June; It's Swell Of You; It's The Animal In Me; Kiss Polka; Kokomo, Indiana; Long Ago Last Night; Love Song Of Tom Jones; Love Thy Neighbor; Loveliness Of You; Lullaby In Blue; Mam'selle; May I; May I Have The Next Romance With You; More I See You; My Heart Tells Me; Never In A Million Years; Oh, My Goodness!; On The Boardwalk At Atlantic City; Once In A Blue Moon; Once Too Often; One Never Knows, Does One?; Orchid To You, An; Paris In The Spring; Play Me An Old Fashioned Melody; Serenade In Blue; She Reminds Me Of You; Sing Me A Song Of The Islands; Somewhere In The Night; Stay As Sweet As You Are; Straight From The Shoulder(right From The Heart); Sweet As A Song; Through A Long And Sleepless Night; Time On My Hands; Two Dreams Met; Underneath The Harlem Moon; Wake Up And Live; Weekend In Havana; Were Your Ears Burning, Baby?; When I'm With You; Wilhelmina; With My Eyes Wide Open I'm Dreaming; Without A Word Of Warning; You Can't Have Everything; You Do; You Gotta Eat Your Spinach Baby; You Hit The Spot; You Make Me Feel So Young; You'll Never Know; You're My Past, Present And Future; You're Such A Comfort To Me

GORDON, MICHAEL Z. — Out Of Limits

GORDON, PAUL — Friends And Lovers(Both To Each Other); Next Time I Fall

GORDON, ROZ — Tracy's Theme

GORDY JR, BERRY — Bells; Come To Me; Do You Love Me?; I Love The Way You Love; I Want You Back; I'll Be Satisfied; I'll Be There; I'm Living In Shame; Lonely Teardrops; Love You Save; Mama's Pearl; Money, That's What I Want; No Matter What Sign You Are; Reet Petite; Shop Around; Sugar Daddy

GORDY, GEORGE — Beechwood 4-5789

GORDY, GWEN — I'll Be Satisfied; Lonely Teardrops; To Be Loved; You Got What It Takes

GORDY, JR, BERRY — To Be Loved; Try It Baby; You Got What It Takes; You've Made Me So Very Happy

GORDY, JR, EMORY — Traces

GORE, CHARLIE — Daddy O

GORE, LESLIE — My Town, My Guy, And Me; Out Here On My Own

GORE, MARTIN K. — People Are People

GORE, MICHAEL — Fame; Out Here On My Own

GORGONI, AL — I Can't Let Go; Step Out Of Your Mind

GORMAN, CHUCK — Seventeen

GORMAN, F. C. — Mashed Potato Time

GORMAN, FREDDY — (Just Like)Romeo And Juliet

GORMAN, FREDDY C. — Please Mr. Postman

GORMAN, ROSS — Rose Of The Rio Grande

GORME, EYDIE — Can't Get Over(the Bossa Nova)

GORNEY, JAY — Baby, Take A Bow; Broadway's Gone Hill Billy; Brother, Can You Spare A Dime?; I'm Laughin'; In Chi-Chi-Castenango; What Wouldn't I Do For That Man!

GORRELL, STUART — Georgia On My Mind

GORRIE, ALAN — Cut The Cake

GOSH, BOBBY — Little Bit More

GOSTING, DICK — Mountain's High

GOTTEHRER, RICHARD — I Want Candy; My Boyfriend's Back; Night Time

GOTTLER, ARCHIE — America, I Love You; Big City Blues; Breakaway; Crazy Feet; Is It Any Wonder

GOULD, BOON — Something About You

GOULD, MORTON — Boogie Woogie Etude; Pavanne

GOULD, PHIL — Something About You

GOULDING, EDMUND — Love, Your Magic Spell Is Everywhere; Mam'selle

GOULDMAN, GRAHAM — Bus Stop; East, West; Heart Full Of Soul; I'm Not In Love; Listen, People; Look Through Any Window

GOUNOD, CHARLES — Ave Maria; Funeral March Of A Marionette; Soldiers Chorus

GRACE, ROCHE — Rocky Mountain Way

GRAFF, JR, GEORGE — When Irish Eyes Are Smiling

GRAFFAGNINO, JAKE — Stop And Think It Over

GRAHAM JR., LEO — Shining Star

GRAHAM, IRVIN — I Believe; You Better Go Now

GRAHAM, ROGER — I Ain't Got Nobody

GRAHAM, RONNY — I'm All I've Got

GRAHAM, STEVE — Dear Old Donegal; Intermission Riff; Off Shore

GRAINGER, GARY — Ain't Love A Bitch; I Was Only Joking; Passion

GRAINGER, M. — Black Is Black

GRAMM, L. — Midnight Blue; Say You Will; Waiting For A Girl Like You

GRAMMATICO, LOU — Blue Morning, Blue Day; Cold As Ice; Dirty White Boy; Double Vision; Head Games; Hot Blooded; Long, Long Way From Home

GRANAHAN, GERRY — No Chemise, Please!

GRANATA, ROCCO — Marina

GRANDE, VINCENTE — Blues Serenade

GRANT, CORNELIUS — (i Know)i'm Losing You; You're My Everything

GRANT, EDDY — Electric Avenue; Romancing The Stone

GRANT, EDMUND — Baby, Come Back

GRANT, HAROLD — Here

GRANT, IAN — Let There Be Love

GRANT, MICKIE — Pink Shoelaces

GRANT, MILT — Rawhide

GRANT, RODGERS — Yeh Yeh

GRASSO, RICHIE — Sweet Cherry Wine

GRAVES, JOHN WOODCOCK — John Peel

GRAY, CHAUNCEY — Bye Bye Blues; You're The One I Care For

GRAY, ED — Crystal Blue Persuasion

GRAY, J. — Buzz Buzz Buzz

GRAY, JERRY — I Dreamt I Dwelt In Harlem; Pennsylvania 6-5000; String Of Pearls

GRAY, THOMAS — Money Changes Everything

GRAY, WAYNE — Cradle Of Love; Crazy

GRAY, YVONNE — Dancin' Man; Lady Love

GRAYDEN, MAC — Everlasting Love

GRAYDON, JAY — Mornin'; Turn Your Love Around; Who's Holding Donna Now

GREAN, CHARLES — I Dreamed; Sweet Violets

GREEN, ADOLPH — All You Need Is A Quarter; Asking For You; Be A Santa; Bells Are Ringing; Close Harmony; Come Up To My Place; Cry Like The Wind; Dance Only With Me; Distant Melody; Fade Out-Fade In; Fireworks; Five Zeros; French Lesson; Girls Like Me; Hold Me-Hold Me-Hold Me; How Can You Describe A Face?; I Can Cook Too; I Get Carried Away; I Know About Love; I Like Myself; I'm Just Taking My Time; I'm With You; Independent(On My Own); It's Love; Just In Time; Legacy; Little Bit In Love; Lonely Town; Long Before I Knew You; Looking Back; Lucky To Be Me; Make Someone Happy; Never-Never Land; New York, New York; Ohio; On The Twentieth Century; Our Private World; Party's Over; Quiet Girl; Ride Through The Night; Right Girl For Me; Right On Track; Say, Darling; Some Other Time; Wendy; What Is This Feeling In The Air?

GREEN, AL — I'm Still In Love With You; L-O-V-E; Let's Stay Together; Livin' For You; Look What You Done For Me; Sha-La-La(Make Me Happy); Tired Of Being Alone; You Ought To Be With Me

GREEN, BUD — Alabamy Bound; Away Down South In Heaven; Congratulations; Flat Foot Floogie; I Love My Baby(My Baby Loves Me); I'll Always Be In Love With You; Once In Awhile; Sentimental Journey; You Showed Me The Way

GREEN, EDDIE — Good Man Is Hard To Find

GREEN, FLORENCE — Soldier Boy

GREEN, GARFIELD — Jealous Kind Of Fellow

GREEN, GEORGE MICHAEL — Crumblin' Down; Hurt So Good

GREEN, HAROLD — I Guess I'll Have To Dream The Rest; It's Make Believe Ballroom Time

GREEN, J. — Can'tcha Say(You Believe In Me)

GREEN, JOHN — Body And Soul; Coquette; Easy Come, Easy Go; Hello, My Lover, Good-bye; I Cover The Waterfront; I Wanna Be Loved; I'm Yours; Out Of Nowhere; You're Mine You

GREEN, LEROY — Disco Inferno

GREEN, PETER — Black Magic Woman; Oh Well

GREEN, SANFORD — Play Me Hearts And Flowers(I Wanna Cry)

GREEN, TONY — Come To Me

GREENALL, RUPERT — One Thing Leads To Another

GREENAWAY, ROGER — Doctor's Orders; Here Comes That Rainy Day Feeling Again; I Was Kaiser Bill's Batman; I'd Like To Teach The World To Sing; Jeans On; Long Cool Woman(In A Black Dress); My Baby Loves Lovin'; Say You'll Stay Until Tomorrow; You've Got Your Troubles

GREENBAUM, NORMAN — Spirit In The Sky

GREENBERG, ELLIOT — Sweet Talkin' Guy

GREENBERG, STEVE — Funkytown

GREENE, JOE — And Her Tears Flowed Like Wine; Outa-Space

GREENE, MORT — Nevada; Sleepy Serenade; When There's A Breeze On Lake Louise

GREENE, TIM — Two Of Hearts

GREENFIELD, HOWARD — Alice In Wonderland; Another Sleepless Night; Bad Girl; Breaking In A Brand New Broken Heart; Breaking Up Is Hard To Do; Calendar Girl; Charms; Crying In The Rain; Diary; Does Goodnight Mean Goodbye; Everybody's Somebody's Fool; Fallin'; Foolish Little Girl; Frankie; Frankie And Johnny; Happy Birthday, Sweet Sixteen; Hungry Years; I Waited Too Long; It Hurts To Be In Love; Let's Go Steady Again; Little Devil; Love Will Keep Us Together; My Heart Has A Mind Of Its Own; Next Door To An Angel; Oh! Carol; Puppet Man; Run Samson Run; Stairway To Heaven; Stupid Cupid; Venus In Blue Jeans; Where The Boys Are; You Mean Everything To Me; You Never Done It Like That

GREENWICH, ELLIE — Be My Baby; Chapel Of Love; Da-Doo Ron Ron; Do Wah Diddy Diddy; Give Us Your Blessing; Hanky Panky; I Can Hear Music; I Wanna Love Him So Bad; Kind Of Boy You Can't Forget; Look Of Love; Maybe I Know; People Say; River Deep-Mountain High; Why Do Lovers Break Each Other's Hearts?

GREER, DAN — Let Me Love You Tonight

GREER, JESSE — Flapperette; Freshie; I'm Making Hay In The Moonlight; Just You, Just Me; Kitty From Kansas City

GRENET, ELISEO — Mama Inez

GRENWICH, ELLIE — Leader Of The Pack

GREVER, MARIA — Magic Is The Moonlight; Ti-Pi-Tin; What A Difference A Day Made

GREY, CLIFFORD — Charming; Dark Night; Dream Lover; Got A Date With An Angel; Hallelujah!; I'm Glad I Waited; If You Were The Only Girl In The World; Ma Belle; March Of The Grenadiers; March Of The Musketeers; My Love Parade; On With The Dance; Rogue Song; Sally; Sometimes I'm Happy; Valencia; When I'm Looking At You; Whip-poor-will; White Dove; Wild Rose

GREY, JOE — Runnin' Wild

GREY, ZANE — Back In Love Again

GRIEG, EDVARD — Anitra's Dance; March Of The Dwarfs; Norwegian Dance

GRIER, JIMMY — Object Of My Affection; What's The Reason (I'm Not Pleasin' You)

GRIFFIN, JAMES — For All We Know

GRIFFIN, KEN — You Can't Be True Dear

GRIFFIN, LEROY — Story Untold

GRIFFITH, ANDY — What It Was, Was Football

GRIFFITH, BILLY — Love Machine(part 1)

GRIMALDI, JERRY — I Can Never Go Home Anymore

GROCE, LARRY — Junk Food Junkie

GROFE, FERDE — Daybreak; Mississippi Suite; On The Trail; Wonderful One (My)

GROGAN, PHIL — Especially For You

GROSS, HENRY — Shannon

GROSSMAN, JULIUS — Tzena, Tzena, Tzena

GROSZ, WILL — Along The Santa Fe Trail; Harbor Lights; In An Old Dutch Garden(By An Old Dutch Mill); Isle Of Capri; Make Believe Island; Tomorrow Night

GROUYA, TED — Flamingo; I Heard You Cried Last Night(and So Did I); In My Arms

GROVES, STEVE — Toast And Marmalade For Tea

GRUBER, EDMUND L. — U.S. Field Artillery March Or The Caissons Go Rolling Along

GRUBER, FRANZ — Silent Night, Holy Night

GRUDEFF, MARIAN — Finding Words For Spring; I'd Do It Again; Married Man

GRUSIN, DAVE — And Then There's Maude; It Might Be You

GRUSKA, JAY — Friends And Lovers(Both To Each Other)

GUADIO, BOB — December 1963(Oh What A Night)

GUARALDI, VINCENT — Cast Your Fate To The Wind

GUARE, JOHN — Love Has Driven Me Sane

GUENTHER, GISELA — Freddy

GUERCIO, JAMES — Distant Shores; Susan

GUEST, WILLIAM — I Don't Want To Do Wrong

GUIDA, CARMELA — If You Wanna Be Happy

GUIDA, FRANK — (Down In)New Orleans; If You Wanna Be Happy; Not Me; Quarter To Three; Twist, Twist Senora

GUIDRY, GREG — Goin' Down

GUIDRY, ROBERT — But I Do; See You Later, Alligator; Walking To New Orleans

GUIFFRIA, GREGG — Call To The Heart

GUINN, JANIS LEE — Chick-A-Boom

GUION, KING — Solitaire

GUMMOE, JOHN — Rhythm Of The Rain

GURVITZ, P. — Who Found Who

GURYAN, MARGO — Lonely Womam; Sunday Mornin'

GUSSIN, DAVID — Envy

GUTHRIE, ARLO — Alice's Restaurant

GUTHRIE, BEVERLY — Love Me Forever

GUTHRIE, WOODY — So Long(It's Been Good To Know Yuh)

GUTIERREZ, L. — Walking Down Your Street

H

HACKADAY, HAL — Shake Me I Rattle(Squeeze Me I Cry)
HADJIDAKIS, MANOS — All Alone Am I; Never On Sunday
HADLER, MARY M. — S h i f t i n g, Whispering Sands
HAENSCHEN, GUSTAVE — Manhattan Merry Go Round
HAGAR, SAMMY — Love Walks In; Why Can't This Be Love
HAGEN, EARLE — Fishin' Hole; Harlem Nocturne
HAGGARD, MERLE — If We Make It Through December; Legend Of Bonnie And Clyde
HAGGART, BOB — Big Noise From Winnetka; Dog Town Blues; I'm Prayin' Humble; South Rampart Street Parade; What's New
HAGUE, ALBERT — Just For Once; Two Faces In The Dark; Young And Foolish
HAGUE, STEVE — So In Love
HAINES, W. G. — Biggest Aspidastra In The World
HAIRSTON, JESTER — Mary's Boy Child
HALDEMAN, OAKLEY — Brush Those Tears From Your Eyes; Here Comes Santa Claus
HALEY, BILL — Crazy Man, Crazy; Skinny Minnie
HALEY, ED — While Strolling Through The Park One Day
HALIFAX, HAL — Penny Serenade
HALL, CAROL — Doatsy Mae
HALL, DARYL — Did It In A Minute; Dreamtime; Every Time You Go Away; I Can't Go For That(No Can Do); It's A Laugh; Kiss On My List; Maneater; Method Of Modern Love; One On One; Out Of Touch; Private Eyes; Rich Girl; Sara Smile; Say It Isn't So; She's Gone; Some Things Are Better Left Unsaid; Swept Away; Swing Low Sweet Chariot; Wait For Me; You Make My Dreams
HALL, FRED — I Got A "code" In My "doze"
HALL, GUY H. — Johnson Rag
HALL, JACK — Keep On Smilin'
HALL, JAMES — Keep On Smilin'
HALL, JOHANNA — Dance With Me; Still The One
HALL, JOHN J. — Dance With Me; Still The One
HALL, OLIVER — Revenge
HALL, REGGIE — You Talk Too Much
HALL, RICH — Cowboy Serenade
HALL, RICK — Sweet And Innocent; Too Weak To Fight
HALL, TOM T. — Harper Valley PTA; I Love
HALL, WENDELL — It Ain't Gonna Rain No Mo'
HALLEY, BOB — Dear Lonely Hearts(I'm Writing To You)
HAM, WILLIAM PETER — Baby Blue; Day After Day; No Matter What; Without You
HAMBLEN, STUART — (Remember Me)I'm The One Who Loves You; It Is No Secret What God Can Do; Open Up Your Heart; Open Your Heart
HAMILTON, ANN — Winners And Losers
HAMILTON, ARTHUR — Cry Me A River; He Needs Me
HAMILTON, BOB — (Just Like)Romeo And Juliet
HAMILTON, CLYDE — Italian Theme
HAMILTON, DANNY — Winners And Losers
HAMILTON, DANNY AND ANN — Fallin' In Love(Again)
HAMILTON, DAVE — Pretty Little Baby
HAMILTON, NANCY — How High The Moon; Old Soft Shoe
HAMILTON, ORD — You're Blase
HAMILTON, RONALD — In A Moment

HAMILTON, RUSS — Rainbow
HAMLIN, ROSE — Angel Baby
HAMLISCH, MARVIN — At The Ballet; Better Than Ever; California Nights; I Still Believe In Love; If You Really Knew Me; If You Remember Me; Just For Tonight; Last Time I Felt Like This; Let Me Dance For You; Life Is What You Make It; Looking Through The Eyes Of Love; Music And The Mirror; Nobody Does It Better; Nothing; One; Sunshine, Lollipops And Roses; Surprise Surprise; Tits And Ass; Way We Were; What I Did For Love
HAMMER, JACK — Great Balls Of Fire; Peek-A-Boo
HAMMER, JAN — Miami Vice Theme
HAMMERSTEIN II, JEROME — 'twas Not So Long Ago
HAMMERSTEIN II, OSCAR — 'Twas Not So Long Ago; All At Once You Love Her; All Er Nothin'; All I Owe Ioway; All In Fun; All The Things You Are; All Through The Day; Allegheny Al; And Love Was Born; Bali Ha'i; Bambalina; Beat Out That Rhythm On A Drum; Big Black Giant; Bill; Bloody Mary; Can I Forget You?; Can't Help Lovin' Dat Man; Climb Ev'ry Mountain; Cock-eyed Optimist; Come Home; Cossack Love Song; D'ye Love Me; Dance, My Darlings; Dat's Love; Dawn; Desert Song; Dites-Moi; Do I Love You Because You're Beautiful; Do-Re-Mi; Don't Ever Leave Me; Door Of My Dreams; Edelweiss; Everybody's Got A Home But Me; Fan Tan Fannie; Far Away; Farmer And The Cowman; Fellow Needs A Girl; Folks Who Live On The Hill; French Marching Song; Gentleman Is A Dope; Getting To Know You; Grant Avenue; Happy Talk; Hay, Straw; Heaven In My Arms; Hello, Young Lovers; High, Wide, And Handsome; Honey Bun; Hundred Million Miracles,a; I Am So Eager; I Built A Dream One Day; I Cain't Say No; I Enjoy Being A Girl; I Have Dreamed; I Have The Room Above; I Haven't Got A Worry In The World; I Might Fall Back On You; I Still Suits Me; I Want A Kiss; I Want A Man; I Whistle A Happy Tune; I Won't Dance; I'll Take Romance; I'm Alone; I'm Gonna Wash That Man Right Outa My Hair; I'm Your Girl; I've Told Every Little Star; If I Loved You; In Egern On The Tegern Sea; In My Own Little Corner; In Other Words, Seventeen; In The Heart Of The Dark; Indian Love Call; Isn't It Kinda Fun; It; It Might As Well Be Spring; It's A Grand Night For Singing; June Is Bustin' Out All Over; Just Once Around The Clock; Kansas City; Keep It Gay; Kiss To Build A Dream On; Last Time I Saw Paris; Let's Say Good Night Till It's Morning; Life Upon The Wicked Stage; Loneliness Of Evening; Lonely Goatherd; Love, Look Away; Lovely Night; Lover, Come Back To Me; Make Believe; Many A New Day; Margot; Maria; Marianne; Marriage Type Love; Mist Over The Moon; Mister Snow; Money Isn't Everything; Mounties; My Favorite Things; My Girl Back Home; Next Time It Happens; No Other Love; Nobody Else But Me; Oh, What A Beautiful Mornin'; Oklahoma; Ol' Man River; One Alone; One Kiss; One More Dance; Out Of My Dreams; People Will Say We're In Love; Poor Jud; Puzzlement; Real Nice Clambake; Reckless; Riff Song; Romance; Rose Marie; Shall We Dance?; Sixteen Going On Seventeen; So Far; Softly, As In A Morning Sunrise; Soliloquy; Some Enchanted Evening; Something Wonderful; Song Is You; Song Of The Flame; Sound Of Music; Stan' Up An' Fight; Stouthearted Men; Sunday; Sunny; Surrey With The Fringe On Top;

Sweet Thursday; Totem Tom Tom; Two Little Bluebirds; Very Special Day; Vodka; Wanting You; We Kiss In A Shadow; We'll Have A Kingdom; What's The Use Of Wond'rin'; When I Grow Too Old To Dream; When I Marry Mister Snow; When The Children Are Asleep; When The Spring Is In The Air; Who; Why Do I Love You; Why Was I Born; Wildflower; Will You Marry Me Tomorrow, Maria; You Are Beautiful; You Are Love; You Are Never Away; You Are Sixteen; You Need Someone, Someone Needs You; You'll Never Walk Alone; You've Got To Be Carefully Taught; Younger Than Springtime

HAMMERSTEIN, ARTHUR — Because Of You

HAMMOND, ALBERT — Gimme Dat Ding; I Need To Be In Love; It Never Rains In Southern California; Little Arrows; Nothing's Gonna Stop Us Now; To All The Girls I've Loved Before; When I Need You

HAMMOND, BARRY — Eighteen With A Bullet

HAMMOND, CLAY — Part Time Love

HAMMOND, CON — Turn Back The Hand Of Time

HAMMOND, RONNIE — Do It Or Die

HAMNER, CURLEY — Hey! Ba-Ba-Re-Bop

HAMPTON, CARL — If Loving You Is Wrong I Don't Want To Be Right; If You're Ready(Come Go With Me)

HAMPTON, LIONEL — Evil Gal Blues; Flying Home; Hamp's Boogie Woogie; Hey! Ba-Ba-Re-Bop; Midnight Sun

HAMPTON, PAUL — You Don't Know What You've Got

HANCOCK, JAMES — Biggest Aspidastra In The World

HANDEL, G. F. — Joy To The World

HANDEL, GEORGE FREDERIC — Hallelujah Chorus

HANDMAN, LOU — Are You Lonesome Tonight?; Blue(and Broken Hearted); Bye Bye Baby; Is My Baby Blue Tonight; Last Night I Dreamed Of You; Me And The Moon; Was It Rain?

HANDY, W. C. — Aunt Hagar's Blues; Beale St. Blues; Careless Love; Loveless Love; Memphis Blues; St. Louis Blues; Yellow Dog Blues

HANIGHEN, BERNIE — 'round Midnight; Baby Doll; Bob White; Dixieland Band; Fare-Thee-Well To Harlem; Here Come The British(Bang! Bang!); If The Moon Turns Green; Weekend Of A Private Secretary; When A Woman Loves A Man

HANKS, LEN — Back In Love Again

HANLEY, JAMES — Zing Went The Strings Of My Heart

HANLEY, JAMES F. — (Back Home Again In)Indiana; As Long As I've Got My Mammy; Born And Bred In Old Kentucky; Cute Little Things You Do; Gee! But I Hate To Go Home Alone; Half A Moon; Hello Tucky; Just A Cottage Small By A Waterfall; Rose Of Washington Square; Second Hand Rose; Somebody Else-Not Me

HANLON, BERT — M-I-S-S-I-S-S-I-P-P-I

HANSEN, RANDY — State Of Shock

HARBACH, OTTO — Allah's Holiday; Bambalina; Cossack Love Song; Cuddle Up A Little Closer, Lovey Mine; D'ye Love Me; Dancing The Devil Away; Dawn; Desert Song; Door Of My Dreams; Every Little Movement(Has A Meaning All It's Own); Far Away; French Marching Song; Giannina Mia; I Want A Kiss; I Watch The Love Parade; I Won't Dance; Indian Love Call; It; Let's Begin; Let's Say Good Night Till It's Morning; Love Nest; Margot; Mounties; New Love Is Old; Night Was Made For Love; No, No, Nanette; One Alone; One Moment Alone; Poor Pierrot; Riff Song; Romance; Rose Marie; She Didn't Say Yes; Smoke

Gets In Your Eyes; Something Had To Happen; Song Of The Flame; Sunny; Totem Tom Tom; Touch Of Your Hand; Try To Forget; Vodka; We'll Have A Kingdom; When A Maid Comes Knocking At Your Heart; Who; Wildflower; Yesterdays; You're Devastating

HARBURG, E. Y. — Ain't It De Truth?; And Russia Is Her Name; Any Moment Now; April In Paris; Begat; Brother, Can You Spare A Dime?; Buds Won't Bud; Californ-I-AY; Can't Help Singing; Chin Up! Cheerio! Carry On!; Cocoanut Sweet; Ding-Dong! The Witch Is Dead; Don't Let It Get You Down; Down With Love; Eagle And Me; Evelina; Fancy Meeting You; Fun To Be Fooled; God's Country; Great Come-and-Get-It Day; Happiness Is A Thing Called Joe; How Are Things In Glocca Morra?; I Am Only Human After All; I Could Go On Singing; I Got A Song; I Like The Likes Of You; I Love To Sing-A; I'll Take Tallulah; I'm Yours; I've Gone Romantic On You; If I Only Had A Brain; If This Isn't Love; In The Shade Of The New Apple Tree; In Your Own Quiet Way; It's Only A Paper Moon; Last Call For Love; Last Night When We Were Young; Let's Put Our Heads Together; Let's Take A Walk Around The Block; Life's A Dance; Life's Full Of Consequence; Little Biscuit; Little Drops Of Rain; Long Before You Came Along; Look To The Rainbow; Lydia, The Tattooed Lady; Merry Old Land Of Oz; Moanin' In The Mornin'; More And More; Napoleon; Necessity; Old Devil Moon; Over The Rainbow; Paris Is A Lonely Town; Poor You; Pretty To Walk With; Push The Button; Right As The Rain; Savannah; Save Me, Sister; Shoein' The Mare; Something Sort Of Grandish; Song Of The Woodman; Suddenly; T'morra, T'morra; The World Is In My Arms; Two Blind Loves; We're Off To See The Wizard; What Can You Say In A Love Song?; What Good Does It Do; What Is There To Say; What Wouldn't I Do For That Man!; When I'm Not Near The Girl I Love; When The Boys Come Home; When The Idle Poor Become The Idle Rich; You're A Builder Upper

HARDAWAY, LILA MAE — Sign O' The Times; Signed, Sealed, Delivered I'm Yours

HARDAWAY, LULA — I Don't Know Why; I Was Made To Love Her; You Met Your Match...

HARDCASTLE, PAUL — 19

HARDEN, MELVIN — Backfield In Motion"

HARDIN, GLEN D. — Count Me In; My Heart's Symphony

HARDIN, TIM — If I Were A Carpenter; Reason To Believe

HARDWICK, OTTO — Down In Our Alley Blues

HARDY, BILL — Amen(Yea-Man)

HARGIS, REGINALD — Dazz; Dusic

HARGRAVE, RON — High School Confidential

HARGREAVES, ROBERT — If; Lady Of Spain; Let's All Sing Like The Birdies Sing; Unless

HARLEN, JACK — Alley Cat

HARLINE, LEIGH — Give A Little Whistle; Hi-Diddle-Dee-Dee(An Actor's Life For Me); I've Got No Strings; Jiminy Cricket; When You Wish Upon A Star; World Owes Me A Living; Wynken, Blynken And Nod

HARLING, W. FRANKE — Beyond The Blue Horizon; Give Me A Moment Please; Sing You Sinners; Tonight Is Mine; Where Was I?

HARMATI, SANDOR — Bluebird Of Happiness

HARNICK, SHELDON — Artificial Flowers; Away From

You; Away In A Manger; Boston Beguine; Days Gone By; Dear Friend; Do You Love Me?; Far From The Home I Love; Fiddler On The Roof; Freddy; Gentleman Jimmy; Good Clean Fun; Grand Knowing You; He Tossed A Coin; Heartbreak Kid; If I Were A Rich Man; Ilona; Little Old New York; Matchmaker, Matchmaker; Miracle Of Miracles; My Gentle Young Johnny; My Miss Mary; Now I Have Everything; Politics And Poker; Sabbath Prayer; She Loves Me; Sunrise, Sunset; Till Tomorrow; To Life Or L'chaim; Tradition; When Did I Fall In Love; Will He Like Me

HAROLD, WILLIAM — Goofus

HARPER, MARJORIE — Jealous Of You; Negra Consentida(My Pet Brunette)

HARRIS III, JAMES — Control; Human; I Didn't Mean To Turn You On; Nasty; What Have You Done For Me Lately; When I Think Of You

HARRIS, ART — What Am I Living For?

HARRIS, BENNY — Ornithology

HARRIS, BOB — Lolita(Love Theme)

HARRIS, DON F. — I'm Leaving It Up To You; Jolly Green Giant

HARRIS, GEORGE — Celery Stalks At Midnight

HARRIS, JAMES — In A Moment; Let's Wait Awhile

HARRIS, JOHN EARL — Surfin' Bird

HARRIS, MAURY COLEMAN — Dear Mom

HARRIS, P. Q. — Touch Me (I Want Your Body)

HARRIS, REMUS — Cry, Baby, Cry; So Long; St. Theresa Of The Roses

HARRIS, ROLF — Tie Me Kangaroo Down Sport

HARRIS, WILL J. — Sweet Sue-Just You

HARRIS, WOODY — Clementine; Queen Of The Hop; Rock-A-Billy

HARRISON, CHARLIE — How Do You Do

HARRISON, GEORGE — All Those Years Ago; Badge; Bangla-Desh; Blow Away; Blue Jay Way; Crackerbox Palace; Dark Horse; Deep Blue; Don't Bother Me; Flying; For You Blue; Give Me Love(Give Me Peace On Earth); Got My Mind Set On You; Here Comes The Sun; I Need You; I Want To Tell You; If I Needed Someone; Inner Light; Isn't It A Pity; It's All Too Much; Long, Long, Long; Love You To; My Sweet Lord; Old Brown Shoe; Only A Northern Song; Photograph; Piggies; Savoy Truffle; Something; What Is Life; While My Guitar Gently Weeps; Within You, Without You; You

HARRISON, JERRY — Burning Down The House

HARRISON, LARRY — (You Don't Know)How Glad I Am; Why Baby Why

HARRISON, NEIL — I Could Never Miss You More Than I Do; I Could Never Take The Place Of Your Man

HARRISON, NIGEL — One Way Or Another

HARRY, DEBBIE — Call Me; Rapture

HARRY, DEBORAH — Dreaming; Heart Of Glass; One Way Or Another

HARSHMAN, DANNY — Something's Wrong With Me

HART, BOBBY — (I'm Not Your)Steppin' Stone; Come A Little Bit Closer; Hurt So Bad; I Wonder What She's Doing Tonight?; Keep On Singing; Last Train To Clarksville; Something's Wrong With Me; Sometimes I Feel Like A Motherless Child; Valleri; Words

HART, BRUCE — Bang The Drum Slowly(theme); You Take My Breath Away

HART, COREY — I Am By Your Side; It Ain't Enough; Never Surrender; Sunglasses At Night

HART, FREDDIE — Loop De Loop

HART, LORENZ — All At Once; All Dark People; All Dressed Up(Spic And Spanish); Amarillo; Any Old Place With You; April Fool; Are You My Love?; Babes In Arms; Baby's Awake Now; Baby's Best Friend; Bewitched; Blue Moon; Blue Ocean Blues; Blue Room; Boy I Left Behind Me; Bye And Bye; Can't You Do A Friend A Favor?; Careless Rhapsody; Circus On Parade; Cuttin' The Cane; Dancing On The Ceiling; Den Of Iniquity; Diavalo; Did You Ever Get Stung?1938); Do I Hear You Saying?; Do It The Hard Way; Don't Tell Your Folks; Down By The River; Ev'ry Sunday Afternoon; Ev'rything I've Got; Falling In Love With Love; From Another World; Girl Friend; Give It Back To The Indians; Glad To Be Unhappy; Hallelujah, I'm A Bum; Happy Hunting Horn; Have You Met Miss Jones?; Heart Is Quicker Than The Eye; Here In My Arms; Here's A Hand; How About It?; How To Win Friends And Influence People; I Could Write A Book; I Didn't Know What Time It Was; I Feel At Home With You; I Like To Recognize The Tune; I Married An Angel; I Must Love You; I Still Believe In You; I Want A Man; I Wish I Were In Love Again; I'd Rather Be Right; I'll Tell The Man In The Street; I've Got Five Dollars; Isn't It Romantic?; It Never Entered My Mind; It's Easy To Remember; It's Got To Be Love; Johnny One Note; Jupiter Forbid; Lady Is A Tramp; Lady Must Live; Like Ordinary People Do; Little Birdie Told Me So; Little Girl Blue; Love Me Tonight; Love Never Went To College; Lover; Manhattan; Mimi; Moon Of My Delight; Most Beautiful Girl In The World; Mountain Greenery; My Funny Valentine; My Heart Stood Still; My Man Is On The Make; My Romance; Nobody's Heart(Belongs To Me); Nothing But You; Oh, Diogenes!; On A Desert Island With Thee; On Your Toes; Over And Over Again; Plant You Now, Dig You Later; Quiet Night; Send For Me; Sentimental Me; Ship Without A Sail; Shortest Day Of The Year; Simpatica; Sing; Sing For Your Supper; Soon; Spring Is Here; Stonewall Moskowitz March; Sweet Peter; Sweet Sixty-Five; Thou Swell; To Keep My Love Alive; Too Good For The Average Man; Tree In The Park; Wait Till You See Her; Way Out West; What's The Use Of Talking; Where Or When; Where's That Rainbow; Why Can't I; Why Do I; Why Do You Suppose; With A Song In My Heart; You Are Too Beautiful; You Have Cast Your Shadow On The Sea; You Mustn't Kick It Around; You Took Advantage Of Me; Yours Sincerely; Zip

HART, ROGER — Just Like Me

HART, SAM C. — When It's Lamp Lightin' Time In The Valley

HART, WILLIAM — Didn't I(Blow Your Mind This Time); Didn't We Almost Have It All; La La La(Means I Love You)

HARTFORD, JOHN — Gentle On My Mind

HARTMAN, DAN — Free Ride; I Can Dream About You; Living In America

HARVEY, ALEX — Delta Dawn; Rings

HASELDON, TONY — Nobody Said It Was Easy

HATCH, EARL — What's The Reason (I'm Not Pleasin' You)

HATCH, TONY — Call Me; Color My World; Don't Sleep In The Subway; Downtown; Forget Him; I Couldn't Live Without Your Love; I Know A Place; Look For A Star; My Love; Other Man's Grass Is Always Greener; Round Every Corner; Sign Of The Times; Who Am

I?; You'd Better Come Home; You're The One
HATCHER, CHARLES — Oh How Happy
HATCHER, HARLEY — All For The Love Of Sunshine
HATHAWAY, DONNY — Come Back Charleston Blue
HATHCOCK, JOHN — Welcome To My World
HAUG, FELIX — Captain Of Her Heart
HAUSMAN, MICHAEL — Voices Carry
HAVEN, GEORGE — (It's No)Sin
HAWES, BESS — M. T. A
HAWES, BRUCE — Mighty Love
HAWKER, KENNETH — Can't You Hear My Heart Beat?
HAWKER, MIKE — I Only Want To Be With You
HAWKINS, CHARLOTTE — With You On My Mind
HAWKINS, COLEMAN — Queer Notions
HAWKINS, DALE — Susie Q
HAWKINS, ERSKINE — Tuxedo Junction
HAWKINS, RON — Mary Lou
HAWTHORNE, ALICE — Whispering Hope
HAY, COLIN — Down Under; It's A Mistake; Overkill; Who Can It Be Now?
HAY, ROY — Church Of The Poison Mind; Do You Really Want To Hurt Me; I'll Tumble 4 Ya; It's A Miracle; Karma Chameleon; Kashmiri Love Song; Miss Me Blind; Time (Clock Of The Heart)
HAYCOCK, PETER — Couldn't Get It Right
HAYDEN, JOSEPH — (There'll Be A)Hot Time In The Old Town Tonight
HAYES, BILLY — Blue Christmas
HAYES, BOB — Is It Any Wonder
HAYES, C. — I Know What I Like
HAYES, CHRIS — Power Of Love; Stuck With You
HAYES, CHRISTOPHER — I Want A New Drug
HAYES, CLANCY — Huggin' And Chalkin'
HAYES, EDGAR — Somebody Stole Gabriel's Horn
HAYES, ISAAC — B-A-B-Y; Deja Vu; Hold On(I'm Coming); I Thank You; Men, The(Theme); Shaft(Theme From); Soul Man; When Something Is Wrong With My Baby; Your Good Thing (Is About To End)
HAYES, KENDALL — Walk On By
HAYES, OTHA — Shake A Tail Feather
HAYES, PETER LIND — Come To Me
HAYES, TONY — Black Is Black; Black Is The Color Of My True Love's Hair
HAYMAN, RICHARD — Dansero
HAYMES, BOB — Lipstick And Candy And Rubber Sole Shoes; My Love, My Love
HAYS, BARRY — Radar Love
HAYS, BILLY — Every Day Of My Life
HAYS, LEE — Badman's Blunder; If I Had A Hammer
HAYWARD, CHARLES — Devil Went Down To Georgia
HAYWARD, JUSTIN — Nights In White Satin; Question; Story In Your Eyes; Your Wildest Dreams
HAYWOOD, LEON — I Want'a Do Something Freaky To You; She's A Bad Mama Jama
HAZARD, ROBERT — Girls Just Want To Have Fun
HAZEL, EDWARD — Shakey Ground
HAZLEWOOD, ALBERT AND MIKE — The Air That I Breathe
HAZLEWOOD, LEE — Bonnie Came Back; Boss Guitar; Cannon Ball; Friday's Child; Houston; How Does That Grab You Darlin'?; Ladybird; Lightning's Girl; Lonely One; Love Eyes; Not The Lovin' Kind; Rebel-Rouser; Some Velvet Morning; Sugar Town
HAZLEWOOD, MIKE — Gimme Dat Ding; It Never Rains In Southern California; Little Arrows; Yes, Yes, Yes

HEAD, ROY — Treat Her Right
HEADON, TOPPER — Rock The Casbah
HEARD, DICK — Kentucky Rain
HEATH, HY — Little Red Fox; Mule Train; Somebody Bigger Than You And I; Uncle Remus Said
HEATHERTON, FRED — I've Got A Lovely Bunch Of Cocoanuts
HEBB, BOBBY — Natural Man; Sunny
HECHT, DON — Walkin' After Midnight
HECHT, KEN — No One Knows
HEFTI, NEAL — Batman Theme; Good Earth; How To Murder Your Wife; Li'l Darlin'; Odd Couple, The(Theme)
HEGEL, ROBERT — Just As I Am
HEINDORF, RAY — Hold Me In Your Arms; Melancholy Rhapsody; Pete Kelly's Blues
HELD, ANNA — It's Delightful To Be Married
HELFMAN, KENNY NOLAN — I Like Dreamin; Lady Marmalade; Love's Grown Deep; My Eyes Adored You
HELLERMAN, FRED — Borning Day; Come Away Melinda; Gotta Travel On; I Never Will Marry
HELLMAN, MARCO H. — Four Or Five Times
HEMERT, VAN — Ronnie Ball
HENDERSON, BRIAN — Summer Nights
HENDERSON, CHARLES — As If I Didn't Have Enough On My Mind; Deep Night; Hold Me In Your Arms; So Beats My Heart For You
HENDERSON, DOUGLAS — Long Lonely Nights
HENDERSON, FLETCHER — Dicty Blues; Down South Blues; Down South Camp Meetin'; Down The Aisle Of Love; Dying With The Blues; Gin House Blues; Henderson Stomp; Kind Lovin' Blues; Stampede; Wrappin' It Up (The Lindy Glide)
HENDERSON, H. — Shake Your Rump To The Funk
HENDERSON, HORACE — Big John's Special; Rug Cutter's Swing
HENDERSON, JOE — Why Don't They Understand
HENDERSON, KNOX — Shame, Shame
HENDERSON, PATRICK — Real Love
HENDERSON, RAY — (There's Something About An)Old Fashioned Girl; Alabamy Bound; Animal Crackers In My Soup; Bam, Bam Bamy Shore; Best Things In Life Are Free; Birth Of The Blues; Black Bottom; Broadway; Button Up Your Overcoat!; Bye Bye Blackbird; Come To Me; Curly Top; Don't Bring Lulu; Don't Hold Everything; Don't Tell Her What's Happened To Me; Five Foot Two, Eyes Of Blue(Has Anybody Seen My Girl); Follow The Swallow; For Old Times' Sake; Georgette; Girl Is You And The Boy Is Me; Girls, Girls, Girls; Good For You, Bad For Me; Good News; He's A Ladies Man; Here Am I-Broken Hearted; Hold My Hand; I Want A Lovable Baby; I Want To Be Bad; I'm A Dreamer, Aren't We All; I'm On The Crest Of A Wave; I'm Sitting On Top Of The World; I've Got To Get Hot; If I Had A Girl Like You; If I Had A Talking Picture Of You; It All Depends On You; Just A Memory; Just Imagine; Life Is Just A Bowl Of Cherries; Little Pal; Lucky Day; Lucky In Love; My Lucky Star; My Sin; My Song; Pickin' Cotton; Sonny Boy; Sunny Side Up; Thrill Is Gone; Together; Turn On The Heat; Varsity Drag; What D'ya Say?; Why Can't You (Birdies Sing In Cages Too); Why Did I Kiss That Girl; Without Love; You Try Somebody Else, And I'll Try Somebody Else; You Wouldn't Fool Me, Would You?; You're The Cream In

My Coffee

HENDLER, HERB — Hot Toddy

HENDRICKS, BELFORD C. — Call Me; It's Just A Matter Of Time; Looking Back

HENDRICKS, JAMES — Summer Rain

HENDRICKS, JON — Desafinado(Slightly Out Of Tune); I Want You To Be My Baby; One Note Samba; Yeh Yeh

HENDRIX, JIMI — Dolly Dagger; Fire; Foxey Lady; Freedom; Purple Haze; Stone Free; The Wind Cries Mary

HENEKER, DAVID — Half A Sixpence; Irma La Douce

HENLEY, DON — Best Of My Love; Boys Of Summer; Brahms' Lullaby; Desperado; Dirty Laundry; Heartache Tonight; Hotel California; I Can't Tell You Why; Life In The Fast Lane; Lyin' Eyes; New Kid In Town; One Of These Nights; Sunset Grill

HENLEY, FRED — You're The Reason

HENNING, PAUL — Ballad Of Jed Clampett

HENNING, ROBERT — Intermezzo(A Love Story); Love Story, A(Intermezzo)

HENRY, CLARENCE — Ain't Got No Home; Evil Ways

HENRY, FRANCIS — Little Girl

HENRY, NORM — You Better Know It

HENRY, S. R. — By Heck

HERBERT, ARTHUR — Broken Down Merry-go-round

HERBERT, TWYLA — Lightnin' Strikes; Rhapsody In The Rain; Two Faces Have I

HERBERT, VICTOR — Because You're You; Eileen; Every Day Is Ladies Day With Me; Fortune Teller; Gypsy Love Song; I'm Falling In Love With Someone; Indian Summer; Italian Street Song; Kiss In The Dark; Kiss Me Again; March Of The Toys; Moonbeams; Neapolitan Love Song; Romany Life; Sweethearts; Toyland; Tramp! Tramp! Tramp! Along The Highway; When You're Away; Woman Is Only A Woman, But A Good Cigar Is A Smoke; Yesterthoughts

HERBSTRITT, LARRY — I Just Fall In Love Again

HERMAN, JERRY — As Simple As That; Before The Parade Passes By; Best Of Times; Dancing; Elegance; Hello, Dolly!; I Am What I Am; I Put My Hand In; I Will Follow You; If He Walked Into My Life; It Only Takes A Moment; It Takes A Woman; Let's Not Waste A Moment; Like A Young Man; Look Over There; Mame; Milk And Honey; Motherhood March; My Best Girl; Open A New Window; Put On Your Sunday Clothes; Ribbons Down My Back; Shalom; So Long, Dearie; We Need A Little Christmas

HERMAN, PINKY — Manhattan Merry Go Round

HERMAN, WOODY — Apple Honey; Blues On Parade; Early Autumn; Northwest Passage

HERNANDEZ, PATRICK — Born To Be Alive

HERNANDEZ, RAFAEL — El Cumbanchero

HERROLD, ERMA — Stood Up

HERRON, JOEL — I'm A Fool To Want You

HERSCHER, LOUIS — Dream Daddy

HERSHEY, JUNE — Deep In The Heart Of Texas

HERZOG JR., ARTHUR — Don't Explain; God Bless The Child

HESTER, TONY — In The Rain; Whatcha See Is Whatcha Get; With This Ring

HEUBERGER, RICHARD — Kiss In Your Eyes

HEWSON, PAUL — Into The Night

HEYES, DOUGLAS — Colt .45

HEYMAN, EDWARD — Blame It On My Youth; Blue Star(the Medic Theme); Bluebird Of Happiness; Body And Soul; Boo-Hoo!; David And Lisa's Love Song; Drums In My Heart; Easy Come, Easy Go; Hello, My Lover, Good-bye; Ho Hum; I Cover The Waterfront; I Wanna Be Loved; If I Steal A Kiss; It's Every Girl's Ambition; Kathleen Mine; Kinda Like You; Love Letters; Moonburn; My Darling; My Silent Love; Out Of Nowhere; Through The Years; What's Wrong With Me?; When I Fall In Love; You Oughta Be In Pictures; You're Everywhere; You're Mine You

HEYNE, JOE — Petite Waltz

HEYWARD, DU BOSE — Bess, You Is My Woman; I Got Plenty O' Nuttin'; I Loves You Porgy; My Man's Gone Now; Oh Bess, Oh Where's My Bess; Red Headed Woman Makes A Choo Choo Jump Its Track; Summertime; Woman Is A Sometime Thing

HEYWOOD, DONALD — I'm Coming Virginia

HEYWOOD, EDDIE — Canadian Sunset; Land Of Dreams; Soft Summer Breeze

HIATT, JOHN — Sure As I'm Sittin' Here

HICKEY, ERSEL — Don't Let The Rain Come Down(Crooked Little Man)

HICKMAN, ART — Hold Me; Rose Room

HICKS, TONY — Carrie-Anne; On A Carousel; Pay You Back With Interest; Stop, Stop, Stop

HIGGENBOTHAM, ROBERT — Hi-Heel Sneakers

HIGGINBOTHAM, IRENE — Fat Meat Is Good Meat; Good Morning Heartache

HIGGINS, BERTIE — Key Largo

HIGGINS, BILLY — Georgia Blues

HILD, R. — You Don't Know

HILDEBRAND, RAY — Hey, Paula; Young Lovers

HILDERBRAND, DIANE — Easy Come, Easy Go

HILL, AL — Let Me Go Lover!

HILL, ALEX — (I Would Do) Anything For You; I'm Crazy 'bout My Baby(And My Baby's Crazy 'bout Me); Rumors

HILL, B. — Can't We Try

HILL, BILLY — Call Of The Canyon; Empty Saddles; Glory Of Love; Have You Ever Been Lonely(Have You Ever Been Blue?); In The Chapel In The Moonlight; Last Round-Up; Lights Out; Old Man Of The Mountain; Old Spinning Wheel; On A Little Street In Singapore; Put On An Old Pair Of Shoes; Rain; Wagon Wheels

HILL, DAN — Can't We Try; Sometimes When We Touch

HILL, DAVID — I Got Stung; Speedy Gonzalez; Start Movin'

HILL, DEDETTE LEE — Old Folks; Put On An Old Pair Of Shoes

HILL, DUSTY — Legs; Sleeping Bag

HILL, JOE — Tush

HILL, MILDRED J. — Happy Birthday To You

HILL, PATTY SMITH — Happy Birthday To You

HILL, ROBERT — Kiss Of Fire

HILL, STANLEY — I'll Pray For You

HILL, TEDDY — Blue Rhythm Fantasy

HILL, TERRY — Our Lips Are Sealed

HILLER, ANTHONY — Save Your Kisses For Me

HILLER, TONY — United We Stand

HILLIARD, BOB — (Don't Go)Please Stay; (Don't Go)Please Stay(; (Why Did I Tell You I Was Going To)Shanghai; Alone At Last; Any Day Now; Be My Life's Companion; Big Brass Band From Brazil; Bouquet Of Roses; Boutonniere; Careless Hands; Castanets And Lace; Coffee Song, The(They've Got An

Awful Lot Of Coffee In Brazil); Dear Hearts And Gentle People; Dearie; Don't Ever Be Afraid To Go Home; Don't You Believe It; Downhearted; English Muffins And Irish Stew; Ev'ry Street's A Boulevard In Old New York; From The Candy Store On The Corner(To The Chapel On The Hill); How Do You Speak To An Angel?; I Feel Like I'm Gonna Live Forever; I'm Late; Mention My Name In Sheboygan; Money Burns A Hole In My Pocket; Moonlight Gambler; My Little Corner Of The World; My Summer Love; Our Day Will Come; Pancho Maximilian Hernandez(The Best President We Ever Had); Poor Man's Roses; Red Silk Stockings And Green Perfume; Sitting In The Back Seat; Somebody Bad Stole De Wedding Bell; Stay With The Happy People; Tower Of Strength; Waiting Game; Wee Small Hours (Of The Morning), In The

HILLMAN, CHRIS — So You Want To Be A Rock 'n Roll Star

HILLMAN, ROC — My Devotion

HIMBER, RICHARD — It Isn't Fair

HINES, EARL — Deep Forest; Rosetta; You Can Depend On Me

HINTON, EDDIE — Choo Choo Train

HINTON, JOE — Gotta Hold On To This Feeling

HIRSCH, LOUIS A. — Hello Frisco Hello; Love Nest; Throw Me A Kiss

HIRSCH, MAURICE — Keep On Smilin'

HIRSCH, WALTER — 'deed I Do; Bye Bye Baby; Last Night I Dreamed Of You; Lullaby In Rhythm; Me And The Moon; Strange Interlude; Was It Rain?; Who's Your Little Who-zis

HIRSCHORN, JOEL — Candle On The Water; Let's Start All Over Again; We May Never Love Like This Again; Will You Be Staying After Sunday?

HIRSH, KEN — I've Never Been To Me

HIRSHHORN, JOEL — Morning After

HITCHINGS, DUANE — Infatuation; Young Turks

HOBGOOD, BUDDY — Get It Together

HODGES, JIMMIE — Someday(You'll Want Me To Want You)

HODGES, JOHNNY — Harmony In Harlem; I'm Beginning To See The Light; Jeep's Blues; Rent Party Blues

HODGES, MABON — L-O-V-E

HODGSON, RED — Music Goes 'round And Around

HODGSON, ROGER — Dreamer; Give A Little Bit; Goodbye Stranger; It's Raining Again; Logical Song

HOEFLE, CARL — Ya Wanna Buy A Bunny?

HOFFMAN, AL — A Dream Is A Wish Your Heart Makes; Ali-Baba Chi-Baba(My Bambino Go To Sleep); Allegheny Moon; Are You Really Mine?; Auf Wiedersehn, My Dear; Bibbidi-Bobbidi-Boo(the Magic Song); Black Eyed Susan Brown; Cinderella; Dennis The Menace; Don't Stay Away Too Long; Don't You Love Me Anymore?; Fit As A Fiddle; Fuzzy Wuzzy; Gilly Gilly Ossenfeffer Katzenellen Bogen By The Sea; Goodnight, Wherever You Are; Hawaiian Wedding Song,the; Heartaches; Hot Diggity; I Apologize; I Can't Tell A Waltz From A Tango; I Saw Stars; I'm A Big Girl Now; I'm Gonna Live Till I Die; I'm In A Dancing Mood; If I Knew You Were Comin' I'd've Baked A Cake; La Plume De Ma Tante; Little Man, You've Had A Busy Day; Mairzy Doats; Mama, Teach Me To Dance; Mi Casa, Su Casa(My House Is Your House); Moon-talk; O Dio Mio; Oh, Oh, I'm Falling

In Love Again; On The Bumpy Road To Love; Papa Loves Mambo; Santo Natale; Secretly; Story Of A Starry Night; Torero; Very Merry Un-Birthday To You

HOFFMAN, HENRY — Bobby's Girl

HOFFS, S. — Walking Down Your Street

HOGAN, DONALD — When We Get Married

HOKENSON, EDWARD — Bad Girls

HOLDEN, RON — Love You So

HOLDEN, SIDNEY — Yankee Rose

HOLDER, NODDY — Cum On Feel The Noize; Run, Runaway

HOLDRIDGE, LEE — Forever Young; Moonlighting

HOLIDAY, BILLIE — Don't Explain; Fine And Mellow; God Bless The Child

HOLIDAY, JIMMY — All I Ever Need Is You; I Chose To Sing The Blues(I Choose To Sing The Blues); Put A Little Love In Your Heart; Understanding (Is The Best Thing In The World)

HOLINER, MANN — I Just Couldn't Take It Baby; Padam-Padam; Until The Real Thing Comes Along; You Can't Stop Me From Lovin' You

HOLLAND, BRIAN — (Come 'round Here)I'm The One You Need; (I'm A)Road Runner; 7 Rooms Of Gloom; Baby Love; Baby, I Need Your Loving; Back In My Arms Again; Bernadette; Can I Get A Witness; Come And Get Those Memories; Come See About Me; Forever Came Today; Give Me Just A Little More Time; Happening; Heat Wave; Heaven Must Have Sent You; How Sweet It Is(To Be Loved By You); I Can't Help Myself(Sugar Pie, Honey Bunch); I Hear A Symphony; I'm Ready For Love; In And Out Of Love; It's The Same Old Song; Jimmy Mack; Just A Little Bit Of You; Little Darling(I Need You); Love Is Here And Now You're Gone; Love Is Like An Itching In My Heart; Mashed Potato Time; Mickey's Monkey; My World Is Empty Without You; Nothing But Heartaches; Nowhere To Run; One, Two, Three(1-2-3); Please Mr. Postman; Quicksand; Reach Out I'll Be There; Reflections; Shake Me, Wake Me(When It's Over); Something About You; Standing In The Shadows Of Love; Stop! In The Name Of Love; Where Did Our Love Go; You Can't Hurry Love; You Keep Me Hangin' On; You Keep Running Away; You're A Wonderful One; Your Unchanging Love

HOLLAND, EDDIE — (Come 'round Here)I'm The One You Need; (i Know)i'm Losing You; (I'm A)Road Runner; (Loneliness Made Me Realize)It's You That I Need; 7 Rooms Of Gloom; Ain't Too Proud To Beg; All I Need; Baby Love; Baby, I Need Your Loving; Back In My Arms Again; Beauty Is Only Skin Deep; Bernadette; Can I Get A Witness; Come And Get Those Memories; Come See About Me; Everybody Needs Love; Forever Came Today; Happening; Heat Wave; Heaven Must Have Sent You; How Sweet It Is(To Be Loved By You); I Can't Help Myself(Sugar Pie, Honey Bunch); I Hear A Symphony; I'm Ready For Love; In And Out Of Love; It's The Same Old Song; Jimmy Mack; Just A Little Bit Of You; Little Darling(I Need You); Little David, Play On Your Harp; Love Is Here And Now You're Gone; Love Is Like An Itching In My Heart; Mickey's Monkey; My World Is Empty Without You; Nothing But Heartaches; Nowhere To Run; Quicksand; Reach Out I'll Be There; Reflections; Shake Me, Wake Me(When It's Over); Something About You; Standing In The Shadows Of Love; Stop! In The Name Of Love; Where

Did Our Love Go; You Can't Hurry Love; You Keep Me Hangin' On; You Keep Running Away; You're A Wonderful One; Your Unchanging Love

HOLLANDER, FREDERICK — Awake In A Dream; Black Market; Boys In The Back Room; House That Jack Built For Jill; I've Been In Love Before; It's Raining Sunbeams; Moon Over Burma; Moonlight And Shadows; My Heart And I; Sammy Lerner; Strange Enchantment; True Confession; Whispers In The Dark; You Leave Me Breathless

HOLLER, RICHARD L. — Snoopy Versus The Red Baron

HOLLINS, LAURA — Why Don't You Write Me

HOLLOWAY, BRENDA — You've Made Me So Very Happy

HOLLOWAY, PATRICE — You've Made Me So Very Happy

HOLLY, BUDDY — Every Day; It's So Easy; Love's Made A Fool Of You; Not Fade Away; Oh Boy; Peggy Sue; True Love Ways; Words Of Love

HOLMES, JACK — Blacksmith Blues

HOLMES, R. — You Got It All

HOLMES, ROBERT — Voices Carry

HOLMES, RUPERT — Escape(The Pina Colada Song); Garden Path To Hell; Him; Moonfall; Never The Luck; Perfect Strangers; Queen Bee; Timothy

HOLMES, WALDO — Rockin' Soul

HOLOFCENER, LARRY — I'm Available; Mr. Wonderful; Too Close For Comfort; Without You I'm Nothing

HOLT, ALAN — Sailor(Your Home Is The Sea)

HOLT, DEREK — Couldn't Get It Right; I Love You

HOLT, JOHN — Tide Is High

HOLT, WILL — Days Of The Waltz; Lemon Tree

HOLVAY, JAMES — Kind Of A Drag; Susan

HOLVAY, JIM — Don't You Care; Hey, Baby! They're Playin' Our Song

HOLYFIELD, WAYLAND — Could I Have This Dance

HOLZER, LOU — When They Played The Polka

HOMBRES, THE — Let It Out

HOMER, BEN — Joltin' Joe Di Maggio; Sentimental Journey

HOOF, VON — Ronnie Ball

HOOKER, BRIAN — Dear Love, My Love; Gather The Rose; Huguette Waltz; Love For Sale; Love Me Tonight; Only A Rose; Some Day; Song Of The Vagabonds; Waltz Huguette Or The Vagabond King Waltz

HOOKER, JAKE — Freedom Overspill; I Love Rock And Roll

HOOKER, JOHN LEE — Boogie Chillun

HOOVEN, JEFF — Cindy's Birthday

HOOVEN, JOSEPH — Any Way The Wind Blows; Gimme Little Sign

HOOVEN, MARILYN — Any Way The Wind Blows

HOPE, LAWRENCE — Kashmiri Love Song

HOPKINS, CLAUDE — (I Would Do)anything For You

HOPKINS, JOHN HENRY — We Three Kings Of Orient

HOPKINS, KENYON — Baby Doll

HOPPEN, LARRY — Love Takes Time

HOPPER, HAL — Colt .45

HOPPER, SEAN — Hip To Be Square

HORLICK, HARRY — Dark Eyes; Two Guitars

HORN, LAWRENCE — Shake And Fingerpop

HORN, TREVOR — Owner Of A Lonely Heart; Video Killed The Radio Star

HORNER, J. — Somewhere Out There

HORNSBY, BRUCE — Every Little Kiss; Jacob's Ladder; Mandolin Rain; Way It Is

HORNSBY, J. — Jacob's Ladder; Mandolin Rain

HORTON, JOHNNY — Sink The Bismarck

HORTON, SAMPSON — Wishing For Your Love

HORTON, VAUGHN — Bar Room Polka; Choo Choo Ch' Boogie; Mockin' Bird Hill

HORWITT, ARNOLD B. — Are You With It?; Young And Foolish

HOSCHNA, KARL — Cuddle Up A Little Closer, Lovey Mine; Every Little Movement(Has A Meaning All It's Own)

HOU, PHILEMON — Grazing In The Grass

HOUDINI, WILMOTH — Gin And Cocoanut Water; Stone Cold Dead In The Market

HOUGH, WILL M. — I Wonder Who's Kissing Her Now

HOUSE, BOB — Could I Have This Dance

HOUSTON, CISCO — Badman's Blunder

HOVEY, RICHARD — It's Always Fair Weather When Good Fellows Get Together

HOWARD, BART — Fly Me To The Moon(In Other Words)

HOWARD, BOB — My Son, My Son

HOWARD, DICK — Somebody Else Is Taking My Place

HOWARD, EDDY — Careless; If I Knew Then(What I Know Now); Million Dreams Ago; My Last Goodbye

HOWARD, HARLAN — Busted; Call Me Mr. In-Between; Chokin' Kind; Heartaches By The Number; I Fall To Pieces; I've Got A Tiger By The Tail; Too Many Rivers; When I Get Thru With You, You'll Love Me Too; Where In The World

HOWARD, JEROME — Midnight Lace

HOWARD, JOSEPH E. — I Wonder Who's Kissing Her Now

HOWARD, KEN — I've Lost You

HOWARD, MEL — Dance Me Loose

HOWARD, PAUL MASON — Gandy Dancers' Ball; Shrimp Boats

HOWARD, ROBERT — Digging Your Scene

HOWE, JULIA WARD — Battle Hymn Of The Republic

HOWE, STEVE — Roundabout

HOWELL, DAN — Even Now; Fan It; Well All Right! (Tonight's The Night)

HOWELL, DON — Open The Door, Richard!

HOYLES, C. — Heartbreak(It's Hurting Me)

HOYT, CHARLES H. — Bowery

HUBBARD, JERRY REED — Ballad Of Gator Mcclusky; East Bound And Down; Legend; Struttin'

HUBBELL, RAYMOND — Poor Butterfly

HUCKNALL, MICK — Holding Back The Years

HUDDLESTON, FLOYD — Idle Gossip; Ready, Willing, And Able; You Started Something

HUDSON, BRETT — Rendezvous

HUDSON, HOWARD — Lady(You Bring Me Up)

HUDSON, JAMES — Goodnight Sweetheart, Well It's Time To Go

HUDSON, MARK — Rendezvous

HUDSON, WILL — Hobo On Park Avenue; Jazznocracy; Mr. Ghost Goes To Town; Organ Grinder's Swing; Sophisticated Swing; Tormented; You're Not The Kind

HUDSON, WILLIAM — Rendezvous

HUDSPETH, WILLIAM GREGORY — Heartbeat-It's A Lovebeat

HUES, JACK — Dance Hall Days

HUFF, LARRY — Easier Said Than Done

HUFF, LEON — Back Stabbers; Close The Door; Cowboys To Girls; Do It Any Way You Wanna; Don't Leave Me This Way; Drowning In The Sea Of Love; Enjoy Yourself; Espressway To Your Heart; Explosion In My Soul; For The Love Of Money; Hey, Western Union Man; I Just Can't Stop Dancing; I Love Music(part 1); If You Don't Know Me By Now; Livin' For The Weekend; Love I Lost; Love Train; Me And Mrs. Jones; Never Give You Up(Never Gonna Give You Up); Only The Strong Survive; Power Of Love; Put Your Hands Together; T.S.O.P. (The Sound Of Philadelphia); United; Use Ta Be My Girl; When Will I See You Again; You'll Never Find Another Love Like Mine

HUGHES, CHRIS — Everybody Wants To Rule The World

HUGHES, JIMMIE — Bless'em All

HUGHES, JIMMY — Steal Away

HUGHES, LANGSTON — Backlash Blues; Boy Like You; Lonely House; Moon-faced, Starry-eyed; What Good Would The Moon Be?

HULL, BUNNY — Breakdance; New Attitude

HUMES, HELEN — Be-Baba-Luba

HUMES, WALDO — Rock The Boat

HUNTER, ALBERTA — Chirpin' The Blues; Down Hearted Blues; Down South Blues

HUNTER, BEATRICE — Guess Who

HUNTER, DON — I Don't Know Why; You Met Your Match...

HUNTER, HANK — Footsteps; Ginger Bread; I'm Gonna Be Warm This Winter; Just For Old Times' Sake; My Empty Arms; Second Hand Love; Vacation

HUNTER, IAN — Ships

HUNTER, IVORY JOE — Don't Fall In Love With Me; Empty Arms; I Almost Lost My Mind; It May Sound Silly; My Wish Came True; Out Of Sight, Out Of Mind; Since I Met You Baby

HUNTER, IVY — Ask The Lonely; My Baby Loves Me; Yesterday's Dreams; You; You've Been In Love Too Long

HUNTER, R. — Touch Of Grey

HUNTER, ROBERT — Uncle John's Band

HUPFELD, HERMAN — Are You Makin' Any Money?; As Time Goes By; Let's Put Out The Lights And Go To Sleep; Sing Something Simple

HUPFIELD, HERMAN — When Yuba Plays The Rumba On His Tuba

HUPP, DEBBIE — You Decorated My Life

HURLEY, JOHN — Land Of Milk And Honey; Son-Of-A-Preacher-Man

HURST, MIKE — Touch Me

HURT, JIM — Love In The First Degree

HUTCH, WILLIE — I'll Be There

HUTCHENCE, M. — Need You Tonight

HUTCHENCE, MICHAEL — What You Need

HUTCHESON, SUSAN — I Love The Nightlife; I Love The Way You Love

HUTCHINS, DARYL — I Wonder, I Wonder, I Wonder

HYDE, MADELINE — Little Girl

HYMAN, ROB — Day By Day; Time After Time

HYNDE, C. — Don't Get Me Wrong

HYNDE, CHRISSIE — Back On The Chain Gang; Brass In Pocket(I'm Special); Middle Of The Road; Show Me

I

IAN, JANIS — At Seventeen; Jesse; Society's Child

IDOL, BILLY — Eyes Without A Face; Hot In The City

IDRISS, RAMEZ — Something Old, Something New; Worry, Worry, Worry

IDRISS, RAMON — Woody Woodpecker

IGLESIAS, JULIO — Cynthia Weil

ILDA, LEWIS — Little Old Mill, The(Went Round And Round)

ILLICA, LUIGI — One Fine Day(Un Bel Di)

IMES, MILDRED — You're The Reason

INGLE, DOUG — In-A-Gadda-Da-Vida

INGMANN, JORGEN — Apache

INGRAHAM, ROY — No Regrets

INGRAM, ARNOLD — Float On

INGRAM, JAMES — P. Y. T. (Pretty Young Thing)

INGRAM, LUTHER — Respect Yourself

INNIS, LOUIE — Daddy O

INSTONE, ANTHONY GORDON — Here Comes That Rainy Day Feeling Again

IRIS, DON — Rapper

IRONS, EDWARD — Dazz

IRWIN, GENE — Five O'clock Whistle

IRWIN, ROY — Yes Tonight, Josephine; You Need Hands

ISBELL, ALVERTIS — I'll Take You There

ISLEY, ERNEST — Fight The Power(part 1); For The Love Of You

ISLEY, MARVIN — Fight The Power(part 1); For The Love Of You

ISLEY, O'KELLY — Fight The Power(part 1); For The Love Of You; Nobody But Me

ISLEY, O'KELLY, RONALD, AND RUDOLPH — I Turned You On; It's Your Thing; Shout(part 1 And 2)

ISLEY, RONALD — Fight The Power(part 1); For The Love Of You

ISLEY, RUDOLPH — Fight The Power(part 1); For The Love Of You; Nobody But Me

IVANOVICI, ION — Waves Of The Danube Or Danube Waves

IVEY, HERBERT — Angel In Your Arms

JABARA, PAUL — Last Dance; Main Event, The(Fight); No More Tears(Enough Is Enough)

JABLECKI, STEVE — Sweet Mary

JACKS, TERRY — Which Way You Goin' Billy

JACKSON JR., AL — Green Onions

JACKSON JR., CHARLES — I've Got Love On My Mind; Our Love; Sophisticated Lady(She's A Different Lady)

JACKSON JR., DAVID — No No Song

JACKSON JR., PAUL M. — Let Me Tickle Your Fancy

JACKSON, AL — I'm Still In Love With You; Let's Stay Together; Look What You Done For Me; Soul-Limbo

JACKSON, AL- — You Ought To Be With Me

JACKSON, ANTHONY — For The Love Of Money

JACKSON, ARTHUR — Drifting Along With The Tide; Scandal Walk; Songs Of Long Ago

JACKSON, B. — Happy

JACKSON, BILLY — Don't Throw Your Love Away

JACKSON, CHARLES — I Don't Want To Cry No More

JACKSON, CHRISTOPHER — You Little Trustmaker

JACKSON, DEON — Love Makes The World Go 'round

JACKSON, G. S. — Northwest Passage

JACKSON, GARY L. — (Your Love Keeps Lifting Me)Higher And Higher; Your Love Keeps Lifting Me Higher And Higher

JACKSON, GEORGE — Double Lovin'; Old Time Rock And Roll; One Bad Apple(Don't Spoil The Whole Bunch); Too Weak To Fight

JACKSON, GERALD — Turn The Beat Around (Love To Hear Percussion)

JACKSON, J. J. — Long Live Our Love

JACKSON, JANET — Control; Let's Wait Awhile; Nasty; What Have You Done For Me Lately; When I Think Of You

JACKSON, JERMAINE — Closest Thing To Perfect; I Think It's Love; Let Me Tickle Your Fancy

JACKSON, JEROME — But It's Alright

JACKSON, JILL — Young Lovers

JACKSON, JOE — Breaking Us In Two; Is She Really Going Out With Him?; Steppin' Out

JACKSON, JR, AL — Time Is Tight

JACKSON, MCKINLEY — Trying To Hold On To My Woman

JACKSON, MICHAEL — Another Part Of Me; Bad; Beat It; Billie Jean; Don't Stop 'til You Get Enough; Eat It; Girl Is Mine; Heartbreak Hotel; I Just Can't Stop Loving You; Muscles; Say Say Say; Shake Your Body(Down To The Ground); State Of Shock; Wanna Be Startin' Somethin'; Way You Make Me Feel; We Are The World

JACKSON, MIKE — Knock Me A Kiss

JACKSON, MILT — Bag's Groove

JACKSON, PETER — Turn The Beat Around (Love To Hear Percussion)

JACKSON, RAYMOND — If Loving You Is Wrong I Don't Want To Be Right; If You're Ready(Come Go With Me); Who's Making Love

JACKSON, RUDY — Hearts Of Stone

JACKSON, STEPHEN — Shake Your Body(Down To The Ground)

JACKSON, STONEWALL — My Song

JACKSON, WANDA — In The Middle Of A Heartache; Right Or Wrong, I'll Be With You

JACKSON, WILLIAM — So Much In Love

JACKSON,JR., CHARLES — Inseparable

JACOBS, AL — But I Did; Every Day Of My Life; Hurt; I Need You Now; If I Give My Heart To You

JACOBS, JIM — Beauty School Dropout; Summer Nights

JACOBS, ROY — Booglie Wooglie Piggy

JACOBSON, KENNY — Put A Light In The Window

JACOBSON, SID — Boy Without A Girl; End; I've Come Of Age; Yogi

JACQUET, ILLINOIS — Don'cha Go 'way Mad; Robbins Nest

JAFFE, MOE — Bell Bottom Trousers; Collegiate; Gypsy In My Soul; I'm My Own Grandpaw; If You Are But A Dream

JAFFEE, BEN — Please No Squeeza Da Banana

JAGGER, MICK — (I Can't Get No)Satisfaction; 19th Nervous Breakdown; Angie; As Tears Go By; Back Street Girl; Beast Of Burden; Black Limousine; Blue Turns To Grey; Brown Sugar; Cool, Calm And Collected; Country Honk; Crazy Mama; Dancing With Mr. D; Dandelion; Dear Doctor; Doo Doo Doo Doo Doo(heartbreaker); Emotional Rescue; Factory Girl; Fool To Cry; Get Off Of My Cloud; Gimme Shelter; Goin' Home; Hang Fire; Happy; Have You Seen Your Mother, Baby, Standing In The Shadow?; Heart Of Stone; Honky Tonk Women; Hot Stuff; I'm Free; It's Not Easy; It's Only Rock 'n' Roll(But I Like It); Jigsaw Puzzle; Jumpin' Jack Flash; Just Another Night; Lady Jane; Last Time; Let It Bleed; Let's Spend The Night Together; Live With Me; Memo From Turner; Midnight Rambler; Miss You; Moonlight Mile; Mother's Little Helper; No Expectations; Out Of Time; Paint It Black; Parachute Woman; Play With Fire; Respectable; Ruby Tuesday; Salt Of The Earth; Shattered; She's A Rainbow; She's So Cold; Sing This All Together; Singer, Not The Song; Sittin' On A Fence; Some Girls; Something Happened To Me Yesterday; Spider And The Fly; Start Me Up; Stray Cat; Street Fighting Man; Stupid Girl; Sympathy For The Devil; Tumbling Dice; Under My Thumb; Undercover Of The Night; Wild Horses; Yesterday's Papers; You Can't Always Get What You Want

JAM, J. — Diamonds

JAMERSON JR., JAMES — Don't Hold Back

JAMES, CASEY — Livin' It Up(Friday Night); Mama Can't Buy You Love

JAMES, DOUG — How Am I Supposed To Live Without You

JAMES, ETTA — Dance With Me Henry

JAMES, FREDDY — Unchain My Heart; Unsuspecting Heart; You Won't Be Satisfied (Until You Break My Heart)

JAMES, HARRY — As If I Didn't Have Enough On My Mind; Back Beat Boogie; Every Day Of My Life; Everything But You; I'm Beginning To See The Light; Life Goes To A Party; Music Makers; Peckin'; Two O'clock Jump

JAMES, INEZ — Come To Baby, Do!; Pillow Talk; Vaya Con Dios; What Do I Have To Do To Make You Love Me?

JAMES, JESSE — Boogaloo Down Broadway; Horse

JAMES, MARK — Always On My Mind; Eyes Of A New York Woman; Hooked On A Feeling; It's Only Love; Moody Blue; One Hell Of A Woman

JAMES, PALMER E. — Back Up, Train

JAMES, PAUL — Can This Be Love; Fine And Dandy;

Freight Train

JAMES, RICK — In My House; Party All The Time

JAMES, SONNY — Satin Pillows

JAMES, TOMMY — Ball Of Fire; Crimson And Clover; Crystal Blue Persuasion; Draggin' The Line; Mony Mony; She; Sweet Cherry Wine; Three Times In Love; Tighter Tighter

JAMESON, TOM — Summertime, Summertime

JANIS, ELSIE — Love, Your Magic Spell Is Everywhere

JANOWSKI, HORST — Walk In The Black Forest

JANS, TOM — Loving Arms

JANSEN, BERNARD — Longing For You

JANSSEN, DANNY — Keep On Singing

JARCZYK, HERBERT — I'm Always Hearing Wedding Bells

JARRE, MAURICE — Lawrence Of Arabia(Theme); Marmalade, Molasses And Honey; Somewhere My Love(Lara's Theme)

JARREAU, AL — Moonlighting; Mornin'

JARRELL, PHIL — Torn Between Two Lovers

JARRETT, TOMMY — How The Time Flies

JASON, WILL — Penthouse Serenade(When We're Alone); When We're Alone Or Penthouse Serenade

JAVITS, JOAN — Santa Baby

JAXON, FRANKIE — Fan It

JAY, FRED — I Cried A Tear; Wedding; What Am I Living For?

JEFFERSON, "BLIND" LEMON — Mojo Woman Blues

JEFFERSON, JOSEPH B. — One Of A Kind(Love Affair)

JEFFERSON, JOSEPH P. — Love Don't Love Nobody; Mighty Love

JEFFREY, ALLAN — Old Cape Cod

JEFFREYS, ALAN — Hopeless

JEFFRIES, HERB — Candy Store Blues

JENKINS, BARRY — Monterey; San Franciscan Nights; Sky Pilot; When I Was Young

JENKINS, DAVID — Cool Love; Don't Want To Live Without It; I Want You Tonight; Love Will Find A Way; Whatcha Gonna Do

JENKINS, GORDON — Blue Evening; Blue Prelude; Good-bye; Homesick-That's All; Married I Can Always Get; New York's My Home; P. S. I Love You; San Fernando Valley; When A Woman Loves A Man; You Have Taken My Heart

JENKINS, REV. ANDREW — Death Of Floyd Collins

JENKINS, T. — Candy

JENKINS, TOMI — Word Up

JENNEY, JACK — Man With A Horn

JENNINGS, DICK — Little Ole Winedrinker Me

JENNINGS, WAYLON — Ain't No Road Too Long; Good Hearted Woman,a; Good King Wenceslas

JENNINGS, WILL — Finer Things; Higher Love; Looks Like We Made It; No Night So Long; Somewhere In The Night; Up Where We Belong; Valerie; While You See A Chance

JENNINGS, WILLIE — I Need Your Lovin'

JENSEN, HARRY — Troglodyte (Cave Man)

JEOPARDI, JEFF — I Wanna Be A Cowboy

JEROME, JOHN — Chincherinchee

JEROME, M. K. — Bright Eyes; Just A Baby's Prayer At Twilight; My Little Buckaroo; Thru The Courtesy Of Love

JEROME, WILLIAM — And The Green Grass Grew All Around; Chinatown, My Chinatown; Get Out And Get Under The Moon

JESSEL, GEORGE — Where Do They Go When They Row, Row, Row?

JESSEL, LEON — Parade Of The Wooden Soldiers

JESSEL, RAYMOND — Finding Words For Spring; I'd Do It Again; Married Man

JILES, JIMMIE — Leaving Me

JOBIM, ANTONIO CARLOS — Desafinado(Slightly Out Of Tune); Girl From Ipanema; How Insensitive; Meditation; One Note Samba; Quiet Nights Of Quiet Stars(Corcovado); Song Of The Jet

JOEL, BILLY — Allentown; Baby Grand; Big Shot; Captain Jack; Don't Ask Me Why; Entertainer; Honesty; Innocent Man, An; It's Still Rock And Roll To Me; Just The Way You Are; Keeping The Faith; Longest Time; Matter Of Trust; Miami 2017(Seen The Lights Go Out On Broadway); Modern Woman; Moving Out(Anthony's Song); My Life; New York State Of Mind; Only The Good Die Young; Piano Man; Pressure; Say Goodbye To Hollywood; Scenes From An Italian Restaurant; She's Always A Woman; She's Got A Way; Uptown Girl; You May Be Right; You're Only Human (Second Wind)

JOHN, DOMINIC — Blossom Fell

JOHN, DUX DE — (My Baby Don't Love Me)No More

JOHN, ELTON — Bennie And The Jets; Bitch Is Back; Blue Eyes; Border Song; Candle In The Wind; Crocodile Rock; Daniel; Don't Go Breaking My Heart; Don't Let The Sun Go Down On Me; Empty Garden(Hey Hey Johnny); Friends; Goodbye Yellow Brick Road; Grow Some Funk Of Your Own; Honky Cat; I Feel Like A Bullet(In The Gun Of Robert Ford); I Guess That's Why They Call It The Blues; I'm Still Standing; Island Girl; Kiss The Bride; Let Me Be Your Car; Levon; Little Jeannie; Nikita; Part-Time Love; Philadelphia Freedom; Rocket Man; Saturday Night's Alright(For Fighting); Someone Saved My Life Tonight; Sorry Seems To Be The Hardest Word; Your Song

JOHN, JULIE DE — (My Baby Don't Love Me)No More

JOHN, LEO J. DE — (My Baby Don't Love Me)No More

JOHN, ROBERT — Sad Eyes

JOHN, ST. — Smooth Operator

JOHNS, LEO — Melodie D'amour

JOHNS, SAMMY — Chevy Van

JOHNSON JR, JAMES — You And I

JOHNSON, ARNOLD — Does Your Heart Beat For Me?; Good-bye Blues

JOHNSON, BRUCE — Beach Girl

JOHNSON, BUDDY — Did You See Jackie Robinson Hit That Ball; Since I Fell For You; When My Man Comes Home

JOHNSON, BUSTER — Wang Wang Blues

JOHNSON, CHICK — Oh! Gee, Oh! Gosh, Oh! Golly, I'm In Love

JOHNSON, CLARENCE — Love Jones

JOHNSON, CLAUDE — What's Your Name

JOHNSON, E. — Jenny, Take A Ride

JOHNSON, EDWARD — Jersey Bounce

JOHNSON, EMANUEL — Gloria

JOHNSON, ENOTRIS — Jenny, Jenny; Long Tall Sally

JOHNSON, GENERAL — Bring The Boys Home; One Monkey Don't Stop No Show; Patches(I'm Depending On You); Pay To The Piper; Somebody's Been Sleeping In My Bed; Stick-Up; Want Ads

JOHNSON, GEORGE — I'll Be Good To You; Stomp

JOHNSON, GEORGE W. — When You And I Were Young Maggie

JOHNSON, HAROLD — You're A Special Part Of Me

JOHNSON, HAVEN — My Last Affair

JOHNSON, HIRAM — Could This Be Magic

JOHNSON, HOWARD — (I Scream, You Scream, We All Scream For)Ice Cream; Gid-Ap, Garibaldi; M-O-T-H-E-R (A Word That Means The World To Me); What Do We Do On A Dew Dew Dewy Day; What Do You Want To Make Those Eyes At Me For; When The Moon Comes Over The Mountain; Where Do We Go From Here!

JOHNSON, J. C. — Believe It, Beloved; Dusky Stevedore; Eavesdropper's Blues; Empty Bed Blues; Haunted House Blues; Louisiana; Patty Cake, Patty Cake(Baker Man); Rhythm And Romance; Trav'lin' All Alone

JOHNSON, J. ROSAMUND — Dry Bones; Under The Bamboo Tree

JOHNSON, JAMES — Stranded In The Jungle

JOHNSON, JAMES C. — Joint Is Jumpin' The

JOHNSON, JAMES P. — Charleston

JOHNSON, JAMES WELDON — Dry Bones

JOHNSON, JANICE — Boogie Oogie Oogie

JOHNSON, JESSE — Jungle Love

JOHNSON, JIMMY — Don't Cry Baby; If I Could Be With You One Hour Tonight

JOHNSON, LOUIS — I'll Be Good To You; Stomp

JOHNSON, LOUIS A. — Sweet Love

JOHNSON, MARV — You Got What It Takes

JOHNSON, MARVIN — Come To Me

JOHNSON, PETE — Boogie Woogie Prayer

JOHNSON, ROBERT — Crossroads

JOHNSON, ROY LEE — Mr. Moonlight

JOHNSON, TERRY — Baby, Baby, Don't Cry; Here I Go Again

JOHNSON, VALERIE — Stomp

JOHNSON, WILLIAM — Pretty Eyed Baby; Relax; Tuxedo Junction

JOHNSTON, ARTHUR — All You Want To Do Is Dance; Between A Kiss And A Sigh; Black Moonlight; Cocktails For Two; Day You Came Along; Down The Old Ox Road; Ebony Rhapsody; I Guess It Had To Be That Way; I'm A Little Blackbird Looking For A Bluebird; I'm Sitting High On A Hilltop; I've Got A Pocketful Of Sunshine; If I Only Had A Match; It's The Natural Thing To Do; Just One More Chance; Learn To Croon; Mandy, Make Up Your Mind; Moon Got In My Eyes; Moon Song(That Wasn't Meant For Me); Moonstruck; My Old Flame; One, Two, Button Your Shoe; Pennies From Heaven; Skeleton In The Closet; Skip To My Lou; So Do I; So Emotional; Song Of The South

JOHNSTON, BOB — Look What You've Done

JOHNSTON, BRUCE — I Write The Songs; Rendezvous

JOHNSTON, PAT — I'll Remember April

JOHNSTON, TOM — China Grove; Listen To The Music; Long Train Running

JOHNSTONE, DAVID — Grow Some Funk Of Your Own; Guaglioni(The Man Who Plays The Mandolin)

JOHSON, JAY — Blue Christmas

JOINER, JAMES — Fallen Star

JOLLEY, STEVE — Cruel Summer

JOLSON, AL — Anniversary Song; Avalon; Back In Your Own Backyard; Bagdad; California, Here I Come; Dirty Hands, Dirty Face; Egg And I; Evangeline; Keep Smiling At Trouble; Me And My Shadow; Sonny Boy; Why Can't You (Birdies Sing In Cages

Too); Year From Today; Yoo-Hoo; You Ain't Heard Nothin' Yet

JONES III, TOM — Old Time Rock And Roll

JONES JR., DAVID — Love Me For A Reason

JONES, AGNES — Unchain My Heart

JONES, ANDREW — When You Dance

JONES, BIFF — Suddenly There's A Valley

JONES, BOOKER T. — Green Onions; Soul-Limbo; Time Is Tight; To Be A Lover

JONES, CHARLES — I Love You Madly

JONES, DORY — Rubberneckin'

JONES, FLOYD — On The Road Again

JONES, FREDERICK — Couldn't Get It Right

JONES, GLORIA — If I Were Your Woman; My Mistake(Was To Love You)

JONES, HOWARD — Life In One Day; No One Is To Blame; You Know I Love You...Don't You

JONES, ISHAM — (There Is)No Greater Love; Broken Hearted Melody; Honestly; I Can't Believe It's True; I'll Never Have To Dream Again; I'll See You In My Dreams; I'm Tired Of Everything But You; Indiana Moon; It Had To Be You; On The Alamo; One I Love Belongs To Somebody Else; Spain; Swingin' Down The Lane; Wooden Soldier And The China Doll; You've Got Me Crying Again

JONES, JACK — Love With The Proper Stranger

JONES, JILL — Get Me To The World On Time

JONES, JIMMY — Handy Man

JONES, JOE — Iko-iko; You Talk Too Much

JONES, JOHN PAUL — Black Dog; Fool In The Rain; Whole Lotta Love

JONES, M. — Say You Will

JONES, MARSHALL — Fire; Funky Worm; Skin Tight; Who'd She Coo

JONES, MARYLIN — Iko-Iko

JONES, MICHAEL — Blue Morning, Blue Day; Cold As Ice; Dirty White Boy; Double Vision; Feels Like The First Time; Head Games; Long, Long Way From Home; Love Come Down

JONES, MICK — I Want To Know What Love Is; Rock The Casbah; Urgent; Waiting For A Girl Like You

JONES, NAT — Bring It Up

JONES, O. DENISE — Trapped By A Thing Called Love

JONES, OLLIE — Love Makes The World Go 'round(Yeah, Yeah); Send For Me; Step By Step; Tiger

JONES, PHALON — Soul Finger

JONES, QUINCY — Come Back Charleston Blue; Do It To It; Eyes Of Love; For Love Of Ivy; In The Heat Of The Night; Love Is In Control; Miss Celie's Blues; P. Y. T. (Pretty Young Thing); Stuff Like That

JONES, RICHARD M — Your Red Wagon

JONES, RICK — I Can Take Or Leave Your Loving

JONES, RICKIE LEE — Chuck E's In Love; Youngblood

JONES, SHARON — Iko-iko

JONES, STAN — Cheyenne; Riders In The Sky(Ghost Riders In The Sky); Wringle, Wrangle

JONES, STEPHEN — What Do You Do Sunday, Mary?

JONES, TOM — Love, Don't Turn Away; My Cup Runneth Over; Try To Remember

JONSON, BEN — Drink To Me Only With Thine Eyes

JOPLIN, JANIS — Down On Me; Kozmic Blues

JOPLIN, SCOTT — Entertainer; Maple Leaf Rag

JORDAN, ARCHIE — It Was Almost Like A Song

JORDAN, JOE — Original Dixieland One Step

JORDAN, LEROY "LONNIE" — Cisco Kid; Gypsy Man; L. A. Sunshine; Low Rider; Me And Baby Brother;

Slipping Into Darkness; Spill The Wine; Summer; World Is A Ghetto

JORDAN, LOUIS — Blue Light Boogie; Is You Is, Or Is You Ain't(Ma' Baby); Saturday Night Fish Fry; You Can't Get That No More

JORDAN, ROBERT — (My Heart Goes)KA-DING-DONG

JOSEA, JOE — Cherry Pie; Oop Shoop

JOSEFOVITS, TERI — Au Revoir Again

JOSEPH, RAY — Kathy-O; Sinner Kissed An Angel

JOSIE, LOU — Midnight Confessions

JOVAN, NICK — City Of Angels

JOYCE, DOROTHEA — Love's Lines, Angles, And Rhymes

JOYCE, JACK — I Wanna Go Home

JOYNER, CAROLE — Young Love

JUDELL, MAXSON — Duel In The Sun(A Duel Of Two Hearts)

JUDGE, JACK — It's A Long Long Way To Tipperary

JULIA, AL — I Cried A Tear

JULIAN, DON — Jerk

JULIEN, MICHAEL — Let's Live For Today

JUNIOR, MARVIN — Oh, What A Night

JUNIORS, DANNY AND THE — Rock And Roll Is Here To Stay

JURGENS, DICK — Careless; Day Dreams Come True At Night; Elmer's Tune; If I Knew Then(What I Know Now); Million Dreams Ago; One Dozen Roses

JURMANN, WALTER — All God's Chillun Got Rhythm; Blue Venetian Waters; Cosi Cosa; San Francisco; Tomorrow Is Another Day; When I Look At You

JUSTIS, BILL — Drownin' My Sorrows; Gitarzan; Raunchy; Ways Of A Woman In Love

JUSTMAN, SETH — Centerfold; Come Back; Freeze-Frame; Give It To Me; Must Of Got Lost; You're The Only One

KABAK, MILTON — Oh Babe!

KAEMPFERT, BERT — Love(L-O-V-E); Spanish Eyes; Strangers In The Night; Swingin' Safari; The World We Knew (Over And Over); Wiederseh'n; Wooden Heart

KAGNA, ERIC — Straight From The Heart

KAHAL, IRVING — (There Ought To Be A)Moonlight Savings Time; Ballad In Blue; By A Waterfall; Corn Silk; Ev'ry Day; I Can Dream, Can't I; I'll Be Seeing You; It Was Only A Sun Shower; Let A Smile Be Your Umbrella; Night Is Young And You're So Beautiful; Three's A Crowd; Wedding Bells Are Breaking Up That Old Gang Of Mine; When I Take My Sugar To Tea; When Tomorrow Comes; You Brought A New Kind Of Love To Me

KAHAN, STANLEY — Girl With The Golden Braids

KAHN, ART — You Don't Like It—Not Much

KAHN, GUS — Ain't We Got Fun; All God's Chillun Got Rhythm; Around The Corner; Beside A Babbling Brook; Bimini Bay; Blue Lovebird; Blue Venetian Waters; Broken Hearted Melody; Carioca; Carolina In The Morning; Charley, My Boy; Chloe; Clouds; Come West, Little Girl, Come West; Coquette; Day Dreaming; Do What You Do!; Dream A Little Dream Of Me; Earful Of Music, An; Flying Down To Rio; Goofus; Guilty; Honolulu; Hour Of Parting; How Strange; I Wonder Where My Baby Is Tonight; I'll Never Be The Same; I'll See You In My Dreams; I'm Bringing A Red, Red Rose; I'm Sitting High On A Hilltop; I'm Thru With Love; I've Got A Pocketful Of Sunshine; It Had To Be You; Josephine; Little Street Where Old Friends Meet; Liza(All The Clouds'll Roll Away); Love Me Forever; Love Me Or Leave Me; Makin' Whoopee; Memories; Music Makes Me; My Baby Just Cares For Me; My Buddy; Nobody's Sweetheart; Now That You've Gone; On The Alamo; One I Love Belongs To Somebody Else; One Night Of Love; Orchids In The Moonlight; San Francisco; Spain; Swingin' Down The Lane; Tomorrow Is Another Love; Tonight Is Mine; Toot Toot Tootsie; Ukelele Lady; Waitin' At The Gate For Katy; Waltz You Saved For Me; Waltzing In The Clouds; When Lights Are Low; When My Ship Comes In; When You And I Were Seventeen; Where The Morning Glories Grow; Where The Shy Little Violets Grow; With All My Heart; Yes Sir, That's My Baby; You Ain't Heard Nothin' Yet; You Stepped Out Of A Dream; You've Got Everything; Your Eyes Have Told Me So

KAHN, KEENE — Charming Little Faker

KAHN, MURL — Petticoats Of Portugal

KAHN, ROGER WOLFE — Crazy Rhythm

KAHNE, D. — Walking Down Your Street

KAIHAN, MAEWA — Now Is The Hour(Maori Farewell Song)

KAILIMAIE, HENRY — On The Beach At Waikiki

KAISERMAN, MAURICIO — Feelings

KALMAN, EMMERICH — Play Gypsies-Dance Gypsies

KALMANOFF, MARTIN — First Name Initial; Just Say I Love Her(Dicitencello Vuie); Utopia

KALMAR, BERT — Dancing The Devil Away; Egg And I; Ev'ryone Says "I Love You"; Hooray For Captain Spaulding; I Wanna Be Loved By You; I'm A Vamp From East Broadway; Keep Romance Alive; Kiss To Build A Dream On; My Sunny Tennessee; Neverthe-

less; So Long! Oh-long(How Long You Gonna Be Gone?); Three Little Words; Timbuctoo; Up In The Clouds; Watching The Clouds Roll By; What A Perfect Combination; Whatever It Is I'm Against It; Where Did You Get That Girl; Where Do They Go When They Row, Row, Row?; Who's Sorry Now

KANDER, JOHN — All The Children In A Row; And All That Jazz; Apple Doesn't Fall,the; Beautiful; Cabaret; Colored Lights; Grass Is Always Greener; How Lucky Can You Get; I Don't Care Much; If You Could See Her(The Gorilla Song); It's The Strangest Thing; Lucky Lady; Married(Heiraten); Maybe This Time; Meeskite; Mein Herr; Money Song, The(Money, Money); My Coloring Book; My Own Best Friend; My Own Space; New York, New York(Theme From); One Of The Boys; Shine It On; Two Ladies; Wilkommen

KANE, ARTIE — Don't Ask To Stay Until Tomorrow

KANNER, HAL — I Guess I'll Get The Papers And Go Home

KANTNER, PAUL — Ballad Of You And Me And Pooneil; Jane; Volunteers; Wooden Ships

KAPER, BRONISLAU — All God's Chillun Got Rhythm; Blue Lovebird; Blue Venetian Waters; Brothers Karamazov, The(Love Theme); Cosi Cosa; Drifting; Forever Darling; Hi-Lili, Hi-lo; Invitation; Long Song From Mutiny On The Bounty; Mutiny On The Bounty(Theme); On Green Dolphin Street; San Francisco; Somebody Up There Likes Me; Tomorrow Is Another Day

KAPP, DAVID — For The First Time(I've Fallen In Love); Hundred And Sixty Acres

KARGER, FRED — Be Prepared; From Here To Eternity; Gidget

KARR, HAROLD — Game Of Love; Mutual Admiration Society; New Fangled Tango

KASENETZ, JERRY — Goody Goody Gumdrops; She

KASHA, AL — Candle On The Water; Gegetta; Let's Start All Over Again; Morning After; My Empty Arms; Switcharoo; We May Never Love Like This Again; Will You Be Staying After Sunday?

KASSEL, ART — Around The Corner; Doodle Doo Doo; Echo Said No

KATSCHER, ROBERT — Good Evening Friends; When Day Is Done

KATZ, BILL — Duke's Place

KATZ, JEFF — Goody Goody Gumdrops; She

KATZ, WILLIAM — Mr. Touchdown U. S. A.

KAUFMAN, AL — Ask Anyone Who Knows; How Many Hearts Have You Broken

KAUFMAN, PAUL — My Town, My Guy, And Me; Poetry In Motion

KAVELIN, AL — I Give You My Word

KAY, JOHN — Magic Carpet Ride; Move Over; Rock Me

KAY, JULIAN — Dum Dot Song

KAYE, BUDDY — "A" You're Adorable(the Alphabet Song); Don't Be A Baby, Baby; Full Moon And Empty Arms; Give Us This Day; Italian Theme; Not As A Stranger; Old Songs,the; Penny A Kiss, A Penny A Hug; Speedy Gonzalez; Till The End Of Time; Walkin' With My Honey (Soon, Soon, Soon), I'll Be

KAYE, FLORENCE — Ask Me; You're The Devil In Disguise

KAYE, SAMMY — Remember Pearl Harbor; Until Tomorrow; Wanderin'

KAYE, TOMMY — One Man Band

KAYLAN, HOWARD — Elenore; Lady Blue

KAZ, ERIC — Beast In Me

KEADY, JOHN THOMAS — As The Backs Go Tearing By

KEAGY, KELLY — Sister Christian

KEANE, T. — Will You Still Love Me?

KEARNEY, RAMSEY — Emotions

KEEFER, GEORGE — Dream Daddy

KEEFER, RUSTY — Skinny Minnie

KEEGAN, SASCHA DISTEL — Good Life

KEENE, KAHN — Scatterbrain

KEHNER, CLARENCE WEY — Bobby Sox To Stockings

KEIFER, T. — Nobody's Fool

KEISER, ROBERT A. — While Strolling Through The Park One Day

KEITH (BERGMAN), MARILYN — Yellow Bird

KEITH, LARRY — Better Love Next Time

KEITH, VIVIAN — Before The Next Teardrop Falls

KELLER, JACK — Almost There; Beats There A Heart So True; Breaking In A Brand New Broken Heart; Does Goodnight Mean Goodbye; Easy Come, Easy Go; Everybody's Somebody's Fool; Just Between You And Me; Just For Old Times' Sake; Let's Turkey Trot; My Heart Has A Mind Of Its Own; Please Don't Ask About Barbara; Run To Him; Venus In Blue Jeans

KELLER, JAMES — 867-5309/jenny

KELLER, JERRY — Here Comes Summer; Man And A Woman; Turn Down The Day

KELLER, LEONARD — Alexander The Swoose

KELLETTE, JOHN — I'm Forever Blowing Bubbles

KELLEY, CHET — Time Won't Let Me

KELLY, CHET — Girl In Love

KELLY, PAUL — Personally

KELLY, R. — I Do You

KELLY, RICH — D.C. Cab

KELLY, SHERMAN — Dancing In The Moonlight

KELLY, T. — Alone

KELLY, TOM — Like A Virgin

KEMP, GARY — True

KEMP, HAL — When Summer Is Gone (Oh, How I'll Miss You)

KEMP, WAYNE — One Piece At A Time

KEMPF, ROLF — Hello-Hooray

KENBROVIN, JEAN — I'm Forever Blowing Bubbles

KENDIS, JAMES — If I Had My Way; When It's Night-Time In Italy, It's Wednesday Over Here

KENNEDY, JIMMY — April In Portugal; Cinderella, Stay In My Arms; Did Your Mother Come From Ireland?; Harbor Lights; Isle Of Capri; Istanbul, Not Constantinople; My Prayer; Red Sails In The Sunset; Serenade In The Night; South Of The Border; Two Bouquets

KENNEDY, JOSEPH HAMILTON — Ole Faithful

KENNEDY, MICHAEL — Heartbeat-It's A Lovebeat

KENNEDY, RAY — Every Time I Think Of You; Isn't It Time

KENNEDY, STEVE — When I Die

KENNER, CHRIS — I Like It Like That; Land Of A Thousand Dances

KENNER, ROY — Run Run Run

KENNY, CHARLES — Dream Valley; While A Cigarette Was Burning

KENNY, GERALD — I Made It Through The Rain

KENNY, NICK — Dream Valley; Drop Me Off In Harlem; While A Cigarette Was Burning

KENNY, NICK AND CHARLES — Cathedral In The Pines; Gone Fishin'; Leanin' On The Ole Top Rail; Love Letters In The Sand; Make Believe Island

KENT, ARTHUR — Don't Go To Strangers; End Of The World; You Never Miss The Water Till The Well Runs Dry

KENT, LEONARD — Hold Tight-Hold Tight(Want Some Sea Food Mama)

KENT, MRS. LARRY — Clapping Song

KENT, WALTER — I Cross My Fingers; I'll Be Home For Christmas; I'm Gonna Live Till I Die; White Cliffs Of Dover, The (There'll Be Bluebirds Over)

KENTON, STAN — And Her Tears Flowed Like Wine; Artistry In Rhythm

KERN, JAMES V. — Little Red Fox

KERN, JEROME — 'Twas Not So Long Ago; All In Fun; All The Things You Are; All Through The Day; Allegheny Al; And Love Was Born; And Russia Is Her Name; Any Moment Now; Bill; Blue Danube Blues; Bojangles Of Harlem; Californ-I-AY; Can I Forget You?; Can't Help Lovin' Dat Man; Can't Help Singing; D'ye Love Me; Day Dreaming; Dearly Beloved; Don't Ever Leave Me; Fine Romance; Folks Who Live On The Hill; Good Morning Dearie; Heaven In My Arms; Heavenly Party; High, Wide, And Handsome; How'd You Like To Spoon With Me; I Am So Eager; I Dream Too Much; I Found You And You Found Me; I Got Love; I Have The Room Above; I Might Fall Back On You; I Still Suits Me; I Watch The Love Parade; I Won't Dance; I'll Be Hard To Handle; I'm Alone; I'm Old Fashioned; I'm The Echo(You're The Song That I Sing); I've Told Every Little Star; In Egern On The Tegern Sea; In Love In Vain; In Love With Love; In Other Words, Seventeen; In The Heart Of The Dark; Jockey On The Carousel; Just Let Me Look At You; Ka-Lu-A; Last Time I Saw Paris; Leave It To Jane; Left All Alone Again Blues; Let's Begin; Let's Say Good Night Till It's Morning; Life Upon The Wicked Stage; Long Ago(And Far Away); Look For The Silver Lining; Lorelei; Lovely To Look At; Make Believe; Make Way For Tomorrow; More And More; Never Gonna Dance; Never Gonna Give You Up; New Love Is Old; Night Was Made For Love; Nobody Else But Me; Ol' Man River; On With The Dance; Once In A Blue Moon; One Moment Alone; One More Dance; Our Song; Pick Yourself Up; Poor Pierrot; Put Me To The Test; Raggedy Ann; Reckless; Remind Me; Sally; She Didn't Say Yes; Smoke Gets In Your Eyes; Something Had To Happen; Song Is You; Song Of India; Sunny; Sure Thing; Till The Clouds Roll By; Touch Of Your Hand; Try To Forget; Two Hearts Are Better Than One; Two Little Bluebirds; Up With The Lark; Waltz In Swing Time; Way You Look Tonight; What's Good About Good Night; When The Spring Is In The Air; Whip-poor-will; Whistling Boy; Who; Whose Baby Are You; Why Do I Love You; Why Don't They Dance The Polka Anymore; Why Was I Born; Wild Rose; Will You Marry Me Tomorrow, Maria; Yesterdays; You Are Love; You Couldn't Be Cuter; You Were Never Lovelier; You're Devastating

KERR, HARRY D. — Do You Ever Think Of Me

KERR, JOE — She Blinded Me With Science

KERR, RICHARD — Looks Like We Made It; Mandy; No Night So Long; Somewhere In The Night

KERSEY, RON — Disco Inferno

KESLER, STANLEY — I Forgot To Remember To Forget

KESSLER, MARY — Baby Love

KESTER, MAX — Love Locked Out

KETELBY, ALBERT — In A Chinese Temple Garden

KETTNER, ALFONS — What You Won't Do For Love

KEY, FRANCIS SCOTT — Star Spangled Banner

KEYES, BERT — Angel Smile; Love On A Two-Way Street

KEYES, JAMES — Sh-Boom(Life Could Be A Dream)

KEYES, JOHN M. — Too Weak To Fight

KHACHATURIAN, ARAM — Sabre Dance Boogie

KHAN, CHAKA — Sweet Thing; You Got The Love

KHENT, ALLISON R. — Sixteen Candles; Trouble In Paradise

KHOURY, GEORGE — Sea Of Love

KIALLMARK, GEORGE — Old Oaken Bucket

KIBBLE, PERRY — Boogie Oogie Oogie

KIDD, JOHNNY — Shakin' All Over

KIHN, GREG — Jeopardy

KILDUFF, FRANK — Little Man With A Candy Cigar

KILGORE, MERLE — Dum-De-Da; Ring Of Fire

KILLEN, BUDDY — Forever; Lady Bird; Sugar Lips

KILLETTE, RONALD B. — Girl Watcher

KILLION, LEO — Hut Sut Song

KILLION, LEO V. — By-U, By-O(the Lou'siana Lullaby)

KILMER, JOYCE — Trees

KIM, ANDY — How'd We Ever Get This Way?; Jingle Jangle; Rock Me Gently; Sugar, Sugar; Sunshine

KING JR., WILLIAM — Brick House; Slippery When Wet; Sweet Love

KING, B. B. — When I'm Wrong; Why I Sing The Blues

KING, BEN E. — Stand By Me

KING, BOB — Tighter Tighter

KING, CAROLE — (You Make Me Feel Like)Natural Woman; At The Club; Beautiful; Been To Canaan; Believe In Humanity; Chicken Soup With Rice; Corazon; Crying In The Rain; Don't Bring Me Down; Don't Say Nothin' Bad(About My Baby); Go Away Little Girl; Halfway To Paradise; Her Royal Majesty; Hey, Girl; Hi-De-Ho(That Old Sweet Roll); I Can't Hear You No More; I Can't Stay Mad At You; I Feel The Earth Move; I Want To Stay Here; I Wasn't Born To Follow; I'm Into Something Good; I've Got Bonnie; It Might As Well Rain Until September; It's Going To Take Some Time; It's Too Late; Jazzman; Just Once In My Life; Keep Your Hands Off My Baby; Loco-Motion; Nightingale; Oh! No, Not My Baby; One Fine Day; Only Love Is Real; Pleasant Valley Sunday; Point Of No Return; Smackwater Jack; So Far Away; Some Kind-A-Wonderful; Sweet Seasons; Up On The Roof; When My Little Girl Is Smiling; Will You Love Me Tomorrow; You've Got A Friend

KING, CHARLES E. — Hawaiian Wedding Song,the; Song Of The Islands

KING, EDWARD — Saturday Night Special; Sweet Home Alabama

KING, FREDDY — Hide Away-1962

KING, IRVING — Show Me The Way To Go Home

KING, J. — Reveille Rock

KING, JACK — How Am I To Know?

KING, JIMMY — Soul Finger

KING, KENNETH — Everyone's Gone To The Moon

KING, MARK — Something About You

KING, PEARL — I Hear You Knocking; I Heard A Rumour; One Night; Witchcraft

KING, PEE WEE — Bonaparte's Retreat; Slow Poke; You Belong To Me

KING, RILEY — Woke Up This Morning

KING, ROBERT A. — (I Scream, You Scream, We All Scream For)Ice Cream; Moonlight On The Colorado; Toot Toot Tootsie; Why Did I Kiss That Girl

KING, ROBERT L. — Draggin' The Line

KING, ROY — I'll Pray For You

KING, S. — Lady(You Bring Me Up)

KING, TOM — Beatnik Fly; Crossfire; Girl In Love; Red River Rock; Time Won't Let Me

KING, WAYNE — Beautiful Love; Corn Silk; Goofus; Josephine; Waltz You Saved For Me

KING, WILLIAM — Lady(You Bring Me Up)

KINGSLEY, GERSHON — Popcorn

KIPLING, RUDYARD — On The Road To Mandalay

KIPNER, NAT — Too Much, Too Little, Too Late

KIPNER, STEVE — Hard Habit To Break; Physical; Twist Of Fate

KIPPS, JR, CHARLES — Walk Away From Love

KIRK, STEVE — Freddy

KIRKEBY, ED — All That Meat And No Potatoes

KIRKLAND, L. — When You Dance

KIRKLAND, LEROY — Good Lovin'

KIRKMAN, TERRY — Cherish; Everything That Touches You

KISCO, CHARLES — It's A Lonesome Old Town When You're Not Around

KLAGES, RAYMOND — Au Revoir But Not Goodbye; Doin' The Raccoon; Just You, Just Me

KLAUBER, MARCY — I Get The Blues When It Rains

KLEBAN, EDWARD — At The Ballet; Let Me Dance For You; Music And The Mirror; Nothing; One; Surprise Surprise; Tits And Ass; What I Did For Love

KLEIN, GARY — Bobby's Girl

KLEIN, LOU — Gay Caballero,a; If I Had My Way

KLEIN, PAUL — Little Blue Man

KLEINKAUF, HENRY — Johnson Rag

KLEINSINGER, GEORGE — Tubby The Tuba

KLENNER, JOHN — Down The River Of Golden Dreams; Heartaches; Japansy; Just Friends

KLINGMAN, MARK — Friends

KLOHR, JOHN N. — Billboard March

KLOSE, OTHMAR — Hear My Song, Violetta

KNAPE, S. — God, Love And Rock 'n' Roll(We Believe)

KNIGHT JR., MERALD — Daddy Could Swear, I Declare; I Don't Want To Do Wrong

KNIGHT, BAKER — I Got A Feeling; Lonesome Town; Never Be Anyone Else But You; Somewhere There's A Someone; Sweeter Than You; Wonder Of You

KNIGHT, FREDEREICK — Ring My Bell

KNIGHT, GARY — River Is Wide

KNIGHT, GLADYS — Daddy Could Swear, I Declare; I Don't Want To Do Wrong

KNIGHT, HOLLY — Invincible; Love Is A Battlefield; Love Touch; Never; Obsession; One Of The Living; Warrior

KNIGHT, JERRY — Breakin'...There's No Stopping Us; Crush On You

KNIGHT, JIMMY DE — Rock Around The Clock

KNIPPER, LEV — Meadowland

KNISS, RICHARD L. — Sunshine On My Shoulders

KNOPFLER, MARK — Money For Nothing; Private Dancer; So Far Away; Sultans Of Swing; Walk Of Life

KNOX, BUDDY — Hula Love; I'm Stickin' With You; Party Doll; Rock Your Little Baby To Sleep

KOCH, JOHN — I Want You All To Myself

KOEHLER, TED — Animal Crackers In My Soup; As Long As I Live; Between The Devil And The Deep Blue Sea; Breakfast Ball; Calico Days; Curly Top; Don't

Worry 'bout Me; Ev'ry Night About This Time; Get Happy; Happy As The Day Is Long; Here Goes(A Fool); Hey, What Did The Bluebird Say?; Hittin' The Bottle; I Gotta Right To Sing The Blues; I Love A Parade; I'm Shooting High; I've Got My Fingers Crossed; I've Got The World On A String; Ill Wind(You're Blowin' Me No Good); Kickin' The Gong Around; Let's Fall In Love; Linda; Lovely Lady; Minnie The Moocher's Wedding Day; Now I Know; Out In The Cold Again; Picture Me Without You; Public Melody Number One; Stay On The Right Side Sister; Stormy Weather; Truckin'; What Are You Doing The Rest Of My Life; When Lights Are Low; When The Sun Comes Out; Wrap Your Troubles In Dreams (And Dream Your Troubles Away)

KOETSCHER, EDMUND — Liechtensteiner Polka

KOFFMAN, MOE — Swingin' Shepherd Blues

KOHLER, DONNA — Hula Hoop Song

KOHLMAN, CHURCHILL — Cry

KOLBER, LARRY — I Love How You Love Me; Patches

KONG, LESLIE — Israelites

KONTE, FRANK — Ride Captain Ride

KOOGMANS, GEORGE — Radar Love

KOOPER, AL — I Must Be Seeing Things And Hearing Things

KOPLOW, DON HOWARD — Oh, Happy Day

KOPPELMAN, CHARLES — Yogi

KORB, ARTHUR — Go On With The Wedding; It Takes Time

KORNFELD, ARTIE — Come On, Let Yourself Go; Dead Man's Curve; Rain, The Park, And Other Things

KORSAKOV, N. RIMSKY — Capriccio Espagnol

KORTCHMAR, DAN — Sunset Grill

KORTCHMAR, DANNY — All She Wants To Do Is Dance; Dirty Laundry; Somebody's Baby

KOSLOFF, IRA — I Want You, I Need You, I Love You

KOSMA, JOSEPH — Autumn Leaves

KOSTELANETZ, ANDRE — Moon Love; On The Isle Of May

KOVEN, REGINALD DE — Oh Promise Me

KRAEMER, PETER — Hello, Hello

KRAMER, ALEX — Ain't Nobody Here But Us Chickens; Candy; Comme Ci, Comme Ca; Far Away Places; High On A Windy Hill; It All Comes Back To Me Now; It's Love, Love, Love!; Love Somebody; Money Is The Root Of All Evil; My Sister And I; No Other Arms, No Other Lips; You'll Never Get Away

KRAMPF, CRAIG — Oh, Sherrie

KREISLER, FRITZ — Caprice Viennois; Liebesfreud; Liebeslied; Old Refrain; Stars In My Eyes

KRENSKI, JOHN MIKE — Cheater

KRETZMER, HERBERT — Yesterday When I Was Young

KREUGER, BENNIE — Sunday

KRIEGER, HENRY — And I Am Telling You I'm Not Going; Cadillac Car; One Night Only

KRIEGER, ROBERT — Hello, I Love You; Light My Fire; Love Her Madly; Love Me Two Times; People Are Strange; Riders On The Storm; Roadhouse Blues; Touch Me; Wishful, Sinful

KRIEGSMAN, JAMES J. — Joey

KRISE, RAY — John Silver

KRISTOFFERSON, KRIS — For The Good Times; Hawk; Help Me Make It Through The Night; Me And Bobby Mcgee; Why Me

KRONDES, JIMMY — End

KRUEGER, JIM — We Just Disagree

KRUGER, JERRIE — I Heard You Cried Last Night(and So Did I)

KRUPA, GENE — Apurksady; Bolero At The Savoy; Boogie Blues; Drumboogie; Drummin' Man

KUHN, LEE — All That Glitters Is Not Gold

KUMMEL, LESLIE — I Will Always Think About You

KUPKA, STEPHEN — So Very Hard To Go; What Is Hip; You're Still A Young Man

KUPPS, MARTY — Two Divided By Love

KUSIK, LARRY — Beyond Tomorrow; Games That Lovers Play; Godfather(Love Theme)(Speak Softly Love); Happy Summer Days

L. A. — Rock Steady
LABOSTRIE, D. — Tutti-Frutti
LACALLE, JOSEPH M. — Amapola (Pretty Little Poppy)
LADD, D. — Rock Steady
LAGO, MARIO — Aurora
LAI, FRANCIS — Love Story (Theme) (Where Do I Begin); Man And A Woman
LAINE, DENNY — Girl's School; Git Along Little Dogies; London Town
LAINE, FRANKIE — Man Ain't Supposed To Cry; We'll Be Together Again
LAIRD, NICK — Life In A Northern Town
LAKE, BONNIE — Man With A Horn; Sandman
LAKE, FRANK — Bless'em All
LAKE, SOL — Lonely Bull
LAMB, ARTHUR — Asleep In The Deep; Bird In A Gilded Cage
LAMBERT, DAVE — What's This
LAMBERT, DENNIS — Ain't No Woman(Like The One I Got); Are You Man Enough; Country Boy(You Got Your Feet In L.A.); Do The Freddie; Don't Pull Your Love; Give It To The People; It Only Takes A Minute; Keeper Of The Castle; Look In My Eyes Pretty Woman; Nightshift; One Tin Soldier; Remember What I Told You To Forget; Two Divided By Love; We Built This City
LAMM, ROBERT — 25 Or 6 To 4; Beginnings; Does Anybody Really Know What Time It Is?; Free; Harry Truman; Questions 67 And 68; Saturday In The Park
LAMPERT, DIANE — Break It To Me Gently
LANCE, BOBBY — House That Jack Built,the
LANCE, MAJOR — Matador
LANCE, MILT — I Want A Little Doggie
LAND, HARRY — Fabulous
LAND, LEON — Lay Down Your Arms
LANDAU, WILLIAM — Sacred
LANDES, BERNIE — Elephants Tango
LANDESMAN, FRAN — Ballad Of The Sad Young Men
LANE, BURTON — Begat; Blue Nightfall; Chin Up! Cheerio! Carry On!; Come Back To Me; Dancing On A Dime; Don't Let It Get You Down; Everything I Have Is Yours; Feudin' And Fightin'; Great Come-and-Get-It Day; Have A Heart; He Wasn't You(He Isn't You); How About You?; How Are Things In Glocca Morra?; How Could You Believe Me When I Said I Love You When You Know I've Been A L; Howdja Like To Love Me; I Hear Music; I Left My Hat In Haiti; I'll Take Tallulah; If This Isn't Love; Lady's In Love With You; Last Call For Love; Let's Go Bavarian; Listen My Children And You Shall Hear; Look To The Rainbow; Melinda; Moments Like This; Necessity; Old Devil Moon; On A Clear Day(You Can See Forever); Poor You; Says My Heart; Something Sort Of Grandish; The World Is In My Arms; Tony's Wife; Too Late Now; What Are You Doing The Rest Of Your Life; What Did I Have That I Don't Have; When I'm Not Near The Girl I Love; When The Idle Poor Become The Idle Rich; You're My Thrill
LANE, GRACE — Clinging Vine
LANE, HERBERT — Disco Nights
LANE, KEN — Everybody Loves Somebody
LANE, RONNIE — Itchycoo Park
LANE, WILLIAM M. — Times Of Your Life

LANEY, KING — Why Don't You Believe Me
LANG, JOHN — Broken Wings
LANGDON, DORY — Bad And The Beautiful; Control Yourself; Faraway Part Of Town
LANGE, EDDIE DE — All I Remember Is You; All This And Heaven Too; Along The Navajo Trail; And So Do I; At Your Beck And Call; Darn That Dream; Deep In A Dream; Do You Know What It Means To Miss New Orleans; Good For Nothin'(But Love); Haunting Me; Heaven Can Wait; I Wish I Were Twins(So I Could Love You Twice As Much); If I'm Lucky; Just As Though You Were Here; Looking For Yesterday; Man With A Horn; Passe; Shake Down The Stars; So Help Me(IF I Don't Love You); Solitude; String Of Pearls
LANGE, HENRY — Hot Lips
LANGE, JOHNNY — Blue Shadows On The Trail; I Lost My Sugar In Salt Lake City; Little Red Fox; Mule Train; Somebody Bigger Than You And I; Uncle Remus Said
LANGE, LEE — Cara Mia
LANGE, R. J. — Get Outta My Dreams, Get Into My Car
LANGE, ROBERT JOHN — Do You Believe In Love; Is It Love; Photograph; Rock Of Ages; When The Going Gets Tough, The Tough Get Going
LANIER, DONNIE H. — Here We Go Again
LARA, AGUSTIN — You Belong To My Heart Or Solamente Una Vez
LARA, AUGUSTIN — Granada
LARA, MARIA TERESA — Sunny Skylar
LARACUENTE, DAVID — Happy Music
LAROCCA, JAMES D. — Barnyard Blues
LARSON, GLEN — Big Man
LARSON, GLENN — Twenty-Six Miles
LARSON, MEL — I Am Love(parts 1 & 2)
LARUSSO, ANDREA — Dress You Up
LASKA, EDWARD — How'd You Like To Spoon With Me
LASLEY, DAVID — Lead Me On
LASLEY, MARK — Too Much Talk (And Not Enough Action)
LAST, JAMES — Games That Lovers Play; Happy Heart
LATHAM, DWIGHT — I'm My Own Grandpaw
LATOUCHE, JOHN — Ballad For Americans; Cabin In The Sky; Day-Dream; Do What You Wanna Do; He Makes Me Believe He's Mine; Honey In The Honeycomb; I've Got Me; Love Me Tomorrow(But Leave Me Alone Today); Maybe I Should Change My Ways; On The Wrong Side Of The Railroad Track; Savannah; When I Walk With You
LAUB, PHOEBE SNOW — Poetry Man
LAUDER, SIR HARRY — It's Nice To Get Up In The Morning; Roamin' In The Gloamin'
LAUPER, CYNDI — Change Of Heart; Goonies 'r' Good Enough; She Bop; Time After Time
LAURENCE, PAUL — Rock Me Tonight(For Old Times Sake)
LAURENTS, ARTHUR — Bonjour Tristesse
LAVA, WILLIAM — Cheyenne
LAVERE, FRANK — Almost Always; Have You Heard; Pretend
LAVOIE, KENT — I'd Love You To Want Me; Me And You And A Dog Named BOO
LAVOIE, ROLAND KENT — Don't Tell Me Goodnight
LAWLOR, CHARLES B. — East Side, West Side(the Sidewalks Of New York)
LAWNHURST, VEE — Cross Patch
LAWRENCE, CHARLES — And Her Tears Flowed Like

Wine
LAWRENCE, ELLIOT — Strange Things Are Happening
LAWRENCE, JACK — (By The)Sleepy Lagoon; All Or Nothing At All; Beyond The Sea; Choo Choo Train; Concerto For Two; Delicado; Hand In Hand; Hand Me Down My Walking Cane; Handful Of Stars; Hold My Hand; Huckleberry Duck; If I Didn't Care; In An Eighteenth Century Drawing Room; It's Funny To Everyone But Me; Johnson Rag; Linda; Moonlight Masquerade; Play, Fiddle, Play; Poor People Of Paris; Sunrise Serenade; Symphony; Vagabond Dreams; What Will I Tell My Heart; What's Your Story, Morning Glory?; With The Wind And The Rain In Your Hair; Yes My Darling Daughter
LAWRENCE, MARK — David And Lisa's Love Song
LAWRENCE, STEPHEN — Bang The Drum Slowly(theme); You Take My Breath Away
LAWRENCE, STEVE — Can't Get Over(the Bossa Nova)
LAWRENCE, TREVOR — I'm So Excited
LAWSON, HERBERT HAPPY — Any Time
LAYTON, TURNER — Dear Old Southland; Way Down Yonder In New Orleans
LAZARUS, EMMA — Give Me Your Tired, Your Poor
LAZER, DAVE — Gotta Travel On
LAZZARO, E. DI — Harold Adamson
LEA, JIM — Cum On Feel The Noize; Run, Runaway
LEADER, MICKEY — Dance With A Dolly(with A Hole In Her Stocking)
LEANDER, MIKE — Another Time, Another Place; Do You Wanna Touch Me; Early In The Morning; Knight In Rusty Armor; Lady Godiva; Rock And Roll(part II)
LEBIEG, EARL — Sleep
LEBISH, LOUIS — Dance With Me
LEBON, SIMON — Election Day; Notorious
LEBOWSKY, STAN — Wayward Wind
LECUONA, ERNESTO — Always In My Heart; Andalucia; Another Night Like This; At The Crossroads; From One Love To Another; Jungle Drums; Malaguena; Say Si Si; Siboney
LECUONA, MARGARITA — S.K. Russell
LEDBETTER, HUDDIE — Cotton Fields; Goodnight Irene; Kisses Sweeter Than Wine
LEDESMA, ISHMAEL — Get Off; Hot Number
LEE JR., JAMES — In A Moment
LEE, BRENDA — Rockin' Around The Christmas Tree
LEE, DICKEY — I Saw Linda Yesterday
LEE, ETHEL — Speedy Gonzalez
LEE, GEDDY — New World Man
LEE, JACK — Hanging On The Telephone
LEE, JAY — Yellow Balloon
LEE, JIM — Let's Dance
LEE, JIMMY — Brush Those Tears From Your Eyes
LEE, LARRY — Jackie Blue
LEE, LEONARD — Feel So Fine; I'm Gone; Let The Good Times Roll
LEE, LESTER — Blue Gardenia; Bride And Groom Polka; Christmas Dreaming; Pennsylvania Polka
LEE, MARTIN — Save Your Kisses For Me
LEE, MICHELLE — He's Good For Me
LEE, NANCY — Stroll
LEE, NORMAN — Champagne Polka
LEE, PEGGY — Blum Blum; Don't Be So Mean To Baby('cause Baby's So Good To You); He's A Tramp; I Don't Know Enough About You; I'm Gonna Go Fishin'; It's A Good Day; Johnny Guitar; Manana(Is Soon Enough For Me); Siamese Cat Song; What More

Can A Woman Do?; Where Can I Go Without You
LEE, SYDNEY — My Love, Forgive Me(Amore, Scusami)
LEE, TOMMY BOYCE AND CURTIS — Pretty Little Angel Eyes
LEEDS, MILTON — Castanets And Lace; Misirlou; Perfidia; You, You, You Are The One
LEEN, THEIS VAN — Hocus Pocus
LEES, GENE — Quiet Nights Of Quiet Stars(Corcovado); Song Of The Jet; Waltz For Debby
LEESON, M. — For Your Eyes Only
LEEUONEN, R. — Venus
LEEWAY, J. — King For A Day
LEEWAY, JOE — Doctor! Doctor!; Hold Me Now; Lay Your Hands On Me
LEGASSICK, S. — One Heartbeat
LEGRAND, MICHEL — Brian's Song; Happy(Love Theme From Lady Sings The Blues); His Eyes-Her Eyes; I Was Born In Love With You; I Will Wait For You; Papa Can You Hear Me; Summer Knows; Watch What Happens; Windmills Of Your Mind, The Or The Theme From The Thomas Crown Affair
LEHAC, NED — You Forgot Your Gloves
LEHAR, FRANZ — Girls, Girls, Girls; Gold And Silver Waltz; Maxim's; Merry Widow Waltz; Vilia; Waltz From The Count Of Luxembourg; White Dove; Yours Is My Heart Alone
LEHMAN, JOHNNY — Alone At Last; First Born; Night; Why Does It Get So Late So Early
LEHMAN, KENNY — Dance, Dance, Dance(yowsah, Yowsah, Yowsah)
LEIBER, JERRY — Bossa Nova Baby; Charlie Brown; D.W. Washburn; Dance With Me; Drip Drop; Hound Dog; I Keep Forgettin'(Every Time You're Near); I Who Have Nothing; I'm A Woman; Is That All There Is?; Jailhouse Rock; Kansas City; Love Me; Love Potion Number Nine; Loving You; Lucky Lips; Marie's The Name, His Latest Flame; On Broadway; Only In America; Poison Ivy; Ruby Baby; Searchin'; She's Not You; Spanish Harlem; Stand By Me; Treat Me Nice; Yakety Yak; Young Blood
LEIGH, CAROLYN — Be A Performer; Best Is Yet To Come; Deep Down Inside; Firefly; Give A Little Whistle; Here's To Us; Hey, Look Me Over; How Little We Know(How Little It Matters How Little We Know); I Won't Grow Up; I'm Flying; I'm Waiting Just For You; I've Got To Crow; I've Got Your Number; Little Me; Other Side Of The Tracks; Poor Little Hollywood Star; Real Live Girl; What Take My Fancy; Witchcraft; Young At Heart
LEIGH, MITCH — Impossible Dream
LEIGH, RICHARD — Don't It Make My Brown Eyes Blue
LEITCH, DONOVAN — Atlantis; Barabajagal; Catch The Wind; Epistle To Dippy; Hurdy Gurdy Man; Jenifer Juniper; Mellow Yellow; Sunshine Superman
LEKA, PAUL — Green Tambourine; Kiss Him Goodbye; Na Na, Hey, Hey, Kiss Him Goodbye
LEMARE, JULES — Sweet And Lovely
LENDELL, MIKE — Mary In The Morning
LENDHURST, PEARL — Be-Bop Baby
LENGSFELDER, H. J. — Perdido
LENK, HARRY — Hayfoot-Strawfoot
LENNON, JOHN — #9 Dream; (P. S.)I Love You; All I've Got To Do; All My Loving; All Together Now; All You Need Is Love; And I Love Her; And Your Bird Can Sing; Another Girl; Any Time At All; Ask Me Why; Baby's In Black; Baby, You're A Rich Man; Back In

The U.S.S.R.; Bad To Me; Ballad Of John And Yoko; Because; Being For The Benefit Of Mr. Kite; Birthday; Blackbird; Can't Buy Me Love; Carry That Weight; Cold Turkey; Come Together; Continuing Story Of Bungalow Bill; Cry Baby Cry; Day In The Life; Day Tripper; Dear Prudence; Do You Want To Know A Secret?; Doctor Robert; Don't Let Me Down; Drive My Car; Eight Days A Week; Eleanor Rigby; End; Every Little Thing; Everybody's Got Something To Hide Except Me And My Monkey; Fame; Fixing A Hole; Flying; Fool On The Hill; For No One; From A Window; From Me To You; Get Back; Getting Better; Gimme Some Truth; Girl; Give Peace A Chance; Glass Onion; Golden Slumbers; Good Day Sunshine; Good Morning, Good Morning; Good Night; Goodbye; Got To Get You Into My Life; Happiness Is A Warm Gun; Hard Day's Night; Hello Little Girl; Hello, Goodbye; Help!; Helter Skelter; Here, There, And Everywhere; Hey Bulldog; Hey Jude; Hold Me Tight; Honey Pie; How Do You Sleep?; I Am The Walrus; I Call Your Name; I Don't Want To See You Again; I Don't Want To Spoil The Party; I Feel Fine; I Saw Her Standing There; I Should Have Known Better; I Wanna Be Your Man; I Want To Hold Your Hand; I Want You(She's So Heavy); I Will; I'll Be Back; I'll Be On My Way; I'll Cry Instead; I'll Follow The Sun; I'll Get You; I'll Keep You Satisfied; I'm A Loser; I'm Happy Just To Dance With You; I'm Looking Through You; I'm Only Sleeping; I'm So Tired; I've Just Seen A Face; If I Fell; Imagine; In My Life; Instant Karma; It Won't Be Long; It's All Down To Goodnight Vienna; It's For You; It's Only Love; Julia; Lady Madonna; Let It Be; Like Dreamers Do; Little Child; Long And Winding Road; Love Me Do; Love Of The Loved; Lovely Rita; Lucy In The Sky With Diamonds; Magical Mystery Tour; Martha My Dear; Maxwell's Silver Hammer; Mean Mr. Mustard; Michelle; Mind Games; Misery; Mother; Mother Nature's Son; Night Before; No Reply; Nobody I Know; Nobody Told Me; Norwegian Wood; Not A Second Time; Nowhere Man; Ob-La-Di, Ob-La-Da; Oh! Darling; P. S. I Love You; Paperback Writer; Penny Lane; Please Please Me; Polythene Pam; Power To The People; Rain; Revolution; Rocky Racoon; Run For Your Life; Sexy Sadie; Sgt. Pepper's Lonely Hearts Club Band; She Came In Through The Bathroom Window; She Loves You; She Said She Said; She's A Woman; She's Leaving Home; Step Inside Love; Strawberry Fields Forever; Sun King; The Word; Ticket To Ride; Watching The Wheels; We Can Work It Out; What You're Doing; Whatever Gets You Through The Night; When I'm Sixty-Four; Why Don't We Do It In The Road; Wild Honey Pie; With A Little Help From My Friends; Woman; Working Class Hero; World Without Love; Yellow Submarine; Yer Blues; Yes It Is; Yesterday; You Can't Do That; You Never Give Me Your Money; You Won't See Me; You're Gonna Lose That Girl; You've Got To Hide Your Love Away; Your Mother Should Know

LENNON, JULIAN — Say You're Wrong; Too Late For Goodbyes

LENNOX, ANNIE — Here Comes The Rain Again; Love Is A Stranger; Missionary Man; Sisters Are Doin' It For Themselves; Sweet Dreams(Are Made Of This); Would I Lie To You?

LENOIR, JEAN — Speak To Me Of Love(Parlez-Moi D'amour)

LENOX, JEAN — I Don't Care

LEON, DAVID — Ride

LEON, ROBERT DE — Can't Get Indiana Off My Mind

LEONARD, ANITA — Sunday Kind Of Love

LEONARD, DUKE — Josephine Please No Lean On The Bell

LEONARD, EDDIE — Ida, Sweet As Apple Cider

LEONARD, GLENN — I'm On Fire

LEONARD, MARK — Missing You

LEONARD, MICHAEL — I'm All Smiles

LEONARD, PAT — La Isla Bonita; Live To Tell; Who's That Girl

LEONCAVALLO, RUGGIERO — Vesti La Giubba

LEOPOLD, GLENN — Back When My Hair Was Short

LERIOS, CORY — Cool Love; Don't Want To Live Without It; I Want You Tonight; Love Will Find A Way; Whatcha Gonna Do

LERNER, ALAN JAY — (I Don't Understand)Parisiens; Another Autumn; Ascot Gavotte; Before I Gaze At You Again; Brigadoon; Camelot; Come Back To Me; Come To Me, Bend To Me; Day Before Spring; Down On Macconnachy Square; Duel For One(The First Lady Of The Land); Fie On Goodness; Follow Me; From This Day On; Get Me To The Church On Time; Gigi; Green-Up Time; Guenevere; He Wasn't You(He Isn't You); Heather On The Hill; Here I'll Stay; How Could You Believe Me When I Said I Love You When You Know I've Been A Louse; How To Handle A Woman; I Could Have Danced All Night; I Left My Hat In Haiti; I Love You This Morning; I Loved You Once In Silence; I Remember It Well; I Still See Elisa; I Talk To The Trees; I Wonder What The King Is Doing Tonight?; I'll Go Home With Bonnie Jean; I'm An Ordinary Man; I'm Glad I'm Not Young Anymore; I'm On My Way; I've Grown Accustomed To Her Face; If Ever I Would Leave You; Jousts; Jug Of Wine; Just You Wait; Little Prince; Love Of My Life; Lusty Month Of May; Melinda; My Last Love; My Mother's Weddin' Day; Night They Invented Champagne; On A Clear Day(You Can See Forever); On The Street Where You Live; Rain In Spain; Seven Deadly Virtues; Show Me; Simple Joys Of Maidenhood; Too Late Now; Waitin' For My Dearie; Wand'rin Star; What Did I Have That I Don't Have; What Do The Simple Folks Do?; Why Can't The English; With A Little Bit Of Luck; Without You; Wouldn't It Be Loverly; You Did It; You Haven't Changed At All

LERNER, SAMMY — (Oh Suzanna)Dust Off That Old Pianna; I'm Popeye The Sailor Man; Is It True What They Say About Dixie?

LESLIE, EDGAR — America, I Love You; Among My Souvenirs; At A Perfume Counter(On The Rue De La Paix); Blue(and Broken Hearted); By The River Sainte Marie; Crazy People; Dirty Hands, Dirty Face; For Me And My Gal; Getting Some Fun Out Of Life; I Wake Up Smiling; In A Little Gypsy Tearoom; It Looks Like Rain In Cherry Blossom Lane; Kansas City Kitty; Little Bit Independent; Lost In A Dream; Me And The Man In The Moon; Moon Over Miami; Oh! What A Pal Was Mary; On Treasure Island; Robins And Roses; Romance; Rose Of The Rio Grande

LESLIE, TOM — Sukiyaki

LESSLIE, THOMAS — Everybody Loves A Clown; She's Just My Style

LESTER, WALTER — Since I Don't Have You

LEVANT, OSCAR — Blame It On My Youth; Lady, Play Your Mandolin; Lovable And Sweet; Until Today; Wacky Dust

LEVAY, SYLVESTER — Fly, Robin, Fly; Get Up And Boogie

LEVEEN, RAYMOND — I Wonder; Ti-Pi-Tin

LEVENSON, NEIL — Denise

LEVIN, IRA — She Touched Me(He Touched Me)

LEVINE, IRWIN — Black Pearl; Candida; I Must Be Seeing Things And Hearing Things; I Woke Up In Love This Morning; Knock Three Times; Say, Has Anybody Seen My Sweet Gypsy Rose; Steppin' Out(I'm Gonna Boogie Tonight); Tie A Yellow Ribbon Round The Ole Oak Tree; Your Husband, My Wife

LEVINE, JOE — Down At Lulu's; Quick Joey Small(Run, Joey, Run); Yummy Yummy Yummy

LEVINE, JOEY — Chewy, Chewy; Gimme, Gimme, Good Lovin'; Make Believe; Mercy

LEVINSON, LOU — Here In My Heart

LEVITAN, LEE OSCAR — Me And Baby Brother; Slipping Into Darkness

LEVITT, ESTELLE — Don't Say You Don't Remember; In The Name Of Love

LEVY, EUNICE — Ko Ko Mo, I Love You So

LEVY, GAIL — Mercy, Mercy, Mercy

LEVY, JACQUES — Hurricane(part 1); Joey; Mozambique

LEVY, MARCY — Lay Down Sally

LEVY, MORRIS — California Sun

LEVY, VINCENT — Mercy, Mercy, Mercy

LEWIS JR., RAMSEY E. — Wade In The Water

LEWIS, AL — Blueberry Hill; Breeze, The(That's Bringin' My Honey Back To Me); Cincinnatti Dancing Pig; Every Now And Then; I'm Ready; Livin' In The Sunlight-Lovin' In The Moonlight; No! No! A Thousand Times No!; Now's The Time To Fall In Love(Potatoes Are Cheaper-Tomatoes Are Cheaper); On The Bumpy Road To Love; Over Somebody Else's Shoulder; Rose O'Day(The Filla-Ga-Dusha Song); Start The Day Right; When I'm The President (We Want Cantor); Why Don't You Fall In Love With Me; You Gotta Be A Football Hero (To Get Along With The Beautiful Girls)

LEWIS, BARBARA — Hello Stranger

LEWIS, BUNNY — Milord

LEWIS, CALVIN — When A Man Loves A Woman

LEWIS, CLARENCE — Ya-Ya

LEWIS, D. — Always

LEWIS, EARLE — Closer You Are

LEWIS, EDNA — I Wish That We Were Married; Judy's Turn To Cry; Lipstick On Your Collar

LEWIS, GARY — Everybody Loves A Clown; She's Just My Style

LEWIS, HUEY — Heart Of Rock And Roll; Hip To Be Square; I Know What I Like; I Want A New Drug; If This Is It; Power Of Love; Stuck With You

LEWIS, HUGH — B.J. The D.J.

LEWIS, J. — Always

LEWIS, JERRY LEE — High School Confidential

LEWIS, KENNETH — Little Bit O' Soul

LEWIS, KENNY ST. — Heaven Must Be Missing An Angel; Hot Line

LEWIS, MARGARET — Reconsider Me

LEWIS, MEADE "LUX" — Boogie Woogie Prayer; Honky Tonk Train

LEWIS, MIRIAM — Port-Au-Prince

LEWIS, MORGAN — How High The Moon; Old Soft Shoe

LEWIS, ROGER — Down By The Winegar Woiks; Love Is The Drug; One Dozen Roses

LEWIS, RUSSELL R. — Groovy Situation

LEWIS, SAM — Beautiful Lady In Blue; Close To Me; Cryin ' For The Carolines; Dinah; Five Foot Two, Eyes Of Blue(Has Anybody Seen My Girl); For All We Know; Gloomy Sunday; Have A Little Faith In Me; How Ya Gonna Keep 'em Down On The Farm; I Believe In Miracles; I Kiss Your Hand, Madame; I Knew You Were Waiting For Me; I'd Love To Fall Asleep And Wake Up In My Mammy's Arms; I'm Sitting On Top Of The World; In A Little Spanish Town; Just A Baby's Prayer At Twilight; Just Friends; Laugh! Clown! Laugh!; Lawd, You Made The Night Too Long; My Mammy; One Minute To One; Rock-A-Bye Your Baby With A Dixie Melody; Singin' The Blues(Till My Daddy Come Home); Street Of Dreams; Tuck Me To Sleep In My Old 'tucky Home; When You're A Long Long Way From Home; Where Did Robinson Crusoe Go With Friday On Saturday Night

LEWIS, STAN — I'll Be Home; Susie Q

LEWIS, T. — Control; Let's Wait Awhile

LEWIS, TED — When My Baby Smiles At Me

LEWIS, TERRY — Human; I Didn't Mean To Turn You On; Nasty; What Have You Done For Me Lately; When I Think Of You

LEWIS, W. — Always

LEYBOURNE, GEORGE — Daring Young Man On The Flying Trapeze

LIBBEY, DEE — Mangos

LICHTY, KATHERINE — Almost Always

LICKLEY, MARK — Look Of Love

LIEBER, JERRY — Along Came Jones; Baby I Don't Care; Bernie's Tune; Black Denim Trousers And Motorcycle Boots; Don't

LIEBLING, HOWARD — California Nights; Sunshine, Lollipops And Roses

LIEBOWITZ, JOSEPH — Wedding Samba, The (Also Known As The Wedding Rhumba)

LIEF, MAX — How Long Will It Last?

LIEURANCE, THURLOW — By The Waters Of Minnetonka

LIFESON, ALEX — New World Man

LIGGINS, JOE — Honeydripper

LIGHTFOOT, GORDON — Carefree Highway; Cotton Jenny; Early Mornin' Rain; For Lovin' Me; If You Could Read My Mind; Rainy Day People; Sundown; Wreck Of The Edmund Fitzgerald

LILIUOKALANI, QUEEN — Aloha Oe

LILLEY, JOSEPH J. — Jingle Jangle Jingle

LIMBO, SONNY — Key Largo

LINCKE, PAUL — Glow Worm

LIND, BOB — Elusive Butterfly

LIND, JON — Crazy For You

LIND, JONATHAN — Boogie Wonderland

LINDE, DENNIS — Burning Love

LINDEMAN, EDITH — Little Things Mean A Lot

LINDEN, DAVE — Love Is A Hurtin' Thing

LINDGREN, ALAN — Hello Again

LINDSAY, MARK — Don't Take It So Hard; Good Thing; Great Airplane Strike Of 1966,the; Him Or Me, What's It Gonna Be?; I Had A Dream; Let Me!; Mr. Sun, Mr. Moon; Steppin' Out

LINDT, R. — Liechtensteiner Polka

LINDUP, MARK — Something About You

LING, SAM — Bad Luck; Eddie, My Love

LINHART, BUZZY — Friends

LINK, HARRY — I'm Just Wild About Animal Crackers; I've Got A Feeling I'm Falling; You're The One I Care For

LINN, ROGER — Promises

LINTON, WILLIAM — Easier Said Than Done

LINZER, SANDY — Attack; Baby,make Your Own Sweet Music; Dawn(Go Away); Keep The Ball Rollin'; Let's Hang On(To What We've Got); Lover's Concerto; Mornin' Beautiful; Native New Yorker; Opus 17(Don't Worry 'bout Me); Working My Way Back To You

LINZNER, SANDY — Fresh

LIPPMAN, SID — "A" You're Adorable(the Alphabet Song); Chickery Chick; House With Love In It; Laroo, Laroo, Lilli Bolero; Too Young; Who Do You Think You Are

LIPSCOMB, BELINDA — Operator

LIPSIUS, FRED — Go Down Gamblin'

LIPTON, LEONARD — Puff(The Magic Dragon)

LISLE, CLAUDE JOSEPH ROUGET DE — Marseillaise, La

LISZT, FRANZ — Hungarian Rhapsody No. 2; Liebestraum

LITTLE, ERIC — My Time Is Your Time

LITTLE, LITTLE JACK — Hold Me; I Wouldn't Trade The Silver In My Mother's Hair(for All The Gold In The Wor; In A Shanty In Old Shanty Town; Jealous; You're A Heavenly Thing

LITTMAN, J. — Strut

LIVGREN, KERRY — Carry On Wayward Son; Dust In The Wind; People Of The South Wind; Play The Game Tonight

LIVINGSTON, ALAN — I Taut I Taw A Puddy Tat(I Thought I Saw A Pussy Cat)

LIVINGSTON, FUD — Aureet; Feelin' No Pain; Humpty Dumpty; I'm Thru With Love

LIVINGSTON, JAY — All The Time; Almost In Your Arms(Love Theme From Houseboat); Angel; Another Time, Another Place; Beside You; Bing! Bang! Bong!; Bonanza!; Bonne Nuit-Goodnight; Buttons And Bows; Cat And The Canary; Copper Canyon; Dear Heart; Eres Tu(Touch The Wind); Ev'rything Beautiful; Femininity; Give It All You've Got; Golden Earrings; Here's To Love; Home Cookin'; In The Arms Of Love; Life Is A Beautiful Thing; Misto Cristofo Columbo; Mona Lisa; Morning Music Of Montmartre; Mr. Lucky; My Own, My Only, My All; Place In The Sun; Que Sera, Sera(Whatever Will Be, Will Be); Silver Bells; Square In A Social Circle; Square In A Social Circle; To Each His Own

LIVINGSTON, JERRY — (Day After Day)I'll Always Love You; (When It's)Darkness On The Delta; 77 Sunset Strip; A Dream Is A Wish Your Heart Makes; Baby,baby,baby; Ballad Of Cat Ballou; Bibbidi-Bobbidi-Boo(the Magic Song); Blue And Sentimental; Bluebell; Bourbon Street Beat; Cinderella; Don't You Love Me Anymore?; Fuzzy Wuzzy; Hanging Tree; Hawaiian Eye; I'm A Big Girl Now; I've Got An Invitation To A Dance; I've Got Sixpence; It's The Talk Of The Town; Mairzy Doats; Story Of A Starry Night; Surfside 6; Twelfth Of Never; Under A Blanket Of Blue; Very Merry Un-Birthday To You; Wait Until Dark; Wake The Town And Tell The People; Wish Me

A Rainbow; Young Emotions

LIVRAGHI, R. — Man Without Love

LLOYD, HARRY — I Just Fall In Love Again

LLOYD, MICHAEL — I Was Made For Dancin'

LOCKE, MATTHEW — Believe Me If All Those Endearing Young Charms

LOCKHART, EUGENE — World Is Waiting For The Sunrise

LOCKLIN, HANK — Send Me The Pillow You Dream On

LODGE, DAVID — Major Tom(Coming Home)

LODGE, JOHN — I'm Just A Singer(in A Rock And Roll Band); Isn't Life Strange

LODWIG, RAY — Since My Best Gal Turned Me Down

LOEB, JOHN JACOB — Boo-Hoo!; Get Out Those Old Records; Got The Jitters; Masquerade; Rosie The Riveter; Sailboat In The Moonlight; Seems Like Old Times

LOESSER, FRANK — "Murder" He Says; Anywhere I Wander; Baby, It's Cold Outside; Big D; Blame It On The Danube; Bloop, Bleep!; Blue Nightfall; Boys In The Back Room; Brotherhood Of Man; Bushel And A Peck; Can't Get Out Of This Mood; College Swing; Company Way; Dancing On A Dime; Dolores; Don't Cry; Dreamer; Faraway Boy; Feathery Feelin' The; Follow The Fold; Fuddy Duddy Watchmaker; Fugue For Tinhorns; Grand Old Ivy; Happy Go Lucky; Happy To Keep His Dinner Warm; Happy To Make Your Acquaintance; Have I Stayed Away Too Long; Heart And Soul; Hoop-Dee-Do; How Sweet You Are; How To Succeed In Business Without Really Trying; Howdja Like To Love Me; I Believe In You; I Don't Want To Walk Without You; I Get The Neck Of The Chicken; I Hear Music; I Said No; I Wish I Didn't Love You So; I Wish I Were Twins(So I Could Love You Twice As Much); I'll Know; I'm Hans Christian Anderson; I'm Ridin' For A Fall; I've Been In Love Before; I've Never Been In Love Before; If I Were A Bell; In My Arms; Inchworm; Jingle Jangle Jingle; Joey, Joey, Joey; Junk Man; Just Another Polka; Kiss The Boys Goodbye; Lady's In Love With You; Leave Us Face It(We're In Love); Let's Get Lost; Lovable Sort Of Person; Love From A Heart Of Gold; Lovelier Than Ever; Luck Be A Lady; Make A Miracle; Moments Like This; Moon Of Manakoora; Moon Over Burma; More I Cannot Wish You; Most Happy Fella; My Darling, My Darling; My Heart Is So Full Of You; My Time Of Day; Never Will I Marry; New Ashmolean Marching Society And Students Conservatory Band; No Two People; Oldest Established; On A Slow Boat To China; Once In Love With Amy; Paris Original; Pernambuco; Pet Me, Poppa; Poppa Don't Preach To Me; Praise The Lord And Pass The Ammunition; Rodger Young; Rumble, Rumble, Rumble; Sand In My Shoes; Say It(Over And Over Again); Says My Heart; Sewing Machine; Sing A Tropical Song; Sit Down, You're Rockin' The Boat; Small Fry; Somebody, Somewhere; Spring Will Be A Little Late This Year; Standing On The Corner; Strange Enchantment; Sue Me; Summertime Love; Thumbelina; Touch Of Texas; Two Sleepy People; Ugly Duckling; Walking Away Whistling; Warm All Over; Wave To Me, My Lady; We're The Couple In The Castle; What Are You Doing New Year's Eve; What Do You Do In The Infantry?; Where Are You Now That I Need You; Why Fight The Feeling; Woman In Love; Wonderful Copenhagen

LOEWE, FREDERICK — Almost Like Being In Love; Another Autumn; Ascot Gavotte; Before I Gaze At You Again; Brigadoon; Camelot; Campbells Are Coming; Come To Me, Bend To Me; Day Before Spring; Down On Macconnachy Square; Fie On Goodness; Follow Me; From This Day On; Get Me To The Church On Time; Gigi; Guenevere; Heather On The Hill; How To Handle A Woman; I Could Have Danced All Night; I Love You This Morning; I Loved You Once In Silence; I Remember It Well; I Still See Elisa; I Talk To The Trees; I Wonder What The King Is Doing Tonight?; I'll Go Home With Bonnie Jean; I'm An Ordinary Man; I'm Glad I'm Not Young Anymore; I'm On My Way; I've Grown Accustomed To Her Face; If Ever I Would Leave You; Jousts; Jug Of Wine; Just You Wait; Little Prince; Love Of My Life; Lusty Month Of May; My Last Love; My Mother's Weddin' Day; Night They Invented Champagne; On The Street Where You Live; Parisiens; Rain In Spain; Seven Deadly Virtues; Show Me; Simple Joys Of Maidenhood; Waitin' For My Dearie; Wand'rin Star; What Do The Simple Folks Do?; Why Can't The English; With A Little Bit Of Luck; Without You; Wouldn't It Be Loverly; You Did It; You Haven't Changed At All

LOFTHOUSE, CHARLIE — Mama Don't Want No Peas An' Rice An' Cocoanut Oil

LOGAN, FREDERICK KNIGHT — Missouri Waltz

LOGAN, HAROLD — Come Into My Heart; I'm Gonna Get Married; Lady Luck; Personality; Stagger Lee

LOGGINS, DANNY — Vahevela

LOGGINS, DAVE — Please Come To Boston

LOGGINS, KENNY — Danny's Song; Don't Fight It; Footloose; Heart To Heart; I Believe In Love; I'm Alright; My Music; What A Fool Believes; Whenever I Call You Friend; Your Mama Don't Dance

LOMAN, JULES — Goodbye Sue; Heavenly Hideaway

LOMAS, BARBARA — Express

LOMAX, ALAN — Inside-Looking Out

LOMAX, JOHN — Goodnight Irene

LOMBARDO, CARMEN — Boo-Hoo!; Coquette; Get Out Those Old Records; Jungle Drums; Oooh! Look-a-There, Ain't She Pretty?; Powder Your Face With Sunshine; Return To Me(Ritorna A Me); Ridin' Around In The Rain; Sailboat In The Moonlight; Seems Like Old Times; Snuggled On Your Shoulder(Cuddled In Your Arms); Sweethearts On Parade; Wake Up And Sing

LONDON, EVE — Envy

LONDON, MARK — Best Of Both Worlds; To Sir With Love

LONG, ANDY IONA — South Sea Island Magic

LONG, BURT — Cindy, Oh Cindy

LONG, FREDERICK — Devil With A Blue Dress On; Here Comes The Judge

LONGSHAW, FRED — Cold In Hand Blues

LOOKOFSKY, MIKE — Walk Away, Renee

LOPES, JOAN CALDERON — Eres Tu(Touch The Wind)

LOPEZ, GILBERT — Happy, Happy Birthday Baby

LOPEZ, VINCENT — Knock, Knock. Who's There?

LORD, JON — Smoke On The Water

LORENZO, ANGE — Sleepy Time Gal

LOTTERMOSER, DANIEL — Vahevela

LOUCHHEIM, STUART F. — Mixed Emotions

LOUDERMILK, JOHN — Ebony Eyes; Rose And A Baby Ruth; Sittin' In The Balcony; Thou Shalt Not Steal; Tobacco Road; Torture; Waterloo

LOUDERMILK, JOHN D. — (He's My)Dreamboat; I Wanna Live; Indian Reservation; James(Hold The Ladder Steady); Norman; Paper Tiger; Sad Movies(Make Me Cry); What A Woman In Love Won't Do

LOUGHRANE, LEE — Call On Me; No Tell Lover

LOUIS, GUY — Don't Forget I Still Love You

LOUIS, KENNY ST. — Boogie Fever

LOUIS, LOUIS ST. — Sandy

LOURGAY, R. S. — Vie En Rose, La

LOVE, GEOFF — He's Got The Whole World In His Hands

LOVE, MIKE — California Saga(Big Sur); Darlin,; Good Vibrations; Surfin' Safari; Wild Honey

LOVEDAY, CARROLL — Shrine Of St. Cecilia

LOVELL, R. — Anchors Aweigh

LOVETT, LEROY — Can't I

LOVETT, WINFRED — Kiss And Say Goodbye

LOWE, — What Have I Done To Deserve This

LOWE, BERNIE — 20 Miles; Butterfly; Ding-A-Ling; Fish; Good Time Baby; Remember You're Mine; Swingin' School; We Got Love; Wild One

LOWE, BERT — I Love You Sweetheart Of All My Dreams

LOWE, C. — It's A Sin

LOWE, CHRIS — Opportunities(Let's Make Lots Of Money); West End Girls

LOWE, JIM — Gambler's Guitar

LOWE, NICK — Cruel To Be Kind

LOWE, RUTH — I'll Never Smile Again; Put Your Dreams Away(For Another Day)

LOWEN, DAVID — We Belong

LOWN, BERT — Bye Bye Blues; You're The One I Care For

LUBAN, FRANCIA — Gay Ranchero

LUBIN, JOE — Inspiration; Midnight Lace; Please Don't Eat The Daisies; Secret; Tutti-Frutti

LUBOFF, NORMAN — Yellow Bird

LUCAS, ANN — Loop De Loop

LUCAS, CARROLL — How Soon(Will I Be Seeing You)

LUCAS, PETER — Crimson And Clover

LUCAS, REGINALD — Borderline; Closer I Get To You; Never Knew Love Like This Before

LUCCHESI, ROGER — Portugese Washerwomen

Lucky — You're

LUGG, MILTON DE — (Why Did I Tell You I Was Going To)Shanghai; Be My Life's Companion; Hoop-Dee-Do; Just Another Polka; My Lady Loves To Dance; Orange Colored Sky; Poor Man's Roses

LUGO, FRANCISCO — I Need Somebody

LUKATHER, STEVE — I Won't Hold You Back; I'll Be Over You; She's A Beauty; Turn Your Love Around

LUKE, ROBIN — Susie Darlin

LULLI, ARTHUR DE — Chopsticks

LUNCEFORD, JIMMIE — (If I Had)Rhythm In My Nursery Rhymes; Dream Of You; Rhythm Is Our Business

LUNSFORD, ORVILLE — All-American Boy,The

LUNT, STEPHEN — Goonies 'r' Good Enough; She Bop

LURIE, ELLIOT — Brandy(You're A Fine Girl)

LUTCHER, NELLIE — He's A Real Gone Guy

LUTHER, FRANK — Barnacle Bill The Sailor

LUTZ, MICHAEL — Smokin' In The Boys Room

LYALL, WILLIAM — Magic

LYLE, G. — What You Get Is What You See

LYLE, GRAHAM — Breakaway; Typical Male; We Don't Need Another Hero (Thunderdome)

LYMAN, ABE — I Cried For You(Now It's Your Turn To Cry Over Me); Mary Lou

LYMON, FRANKIE — Why Do Fools Fall In Love

LYN, MERRIL — I Give You My Word

LYNES, GARY — Love Me Forever

LYNN, CHERYL — Got To Be Real

LYNN, LORETTA — Coal Miner's Daughter

LYNNE, JEFF — All Over The World; Can't Get It Out Of My Head; Do Ya; Don't Bring Me Down; Evil Woman; Hold On Tight; Livin' Thing; Rock 'n Roll Is King; Rock Of Ages; Strange Magic; Sweet Talkin' Woman; Turn To Stone; Xanadu

LYNOTT, PHIL — Boys Are Back In Town

LYNTON, EVERETT — I Never See Maggie Alone

LYON, DEL — One Rose, The(That's Left In My Heart)

LYON, JAMES — Baby Hold On

LYONS, JOE — On The Alamo; When It's Lamp Lightin' Time In The Valley

LYTELL, JIMMY — Blues Serenade

MACAULEY, TONY — (Last Night)I Didn't Get To Sleep At All; Baby, Now That I've Found You; Baby, Take Me In Your Arms; Don't Give Up On Us; Love Grows(Where My Rosemary Goes); Smile A Little Smile For Me

MACDERMOT, GALT — Ain't Got No; Air; Aquarius; Dead End; Don't Put It Down; Easy To Be Hard; Frank Mills; Good Morning Starshine; Hair; Hare Krishna; I Got Life; Let The Sunshine In; Love Has Driven Me Sane; Walking In Space; Where Do I Go

MACDONALD, BALLARD — (Back Home Again In)Indiana; Beautiful Ohio; Bend Down Sister; Clap Hands! Here Comes Charley!; Parade Of The Wooden Soldiers; Rose Of Washington Square; Somebody Else-Not Me; Somebody Loves Me; Trail Of The Lonesome Pine; Year From Today

MACDONALD, PAT — Future's So Bright, I Gotta Wear Shades

MACDONALD, RALPH — Just The Two Of Us

MACDONOUGH, GLEN — Toyland

MACDOWELL, EDWARD — To A Water Lily; To A Wild Rose

MACGIMSEY, ROBERT — Shadrack(Shadrach)

MACGREGOR, CHUMMY — It Must Be Jelly('Cause Jam Don't Shake Like That)

MACK, CECIL — Charleston; S-H-I-N-E

MACK, IRA — Beatnik Fly; Red River Rock; Reveille Rock

MACK, RONNIE — He's So Fine

MACKENZIE, LEONARD — Chiquita Banana

MACKINTOSH, BILL AND ROMA — Gods Were Angry With Me

MACLEAN, ROSS — Too Fat Polka

MACLELLAN, GENE — Put Your Hand In The Hand; Snowbird

MACLEOD, JOHN — Baby, Now That I've Found You; Baby, Take Me In Your Arms

MACLEOD, MURRAY — Sunshine Girl

MACMURROUGH, DERMOT — Macushla

MACNEIL, TERRY — Hello, Hello

MADARA, JOHN — One, Two, Three(1-2-3); You Don't Own Me

MADDEN, EDWARD — (Look Out For)Jimmy Valentine; (On)Moonlight Bay; By The Light Of The Silvery Moon

MADDEN, FRANK — Maybe

MADDUX, PETE — Wishing Ring

MADEIRA, PAUL — I'm Glad There Is You

MADERA, JOHN — Fly; Like A Baby

MADISON, FRED — Don't Be Angry

MADONALD, JIMMY — Crocodile Tears

MADONNA, — True Blue

MADURI, CARL — Hula Hoop Song

MAGIDSON, HERB — (I'm Afraid)Masquerade Is Over; Barrelhouse Bessie From Basin Street; Black Eyed Susan Brown; Conchita, Marquita, Lolita, Pepita, Rosita, Juanita Lopez; Continental; Enjoy Yourself(It's Later Than You Think); Gone With The Wind; Good Night Angel; Here's To Romance; I Can't Love You Any More(Any More Than I Do); I'll Buy That Dream; I'll Dance At Your Wedding; I'm Stepping Out With A Memory Tonight; Midnight In Paris; Music, Maestro, Please!; Say A Pray'r For The Boys Over

There; Twinkle, Twinkle Little Star; Violins From Nowhere

MAGILL, JACQUELINE — Mary Lou

MAGNESS, CLIFTON — All I Need

MAHONEY, EDWARD — Baby Hold On; Maybe I'm A Fool

MAIDEN, TONY — Sweet Thing

MAINEGRA, RICHARD — Separate Ways

MAKEBA, MIRIAM — Pata Pata

MALIE, TOMMY — Jealous; Looking At The World Thru Rose Colored Glasses

MALKIN, NORMAN — Hey, Mr. Banjo

MALLAH, L. — I Do You

MALLETTE, WANDA — Lookin' For Love

MALLOY, DAVID — I Love A Rainy Night; I Love Life; Love Will Turn You Around; Someone Could Lose A Heart Tonight; Step By Step; Suspicions

MALNECK, MATTY — Eeny, Meeny, Meiny, Mo; Goody-Goody; I Saw Her At Eight O'clock; I'll Never Be The Same; I'm Thru With Love; Pardon My Southern Accent; Shangri-La; Stairway To The Stars

MALONE, DEADRIC — Ain't Nothing You Can Do; Ain't That Loving You; Call On Me; Share Your Love With Me

MALONE, GEORGE — Book Of Love

MALONE, JOHNNY — Please Love Me Forever

MALOO, KURT — Captain Of Her Heart

MALOTTE, ALBERT HAY — Ferdinand The Bull

MALSBY, LYNN — I Miss You

MALTBY JR., RICHARD — Autumn

MANA, MME. — I Love Life

MANASCALCO, JOHN — Goodnight My Love

MANCHESTER, MELISSA — Better Days; Come In From The Rain; Just Too Many People; Midnight Blue; Whenever I Call You Friend

MANCINI, HENRY — All His Children; Baby Elephant Walk; Bachelor In Paradise; Charade; Chariots Of Fire; Chicago, Illinois; Come To Me; Crazy World; Days Of Wine And Roses; Dear Heart; Don't You Forget It; Great Imposter; Hatari!; In The Arms Of Love; It's Easy To Say; Moon River; Mr. Lucky; Peter Gunn Theme; Pink Panther Theme; Sweetheart Tree; Two For The Road (Theme From); Wait Until Dark; Whistling Away The Dark

MANDEL, JOHNNY — Emily; M*A*S*H (song From) (Suicide Is Painless); Shadow Of Your Smile

MANGIONE, CHUCK — Feels So Good; Give It All You Got

MANGOLD, M. — I Found Someone

MANIGAULT, ROBERT — Troglodyte (Cave Man)

MANILOW, BARRY — Copacabana; Could It Be Magic; Daybreak; Even Now; I Made It Through The Rain; It's A Miracle; Some Kind Of Friend

MANKER, SIDNEY — Raunchy

MANN, AIMEE — Voices Carry

MANN, BARRY — (You're My)Soul And Inspiration; Blame It On The Bossa Nova; Bless You; Brown Eyed Woman; Conscience; Don't Be Afraid, Little Darlin'; Footsteps; Grass Is Greener; He's Sure The Boy I Love; Here You Come Again; Home Of The Brave; Home On The Range; How Much Love; Hungry; I Love How You Love Me; I'll Never Dance Again; I'll Take You Home; I'm Gonna Be Strong; It's Getting Better; Johnny Loves Me; Kicks; Looking Through The Eyes Of Love; Magic Town; Make Your Own Kind Of Music; Mary's Little Lamb; My Dad; Never Gonna

Let You Go; On Broadway; Only In America; Patches; Proud; Rock And Roll Lullabye; Saturday Night At The Movies; Shape Of Things To Come; She Say(Oom Dooby Doom); Sometimes When We Touch; Somewhere Out There; Uptown; Walking In The Rain; We Gotta Get Out Of This Place; Who Put The Bomp (In The Bomp-Bomp-Bomp); You've Lost That Lovin' Feelin'

MANN, DAVE — Boutonniere; Castanets And Lace; Dearie; Don't Go To Strangers; Downhearted; I've Only Myself To Blame; No Moon At All; Somebody Bad Stole De Wedding Bell; Wee Small Hours (Of The Morning), In The

MANN, KAL — 20 Miles; Bristol Stomp; Butterfly; Cha Cha Cha; Dancin' Party; Ding-A-Ling; Do The Bird; Don't Hang Up; Fish; Good Time Baby; Gravy; Hey Bobba Beedle; Let's Twist Again; Popeye(The Hitchhiker); Remember You're Mine; South Street; Swingin' School; Twistin' U.S.A.; Wah Watusi; We Got Love; Wild One; Wildwood Days; You Can't Sit Down

MANN, LORENE — Don't Go Near The Indians; It Keeps Right On A-hurtin' Since I Left

MANN, PAUL — And So Do I; Angel In Disguise; Put Your Dreams Away(For Another Day)

MANNERS, HENRY — Delilah; We Could Make Such Beautiful Music (Together)

MANNERS, ZEKE — Pennsylvania Polka

MANNING, DICK — Allegheny Moon; Are You Really Mine?; Dennis The Menace; Don't Stay Away Too Long; Fascination; Gilly Gilly Ossenfeffer Katzenellen Bogen By The Sea; Hawaiian Wedding Song; Hot Diggity; I Can't Tell A Waltz From A Tango; Jilted; La Plume De Ma Tante; Mama, Teach Me To Dance; Mi Casa, Su Casa(My House Is Your House); Moon-talk; Morningside Of The Mountain; O Dio Mio; Oh, Oh, I'm Falling In Love Again; Papa Loves Mambo; Pussy Cat Song, The(Nyow! Nyot! Nyow!); Santo Natale; Secretly; Torero; While The Angelus Was Ringing Or The Three Bells Or The Jimmy Brown Song

MANNING, PAUL — Petticoat Junction

MANSON, EDDY — Joey's Theme

MANTZ, NANCIE — I Had Too Much To Dream(Last Night)

MANUS, JACK — Hills Of Colorado; Vanity

MANZANERO, ARMANDO — It's Impossible

MANZAREK, RAY — Hello, I Love You; Light My Fire; Love Her Madly; Love Me Two Times; People Are Strange; Riders On The Storm; Roadhouse Blues; Touch Me; Wishful, Sinful

MAR, THE — Last Night

MARAIS, JOSEF — Ma Says, Pa Says

MARASCALCO, JOHN — Good Golly, Miss Molly; Ready Teddy; Rip It Up; Send Me Some Lovin'

MARBOT, ROLF — Call Me Darling(Call Me Sweetheart, Call Me Dear)

MARCELLINO, GERALD — I Am Love(parts 1 & 2)

MARCHETTI, F. D. — Fascination

MARCOTTE, DON — I Think Of You

MARCUCCI, BOB — Dede Dinah; I'll Wait For You; Why; With All My Heart

MARCUS, BOB — Patricia

MARCUS, SOL — Ask Anyone Who Knows; Cancel The Flowers; Don't Let Me Be Misunderstood; Fabulous Character; I Don't Want To Set The World On Fire; Strictly Instrumental; Till Then; When The Lights Go

On Again (All Over The World)

MARDEN, PAULINE — Pack Up Your Sorrows

MARENO, RICCI — I Believe You

MARES, PAUL — Farewell Blues; Make Love To Me; Milenberg Joys; Tin Roof Blues

MARESCA, ERNEST — Lovers Who Wander; Runaround Sue; Wanderer

MARESCA, ERNIE — Child Of Clay; Donna The Prima Donna; No One Knows; Shout! Shout! Knock Yourself Out!; Whenever A Teenagre Cries

MARGO, MITCHELL — I Hear Trumpets Blow

MARGO, PHILIP — I Hear Trumpets Blow

MARIA, ANTONIO — Manha De Carnival; Samba De Orfeu

MARIE, BUFFY SAINTE — Cod'ine

MARIE, GABRIEL P. — Cinquantaine, La

MARILYN, GIMS — Can't Get Over(the Bossa Nova)

MARINELL, LEROY — Werewolves Of London

MARION JR., GEORGE — It Seems To Be Spring; My Future Just Passed

MARKES, LARRY — Along The Navajo Trail; Casanova Cricket; Mad About Him, Sad Without Him, How Can I Be Glad Without Him Blues; May You Always

MARKOWITZ, D. — Time Of My Life

MARKS, CHARLEY — Where Do You Work-a-John

MARKS, GERALD — (Oh Suzanna)Dust Off That Old Pianna; All Of Me; Is It True What They Say About Dixie?

MARKS, GODFREY — Sailing Over The Bounding Main

MARKS, JOHNNY — Holly Jolly Christmas; Rudolph The Red Nosed Reindeer

MARKS, ROSE — Sixty Minute Man

MARKS, WALTER — I Can; I've Gotta Be Me; Love Is A Chance; Love-Line

MARKWELL, MARK — Are You Really Mine?; Secretly

MARLEY, BOB — I Shot The Sheriff; Lively Up Yourself; Stir It Up

MARRIOTT, STEVE — Itchycoo Park

MARSALA, ADELE GIRARD — Little Sir Echo

MARSALA, JOE — And So To Sleep Again; Don't Cry Joe(Let Her Go, Let Her Go, Let Her Go); Little Sir Echo

MARSDEN, GERRARD — Don't Let The Sun Catch You Crying; It's Gonna Be All Right

MARSDEN, GERRY — Ferry Cross The Mersey

MARSH, ROY — I Never Knew I Could Love Anybody Like I'm Loving You

MARSHALL, ED — Venus

MARSHALL, HENRY I. — Be My Little Baby Bumblebee

MARSHALL, JACK — Munster's Theme

MARSHALL, MICHAEL — Rumors

MARSHALL, SHERMAN — I'm Doin' Fine Now; Lady Love

MARTELL, PAUL — I Wuv A Wabbit

MARTIN, BILL — My Boy; Saturday Night

MARTIN, BILLY — Till We Two Are One

MARTIN, BOBBI — For The Love Of Him

MARTIN, D. — Goin' Down

MARTIN, DAVID — Can't Smile Without You

MARTIN, FREDDY — I Look At Heaven(When I Look At You); Tonight We Love

MARTIN, GRADY — Snap Your Fingers

MARTIN, HERBERT — I'm All Smiles

MARTIN, HUGH — Athena; Birmin'ham; Boy Next Door; Buckle Down, Winsocki; Ev'ry Time; Have Yourself A Merry Little Christmas; I Know You By

Heart; I'm The First Girl In The Second Row; I'm Tired Of Texas; Joint Is Really Jumpin' In Carnegie Hall; Just A Little Joint With A Juke Box; Little Boy Blues; Love; Shady Lady Bird; Trolley Song

MARTIN, JOHN — Bad Case Of Lovin' You

MARTIN, LARRY — Till We Two Are One

MARTIN, LINDA — Chick-A-Boom

MARTIN, MOON — Rolene

MARTIN, RAY — Blue Violins

MARTIN, SAM — You Call Everybody Darling

MARTIN, STEVE — King Tut

MARTINE JR., LAYNG — Rub It In; Should I Do It; Way Down

MARTINEE, L. A. — Come Go With Me; Let Me Be The One; Seasons Change

MARTINEZ, RUDY — 96 Tears; I Need Somebody

MARVELL, HOLT — World Is Mine (tonight)

MARVIN, HANK — Same

MARVIN, JOHNNY — Dust

MARX, RICHARD — Don't Mean Nothing; Should've Known Better

MASCAGNI, PIETRO — Intermezzo

MASCARI, EDDIE — I Got A Wife

MASCHERONI, VITTORIO — Jealous Of You

MASCHWITZ, ERIC — At The Balalaika; He Wears A Pair Of Silver Wings; Nightingale Sang In Berkeley Square

MASON, BARBARA — Sad, Sad Girl

MASON, BARRY — Delilah; Here It Comes Again; Kiss Me Goodbye; Last Waltz; Les Bicyclettes De Belsize; Love Grows(Where My Rosemary Goes); Love Me Tonight; Man Without Love; Say You'll Stay Until Tomorrow; Winter World Of Love

MASON, DAVID — Feelin' Alright; Only You Know And I Know; You Can All Join In

MASON, JAMES — I Dig Rock And Roll Music

MASON, JOHN — Open The Door, Richard!

MASON, MARILYN — Love Takes Time

MASON, MELVIN — I Do

MASON, NIKKI — Au Revoir Again

MASSANET, JULES — Elegie

MASSER, MICHAEL — All At Once; Didn't We Almost Have It All; Do You Know Where You're Going To; Greatest Love Of All; If Ever You're In My Arms Again; It's My Turn; Last Time I Saw Him; Nothing's Gonna Change My Love For You; Saving All My Love For You; Someone That I Used To Love; Touch Me In The Morning

MASSEY, CURT — Petticoat Junction

MASSEY, GUY — Prisoner's Song, The(If I Had The Wings Of An Angel)

MASSEY, LOUISE — My Adobe Hacienda

MASTELLOTTO, PAT — Is It Love

MASTERS, FRANKIE — Charming Little Faker; Scatterbrain

MATASSA, COSMO — Just A Dream

MATHER, ROBERT — Sexy Eyes

MATHIESON, GREGG — Heaven Knows

MATKOSKY, DENNIS — Maniac

MATSON, VERA — Daniel Boone; Love Me Tender

MATTHEWMAN, STUART — Never As Good As The First Time

MATTHEWS, CHARLES G. — White Silver Sands

MATZ, PETER — Gotta Move

MAUDLEY, FRANK — I Ran

MAUGERI, RUDI — Crazy 'bout Ya, Baby

MAXTED, BILLY — Manhattan Spiritual

MAXWELL, RAY — Marina

MAXWELL, ROBERT — Ebb Tide; Little Dipper; Shangri-La

MAY, BILLY — I Taut I Taw A Puddy Tat(I Thought I Saw A Pussy Cat)

MAYER, HENRY — Summer Wind

MAYFIELD, CURTIS — Amen; Choice Of Colors; Find Another Girl; Fool For You; Freddie's Dead(Theme From Superfly); Gypsy Woman; He Don't Love You(Like I Love You); Hey Little Girl; I'm So Proud; It's All Right!; Jump; Keep On Pushing; Let's Do It Again; Look Into Your Heart; Monkey Time; Nothing Can Stop Me; On And On; People, Get Ready; Rhythm; Something He Can Feel; Superfly; Um, Um, Um, Um, Um, Um; Woman's Got Soul; You've Been Cheatin'

MAYFIELD, PERCY — Hit The Road, Jack; Please Send Me Someone To Love

MAYHEW, BILLY — It's A Sin To Tell A Lie

MAYNE, MARTYN — I Remember The Cornfields

MCBROOM, AMANDA — Rose

MCCANN, PETER — Do You Wanna Make Love; Right Time Of The Night

MCCARRON, CHARLES — Blues My Naughty Sweetie Gives To Me

MCCARTHY, JOSEPH — Alice Blue Gown; Following The Sun Around; If You're In Love, You'll Waltz; Irene; Irish Washerwoman; Kinkajou; Kiss; Rangers Song; Rio Rita; Through (How Can You Say We're Through); Underneath The Arches; What Do You Want To Make Those Eyes At Me For; You Made Me Love You (I Didn't Want To Do It)

MCCARTHY, JOSEPH A. — Why Try To Change Me Now

MCCARTHY, MRS. JAMES — Clapping Song

MCCARTNEY, LINDA — Uncle Albert/ Admiral Halsey; With A Little Luck

MCCARTNEY, PAUL — (P. S.)I Love You; All I've Got To Do; All My Loving; All Together Now; All You Need Is Love; And I Love Her; And Your Bird Can Sing; Another Girl; Any Time At All; Arrow Through Me; Ask Me Why; Baby's In Black; Baby, You're A Rich Man; Back In The U.S.S.R.; Bad To Me; Ballad Of John And Yoko; Because; Being For The Benefit Of Mr. Kite; Believe In Me; Birthday; Blackbird; Can't Buy Me Love; Carry That Weight; Come And Get It; Come Together; Coming Up; Continuing Story Of Bungalow Bill; Cry Baby Cry; Day In The Life; Day Tripper; Dear Prudence; Do You Want To Know A Secret?; Doctor Robert; Don't Let Me Down; Drive My Car; Ebony And Ivory; Eight Days A Week; Eleanor Rigby; End; Every Little Thing; Everybody's Got Something To Hide Except Me And My Monkey; Fixing A Hole; Flying; Fool On The Hill; For No One; From A Window; From Me To You; Get Back; Getting Better; Getting Closer; Girl; Girl's School; Give Peace A Chance; Glass Onion; Golden Slumbers; Good Day Sunshine; Good Morning, Good Morning; Good Night; Goodbye; Goodnight Tonight; Got To Get You Into My Life; Happiness Is A Warm Gun; Hard Day's Night; Hello Little Girl; Hello, Goodbye; Help!; Helter Skelter; Here, There, And Everywhere; Hey Bulldog; Hey Jude; Hold Me Tight; Honey Pie; I Am The Walrus; I Call Your Name; I Don't Want To See You Again; I Don't Want To Spoil The Party; I

Feel Fine; I Saw Her Standing There; I Should Have Known Better; I Wanna Be Your Man; I Want To Hold Your Hand; I Want You(She's So Heavy); I Will; I'll Be Back; I'll Be On My Way; I'll Cry Instead; I'll Follow The Sun; I'll Get You; I'll Keep You Satisfied; I'm A Loser; I'm Happy Just To Dance With You; I'm Looking Through You; I'm Only Sleeping; I'm So Tired; I've Had Enough; I've Just Seen A Face; If I Fell; In My Life; It Won't Be Long; It's For You; It's Only Love; Julia; Lady Madonna; Let It Be; Like Dreamers Do; Little Child; London Town; Londonderry Air; Long And Winding Road; Love Me Do; Love Of The Loved; Lovely Rita; Lucy In The Sky With Diamonds; Magical Mystery Tour; Martha My Dear; Maxwell's Silver Hammer; Maybe I'm Amazed; Mean Mr. Mustard; Michelle; Mind For Me; Misery; Mother Nature's Son; Night Before; No More Lonely Nights; No Reply; Nobody I Know; Norwegian Wood; Not A Second Time; Nowhere Man; Ob-La-Di, Ob-La-Da; Oh! Darling; P. S. I Love You; Paperback Writer; Penny Lane; Please Please Me; Polythene Pam; Press; Rain; Revolution; Rocky Racoon; Run For Your Life; Say Say Say; Sexy Sadie; Sgt. Pepper's Lonely Hearts Club Band; She Came In Through The Bathroom Window; She Loves You; She Said She Said; She's A Woman; She's Leaving Home; So Bad; Spies Like Us; Step Inside Love; Strawberry Fields Forever; Sun King; The Word; Ticket To Ride; Uncle Albert/ Admiral Halsey; Venus And Mars/rock Show; We Can Work It Out; What You're Doing; When I'm Sixty-Four; Why Don't We Do It In The Road; Wild Honey Pie; With A Little Help From My Friends; With A Little Luck; World Without Love; Yellow Submarine; Yer Blues; Yes It Is; Yesterday; You Can't Do That; You Never Give Me Your Money; You Won't See Me; You're Gonna Lose That Girl; You've Got To Hide Your Love Away; Your Mother Should Know

MCCARTNEY, PAUL AND LINDA — Another Day; Band On The Run; Give Ireland Back To The Irish; Heart Of The Country; Helen Wheels; Hi Hi Hi; Jet; Junior's Farm; Let 'em In; Listen To What The Man Said; Live And Let Die; Mary Had A Little Lamb; My Love; Sally G; Silly Love Songs

MCCARTY, CHRIS — Swingtown

MCCARTY, JAMES — Happenings Ten Years Time Ago; Over Under Sideways Down; Shapes Of Things

MCCAULEY, TONY — Build Me Up, Buttercup

MCCLARY, THOMAS — Brick House; Sweet Love

MCCLURG, MARION — My Bonnie Lassie

MCCLUSKEY, BUDDY — Chiquitita

MCCOLL, DEBORAH — Fins

MCCOLLOCH, JAMES — Hot Child In The City

MCCORD, J. — 19

MCCORMACK, KEITH — Sugar Shack

MCCORMICK, CHARLES E. — Natural High

MCCORMICK, RANDY — Suspicions

MCCOY, JOE — Why Don't You Do Right

MCCOY, ROSE MARIE — Don't Be Angry; I Beg Of You; If I May; It's Gonna Work Out Fine; Mambo Baby

MCCOY, VAN — Baby, I'm Yours; Before And After; Giving Up; Hustle; I Get The Sweetest Feeling; When You're Young And In Love

MCCREE, JUNIE — Put Your Arms Around Me Honey

MCCULLOCH, DANNY — Monterey; San Franciscan Nights; Sky Pilot; When I Was Young

MCCULLOUGH, JAMES — Return Of The Red Baron

MCCULLOUGH, JOHN — Return Of The Red Baron

MCDANIEL, E. — Bo Diddley; I'm A Man; Say, Man

MCDANIEL, ELLAS — Oh Yeah

MCDANIELS, GENE — Feel Like Makin' Love

MCDERMOTT JR., JOHN J. — (My Heart Goes)KA-DING-DONG

MCDONALD, IAN — Long, Long Way From Home

MCDONALD, MICHAEL — Dependin' On You; Heart To Heart; I'll Wait; It Keeps You Running; Minute By Minute; Real Love; What A Fool Believes; You Belong To Me

MCDONALD, RALPH — Where Is The Love

MCDOWELL, RONNIE — King Is Gone

MCELHONE, J. — Honeythief

MCFADDEN, GENE — Ain't No Stopping Us Now; Back Stabbers; Bad Luck(part 1); Wake Up, Everybody (Part 1)

MCFADDIN, THERESA — One Love In My Lifetime

MCFARLAND, J. LESLIE — Little Children; Stuck On You

MCGEE, PARKER — American Music; I'd Really Love To See You Tonight; Nights Are Forever Without You

MCGHEE, GRANVILLE — Drinkin' Wine, Spo-Dee-O-Dee

MCGILL, JOSEPHINE — Duna

MCGRANE, PAUL — Hayfoot-Strawfoot; Juke Box Saturday Night

MCGRIFF, EDNA — Heavenly Father

MCGUINN, JIM — Eight Miles High; Mr. Spaceman; So You Want To Be A Rock 'n Roll Star; You Showed Me

MCGUINN, ROGER — Ballad Of Easy Rider

MCGUIRE, BARRY — Green Green

MCHUGH, JIMMY — "Murder" He Says; As The Girls Go; Be A Good Scout; Blame It On The Rhumba; Blue Again; Broadway Jamboree; Button Up Your Heart; Can't Get Out Of This Mood; Candlelight And Wine; Change Of Heart; Chapel Bells; Clear Out Of This World; Comin' In On A Wing And A Prayer; Crazy As A Loon; Cuban Love Song; Dig You Later(a Hubba-hubba-hubba); Diga Diga Doo; Dinner At Eight; Doin' The New Low-down; Don't Believe Everything You Dream; Don't Blame Me; Don't Think It Ain't Been Charming; Dream, Dream, Dream; Ev'rything Is Hotsy Totsy Now; Exactly Like You; Fuddy Duddy Watchmaker; Futuristic Rhythm; Go Home And Tell Your Mother; Good-bye Blues; Happy Go Lucky; Here Comes Heaven Again; Hey, What Did The Bluebird Say?; Hooray For Love; How Blue The Night; How Many Times Do I Have To Tell You; How Would You Like To Kiss Me In The Moonlight?; Hush-A-Bye Island; I Can't Believe That You're In Love With Me; I Can't Give You Anything But Love; I Couldn't Sleep A Wink Last Night; I Don't Care Who Knows It; I Feel A Song Comin' On; I Get The Neck Of The Chicken; I Got Lucky In The Rain; I Hit A New High; I Love To Whistle; I Must Have That Man; I Walked In(With My Eyes Wide Open); I'd Know You Anywhere; I'm Feelin' Blue('cause I Got Nobody); I'm In The Mood For Love; I'm Living In A Great Big Way; I'm Shooting High; I've Got My Fingers Crossed; In A Moment Of Madness; It's A Most Unusual Day; Latin Tune, A Manhattan Moon And You; Let's Get Lost; Like The Fella Once Said; Lonesomest Girl In Town; Lost In A Fog; Lovely Lady; Lovely To Look At; Lovely Way To Spend An Evening; Music Stopped;

My Dancing Lady; My Fine Feathered Friend; On The Old Park Bench; On The Sunny Side Of The Street; Picture Me Without You; Say A Pray'r For The Boys Over There; Say It(Over And Over Again); Serenade For A Wealthy Widow; Sing A Tropical Song; South American Way; Too Young To Go Steady; Touch Of Texas; What Has Become Of Hinky Dinky Parlay Voo; When Love Is Young; When My Sugar Walks Down The Street; Where Are You; Where The Lazy River Goes By; With All My Heart; You Say The Nicest Things, Baby; You're A Sweetheart; You're An Angel; You're The One (For Me); You've Got Me This Way (Whatta-Ya-Gonna Do About It)

MCINTIRE, LANI — One Rose, The(That's Left In My Heart)

MCINTOSH, ROBBIE — Cut The Cake; Pick Up The Pieces

MCINTOSH, WINSTON — Four Hundred Years

MCINTYRE, MARK — Money Tree

MCINTYRE, OWEN — Cut The Cake; Pick Up The Pieces

MCKAY, ALBERT — Best Of My Love; Saturday Nite; September; Singasong

MCKENZIE, MARION — Little Town Flirt

MCKINLEY, RAY — Hoodle Addle; My Guy's Come Back

MCKINNEY, SYLVIA — It's Gonna Work Out Fine

MCKUEN, ROD — Forever Young; If You Go Away; Jean; Seasons In The Sun; Sing Boy, Sing

MCLEAN, DON — American Pie; And I Love You So; Castles In The Air; Dreidel; Vincent

MCLEOD, A. — Honeythief The

MCLEOD, MARILYN — Let Me Tickle Your Fancy; Love Hangover; You Can't Turn Me Off

MCMICHAEL, TED — By-U, By-O(the Lou'siana Lullaby); Hut Sut Song

MCMURRAY, CLAY — If I Were Your Woman; Make Me The Woman That You Go Home To

MCNALLY, LARRY JOHN — D.C. Cab

MCNAMARA, TED — Sooner Or Later

MCNAUGHTON, F. — Rivers Of Babylon

MCNEILL, LANDY — If I Could Reach You

MCNICOL, STEVE — You, I

MCPHAIL, LINDSAY — San

MCPHATTER, CLYDE — Honey Love

MCPHERSON, HERBERT — Backfield In Motion"

MCPHERSON, JIM — Jane

MCRAE, FLOYD — Sh-Boom(Life Could Be A Dream)

MCRAE, TEDDY — Back Bay Shuffle; Broadway; Love! Love! Love!; Traffic Jam; You Showed Me The Way

MCREE, BOB — Pickin' Wild Mountain Berries

MCSHANN, JAY — Confessin' The Blues; Hootie Blues

MCVEA, JACK — Open The Door, Richard!

MCVIE, CHRISTINE — Don't Stop; Got A Hold On Me; Hold Me; Little Lies; Over My Head; Say You Love Me; You Make Loving Fun

MEACHAM, F. W. — American Patrol

MEADE, NORMAN — Cry Baby

MEADOWS, FRED — You Were Only Fooling

MEAUX, HUEY P. — Rains Came

MECUM, DUDLEY — Angry; Animalclark

MEDLEY, BILL — Go Ahead And Cry; Little Latin Lupe Lu

MEDLEY, PHIL — Million To One; Twist And Shout

MEDOFF, SAM — Walkin' With My Honey (Soon, Soon, Soon), I'll Be

MEDORA, J. — At The Hop

MEDRESS, HENRY — I Hear Trumpets Blow; I Heard A Rumour

MEEHAN, DANNY — Where Are You Going

MEINE, KLAUS — Rock You Like A Hurricane

MEINKEN, FRED — Wabash Blues

MEKLER, GABRIEL — Kozmic Blues; Move Over

MELCHER, TERRY — Beach Girl; Good Thing; Great Airplane Strike Of 1966; Him Or Me, What's It Gonna Be?; I Had A Dream

MELLENCAMP, JOHN COUGAR — Authority Song; Check It Out; Cherry Bomb; Crumblin' Down; Hand To Hold Onto; Hurt So Good; I Need A Lover; Jack And Diane; Lonely Ol' Night; Paper In Fire; Pink Houses; R-O-C-K(In The U. S. A.); Rain On The Scarecrow; Small Town

MELLIN, ROBERT — Cornbelt Symphony; I'm Always Hearing Wedding Bells; I'm Yours; It Isn't Right; Man With The Banjo; My One And Only Love; River; Stranger On The Shore; You, You, You

MELODY, LORD — Mama Look A Booboo

MELROSE, WALTER — Copenhagen; Doctor Jazz; High Society; Milenberg Joys; Sugar Foot Stomp(Dipper Mouth Blues); Tin Roof Blues

MELSHER, IRVING — Cry, Baby, Cry; I May Never Pass This Way Again; So Long

MELSON, JOE — Blue Bayou; Crowd; Crying; Only The Lonely(Know The Way I Feel); Run, Baby, Run(Back Into My Arms); Running Scared

MENCHER, MURRAY — Flowers For Madame; I Want A Little Girl; On The Bumpy Road To Love; Throw Another Log On The Fire; You Can't Pull The Wool Over My Eyes

MENDE, G. — Power Of Love

MENDELSOHN, FRED — Red River Rock

MENDELSSOHN, FELIX — Hark The Herald Angels Sing; On Wings Of Song; Spring Song; Wedding March

MENENDEZ, NILO — Green Eyes

MERCER, JOHNNY — (Love's Got Me In A)Lazy Mood; A Woman's Prerogative; And So To Bed; And The Angels Sing; Any Place I Hang My Hat Is Home; Arthur Murray Taught Me Dancing In A Hurry; Autumn Leaves; Bernadine; Big Movie Show In The Sky; Bilbao Song; Bless Your Beautiful Hide; Blue Rain; Blues In The Night; Bob White; Bobby Shafto; Cakewalk Your Lady; Captains Of The Clouds; Charade; Come Rain Or Come Shine; Confidentially; Could Be; Cowboy From Brooklyn; Cuckoo In The Clock; Day In-Day Out; Daydreaming(All Night Long); Days Of Wine And Roses; Dearly Beloved; Dixieland Band; Don't Think It Ain't Been Charming; Dream; Early Autumn; Eeny, Meeny, Meiny, Mo; Emily; Empty Tables; Everything Happens To Me; Facts Of Life; Fancy Free; Fare-Thee-Well To Harlem; Fleet's In; Fools Rush In(Where Angels Fear To Tread); Forever Amber; G. I. Jive; Garden Of The Moon; Girl Friend Of The Whirling Dervish; Glow Worm; Goody-Goody; Have You Got Any Castles, Baby?; Here Come The British(Bang! Bang!); Here's To My Lady; Hit The Road To Dreamland; Hooray For Hollywood; Hooray For Spinach; How Little We Know; I Had Myself A True Love; I Promise You; I Remember You; I Saw Her At Eight O'clock; I Thought About You; I Walk With Music; I Wanna Be Around; I'd Know You Anywhere; I'll Cry Tomorrow; I'll Dream Tonight; I'm An Old Cow Hand(From The

Rio Grande); I'm Building Up To An Awful Letdown; I'm Happy About The Whole Thing; I'm Old Fashioned; I've Hitched My Wagon To A Star; If I Had My Druthers; If You Build A Better Mousetrap; In A Moment Of Weakness; In The Cool, Cool, Cool Of The Evening; In The Valley(Where The Evening Sun Goes Down); It's A Great Big World; Jeepers Creepers; Jubilation T. Cornpone; June Comes Around Every Year; Laura; Lazybones; Legalize My Name; Let's Take The Long Way Home; Life Is What You Make It; Like The Fella Once Said; Lonesome Polecat; Lost; Love Held Lightly; Love In A Home; Love Is Where You Find It; Love Of My Life; Midnight Sun; Mister Meadowlark; Moon Country; Moon River; My Shining Hour; N T'uncle Bills"; Namely You; On Behalf Of The Visiting Firemen; On The Atchison, Topeka, And The Santa Fe; One For My Baby(And One More For The Road); Ooh! What You Said; Out Of This World; P. S. I Love You; Pardon My Southern Accent; Pink Panther Theme; Ride, Tenderfoot, Ride; Ridin' On The Moon; Satin Doll; Sentimental And Melancholy; Skylark; Sluefoot; Sobbin' Women; Something's Gotta Give; Spring Spring Spring; Strip Polka(Take It Off-Take It Off); Summer Wind; Sweetheart Tree; Swing Your Partner Round And Round; Too Marvelous For Words; True Love (I Had Myself A); Wait And See; Waiter And The Porter And The Upstairs Maid; Weekend Of A Private Secretary; What's Good For General Bullmoose; When A Woman Loves A Man; When The World Was Young (Ah The Apple Trees); When You're In Love; Whistling Away The Dark; You Can't Run Away From It; You Have Taken My Heart; You Must Have Been A Beautiful Baby; You Were Never Lovelier; You're The One (For Me); You've Got Me This Way (Whatta-Ya-Gonna Do About It)

MERCURY, FREDDIE — Bicycle Race; Killer Queen; Somebody To Love; We Are The Champions

MERCURY, FREDDY — Body Language; Bohemian Rhapsody; Crazy Little Thing Called Love

MERRELL, WANDRA — Pepino, The Italian Mouse

MERRICK, BOB — New Girl In Town

MERRILL, ALAN — I Love Rock And Roll

MERRILL, BEB — Sadie, Sadie

MERRILL, BLANCHE — I'm An Indian

MERRILL, BOB — (How Much Is That)Doggie In The Window; Beautiful Candy; Belle, Belle(My Liberty Belle); Butterflies; Candy And Cake; Carnival(theme From)(Also Called Love Makes The World Go 'round); Chicken Song; Cornet Man; Don't Rain On My Parade; Feet Up(Pat Him On The Po-Po); Find Yourself A Man; Fool's Paradise; Funny Girl; Honeycomb; I'm The Greatest Star; If I Knew You Were Comin' I'd've Baked A Cake; It Was Always You; It's Good To Be Alive; Let Me In; Let's Always Love; Look At 'er; Lover's Gold; Make Yourself Comfortable; Mambo Italiano; Mira(Can You Imagine That?); Miracle Of Love; Music That Makes Me Dance; My Truly, Truly Fair; People; Pittsburgh, Pennsylvania; She's My Love; Sparrow In The Treetop; Sweet Old Fashioned Girl; Tina Marie; Walkin' To Missouri; When The Boys Talk About The Girls; You Are Woman (I Am Man)

MERRILL, GARY — How Will I Know

MERRITT, NEAL — May The Bird Of Paradise Fly Up Your Nose

MERSON, BILLY — Spaniard That Blighted My Wife

MESCOLI, GINO — My Love, Forgive Me(Amore, Scusami)

MESKILL, JACK — I Was Lucky; On The Beach At Bali-Bali; Rhythm Of The Rain; Smile, Darn Ya, Smile

MESSENHEIMER, SAM — Singing A Vagabond Song

MESSINA, JIM — My Music; You Better Think Twice; Your Mama Don't Dance

METCALFE, CLIVE — Summer Song

METIS, FRANK — Enchanted Sea

METRIUS, CLAUDE DE — Hard Headed Woman; I Was The One

METZ, THEODORE M. — (There'll Be A)Hot Time In The Old Town Tonight

MEYER, CHUCK — Suddenly There's A Valley

MEYER, GEORGE — In A Little Bookshop

MEYER, GEORGE W. — Brown Eyes, Why Are You Blue?; Everything Is Peaches Down In Georgia; For Me And My Gal; I Believe In Miracles; I'm A Little Blackbird Looking For A Bluebird; If I Only Had A Match; In The Land Of Beginning Again; Mandy, Make Up Your Mind; Tuck Me To Sleep In My Old 'tucky Home; When You're A Long Long Way From Home; Where Did Robinson Crusoe Go With Friday On Saturday Night

MEYER, JOSEPH — As Long As I've Got My Mammy; Born And Bred In Old Kentucky; But I Did; California, Here I Come; Clap Hands! Here Comes Charley!; Crazy Rhythm; Cup Of Coffee, A Sandwich And You; Fancy Our Meeting; Hello Tucky; How Long Will It Last?; I Wish I Were Twins(So I Could Love You Twice As Much); Idle Gossip; If You Knew Susie Like I Knew Susie; It's An Old Southern Custom; Junk Man; Love Lies; Mickey Mouse's Birthday Party; My Honey's Lovin' Arms; Passe

MEYERS, BILLY — Bugle Call Rag; Nobody's Sweetheart

MEYERS, BUBSY — What's The Use Of Getting Sober

MICHAEL, GEORGE — Careless Whisper; Different Corner; Edge Of Heaven; Everything She Wants; Faith; Father Figure; Freedom; I Want Your Sex; Wake Me Up Before You Go-Go

MICHAELI, M. — Carrie

MICHAELS, LEE — Do You Know What I Mean

MICHAELS, SIDNEY — Look For Small Pleasures

MICHAELS, STEVEN — Someone You Love

MICHALSKI, JOHN — Psychotic Reaction

MICHELS, WALTER — San

MICKENS, ROBERT — Get Down On It

MIDDLEBROOKS, HARRY — Spooky

MIDDLEBROOKS, RALPH — Funky Worm; Love Rollercoaster

MIDDLEBROOKS, RONALD — Skin Tight

MIDLER, BETTE — You're Moving Out Today

MIDNIGHT, CHARLIE — Living In America

MIKETTA, BOB — Robin Hood

MILBURN, RICHARD — Listen To The Mocking Bird

MILES, ALFRED HART — Anchors Aweigh

MILES, C. AUSTIN — In The Garden

MILES, DICK — Coffee Song, The(They've Got An Awful Lot Of Coffee In Brazil)

MILES, FLORENCE — At Last! At Last!

MILES, RICHARD — Jack, You're Dead

MILEY, BUBBER — Black And Tan Fantasy; Doin' The Voom Voom; East St. Louis Toodle-O

MILLAS, — You Wouldn't Listen

MILLER, BERNARD — I Can't Stand The Rain

MILLER, BERNIE — Bernie's Tune

MILLER, BOBBY — Always Together; Stay In My Corner

MILLER, CHARLES — Cisco Kid; Spill The Wine

MILLER, CHARLES W. — Gypsy Man

MILLER, ED — Don't Let The Rain Come Down(Crooked Little Man)

MILLER, EDDIE — (Love's Got Me In A)Lazy Mood

MILLER, FRANK — Green Fields; Love Is A Golden Ring; Marianne; Memories Are Made Of This

MILLER, GLENN — Moonlight Serenade

MILLER, HELEN — Am I Asking Too Much; Charms; Don't Say You Don't Remember; Foolish Little Girl; It Hurts To Be In Love; Make Me Your Baby

MILLER, HERB — Night

MILLER, JIMMY — I'm A Man

MILLER, KIM — I Got My Mind Made Up

MILLER, MELVIN — Burning Bridges

MILLER, NED — Dark Moon; Don't Mind The Rain; From A Jack To A King; Invisible Tears; Sunday; Why Should I Cry Over You?; You Don't Like It—Not Much

MILLER, ROGER — Chug-A-Lug; Dang Me; Do-Wacka-Do; Engine, Engine Number Nine; England Swings; Husbands And Wives; Kansas City Star; King Of The Road; Muddy Water

MILLER, RON — I've Never Been To Me; Touch Me In The Morning; Yester-Me Yester-You Yesterday

MILLER, RONALD — For Once In My Life; Heaven Help Us All; Place In The Sun

MILLER, SCOTT — I Got My Mind Made Up

MILLER, SIDNEY — Come To Baby, Do!; I Waited A Little Too Long; What Do I Have To Do To Make You Love Me?

MILLER, SONNY — Got A Date With An Angel

MILLER, STEVE — Fly Like An Eagle; Joker; Swingtown

MILLER, SUE — Invisible Tears

MILLER, WILLIAM — Daddy's Home

MILLINDER, LUCKY — I'm Waiting Just For You; Who Threw The Whiskey In The Well?

MILLROSE, VIC — I'll Try Anything(To Get You); Last Chance(To Turn Around)

MILLS, ANNETTE — Boomps-A-Daisy

MILLS, CHARLES — Knight In Rusty Armor; Lady Godiva

MILLS, FRANK — Music Box Dancer

MILLS, GORDON — It's Not Unusual

MILLS, IRVING — Black Butterfly; Blame It On My Last Affair; Blue Lou; Blues In My Heart; Boneyard Shuffle; Boy Meets Horn; Caravan; Double Check Stomp; Down South Camp Meetin'; Dusk On The Desert; Ev'rything Is Hotsy Totsy Now; Gal From Joe's; Harmony In Harlem; I Let A Song Go Out Of My Heart; I'm A Hundred Percent For You; If Dreams Come True; If You Were In My Place(What Would You Do?); It Don't Mean A Thing(If It Ain't Got That Swing); Jitter Bug; Lonesome Nights; Lonesomest Girl In Town; Lost In Meditation; Minnie The Moocher; Mooche; Mood Indigo; Mr. Ghost Goes To Town; Organ Grinder's Swing; Prelude To A Kiss; Ring Dem Bells; Riverboat Shuffle; Rockin' In Rhythm; Scattin' At The Kit Kat; Sidewalks Of Cuba; Solitude; Somebody Stole Gabriel's Horn; Sophisticated Lady; St. James Infirmary; Steppin' Into Swing Society; Straighten Up And Fly Right; Symphony In Riffs; Washboard

Blues; What Has Become Of Hinky Dinky Parlay Voo; When My Sugar Walks Down The Street; Yearning For Love; You're Not The Kind

MILLS, KERRY — At A Georgia Camp Meeting; Meet Me In St. Louis, Louis

MILTON, JAY — Don't Forget Tonight, Tomorrow

MIMS, JOE — Get On The Good Foot

MINDS, SIMPLE — Alive And Kicking; Sanctify Yourself

MINER, RAYNARD — (Your Love Keeps Lifting Me) Higher And Higher; Rescue Me; Who's Cheating Who?; Your Love Keeps Lifting Me Higher And Higher

MINKOFF, FRAN — Borning Day; Come Away Melinda

MINNIGERODE, MEADE — Whiffenpoof Song

MINNO, DANNY DI — I Can't Get You Out Of My Heart(Ti Amo-ti Voglio Amor); Return To Me(Ritorna A Me)

MINUCCI, ULPIO — Domani(Tomorrow)

MIRANDA, BOB — Girl On A Swing

MIRO, JOSE — Hijack

MIRON, ISSACHAR — Tzena, Tzena, Tzena

MITCHELL JR., JAMES — Float On

MITCHELL, CHARLES — You Are My Sunshine

MITCHELL, JOHN — Two Of Hearts

MITCHELL, JONI — Amelia; Big Yellow Taxi; Blonde In The Bleachers; Blue; Both Sides Now(also known as Clouds); Cactus Tree; Car On A Hill; Carey; Chelsea Morning; Circle Game; Cold Blue Steel And Sweet Fire; For The Roses; Free Man In Paris; Furry Sings The Blues; Help Me; Help Me, Girl; Song To A Seagull; Urge For Going; Woodstock; You Turn Me On, I'm A Radio

MITCHELL, LEWIS — Kind Lovin' Blues

MITCHELL, MEL — Petticoats Of Portugal; Poor Boy

MITCHELL, PAUL — Tryin' To Love Two

MITCHELL, PHILLIP — Starting All Over Again

MITCHELL, SIDNEY — All My Life; At The Codfish Ball; Balboa; Big City Blues; Breakaway; Crazy Feet; Early Bird; Melody From The Sky; S Love I'm After; Sugar(That Sugar Baby O' Mine); Toy Trumpet; Who's Afraid Of Love; You Do The Darndest Things, Baby; You Turned The Tables On Me; You're Slightly Terrific

MITCHELL, STEVE — Jump(For My Love)

MITCHELL, TEEPEE — You Told A Lie (I Believed You)

MITCHELL, WILLIE — I'm Still In Love With You; L-O-V-E; Let's Stay Together; Livin' For You; Look What You Done For Me; You Ought To Be With Me

MITOO, JACKIE — Pass The Dutchie

MIZELL, AL — I Want You Back

MIZELL, FONCE — Love You Save; Mama's Pearl; Sugar Daddy

MIZZY, VIC — Choo'n Gum; Didja Ever?; Enchanted Melody; Hotta Chocolotta; I Like It, I Like It; Jones Boy; My Dreams Are Getting Better All The Time; Three Little Sisters; Whole World Is Singing My Song

MOCKRIDGE, CYRIL — It's A Woman's World

MODELISTE JR., JOSEPH — Cissy Strut

MODUGNO, DOMENICO — Ask Me; Volare Or Nel Blu, Dipinto Di Blu

MOELLER, FRIEDRICH WILHELM — Happy Wanderer

MOELLER, TOMMY — Concrete And Clay

MOFFETT, PAMELA — Baby Come Close

MOFFITT, KENNETH R. — Oh Julie

MOHAWK, ESSRA — Change Of Heart

MOHR, JOSEPH — Silent Night, Holy Night

MOIR, M. — Pleasure Principle

MOLINARE, NICANOR — Chiu, Chiu

MOLL, BILLY — (I Scream, You Scream, We All Scream For)Ice Cream; Gid-Ap, Garibaldi; I Want A Little Girl; Moonlight On The Colorado; Wrap Your Troubles In Dreams (And Dream Your Troubles Away)

MOMAN, CHIPS — (Hey Won't You Play)Another Somebody Done Somebody Wrong Song); Luckenbach, Texas

MONACO, JAMES V. — (All Of A Sudden)My Heart Sings; An Apple For The Teacher; April Played The Fiddle; Crazy People; Crying For Joy; Dirty Hands, Dirty Face; Don't Let That Moon Get Away; East Side Of Heaven; Ev'ry Night About This Time; Hang Your Heart On A Hickory Limb; I Can't Begin To Tell You; I Haven't Time To Be A Millionaire; I'll Take Care Of Your Cares; I'm Making Believe; I've Got A Pocketful Of Dreams; Laugh And Call It Love; Man And His Dream; Me And The Man In The Moon; My Heart Is Taking Lessons; On The Sentimental Side; Once Too Often; Only Forever; Rhythm On The River; Six Lessons From Madame La Zonga; Through (How Can You Say We're Through); Time Alone Will Tell; Too Romantic; We Mustn't Say Goodbye; What Do You Want To Make Those Eyes At Me For; When The Moor Comes Over Madison Square (The Love Lament Of A Western Gent); You Know You Belong To Somebody Else So Why Don't You Leaveme Alone; You Made Me Love You (I Didn't Want To Do It); You're Gonna Lose Your Gal

MONK, THELONIUS — 'round Midnight; Blue Monk; Epistrophy; Well, You Needn't

MONNOT, MARGUERITE — If You Love Me(Really Love Me); Irma La Douce; Milord; Poor People Of Paris

MONROE, BILL — Blue Moon Of Kentucky; Uncle Pen

MONROE, VAUGHN — Racing With The Moon

MONTANA JR., VINCENT — Nice 'n' Nasty

MONTGOMERY, BOB — Love's Made A Fool Of You; Misty Blue

MONTGOMERY, GARTH — Chiquita Banana

MONTGOMERY, MARSHALL — Pal Of My Cradle Days

MONTI, VITTORIO — Czardas

MONTROSE, PERCY — (Oh My Darling)Clementine

MOODY, RUSSELL — Wear My Ring Around Your Neck

MOONEY, HAROLD — Swamp Fire

MOORE, CONNIE — Slow Walk

MOORE, DANIEL — My Maria; Shambala

MOORE, DEBRA MAE — Heaven In Your Eyes

MOORE, ELIZABETH — Laroo, Laroo, Lilli Bolero

MOORE, FLEECIE — Ain't That Just Like A Woman; Beans And Cornbread; Buzz Me; Caldonia(what Makes Your Big Head So Hard?)

MOORE, GLEN — You're All I Want For Christmas

MOORE, HAYWARD — America Is My Home

MOORE, J. B. — Got To Get You Off My Mind

MOORE, JAMES — Baby, Scratch My Back

MOORE, JOHNNY — Merry Christmas Baby

MOORE, MARVIN — Four Walls; Green Door; I Dreamed

MOORE, PETER — Love Machine(part 1)

MOORE, PHIL — Blow Out The Candle; Blow The Man Down; I Feel So Smoochie; I Want A Little Doggie; I'm Gonna See My Baby; Shoo-Shoo-Baby

MOORE, RICHARD — Earache My Eye

MOORE, ROBERT — Searching For My Love

MOORE, ROBIN — Ballad Of The Green Berets

MOORE, THOMAS — Believe Me If All Those Endearing Young Charms

MOORE, WARREN — Ain't That Peculiar; Going To A Go-Go; Here I Go Again; I'll Be Doggone; It's Growing; My Baby; My Girl Has Gone; One More Heartache; Ooh Baby Baby; Tracks Of My Tears

MOORER, GILBERT — Get On Up

MORAINE, LYLE L. — Christmas Island

MORAKIS, TAKIS — Boy On A Dolphin

MORALES, ESY — Jungle Fantasy

MORALI, JACQUES — In The Navy; Macho Man; Y.M.C.A.

MORAN, EDWARD P. — Dream Of You

MORAN, JACK — Skip A Rope

MORE, JULIAN — Irma La Douce

MOREHEAD, JIM — Sentimental Me

MORET, NEIL — (I Got A Woman, Crazy For Me)She's Funny That Way; Chloe; Moonlight And Roses Bring Mem'ries Of You; Song Of The Wanderer(Where Shall I Go?)

MOREY, LARRY — Ferdinand The Bull; Heigh-Ho(The Dwarfs' Marching Song); I'm Wishing; Lavender Blue(Dilly Dilly); One Song; Someday My Prince Will Come; Whistle While You Work; With A Smile And A Song; World Owes Me A Living

MORGAN, AL — Half A Heart

MORGAN, CAREY — Blues My Naughty Sweetie Gives To Me

MORGAN, DENNIS — I Wouldn't Have Missed It For The World; Nobody; Years

MORGAN, FREDDY — Hey, Mr. Banjo

MORGAN, GEORGE — Candy Kisses

MORGAN, LEE — King Is Gone

MORGAN, RUSS — Does Your Heart Beat For Me?; So Long; So Tired; Somebody Else Is Taking My Place; Sweet Eloise; You're Nobody 'til Somebody Loves You

MORGAN, W. ASTOR — Dying With The Blues

MORODER, GIORGIO — Breakdance; Call Me; Cat People(Putting Out Fire); Chase; Danger Zone; Flashdance(What A Feeling); Heaven Knows; I Feel Love; Love To Love You Baby; Meet Me Halfway; Never Ending Story; On The Radio; Wanderer

MORRICONE, ENNIO — Good, The Bad, And The Ugly

MORRIS, DOUG — Sweet Talkin' Guy

MORRIS, JOE — Shake A Hand

MORRIS, JOHN — Blazing Saddles

MORRIS, JOHNNY — Knock, Knock. Who's There?; Paradiddle Joe

MORRIS, LEE — Blue Velvet; If I Only Had A Match

MORRIS, RICHARD — Honey Chile; Love Bug Leave My Heart Alone

MORRISON, BOB — Lookin' For Love; Love The World Away; You Decorated My Life

MORRISON, EDDIE — Madison Time

MORRISON, JAMES — Hello, I Love You; Love Me Two Times; People Are Strange; Riders On The Storm; Roadhouse Blues; Touch Me; Wishful, Sinful; You Make Me Real

MORRISON, JIM — Light My Fire

MORRISON, VAN — Blue Money; Brown Eyed Girl; Come Running; Gloria; I Shall Sing; Wavelength; Wild Night

MORRISON, WALTER — Funky Worm; One Nation Under A Groove

MORROW, GEOFF — Can't Smile Without You; Can't Stay Away From You

MORROW, MARVIN — Beast In Me

MORSE, DOLLY — Siboney

MORSE, STEVE — All I Wanted

MORSE, THEODORE — Dear Old Girl; Hail, Hail, The Gang's All Here; M-O-T-H-E-R (A Word That Means The World To Me); Mother Machree

MORTIMER, AL — For The Love Of Him

MORTON, FERDINAND "JELLY ROLL" — King Porter Stomp; Milenberg Joys; Wild Man Blues; Wolverine Blues

MORTON, GEORGE — Give Him A Great Big Kiss; I Can Never Go Home Anymore; Leader Of The Pack

MORTON, GEORGE F. — Remember(Walking In The Sand)

MOSELY, BOB — Aureet

MOSELY, SNUB — Pretty Eyed Baby

MOSHER, BOB — Munster's Theme

MOSLEY, ROBERT — Sha-La-La

MOSS, JEFFREY — Rubber Duckie

MOSS, JOHN — Church Of The Poison Mind; Do You Really Want To Hurt Me; I'll Tumble 4 Ya; It's A Miracle; Karma Chameleon; Miss Me Blind; Time (Clock Of The Heart)

MOSS, NEIL — Holding Back The Years

MOSS, TYRONE — Everybody's Everything

MOSSER, PETER — Morgen(One More Sunrise)

MOSSMAN, TED — Full Moon And Empty Arms; Till The End Of Time

MOTEN, BENNIE — Moten Stomp; Moten Swing; Moten's Blues

MOTEN, BUSTER — Moten Swing

MOTLOBELOS, FORERE — Boy In The Bubble

MOTOLA, GEORGE — Goodnight My Love

MOTZAN, OTTO — Bright Eyes

MOY, SYLVIA — Honey Chile; I'm Wondering; It Takes Two; Little Ole Man(Uptight Everything's Alright); Love Bug Leave My Heart Alone; My Baby Loves Me; My Cherie Amour; Nothing's Too Good For My Baby; Shoo-Be-Foo-Be-Doo-Da-Day; Uptight (Everything's Alright)

MOZART, WOLFGANG AMADEUS — Marriage Of Figaro(Overture)

MOZIAN, ROGER KING — Asia Minor

MSARURGWA, AUGUST — Skokiaan

MTUME, JAMES — Closer I Get To You; Never Knew Love Like This Before

MUCCI, DION DI — Donna The Prima Donna; Little Diane; Love Came To Me; Lovers Who Wander; Runaround Sue

MUELLER, MARK — Nothin' At All

MUIR, LEWIS — Ragtime Cowboy Joe

MUIR, LEWIS F. — Waiting For The Robert E. Lee

MULDROW, CORNELL — You Can't Sit Down

MULLAN, JACK — He

MULLER, GUS — Wang Wang Blues

MULLER, RANDY — Call Me; Movin'

MULLERN, LARRY — Into The Night

MULLICAN, MOON — New Pretty Blonde(New Jole Blon)

MULLIGAN, GERRY — Jeru

MUNDY, JIMMY — Air Mail Special; Bolero At The Savoy; Don'cha Go 'way Mad; Solo Flight; Swingtime In The Rockies

MUNNINGS, RALPH — Funky Nassau

MUNRO, BILL — When My Baby Smiles At Me

MUNSON, EDDIE — Ida, Sweet As Apple Cider

MURDEN, ORLANDO — For Once In My Life

MURPH, RANDOLPH — Love Jones

MURPHEY, MICHAEL — Carolina In The Pines; Wildfire

MURPHY, AUDIE — Shutters And Boards

MURPHY, M. — Don't Disturb This Groove

MURPHY, MICHAEL — Geronimo's Cadillac

MURPHY, RALPH — Half The Way

MURPHY, STANLEY — Be My Little Baby Bumblebee

MURPHY, WALTER — Fifth Of Beethoven

MURRAY, FRED — I'm Henry Viii, I Am

MURRAY, J. P. — Do The New York; Two Loves Have I

MURRAY, JACK — If I Love Again

MURRAY, JAMES RAMSEY — Away In A Manger

MURRAY, JEAN — Splish Splash

MURRAY, LYN — Bridges At Toko-Ri

MURRAY, MAURICE — Crazy Heart

MURRAY, MITCH — Ballad Of Bonnie And Clyde; Billy, Don't Be A Hero; Hitchin' A Ride; How Do You Do It; I'm Telling You Now

MURRAY, TED — Don't Break The Heart That Loves You; Follow The Boys; Whose Heart Are You Breaking Tonight?

MUSE, CLARENCE — When It's Sleepy Time Down South

MUSEL, BOB — Band Of Gold; Earthbound

MUSKER, FRANK — Every Woman In The World; Heaven On The Seventh Floor; Married Men; Modern Girl

MYERS, FRANK — You And I

MYERS, HENRY — In Chi-Chi-Castenango

MYERS, RANDY — Put A Little Love In Your Heart

MYERS, RICHARD — Hold My Hand; My Darling

MYERS, SHERMAN — Moonlight On The Ganges

MYLES, BILLY — u Were Made For)All My Love; $MYLES, BILLY — Joker; No Love(But Your Love)

MYROW, JOSEF — Autumn Nocturne; By The Way; Comment Allez-vous?; Fable Of The Rose; Five O'clock Whistle; Haunting Me; I Like Mike; I Never Felt This Way Before; If I'm Lucky; It Happens Every Spring; Kokomo, Indiana; Lullaby In Blue; On The Boardwalk At Atlantic City; Somewhere In The Night; Velvet Moon; You Do; You Make Me Feel So Young

MYROW, JOSEPH — Wilhelmina

MYSELS, GEORGE — Heaven Drops Her Curtain Down; One Little Candle

MYSELS, MAURICE — I Want You, I Need You, I Love You

MYSELS, SAMMY — Bim Bam Baby; Heaven Drops Her Curtain Down; His Feet Too Big For De Bed; Mention My Name In Sheboygan; Red Silk Stockings And Green Perfume; Singing Hills; We Three - My Echo, My Shadow And Me; Yesterday's Gardenias

MYX JR., JAMES — Inner City Blues(Make Me Wanna Holler)

NABBIE, JIMMIE — You Are My Love

NACHO, TATA — I'll Never Love Again

NADER, NEVAL — Mecca

NAHAN, IRV — Dance With Me

NAKAMURA, HACHIDAI— Sukiyaki

NANCE, DOLORES — Endless Sleep

NANCE, JACK — It's Only Make Believe; Story Of My Love

NAPIER-BELL, SIMON — You Don't Have To Say You Love Me

NAPTON, JOHNNY — My Devotion

NARDONE, BELLE — Santo Natale

NASCIMBENE, MARIO — Barabbas; Farewell To Arms, A(Love Theme); Song Of The Barefoot Contessa

NASH, GRAHAM — Carrie-Anne; Chicago; Just A Song Before I Go; Marrakesh Express; On A Carousel; Our House; Pay You Back With Interest; Stop, Stop, Stop; Wasted On The Way

NASH, JOHNNY — Hold Me Tight; I Can See Clearly Now; What Kind Of Love Is This?

NASH, OGDEN — Foolish Heart; How Much I Love You; I'm A Stranger Here Myself; Just Like A Man; Round About; Speak Low

NATHAN, SIDNEY — New Pretty Blonde(New Jole Blon)

NATKOSKY, DENNIS — Mirror, Mirror

NAUMAN, PAUL — Ball Of Fire

NAVARRO, DANIEL — We Belong

NAVARRO, ESTHER — Speedoo

NAYLOR, CHARLES — Shake Me I Rattle(Squeeze Me I Cry)

NAZARETH, ERNESTO — Blame It On The Samba

NEBB, JIMMY — No Arms Can Ever Hold You(Like These Arms Of Mine)

NEIBERG, AL — (When It's)Darkness On The Delta; I'm Confessin'(That I Love You); I've Got An Invitation To A Dance; It's The Talk Of The Town; Under A Blanket Of Blue

NEIL, CHRISTOPHER — All I Need Is A Miracle

NEIL, FRED — Candy Man; Everybody's Talkin

NELSOM, STEVE — Peter Cottontail

NELSON, BETTY — Don't Play That Song

NELSON, EARL — Duck; Harlem Shuffle

NELSON, ED — Auf Wiedersehn, My Dear; I Apologize; Josephine Please No Lean On The Bell; Joshua Fit De Battle Of Jericho; Peggy O'neil

NELSON, GERALD H. — Tragedy

NELSON, OZZIE — I'm Looking For A Guy Who Plays Alto And Baritone And Doubles On A Clarinet

NELSON, PRINCE ROGERS — 1999; Delirious; Glamorous Life; I Feel For You; I Wanna Be Your Lover; I Would Die 4 U; Jungle Love; Let's Go Crazy; Little Red Corvette; Love Bizarre; Manic Monday; Pop Life; Purple Rain; Raspberry Beret; Stand Back; Sugar Walls

NELSON, RICK — Garden Party

NELSON, SANDY — Let There Be Drums

NELSON, STEPHEN — Songbird

NELSON, STEVE — Bouquet Of Roses; Frosty The Snow Man

NELSON, WILLIE — Crazy; Funny(How Time Slips Away); Good Hearted Woman,a; Hello Walls; On The Road Again

NEMO, HENRY — 'Tis Autumn; Blame It On My Last Affair; Don't Take Your Love From Me; I Let A Song Go Out Of My Heart; If You Were In My Place(What Would You Do?); Steppin' Into Swing Society

NERO, PAUL — Hot Canary

NESBITT, HARRY — Without That Certain Thing

NESBITT, MAX — Without That Certain Thing

NESMITH, MICHAEL — Joanne

NEUMANN, KLAUS GUNTER — Wonderland By Night

NEVIL, ROBBIE — Dominoes; It's Not Over('Til It's Over); Wot's It To Ya

NEVILLE, ARTHUR — Cissy Strut

NEVILLE, NAOMI — Ride Your Pony; Whipped Cream

NEVIN, ETHELBERT — Mighty Lak' A Rose; Narcissus; Rosary

NEVINS, AL — Twilight Time

NEVINS, MORTY — Lover's Gold; Twilight Time

NEWELL, NORMAN — Forget Domani; More(Theme From Mondo Cane); To The Door Of The Sun (Alle Porte Del Sole)

NEWLEY, ANTHONY — Beautiful Land; Candy Man; Feeling Good; Goldfinger; Gonna Build A Mountain; Joker; Look At That Face; Lumbered; My First Love Song; Nothing Can Stop Me Now; Once In A Lifetime; Someone Nice Like You; Sweet Beginning; What Kind Of Fool Am I; Where Would You Be Without Me; Who Can I Turn To (When Nobody Needs Me); Wonderful Day Like Today, On A

NEWMAN, ALFRED — Airport Love Theme; Anastasia; Best Of Everything; Girl Upstairs; How Green Was My Valley; How The West Was Won; Moon Of Manakoora; Street Scene; Through A Long And Sleepless Night

NEWMAN, CHARLES — Flowers For Madame; Honestly; I Can't Believe It's True; I Met Her On Monday; I'll Never Have To Dream Again; Six Lessons From Madame La Zonga; Sweethearts On Parade; Tiny Little Fingerprints; Why Don't We Do This More Often; Wooden Soldier And The China Doll; You Can't Pull The Wool Over My Eyes; You've Got Me Crying Again

NEWMAN, HERBERT — Birds And The Bees; So This Is Love; Wayward Wind

NEWMAN, JOHN HENRY — Lead, Kindly Light

NEWMAN, LIONEL — As If I Didn't Have Enough On My Mind; Cowboy And The Lady,the; Daniel Boone; Never

NEWMAN, RANDY — Baltimore; Birmingham; Burn On, Big River; He Gives Us All His Love; I Think It's Going To Rain Today; Mama Told Me(Not To Come); Natural; One More Hour; Short People

NEWSOME, BETTY JEAN — It's A Man's, Man's, Man's World(But It Wouldn't Be Without A Woman)

NEWTON, EDDIE — Casey Jones

NEWTON, JOHN — Amazing Grace

NICHOL, AL — Elenore

NICHOLLS, HORATIO — Among My Souvenirs

NICHOLS, ALBERTA — I Just Couldn't Take It Baby; Padam-Padam; You Can't Stop Me From Lovin' You

NICHOLS, BILLY — Do It('Til You're Satisfied)

NICHOLS, RED — Five Pennies

NICHOLS, ROGER — I Won't Last A Day Without You; Out In The Country; Rainy Days And Mondays

NICHOLS, ROGER S. — Times Of Your Life

NICHTERN, DAVID — Midnight At The Oasis

NICKS, STEPHANIE — Dreams; If Anyone Falls; Leather And Lace; Rhiannon(Will You Ever Win); Sara; Stand Back

NICKS, STEVIE — I Can't Wait

NICOLAI, OTTO — Merry Wives Of Windsor, The(Overture)

NIELSEN, RICK — I Want You To Want Me

NIGHTINGALE, FRED — Sugar And Spice

NILSSON, HARRY — Coconut; Jump Into The Fire; Me And My Arrow; One; Spaceman; Without Her

NIMS, WALTER — Precious And Few

NITZSCHE, JACK — Needles And Pins; Up Where We Belong

NIX, ROBERT — Cherryhill Park; I'm Not Gonna Let It Bother Me Tonight; Imaginary Lover; So Into You

NO ARTIST — Billy(For When I Walk)

NOBLE, HARRY — Hold Me, Thrill Me, Kiss Me

NOBLE, JIMMY — Blue Flame

NOBLE, KEITH — Summer Song,a

NOBLE, RAY — By The Fireside; Change Your Mind; Cherokee; Goodnight Sweetheart; I Hadn't Anyone Till You; Love Is The Sweetest Thing; Love Locked Out; Touch Of Your Lips; Very Thought Of You; What More Can I Ask?

NOBLE-LELEIOHAKU, JOHNNY — Hawaiian War Chant

NOCENTELLI, LEO — Cissy Strut

NOLAN, BOB — Cool Water; Tumbling Tumbleweeds

NOLAN, KENNY — Get Dancin'

NOLAN, MICHAEL — Little Annie Roonie

NOLAND, ANDREW — Funky Worm

NOONAN, STEVE — Buy For Me The Rain

NORMAN, JOSE — Cuban Pete; Cucaracha, La

NORMAN, MONTY — Irma La Douce; James Bond Theme

NORTH, ALEX — Antony And Cleopatra Theme; I'll Cry Tomorrow; Long Hot Summer; Spartacus(Love Theme); Unchained Melody

NORTHERN, JOHNNY — My Angel Baby

NORTON, DANIEL — Gee!

NORTON, GEORGE A. — Memphis Blues; My Melancholy Baby

NORVAS, BILL — Make Love To Me

NORWOOD, DENNISE HAAS — Garden Of Eden

NORWORTH, JACK — Shine On Harvest Moon

NOTA, DIANE DE — Just Ask Your Heart

NOVELLO, IVOR — We'll Gather Lilacs

NOWELS, R. — Heaven Is A Place On Earth; I Can't Wait

NUGENT, MAUDE — Sweet Rosie O'grady

NUGENT, TED — Cat Scratch Fever; Journey To The Center Of The Mind; Yank Me, Crank Me

NUMAN, GARY — Cars

NUNN, B. — Rocket 2 U

NUNN, TREVOR — Memory

NUTTER, CARL — Solitaire

NYRO, LAURA — And When I Die; Been On A Train; Blowing Away; Brown Earth; Buy And Sell; Child In A Universe; Eli's Coming; Flim Flam Man; Save The Country; Stoned Soul Picnic; Stony End; Sweet Blindness; Wedding Bell Blues; You Don't Love Me When I Cry

O'BRIEN, BOB — Zoot Suit (For My Sunday Gal)

O'CONNOR, CALEB — Down The Field

O'CONNOR, DONALD — I Waited A Little Too Long

O'CONNOR, GARY — Back Where You Belong

O'CONNOR, SHAMUS — Macnamara's Band

O'DAY, ALAN — Angie Baby; Undercover Angel

O'DELL, KENNY — Beautiful People; Behind Closed Doors

O'DOWD, GEORGE — Church Of The Poison Mind; Do You Really Want To Hurt Me; I'll Tumble 4 Ya; It's A Miracle; Karma Chameleon; Miss Me Blind

O'FLYNN, CHARLES — Jungle Drums; Smile, Darn Ya, Smile; Swingin' In A Hammock

O'HARA, GEOFFREY — K-K-K-Katy

O'KEEFE, DANNY — Good Time Charlie's Got The Blues

O'KEEFE, JIMMY — Quien Sabe?(Who Knows?)

O'KEEFE, WALTER — Little By Little; Man On The Flying Trapeze

O'NEAL, MARGE — Calypso Joe

O'SULLIVAN, RAYMOND — Alone Again(Naturally); Clair; Out Of The Question

O'TOOLE, MARK — Relax

OAKELEY, FREDERICK — O Come All Ye Faithful(Adeste Fidelis)

OAKEY, PHIL — (Keep Feeling)Fascination

OAKLAND, BEN — Champagne Waltz; Do The New York; I'll Dance At Your Wedding; I'll Take Romance; I'm A Hundred Percent For You; If I Love Again; Java Jive; Mist Over The Moon; Sidewalks Of Cuba; Twinkle, Twinkle Little Star

OATES, JOHN — I Can't Go For That(No Can Do); Maneater; Out Of Touch; Sara Smile; She's Gone; You Make My Dreams

OCASEK, RIC — Drive; Emotion In Motion; Hello Again; Just What I Needed; Let's Go; Magic; Tonight She Comes; You Are The Girl; You Might Think

OCEAN, B. — Get Outta My Dreams, Get Into My Car

OCEAN, BILLY — Caribbean Queen; Love Is Forever; Love Zone; Mystery Lady; Suddenly; When The Going Gets Tough, The Tough Get Going

OCHS, PHIL — Bells; Bound For Glory

ODETTE, MARCELENE — Full Moon

OFFENBACH, JACQUES — Apache Dance; Can Can

OHMAN, PHIL — Lost

OLCOTT, CHAUNCEY — My Wild Irish Rose; When Irish Eyes Are Smiling

OLDFIELD, MIKE — Family Man; Tubular Bells (Exorcist Theme)

OLDHAM, ANDREW — As Tears Go By

OLDHAM, LINDON — I'm Your Puppet; It Tears Me Up; Wish You Didn't Have To Go

OLDHAM, SPOONER — Cry Like A Baby; Sweet Inspirations

OLIAS, LOTAR — Blue Mirage; You, You, You

OLIVEIRA, MILTON DE — Come To The Mardi Gras

OLIVER, JAMES — Itchy Twitchy Feeling

OLIVER, JOE "KING" — Doctor Jazz; Sugar Foot Stomp(Dipper Mouth Blues); West End Blues

OLIVER, S. — Wishing Well

OLIVER, SY — Dream Of You; Easy Does It; For Dancers Only; Neiani; Opus One; Quiet Please; Rumble; Well, Git It; Yes Indeed

OLIVIERI, DINO — I'll Be Yours(J'attendrai)

OLIVIERO, N. — More(Theme From Mondo Cane)

OLMAN, ABE — Down Among The Sheltering Palms; Down By The O-HI-O; Oh Johnny, Oh Johnny Oh!

OLSEN, OLE — Oh! Gee, Oh! Gosh, Oh! Golly, I'm In Love

OLSEN, PHILLIPS — Gonna Build A Big Fence Around Texas

OLSHEY, ALEX — I Love You Much Too Much

OMARTIAN, MICHAEL — Closest Thing To Perfect; Get Used To It; I Think It's Love; Infatuation; She Works Hard For The Money

ONO, YOKO — Whatever Gets You Through The Night

ONORATI, HENRY — Little Drummer Boy

OPENSHAW, JOHN — Love Sends A Little Gift Of Roses

OPPENHEIM, DAVE — Hold Me; It's The Girl

OPPENHEIMER, GEORGE — I Feel A Song Comin' On

ORANGE, WALTER LEE — Brick House; Nightshift; Sweet Love

ORBISON, ROY — Blue Bayou; Crowd; Crying; Goodnight; In Dreams; It's Over; Oh Pretty Woman; Only The Lonely(Know The Way I Feel); Ride Away; Running Scared; Working For The Man

ORCHESTRAL MANOEUVRES IN THE DARK — If You Leave

ORENT, MILTON — In The Land Of Oo-Bla-Dee

ORLOB, HAROLD — I Wonder Who's Kissing Her Now

ORLOWSKI, ANNE — Rubber Ball

ORNADEL, CYRIL — I Ruled The World"; Portrait Of My Love

ORR, BENJAMIN — Stay The Night

ORSBORN, VICTOR — Dance(Disco Heat)

ORTOLANI, RIZ — Forget Domani; More(Theme From Mondo Cane)

ORY, EDWARD "KID" — Muskrat Ramble

ORZABAL, ROLAND — Shout

ORZABAL, ROY — Everybody Wants To Rule The World

OSBORNE, GARY — Blue Eyes; Little Jeannie; Part-Time Love

OSBORNE, JEFFREY — All At Once; On The Wings Of Love

OSBORNE, JIMMY — Death Of Little Kathy Fiscus

OSBORNE, WILL — Beside An Open Fireplace; Between 18th And 19th On Chestnut Street; Pompton Turnpike

OSMOND, ALAN, WAYNE, AND MERRIL — Hold Her Tight

OSMOND, ALAN — Crazy Horses; Down By The Lazy River

OSMOND, MERRILL — Crazy Horses; Down By The Lazy River

OSMOND, WAYNE — Crazy Horses

OSSER, EDNA — I Dream Of You(More Than You Dream I Do)

OTIS, CLYDE — Baby(You've Got What It Takes); Boll Weevil Song; Call Me; Doncha' Think It's Time; Endlessly; For My Baby; It's Just A Matter Of Time; Kiddio; Looking Back; Out Of Sight, Out Of Mind; Stroll

OTIS, JOHNNY — Dance With Me Henry; Every Beat Of My Heart; So Fine

OTIS, SHUGGIE — Strawberry Letter 23

OTTNER, M. — 'round Her Neck She Wore A Yellow Ribbon

OUSLEY, CURTIS — Soul Serenade; Soul Twist

OVERSTREET, W. BENTON — Georgia Blues

OWENS, BONNIE — Legend Of Bonnie And Clyde
OWENS, BUCK — Crying Time; I've Got A Tiger By The Tail; Together Again; Under Your Spell Again
OWENS, CLIFF — Any Way You Want Me
OWENS, HARRY — Cocoanut Grove; Dreamy Hawaiian Moon; Linger Awhile; Sing Me A Song Of The Islands; Sweet Leilani; To You Sweetheart Aloha

OWENS, JACK — By-U, By-O(the Lou'siana Lullaby); Cynthia's In Love; Hi, Neighbor; How Soon(Will I Be Seeing You); Hut Sut Song; Hysteria
OWENS, KELLY — I Beg Of You
OWENS, TEX — Cattle Call
OZEN, BARBARA LYNN — You'll Lose A Good Thing

PACE, D. — Man Without Love

PACE, L. — Serious

PACK, DAVID — Biggest Part Of Me; Holdin' On To Yesterday; How Much I Feel

PADEN, FRANK — I Do

PADEN, JOHNNY — I Do

PADEREWSKI, IGNACE — Minuet In G

PADILLA, JOSE — My Toreador(El Relicario); Paree!; Valencia

PAGE, BILLY — "in" Crowd; In Crowd

PAGE, D. G. — Stay The Night

PAGE, JIMMY — Black Dog; Fool In The Rain; Happenings Ten Years Time Ago; Immigrant Song; Stairway To Heaven; Whole Lotta Love

PAGE, MARTIN — We Built This City

PAGE, RICHARD — Broken Wings; Is It Love; Kyrie

PAICE, IAN — Smoke On The Water

PAICH, DAVID — 99; Got To Be Real; Hold The Line; Lido Shuffle; Lowdown; Rosanna

PAIVA, JARARACA — I Want My Mama(Mama Yo Quiero)

PAIVA, VINCENTE — I Want My Mama(Mama Yo Quiero)

PALITZ, MORTY — While We're Young

PALLINI, BRUNO — Rockin' Soul

PALMER, DAVID — Look Of Love; Nightingale

PALMER, DONALD — Jazzman

PALMER, FLORRIE — Morning Train

PALMER, JACK — Boog-It; Everybody Loves My Baby, But My Baby Don't Love Nobody But Me; I've Found A New Baby; Jumpin' Jive

PALMER, JOHN — Band Played On

PALMER, KING — 11th Hour Melody

PALMER, ROBERT — Some Like It Hot

PAN, PETER — Freddy

PANKOW, JAMES — (I've Been)Searchin' So Long; Alive Again; Feelin' Stronger Every Day; Just You 'n' Me; Make Me Smile; Old Days

PANZER, MARTY — Even Now; It's A Miracle

PANZERI, M. — Love Me Tonight; Man Without Love

PANZERI, MARIO — To The Door Of The Sun (Alle Porte Del Sole)

PAOLA, DI — Come Prima(For The First Time)

PAOLI, GINO — Phoenix Love Theme; You're My World

PAPARELLI, FRANK — Blue 'n Boogie; Night In Tunisia,a

PARDAVE, JOAQUIN — Negra Consentida(My Pet Brunette)

PARDIN, L. — Just To See Her

PARHAM, TINY — Drummin' Man

PARIS, ADENYI — Sooner Or Later

PARIS, EKUNDAYO — It's Ecstasy When You Lay Down Next To Me; Sooner Or Later

PARISH, MITCHELL — All I Need Is You; All My Love; Baby, When You Ain't There; Belle Of The Ball; Blue Tango; Blues Serenade; Cabin In The Cotton; Ciao, Ciao, Bambina; Deep Purple; Deep River; Does Your Heart Beat For Me?; Don't Be That Way; Dream, Dream, Dream; Emaline; Hands Across The Table; I'm A Hundred Percent For You; I'm Satisfied; Is That Religion?; Lamp Is Low; Lazy Rhapsody; Let Me Love You Tonight(No Te Importe Saber); Lilacs In The Rain; Mademoiselle De Paree; Moonlight Serenade; Mr. Ghost Goes To Town; One Morning In May; Orchids For Remembrance; Organ Grinder's Swing; Riverboat Shuffle; Ruby; Scat Song; Sentimental Gentleman From Georgia; Sidewalks Of Cuba; Sleigh Ride; Sophisticated Lady; Sophisticated Swing; Stairway To The Stars; Star Dust; Starlit Hour; Stars Fell On Alabama; Sweet Lorraine; Tzena, Tzena, Tzena; Volare Or Nel Blu, Dipinto Di Blu; Yearning For Love

PARISSI, ROBERT — Play That Funky Music

PARKER, BRIAN — Concrete And Clay

PARKER, CHARLIE — Billie's Bounce; Confirmation; Donna Lee; Hootie Blues; Now's The Time; Ornithology; Yardbird Suite

PARKER, DOROTHY — How Am I To Know?; I Wished On The Moon

PARKER, EULA — Village Of Saint Bernadette

PARKER, GRAHAM — (Let Me Get)Sweet On You

PARKER, JOHN — Hard Habit To Break

PARKER, JOHNNY — Baby Sittin' Boogie

PARKER, JR., RAY — Ghostbusters; I Still Can't Get Over Loving You; Jack And Jill; Jamie; Mr. Telephone Man; Other Woman; Woman Needs Love; You Can't Change That; You Got The Love

PARKER, JUDY — December 1963(Oh What A Night); Who Loves You

PARKER, LEROY — 'round Her Neck She Wore A Yellow Ribbon

PARKER, RICHARD — Comin' In And Out Of Your Life

PARKER, ROBERT — Barefootin'

PARKER, ROSS — Joy(Song Of Joy); We'll Meet Again

PARKER, SOL — Dansero

PARKS, CARSON — Cab Driver

PARKS, CARSON C. — Somethin' Stupid

PARKS, LARRY — Bread And Butter

PARKS, VAN DYKE — Available Space; Come To The Sunshine; Heroes And Villains

PARKS, WELDON — Dancing Machine

PARMAN, CLIFF — Pretend

PARNES, PAUL — Next Step Is Love

PARR, JOHN — St. Elmo's Fire(Man In Motion)

PARRIES, FRED — Paradiddle Joe

PARRIS, FREDERICKE — I'll Remember(In The Still Of The Nite)

PARSONS, ALAN — Eye In The Sky; Games People Play

PARSONS, BILL — All-American Boy,The

PARSONS, GEOFFREY — Chee Che-OO Chee(Sang The Little Bird); Eternally(Limelight); If You Love Me(Really Love Me); Little Shoemaker; Oh! My Pa-Pa; Smile

PARTON, DES — Sad Sweet Dreamer

PARTON, DOLLY — 9 To 5; Two Doors Down

PASCAL, MILTON — I Wanna Get Married

PASH, WARREN — Private Eyes

PASQUALE, CHARLES — Magic Is The Moonlight

PASSARELLI, KENNY — Rocky Mountain Way

PATE SR., JOHN W. — Amen

PATERSON, JIM — Come On Eileen

PATRICI, ANITA, RUTH, JUNE, AN — How Long(Betcha' Got A Chick On The Side)

PATRICK, CHARLES — Book Of Love

PATRICK, PAT — Yeh Yeh

PATTERSON, A.B. — Waltzing Matilda

PATTON, JOHN — Big John(ain't You Gonna Marry Me?)

PATTON, ROBBIE — Hold Me

PAUL, CLARENCE — Fingertips; I Need Your Lovin';

Pretty Little Baby; Until You Come Back To Me; You've Been In Love Too Long

PAUL, GENE DE — Ain't That Just Like A Man; Bless Your Beautiful Hide; Cow-Cow Boogie; Daddy-O(I'm Gonna Teach You Some Blues); He's My Guy; I'll Remember April; If I Had My Druthers; Jubilation T. Cornpone; Lonesome Polecat; Love In A Home; Milkman, Keep Those Bottles Quiet; Mr. Five By Five; Namely You; Sobbin' Women; Song Was Born; Spring Spring Spring; Star Eyes

PAUL, MORRIS — The Untouchables (Theme From)

PAULING, LOWMAN — Dedicated To The One I Love

PAXTON, GARY — It Was I

PAXTON, TOM — Bottle Of Wine; What Did You Learn In School Today?

PAYNE, DORIS — Just One Look

PAYNE, JAMES O. — Woman, Woman

PAYNE, JOHN HOWARD — Home Sweet Home

PAYNE, KIM — Midnight Rider

PAYNE, LEON — I Love You Because

PAYTON, BRENDA — Dry Your Eyes

PAYTON, DAVID — Magic

PEACOCK, TREVOR — Mrs. Brown, You've Got A Lovely Daughter

PEARCY, STEPHEN — Body Talk; Round And Round

PEARSON, EUGENE — Thousand Stars

PEART, NEIL — New World Man

PEASE, HARRY — Josephine Please No Lean On The Bell; Peggy O'neil

PEEBLES, ANN — I Can't Stand The Rain

PEEK, CATHERINE — Lonely People

PEEK, DAN — Lonely People

PELLETTIERI, VITO — Unloved And Unclaimed

PELOSI, DON — Little Old Mill, The(Went Round And Round)

PENA, PAUL — Jet Airliner

PENN, DAN — Cry Like A Baby; It Tears Me Up; Sweet Inspirations

PENNIMAN, RICHARD — Jenny, Jenny; Jenny, Take A Ride; Keep A-Knockin'; Long Tall Sally; Lucille; Slippin' And Slidin'; Tutti-Frutti

PENNINGTON, DAN — I'm Your Puppet; Wish You Didn't Have To Go

PENNY, ED — Somebody's Knockin'; Somebody's Watching Me

PENNY, JOE — Angel Baby

PENNY, LEE — My Adobe Hacienda

PENRIDGE, STANLEY — Beth

PENZABENE, ROGER — End Of Our Road; I Could Never Love Another(After Loving You); I Wish It Would Rain; You're My Everything

PEOPLES, ALISA — Don't Stop The Music

PEPPER, BUDDY — Don't Tell Me; Pillow Talk; Sorry; Vaya Con Dios

PEPPERS, BILL — I Was The One

PEREN, FREDDY — Makin' It

PERETTI, HUGO — Bimbombey; Can't Help Falling In Love; Crazy Otto Rag; Experience Unnecessary; Let's Put It All Together; Oh, Oh, I'm Falling In Love Again; Wild In The Country

PERKINS, BARNEY — Want Ads

PERKINS, CARL — Daddy Sang Bass; Matchbox; Your True Love

PERKINS, FRANK — Cabin In The Cotton; Emaline; Scat Song; Sentimental Gentleman From Georgia; Stars Fell On Alabama

PERKINS, RAY — Under A Texas Moon

PERREN, FREDDY — Boogie Fever; Do It Baby; Heaven Must Be Missing An Angel; Hot Line; I Pledge My Love; I Want You Back; I Will Survive; Love You Save; Mama's Pearl; Reunited; Shake Your Groove Thing; Sugar Daddy; Whodunit

PERRICONE, JACK — Run Joey Run

PERRY, BARNEY — Walking In Rhythm

PERRY, GREG — Bring The Boys Home; One Monkey Don't Stop No Show; Pay To The Piper; Somebody's Been Sleeping In My Bed; Stick-Up; Want Ads

PERRY, J. — Dude(Looks Like A Lady); Walk This Way

PERRY, LEONARD — One Love In My Lifetime

PERRY, STEVE — Any Way You Want It; Be Good To Yourself; Don't Fight It; Don't Stop Believin'; Foolish Heart; Girl Can't Help It; I'll Be Alright Without You; Lovin', Touchin', Squeezin'; Oh, Sherrie; Only The Young; Open Arms; Still They Ride; Suzanne; Who's Crying Now

PERRYMAN, WILLIE — Bald Headed Lena

PERT, MORRIS — Family Man

PESCE, JOSEPH — Voices Carry

PESTALOZZA, ALBERTO — Ciribiribin

PETERBURSKI, J. — Oh, Donna Clara

PETERIK, JIM — American Heartbeat; Burning Heart; Caught Up In You; Eye Of The Tiger; High On You; I Can't Hold Back; Is This Love; Vehicle; You Wouldn't Listen

PETERS, BEN — Before The Next Teardrop Falls; Daytime Friends; Kiss An Angel Good Morning

PETERS, JERRY — Going In Circles

PETERSON, BETTY — My Happiness

PETERSON, ERNIE — I Want To Be The Only One

PETKERE, BERNICE — Close Your Eyes; Lullaby Of The Leaves

PETRIE, HENRY — Asleep In The Deep

PETRILLO, CAESAR — Jim

PETTIS, JACK — Bugle Call Rag

PETTY, NORMAN — Almost Paradise; Every Day; It's So Easy; Not Fade Away; Oh Boy; Peggy Sue; True Love Ways

PETTY, TOM — Breakdown; Don't Come Around Here No More; Don't Do Me Like That; Jammin' Me; Refugee; Stop Draggin' My Heart Around

PEVERETT, DAVE — Slow Ride

PEYTON, DAVE — I Ain't Got Nobody

PHILLINGANES, GREG — Love Will Conquer All; Se La

PHILLIPS, CHARLIE — Sugartime

PHILLIPS, J. C. — Green Eyed Lady

PHILLIPS, JOHN — Creeque Alley; Go Where You Wanna Go; I Saw Her Again Last Night; Like An Old Time Movie; San Francisco(Be Sure To Wear Some Flowers In Your Hair); Twelve Thirty (Young Girls Are Coming To The Canyon); Words Of Love

PHILLIPS, JOHN AND MICHELLE — California Dreaming

PHILLIPS, JOHN E. A. — Look Through My Window; Monday, Monday

PHILLIPS, KATHERINE — Gonna Build A Big Fence Around Texas

PHILLIPS, MARVIN — Cherry Pie; Cherry Pink And Apple Blossom White

PHILLIPS, MIKE — North To Alaska

PHILLIPS, MILDRED — Mambo Rock

PHILLIPS, STU — Beyond The Valley Of The Dolls

PIAF, EDITH — I'll Remember Today; Vie En Rose, La

PIANTADOSI, AL — I Didn't Raise My Boy To Be A Soldier; Pal Of My Cradle Days

PICCOLO, STEVE — Self Control

PICKETT, BOBBY — Monster Mash

PICKETT, PHIL — It's A Miracle; Karma Chameleon; Move Away

PICKETT, WILSON — Don't Knock My Love; I Found A Love; I'm A Midnight Mover; If You Need Me; In The Midnight Hour

PICKHALL, MARJORIE — Duna

PICONE, VITO — Little Star

PIERCE, D. — I Need Love

PIERCE, JOHN — Cool Love

PIERCE, MARVIN — Love Rollercoaster; Skin Tight; Who'd She Coo

PIERCE, T. — Cross My Broken Heart

PIERCE, WEBB — I Ain't Never

PIERCY, ANDREW — Der Kommissar

PIERPONT, J. S. — Jingle Bells

PIGFORD, NELSON — It's Ecstasy When You Lay Down Next To Me

PILAT, LORENZO — To The Door Of The Sun (Alle Porte Del Sole)

PILLAR, GENE — Mr. Touchdown U. S. A.

PINERA, CARLOS — Ride Captain Ride

PINKARD JR., JAMES S. — Coca Cola Cowboy

PINKARD, MACEO — Congratulations; Gimme A Little Kiss, Will Ya Huh?; Here Comes The Show Boat; Is That Religion?; Sugar(That Sugar Baby O' Mine); Sweet Georgia Brown

PINZ, SHELLEY — Green Tambourine

PIPPA, SALVATORE — Lonely Teenager

PIPPIN, DON — Hold Me In Your Arms

PIPPIN, STEVE — Better Love Next Time

PIRON, ARMAND — I Wish I Could Shimmy Like My Sister Kate

PIRONE, HARRY — I Want To Cry

PIRRONI, MARCO — Goody Two Shoes

PISTILLI, GENE — Medicine Man

PITCHFORD, DEAN — Almost Paradise(Love Theme From Footloose); Dancing In The Sheets; Fame; Footloose; Let's Hear It For The Boy

PITMAN, JACK — Beyond The Reef

PITNEY, GENE — He's A Rebel; Hello, Mary Lou

PITT, EUGENE — My True Story

PITTS, TOM — I Never Knew I Could Love Anybody Like I'm Loving You

PLACE, MARY KAY — Baby Boy

PLANT, ROBERT — Big Log; Black Dog; D'yer Maker; Fool In The Rain; Immigrant Song; Stairway To Heaven; Whole Lotta Love

PLATER, BOBBY — Jersey Bounce

PLUMMER JR., HOWARD — I Can't Love You Enough

POBER, LEON — Pearly Shells; Tiny Bubbles

POCKRISS, LEE — All For You; Big Daddy; Calcutta; Catch A Falling Star; I Go To Bed; I Know The Feeling; Itsy Bitsy Teenie Weenie Yellow Polkadot Bikini; Jimmy's Girl; Johhny Angel; Leader Of The Laundromat; My Heart Is An Open Book; My Little Corner Of The World; Only One; Playground In My Mind; Sitting In The Back Seat; Starbright; Tracy; What Is Love?

PODOLOR, RICHARD — Let There Be Drums

POE, COY — Object Of My Affection; What's The Reason (I'm Not Pleasin' You)

POE, EDGAR ALLEN — Bells

POINDEXTER, RICHARD — Hypnotized; Hysteria

POINTER, ANITA — I'm So Excited

POINTER, ANITA AND BONNIE — Fairytale

POINTER, JUNE — I'm So Excited

POINTER, RUTH — I'm So Excited

POLA, EDDIE — Caramba! It's The Samba!; I Didn't Slip, I Wasn't Pushed, I Fell; I Love The Way You Say Goodnight; I Said My Pajamas(And Put On My Pray'rs); Longest Walk

POLA, EDWARD — Marching Along Together

POLL, RUTH — Bring Back The Thrill; New Shade Of Blue

POLLA, W. C. — Dancing Tambourine

POLLACK, BEN — Make Love To Me; Peckin'

POLLACK, BERT — Athena

POLLACK, LEW — (I'm In Heaven When I See You Smile)Diane; Angela Mia(My Angel); At The Codfish Ball; Balboa; Charmaine; Cheatin' On Me; Early Bird; Love Will Tell; My Yiddishe Momme; Right Somebody To Love; S Love I'm After; Sing, Baby, Sing; Toy Trumpet; Two Cigarettes In The Dark; Who's Afraid Of Love; You Do The Darndest Things, Baby; You're Slightly Terrific

POLLOCK, CHANNING — My Man

POMERANZ, DAVID — Old Songs,the; Tryin' To Get The Feelin' Again

POMEROY, GEORGE S. — Whiffenpoof Song

POMUS, DOC — Can't Get Used To Losing You; Go, Jimmy, Go; His Latest Flame(Marie's The Name); Hopeless; Hound Dog Man; Hushabye; I'm A Man; Kiss Me Quick; Little Sister; Mess O' Blues; No One; Save The Last Dance For Me; Seven Day Weekend; She's Not You; Surrender; Suspicion; Sweets For My Sweet

POMUS, JEROME "DOC" — Turn Me Loose

PONCE, PHIL — Dancing Tambourine

PONCHIELLI, A. — Dance Of The Hours

PONCIA, VINI — I Was Made For Loving You; Just Too Many People; You Make Me Feel Like Dancing

PONGER, ROBERT — Der Kommissar

PONS, JIM — Elenore

POP, IGGY — China Girl

POPE, PAULINE — Racing With The Moon

POPP, ANDRE — Love Is Blue; Portugese Washerwomen

POPU, CHARLES WAKEFIELD CADMAN — At Dawning

POPULAR — Daring Young Man On The Flying Trapeze

POPULAR STANDARD — Can't You Hear Me Calling Caroline

PORCARO, JEFF — Human Nature

PORCE, ANITA — Going In Circles

POREE, ANITA — Boogie Down; Keep On Truckin'; Love Or Let Me Be Lonely

PORTAL, OTILIO — Sweet And Gentle

PORTELA, RAUL — Lisbon Antigua(In Old Lisbon)

PORTER JR., GEORGE — Cissy Strut

PORTER, ANDREW — You're A Special Part Of Me

PORTER, COLE — All I've Got To Get Now Is My Man; All Of You; All Through The Night; Allez-Vous-En, Go Away; Always True To You In My Fashion; Another Op'nin, Another Show; Anything Goes; At Long Last Love; Be A Clown; Begin The Beguine; Between You And Me; Bianca; Blow, Gabriel, Blow; Brush Up Your Shakespeare; Buddie, Beware; Bulldog, Bulldog; But In The Morning, No!; By The

Mississinewah; C'est Magnifique; Can-Can; Cherry Pies Ought To Be You; Close; Come Along With Me; Come On In; Come To The Supermarket(In Old Peking); Could It Be You?; Count Your Blessings; Do I Love You?; Don't Fence Me In; Don't Look At Me That Way; Down In The Depths, On The Ninetieth Floor; Dream Dancing; Easy To Love; Ev'ry Day A Holiday; Ev'ry Time We Say Goodbye; Ev'rything I Love; Experiment; Far, Far Away; Farewell Amanda; Farming; Find Me A Primitive Man; For No Rhyme Or Reason; Fresh As A Daisy; Friendship; From Alpha To Omega; From Now On; From This Moment On; Get Out Of Town; Give Him The Oo-La-La; Goodbye, Little Dream, Goodbye; Great Indoors; Gypsy In Me; Heaven Hop; Hey, Babe, Hey!(I'm Nuts About You); Hey, Good Lookin'; How Could We Be Wrong; How's Your Romance?; I Adore You; I Always Knew; I Am Ashamed That Women Are So Simple; I Am In Love; I Am Loved; I Concentrate On You; I Get A Kick Out Of You; I Happen To Like New York; I Hate Men; I Hate You, Darling; I Love Paris; I Love You; I Love You, Samantha; I Want To Go Home; I Worship You; I'm A Gigolo; I'm Getting Myself Ready For You; I'm In Love; I'm In Love Again; I'm Unlucky At Gambling; I've A Strange New Rhythm In My Heart; I've Come To Wive It Wealthily In Padua.; I've Got My Eyes On You; I've Got You On My Mind; I've Got You Under My Skin; I've Still Got My Health; If You Loved Me Truly; If You Smile At Me; In The Still Of The Night; It Might Have Been; It Was Written In The Stars; It's A Chemical Reaction; It's All Right With Me; It's D'lovely; Josephine; Just One Of Those Things; Katie Went To Haiti; Laziest Gal In Town; Let's Be Buddies; Let's Do It(Let's Fall In Love); Let's Fly Away; Let's Misbehave; Let's Not Talk About Love; Let's Step Out; Little Skipper From Heaven Above; Live And Let Live; Live To Tell; Look What I Found; Looking At You; Love For Sale; Love Me, Love My Pekinese; Love Of My Life; Mack The Black; Make It Another Old Fashioned, Please; Maria; Me And Marie; Mind If I Make Love To You; Miss Otis Regrets; Mister And Missus Fitch; Most Gentlemen Don't Like Love; My Heart Belongs To Daddy; My Mother Would Love You; Never Give Anything Away; Night And Day; Nina; Nobody's Chasing Me; Now You Has Jazz; Old Fashioned Garden; Ours; Ozarks Are Calling Me Home; Paree, What Did You Do To Me?; Paris Loves Lovers; Physician; Picture Of Me Without You; Pipe-Dreaming; Rap Tap On Wood; Red, Hot And Blue; Ridin' High; Rolling Home; Rosalie; Satin And Silk; Since I Kissed My Baby Goodbye; Sing To Me, Guitar; So In Love; So Near And Yet So Far; Solomon; Something For The Boys; Something To Shout About; Stereophonic Sound; Swingin' The Jinx Away; Tomorrow; Too Bad; Too Darn Hot; True Love; Two Little Babes In The Woods; Use Your Imagination; Visit Panama; We Open In Venice; Well, Did You Evah; Were Thine That Special Face; What Is This Thing Called Love; When I Was A Little Cuckoo; Where Have You Been; Where Is The Life That Late I Led?; Where, Oh Where?; Who Wants To Be A Millionaire; Who Would Have Dreamed?; Why Can't You Behave; Why Should I Care; Why Shouldn't I; Without Love; Wunderbar; You Can Do No Wrong; You Do Something To Me; You Don't Know Paree;

You Irritate Me So; You Never Know; You'd Be So Nice To Come Home To; You're Just Too Too; You're Sensational; You're The Top; You've Got That Thing

PORTER, DAVID — B-A-B-Y; Hold On(I'm Coming); I Thank You; Soul Man; When Something Is Wrong With My Baby; Your Good Thing (Is About To End)

PORTER, DEL — Ya Wanna Buy A Bunny?

PORTER, JAKE — Ko Ko Mo, I Love You So

PORTER, LEW — Little Red Fox; You Told A Lie (I Believed You)

POSFORD, GEORGE — At The Balalaika; World Is Mine (tonight)

POST, BILL — Sixteen Reasons(Why I Love You)

POST, DOREE — Sixteen Reasons(Why I Love You)

POST, JIM — Reach Out In The Darkness

POST, MIKE — Rockford Files

POTTER, BRIAN — Ain't No Woman(Like The One I Got); Are You Man Enough; Country Boy(You Got Your Feet In L.A.); Don't Pull Your Love; Give It To The People; It Only Takes A Minute; Keeper Of The Castle; Look In My Eyes Pretty Woman; One Tin Soldier; Remember What I Told You To Forget; Two Divided By Love

POUGHT, EMMA RUTH — Mr. Lee

POUGHT, JANNIE — Mr. Lee

POULTON, GEORGE R. — Aura Lee

POWELL, ARCHIE — 5-10-15-20(25-30 Years Of Love)

POWELL, FELIX — Pack Up Your Troubles In Your Old Kit Bag And Smile, Smile, Smile

POWELL, MEL — Mission To Moscow; My Guy's Come Back

POWELL, ROGER — Set Me Free

POWELL, TEDDY — Bewildered; I Couldn't Believe My Eyes; Love Has Joined Us Together

POWERS, CHESTER — Get Together

POWERS, TONY — 98. 6; Lazy Day; Why Do Lovers Break Each Other's Hearts?

PRADO, MIGUEL — Time Was

PRADO, PEREZ — Mambo, No. 5; Patricia

PRAGER, STEPHEN — Fly, Robin, Fly; Get Up And Boogie

PRATT, HARRY — See-Saw

PREAD, RONALD LA — Brick House; Sweet Love

PRESLEY, ELVIS — All Shook Up; Don't Be Cruel(to A Heart That's True); Heartbreak Hotel; Love Me Tender

PRESLEY, REG — Love Is All Around

PRESSLY, ERIS — I Can't Wait

PRESTON, BILLY — Nothing From Nothing; Outa-Space; Space Race; Will It Go Round In Circles; You Are So Beautiful

PRESTOPINO, GREG — Break My Stride

PREVIN, ANDRE — Control Yourself; Faraway Part Of Town; I Like Myself; I Live For Your Love; I'll Plant My Own Tree; Long Day's Journey Into Night; Valley Of The Dolls (Theme From)

PREVIN, DORY — Come Saturday Morning; I'll Plant My Own Tree; Last Tango In Paris; Valley Of The Dolls (Theme From)

PREVITE, FRANKIE — Hungry Eyes; Sweetheart; Time Of My Life

PRICE JR, DOCK — Your Time To Cry

PRICE, ALAN — House Of The Rising Sun; I'm Crying

PRICE, CHILTON — Slow Poke; You Belong To Me

PRICE, HARVEY — Heaven Knows

PRICE, LEO — Send Me Some Lovin'

PRICE, LLOYD — Come Into My Heart; I'm Gonna Get Married; Just Because; Lady Luck; Lawdy Miss Clawdy; Personality; Stagger Lee

PRIEST, STEPHEN — Fox On The Run

PRIETO, JOAQUIN — Wedding

PRIMA, LOUIS — Oh Babe!; Robin Hood; Sing, Sing, Sing; Sunday Kind Of Love

PRINCE — U Got The Look; When Doves Cry

PRINCE, HUGHIE — Beat Me Daddy, Eight To The Bar; Boogie Woogie Bugle Boy; Bounce Me Brother With A Solid Four; I Guess I'll Get The Papers And Go Home; Rhumboogie; She Had To Go And Lose It At The Astor

PRINCE, WILLIAM RODNEY — Hot Smoke And Sassafras

PRINE, JOHN — Chinatown

PRITCHARD JR., JOHN — Can't Stop Dancin

PROCTOR, ADELAIDE — Lost Chord

PROFIT, CLARENCE — Lullaby In Rhythm

PROKOFIEFF, SERGE — Love Of Three Oranges

PROKOP, SKIP — One Fine Morning

PROMUS, DOC — Young Blood

PROSEN, SIDNEY — Till I Waltz Again With You

PROVOST, HEINZ — Intermezzo(A Love Story); Love Story, A(Intermezzo)

PRUITT, JOHNNIE — Bertha Butt Boogie; Hey, Leroy, You're Mama's Callin' You

PRYOR, ARTHUR — Whistler And His Dog

PRYOR, CACTUS — Don't Let The Stars Get In Your Eyes

PUCCINI, GIACOMO — Musetta's Waltz; One Fine Day(Un Bel Di); Un Bel Di Or One Fine Day

PUCK, HARRY — Where Did You Get That Girl

PUENTE, TITO — Oye Come Va

PUERTA JR., JOSEPH — Holdin' On To Yesterday

PUGSLEY, JERRY — Paradiddle Joe

PURVIS, CHARLES — Go On With The Wedding

PURVIS, KATHERINE E. — When The Saints Go Marching In

PUTNAM, CLAUDE — My Elusive Dreams

PUTNAM, CURLY — Green, Green Grass Of Home

PYLES, FROSTY — Voo-It! Voo-It!

QUADLING, LEW — Careless; Million Dreams Ago; Sam's Song(The Happy Tune)

QUARTO, CHARLES — Geronimo's Cadillac

QUASHA, SOL — Chain Gang

QUENZER, ARTHUR — Cowboy And The Lady,the

QUICK, C. E. — Come Go With Me; Whispering Bells

QUICKSELL, HOWARD — Since My Best Gal Turned Me Down

QUILLAN, CHARLES — I Wouldn't Have Missed It For The World

QUIN, THE — Down The Aisle Of Love

QUINE, RICHARD — Be Prepared; Be Still My Beating Heart

QUINN, PETER — Curly Shuffle

QUINTELA, E. — Little Lies

QUITTENTON, MARTIN — Maggie May; You Wear It Well

RABBITT, EDDIE — I Love A Rainy Night; Kentucky Rain; Someone Could Lose A Heart Tonight; Step By Step; Suspicions

RABIN, TREVOR — Owner Of A Lonely Heart

RABON, MIKE — I See The Light; Zip Code

RACHMANINOFF, SERGEI — Prelude In C Sharp Minor

RADCLIFFE, PETER — You're The First, The Last, My Everything

RADFORD, DAVE — Where The Black Eyed Susans Grow

RADO, JAMES — Ain't Got No; Air; Aquarius; Dead End; Don't Put It Down; Easy To Be Hard; Frank Mills; Good Morning Starshine; Hair; Hare Krishna; I Got Life; Let The Sunshine In; Walking In Space; Where Do I Go

RAE, JACKIE — Happy Heart; When There's No You

RAFELSON, PETER — Open Your Heart

RAFFERTY, GERRY — Baker Street; Days Gone Down(Still Got The Light In Your Eyes); Get It Right Next Time; Right Down The Line; Stuck In The Middle With You

RAGGI, LORENZO — Rockin' Soul

RAGNI, GEROME — Ain't Got No; Air; Aquarius; Dead End; Don't Put It Down; Easy To Be Hard; Frank Mills; Good Morning Starshine; Hair; Hare Krishna; I Got Life; Let The Sunshine In; Walking In Space; Where Do I Go

RAGOVOY, JERRY — I'll Take Good Care Of You; Pata Pata; Piece Of My Heart; Time Is On My Side; What's It Gonna Be?

RAINEY, GERTRUDE "MA" — Hear Me Talkin' To Ya; Weeping Woman Blues

RAINEY, MA — See See Rider

RAINGER, RALPH — Blossoms On Broadway; Blue Hawaii; Double Trouble; Faithful Forever; Funny Old Hills; Give Me Liberty Or Give Me Love; Guy What Takes His Time; Havin' Myself A Time; Here Lies Love; Here's Love In Your Eye; I Don't Want To Make History(I Just Want To Make Love); I Have Eyes; I Wished On The Moon; I'll Take An Option On You; If I Should Lose You; In A Little Hula Heaven; In The Park In Paree; Joobalai; June In January; Little Kiss At Twilight; Love In Bloom; Miss Brown To You; Moanin' Low; Please; What Goes On Here In My Heart; What Have You Got That Gets Me?; When A Woman Loves A Man; Why Dream?; With Every Breath I Take; You Started Something; You're A Sweet Little Headache

RAINWATER, MARVIN — Gonna Find Me A Bluebird

RAKSIN, DAVID — Bad And The Beautiful; Ben Casey, Theme From; Forever Amber; Laura

RALEIGH, BEN — Baion; Blue Winter; Dead End Street; Dungaree Doll; El Rancho Rock; Faith Can Move Mountains; Laughing On The Outside(Crying On The Inside); Love Is A Hurtin' Thing; Love Is All We Need; Midnight Mary; Wonderful, Wonderful; You Walk By; You're So Understanding

RALPHS, MICK — Can't Get Enough; Feel Like Makin' Love; Movin' On

RALTON, HARRY — I Remember The Cornfields

RAM, BUCK — At Your Beck And Call; Boog-It; Chew-Chew-Chew(Chew Your Bubble Gum); Come Prima(For The First Time); Enchanted; Great Pretender; Have Mercy; I'll Be Home For Christmas; Only You; Twilight Time

RAMAL, B. — Mr. Jaws

RAMBEAU, EDDIE — Kiss Me, Sailor

RAMIN, SID — Music To Watch Girls By; Patty Duke Theme

RAMIREZ, ROGER — Lover Man(Oh, Where Can You Be?)

RAMOS, SILVANO R. — (alla En)el Rancho Grande; El Rancho Rock

RAMSDEN, NICO — I Wanna Be A Cowboy

RAMSEY, KEN — Greenback Dollar

RAMSEY, WILLIS ALAN — Muskrat Love

RANCIFER, RODERICK — I Am Love(parts 1 & 2)

RAND, ANDE — Only You

RAND, LIONEL — Let There Be Love

RANDALL, JAMES RYDER — Maryland, My Maryland

RANDALL, LILLE — I Want To Cry

RANDAZZO, TEDDY — Big Wide World; Goin' Out Of My Head; Have You Looked Into Your Heart; Hurt So Bad; I'm On The Outside(Looking In); It's Gonna Take A Miracle; Pretty Blue Eyes

RANDELL, BUDDY — Lies(Are Breakin' My Heart)

RANDELL, DENNY — Attack; Baby,make Your Own Sweet Music; I Wanna Dance Wit' Choo(Doo Dat Dance); I Wanna Dance With Somebody(Who Loves Me); Keep The Ball Rollin'; Let's Hang On(To What We've Got); Lover's Concerto; Native New Yorker; Opus 17(Don't Worry 'bout Me); Swearin' To God; Working My Way Back To You

RANDLE, EARL — I'll Be Around; I'm Gonna Tear Your Playhouse Down

RANDOLPH, RANDY — Yakety Sax (Yakety Axe)

RANDOLPH, ZILNER — Ol' Man Mose

RANEY, WAYNE — Why Don't You Haul Off And Love Me?

RANKIN, KENNY — In The Name Of Love; Peaceful

RANS, ROBERT — Dance With Me; Do Ya Wanna Get Funky With Me; Material Girl

RANSOM JR., R. — Dusic

RANSOM, JR., R. — Dazz

RAPEE, ERNO — (I'm In Heaven When I See You Smile)Diane; Angela Mia(My Angel); Charmaine

RAPOSO, JOE — Bein' Green; First Time It Happens,the; Gingham And Yarn; Sing

RAPPAPORT, ROBERT LAWRENCE — Martian Hop

RAPPAPORT, STEVE — Martian Hop

RAPPOLO, LEON — Farewell Blues; Make Love To Me; Milenberg Joys; Tin Roof Blues

RAREBELL, HERMAN — Rock You Like A Hurricane

RASBACH, OSCAR — Trees

RASCEL, RENATO — Arrivederci, Roma

RASKIN, WILLIE — Fifty Million Frenchmen Can't Be Wrong; Wedding Bells Are Breaking Up That Old Gang Of Mine

RATH, FRED — Just A Girl That Men Forget

RAUCH, FRED — Answer Me, My Love

RAVEL, MAURICE — Bolero

RAVEN, CAROL — Cumparsita, La

RAY, ALAN — You Don't Love Me Anymore

RAY, B. — One Heartbeat

RAY, EDDY — Hearts Of Stone

RAY, HAROLD — Special Lady

RAY, HARRY MILTON — Sexy Mama

RAY, JOHNNIE — Little White Cloud That Cried

RAY, MICHAEL — Big Fun

RAYBURN, GENE — Hop Scotch Polka

RAYE, DON — (If I Had)Rhythm In My Nursery Rhymes; Ain't That Just Like A Man; Beat Me Daddy, Eight To The Bar; Boogie Woogie Bugle Boy; Bounce Me Brother With A Solid Four; Cow-Cow Boogie; Daddy-O(I'm Gonna Teach You Some Blues); Domino; Down The Road A Piece; For Dancers Only; He's My Guy; Hey, Mr. Postman; House Of Blue Lights; I Love You Much Too Much; I'll Remember April; Milkman, Keep Those Bottles Quiet; Mr. Five By Five; Music Makers; Rhumboogie; Scrub Me Mama(With A Boogie Beat); She Had To Go And Lose It At The Astor; Song Was Born; Star Eyes; Well All Right! (Tonight's The Night); You Don't Know What Love Is; Your Red Wagon

RAYMOND, JEFFREY — You Don't Love Me Anymore

RAYMONDE, IVOR — I Only Want To Be With You

RAZAF, ANDY — Ain't Misbehavin'; Big Chief De Sota; Blue Turning Gray Over You; Christopher Columbus; Concentratin' On You; Deep Forest; Dusky Stevedore; Gee Baby, Ain't I Good To You; Honeysuckle Rose; In The Mood; Joint Is Jumpin' The; Keeping Out Of Mischief Now; Knock Me A Kiss; Louisiana; Lover's Lullaby; Memories Of You; Milkmen's Matinee; My Fate Is In Your Hands; On Revival Day; Patty Cake, Patty Cake(Baker Man); Reefer Man; S'posin'; Stealin' Apples; Stompin' At The Savoy; What Did I Do To Be So Black And Blue; Zonky

REA, CHRIS — Fool(If You Think It's Over)

REARDON, FRANK — Same Old Saturday Night

REARDON, JACK — Good Life; When

REB, JOHNNY — Goober Peas

REBENNACK, MAC — Such A Night

RECORD, EUGENE — Have You Seen Her; Love Makes A Woman; Oh Girl; Soulful Strut

REDD, GENE — Please Come Home For Christmas

REDD, HENRY J. — Free

REDDICK, JAMES — Trying To Hold On To My Woman

REDDING, EDWARD C. — End Of A Love Affair

REDDING, OTIS — Amen; Fa-Fa-Fa-Fa-Fa(Sad Song); Happy Song(Dum Dum); I've Been Loving You Too Long; Mr. Pitiful; Respect; Sittin' On The Dock Of The Bay; Sweet Soul Music

REDDY, HELEN — I Am Woman

REDI, P. G. — Non Dimenticar

REDMAN, DON — Chant Of The Weed; Cherry; Gee Baby, Ain't I Good To You; How'm I Doin?(Hey, Hey!)

REDMOND, JOHN — Christmas In Killarney; Crosstown; Dream, Dream, Dream; Gaucho Serenade; I Let A Song Go Out Of My Heart

REDNER, LEWIS H. — O Little Town Of Bethlehem

REED, JERRY — Guitar Man; When You're Hot, You're Hot

REED, JIMMY — Ain't That Lovin' You Baby; Honest I Do

REED, LES — Daughter Of Darkness; Delilah; Here It Comes Again; It's Not Unusual; Kiss Me Goodbye; Last Waltz; Les Bicyclettes De Belsize; When There's No You; Winter World Of Love

REED, LOU — Walk On The Wild Side

REED, NANCY BINNS — Oh, Happy Day

REEVE, IVAN — Don't Blame The Children

REEVES, EDDIE — All I Ever Need Is You; Rings

REGAN, RUSS — Cinnamon Cinder

REGNEY, NOEL — Dominique; Rain, Rain Go Away

REHAK, BUD — Kiss Me, Sailor

REHBEIN, HERBERT — The World We Knew (Over And Over); Wiederseh'n

REICHNER, BICKLEY — Fable Of The Rose; Stop Beatin' 'round The Mulberry Bush

REICHNER, BIX — I Need Your Love Tonight; Mambo Rock; Papa Loves Mambo; You Better Go Now

REID, BILLY — Gypsy; I'm Walking Behind You; It's A Pity To Say Goodnight; Tree In The Meadow

REID, CLARENCE — Clean Up Woman; Girls Can't Do What The Guys Do

REID, DON — Green Years; Remember Pearl Harbor

REID, IRVING — Man Ain't Supposed To Cry

REID, KEITH — Conquistador; Whiter Shade Of Pale

REID, L. A. — Girlfriend

REID, MIKE — Stranger In My House

REINE, JOHNNY — Wedding Of Lilli Marlene

REISFELD, BERT — Call Me Darling(Call Me Sweetheart, Call Me Dear)

REISNER, C. FRANCIS — Good-bye Broadway, Hello France

RELF, KEITH — Happenings Ten Years Time Ago; Harlem Shuffle; Over Under Sideways Down; Shapes Of Things

RENARD, JEAN — Losing You

RENE JR., OTIS — I Sold My Heart To The Junk Man

RENE, HENRI — Wagon Train

RENE, LEON — I Lost My Sugar In Salt Lake City; I Sold My Heart To The Junk Man; Someone's Rocking My Dreamboat; When It's Sleepy Time Down South; When The Swallows Come Back To Capistrano

RENE, MALOU — Tossin' And Turnin'

RENE, OTIS — Someone's Rocking My Dreamboat; When It's Sleepy Time Down South

RENIS, TONY — Cynthia Weil; Quando, Quando, Quando(Tell Me When)

RENO, MIKE — Heaven In Your Eyes

RESNICK, ARTHUR — Chip Chip; Good Lovin'; Little Bit Of Heaven; One Kiss For Old Times' Sake; Quick Joey Small(Run, Joey, Run); Under The Boardwalk; Yummy Yummy Yummy

RESNICK, KRIS — Chewy, Chewy; Down At Lulu's

REVAUX, JACQUES — My Way

REVEL, HARRY — Are You With It?; Broadway's Gone Hawaii; But Definitely; Cigarettes, Cigars; College Rhythm; Danger-Love At Work; Did You Ever See A Dream Walking?; Doin' The Uptown Lowdown; Don't Let It Bother You; From The Top Of Your Head To The Tip Of Your Toes; Good Morning Glory; Good Night Lovely Little Lady; Goodnight, My Love; Head Over Heels In Love; Hear My Song, Violetta; Help Yourself To Happiness; I Feel Like A Feather In The Breeze; I Hum A Waltz; I Never Knew Heaven Could Speak; I Played Fiddle For The Czar; I Wanna Be In Winchell's Column; I Wanna Go To The Zoo; I Wish I Were Aladdin; I'd Like To Set You To Music; I'm Like A Fish Out Of Water; I've Got A Date With A Dream; If I Had A Dozen Hearts; It Takes Two To Make A Bargain; It Was A Night In June; It's Swell Of You; It's The Animal In Me; Jet; Love Thy Neighbor; Loveliness Of You; May I; May I Have The Next Romance With You; Never In A Million Years; Oh, My Goodness!; Once In A Blue Moon; One Never Knows, Does One?; Orchid To You, An; Paris In The Spring; She Reminds Me Of You; Stay As Sweet As You Are; Straight From The Shoulder(right From The Heart);

Sweet As A Song; Underneath The Harlem Moon; Wake Up And Live; Were Your Ears Burning, Baby?; When I'm With You; When There's A Breeze On Lake Louise; With My Eyes Wide Open I'm Dreaming; Without A Word Of Warning; You Can't Have Everything; You Gotta Eat Your Spinach Baby; You Hit The Spot; You're Everywhere; You're My Past, Present And Future; You're Such A Comfort To Me

REVERE, PAUL — Good Thing; Great Airplane Strike Of 1966,the; Steppin' Out; Who Takes Care Of The Caretaker's Daughter (While The Caretaker's Busy Taking Care)

REVIL, RUDI — Little Shoemaker

REW, KIMBERLY — Walking On Sunshine

REXFORD, EBEN E. — Silver Threads Among The Gold

REYAM, G. — Rivers Of Babylon

REYNOLDS, ALLEN — Five O'clock World; I Saw Linda Yesterday

REYNOLDS, DICK — If I Ever Love Again; Silver Threads And Golden Needles

REYNOLDS, ELLIS — I'm Confessin'(That I Love You)

REYNOLDS, HERBERT — Auf Wiedersehn; Half A Moon; Valentine

REYNOLDS, J. J. — Battle Of Kookamonga

REYNOLDS, JODY — Endless Sleep

REYNOLDS, MALVINA — What Have They Done To The Rain?

REYNOLDS, PAUL — I Ran

RHODES, DUSTY — Under Your Spell Again

RHODES, JACK — Silver Threads And Golden Needles

RHODES, NICK — Election Day; Notorious

RHODES, STAN — Sunday Kind Of Love

RICARDEL, JOE — Frim Fram Sauce; Wise Old Owl

RICCA, LOU — Dream, Dream, Dream; Goodbye Sue; Heavenly Hideaway

RICCI, JOE — Just Ask Your Heart

RICE, BONNY — Mustang Sally

RICE, MACK — Cheaper To Keep Her; Respect Yourself

RICE, RONALD — I Will Always Think About You

RICE, SEYMOUR — You Tell Me Your Dream Or I Had A Dream, Dear

RICE, TIM — Buenos Aires; Christmas Dream; Don't Cry For Me Argentina; Everything's Alright; I Don't Know How To Love Him; One Night In Bangkok

RICE, VERLIE — Shake A Tail Feather; Twine Time

RICH, CHARLIE — Every Time You Touch Me(I Get High); Lonely Weekends; Ways Of A Woman In Love

RICH, FREDDIE — I'm Just Wild About Animal Crackers

RICH, JAMES — Yakety Sax (Yakety Axe)

RICH, MAX — Smile, Darn Ya, Smile

RICHARD, CLIFF — Bachelor Boy; Living Doll; Living In A Box

RICHARD, KEITH — (I Can't Get No)Satisfaction; 19th Nervous Breakdown; Back Street Girl; Blue Turns To Grey; Cool, Calm And Collected; Country Honk; Dear Doctor; Factory Girl; Get Off Of My Cloud; Gimme Shelter; Goin' Home; Hang Fire; Happy; Have You Seen Your Mother, Baby, Standing In The Shadow?; Heart Of Stone; Honky Tonk Women; Hot Stuff; I'm Free; It's Not Easy; It's Only Rock 'n' Roll(But I Like It); Jig-saw Puzzle; Jumpin' Jack Flash; Lady Jane; Last Time; Let It Bleed; Let's Spend The Night Together; Live With Me; Memo From Turner; Midnight Rambler; Miss You; Mother's Little Helper; No Expectations; Out Of Time; Paint It

Black; Parachute Woman; Play With Fire; Respectable; Ruby Tuesday; Salt Of The Earth; Shattered; She's A Rainbow; She's So Cold; Sing This All Together; Singer, Not The Song; Sittin' On A Fence; Some Girls; Something Happened To Me Yesterday; Spider And The Fly; Start Me Up; Stray Cat; Street Fighting Man; Stupid Girl; Sympathy For The Devil; Under My Thumb; Yesterday's Papers; You Can't Always Get What You Want

RICHARD, RENALD — Greenbacks; I Got A Woman(I Got A Sweetie)

RICHARDS, DEKE — I Want You Back; Love Child; Love You Save; Mama's Pearl; Sugar Daddy

RICHARDS, GREG — She Cried

RICHARDS, JACK — He

RICHARDS, JOHNNY — Young At Heart

RICHARDS, KEITH — Angie; As Tears Go By; Beast Of Burden; Black Limousine; Brown Sugar; Crazy Mama; Dancing With Mr. D; Dandelion; Doo Doo Doo Doo Doo(heartbreaker); Emotional Rescue; Fool To Cry; Tumbling Dice; Undercover Of The Night; Wild Horses

RICHARDS, NICK — I Wanna Be A Cowboy

RICHARDS, REGINA — Baby Love

RICHARDSON, ARTHUR — Too Fat Polka

RICHARDSON, CLIVE — Earthbound

RICHARDSON, DAVID — Wildflower

RICHARDSON, J. P. — Chantilly Lace; Running Bear

RICHIE JR, LIONEL B. — Three Times A Lady

RICHIE, BRENDA — You Are

RICHIE, BRENDA HARVEY — Penny Lover

RICHIE, LIONEL — All Night Long(All Night); Ballerina Girl; Brick House; Dancing On The Ceiling; Easy; Endless Love; Hello; Just To Be Close To You; Lady; Love Will Conquer All; Miss Celie's Blues; Missing You; Oh No; Penny Lover; Running With The Night; Sail On; Say You, Say Me; Se La; Still; Stuck On You; Sweet Love; Truly; We Are The World; You Are

RICHMAN, BILLY HILL,DANIEL — Alone At A Table For Two

RICHMAN, HARRY — (There Ought To Be A)Moonlight Savings Time; Help Yourself To Happiness; Muddy Waters; Singing A Vagabond Song

RICHMOND, PAUL — Shining Star

RICKS, LEE — Cement Mixer(Put-ti, Put-ti); Down By The Station

RICRATH, GARY — In Your Letter

RIDDLE, NELSON — Route 66(theme); Untouchables, The (Theme From)

RIDGE, ANTONIA — Happy Wanderer

RIDGELY, ANDREW — Careless Whisper

RIEFOLI, RAFFAELE — Self Control

RILEY JR., M. — Love You Down

RILEY, MEL — Oh Sheila

RILEY, MIKE — Music Goes 'round And Around

RILEY, ROBERT S. — Just Walking In The Rain; Rollin' Stone

RILEY, T. — I Want Her

RIMBAULT, EDWARD F. — How Dry I Am

RIMSKY KORSAKOV, NIKOLAI — Flight Of The Bumble Bee; Scheherazade; Song Of India

RINGLE, DAVE — Ragging The Scale; Wabash Blues

RINKER, AL — Ready, Willing, And Able; You Started Something

RIOPELLE, JERRY — Sunshine Girl

RIORDAN, DAVID — Green Eyed Lady

RIOS, CARLOS — Dancing On The Ceiling

RIPPERTON, MINNIE — Lovin' You

RISBROOK, LOUIS — Express

RISBROOK, WILLIAM — Express

RISER, PAUL — I Don't Know Why; What Becomes Of The Broken Hearted?

RITENOUR, LEE — Is It You

RITTER, TEX — You Will Have To Pay For Your Yesterday

RIVERA, E. — Green Eyes

RIVERS, JOHNNY — Midnight Special; Poor Side Of Town

RIVES, TUBBY — Half A Heart

ROACH, JAMES MALOY — One Little Candle

ROACH, JIMMY — My Whole World Ended

ROBBINS, AYN — Gonna Fly Now(Theme From Rocky)

ROBBINS, C. A. — Washington And Lee Swing

ROBBINS, CORKY — Whispering Winds

ROBBINS, FRAN — House That Jack Built,the

ROBBINS, MARTY — Big Iron; Devil Woman; Don't Worry; El Paso; My Woman, My Woman, My Wife; White Sport Coat And A Pink Carnation; You Don't Owe Me A Thing; You Gave Me A Mountain

ROBERDS, FRED — Sunshine Girl

ROBERT, CAMILLE — Madelon

ROBERTI, ROBERTO — Aurora

ROBERTS, ALLAN — Bride And Groom Polka; Good, Good, Good; I Wish; Into Each Life Some Rain Must Fall; Invitation To The Blues; Kissin' Bug Boogie; Noodlin' Rag; Put The Blame On Mame; Rainbow Rhapsody; Tired; To Know You Is To Love You; You Always Hurt The One You Love

ROBERTS, ALLEN — Angelina(the Waitress At The Pizzeria); You Can't See The Sun When You're Cryin'

ROBERTS, BOB — King Of The Whole Wide World

ROBERTS, BRUCE — Dynamite; Main Event, The (Fight); Making Love; No More Tears(Enough Is Enough); You're Moving Out Today

ROBERTS, DON — Practice Makes Perfect

ROBERTS, JAY — Oop Bop Sh-bam

ROBERTS, LEE G. — (There Are)Smiles

ROBERTS, LUCKY — Moonlight Cocktail

ROBERTS, PADDY — Lay Down Your Arms

ROBERTS, PAUL — Driver's Seat

ROBERTS, RHODA — Put A Light In The Window

ROBERTS, RICHARD — You Are The Woman

ROBERTS, RICK — Colorado; Just Remember I Love You; Strange Way

ROBERTS, RUTH — Duke's Place; Mr. Touchdown U. S. A.

ROBERTSON, BRIAN — Silent Running

ROBERTSON, DICK — Goodnight, Wherever You Are; Little On The Lonely Side; We Three - My Echo, My Shadow And Me; Yesterday's Gardenias

ROBERTSON, DON — Anything That's Part Of You; Born To Be With You; Happy Whistler; Hummingbird; I Love You More And More Every Day; I Really Don' T Want To Know; I'm Yours; Please Help Me, I'm Falling; Ringo

ROBERTSON, JAIME ROBBIE — Night They Drove Old Dixie Down; Up On Cripple Creek; Weight

ROBEY, DON — Pledging My Love

ROBIN, LEO — (I'd Love To Spend)One Hour With You; Always In All Ways; Awake In A Dream; Beyond The Blue Horizon; Blossoms On Broadway; Blue Hawaii; Bye Bye Baby; Diamonds Are A Girl's Best Friend; Double Trouble; Faithful Forever; For Every Man There's A Woman; Funny Old Hills; Gal In Calico; Give Me A Moment Please; Give Me Liberty Or Give Me Love; Hallelujah!; Havin' Myself A Time; Here Lies Love; Here's Love In Your Eye; Hooray For Love; House That Jack Built For Jill; I Can't Escape From You; I Don't Want To Make History(I Just Want To Make Love); I Have Eyes; I Have To Have You; I'll Take An Option On You; If I Should Lose You; If I Were King; In A Little Hula Heaven; In Love In Vain; In Paris And In Love; In The Park In Paree; It Was Written In The Stars; It's A Great Life(If You Don't Weaken); It's Delightful Down In Chile; It's High Time; Joobalai; Journey To A Star; June In January; Just A Kiss Apart; Kind'a Lonesome; Little Girl From Little Rock; Little Kiss At Twilight; Lost In Loveliness; Louise; Love In Bloom; Love Is Just Around The Corner; Mamie Is Mimi; Miss Brown To You; Moonlight And Shadows; My Heart And I; My Ideal; No Love, No Nothin'; Paree!; Please; Prisoner Of Love; Rainy Night In Rio; Sailor Beware; Sometimes I'm Happy; Through A Thousand Dreams; Two Hearts Are Better Than One; Up With The Lark; Wait 'Til You See "Ma Cherie"; We Will Always Be Sweethearts; What Goes On Here In My Heart; What Have You Got That Gets Me?; What's Good About Goodbye; Whispers In The Dark; Why Dream?; With Every Breath I Take; You Started Something; You're A Sweet Little Headache; Zing A Little Zong

ROBIN, SID — Congratulations; Flying Home

ROBINSON JR., WM. "SMOKEY" — Baby That's Backatcha; Being With You; Composer; Doggone Right; Floy Joy; Love I Saw In You Was Just A Mirage; Two Lovers; Your Old Standby

ROBINSON, AVERY — Water Boy

ROBINSON, BOBBY — Warm And Tender Love (Wrap Me In Your Warm And Tender Love)

ROBINSON, EARL — Ballad For Americans; Black & White; House I Live In, The(That's America To Me)

ROBINSON, EDWARD — Hold Tight-Hold Tight(Want Some Sea Food Mama)

ROBINSON, ERIC — Dance(Disco Heat)

ROBINSON, FLOYD — Makin' Love

ROBINSON, FRANK K. — I've Found Someone Of My Own

ROBINSON, J. RUSSEL — Beale Street Mamma; Margie; Mary Lou; Original Dixieland One Step; Palesteena; Reefer Man; Singin' The Blues(Till My Daddy Come Home)

ROBINSON, JESSIE MAE — Blue Light Boogie; I Went To Your Wedding; Keep It A Secret

ROBINSON, MORGAN — Closer You Are; Ya-Ya

ROBINSON, SHARON — New Attitude

ROBINSON, SYLVIA — Love On A Two-Way Street; Pillow Talk; Sexy Mama; Shame, Shame, Shame

ROBINSON, WILLIAM — Ain't That Peculiar; Baby Come Close; Baby, Baby, Don't Cry; Cruisin'; Don't Mess With Bill; Get Ready; Going To A Go-Go; Happy(Love Theme From Lady Sings The Blues); Here I Go Again; Hunter Gets Captured By The Game; I Don't Blame You At All; I Second That Emotion; I'll Be Doggone; I'll Try Something New; If You Can Want; It's Growing; Laughing Boy; Love She Can Count On; More Love; My Baby; My Baby Must Be A Magician; My Girl; My Girl Has Gone; My Guy; One More Heartache; One Who Really Loves You; Ooh

Baby Baby; Shop Around; Special Occasion; Still Water; Way You Do The Things You Do; You're The One

ROBINSON, WILLIAM "SMOKEY"- Yester Love

ROBINSON, WM. "SMOKEY" — Tracks Of My Tears; You Beat Me To The Punch

ROBISON, CARSON — Barnacle Bill The Sailor

ROBISON, CARSON J. — Carry Me Back To The Lone Prairie

ROBISON, WILLARD — Cottage For Sale; Old Folks

ROBLEDO, JULIAN — Three O'clock In The Morning

ROCCA, JAMES LA — At The Jazz Band Ball; Clarinet Marmalade; Original Dixieland One Step

ROCHINSKI, STANLEY — Powder Your Face With Sunshine

RODA, MICHAEL — Smokin' In The Boys Room

RODDE, ROY — Have You Heard; Is It Any Wonder; Why Don't You Believe Me

RODEMICH, GENE — Shanghai Shuffle

RODGERS, BERNARD — We Are Family

RODGERS, GABY — Jackson

RODGERS, JIMMIE — In The Jailhouse Now; Mule Skinner Blues

RODGERS, MARY — Very Soft Shoes

RODGERS, NILE — Dance, Dance, Dance(yowsah, Yowsah, Yowsah); Good Times; He's The Greatest Dancer; I Want Your Love; I'm Coming Out; Le Freak; Upside Down; We Are Family

RODGERS, PAUL — All Right Now; Feel Like Makin' Love; Rock 'n Roll Fantasy

RODGERS, RICHARD — All At Once; All At Once You Love Her; All Dark People; All Dressed Up(Spic And Spanish); All Er Nothin'; All I Owe Ioway; Amarillo; Any Old Place With You; April Fool; Are You My Love?; Away From You; Babes In Arms; Baby's Awake Now; Baby's Best Friend; Bali Ha'i; Be My Host; Bewitched; Big Black Giant; Bloody Mary; Blue Moon; Blue Ocean Blues; Blue Room; Boy I Left Behind Me; Bye And Bye; Can't You Do A Friend A Favor?; Careless Rhapsody; Carousel Waltz; Circus On Parade; Climb Ev'ry Mountain; Cock-eyed Optimist; Come Home; Cuttin' The Cane; Dancing On The Ceiling; Den Of Iniquity; Diavalo; Did You Ever Get Stung?1938); Dites-Moi; Do I Hear A Waltz?; Do I Hear You Saying?; Do I Love You Because You're Beautiful; Do It The Hard Way; Do-Re-Mi; Don't Tell Your Folks; Down By The River; Eager Beaver; Edelweiss; Ev'ry Sunday Afternoon; Ev'rything I've Got; Everybody's Got A Home But Me; Falling In Love With Love; Fan Tan Fannie; Farmer And The Cowman; Fellow Needs A Girl; From Another World; Gentleman Is A Dope; Getting To Know You; Girl Friend; Give It Back To The Indians; Glad To Be Unhappy; Grant Avenue; Hallelujah, I'm A Bum; Happy Hunting Horn; Happy Talk; Have You Met Miss Jones?; Heart Is Quicker Than The Eye; Hello, Young Lovers; Here In My Arms; Here's A Hand; Honey Bun; How About It?; How Sad; How To Win Friends And Influence People; Hundred Million Miracles,a; I Cain't Say No; I Could Write A Book; I Didn't Know What Time It Was; I Do Not Know A Day I Did Not Love You; I Enjoy Being A Girl; I Feel At Home With You; I Have Dreamed; I Haven't Got A Worry In The World; I Like To Recognize The Tune; I Live For Your Love; I Married An Angel; I Must Love You; I Still Believe In You; I Want A Man; I Whistle

A Happy Tune; I Wish I Were In Love Again; I'd Rather Be Right; I'll Tell The Man In The Street; I'm Gonna Wash That Man Right Outa My Hair; I'm Your Girl; I've Got Five Dollars; If I Loved You; In My Own Little Corner; Isn't It Kinda Fun; Isn't It Romantic?; It Might As Well Be Spring; It Never Entered My Mind; It's A Grand Night For Singing; It's Easy To Remember; It's Got To Be Love; It's The Little Things In Texas; Johnny One Note; June Is Bustin' Out All Over; Jupiter Forbid; Kansas City; Keep It Gay; La La La; Lady Is A Tramp; Lady Must Live; Like Ordinary People Do; Little Birdie Told Me So; Little Girl Blue; Loads Of Love; Loch Lomond; Loneliness Of Evening; Lonely Goatherd; Look No Further; Love Makes The World Go; Love Me Tonight; Love Never Went To College; Love, Look Away; Lovely Night; Lover; Maine; Man Who Has Everything; Manhattan; Many A New Day; March Of The Siamese Children; Maria; Marriage Type Love; Mimi; Mister Snow; Money Isn't Everything; Moon Of My Delight; Most Beautiful Girl In The World; Mountain Greenery; My Favorite Things; My Funny Valentine; My Girl Back Home; My Heart Stood Still; My Man Is On The Make; My Romance; Never Say "No"(To A Man); Next Time It Happens; No Other Love; No Strings; Nobody Told Me; Nobody's Heart(Belongs To Me); Nothing But You; Oh, Diogenes!; Oh, What A Beautiful Mornin'; Oklahoma; On A Desert Island With Thee; On Your Toes; Orthodox Fool, An; Out Of My Dreams; Over And Over Again; People Will Say We're In Love; Plant You Now, Dig You Later; Poor Jud; Puzzlement; Quiet Night; Real Nice Clambake; Send For Me; Sentimental Me; Shall We Dance?; Ship Without A Sail; Shortest Day Of The Year; Simpatica; Sing; Sing For Your Supper; Sixteen Going On Seventeen; Slaughter On Tenth Avenue; So Far; Soliloquy; Some Enchanted Evening; Something Wonderful; Soon; Sound Of Music; Spring Is Here; Stonewall Moskowitz March; Sunday; Surrey With The Fringe On Top; Sweet Peter; Sweet Sixty-Five; Sweet Thursday; Sweetest Sounds; Thou Swell; To Keep My Love Alive; Too Good For The Average Man; Tree In The Park; Very Special Day; Wait Till You See Her; Way Out West; We Kiss In A Shadow; We're Gonna Be All Right; What's The Use Of Talking; What's The Use Of Wond'rin'; When I Marry Mister Snow; When The Children Are Asleep; Where Or When; Where's That Rainbow; Why Can't I; Why Do I; Why Do You Suppose; With A Song In My Heart; You Are Beautiful; You Are Never Away; You Are Sixteen; You Are Too Beautiful; You Have Cast Your Shadow On The Sea; You Mustn't Kick It Around; You Took Advantage Of Me; You'll Never Walk Alone; You've Got To Be Carefully Taught; Younger Than Springtime; Yours Sincerely; Zip

RODIN, GIL — Big Noise From Winnetka; Big Rock Candy Mountain; Boogie Woogie Maxixe

RODNEY, DON — Four Winds And The Seven Seas

RODOR, JEAN — Under The Bridges Of Paris

RODRIGUEZ, FRANK — I Need Somebody

RODRIGUEZ, MATOS — Cumparsita, La

ROE, TOMMY — Dizzy; Everybody; Heather Honey; Hooray For Hazel; It's Now Winter's Day; Jam Up And Jelly Tight; She'll Be Comin' Round The Mountain; Sheila; Sweet Pea

ROEMHELD, HEINZ — Ruby

ROGAN, JIMMY — When A Gypsy Makes His Violin Cry
ROGER, KAY — Hundred Pounds Of Clay
ROGERS, ALEX — Nobody
ROGERS, BOBBY — Way You Do The Things You Do
ROGERS, CURTIS — Back Up, Train
ROGERS, DICK — Between 18th And 19th On Chestnut Street; Pompton Turnpike
ROGERS, KENNY — Love Or Something Like It; Love Will Turn You Around
ROGERS, R. — Heart And Soul
ROGERS, ROBERT — Ain't That Peculiar; Going To A Go-Go; My Baby; One More Heartache; One Thing Leads To Another
ROGERS, ROBERT CAMERON — Rosary
ROGERS, SMOKEY — Gone
ROKUSUKE, EI — Sukiyaki
ROLFE, SAM — Ballad Of Paladin
ROLLINS, DON — Race Is On
ROLLINS, JACK — Frosty The Snow Man; Peter Cottontail
ROMA, DEL — I Will Follow Him
ROMAN, A. — Prove Your Love
ROMANS, ALAIN — Padre
ROMBERG, SIGMUND — "it"; April Snow; Auf Wiedersehn; Big Back Yard; Carrousel In The Park; Close As Pages In A Book; Dance, My Darlings; Deep In My Heart, Dear; Desert Song; Drinking Song; French Marching Song; Golden Days; I Built A Dream One Day; I Want A Kiss; In Paris And In Love; Just Once Around The Clock; Just We Two; Lost In Loveliness; Lover, Come Back To Me; Margot; Marianne; Mother; One Alone; One Kiss; Riff Song; Romance; Serenade; Softly, As In A Morning Sunrise; Song Of Love; Stouthearted Men; Wanting You; When Hearts Are Young; When I Grow Too Old To Dream; When She Walks In The Room; Will You Remember (Sweetheart); Your Land And My Land; Zing Zing -- Zoom Zoom
ROME, HAROLD — (All Of A Sudden)My Heart Sings; Along With Me; Anyone Would Love You; Be Kind To Your Parents; Chain Store Daisy; Doing The Reactionary; F. D. R. Jones; Face On The Dime; Fair Warning; Fanny; Four Little Angels Of Peace; Funny Thing Happened; Gift Today; Have I Told You Lately; I Have To Tell You; I Like You; I Say Hello; It's Better With A Union Man; Love Is A Very Light Thing; Meadowland; Military Life(The Jerk Song); Miss Marmelstein; Momma Momma!; Nobody Makes A Pass At Me; Once Knew A Fella; One Big Union For Two; Red Ball Express; Restless Heart; Sing Me A Song With Social Significance; South America, Take It Away; Sunday In The Park; Welcome Home; Wish You Were Here
ROMEO, TONY — I Think I Love You; I'm Gonna Make You Mine; Indian Lake
RONELL, ANN — (Don't Look Now, But)My Heart Is Showing; Rain On The Roof; Willow Weep For Me
RONNELL, ANN — Baby's Birthday Party
ROOT, GEORGE FREDERIC — Tramp, Tramp, Tramp (The Boys Are Marching)
ROSA, FRANCIS DE — Big Guitar
ROSA, JULIUS LA — Eh, Cumpari!
ROSA, MALIA — Forever And Ever
ROSAS, JUVENTINO — Over The Waves
ROSE, BILLY — Back In Your Own Backyard; Barney Google; Cheerful Little Earful; Clap Hands! Here Comes Charley!; Cooking Breakfast For The One I Love; Crying For Joy; Cup Of Coffee, A Sandwich And You; Does Your Chewing Gum Lose It's Flavor On The Bedpost Over Night?; Don't Bring Lulu; Evangeline; Fifty Million Frenchmen Can't Be Wrong; Follow The Swallow; Got The Jitters; Great Day!; Happy Days And Lonely Nights; Here Comes The Show Boat; House Is Haunted; I Found A Million Dollar Baby(in A Five And Ten Cent Store); I Got A "code" In My "doze"; I Wanna Be Loved; I'd Rather Be Blue Over You(Than Be Happy With Somebody Else); I've Got A Feeling I'm Falling; If I Had A Girl Like You; In The Merry Month Of Maybe; It Happened In Monterey; It's Only A Paper Moon; Me And My Shadow; More Than You Know; Night Is Young And You're So Beautiful; Suddenly; Tonight You Belong To Me; When A Woman Loves A Man; Without A Song; Would You Like To Take A Walk; You've Got To See Mamma Ev'ry Night Or You Can't See Mamma At All; Yours For A Song
ROSE, DAVID — Dance Of The Spanish Onion; Holiday For Strings; Our Waltz; Stripper
ROSE, ED — Oh Johnny, Oh Johnny Oh!
ROSE, FRED — 'deed I Do; Be Honest With Me; Blue Eyes Crying In The Rain; Crazy Heart; Flamin' Mamie; Honest And Truly; Kaw-Liga; Red Hot Mamma; Tweedle-o-Twill; We Live In Two Different Worlds; You'll Be Sorry
ROSE, HARRY — Kitty From Kansas City
ROSE, HENRY — Cooking Breakfast For The One I Love
ROSE, PETER DE — All I Need Is You; Autumn Serenade; Close To Me; Deep Purple; Have You Ever Been Lonely(Have You Ever Been Blue?); Lamp Is Low; Lilacs In The Rain; Love Ya; Manhattan Mood; Marshmallow World; Moonlight Mood; Muddy Waters; On A Little Street In Singapore; Orchids For Remembrance; Rain; Somebody Loves You; Starlit Hour
ROSE, VINCENT — Avalon; Blueberry Hill; Linger Awhile; Umbrella Man; Whispering
ROSELAND, DON — Hit And Run Affair
ROSENBERG, MARVIN — Image Of A Girl
ROSENMAN, LEONARD — East Of Eden(theme From)
ROSENSTOCK, L. — In A Little Dutch Garden(Down By The Zuider Zee)
ROSNER, GEORGE — Nightingale
ROSOFF, CHARLES — When You And I Were Seventeen
ROSS, ADAM — Sacred
ROSS, ADRIAN — Girls, Girls, Girls; Love Here Is My Heart; Maxim's; Merry Widow Waltz; Vilia; Waltz Dream
ROSS, ARTHUR — I Wanna Be Where You Are
ROSS, BERNICE — Don't Just Stand There(What's On Your Mind?); I'll Make All Your Dreams Come True; Say Something Funny; White On White
ROSS, BEVERLY — Candy Man; Dim, Dim The Lights; Judy's Turn To Cry; Lollipop
ROSS, EDWARD — Jim
ROSS, JERRY — (When You're)Racing With The Clock; Dream Merchant; Even Now; Everybody Loves A Lover; Fini; Goodbye, Old Girl; Heart; Hernando's Hideaway; Hey There; I'm Gonna Make You Love Me; I'm Not At All In Love; Man Doesn't Know,a; Near To You; New Town Is A Blue Town; Rags To Riches; Shoeless Joe From Hannibal Mo.; Small Talk; Steam

Heat; Two Lost Souls; Whatever Lola Wants

ROSS, LEWIS — Keep On Smilin'

ROSS, MARV — Find Another Fool; Harden My Heart

ROSS, MERRIA — Love Is In Control

ROSSI, FRANCIS MICHAEL — Pictures Of Matchstick Men

ROSSINGTON, GARY — Sweet Home Alabama; What's Your Name

ROSSINI, G. — Barber Of Seville, The(overture); William Tell Overture

ROSSITER, WILL — I'd Love To Live In Loveland

ROSTILL, JOHN — If You Love Me(Let Me Know); Let Me Be There; Please Mr. Please

ROTA, NINO — 8 1/2(theme From); Godfather(Love Theme)(Speak Softly Love); La Dolce Vita(The Sweet Life); La Strada(Love Theme); War And Peace

ROTH, BERNIE — Forty Days And Forty Nights

ROTH, DAVID LEE — Dance The Night Away; I'll Wait; Jump; Just Like Paradise

ROTH, I. J. — Inspiration; Secret

ROTHBERG, BOB — Mickey Mouse's Birthday Party

ROTHERMEL, JIM — Banana Republic

ROTHROCK, CLAIRE — Old Cape Cod; Old Chisholm Trail

ROUBANIS, N. — Misirlou

ROWE, JOSEPHINE V. — Macushla

ROWLAND, KEVIN — Come On Eileen

ROX, JOHN — Earth And The Sky; It's A Big Wide Wonderful World

ROYER, ROBB — For All We Know

ROYSTER, JOSEPH — (Down In)New Orleans; If You Wanna Be Happy; Quarter To Three; Twist, Twist Senora

ROZIER, DESSIE — Hot Pastrami

ROZSA, MIKLOS — Ben Hur, Love Theme From; El Cid(love Theme)(the Falcon And The Dove); King Of Kings Theme; Lygia; Spellbound

RUBENSTEIN, ANTON — Melody In F

RUBICAM, SHANNON — How Will I Know

RUBINSTEIN, ARTUR — Kamennoi Ostrow

RUBY, HARRY — Another Night Like This; Dancing The Devil Away; Do You Love Me; Ev'ryone Says "I Love You"; Give Me The Simple Life; Hooray For Captain Spaulding; I Wanna Be Loved By You; I Wish I Could Tell You; I'm A Vamp From East Broadway; Keep Romance Alive; Kiss To Build A Dream On; Maybe It's Because; My Sunny Tennessee; Nevertheless; So Long! Oh-long(How Long You Gonna Be Gone?); Three Little Words; Timbuctoo; Up In The Clouds; Watching The Clouds Roll By; What A Perfect Combination; Whatever It Is I'm Against It; Where Do They Go When They Row, Row, Row?; Who's Sorry Now

RUBY, HERMAN — Cecilia; Egg And I; I'll Always Be In Love With You; My Honey's Lovin' Arms; My Sunny Tennessee

RUDOLPH, RICHARD — Lovin' You

RUGOLO, PETE — Bring Back The Thrill; Dr. Kil-

dare(Theme from)(Three Stars Will Shine Tonight)

RUIZ, GABRIEL — Amor; Ray Gilbert

RUIZ, MARIANO — Way Of Love

RUIZ, PABLO BELTRAN — Sway(Quien Sera)

RULE, JIMMY — Goodbye Sue

RUNDGREN, TODD — Be Nice To Me; Can We Still Be Friends; Hello, It's Me; I Saw The Light; Love Is The Answer; Set Me Free; We Got To Get You A Woman

RUSH, J. — Power Of Love

RUSHING, JIMMY — Baby, Don't Tell On Me; Don't You Miss Your Baby; Goin' To Chicago Blues; Good Morning Blues; Sent For You Yesterday(And Here You Come Today)

RUSHTON, MOREVE — Magic Carpet Ride

RUSKIN, HARRY — I May Be Wrong(But I Think You're Wonderful)

RUSSELL, AL — Cabaret; It's Like Takin' Candy From A Baby

RUSSELL, ARTHUR — Aureet

RUSSELL, BERT — Cry Baby; Cry To Me; Hang On Sloopy; Twist And Shout

RUSSELL, BOB — At The Crossroads; Ballerina; Blue Gardenia; Carnival; Carnival Of Venice; Circus; Crazy, He Calls Me; Do Nothin' Till You Hear From Me; Don't Get Around Much Anymore; Eyes Of Love; For Love Of Ivy; Full Moon; Half A Photograph; He Ain't Heavy. . . He's My Brother; I Didn't Know About You; Illusion; It's Like Takin' Candy From A Baby; Matinee; Wagon Train; Would I Love You (Love You, Love You); You Came A Long Way From St. Louis

RUSSELL, BOBBY — 1432 Franklin Pike Circle Hero; Honey; Joker Went Wild; Little Green Apples; Night The Lights Went Out In Georgia; Popsicle; Sure Gonna Miss Her

RUSSELL, GRAHAM — All Out Of Love; Lost In Love; One That You Love; Sweet Dreams

RUSSELL, LARRY — Vaya Con Dios

RUSSELL, LEON — Back To The Island; Bluebird; Everybody Loves A Clown; She's Just My Style; Superstar; You Don't Have To Paint Me A Picture

RUSSELL, LUIS — Back O' Town Blues; Come Back Sweet Papa

RUSSELL, S. K. — Brazil; Frenesi; Maria Elena; Misirlou; Time Was

RUTHERFORD, M. — Tonight, Tonight, Tonight

RUTHERFORD, MIKE — All I Need Is A Miracle; Follow You, Follow Me; In Too Deep; Invisible Touch; Land Of Confusion; Silent Running; Throwing It All Away; Your Own Special Way

RYAN, BEN — (The Gang That Sang)Heart Of My Heart; Inka Dinka Doo; M-I-S-S-I-S-S-I-P-P-I; When Francis Dances With Me

RYAN, CHARLES — Hot Rod Lincoln

RYAN, PATTI — Lookin' For Love

RYERSON, FRANK — Blue Champagne

RYSKIND, MORRIE — Why Do Ya Roll Those Eyes?

SACCO, LOU — Two Faces Have I

SACCO, TONY — Breeze, The(That's Bringin' My Honey Back To Me)

SADLER, BARRY — Ballad Of The Green Berets

SAFFER, BOB — Buon Natale(Means Merry Xmas To You)

SAFKA, MELANIE — Bitter Bad; Brand New Key; Peace Will Come(According To Plan); Ring The Living Bell

SAGER, CAROLE BAYER — Arthur's Theme; Better Days; Better Than Ever; Come In From The Rain; Don't Cry Out Loud; Groovy Kind Of Love,a; Heartbreaker; I Still Believe In Love; I'd Rather Leave While I'm In Love; If You Really Knew Me; If You Remember Me; It's My Turn; Just For Tonight; Looking Through The Eyes Of Love; Love Power; Making Love; Midnight Blue; Nobody Does It Better; On My Own; When I Need You; You're Moving Out Today

SAHM, DOUGLAS — Mendocino; She's About A Mover

SAIN, OLIVER — Don't Mess Up A Good Thing

SAINT, CAMILLE — Danse Macabre; My Heart At Thy Sweet Voice; Swan

SAINTE MARIE, BUFFY — Universal Soldier; Until It's Time For You To Go; Up Where We Belong

SALLITT, NORMAN — Here I Am

SALTER, WILLIAM — Just The Two Of Us; Where Is The Love

SALVADOR, HENRI — Melodie D'amour

SAM, SENORA — I'll Be Good To You

SAMBORA, RITCHIE — Livin' On A Prayer; Wanted Dead Or Alive; You Give Love A Bad Name

SAMOHT, YENNIK — Stoned Love

SAMPSON, EDGAR — Blue Lou; Don't Be That Way; If Dreams Come True; Lullaby In Rhythm; Stompin' At The Savoy

SAMUDIO, DOMINGO — Ju Ju Hand; Wooly Bully

SAMUELS, JERRY — Shelter Of Your Arms; Shenandoah(Across The Wide Missouri)

SAMUELS, WALTER G. — I Couldn't Believe My Eyes; True

SAMUELS, ZELDA — Lookin' For A Love

SAMWELL, PAUL — Shapes Of Things

SANCHEZ, AL — Come What May

SANDERS, JULIO — I Get Ideas

SANDERS, SONNY — If You Need Me; Soulful Strut

SANDERS, WILLIAM — Love Makes A Woman

SANDERS, ZELL — Sally Go 'round The Roses

SANDERSON, DAVID R. — Poor Boy

SANDLER, GEORGE — Pa-Paya Mama

SANDRICH JR., MARK — Look For Small Pleasures

SANDS, TOMMY — Sing Boy, Sing

SANFORD, CHAS — Missing You

SANFORD, DICK — His Feet Too Big For De Bed; Mention My Name In Sheboygan; Red Silk Stockings And Green Perfume; Singing Hills

SANFORD, ED — Smoke From A Distant Fire

SANSON, VERONIQUE MARIE — Emotion

SANSONE, TONY — Walk Away, Renee

SANTANA, CARLOS — Everybody's Everything

SANTLY, LESTER — I'm Nobody's Baby

SANTOS, LARRY — Candy Girl

SAROYAN, WILLIAM — Come On-A My House

SATCHELL, CLARENCE — Fire; Love Rollercoaster

SAUER, ROBERT — When It's Springtime In The Rockies

SAUNDERS, RED — Hambone

SAUSSY, TUPPER — Morning Girl

SAUTER, EDDIE — All The Cats Join In

SAVAGE, JOHN — Photograph

SAVIGAR, KEVIN — Passion; Young Turks

SAVITT, JAN — It's A Wonderful World; Now And Forever; Quaker City Jazz; Seven Twenty In The Books

SAWYER, JEAN — Painted, Tainted Rose

SAWYER, PAM — Gotta Hold On To This Feeling; I'm Living In Shame; If I Were Your Woman; Last Time I Saw Him; Let Me Tickle Your Fancy; Let Me Try Again; Love Child; Love Hangover; My Mistake(Was To Love You); My Whole World Ended; Yesterday's Dreams; You Can't Turn Me Off

SAXON, DAVID — Free

SAYER, LEO — Dreaming; How Much Love; Long Tall Glasses(I Can Dance); Show Must Go On; You Make Me Feel Like Dancing

SCAGGS, WILLIAM "BOZ" — Breakdown Dead Ahead; Lido Shuffle; Look What You Done To Me; Lowdown; Miss Sun; We're All Alone

SCAIFE, RONNY — Men, The(Theme)

SCALA, RALPH — We Ain't Got Nothing Yet

SCALES, HARVEY — Disco Lady

SCARBOROUGH, SKIP — Love Ballad; Love Or Let Me Be Lonely

SCHAFER, BOB — Louisiana; Walk, Jenny, Walk

SCHAFER, JACK — Wondering

SCHAFER, MILTON — I'm All I've Got; She Touched Me(He Touched Me)

SCHARF, STUART — Like To Get To Know You

SCHARF, WALTER — Ben

SCHARFENBERGER, WERNER — Sailor(Your Home Is The Sea)

SCHENKER, RUDOLF — Rock You Like A Hurricane

SCHERTZINGER, VICTOR — Arthur Murray Taught Me Dancing In A Hurry; Dream Lover; Fleet's In; Flight Of The Bumble Bee; I Remember You; If You Build A Better Mousetrap; Kiss The Boys Goodbye; Love Me Forever; March Of The Grenadiers; Marcheta; My Love Parade; One Night Of Love; Sand In My Shoes

SCHIFF, ABE — Time Out For Tears

SCHIFF, STEVE — Don't You(Forget About Me)

SCHIFRIN, LALO — All For The Love Of Sunshine; Cat; Cincinnati Kid; Mission: Impossible

SCHILLER, ALLEN — Come What May

SCHLESS, PETER — On The Wings Of Love

SCHLITZ, DON — Gambler

SCHMIDT, ERWIN — Drifting And Dreaming

SCHMIDT, HARVEY — Love, Don't Turn Away; My Cup Runneth Over; Try To Remember

SCHMIT, TIMOTHY — I Can't Tell You Why

SCHOEBEL, ELMER — Bugle Call Rag; Farewell Blues; Nobody's Sweetheart; Stomp Off, Let's Go

SCHOEN, VIC — Amen(Yea-Man); For Dancers Only

SCHOFIELD, WILLIE — I Found A Love; You're So Fine

SCHOLL, JACK — My Little Buckaroo; Throw Another Log On The Fire; Thru The Courtesy Of Love

SCHOLZ, TOM — Amanda; Can'tcha Say(You Believe In Me); Capriccio Espagnol; Don't Look Back; Long Time; More Than A Feeling; We're Ready

SCHON, NEAL — Any Way You Want It; Be Good To Yourself; Don't Stop Believin'; Girl Can't Help It; I'll Be Alright Without You; Only The Young; Still They

Ride
SCHONBERGER, JOHN — Whispering
SCHRAUBSTADER, CARL — Last Night On The Back Porch, I Loved Her Best Of All
SCHROEDER, AARON — Any Way You Want Me; Because They're Young; Big Hunk 'o Love; Don't Let Her Go; First Name Initial; First Noel; Fools' Hall Of Fame; French Foreign Legion; Good Luck Charm; I Got Stung; I Was The One; I'm Gonna Knock On Your Door; It's Now Or Never; Rubber Ball; Stuck On You; Twixt Twelve And Twenty; Utopia
SCHUBERT, FRANZ — Ave Maria; Marche Militaire; Moment Musicale; Serenade
SCHULBERG, BUDD — Face In The Crowd
SCHULTZ, JIMMY — Quaker City Jazz
SCHULTZE, NORBERT — Lilli Marlene
SCHULZ, FRITZ — Man With The Banjo
SCHUMANN, ROBERT — Happy Farmer; Traumerei
SCHUMANN, WALTER — Dragnet; St. George And The Dragonet
SCHUSTER, IRA — (Shout! Wherever You May Be)I Am An American; Did You Ever Get That Feeling In The Moonlight; Hold Me
SCHUYLER, THOM — Love Will Turn You Around
SCHWANDT, WILBUR — Dream A Little Dream Of Me
SCHWARTZ, ARTHUR — Alone Together; Alone Too Long; Before I Kiss The World Goodbye; Born Again; By Myself; Confession; Dancing In The Dark; Don't Be A Woman If You Can; Dreamer; Farewell, My Lovely; For The First Time; Gal In Calico; Good-bye Jonah; Got A Bran' New Suit; Hang Up; Happy Habit; Haunted Heart; High And Low(I've Been Looking For You); Hoops; Hottentate Potentate; How Sweet You Are; I Guess I'll Have To Change My Plan(the Blue Pajama Song); I Love Louisa; I See Your Face Before Me; I Still Look At You That Way; I'll Buy You A Star; I'm Like A New Broom; I'm Ridin' For A Fall; If There Is Someone Lovelier Than You"; Look Who's Dancing; Louisiana Hayride; Love Is A Dancing Thing; Love Is The Reason; Lucky Seven; Magic Moment; Make The Man Love Me; Moment I Saw You; More Love Than Your Love; New Sun In The Sky; Rainy Day; Rainy Night In Rio; Relax-Ay-Voo; Shine On Your Shoes; Smokin' Reefers; Something To Remember You By; Through A Thousand Dreams; You And I Know; You And The Night And The Music; You Have Everything
SCHWARTZ, EDDIE — Hit Me With Your Best Shot
SCHWARTZ, JEAN — Au Revoir, Pleasant Dreams; Chinatown, My Chinatown; Rock Me Amadeus; Rock-A-Bye Your Baby With A Dixie Melody; Trust In Me
SCHWARTZ, MELVIN H. — Baby Talk
SCHWARTZ, NAT — Believe It, Belovedgeorge Whiting; Rhythm And Romance
SCHWARTZ, ROBERT — Sweet Talkin' Guy
SCHWARTZ, SHERWOOD — Ballad Of Gilligan's Isle,the
SCHWARTZ, STEPHEN — Corner Of The Sky; Day By Day
SCOLLARD, CLINTON — Sylvia
SCORE, ALI — I Ran
SCORE, MIKE — I Ran
SCOTT, ANDREW — Fox On The Run
SCOTT, BOBBY — He Ain't Heavy. . . He's My Brother; Where Are You Going

SCOTT, C. K. — Who Do You Know In Heaven (That Made You The Angel You Are?)
SCOTT, CLEMENT — Now Is The Hour(Maori Farewell Song); Oh Promise Me
SCOTT, CLIFFORD — Honky Tonk
SCOTT, CLIVE — Sky High
SCOTT, DAVID — The Whisper's Getting Louder (Whispers)
SCOTT, EMERSON — Someone's Rocking My Dreamboat
SCOTT, HOWARD — Slipping Into Darkness; Spill The Wine
SCOTT, JACK — Goodbye Baby; My True Love; What In The World's Come Over You
SCOTT, JAMES — Brass In Pocket(I'm Special)
SCOTT, JOHNNIE — I'm Sorry Dear; Maybe It's Because
SCOTT, JOSEPH W. — Ain't Nothing You Can Do
SCOTT, LADY JOHN — Annie Laurie
SCOTT, LINDA — Don't Bet Money, Honey
SCOTT, MAURICE — I've Got Rings On My Fingers(Bells On My Toes); I've Got Sixpence
SCOTT, RAYMOND — Dinner Music For A Pack Of Hungry Cannibals; Huckleberry Duck; In An Eighteenth Century Drawing Room; Powerhouse; Toy Trumpet; Twilight In Turkey
SCOTT, ROBIN — Pop Muzik
SCOTT, RONNIE — It's A Heartache
SCOTT, WINFIELD — (such An)Easy Question; Bop-Ting-A-Ling; Burn That Candle; Many Tears Ago; One Broken Heart For Sale; Return To Sender; Tweedlee Dee
SCOTT-HERON, GIL — We Almost Lost Detroit
SCOTTI, WILLIAM — My Moonlight Madonna
SCOTTO, VINCENT — It's Delightful To Be Married; Two Loves Have I; Under The Bridges Of Paris; Vieni, Vieni
SCRUGGS, EARL — Foggy Mountain Breakdown(Ballad Of Bonnie And Clyde)
SEAGO, EDWARD — Another Time, Another Place; Early In The Morning
SEALS, JAMES — Diamond Girl; Get Closer; Hummingbird; I'll Play For You; Summer Breeze; Unborn Child; We May Never Pass This Way (Again)
SEALS, TROY — I've Got A Rock And Roll Heart
SEARS, AL — Castle Rock
SEARS, EDMUND HAMILTON — It Came Upon A Midnight Clear
SEARS, JERRY — And When I Die
SEBASTIAN, JOHN — Darling Be Home Soon; Daydream; Did You Ever Have To Make Up Your Mind?; Do You Believe In Magic; Nashville Cats; Rain On The Roof(You And Me And Rain On The Roof); She Is Still A Mystery; She's A Lady; Six O'clock; Summer In The City; Welcome Back; You Didn't Have To Be So Nice; Younger Girl
SEBASTIAN, MARK — Summer In The City
SECKLER, BILL — Who's Yehoodi
SECON, PAUL — You Never Miss The Water Till The Well Runs Dry
SECUNDA, SHOLOM — Bei Mir Bist Du Schon
SEDAKA, NEIL — Alice In Wonderland; Another Sleepless Night; Bad Blood; Bad Girl; Breaking Up Is Hard To Do; Calendar Girl; Diary; Fallin'; Frankie; Happy Birthday, Sweet Sixteen; Hungry Years; I Waited Too Long; Immigrant; Laughter In The Rain; Let's Go

Steady Again; Little Devil; Lonely Night(Angel Face); Love In The Shadows; Love Will Keep Us Together; Next Door To An Angel; Oh! Carol; Puppet Man; Run Samson Run; Should've Never Let You Go; Solitaire; Stairway To Heaven; Stupid Cupid; Where The Boys Are; Workin' On A Groovy Thing; You Mean Everything To Me; You Never Done It Like That

SEEGER, PETE — Bells Of Rhymney; Gotta Travel On; Guantanamera; If I Had A Hammer; On Top Of Old Smokey; Turn! Turn! Turn!; Where Have All The Flowers Gone

SEELEN, JERRY — C'est Si Bon

SEGAL, JACK — Scarlet Ribbons(For Her Hair); When Sunny Gets Blue

SEGER, BOB — American Storm; Beautiful Loser; Even Now; Fire Lake; Heartache Tonight; Hollywood Nights; Like A Rock; Mainstreet; Night Moves; Ramblin' Gamblin' Man; Roll Me Away; Shakedown; Still The Same; We've Got Tonite

SEGURE, ROGER — Amen(Yea-Man)

SEIBERT, T. LAWRENCE — Casey Jones

SEILER, EDDIE — Ask Anyone Who Knows; Cancel The Flowers; I Don't Want To Set The World On Fire; Strictly Instrumental; Till Then; When The Lights Go On Again (All Over The World)

SEITZ, ERNEST — World Is Waiting For The Sunrise

SELF, RONNIE — Anybody But Me; Everybody Loves Me But You; I'm Sorry; Sweet Nothin's

SELSMAN, VICTOR — Do You Wanna Jump, Children?

SEMBELLO, DAVID — Neutron Dance

SEMBELLO, MICHAEL — Gravity; Maniac; Mirror, Mirror

SENDAK, MAURICE — Chicken Soup With Rice

SENECA, JOE — Break It To Me Gently

SEPE, TONY — You're The First, The Last, My Everything

SEPTEMBER, ANTHONY — Ninety-nine Ways

SERACINI, SEVERIO — Chee Che-OO Chee(Sang The Little Bird)

SERAPHINE, DANIEL — No Tell Lover

SERESS, REZSO — Gloomy Sunday

SEROTA, RICK — Three Times In Love

SERRADELL, NARCISCO — Golondrina, La

SERRATO, EDWARD — I Need Somebody

SERVICE, PAUL — Disco Nights

SETSER, EDDIE — I've Got A Rock And Roll Heart

SETTLE, MIKE — But You Know I Love You

SETZER, BRIAN — Rock This Town; She's Sexy & 17; Stray Cat Strut

SEVERINSEN, DOC — Stop And Smell The Roses

SEXTER, RUTH — Boy Without A Girl

SEXTON, JOHN — Auf Wiedersehn, Sweetheart

SEYMOUR, TOT — Cross Patch; I'm Making Hay In The Moonlight; Swingin' In A Hammock

SHABALALA, JOSEPH — Homeless

SHADDICK, TERRY — Physical

SHAFFNER, CATHERINE — I Don't Want To Do Wrong; I Heard A Rumour

SHAFTEL, ARTHUR — Atlanta, G. A.; Just A Little Bit South Of North Carolina

SHAKESPEARE, JOHN — Can't You Hear My Heart Beat?; Little Bit O' Soul; Sunday For Tea

SHAND, TERRY — Chicken Song; Cry, Baby, Cry; Dance With A Dolly(with A Hole In Her Stocking); I Double Dare You; I'm Gonna Lock My Heart(and Throw Away The Key); If You're Ever Down In Texas(Look Me Up)

SHANK, JOE — Unsuspecting Heart

SHANKLIN, WAYNE — Big Hurt; Jezebel; Little Boy And The Old Man; Primrose Lane

SHANNON, DEL — Hats Off To Larry; I Go To Pieces; Keep Searchin'; Little Town Flirt; Runaway; Stranger In Town

SHANNON, JAMES R. — Missouri Waltz; Too-Ra-Loo-Ra-Loo-Ral (That's An Irish Lullaby)

SHANNON, RONNIE — Baby, I Love You; I Can't See Myself Leaving You; I Never Loved A Man(The Way I Love You)

SHANNON, TOM — Wild Weekend

SHAPER, HAL — Softly, As I Leave You

SHAPIRO, BRAD — Don't Knock My Love

SHAPIRO, D. — Let's Live For Today

SHAPIRO, DAN — I Wanna Get Married

SHAPIRO, ELLIOTT — Sierra Sue

SHAPIRO, J. — Treasure Of Love

SHAPIRO, JOE — Round And Round

SHAPIRO, MIKE — Spooky

SHAPIRO, MR. AND MRS. TED — Ask Anyone In Love

SHAPIRO, TED — Handful Of Stars; If I Had You; Winter Weather

SHARP, MARTHA — Born A Woman; Come Back When You Grow Up; Single Girl

SHARP, TODD — Got A Hold On Me

SHARRON, MARTI — Jump(For My Love)

SHAW, ARTIE — Back Bay Shuffle; Concerto For Clarinet; Love Of My Life; Nightmare; Non-stop Flight; Summit Ridge Drive; Traffic Jam

SHAW, DAVID T. — Columbia, The Gem Of The Ocean

SHAW, SYDNEY — Heavenly

SHAW, TOMMY — Blue Collar Man; Renegade; Too Much Time On My Hands

SHAWN, NELSON — Jim

SHAY, LARRY — Everywhere You Go; Get Out And Get Under The Moon; When You're Smiling (The Whole World Smiles With You)

SHAYNE, GLORIA — Almost There; Goodbye Cruel World; Men In My Little Girl's Life; Rain, Rain Go Away

SHEAFE, M. W. — Washington And Lee Swing

SHEAN, AL — Mister Gallagher And Mister Shean

SHEAR, JULES — All Through The Night

SHEARING, GEORGE — Man From Minton's

SHEEHY, ELEANORE — Beat Me Daddy, Eight To The Bar

SHEELEY, SHARON — Breakaway; Dum Dum; Heart In Hand; Poor Little Fool

SHEFTER, BERT — Lamp Is Low

SHELBY, WILLIAM — And The Beat Goes On

SHELDON, ERNIE — Baby, The Rain Must Fall; Sons Of Katie Elder

SHELDON, JOHN — Ride

SHELDON, JON — Fabulous; Limbo Rock; Slow Twistin'

SHELLEY, GLADYS — Experience Unnecessary; Pavanne

SHELTON, JAMES — Lamplight

SHELTON, MARIA — Black Lace

SHEPPARD, BILL — Get On Up

SHEPPARD, DREY — I Made It Through The Rain

SHEPPARD, JAMES — Daddy's Home

SHEPPARD, SHAPE — Honky Tonk; Hysteria

SHER, JACK — Kathy-O

SHERIDAN, LEE — Save Your Kisses For Me

SHERIN, UKIE — Don't Forget Tonight, Tomorrow

SHERMAN, AL — Comes A-Long A-Love; Every Now And Then; Livin' In The Sunlight-Lovin' In The Moonlight; Mood That I'm In; No! No! A Thousand Times No!; Now's The Time To Fall In Love(Potatoes Are Cheaper-Tomatoes Are Cheaper); On The Beach At Bali-Bali; Over Somebody Else's Shoulder; What Do We Do On A Dew Dew Dewy Day; When I'm The President (We Want Cantor); You Gotta Be A Football Hero (To Get Along With The Beautiful Girls)

SHERMAN, ALLEN — Hello Muddah, Hello Fadduh

SHERMAN, BOB — Pineapple Princess

SHERMAN, DICK — Pineapple Princess

SHERMAN, JIMMY — Lover Man(Oh, Where Can You Be?)

SHERMAN, JOE — Anything Can Happen-Mambo; Eso Beso(That Kiss); Graduation Day; Juke Box Baby; Por Favor; Ramblin' Rose

SHERMAN, NOEL — Beats There A Heart So True; Eso Beso(That Kiss); Graduation Day; Juke Box Baby; Morgen(One More Sunrise); Por Favor; Ramblin' Rose

SHERMAN, RICHARD — Chim Chim Cher-ee; Chitty Chitty Bang Bang; Feed The Birds(Tuppence A Bag); Hushabye Mountain; I Love To Laugh; Jolly Holiday; Let's Go Fly A Kite; Life I Lead; Sister Suffragette; Spoonful Of Sugar; Stay Awake; Step In Time; Supercalifragilisticexpialidocious; You're Sixteen

SHERMAN, ROBERT — Chim Chim Cher-ee; Chitty Chitty Bang Bang; Feed The Birds(Tuppence A Bag); Hushabye Mountain; I Love To Laugh; Jolly Holiday; Let's Go Fly A Kite; Life I Lead; Life In A Northern Town; Sister Suffragette; Spoonful Of Sugar; Stay Awake; Step In Time; Supercalifragilisticexpialidocious; You're Sixteen

SHERRILL, BILLY — Almost Persuaded; Every Time You Touch Me(I Get High); I Love My Friend; Kiss Away; Lady Bird; Most Beautiful Girl; My Elusive Dreams; Southtown, U. S. A.; Stand By Your Man; Sugar Lips; Sweet And Innocent; Very Special Love Song

SHERWIN, MANNING — Nightingale Sang In Berkeley Square,a

SHERWOOD, LEW — My Twilight Dream

SHIDER, GARY — One Nation Under A Groove

SHIELDS, HARVEY — Way I Feel Tonight

SHIELDS, LARRY — Barnyard Blues; Clarinet Marmalade

SHIELDS, REN — In The Good Old Summertime; Steamboat Bill; Waltz Me Around Again Willie

SHILKRET, NATHANIEL — Down The River Of Golden Dreams; First Time I Saw You; Jeannine, I Dream Of Lilac Time; Lonesome Road

SHILLING, PETER — Major Tom(Coming Home)

SHIPLEY, E. — Heaven Is A Place On Earth

SHIRE, DAVID — Autumn; It Goes Like It Goes; Washington Square; With You I'm Born Again

SHIRL, JIMMY — Beloved, Be Faithful; Castle Rock; Come To The Mardi Gras; Delilah; I Believe; Meet Mister Callaghan; Sonata

SHOCK, HARRIET — Ain't No Way To Treat A Lady

SHOCKLEY, STEPHEN — And The Beat Goes On

SHORROCK, GLENN — Cool Change; Help Is On Its Way; Man On Your Mind

SHREEVE, M. — Touch Me (I Want Your Body)

SHULL, CHESTER R. — (It's No)Sin

SHUMAN, ALDEN — Banjo's Back In Town; Seven Lonely Days

SHUMAN, EARL — (Hey There)Lonely Boy; Another Cup Of Coffee; Banjo's Back In Town; Barabbas; Caterina; Clinging Vine; Close To Cathy; Confidence; Disorderly Orderly; Dondi; Fan The Flame; Hello, I Love You, Goodbye; Hey There Lonely Boy; Hotel Happiness; I've Been Here!; Left Right Out Of Your Heart; Most People Get Married; Seven Lonely Days; Walkin' With Peninnah

SHUMAN, FRANK — Penguin At The Waldorf

SHUMAN, MORT — Amsterdam; Can't Get Used To Losing You; Go, Jimmy, Go; His Latest Flame(Marie's The Name); Hound Dog Man; Hushabye; I'm A Man; If We Only Have Love; If You Only Have Love; Kiss Me Quick; Little Children; Little Sister; Mess O' Blues; No One; Save The Last Dance For Me; Seven Day Weekend; Surrender; Suspicion; Sweets For My Sweet; Turn Me Loose; What's It Gonna Be?

SHURY, GERALD — Up In A Puff Of Smoke

SIBELIUS, JEAN — Finlandia

SIDERS, IRVING — Slow Walk

SIDMOS, JOHN — Do You Feel Like We Do

SIEGEL, ARTHUR — Love Is A Simple Thing; Miracle Worker, The(Theme)(Hush, Little Baby)

SIEGEL, JAY — I Hear Trumpets Blow; I Heard A Rumour

SIEGEL, PAUL — Autumn Concerto

SIEVIER, BRUCE — Speak To Me Of Love(Parlez-Moi D'amour)

SIGLER, JACK — Love(Can Make You Happy)

SIGLER, MAURICE — I Saw Stars; I Want To Ring Bells; I'm In A Dancing Mood; Little Man, You've Had A Busy Day

SIGMAN, CARL — 11th Hour Melody; All Too Soon; Answer Me, My Love; Arrivederci, Roma; Ballerina; Band Of Angels; Believe In Me; Big Brass Band From Brazil; Blossoms On The Bough; Careless Hands; Crazy, He Calls Me; Day The Rains Came; Don't Ever Be Afraid To Go Home; Dream Along With Me; Ebb Tide; Enjoy Yourself(It's Later Than You Think); Funny Thing; Hop Scotch Polka; If You Could See Me Now; It's All In The Game; Losing You; Love Lies; Love Story(Theme)(Where Do I Begin); Marshmallow World; Matinee; Mountains Beyond The Moon; My Heart Cries For You; Passe; Pennsylvania 6-5000; Shangri-La; Summertime In Venice; The World We Knew (Over And Over); Till; Twenty-Four Hours Of Sunshine; What Now My Love; You're My World

SIGNORELLI, FRANK — Blues Serenade; I'll Never Be The Same; Stairway To The Stars

SILESU, LAO — Love Here Is My Heart

SILHOUETTES, THE — Get A Job

SILVER, ABNER — Bebe; Chasing Shadows; Don't Let Her Go; Every Now And Then; Farewell To Arms; I'm Goin' South; Mood That I'm In; No! No! A Thousand Times No!; On The Beach At Bali-Bali; With These Hands

SILVER, FRANK — Yes! We Have No Bananas

SILVERMAN, CHARLES — Look Through Any Window

SILVERS, DOLORES VICKI — Learnin' The Blues

SILVERS, LOUIS — April Showers; Weary River

SILVERS, PHIL — Nancy(With The Laughing Face)

SILVERSTEIN, DAVE — Bend Down Sister

SILVERSTEIN, SHEL — Boa Constrictor; Boy Named Sue; Cover Of Rolling Stone; Free As A Bird; I Got Stoned And I Missed It; Sylvia's Mother; Unicorn
SILVESTRE, PAUL — Berceuse
SIMEONE, HARRY — Little Drummer Boy
SIMMONS, CHARLES — Love Don't Love Nobody; Mighty Love
SIMMONS, GENE — Calling Dr. Love; Christine Sixteen; Rock And Roll All Night
SIMMONS, LONNIE — Don't Stop The Music; Early In The Morning
SIMMONS, PAT — Black Water; Dependin' On You
SIMMS, ALICE D. — Encore, Cherie
SIMMS, EARL — Funky Street
SIMON, CARLY — Anticipation; Attitude Dancing; Coming Around Again; Haven't Got Time For The Pain; Right Thing To Do; You're So Vain
SIMON, D. — I Need Love
SIMON, JOE — Cleopatra Jones; Get Down, Get Down(Get On The Floor); Power Of Love; Your Time To Cry
SIMON, NAT — Bamboo; Cocoanut Song; Crosstown; Gaucho Serenade; Goody Goodbye; Istanbul, Not Constantinople; Little Curly Hair In A High Chair; Little Lady Make Believe; Mama Doll Song,the; No Can Do; Old Lamp-Lighter; Poinciana; Wait For Me Baby; Wait For Me, Mary
SIMON, PAUL — 59th Street Bridge Song, The(Feelin' Groovy); Allergies; America; American Tune; At The Zoo; Big, Bright Green Pleasure Machine; Bleecker Street; Boxer; Boy In The Bubble; Bridge Over Troubled Water; Cecilia; Dangling Conversation; Fakin' It; Fifty Ways To Leave Your Lover; For Emily, Whenever I May Find Her; Gone At Last; Graceland; Hazy Shade Of Winter; He Was My Brother; Hey, Schoolgirl; Homeless; Homeward Bound; I Am A Rock; I Do It For Your Love; Kodachrome; Late In The Evening; Leaves That Are Green; Loves Me Like A Rock; Me And Julio Down By The School Yard; Mother And Child Reunion; Mrs. Robinson; My Little Town; One Trick Pony; Peace Like A River; Red River Valley; Red Rubber Ball; Scarborough Fair-Canticle; Slip Slidin Away; Sounds Of Silence
SIMON, SCOTT — Sandy
SIMONE, NINA — Backlash Blues
SIMONON, PAUL — Rock The Casbah
SIMONS, MOISES — Marta; Peanut Vendor
SIMONS, NEV — Cornbelt Symphony
SIMONS, PETER — United We Stand
SIMONS, SEYMOUR — All Of Me; Breezin' Along With The Breeze; Honey; Why Worry?
SIMPKINS, LEWIS C. — Night Train
SIMPSON, FITZROY — Pass The Dutchie
SIMPSON, VALERIE — Ain't No Mountain High Enough; Ain't Nothing Like The Real Thing; Boss; California Soul; Count Your Blessings; Good Lovin' Ain't Easy To Come By; I Don't Need No Doctor; I'm Every Woman; Let's Go Get Stoned; Reach Out And Touch(Somebody's Hand); Remember Me; Solid; Some Things You Never Get Used To; Stuff Like That; What You Gave Me; Who's Gonna Take The Blame; You're All I Need To Get By; Your Precious Love
SINATRA, FRANK — I'm A Fool To Want You
SINCLAIR, JOHN L. — Eyes Of Texas
SINGER, A. — At The Hop
SINGER, BOB — Unsuspecting Heart

SINGER, GUY — Whither Thou Goest
SINGER, LOU — Gypsy Without A Song; Lost In Meditation; One Meat Ball; Sleepy Serenade; Young And Warm And Wonderful
SINGLETON, CHARLES — Don't Forbid Me; For A Penny; If I May; Just As Much As Ever; Mambo Baby; Spanish Eyes; Strangers In The Night; Wheel Of Hurt
SINGLETON, MARGIE — Dum-De-Da; Lie To Me
SINGLETON, SHELBY — Am I That Easy To Forget
SINGLETON, STEPHEN — Look Of Love
SIRAS, JOHN — In A Shanty In Old Shanty Town
SISSLE, NOBLE — Baltimore Buzz; Bandana Days; Gypsy Blues; I'm Craving For That Kind Of Love; I'm Just Wild About Harry; Shuffle Along; You Were Meant For Me
SIVIER, BRUCE — You're Blase
SKARDINA, GARY — Jump(For My Love)
SKINNER, ALBERT — Away All Boats
SKINNER, FRANK — Away All Boats; Back Street
SKINNER, G. — Honeythief The
SKINNER, TERRY — Even The Nights Are Better
SKLEROV, GLORIA — I Just Fall In Love Again
SKYLAR, SUNNY — Amor; And So To Sleep Again; Ask Me; Atlanta, G. A.; Besame Mucho; Don't Wait Too Long; Fifteen Minute Intermission; Gotta Be This Or That; Hair Of Gold, Eyes Of Blue; It Must Be Jelly('Cause Jam Don't Shake Like That); Just A Little Bit South Of North Carolina; Pussy Cat; Ruby-Du-Du; Waitin' For The Train To Come In; You'll Always Be The One I Love; You're Breaking My Heart
SLACK, FREDDIE — House Of Blue Lights
SLATE, JOHNNY — Better Love Next Time
SLAY JR., FRANK C. — La Dee Dah; Lucky Ladybug; Silhouettes
SLICK, DARBY — Somebody To Love
SLICK, GRACE — White Rabbit
SLOAN, LLOYD — Did Anyone Ever Tell You Mrs. Murphy
SLOAN, PHIL F. — Eve Of Destruction; I Found A Girl; Let Me Be; Must To Avoid; Secret Agent Man; You, Baby (Nobody But You)
SLOANE, A. BALDWIN — Heaven Will Protect The Working Girl
SLOANE, EVERETT — Fishin' Hole
SMALL, ALLAN — Wedding Samba, The (Also Known As The Wedding Rhumba)
SMALL, CHARLIE — Home
SMALL, DANNY — Without Love
SMALLS, CHARLIE — Ease On Down The Road
SMETENA, BEDRICH — Bartered Bride, The(overture); Moldau, Die; Molly Malone
SMITH, "STUFF" — I'se A-Muggin'
SMITH, AL — Big Boss Man
SMITH, ALFRED — Gimme Little Sign
SMITH, ARTHUR — Beautiful Brown Eyes; Dueling Banjos; Guitar Boogie
SMITH, BEASLEY — Beg Your Pardon; Old Master Painter
SMITH, BEN — I Dreamt I Dwelt In Harlem
SMITH, BESSIE — Baby Doll; Back Water Blues; Jail House Blues; Weeping Woman Blues
SMITH, BILLY DAWN — Angel Smile; Love Has Joined Us Together; Step By Step; Trouble In Paradise
SMITH, BOB — Shimmy, Shimmy, Ko-Ko-Bop
SMITH, BOBBY — Tippin' In
SMITH, CARL — (Your Love Keeps Lifting Me)Higher

And Higher; Who's Cheating Who?; Your Love Keeps Lifting Me Higher And Higher

SMITH, CARL WILLIAM — Rescue Me

SMITH, CHARLES — Cherish; Emergency; Fresh; Get Down On It; Joanna; Misled

SMITH, CHRIS — Ballin' The Jack; Cake Walking Babies From Home; Constantly

SMITH, CLARENCE "PINE TOP" — Boogie Woogie

SMITH, CLAYDES — Celebration; Hollywood Swinging; Ladies Night

SMITH, CLAYTON — Jungle Boogie

SMITH, DICK — Breeze, The(That's Bringin' My Honey Back To Me); When A Gypsy Makes His Violin Cry

SMITH, DON — Double Shot(of My Baby's Love)

SMITH, E. B. — Oh Babe, What Would You Say

SMITH, EDGAR — Heaven Will Protect The Working Girl

SMITH, ERNESTINE — Stranded In The Jungle

SMITH, ETHEL — Love Is Strange

SMITH, FRED — Duck; Peanut Butter; Western Movies

SMITH, HARRY — Bright Eyes; Gypsy Love Song; I Wonder If You Still Care For Me; Romany Life

SMITH, HARRY B. — Dancing Fool; Fortune Teller; Play Gypsies-Dance Gypsies; Sheik Of Araby; Why Don't They Dance The Polka Anymore; Woman Is Only A Woman, But A Good Cigar Is A Smoke; Yours Is My Heart Alone

SMITH, J. T. — I Need Love

SMITH, JACK — Gimme A Little Kiss, Will Ya Huh?

SMITH, JAMES — Battle Hymn Of Lieutenant Calley; Slippin' And Slidin'

SMITH, JERRY DEAN — (Down At)Papa Joe's

SMITH, JESSE — I Do

SMITH, JOHN STAFFORD — Star Spangled Banner

SMITH, JOHNNY — Walk - Don't Run

SMITH, LAURA — Little Sir Echo

SMITH, MIKE — Bits And Pieces; Can't You See That She's Mine?; Come Home; Glad All Over; Please Tell Me Why; Try Too Hard

SMITH, MYRA — Reconsider Me

SMITH, NEAL — Eighteen

SMITH, PATTI — Because The Night

SMITH, PAUL SAMWELL — Over Under Sideways Down

SMITH, REV. GUY — Great Speckled Bird

SMITH, RICHARD B. — Winter Wonderland

SMITH, ROBERT B. — Sweethearts

SMITH, TAB — Harvard Blues

SMITH, VICTOR — With Your Love

SMITH, WHISPERING — Mean Woman Blues

SMITH, WILLIAM — When I Die

SMITH, WILLIAM H. — Stuff Is Here, The(and It's Mellow)

SMYTH, CHARLES — Our House

SNEED, EDWARD — Bald Headed Lena

SNOW, TOM — All The Right Moves; Deeper Than The Night; He's So Shy; If Ever You're In My Arms Again; Let's Hear It For The Boy; Make A Move On Me; Somewhere Down The Road; You

SNYDER, EDDIE — Games That Lovers Play; Girl With The Golden Braids; Girlfriend; Spanish Eyes; Strangers In The Night; What Will My Mary Say; Wheel Of Hurt

SNYDER, TED — Dancing Fool; I Wonder If You Still Care For Me; It Was Only A Sun Shower; Next To Your Mother, Who Do You Love?; Oh, That Beautiful Rag; Sheik Of Araby; Who's Sorry Now

SOBOLEWSKI, MICHAEL — Dance The Night Away

SOBOTKA, JOE — Let Love Come Between Us

SOLOWAY, SY — Lips Of Wine

SONDHEIM, STEPHEN — All I Need Is The Girl; America; Another Hundred People; Anyone Can Whistle; Barcelona; Beautiful; Being Alive; Children And Art; Chrysanthemum Tea; Comedy Tonight; Cool; Do I Hear A Waltz?; Everybody Ought To Have A Maid; Everybody Says Don't; Everything's Coming Up Roses; Finishing The Hat; Franklin Shepard, Inc.; Gee, Officer Krupke; Girls Of Summer; Good Thing Going(Going Gone); Hills Of Tomorrow; I Feel Pretty; I've Got You To Lean On; It Would Have Been Wonderful; Johanna; John Henry; Ladies Who Lunch; Let Me Entertain You; Liaisons; Little Lamb; Love, I Hear; Lovely; Maria; Move On; Night Waltz; Not A Day Goes By; Not While I'm Around; One Hand, One Heart; Our Time; Parade In Town; Pretty Women; Putting It Together; Road You Didn't Take; Rose's Turn; See What It Gets You; Send In The Clowns; Side By Side By Side; Small World; Some People; Something's Coming; Somewhere; Together Wherever We Go; Tonight; Too Many Mornings; Waiting For The Girls Upstairs; We're Gonna Be All Right; Weekend In The Country; What Would We Do Without You; Worst Pies In London; You Could Drive A Person Crazy; You Gotta Have A Gimmick; You Must Meet My Wife; You'll Never Get Away From Me

SONG, BASED ON A SICILIAN — Home Sweet Home

SOSENKO, ANNA — Darling. Je Vous Aime Beaucoup; I'll Be Yours(J'attendrai)

SOTHERN, HAL — I Dreamed Of A Hillbilly Heaven

SOUR, ROBERT — Body And Soul; I See A Million People(But All I Can See Is You); Walkin' By The River; We Could Make Such Beautiful Music (Together)

SOURIRE, SOEUR — Dominique

SOUSA, JOHN PHILIP — Capitan, El; Gladiator March; Hands Across The Sea; High School Cadets; King Cotton; Liberty Bell; Semper Fidelis; Stars And Stripes Forever; Thunderer; Washington Post March

SOUTH, JOE — (I Never Promised You A)Rose Garden; Don't It Make You Want To Go Home; Down In The Boondocks; Games People Play; I Knew You When; Walk A Mile In My Shoes; Yo-Yo

SOUTHER, JOHN D. — Her Town Too

SOUTHER, JOHN DAVID — Best Of My Love; Heartache Tonight; New Kid In Town; You're Only Lonely

SOWDER, KENNY — Lonely Street

SPAIN, IRENE — Death Of Floyd Collins

SPARBARO, TONY — Barnyard Blues; Clarinet Marmalade

SPARKS, RANDY — Green Green; Today

SPEAKS, OLEY — On The Road To Mandalay; Sylvia

SPEAR, ERIC — Meet Mister Callaghan

SPECTOR, ABNER — Smoky Places

SPECTOR, LONA — Sally Go 'round The Roses

SPECTOR, PHIL — Be My Baby; Black Pearl; Chapel Of Love; Da-Doo Ron Ron; I Can Hear Music; Just Once In My Life; River Deep-Mountain High; Second Hand Love; Spanish Harlem; To Know Him Is To Love Him; Walking In The Rain; Why Do Lovers Break Each Other's Hearts?; You've Lost That Lovin' Feelin'

SPENCE, LEW — Nice 'n' Easy

SPENCER, C. MORDAUNT — Rose Of Tralee
SPENCER, HERB — Fishin' Hole
SPENCER, JUDY — Soft Summer Breeze
SPENCER, OTIS — Broadway Rose
SPENCER, RICHARD — Color Him Father
SPENCER, TIM — Careless Kisses; Room Full Of Roses
SPICKARD, BOB — Pipeline
SPIELMAN, FRED — Go To Sleep, Go To Sleep, Go To Sleep; It Only Hurts For A Little While; Longest Walk; Paper Roses; Shepherd Serenade
SPIER, LARRY — Put Your Little Foot Right Out; Was It A Dream
SPIKES, BENJAMIN — Wolverine Blues
SPIKES, JOHN — Wolverine Blues
SPILMAN, JAMES E. — Flow Gently, Sweet Afton
SPILTON, ALAN — Lover Come Back
SPINA, HAROLD — Annie Doesn't Live Here Anymore; Be Mine; Beat Of My Heart; Half Moon On The Hudson; I Could Use A Dream; I Love To Walk In The Rain; I Still Love To Kiss You Goodnight; It's Dark On Observatory Hill; It's So Nice To Have A Man Around The House.; Lazy Summer Night; My Very Good Friend, The Milkman; The Velvet Glove; Would I Love You (Love You, Love You)
SPINKS, JOHN — All The Love In The World; Your Love
SPIRT, JOHN — Martian Hop
SPITALNY, MAURICE — Start The Day Right
SPIVEY, WILLIAM — Operator
SPOLAN, GLORIA A. — Hypnotized; Hysteria
SPOLIANSKY, MISCHA — Hour Of Parting
SPOTTI, PINO — I Want To Be Wanted
SPOTTSWOOD, WILLIE — Hold Tight-Hold Tight(Want Some Sea Food Mama)
SPRIGATO, SYLVESTER — It Isn't Fair
SPRINGER, GEORGE E. — Lies
SPRINGER, PHIL — How Little We Know(How Little It Matters How Little We Know); Moonlight Gambler; Santa Baby
SPRINGER, TONY — Santa Baby
SPRINGFIELD, RICK — Bruce; Human Touch; I've Done Everything For You; Jessie's Girl; Love Is Alrite Tonite; Love Somebody; Souls; State Of The Heart
SPRINGFIELD, TOM — Georgy Girl; I'll Never Find Another You; World Of Our Own
SPRINGSTEEN, BRUCE — 4th Of July, Asbury Park(Sandy); Backstreets; Badlands; Because The Night; Blinded By The Light; Born In The U.S.A.; Born To Run; Brilliant Disguise; Cover Me; Dancing In The Dark; Darkness On The Edge Of Town; Fade Away; Fire; For You; Glory Days; Growin' Up; Hearts Of Stone; Hungry Heart; I'm Goin' Down; I'm On Fire; Independence Day; Jungleland; Lost In The Flood; My Father's House; My Hometown; One Step Up; Out Of Work; Pink Cadillac; Prove It All Night; Rosalita(Come Out Tonight); Spirit In The Night; Tunnel Of Love; Wild Billy's Circus Story
SPRINGTHORPE, RICHARD — Speak To The Sky
SQUIER, BILLY — Rock Me Tonite; Stroke
SQUIRE, CHRIS — Owner Of A Lonely Heart
ST. JOHN, DICK — Yellow Balloon
ST. LEWIS, KENNY — Whodunit
STAFFORD JR., JOSEPH — My Pledge Of Love
STAFFORD, JIM — My Girl Bill; Spiders And Snakes; Wildwood Weed; Your Bulldog Drinks Champagne
STAHL, FELIX — Many Times

STALLINGS, LAURENCE — You And I Know
STALLMAN, LOU — Everybody's Got The Right To Love; I've Come Of Age; It's Gonna Take A Miracle; Round And Round; Treasure Of Love; Yogi
STALLONE, FRANK — Far From Over
STAMFORD, JOHN J. — Macnamara's Band
STAMPER, DAVE — Throw Me A Kiss
STANDLEY, JOHNNY — It's In The Book
STANGE, STANISLAUS — My Hero
STANLEY, EDDIE Y. — Botch-A-Me
STANLEY, HAL — Half A Photograph
STANLEY, IAN — Everybody Wants To Rule The World; Shout
STANLEY, PAUL — Detroit Rock City; Hard Luck Woman; I Was Made For Loving You
STANLEY, RAY — Glendora
STANTON, ARNOLD — Roving Kind
STANTON, FRANK — Just A Wearyin' For You; Mighty Lak' A Rose
STANTON, FRANK H. — Face It Girl, It's Over
STANZIALE, PEGGY — Dress You Up
STAPP, JACK — Chattanoogie Shoe Shine Boy
STARKEY, RICHARD — Back Off Boogaloo
STARKS, JOHN — Payback
STARLING, J. — Catch Me(I'm Falling)
STARR, EDWIN — Twenty-Five Miles
STARR, RANDY — Enchanted Sea; Kissin' Cousins
STARR, RINGO — Don't Pass Me By; Flying; It Don't Come Easy; Octopus's Garden; Photograph
STEAD, ARTHUR — Goonies 'r' Good Enough
STEAGALL, RUSSELL DON — Here We Go Again
STEALS, MELVIN — Could It Be I'm Falling In Love
STEEDEN, PETER VAN — Home(When Shadows Fall)
STEELE, LARRY — If I'd Been The One
STEELE, LOIS — Ivory Tower; Wanted
STEELE, PORTER — High Society
STEFFE, WILLIAM — Battle Hymn Of The Republic
STEGALL, KEITH — Sexy Eyes
STEIGER, JIMMY — Looking At The World Thru Rose Colored Glasses
STEIN, CHRIS — Dreaming; Fade Away And Radiate; Heart Of Glass; Rapture
STEIN, MURRAY — Baby(You've Got What It Takes)
STEIN, WILLIAM — Wave To Me, My Lady
STEIN, WILLIE — Orange Colored Sky
STEINBERG, B. — Alone; How Do I Make You; Like A Virgin; So Emotional
STEINBERG, LEWIE — Green Onions
STEINBERG, SAM — Joseph! Joseph!
STEINER, HOWARD — Don't Be A Baby, Baby
STEINER, JACQUELINE — M. T. A
STEINER, MAX — Allison's Theme From Parrish; Angel; As Long As I Live; Band Of Angels; Come Next Spring; Honey-Babe; It Can't Be Wrong; Lucy's Theme; My Own True Love; Summer Place, A(Theme From)
STEININGER, FRANZ — Marching Along Together
STEINMAN, JIM — Making Love Out Of Nothing At All; Read' Em And Weep; Total Eclipse Of The Heart; Two Out Of Three Ain't Bad; You Took The Words Right Out Of My Mouth
STEPHENS, EVEN — Someone Could Lose A Heart Tonight
STEPHENS, GEOFF — Daddy Don't You Walk So Fast; Daughter Of Darkness; Doctor's Orders; Smile A Little Smile For Me; Winchester Cathedral

STEPHENS, RICHARD — Wheels

STEPHENSON, WILLIE — I Do

STEPT, SAM H. — All My Life; Breakin' In A Pair Of Shoes; Comes Love; Congratulations; Don't Sit Under The Apple Tree(With Anyone Else But Me); I Came Here To Talk For Joe; I Fall In Love With You Ev'ry Day; I'll Always Be In Love With You; It Seems Like Old Times; Please Don't Talk About Me When I'm Gone; Tiny Little Fingerprints; When They Ask About You

STERLING, ANDREW B. — Meet Me In St. Louis, Louis; Under The Yum Yum Tree; Wait 'Til The Sun Shines Nellie; When My Baby Smiles At Me

STERN, HAROLD — I'm All Dressed Up With A Broken Heart

STERN, JACK — I Was Lucky; Rhythm Of The Rain

STERN, TONI — It's Going To Take Some Time; It's Too Late; Sweet Seasons

STERNBERG, L. — Walk Like An Egyptian

STEVENS, CAT — First Cut Is The Deepest; Here Comes My Baby; Moon Shadow; Morning Has Broken; Oh Very Young; Peace Train; Ready; Sitting; Wild World

STEVENS, EVAN — I Love A Rainy Night; Love Will Turn You Around; Step By Step; Suspicions; When You're In Love With A Beautiful Woman

STEVENS, HUNT — Lasting Love

STEVENS, JAY — Rocky

STEVENS, LEONARD — I Faw Down And Go Boom!

STEVENS, MORT — Hawaii Five-O

STEVENS, RAY — Can't Stop Dancin; Everything Is Beautiful; Gitarzan; Mr. Businessman; Streak

STEVENS, STEVE — Eyes Without A Face

STEVENSON, B. W. — My Maria

STEVENSON, BOBBY — For My Good Fortune; Hey, Little Girl; So Many Ways; Start Movin'

STEVENSON, W. S. — Am I That Easy To Forget; Hot Rod Lincoln; I'm Tired; Lonely Street

STEVENSON, WILLIAM — Ask The Lonely; Beechwood 4-5789; Dancing In The Street; Devil With A Blue Dress On; It Takes Two; Jamie; My Baby Loves Me; Nothing's Too Good For My Baby; Pride And Joy; You've Been In Love Too Long

STEWART, AL — Come Closer To Me(Acerate Mas); I'll Never Love Again; Song On The Radio; Time Passages; Year Of The Cat

STEWART, BILLY — I Do Love You; Sitting In The Park

STEWART, DAVID — Don't Come Around Here No More; Here Comes The Rain Again; Love Is A Stranger; Missionary Man; Sisters Are Doin' It For Themselves; Sweet Dreams(Are Made Of This); Would I Lie To You?

STEWART, DOROTHY — Now Is The Hour(Maori Farewell Song)

STEWART, ERIC — I'm Not In Love

STEWART, JOHN — Daydream Believer; Gold

STEWART, MICHAEL — Colors Of My Life,the; Love Makes Such Fools Of Us All

STEWART, REDD — Slow Poke

STEWART, REX — Boy Meets Horn

STEWART, ROD — Ain't Love A Bitch; Baby Jane; Do(Da)You Think I'm Sexy; Hot Legs; I Was Only Joking; Infatuation; Killing Of Georgie; Maggie May; Passion; Stay With Me; Tonight's The Night (It's Gonna Be Alright); You Belong To Me; You Wear It Well; You're In My Heart; Young Turks

STEWART, SANDY — If Anyone Falls

STEWART, SLAM — Flat Foot Floogie

STEWART, STEVEN — Smoke From A Distant Fire

STEWART, SYLVESTER — C'mon And Swim; Dance To The Music; Everybody Is A Star; Everyday People; Family Affair; Hot Fun In The Summertime; I Want To Take You Higher; If You Want Me To Stay; M'lady; Runnin' Away; Stand

STEWART, W. — Shake Your Rump To The Funk

STILLMAN, AL — (There's No Place Like)Home For The Holidays; Bless'em All; Breeze And I; Can You Find It In Your Heart; Chances Are; Cockeyed Mayor Of Kaunakakai; Don'cha Go 'way Mad; Don't You Forget It; Enchanted Island; Every Step Of The Way; Good-bye Jonah; Great Escape March; Happy Anniversary; I Believe; I Want My Mama(Mama Yo Quiero); If Dreams Come True; It's Not For Me To Say; Juke Box Saturday Night; Moments To Remember; My One And Only Heart; No Not Much; Now And Forever; One-Two-Three-Kick; Room With A View; Say Si Si; Way Of Love; Who Needs You; You Alone (Sole Tu); You And I Know

STILLS, STEPHEN — For What It's Worth; Suite: Judy Blue Eyes; Wooden Ships

STILLS, STEVE — Southern Cross

STING — We'll Be Together; Wrapped Around Your Finger

STITCHER, LIONEL — Night Chicago Died

STITES, GARY — Lonely For You

STITZEL, MEL — Doodle Doo Doo

STOCK, LARRY — Blueberry Hill; Did You Ever Get That Feeling In The Moonlight; Morningside Of The Mountain; Umbrella Man; You Won't Be Satisfied (Until You Break My Heart); You're Nobody 'til Somebody Loves You

STODDARD, HARRY — I Get The Blues When It Rains

STOKES, BRYAN — Sweetheart Of Sigma Chi

STOKES, MICHAEL — Gloria

STOKEY, PAUL — I Dig Rock And Roll Music

STOLE, J. W. — I Will Follow Him

STOLLER, MIKE — Along Came Jones; Baby I Don't Care; Bernie's Tune; Black Denim Trousers And Motorcycle Boots; Bossa Nova Baby; Charlie Brown; D.W. Washburn; Dance With Me; Don't; Drip Drop; Hound Dog; I Keep Forgettin'(Every Time You're Near); I Who Have Nothing; I'm A Woman; Is That All There Is?; Jailhouse Rock; Kansas City; Love Me; Love Potion Number Nine; Loving You; Lucky Lips; Marie's The Name, His Latest Flame; On Broadway; Only In America; Poison Ivy; Ruby Baby; Searchin'; She's Not You; Stand By Me; Treat Me Nice; Yakety Yak; Young Blood

STOLZ, ROBERT — Dawn; Two Hearts In Three Quarter Time; Waltzing In The Clouds

STONE, BOB — Beyond The Valley Of The Dolls

STONE, GREGORY — Let's Dance

STONE, HELEN — Mexicali Rose; Mexican Hat Dance(Jarabe Tapatio)

STONE, HENRY — Chattanoogie Shoe Shine Boy; Two Hearts

STONE, JESSE — Cole Slaw; Don't Let Go; Good Lovin'; Idaho; Money Honey; Sorghum Switch

STONE, JOSEPH — I Just Don't Know

STONE, ROBERT — Gypsies, Tramps, And Thieves

STONE, WILSON — War And Peace

STONER, MICKEY — I Guess I'll Have To Dream The

Rest; It's Make Believe Ballroom Time
STORBALL, DONALD — Cool Jerk
STORCH, EBERHARD — Auf Wiedersehn, Sweetheart
STORDAHL, AXEL — Day By Day; I Should Care; Neiani
STORIE, CARL — Dancin' Shoes
STOTHART, HERBERT — At The Balalaika; Bambalina; Charming; Cossack Love Song; Cuban Love Song; Dark Night; Dawn; Donkey Serenade,the; Far Away; How Strange; I Wanna Be Loved By You; Rogue Song; Song Of The Flame; Vodka; When I'm Looking At You; Wildflower
STOTT, HAROLD — Chirpy Chirpy Cheep Cheep
STOVALL, MARY — First Date, First Kiss, First Love
STOVER, ELGIE — Bells
STOVER, G. H. — On The Beach At Waikiki
STRACHEY, JACK — No Orchids For My Lady
STRAIGIS, ROY — So Much In Love
STRALS, ARNOLD — Lord's Prayer
STRANGE, BILLY — Clean Up Your Own Back Yard; Limbo Rock; Memories
STRANKS, ALAN — No Orchids For My Lady
STRAUSS, ARTHUR — St. Theresa Of The Roses
STRAUSS, JOHANN — Artists Life; Blue Danube Waltz; Du Und Du(You And You Waltz); Vienna Life; Voices Of Spring; Wine, Women And Song
STRAUSS, OSCAR — Make A Wish; My Hero; Waltz Dream; We Will Always Be Sweethearts
STRAUSS, RICHARD — Till Eulenspiegel
STRAVINSKY, IGOR — Firebird Ballet Suite; Rites Of Spring
STRAYHORN, BILLY — Chelsea Bridge; Day-Dream; Grievin'; I'm Checking Out Goombye; Just A-Sittin' And A-Rockin'; Little Brown Book; Lush Life; Paris Blues; Satin Doll; Something To Live For
STREET, RICHARD — I'm On Fire
STREISAND, BARBRA — Evergreen
STRIKE, LIZA — Summer Nights
STROLL, JON — Sweet Cream Ladies, Forward March
STRONG, BARRETT — Ball Of Confusion; Cloud Nine; Don't Let The Joneses Get You Down; End Of Our Road; Friendship Train; Gonna Give Her All The Love I've Got; I Can't Get Next To You; I Could Never Love Another(After Loving You); I Heard It Through The Grapevine; I Wish It Would Rain; Jamie; Just My Imagination(Running Away With Me); Papa Was A Rollin' Stone; Please Return Your Love To Me; Psychedelic Shack; Stay In My Corner; Superstar Remember How You Got Where You Are; Too Busy Thinking About My Baby; War
STROTHER, CYNTHIA — Bermuda
STROTHER, EUGENE R. — Bermuda
STROUSE, CHARLES — Baby, Talk To Me; Born Too Late; Bye Bye Birdie; Can't You See It?; Central Park Ballad; Colorful; Don't Forget 127th Street; Easy Street; English Teacher, An; Everything's Great; Gimme Some; Golden Boy; Have A Dream; Honestly Sincere; How Lovely To Be A Woman; How'm I Doin'; Hymn For A Sunday Evening; I Don't Need Anything But You; I Want To Be With You; I'm Fascinating; I've Just Seen Her; If I Were You; Kids; Lorna's Here; Lot Of Livin' To Do; March Of The Yuppies; Mating Game; Maybe; N. Y. C.; Night Song; No More; Normal American Boy; Once Upon A Time; One Boy; One Last Kiss; Our Children; Put On A Happy Face; Rosie; Spanish Rose; Stick Around;

Those Were The Days Or Theme From All In The Family; Tomorrow
STROZIER, GORDON — Oh Sheila
STRUMMER, JOE — Rock The Casbah
STRUNK, JUD — Daisy A Day
STRUZICK, EDWARD — Falling; Sharing The Night Together
STRYKER, FRED — Broken Down Merry-go-round
STRYKERT, ROY — Down Under
STUART, ALLAN — La Rosita; Rosita, La
STUART, DAVID — Summer Song,a
STUART, JACK — So Tired
STUTZ, CARL — Danger! Heartbreak Ahead; Little Things Mean A Lot
STYNE, JULE — All I Need Is The Girl; All You Need Is A Quarter; And Then You Kissed Me; Anywhere; As Long As There's Music; Asking For You; Barrelhouse Bessie From Basin Street; Be A Santa; Bells Are Ringing; Bop! Goes My Heart; Brooklyn Bridge; Bye Bye Baby; Can't You Just See Yourself; Can't You Read Between The Lines?; Charm Of You; Close Harmony; Conchita, Marquita, Lolita, Pepita, Rosita, Juanita Lopez; Cornet Man; Cry Like The Wind; Dance Only With Me; Diamonds Are A Girl's Best Friend; Distant Melody; Don't Rain On My Parade; Ev'ry Day I Love You(Just A Little Bit More); Ev'ry Street's A Boulevard In Old New York; Everything's Coming Up Roses; Fade Out-Fade In; Find Yourself A Man; Fireworks; Five Minutes More; Five Zeros; Funny Girl; Get Away For A Day(In The Country); Girls Like Me; Give Me A Song With A Beautiful Melody; Guess I'll Hang My Tears Out To Dry; Hold Me-Hold Me-Hold Me; How Can You Describe A Face?; How Do You Speak To An Angel?; I Begged Her; I Believe; I Don't Want To Walk Without You; I Fall In Love Too Easily; I Feel Like I'm Gonna Live Forever; I Gotta Gal I Love(in North And South Dakota); I Know About Love; I Said No; I Still Get Jealous; I'll Walk Alone; I'm In Love; I'm Just Taking My Time; I'm The Greatest Star; I'm With You; I've Heard That Song Before; I've Never Forgotten; I, Yes Me, That's Who; Independent(On My Own); It's A Great Feeling; It's Been A Long, Long Time; It's Delighful Down In Chile; It's High Time; It's Magic; It's The Same Old Dream; It's You Or No One; Just A Kiss Apart; Just In Time; Let It Snow! Let It Snow! Let It Snow!; Let Me Entertain You; Let's Always Love; Little Girl From Little Rock; Little Lamb; Long Before I Knew You; Looking Back; Love Me; Make Someone Happy; Mamie Is Mimi; Money Burns A Hole In My Pocket; Music That Makes Me Dance; Never-Never Land; Papa, Won't You Dance With Me; Party's Over; People; Poor Little Rhode Island; Put It In A Box(Tie 'em With A Ribbon And Throw 'em In The Deep Blue Sea); Ride Through The Night; Rose's Turn; Sadie, Sadie; Saturday Night(Is The Loneliest Night In The Week); Say, Darling; Small World; Some People; Songs Gotta Come From The Heart; Stay With The Happy People; Sunday; Swing Low Sweet Rhythm; Three Coins In The Fountain; Time After Time; Together Wherever We Go; Vict'ry Polka; Wendy; What Is This Feeling In The Air?; What Makes The Sunset; When The One You Love (Simply Won't Come Back); You Are Woman (I Am Man); You'll Never Get Away From Me; You're My Girl; Zuyder Zee

SUDANO, BRUCE — Bad Girls; Ball Of Fire; Closest Thing To Perfect

SUDDOTH, J. GUY — Booze And Blues

SUESSDORF, KARL — Did Anyone Ever Tell You Mrs. Murphy; Moonlight In Vermont

SUESSE, DANA — Ho Hum; My Silent Love; Night Is Young And You're So Beautiful; Whistling In The Dark; You Oughta Be In Pictures; Yours For A Song

SULLAVAN, JERI — Rum And Coca Cola

SULLIVAN, ARTHUR — He Is An Englishman; I'm Called Little Buttercup; Tit-Willow; When I Was A Lad

SULLIVAN, FRANK — American Heartbeat; Burning Heart; Caught Up In You; Eye Of The Tiger; High On You; I Can't Hold Back; Is This Love

SULLIVAN, HENRY — I May Be Wrong(But I Think You're Wonderful)

SULLIVAN, JOE — Gin Mill Blues; Little Rock Getaway

SULLIVAN, LARRY — Cinco Robles

SULLIVAN, RAYMOND O' — Get Down

SULLIVAN, SIR ARTHUR — Lost Chord; Onward Christian Soldiers

SULTON, KASIM — Set Me Free

SUMMER, DONNA — Bad Girls; Dim All The Lights; Heaven Knows; I Feel Love; Love To Love You Baby; On The Radio; She Works Hard For The Money; Wanderer

SUMMERS, AMIEL — Big John(ain't You Gonna Marry Me?)

SUMNER(STING), GORDON — De Do Do Do, De Da Da Da; Don't Stand So Close To Me; Every Breath You Take; Every Little Thing She Does Is Magic; Fortress Around Your Heart; If You Love Somebody Set Them Free; King Of Pain; Love Is The Seventh Wave; Money For Nothing; Russians; Spirits In The Material World

SUNSHINE, MARION — Peanut Vendor

SUPPE, FRANZ VON — Light Cavalry(Overture); Poet And Peasant Overture

SURGAL, ALAN — Chiu, Chiu

SUSSMAN, BRUCE — Copacabana; I Made It Through The Rain

SUTTON, CHARLES — See-Saw

SUTTON, GLENN — Almost Persuaded; Kiss Away

SUTTON, HARRY O. — I Don't Care

SWAIN, ROYCE — (I Love You) Twice As Much

SWAIN, TONY — Cruel Summer

SWAN, BILL — Lover, Please

SWAN, BILLY — I Can Help

SWAN, E. A. — When Your Lover Has Gone

SWAN, EINAR — Room With A View

SWANDER, DON — Deep In The Heart Of Texas

SWANSTROM, ARTHUR — Blues My Naughty Sweetie Gives To Me; Come Up And See Me Sometime; Cross Your Fingers; Why (Is There A Rainbow In The Sky)

SWAYZE, ED — Jitter Bug

SWAYZE, P. — She's Like The Wind

SWEAT, K. — I Want Her

SWEENEY, CHUCK — Young Ideas

SWEET, SAM — Midnight Hour

SWERN, PHILIP — Up In A Puff Of Smoke

SWIFT, KAY — Can This Be Love; Can't We Be Friends?; Fine And Dandy

SWIRSKY, S. — Prove Your Love

SYKES, JOHN — Is This Love

SYLVA, B. G. DE — (There's Something About An)Old Fashioned Girl; Alabamy Bound; April Showers; As Long As I've Got My Mammy; Best Things In Life Are Free; Birth Of The Blues; Black Bottom; Born And Bred In Old Kentucky; Broadway; Button Up Your Overcoat!; California, Here I Come; Come To Me; Cross Your Heart; Do It Again; Don't Hold Everything; Don't Send Your Wife To The Country; Don't Tell Her What's Happened To Me; Down South; Eady Was A Lady; For Old Times' Sake; Gentlemen Prefer Blondes 1926); Girl Is You And The Boy Is Me; Give Me My Mammy; Good For You, Bad For Me; Good News; He's A Ladies Man; Hello Tucky; Here Am I-Broken Hearted; I Found A Four Leaf Clover; I Want A Lovable Baby; I Want To Be Bad; I Won't Say I Will But I Won't Say I Won't; I'll Build A Stairway To Paradise; I'm A Dreamer, Aren't We All; I'm On The Crest Of A Wave; If I Had A Talking Picture Of You; If You Knew Susie Like I Knew Susie; It All Depends On You; Just A Cottage Small By A Waterfall; Just A Memory; Just Imagine; Keep Smiling At Trouble; Kiss In The Dark; Life Of A Rose; Little Pal; Look For The Silver Lining; Lucky Day; Lucky In Love; My Lucky Star; My Sin; Nobody But You; Oh How I Long To Belong To You; Pickin' Cotton; Rise 'n Shine; Rose Of Madrid; Should I Be Sweet?; So Do I; Somebody Loves Me; Someone Who Believes In You; Sonny Boy; Sunny Side Up; Together

SYLVERS, LEON — And The Beat Goes On

SYLVIA, MARGO — Happy, Happy Birthday Baby

SYMES, MARTY — (There Is)No Greater Love; (When It's)Darkness On The Delta; By The River Of The Roses; How Many Hearts Have You Broken; I Have But One Heart; I've Got An Invitation To A Dance; It's The Talk Of The Town; Tippin' In; Under A Blanket Of Blue

TAGG, ERIC — Is It You
TALLARICO, STEVE — Dream On
TARNEY, ALAN — Dreaming; Little In Love; We Don't Talk Anymore
TARPLIN, MARVIN — Ain't That Peculiar; Baby Come Close; Cruisin'; Doggone Right; Dominoes; Going To A Go-Go; I'll Be Doggone; Love I Saw In You Was Just A Mirage; My Girl Has Gone; One More Heartache; Tracks Of My Tears
TAUB, JULES — Bad Luck; Woke Up This Morning
TAUBER, DORIS — Fooled
TAUPIN, BERNIE — Bennie And The Jets; Bitch Is Back; Border Song; Candle In The Wind; Crocodile Rock; Daniel; Don't Go Breaking My Heart; Don't Let The Sun Go Down On Me; Empty Garden(Hey Hey Johnny); Friends; Goodbye Yellow Brick Road; Grow Some Funk Of Your Own; Honky Cat; How You Gonna See Me Now; I Feel Like A Bullet(In The Gun Of Robert Ford); I Guess That's Why They Call It The Blues; I'm Still Standing; Island Girl; Kiss The Bride; Let Me Be Your Car; Levon; Nikita; Philadelphia Freedom; Rocket Man; Saturday Night's Alright(For Fighting); Someone Saved My Life Tonight; We Built This City; Your Song
TAYLOR, ANDY — Some Like It Hot
TAYLOR, BELOYD — Getaway
TAYLOR, CARMEN — Little Mama; Seven Days
TAYLOR, CHIP — Angel Of The Morning; Country Girl-City Man; I Can Make It With You; I Can't Let Go; Make Me Belong To You; Step Out Of Your Mind; Wild Thing
TAYLOR, CHUCK — Burning Of Atlanta
TAYLOR, DANNY — Good Lovin'
TAYLOR, DERON — I Wanna Testify
TAYLOR, IRVING — Caramba! It's The Samba!; Everybody Loves Somebody; Kookie, Kookie, Lend Me Your Comb; Lily Belle; So Dear To My Heart; Three Little Sisters
TAYLOR, J. — Victory
TAYLOR, JACK — Band Of Gold; Earthbound
TAYLOR, JAMES — Big Fun; Celebration; Cherish; Country Road; Don't Let Me Be Lonely Tonight; Emergency; Fire And Rain; Fresh; Get Down On It; Her Town Too; Joanna; Ladies Night; Misled; Shower The People; Steamroller Blues; Sweet Baby James; Your Smiling Face
TAYLOR, JOHN — Boy From New York City; Notorious; Since I Don't Have You; Some Like It Hot
TAYLOR, JOHNNY — Get On Up
TAYLOR, MICHAEL — Rocky Mountain High; Sunshine On My Shoulders
TAYLOR, R. DEAN — All I Need; I'm Living In Shame; Indiana Wants Me; Love Child
TAYLOR, ROBERT — Maybe I'm A Fool; Sha-La-La
TAYLOR, ROGER — Election Day
TAYLOR, RUDOLPH — Early In The Morning
TAYLOR, TELL — Down By The Old Mill Stream; Down By The Riverside
TCHAIKOVSKY, PETER I. — 1812 Overture; Marche Slav; None But The Lonely Heart; Nutcracker Suite; Romeo And Juliet(Overture); Song Without Words; Waltz Of The Flowers
TEBELAK, JOHN MICHAEL — Day By Day
TEEGARDEN, D. — God, Love And Rock 'n' Roll(We Believe)
TEETOR, MACY O. — Lost
TELLEZ, PABLO — Suavecito
TEMPCHIN, JACK — One You Love; Peaceful Easy Feeling; Sexy Girl; Slow Dancing(Swayin' To The Music); Smuggler's Blues
TEMPERTON, ROD — Always And Forever; Baby, Come To Me; Boogie Nights; Give Me The Night; Groove Line; Love Is In Control; Man Size Love; Miss Celie's Blues; Off The Wall; Rock With You; Stomp; Sweet Freedom; Thriller
TEMPEST, J. — Carrie; Final Countdown,the
TEMPLETON, ALEC — Bach Goes To Town
TENCH, BEN — Sunset Grill
TENILLE, TONI — Way I Want To Touch You
TENNANT, NICK — It's A Sin; Opportunities(Let's Make Lots Of Money); West End Girls; What Have I Done To Deserve This
TENNEY, JACK B. — Mexicali Rose
TENNILLE, TONI — Do That To Me One More Time
TENNYSON, ALFRED — Sweet And Low
TEPPER, SID — All That I Am; If I Had A Girl; Kewpie Doll; My Bonnie Lassie; Naughty Lady Of Shady Lane; Nuttin' For Christmas; Puppet On A String; Red Roses For A Blue Lady; Suzy Snowflake; When The Boy In Your Arms
TERRELL, WILBUR — Slip Away
TERRISS, DOROTHY — Three O'clock In The Morning; Wonderful One (My)
TERRY, DEWEY — I'm Leaving It Up To You; Jolly Green Giant
TERRY, GEORGE — Lay Down Sally
TESCHEMACHER, EDWARD — Because
TETTEROO, PETER — Ma Belle Amie
TEX, JOE — Baby, You're Right; Hold What You've Got; I Gotcha; I Want To(Do Everything For You); Men Are Gettin' Scarce; Skinny Legs And All; Sweet Woman Like You; You Better Get It; You Said A Bad Word
THALER, RUDOLF — Ciribiribin
THARP, WINSTON C. — Out Of Space
THARPE, SISTER ROSETTA — Up Above My Head, I Hear Music In The Air
THEARD, SAM — You Can't Get That No More; You Rascal You (I'll Be Glad When You're Dead)
THEODORAKIS, MIKIS — Beyond Tomorrow
THEODORAKIS, MIKOS — Zorba The Greek (Theme From)
THIELE, BOB — Duke's Place
THIELEMANS, JEAN — Bluesette
THIELHELM, EMIL — We Ain't Got Nothing Yet
THOMAS, ARTHUR — Signs
THOMAS, CARLA — Gee Whiz!(Look At His Eyes)
THOMAS, CLIFTON — Pickin' Wild Mountain Berries
THOMAS, DAVID CLAYTON — Go Down Gamblin'; Go Down Moses; Spinning Wheel
THOMAS, DICK — Sioux City Sue
THOMAS, EDWARD — Pickin' Wild Mountain Berries
THOMAS, F. — Shake Your Rump To The Funk
THOMAS, GENE — Playboy
THOMAS, GERALD — Troglodyte (Cave Man)
THOMAS, HARRY — Hold 'em Joe; Matilda, Matilda
THOMAS, IAN — Runner
THOMAS, JESSIE — Iko-iko
THOMAS, JIMMIE — Rockin' Robin
THOMAS, JOE — Melancholy Me
THOMAS, JOHN — Heartbreak(It's Hurting Me)

THOMAS, MICHAEL — Hawaii Tattoo

THOMAS, RONALD — Girl Of My Dreams

THOMAS, RUFUS — Walking The Dog

THOMAS, TIMMY — Why Can't We Live Together

THOMPSON, BONNIE — Turn Back The Hands Of Time

THOMPSON, DENNY — Tijuana Jail

THOMPSON, HARLAN — Ending With A Kiss; I Love You

THOMPSON, JANE BROWN — I Get Along Without You Very Well

THOMPSON, KAY — Promise Me Love

THOMPSON, MARCUS — Rumors

THOMPSON, RICHARD — Express

THOMPSON, SIR CHALRES — Robbins Nest

THOMPSON, SONNY — Hide Away-1962

THOMPSON, WAYNE CARSON — Always On My Mind; Do It Again-A Little Bit Slower; Letter; Neon Rainbow; No Love At All; Soul Deep

THOMSON, ALI — Really Wanna Know You

THORN, GEORGE — Sweet And Gentle

THORNHILL, CLAUDE — Snowfall

THORNTON, WILLIE MAE — Ball And Chain

THORSEN, ART — It's In The Book

THROCKMORTON, SONNY — I Wish I Was Eighteen Again

TIBBLES, GEORGE — Something Old, Something New; Woody Woodpecker; Worry, Worry, Worry

TIERNEY, HARRY — Alice Blue Gown; Following The Sun Around; If You're In Love, You'll Waltz; Irene; Kinkajou; M-I-S-S-I-S-S-I-P-P-I; Rangers Song; Rio Rita

TIGER, GLASS — Someday

TILLIS, MEL — Detroit City; Emotions; I Ain't Never; Ruby, Don't Take Your Love To Town

TILLISON, ROGER CARROLL — You Don't Have To Paint Me A Picture

TILLMAN, FLOYD — I Love You So Much It Hurts; Slipping Around

TILLOTSON, JOHNNY — It Keeps Right On A-hurtin' Since I Left

TILSLEY, HENRY — I Never See Maggie Alone; Lady Of Spain; Unless

TILZER, ALBERT VON — I Used To Love You But It's All Over Now; I'll Be With You In Apple Blossom Time; Oh By Jingo, Oh By Gee, You're The Only Girl For Me; Put Your Arms Around Me Honey

TILZER, HARRY VON — And The Green Grass Grew All Around; Bird In A Gilded Cage; In The Sweet Bye And Bye

TIMAS, RICK — Cool It Now

TINTURIN, PETER — What Will I Tell My Heart

TIOMKIN, DIMITRI — Ballad Of The Alamo; Duel In The Sun(A Duel Of Two Hearts); Friendly Persuasion(Thee I Love); Giant(This Then Is Texas); Green Leaves Of Summer; Guns Of Navarone; Hajji Baba; High And The Mighty; High Noon(Do Not Forsake Me); Land Of The Pharaohs; Old Man And The Sea; Rawhide; Return To Paradise; Rio Bravo; Sundowners,theme From; Town Without Pity; Unforgiven, The (The Need For Love); Wild Is The Wind

TIPTON, BILL — Knock, Knock. Who's There?

TIZOL, JUAN — Caravan; Gypsy Without A Song; Lost In Meditation; Perdido

TOBANI, THEODORE MOSES — Hearts And Flowers

TOBIAS, CHARLES — All Over The World; As Long As I Live; Broken Record; Cocoanut Song; Comes Love; For The First Time(I've Fallen In Love); Good Night Little Girl Of My Dreams; I Came Here To Talk For Joe; I Remember Mama; It Seems Like Old Times; Kathy-O; Little Curly Hair In A High Chair; Little Lady Make Believe; Love Ya; Mama Doll Song,the; May I Sing To You; Mickey Mouse's Birthday Party; No Can Do; Old Lamp-Lighter; Old Macdonald Had A Farm; Rose O'Day(The Filla-Ga-Dusha Song); Somebody Loves You; Start The Day Right; Throw Another Log On The Fire; Tiny Little Fingerprints; Trade Winds; Two Tickets To Georgia; Wait For Me, Mary; Wake Up And Sing; What Do We Do On A Dew Dew Dewy Day; When Your Hair Has Turned To Silver I Will Love You Just The; Zing Zing -- Zoom Zoom

TOBIAS, CHARLES AND HARRY — Miss You

TOBIAS, CHARLIE — Don't Sit Under The Apple Tree(With Anyone Else But Me); Don't Sweetheart Me; Flowers For Madame; Gee! But You're Swell; Get Out And Get Under The Moon; Time Waits For No One; Wait For Me Baby; We Did It Before (and We Can Do It Again)

TOBIAS, FRED — Born Too Late; Good Timin'; Litty Bitty Girl; One Of Us(Will Weep Tonight)

TOBIAS, HARRY — At Your Command; I'm Sorry Dear; It's A Lonesome Old Town When You're Not Around; No Regrets; Sail Along Silv'ry Moon; Sweet And Lovely; Wait For Me Baby; Wait For Me, Mary

TOBIAS, HENRY — I Remember Mama; Miss You

TOBIN, GEORGE — Cinnamin

TODARO, PHIL — Wild Weekend

TODD, CLARENCE — Oooh! Look-a-There, Ain't She Pretty?

TOLHURST, KERRYN — Man On Your Mind

TOLLERTON, NEIL — Cruising Down The River

TOMES, JIMMY — Wheels

TOMLIN, PINKY — Love Bug Will Bite You, The(If You Don't Watch Out); Object Of My Affection; What's The Reason (I'm Not Pleasin' You)

TOMPSON, ROBERT — Open Letter To My Teenage Son, An

TOMSCO, BARBARA — Say I Am(What I Am)

TOMSCO, GEORGE — Say I Am(What I Am)

TONGEREN, J. VAN — It's Not Over('Til It's Over)

TOOMBS, RUDY — Gum Drop; One Mint Julep

TOP, Z. Z. — Rough Boy

TORME, MEL — Born To Be Blue; Christmas Song, The(Chestnuts Roasting On An Open Fire)

TOROK, MITCHELL — Caribbean

TORRE, JANICE — Paper Roses

TOSELLI, ENRICO — Serenade

TOUSSAINT, ALLAN — Holy Cow; I Like It Like That; Java; Mother-in-Law; Southern Nights; Working In The Coal Mine; Yes We Can Can

TOUZET, RENE — Let Me Love You Tonight(No Te Importe Saber)

TOWBER, CHAIM — I Love You Much Too Much

TOWERS, LEO — Little Old Mill, The(Went Round And Round)

TOWNE, BILLY — Never On Sunday

TOWNSEND, D. — Happy

TOWNSEND, ED — For Your Love; Love Of My Man

TOWNSEND, JOHN — Smoke From A Distant Fire

TOWNSEND, PETER — Who Are You

TOWNSHEND, EDWARD — Finally Got Myself Together(I'm A Changed Man); Let's Get It On

TOWNSHEND, PETER — Bargain; Behind Blue Eyes; Blue, Red And Gray; Champagne; Go To The Mirror, Boy; Happy Jack; I Can See For Miles; It's A Boy(Overture From Tommy); Join Together; Let My Love Open The Door; Magic Bus; Pinball Wizard; Squeeze Box

TOZZ, GIANCARLO BIGAZZI-UMBERT — Gloria

TRACE, AL — Brush Those Tears From Your Eyes

TRACE, BEN — You Call Everybody Darling

TRACEY, WILLIAM — Is My Baby Blue Tonight

TRADER, BILL — Fool Such As I

TRADITIONAL — Auld Lang Syne; Comin' Thro' The Rye

TRAMMEL, BARBARA — Don't Let The Stars Get In Your Eyes; Don't Make Me Wait For Love

TRAPANI, TULIO — Cara Mia

TRAVERS, H. — Honeythief The

TRAVIS, MERLE — Sixteen Tons; Smoke! Smoke! Smoke!(That Cigarette)

TREADWELL, GEORGE — Dance With Me

TRENET, CHARLES — At Last! At Last!; Beyond The Sea; I Wish You Love

TRENT, JACKIE — Color My World; Don't Sleep In The Subway; I Couldn't Live Without Your Love; Other Man's Grass Is Always Greener; Who Am I?

TRENT, JO — Blind Man's Buff; Georgia Bo Bo; Gotta Feelin' For You; Jig Walk; Jim Dandy; Muddy Waters

TRIMACHI, BOBBI — 1,2,3, Red Light

TRIMACHI, SAL — 1,2,3, Red Light

TRIPP, PAUL — Tubby The Tuba

TRIVERS, BARRY — Do The New York; Two Loves Have I

TROIANO, DOMINIC — Run Run Run

TROLLI, JOE — Blue Bird Waltz

TROUP, BOBBY — (Get Your Kicks On)Route 66!; (You're A)Snootie Little Cutie; Baby, Baby All The Time; Daddy

TROUTMAN, L. — I Want To Be Your Man

TROXEL, GARY — Come Softly To Me

TROY, HENRY — Cake Walking Babies From Home; Gin House Blues

TUBB, ERNEST — Try Me One More Time; Walking The Floor Over You; Yesterday's Tears

TUBB, GLENN D. — Skip A Rope

TUBBS, PIERRE — But It's Alright; Right Back Where We Started From

TUBERT, BOB — Our Winter Love; Satin Pillows

TUCKER, ALONZO — Baby Workout; Switcharoo

TUCKER, ANNETTE — Get Me To The World On Time; I Had Too Much To Dream(Last Night)

TUCKER, BEN — Comin' Back Baby

TUCKER, HENRY — Sweet Genevieve

TUCKER, MICHAEL — Fox On The Run

TUCKER, ORRIN — Especially For You

TUGGLE, B. — Just Like Paradise

TUNBRIDGE, JOSEPH — Got A Date With An Angel

TURGON, B. — Midnight Blue

TURK, ROY — Are You Lonesome Tonight?; Beale Street Mamma; Contented; Free And Easy; Gimme A Little Kiss, Will Ya Huh?; I Don't Know Why(I Just Do); I'll Get By(As Long As I Have You); I'm A Little Blackbird Looking For A Bluebird; Into My Heart; It Must Be You; Love, You Funny Thing; Mandy, Make Up Your Mind; Mean To Me; Walkin' My Baby Back Home; Where The Blue Of The Night Meets The Gold Of The Day; With Summer Coming On (I'm Still A Sweetheart)

TURNBOW, JAY — Bread And Butter

TURNER, CHARLES — Let It Ride; Roll On Down The Highway

TURNER, IKE — Fool In Love, A(Tell Me What's Wrong); I'm Blue(The Gong Gong Song); Poor Fool

TURNER, JOHN — Auf Wiedersehn, Sweetheart; Chee Che-OO Chee(Sang The Little Bird); Little Shoemaker; Oh! My Pa-Pa; Smile

TURNER, LEONARD — Jungle Love

TURNER, LOU WILLIE — Flip Flop And Fly

TURNER, REGINALD — Don't Let The Green Grass Fool You

TURNER, SCOTT — Shutters And Boards

TURNER, TINA — Nutbush City Limits

TURNER, TITUS — Hey, Doll Baby

TUVIM, ABE — Gay Ranchero

TWIGGS, CHARLES — Pop Goes The Weasel

TWILLEY, DWIGHT — Girls; I'm On Fire

TWITTY, CONWAY — It's Only Make Believe; Story Of My Love

TWOMEY, KAY — Hey! Jealous Lover; In A Little Bookshop; Johnny Doughboy Found A Rose In Ireland; Serenade Of The Bells; Wooden Heart

TYLER, ALVIN — Java

TYLER, S. — Angel; Du, Du, Liegst Mir In Herzen; Dude(Looks Like A Lady); Walk This Way

TYLER, STEPHEN — Last Child

TYLER, T. TEXAS — Deck Of Cards; Deck The Halls With Boughs Of Holly

TYLER, TOBY — Blues On Parade

TYME, JANUARY — One Man Band

TYRELL, STEVE — It's Only Love

TYSON, IAN — Someday Soon

U2 — Where The Streets Have No Name; With Or Without You

UDELL, PETER — Big Daddy; Ginny Come Lately; Hurting Each Other; I Got Love; Let Me Belong To You; Purlie; Save Your Heart For Me; Sealed With A Kiss; Why Am I Me

ULVAEUS, BJORN — Chiquitita; Dancing Queen; Does Your Mother Know; Fernando; I Do, I Do, I Do, I Do, I Do; Knowing Me, Knowing You; Mamma Mia; Name Of The Game; One Night In Bangkok; S. O. S.; Waterloo; Winner Takes It All

UNGER, STELLA — C'est La Vie; Don't Cry Baby; I'm All Dressed Up With A Broken Heart; Man With A Dream

UNIMAN, MIMI — Long Lonely Nights

UNKNOWN — Drink To Me Only With Thine Eyes

UPOON, DEAN — When It's Lamp Lightin' Time In The Valley

UPTON, PATRICK N. — More Today Than Yesterday

URBANO, AL — Serenade Of The Bells

URE, MIDGE — Do They Know It's Christmas

USHER, GARY — Don't Give In To Him; In My Room

ALL THE WAY
BUT BEAUTIFUL
CALL ME IRRESPONSIBLE
HERE'S THAT RAINY DAY
DARN THAT DREAM
I THOUGHT ABOUT YOU
IMAGINATION
IT COULD HAPPEN TO YOU
LIKE SOMEONE IN LOVE
LOVE AND MARRIAGE
MOONLIGHT BECOMES YOU
NANCY (with the laughing face)

POLKA DOT AND MOONBEAMS
SECOND TIME AROUND

DEEP IN A DREAM

VAL, JACK — Just Say I Love Her(Dicitencello Vuie)
VALANCE, JIM — It's Only Love
VALE, MIKE — Ball Of Fire; Crystal Blue Persuasion; She
VALENS, RITCHIE — Donna; La Bamba; La Cucaracha(Date Of Origin Unknown)
VALENTI, DINO — Hey Joe
VALENTINE, GERALD — Oh Sheila
VALENTINE, KATHY — Head Over Heels
VALENZUELA, RICHARD — Come On, Let's Go
VALLANCE, JIM — Heat Of The Night; Heaven; Like No Other Night; One Night Love Affair; Run To You; Somebody; Someday; What About Love?
VALLE, MARCOS — Summer Samba
VALLE, PAULO SERGIO — Summer Samba
VALLEE, RUDY — Betty Co-ed; Deep Night; Goodnight Sweetheart; I'm Just A Vagabond Lover; Kitty From Kansas City; Oh! Ma-Ma(The Butcher Boy); Old Man Harlem; Toodle-oo, So Long, Good-bye; Vieni, Vieni
VALLINS, JOHN — Too Much, Too Little, Too Late
VAN ALSTYNE, EGBERT — Your Eyes Have Told Me So
VAN HALEN, ALEX — I'll Wait; Jump; Love Walks In; Why Can't This Be Love
VAN HALEN, EDDIE — Dance The Night Away; I'll Wait; Jump; Love Walks In; Why Can't This Be Love
VAN HEUSEN, JIMMY — All I Remember Is You; All The Way; All This And Heaven Too; And You'll Be Home; Apalachicola, Fla.; Aren't You Glad You're You; As Long As I'm Dreaming; Be Beautiful; Birds Of A Feather; Blue Rain; Bluebirds In My Belfry; Boys' Night Out; Busy Doing Nothing; Call Me Irresponsible; Chicago Style; Closer Than A Kiss; Constantly; Country Style; Darn That Dream; Day After Forever; Dearest, Darest I; Deep In A Dream; Do You Know Why; Do You Wanna Jump, Children?; Empty Tables; Ev'ry Girl Is Diff'rent; Everything Makes Music When You're In Love; Experience; For The First Hundred Years; Friend Of Yours; Going My Way; Good For Nothin'(But Love); Got The Moon In My Pocket; Hard Way; Harmony; Heaven Can Wait; Here's That Rainy Day; High Hopes; His Rocking Horse Ran Away; Horse Told Me; How D'ye Talk To A Girl; Humpty Dumpty Heart; I Don't Think I'm In Love; I Thought About You; I'll Make A Man Of The Man; If You Please; If You Stub Your Toe On The Moon; Imagination; Impatient Years; Indiscreet; Isn't That Just Like Love; It Could Happen To You; It's Always You; It's Anybody's Spring; It's The Dreamer In Me; Just My Luck; Just Plain Lonesome; Last Dance; Let's Not Be Sensible; Life Is So Peculiar; Like Someone In Love; Looking For Yesterday; Love And Marriage; Love Is A Bore; Love Is The Darndest Thing; Moonlight Becomes You; My Heart Is A Hobo; My Kind Of Town; Nancy(With The Laughing Face); Not As A Stranger; Nothing In Common; Oh, You Crazy Moon; Once And For Always; Only The Lonely; Personality; Pleasure Seekers; Pocketful Of Miracles; Polka Dots And Moonbeams; Put It There, Pal; Road To Hong Kong; Road To Morocco; Second Time Around; September Of My Years; Shake Down The Stars; So Help Me(IF I Don't Love You); Song From Some Came Running(To Love And Be Loved); Star!; Suddenly It's Spring; Sunday, Monday, Or Always; Swinging On A Star; Wake Me When It's Over; Walking Happy; Welcome To My Dream; When Is Sometime?; Where Love Has Gone; Yah-Ta-Ta, Yah-Ta-Ta (Talk, Talk, Talk); You Don't Have To Know The Language
VAN ZANT, RONNIE — Free Bird; If I'd Been The One; Saturday Night Special; Sweet Home Alabama; What's Your Name
VAN, MEL — Hit And Run Affair
VANCE, ALBERT — Disco Lady
VANCE, PAUL J. — Calcutta; Catch A Falling Star; Gina; Itsy Bitsy Teenie Weenie Yellow Polkadot Bikini; Jimmy's Girl; Leader Of The Laundromat; Playground In My Mind; Run Joey Run; Starbright; Tracy; What Is Love?; What Will My Mary Say
VANDA, HARRY — Love Is In The Air; Yesterday's Hero
VANDROSS, LUTHER — Stop To Love
VANDYKE, LES — La Dolce Vita(The Sweet Life); La Isla Bonita
VANELLI, GINO — Living Inside Myself
VANN, TEDDY — Love Power
VANNELLI, ROSS — I Just Wanna Stop
VARNICK, TED — Am I In Love?; Ghost Town; In The Middle Of An Island
VASTANO, JOHN — Deeper Than The Night
VATRO, R. — Anna(El Negro Zambon)
VAUGHAN, SHARON — My Heroes Have Always Been Cowboys
VAUGHN, BILLY — Trying
VAUGHN, D. — Fall In Love With Me
VAUGHN, GEORGE — Mule Skinner Blues
VAUGHN, WAYNE — Fall In Love With Me; Let's Groove
VEGA, SUZANNE — Luka
VEGAS, LOLLY — Come And Get Your Love; Niki Hoeky; Witch Queen Of New Orleans
VEGAS, PATRICK — Niki Hoeky; Witch Queen Of New Orleans
VEITCH, TREVOR — Gloria
VEJVODA, JAROMIR — Beer Barrel Polka
VELAZQUEZ, CONSUELO — Besame Mucho
VELONA, TONY — Domani(Tomorrow); Lollipops And Roses; Music To Watch Girls By
VENABLE, PERCY — I Want A Big Butter And Egg Man
VENOSA, ARTHUR — Little Star
VERA, BILLY — At This Moment; Make Me Belong To You
VERDI, GIUSEPPE — Anvil Chorus
VERNOR, F. DUDLEIGH — Sweetheart Of Sigma Chi
VERSCHAREN, JOSEPH — Since I Don't Have You
VETTER, CYRIL E. — Double Shot(of My Baby's Love)
VIAN, A. — Luna Rossa(Blushing Moon)
VIGIL, RAFAEL — Bad Boy
VILLARD, JEAN — While The Angelus Was Ringing Or The Three Bells Or The Jimmy Brown Song
VILLODO, A. G. — Kiss Of Fire
VIMMERSTEDT, SADIE — I Wanna Be Around
VINCENT, GENE — Be-Bop-A-Lula
VINCENT, HUNTER — Drownin' My Sorrows
VINCENT, STAN — O-O-H Child
VINTON, BOBBY — Comin' Home Soldier; L-O-N-E-L-Y; Mr. Lonely; My Melody Of Love
VIOLINSKY, SOL — When Francis Dances With Me
VITALE, JOEY — Rocky Mountain Way
VITO, HANK DE — Queen Of Hearts
VOGEL, JANET — Since I Don't Have You
VOIE, KENT LA — Don't Expect Me To Be Your Friend
VOL, FRANK DE — Friendly Tavern Polka; Hush Hush,

Sweet Charlotte; Lover Come Back
VOLL, CAL DE — How Do You Do
VOLMAN, MARK — Elenore
VON TILZER, HARRY — Under The Yum Yum Tree; Wait 'Til The Sun Shines Nellie
VORZON, BARRY DE — S. W. A. T. (Theme From)

VOSS, FAYE — Sugar Shack
VOUDOURIS, ROGER — Get Used To It
VOYNOW, DICK — Riverboat Shuffle
VRIES, JOHN DE — (There'll Be A)Hot Time In The Town Of Berlin; Oh! Look At Me Now!

More I See You; Muchacha; My Dream Is Yours; My Heart Tells Me; My One And Only Highland Fling; Nagasaki; No Love, No Nothin'; No More Love; On The Atchison, Topeka, And The Santa Fe; One Sweet Letter From You; Ooh That Kiss; Page Miss Glory; Play Me An Old Fashioned Melody; Remember Me; Remember My Forgotten Man; Rose Of The Rio Grande; Rose, Rose, I Love You; September In The Rain; Serenade In Blue; Shadow Waltz; Shanghai Lil; She's A Latin From Manhattan; Shoes With Wings On; Shuffle Off To Buffalo; Somebody; Stanley Steamer; Swing Your Partner Round And Round; Three's A Crowd; Time Alone Will Tell; Too Many Tears; Torch Song; Two Dreams Met; Wait And See; We're In The Money Or The Gold Digger Song; Weekend In Havana; Where Am I? (Am I In Heaven?); Where Do You Work-a-John; Where The Shy Little Violets Grow; Why Do I Dream Those Dreams; With Plenty Of Money And You; Wonder Bar; Words Are In My Heart; Would You Like To Take A Walk; You Let Me Down; You Must Have Been A Beautiful Baby; You Wonderful You; You'll Never Know; You're Getting To Be A Habit With Me; You're My Everything; Young And Healthy; Zing A Little Zong

WARREN, JAMES — Everybody's Got To Learn Sometime

WARREN, W. — Wild Side Of Life

WARSHAUER, FRANK — It Isn't Fair

WASHBURN, COUNTRY — One Dozen Roses

WASHINGTON, CARROL — Mr. Big Stuff

WASHINGTON, FERDINAND — I'll Be Home; Pledging My Love

WASHINGTON, LEON — Hambone

WASHINGTON, NED — (I Don't Stand A)Ghost Of A Chance With You; Baby Mine; Breakin' In A Pair Of Shoes; Can't We Talk It Over; Casey Junior; Cosi Cosa; Don't Call It Love; Give A Little Whistle; Greatest Show On Earth; Hajji Baba; Hands Across The Border; Hi-Diddle-Dee-Dee(An Actor's Life For Me); High And The Mighty; High Noon(Do Not Forsake Me); Hundred Years From Today; I'm Gettin' Sentimental Over You; I've Got No Strings; Jiminy Cricket; Land Of The Pharaohs; Love Is The Thing; Love Me; Love Me Tonight; My Foolish Heart; Nearness Of You; On Green Dolphin Street; Rawhide; Return To Paradise; Saludos Amigos; Smoke Rings; Somebody Stole Gabriel's Horn; Stella By Starlight; Town Without Pity; Unforgiven, The (The Need For Love); Waltzing In A Dream; When I See An Elephant Fly; When You Wish Upon A Star; Wild Is The Wind; You're My Thrill

WASHINGTON, OSCAR — Night Train

WASHINGTON, PATTI — Gidget

WATERS, ETHEL — Down South Blues; Kind Lovin' Blues

WATERS, ROGER — Another Brick In The Wall; Money

WATKINS, VIOLA — Gee!

WATLEY, JODY — Don't You Want Me; Looking For A New Love; Some Kind Of Lover

WATSON, B. — Rock Steady

WATSON, BOAZ — Operator

WATSON, DEEK — (I Love You)For Sentimental Reasons

WATSON, JEFF — Goodbye

WATSON, JOHNNY — It's A Wonderful World; Seven Twenty In The Books

WATTS, CLEM — If I Knew You Were Comin' I'd've Baked A Cake; You Call Everybody Darling

WATTS, GRADY — Blue Champagne

WATTS, MAYME — Alright, Okay, You Win

WATTS, NATHAN L. — Free

WAXMAN, FRANZ — Katsumi Love Theme; Mountains Beyond The Moon; Place In The Sun

WAYBILL, FEE — She's A Beauty

WAYNE, ARTIE — Mahzel(Means Good Luck); Midnight Mary

WAYNE, BERNIE — Blue Velvet; Laughing On The Outside(Crying On The Inside); Miss America; Port-Au-Prince; Tropicana; Vanessa; You Walk By; You're So Understanding; Zsa Zsa

WAYNE, EDYTHE — Band Of Gold; Give Me Just A Little More Time; Mind, Body And Soul; You've Got Me Dangling On A String

WAYNE, MABEL — Chiquita; Don't Wake Me Up(Let Me Dream); Dreamers Holiday; I Understand; In A Little Spanish Town; It Happened In Monterey; Little Man, You've Had A Busy Day; Ramona

WAYNE, MABLE — Why Don't You Fall In Love With Me

WAYNE, SID — Anything Can Happen-Mambo; Do The Clam; I Need Your Love Tonight; I'm Gonna Knock On Your Door; It's Impossible; Mangos; Ninety Nine Years(Dead Or Alive); See You In September; Two Different Worlds

WEATHERLY, FRED — Danny Boy; Roses Of Picardy

WEATHERLY, JIM — Midnight Train To Georgia; Need To Be; Neither One Of Us(Wants To Be The First To Say Goodbye)

WEATHERSPOON, WILLIAM — What Becomes Of The Broken Hearted?

WEAVER, BLUE — (Our Love)Don't Throw It Away; Hold Onto My Love

WEBB, BERNARD — Woman

WEBB, CHICK — Chew-Chew-Chew(Chew Your Bubble Gum); Have Mercy; Let's Get Together; Stompin' At The Savoy; You Showed Me The Way

WEBB, DANNY — One Summer Night

WEBB, JIM — All I Know; By The Time I Get To Phoenix; Carpet Man; Didn't We?; Highwayman; Honey Come Back; It's A Sin When You Love Somebody; Macarthur Park; Up, Up And Away Or My Beautiful Balloon; Wichita Lineman; Worst That Could Happen; Yard Went On Forever

WEBB, JIMMY — Galveston

WEBB, LAURA — Mr. Lee

WEBBER, ANDREW LLOYD — Buenos Aires; Christmas Dream; Come Back With The Same Look In Your Eyes; Don't Cry For Me Argentina; Everything's Alright; I Don't Know How To Love Him; I Have Never Felt This Way Before; Memory

WEBER, BILLIE — Crocodile Tears

WEBER, CARL MARIA VON — Invitation To The Dance

WEBSTER, PAUL FRANCIS — Airport Love Theme; Anastasia; April Love; Ballad Of The Alamo; Baltimore Oriole; Beloved; Black Coffee; Bluebell; Boy On A Dolphin; Bubble-Loo, Bubble-Loo; Certain Smile; Chocolate Shake; Doctor, Lawyer, Indian Chief; El Cid(love Theme)(the Falcon And The Dove); Follow The Swallow(To Hideaway Hollow); Friendly Persuasion(Thee I Love); Giant(This Then Is Texas); Got The Jitters; Green Leaves Of Summer; Guns Of Navarone; Honey-Babe; How Green Was My Valley; How It Lies, How It Lies, How It Lies; I Got It Bad(and

That Ain't Good); I Speak To The Stars; I'd Like To Set You To Music; I'm Like A Fish Out Of Water; If I Had A Dozen Hearts; Imitation Of Life; Jump For Joy; Lamplighter's Serenade; Lily Of Laguna; Little Love Can Go A Long, Long Way; Long Song From Mutiny On The Bounty; Love Is A Many Splendored Thing; Loveliest Night Of The Year; Lygia; Make A Wish; Masquerade; Maverick; Memphis In June; My Moonlight Madonna; Padre; Rainbow On The River; Rio Bravo; Secret Love; Shadow Of Your Smile; Somewhere My Love(Lara's Theme); Song Of Raintree County; Twelfth Of Never; Two Cigarettes In The Dark; Very Precious Love; Watermelon Weather; What's Your Story, Morning Glory?; When I Look At You; You Was; You're Everywhere

WEBSTER, R. A. — Last Farewell

WEBSTER, WARWICK — Man In The Raincoat

WECHTER, JULIUS — Spanish Flea

WEEKS, ANSON — I'm Sorry Dear

WEEKS, RICARDO — I Wonder Why

WEEMS, TED — Martins And The Coys

WEERSMA, MELLE — Penny Serenade

WEIDER, JOHN — San Franciscan Nights

WEIDER, JOHNNY — Monterey; Sky Pilot

WEIDLIN, JANE — Our Lips Are Sealed

WEIL, CYNTHIA — (You're My)Soul And Inspiration; Blame It On The Bossa Nova; Bless You; Brown Eyed Woman; Conscience; Don't Be Afraid, Little Darlin'; He's So Shy; He's Sure The Boy I Love; Here You Come Again; Home Of The Brave; Hungry; I'll Take You Home; I'm Gonna Be Strong; If Ever You're In My Arms Again; It's Getting Better; Johnny Loves Me; Kicks; Looking Through The Eyes Of Love; Love Will Conquer All; Magic Town; Make Your Own Kind Of Music; Mary's Little Lamb; My Dad; Never Gonna Let You Go; On Broadway; Only In America; Proud; Rock And Roll Lullabye; Running With The Night; Saturday Night At The Movies; Shape Of Things To Come; Shapes Of Things; Somewhere Down The Road; Somewhere Out There; Uptown; Walking In The Rain; We Gotta Get Out Of This Place; You've Lost That Lovin' Feelin'

WEILL, KURT — (All Of A Sudden)My Heart Sings; (Don't Look Now, But)My Heart Is Showing; Alabama-Song; All At Once; Big Mole; Bilbao Song; Boy Like You; Catfish Song; Come In, Mornin'; Foolish Heart; Girl Of The Moment; Green-Up Time; Here I'll Stay; How Can You Tell An American?; How Much I Love You; I'm A Stranger Here Myself; If Love Remains; It Never Was You; Jenny(The Saga Of Jenny); Little Gray House; Lonely House; Lost In The Stars; Mack The Knife(Moritat); Moon-faced, Starry-eyed; My Ship; Nina, The Pinta, The Santa Maria; One Life To Live; Pirate Jenny; Princess Of Pure Delight; River Chanty; September Song; Speak Low; Tschaikowsky; What Good Would The Moon Be?

WEINBERG, MORTIMER — Where Do You Work-a-John

WEINER, HERB — It's My Party

WEINMAN, BERNARD — Too Much

WEINSTEIN, BOBBY — Big Wide World; Goin' Out Of My Head; Have You Looked Into Your Heart; I'm On The Outside(Looking In); It's Gonna Take A Miracle; Pretty Blue Eyes; Sweet Cream Ladies, Forward March

WEISMAN, BEN — All I See Is You; Do The Clam; Don't Ask Me Why; Fame And Fortune; Rock-A-Hula-Baby; Wooden Heart

WEISS, DONNA — Bette Davis Eyes

WEISS, GEORGE — Can Anyone Explain(No! No! No!); Can't Help Falling In Love; Confess; Cross Over The Bridge; Dancin' With Someone(longin' For You); Don't Call My Name; Echoes; Gegetta; How Important Can It Be?; I Don't See Me In Your Eyes Anymore; I Ran All The Way Home; I Want To Thank Your Folks; I'll Never Be Free; I'm Available; Jet; Let's Put It All Together; Magic Circle; Mr. Wonderful; Oh! What It Seemed To Be; Pianissimo; Rumors Are Flying; Surrender; To Think You've Chosen Me; Too Close For Comfort; What A Wonderful World; Wheel Of Fortune; Wild In The Country; Without You I'm Nothing

WEISS, LARRY — Dream Merchant; Rhinestone Cowboy

WEISS, LAURENCE — Bend Me, Shape Me

WEISS, MARION — I Wish That We Were Married

WEISS, STEPHAN — Music! Music! Music!(Put Another Nickel In); Put Your Dreams Away(For Another Day); While You Danced, Danced, Danced

WEISS, STEPHEN — And So Do I; Angel In Disguise

WELCH, BRUCE — Bachelor Boy; Please Mr. Please

WELCH, DAN — First Date, First Kiss, First Love

WELCH, ROBERT — Ebony Eyes; Precious Love; Sentimental Lady

WELDON, FRANK — Christmas In Killarney; Goodnight, Wherever You Are; I Like Mountain Music; Little On The Lonely Side

WELK, LAWRENCE — Champagne Polka

WELLER, FREDDY — Dizzy; Jam Up And Jelly Tight

WELLS, BOB — From Here To Eternity; Patty Duke Theme

WELLS, BRYAN — Place In The Sun; Yester-Me Yester-You Yesterday

WELLS, ED — Casual Look

WELLS, GILBERT — Red Hot Mamma

WELLS, JOHNNIE LEE — Rag Mop

WELLS, ROBERT — Born To Be Blue; Christmas Song, The(Chestnuts Roasting On An Open Fire); Comment Allez-vous?; It's Easy To Say

WELLS, ROY — Lonely Wine

WELLS, VAN — Chains Of Love

WENDLING, PETE — By The Sycamore Tree; I Believe In Miracles; Oh! What A Pal Was Mary; Swingin' In A Hammock; Yaaka Hulaa Hickey Dula

WENRICH, PERCY — (On)Moonlight Bay; Sail Along Silv'ry Moon; Where Do We Go From Here!

WENZLAFF, ERWIN — I Got A Wife

WERBER, CAREL — Cast Your Fate To The Wind

WERNER JR., FRED — Desiderata

WERNER, JOE — Wondering

WERNER, KAY — My Wubba Dolly

WERNER, SUE — My Wubba Dolly

WESLEY, CHARLES — Hark The Herald Angels Sing

WESLEY, FRED — Get On The Good Foot; Payback

WEST, BOBBY — I'll Be There; If You Talk In Your Sleep; Separate Ways; You're So Fine

WEST, DAVID — Portrait Of My Love

WEST, EUGENE — Broadway Rose; You Know You Belong To Somebody Else So Why Don't You Leaveme Alone

WEST, HEDY — 500 Miles Away From Home

WEST, JAMIE — One Thing Leads To Another

WEST, JERRY — Mean Woman Blues
WEST, RED — I'm A Fool
WEST, RICKY — Hollywood Swinging
WEST, ROBERT — I Found A Love
WEST, T. P. — Medicine Man
WESTBURY, KENT — I Just Don't Understand
WESTENDORF, THOMAS — I'll Take You Home Again Kathleen
WESTERN, JOHNNY — Ballad Of Paladin
WESTFIELD, RICHARD — Jungle Boogie
WESTLAKE, CLIVE — All I See Is You
WESTMORELAND, PAUL — Detour
WESTON, GARY — Vacation
WESTON, PAUL — Autumn In Rome; Congratulations; Day By Day; Gandy Dancers' Ball; Hey, Mr. Postman; I Should Care; Indiscretion; Shrimp Boats; Shrine Of St. Cecilia
WESTON, R. P. — I'm Henry Viii, I Am; I've Got Rings On My Fingers(Bells On My Toes); I've Got Sixpence
WETTEN, JOHN — Don't Cry
WETZEL, RAY — Intermission Riff
WEVER, NED — Trust In Me
WEXLER, JERRY — (You Make Me Feel Like)Natural Woman; Everybody Needs Somebody To Love; Little Mama; Twenty-Five Miles
WEYMOUTH, TINA — Burning Down The House
WHEELER, BILLY — Coward Of The County; Jackson; Reverend Mr. Black
WHEELER, FRANCIS — Dancing Fool; I Wonder If You Still Care For Me; It Was Only A Sun Shower; Let A Smile Be Your Umbrella; Sheik Of Araby
WHELAN, JAMES — Mad About You
WHETSOL, ARTHUR — Misty Mornin'
WHIPPLE, STERLING — Last Game Of The Season, The(A Blind Man In The Bleachers)
WHITCOMB, IAN — You Turn Me On
WHITCUP, LEONARD — (Shout! Wherever You May Be)I Am An American; Bewildered; From The Vine Came The Grape; I Couldn't Believe My Eyes; True
WHITE, BARRY — Can't Get Enough Of Your Love, Babe; I Belong To You(and Only You); I'm Gonna Love You Just A Little Bit More Babe; Love's Theme; Never, Never Gonna Give Ya Up; Oh What A Night For Dancing; Satin Soul; Walkin' In The Rain With The One I Love; What Am I Gonna Do With You?; You're The First, The Last, My Everything
WHITE, CARL — Surfin' Bird
WHITE, CHRIS — Hold Your Head Up; I Love You
WHITE, COOL — Buffalo Gals
WHITE, DAVID — At The Hop; Fly; Like A Baby; One, Two, Three(1-2-3); You Don't Own Me
WHITE, EARL — Cynthia's In Love
WHITE, EDWARD R. — C'est La Vie; Crazy Otto Rag; Flowers Mean Forgiveness; Happiness Street(Corner Sunshine Square)
WHITE, GARY — Long Long Time
WHITE, GUS — Canadian Capers
WHITE, M. — When Smokey Sings
WHITE, MARK — (How To Be A)Millionaire; Be Near Me
WHITE, MAURICE — Best Of My Love; Fall In Love With Me; Fantasy; Let's Groove; Saturday Nite; September; Serpentine Fire; Shining Star; Singasong
WHITE, PAT — It's The Same Old Shillelagh
WHITE, PETER — Time Passages
WHITE, RONALD — My Girl; My Girl Has Gone; One More Heartache; You Beat Me To The Punch

WHITE, TED — Since You've Been Gone(Sweet, Sweet Baby)
WHITE, TONY JOE — Polk Salad Annie; Rainy Night In Georgia
WHITE, VERDINE — Fantasy; Serpentine Fire
WHITEHEAD, JOHN — Ain't No Stopping Us Now; Back Stabbers; Bad Luck(part 1); Wake Up, Everybody (Part 1)
WHITEHEAD, PETER — Macho Man
WHITELAW, REID — Goody Goody Gumdrops
WHITEMAN, PAUL — Flamin' Mamie; Wonderful One (My)
WHITESIDE, BOBBY — Comin' In And Out Of Your Life
WHITFIELD, NORMAN — (I Know)I'm Losing You; (Loneliness Made Me Realize)It's You That I Need; Ain't Too Proud To Beg; Ball Of Confusion; Beauty Is Only Skin Deep; Car Wash; Cloud Nine; Don't Let The Joneses Get You Down; End Of Our Road; Everybody Needs Love; Friendship Train; Gonna Give Her All The Love I've Got; I Can't Get Next To You; I Could Never Love Another(After Loving You); I Heard It Through The Grapevine; I Wish It Would Rain; Just My Imagination(Running Away With Me); Papa Was A Rollin' Stone; Please Return Your Love To Me; Pride And Joy; Psychedelic Shack; Superstar Remember How You Got Where You Are; Too Busy Thinking About My Baby; War; You're My Everything
WHITFORD, BRAD — Last Child
WHITING, GEORGE — My Blue Heaven; Rhythm And Romance; West Of The Great Divide
WHITING, RICHARD A. — (I Got A Woman, Crazy For Me)She's Funny That Way; (I'd Love To Spend)One Hour With You; Ain't We Got Fun; Always In All Ways; Beyond The Blue Horizon; Bimini Bay; Breezin' Along With The Breeze; Double Trouble; Eady Was A Lady; Give Me A Moment Please; Guilty; Have You Got Any Castles, Baby?; Honey; Hooray For Hollywood; Horses; I Can't Escape From You; I Have To Have You; I'll Dream Tonight; I've Hitched My Wagon To A Star; It Seems To Be Spring; It's A Great Life(If You Don't Weaken); Japanese Sandman; Louise; Miss Brown To You; My Future Just Passed; My Ideal; On The Good Ship Lollipop; Ride, Tenderfoot, Ride; Sailor Beware; Sentimental And Melancholy; Sleepy Time Gal; Song Of Raintree County; Sorry; Till We Meet Again; Too Marvelous For Words; True Blue Lou; Turn Out The Light; Ukelele Lady; Wait 'Til You See "Ma Cherie"; Waitin' At The Gate For Katy; When Did You Leave Heaven; When Shall We Meet Again; Where The Black Eyed Susans Grow; Where The Morning Glories Grow; Why Dream?; You're An Old Smoothie
WHITLEY, RAY — Run, Run, Look And See; What Kind Of Fool (Do You Think I Am)
WHITLOCK, TOM — Danger Zone; Meet Me Halfway
WHITLOCK, WILLIAM — Hop Scotch Polka
WHITMAN, FAY — Am I Asking Too Much
WHITNEY, JOAN — Ain't Nobody Here But Us Chickens; Candy; Comme Ci, Comme Ca; Far Away Places; High On A Windy Hill; It All Comes Back To Me Now; It's Love, Love, Love!; Love Somebody; Money Is The Root Of All Evil; My Sister And I; No Other Arms, No Other Lips; You'll Never Get Away
WHITSON, BETH SLATER — Let Me Call You Sweetheart; Meet Me Tonight In Dreamland
WHITTAKER, ROGER — Last Farewell; Last Night

WICKHAM, VICKI — You Don't Have To Say You Love Me

WIDELITZ, S. — She's Like The Wind

WIEGAND, LARRY — Evil Woman

WIEGAND, RICHARD — Evil Woman

WIENER, HERB — Joey

WILCOX, HARLOW — Groovy Grubworm

WILCOX, JOHN — Set Me Free

WILDER, ALEC — All The Cats Join In; All The King's Horses; Goodbye, John; I'll Be Around; If She Should Come To You(La Montana); It's So Peaceful In The Country; Love Among The Young; Phoenix Love Theme; Soft As Spring; While We're Young; Who Can I Turn To?

WILDER, MATTHEW — Break My Stride

WILDING, BOBBY — Hurt So Bad

WILKIN, JOHN — G. T. O.

WILKINS, A. E. — What More Can I Ask?

WILKINS, DAVID — Coming On Strong

WILKINS, MARIJOHN — I Just Don't Understand; P. T. 109; Waterloo

WILKINS, RONNIE — Land Of Milk And Honey; Son-Of-A-Preacher-Man

WILKINSON, DUDLEY — Because Of You

WILLENSKY, ELLIOTT — Got To Be There

WILLET, CHAPPIE — Apurksady; Blue Rhythm Fantasy

WILLET, SLIM — Don't Let The Stars Get In Your Eyes

WILLIAMS, ANDRE — Shake A Tail Feather; Twine Time

WILLIAMS, ARTHUR — Funny Thing

WILLIAMS, ASTON ""DEACON"" — Where The Mountains Meet The Sky (I'm Headin' For The Blue Horizon)

WILLIAMS, BARNEY — Baby, It's You

WILLIAMS, BERNIE — Duke Of Earl

WILLIAMS, BERT — Constantly; Nobody

WILLIAMS, BOB — Would Do)anything For You

WILLIAMS, CHARLES — Jealous Lover

WILLIAMS, CHARLIE — 500 Miles Away From Home

WILLIAMS, CLARENCE — Baby, Won't You Please Come Home; Cake Walking Babies From Home; Gulf Coast Blues; Jail House Blues; Royal Garden Blues; Squeeze Me; Stuff Is Here, The(and It's Mellow); Sugar Blues; West End Blues

WILLIAMS, COOTIE — 'round Midnight; Epistrophy

WILLIAMS, CURLEY — Half As Much

WILLIAMS, CURTIS — Big Fun; Fresh; Joanna

WILLIAMS, DAVE — Whole Lot Of Shakin' Going On

WILLIAMS, DAVID — Don't Hold Back

WILLIAMS, EUGENE — Tryin' To Live My Life Without You

WILLIAMS, FRED — Freight Train

WILLIAMS, GEORGE — It Must Be Jelly('Cause Jam Don't Shake Like That); So Much In Love

WILLIAMS, HANK — Cold, Cold Heart; Hey Good Lookin'; I Can't Help It(If I'm Still In Love With You); I'm So Lonesome I Could Cry; Jambalaya(On The Bayou); Kaw-Liga; Your Cheatin' Heart

WILLIAMS, HARRY — It's A Long Long Way To Tipperary; Rose Room

WILLIAMS, HARRY H. — In The Shade Of The Old Apple Tree

WILLIAMS, HUGH — Red Sails In The Sunset

WILLIAMS, IRA — Ballad For D

WILLIAMS, J. MAYO — Corrine, Corrina; Drinkin' Wine, Spo-Dee-O-Dee; Fine Brown Frame; When My Man Comes Home

WILLIAMS, JAMES — Skin Tight

WILLIAMS, JERRY — Giving It Up For Your Love; I'm Gonna Make You Love Me; She's A Heartbreaker

WILLIAMS, JIM — Fire; Who'd She Coo

WILLIAMS, JIMMY — (You Don't Know)How Glad I Am; Lover's Question

WILLIAMS, JOE — Baby, Please Don't Go

WILLIAMS, JOHN — Can You Read My Mind(Love Theme From Superman); Close Encounters Of The Third Kind(Theme from); Empire Strikes Back; Froggy Bottom; If We Were In Love; Jaws(Theme From); Star Wars Title Theme

WILLIAMS, KENNETH — Everybody Plays The Fool

WILLIAMS, LARRY — Bony Moronie; Short Fat Fannie

WILLIAMS, LAWRENCE — Let Your Love Flow

WILLIAMS, LAWRENCE E. — Slow Down

WILLIAMS, LAWTON — Fraulein

WILLIAMS, MARY LOU — Camel Hop; In The Land Of Oo-Bla-Dee; Pretty Eyed Baby; Roll 'em; What's Your Story, Morning Glory?

WILLIAMS, MASON — Classical Gas

WILLIAMS, MATT — I Gotta Know

WILLIAMS, MAURICE — Little Darlin'; Stay

WILLIAMS, MENTOR — Drift Away

WILLIAMS, MILAN — Machine Gun; Old-Fashion Love

WILLIAMS, OTIS — I'm On Fire; Two Hearts

WILLIAMS, PAUL — Cried Like A Baby; Evergreen; Family Of Man; I Won't Last A Day Without You; Love Boat Theme; My Fair Share; Old Fashioned Love Song, An; Out In The Country; Rainbow Connection; Rainy Days And Mondays; We've Only Just Begun; You And Me Against The World

WILLIAMS, RALPH — Mr. Big Stuff

WILLIAMS, RICHARD — Play The Game Tonight

WILLIAMS, SPENCER — Basin Street Blues; Black Bottom Ball; Careless Love; Everybody Loves My Baby, But My Baby Don't Love Nobody But Me; I Ain't Got Nobody; I've Found A New Baby; Royal Garden Blues; Tishomingo Blues

WILLIAMS, TEX — Smoke! Smoke! Smoke!(That Cigarette)

WILLIAMSTON, WADE — Movin'

WILLIS, — What Have I Done To Deserve This

WILLIS, ALLEE — Boogie Wonderland; I Want You Tonight; Lead Me On; Neutron Dance; September

WILLIS, CHUCK — Close Your Eyes; Door Is Still Open To My Heart; Hang Up My Rock And Roll Shoes; I Feel So Bad; What A Dream (Oh What A Dream)

WILLIS, MARVIN — Float On

WILLIS, RICHARD STORRS — It Came Upon A Midnight Clear

WILLIS, VICTOR — In The Navy; Macho Man; Y.M.C.A.

WILLS, BOB — San Antonio Rose

WILLS, RICK — Do You Feel Like We Do

WILLSON, MEREDITH — Are You Sure; Arm In Arm; Being In Love; Belly Up To The Bar, Boys; Big Clown Balloons; Colorado, My Home; Dolce Far Niente; Goodnight My Someone; He's My Friend; I Ain't Down Yet; I'll Never Say No; If I Knew; It's Beginning To Look Like Christmas; It's You; Lida Rose; Marian The Librarian; May The Good Lord Bless And Keep You; Seventy Six Trombones; Till There Was You; Trouble In River City; Two In Love; You And I

WILSON, AL — In The Little Red School House

WILSON, ALLEN — Going Up The Country; On The Road Again

WILSON, ANN — Barracuda; Best Man In The World; Crazy On You; Heartless; Magic Man; Never; Straight On

WILSON, ANTHONY — Brother Louie; Disco Queen

WILSON, BRIAN — Be True To Your School; California Girls; Caroline, No; Dance, Dance, Dance; Darlin,; Don't Worry Baby; Drag City; Fun, Fun, Fun; God Only Knows; Good Vibrations; Help Me, Rhonda; Heroes And Villains; I Get Around; In My Room; Little Girl I Once Knew; Little Honda; Shut Down; Sloop John B.; Surf City; Surfer Girl; Surfin' Safari; Surfin' U. S. A.; When I Grow Up (To Be A Man); Wild Honey; Wouldn't It Be Nice

WILSON, CARL — Dance, Dance, Dance

WILSON, CHARLES — Early In The Morning

WILSON, CLYDE — She's Not Just Another Woman

WILSON, FOREST — Ko Ko Mo, I Love You So

WILSON, FRANK — All I Need; Boogie Down; Chained; I'm Living In Shame; Keep On Truckin'; Love Child; Still Water; Stoned Love; Up The Ladder To The Roof; Whole Lot Of Shakin' In My Heart (Since I Met You); You've Made Me So Very Happy

WILSON, JACKIE — (You Were Made For)All My Love; Baby Workout; You Better Know It

WILSON, JEFF — Let Me Love You Tonight

WILSON, JOHNNY — Love The World Away

WILSON, JULIAN — Battle Hymn Of Lieutenant Calley

WILSON, K. — Tuff Enuf

WILSON, LEE — I Wish You Love

WILSON, MARTY — Story Untold

WILSON, NANCY — Barracuda; Best Man In The World; Crazy On You; Heartless; Magic Man; Straight On

WILSON, NORRO — I Love My Friend; Most Beautiful Girl; Very Special Love Song

WILSON, RON — Wipe Out

WILSON, SANDY — I Could Be Happy With You

WILSON, TONY — Emma; You Sexy Thing

WILSON, TURNER — Surfin' Bird

WILSON, VANCE — Oh What A Night For Dancing

WILSON, WESLEY — Gimme A Pigfoot

WILSON, WOODY — Ball Of Fire

WINE, TONI — Black Pearl; Candida; Groovy Kind Of Love,a; Your Husband, My Wife

WINEGAR, FRANK — When A Gypsy Makes His Violin Cry

WINFREE, DICK — China Boy

WINGFIELD, WILLIAM — Eighteen With A Bullet

WINKLE, JOSEPH VAN — Mr. Custer

WINKLER, FRANZ — Forever And Ever

WINKLER, GERHARD — Answer Me, My Love; Don Pelosi-Leo Towers

WINKLER, RAY — Welcome To My World

WINLEY, PAUL — I've Got My Eyes On You; Rinky Dink

WINN, HAL — Cindy's Birthday; Dr. Kildare(Theme from)(Three Stars Will Shine Tonight)

WINN, JERRY — Gimme Little Sign

WINNER, JOSEPH E. — Little Brown Jug

WINNER, SEPTIMUS — Listen To The Mocking Bird

WINTER, EDGAR — Frankenstein

WINTER, KURT — Clap For The Wolfman; Hand Me Down World; Rain Dance

WINTERHALTER, HUGO — Diamond Head; Diamonds

WINWOOD, MUFF — Gimme Some Lovin'

WINWOOD, STEVE — Finer Things; Freedom Over-spill; Gimme Some Lovin'; Higher Love; I'm A Man; Paper Sun; Valerie; While You See A Chance

WIRGES, WILLIAM — Chiquita Banana

WISE, FRED — "A" You're Adorable (the Alphabet Song); Best Man; Don't Ask Me Why; Fame And Fortune; I Won't Cry Anymore; Kissin' Cousins; Lonely Blue Boy; Misirlou; Nightingale; Roses In The Rain; Wooden Heart; You, You, You Are The One

WISEMAN, BEN — Lonely Blue Boy

WISEMAN, SCOTT — Have I Told You Lately That I Love You

WISNER, JIM — Don't Throw Your Love Away

WITHERS, BILL — Ain't No Sunshine; Just The Two Of Us; Lean On Me; Use Me

WITHERSPOON, WILLIAM — I've Passed This Way Before

WITT, FRANCIS DE — Moon Shines On The Moonshine

WIZELL, MURRAY — I May Never Pass This Way Again

WODEHOUSE, P. G. — Bill; I Found You And You Found Me; Leave It To Jane; March Of The Musketeers; Oh Gee! Oh Joy!; Say So!; Till The Clouds Roll By

WOLCOTT, CHARLES — Ruby-Du-Du;   Saludos Amigos; Sooner Or Later; Two Silhouettes

WOLF, DANNY — Sugar Moon

WOLF, DON — Love Is All We Need

WOLF, INA — No Way Out; Sara; Who's Johnny ("Short Circuit" Theme)

WOLF, JACK — I'm A Fool To Want You

WOLF, PETER — Come Back; Everybody Have Fun Tonight; Freeze-Frame; Give It To Me; Lights Out; Must Of Got Lost; No Way Out; Sara; We Built This City; Who's Johnny ("Short Circuit" Theme); You're The Only One

WOLF, TOMMY — Ballad Of The Sad Young Men

WOLFE, JACQUES — Shortnin' Bread

WOLFE, SHIRLEY — Lips Of Wine

WOLFE, STEVE — It's A Heartache

WOLFER, BILL — Dancing In The Sheets

WOLFERT, DAVE — Heartbreaker; Songbird

WOLFOLK, CARL — Can I Change My Mind?; Is It Something You've Got?wm)barry Dispenza

WOLFSON, MACK — C'est La Vie; Crazy Otto Rag; Flowers Mean Forgiveness; Happiness Street(Corner Sunshine Square)

WOLINSKI, DAVID — Ain't Nobody; Do You Love What You Feel

WOLOSCHUK, JOHN — Calling Occupants Of Interplanetary Craft

WOMACK, BOBBY — Breezin'; I'm A Midnight Mover; I'm In Love

WONDER, STEVIE — All In Love Is Fair; Black Man; Boogie On Reggae Woman; Do I Do; Don't You Worry 'bout A Thing; Go Home; Higher Ground; I Ain't Gonna Stand For It; I Don't Know Why; I Just Called To Say I Love You; I Think It's Love; I Was Made To Love Her; I Wish; I'm Wondering; If You Really Love Me; Isn't She Lovely; It's A Shame; Let's Get Serious; Little Ole Man(Uptight Everything's Alright); Living For The City; Living In A Box; Love Light In Flight; Master Blaster; My Cherie Amour; Overjoyed; Part Time Lover; Send One Your Love; Shoo-Be-Foo-Be-Doo-Da-Day; Signed, Sealed, Delivered I'm Yours; Sir Duke; Skeletons; Superstition; Superwoman(Where Were You When I Needed You); Uptight (Everything's Alright); You Are The Sunshine

Of My Life; You Haven't Done Nothin'; You Met Your Match...
WOOD, BOBBY — Half The Way
WOOD, CHARLES — Black Is Beautiful
WOOD, CLEMENT — De Glory Road; Shortnin' Bread
WOOD, GUY — Cincinnati Dancing Pig; Faith Can Move Mountains; French Foreign Legion; My One And Only Love; Shoo-Fly-Pie And Apple Pan Dowdy; Till Then; Vanity
WOOD, HAYDN — Roses Of Picardy
WOOD, KEN — Happy Organ
WOOD, LAUREN — Please Don't Leave
WOOD, LEO — Cherie; Honest And Truly; Runnin' Wild; Somebody Stole My Gal; Wang Wang Blues
WOOD, PETER — Year Of The Cat
WOOD, RON — Black Limousine; Stay With Me
WOODARD, STEVE — Let Me Love You Tonight
WOODE, HENRY — Broadway; Rosetta
WOODEFORDE, AMY — Kashmiri Love Song
WOODFORD, TERRY — Angel In Your Arms
WOODING, SAM — Walk, Jenny, Walk
WOODLEY, BRUCE — Red Rubber Ball
WOODLEY, JAMES — Mystery Lady
WOODS, ADAM — One Thing Leads To Another
WOODS, EDDIE — Green Eyes
WOODS, H. — Walk Right In
WOODS, HARRY — Here Comes The Sun; I'll Never Say "Never Again" Again; I'm Goin' South; I'm Looking Over A Four Leaf Clover; Just An Echo In The Valley; Just Like A Butterfly That's Caught In The Rain; Little Kiss Each Morning, A(A Little Kiss Each Night); Little Street Where Old Friends Meet; Man From The South(With A Big Cigar In His Mouth); Paddlin' Madelin' Home; River Stay 'way From My Door; Side By Side; Try A Little Tenderness; We Just Couldn't Say Goodbye; What A Little Moonlight Can Do (Ooh); When The Moon Comes Over The Mountain; When The Red, Red Robin Comes Bob, Bob Bobbin' Along
WOODS, ORLANDO — Express
WOODS, SONNY — I Need Your Lovin'
WOODS, STUART — Money Honey
WOODS, WILLIE — Shake And Fingerpop
WOODWORTH, SAMUEL — Old Oaken Bucket
WOOLEY, SHEB — Purple People Eater,the
WOOLFSON, ERIC — Damned If I Do; Eye In The Sky; Games People Play
WOOLLEY, BRUCE — Video Killed The Radio Star
WOOLSEY, MARY HALE — When It's Springtime In The Rockies
WORK, HENRY CLAY — Grandfather's Clock; Marching Through Georgia
WORRELL, BERNIE — Flash Light
WORTH, BOBBY — 'Til Reveille; Do I Worry?; Don't You Know; Fellow On A Furlough,a; I Look At Heaven(When I Look At You); Tonight We Love
WORTH, LEAH — Corns For My Country; Did Anyone

Ever Tell You Mrs. Murphy
WRAY, LINK — Rawhide
WRIGHT, ANDREW — When A Man Loves A Woman
WRIGHT, BENJAMIN — I'm On Fire; One Hundred Ways; One I Love
WRIGHT, BETTY — Where Is The Love
WRIGHT, BOB — Always And Always; At The Balalaika; Horse With The Dreamy Eyes
WRIGHT, CHARLES — Do Your Thing; Express Yourself
WRIGHT, DOROTHY — Cinco Robles
WRIGHT, GARY — Dream Weaver; Love Is Alive; Really Wanna Know You
WRIGHT, GAVIN — Once You Get Started
WRIGHT, GREGORY — You're A Special Part Of Me
WRIGHT, RICHARD — King Joe
WRIGHT, ROBERT — And This Is My Beloved; Baubles, Bangles And Beads; Chime In!; Donkey Serenade,the; Elena; Fate; Fog And The Grog; Freddy And His Fiddle; He's In Love; I Love You; It's A Blue World; Midsummer's Eve; Night Of My Nights; Not Since Ninevah; Now; Sands Of Time; Strange Music; Stranger In Paradise
WRIGHT, ROBERT B. — I Dreamt I Dwelt In Harlem; Jersey Bounce
WRIGHT, STEVEN — Jeopardy
WRIGHT, SYREETA — If You Really Love Me; It's A Shame; Signed, Sealed, Delivered I'm Yours
WRUBEL, ALLIE — (I'm Afraid)Masquerade Is Over; As You Desire Me; At The Flying "W"; Don't Call It Love; Everybody Has A Laughing Place; Fare Thee Well Annabelle; Farewell To Arms; First Time I Saw You; Flirtation Walk; Gone With The Wind; Good Night Angel; Good Night Ladies(Merrily We Roll Along); Gotta Get Me Somebody To Love; I Can't Love You Any More(Any More Than I Do); I Met Her On Monday; I See Two Lovers; I'll Buy That Dream; I'm Stepping Out With A Memory Tonight; Lady From 29 Palms; Lady In Red; Little Things You Used To Do; Mr. And Mrs. Is The Name; Music, Maestro, Please!; Why Does It Get So Late So Early; Why Don't We Do This More Often; Zip-A-Dee-Doo-Dah
WWTTON, JOHN — Only Time Will Tell
WYCHE, SID — A Woman, A Lover, A Friend; Alright, Okay, You Win; Big Hunk 'o Love; Love! Love! Love!
WYKER III, JOHNNY — Let Love Come Between Us
WYKER, JOHN — Motorcycle Mama
WYLE, GEORGE — Ballad Of Gilligan's Isle,the; Caramba! It's The Samba!; I Didn't Slip, I Wasn't Pushed, I Fell; I Love The Way You Say Goodnight; I Said My Pajamas(And Put On My Pray'rs)
WYLIE, RICHARD — With This Ring
WYMAN, BILL — Play With Fire
WYNETTE, TAMMY — Stand By Your Man
WYNN, LARRY — Five Guys Named Moe

YAKUS, HERB — Chain Gang
YAKUS, MILT — Old Cape Cod
YAKUS, MILTON — Go On With The Wedding
YANCY, MARVIN — I've Got Love On My Mind; Inseparable; Our Love; Sophisticated Lady(She's A Different Lady)
YANKOVIC, AL — Eat It
YANKOVIC, FRANK — Blue Bird Waltz
YARIAN, CHRISTINE — Do It Baby
YARROW, PETER — Day Is Done; Puff(The Magic Dragon); Torn Between Two Lovers
YELLEN, JACK — Ain't She Sweet; Alabama Jubilee; Are You Havin' Any Fun?; Bagdad; Bench In The Park; Cheatin' On Me; Crazy Words-Crazy Tune; Down By The O-HI-O; Forever And Ever; Forgive Me; Glad Rag Doll; Happy Days Are Here Again; Happy Feet; Happy In Love; Hard Hearted Hannah, The Vamp Of Savannah; He's A Good Man To Have Around; Hold My Hand; I Wonder What's Become Of Sally; I'm The Last Of The Red Hot Mammas; I've Got To Get Hot; It's An Old Southern Custom; Louisville Lou, The Vampin' Lady; Love Will Tell; Mamma Goes Where Papa Goes Or Papa Don't Go Out Tonight; My Yiddishe Momme; Right Somebody To Love; Sing, Baby, Sing; Sweet And Hot; Who Cares; Wildest Gal In Town; Young Man's Fancy
YESTON, MAURY — Be Italian
YOUMANS, VINCENT — Bambalina; Carioca; Drums In My Heart; Flying Down To Rio; Great Day!; Hallelujah!; Hay, Straw; I Know That You Know; I Want A Man; I Want To Be Happy; I'm Glad I Waited; It's Every Girl's Ambition; Kathleen Mine; Keepin' Myself For You; Kinda Like You; Like He Loves Me; More Than You Know; Music Makes Me; No, No, Nanette; Oh How I Long To Belong To You; Oh Me! Oh My!; Orchids In The Moonlight; Rise 'n Shine; Should I Be Sweet?; So Do I; Sometimes I'm Happy; Through The Years; Time On My Hands; Too Many Rings Around Rosie; Wildflower; Without A Song; You're Everywhere
YOUNG JR., JOHN — My Boy, Flat Top; Seventeen
YOUNG, CYRUS — When Hearts Are Young
YOUNG, DENNIS DE — Come Sail Away; Desert Moon; Don't Let It End; Lady; Mr. Roboto
YOUNG, GEORGE — Friday On My Mind; Love Is In The Air; Yesterday's Hero
YOUNG, JAMES "TRUMMY" — Whatcha Know Joe
YOUNG, JIMMY — Easy Does It
YOUNG, JOE — Annie Doesn't Live Here Anymore; Cryin ' For The Carolines; Dinah; Five Foot Two, Eyes Of Blue(Has Anybody Seen My Girl); Have A Lit-

tle Faith In Me; How Ya Gonna Keep 'em Down On The Farm; Hundred Years From Today; I Kiss Your Hand, Madame; I Knew You Were Waiting For Me; I'd Love To Fall Asleep And Wake Up In My Mammy's Arms; I'm Gonna Sit Right Down And Write Myself A Letter; I'm Sitting On Top Of The World; In A Little Spanish Town; In A Shanty In Old Shanty Town; Just A Baby's Prayer At Twilight; Laugh! Clown! Laugh!; Life Is A Song(Let's Sing It Together); Lullaby Of The Leaves; My Mammy; Ooh That Kiss; Rock-A-Bye Your Baby With A Dixie Melody; Singin' The Blues(Till My Daddy Come Home); Snuggled On Your Shoulder(Cuddled In Your Arms); Torch Song; Tuck Me To Sleep In My Old 'tucky Home; Two Hearts In Three Quarter Time; Two Tickets To Georgia; Was That The Human Thing To Do; Where Did Robinson Crusoe Go With Friday On Saturday Night; Yaaka Hulaa Hickey Dula; You're A Heavenly Thing; You're Gonna Lose Your Gal; You're My Everything
YOUNG, KENNY — Arizona; Arkansas Traveler,The; Don't Go Out Into The Rain; Just A Little Bit Better; Little Bit Of Heaven; One Kiss For Old Times' Sake; Under The Boardwalk; When Liking Turns To Loving
YOUNG, LESTER — Baby, Don't Tell On Me
YOUNG, M. — Pump Up The Volume
YOUNG, NEIL — Heart Of Gold; Lotta Love; Love Is A Rose; Ohio; Old Man; Walk On
YOUNG, OTHA — Sweetest Thing I've Ever Known
YOUNG, RIDA JOHNSON — I'm Falling In Love With Someone; Italian Street Song; Mother Machree; Tramp! Tramp! Tramp! Along The Highway; Will You Remember (Sweetheart)
YOUNG, RUSSELL — Crazy Love
YOUNG, S. — Pump Up The Volume
YOUNG, SHEILA — I Love You For All Seasons
YOUNG, VICTOR — (I Don't Stand A)Ghost Of A Chance With You; Alone At Last; Around The World; Beautiful Love; Blue Star(the Medic Theme); C'est La Vie; Call Of The Far-Away Hills; Can't We Talk It Over; China Gate; Golden Earrings; Greatest Show On Earth; Hundred Years From Today; Johnny Guitar; Lawd, You Made The Night Too Long; Lovable Sort Of Person; Love Is The Thing; Love Letters; Love Me; Love Me Tonight; Man With A Dream; My Foolish Heart; Old Man Of The Mountain; Stella By Starlight; Street Of Dreams; Sweet Sue-Just You; Waltzing In A Dream; Weaver Of Dreams; When I Fall In Love; Where Can I Go Without You; Written On The Wind
YOUNG, WILLIE DAVID — Keep On Dancing
YRADIER, SEBASTIAN — Paloma, La(The Dove)
YVAIN, MAURICE — My Man; Throw Me A Kiss

ZAMBON, FRED — Suspicious Minds

ZANETIS, ALEX — Snap Your Fingers

ZANY, KING — Coral Sea

ZAPPA, FRANK — Dancin' Fool

ZARATE, ABEL — Suavecito

ZARET, HY — Dedicated To You; It All Comes Back To Me Now; My Sister And I; No Other Arms, No Other Lips; One Meat Ball; Unchained Melody; You'll Never Get Away; Young And Warm And Wonderful

ZAWINUL, JOSEPH — Mercy, Mercy, Mercy

ZEKLEY, GARY — Sooner Or Later; Yellow Balloon

ZELLER, PHIL — Hang 'em High; I Can't Believe I'm Losing You

ZERATO, LOU — Beg, Borrow And Steal

ZERO, JACK — Please No Squeeza Da Banana

ZESSES, NICK — Hey Big Brother

ZEVON, WARREN — Poor Poor Pitiful Me; Werewolves Of London

ZIGMAN, AARON — Crush On You

ZIMMERMAN, CHARLES A. — Anchors Aweigh

ZIMMERMAN, LEON — I'm Just A Vagabond Lover

ZWIRN, ARTIE — Sorry, I Ran All The Way Home

The Award Winners

Academy Award Winners

The Oscar is awarded by the Academy of Motion Picture Arts and Sciences. Listed here, by year, are the awardwinning titles, the motion picture in which each was featured, and the composers of each song.

Year	Song	Film	Composers
1934	*The Continental*	*The Gay Divorcee*	Herb Magidson and Con Conrad
1935	*Lullaby of Broadway*	*Gold Diggers of 1935*	Al Dubin and Harry Warren
1936	*The Way You Look Tonight*	*Swingtime*	Dorothy Fields and Jerome Kern
1937	*Sweet Leilani*	*Waikiki Wedding*	Harry Owens
1938	*Thanks for the Memory*	*The Big Broadcast of 1938*	Leo Robin and Ralph Rainger
1939	*Over the Rainbow*	*The Wizard of Oz*	E.Y. Harburg and Harold Arlen
1940	*When You Wish Upon a Star*	*Pinocchio*	Ned Washington and Leigh Harline
1941	*The Last Time I Saw Paris*	*Lady, Be Good*	Oscar Hammerstein II and Jerome Kern
1942	*White Christmas*	*Holiday Inn*	Irving Berlin
1943	*You'll Never Know*	*Hello Frisco, Hello*	Mack Gordon and Harry Warren
1944	*Swinging on a Star*	*Going My Way*	Johnny Burke and Jimmy Van Heusen
1945	*It Might As Well Be Spring*	*State Fair*	Oscar Hammerstein II and Richard Rodgers
1946	*On the Atchison, Topeka and the Santa Fe*	*The Harvey Girls*	Johnny Mercer and Harry Warren
1947	*ZipADeeDooDah*	*Song of the South*	Ray Gilbert and Allie Wrubel
1948	*Buttons and Bows*	*Paleface*	Ray Evans and Jay Livingston
1949	*Baby, It's Cold Outside*	*Neptune's Daughter*	Frank Loesser
1950	*Mona Lisa*	*Captain Carey, U.S.A.*	Ray Evans and Jay Livingston
1951	*In the Cool, Cool, Cool of the Evening*	*Here Comes the Groom*	Johnny Mercer and Hoagy Carmichael
1952	*High Noon*	*High Noon*	Ned Washington and Dimitri Tiomkin
1953	*Secret Love*	*Calamity Jane*	Paul Francis Webster and Sammy Fain
1954	*Three Coins in the Fountain*	*Three Coins in the Fountain*	Sammy Cahn and Jule Styne
1955	*Love Is a ManySplendored Thing*	*Love Is a ManySplendored Thing*	Paul Francis Webster and Sammy Fain
1956	*Que Sera, Sera*	*The Man Who Knew Too Much*	Ray Evans and Jay Livingston
1957	*All the Way*	*The Joker Is Wild*	Sammy Cahn and Jimmy Van Heusen
1958	*Gigi*	*Gigi*	Alan Jay Lerner and Frederick Loewe
1959	*High Hopes*	*Hole in the Head*	Sammy Cahn and Jimmy Van Heusen
1960	*Never on Sunday*	*Never on Sunday*	Manos Hadjidakis
1961	*Moon River*	*Breakfast at Tiffany's*	Johnny Mercer and Henry Mancini

Year	Song	Film	Composers
1962	Days of Wine and Roses	Days of Wine and Roses	Johnny Mercer and Henry Mancini
1963	Call Me Irresponsible	Papa's Delicate Condition	Sammy Cahn and Jimmy Van Heusen
1964	Chim Chim Cheree	Mary Poppins	Richard M. Sherman and Robert B. Sherman
1965	The Shadow of Your Smile	The Sandpiper	Paul Francis Webster and Johnny Mandel
1966	Born Free	Born Free	Don Black and John Barry
1967	Talk to the Animals	Doctor Dolittle	Leslie Bricusse
1968	The Windmills of Your Mind	The Thomas Crown Affair	Alan Bergman, Marilyn Bergman, and Michel Legrand
1969	Raindrops Keep Fallin' on My Head	Butch Cassidy and the Sundance Kid	Hal David and Burt Bacharach
1970	For All We Know	Lovers and Other Strangers	Arthur James, Robb Wilson, and Fred Karlin
1971	Theme from Shaft	Shaft	Isaac Hayes
1972	The Morning After	The Poseidon Adventure	Al Kasha and Joel Hirschorn
1973	The Way We Were	The Way We Were	Alan Bergman, Marilyn Bergman, and Marvin Hamlisch
1974	We May Never Love Like This Again	The Towering Inferno	Al Kasha and Joel Hirschorn
1975	I'm Easy	Nashville	Keith Carradine
1976	Evergreen	A Star Is Born	Paul Williams and Barbra Streisand
1977	You Light Up My Life	You Light Up My Life	Joseph Brooks
1978	Last Dance	Thank God It's Friday	Paul Jabara
1979	It Goes Like It Goes	Norma Rae	Norman Gimbel
1980	9 to 5	9 to 5	Dolly Parton
1981	Arthur's Theme (The Best That You Can Do)	Arthur	Carole Bayer Sager, Christopher Cross, Peter Allen, and Burt Bacharach
1982	Up Where We Belong	An Officer and a Gentleman	Jack Nitzsche, Will Jennings, and Buffy SainteMarie
1983	Flashdance...What a Feeling	Flashdance	Keith Forsey, Irene Cara, and Giorgio Moroder
1984	I Just Called to Say I Love You	The Lady in Red	Stevie Wonder
1985	Say You, Say Me (Title Song from White Knights)	White Knights	Lionel Richie
1986	Take My Breath Away (Love Theme from Top Gun)	Top Gun	Giorgio Moroder and Tom Whitlock

NARAS Award Winners

The Grammy is awarded by the National Academy of Recording Arts and Sciences. Listed here, by year, are the award winners in the categories of Song, Record, Rhythm and Blues (R & B) Song, and Country and Western (C & W) or Country Song, along with the composers of each song and the artist performing on each record.

Year	Song	Record	R &B Song	C & W Song
1958	*Volare (Nel Blu Dipinto Di Blu)* / Domenico Modugno	*Volare (Nel Blu Dipinto Di Blu)* / Domenico Modugno, artist	*Tequila* / Chuck Rio	*Tom Dooley* / Traditional
1959	*The Battle of New Orleans* / Jimmy Driftwood	*Mack the Knife* / Bobby Darin, artist	*What a Diff'rence a Day Makes* / Maria Grever and Stanley Adams	*The Battle of New Orleans* / Jimmy Driftwood
1960	*Theme from Exodus* / Ernest Gold	*Theme from A Summer Place* / Percy Faith, artist	*Let the Good Times Roll* / Leonard Lee	*El Paso* / Marty Robbins
1961	*Moon River* / Johnny Mercer and Henry Mancini	*Moon River* / Johnny Mercer and Henry Mancini	*Hit the Road, Jack* / Percy Mayfield	*Big Bad John* / Jimmy Dean
1962	*What Kind of Fool Am I* / Leslie Bricusse and Anthony Newley	*I Left My Heart in San Francisco* / Tony Bennett, artist	*I Can't Stop Loving You* / Don Gibson	*Funny Way of Laughing* / Hank Cochran
1963	*The Days of Wine and Roses* / Johnny Mercer and Henry Mancini	*The Days of Wine and Roses* / Henry Mancini, artist	*Busted* / Harlan Howard	*Detroit City* / Danny Dill and Mel Tillis
1964	*Hello, Dolly!* / Jerry Herman	*The Girl From Ipanema* / Stan Getz and Astrud Gilberto, artists	*How Glad I Am* / Jimmy T. Williams and Larry Harrison	*Dang Me* / Roger Miller
1965	*The Shadow of Your Smile* / Paul Francis Webster and Johnny Mandel	*A Taste of Honey* / Herb Alpert and the Tijuana Brass, artist	*Papa's Got a Brand New Bag* / James Brown	*King of the Road* / Roger Miller
1966	*Michelle* / John Lennon and Paul McCartney	*Strangers in the Night* / Frank Sinatra, artist	*Crying Time* / Buck Owens	*Almost Persuaded* / Glen Sutton and Billy Sherrill
1967	*Up, Up and Away* / Jim Webb	*Up, Up and Away* / The 5th Dimension, artist	*Respect* / Otis Redding	*Gentle on My Mind* / John Hartford
1968	*Little Green Apples* / Bobby Russell	*Mrs. Robinson* / Simon and Garfunkel, artist	*(Sittin' on) The Dock of the Bay* / Steve Cropper and Otis Redding	*Little Green Apples* / Bobby Russell
1969	*Games People Play* / Joe South	*AquariusLet the Sunshine In* / The 5th Dimension, artist	*Color Him Father* / Richard Spencer	*A Boy Named Sue* / Shel Silverstein
1970	*Bridge Over Troubled Water* / Paul Simon	*Bridge Over Troubled Water* / Simon and Garfunkel, artist	*Patches (I'm Depending on You)* / General Johnson and Ronald Dunbar	*My Woman, My Woman, My Wife* / Marty Robbins
1971	*You've Got a Friend* / Carole King	*It's Too Late* / Carole King, artist	*Ain't No Sunshine* / Bill Withers	*Help Me Make it Through the Night* / Kris Kristofferson and Fred Foster

Year	Song	Record	R &B Song	C & W Song
1972	*The First Time Ever I Saw Your Face* / Ewan MacColl	*The First Time Ever I Saw Your Face* / Roberta Flack, artist	*Papa Was A Rolling Stone* / Barrett Strong and Norman Whitfield	*Kiss an Angel Good Mornin'* / Ben Peters
1973	*Killing Me Softly With His Song* / Charles Fox and Norman Gimbel	*Killing Me Softly With His Song* / Roberta Flack, artist	*Superstition* / Stevie Wonder	*Behind Closed Doors* / Kenny O'Dell
1974	*The Way We Were* / Marilyn Bergman, Alan Bergman, and Marvin Hamlisch	*I Honestly Love You* / Olivia NewtonJohn, artist	*Living for the City* / Stevie Wonder	*A Very Special Love Song* / Norris Wilson and Billy Sherrill
1975	*Send in the Clowns* / Stephen Sondheim	*Love Will Keep Us Together* / Captain and Tennille, artist	*Where Is the Love* / Harry Wayne Casey, Richard Finch, Wille Clark, and Betty Wright	*(Hey Won't You Play) Another Somebody Done Somebody Wrong Song* / Chips Moman and Larry Butler
1976	*I Write the Songs* / Bruce Johnston	*This Masquerade* / George Benson, artist	*Lowdown* / Boz Scaggs and David Paich	*Broken Lady* / Larry Gatlin
1977	*Love Theme from A Star Is Born (Evergreen)* / Barbra Streisand and Paul Williams	*Hotel California* / Eagles, artist	*You Make Me Feel Like Dancing* / Leo Sayer and Vini Poncia	*Don't it make My Brown Eyes Blue* / Richard Leigh
1978	*Just the Way You Are* / Billy Joel	*Just the Way You Are* / Billy Joel, artist	*Last Dance* / Paul Jabara	*The Gambler* / Don Schlitz
1979	*What a Fool Believes* / Kenny Loggins and Michael McDonald	*What a Fool Believes* / The Doobie Brothers, artist	*After the Love is Gone* / David Foster, Jay Graydon, and Bill Champlin	*You Decorated My Life* / Bob Morrison and Debbie Hupp
1980	*Sailing* / Christopher Cross	*Sailing* / Christopher Cross, artist	*Never Knew Love Like This Before* / James Mtume and Reginald Lucas	*On the Road Again* / Willie Nelson
1981	*Bette Davis Eyes* / Donna Weiss and Jackie DeShannon	*Bette Davis Eyes* / Kim Carnes, artist	*Just the Two of Us* / Bill Withers, William Salter, and Ralph MacDonald	*9 to 5* / Dolly Parton
1982	*Always On My Mind* / Johnny Christopher, Wayne Thompson, and Mark James	*Rosanna* / Toto, artist	*Turn Your Love Around* / Jay Graydon, Steve Lukather, and Bill Champlin	*Always On My Mind* / Johnny Christopher, Wayne Thompson, and Mark James
1983	*Every Breath You Take* / Sting	*Beat It* / Michael Jackson, artist	*Billie Jean* / Michael Jackson	*Stranger in My House* / Mike Reid
1984	*I Just Called to Say I Love You* / Stevie Wonder	*What's Love Got to Do With It* / Tina Turner, artist	*I Feel For You* / Prince Rogers Nelson	*City of New Orleans* / Steve Goodman
1985	*We Are the World* / Michael Jackson and Lionel Richie	*We Are the World* / U.S.A. for Africa, artist	*Freeway of Love* / Narada Michael Walden and Jeffrey Cohen	*Highwayman* / Jim Webb
1986	*That's What Friends Are For* / Carole Bayer Sager and Burt Bacharach	*Higher Love* / Steve Winwood, artist	*Sweet Love* / Anita Baker, Louis A. Johnson, and Gary Bias	*Grandpa (Tell Me 'Bout the Good Old Days)* / Jamie O'Hara

The National Academy of Popular Music
Songwriters' Hall of Fame

The National Academy of Popular Music was founded in 1969. In 1977, this organization opened the Songwriters' Hall of Fame. Each year, a nominating committee selects candidates for the Hall, and NAPM members, as well as the music press, receive ballots. The inductees as of 1988 are listed below.

Harold Adamson
Richard Adler
Milton Ager
Fred Ahlert
Harry Akst
Lewis Alter
Leroy Anderson
Harold Arlen
Burt Bacharach
Ernest Ball
Katherine Lee Bates
William Becket
Bennie Benjamin
Alan Bergman
Marilyn Bergman
Irving Berlin
Leonard Bernstein
Chuck Berry
William Billings
James Bland
Ralph Blane
Rube Bloom
Jerry Bock
James Brockman
Lew Brown
Nacio Herb Brown
Boudleaux Bryant
Felice Bryant
Alfred Bryan
Joe Burke
Johnny Burke
Irving Caesar
Sammy Cahn
Anne Caldwell
Hoagy Carmichael
Harry Carroll
Saul Chaplin
Sidney Clare
Will D. Cobb
George M. Cohan
Cy Coleman
Betty Comden
Con Conrad
Sam Cooke
J. Fred Coots
Sam Coslow
Noel Coward
Hart P. Danks
Hal David
Mack David
Benny Davis
Reginald De Koven
Gene De Paul
Peter De Rose
Buddy De Sylva
Neil Diamond
Howard Dietz
Mort Dixon
Walter Donaldson
Lamont Dozier
Ervin Drake

Paul Dresser
Dave Dreyer
Al Dubin
Vernon Duke
Bob Dylan
Fred Ebb
Gus Edwards
Raymond B. Egan
Edward Eliscu
Duke Ellington
Daniel Decatur Emmet
Ray Evans
Sammy Fain
Dorothy Fields
Ted Fio Rito
Fred Fisher
Stephen Foster
Arthur Freed
Rudolph Friml
George Gershwin
Ira Gershwin
L. Wolfe Gilbert
Haven Gillespie
Patrick S. Gilmore
Norman Gimbel
Gerry Goffin
Mack Gordon
Adolph Greeen
Bud Green
John Green
Ferde Grofe
Woody Guthrie
Marvin Hamlisch
Oscar Hammerstein II
Lou Handman
W. C. Handy
James F. Hanley
Otto Harbach
E. Y. Harburg
Sheldon Harnick
Charles K. Harris
Lorenz Hart
Ray Henderson
Victor Herbert
Jerry Herman
Edward Heyman
Billy Hill
Bob Hilliard
Al Hoffman
Brian Holland
Edward Holland
Buddy Holly
Joe Howard
Julia Ward Howe
Carrie Jacobs-Bond
Gordon Jenkins
Howard Johnson
James P. Johnson
James Weldon Johnson
Arthur Johnston
Isham Jones

Scott Joplin
Irving Kahl
Gus Kahn
Burt Kalmar
John Kander
Jerome Kern
Francis Scott Key
Carole King
Ted Koehler
Kris Kristofferson
Burton Lane
Jack Lawrence
Huddie Ledbetter
Jerry Leiber
Carolyn Leigh
John Lennon
Allan Jay Lerner
Edgar Leslie
Sam Lewis
Jay Livingston
Jerry Livingston
Fred Loesser
Frederick Loewe
Ballard MacDonald
Edward Madden
Herb Magidson
Henry Mancini
Barry Mann
Johnny Marks
Hugh Martin
Paul McCartney
Joseph McCarthy
Jimmy McHugh
Johnny Mercer
Bob Merrill
George W. Meyer
Joseph Meyer
Jimmy Monaco
Neil Moret
Theodore Morse
Lewis F. Muir
Ethelbert Nevin
Jack Norworth
Chauncey Olcott
Mitchell Parish
John Howard Payne
J. S. Pierpont
Maceo Pinkard
Lew Pollack
Cole Porter
Ralph Rainger
Don Raye
Andy Razaf
Harry Revel
Eben E. Rexford
Leo Robin
Jimmie Rodgers
Richard Rodgers
Sigmund Romberg
Harold Rome
George F. Root

Billy Rose
Fred Rose
Vincent Rose
Jerry Ross
Harry Ruby
Bob Russell
Carole Bayer Sager
Arthur Schwartz
Jean Schwartz
Neil Sedaka
Pete Seeger
Carl Sigman
Paul Simon
Seymour Simons
Harry B. Smith
Samuel Francis Smith
Ted Snyder
Stephen Sondheim
John Phillip Sousa
Andrew B. Sterling
Al Stillman
Mike Stoller
Billy Strayhorn
Charles Strouse
Jule Styne
Harry A. Tierney
Charles Tobias
Harry Tobias
Roy Turk
Egbert Van Alstyne
Jimmy Van Heusen
Albert Von Tilzer
Harry Von Tilzer
Fats Waller
Samuel A. Ward
Harry Warren
Ned Washington
Mabel Wayne
Paul Francis Webster
Jimmy Webb
Cynthia Weil
Kurt Weill
George David Weiss
Percy Weinrich
Richard Whiting
Alec Wilding
Clarence Williams
Hank Williams
Spencer Williams
Meredith Willson
Septimus Winner
Stevie Wonder
Harry MacGregor Woods
Henry C. Work
Allie Wrubel
Jack Yellen
Vincent Youmans
Joe Young
Rida Johnson Young
Victor Young

Testing 1...2...3...

A popular music quiz with more than 450 questions.
(Answers begin on page 409)

Testing 1...2...3...

See Page 409 for Answers

Q1. What William Bell—Booker T. Jones composition was popularized by Gene Chandler (1962) and revived by Billy Idol (1986)?

Q2. Who composed and introduced the 1967 song *Chelsea Morning*?

Q3. Who composed *Smoke Gets in Your Eyes*?

Q4. What Willie Nelson composition was the NARAS Country Song of the Year in 1980?

Q5. Who composed the Rosemary Clooney hit, *Come Ona My House*?

Q6. Who composed the 1931 song *Mad Dogs and Englishmen*?

Q7. Who composed *Someday We'll Be Together*?

Q8. Who popularized the 1955 song *I Hear You Knocking*?

Q9. Who composed the Three Dog Night hit *Mama Told Me (Not to Come)*?

Q10. What General Johnson—Ronald Dunbar composition was the NARAS R & B Song of the Year in 1970?

Q11. Who popularized *Into Each Life Some Rain Must Fall*?

Q12. What Dolly Parton composition was the NARAS Country Song of the Year in 1981?

Q13. In what film did Doris Day introduce the Webster-Fain title *Secret Love*?

Q14. Who composed *How Long Has This Been Going On*?

Q15. Who composed *Bluesette*?

Q16. Who composed *I Left My Heart in San Francisco*?

Q17. Who composed *I'm Beginning to See the Light*?

Q18. Who popularized Turk and Ahlert's *Mean to Me*?

Q19. What Carole King composition was the NARAS Song of the Year in 1971?

Q20. Who popularized the 1985 song *Living in America*?

Q21. Who introduced *The Look of Love* in the film *Casino Royale*?

Q22. Who popularized *Maria Elena*?

Q23. Who wrote *Star Dust*?

Q24. Who wrote the Academy Awardwinning song *I'm Easy*?

Q25. Who, in 1878, wrote the words and music for *Aloha Oe*?

Q26. What 1939 Irving Berlin song was popularized by Kate Smith?

Q27. Who introduced Gordon Jenkins' *This Is All I Ask*?

Q28. Who composed Nilsson's hit *Everybody's Talkin' (Echoes)*, introduced in the film *Midnight Cowboy*?

Q29. Who wrote *Traces*, popularized by The Classics IV?

Q30. For whom was *Cherry Pink and Apple Blossom White* a number one recording?

Q31. Who wrote *Spanish Harlem*?

Q32. What Withers—Salter—MacDonald composition was the NARAS R & B Song of the Year in 1981?

Q33. Who composed *Don't Think Twice, It's All Right*?

Q34. What song written by Rickie Lee Jones was nominated for a NARAS Award (Song of the Year) in 1979?

Q35. What Casey—Finch—Clark—Wright composition was the NARAS R & B Song of the Year in 1975?

Q36. Who composed The Teddy Bears' number one hit *To Know Him Is to Love Him*?

Q37. Who was the vocalist on Harry James and his Orchestra's recording of *I've Heard That Song Before*?

Q38. Who wrote *Baby Face*?

Q39. Who composed *Laura*?

Q40. Who wrote *Sing, Sing, Sing*, popularized by Benny Goodman and his Orchestra?

Q41. What Kahn—Eliscu—Youmans song, introduced in the film *Flying Down to Rio*, was nominated for an Academy Award in 1934?

Q42. What Kenneth Williams—Rudy Clark—Jim Bailey song, popularized by The Main Ingredient, was nominated for a NARAS Award in 1972?

Q43. Who composed *California, Here I Come* and in what musical was it introduced?

Q44. What Graydon—Lukather—Champlin composition was the NARAS R & B Song of the Year in 1982?

Q45. What Leslie Bricusse song featured in the film *Doctor Dolittle* won an Academy Award in 1967?

Q46. Who wrote the Three Dog Night hit *Eli's Coming*?

Q47. Who wrote *Willow Weep for Me*?

Q48. Who wrote *Young at Heart*?

Q49. Who composed *Solitude*?

Q50. Who wrote Gale Garnett's hit *We'll Sing in the Sunshine*?

Q51. Who wrote *When Sunny Gets Blue*?

Q52. Who composed *Something*?

Q53. Who wrote *Wonderful Copenhagen*?

Q54. What song written and originally popularized by Sam Cooke was revived in 1974 by Cat Stevens?

Q55. Who composed *My Way*, popularized by Frank Sinatra?

Q56. Who composed the 1977 song *New York, New York*?

Q57. Who wrote *After Midnight*?

Q58. What Don Raye—Hughie Prince song, introduced in the film *Buck Privates*, was nominated for an Academy Award in 1941?

Q59. What Marty Robbins composition won a Grammy for C & W Song of the Year in 1960?

Q60. What two artists each had a number one record with the Gerry Goffin—Carole King song *Go Away Little Girl*?

Q61. Who composed *Misty*?

Q62. Who popularized *My Heart Tells Me*?

Q63. What Shel Silverstein composition was the NARAS C & W Song of the Year in 1969?

Q64. What song was featured on Ella Fitzgerald's first record, and how old was Ella when she recorded it?

Q65. What was the theme song of Jimmy Dorsey and

his Orchestra?

Q66. Who composed *On Broadway?*

Q67. Who composed *Sincerely*, popularized by The Mc-Guire Sisters?

Q68. What Leo Sayer—Vini Poncia composition was the NARAS R & B Song of the Year in 1977?

Q69. Who cowrote both *Those Were the Days* (theme from *All in the Family*) and *Tomorrow* (from the musical *Annie*)?

Q70. Who wrote *Too Young?*

Q71. Who wrote Starship's hit *We Built This City?*

Q72. Who composed *A Night in Tunisia?*

Q73. Who composed *Diamonds Are a Girl's Best Friend?*

Q74. Who composed *Theme from The Untouchables?*

Q75. Who wrote *You Belong to Me*, popularized by Carly Simon?

Q76. For whom was the 1938 song *Don't Be That Way* a number one record?

Q77. In what musical was the Webster—Ellington song *I Got It Bad (And That Ain't Good)* introduced?

Q78. What Narada Michael Walden—Jeffrey Cohen compostition was the NARAS R&B Song of the Year in 1985?

Q79. Who composed the Academy Awardwinning song *Born Free?*

Q80. What song, written by Sol Quasha and Herb Yakus, was popularized in 1956 by Bobby Scott and revived in 1960 by Sam Cooke and in 1968 by Jackie Wilson with Count Basie and his Orchestra?

Q81. Who composed *Prisoner of Love*, popularized by Russ Columbo?

Q82. Who composed *Try a Little Tenderness*, revived most recently by Otis Redding?

Q83. What Ernest Gold composition won a Grammy for Best Song of the Year in 1960?

Q84. Who were the four saxophonists in Woody Herman's Second Herd's recording of Jimmy Giuffre's *Four Brothers?*

Q85. What was the title of Duke Ellington's *Do Nothin' Till You Hear From Me* before lyrics were added?

Q86. Who composed the 1951 song *It's All in the Game*, a number one record for Tommy Edwards?

Q87. Who composed *Goodnight Irene?*

Q88. What Phil F. Sloane—Steve Barri composition was brought to the top of the chart by Barry McGuire?

Q89. Who wrote *The Shadow of Your Smile?*

Q90. Who composed *This Love of Mine*, popularized by Tommy Dorsey and his Orchestra, with vocal by Frank Sinatra?

Q91. Who composed *Day InDay Out*, brought to the top of the chart by Bob Crosby and his Orchestra with vocal by Helen Ward and subsequently revived by Frank Sinatra?

Q92. Who brought *Ain't That a Shame* to the top of the chart?

Q93. Who had a number one hit with *Gimme a Little Kiss, Will Ya Huh?*

Q94. Who composed the 1960 song *I'm Sorry?*

Q95. Who introduced *Blueberry Hill?*

Q96. Who wrote *Respect*, brought to number one by Aretha Franklin?

Q97. Who had a number one hit with *Frenest?*

Q98. Who composed the 1954 song *I Never Has Seen Snow?*

Q99. Who popularized *Riders in the Sky (Ghost Riders in the Sky)*, and who wrote it?

Q100. Who composed the David Bowie hit *China Girl?*

Q101. What Jimmy Dean composition was the NARAS C & W Song of the Year in 1961?

Q102. Who composed *Here's That Rainy Day?*

Q103. In what film was *The Long and Winding Road* introduced?

Q104. Who composed *Mercy, Mercy, Mercy?*

Q105. Who composed *Round Midnight?*

Q106. Who composed *Cry Me a River?*

Q107. Who composed *No, No, Nanette?*

Q108. What Roger Miller composition was the NARAS C & W Song of the Year in 1964?

Q109. Who composed *You Made Me Love You (I Didn't Want to Do It)?*

Q110. What Gordon Jenkins song, revived by Linda Ronstadt with Nelson Riddle and his Orchestra in 1985, was the closing theme for Benny Goodman and his Orchestra?

Q111. What song popularized and cowritten by Al Green was revived in 1984 by Tina Turner?

Q112. What Chuck Rio composition was the NARAS R & B Song of the Year in 1958?

Q113. Who wrote The Byrds *Turn! Turn! Turn!?*

Q114. Who composed *Me and My Shadow?*

Q115. Who composed *The Mighty Quinn?*

Q116. Who wrote *All of Me?*

Q117. What Gamble—Huff—Jackson song, popularized by The O'Jays, was nominated for a NARAS Award in 1974?

Q118. Who composed the 1959 song *Desafinado (Slightly Out of Tune)?*

Q119. What James—Wilson—Karlin composition featured in the film *Lovers and Other Strangers* won an Academy Award in 1970?

Q120. Who composed *Seasons in the Sun*, a number one hit for Terry Jacks in 1974?

Q121. What Foster—Graydon—Champlin composition was the NARAS R & B Song of the Year in 1979?

Q122. Who wrote the words and music for *America the Beautiful?*

Q123. What Joe South composition was the NARAS Song of the Year in 1969?

Q124. Who wrote *Stand By Me?*

Q125. Who composed *I Love to Singa?*

Q126. Who composed *Love Is a Many Splendored Thing?*

Q127. What Christopher Cross composition was the NARAS Song of the Year in 1980?

Q128. What song written in 1926 by Roy Turk and Lou Handman did Elvis Presley bring to the top of the chart in 1960?

Q129. Who composed the 1984 NARAS Award-winning song *I Feel For You*, popularized by Chaka Khan?

Q130. Who wrote *My Cherie Amour?*

Q131. What song written by Brian Holland and Freddy C. Gorman was brought to the top of the chart by both the Marvelettes (1961) and the Carpenters (1975)?

Q132. Who composed the Zombies' hit *She's Not There*?

Q133. For whom was Cole Porter's *Don't Fence Me In* a number one record?

Q134. Who composed Eric Clapton's number one hit *I Shot the Sheriff*?

Q135. What Academy Awardwinning Frank Loesser song was introduced in the film *Neptune's Daughter* by Esther Williams and Ricardo Montalban?

Q136. Who performed Irving Berlin's *Couple of Song and Dance Men* in the film *Blue Skies*?

Q137. Who composed *Octopus's Garden*?

Q138. Who wrote *The Best Is Yet to Come*?

Q139. What Maurice White—Albert McKay song, popularized by the Emotions, was nominated for a NARAS Award in 1977?

Q140. Who composed The Spinners' hit *The Rubberband Man*?

Q141. What Kenny O'Dell composition was the NARAS C & W Song of the Year in 1973?

Q142. Who wrote *You Always Hurt the One You Love*, popularized by The Mills Brothers?

Q143. In what musical was *I Get a Kick Out of You* introduced?

Q144. Who composed *Hey! BaBaReBop*?

Q145. Who popularized *(There is) No Greater Love*?

Q146. Who composed the Kim Carnes hit *Bette Davis Eyes*?

Q147. What was Edward Kennedy "Duke" Ellington's first published composition?

Q148. What Grever—Adams composition was the NARAS R & B Song of the Year in 1959?

Q149. Who composed *Potato Head Blues*?

Q150. Who wrote *Boll Weevil Song*?

Q151. Who wrote *Satin Doll*?

Q152. What Strong—Whitfield composition was the NARAS R & B Song of the Year in 1972?

Q153. Who composed the Elvis Presley number one hit *Don't Be Cruel (To a Heart That's True)*?

Q154. Who composed the 1938 song *Heart and Soul*?

Q155. Who composed *Minnie the Moocher*?

Q156. Who composed *Caldonia (What Makes Your Big Head So Hard)*, popularized by Louis Jordan and Woody Herman and his Orchestra?

Q157. Who wrote *Call Me*, popularized by Chris Montez?

Q158. What Hank Cochran composition was the NARAS C & W Song of the Year in 1962?

Q159. Who composed *The Glory of Love*?

Q160. What was the theme song of Jack Teagarden and his Orchestra?

Q161. Who composed *Save the Last Dance for Me*?

Q162. Who wrote *Chitty Chitty Bang Bang*?

Q163. What Stephen Sondheim composition was the NARAS Song of the Year in 1975?

Q164. What Buddy Holly—Norman Petty song was revived in 1985 by James Taylor?

Q165. Who wrote *The Twelfth of Never*, popularized by Johnny Mathis?

Q166. What song was the theme for Stan Kenton and his Orchestra?

Q167. In what film did Fred Astaire and Ginger Rogers perform *I Won't Dance*?

Q168. Who wrote *The Very Thought of You*?

Q169. What song popularized by The Skyliners was revived by Chuck Jackson (1964), Art Garfunkel (1979), and Don McLean (1981)?

Q170. What Al Kasha—Joel Hirschorn composition featured in the film *The Poseidon Adventure* won an Academy Award in 1972?

Q171. In what musical was George and Ira Gershwin's *Fascinating Rhythm* introduced?

Q172. What Boz Scaggs—David Paich composition was the NARAS R & B Song of the Year in 1976?

Q173. Who composed *Good Morning Heartache*?

Q174. Who popularized the 1959 song *Alvin's Harmonica*?

Q175. Who wrote *Stir It Up*, popularized by Johnny Nash?

Q176. In what musical was Cole Porter's *Do I Love You*? introduced and by whom?

Q177. What Streisand—Williams composition was the NARAS Song of the Year in 1977?

Q178. What Jimmy Driftwood composition was the NARAS Song of the Year in 1959?

Q179. What Percy Mayfield composition was the NARAS R & B Song of the Year in 1961?

Q180. Who revived *The Lady Is a Tramp* in the 1939 film *Words and Music*?

Q181. Who composed the 1927 song *Bill*?

Q182. What Kristofferson—Foster composition was the NARAS C & W Song of the Year in 1971?

Q183. Who composed *Islands in the Stream*, a number one record for Kenny Rogers and Dolly Parton?

Q184. Who composed *September Song*, popularized by Bing Crosby and revived (1984) by Willie Nelson?

Q185. What Norman Gimbel composition featured in the film *Norma Rae* won an Academy Award in 1979?

Q186. Who composed *Don't Get Around Much Anymore*?

Q187. Who composed *Stranger in Paradise*?

Q188. Who besides Stevie Wonder had a bestselling recording of the Ronald Miller—Orlando Murden song *For Once in My Life*?

Q189. What Lionel Richie composition featured in the film *White Nights* won an Academy Award in 1985?

Q190. Who composed The Supremes' number one hit *Baby Love*?

Q191. What Jim Weatherly song, popularized by Gladys Knight & The Pips, was nominated for a NARAS Award in 1973?

Q192. Who wrote *Someday My Prince Will Come*?

Q193. Who wrote *Tradition* from the musical *Fiddler on the Roof*?

Q194. Who composed *The Jitterbug Waltz*?

Q195. What 1979 song popularized by England Dan and John Ford Coley was written by Todd Rundgren?

Q196. What Bergman—Bergman—Hamlisch composition was the NARAS Song of the Year in 1974?

Q197. Who composed *You're Blasé*?

Q198. Who wrote the words and music for the Badfinger hit *Come and Get It*?

Q199. Who popularized the 1931 Kahn—Akst—Whiting collaboration *Guilty*?

Q200. What Ewan MacColl composition was the NARAS Song of the Year in 1972?

Q201. Who popularized *The Dicty Blues*?

Q202. Who popularized Koehler and Arlen's *Let's Fall in Love*?

Q203. Who wrote *St. Louis Blues*, popularized by Marion Harris?

Q204. Who composed the 1938 song *I'm Building Up to an Awful Letdown*, popularized by Fred Astaire?

Q205. Who wrote Art Garfunkel's hit *All I Know*?

Q206. What James Brown composition was the NARAS R & B Song of the Year in 1965?

Q207. Who composed *Um, Um, Um, Um, Um, Um*?

Q208. Who wrote *The Unicorn*?

Q209. Who wrote *Wake Up Little Susie*?

Q210. With what 1938 Irving Berlin song, introduced in the film *Carefree*, did both Fred Astaire and Jimmy Dorsey and his Orchestra have number one recordings?

Q211. Who wrote *Every Time You Go Away*, a number one record for Paul Young?

Q212. Who wrote the 1986 song *Walk of Life*?

Q213. Who wrote *You've Made Me So Very Happy*, popularized by Blood, Sweat & Tears?

Q214. What Stevie Wonder composition was the NARAS Song of the Year in 1984?

Q215. Who wrote the words and music for *Ain't Too Proud to Beg*, popularized by The Temptations (1966) and revived by The Rolling Stones (1974)?

Q216. Who composed *Mairzy Doats*?

Q217. What Evans—Livingston song featured in the film *Paleface* won an Academy Award in 1948?

Q218. Who introduced *Lulu's Back in Town*?

Q219. Who composed the Jackie Wilson hit *Lonely Teardrops*?

Q220. Who popularized Irving Berlin's *Some Sunny Day*?

Q221. Who composed *In the Mood*?

Q222. What Steven Schwartz song from the film *Pippin* was popularized by The Jackson Five?

Q223. What Al Dubin—Harry Warren song, introduced in the film *Dames*, has been revived by The Lettermen (1966) and Art Garfunkel (1975)?

Q224. Who composed *Lullaby of Broadway*?

Q225. Who wrote the Academy Awardwinning *Up Where We Belong*?

Q226. What Roger Miller composition was the NARAS C & W Song of the Year in 1965?

Q227. What Lennon—McCartney collaboration, originally performed by The Beatles, was revived by Earth, Wind and Fire in 1978?

Q228. Who popularized *I'm in the Mood for Love*?

Q229. Who composed *I Didn't Know What Time It Was*?

Q230. Who wrote Gary Lewis and The Playboys' *Everybody Loves a Clown*?

Q231. Who popularized the Mercer—de Paul song *Lonesome Polecat*?

Q232. Who wrote *Stop and Smell the Roses*, along with Mac Davis?

Q233. What Sylvester Allena—Harold R. Brown—Morris Dickerson—Leroy "Lonnie" Jordan—Charles W. Miller—Lee Oscar Levitin—Howard Scott song, popularized by the group comprising the same, was nominated for a NARAS Award in 1974?

Q234. What George Harrison—Eric Clapton collabora-

tion produced a hit for Cream in 1969?

Q235. Who composed *High Noon (Do Not Forsake Me)*?

Q236. Who wrote the music for *Somewhere My Love (Lara's Theme)*?

Q237. What Harry Owens song introduced in the film *Waikiki Wedding* won an Academy Award in 1937?

Q238. Who composed *Moonlight in Vermont*?

Q239. Who composed *Confirmation*?

Q240. Who composed *It Was a Very Good Year*?

Q241. What Lennon—McCartney composition was the NARAS Song of the Year in 1966?

Q242. Who performed the soundtrack version of *Alfie* in the film of the same name?

Q243. Who wrote *Stay*?

Q244. What song composed by Alan and Marilyn Bergman and Michel Legrand and featured in the film *The Thomas Crown Affair* won an Academy Award in 1968?

Q245. What Buck Owens composition was the NARAS R & B Song of the Year in 1966?

Q246. Who composed the David Bowie hit *Fame*?

Q247. What song, introduced in the film *The Goldwyn Follies*, was George Gershwin's last?

Q248. Who wrote The Rolling Stones' hit *Time Is on My Side*?

Q249. For whom was *Didn't We Almost Have it All* a number one record?

Q250. What Cahn—Styne song, introduced in the film *Follow the Boys*, was nominated for an Academy Award in 1944?

Q251. What Jackson—Richie composition was the NARAS Song of the Year in 1985?

Q252. Who composed *The Continental* and who introduced it?

Q253. Who composed *I'm Looking for a Guy Who Plays Alto and Baritone and Doubles on a Clarinet and Wears a Size 37 Suit*?

Q254. Who popularized the Webster—Mills song *Black Coffee*?

Q255. Who popularized *Miss Otis Regrets*?

Q256. Who introduced Rodgers and Hammerstein's *Oh, What a Beautiful Mornin'*?

Q257. Who popularized Lawrence E. Williams' *Slow Down*?

Q258. What Jim Webb composition was the NARAS Song of the Year in 1967?

Q259. Who popularized *Blues in the Night*?

Q260. Who popularized the Carmichael—Brooks song *Ole Buttermilk Sky*?

Q261. Who popularized Jimmy Drake's *Transfusion*?

Q262. Who wrote *You Send Me*?

Q263. What Leonard Lee composition won a Grammy for R & B Song of the Year in 1960?

Q264. Who composed *Toyland*?

Q265. Who composed *Chattanooga Choo Choo*?

Q266. Who composed *Indian Love Call*?

Q267. Who composed *Shop Around*?

Q268. Who performed *Always True to You in My Fashion* in the 1953 film version of *Kiss Me, Kate*?

Q269. Who composed the Three Dog Night hit *One*?

Q270. Who composed *Soul Man*, popularized by Sam and Dave and revived (1979) by the Blues Brothers?

Q271. What Evans—Livingston song featured in the film

The Man Who Knew Too Much won an Academy Award in 1956?

Q272.By whom was the Rodgers and Hammerstein song *Whistle a Happy Tune* introduced?

Q273.Who composed *Paris in the Spring*?

Q274.What Otis Redding composition was the NARAS R & B Song of the Year in 1967?

Q275.Who brought *Amapola (Pretty Little Poppy)* to the top of the chart in 1940?

Q276.Who wrote *Break Up to Make Up*, popularized by The Stylistics?

Q277.What Bricusse—Newley song was the NARAS Song of the Year in 1962?

Q278.Who collaborated with Brian Wilson on *Surfin' U.S.A.*?

Q279.What Gerry Goffin—Carole King collaboration was brought to the top of the chart by both Little Eva and Grand Funk?

Q280.Who wrote *Rock Around the Clock*, and in what film was it introduced?

Q281.What Jim Webb song was the NARAS Country Song of the Year in 1985?

Q282.With what 1957 song, written by Al Stillman and Robert Allen, did Johnny Mathis have a number one recording?

Q283.What Jimmy T. Williams—Larry Harrison composition was the NARAS R & B Song of the Year in 1964?

Q284.Who composed *Happy Days Are Here Again*?

Q285.Who popularized *Shout (Part 1 and 2)*, and who wrote it?

Q286.Who introduced Robin and Rainger's *Thanks for the Memory*?

Q287.What John Hartford composition was the NARAS C & W Song of the Year in 1967?

Q288.Who composed *Moon Love*, popularized by Glenn Miller and his Orchestra, and from what classical composition is it adapted?

Q289.Who wrote *Pennies from Heaven*?

Q290.Who wrote *Poor Poor Pitiful Me*, popularized by Linda Ronstadt?

Q291.In what musical was *I Got Rhythm* introduced?

Q292.What song written and performed by Bill Withers won a NARAS Award in 1971?

Q293.Who composed *Cherokee*?

Q294.What Billy Joel composition was the NARAS Song of the Year in 1978?

Q295.Who popularized the Green—Brown—Homer composition *Sentimental Journey*?

Q296.Who wrote *The Tears of a Clown*, popularized by The Miracles?

Q297.Who composed *I Keep Forgettin' (Every Time You're Near)*, revived in 1982 by Michael McDonald?

Q298.Who wrote the music for and performed the 1931 song *Concentratin' on You*?

Q299.Who introduced *I Could Have Danced All Night* in the musical *My Fair Lady*?

Q300.Who composed *Silhouettes*?

Q301.Who composed *That's Life*?

Q302.What Bobby Russell composition was the NARAS Song of the Year in 1968?

Q303.Who composed The Platters' number one song *The Great Pretender*?

Q304.Who composed *Old Folks at Home (Way Down Upon the Swanee River)*?

Q305.What 1930 Irving Berlin song was popularized by Harry Richman and revived by Fred Astaire (1946) and Taco (1983)?

Q306.What Cahn—Styne song introduced in the film *Anchors Aweigh* was nominated for an Academy Award in 1945?

Q307.Who composed the 1933 song *Flying Down to Rio*?

Q308.Who wrote *Tell Me Something Good*, popularized by Rufus?

Q309.What Kenny Loggins—Michael McDonald composition was the NARAS Song of the Year in 1978?

Q310.Who composed the 1933 song *Heat Wave*?

Q311.Who composed The Spinners' hit *It's a Shame*?

Q312.Who wrote *You Are So Beautiful*, popularized by Joe Cocker?

Q313.What 1981 song was written by George Harrison as a tribute to John Lennon?

Q314.Who composed *The Christmas Song (Chestnuts Roasting on an Open Fire)*?

Q315.Who wrote *Singin' in the Rain*?

Q316.What Hy Zaret—Alex North song introduced in the film *Unchained* was nominated for an Academy Award in 1955?

Q317.Who performed the Clarke—Akst song *Am I Blue* in the film *On With the Show*?

Q318.What Terry Gilkyson song introduced in the animated film *The Jungle Book* was nominated for an Academy Award in 1967?

Q319.What Harlan Howard composition was the NARAS R & B Song of the Year in 1963?

Q320.Who wrote *Yesterday When I Was Young*, popularized by Roy Clark?

Q321.What 1938 Irving Kahal—Sammy Fain collaboration was brought to the top of the chart by Bing Crosby and later became Liberace's theme song?

Q322.Who composed the music for *Autumn Leaves*?

Q323.Who wrote *Stoned Soul Picnic*, popularized by The 5th Dimension?

Q324.What Stevie Wonder composition was the NARAS R & B Song of the Year in 1973?

Q325.Who composed *Darn That Dream*, a number one record for Benny Goodman and his Orchestra?

Q326.Who popularized the Gershwin's *Someone to Watch Over Me*?

Q327.Who composed Gene Autry's theme song *Back in the Saddle Again*?

Q328.Who wrote *You're Getting to Be a Habit With Me*?

Q329.What Roy Orbison—Joe Melson collaboration was introduced by Orbison and revived by Jay and The Americans (1966) and Don McLean (1981)?

Q330.Who collaborated with Stephanie (Stevie) Nicks in the writing of *Stand Back*?

Q331.Who composed the Academy Awardwinning *Never on Sunday*?

Q332.Who wrote *We Need a Little Christmas*?

Q333.Who composed *Dancing in the Street*, most recently revived by Mick Jagger and David Bowie?

Q334.What Stevie Wonder composition was the NARAS R & B Song of the Year in 1974?

Q335.Who composed *How High the Moon*?

Q336.Who composed the 1921 song *I'm Just Wild About Harry*?

Q337. Who popularized *Bei Mir Bist Du Schon*?

Q338. What Paul Jabara composition featured in the film *Thank God It's Friday* won an Academy Award in 1978?

Q339. Who wrote the words for the vocal version of the 1981 song *Chariots of Fire*, and who performed it?

Q340. Who composed *Santa Claus Is Coming to Town*?

Q341. What Fox—Gimbel composition was the NARAS Song of the Year in 1973?

Q342. Who composed *I Can't Give You Anything But Love (Baby)*?

Q343. What Academy Awardwinning song was introduced in the film *The Joker Is Wild*?

Q344. Who composed *Have You Met Miss Jones*?

Q345. What song introduced in the film *Now, Voyager* became a number one record for Dick Haymes?

Q346. Who popularized *Boogie Woogie Etude*?

Q347. Who composed *Strangers in the Night*?

Q348. Who composed *Don't Explain*, popularized by Billie Holiday?

Q349. Who composed The O'Jays' *Love Train*?

Q350. Who cowrote both *Touch Me in the Morning* and *All at Once*?

Q351. Who wrote and popularized *Foxy Lady*?

Q352. Who composed *Moonlight Serenade*?

Q353. Who introduced George Gershwin's *Concerto in F*?

Q354. Who composed *Chopsticks*?

Q355. Who composed *MacArthur Park*?

Q356. What Mercer—Warren song featured in *The Harvey Girls* won an Academy Award in 1946?

Q357. Who composed *Ships*, popularized by Barry Manilow?

Q358. Who wrote the Academy Awardwinning *You Light Up My Life*?

Q359. Who composed the 1936 song *A Fine Romance*?

Q360. What Moroder—Whitlock composition featured in the film *Top Gun* won an Academy Award in 1986?

Q361. Who popularized the Bob Troup song *(Get Your Kicks on) Route 66*?

Q362. Who wrote *Tennessee Waltz*?

Q363. For whom was the 1921 Leo Wood—Irving Bibo song *Cherie* a number one recording?

Q364. Who composed *Bye Bye Blackbird*?

Q365. Who composed *Have You Ever Seen the Rain*?

Q366. Who composed the 1971 song *American Pie*, and to whom is it a tribute?

Q367. What Jerry Herman composition was the NARAS Song of the Year in 1964?

Q368. Who wrote and popularized the number one recording *Sheila*?

Q369. What Gordon Sumner composition was the NARAS Song of the Year in 1983?

Q370. What Deek Watson—William Best collaboration did Nat "King" Cole bring to number one in 1947?

Q371. Who composed *My Ideal*?

Q372. Who introduced the Comden—Green—Styne composition *The Party's Over*?

Q373. Who composed *The Payback*?

Q374. What Christopher—Thompson—James composition was the NARAS Song of the Year in 1982?

Q375. Who popularized *Mack the Knife (Moritat)*?

Q376. Who wrote *That's What Friends Are For*?

Q377. What Leslie Bricusse song introduced in the film *Scrooge* was nominated for an Academy Award in 1970?

Q378. What song, not mentioned anywhere else in this book, written by Paul Craft and popularized by Bobby Bare was nominated for a NARAS Award (Country Song) in 1976?

Q379. Who composed *Being in Love*?

Q380. What James Mtume—Reginald Lucas composition was the NARAS R & B Song of the Year in 1980?

Q381. Who wrote *You've Lost That Lovin' Feelin'*?

Q382. What 1934 song was introduced by Ethel Merman, covered by Paul Whiteman and his Orchestra, and revived by Harper's Bizarre, and who wrote it?

Q383. Who wrote Kool & The Gang's *Celebration*?

Q384. What Stevie Wonder composition featured in the film *The Lady in Red* won an Academy Award in 1984?

Q385. Who composed Billie Holiday's *Crazy, He Calls Me*?

Q386. Who wrote *Groovin'*?

Q387. Who composed *Shine on Harvest Moon*?

Q388. What Paul Simon composition was the NARAS Song of the Year in 1970?

Q390. Who composed *As Time Goes By*?

Q391. Who wrote *The Man Who Shot Liberty Valence*?

Q392. What Ray Gilbert—Allie Wrubel song featured in the film *Song of the South* won an Academy Award in 1947?

Q393. Who composed The Monkees' hit *A Little Bit You, A Little Bit Me*?

Q394. Who composed George Benson's *Breezin'*?

Q395. Who wrote *What Does It Take (To Win Your Love)*, popularized by Jr. Walker and The All Stars?

Q396. Who popularized and collaborated in the composition of the awardwinning *Gravy Waltz*?

Q397. Who composed *I Wanna Be Around*, popularized by Tony Bennett?

Q398. Who introduced George Gershwin's *Rhapsody in Blue*?

Q399. Who composed the Academy Award and NARAS Awardwinning song *Days of Wine and Roses*?

Q400. Who introduced the Fields—McHugh—Kern song *Lovely to Look At*?

Q401. Who wrote *Do They Know It's Christmas*?

Q402. Who wrote *Bein' Green*?

Q403. Who composed *I'm Gonna Sit Right Down and Write Myself a Letter*?

Q404. In what film was the Harburg—Arlen song *Happiness is a Thing Called Joe* introduced, and by whom?

Q405. What Webster—Mandel composition was the NARAS Song of the Year in 1965?

Q406. Who composed the 1943 song *Lonesome Nights*?

Q407. Who introduced *The Sounds of Silence*?

Q408. Who popularized the Ted Koehler—Harold Arlen song *I've Got the World on a String*?

Q409. What Michael Jackson composition was the NARAS R & B Song of the Year in 1983?

Q410. What 1931 Lew Brown—Ray Henderson song

was revived by B.B. King in 1970?

Q411. Who composed *(They Long to Be) Close to You*, a number one recording for The Carpenters?

Q412. Who composed *I Don't Need No Doctor*?

Q413. What awardwinning Johnny Mercer—Hoagy Carmichael song was introduced in the film *Here Comes the Groom*?

Q414. Who composed *Lush Life*?

Q415. What Cole Porter song, introduced in the film *Born to Dance*, was nominated for an Academy Award in 1936?

Q416. What Glen Frey—Don Henley song, popularized by The Eagles, was nominated for a NARAS Award in 1975?

Q417. Who composed *Georgia on My Mind*?

Q418. In what musical was the Oscar Hammerstein II—Jerome Kern song *All the Things You Are* introduced?

Q419. Who composed *Get Ready*, popularized by The Temptations and revived by Rare Earth?

Q420. Who popularized the Lord Burgess composition *Jamaica Farewell*?

Q421. Who popularized *Smoke Rings*?

Q422. What Roy Orbison—Joe Melson song, written in 1963, was nominated for a NARAS Award in 1977?

Q423. Who brought Bruce Springsteen's *Blinded By the Light* to the top of the chart?

Q424. Who composed the Michael McDonald—Patti Labelle hit *On My Own*?

Q425. What Bruce Johnston composition was the NARAS Song of the Year in 1976?

Q426. Who popularized *Layla*?

Q427. Who composed the Buddy Holly hit *It Doesn't Matter Anymore*?

Q428. Who composed and performed the 1960 hit *Cathy's Clown*?

Q429. Who introduced *I've Got a Crush on You* in the musical *Treasure Girl*?

Q430. Who was the vocalist on Jimmy Dorsey and his Orchestra's recording of *Blue Champagne*?

Q431. What Lerner—Loewe song featured in the film *Gigi* won an Academy Award in 1958?

Q432. What Don Gibson composition was the NARAS R & B Song of the Year in 1962?

Q433. Who introduced the song *Jeepers Creepers* in the film *Going Places*?

Q434. What Cropper—Redding composition was the

NARAS R & B Song of the Year in 1968?

Q435. Who introduced Stephen Sondheim's *Send in the Clowns*?

Q436. Who wrote *Tangerine*?

Q437. Who wrote *You Stepped Out of a Dream*?

Q438. In what film was the Hugh Martin—Ralph Blane song *Have Yourself a Merry Little Christmas* introduced?

Q439. Who performed *The Ballad of Cat Ballou* in the film *Cat Ballou*?

Q440. What Al Kasha—Joel Hirschorn composition featured in the film *The Towering Inferno* won an Academy Award in 1974?

Q441. Who wrote *Stella By Starlight*?

Q442. Who wrote *Ghostbusters*?

Q443. Who wrote *Baby, the Rain Must Fall*?

Q444. Who composed the *Batman Theme*?

Q445. Who composed *I Heard It Through the Grapevine*?

Q446. Who introduced the Kern—Hammerstein song *The Last Time I Saw Paris* in the film *Lady, Be Good*?

Q447. What Steve Goodman composition was the NARAS Country Song of the Year in 1984?

Q448. Who wrote *Worst That Could Happen*, popularized by Brooklyn Bridge?

Q449. Who composed *To All the Girls I've Loved Before*, popularized by Julio Iglesias and Willie Nelson?

Q450. From what Civil War era song was Elvis Presley's *Love Me Tender* derived?

Q451. Who composed *Miss Celie's Blues*, introduced in the film *The Color Purple*?

Q452. What Paul Simon song was revived by Yes in 1972?

Q453. Who composed *Cheek to Cheek*, introduced in the film *Top Hat* by Fred Astaire?

Q454. Who wrote the Blondie hit *Call Me*?

Q455. What Herman Davis—Russell R. Lewis song, popularized by Gene Chandler, was nominated for a NARAS Award in 1970?

Q456. What Irving Berlin song featured in the film *Holiday Inn* won an Academy Award in 1942?

Q457. Who introduced *Be My Love* in the film *The Toast of New Orleans*?

Q458. Who performed *The Ballad of Cat Ballou* in the film *Cat Ballou*?

Answers to Testing 1...2...3...

A1. *To Be A Lover*
A2. Joni Mitchell
A3. Otto Harbach (w) and Jerome Kern (m)
A4. *On the Road Again*
A5. William Saroyan and Ross Bagdasarian (the latter being "David Seville" from Dave and the Chipmunks
A6. Noel Coward
A7. Jackey Beavers, Johnny Bristol, and Harvey Fuqua
A8. Gale Storm
A9. Randy Newman
A10. *Patches (I'm Depending On You)*
A11. Ella Fitzgerald and The Ink Spots
A12. *9 to 5*
A13. *Calamity Jane*
A14. George and Ira Gershwin
A15. Norman Gimbel (w) and Jean Thielemans (m)
A16. Douglas Cross (w) and George Corey (m)
A17. Harry James, Duke Ellington, Johnny Hodges, and Don George
A18. Ruth Etting
A19. *You've Got a Friend*
A20. James Brown
A21. Dusty Springfield
A22. Jimmy Dorsey and his Orchestra, with vocal by Bob Eberly
A23. Mitchell Parish (w) and Hoagy Carmichael (m)
A24. Keith Carradine
A25. Queen Liliuokalani
A26. *God Bless America*
A27. Burl Ives
A28. Fred Neil
A29. Buddy Buie, Emery Gordy, Jr., and James B. Cobb, Jr.
A30. Perez Prado and his Orchestra
A31. Jerry Leiber and Phil Spector
A32. *Just the Two of Us*
A33. Bob Dylan
A34. *Chuck E's in Love*
A35. *Where Is the Love*
A36. Phil Spector
A37. Helen Forrest
A38. Benny Davis and Harry Akst
A39. Johnny Mercer (w) and David Raskin (m)
A40. Louis Prima
A41. *Carioca*
A42. *Everybody Plays the Fool*
A43. Al Jolson, B.G.De Sylva, and Joseph Meyer; *Bombo*
A44. *Turn Your Love Around*
A45. *Talk to the Animals*
A46. Laura Nyro
A47. Ann Ronell
A48. Carolyn Leigh (w) and Johnny Richards (m)
A49. Eddie De Lange and Irving Mills (w) and Duke Ellington (m)
A50. Gale Garnett
A51. Jack Segal (w) and Marvin Fisher (m)
A52. George Harrison
A53. Frank Loesser
A54. *Another Saturday Night*
A55. Paul Anka (wEng) and Jacques Revaux (m)

A56. Fred Ebb and John Kander
A57. John J.Cale
A58. *Boogie Woogie Bugle Boy*
A59. *El Paso*
A60. Steve Lawrence and Donny Osmond
A61. Johnny Burke (w) and Errol Garner (m)
A62. Glen Gray and the Casa Loma Orchestra, with vocal by Eugenie Baird
A63. *A Boy Named Sue*
A64. *ATisket ATasket*; 15
A65. *Contrasts*
A66. Barry Mann, Cynthia Weil, Jerry Lieber, and Mike Stoller
A67. Harvey Fuqua and Alan Freed
A68. *You Make Me Feel Like Dancing*
A69. Charles Strouse
A70. Sylvia Dee (w) and Sid Lippman (m)
A71. Bernie Taupin, Martin Page, Dennis Lambert, and Peter Wolf
A72. John Birks Gillespie and Frank Paparelli
A73. Leo Robin (w) and Jule Styne (m)
A74. Nelson Riddle
A75. Michael McDonald
A76. Benny Goodman and his Orchestra
A77. *Jump for Joy*
A78. *Freeway of Loven*
A79. Don Black and John Barry
A80. *Chain Gang*
A81. Leo Robin (w) and Russ Columbo and Clarence Gaskill (m)
A82. Harry Woods, Jimmy Campbell, and Reg Connelley (1932)
A83. *Theme from Exodus*
A84. Zoot Sims, Stan Getz, Herbie Steward, and Serge Chaloff
A85. *Concerto for Cootie*, which, in recorded form, featured Cootie Williams on trumpet
A86. Carl Sigman (w) and Charles Gates Dawes (m).The music is from Dawes' *Melody*, published in 1912; Dawes was to be Vice President of the United States (192528).
A87. Huddie Ledbetter ("Leadbelly") and John Lomax
A88. *Eve of Destruction*
A89. Paul Francis Webster (w) and Johnny Mandel (m)
A90. Frank Sinatra (w) and Sol Parker and Henry Sanicola (m)
A91. Johnny Mercer (w) and Rube Bloom (m)
A92. Pat Boone
A93. Whispering Jack Smith
A94. Ronnie Self and Dub Allbritten
A95. Gene Autry, in the film *Singing Hill*
A96. Otis Redding
A97. Artie Shaw and his Orchestra
A98. Truman Capote and Harold Arlen
A99. Vaughn Monroe and his Orchestra; Stan Jones
A100. David Bowie and Iggy Pop
A101. *Big Bad John*
A102. Johnny Burke (w) and Jimmy Van Heusen (m)
A103. *Let It Be*
A104. Gail Levy, Vincent Levy, and Joseph Zawinul
A105. Bernie Hanighen (w) and Cootie Williams and Thelonius Monk (m)
A106. Arthur Hamilton

A107.Otto Harbach (w) and Vincent Youmans (m)
A108.*Dang Me*
A109.Joseph McCarthy (w) and James V.Monaco (m)
A110.*GoodBye*
A111.*Let's Stay Together*
A112.*Tequila*
A113.Pete Seeger
A114.Billy Rose (w) and Al Jolson and Dave Dreyer (m)
A115.Bob Dylan
A116.Seymour Simons and Gerald Marks
A117.*For the Love of Money*
A118.Jon Hendricks and Jessie Cavanaugh (wEng) and Antonio Carlos Jobim (Portuguese words and music)
A119.*For All We Know*
A120.Rod McKuen (wEng) and Jacques Brel (wFr, m)
A121.*After the Love Has Gone*
A122.Katherine Lee Bates (w) and Samuel Ward (m)
A123.*Games People Play*
A124.Ben E.King, Jerry Leiber, and Mike Stoller
A125.E.Y.Harburg (w) and Harold Arlen (m)
A126.Paul Francis Webster (w) and Sammy Fain (m)
A127.*Sailing*
A128.*Are You Lonesome Tonight?*
A129.Prince Rogers Nelson (i.e., "Prince")
A130.Stevie Wonder, Henry Cosby, and Sylvia Moy
A131.*Please Mr.Postman*
A132.Rod Argent
A133.Bing Crosby and The Andrews Sisters
A134.Bob Marley
A135.*Baby, It's Cold Outside*
A136.Fred Astaire and Bing Crosby
A137.Ringo Starr
A138.Carolyn Leigh (w) and Cy Coleman (m)
A139.*The Best of My Love*
A140.Thom Bell and Linda Creed
A141.*Behind Closed Doors*
A142.Allan Roberts and Doris Fisher
A143.*Anything Goes*
A144.Lionel Hampton and Curly Hamner
A145.Isham Jones and his Orchestra
A146.Donna Weiss (w) and Jackie DeShannon (m)
A147.*Blind Man's Buff*
A148.*What a Diff'rence a Day Makes*
A149.Louis Armstrong
A150.Clyde Otis and Brook Benton
A151.Johnny Mercer (w) and Billy Strayhorn and Duke Ellington (m)
A152.*Papa Was a Rolling Stone*
A153.Otis Blackwell and Elvis Presley
A154.Frank Loesser (w) and Hoagy Carmichael (m)
A155.Cab Calloway, Irving Mills, and Clarence Gaskill
A156.Fleecie Moore
A157.Tony Hatch
A158.*Funny Way of Laughing*
A159.Billy Hill
A160.*I Gotta Right to Sing the Blues*
A161.Doc Pomus and Mort Shuman
A162.Richard M.Sherman and Robert B.Sherman
A163.*Send in the Clowns*
A164.*Every Day*
A165.Paul Francis Webster (w) and Jerry Livingston (m)
A166.*Artistry in Rhythm*
A167.*Roberta*
A168.Ray Noble
A169.*Since I Don't Have You*

A170.*The Morning After*
A171.*Lady, Be Good!*
A172.*Lowdown*
A173.Irene Higginbotham, Ervin Drake, and Dan Fisher
A174.David Seville and the Chipmunks
A175.Bob Marley
A176.*DuBarry Was A Lady*; Ethel Merman and Ronald Graham
A177.*Love Theme from A Star Is Born (Evergreen)*
A178.*The Battle of New Orleans*
A179.*Hit the Road, Jack*
A180.Lena Horne
A181.P.G.Wodehouse and Oscar Hammerstein II (w) and Jerome Kern (m)
A182.*Help Me Make it Through the Night*
A183.Barry, Robin, and Maurice Gibb (The Bee Gees)
A184.Maxwell Anderson (w) and Kurt Weill (m)
A185.*It Goes Like It Goes*
A186.Bob Russell (w) and Duke Ellington (m)
A187.Robert Wright and George Forrest
A188.Tony Bennett
A189.*Say You, Say Me*
A190.Eddie Holland, Brian Holland, and Lamont Dozier
A191.*Midnight Train to Georgia*
A193.Larry Morey and Frank Churchill
A193.Sheldon Harnick (w) and Jerry Bock (m)
A194.Thomas "Fats" Waller
A195.*Love Is the Answer*
A196.*The Way We Were*
A197.Bruce Sivier (w) and Ord Hamilton (m)
A198.Paul McCartney
A199.Russ Columbo
A200.*The First Time Ever I Saw Your Face*
A201.Fletcher Henderson and his Orchestra
A202.Eddy Duchin and his Orchestra
A203.W.C.Handy
A204.Johnny Mercer (w) and Fred Astaire (m)
A205.Jim Webb
A206.*Papa's Got a Brand New Bag*
A207.Curtis Mayfield
A208.Shel Silverstein
A209.Boudleaux and Felice Bryant
A210.*Change Partners*
A211.Daryl Hall
A212.Mark Knopfler
A213.Berry Gordy, Jr., Frank E.Wilson, Brenda Holloway, and Patrice Holloway
A214.*I Just Called to Say I Love You*
A215.Eddie Holland and Norman Whitfield
A216.Milton Drake, Al Hoffman, and Jerry Livingston
A217.*Buttons and Bows*
A218.Dick Powell and the Mills Brothers in the film *Broadway Gondolier*
A219.Berry Gordy, Jr., Gwen Gordy, and Tyran Carlo
A220.Marion Harris
A221.Andy Razaf (w) and Joe Garland (m)
A222.*Corner of the Sky*
A223.*I Only Have Eyes For You*
A224.Al Dubin (w) and Harry Warren (m)
A225.Jack Nitzsche, Will Jennings, and Buffy Sainte-Marie
A226.*King of the Road*
A227.*Got to Get You Into My Life*
A228.Little Jack Little and his Orchestra
A229.Lorenz Hart (w) and Richard Rodgers (m)
A230.Gary Lewis, Thomas Leslie, and Leon Russell

A231.The McGuire Sisters
A232.Doc Severinsen
A233.*Cisco Kid*; the group is War
A234.*Badge*
A235.Ned Washington (w) and Dimitri Tiomkin (m)
A236.Maurice Jarre
A237.*Sweet Leilani*
A238.John Blackburn (w) and Karl Suessdorf (m)
A239.Charlie Parker
A240.Ervin Drake
A241.*Michelle*
A242.Cher
A243.Maurice Williams
A244.*The Windmills of Your Mind*
A245.*Crying Time*
A246.John Lennon, David Bowie, and Carlos Alomar
A247.*(Our) Love Is Here to Stay*
A248.Jerry Ragovay
A249.Whitney Houston
A250.*I'll Walk Alone*
A251.*We Are the World*
A252.Herb Magidson (w) and Con Conrad (m); Ginger Rogers, in the film *Gay Divorcee*
A253.Ozzie Nelson
A254.Sarah Vaughan
A255.Ethel Waters
A256.Alfred Drake
A257.The Beatles
A258.*Up, Up and Away*
A259.Jimmy Lunceford and his Orchestra
A260.Kay Kyser and his Orchestra
A261.Nervous Norvus
A262.L.C.Cooke
A263.*Let the Good Times Roll*
A264.Glen MacDonough (w) and Victor Herbert (m)
A265.Mack Gordon (w) and Harry Warden (m)
A266.Otto Harbach and Oscar Hammerstein II (w) and Rudolf Friml (m)
A267.Berry Gordy, Jr.and William "Smokey" Robinson
A268.Ann Miller and Tommy Rall
A269.Harry Nilsson
A270.Isaac Hayes and David Porter
A271.*Que Sera Sera*
A272.Gertrude Lawrence
A273.Mack Gordon (w) and Harry Revel (m)
A274.*Respect*
A275.Helen O'Connell and Bob Eberly, backed by Jimmy Dorsey and his Orchestra
A276.Thom Bell, Kenny Gamble, and Linda Creed
A277.*What Kind of Fool Am I?*
A278.Chuck Berry
A279.*The LocoMotion*
A280.Max Freedman and Jimmy De Knight (1953); *The Blackboard Jungle* (1955)
A281.*The Highwayman*
A282.*Chances Are*
A283.*How Glad I Am*
A284.Jack Yellen (w) and Milton Ager (m)
A285.The Isley Brothers; O'Kelly, Ronald, and Rudolph Isley
A286.Bob Hope and Shirley Ross in the film *Big Broadcast of 1938*
A287.*Gentle on My Mind*
A288.Mack David, Mack Davis, and Andre Kostelanetz; Tchaikovsky's Fifth Symphony
A289.Johnny Burke and Arthur Johnston

A290.Warren Zevon
A291.*Girl Crazy*
A292.*Ain't No Sunshine*
A293.Ray Noble
A294.*Just the Way You Are*
A295.Les Brown and his Orchestra, with vocal by Doris Day
A296.Henry Cosby, Stevie Wonder, and William Robinson
A297.Jerry Lieber and Mike Stoller
A298.Thomas "Fats" Waller
A299.Julie Andrews
A300.Frank C.Slay, Jr.and Bob Crewe
A301.Dean Kay and Kelly Gordon
A302.*Little Green Apples*
A303.Buck Ram
A304.Stephen Collins Foster
A305.*Puttin' on the Ritz*
A306.*I Fall in Love Too Easily*
A307.Gus Kahn and Edward Eliscu (w) and Vincent Youmans (m)
A308.Stevie Wonder
A309.*What a Fool Believes*
A310.Irving Berlin
A311.Stevie Wonder, Lee Garrett, and Syreeta Wright
A312.Billy Preston and Bruce Fisher
A313.*All Those Years Ago*
A314.Mel Torme and Robert Wells
A315.Arthur Freed (w) and Nacio Herb Brown (m)
A316.*Unchained Melody*
A317.Ethel Waters
A318.*The Bare Necessities*
A319.*Busted*
A320.Charles Aznavour and Herbert Kretzmer
A321.*I'll Be Seeing You*
A322.Joseph Kosma
A323.Laura Nyro
A324.*Superstition*
A325.Eddie De Lange (w) and Jimmy Van Heusen (m)
A326.George Olsen and his Orchestra
A327.Gene Autry
A328.Al Dubin (w) and Harry Warren (m)
A329.*Crying*
A330.Prince Rogers Nelson
A331.Manos Hadjidakis
A332.Jerry Herman
A333.William Stevenson and Marvin Gaye
A334.*Living for the City*
A335.Nancy Hamilton (w) and Morgan Lewis (m)
A336.Noble Sissle and Eubie Blake
A337.The Andrews Sisters
A338.*Last Dance*
A339.Jon Anderson; Melissa Manchester
A340.Haven Gillespie and J.Fred Coots
A341.*Killing Me Softly With His Song*
A342.Dorothy Fields (w) and Jimmy McHugh (m)
A343.*All the Way*
A344.Lorenz Hart (w) and Richard Rodgers (m)
A345.*It Can't Be Wrong*
A346.Jose Iturbi
A347.Charles Singleton and Eddie Snyder (w) and Bert Kaempfert (m)
A348.Arthur Herzog, Jr.(w) and Billie Holiday (m)
A349.Kenny Gamble and Leon Huff
A350.Michael Masser
A351.Jimi Hendrix

A352.Mitchell Parish (w) and Glenn Miller (m)
A353.Paul Whiteman and his Orchestra
A354.Arthur de Lulli
A355.Jim Webb
A356.*On the Atchison, Topeka and the Santa Fe*
A357.Ian Hunter
A358.Joseph Brooks
A359.Dorothy Fields (w) and Jerome Kern (m)
A360.*Take My Breath Away*
A361.The King Cole Trio
A362.Redd Stewart and Pee Wee King
A363.Paul Whiteman and his Orchestra
A364.Mort Dixon (w) and Ray Henderson (m)
A365.John C.Fogerty
A366.Don McLean; Buddy Holly
A367.*Hello, Dolly!*
A368.Tommy Roe
A369.*Every Breath You Take*
A370.*(I Love You) For Sentimental Reasons*
A371.Leo Robin (w) and Richard A.Whiting and Newell Chase (m)
A372.Judy Holliday in the musical *Bells Are Ringing*
A373.James Brown, Fred Wesley, and John Starks
A374.*Always on My Mind*
A375.Lotte Lenya
A376.Carole Bayer Sager and Burt Bacharach
A377.*Thank You Very Much*
A378.*Dropkick Me, Jesus*
A379.Meredith Willson
A380.*Never Knew Love Like This Before*
A381.Barry Mann, Cynthia Weill, and Phil Spector
A382.*Anything Goes*; Cole Porter
A383.Ronald Bell, Claydes Smith, Robert "Kool" Bell, James Taylor, Eumir Deodato, Robert Mickens, Earl Toon, and Dennis Thomas
A384.*I Just Called to Say I Love You*
A385.Bob Russell (w) and Carl Sigman (m)
A386.Felix Cavaliere and Eddie Brigati, Jr.
A387.Jack Norworth and Nora Bayes
A389.*Bridge Over Troubled Water*
A390.Herman Hupfeld
A391.Hal David (w) and Burt Bacharach (m)
A392.*ZipADeeDooDah*
A393.Neil Diamond
A394.Bobby Womack
A395.Harvey Fuqua, Vernon Bullock, and Johnny Bristol
A396.Steve Allen
A397.Johnny Mercer and Sadie Vimmerstedt
A398.Paul Whiteman and his Orchestra, with Gershwin at the piano
A399.Johnny Mercer (w) and Henry Mancini (m)
A400.Irene Dunne in the film *Roberta*
A401.Bob Geldof and Midge Ure
A402.Joe Raposo
A403.Joe Young (w) and Fred E.Ahlert (m)
A404.*Cabin in the Sky*; Ethel Waters

A405.*The Shadow of Your Smile*
A406.Irving Mills (w) and Benny Carter (m)
A407.Tom and Jerry (Simon and Garfunkel)
A408.Cab Calloway
A409.*Billie Jean*
A410.*The Thrill Is Gone*
A411.Hal David (w) and Burt Bacharach (m)
A412.Nick Ashford and Valerie Simpson
A413.*In the Cool, Cool, Cool of the Evening*
A414.Billy Strayhorn
A415.*I've Got You Under My Skin*
A416.*Lyin' Eyes*
A417.Stuart Gorrell (w) and Hoagy Carmichael (m)
A418.*Very Warm for May*
A419.William "Smokey" Robinson
A420.Harry Belafonte
A421.Glen Gray and the Casa Loma Orchestra
A422.*Blue Bayou*, on the strength of Linda Ronstadt's revival
A423.Manfred Mann
A424.Carole Bayer Sager and Burt Bacharach
A425.*I Write the Songs*
A426.Derek and The Dominoes
A427.Paul Anka
A428.Don and Phil Everly, the Everly Brothers
A429.Clifton Webb and Mary Hay
A430.Bob Eberly
A431.*Gigi*
A432.*I Can't Stop Loving You*
A433.Louis Armstrong
A434.*Sittin' on the Dock of the Bay*
A435.Glynis Johns, in the musical *A Little Night Music*
A436.Johnny Mercer (w) and Victor Schertzinger (m)
A437.Gus Kahn (w) and Nacio Herb Brown (m)
A438.*Meet Me in St.Louis*, by Judy Garland
A439.Nat "King" Cole and Stubby Kaye
A440.*We May Never Love Like This Again*
A441.Ned Washington (w) and Victor Young (m)
A442.Ray Parker, Jr.
A443.Ernie Sheldon (w) and Elmer Bernstein (m)
A444.Neil Hefti
A445.Norman Whitfield and Barrett Strong
A446.Ann Sothern
A447.*City of New Orleans*
A448.Jim Webb
A449.Hal David (w) and Albert Hammond (m)
A450.*Aura Lee*
A451.Quincy Jones, Rod Temperton, and Lionel Richie
A452.*America*
A453.Irving Berlin
A454.Giorgio Moroder and Debbie Harry
A455.*Groovy Situation*
A456.*White Christmas*
A457.Mario Lanza
A458.Nat "King" Cole and Stubby Kaye

Index

Index